Mathematics for the IB Diploma

Standard Level

Hugh Neill and Douglas Quadling

Series editor Hugh Neill

CAMBRIDGE UNIVERSITY PRESS
Cambridge, New York, Melbourne, Madrid, Cape Town, Singapore, São Paulo, Delhi

Cambridge University Press
The Edinburgh Building, Cambridge CB2 8RU, UK

www.cambridge.org
Information on this title: www.cambridge.org/9780521699280

© Cambridge University Press 2007

This publication is in copyright. Subject to statutory exception and to the provisions of relevant collective licensing agreements, no reproduction of any part may take place without the written permission of Cambridge University Press.

First published 2007

Printed in the United Kingdom at the University Press, Cambridge

A catalogue record for this publication is available from the British Library

ISBN 978-0-521-69928-0 paperback

The authors and publisher are grateful to the following examination boards for permission to reproduce questions from past examination papers, identified in the text as follows.

OCR Oxford, Cambridge and RSA Examinations
IBO International Baccalaureate Organization

The authors, and not the examination boards, are responsible for the method and accuracy of the answers to examination questions given; these may not necessarily constitute the only possible solutions.

This material has been developed independently of the International Baccalaureate Organization (IBO). The text is in no way connected with, nor endorsed by, the IBO.

Cambridge University Press has no responsibility for the persistence or accuracy of URLs for external or third-party internet websites referred to in this publication, and does not guarantee that any content on such websites is, or will remain, accurate or appropriate.

Contents

Introduction

Mathematics Standard Level has been written especially for the International Baccalaureate Mathematics SL examination.

The book is divided into small groups of connected chapters, each covering one part of the syllabus. There is a small amount of material which extends a topic beyond the syllabus as printed, with the aim of enhancing students' appreciation of the subject. This is indicated by an asterisk (∗) at the appropriate place in the text.

Occasionally within the text paragraphs appear in a grey box. These paragraphs may help to give insight, suggest different approaches or provide background to a topic.

Students are expected to have access to graphic display calculators and the text places considerable emphasis on their potential for supporting the learning of mathematics.

Numerical work is presented in a form intended to discourage premature approximation. In ongoing calculations inexact numbers appear in decimal form like 3.456... , signifying that the number is held in a calculator to more places than are given. Numbers are not rounded at this stage; the full display could be, for example, 3.456 123 or 3.456 789. Final answers are then stated with some indication that they are approximate, for example '3.46 correct to 3 significant figures'.

There are plenty of exercises. After each group of connected chapters there is a Review exercise which includes some questions from past International Baccalaureate examinations, but on a different syllabus. At the time of writing, there are no current versions of the Standard Level examinations, so there is no backlog of examination questions on the newer parts of the syllabus.

The authors thank Steve Dobbs and Jane Miller who gave permission to use work from their statistics books. The authors also thank the International Baccalaureate Organization (IBO) and Oxford, Cambridge and RSA Examinations (OCR) for permission to reproduce IBO and OCR intellectual property and Cambridge University Press for their help in producing this book. Particular thanks are due to Sharon Dunkley, for her considerable help and advice. However, the responsibility for the text, and for any errors, remains with the authors.

1 Numbers

One thread in the history of mathematics has been the extension of what is meant by a number. This has led to the invention of new symbols and techniques of calculation. When you have completed this chapter, you should

- be able to recognise various number systems, and know the notation for them
- understand inequality relations, and the rules for calculating with them
- know what is meant by the modulus of a number, and how it can be used
- be familiar with techniques for calculating with surds.

1.1 Different kinds of number

At first numbers were used only for counting, and 1, 2, 3, ... were all that was needed. These are called **positive integers**.

Sometimes you also need the number 0, or 'zero'. For example, suppose you are recording the number of sisters of every person in the class. Some will have one, two, three, ... sisters, but some will have none. The numbers 0, 1, 2, 3, ... are called **natural numbers**.

Then people found that numbers could also be useful for measurement and in commerce. For these purposes they also needed fractions. Integers and fractions together make up the **rational numbers**. These are numbers which can be expressed in the form $\frac{p}{q}$ where p and q are integers, and q is not 0.

One of the most remarkable discoveries of the ancient Greek mathematicians was that there are numbers which cannot be expressed like this. These are called **irrational numbers**. The first such number to be found was $\sqrt{2}$, which is the length of the diagonal of a square with side 1 unit, by Pythagoras' theorem (see Fig. 1.1).

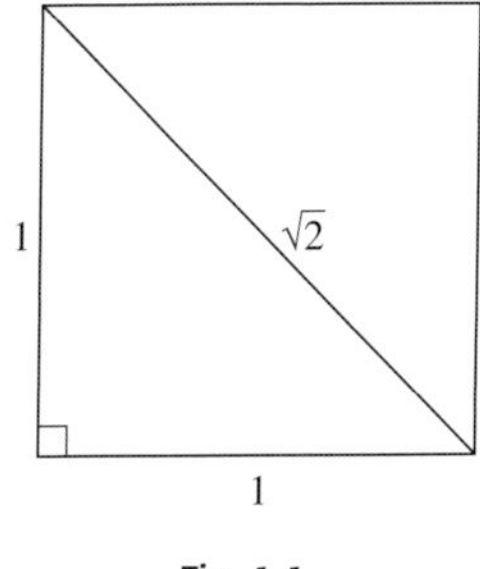

Fig. 1.1

The argument that the Greeks used to prove this can be adapted to show that the square root, cube root, ... of any positive integer is either an integer or an irrational number. For example, the square root of 8 is an irrational number, but the cube root of 8 is the integer 2. Many other numbers are now known to be irrational, of which the most famous is π.

Rational and irrational numbers together make up the **real numbers**.

When rational numbers are written as decimals, they either come to a stop after a number of places, or the sequence of decimal digits eventually starts repeating in a regular pattern. For example,

$$\tfrac{7}{10} = 0.7,\quad \tfrac{7}{11} = 0.6363...,\quad \tfrac{7}{12} = 0.5833...,\quad \tfrac{7}{13} = 0.538\,461\,538\,461\,53...,$$
$$\tfrac{7}{14} = 0.5,\quad \tfrac{7}{15} = 0.466...,\quad \tfrac{7}{16} = 0.4375,\quad \tfrac{7}{17} = 0.411\,764\,705\,882\,352\,941\,176... .$$

The reverse is also true. If a decimal number stops or repeats indefinitely then it is a rational number. So if an irrational number is written as a decimal, the pattern of the decimal digits never repeats however long you continue the calculation.

Integers, rational and irrational numbers and real numbers can all be either positive or negative.

It is helpful to have special symbols to denote the different kinds of number. The set of integers $\{\ldots, -3, -2, -1, 0, 1, 2, 3, \ldots\}$ is written as $\mathbb{Z}$; the set of (positive and negative) rational numbers is $\mathbb{Q}$; and the set of real numbers is $\mathbb{R}$. If you want just the positive numbers, you use the symbols $\mathbb{Z}^+$, $\mathbb{Q}^+$, $\mathbb{R}^+$. The set of natural numbers, $\{0, 1, 2, 3, \ldots\}$, is written as $\mathbb{N}$; there are no negative natural numbers.

You may wonder why these letters were chosen. The notation was first used by German mathematicians in the 19th century, and the German word for number is *Zahl*. Hence the choice of $\mathbb{Z}$ for the integers. The letter $\mathbb{Q}$ probably came from Quotient, which is the result of dividing one number by another.

You probably know the symbol $\in$, which stands for 'is an element of'. The statement '$x \in \mathbb{Z}^+$' means 'x belongs to the set of positive integers'; that is, 'x is a positive integer'. So

'$x \in \mathbb{Z}^+$' and 'x is a positive integer'

are two ways of saying the same thing.

You can also draw diagrams of these sets of numbers on a **number line**, as in Fig. 1.2. The arrows at the ends of the lines indicate the positive direction; the usual convention is for this to point to the right. The larger the number, the further it is to the right on the line.

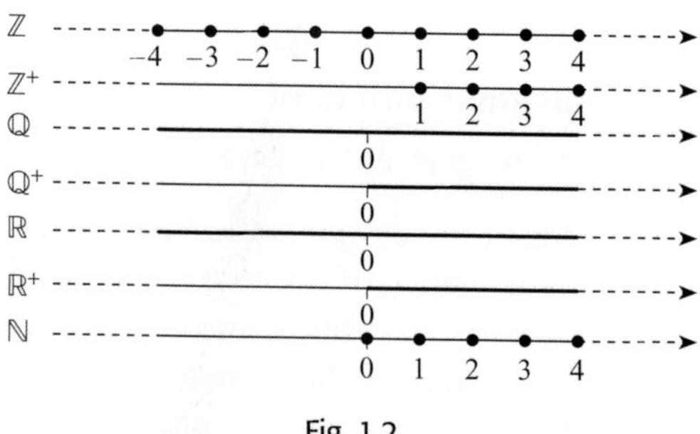

Fig. 1.2

The point which represents 0 is called the **origin** on the number line. It is usually denoted by the letter O.

But you will notice a snag. There are more real numbers than rational numbers. But in the figure $\mathbb{R}$ and $\mathbb{Q}$, and $\mathbb{R}^+$ and $\mathbb{Q}^+$, look the same. This is because there are rational numbers as close as you like to any real number. For example, $\pi \in \mathbb{R}$, but π is not a member of $\mathbb{Q}$. However, 3.141 592 65 (which is the 8 decimal place approximation to π) is a member of $\mathbb{Q}$, and you can't distinguish π from 3.141 592 65 in the figure.

All the numbers that can be shown on a calculator are rational numbers. Calculators can't handle irrational numbers. So when you key in $\sqrt{2}$ on your calculator, and it displays 1.414 213 562, this is only an approximation to $\sqrt{2}$. If you square the rational number 1.414 213 562, you get

$$1.414\,213\,562^2 = 1.999\,999\,998\,944\,727\,844,$$

but $\sqrt{2}^2 = 2$ exactly.

1.2 Notation for inequalities

You often want to compare one number with another and say which is the bigger. This comparison is expressed by using the inequality symbols $>$, $<$, $\leq$ and $\geq$.

The symbol $a > b$ means that a is greater than b. You can visualise this geometrically as in Fig. 1.3, which shows three number lines, with a to the right of b.

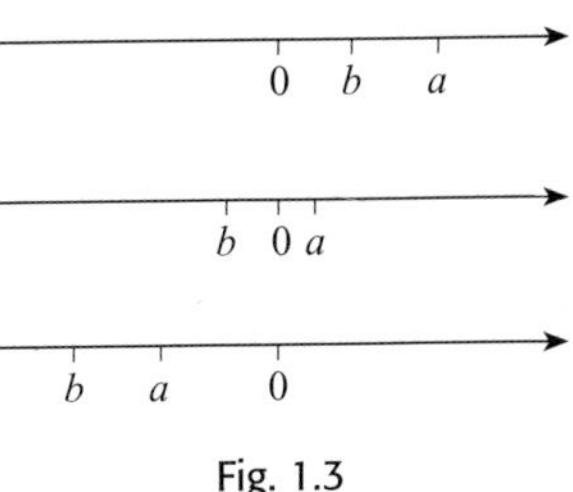

Fig. 1.3

Notice that it does not matter whether a and b are positive or negative. The position of a and b in relation to zero on the number line is irrelevant. In all three lines, $a > b$. As an example, in the bottom line, $-4 > -7$.

Similarly, the symbol $a < b$ means that a is less than b. You can visualise this geometrically on a number line, with a to the left of b.

> These four expressions are equivalent.
>
> $a > b$ a is greater than b
>
> $b < a$ b is less than a

The symbol $a \geq b$ means 'either $a > b$ or $a = b$'; that is, a is greater than or equal to, but not less than, b. Similarly, the symbol $a \leq b$ means 'either $a < b$ or $a = b$' ; that is, a is less than or equal to, but not greater than, b.

> These expressions are equivalent.
>
> $a \geq b$ a is greater than or equal to b
>
> $b \leq a$ b is less than or equal to a

> Some books use the symbols $\geqslant$ and $\leqslant$ in place of $\geq$ and $\leq$.

Since, for any two numbers a and b, a must be either greater than, equal to, or less than b, it follows that another way of writing

a is greater than or equal to b

is to say that

a is not less than b.

Similarly,

b is less than or equal to a

is equivalent to

b is not greater than a,

The symbols $<$ and $>$ are called **strict** inequalities, and the symbols $\leq$ and $\geq$ are called **weak** inequalities.

Example 1.2.1

Write down the set of numbers x such that $x \in \mathbb{N}$ and $x < 6$.

$\mathbb{N}$ is the set of natural numbers $\{0, 1, 2, 3, ...\}$. The largest number in $\mathbb{N}$ less than 6 is 5. So the set of numbers such that $x \in \mathbb{N}$ and $x < 6$ is $\{0, 1, 2, 3, 4, 5\}$.

Example 1.2.2

The points A and B on the number line represent the numbers -2 and 3. Use inequalities to describe the numbers represented by the line segment [AB] shown in Fig. 1.4.

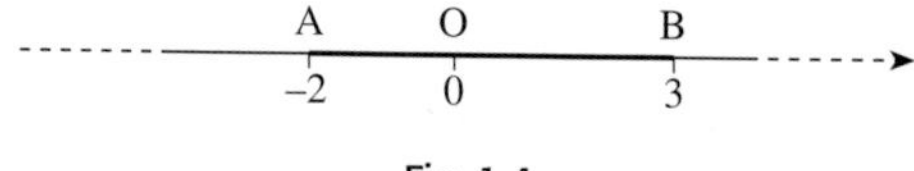

Fig. 1.4

> The notation [AB] is explained in Section 7.2.

All the points of the line segment, except A itself, are to the right of A. So the numbers they represent satisfy the inequality $x \geq -2$. They are also, except B itself, to the left of B, so the numbers satisfy $x \leq 3$.

You could also write $x \geq -2$ as $-2 \leq x$. So $-2 \leq x$ and $x \leq 3$.

These two inequalities can be combined in a single statement as $-2 \leq x \leq 3$.

> When you write an inequality of the kind $r < x$ and $x < s$ in the form $r < x < s$, it is essential that $r < s$. It makes no sense to write $7 < x < 3$; how can x be both greater than 7 and less than 3?

An inequality of the type $r < x < s$ (or $r < x \leq s$ or $r \leq x < s$ or $r \leq x \leq s$) is called an **interval**. It consists of all the numbers between r and s (including r or s where the sign adjacent to them is $\leq$).

The word 'interval' is also used for an inequality such as $x > r$, which consists of all the numbers greater than r (and similarly for $x \geq r$, $x < s$ and $x \leq s$).

1.3 Solving linear inequalities

When you solve an equation like $3x + 7 = -5$, you use two rules:

- you can add (or subtract) the same number on both sides of the equation
- you can multiply (or divide) both sides of the equation by the same number.

In this example, subtracting 7 from both sides and then dividing by 3 leads to the solution $x = -4$.

An inequality like $3x + 7 > -5$ doesn't have a single solution for x, but it can be replaced by a simpler statement about the value of x. To find this, you need rules for working with inequalities. These are similar to those for equations, but with one very important difference.

Adding or subtracting the same number on both sides

You can add or subtract the same number on both sides of an inequality. Justifying such a step involves showing that, for any number c, 'if $a > b$ then $a + c > b + c$'.

This is saying that if a is to the right of b on the number line, then $a + c$ is to the right of $b + c$. Fig. 1.5 shows that this is true whether c is positive or negative.

Since subtracting c is the same as adding $-c$, you can also subtract the same number from both sides.

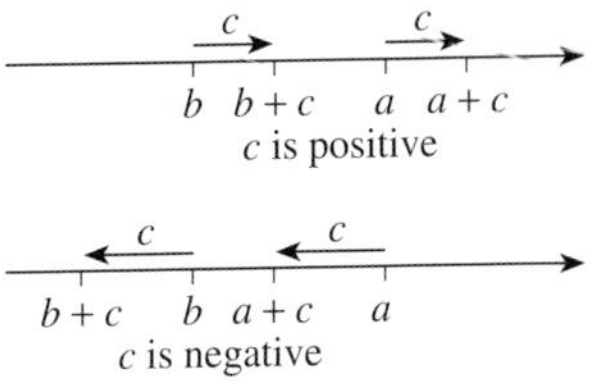

c c
b $b+c$ a $a+c$
c is positive

c c
$b+c$ b $a+c$ a
c is negative

Fig. 1.5

Example 1.3.1

If $x - 3 < -4$, what can you say about the value of x?

You can add 3 on both sides of the inequality, which gives

$$x - 3 + 3 < -4 + 3,$$

that is

$$x < -1.$$

In this example, the inequality $x < -1$ is called the **solution** of the inequality $x - 3 < -4$. It is the simplest statement you can make about x which is equivalent to the given inequality.

Multiplying both sides by a positive number

You can multiply (or divide) both sides of an inequality by a positive number. That is, if $a > b$ and $c > 0$, then $ca > cb$. Here is a justification.

As $a > b$, a is to the right of b on the number line.

As $c > 0$, ca and cb are enlargements of the positions of a and b relative to the number 0.

Fig. 1.6 shows that, whether a and b are positive or negative, ca is to the right of cb, so $ca > cb$.

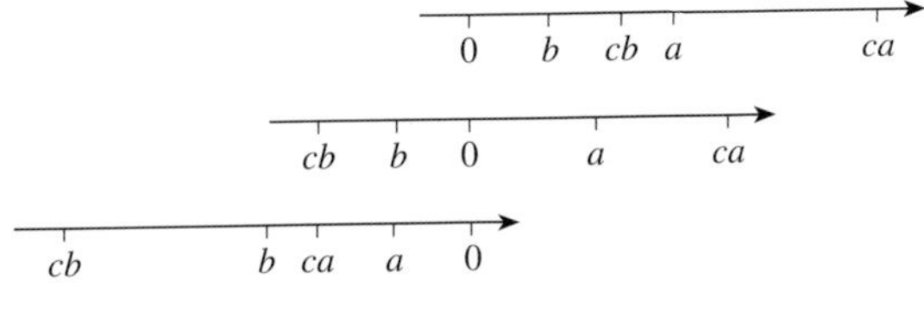

Fig. 1.6

Example 1.3.2
Solve the inequality $\frac{1}{3}x \geq 2$.

Multiply both sides of the inequality by 3. This gives the equivalent inequality

$$3 \times \left(\tfrac{1}{3}x\right) \geq 3 \times 2,$$

that is

$$x \geq 6.$$

Multiplying both sides by a negative number
If $a > b$, and you subtract $a + b$ from both sides, then you get $-b > -a$, which is the same as $-a < -b$. This shows that if you multiply both sides of an inequality by -1, then you change the direction of the inequality.

Suppose that you wish to multiply the inequality $a > b$ by -2. This is the same as multiplying $-a < -b$ by 2, so $-2a < -2b$.

You can also think of multiplying by -2 as reflecting the points corresponding to a and b in the origin, and then multiplying by 2 as an enlargement (see Fig. 1.7).

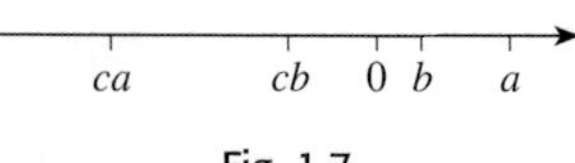

Fig. 1.7

You can summarise this by saying that if you multiply (or divide) both sides of an inequality by a negative number, you must change the direction of the inequality. Thus if $a > b$ and $c < 0$, then $ca < cb$.

Example 1.3.3
Solve the inequality $-3x < 21$.

In this example you need to divide both sides by -3. Remembering to change the direction of the inequality, $-3x < 21$ becomes $x > -7$.

Summary of operations on inequalities
- You can add or subtract a number on both sides of an inequality.
- You can multiply or divide an inequality by a positive number.
- You can multiply or divide an inequality by a negative number, but you must change the direction of the inequality.

Solving inequalities is simply a matter of exploiting these three rules.

You can link the inequality operation involving multiplication with '$+ \times + = +$'. For if $a > b$ and $c > 0$, both $a - b$ and c are positive numbers, so $c(a - b)$ is also positive. So $ca - cb$ is positive, $ca - cb > 0$ and $ca > cb$.

Example 1.3.4
Solve the inequality $3 - \frac{1}{2}x \le 5$.

Begin by subtracting 3 from both sides, to get

$$-\tfrac{1}{2}x \le 2.$$

Now multiply both sides by -2, remembering to change the direction of the inequality. This gives

$$x \ge -4.$$

Example 1.3.5
Solve the inequality $4 - 2x > 3x$.

Begin by adding $2x$ on both sides, to get

$$4 > 5x.$$

Dividing both sides by 5 then gives

$$0.8 > x.$$

The answer is usually written with x on the left side, as

$$x < 0.8.$$

Exercise 1A

1 Which of the number systems $\mathbb{N}$, $\mathbb{Z}$, $\mathbb{Q}$, $\mathbb{R}$, $\mathbb{Z}^+$, $\mathbb{Q}^+$ and $\mathbb{R}^+$ contain the following numbers?

(a) 6 (b) 6.6 (c) 0.666... (continued indefinitely) (d) $\sqrt[3]{125}$

(e) $\sqrt{125}$ (f) 0 (g) $-\pi$ (h) -2

2 State in list form the sets of numbers x which satisfy the following.

(a) $x \in \mathbb{Z}^+$ and $x \le 3$ (b) $x \in \mathbb{N}$ and $2x < 9$ (c) $x \in \mathbb{Z}$ and $-2 \le x < 2$

(d) $x \in \mathbb{N}$ and $3 - x > 1$ (e) $x \in \mathbb{Z}^+$ and $4x - 7 < 9$ (f) $x \in \mathbb{N}$ and $10 - 3x > 1$

3 Solve the following inequalities, where $x \in \mathbb{R}$.

(a) $x - 3 > 11$ (b) $2x + 3 \le 8$ (c) $5x + 6 \le -10$ (d) $3x - 1 \le -13$

(e) $-5x \le 20$ (f) $-3x \ge -12$ (g) $\dfrac{x-4}{6} \le 3$ (h) $\dfrac{3x+2}{5} \le 4$

(i) $\dfrac{5x+1}{3} > -3$ (j) $4 - 3x \le 10$ (k) $2 - 6x \le 0$ (l) $6 - 5x > 1$

(m) $\dfrac{7-3x}{2} < -1$ (n) $x - 4 \le 5 + 2x$ (o) $2x + 5 < 4x - 7$ (p) $4x \le 3(2 - x)$

(q) $3x \ge 5 - 2(3 - x)$

1.4 Modulus notation

Suppose that you want to find the difference between the heights of two children. With numerical information, the answer is quite straightforward: if their heights are 90 cm and 100 cm, you would answer 10 cm; and if their heights were 100 cm and 90 cm, you would still answer 10 cm.

But how would you answer the question if their heights were H cm and h cm? The answer is, it depends which is bigger: if $H > h$, you would answer $(H - h)$ cm; if $h > H$ you would answer $(h - H)$ cm; and if $h = H$ you would answer 0 cm, which is either $(H - h)$ cm or $(h - H)$ cm.

Questions like this, in which you want an answer which is always positive or zero, lead to the idea of the modulus of a number. This is a quantity which tells you the 'size' of a number regardless of its sign. For example, the modulus of 15 is 15, but the modulus of -15 is also 15.

The notation for modulus is to write the number between a pair of vertical lines. So you would write $|15| = 15$ and $|-15| = 15$.

The modulus is sometimes called the 'absolute value' of the number. Some calculators have a key marked 'abs' which produces the modulus. If yours has, try using it with a variety of inputs.

The modulus can be defined formally like this:

The **modulus** of x, written $|x|$ and pronounced 'mod x', is defined by

$$|x| = x \qquad \text{if } x \geq 0,$$
$$|x| = -x \qquad \text{if } x < 0.$$

Using the modulus notation, you can now write the difference in heights as $|H - h|$ whether $H > h$, $h > H$ or $h = H$.

Another situation when the modulus is useful is when you talk about numbers which are large numerically, but which are negative, such as -1000 or $-1\,000\,000$. These are 'negative numbers with large modulus'.

For example, for large positive values of x, the value of $\frac{1}{x}$ is close to 0. The same is true for negative values of x with large modulus. So you can say that, when $|x|$ is large, $\left|\frac{1}{x}\right|$ is close to zero; or in a numerical example, when $|x| > 1000$, $\left|\frac{1}{x}\right| < 0.001$.

1.5 Modulus on the number line

In Fig. 1.8 A and B are points on a number line with coordinates a and b. How can you express the distance AB in terms of a and b?

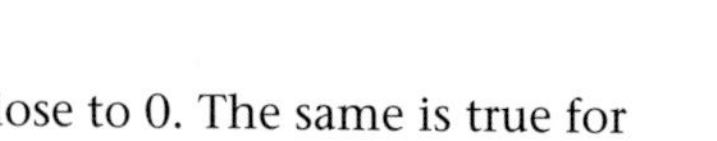

O A B
0 a b

Fig. 1.8

- If B is to the right of A, then $b > a$, so $b - a > 0$ and the distance is $b - a$.
- If B is to the left of A, then $b < a$, so $b - a < 0$ and the distance is $a - b = -(b - a)$.
- If B and A coincide, then $b = a$, so $b - a = 0$ and the distance is 0.

You will recognise this as the definition of $|b - a|$.

> The distance between points on the number line representing numbers a and b is $|b - a|$.

As a special case, if a point X has coordinate x, then $|x|$ is the distance of X from the origin.

Now suppose that $|x| = 3$. What can you say about X?

There are two possibilities: since the distance OX = 3, either X is 3 units to the right of O so that $x = 3$, or X is 3 units to the left of O so that $x = -3$.

This is also true in reverse. If $x = 3$ or $x = -3$, then X is 3 units from O, so $|x| = 3$.

A convenient way of summarising this is to write

$$|x| = 3 \quad \text{means that} \quad x = 3 \ \text{ or } x = -3.$$

Similarly you can write

$$|x| \le 3 \quad \text{as} \quad -3 \le x \le 3,$$

since these are two different ways of saying that X is within 3 units of O on the number line.

In this example there is nothing special about the number 3. You could use the same argument with 3 replaced by any positive number a to show that

$$|x| \le a \quad \text{means that} \quad -a \le x \le a.$$

You can get a useful generalisation by replacing x in this statement by $x - k$, where k is a constant:

$$\text{If } a \text{ is a positive number,} \quad |x - k| \le a \quad \text{means that} \quad -a \le x - k \le a.$$

Now add k to each side of the inequalities $-a \le x - k$ and $x - k \le a$. You then get $k - a \le x$ and $x \le k + a$.

That is,

$$k - a \le x \le k + a.$$

The equivalence then becomes:

> If a is a positive number,
>
> $$|x - k| \le a \quad \text{means that} \quad k - a \le x \le k + a.$$

This result is used when you give a number correct to a certain number of decimal places. For example, to say that $x = 3.87$ 'correct to 2 decimal places' is in effect saying that $|x - 3.87| \le 0.005$.

Fig. 1.9 shows that $|x - 3.87| \le 0.005$ means

$$3.87 - 0.005 \le x \le 3.87 + 0.005,$$

or $$3.865 \le x \le 3.875.$$

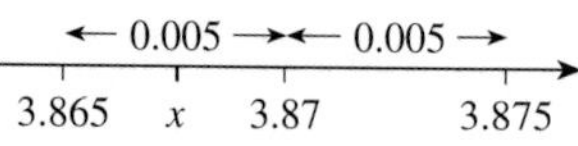

Fig. 1.9

Exercise 1B

1 Write down the values of

(a) $|-6|$, (b) $|13 - 15|$, (c) $|13| + |-15|$.

2 If $|x| > 100$, what can you say about $\frac{1}{x^2}$? Write your answer using inequality notation.

3 The mass of a prize pumpkin is 4.76 kg correct to 2 decimal places. Denoting the mass by m kg, write this statement in mathematical form

(a) without modulus notation, (b) using modulus notation.

4 The length and width of a rectangle are measured as 4.8 cm and 3.6 cm, both correct to 1 decimal place. Write a statement about the perimeter, P cm, in mathematical form

(a) without modulus notation, (b) using modulus notation.

5 Repeat Question 4 for the area, $A\,\text{cm}^2$.

6 Write the given inequalities in an equivalent form of the type $a < x < b$ or $a \le x \le b$.

(a) $|x - 3| < 1$ (b) $|x + 2| \le 0.1$ (c) $|2x - 3| \le 0.001$ (d) $|4x - 3| \le 8$

7 Rewrite the given inequalities using modulus notation.

(a) $1 \le x \le 2$ (b) $-1 < x < 3$ (c) $-3.8 \le x \le -3.5$ (d) $2.3 < x < 3.4$

8 What can you say about $|x|$ if $x \in \mathbb{Z}$?

1.6 Surds and their properties

When you have met expressions such as $\sqrt{2}$, $\sqrt{8}$ and $\sqrt{12}$ before, it is likely that you have used a calculator to express them in decimal form. You might have written

$$\sqrt{2} = 1.414\ldots \text{ or } \sqrt{2} = 1.414 \text{ correct to 3 decimal places or } \sqrt{2} \approx 1.414.$$

Why is the statement '$\sqrt{2} = 1.414$' incorrect?

Expressions like $\sqrt{2}$ or $\sqrt[3]{9}$ are called **surds**. However, expressions like $\sqrt{4}$ or $\sqrt[3]{27}$, which are whole numbers, are not surds.

This section is about calculating with surds. You need to remember that $\sqrt{x}$ always means the **positive** square root of x, or 0 if x is 0.

The main properties that you will use are:

> If x and y are positive numbers, then
>
> $$\sqrt{xy} = \sqrt{x} \times \sqrt{y} \quad \text{and} \quad \sqrt{\frac{x}{y}} = \frac{\sqrt{x}}{\sqrt{y}}.$$

You can use these properties to express square roots like $\sqrt{8}$ and $\sqrt{12}$ in terms of smaller surds:

$$\sqrt{8} = \sqrt{4 \times 2} = \sqrt{4} \times \sqrt{2} = 2\sqrt{2}; \qquad \sqrt{12} = \sqrt{4 \times 3} = \sqrt{4} \times \sqrt{3} = 2\sqrt{3}.$$

You can also simplify products and quotients of square roots:

$$\sqrt{18} \times \sqrt{2} = \sqrt{18 \times 2} = \sqrt{36} = 6; \qquad \frac{\sqrt{27}}{\sqrt{3}} = \sqrt{\frac{27}{3}} = \sqrt{9} = 3.$$

Use a calculator to check the results of these calculations.

Example 1.6.1
Simplify (a) $\sqrt{28} + \sqrt{63}$, (b) $\sqrt{5} \times \sqrt{10}$.

> Notice that alternative methods of solution may be possible, as in part (b).

(a) $$\begin{aligned}\sqrt{28} + \sqrt{63} &= \sqrt{4 \times 7} + \sqrt{9 \times 7} \\ &= (\sqrt{4} \times \sqrt{7}) + (\sqrt{9} \times \sqrt{7}) \\ &= 2\sqrt{7} + 3\sqrt{7} = 5\sqrt{7}.\end{aligned}$$

(b) **Method 1** $$\begin{aligned}\sqrt{5} \times \sqrt{10} &= \sqrt{5 \times 10} = \sqrt{50} \\ &= \sqrt{25 \times 2} = 5\sqrt{2}.\end{aligned}$$

Method 2 $$\begin{aligned}\sqrt{5} \times \sqrt{10} &= \sqrt{5} \times \sqrt{5 \times 2} = \sqrt{5} \times (\sqrt{5} \times \sqrt{2}) \\ &= (\sqrt{5} \times \sqrt{5}) \times \sqrt{2} = 5\sqrt{2}.\end{aligned}$$

Example 1.6.2
Simplify (a) $\dfrac{\sqrt{32}}{\sqrt{2}}$, (b) $(\sqrt{8} - \sqrt{3})(\sqrt{8} + \sqrt{3})$.

(a) **Method 1** $$\begin{aligned}\frac{\sqrt{32}}{\sqrt{2}} &= \frac{\sqrt{2} \times \sqrt{16}}{\sqrt{2}} \\ &= \frac{\sqrt{2} \times 4}{\sqrt{2}} \\ &= 4.\end{aligned}$$

Method 2 $$\begin{aligned}\frac{\sqrt{32}}{\sqrt{2}} &= \sqrt{\frac{32}{2}} \\ &= \sqrt{16} \\ &= 4.\end{aligned}$$

(b) $$\begin{aligned}(\sqrt{8} - \sqrt{3})(\sqrt{8} + \sqrt{3}) &= (\sqrt{8})^2 - (\sqrt{3})^2 \\ &= 8 - 3 = 5.\end{aligned}$$

Example 1.6.2(b) uses the formula for the difference of two squares:

The difference of two squares

$$p^2 - q^2 = (p - q)(p + q).$$

However, it is written with $p = \sqrt{x}$ and $q = \sqrt{y}$, so it appears as

$$x - y = (\sqrt{x} - \sqrt{y})(\sqrt{x} + \sqrt{y}).$$

Similar rules to those for square roots also apply to cube roots and higher roots.

Example 1.6.3

Simplify (a) $\sqrt[3]{16}$, (b) $\sqrt[3]{12} \times \sqrt[3]{18}$.

$$\begin{aligned}\text{(a) } \sqrt[3]{16} &= \sqrt[3]{8 \times 2}\\ &= \sqrt[3]{8} \times \sqrt[3]{2}\\ &= 2 \times \sqrt[3]{2}.\end{aligned}$$

$$\begin{aligned}\text{(b) } \sqrt[3]{12} \times \sqrt[3]{18} &= \sqrt[3]{12 \times 18}\\ &= \sqrt[3]{216}\\ &= 6.\end{aligned}$$

Example 1.6.4

Show that if neither x nor y is equal to 0, then $\sqrt{x + y}$ is never equal to $\sqrt{x} + \sqrt{y}$.

If you square the left side, you get $x + y$.

If you square the right side, you get

$$\begin{aligned}(\sqrt{x} + \sqrt{y})(\sqrt{x} + \sqrt{y}) &= (\sqrt{x})^2 + 2\sqrt{x}\sqrt{y} + (\sqrt{y})^2\\ &= x + 2\sqrt{xy} + y.\end{aligned}$$

But neither x nor y is equal to 0, so xy is not equal to 0, so $\sqrt{xy}$ is not equal to 0.

Hence the square of the left side is less than the square of the right side.

Therefore, if neither x nor y is equal to 0, then $\sqrt{x + y}$ is never equal to $\sqrt{x} + \sqrt{y}$.

It is also true that if neither x nor y is equal to 0, then $\sqrt{x - y}$ is never equal to $\sqrt{x} - \sqrt{y}$.

So beware, and do not be tempted!

If x and y are positive numbers, then

$$\sqrt{x + y} \neq \sqrt{x} + \sqrt{y} \quad \text{and} \quad \sqrt{x - y} \neq \sqrt{x} - \sqrt{y}.$$

Exercise 1C

1 Simplify the following without using a calculator.

(a) $\sqrt{3} \times \sqrt{3}$ (b) $\sqrt{10} \times \sqrt{10}$ (c) $\sqrt{8} \times \sqrt{2}$ (d) $\sqrt{32} \times \sqrt{2}$

(e) $\sqrt{3} \times \sqrt{12}$ (f) $5\sqrt{3} \times \sqrt{3}$ (g) $2\sqrt{5} \times 3\sqrt{5}$ (h) $2\sqrt{20} \times 3\sqrt{5}$

(i) $(2\sqrt{7})^2$ (j) $(3\sqrt{3})^2$ (k) $\sqrt[3]{5} \times \sqrt[3]{5} \times \sqrt[3]{5}$ (l) $(2\sqrt[4]{3})^4$

2 Write the following in the form $a\sqrt{b}$.

(a) $\sqrt{18}$ (b) $\sqrt{20}$ (c) $\sqrt{24}$ (d) $\sqrt{32}$

(e) $\sqrt{40}$ (f) $\sqrt{45}$ (g) $\sqrt{48}$ (h) $\sqrt{50}$

3 Simplify the following without using a calculator.

(a) $\sqrt{8}+\sqrt{18}$ (b) $\sqrt{3}+\sqrt{12}$ (c) $\sqrt{20}-\sqrt{5}$

(d) $\sqrt{32}-\sqrt{8}$ (e) $\sqrt{50}-\sqrt{18}-\sqrt{8}$ (f) $2\sqrt{20}+3\sqrt{45}$

4 Simplify the following without using a calculator.

(a) $\dfrac{\sqrt{8}}{\sqrt{2}}$ (b) $\dfrac{\sqrt{27}}{\sqrt{3}}$ (c) $\dfrac{\sqrt{40}}{\sqrt{10}}$ (d) $\dfrac{\sqrt{50}}{\sqrt{2}}$

(e) $\dfrac{\sqrt{125}}{\sqrt{5}}$ (f) $\dfrac{\sqrt{54}}{\sqrt{6}}$ (g) $\dfrac{\sqrt{3}}{\sqrt{48}}$ (h) $\dfrac{\sqrt{50}}{\sqrt{200}}$

5 Simplify

(a) $(\sqrt{2}-1)(\sqrt{2}+1)$, (b) $(3-\sqrt{2})(3+\sqrt{2})$,

(c) $(\sqrt{7}+\sqrt{3})(\sqrt{7}-\sqrt{3})$, (d) $(2\sqrt{2}+1)(2\sqrt{2}-1)$,

(e) $(4\sqrt{3}-\sqrt{2})(4\sqrt{3}+\sqrt{2})$, (f) $(\sqrt{10}+\sqrt{5})(\sqrt{10}-\sqrt{5})$,

(g) $(4\sqrt{7}-\sqrt{5})(4\sqrt{7}+\sqrt{5})$, (h) $(2\sqrt{6}-3\sqrt{3})(2\sqrt{6}+3\sqrt{3})$.

1.7 Rationalising denominators

If you are using a calculator, then it is easy to calculate $\dfrac{1}{\sqrt{2}}$ directly. But without a calculator, if you know that $\sqrt{2}=1.414\,213\,562\ldots$, finding $\dfrac{1}{\sqrt{2}}$ as a decimal is a very unpleasant calculation.

Calculating $\dfrac{1}{\sqrt{2}}$ can be greatly simplified by multiplying top and bottom by $\sqrt{2}$, giving

$$\frac{1}{\sqrt{2}}=\frac{1}{\sqrt{2}}\times\frac{\sqrt{2}}{\sqrt{2}}=\frac{1\times\sqrt{2}}{\sqrt{2}\times\sqrt{2}}=\frac{\sqrt{2}}{2}.$$

Using this, from $\sqrt{2}=1.414\,213\,562\ldots$ you can find at once that

$$\frac{1}{\sqrt{2}}=0.707\,106\,781\ldots.$$

You can see that the result $\dfrac{1}{\sqrt{2}}=\dfrac{\sqrt{2}}{2}$ is just another way of writing $\sqrt{2}\times\sqrt{2}=2$.

Generalising, you can deduce the following:

> To remove the surd $\sqrt{x}$ from the denominator of a fraction, multiply by $\dfrac{\sqrt{x}}{\sqrt{x}}$ to get
>
> $$\frac{1}{\sqrt{x}}\times\frac{\sqrt{x}}{\sqrt{x}}=\frac{\sqrt{x}}{x}.$$

Removing the surd from the denominator is called **rationalising the denominator**.

Example 1.7.1

Rationalise the denominator in the expressions (a) $\dfrac{6}{\sqrt{2}}$, (b) $\dfrac{3\sqrt{2}}{\sqrt{10}}$, (c) $\dfrac{2}{3\sqrt{2}}$.

(a) $\dfrac{6}{\sqrt{2}} = \dfrac{6}{\sqrt{2}} \times \dfrac{\sqrt{2}}{\sqrt{2}} = \dfrac{6 \times \sqrt{2}}{\sqrt{2} \times \sqrt{2}} = \dfrac{6\sqrt{2}}{2} = 3\sqrt{2}.$

(b) **Method 1** $\dfrac{3\sqrt{2}}{\sqrt{10}} = 3\sqrt{\dfrac{2}{10}} = \dfrac{3}{\sqrt{5}} = \dfrac{3}{\sqrt{5}} \times \dfrac{\sqrt{5}}{\sqrt{5}} = \dfrac{3\sqrt{5}}{5}.$

Method 2 $\dfrac{3\sqrt{2}}{\sqrt{10}} = \dfrac{3\sqrt{2}}{\sqrt{10}} \times \dfrac{\sqrt{10}}{\sqrt{10}} = \dfrac{3\sqrt{2} \times \sqrt{10}}{\sqrt{10} \times \sqrt{10}}$

$= \dfrac{3\sqrt{20}}{10} = \dfrac{3\sqrt{4} \times \sqrt{5}}{10} = \dfrac{6\sqrt{5}}{10} = \dfrac{3\sqrt{5}}{5}.$

(c) $\dfrac{2}{3\sqrt{2}} \times \dfrac{\sqrt{2}}{\sqrt{2}} = \dfrac{2\sqrt{2}}{3\sqrt{2} \times \sqrt{2}} = \dfrac{2\sqrt{2}}{3 \times 2} = \dfrac{\sqrt{2}}{3}.$

Expressions like those in parts (b) and (c) are often written in the form $\frac{3}{5}\sqrt{5}$, $\frac{1}{3}\sqrt{2}$.

Calculating with surds using these rules is often useful in geometry, especially when Pythagoras' theorem is involved.

Example 1.7.2

Fig. 1.10 shows the vertical cross-section of a roof of a building as a right-angled triangle ABC, with AB = 15 m. The height of the roof, BD, is 10 m.

Calculate (a) z, (b) cos DÂB, (c) x, (d) y.

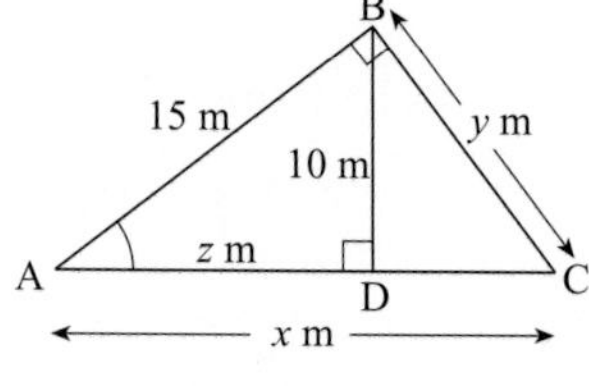

Fig. 1.10

(a) Use Pythagoras' theorem in triangle ADB.

$$z^2 + 10^2 = 15^2,$$
$$z^2 = 225 - 100 = 125,$$
$$z = \sqrt{125} = \sqrt{25 \times 5} = 5\sqrt{5}.$$

(b) In triangle ADB,

$$\cos D\hat{A}B = \frac{AD}{AB} = \frac{z}{15} = \frac{5\sqrt{5}}{15} = \frac{\sqrt{5}}{3}.$$

(c) Angle BÂC in triangle ABC is the same as angle DÂB in triangle ADB. So, in triangle ABC,

$$\frac{AB}{AC} = \cos B\hat{A}C = \cos D\hat{A}B = \frac{\sqrt{5}}{3}.$$

That is,

$$\frac{15}{x} = \frac{\sqrt{5}}{3}.$$

Multiplying both sides of the equation by $3x$,

$$45 = x \times \sqrt{5},$$

$$x = \frac{45}{\sqrt{5}} = \frac{9 \times 5}{\sqrt{5}} = 9 \times \sqrt{5} = 9\sqrt{5}.$$

(d) Use Pythagoras' theorem in triangle ABC.

$$15^2 + y^2 = (9\sqrt{5})^2,$$

$$y^2 = 81 \times 5 - 15^2 = 405 - 225 = 180.$$

So $\quad y = \sqrt{180} = \sqrt{36 \times 5} = 6\sqrt{5}.$

Exercise 1D

1 Rationalise the denominator in each of the following expressions, and simplify them.

(a) $\frac{1}{\sqrt{3}}$ (b) $\frac{1}{\sqrt{5}}$ (c) $\frac{4}{\sqrt{2}}$ (d) $\frac{6}{\sqrt{6}}$

(e) $\frac{11}{\sqrt{11}}$ (f) $\frac{2}{\sqrt{8}}$ (g) $\frac{12}{\sqrt{3}}$ (h) $\frac{14}{\sqrt{7}}$

(i) $\frac{\sqrt{6}}{\sqrt{2}}$ (j) $\frac{\sqrt{2}}{\sqrt{6}}$ (k) $\frac{3\sqrt{5}}{\sqrt{3}}$ (l) $\frac{4\sqrt{6}}{\sqrt{5}}$

2 ABCD is a rectangle in which $AB = 4\sqrt{5}$ cm and $BC = \sqrt{10}$ cm. Giving each answer in simplified surd form, find

(a) the area of the rectangle, (b) the length of the diagonal AC.

3 You are given that, correct to 12 decimal places, $\sqrt{26} = 5.099\,019\,513\,593$. Find

(a) $\sqrt{104}$, (b) $\sqrt{650}$, (c) $\frac{13}{\sqrt{26}}$, each correct to 10 decimal places.

4 Find the length of the third side in each of the following right-angled triangles, giving each answer in simplified surd form.

(a)

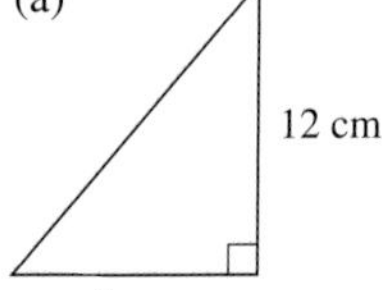

(b)

10√2 cm

5√3 cm

(c)

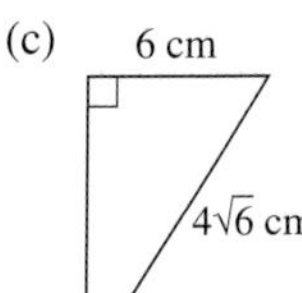

(d)

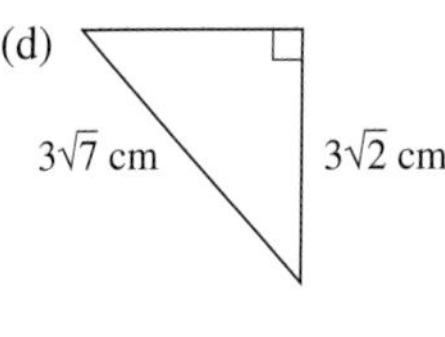

2 Sequences

This chapter is about sequences of numbers. When you have completed it, you should

- know that a sequence can be constructed from a formula or an inductive definition
- be familiar with triangle and arithmetic sequences
- know how to find the sum of an arithmetic series
- know how to use a graphic display calculator to find terms of sequences and sums of series
- be able to use sigma notation.

From here on 'calculator' is taken to mean 'graphic display calculator'.

2.1 Constructing sequences

Here are six rows of numbers, each forming a pattern of some kind. What are the next three numbers in each row?

(a) 1, 4, 9, 16, 25, ... (b) $\frac{1}{2}$, $\frac{2}{3}$, $\frac{3}{4}$, $\frac{4}{5}$, $\frac{5}{6}$, ...

(c) 99, 97, 95, 93, 91, ... (d) 1, 1.1, 1.21, 1.331, 1.4641, ...

(e) 2, 4, 8, 14, 22, ... (f) 3, 1, 4, 1, 5, ...

Rows of this kind are called **sequences**, and the separate numbers are called **terms**.

The usual notation for the first, second, third, ... terms of a sequence is u_1, u_2, u_3, and so on. If n is a positive integer, then the nth term is written as u_n. In this notation, the letter n is called a **suffix**.

In (a) and (b) you would have no difficulty in writing a formula for the nth term of the sequence. The numbers in (a) could be rewritten as 1^2, 2^2, 3^2, 4^2, 5^2, and the pattern could be summed up by writing

$$u_n = n^2.$$

The terms of (b) are $\frac{1}{1+1}, \frac{2}{2+1}, \frac{3}{3+1}, \frac{4}{4+1}, \frac{5}{5+1}$, so $u_n = \frac{n}{n+1}$.

In (c), (d) and (e) you probably expect that there is a formula, but it is not so easy to find it. What is more obvious is how to get each term from the one before. For example, in (c) the terms go down by 2 at each step, so that $u_2 = u_1 - 2$, $u_3 = u_2 - 2$, $u_4 = u_3 - 2$, and so on. These steps can be summarised by the single equation

$$u_n = u_{n-1} - 2.$$

The terms in (d) are multiplied by 1.1 at each step, so the rule is

$$u_n = 1.1u_{n-1}.$$

Unfortunately, there are many other sequences which satisfy the equation $u_n = u_{n-1} - 2$. Other examples are 10, 8, 6, 4, 2, ... and −2, −4, −6, −8, −10, ...

The definition is not complete until you know the first term. So to complete the definitions of the sequences (c) and (d) you have to write

(c) $u_1 = 99$ and $u_n = u_{n-1} - 2$,

(d) $u_1 = 1$ and $u_n = 1.1u_{n-1}$.

Definitions like these are called **inductive definitions**, or sometimes 'recursive defintions'.

Sequence (e) comes from geometry. It gives the greatest number of regions into which a plane can be split by different numbers of circles. (Try drawing your own diagrams with 1, 2, 3, 4, ... circles.) This sequence is developed as $u_2 = u_1 + 2$, $u_3 = u_2 + 4$, $u_4 = u_3 + 6$, and so on. You will see that the increases 2, 4, 6, ... are themselves double the suffixes on the right of each equation; thus $u_2 = u_1 + 2 \times 1$, $u_3 = u_2 + 2 \times 2$, $u_4 = u_3 + 2 \times 3$, and so on. These equations can be summarised by the inductive definition

$$u_1 = 2 \text{ and } u_n = u_{n-1} + 2(n-1).$$

For (f) you may have given the next three terms as 1, 6, 1 (expecting the even-placed terms all to be 1, and the odd-placed terms to go up by 1 at each step). In fact this sequence had a quite different origin, as the first five digits of π in decimal form! With this meaning, the next three terms would be 9, 2, 6.

This illustrates an important point, that a sequence can never be uniquely defined by giving just the first few terms. Try, for example, working out the first eight terms of the sequence defined by

$$u_n = n^2 + (n-1)(n-2)(n-3)(n-4)(n-5).$$

You will find that the first five terms are the same as those given in (a), but the next three are probably very different from your original guess.

A sequence can only be described unambiguously by giving a formula, an inductive definition in terms of a general natural number n, or some other general rule.

> There is nothing special about the choice of the letter u for a sequence. Other letters such as v, x, t and I are often used instead, especially if the sequence appears in some application. The nth term is then v_n, x_n, t_n or I_n.
>
> You will also sometimes find different letters used in place of n for the suffix. The most common alternatives are i and r, so that a term of the sequence may be written as u_i or u_r.
>
> Sometimes it is convenient to number the terms u_0, u_1, u_2, ... , starting with $n = 0$, but you then have to be careful in referring to 'the first term': do you mean u_0 or u_1?

2.2 Sequences on a calculator

If you know the definition of a sequence, your calculator can produce a table of values of u_n for different values of n.

- If the sequence is defined by a formula, you will have to enter the formula for u_n and the first value of n for which the value is required.
- If the definition is inductive, you will also have to enter the value of the first term of the sequence.

The actual key sequence varies for different calculators, so you will need to consult the instruction manual for your particular model.

Exercise 2A

1 Write down the first five terms of the sequences with the following definitions.

(a) $u_1 = 7, \quad u_n = u_{n-1} + 7$ (b) $u_1 = 13, \quad u_n = u_{n-1} - 5$

(c) $u_1 = 4, \quad u_n = 3u_{n-1}$ (d) $u_1 = 6, \quad u_n = \frac{1}{2}u_{n-1}$

(e) $u_1 = 2, \quad u_n = 3u_{n-1} + 1$ (f) $u_1 = 1, \quad u_n = u_{n-1}{}^2 + 3$

Use a calculator to check your answers.

2 Suggest inductive definitions which would produce the following sequences.

(a) $2, \quad 4, \quad 6, \quad 8, \quad 10, \quad \ldots$ (b) $11, \quad 9, \quad 7, \quad 5, \quad 3, \quad \ldots$

(c) $2, \quad 6, \quad 10, \quad 14, \quad 18, \quad \ldots$ (d) $2, \quad 6, \quad 18, \quad 54, \quad 162, \quad \ldots$

(e) $\frac{1}{3}, \quad \frac{1}{9}, \quad \frac{1}{27}, \quad \frac{1}{81}, \quad \ldots$ (f) $\frac{1}{2}a, \quad \frac{1}{4}a, \quad \frac{1}{8}a, \quad \frac{1}{16}a, \quad \ldots$

(g) $1, \quad -1, \quad 1, \quad -1, \quad 1, \quad \ldots$ (h) $1, \quad 1+x, \quad (1+x)^2, \quad (1+x)^3, \quad \ldots$

Use a calculator to check your answers to parts (a) to (d).

3 Write down the first five terms of each sequence and give an inductive definition for it.

(a) $u_n = 2n + 3$ (b) $u_n = n^2$ (c) $u_n = \frac{1}{2}n(n+1)$

(d) $u_n = \frac{1}{6}n(n+1)(2n+1)$ (e) $u_n = 2 \times 3^n$ (f) $u_n = \frac{3}{5} \times 5^n$

Use a calculator to show that the given formula and your inductive definition give the same table of values.

4 For each of the following sequences give a possible formula for the nth term.

(a) $9, \quad 8, \quad 7, \quad 6, \quad \ldots$ (b) $6, \quad 18, \quad 54, \quad 162, \quad \ldots$

(c) $4, \quad 7, \quad 12, \quad 19, \quad \ldots$ (d) $4, \quad 12, \quad 24, \quad 40, \quad 60, \quad \ldots$

(e) $\frac{1}{4}, \quad \frac{3}{5}, \quad \frac{5}{6}, \quad \frac{7}{7}, \quad \ldots$ (f) $\frac{2}{2}, \quad \frac{5}{4}, \quad \frac{10}{8}, \quad \frac{17}{16}, \quad \ldots$

2.3 The triangle number sequence

The numbers of crosses in the triangular patterns in Fig. 2.1 are called triangle numbers. If t_n denotes the nth triangle number, you can see by counting the numbers of crosses in successive rows that

$$t_1 = 1, \quad t_2 = 1 + 2 = 3, \quad t_3 = 1 + 2 + 3 = 6,$$

Fig. 2.1

and in general $t_n = 1 + 2 + 3 + \ldots + n$, where the dots indicate that all the positive integers between 3 and n have to be included in the addition.

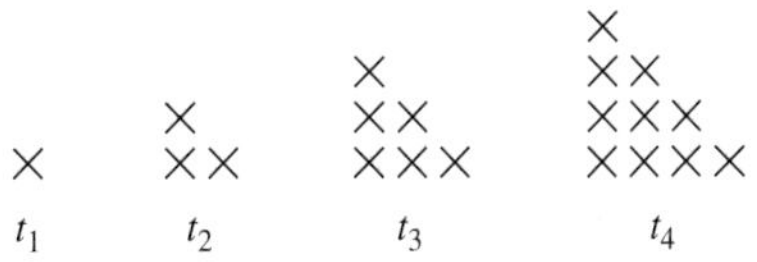

Fig. 2.2 shows a typical pattern of crosses forming a triangle number t_n. (It is in fact drawn for $n = 8$, but any other value of n could have been chosen.) An easy way of finding a formula for t_n is to make a similar pattern of 'noughts', and then to turn it upside down and place it alongside the pattern of crosses, as in Fig. 2.3. The noughts and crosses together then make a rectangular pattern, $n + 1$ objects wide and n objects high. So the total number of objects is $n(n + 1)$, half of them crosses and half noughts. The number of crosses alone is therefore

$$t_n = \tfrac{1}{2}n(n + 1).$$

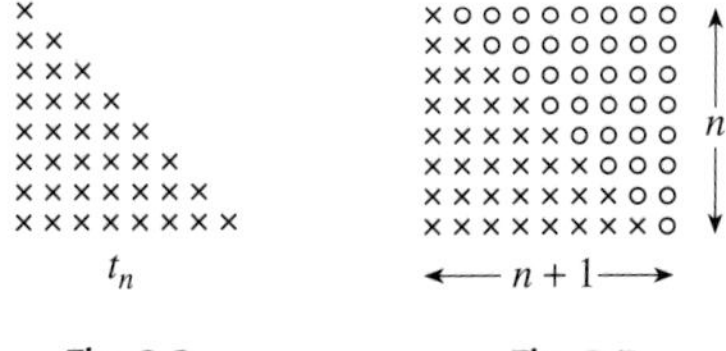

Fig. 2.2 Fig. 2.3

This shows that:

> The sum of all the positive integers from 1 to n is $\frac{1}{2}n(n + 1)$.

Example 2.3.1
Find (a) the sum of the first 50 positive integers,
(b) the sum of the positive integers from 31 to 50 inclusive,
(c) the sum of the first 30 even numbers.

(a) Using the result in the box, the sum of the first 50 positive integers is

$$1 + 2 + \ldots + 50 = \tfrac{1}{2} \times 50 \times (50 + 1) = 25 \times 51 = 1275.$$

(b) Using an 'add and subtract method',

$$\begin{aligned} 31 + 32 + \ldots + 50 &= (1 + 2 + \ldots + 50) - (1 + 2 + \ldots + 30) \\ &= 1275 - \tfrac{1}{2} \times 30 \times (30 + 1) \\ &= 1275 - 15 \times 31 = 810. \end{aligned}$$

(c) The 30th even number is 60, so

$$\begin{aligned} 2+4+\ldots+60 &= 2(1+2+\ldots+30) \\ &= 2 \times \tfrac{1}{2} \times 30 \times (30+1) \\ &= 30 \times 31 = 930. \end{aligned}$$

You can put the geometric argument which gives the result in the box into algebraic form. If you count the crosses in Fig. 2.2 from the top downwards you get

$$t_n = 1 + 2 + 3 + \ldots + (n-2) + (n-1) + n.$$

But if you count the noughts from the top downwards you get

$$t_n = n + (n-1) + (n-2) + \ldots + 3 + 2 + 1.$$

Counting all the objects in the rectangle is equivalent to adding these two equations:

$$2t_n = (n+1) + (n+1) + (n+1) + \ldots + (n+1) + (n+1) + (n+1),$$

with one $(n+1)$ bracket for each of the n rows. It follows that $2t_n = n(n+1)$, so that

$$t_n = \tfrac{1}{2}n(n+1).$$

It is also possible to give an inductive definition for the sequence t_n. Fig. 2.1 shows that to get from any triangle number to the next you simply add an extra row of crosses underneath. Thus $t_2 = t_1 + 2$, $t_3 = t_2 + 3$, $t_4 = t_3 + 4$, and in general

$$t_n = t_{n-1} + n.$$

You can complete this definition by starting either with $t_1 = 1$ or $t_0 = 0$. If you choose $t_0 = 0$, then you can find t_1 by putting $n = 1$ in the general equation, as $t_1 = t_0 + 1 = 0 + 1 = 1$. So you may as well define the triangle number sequence by

$$t_0 = 0 \quad \text{and} \quad t_n = t_{n-1} + n, \quad \text{where } n = 1, 2, 3, \ldots .$$

Exercise 2B

1 Calculate

(a) $1 + 2 +$ (all the integers up to) $+ 40$,

(b) $21 + 22 +$ (all the integers up to) $+ 40$,

(c) $2 + 4 +$ (all the even integers up to) $+ 40$,

(d) $1 + 3 +$ (all the odd integers up to) $+ 39$.

2 Using Fig. 2.3 as an example,

(a) draw a pattern of crosses to represent the nth triangle number t_n,

(b) draw another pattern of noughts to represent t_{n-1},

(c) combine these two patterns to show that $t_n + t_{n-1} = n^2$.

(d) Use the fact that $t_n = \tfrac{1}{2}n(n+1)$ to show the result in part (c) algebraically.

3 (a) Find an expression in terms of n for $t_n - t_{n-1}$ for all $n \geq 1$.

(b) Use this result and that in Question 2(c) to show that $t_n^2 - t_{n-1}^2 = n^3$.

(c) Use part (b) to write expressions in terms of triangle numbers for $1^3, 2^3, 3^3, \ldots, n^3$.

Hence show that $1^3 + 2^3 + 3^3 + \ldots + n^3 = \frac{1}{4}n^2(n+1)^2$.

2.4 Arithmetic sequences

An **arithmetic sequence**, or **arithmetic progression**, is a sequence whose terms go up or down by constant steps.

Here are some examples.

(a) 1, 3, 5, 7, 9, ... (b) 2, 5, 8, 11, 14, ...

(c) 99, 97, 95, 93, 91, ... (d) 3, 1.5, 0, −1.5, −3, ...

It is easy to write down inductive definitions for these sequences. In sequence (a), for example, the step from each term to the next is +2. You can write this as an equation, $u_n = u_{n-1} + 2$. You also need to state that the first term, u_1, is 1. The complete definition is then

$$u_1 = 1, \quad u_n = u_{n-1} + 2.$$

Check for yourself that the other three sequences have inductive definitions

(b) $u_1 = 2, \quad u_n = u_{n-1} + 3,$

(c) $u_1 = 99, \quad u_n = u_{n-1} - 2,$

(d) $u_1 = 3, \quad u_n = u_{n-1} - 1.5.$

You will see that these definitions all have the form

$$u_1 = a, \quad u_n = u_{n-1} + d$$

for different values of a and d. The letter a is usually chosen for the first term of the sequence. The step d is called the **common difference**.

Example 2.4.1
An arithmetic sequence is defined by

$$u_1 = 5, \quad u_n = u_{n-1} + 7.$$

Find (a) the fifth term, (b) the fiftieth term.

(a) It is simple to count up

$$u_2 = u_1 + 7 = 5 + 7 = 12, \quad u_3 = u_2 + 7 = 12 + 7 = 19,$$
$$u_4 = u_3 + 7 = 19 + 7 = 26, \quad u_5 = u_4 + 7 = 26 + 7 = 33.$$

The fifth term of the sequence is 33.

(b) You certainly wouldn't want to carry on as in part (a) until you reach u_{50}. It is simpler to note that, in going from the first term to the fiftieth, you have to add 7 on 49 times. So

$$u_{50} = u_1 + 49 \times 7 = 5 + 343 = 348.$$

The fiftieth term of the sequence is 348.

The method used in part (b) of Example 2.4.1 can be applied to any sequence with first term a and common difference d to find a formula for u_n, the nth term. In going from the first term to the nth term you have to add the step d on $(n-1)$ times. Since the first term is a, the nth term is

$$u_n = a + (n-1)d.$$

> An arithmetic sequence with first term a and common difference d is defined inductively by
>
> $$u_1 = a, \quad u_n = u_{n-1} + d.$$
>
> The nth term of the sequence is given by
>
> $$u_n = a + (n-1)d.$$

Example 2.4.2
The 10th term of the sequence (b) at the beginning of this section is also a term of the sequence (c). Which term is it?

For the sequence (b), $a = 2$ and $d = 3$, so the 10th term is

$$2 + (10-1) \times 3 = 2 + 27 = 29.$$

For the sequence (c), $a = 99$ and $d = -2$, so the nth term is

$$\begin{aligned} 99 + (n-1) \times (-2) &= 99 - 2n + 2 \\ &= 101 - 2n. \end{aligned}$$

This has to equal 29, so

$$101 - 2n = 29,$$

giving

$$n = 36.$$

The 10th term of sequence (b) is the 36th term of sequence (c).

Example 2.4.3
The 12th term of an arithmetic sequence is 23 and the 19th term is 65. Find the first term and the common difference.

You can either reason this out arithmetically or use algebra, whichever you prefer.

Method 1 In getting from the 12th term to the 19th you take 7 steps of the common difference. In doing this the terms increase by 65 – 23, which is 42. So each step is of amount $42 \div 7$, which is 6.

Therefore, in getting from the first term to the 12th the terms increase by 11 steps of 6, a total increase of 66. So the first term is $23 - 66 = -43$.

Method 2 Let the first term be a and the common difference d. Then, using the formula for the nth term,

$$a + (12 - 1)d = 23 \quad \text{and} \quad a + (19 - 1)d = 65.$$

So a and d can be found from the simultaneous equations

$$a + 11d = 23,$$
$$a + 18d = 65.$$

Subtracting the first equation from the second,

$$7d = 42,$$

which gives $d = 6$. Substituting this in the first equation gives

$$a + 11 \times 6 = 23,$$

so $a = -43$.

The first term is -43 and the common difference is 6.

Example 2.4.4
A person who usually eats 600 grams of bread a day tries to lose weight by reducing his consumption by 15 grams each day. After how many days will his consumption be less than 200 grams?

After 1, 2, 3, ... days his consumption (in grams) will be 585, 570, 555, ... This is an arithmetic sequence with first term $a = 585$ and common difference $d = -15$. Using the formula, his consumption on the nth day will be

$$\begin{aligned} 585 + (n - 1) \times (-15) &= 585 - 15(n - 1) \\ &= 600 - 15n. \end{aligned}$$

The questions asks for the smallest value of n for which this is less than 200. This is found by solving the inequality

$$600 - 15n < 200,$$

which gives

$$\begin{aligned}-15n &< 200 - 600 \\ &= -400.\end{aligned}$$

Dividing both sides by -15, remembering to change the direction of the inequality,

$$n > \frac{-400}{-15} = 26\tfrac{2}{3}.$$

The smallest integer value for n for which this is true is 27.

He will get his consumption down below 200 grams after 27 days.

2.5 Finding the sum of arithmetic series

Example 2.5.1

Sarah would like to give a sum of money to a charity each year for 10 years. She decides to give \$100 in the first year, and to increase her contribution by \$20 each year. How much does she give in the last year, and how much does the charity receive from her altogether?

Although she makes 10 contributions, there are only 9 increases. So in the last year she gives $\$(100 + 9 \times 20) = \$280$.

If the total amount the charity receives is $\$S$, then

$$S = 100 + 120 + 140 + ... + 240 + 260 + 280.$$

With only 10 numbers it is easy enough to add these up, but you can also find the sum by a method similar to that used in Section 2.3 to find a formula for t_n. If you add up the numbers in reverse order, you get

$$S = 280 + 260 + 240 + ... + 140 + 120 + 100.$$

Adding the two equations then gives

$$2S = 380 + 380 + 380 + ... + 380 + 380 + 380,$$

where the number 380 occurs 10 times. So

$$2S = 380 \times 10 = 3800, \text{ giving } S = 1900.$$

Over the 10 years the charity receives \$1900.

This calculation can be illustrated with diagrams similar to Figs. 2.2 and 2.3. Sarah's contributions are shown by Fig. 2.4, with the first year in the top row. (Each cross is worth \$20.) In Fig. 2.5 a second copy, with noughts instead of crosses, is put alongside it, but turned upside down. There are then 10 rows, each with 19 crosses or noughts and worth \$380.

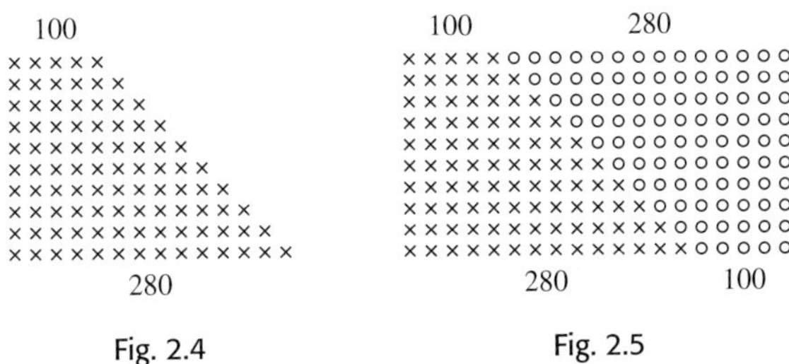

Fig. 2.4

Fig. 2.5

Two features of Example 2.5.1 are typical of arithmetic progressions.

- They usually only continue for a finite number of terms.
- It is often interesting to know the sum of all the terms. In this case, it is usual to describe the sequence as a **series**.

In Example 2.5.1, the annual contributions

$$100, 120, 140, \dots, 240, 260, 280$$

form an arithmetic sequence, but if they are added as

$$100 + 120 + 140 + \dots + 240 + 260 + 280$$

they become an **arithmetic series**.

You can use a method similar to that in Example 2.5.1 to find a formula for the sum of any arithmetic series with first term a and common difference d.

Suppose that the general arithmetic sequence

$$a,\ a + d,\ a + 2d,\ a + 3d, \dots$$

has n terms in all. Denote the last term, u_n, by l. Then you know that

$$l = a + (n - 1)\,d.$$

From this equation you can calculate any one of the four quantities a, l, n, d if you know the other three.

Let S be the sum of the arithmetic series formed by adding these terms. Then it is possible to find a formula for S in terms of a, n and either d or l.

Method 1 This generalises the argument used in Example 2.5.1.

If the last term is l, the last but one term is $l - d$, and the term before that is $l - 2d$. So the series can be written as

$$S = \quad a \quad + (a + d) + (a + 2d) + \dots + (l - 2d) + (l - d) + l.$$

Turning this back to front,

$$S = \quad l \quad + (l - d) + (l - 2d) + \dots + (a + 2d) + (a + d) + a.$$

Adding these,

$$2S = (a + l) + (a + l) + (a + l) + ... + (a + l) + (a + l) + (a + l),$$

where the bracket $(a + l)$ occurs n times. So

$$2S = n(a + l), \text{ which gives } S = \tfrac{1}{2}n(a + l).$$

Method 2 This uses the formula for triangle numbers found in Section 2.3.

In the series

$$S = a + (a + d) + (a + 2d) + ... + (a + (n - 1)d)$$

you can collect separately the terms involving a and those involving d:

$$S = (a + a + ... + a) + (1 + 2 + 3 + ... + (n - 1))d.$$

In the first bracket a occurs n times. The second bracket is the sum of the positive integers from 1 to $n - 1$, or t_{n-1}; using the formula $t_n = \frac{1}{2}n(n + 1)$ with n replaced by $n - 1$ gives this sum as

$$\begin{aligned} t_{n-1} &= \tfrac{1}{2}(n - 1)((n - 1) + 1) \\ &= \tfrac{1}{2}(n - 1)n. \end{aligned}$$

Therefore

$$\begin{aligned} S &= na + \tfrac{1}{2}(n - 1)nd \\ &= \tfrac{1}{2}n(2a + (n - 1)d). \end{aligned}$$

Since $l = a + (n - 1)d$, this is the same answer as that given by Method 1.

Here is a summary of the results about arithmetic series.

> An arithmetic series of n terms with first term a and common difference d has nth term
>
> $$l = a + (n - 1)d$$
>
> and sum
>
> $$S = \tfrac{1}{2}n(a + l) = \tfrac{1}{2}n(2a + (n - 1)d).$$

Example 2.5.2
Find a formula for the nth term and the sum of n terms for the arithmetic sequence 1, 4, 7, 10, 13, ...

In this sequence $a = 1$ and $d = 3$.

Using the formulae in the blue box,

the nth term is $1 + (n - 1) \times 3 = 3n - 2$,
the sum of n terms is $\frac{1}{2}n(2 \times 1 + (n - 1) \times 3) = \frac{1}{2}n(2 + 3n - 3) = \frac{1}{2}n(3n - 1)$.

It is worth checking the sum by putting n equal to a small number, say 3. In that case you can check whether the answer gives $1 + 4 + 7 = 12$.

Example 2.5.3
The first two terms of an arithmetic sequence are 4 and 2. The nth term is -36. Find the number of terms.

For this sequence, $a = 4$ and $d = -2$.

Using the formula for the nth term, $l = a + (n - 1)d$,

$$\begin{aligned} -36 &= 4 + (n - 1) \times (-2) \\ -36 &= 4 - 2n + 2 \\ -36 &= 6 - 2n \\ n &= 21. \end{aligned}$$

The sequence has 21 terms.

Example 2.5.4
Find the sum of the first n odd positive integers.

Method 1 The odd numbers 1, 3, 5, ... form an arithmetic series with first term $a = 1$ and common difference $d = 2$. So

$$\begin{aligned} S &= \tfrac{1}{2}n(2a + (n - 1)d) \\ &= \tfrac{1}{2}n(2 + (n - 1) \times 2), \\ &= \tfrac{1}{2}n(2n) = n^2. \end{aligned}$$

Method 2 Take the positive integers from 1 to $2n$, and remove the n even numbers $2, 4, 6, \ldots, 2n$. You are left with the first n odd numbers.

To find the sum of the numbers from 1 to $2n$, use the formula $t_n = \frac{1}{2}n(n + 1)$ with n replaced by $2n$; that is,

$$\begin{aligned} t_{2n} &= \tfrac{1}{2}(2n)(2n + 1) \\ &= n(2n + 1). \end{aligned}$$

The sum of the n even numbers is

$$\begin{aligned} 2 + 4 + 6 + \ldots + 2n &= 2(1 + 2 + 3 + \ldots + n) \\ &= 2t_n \\ &= n(n + 1). \end{aligned}$$

So the sum of the first n odd numbers is

$$\begin{aligned} n(2n + 1) - n(n + 1) &= n((2n + 1) - (n + 1)) \\ &= n(n) \\ &= n^2. \end{aligned}$$

Method 3 Fig. 2.6 shows a square of n rows with n crosses in each row (drawn for $n = 7$).

You can count the crosses in the square by adding the numbers in the 'channels' between the dotted L-shaped lines, which gives

$$n^2 = 1 + 3 + 5 + \ldots \text{ (to } n \text{ terms).}$$

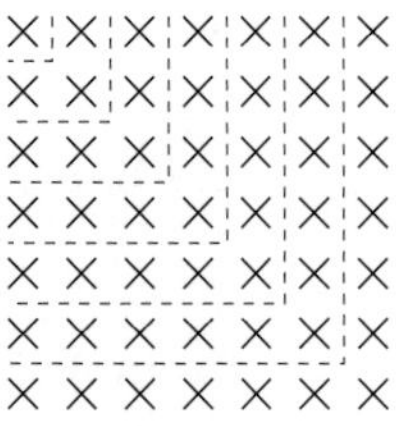

Fig. 2.6

Example 2.5.5

A student reading a 426-page book finds that he reads faster as he gets into the subject. He reads 19 pages on the first day, and his rate of reading then goes up by 3 pages each day. How long does he take to finish the book?

You are given that $a = 19$ and $d = 3$. The formula $S = \frac{1}{2}n(2a + (n - 1)d)$ gives

$$\begin{aligned} S &= \tfrac{1}{2}n(38 + (n - 1) \times 3) \\ &= \tfrac{1}{2}n(3n + 35). \end{aligned}$$

You may recognise that, when you put S equal to 426, you get a quadratic equation. If so, you could rearrange it in the usual form as $3n^2 + 35n - 852 = 0$ and then solve it by using the standard formula (see Section 10.4).

But if not, you can use your calculator to display a table of values of the sequence $u_n = \frac{1}{2}n(3n + 35)$ for different values of n. Scroll through the table until you reach the entries

n	u_n
...	...
10	325
11	374
12	426
13	481
...	...

You can see that $u_n = 426$ when $n = 12$.

The student takes 12 days to finish the book.

In this section the letters a, l and S have been used to keep the algebra simple. But since a is the first term and l is the last, a could have been written as u_1 and l as u_n. It is also quite common to use S_n (rather than simply S) for the sum of n terms. The formulae for an arithmetic series would then take the form:

$$u_n = u_1 + (n - 1)d,$$

$$S_n = \tfrac{1}{2}n(u_1 + u_n) = \tfrac{1}{2}n(2u_1 + (n - 1)d).$$

Your calculator also has a procedure for finding the sum of the terms of a sequence. If you key in the formula for the nth term, and the first and last values of n for which you want to add up the terms, the calculator will give the sum. You will find detailed instructions in the calculator manual.

The procedure is not restricted to arithmetic sequences; it works for any sequence, provided that you know a formula for u_n. But of course you can only use it for sequences with numerical terms.

Exercise 2C

1 Which of the following sequences are the first four terms of an arithmetic sequence? For those that are, write down the value of the common difference.

(a) 7 10 13 16 ...
(b) 3 5 9 15 ...
(c) 1 0.1 0.01 0.001 ...
(d) 4 2 0 −2 ...
(e) 2 −3 4 −5 ...
(f) $p-2q$ $p-q$ p $p+q$ ...
(g) $\frac{1}{2}a$ $\frac{1}{3}a$ $\frac{1}{4}a$ $\frac{1}{5}a$ ...
(h) x $2x$ $3x$ $4x$ ...

2 Write down the sixth term, and an expression for the nth term, of the arithmetic sequences which begin as follows.

(a) 2 4 6 ...
(b) 17 20 23 ...
(c) 5 2 −1 ...
(d) 1.3 1.7 2.1 ...
(e) 1 $1\frac{1}{2}$ 2 ...
(f) 73 67 61 ...
(g) x $x+2$ $x+4$ ...
(h) $1-x$ 1 $1+x$ ...

3 In the following arithmetic progressions, the first three terms and the last term are given. Find the number of terms.

(a) 4 5 6 ... 17
(b) 3 9 15 ... 525
(c) 8 2 −4 ... −202
(d) $2\frac{1}{8}$ $3\frac{1}{4}$ $4\frac{3}{8}$ ... $13\frac{3}{8}$

4 Find the sum of the given number of terms of the following arithmetic series.

(a) $2+5+8+...$ (20 terms)
(b) $4+11+18+...$ (15 terms)
(c) $8+5+2+...$ (12 terms)
(d) $\frac{1}{2}+1+1\frac{1}{2}+...$ (58 terms)
(e) $7+3+(-1)+...$ (25 terms)
(f) $1+3+5+...$ (999 terms)

Use your calculator to check your answers.

5 Find the number of terms and the sum of each of the following arithmetic series.

(a) $5+7+9+...+111$
(b) $8+12+16+...+84$
(c) $7+13+19+...+277$
(d) $8+5+2+...+(-73)$
(e) $-14-10-6-...+94$
(f) $157+160+163+...+529$
(g) $10+20+30+...+10\,000$
(h) $1.8+1.2+0.6+...+(-34.2)$

6 In each of the following arithmetic sequences you are given two terms. Find the first term and the common difference.

(a) 4th term $= 15$, 9th term $= 35$ (b) 3rd term $= 12$, 10th term $= 47$

(c) 8th term $= 3.5$, 13th term $= 5.0$ (d) 5th term $= 2$, 11th term $= -13$

(e) 12th term $= -8$, 20th term $= -32$ (f) 3rd term $= -3$, 7th term $= 5$

7 Find how many terms of the given arithmetic series must be taken to reach the given sum.

(a) $3 + 7 + 11 + \ldots$, sum $= 820$ (b) $8 + 9 + 10 + \ldots$, sum $= 162$

(c) $20 + 23 + 26 + \ldots$, sum $= 680$

8 A squirrel is collecting nuts. It collects 5 nuts on the first day of the month, 8 nuts on the second, 11 on the third and so on in arithmetic progression.

(a) How many nuts will it collect on the 20th day?

(b) After how many days will it have collected more than 1000 nuts?

9 Kulsum is given an interest-free loan to buy a car. She repays the loan in unequal monthly instalments; these start at \$30 in the first month and increase by \$2 each month after that. She makes 24 payments.

(a) Find the amount of her final payment.

(b) Find the amount of her loan.

10 (a) Find the sum of the positive integers from 1 to 100 inclusive.

(b) Find the sum of the positive integers from 101 to 200 inclusive.

(c) Find and simplify an expression for the sum of the positive integers from $n + 1$ to $2n$ inclusive.

11 An employee started work on 1 January 2000 on an annual salary of \$30 000. His pay scale will give him an increase of \$800 per annum on the first of January until 1 January 2015 inclusive. He remains on this salary until he retires on 31 December 2040. How much will he earn during his working life?

2.6 Sigma notation

This section is about a notation for sums of sequences. You know that $u_1, u_2, \ldots$ is called a sequence, and if you need to add the terms to get $u_1 + u_2 + \ldots + u_n$, the sequence changes its name and is called a series.

The first thing you need is a way of referring to any of the n terms of the series. So far you have used u_n to stand for a term of a sequence, where n can be any of the positive integers $1, 2, 3, \ldots$. But if you write the series as $u_1 + u_2 + \ldots + u_n$, n stands for the number of terms of the series, and u_n is the last term. You must therefore find some other way of referring to *any* term of the series. This can be done by using some different letter for the suffix, such as i. Then u_i is called the **general term** of the series, and i can take any of the values $1, 2, 3, \ldots, n$.

The sum $u_1 + u_2 + ... + u_n$ is then written as

$$\sum_{i=1}^{n} u_i.$$

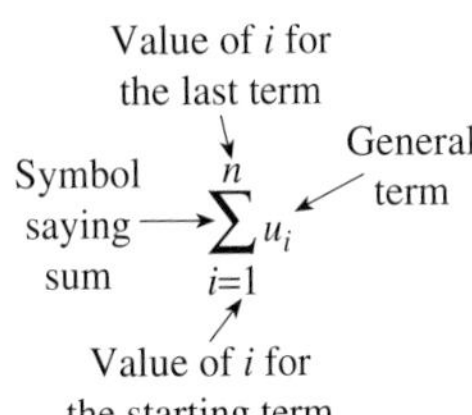

Fig. 2.7

This means 'the sum of the terms of the sequence u_i from $i = 1$ to $i = n$'.

This is called **sigma notation**. It is illustrated in more detail in Fig. 2.7. The letter sigma, $\sum$, is the Greek capital letter S.

- The symbol $\sum$ is an instruction to add.
- Following the $\sum$ symbol is an expression for the general term of a series.
- Below the $\sum$ symbol is the value of i corresponding to the starting term.
- Above the $\sum$ symbol is the value of i corresponding to the last term.

The expression $\sum_{i=1}^{n} u_i$ is read as 'sigma from 1 to n of u_i'.

Although the notation is most often used with a starting term of u_1 (or sometimes u_0), you occasionally want to use it with other starting terms. For example, $\sum_{i=3}^{6} u_i$ stands for $u_3 + u_4 + u_5 + u_6$.

Example 2.6.1
Express as addition sums (a) $\sum_{i=1}^{3} i$, (b) $\sum_{i=4}^{7} (2i - 1)$, (c) $\sum_{i=0}^{4} 1$, (d) $\sum_{i=3}^{8} i^2$.

(a) The ith term is i and, as the first term has $i = 1$, the first term is 1. For the second term, put $i = 2$, so the second term is 2. The last term is the term for which $i = 3$, so the last term is 3. The $\sum$ symbol means add, so

$$\sum_{i=1}^{3} i = 1 + 2 + 3.$$

(b) The first term is $(2 \times 4 - 1) = 7$, corresponding to $i = 4$. The second term, corresponding to $i = 5$, is $(2 \times 5 - 1) = 9$. Continuing in this way,

$$\sum_{i=4}^{7} (2i - 1) = 7 + 9 + 11 + 13.$$

(c) In this case, the ith term is 1, independent of the value of i. That is, $u_0 = u_1 = u_2 = u_3 = u_4 = 1$, so

$$\sum_{i=0}^{4} 1 = 1 + 1 + 1 + 1 + 1.$$

(d) The first term is 3^2, corresponding to $i = 3$. The second term, corresponding to $i = 4$, is 4^2. Continuing in this way,

$$\sum_{i=3}^{8} i^2 = 3^2 + 4^2 + 5^2 + 6^2 + 7^2 + 8^2.$$

Notice that, in part (c), there are 5 terms and in part (d) there are 6 terms. In general the number of terms in the series $\sum_{i=m}^{n} u_i$ is $n - m + 1$.

There is more than one way to describe a series using sigma notation. For example,

$$\sum_{i=0}^{2} (i+1) = (0+1) + (1+1) + (2+1) = 1 + 2 + 3,$$

which is the same as $\sum_{i=1}^{3} i$ in Example 2.6.1(a).

Example 2.6.2
Express each of the following sums in $\sum$ notation.

(a) $2+4+6+8+10$ (b) $\frac{1}{2}+\frac{1}{3}+\frac{1}{4}+\frac{1}{5}$ (c) $6^3+7^3+8^3$

(a) The general term of this sequence is $2i$. The first term corresponds to $i = 1$, and the last to $i = 5$. So the sum can be written as $\sum_{i=1}^{5} 2i$.

(b) The general term of this sequence is $\frac{1}{i+1}$. The first term corresponds to $i = 1$, and the last to $i = 4$. So the sum can be written as $\sum_{i=1}^{4} \frac{1}{i+1}$.

(c) The general term of this sequence is i^3. The first term corresponds to $i = 6$, and the last to $i = 8$. So the sum can be written as $\sum_{i=6}^{8} i^3$.

These answers are not unique; they are not the only answers possible. In part (b), for example, you could easily argue that the general term is $\frac{1}{i}$, with the first term corresponding to $i = 2$ and the last to $i = 5$. So the sum can be written $\sum_{i=2}^{5} \frac{1}{i}$.

Sometimes you can break up a complicated series into simpler series. For example, you can write the sum $\sum_{i=1}^{200} (2i+1)$ in the form

$$\begin{aligned}\sum_{i=1}^{200} (2i+1) &= (2\times 1+1) + (2\times 2+1) + (2\times 3+1) + \ldots + (2\times 200+1)\\ &= (2\times 1 + 2\times 2 + 2\times 3 + \ldots + 2\times 200) + \overbrace{1+1+1+\ldots+1}^{200 \text{ of these}}\\ &= 2\times(1+2+3+\ldots+200) + \overbrace{1+1+1+\ldots+1}^{200 \text{ of these}}\\ &= 2\sum_{i=1}^{200} i + \sum_{i=1}^{200} 1.\end{aligned}$$

You can now go on and sum the series, using the formula for the nth triangle number in Section 2.3, since the sum $\sum_{i=1}^{200} i$ is the same as t_{200}. Using $t_n = \frac{1}{2}n(n+1)$,

$$t_{200} = \tfrac{1}{2} \times 200 \times 201 = 20\,100.$$

Therefore

$$\begin{aligned}\sum_{i=1}^{200}(2i+1) &= 2\sum_{i=1}^{200} i + \sum_{i=1}^{200} 1 \\ &= 2 \times 20\,100 + 200 = 40\,400.\end{aligned}$$

In the example above, two important rules about sigma notation were used.

The first rule is called the **addition rule** for sums:

$$\begin{aligned}\sum_{i=1}^{n}(u_i + v_i) &= (u_1 + v_1) + (u_2 + v_2) + \ldots + (u_n + v_n) \\ &= (u_1 + u_2 + \ldots + u_n) + (v_1 + v_2 + \ldots + v_n) \\ &= \sum_{i=1}^{n} u_i + \sum_{i=1}^{n} v_i.\end{aligned}$$

The second rule deals with the effect of multiplying each term by a constant k. It is called the **multiple rule** for sums:

$$\begin{aligned}\sum_{i=1}^{n}(ku_i) &= (ku_1 + ku_2 + \ldots + ku_n) \\ &= k(u_1 + u_2 + \ldots + u_n) \\ &= k\sum_{i=1}^{n} u_i.\end{aligned}$$

Addition rule $\sum_{i=1}^{n}(u_i + v_i) = \sum_{i=1}^{n} u_i + \sum_{i=1}^{n} v_i.$

Multiple rule For any number k, $\sum_{i=1}^{n}(ku_i) = k\sum_{i=1}^{n} u_i.$

Example 2.6.3

Find $\sum_{1=1}^{4}(2i + 2^i)$.

Using the addition rule,

$$\begin{aligned}\sum_{1=1}^{4}(2i + 2^i) &= \sum_{i=1}^{4} 2i + \sum_{i=1}^{4} 2^i \\ &= (2 + 4 + 6 + 8) + (2 + 4 + 8 + 16) \\ &= 20 + 30 = 50.\end{aligned}$$

Another important fact to notice about sigma notation is that the final result is nothing to do with i. For example,

$$\sum_{i=0}^{2}(3+2i+i^2) = 3+(3+2\times 1+1^2)+(3+2\times 2+2^2)$$
$$= 3+6+11 = 20.$$

So it doesn't matter what letter you use. Thus $\sum_{i=0}^{2}(3+2i+i^2)$ is precisely the same sum as $\sum_{r=0}^{2}(3+2r+r^2)$. For this reason i is called a **dummy variable**.

Exercise 2D

1 Express each of the following as addition sums.

(a) $\sum_{i=2}^{3} i$ (b) $\sum_{i=3}^{5} 2$ (c) $\sum_{i=1}^{4} \frac{1}{i}$

(d) $\sum_{i=1}^{4} i^2$ (e) $\sum_{i=2}^{5} (2i+1)$ (f) $\sum_{i=0}^{2} u_i$

2 Write each of the following sums using sigma notation. (Note that your answers could differ from those given.)

(a) $2+3+4$ (b) $1+4+9+16$ (c) $3^3+4^3+5^3+6^3+7^3$

(d) $\frac{1}{2}+\frac{1}{4}+\frac{1}{6}$ (e) $3+5+7+9$ (f) $2+5+8+11+14$

3 (a) Use your calculator to check that

$\sum_{i=1}^{20} i^2 = 2870,$ $\sum_{i=1}^{20} i^3 = 44\,100,$ $\sum_{i=1}^{20} i^4 = 722\,666.$

(b) Then use the addition and multiple rules to calculate

$\sum_{i=1}^{20} i^2(i-1),$ $\sum_{i=1}^{20} i^2(i-1)^2,$ $\sum_{i=1}^{20} (i^2-1)^2.$

(c) Use your calculator to check your answers to part (b).

3 The binomial theorem

This chapter is about the expansion of $(a+b)^n$, where n is a positive integer. When you have completed it, you should

- be able to use Pascal's triangle to find the expansion of $(a+b)^n$ when n is small
- know how to use a calculator to find the coefficients in the expansion of $(a+b)^n$ when n is large
- be able to use the notation $\binom{n}{r}$ or ${}^nC_r$ in the context of the binomial theorem.

3.1 Expanding $(a+b)^n$

The binomial theorem is a quick and easy rule for multiplying out $(a+b)^n$ where n is a positive integer. (The word 'binomial' refers to the expression $a+b$, which is the sum of two terms.)

You know that $(a+b)^2 = a^2 + 2ab + b^2$. This is proved by writing $(a+b)^2$ as $(a+b)(a+b)$. First, treating the second $(a+b)$ as a single object and using the rule $(x+y)z = xz + yz$ for multiplying out brackets,

$$(a+b)(a+b) = a(a+b) + b(a+b).$$

Then, using the rule again in the form $z(x+y) = zx + zy$,

$$a(a+b) + b(a+b) = (a^2 + ab) + (ba + b^2).$$

Since ab is the same as ba, you can set this out as

$$\begin{aligned}(a+b)^2 &= a^2 + ab \\ &\quad\;\; + ab + b^2 \\ &= a^2 + 2ab + b^2.\end{aligned}$$

This expression is called the **expansion** of $(a+b)^2$.

You can use a similar method to find expansions of $(a+b)^3$ and $(a+b)^4$:

$$\begin{aligned}(a+b)^3 &= (a+b)(a+b)^2 \\ &= (a+b)(a^2+2ab+b^2) \\ &= a(a^2+2ab+b^2) + b(a^2+2ab+b^2) \\ &= a^3 + 2a^2b + ab^2 \\ &\quad\;\; + a^2b + 2ab^2 + b^3 \\ &= a^3 + 3a^2b + 3ab^2 + b^3.\end{aligned}$$

$$\begin{aligned}(a+b)^4 &= (a+b)(a+b)^3 \\ &= (a+b)(a^3+3a^2b+3ab^2+b^3) \\ &= a(a^3+3a^2b+3ab^2+b^3) + b(a^3+3a^2b+3ab^2+b^3) \\ &= a^4 + 3a^3b + 3a^2b^2 + ab^3 \\ &\quad\;\; + a^3b + 3a^2b^2 + 3ab^3 + b^4 \\ &= a^4 + 4a^3b + 6a^2b^2 + 4ab^3 + b^4.\end{aligned}$$

Notice that, when you multiply out $b(...)$, the factors in each term have been written in alphabetical order. For example, $b \times (2ab)$ becomes $2ab^2$ and $b \times (3a^2b)$ becomes $3a^2b^2$.

You can summarise these results, including $(a+b)^1$, as follows. The numbers in bold type are called **binomial coefficients**.

$$(a+b)^1 = \mathbf{1}a + \mathbf{1}b$$
$$(a+b)^2 = \mathbf{1}a^2 + \mathbf{2}ab + \mathbf{1}b^2$$
$$(a+b)^3 = \mathbf{1}a^3 + \mathbf{3}a^2b + \mathbf{3}ab^2 + \mathbf{1}b^3$$
$$(a+b)^4 = \mathbf{1}a^4 + \mathbf{4}a^3b + \mathbf{6}a^2b^2 + \mathbf{4}ab^3 + \mathbf{1}b^4$$

Study these expansions carefully. You will see that there are two parts to the rule for writing out the expressions:

- The 'a and b' rule. Each row starts on the left with a^n. Moving from one term to the next, the powers of a successively go down by 1, and the powers of b go up by 1, until you reach the last term b^n.

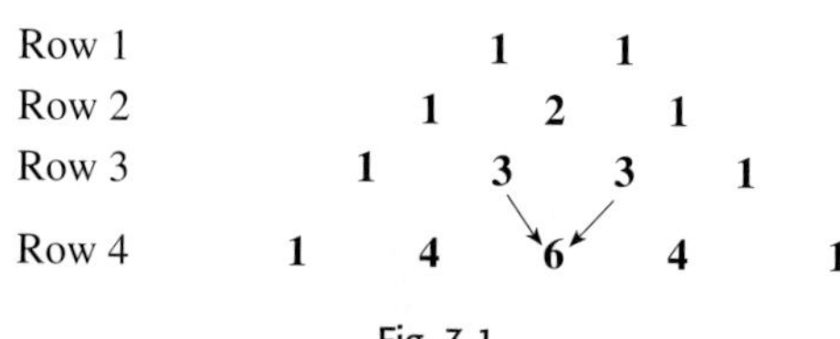

Fig. 3.1

- The coefficient rule. The coefficients form the pattern in Fig. 3.1. This is called **Pascal's triangle**. (The pattern first appeared in a Chinese manuscript by Yang Hui in the 13th century, but Blaise Pascal was one of the first Europeans to use it.)

A simple way of building up Pascal's triangle is as follows:

- start each row with 1,
- then add pairs of numbers in the row above to get the entry positioned below and between them (the arrows in Fig. 3.1 show the number 6 in Row 4 obtained as $3+3$ from Row 3),
- complete the row with a 1.

This corresponds to the way in which the two rows of algebra are added to give the final result when you expand $(a+b)^2$, $(a+b)^3$ and $(a+b)^4$.

You should now be able to predict that the coefficients in the fifth row are

1 5 10 10 5 1

and that

$$(a+b)^5 = a^5 + 5a^4b + 10a^3b^2 + 10a^2b^3 + 5ab^4 + b^5.$$

3.2 Substitution

You also know that $(a-b)^2 = a^2 - 2ab + b^2$.

You could prove this by a method similar to that used in Section 3.1 for $(a+b)^2$, writing

$$\begin{aligned}(a-b)^2 &= (a-b)(a-b)\\ &= a(a-b) - b(a-b)\\ &= (a^2 - ab) - (ba - b^2)\\ &= a^2 - ab\\ & - ab + b^2\\ \hline &= a^2 - 2ab + b^2.\end{aligned}$$

But there is no need to do this. It is easier to write $a+b$ as $a+(-b)$, so

$$(a-b)^2 = (a+(-b))^2.$$

This is just like $(a+b)^2$ but with $(-b)$ written in place of b. So

$$(a+(-b))^2 = a^2 + 2a \times (-b) + (-b)^2.$$

Since $2a \times (-b) = -2ab$ and $(-b)^2 = b^2$,

$$(a-b)^2 = a^2 - 2ab + b^2.$$

This process is called **substitution**. You expand $(a-b)^2$ by substituting $-b$ in place of b in the expansion of $(a+b)^2$.

In Examples 3.2.1 to 3.2.4 the coefficients from Pascal's triangle are shown in bold-faced type to help you to keep track of them.

Example 3.2.1
Write down the expansion of $(1+b)^6$.

Use the next row of Pascal's triangle, continuing the pattern of powers and replacing a by 1:

$$\begin{aligned}(1+b)^6 &= \mathbf{1}(1)^6 + \mathbf{6}(1)^5 b + \mathbf{15}(1)^4 b^2 + \mathbf{20}(1)^3 b^3 + \mathbf{15}(1)^2 b^4 + \mathbf{6}(1) b^5 + \mathbf{1} b^6\\ &= 1 + 6b + 15b^2 + 20b^3 + 15b^4 + 6b^5 + b^6.\end{aligned}$$

Example 3.2.2
Multiply out the brackets in the expression $(2x+3)^4$.

Use the expansion of $(a+b)^4$, substituting $(2x)$ for a and 3 for b:

$$\begin{aligned}(2x+3)^4 &= \mathbf{1} \times (2x)^4 + \mathbf{4} \times (2x)^3 \times 3 + \mathbf{6} \times (2x)^2 \times 3^2 + \mathbf{4} \times (2x) \times 3^3 + \mathbf{1} \times 3^4\\ &= 16x^4 + 96x^3 + 216x^2 + 216x + 81.\end{aligned}$$

Example 3.2.3
Expand $(x^2+2)^3$.

In $(a+b)^3$, substitute x^2 for a and 2 for b.

$$\begin{aligned}(x^2+2)^3 &= \mathbf{1}\times(x^2)^3+\mathbf{3}\times(x^2)^2\times 2+\mathbf{3}\times x^2\times 2^2+\mathbf{1}\times 2^3\\ &= x^6+6x^4+12x^2+8.\end{aligned}$$

Example 3.2.4
Expand $(2p-3)^6$.

In $(a+b)^6$, replace a by $2p$ and b by (-3).

Don't be tempted to economise on brackets!

$$\begin{aligned}(2p-3)^6 &= \mathbf{1}\times(2p)^6+\mathbf{6}\times(2p)^5\times(-3)+\mathbf{15}\times(2p)^4\times(-3)^2+\mathbf{20}\times(2p)^3\times(-3)^3\\ &\qquad+\mathbf{15}\times(2p)^2\times(-3)^4+\mathbf{6}\times(2p)\times(-3)^5+\mathbf{1}\times(-3)^6\\ &= 64p^6+6\times 32p^5\times(-3)+15\times 16p^4\times 9+20\times 8p^3\times(-27)\\ &\qquad+15\times 4p^2\times 81+6\times 2p\times(-243)+729\\ &= 64p^6-576p^5+2160p^4-4320p^3+4860p^2-2916p+729.\end{aligned}$$

Example 3.2.5
Find the coefficient of x^3 in the expansion of $(3x-4)^5$.

The term which involves x^3 comes third in the row with coefficients 1, 5, 10, ... So this term is

$$10\times(3x)^3\times(-4)^2=10\times 27x^3\times 16=4320x^3.$$

The required coefficient is therefore 4320.

In this example notice the difference between 'the coefficient of x^3' and the 'binomial coefficient'. The first is the number which multiplies x^3 when the expansion is written out in full, but the second refers to just the number 10.

Exercise 3A

1 Write down the expansion of each of the following.

(a) $(x+1)^3$ (b) $(2x+1)^3$ (c) $(4+p)^3$ (d) $(x-1)^3$

(e) $(x+2)^3$ (f) $(2p+3q)^3$ (g) $(1-4x)^3$ (h) $(1+\frac{1}{2}x)^4$

(i) $(x^2+2)^3$ (j) $(1-5x^2)^3$ (k) $(x^2+y^3)^3$ (l) $(1-x^3)^3$

2 Find the coefficient of x in the expansion of (a) $(3x+1)^4$, (b) $(2x+5)^3$.

3 Find the coefficient of x^2 in the expansion of (a) $(4x+5)^3$, (b) $(1-3x)^4$.

4 Find the coefficient of x^3 in the expansion of (a) $(1+3x)^5$, (b) $(2-5x)^4$.

5 Write down the expansion of $(m+4)^3$ and hence expand $(m+1)(m+4)^3$.

6 Expand $(3r+2)(2r+3)^3$.

7 In the expansion of $(1+ax)^4$, the coefficient of x^3 is 1372. Find the constant a.

8 Expand $(a+b)^9$.

9 Find the coefficient of x^5y^5 in the expansion of $(2x+y)^{10}$.

3.3 The binomial theorem

The treatment given in Section 3.1 is fine for calculating the coefficients in the expansion of $(a+b)^n$ where n is small, but it is hopelessly inefficient for finding the coefficient of $a^{11}b^4$ in the expansion of $(a+b)^{15}$. Just think of all the rows of Pascal's triangle which you would have to write out! What you need is a way of finding any term in the expansion of $(a+b)^n$ for any positive integer n.

Notice first how to generalise the 'a and b' rule. The first term is just a^n. For the next term, the power of a goes down by 1 and the power of b goes up by 1. It is therefore

$$\text{coefficient} \times a^{n-1}b^1.$$

The term after that is coefficient $\times\, a^{n-2}b^2$, and so on.
You will see that the powers of a and b always add up to n. So a typical term will have the form

$$\text{coefficient} \times a^{n-r}b^r.$$

The coefficient depends on the values of n and r. You will find two different symbols used for it, either $\binom{n}{r}$ or ${}^nC_r$ (or sometimes ${}_nC_r$). In written mathematics $\binom{n}{r}$ is commonly used, but on your calculator it is probably shown as nCr. (The reason for this is explained in Section 3.4.) These are the binomial coefficients. You can find them by using a calculator.

You will have to look at the instruction manual to find precisely how to calculate a binomial coefficient ${}^nC_r$. Typically you begin by entering the number n, then use keys to identify the instruction ${}^nC_r$, and finally you enter the number r. That is, you first show that you are interested in the expansion $(a+b)^n$, and then you show which of the coefficients you want. Try it in the following example.

Example 3.3.1
Calculate the coefficient of $a^{11}b^4$ in the expansion of $(a+b)^{15}$.

The coefficient is ${}^{15}C_4$. The calculator gives ${}^{15}C_4 = 1365$.

All the numbers in Pascal's triangle can therefore be written in the form $\binom{n}{r}$. For example, Row 3 gives the coefficients in the expansion of $(a+b)^3$, so $n=3$. The coefficient of ab^2, which is $a^{3-2}b^2$, has $r=2$. So this coefficient is $\binom{3}{2}$.

Pascal's triangle can then be written as

$$\begin{array}{lccccccccc}
\text{Row 1} & & & & \binom{1}{0} & & \binom{1}{1} & & & \\
\text{Row 2} & & & \binom{2}{0} & & \binom{2}{1} & & \binom{2}{2} & & \\
\text{Row 3} & & \binom{3}{0} & & \binom{3}{1} & & \binom{3}{2} & & \binom{3}{3} & \\
\text{Row 4} & \binom{4}{0} & & \binom{4}{1} & & \binom{4}{2} & & \binom{4}{3} & & \binom{4}{4}
\end{array}$$

and so on.

This enables you to write down a neater form of the expansion of $(a+b)^n$.

The **binomial theorem** states that, if n is a positive integer,

$$(a+b)^n = \binom{n}{0}a^n + \binom{n}{1}a^{n-1}b + \binom{n}{2}a^{n-2}b^2 + \ldots + \binom{n}{n}b^n.$$

Some special cases are worth mention. The coefficients of the first term a^n and the last term b^n are written as $\binom{n}{0}$ and $\binom{n}{n}$, and both of these are equal to 1. You may already have noticed that the coefficients of the second term and the last but one term, which are $\binom{n}{1}$ and $\binom{n}{n-1}$, are both equal to n.

Notice also that each row of Pascal's triangle is symmetrical. That is, if you read the numbers from right to left you get exactly the same sequence as if you read it from left to right. This means that $\binom{n}{n-r}$ is equal to $\binom{n}{r}$ whatever the values of n and r.

Example 3.3.2

Find the coefficient of a^5 in the expansion of $(a-2)^8$.

Substituting (-2) for b, the term you want is the one involving a^5b^3. The binomial coefficient is therefore $\binom{8}{3} = 56$.

The corresponding term is

$$56 \times a^5 \times (-2)^3,$$

so the coefficient of a^5 is

$$56 \times (-8) = -448.$$

The next example is one in which the value of x is assumed to be small. When this is the case, say for $x = 0.01$, the successive powers of x decrease by a factor of 100 each time and become very small indeed. So higher powers can be neglected in approximations, even though for some time the binomial coefficients are still getting larger.

For this reason you are asked to put the terms of a binomial expansion in order of **ascending powers** of x. This means that you start with the term with the smallest power of x, then move to the next smallest, and so on. In this way the terms likely to have the largest absolute value are written first.

Example 3.3.3
Find the first four terms in the expansion of $(2-3x)^{10}$ in ascending powers of x. By putting $x = 0.01$, find an approximation to 1.97^{10} correct to the nearest whole number.

You know that $\binom{10}{0} = 1$ and $\binom{10}{1} = 10$. The calculator gives $\binom{10}{2} = 45$ and $\binom{10}{3} = 120$.

$$\begin{aligned}(2-3x)^{10} &= \binom{10}{0} \times 2^{10} + \binom{10}{1} \times 2^9 \times (-3x) + \binom{10}{2} \times 2^8 \times (-3x)^2 \\ &\quad + \binom{10}{3} \times 2^7 \times (-3x)^3 + \ldots \\ &= 1024 - 10 \times 512 \times 3x + 45 \times 256 \times 9x^2 - 120 \times 128 \times 27x^3 + \ldots \\ &= 1024 - 15\,360x + 103\,680x^2 - 414\,720x^3 + \ldots .\end{aligned}$$

The first four terms are therefore $1024 - 15\,360x + 103\,680x^2 - 414\,720x^3$.

The dots at the ends of the lines indicate that the expression continues but that you are not interested in the remaining terms.

Putting $x = 0.01$ gives

$$\begin{aligned}1.97^{10} &\approx 1024 - 15\,360 \times 0.01 + 103\,680 \times 0.01^2 - 414\,720 \times 0.01^3 \\ &= 880.353\,28.\end{aligned}$$

Therefore $1.97^{10} \approx 880$.

The next term is actually $\binom{10}{4} \times 2^6 \times (3x)^4 = 1\,088\,640x^4 = 0.010\,886\,4$ and the rest are very small indeed. So, by taking the first four terms of the expansion, you can be sure that $1.97^{10} \approx 880$ correct to the nearest whole number. Check this directly from your calculator.

3.4* The notation ^nC_r

This section explains why the alternative notation ^nC_r is sometimes used instead of $\binom{n}{r}$. It is purely for interest, and you may leave it out if you wish.

In Section 3.1 the expansion of $(a+b)^4$ was found by using $(a+b)^3$, which you had already found. But there is another way of getting the expansion, starting with the definition as the product of four factors,

$$(a+b)^4 = (a+b)(a+b)(a+b)(a+b).$$

To expand the right side you have to take either an a or a b out of each bracket, and multiply them together. So to get a^4 you have to take the a from each of the four brackets; there is only one way of doing this, so the expansion contains just $1a^4$.

But there are four ways of getting a^3b, since you can choose any one of the four brackets for the b, and then take the a from each of the others. That is, the term involving a^3b in the expansion is

$$baaa + abaa + aaba + aaab = a^3b + a^3b + a^3b + a^3b = 4a^3b.$$

This shows that $\binom{4}{1} = 4$.

The notation ${}^4C_1$ stands for the number of ways in which you can pick 1 b-bracket out of the total of 4 brackets. You can read it as '4 choose 1', where the first number tells you how many brackets there are, and the second number tells you how many b-brackets you need so as to get the term of the expansion you are interested in.

Exercise 3B

1 Use your calculator to find the value of each of the following.

(a) $\binom{7}{3}$ (b) $\binom{8}{6}$ (c) $\binom{9}{5}$ (d) $\binom{13}{4}$

(e) $\binom{6}{4}$ (f) $\binom{10}{2}$ (g) $\binom{11}{10}$ (h) $\binom{50}{2}$

2 Find the coefficient of b^3 in the expansion of each of the following.

(a) $(1 + b)^5$ (b) $(1 - b)^8$ (c) $(1 + b)^{11}$ (d) $(1 - b)^{16}$

3 Find the coefficient of x^5 in the expansion of each of the following.

(a) $(2 + x)^7$ (b) $(3 - x)^8$ (c) $(1 + 2x)^9$ (d) $\left(1 - \frac{1}{2}x\right)^{12}$

4 Find the coefficient of x^6y^8 in the expansion of each of the following.

(a) $(x + y)^{14}$ (b) $(2x + y)^{14}$ (c) $(3x - 2y)^{14}$ (d) $\left(4x + \frac{1}{2}y\right)^{14}$

5 Find the first four terms in the expansion in ascending powers of x of the following.

(a) $(1 + x)^{13}$ (b) $(1 - x)^{15}$ (c) $(1 + 3x)^{10}$ (d) $(2 - 5x)^7$

6 Find the first three terms in the expansion in ascending powers of x of the following.

(a) $(1 + x)^{22}$ (b) $(1 - x)^{30}$ (c) $(1 - 4x)^{18}$ (d) $(1 + 6x)^{19}$

7 Find the first three terms in the expansion, in ascending powers of x, of $(1 + 2x)^8$. By substituting $x = 0.01$, find an approximation to 1.02^8.

8 Find the first three terms in the expansion, in ascending powers of x, of $(2 + 5x)^{12}$. By substituting a suitable value for x, find an approximation to 2.005^{12} to 2 decimal places.

9 Simplify $(1 - x)^8 + (1 + x)^8$. Substitute a suitable value of x to find the exact value of $0.99^8 + 1.01^8$.

10* Use an argument like that in Section 3.4 to show that

(a) $\binom{3}{2} = 3$, (b) $\binom{4}{2} = 6$, (c) $\binom{5}{2} = 10$.

Review exercise 1

1 Simplify

(a) $\sqrt{27}+\sqrt{12}-\sqrt{3}$, (b) $\sqrt{63}-\sqrt{28}$,

(c) $\sqrt{100\,000}+\sqrt{1000}+\sqrt{10}$, (d) $\sqrt[3]{2}+\sqrt[3]{16}$.

2 Rationalise the denominators of the following.

(a) $\dfrac{9}{2\sqrt{3}}$ (b) $\dfrac{1}{5\sqrt{5}}$ (c) $\dfrac{2\sqrt{5}}{3\sqrt{10}}$ (d) $\dfrac{\sqrt{8}}{\sqrt{15}}$

3 In the diagram, angles $\hat{ABC}$ and $\hat{ACD}$ are right angles. Given that $AB = CD = 2\sqrt{6}$ cm and $BC = 7$ cm, show that the length of [AD] is between $4\sqrt{6}$ cm and $7\sqrt{2}$ cm.

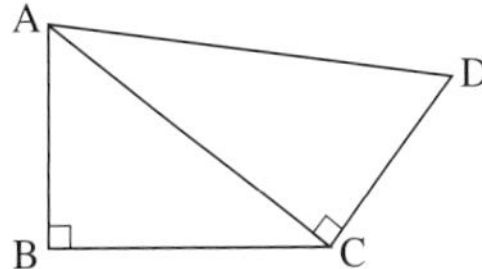

4 In the triangle PQR, $\hat{Q}$ is a right angle, $PQ = (6-2\sqrt{2})$ cm and $QR = (6+2\sqrt{2})$ cm.

(a) Find the area of the triangle. (b) Show that the length of [PR] is $2\sqrt{22}$ cm.

5 Simplify (a) $3\sqrt{3}+3\sqrt{27}$, (b) $3\sqrt{2}\times 4\sqrt{8}$.

6 Solve the inequality $2(3-x) < 4-(2-x)$.

7 The sequence $u_1, u_2, u_3, \ldots$ is defined by

$$u_1 = 0, \quad u_n = (2+u_{n-1})^2.$$

Find the value of u_4.

8 Find the first four terms in the binomial expansion of $(2-x)^7$. Use your answer to calculate 1.99^7 correct to 2 places of decimals.

9 (a) Find the sum of all the integers between 1 and 100 which are divisible by 3.

(b) Find the sum of all the integers from 1 to 100 which are not divisible by 3.

10 Expand $\left(a^2+\dfrac{2}{a}\right)^5$.

11 A small company producing children's toys plans an increase in output. The number of toys produced is to be increased by 8 each week until the weekly number produced reaches 1000. In week 1, the number to be produced is 280; in week 2, the number is 288; etc. Show that the weekly number produced will be 1000 in week 91.

From week 91 onwards, the number produced each week is to remain at 1000. Find the total number of toys to be produced over the first 104 weeks of the plan. (OCR)

12 The ith term of an arithmetic progression is $1+4i$. Find, in terms of n, the sum of the first n terms of the progression. (OCR)

13 The sum of the first two terms of an arithmetic progression is 18 and the sum of the first four terms is 52. Find the sum of the first eight terms. (OCR)

14 Find the sum of the arithmetic progression 1, 4, 7, 10, 13, 16, ... , 1000.

Every third term of the above progression is removed, i.e. 7, 16, etc. Find the sum of the remaining terms. (OCR)

15 The tenth term of an arithmetic progression is 125 and the sum of the first ten terms is 260.

(a) Show that the first term in the progression is -73.

(b) Find the common difference. (OCR)

16 The binomial expansion of $(1 + ax)^n$, where n is a positive integer, has six terms.

(a) Write down the value of n.

The coefficient of the x^3 term is $\frac{5}{4}$.

(b) Find a. (OCR)

Examination questions

1 Given that $(3 + \sqrt{7})^3 = p + q\sqrt{7}$ where p and q are integers, find

(a) p, (b) q. (© IBO 2005)

2 Gwendolyn added the multiples of 3, from 3 to 3750 and found that $3 + 6 + 9 + ... + 3750 = s$. Calculate s. (© IBO 2003)

3 Find the term containing x^{10} in the expansion of $(5 + 2x^2)^7$. (© IBO 2003)

4 Arturo goes swimming every week. He swims 200 metres in the first week. Each week he swims 30 metres more than the previous week. He continues for one year (52 weeks).

(a) How far does Arturo swim in the final week?

(b) How far does he swim altogether? (© IBO 2003)

5 Let S_n be the sum of the first n terms of an arithmetic sequence, whose first three terms are u_1, u_2 and u_3. It is known that $S_1 = 7$ and $S_2 = 18$.

(a) Write down u_1.

(b) Calculate the common difference of the sequence.

(c) Calculate u_4. (© IBO 2005)

6 When the expression $(2 + ax)^{10}$ is expanded, the coefficient of the term in x^3 is 414 720. Find the value of a. (© IBO 2004)

7 Consider the expansion of $\left(3x^2 - \frac{1}{x}\right)^9$.

(a) How many terms are there in this expansion?

(b) Find the constant term in this expansion. (© IBO 2002)

4 Representation of statistical data

This chapter looks at ways of displaying numerical data using diagrams. When you have completed it, you should

- know the difference between quantitative and qualitative data
- be able to construct grouped frequency tables
- be able to draw a frequency histogram from a grouped frequency table
- be able to construct a cumulative frequency diagram from a frequency distribution table
- be able to make comparisons between sets of data by using diagrams.

4.1 Introduction

The collection, organisation and analysis of numerical information are all part of the subject called **statistics**. Pieces of numerical and other information are called **data**. A more helpful definition of 'data' is 'a series of facts from which conclusions may be drawn'.

In order to collect data you need to observe or to measure some property. This property is called a **variable**. The data which follow were taken from the internet, which has many sites containing data sources. In this example a variety of measurements was taken on brain sizes. Each column represents a variable. So, for example, 'gender', 'FSIQ' and 'height' are all variables.

Datafile name Brain size (Data reprinted from *Intelligence*, Vol. 15, Willerman et al, 'In vivo brain size ...', 1991, with permission from Elsevier Science.)

Description A team of researchers used a sample of 40 students at a university. The subjects took four subtests from the 'Wechsler (1981) Adult Intelligence Scale – Revised' test. Magnetic Resonance Imaging (MRI) was then used to measure the brain sizes of the subjects. The subjects' genders, heights and body masses are also included. The researchers withheld the masses of two subjects and the height of one subject for reasons of confidentiality.

Number of cases 40

Variable names

1 Gender: male or female

2 FSIQ: full scale IQ scores based on the four Wechsler (1981) subtests

3 VIQ: verbal IQ scores based on the four Wechsler (1981) subtests

4 PIQ: performance IQ scores based on the four Wechsler (1981) subtests

5 Mass: body mass in pounds

6 Height: height in inches (1 inch = 2.54 cm)

7 MRI_count: total pixel count from 18 MRI scans

Brain size						
Gender	FSIQ	VIQ	PIQ	Mass	Height	MRI_count
Female	133	132	124	118	64.5	816 932
Male	140	150	124	–	72.5	1 001 121
Male	139	123	150	143	73.3	1 038 437
Male	133	129	128	172	68.8	965 353
Female	137	132	134	147	65.0	951 545
Female	99	90	110	146	69.0	928 799
Female	138	136	131	138	64.5	991 305
Female	92	90	98	175	66.0	854 258
Male	89	93	84	134	66.3	904 858
Male	133	114	147	172	68.8	955 466
Female	132	129	124	118	64.5	833 868
Male	141	150	128	151	70.0	1 079 549
Male	135	129	124	155	69.0	924 059
Female	140	120	147	155	70.5	856 472
Female	96	100	90	146	66.0	878 897
Female	83	71	96	135	68.0	865 363
Female	132	132	120	127	68.5	852 244
Male	100	96	102	178	73.5	945 088
Female	101	112	84	136	66.3	808 020
Male	80	77	86	180	70.0	889 083
Male	83	83	86	–	–	892 420
Male	97	107	84	186	76.5	905 940
Female	135	129	134	122	62.0	790 619
Male	139	145	128	132	68.0	955 003
Female	91	86	102	114	63.0	831 722
Male	141	145	131	171	72.0	935 494
Female	85	90	84	140	68.0	798 612
Male	103	96	110	187	77.0	1 062 462
Female	77	83	72	106	63.0	793 549
Female	130	126	124	159	66.5	866 662
Female	133	126	132	127	62.5	857 782
Male	144	145	137	191	67.0	949 589
Male	103	96	110	192	75.5	997 925
Male	90	96	86	181	69.0	879 987
Female	83	90	81	143	66.5	834 344
Female	133	129	128	153	66.5	948 066
Male	140	150	124	144	70.5	949 395
Female	88	86	94	139	64.5	893 983
Male	81	90	74	148	74.0	930 016
Male	89	91	89	179	75.5	935 863

Table 4.1

You can see that there are different types of variable. The variable 'gender' is non-numerical: such variables are usually called **qualitative**. The other variables are called **quantitative**, because the values they take are numerical.

Quantitative numerical data can be subdivided into two categories. For example the height of a person in inches, which can take any value in a particular range, is called a **continuous** variable. 'MRI_count', on the other hand, is a **discrete** variable: it can only take the integer values because it counts pixels, and there is a clear step between each possible value. It would not be sensible, for example, to refer to an MRI_count of 1 000 000.3.

In summary:

A variable is **qualitative** if it is not possible for it to take a numerical value.

A variable is **quantitative** if it can take a numerical value.

A quantitative variable which can take any value in a given range is **continuous**.

A quantitative variable which has clear steps between its possible values is **discrete**.

4.2 Frequency histograms

Sometimes, for example if the data set is large, you may wish to divide the data into groups, called **class intervals**.

In the 'Brain size' data, the verbal IQ scores (VIQ) may be grouped into class intervals as in Table 4.2.

Verbal IQ	Tally	Frequency
71–80	||	2
81–90	卌 ||||	9
91–100	卌 ||	7
101–110	|	1
111–120	|||	3
121–130	卌 |||	8
131–140	||||	4
141–150	卌 |	6

Table 4.2

Table 4.2 is called a **grouped frequency table**. It shows how many values of the variable lie in each class interval. The pattern of a grouped frequency distribution is decided to some extent by the choice of class intervals. There would have been a different appearance to the distribution if the class intervals 71–90, 91–110, 111–130 and 131–150 had been chosen. There is no clear rule about how many class intervals should be chosen or what size they should be, but it is usual to have from 5 to 10 class intervals.

Grouping the data into class intervals inevitably means losing some information. For example, someone looking at the table would not know the exact values of the observations in the 71–80 category. All he or she would know for certain is that there were two such observations.

Suppose now that you were considering the mass data from the 'Brain size' data set and that you had a class interval 141–150. This refers to weights which are measured and then rounded to between 141 and 150 pounds. The class interval labelled as 141–150 actually contains values from 140.5 up to (but not including) 150.5. These real endpoints, 140.5 and 150.5, are referred to as the **interval boundaries**.

Notice that the upper interval boundary of the class interval 141–150, which is 150.5, is the lower interval boundary of the next class interval.

Example 4.2.1

For each case below give the interval boundaries of the first class interval.

(a) The heights of 100 students were recorded to the nearest centimetre.

Height, h (cm)	160–164	165–169	170–174	...
Frequency	7	9	13	...

Table 4.3

(b) The masses in kilograms of 40 patients entering a doctor's surgery on one day were recorded to the nearest kilogram.

Mass, m (kg)	55–	60–	65–	...
Frequency	9	15	12	...

Table 4.4

(c) A group of 40 motorists was asked to state the ages at which they passed their driving tests.

Age, a (years)	17–	20–	23–	...
Frequency	6	11	7	...

Table 4.5

(a) The minimum and maximum heights for someone in the first class interval are 159.5 cm and 164.5 cm. The interval boundaries are given by $159.5 \le h < 164.5$.

(b) The first class interval appears to go from 55 kg up to but not including 60 kg, but as the measurement has been made to the nearest kilogram the lower and upper interval boundaries are 54.5 kg and 59.5 kg. The interval boundaries are given by $54.5 \le m < 59.5$.

(c) Age is recorded to the number of completed years, so 17– contains those who passed their tests from the day of their 17th birthday up to, but not including, the day of their 20th birthday. The interval boundaries are given by $17 \le a < 20$.

Sometimes discrete data are grouped into class intervals. For example, the test scores of 40 students might appear as in Table 4.6.

Score	0–9	10–19	20–29	30–39	40–49	50–59
Frequency	14	9	9	3	3	2

Table 4.6

What are the interval boundaries? There is no universally accepted answer, but a common convention is to use 9.5 and 19.5 as the interval boundaries for the second class interval. Although it may appear strange, the interval boundaries for the first class interval would be −0.5 and 9.5. The **interval width** is given by

interval width = upper interval boundary − lower interval boundary.

When a grouped frequency distribution contains continuous data, one of the most common forms of graphical display is the **frequency histogram**.

A **frequency histogram** is a bar chart with the following properties:

- it has equal class intervals
- there are no spaces between the bars (though there may be bars of height zero, which look like spaces)
- the area of each bar is proportional to the frequency.

Since all the bars of a frequency histogram have the same width, the last property becomes *the height of each bar is proportional to the frequency.*

Given that the blocks have equal widths, the simplest way of making the area of a block proportional to the frequency is to make the height equal to the frequency. This means that

width of class × height is proportional to frequency.

Example 4.2.2

The grouped frequency distribution in Table 4.7 represents the heights in inches of a sample of 39 of the people from the 'Brain size' data (see the previous section). Represent these data in a frequency histogram.

Height (inches)	Frequency
62–63	4
64–65	5
66–67	8
68–69	9
70–71	4
72–73	3
74–75	2
76–77	4
78–79	0

Table 4.7

You need to check that all the class interval widths are equal.

Height, h (inches)	Interval boundaries	Interval width	Frequency
62–63	$61.5 \le h < 63.5$	2	4
64–65	$63.5 \le h < 65.5$	2	5
66–67	$65.5 \le h < 67.5$	2	8
68–69	$67.5 \le h < 69.5$	2	9
70–71	$69.5 \le h < 71.5$	2	4
72–73	$71.5 \le h < 73.5$	2	3
74–75	$73.5 \le h < 75.5$	2	2
76–77	$75.5 \le h < 77.5$	2	4
78–79	$77.5 \le h < 79.5$	2	0

Table 4.8

The frequency histogram is shown in Fig. 4.9.

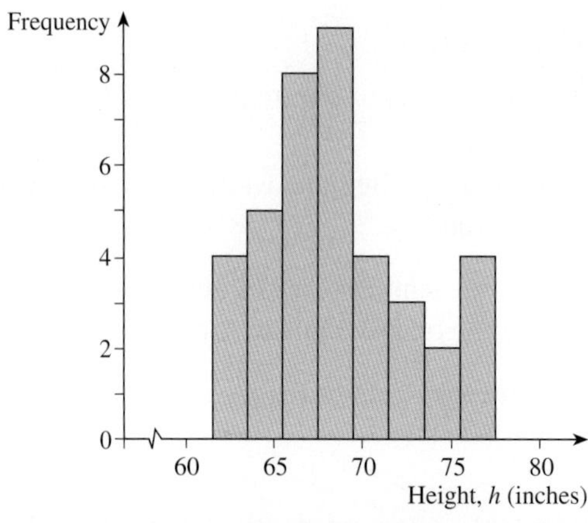

Fig. 4.9

The previous example of a frequency histogram has involved continuous data. You can also represent grouped discrete data in a frequency histogram. Table 4.10 gives the interval boundaries for the data in Table 4.6, which were the test scores of 40 students. Recall that the convention used is to take the class interval with limits 10 and 19 as having interval boundaries 9.5 and 19.5.

Score	Interval boundaries	Frequency
0–9	−0.5–9.5	14
10–19	9.5–19.5	9
20–29	19.5–29.5	9
30–39	29.5–39.5	3
40–49	39.5–49–5	3
50–59	49.5–59.5	2

Table 4.10

Fig. 4.11 shows the frequency histogram for the data. Notice that the left bar extends slightly to the left of the vertical axis, to the point −0.5. This accounts for the apparent thickness of the vertical axis.

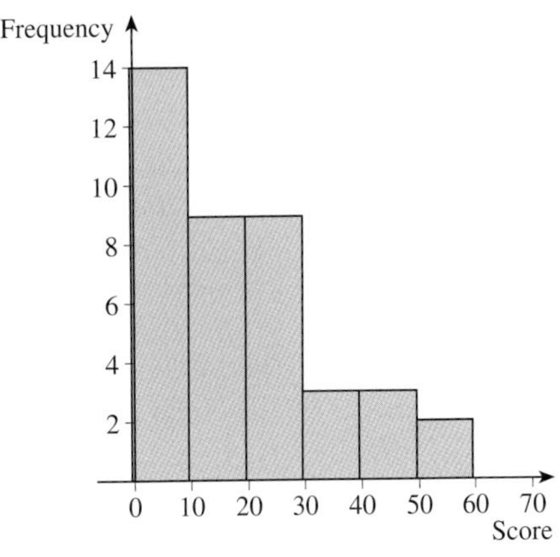

Fig. 4.11

Exercise 4A

In Question 1 below, the upper class boundary of one class is identical to the lower class boundary of the next class. If you were measuring speeds to the nearest m.p.h., then you might record a result of 40 m.p.h., and you would not know which class to put it in. This is not a problem in Question 1. You may come across data like these in examination questions, but it will be made clear what to do with them.

1 The speeds, in miles per hour, of 200 vehicles travelling on a motorway were measured by a radar device. The results are summarised in the following table.

Speed	30–40	40–50	50–60	60–70	70–80	80–90
Frequency	12	32	56	72	20	8

Draw a frequency histogram to illustrate the data.

2 The mass of each of 60 pebbles collected from a beach was measured. The results, correct to the nearest gram, are summarised in the following table.

Mass	5–9	10–14	15–19	20–24	25–29	30–34	35–39
Frequency	2	5	8	14	17	11	3

Draw a frequency histogram of the data.

3 A frequency histogram is drawn to represent a set of data.

(a) The first two class intervals have boundaries 2.0 and 2.25, and 2.25 and 2.5, with frequencies 5 and 12. The height of the first bar drawn is 2.5 cm. What is the height of the second bar?

(b) The interval boundaries of the third bar are 2.5 and 2.75. What is the corresponding frequency if the bar drawn has height 3.5 cm?

4 The grouped frequency table shows the score received by 275 students who sat an examination. Taking the interval boundaries for 0–9 as −0.5 and 9.5, draw a frequency histogram of the data.

Score	0–9	10–19	20–29	30–39	40–49	50–59
Frequency	6	21	51	84	82	31

5 The haemoglobin levels in the blood of 45 hospital patients were measured. The results, correct to 1 decimal place, and ordered for convenience, are as follows.

9.1	10.1	10.7	10.7	10.9	11.3	11.3	11.4	11.4	11.4	11.6	11.8	12.0	12.1	12.3
12.4	12.7	12.9	13.1	13.2	13.4	13.5	13.5	13.6	13.7	13.8	13.8	14.0	14.2	14.2
14.2	14.6	14.6	14.8	14.8	15.0	15.0	15.0	15.1	15.4	15.6	15.7	16.2	16.3	16.9

(a) Form a grouped frequency table with 8 class intervals.

(b) Draw a frequency histogram of the data.

6 Each of the 34 children in a Year 3 class was given a task to perform. The times taken in minutes, correct to the nearest quarter of a minute, were as follows.

4	$3\frac{3}{4}$	5	$6\frac{1}{4}$	7	3	7	$5\frac{1}{4}$	$7\frac{1}{2}$	$8\frac{3}{4}$	$7\frac{1}{2}$	$4\frac{1}{2}$
$6\frac{1}{2}$	$4\frac{1}{4}$	8	$7\frac{1}{4}$	$6\frac{3}{4}$	$5\frac{3}{4}$	$4\frac{3}{4}$	$8\frac{1}{4}$	7	$3\frac{1}{2}$	$5\frac{1}{2}$	$7\frac{3}{4}$
$8\frac{1}{2}$	$6\frac{1}{2}$	5	$7\frac{1}{4}$	$6\frac{3}{4}$	$7\frac{3}{4}$	$5\frac{3}{4}$	6	$7\frac{3}{4}$	$6\frac{1}{2}$		

(a) Form a grouped frequency table with 6 equal class intervals beginning with $3\text{–}3\frac{3}{4}$.

(b) What are the boundaries of the first class interval?

(c) Draw a frequency histogram of the data.

7 The table shows the age distribution of the 200 members of a golf club.

Age	10–19	20–29	30–39	40–49	50–59	60–69	70–79
Number of members	12	40	44	47	32	15	10

(a) Form a table showing the interval boundaries.

(b) Draw a frequency histogram of the data.

4.3 Cumulative frequency diagrams

An alternative method of representing continuous data is a **cumulative frequency diagram**. This is a graph in which the cumulative frequencies are plotted against the upper interval boundaries of the corresponding class interval. Consider the data from Example 4.2.2, reproduced in a slightly different form in Table 4.12.

Height, h (inches)	62–63	64–65	66–67	68–71	72–75	76–79
Frequency	4	5	8	13	5	4

Table 4.12

There are 0 observations less than 61.5.
There are 4 observations less than 63.5.
There are 4 + 5, or 9, observations less than 65.5.
There are 4 + 5 + 8, or 17, observations less than 67.5.

⋮ ⋮ ⋮

There are 39 observations less than 79.5.

This results in Table 4.13, which shows the cumulative frequency.

Height, h (inches)	<61.5	<63.5	<65.5	<67.5	<71.5	<75.5	<79.5
Cumulative frequency	0	4	9	17	30	35	39

Table 4.13

The points (61.5,0), (63.5,4), ..., (79.5,39) are then plotted and are joined with a smooth curve, as shown in Fig. 4.14.

Sometimes you may see cumulative frequency graphs in which the points are joined by line segments.

You can also use the graph to read off other information. For example, you can estimate the proportion of the sample whose heights are under 69 inches. Read off the cumulative frequency corresponding to a height of 69 in Fig. 4.14. This is approximately 21.9. Therefore an estimate of the proportion of the sample whose heights were under 69 inches would be $\frac{21.9}{39} \approx 0.56$, or 56%.

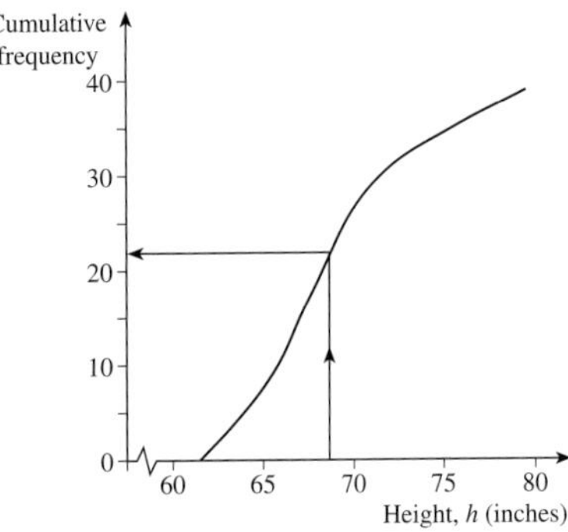

Fig. 4.14

Exercise 4B

1 Draw a cumulative frequency diagram for the data in Question 1 of Exercise 4A. With the help of the diagram estimate

(a) the percentage of cars that were travelling at more than 65 m.p.h.,

(b) the speed below which 25% of the cars were travelling.

2 Draw a cumulative frequency diagram for the examination marks in Question 4 of Exercise 4A.

(a) Candidates with at least 44 marks received Grade A. Find the percentage of the students that received Grade A.

(b) It is known that 81.8% of these students gained Grade E or better. Find the lowest Grade E mark for these students.

3 Estimates of the age distribution of a European country for the year 2010 are given in the following table.

Age	under 16	16–39	40–64	65–79	80–99
Percentage	14.3	33.1	35.3	11.9	5.4

(a) Draw a percentage cumulative frequency diagram.

(b) It is expected that people who have reached the age of 60 will be drawing a state pension in 2010. If the projected population of the country is 42.5 million, estimate the number who will then be drawing this pension.

4 The records of the sales in a small grocery store for the 360 days that it opened during the year 2006 are summarised in the following table.

Sales, x (in £100s)	$x < 2$	$2 \le x < 3$	$3 \le x < 4$	$4 \le x < 5$
Number of days	15	27	64	72

Sales, x (in £100s)	$5 \le x < 6$	$6 \le x < 7$	$7 \le x < 8$	$8 \le x < 9$
Number of days	86	70	16	10

Days for which sales fall below £325 are classified as 'poor' and those for which the sales exceed £775 are classified as 'good'. With the help of a cumulative frequency diagram estimate the number of poor days and the number of good days in 2006.

Keep your cumulative frequency diagram for Exercise 5A Question 4.

5 A company has 132 employees who work in its city branch. The distances, x miles, measured to the nearest mile, that employees travel to work are summarised in the following grouped frequency table.

x	<5	5–9	10–14	15–19	20–24	25–29
Frequency	12	29	63	13	12	3

Draw a cumulative frequency diagram and use it to find the number of miles below which

(a) one-quarter (b) three-quarters

of the employees travel to work.

5 Measures of location

This chapter describes three different measures of location and their method of calculation. When you have completed it, you should

- know what the median is, and be able to calculate it using a calculator if necessary
- know what the mean is, and be able to calculate it using a calculator if necessary
- know what the mode and the modal class are, and be able to find them
- be able to choose which is the appropriate measure to use in a given situation.

5.1 Introduction

Suppose that you wanted to know the typical playing time for a compact disc (CD). You cannot possibly find the playing times of all CDs, that is, the **population** of CDs, but you could start by taking a few CDs (a **sample**) and finding out the playing time for each one. You might obtain a list of values such as

49, 56, 55, 68, 61, 57, 61, 52, 63

where the values have been given in minutes, to the nearest whole minute.

You can see that the values are located roughly in the region of 1 hour (rather than, say, 2 hours or 10 minutes). It would be useful to have a single value which gave some idea of this location. A single value would condense the information contained in the data set into a 'typical' value, and would allow you to compare this data set with another one. Such a value is called a **measure of location**, or a **measure of central tendency**, or, in everyday language, an **average**.

If you have chosen the sample using a method in which every CD in the population of CDs is equally likely to be picked, your sample would be a **random sample**. In this case the sample is clearly not random – almost certainly you have no CDs of, say, Japanese music and could not have picked one.

5.2 The median

You can get a clearer picture of the location of the playing times by arranging them in ascending order of size:

49, 52, 55, 56, 57, 61, 61, 63, 68.

A simple measure of location is the middle value. There are equal numbers of values above and below it. In this case there are nine values and the middle one is 57. This value is called the **median**.

If the number of values is even then there is no single 'middle' value. In the case of the six values

47, 49, 59, 62, 65, 68,

which are the playing times of another six CDs (in order), the median is taken to be halfway between the third and fourth values, which is $\frac{1}{2}(59 + 62)$, or 60.5. Again, there are equal numbers of values below and above this value: in this case, three.

> To find the median of a data set of n values, arrange the values in order of increasing size.
>
> If n is odd, the median is the $\frac{1}{2}(n + 1)$th value. If n is even, the median is halfway between the $\frac{1}{2}n$th value and the following value.

Here is a list of the masses of the female students from the 'Brain size' datafile in Table 4.1.

118 147 146 138 175 118 155 146 135 127 136 122 114 140
106 159 127 143 153 139

First, put them in order.

106 114 118 118 122 127 127 135 136 **138** **139** 140 143 146
146 147 153 155 159 175

There are 20 students so the median is calculated from the 10th and 11th values. These two values are shown in bold type. The median is $\frac{1}{2}(138 + 139)$, or 138.5 pounds.

Your calculator probably has a built-in routine for finding the median. Consult the manual to find out how to use it.

5.3 Finding the median from a frequency table

Data sets are often much larger than the ones in the previous section and the values will often have been organised in some way, maybe in a frequency table. As an example, Table 5.1 gives the number of brothers and sisters of the children in Year 8 at a school.

Number of brothers and sisters	Frequency	Cumulative frequency
0	36	36
1	94	130
2	48	178
3	15	193
4	7	200
5	3	203
6	1	204
	Total: 204	

Table 5.1

One way of finding the median is to write out a list of all the individual values, starting with 36 '0's, then 94 '1's and so on, and find the $\frac{1}{2} \times 204$, or 102nd value and the 103rd value. A much easier method is to insert a column of cumulative frequencies, as in Table 5.1. From this you can see that when you have come to the end of the '0's you have not yet reached the 102nd value but, by the end of the '1's, you have reached the 130th value. This means that the 102nd and 103rd values are both 1, so the median is also 1.

You can also use your calculator to find the median from a frequency table.

In this example the data had not been grouped, so it was possible to count to the median. Large data sets for continuous variables, however, are nearly always grouped, and the individual values are lost. This means that you cannot find the median exactly and you have to estimate it. Table 5.2 gives the frequency distribution for the playing time of a much larger selection of CDs.

Playing time, x (min)	Interval boundaries	Frequency	Cumulative frequency
40–44	$39.5 \le x < 44.5$	1	1
45–49	$44.5 \le x < 49.5$	7	8
50–54	$49.5 \le x < 54.5$	12	20
55–59	$54.5 \le x < 59.5$	24	44
60–64	$59.5 \le x < 64.5$	29	73
65–69	$64.5 \le x < 69.5$	14	87
70–74	$69.5 \le x < 74.5$	5	92
75–79	$74.5 \le x < 79.5$	3	95
		Total: 95	

Table 5.2

A column for cumulative frequency has been added to the table, and Fig. 5.3 shows a cumulative frequency graph for the data.

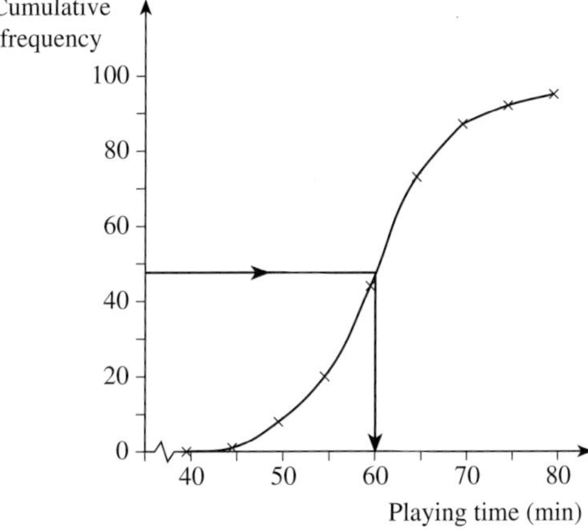

Fig. 5.3

Reminder: cumulative frequency is plotted against the upper interval boundary of each class interval.

The cumulative frequency curve allows you to find the number of CDs with a playing time less than a given value. To obtain the median playing time from the cumulative frequency graph, you read off the value corresponding to a cumulative frequency equal to half the total frequency, in this case $\frac{1}{2} \times 95$, or 47.5. This gives a playing time of 60 minutes. This value is taken as an estimate of the median, because roughly half the playing times will be below it and consequently about half will be above it.

To find the median value for grouped data from a cumulative frequency graph, read off the value of the variable corresponding to a cumulative frequency equal to half the total frequency.

Some books suggest reading off the value from the cumulative frequency graph which corresponds to a cumulative frequency of $\frac{1}{2}(n+1)$ rather than $\frac{1}{2}n$. This will give a slightly different value but the difference is not important.

Sometimes discrete data are grouped into classes so that, once again, you cannot list the individual values. An example was given in Table 4.6. To estimate the median for such data, treat the variable as though it were continuous and find the median from the cumulative frequency graph or from a calculator.

When you use your calculator to calculate the median, or any other statistical calculation, it is crucial to make sure that you enter the data correctly.

Exercise 5A

1 Find the median weight of 6.6 kg, 3.2 kg, 4.8 kg, 7.6 kg, 5.4 kg, 7.1 kg, 2.0 kg , 6.3 kg and 4.3 kg.

A weight of 6.0 kg is added to the set. What is the median of the 10 weights?

2 Obtain the medians for the following data sets.

(a) The speeds, in miles per hour, of 20 cars, measured on a city street.

41 15 4 27 21 32 43 37 18 25 29 34 28 30 25 52 12 36 6 25

(b) The times taken, in hours (to the nearest tenth), to carry out repairs to 17 pieces of machinery.

0.9 1.0 2.1 4.2 0.7 1.1 0.9 1.8 0.9 1.2 2.3 1.6 2.1 0.3 0.8 2.7 0.4

3 Obtain the median of the haemoglobin levels in Exercise 4A Question 5.

4 Using your cumulative frequency diagram from Exercise 4B Question 4, obtain an estimate of the median value of the sales.

5 The following are ignition times in seconds, correct to the nearest 0.1 s, of samples of 80 flammable materials. They are arranged in numerical order by rows.

1.2	1.4	1.4	1.5	1.5	1.6	1.7	1.8	1.8	1.9	2.1	2.2	2.3	2.5	2.5	2.5
2.5	2.6	2.7	2.8	3.1	3.2	3.5	3.6	3.7	3.8	3.8	3.9	3.9	4.0	4.1	4.2
4.3	4.5	4.5	4.6	4.7	4.7	4.8	4.9	5.1	5.1	5.1	5.2	5.2	5.3	5.4	5.5
5.6	5.8	5.9	5.9	6.0	6.3	6.4	6.4	6.4	6.4	6.7	6.8	6.8	6.9	7.3	7.4
7.4	7.6	7.9	8.0	8.6	8.8	8.8	9.2	9.4	9.6	9.7	9.8	10.6	11.2	11.8	12.8

(a) Group the data into 8 equal classes, starting with 1.0–2.4 and 2.5–3.9, and form a grouped frequency table. Draw a frequency histogram. State what it indicates about the ignition times.

(b) From the grouped frequency table draw a cumulative frequency diagram and use it to estimate the median ignition time.

(c) Find the exact median from the data set, and account for any difference in your two answers.

6 The number of rejected CDs produced each day by a machine was monitored for 100 days. The results are summarised in the following table.

Number of rejects	0–9	10–19	20–29	30–39	40–49	50–59
Number of days	5	8	19	37	22	9

Estimate the median number of rejects.

7 For the 'Brain size' data in Table 4.1, find and compare the median heights of

(a) the men, (b) the women.

5.4 The mean

The median does not use the actual values of the observations in a data set, apart from the middle value(s) when the data are arranged in order of increasing size. A measure of location which does make use of the values of all the observations is the **mean**. This is the quantity which most people are referring to when they talk about the 'average'. The mean is found by adding all the values and dividing by the number of values. For the nine CDs in Section 5.1,

$$\text{mean} = \frac{49 + 56 + 55 + 68 + 61 + 57 + 61 + 52 + 63}{9} = \frac{522}{9} = 58 \text{ minutes.}$$

The **mean** of a data set is equal to the sum of the values in the data set divided by the number of values.

You can also use your calculator to find the mean. Refer to your calculator manual.

5.5 Samples and populations

You should realise that the calculation of the mean of the nine CDs in Section 5.4 can only give you an **estimate** of the mean of the whole population of CDs. The true mean playing time of CDs can only be found by testing the playing times of the whole population of CDs. This is clearly impossible, so you have to use a sample of CDs, which gives you an approximation to the true mean.

When you are finding the mean of a population, the symbol μ is used. (The letter μ is the greek letter 'm', and is pronounced 'mu'.) If you are finding the mean of a sample to get an approximation to the mean of a population, the symbol $\overline{x}$ (pronounced 'x-bar') is used.

The fact that the sample mean is the best possible approximation to the population mean in the sense that it is an unbiased approximation is an important issue which cannot be addressed in this book.

The word 'unbiased' is a technical word with a specific meaning, but it is being used in both in its technical and untechnical senses here.

Note that although a population sounds as though it ought to be large, it need not be so. For example, it may be that the population you are concerned with is the total number of people in your mathematics class.

It is possible to express the definition of the mean as a mathematical formula by using the Σ-notation you met in Section 2.6. Suppose you have n data values. The symbol x_i denotes the ith value in the data set. For the playing times of the nine CDs in the previous section, $x_1 = 49$, $x_2 = 56$, $x_3 = 55$ and so on. The sum of these values is

$$x_1 + x_2 + x_3 + x_4 + x_5 + x_6 + x_7 + x_8 + x_9.$$

The population mean, μ, of a data set of n values is given by

$$\mu = \frac{x_1 + x_2 + \ldots + x_n}{n} = \frac{\sum_{i=1}^{n} x_i}{n}.$$

The sample mean, $\overline{x}$, of a sample with n values is given by

$$\overline{x} = \frac{x_1 + x_2 + \ldots + x_n}{n} = \frac{\sum_{i=1}^{n} x_i}{n}.$$

Sometimes the equation $\overline{x} = \dfrac{\sum_{i=1}^{n} x_i}{n}$ is written $\overline{x} = \dfrac{\sum x}{n}$.

Although the two formulae above look identical, it is important to make sure that you know when you are dealing with a population and when you are dealing with a sample, which gives an approximation to the mean of the population.

When you use your calculator to calculate the mean, you can either use the formulae above, or you can use the calculator's own built-in routine. If you use the formulae above, you can be prone to errors as you carry out the calculation; whichever method you use, ensure that you enter the data correctly.

5.6 Calculating the mean from a frequency table

Table 5.4 contains a copy of the data in Table 5.1, which was the frequency distribution of the number of brothers and sisters of the children in Year 8 at a school. Of the 204 values, 36 are '0's, 94 are '1's, 48 are '2's and so on. Their sum will be

$$(0 \times 36) + (1 \times 94) + (2 \times 48) + (3 \times 15) + (4 \times 7) + (5 \times 3) + (6 \times 1).$$

You can include this calculation in the table by adding a third column in which each value of the variable, x_i, is multiplied by its frequency, f_i.

Number of brothers and sisters, x_i	Frequency, f_i	$f_i x_i$
0	36	0
1	94	94
2	48	96
3	15	45
4	7	28
5	3	15
6	1	6
	Totals: $\sum_{i=1}^{n} f_i = 204$	$\sum_{i=1}^{n} f_i x_i = 284$

Table 5.4

The mean is equal to $\dfrac{284}{204} = 1.39$, correct to 3 significant figures.

Although the number of brothers and sisters of each child must be a whole number, the mean of the data values need not be a whole number.

In this example the answer is a recurring decimal, and so the answer has been rounded to 3 significant figures. This degree of accuracy is suitable for the answers to most statistical calculations. However, it is important to keep more significant figures when values are carried forward for use in further calculations.

The calculation of the mean can be expressed in Σ-notation as follows:

The population mean, μ, of a data set in which the variable takes the value x_1 with frequency f_1, x_2 with frequency f_2 and so on is given by

$$\mu = \frac{f_1x_1 + f_2x_2 + \ldots + f_nx_n}{f_1 + f_2 + \ldots + f_n} = \frac{\sum_{i=1}^{n} f_ix_i}{\sum_{i=1}^{n} f_i}.$$

The sample mean, $\bar{x}$, of a sample in which the variable takes the value x_1 with frequency f_1, x_2 with frequency f_2 and so on is given by

$$\bar{x} = \frac{f_1x_1 + f_2x_2 + \ldots + f_nx_n}{f_1 + f_2 + \ldots + f_n} = \frac{\sum_{i=1}^{n} f_ix_i}{\sum_{i=1}^{n} f_i}.$$

If the data in a frequency table are grouped, you need a single value to represent each class before you can calculate an estimate of the mean using either of the equations in the blue box. A reasonable choice is to take the value halfway between the class boundaries. This is called the **mid-interval value**. Table 5.5 reproduces Table 5.2 for the playing times of 95 CDs. Two other columns have been included, one giving the mid-interval value for each class and the other the product of this mid-interval value and the frequency.

Playing time, x (min)	Class boundaries	Frequency, f_i	Mid-interval value, x_i	f_ix_i
40–44	$39.5 \leq x < 44.5$	1	42	42
45–49	$44.5 \leq x < 49.5$	7	47	329
50–54	$49.5 \leq x < 54.5$	12	52	624
55–59	$54.5 \leq x < 59.5$	24	57	1368
60–64	$59.5 \leq x < 64.5$	29	62	1798
65–69	$64.5 \leq x < 69.5$	14	67	938
70–74	$69.5 \leq x < 74.5$	5	72	360
75–79	$74.5 \leq x < 79.5$	3	77	231
		Totals: $\sum_{i=1}^{8} f_i = 95$		$\sum_{i=1}^{8} f_ix_i = 5690$

Table 5.5

Thus the estimate of the mean is $\dfrac{\sum_{i=1}^{8} f_ix_i}{\sum_{i=1}^{8} f_i} = \dfrac{5690}{95} = 59.9$ min, correct to 3 significant figures.

This value is only an estimate of the mean playing time for the CDs, because individual values have been replaced by mid-interval values: some information has been lost by grouping the data.

Exercise 5B

1 The test marks of 8 students were 18, 2, 5, 0, 17, 15, 16 and 11. Find the mean score.

2 For the data set in Table 4.1, find the mean height of the male students.

The mean height of adult males is about 69 inches. Comment on your answer in the light of this information.

3 (a) Find $\bar{x}$ given that $\sum_{i=1}^{20} x_i = 226$. (b) Find $\bar{y}$ given that $\sum_{i=1}^{12} (y_i - 100) = 66$.

4 The number of misprints on each page of the draft of a book containing 182 pages is summarised in the following table. Find the mean number of misprints on a page.

Number of misprints	0	1	2	3	4
Number of pages	144	24	10	2	2

5 The following table gives the frequency distribution for the lengths of rallies (measured by the number of shots) in a tennis match. Find the mean length of a rally.

Length of rally	1	2	3	4	5	6	7	8
Frequency	2	20	15	12	10	5	3	1

6 The table below gives the number of shoots produced by 50 plants in a botanical research laboratory. Calculate the mean number of shoots per plant.

No. of shoots	0–4	5–9	10–14	15–19	20–24	25–29	30–34	35–39	40–44
Frequency	1	1	1	6	17	16	4	2	2

7 The speeds, in miles per hour, of 200 vehicles travelling on a motorway were measured using a radar device. The results are summarised in the following grouped frequency table. Estimate the mean speed.

Speed (m.p.h.)	30–40	40–50	50–60	60–70	70–80	80–90
Frequency	12	32	56	72	20	8

8 Calls made by a telephone saleswoman were monitored. The lengths (in minutes, to the nearest minute) of 30 calls are summarised in the following table.

Length of call	0–2	3–5	6–8	9–11	12–14
Number of calls	17	6	4	2	1

(a) Write down the class interval boundaries.

(b) Estimate the mean length of the calls.

9 The price of a CD is denoted by $\$x$. For 60 CDs bought in different stores it is found that

$$\sum_{i=1}^{60}(x-12) = 53.40.$$

Calculate the mean price of these CDs. The mean price of a further 40 CDs is found to be \$11.64. Find the mean price of the 100 CDs.

10 The mean weight of eight oarsmen is 100 kg. They are joined by a cox of weight 55 kg. Calculate the mean weight of all nine people.

11 When a tug of war team of six members is joined by another member, the mean weight goes up from 110 kg to 111 kg. Find the weight of the new member.

5.7 The mode and the modal class

A third measure of location is the **mode**, sometimes called the **modal value**. This is defined to be the most frequently occurring value. You can pick it out from a frequency table (if the data have not been grouped) by looking for the value with the highest frequency. If you look back to Table 5.1 you will see that the mode for the number of brothers and sisters is 1.

If the data have been grouped then it only possible to estimate the mode. Alternatively, you can give the **modal class interval**, which is the class interval with the highest frequency. For example, the modal class for the playing time in Table 5.2 is 60–64 minutes.

If you are given a small data set then you can find the mode just by looking at the data. For the first nine CDs in Section 5.2, with playing times

$$49, 52, 55, 56, 57, 61, 61, 63, 68$$

the mode is 61.

It is not uncommon for all the values to occur only once, so that there is no mode. For example, the next six CDs had playing times

$$47, 49, 59, 62, 65, 68,$$

and there is no modal value. Combining the two data sets gives

$$47, 49, 49, 52, 55, 56, 57, 59, 61, 61, 62, 63, 65, 68, 68.$$

Now there are three values which have a frequency of 2, giving three modes: 49, 61 and 68. One of these values is low, one high and the other is near the centre of the data set. In this case, the mode fails to provide only one measure of location to represent the data set. You can see that the mode is not a very useful measure of location for small data sets.

In contrast to the mean and median, the mode can be found for qualitative data. For example, for the datafile 'Brain size' in Table 4.1 the mode for the variable 'gender' can be found. However, since the number of males is equal to the number of females (both 20), both 'males' and 'females' are modes.

> The **mode** of a data set is the value which occurs with the highest frequency. A data set can have more than one mode if two or more values have the same maximum frequency. A data set has no mode if all the values have the same frequency.
>
> The **modal class** for a grouped frequency table is the class with the highest frequency.

5.8 Comparison of the mean, median and mode

The examples in this chapter show that the mean, median and mode of a data set can differ from each other. For example, for the first nine CDs, the median was 57, the mean 58 and the mode 61. The question then arises as to why there are different ways of calculating the average of a data set. The answer is that an average describes a large amount of information with a single value, and there is no completely satisfactory way of doing this. Each average conveys different information and each has its advantages and disadvantages. You can see this by comparing the mean, median and mode for the following data set, which gives the monthly salaries of the thirteen employees in a small firm.

\$1000 \$1000 \$1000 \$1000 \$1100 \$1200 \$1250
\$1400 \$1600 \$1600 \$1700 \$2900 \$4200

Median = $\frac{1}{2}(n+1)$th value = $\frac{1}{2}(13+1)$th value = 7th value = \$1250.

Mean = sum of the values $\div\, n = \frac{20\,950}{13}$ = \$1612, correct to the nearest dollar.

Mode = value with the highest frequency = \$1000.

A new employee who had been told that the 'average' wage was \$1612 (the mean) would probably be disappointed when he learnt his own salary, because 10 out of the 13 employees earn less than \$1612. In this example the median would measure the centre of the distribution better because the median is not affected by the large distance of the last two salaries from the other salaries, whereas the mean is 'pulled up' by them. Normally the median is preferable to the mean as an average when there are values which are not typical. Such values are called **outliers**. The mode is not a very useful measure of the centre in this example, because it is \$1000, the lowest salary: 9 of the 13 employees earn more than this.

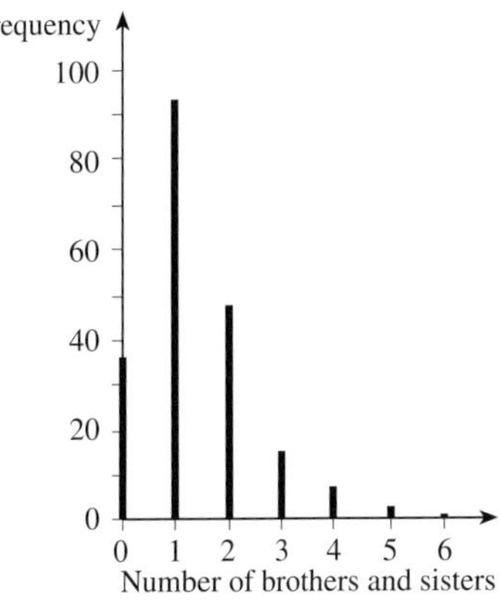

Fig. 5.6

You can see the same effect of a few high values on the mean for the data set in Table 5.4. The frequency distribution is illustrated in Fig. 5.6. The distribution is not symmetrical but is said to be **skewed**. The 'tail' of high values on the right of the distribution has the effect of making the mean (approximately 1.4) higher than the median (1).

A distribution which has a 'tail' of low values on the left will have a mean which is less than the median.

Distributions which are roughly symmetrical will have similar values for the mean and the median. The data for the CD playing times in Table 5.2 illustrate this. The frequency histogram in Fig. 5.7, which illustrates this distribution, is approximately symmetrical; the estimates for the mean (59.9) and median (60) are nearly equal. For such a distribution the mean might be considered the 'best' average, because it uses all the information in the data set.

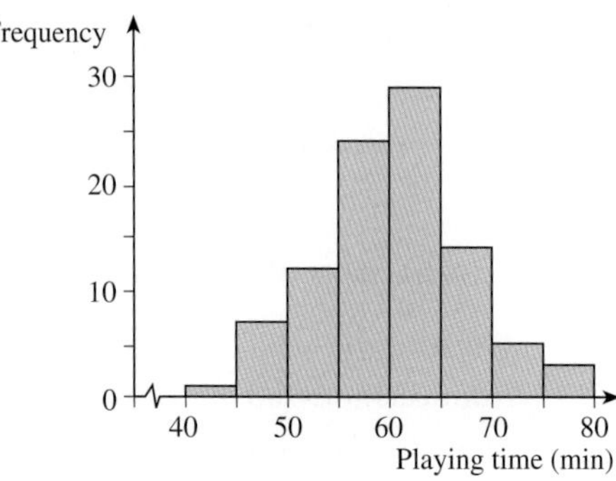

Fig. 5.7

From these examples it should be clear that the mean, median and mode often provide different information. When you are given an 'average' it is important to know whether it is the mean, the median or the mode. When you calculate an average, it is important to choose the average which is the most 'typical' value.

Example 5.8.1

A commuter who travels to work by car has a choice of two different routes, V and W. She decides to compare her journey times for each route. So she records the journey times, in minutes, for 10 consecutive working days, for each route. The results are:

Route V	53	52	48	51	49	47	42	48	57	53
Route W	43	41	39	108	52	42	38	45	39	51

Calculate the mean and median for route V, and the mean and median for route W. Which average do you think is more suitable for comparing the time taken on each route?

For route V, $\bar{v} = \dfrac{\sum_{i=1}^{10} v_i}{n} = \dfrac{500}{10} = 50$. For route W, $\bar{w} = \dfrac{\sum_{i=1}^{10} w_i}{n} = \dfrac{498}{10} = 49.8$.

Arranging the values in order of increasing size gives:

Route V	42	47	48	48	49	51	52	53	53	57
Route W	38	39	39	41	42	43	45	51	52	108

For route V, median $= \frac{1}{2}(5\text{th} + 6\text{th})$ values $= \frac{1}{2}(49 + 51) = 50$.

For route W, median $= \frac{1}{2}(5\text{th} + 6\text{th})$ values $= \frac{1}{2}(42 + 43) = 42.5$.

For route V, the mean and the median are equal. For route W the mean is greater than the median, because one high value (108) pulls up the mean. This unusual value was perhaps due to bad weather or an accident and is not typical. So it is better to use the median as the average journey time, because it is not affected by such outliers.

This suggests that route W, with median 42.5 minutes, is quicker than route V, with median 50 minutes.

Exercise 5C

1 For the following distributions state, where possible, the mode or the modal class.

(a)

x	0	1	2	3	4
f	7	4	2	5	1

(b)

x	70	75	80	85	90
f	5	5	5	5	5

(c)

x	2–3	4–5	6–7	8–9	10–11
f	7	4	4	4	1

(d)

Eye colour	Blue	Brown	Green
f	23	39	3

2 State, giving a reason, which of the mean, median or mode would be most useful in the following situations.

(a) The manager of a shoe shop wishes to stock shoes of various sizes.

(b) A City Council wishes to plan for a school to serve a new housing estate. In order to estimate the number of pupils, it studies family sizes on similar estates.

(c) A person travels by car from York to Crewe regularly and has kept a record of the times taken. She wishes to make an estimate of the time that her next journey will take.

3 An estate agent makes the following statement.

'Over 60% of houses sold this month were sold for more than the average selling price.'

Consider the possible truth of this statement, and what is meant by 'average'.

4 State whether you would expect the following variables to have distributions which are skewed, or which are roughly symmetrical.

(a) The heights of female students in a university.

(b) The running times of competitors in a marathon race.

(c) The scores obtained by candidates in an easy examination.

(d) The numbers of pages in the books in a library.

5 A mental arithmetic test of 8 questions was given to a class of 32 pupils. The results are summarised in the following table.

Number of correct answers	0	1	2	3	4	5	6	7	8
Number of pupils	1	2	1	4	4	6	7	4	3

(a) Find the mean, median and mode of the number of correct answers. Interpret the median and mode in the context of this maths test.

(b) Describe the shape of the distribution.

6 Measures of spread

This chapter describes three different measures of spread and their methods of calculation. When you have completed it, you should

- know what the range is, and be able to calculate it
- know what the quartiles are and how to find the interquartile range from them
- be able to construct a box and whisker plot from a set of data
- know what the variance and standard deviation are, and be able to calculate them
- be able to select an appropriate measure of spread to use in a given situation.

6.1 Introduction

You saw in Chapter 5 how a set of data could be summarised by choosing an appropriate typical value, or 'measure of location' as it is more correctly known. Three different measures of location, the mean, the median and the mode, were introduced.

Now consider the two sets of data A and B given below.

A:	48	52	60	60	60	68	72
B:	0	10	60	60	60	110	120

For both data sets A and B, mean = median = mode = 60. If you were only given a measure of location for each set you might think that A and B were similar. Yet looking in detail at A and B shows that they are quite different. The most striking difference between the two data sets is that B is much more spread out than A. Measures of location give no indication of these differences in spread, so new measures are needed to summarise the spread of data.

6.2 The range

The most obvious method of measuring spread is to calculate the difference between the lowest value and the highest value. This difference is called the **range**.

> The **range** of a set of data values is defined by the equation
>
> range = largest value − smallest value.

The range of data set A is $72 - 48 = 24$, whereas the range of data set B is $120 - 0 = 120$. Calculating the ranges shows clearly that data set B is more spread out than data set A.

> Students often give the range as an interval. This would mean, for instance, that the range of data set A would be given as 48 to 72, or 48–72, or $48 \rightarrow 72$. In statistics the range is a single value.

If you are going to use the range as a measure of spread it is helpful to realise its limitations. If you consider the two further data sets C and D shown below, you will see that they both have the same range, 8.

C: 2 4 6 8 10
D: 2 6 6 6 10

Although both data sets C and D have the same range, the patterns of their distributions are quite different from one another. Data set C is evenly spread within the interval 2 to 10 whereas data set D has more of its values 'bunched' centrally. Because the range is calculated from extreme values it ignores the pattern of spread for the rest of the values. This is a major criticism of using the range as a measure of spread. Although the range is easy to calculate, it ignores the pattern of spread and considers only the extreme values.

6.3 The interquartile range

Since the range ignores the internal spread of the values in a data set, an alternative measure is needed. One possibility is to look at the spread between two values which are at some fixed, but interior, position. A sensible choice, which is associated naturally with the median, is to choose the values that are at the positions one-quarter and three-quarters of the way through the data when the values are arranged in order. These points are known as the **lower quartile** and the **upper quartile** respectively, and they are usually denoted by the symbols Q_1 and Q_3 respectively. The difference between these values is called the **interquartile range**.

Interquartile range = upper quartile − lower quartile = $Q_3 - Q_1$.

The interquartile range is really just the range of the middle 50% of the distribution.

Notice that there is also a **middle quartile**, Q_2, which is the median.

To find the position of the quartiles for small data sets there are several possible methods that you might see in textbooks. The one suggested below is fairly easy to apply.

Finding the quartiles

- First arrange the data in ascending order.

Case 1 An even number of data values

- Split the data into their upper half and lower half.
- Then the median of the upper half is Q_3, and the median of the lower half is Q_1.

Case 2 An odd number of data values

- Find the median, Q_2, and delete it from the list.
- Split the remaining data into their upper half and lower half.
- Then the median of the upper half is Q_3, and the median of the lower half is Q_1.

Example 6.3.1

Find the quartiles and the interquartile range for each of the two sets of data below.

(a) 7 9 12 13 8 11 (b) 7 8 22 20 15 18 19 13 11

(a) First, arrange the data in numerical order.

7 8 9 11 12 13

The number of data values is even, so divide the data into its two halves:

Lower half: 7 8 9 Upper half: 11 12 13

The lower quartile Q_1 is the median of the lower half, which is 8. The upper quartile Q_3 is the median of the upper half, which is 12. So

$$\text{interquartile range} = Q_3 - Q_1 = 12 - 8 = 4.$$

(b) Arrange the data in numerical order.

7 8 11 13 15 18 19 20 22

Since the number of data values (9) is odd, find the median $Q_2 = 15$ and delete it.

7 8 11 13 18 19 20 22

This automatically divides the data into lower and upper halves.

The median of the lower half is the lower quartile, so $Q_1 = \frac{1}{2}(8 + 11) = 9.5$, and the median of the upper half is the upper quartile, so $Q_3 = \frac{1}{2}(19 + 20) = 19.5$.

The interquartile range is $Q_3 - Q_1 = 19.5 - 9.5 = 10$.

In Chapter 5 you saw how the median of the masses of female students taken from the 'Brain size' datafile could be found by arranging the masses from Section 5.2 in order.

106 114 118 118 **122** **127** 127 135 136 **138** **139** 140 143 146 **146** **147** 153 155 159 175

As there are 20 students, the upper and lower halves of the data set each contain 10 values. The lower quartile is at the position which is equivalent to the median of the lower half. This is halfway between the 5th and 6th values (in ascending order). These are shown in bold type.

Therefore $Q_1 = \frac{1}{2}(122 + 127) = 124.5$.

Similarly the upper quartile is at the position which is equivalent to the median of the upper half of the data set. This is halfway between the 15th and 16th values (in ascending order). These are also shown in bold type.

Therefore $Q_3 = \frac{1}{2}(146 + 147) = 146.5$.

The interquartile range is therefore $Q_3 - Q_1 = 146.5 - 124.5 = 22$.

It is quite likely that the size of a data set will be much larger than the ones which have so far been considered. Larger data sets are usually organised into frequency tables and it is then necessary to think carefully about how to find the position of the quartiles. In Chapter 5 you saw how to find the median of a set of data which referred to the numbers of brothers and sisters of children in a year at a school. Table 6.1 below reproduces Table 5.1.

Number of brothers and sisters	Frequency	Cumulative frequency
0	36	36
1	94	130
2	48	178
3	15	193
4	7	200
5	3	203
6	1	204
	Total: 204	

Table 6.1

There were 204 observations. This means that each half will have 102 data values.

The position of the lower quartile, Q_1, will be halfway between the 51st and 52nd values (in ascending order). From the cumulative frequency column you can see that both values are 1s, so $Q_1 = 1$. The position of the upper quartile, Q_3, will be halfway between the $(102 + 51)$th and $(102 + 52)$th values (in ascending order); that is, between the 153rd and 154th values. From the cumulative frequency column that both values are 2s, so $Q_3 = 2$.

For continuous variables, large data sets are usually grouped and so the individual values are lost. The quartiles are estimated from a cumulative frequency graph using a method similar to that described in Chapter 5 to find the median.

Table 6.2 gives the frequency distribution for the playing times of the selection of CDs which you first met in Table 5.2.

Playing time, x (min)	Class boundaries	Frequency	Cumulative frequency
40–44	$39.5 \le x < 44.5$	1	1
45–49	$44.5 \le x < 49.5$	7	8
50–54	$49.5 \le x < 54.5$	12	20
55–59	$54.5 \le x < 59.5$	24	44
60–64	$59.5 \le x < 64.5$	29	73
65–69	$64.5 \le x < 69.5$	14	87
70–74	$69.5 \le x < 74.5$	5	92
75–79	$74.5 \le x < 79.5$	3	95
		Total: 95	

Table 6.2

To obtain an estimate of the lower quartile of the playing times you read off the value corresponding to a cumulative frequency equal to one-quarter of the total frequency, which in this case is $\frac{1}{4} \times 95 = 23.75$. From the cumulative frequency graph in Fig. 6.3 you can see that $Q_1 \approx 56$ minutes. Similarly you find an estimate of the upper quartile by reading off the value corresponding to a cumulative frequency equal to three-quarters of the total frequency, which is $\frac{3}{4} \times 95 = 71.25$. From the cumulative frequency graph in Fig. 6.3 this gives $Q_3 \approx 64$ minutes.

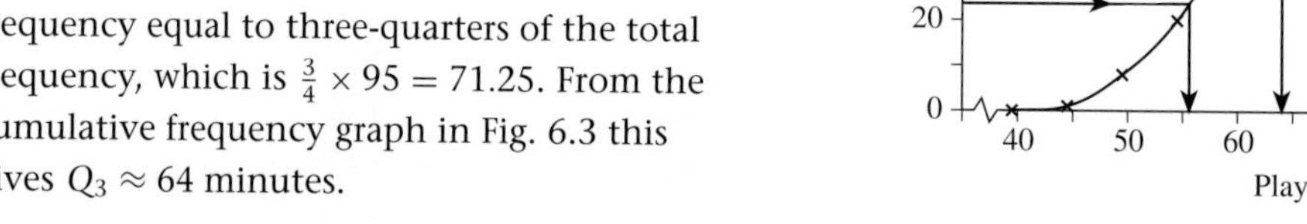

Fig. 6.3

Then the interquartile range is

$$Q_3 - Q_1 \approx 64 - 56 = 8,$$

so the interquartile range is approximately 8 minutes.

Note that you can also use your calculator to find quartiles.

Sometimes there is a need to find the data value which occupies a position other than the median or the upper and lower quartiles. For example, you might want to know the value which has 90% of the data below it. This is an example of a **percentile**; this particular percentile is called the 90th percentile. You can find its value from the cumulative frequency diagram in a similar way to that used for finding the quartiles. For example, in Fig. 6.3, the 90th percentile is found by first finding 90% of the total frequency, that is, $\frac{90}{100} \times 95 = 85.5$. From the cumulative frequency graph in Fig. 6.3, you will see that the 90th percentile is about 69 minutes. You can use a similar method to find the 95th percentile, the 40th percentile or any other percentile.

You may be wondering how to interpret the interquartile range for a set of data. For example, is the value of 8 in the example above large or small? The answer is that you cannot tell without more information. Normally you would be comparing the spread of two or more data sets. You can then make a more sensible comment on whether a particular interquartile range is large or small by comparing its size with the other interquartile ranges. The following example illustrates this idea.

Example 6.3.2

Two people did separate traffic surveys, using a radar gun, at different locations, A and B. Each person noted down the speed of 50 cars which passed their observation point. The results are given in Table 6.4.

Speed, v (km h^{-1})	A frequency	B frequency
$0 \le v < 20$	7	1
$20 \le v < 40$	11	3
$40 \le v < 60$	13	5
$60 \le v < 80$	12	20
$80 \le v < 100$	5	18
$100 \le v < 120$	2	3
	Totals: 50	50

Table 6.4

(a) Draw a cumulative frequency diagram for each set of data and use it to estimate the median speed and the interquartile range of speeds at each observation point.

(b) Use your results to part (a) to comment on the locations.

(a) From Fig. 6.5, you can estimate the median and quartiles for the cars at location A. The median corresponds to a cumulative frequency of 25 and, from Fig. 6.5, it is approximately 51. The lower quartile corresponds to a cumulative frequency of 12.5, and it is approximately 30. The upper quartile corresponds to a cumulative frequency of 37.5, and it is approximately 69.

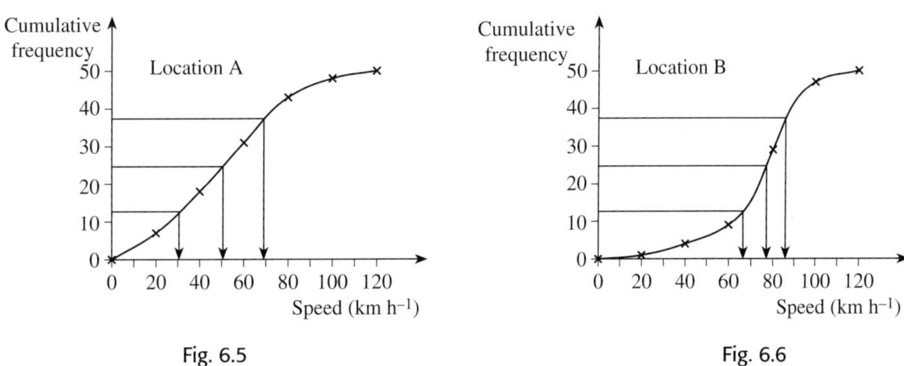

Fig. 6.5

Fig. 6.6

From Fig. 6.6, you can estimate the median and quartiles for the cars at location B. The values of the median and the quartiles are approximately 76, 66 and 86.

(b) You can now compare the medians and the interquartile ranges.

For A the median is 51 and the interquartile range is $69 - 30 = 39$.

For B the median is 76 and the interquartile range is $86 - 66 = 20$.

The median speed at A is lower than the median speed at B and the interquartile range at A is higher than the interquartile range at B. So at location A the cars go more slowly and there is a greater variation in their speeds. Perhaps B is on or near a motorway, and A may be in a town near some point of congestion. You cannot say for certain what types of location A and B are but the summary values do give you an idea of the type of road at each position.

6.4 The five-number summary

One helpful way of summarising data is to give values which provide essential information about the data set. One such summary is called the **five-number summary**. This summary gives the median, Q_2, the lower quartile Q_1, the upper quartile Q_3, the minimum value and the maximum value. These five values are usually given in numerical order.

Example 6.4.1
The data below give the number of fish caught each day over a period of 11 days by an angler. Give a five-number summary of the data.

0 2 5 2 0 4 4 8 9 8 8

Rearranging the data in order gives:

0 0 2 2 4 4 5 8 8 8 9

The median value is $Q_2 = 4$. As the number of data values is odd, deleting the middle one and finding the medians of the lower and upper halves gives

$$Q_1 = 2 \quad \text{and} \quad Q_3 = 8.$$

The five-number summary is then the minimum value, 0, the lower quartile, 2, the median, 4, the upper quartile, 8, and the maximum value, 9.

The five-number summary can also be usefully presented as a table, as in Table 6.7.

Minimum	0
Q_1	2
Q_2	4
Q_3	8
Maximum	9

Table 6.7

6.5 Box and whisker plots

You can convert this five-number summary into a useful diagram, called a **box and whisker plot**. To draw a box and whisker plot, first draw a scale, preferably using graph paper. You can draw the scale vertically or horizontally, but in this book, the scale and the diagram are always drawn horizontally. Above the scale draw a box (or rectangle) in which the left side is above the point corresponding to the lower quartile and the right side is above the point corresponding to the upper quartile. Then mark a third line inside the box above the point which corresponds to the median value. After this you draw the two whiskers. The left whisker extends from the lower quartile to the minimum value and the right whisker extends from the upper quartile to the maximum. Fig. 6.8 shows the box and whisker plot for the data in Example 6.4.1.

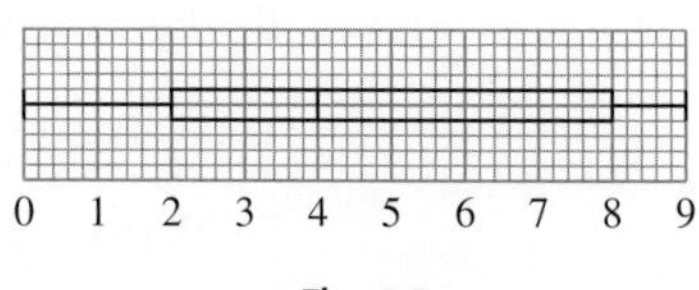

Fig. 6.8

In a box and whisker plot the box itself indicates the location of the middle 50% of the data. The whiskers then show how the data is spread overall.

Another important feature of a set of data is its shape when represented as a frequency diagram. The three pictures below in Fig. 6.9 show three different shapes which commonly occur when you draw frequency diagrams.

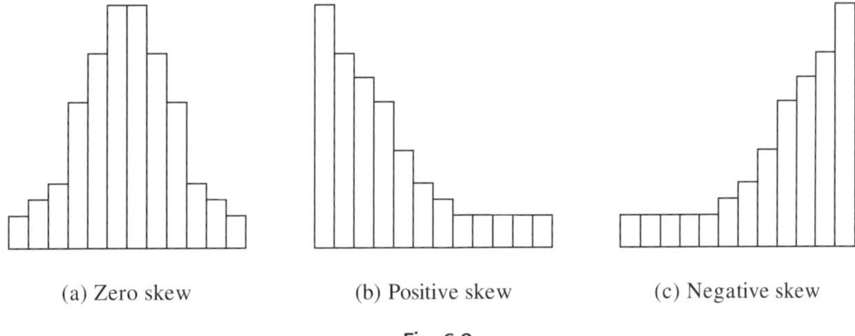

(a) Zero skew (b) Positive skew (c) Negative skew

Fig. 6.9

The distribution in Fig. 6.9a is symmetrical. If a distribution lacks symmetry it is said to be **skew**, or to have **skewness**. The distribution in Fig. 6.9a may therefore be said to have zero skewness. You were briefly introduced to the term 'skewness' in Section 5.8.

The distribution in Fig. 6.9b is not symmetrical, with a 'tail' which stretches towards the higher values. This distribution is said to have **positive skew**, or to be **skewed positively**.

The distribution in Fig. 6.9c is also not symmetrical, with a 'tail' which stretches towards the lower values. This distribution is said to have **negative skew**, or to be **skewed negatively**.

Another method of assessing the skewness of a distribution uses the quartiles Q_1, Q_2 and Q_3.

If $Q_3 - Q_2 \approx Q_2 - Q_1$ then the distribution is said to be (almost) symmetrical, and a box and whisker plot of such data, as in Fig. 6.10, would show a box in which the line corresponding to the median was in the centre of the box.

If $Q_3 - Q_2 > Q_2 - Q_1$, as in Fig. 6.11, then the data is said to have positive skew, and the line representing the median would be nearer to the left side of the box.

If $Q_3 - Q_2 < Q_2 - Q_1$, as in Fig. 6.12, then the data would be said to have negative skew, and the line representing the median would be nearer to the right side of the box.

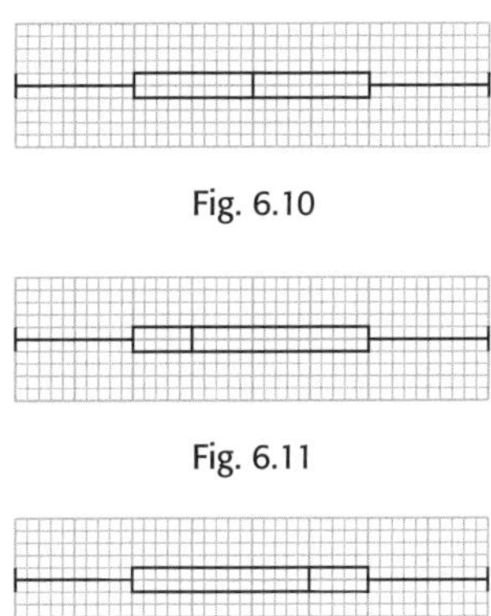

Fig. 6.10

Fig. 6.11

Fig. 6.12

For the data in Example 6.4.1, $Q_1 = 2$, $Q_2 = 4$ and $Q_3 = 8$, so $Q_3 - Q_2 = 8 - 4 = 4$ and $Q_2 - Q_1 = 4 - 2 = 2$. The set of data in Example 6.4.1 therefore has positive skew.

The length of the whiskers can also give some indication of skewness. If the left whisker is shorter than the right whisker then that would tend to indicate positive skew, whereas if the right whisker is shorter than the left whisker, negative skew would be implied.

It is possible for the data to give different results for skewness depending on what measure you use. For example, it is perfectly possible for a box and whisker plot to have $Q_3 - Q_2 > Q_2 - Q_1$, indicating positive skew, but for the left whisker to be longer than the right whisker, which would tend to suggest negative skew. In such cases you must make a judgement about which method of assessing skewness you think is the more important. Fortunately data of this sort do not occur commonly.

Exercise 6A

1 Find the range and the interquartile range of each of the following data sets.

(a) 7 4 14 9 12 2 19 6 15
(b) 7.6 4.8 1.2 6.9 4.8 7.2 8.1 10.3 4.8 6.7

2 The number of times a factory machine broke down was noted over a period of 50 consecutive weeks. The results are given in the following table.

Number of breakdowns	0	1	2	3	4	5	6
Number of weeks	2	12	14	8	8	4	2

(a) Find the interquartile range of the number of breakdowns in a week.

(b) Find the 95th percentile of the number of breakdowns in a week.

3 The audience size in a theatre performing a long-running detective play was monitored over a period of 1 year. The sizes for Monday and Wednesday nights are summarised below.

Audience size	50–99	100–199	200–299	300–399	400–499	500–599
Number of Mondays	12	20	12	5	3	0
Number of Wednesdays	2	3	20	18	5	4

Compare the audience sizes on Mondays and Wednesdays.

4 Draw box and whisker plots for data which have the following five-number summaries, and in each case describe the shape of the data.

(a) 6.0 kg 10.2 kg 12.7 kg 13.2 kg 15.7 kg
(b) −12 °C −8 °C −6 °C 3 °C 11 °C
(c) 37 m 48 m 60 m 72 m 82 m

5 The following figures are the amounts spent in a supermarket by a family for 13 weeks.

£48.25 £43.70 £52.83 £49.24 £58.28 £55.47 £47.29
£51.82 £58.42 £38.73 £42.76 £50.42 £40.85

(a) Obtain a five-number summary of the data.

(b) Construct a box and whisker plot of the data.

(c) Describe any skewness of the data.

6 State, with reasons, whether box and whisker plots or histograms are better for comparing two distributions.

6.6 Variance and standard deviation

One of the reasons for using the interquartile range in preference to the range as a measure of spread was that it took some account of how the more central values were spread rather than concentrating solely on the spread of the extreme values. The interquartile range, however, does not take account of the spread of all of the data values and so, in some sense, it is still an inadequate measure. An alternative measure of spread which does take into account the spread of all the values can be devised by finding how far each data value is from the mean. To do this you would calculate the quantities $x_i - \mu$ for each x_i.

An example in Section 5.4 used the playing times, in minutes, of nine CDs.

49 56 55 68 61 57 61 52 63

The mean of these times was found to be 58 minutes. If the mean is subtracted from each of the original values you get the following values.

−9 −2 −3 10 3 −1 3 −6 5

The negative signs cause a problem, and a simple way to remove them is to square all the numbers to get

81 4 9 100 9 1 9 36 25.

The mean of these squared distances would be a sensible measure of spread. It would represent the mean of the squared distance from the mean.

In this case the mean squared distance from the mean would be

$$\frac{81+4+9+100+9+1+9+36+25}{9} = \frac{274}{9} = 30.4\ldots .$$

Generalising, this leads to the expression $\dfrac{\sum_{i=1}^{n}(x_i - \mu)^2}{n}$ as a measure of spread.

This quantity is called the **variance** of the data values. It is the mean of the squared distances from the mean. So for the data on playing times of CDs,

$$\begin{aligned} \text{variance} &= \frac{\sum_{i=1}^{n}(x_i - \mu)^2}{n} \\ &= \frac{274}{9} = 30.4\ldots . \end{aligned}$$

If the data values $x_1, x_2, \ldots, x_n$ have units associated with them then the variance will be measured in units^2. In the example the data values were measured in minutes and therefore the variance would be measured in minutes^2. This is something which can be avoided by taking the positive square root of the variance. The positive square root of the variance is known as the **standard deviation**, often shortened to 'SD', and it always has the same units as the original data values. The formula for standard deviation is

$$\sqrt{\frac{\sum_{i=1}^{n}(x_i-\mu)^2}{n}}.$$

So the standard deviation of the playing times of the nine CDs is $\sqrt{30.4...} = 5.52$, correct to 3 significant figures.

The symbol σ^2 is used for variance and the symbol σ is used for the standard deviation. (The letter σ is the small greek letter 'sigma'.)

The **variance** of a set of data values $x_1, x_2, \dots, x_n$ whose mean is

$$\mu = \frac{x_1 + x_2 + ... + x_n}{n} = \frac{\sum_{i=1}^{n} x_i}{n}$$

is given by the formula

$$\sigma^2 = \frac{\sum_{i=1}^{n}(x_i-\mu)^2}{n}.$$

The **standard deviation** is the positive square root of the variance.

You can use your calculator to calculate variance or standard deviation.

6.7 Samples and populations

In Section 5.5 your attention was drawn to the difference between finding the mean of a population and the mean of a sample which gives an estimate of the mean of a population. The distinction is similar when calculating variance and standard deviation.

The formula for variance in the blue box above refers to a population. If you have a sample and need to estimate the variance or the standard deviation of the underlying population, then the sample variance or the sample standard deviation gives such an estimate. The estimate of population variance obtained from a sample of size n is called s_n^2, and the corresponding standard deviation is called s_n.

The **variance** of a **sample** of size n is given by

$$s_n^2 = \frac{\sum_{i=1}^{n}(x_i-\bar{x})^2}{n}.$$

The **standard deviation** of the **sample** is the positive square root of the variance.

Notice that in the example of the nine CDs

49 56 55 68 61 57 61 52 63

used at the beginning of Section 6.6, the estimate of the standard deviation of the population is given by $s_n = 5.52$ correct to 3 significant figures. The symbol s_n is used because it is the standard deviation of a sample of the whole population of CDs.

6.8 Calculating variance

Your calculator has a routine for calculating the variance directly from the data, so you do not need to be able to use the formulae of the previous section in situations when you are given numerical data. You will need to consult the manual for your particular calculator.

You may find that your calculator gives two values for the variance. You should always use the **lower** one. If it gives only one value, check that the value it gives is s_n^2. Your teacher may be able to help.

Exercise 6B

1 State or find the mean of

(a) 1, 2, 3, 4, 5, 6, 7 (b) 4, 12, −2, 7, 0, 9.

Use your calculator to find the standard deviation of each data set.

2 Use your calculator to find the standard deviation of the following data sets.

(a) 2, 1, 5.3, −4.2 , 6.7, 3.1 (b) 15.2, 12.3, 5.7, 4.3, 11.2, 2.5, 8.7

3 The masses, x grams, of the contents of 25 tins of Brand A anchovies are summarised by $\sum_{i=1}^{25} x_i = 1268.2$ and $\sum_{i=1}^{25} x_i^2 = 64\,585.16$. Find the mean and variance of the masses. What is the unit of measurement of the variance?

4 The runs made by two batsmen, Anwar and Brian, in 12 innings during the 2006 cricket season are shown in the following table.

Anwar	23	83	40	0	89	98	71	31	102	48	15	18
Brian	43	32	61	75	68	92	17	15	25	43	86	12

Giving your reasons, state which batsman you consider to be

(a) better, (b) more consistent.

6.9 Calculating variance from a frequency table

Table 6.13 reproduces Table 5.4, which gave the frequency distribution of the numbers of brothers and sisters of children in Year 8 in a school.

Number of brothers and sisters, x_i	Frequency, f_i
0	36
1	94
2	48
3	15
4	7
5	3
6	1

Table 6.13

To find the variance, use the programmed routine in your calculator. You then find that the variance is 1.218... = 1.22 correct to 3 significant figures.

The standard deviation is then $\sqrt{1.218\ldots} = 1.10$ correct to 3 significant figures.

If you had to calculate the variance without the built-in calculator routine, you would proceed as follows.

First calculate the mean. From Section 5.6, the mean is $\bar{x} = \dfrac{284}{204} = 1.39\ldots$.

To calculate $\sigma^2 = \dfrac{\sum_{i=1}^{n}(x_i - \bar{x})^2}{n}$ for these data, you need to calculate

$$\begin{aligned}\sum_{i=1}^{n}(x_i - \bar{x})^2 &= \overbrace{(0-\bar{x})^2 + \ldots + (0-\bar{x})^2}^{\text{36 of these}} + \overbrace{(1-\bar{x})^2 + \ldots + (1-\bar{x})^2}^{\text{94 of these}} + \ldots \\ &\quad + \overbrace{(5-\bar{x})^2 + \ldots + (5-\bar{x})^2}^{\text{3 of these}} + \overbrace{(1-\bar{x})^2}^{\text{1 of these}} \\ &= 248.62\ldots.\end{aligned}$$

Then, dividing by $n = 204$, you find that the variance is 1.218... = 1.22 correct to 3 significant figures, as before.

You should try this calculation on your calculator. It will quickly convince you that the built-in routine is better.

Here is a summary the method used to find the variance:

The variance of data given in a frequency table in which the variable takes the value x_1 with frequency f_1, the value x_2 with frequency f_2 and so on is given by the formula

$$\sigma^2 = \frac{\sum_{i=1}^{n} f_i(x_i - \mu)^2}{\sum_{i=1}^{n} f_i}.$$

If the data in the frequency table is a sample from the population, and you need to estimate the variance of the population, the estimate is given by

$$s_n^2 = \frac{\sum_{i=1}^{n} f_i(x_i - \bar{x})^2}{\sum_{i=1}^{n} f_i}.$$

If the data are grouped you need a single value to represent each class. In Section 5.6 you saw that the most reasonable choice was the mid-interval value. After you have made this simplifying assumption, use the in-built routine in your calculator.

Example 6.9.1
Calculate an estimate of the variance of the data given in Table 5.5.

Table 6.14 reproduces the first four columns of Table 5.5.

Playing time, x (min)	Interval boundaries	Frequency, f_i	Mid-interval value, x_i
40–44	$39.5 \le x < 44.5$	1	42
45–49	$44.5 \le x < 49.5$	7	47
50–54	$49.5 \le x < 54.5$	12	52
55–59	$54.5 \le x < 59.5$	24	57
60–64	$59.5 \le x < 64.5$	29	62
65–69	$64.5 \le x < 69.5$	14	67
70–74	$69.5 \le x < 74.5$	5	72
75–79	$74.5 \le x < 79.5$	3	77

Table 6.14

Using the in-built calculator routine,

variance $= 51.4$, correct to 3 significant figures.

You should remember that, just as with the mean calculation in Section 5.6, this value is only an estimate, because the individual values have been replaced by mid-interval values.

Exercise 6C

1 The number of absences by employees in an office was recorded over a period of 96 days, with the following results.

Number of absences	0	1	2	3	4	5
Number of days	54	24	11	4	2	1

Use your calculator to find the mean and variance of the number of daily absences, setting out your work in a table similar to Table 6.14.

2 Plates of a certain design are painted by a particular factory employee. At the end of each day the plates are inspected and some are rejected. The table shows the number of plates rejected over a period of 30 days.

Number of rejects	0	1	2	3	4	5	6
Number of days	18	5	3	1	1	1	1

Show that the standard deviation of the daily number of rejects is approximately equal to one quarter of the range.

3 The times taken in a 20 km race were noted for 80 people. The results are summarised below.

Time (minutes)	60–80	80–100	100–120	120–140	140–160	160–180	180–200
Number of people	1	4	26	24	10	7	8

Use your calculator to estimate the variance of the times of the 80 people in the race.

4 The mass of coffee in each of 80 packets of a certain brand was measured correct to the nearest gram. The results are shown in the following table.

Mass (grams)	244–246	247–249	250–252	253–255	256–258
Number of packets	10	20	24	18	8

Use your calculator to estimate the mean and standard deviation of the masses.

State two ways in which the accuracy of these estimates could be improved.

5 The ages, in completed years, of the 104 workers in a company are summarised as follows.

Age (years)	16–20	21–25	26–30	31–35	36–40	41–50	51–60	61–70
Frequency	5	12	18	14	25	16	8	6

Estimate the mean and standard deviation of the workers' ages.

In another company, with a similar number of workers, the mean age is 28.4 years and the standard deviation is 9.9 years. Briefly compare the two age distributions.

Review exercise 2

1 Certain insects can cause small growths, called 'galls', on the leaves of trees. The numbers of galls found on 60 leaves of an oak tree are given below.

5	19	21	4	17	10	0	61	3	31	15	39	16	27	48
51	69	32	1	25	51	22	28	29	73	14	23	9	2	0
1	37	31	95	10	24	7	89	1	2	50	33	22	0	75
7	23	9	18	39	44	10	33	9	11	51	8	36	44	10

(a) Put the data into a grouped frequency table with classes 0–9, 10–19, … , 90–99.

(b) Draw a frequency histogram of the data.

(c) Draw a cumulative frequency diagram and use it to estimate the number of leaves with fewer than 34 galls.

2 The following table summarises the maximum daily temperatures in two holiday resorts in July and August 2005.

Temperature (°C)	18.0–19.9	20.0–21.9	22.0–23.9	24.0–25.9	26.0–27.9	28.0–29.9
Resort 1 frequency	9	13	18	10	7	5
Resort 2 frequency	6	21	23	8	3	1

(a) State the modal classes for the two resorts.

(b) A student analysed the data and came to the conclusion that, on average, Resort 1 was hotter than Resort 2 during July and August 2005. Is this conclusion supported by your answer to part (a)? If not, then obtain some evidence that does support the conclusion.

3 The costs, $\$x$, of 31 mobile telephone calls costing over \$0.50 made during a period of 1 month are as follows.

1.02	0.76	0.56	0.52	0.64	0.51	0.59	0.69	0.85	0.62	0.52
0.50	0.59	0.62	0.74	0.58	0.67	0.56	0.59	0.52	0.75	0.83
0.50	1.22	1.04	0.86	0.58	0.95	1.76	0.50	0.60		

$$\sum_{i=1}^{31} x_i = 22.24$$

(a) Obtain the median, the mean and the mode for the data.

(b) Which of the median, mean and mode would be best used to give the average cost of a call costing over \$0.50? Give a reason for your answer.

(c) In the same period, the number of calls which cost \$0.50 or under was 125, with mean cost \$0.242. Find the mean cost of all calls for the period.

4 Seven mature robins (*Erithacus rubecula*) were caught and their wingspans were measured. The results, in centimetres, were as follows.

23.1 22.7 22.1 24.2 23.9 20.9 25.2

Here are the corresponding figures for seven mature house sparrows (*Passer domesticos*).

22.6 24.1 23.5 21.8 21.0 24.4 22.8

Find the mean and standard deviation of each species' wingspan, and use these statistics to compare the two sets of figures.

5 The lengths of 120 nails of nominal length 3 cm were measured, each correct to the nearest 0.05 cm. The results are summarised in the following table.

Length (cm)	2.85	2.90	2.95	3.00	3.05	3.10	3.15
Frequency	1	11	27	41	26	12	2

(a) Draw a box and whisker plot of these results, taking the extremes as 2.825 cm and 3.175 cm.

(b) Estimate the standard deviation.

(c) It is claimed that for a roughly symmetrical distribution the statistic obtained by dividing the interquartile range by the standard deviation is approximately 1.3. Calculate the value of this statistic for these data, and comment.

6 There are 30 girls in a class. The weights of five of them, chosen at random, in kilograms are 64, 73, 57, 54 and 75. Calculate the mean and standard deviation of the sample, and hence estimate the mean and standard deviation of the 30 girls.

Examination questions

1 The table below shows the marks gained in a test by a group of students.

Mark	1	2	3	4	5
Number of students	5	10	p	6	2

The median is 3 and the mode is 2. Find the **two** possible values of p. (© IBO 2004)

2 A collection of five whole numbers has a mode of 3, a median of 4 and a mean of 5. List all the possible collections of five numbers. (© IBO 2004)

3 The number of hours of sleep of 21 students are shown in the frequency table below.

Hours of sleep	4	5	6	7	8	10	12
Number of students	2	5	4	3	4	2	1

Find (a) the median, (b) the lower quartile, (c) the interquartile range. (© IBO 2003)

4 Three positive integers, a, b and c, where $a < b < c$, are such that their median is 11, their mean is 9 and their range is 10. Find the value of a. (© IBO 2002)

5 A taxi company has 200 taxi cabs. The cumulative frequency curve below shows the fares in dollars ($) taken by the cabs on a particular morning.

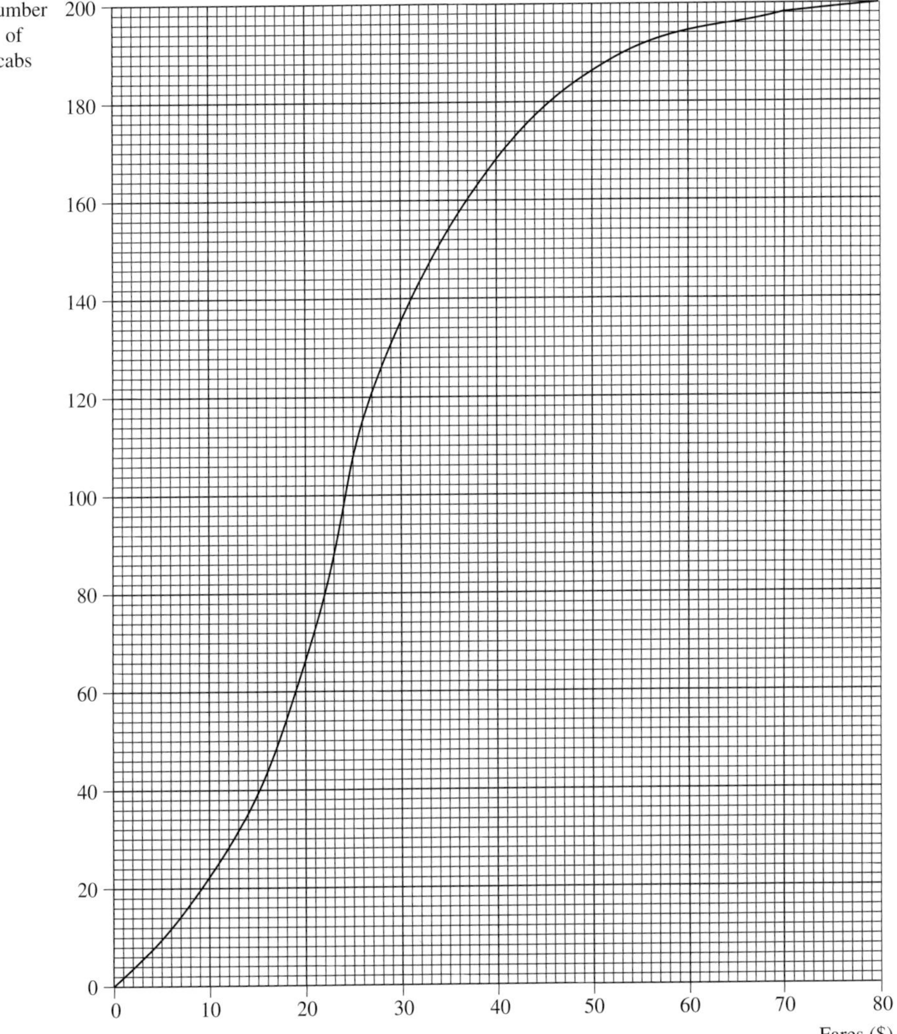

(a) Use the curve to estimate

(i) the median fare,

(ii) the number of cabs in which the fare taken is $35 or less.

The company charges 55 cents per kilometre for distance travelled. There are no other charges. Use the curve to answer the following.

(b) On that morning, 40% of the cabs travel less than a km. Find the value of a.

(c) What percentage of cabs travel more than 90 km on that morning? (© IBO 2002)

6 In a suburb of a large city, 100 houses were sold in a three-month period. The following cumulative frequency table shows the distribution of selling prices (in thousands of dollars).

Total number of houses	12	58	87	94	100
Selling price P (\$1000)	$P \leq 100$	$P \leq 200$	$P \leq 300$	$P \leq 400$	$P \leq 500$

(a) Represent this information on a cumulative frequency curve, using a scale of 1 cm represent \$50 000 on the horizontal axis and 1 cm to represent 5 houses on the vertical axis.

(b) Use your curve to find the interquartile range.

The information above is represented in the following frequency distribution.

Selling price P (\$1000)	Number of houses
$0 < P \leq 100$	12
$100 < P \leq 200$	46
$200 < P \leq 300$	29
$300 < P \leq 400$	a
$400 < P \leq 500$	b

(c) Find the value of a and of b.

(d) Use mid-interval values to calculate an estimate for the mean selling price.

(e) Houses which sell for more than \$350 000 are described as De Luxe. Use your graph to estimate the number of De Luxe houses sold. Give your answer to the nearest integer. (© IBO 2002)

7 Let a, b, c and d be integers such that $a < b$, $b < c$ and $c = d$.

The mode of these four numbers is 11.

The range of these four numbers is 8.

The mean of these four numbers is 8.

Calculate the value of each of the integers a, b, c, d. (© IBO 2004)

8 The 45 students in a class each recorded the number of whole minutes, x, spent doing experiments on Monday. The results are $\sum x = 2230$.

(a) Find the mean number of minutes the students spent doing experiments on Monday.

Two new students joined the class and reported that they spent 37 minutes and 30 minutes respectively.

(b) Calculate the new mean including these two students. (© IBO 2005)

7 Coordinates, points and lines

This chapter uses coordinates to describe points and lines in two dimensions. When you have completed it, you should be able to

- find the length, the mid-point and the gradient of a line segment, given the coordinates of its end points
- find the equation of the line through a given point with a given gradient
- recognise the equations of lines
- tell from their gradients if two lines are parallel or perpendicular.

7.1 The distance between two points

When you draw an x-axis and a y-axis intersecting at an origin O, and choose a scale for the axes, you are setting up a coordinate system. The coordinates of this system are called **Cartesian coordinates** after the French mathematician René Descartes, who lived in the 17th century.

The reason for the word 'Cartesian' is that, at that time, Descartes would normally have been spelt as 'des Cartes'.

The axes divide the plane of the paper or screen into four quadrants, numbered as shown in Fig. 7.1.

The first quadrant is in the top right corner, where x and y are both positive. The other quadrants then follow in order going anticlockwise round the origin.

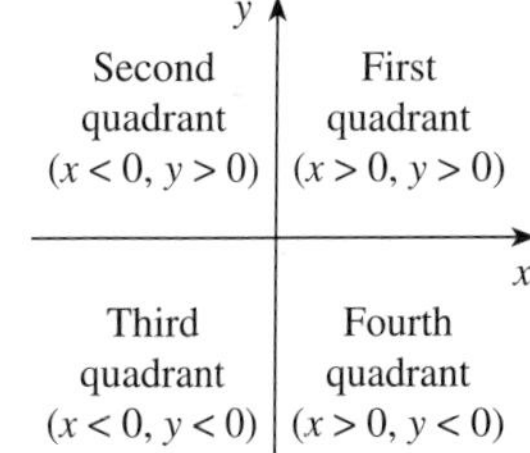

Fig. 7.1

Example 7.1.1
In which quadrants is $xy > 0$?

If the product of two numbers is positive, either both are positive or both are negative. So either $x > 0$ and $y > 0$, or $x < 0$ and $y < 0$. The point (x, y) therefore lies in either the first or the third quadrant.

Calculations with coordinates are often simplest if the points are in the first quadrant.

Example 7.1.2
The points A and B have coordinates (4, 3) and (10, 7). The point M is the mid-point of the line segment [AB].

Find (a) the length of the line segment, (b) the coordinates of M.

(a) Fig. 7.2 shows the points A and B. A third point C has been added to form a right-angled triangle. You can see that C has the same x-coordinate as B and the same y-coordinate as A; that is, C has coordinates (10, 3).

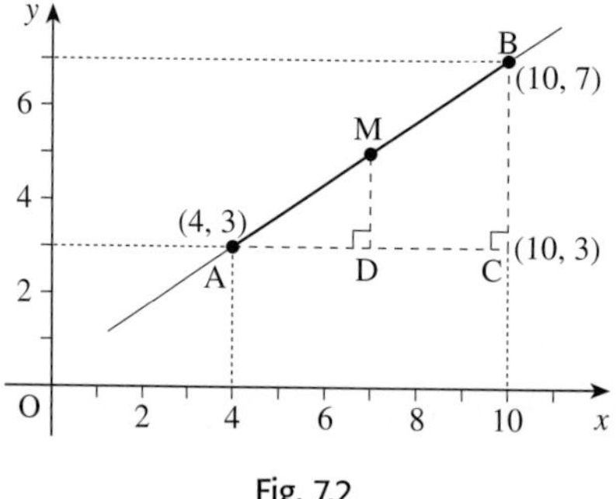

Fig. 7.2

It is possible to use your calculator to produce a figure like Fig. 7.2, but it isn't often worth doing. If you want an accurate diagram, it is best to draw it on paper ruled in squares. But usually all you need is a sketch, with the points shown in roughly the right position.

If you do use a calculator, you will only get a geometrically accurate diagram if you choose a window which gives the same scale on both axes.

It is easy to see that $AC = 10 - 4 = 6$, and $CB = 7 - 3 = 4$. Using Pythagoras' theorem in triangle ABC shows that the length of the line segment [AB] is

$$\sqrt{(10-4)^2 + (7-3)^2} = \sqrt{6^2 + 4^2} = \sqrt{36 + 16} = \sqrt{52}.$$

You can give this answer as 7.21... , if you need to, but often it is better to leave it as $\sqrt{52}$, or better still as $2\sqrt{13}$.

(b) In Fig. 7.2, M is the point of the line segment such that AM = MB, so that $AM = \frac{1}{2}AB$. The lines [MD] and [BC] have been drawn parallel to the y-axis, so they are parallel to each other. Then $AD = \frac{1}{2}AC$ and $DM = \frac{1}{2}CB$. So

$$AD = \tfrac{1}{2}AC = \tfrac{1}{2}(10 - 4) = \tfrac{1}{2}(6) = 3,$$

$$DM = \tfrac{1}{2}CB = \tfrac{1}{2}(7 - 3) = \tfrac{1}{2}(4) = 2.$$

The x-coordinate of M is the same as the x-coordinate of D, which is

$$4 + AD = 4 + \tfrac{1}{2}(10 - 4) = 4 + 3 = 7.$$

The y-coordinate of M is

$$3 + DM = 3 + \tfrac{1}{2}(7 - 3) = 3 + 2 = 5.$$

So the mid-point M has coordinates (7, 5).

The idea of coordinate geometry is to use algebra so that you can do calculations like this when A and B are any points, and not just the particular points in Fig. 7.2. It often helps to use a notation which shows at a glance which point a coordinate refers to. One way of doing this is with **suffixes**, calling the coordinates of the first point (x_1, y_1), and the coordinates of the second point (x_2, y_2). So, for example, x_1 stands for 'the x-coordinate of the first point'.

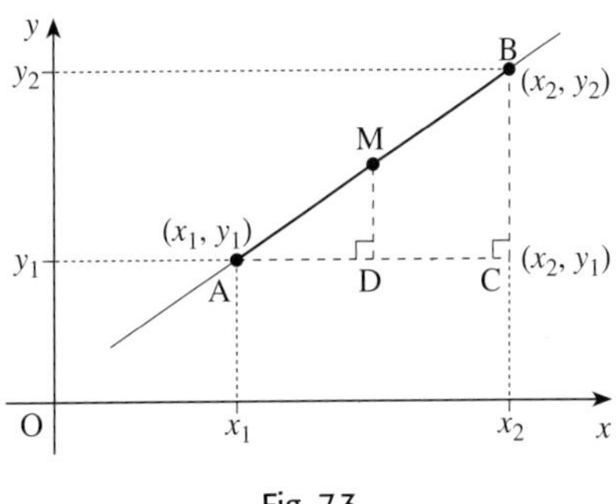

Fig. 7.3

Fig. 7.3 shows these two general points, and the point C such that ACB is a right-angled triangle.

You can see that C now has coordinates (x_2, y_1), and that $\text{AC} = x_2 - x_1$ and $\text{CB} = y_2 - y_1$. Pythagoras' theorem now gives

$$\text{AB} = \sqrt{(x_2 - x_1)^2 + (y_2 - y_1)^2}.$$

The coordinates of the mid-point M can be found exactly as in Example 7.1.2. From Fig. 7.3, the x-coordinate of M is $x_1 + \text{AD}$, and the y-coordinate is $y_1 + \text{DM}$.

Then

$$\begin{aligned} x_1 + \text{AD} &= x_1 + \tfrac{1}{2}(x_2 - x_1) \\ &= x_1 + \tfrac{1}{2}x_2 - \tfrac{1}{2}x_1 \\ &= \tfrac{1}{2}x_1 + \tfrac{1}{2}x_2 \\ &= \tfrac{1}{2}(x_1 + x_2), \end{aligned} \qquad \begin{aligned} y_1 + \text{DM} &= y_1 + \tfrac{1}{2}(y_2 - y_1) \\ &= y_1 + \tfrac{1}{2}y_2 - \tfrac{1}{2}y_1 \\ &= \tfrac{1}{2}y_1 + \tfrac{1}{2}y_2 \\ &= \tfrac{1}{2}(y_1 + y_2). \end{aligned}$$

So, to find the mid-point you take the average of the x-coordinates and the average of the y-coordinates.

> The length of the line segment joining the points (x_1, y_1) and (x_2, y_2) is
>
> $$\sqrt{(x_2 - x_1)^2 + (y_2 - y_1)^2}.$$
>
> The mid-point of the line segment has coordinates
>
> $$\left(\frac{x_1 + x_2}{2}, \frac{y_1 + y_2}{2}\right).$$

An advantage of using algebra is that these formulae work whatever the shape and position of the triangle. In Fig. 7.4 the coordinates of A are negative, and in Fig. 7.5 the line slopes downhill rather than uphill as you move from left to right. Use these two figures to work out for yourself the length AB in each case. You can then use the formula to check your answers.

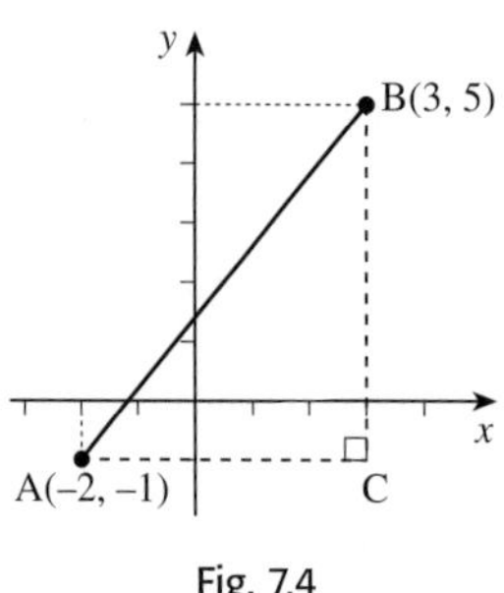

Fig. 7.4

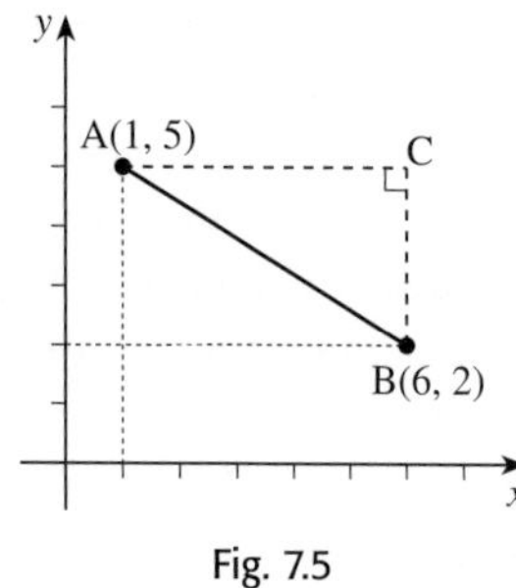

Fig. 7.5

Also, it doesn't matter which way round you label the points A and B. If you think of B as 'the first point' (x_1, y_1) and A as 'the second point' (x_2, y_2), the formulae don't change. For example, in Fig. 7.2, they would give

$$\begin{aligned} BA &= \sqrt{(4-10)^2+(3-7)^2} \\ &= \sqrt{(-6)^2+(-4)^2} \\ &= \sqrt{36+16} = \sqrt{52}, \end{aligned}$$

and the coordinates of M as

$$\left(\frac{10+4}{2}, \frac{7+3}{2}\right) = (7, 5)\text{, as in Example 7.1.2.}$$

There is one more point to notice. Suppose that in Fig. 7.3 the line segment [AB] slopes downhill (as in Fig. 7.5). Then $x_2 > x_1$ but $y_2 < y_1$. This means that the length CB is not $y_2 - y_1$ but $y_1 - y_2$. You could use modulus notation (see Section 1.4) to write $CB = |y_2 - y_1|$, which is true whether $y_2 > y_1$ or $y_2 < y_1$.

However, the formulae are still valid. In finding the length you have $(y_1 - y_2)^2$ instead of $(y_2 - y_1)^2$, but these are equal; the square of a negative number is the square of its modulus. And the y-coordinate of M is $y_1 - \text{DM}$ instead of $y_1 + \text{DM}$, but this is $y_1 - \frac{1}{2}(y_1 - y_2)$, which is still equal to $\frac{1}{2}(y_1 + y_2)$.

7.2 The gradient of a line

You will have noticed in Section 7.1 that the line segment joining A to B is denoted by [AB], with square brackets. If you want to refer to the whole line, of which the line segment is a part, you use the symbol (AB) with round brackets. The symbol AB without brackets is used for the length of [AB]. This is illustrated in Fig. 7.6.

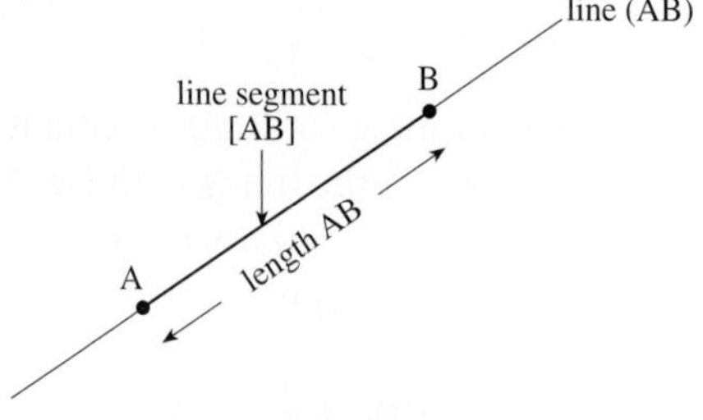

Fig. 7.6

Lines can be drawn in many different directions, and when you use coordinates you need a number to describe the direction of a line. In ordinary geometry you do this by giving the angle which the line makes with a fixed direction (such as a bearing). But this doesn't work well with coordinates, since it involves trigonometry. It is simpler to use instead the idea of 'gradient'.

The gradient of a line is a measure of its steepness. A line which goes up as you move from left to right is said to have a positive gradient. The steeper the line, the larger the gradient. A line which goes down from left to right has a negative gradient.

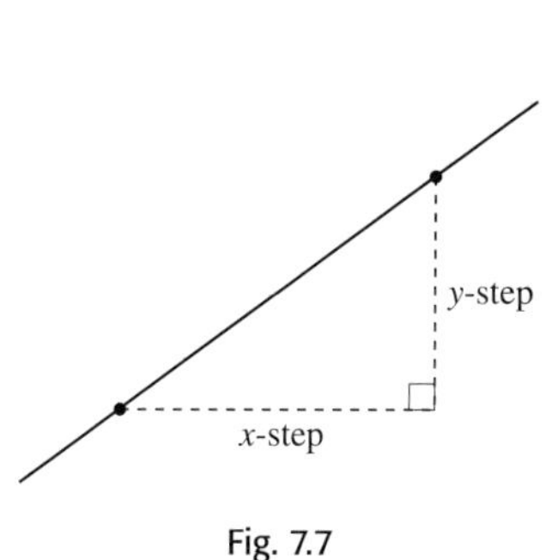

Fig. 7.7

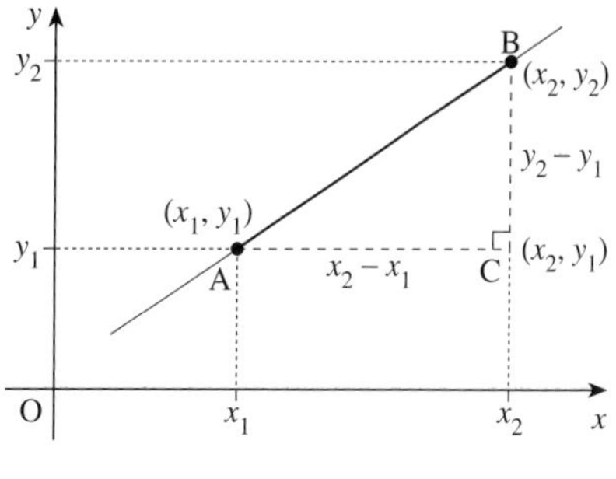

Fig. 7.8

Unlike the distance and the mid-point, the gradient is a property of the whole line, not just of a particular line segment. If you take any two points on the line and find the increases in the x- and y-coordinates as you go from one to the other, as in Fig. 7.7, then the value of the fraction

$$\frac{y\text{-step}}{x\text{-step}}$$

is the same whichever points you choose. This is the **gradient** of the line.

In Fig. 7.8 the x-step and y-step are $x_2 - x_1$ and $y_2 - y_1$, so that:

> The gradient of the line joining (x_1, y_1) to (x_2, y_2) is $\dfrac{y_2 - y_1}{x_2 - x_1}$.

The formula in the blue box applies whether the coordinates are positive or negative. In Fig. 7.4, for example, the gradient of AB is $\dfrac{5-(-1)}{3-(-2)} = \dfrac{5+1}{3+2} = \frac{6}{5}$.

But notice that in Fig. 7.5 the gradient is $\dfrac{2-5}{6-1} = \dfrac{-3}{5} = -\frac{3}{5}$; the negative gradient tells you that the line slopes downhill as you move from left to right.

As with the other formulae, it doesn't matter which point has the suffix 1 and which has the suffix 2. In Fig. 7.2, you can calculate the gradient as either $\dfrac{7-3}{10-4} = \dfrac{4}{6} = \frac{2}{3}$, or $\dfrac{3-7}{4-10} = \dfrac{-4}{-6} = \frac{2}{3}$.

Two lines are **parallel** if they have the same gradient.

Example 7.2.1

Find the gradient of the line which passes through the points

(a) $(1, 3)$ and $(6, 2)$, (b) $(-2, -5)$ and $(-6, -10)$.

State which of the lines slopes downwards to the right.

(a) Using the formula in the box the gradient is

$$\frac{2-3}{6-1}=\frac{-1}{5}=-\tfrac{1}{5}.$$

(b) Using the formula in the box the gradient is

$$\frac{-10-(-5)}{(-6)-(-2)}=\frac{-10+5}{-6+2}=\frac{-5}{-4}=\tfrac{5}{4}.$$

As the gradient of the first line is negative, it slopes downwards to the right.

Example 7.2.2

Show that the points P(1, 3), Q(2, 6), R(4, −3) and S(1, −12) form a trapezium but not a parallelogram.

It is a great help to draw a sketch. Fig. 7.9 is an example of a sketch where the points are not accurately placed, but good enough to suggest that the parallel sides are [PQ] and [RS].

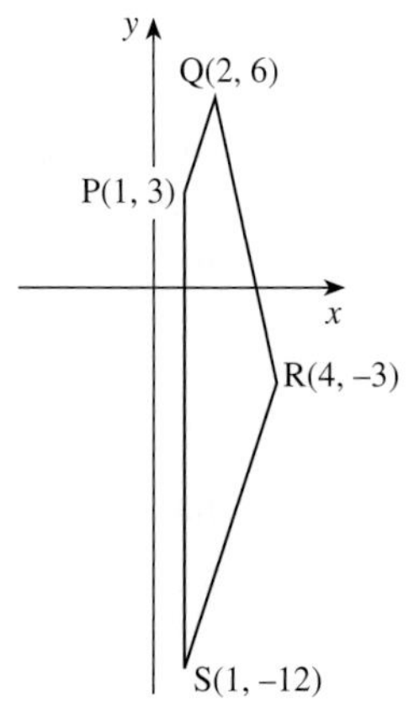

Fig. 7.9

The gradient of [PQ] is $\dfrac{6-3}{2-1}=3$.

The gradient of [QR] is $\dfrac{(-3)-6}{4-2}=\dfrac{-9}{2}=-4\tfrac{1}{2}$.

The gradient of [RS] is $\dfrac{(-12)-(-3)}{1-4}=\dfrac{-9}{-3}=3$.

When you try to find the gradient of [SP] you get $\dfrac{(-12)-3}{1-1}$ which you cannot calculate because it involves division by 0. Fig. 7.9 shows that [SP] is parallel to the y-axis.

From the gradients, [PQ] and [RS] are parallel and [QR] and [SP] are not parallel, so PQRS is a trapezium but not a parallelogram.

You should take note of the difficulty that arises with the side [PS] in Example 7.2.2. If two points have equal x-coordinates but unequal y-coordinates, say (p, q) and (p, r) the gradient formula takes the form $\dfrac{r-q}{p-p}$, or $\dfrac{r-q}{0}$. Division by 0 is meaningless, so that the gradient is not defined.

But if two points have equal y-coordinates but unequal x-coordinates, say (r, p) and (s, p), then the gradient formula gives $\dfrac{p-p}{s-r}=\dfrac{0}{s-r}$, which is equal to 0.

> Lines parallel to the x-axis have gradient 0.
>
> The gradient is not defined for lines parallel to the y-axis.

Exercise 7A

Start each question by drawing a sketch. Do not use a calculator. Where appropriate, leave your answers in surd form.

1 Find the lengths and mid-points of the line segments joining these pairs of points.

(a) $(2, 5)$ and $(7, 17)$ (b) $(6, 5)$ and $(2, 2)$

(c) $(10, 9)$ and $(4, 1)$ (d) $(-3, 2)$ and $(1, -1)$

(e) $(4, -5)$ and $(-1, 0)$ (f) $(-3, -3)$ and $(-7, 3)$

2 Show that the points $(7, 12)$, $(-3, -12)$, $(15, 0)$, $(2, 13)$ and $(14, -5)$ lie on a circle with centre $(2, 0)$.

3 Show that the points $(3, 1)$, $(-3, -7)$ and $(11, -5)$ form an isosceles triangle. Find the mid-point of the side which is not one of the equal sides.

4 Find the gradients of the lines joining the following pairs of points.

(a) $(3, 8)$, $(5, 12)$ (b) $(1, -3)$, $(-2, 6)$

(c) $(-4, -3)$, $(0, -1)$ (d) $(-5, -3)$, $(3, -9)$

5 Find the gradients of the lines (AB) and (BC) where A is $(3, 4)$, B is $(7, 6)$ and C is $(-3, 1)$. What can you deduce about the points A, B and C?

6 The points A, B, C and D have coordinates $(2, 3)$, $(-3, 11)$, $(4, -2)$ and $(1, 8)$ respectively. Is (AB) parallel to (CD)?

7 The vertices of a quadrilateral ABCD are A$(1, 1)$, B$(7, 3)$, C$(9, -7)$ and D$(-3, -3)$. The points P, Q, R and S are the mid-points of [AB], [BC], [CD] and [DA] respectively.

(a) Find the gradient of each side of PQRS.

(b) Find the length of each side of PQRS.

(c) Find the mid-points of [PR] and [QS].

Parts (a), (b) and (c) all lead to the same conclusion about PQRS.

(d) What type of quadrilateral is PQRS?

7.3 The equation of a line

The x- and y-axes define a plane, which is the plane of the paper (or the calculator window) extended indefinitely in all directions. By giving different real number values to the coordinates x and y you can get all the points which make up the plane. The letters x and y are called **variables**.

If x and y are connected by an equation, such as $2y = 3x - 1$, then some points of the plane will have coordinates which **satisfy** the equation. For example, putting $x = 3$ and $y = 4$, the left side is $2 \times 4 = 8$ and the right side is $3 \times 3 - 1 = 8$; so the coordinates of the point $(3, 4)$ satisfy the equation. But the coordinates of the point $(4, 3)$ don't satisfy the equation, because $2 \times 3 = 6$ and $3 \times 4 - 1 = 11$, and $6 \neq 11$.

Example 7.3.1

Mark on an accurate diagram the points A(1, 1), B(−1, − 4), C(0, −2), D($\frac{3}{2}$, $\frac{4}{3}$), E($\frac{2}{3}$, 0). Which three of these points have coordinates which satisfy the equation $y = 3x - 2$? Show that these three points are in a straight line.

The points are shown in Fig. 7.10.

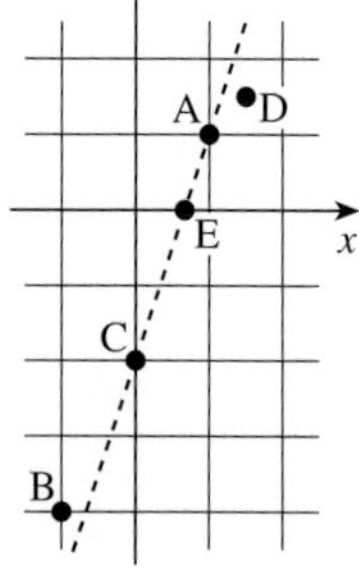

Fig. 7.10

You can easily check that

for A, $\quad 1 = 3 \times 1 - 2,$
for B, $\quad -4 \neq 3 \times (-1) - 2,$
for C, $\quad -2 = 3 \times 0 - 2,$
for D, $\quad \frac{4}{3} \neq 3 \times \frac{3}{2} - 2,$
for E, $\quad 0 = 3 \times \frac{2}{3} - 2.$

So the coordinates of A, C and E satisfy the equation.

In Fig. 7.10 it looks as if A, E and C are in a straight line. To check this, calculate the gradients of [CE] and [EA]:

$$\text{gradient of [CE]} = \frac{0-(-2)}{\frac{2}{3}-0} = \frac{2}{\frac{2}{3}} = 3, \quad \text{gradient of [EA]} = \frac{1-0}{1-\frac{2}{3}} = \frac{1}{\frac{1}{3}} = 3.$$

Since the line segments [CE] and [EA] have the same gradient, and both line segments share the same point E, the points A, E and C are in a straight line (drawn dotted in Fig. 7.10).

If three or more points are in a straight line, they are said to be **collinear**. In Example 7.3.1 the points A, C and E are collinear, and the equation $y = 3x - 2$ is the **equation of the line** through them.

You will notice that two of the points in Fig. 7.10, C and E, are on one or other of the axes. The y-coordinate of C, where the line cuts the y-axis, is called the ***y*-intercept** of the line. Similarly the x-coordinate of E, where the line cuts the x-axis, is the ***x*-intercept** of the line. So for the line with equation $y = 3x - 2$, the x-intercept is $\frac{2}{3}$ and the y-intercept is −2.

> To find the y-intercept of a straight line, put $x = 0$ in the equation of the line and solve for y.
>
> To find the x-intercept of a straight line, put $y = 0$ in the equation of the line and solve for x.

The question that now needs to be answered is: given a particular line, what is its equation?

Begin by asking how you might describe the line. First, you need to know its direction, and this is given by the gradient. But that isn't enough; there are many lines in any direction. To fix a particular line, you need something more. One possibility is to give the y-intercept.

Example 7.3.2
Find the equation of the line with gradient 2 and y-intercept 3.

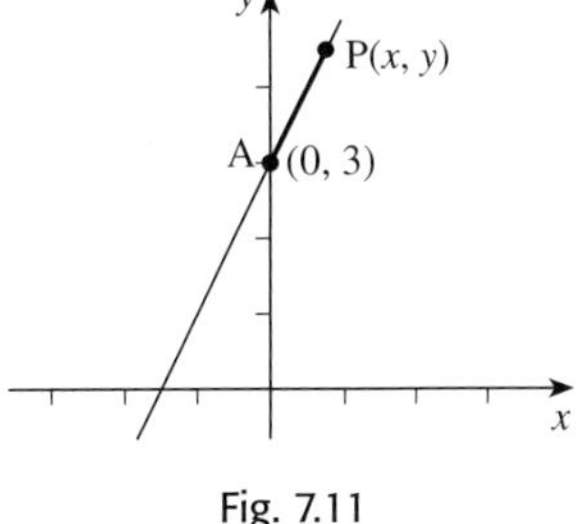

Fig. 7.11

The line is drawn in Fig. 7.11, passing through A(0, 3). The figure also shows another point P on the line, with coordinates (x, y). You want to find an equation connecting x with y.

The equation has to express the fact that the line segment [AP] has gradient 2. Using the gradient formula in Section 7.2,

$$\frac{y-3}{x-0} = 2.$$

This can be written more simply as

$$y - 3 = 2x, \quad \text{or} \quad y = 2x + 3.$$

The method used in Example 7.3.2 can be generalised to find the equation of any line with gradient m and y-intercept c. If the line segment joining $(0, c)$ to (x, y) has gradient m, then

$$\frac{y-c}{x-0} = m.$$

This can be simplified as

$$y - c = mx, \quad \text{or} \quad y = mx + c.$$

This is called the **gradient–intercept form** for the equation of a line.

> The equation of the line with gradient m through the point $(0, c)$ is
>
> $$y = mx + c.$$

Compare this with Example 7.3.1, where the gradient is 3, the y-intercept is -2, and the equation is $y = 3x - 2$.

This is the simplest form for the equation of a straight line, but you can't always use it. Sometimes you don't know the y-intercept, but you know that the line passes through some other point B, with coordinates (x_1, y_1). In that case, you want an equation to express the fact that the line segment [BP] joining (x_1, y_1) to (x, y) has gradient m (see Fig. 7.12). That is,

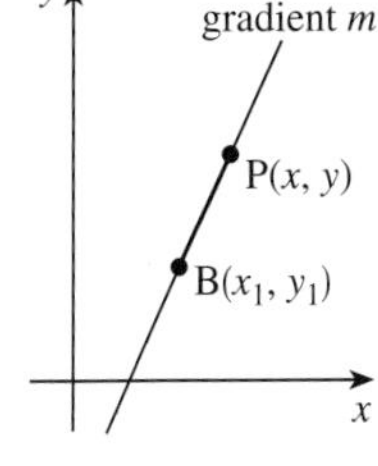

Fig. 7.12

$$\frac{y-y_1}{x-x_1} = m,$$

or

$$y - y_1 = m(x - x_1).$$

> The equation of the line through (x_1, y_1) with gradient m is
>
> $$y - y_1 = m(x - x_1).$$

Example 7.3.3

(a) Find the equation of the line with gradient 2 which passes through the point (3, 1).

(b) Find the y-intercept of this line.

(a) Using the equation $y - y_1 = m(x - x_1)$, the equation of the line is

$$y - 1 = 2(x - 3).$$

Multiplying out the bracket and simplifying, you get $y - 1 = 2x - 6$, or

$$y = 2x - 5.$$

As a check, substitute the coordinates (3, 1) into both sides of the equation, to make sure that the given point does actually lie on the line.

(b) The equation $y = 2x - 5$ is in the form $y = mx + c$ with $c = -5$.

So the y-intercept is -5.

There is one more special case to consider, when the line is parallel to one of the axes.

For a line parallel to the x-axis the gradient is 0. Putting $m = 0$ in the equation $y = mx + c$ gives $y = c$. That is, all the points on the line have coordinates of the form (something, c). Thus the points (1, 2), (−1, 2), (5, 2), ... all lie on the straight line $y = 2$, shown in Fig. 7.13. As a special case, the x-axis has equation $y = 0$.

Similarly, a straight line parallel to the y-axis has an equation of the form $x = k$. All points on it have coordinates (k, something). Thus the points (3, 0), (3, 2), (3, 4), ... all lie on the line $x = 3$, shown in Fig. 7.14. The y-axis itself has equation $x = 0$.

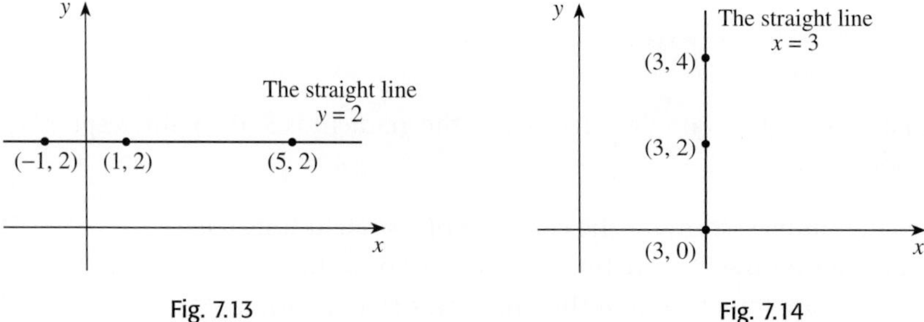

Fig. 7.13 Fig. 7.14

The line $x = k$ does not have a gradient; its gradient is undefined. Its equation cannot be written in the form $y = mx + c$.

Example 7.3.4
Find the equation of the straight line through (3, 2) parallel to

(a) $y = 3x - 2$, (b) $x = 2$.

(a) The line $y = 3x - 2$ has gradient 3, so the equation of a line parallel to it also has gradient 3. If this line passes through (3, 2), then its equation is

$$y - 2 = 3(x - 3).$$

Multiplying out the brackets,

$$\begin{aligned} y - 2 &= 3x - 9, \\ y &= 3x - 7. \end{aligned}$$

The equation of the line is $y = 3x - 7$.

(b) The line $x = 2$ is parallel to the y-axis. The equation of any line parallel to this has the form $x = c$.

If this line passes through then (3, 2) must satisfy the equation, so

$$3 = c.$$

The equation of the line is $x = 3$.

Example 7.3.5
Find the equation of the line joining the points (3, 4) and (−1, 2).

First find the gradient of the line joining (3, 4) to (−1, 2). Then you can use the equation $y - y_1 = m(x - x_1)$.

The gradient of the line joining (3, 4) to (−1, 2) is $\dfrac{2-4}{(-1)-3} = \dfrac{-2}{-4} = \frac{1}{2}$.

The equation of the line through (3, 4) with gradient $\frac{1}{2}$ is $y - 4 = \frac{1}{2}(x - 3)$. After multiplying out you get

$$2y - 8 = x - 3,$$

which is

$$2y = x + 5.$$

Since you used the point (3, 4) to find the equation, it is a good idea to check your answer by using the point (−1, 2). When $x = -1$ and $y = 2$, the left side is $2 \times 2 = 4$ and the right side is $-1 + 5 = 4$.

Exercise 7B

1 Test whether the given point lies on the straight line with the given equation.

(a) $(1, 2)$ on $y = 5x - 3$ (b) $(3, -2)$ on $y = 3x - 7$

2 Find the equations of the straight lines through the given points with the gradients shown. Your final answers should not contain any fractions.

(a) $(2, 3)$, gradient 5 (b) $(1, -2)$, gradient -3

(c) $(0, 4)$, gradient $\frac{1}{2}$ (d) $(-2, 1)$, gradient $-\frac{3}{8}$

(e) $(0, 0)$, gradient -3 (f) $(3, 8)$, gradient 0

(g) $(-5, -1)$, gradient $-\frac{3}{4}$ (h) $(-3, 0)$, gradient $\frac{1}{2}$

(i) $(-3, -1)$, gradient $\frac{3}{8}$ (j) $(3, 4)$, gradient $-\frac{1}{2}$

(k) $(2, -1)$, gradient -2 (l) $(-2, -5)$, gradient 3

(m) $(0, -4)$, gradient 7 (n) $(0, 2)$, gradient -1

3 Find the equations of the lines joining the following pairs of points.

(a) $(1, 4)$ and $(3, 10)$ (b) $(4, 5)$ and $(-2, -7)$

(c) $(3, 2)$ and $(0, 4)$ (d) $(3,7)$ and $(3,12)$

(e) $(10, -3)$ and $(-5, -12)$ (f) $(3, -1)$ and $(-4, 20)$

(g) $(2, -3)$ and $(11, -3)$ (h) $(2, 0)$ and $(5, -1)$

(i) $(-4, 2)$ and $(-1, -3)$ (j) $(-2, -1)$ and $(5, -3)$

(k) $(-3, 4)$ and $(-3, 9)$ (l) $(-1, 0)$ and $(0, -1)$

(m) $(2, 7)$ and $(3, 10)$ (n) $(-5, 4)$ and $(-2, -1)$

(o) $(0, 0)$ and $(5, -3)$ (p) $(0, 0)$ and (p, q)

4 Find the gradients, x-intercepts and y-intercepts of the following lines.

(a) $y = -x - 3$ (b) $y = 3(x + 4)$ (c) $5x + 2y + 3 = 0$

(d) $y = 5$ (e) $2y = 3x + 4$ (f) $5x = 7$

(g) $2x + y = 7$ (h) $4y = 3x - 8$ (i) $2y = 7 - x$

5 Find the equation of the line through $(-2, 1)$ parallel to $y = \frac{1}{2}x - 3$.

6 Find the equation of the line through $(4, -3)$ parallel to $y = -2x + 7$.

7.4 The gradients of perpendicular lines

In Section 7.2 it is stated that two lines are parallel if they have the same gradient. But what can you say about the gradients of two lines which are perpendicular?

First, if a line has a positive gradient, then the perpendicular line has a negative gradient, and vice versa. But you can be more exact than this.

In Fig. 7.15 if the gradient of (PB) is m, you can draw a 'gradient triangle' PAB in which PA is one unit and AB is m units.

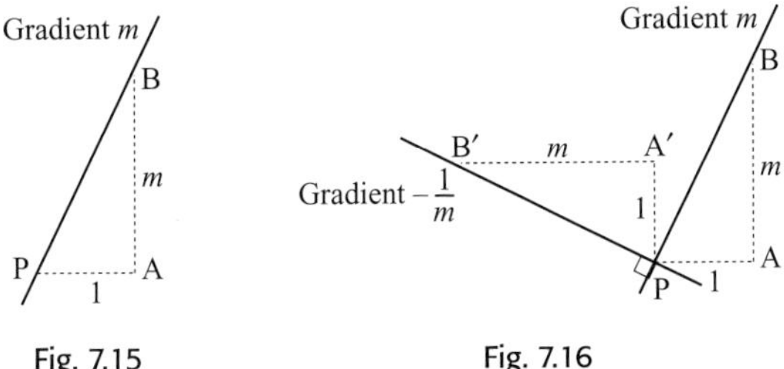

Fig. 7.15

Fig. 7.16

In Fig 7.16, the gradient triangle PAB has been rotated through a right-angle to PA′B′, so that (PB′) is perpendicular to (PB). The y-step for triangle PA′B′ is 1 and the x-step is $-m$, so

$$\text{gradient of (PB}') = \frac{y\text{-step}}{x\text{-step}} = \frac{1}{-m} = -\frac{1}{m}.$$

Therefore the gradient of the line perpendicular to (PB) is $-\frac{1}{m}$.

Thus if the gradients of the two perpendicular lines are m_1 and m_2, then $m_2 = -\frac{1}{m_1}$, so $m_1 m_2 = -1$. It is also true in reverse: if two lines have gradients m_1 and m_2, and if $m_1 m_2 = -1$, then the lines are perpendicular.

> If a line has gradient m, the gradient of the line perpendicular to it is $-\frac{1}{m}$.
>
> Two lines with gradients m_1 and m_2 are perpendicular if
> $m_1 m_2 = -1$.

Notice that the condition does not work if the lines are parallel to the axes. However, you can see that a line x = constant is perpendicular to one of the form y = constant.

Example 7.4.1
The gradients of four lines are 2, $\frac{2}{3}$, -3 and $-\frac{4}{3}$. Find the gradients of the four lines at right angles to them.

Using the rule $m_2 = -\frac{1}{m_1}$ the gradients of the perpendicular lines are, in turn, $-\frac{1}{2}$, $-\frac{1}{\frac{2}{3}}$, $-\frac{1}{-3}$ and $-\frac{1}{-\frac{4}{3}}$. These simplify to $-\frac{1}{2}$, $-\frac{3}{2}$, $\frac{1}{3}$ and $\frac{3}{4}$.

The gradients of the four lines are $-\frac{1}{2}$, $-\frac{3}{2}$, $\frac{1}{3}$ and $\frac{3}{4}$.

Example 7.4.2
A line is perpendicular to $3y = 2x - 4$. Find its gradient.

The line $3y = 2x - 4$ can be written as $y = \frac{2}{3}x - \frac{4}{3}$.

The gradient of this line is $\frac{2}{3}$, so the gradient of the line perpendicular to it is $-\frac{3}{2}$.

Example 7.4.3
Find the equation of the line through $(1, 6)$ which is perpendicular to $y = 2x + 3$.

The line $y = 2x + 3$ has gradient 2, so the perpendicular line has gradient $-\frac{1}{2}$.

Using $y - y_1 = m(x - x_1)$, the line through $(1, 6)$ with gradient $-\frac{1}{2}$ is

$$y - 6 = -\tfrac{1}{2}(x - 1).$$

This simplifies to $2y - 12 = -x + 1$, which is $2y = -x + 13$.

Example 7.4.4
Find the equation of the perpendicular bisector of the points A(3, 6) and B(−1, 4).

Fig. 7.17 shows the situation. The perpendicular bisector of two points A and B is the line which passes through the mid-point of [AB] at right angles to [AB].

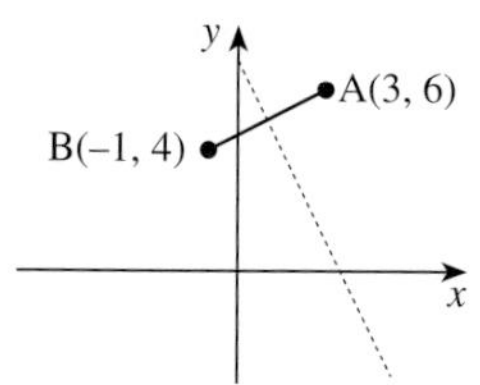

Fig. 7.17

The mid-point of [AB] is $\left(\frac{3+(-1)}{2}, \frac{6+4}{2}\right)$, which is $(1, 5)$.

The gradient of [AB] is $\frac{4-6}{(-1)-3} = \frac{-2}{-4} = \frac{1}{2}$.

The gradient of the line perpendicular to [AB] is $-\frac{1}{\frac{1}{2}} = -2$.

The equation of the perpendicular bisector is therefore

$$y - 5 = -2(x - 1), \text{ or } y - 5 = -2x + 2.$$

This can be simplified to $y = -2x + 7$.

Exercise 7C

1 In each part write down the gradient of a line which is perpendicular to one with the given gradient.

(a) 2 (b) -3 (c) $\frac{3}{4}$ (d) $-\frac{5}{6}$
(e) -1 (f) $1\frac{3}{4}$ (g) $-\frac{1}{m}$ (h) m
(i) $\frac{p}{q}$ (j) 0 (k) $-m$ (l) $\frac{a}{b-c}$

2 In each part find the equation of the line through the given point which is perpendicular to the given line. Write your final answer so that it doesn't contain fractions.

(a) $(2, 3)$, $y = 4x + 3$ (b) $(-3, 1)$, $y = -\frac{1}{2}x + 3$
(c) $(2, -5)$, $y = -5x - 2$ (d) $(7, -4)$, $y = 2\frac{1}{2}$
(e) $(-1, 4)$, $3y = -2x + 8$ (f) $(4, 3)$, $5y = 3x - 8$
(g) $(5, -3)$, $2x = 3$ (h) $(0, 3)$, $y = 2x - 1$

3 A line through a vertex of a triangle which is perpendicular to the opposite side is called an altitude. Find the equation of the altitude through the vertex A of the triangle ABC where A is the point $(2, 3)$, B is $(1, -7)$ and C is $(4, -1)$.

8 Functions and graphs

This chapter introduces the idea of a function and investigates the graphs representing functions of various kinds. When you have completed it, you should

- understand function notation
- be able to use a calculator to display the shape of a graph with a given equation
- understand what is meant by an asymptote
- understand the terms 'domain' and 'range', and appreciate the importance of defining the domain of a function
- understand that a sequence is a function whose domain is the set of positive integers or natural numbers
- be able to use a calculator to display the graph of a sequence
- understand that a sequence u_n may converge to a limit as n tends to infinity.

8.1 The idea of a function

If you need to carry out a particular calculation frequently, it is useful to summarise it with a formula. For example:

the area of a circle with radius x metres is πx^2 square metres;

the volume of a cube of side x metres is x^3 cubic metres;

the time that it takes to travel k kilometres at x kilometres per hour is $\frac{k}{x}$ hours.

You will often have used different letters from x in these formulae, such as r for radius or s for speed, but in most of this chapter x will always be used for the letter in the formula, and y for the quantity you want to calculate. Notice that some formulae also involve other letters, called **constants**; these might be either a number like π, which is irrational and cannot be written out in full, or a quantity like the distance k, which you choose for yourself depending on the distance you intend to travel.

Expressions such as πx^2, x^3 and $\frac{k}{x}$ are examples of **functions** of x. The essential feature of a function is that, having chosen x, you can get a *unique* value of y from it.

It is often useful to have a way of writing functions in general, rather than always having to refer to particular functions. The notation which is used for this is $f(x)$ (read 'f of x', or sometimes just 'f x'). The letter f stands for the function itself, and x for the number you choose for its evaluation.

If you want to refer to the value of the function when x has a particular value, say $x = 2$, then you write the value as $f(2)$. For example, if $f(x)$ stands for the function x^3, then $f(2) = 2^3 = 8$.

If a problem involves more than one function, you can use different letters for each function. Two functions can, for example, be written as $f(x)$ and $g(x)$.

Example 8.1.1

(a) If $f(x) = \sqrt{x}$ and $g(x) = \frac{1}{x}$, find $f(100)$ and $g(100)$.

(b) Are there any real numbers for which $f(x)$ or $g(x)$ cannot be calculated?

(a) Remember that $\sqrt{x}$ stands for the positive square root. So

$$f(100) = \sqrt{100} = 10, \text{ and } g(x) = \frac{1}{100} = 0.01.$$

(b) Whenever you square a number, the result is a positive number or zero. So a negative number cannot have a square root. That is, $\sqrt{x}$ can't be calculated if x is a negative real number.

By $\frac{1}{x}$ you mean the number y such that $x \times y = 1$. But if $x = 0$, then $x \times y = 0$ for every number y. So $\frac{1}{x}$ has no meaning if $x = 0$.

Investigate what happens when you try to find $\sqrt{-100}$ or $\frac{1}{0}$ with a calculator.

Functions are not always defined by algebraic formulae. Sometimes it is easier to describe them in words, or to define them using a flow chart or a computer program. All that matters is that each value of x chosen leads to a unique value of $y = f(x)$.

8.2 Graphs

You are familiar with drawing graphs. You set up a coordinate system for Cartesian coordinates using x- and y-axes, and choose the scales on each axis.

The graph of a function $f(x)$ is made up of all the points whose coordinates (x, y) satisfy the equation $y = f(x)$. When you draw such a graph on graph paper, you choose a few values of x and work out $y = f(x)$ for these. You then plot the points with coordinates (x, y), and join up these points by eye, usually with a smooth curve. If you have done this accurately, the coordinates of other points of the curve will also satisfy the equation $y = f(x)$. Calculators and computers make graphs in much the same way, but they can plot many more points much more quickly.

It is important to become proficient in using your calculator to display graphs. To do this you must enter the formula for the function, probably in the form '$y = \ldots$'. You also have to specify a 'window', stating intervals of values of x and y which you want to appear in the display. Obviously you can't show the whole plane in a small window, so the choice of which part of the plane to display can be very significant.

Example 8.2.1
Use your calculator to display the graph of the function $3x - \frac{1}{5}x^3$ with the following windows:

(a) $-1 \le x \le 1,\ -0.6 \le y \le 0.6$, (b) $-5 \le x \le 5, -3 \le y \le 3$, (c) $-5 \le x \le 5, -5 \le y \le 5$.

You should get displays like those in Fig. 8.1. In (a) the graph looks like a straight line, and there is no indication that it will go in quite different directions for larger values of $|x|$. The graph in (b) seems to be in three separate parts, which is improbable; there must be a value for $x = 2$, for example, but it doesn't show up in the display.

Reducing the y-scale as in (c) reveals all the important features of the graph. Although only a small part of the complete graph appears in the window, you will probably agree that it tells you as much as you need to know about the function.

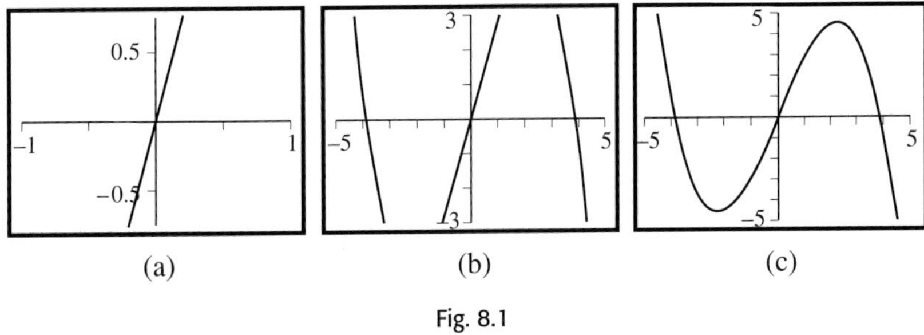

Fig. 8.1

Example 8.2.1 illustrates the importance of choosing a suitable window. You will often find that you need to experiment with several different windows before you are satisfied that the graph shows all the important features of the function.

The problem doesn't only arise when you use a calculator to draw graphs. Exactly the same considerations apply when you draw graphs by hand on graph paper.

Notice that when graphing functions it isn't usually important to use the same scale on both axes. If you can, do; but if the spread of the y-values is greater than the spread of the x-values, it is quite acceptable to squash the y-axis so as to fit the graph into the window.

This is different from the advice in Chapter 7, where you were concerned with geometrical figures such as isosceles triangles and perpendicular lines. These will appear distorted unless you use equal scales on the two axes.

In Example 8.2.1 you will probably find that in parts (a) and (b) the scales are almost equal on the two axes, but in part (c) the y-scale is smaller than the x-scale.

Example 8.2.2
Use your calculator to display the graphs of

(a) $f(x) = 1 - \frac{1}{4}x^2$, (b) $g(x) = \sqrt{1 - \frac{1}{4}x^2}$, with a window of $-3 \le x \le 3, -2 \le y \le 2$.

Describe and explain their principal features.

The two graphs are shown in Fig. 8.2.

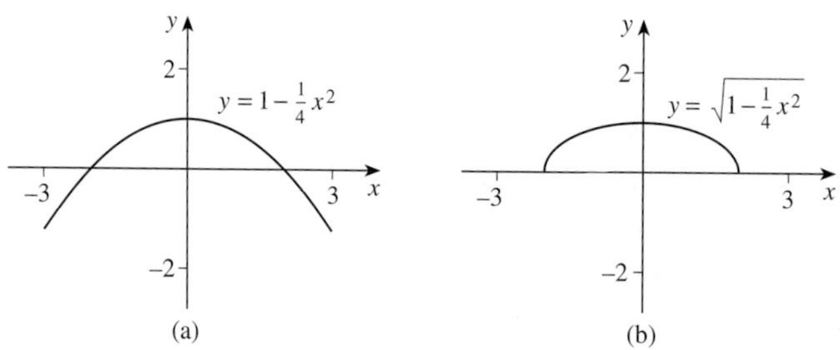

Fig. 8.2

(a) The window is large enough to show the main features. Since $x^2 \geq 0$ for all real numbers x, $1 - \frac{1}{4}x^2$ is always less than or equal to 1. But, when $|x|$ is large, $f(x)$ is a very large negative number. So the graph extends indefinitely to the left and right, and at the foot of the window. However small the scale, the window can never contain the whole graph.

Since $f(2) = f(-2) = 0$, the graph crosses the x-axis at $(2, 0)$ and $(-2, 0)$. The sign of $f(x)$ is positive if $-2 < x < 2$, and negative if $x > 2$ or $x < -2$ (that is, if $|x| > 2$).

(b) Since negative numbers don't have square roots, and $1 - \frac{1}{4}x^2 < 0$ if $|x| > 2$, the graph cannot exist outside the interval $-2 \leq x \leq 2$. In that interval $0 \leq 1 - \frac{1}{4}x^2 \leq 1$, so $0 \leq \sqrt{1 - \frac{1}{4}x^2} \leq 1$.The whole graph therefore lies in the box defined by the inequalities $-2 \leq x \leq 2$, $0 \leq y \leq 1$. It follows that, by defining a suitable window, you can display the whole graph on the calculator or on a sheet of graph paper.

Example 8.2.3

Use your calculator to display the graph of $f(x) = \dfrac{2x}{x-1}$ with a window of $-10 \leq x \leq 10$, $-10 \leq y \leq 10$. Investigate any special features of the graph.

The graph is shown in Fig. 8.3a. You can see that, even with such a small scale, the window can't contain the whole graph. The graph extends indefinitely to the left and right, and also upwards and downwards. Notice that the graph passes through the origin, because $f(0) = 0$.

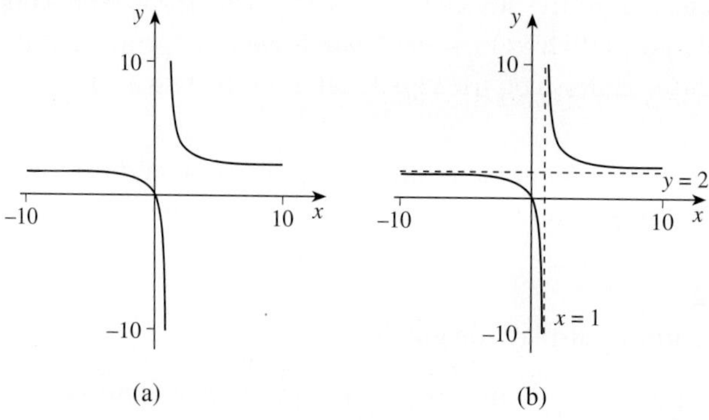

Fig. 8.3

The most obvious peculiarity of the graph occurs where $x = 1$. If you try to calculate $f(1)$ you get the form $\frac{2 \times 1}{1 - 1}$, or $\frac{2}{0}$ which has no meaning. So there is no point on the graph corresponding to $x = 1$.

To see what is happening in more detail, try evaluating $f(x)$ when x is slightly less or slightly greater than 1. For example, find $f(0.99)$, $f(0.999)$, $f(1.01)$ and $f(1.001)$. You will find that if $x - 1$ is a small positive number, $f(x)$ is a large positive number; and if $x - 1$ is a negative number with small modulus, $f(x)$ is a negative number with large modulus. Either way, if $|x - 1|$ is small, then $|f(x)|$ is large.

Another interesting feature is that the curve seems to flatten out when $|x|$ is large. To investigate this, try evaluating $f(10)$, $f(100)$, $f(-10)$ and $f(-100)$.You will find that if x is a large positive number, then $f(x)$ is slightly greater than 2; and if x is a negative number with large modulus, then $f(x)$ is slightly less than 2. But if you try to find a value of x for which $f(x) = 2$, you get the equation

$$\frac{2x}{x - 1} = 2,$$

which when simplified becomes $0 = -2$! This means that there are no values of x for which $f(x) = 2$.

You will see this clearly if you add the graph with equation $y = 2$ to your calculator display.

Fig. 8.3b reproduces Fig. 8.3a with the lines $x = 1$ and $y = 2$ added. These lines are called **asymptotes** of the graph with equation $y = \frac{2x}{x - 1}$. They are lines which the graph approaches indefinitely closely when either $|x|$ or $|y|$ is large.

It is conventional to describe $x = 1$ as a 'vertical' asymptote and $y = 2$ as a 'horizontal' asymptote, although these terms are only really appropriate if the graph is mounted on a vertical surface.

Exercise 8A

1 Given $f(x) = 2x + 5$, find the values of

(a) $f(3)$, (b) $f(0)$, (c) $f(-4)$, (d) $f\left(-2\frac{1}{2}\right)$.

2 Given $f(x) = 3x^2 + 2$, find the values of

(a) $f(4)$, (b) $f(-1)$, (c) $f(-3)$, (d) $f(3)$.

3 Given $f(x) = x^2 + 4x + 3$, find the values of

(a) $f(2)$, (b) $f(\frac{1}{2})$, (c) $f(-1)$, (d) $f(-3)$.

4 Given $g(x) = x^3$ and $h(x) = 4x + 1$,

(a) find the value of $g(2) + h(2)$, (b) find the value of $3g(-1) - 4h(-1)$,

(c) show that $g(5) = h(31)$.

5 With a window of $-2 \le x \le 3$, $-3 \le y \le 4$, display the graph of $f(x) = x^2 - x$. Estimate from the graph the value of x for which $f(x)$ has its smallest value.

6 With a window from -2 to 4 for both x and y, display the graph of $y = f(x)$, where $f(x) = x^2(3 - x)$. Estimate from your graph the largest value taken by $f(x)$ in the interval $0 \le x \le 3$, and the value of x when $f(x)$ takes this value.

7 Use your calculator with a window of $-1 \le x \le 5$, $-1 \le y \le 3$ with equal scales on both axes to display the graphs of $y = x(3 - x)$ and $y = \sqrt{x(3 - x)}$. Suggest a name to describe the shape of the second graph.

8 With a window of $-5 \le x \le 5$, $-5 \le y \le 5$ display the graph of $y = \dfrac{x^2 + 1}{x^2 - 1}$. Suggest the equations of the three asymptotes, and check your answers with suitable calculations.

9 Choose a suitable window to show the main features of the graph of $f(x) = (x^2 - 2x)^2$.

10 Find the equations of the asymptotes of the graph of $y = \dfrac{1 - 2x}{x - 3}$.

8.3 Positive integer powers of *x*

This section looks at graphs of functions of the form $f(x) = x^n$, where n is a positive integer.

First look at the graphs when x is positive, using a window of $0 \le x \le 2$, $0 \le y \le 2$ with equal scales on the two axes. Then x^n is also positive, so that the graphs lie entirely in the first quadrant. Begin by showing each graph separately. Fig. 8.4 shows the graphs for $n = 1, 2, 3$ and 4 for values of x from 0 to somewhere beyond 1.

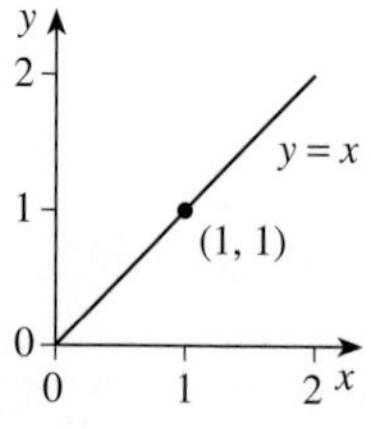

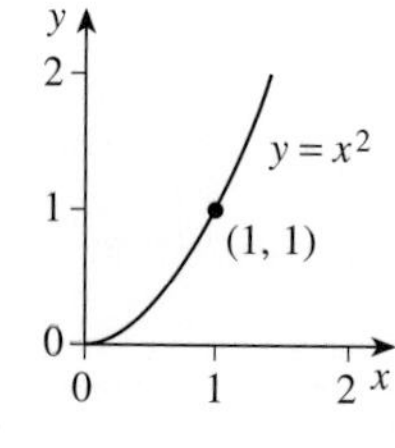

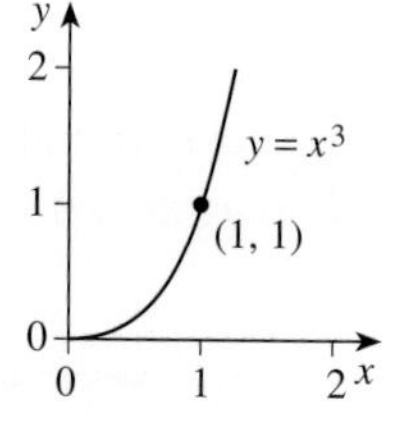

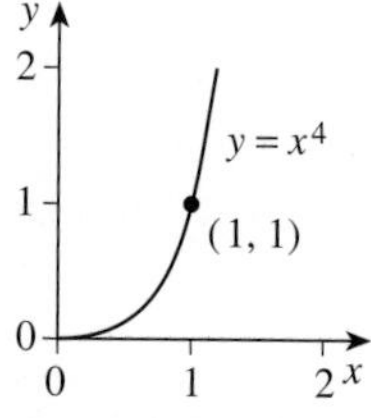

Fig. 8.4

Now put the graphs together in a single display. Points to notice are:

- (0, 0) and (1, 1) satisfy the equation $y = x^n$ for all these values of n, so that all the graphs include the points (0, 0) and (1, 1).
- $n = 1$ is a special case: it gives the straight line $y = x$ through the origin, which makes an angle of 45° with each axis.
- For $n > 1$ the x-axis is a tangent to the graphs at the origin. This is because, when x is small, x^n is very small. For example, $0.1^2 = 0.01$, $0.1^3 = 0.001$, $0.1^4 = 0.0001$.
- For each increase in the index n, the graph stays closer to the x-axis between $x = 0$ and $x = 1$, but then climbs more steeply beyond $x = 1$. This is because $x^{n+1} = x \times x^n$, so that $x^{n+1} < x^n$ when $0 < x < 1$ and $x^{n+1} > x^n$ when $x > 1$.

Now display the graphs again, using a window of $-2 \le x \le 2$, $-2 \le y \le 2$ with equal scales on both axes.

You will notice that what happens when x is negative depends on whether n is odd or even. To see this, suppose $x = -a$, where a is a positive number.

If n is even, $(-a)^n = a^n$. (Think of $n = 2$ or $n = 4$.)

So for the graph $y = f(x)$ where $f(x) = x^n$,

$$\begin{aligned} f(-a) &= (-a)^n \\ &= a^n \qquad \text{(since } n \text{ is even)}, \\ &= f(a). \end{aligned}$$

So the value of y on the graph is the same for $x = -a$ and $x = a$. This means that the graph is symmetrical about the y-axis. This is illustrated in Fig. 8.5 for the graphs of $y = x^2$ and $y = x^4$. Functions with the property that $f(-a) = f(a)$ for all values of a are called **even functions**.

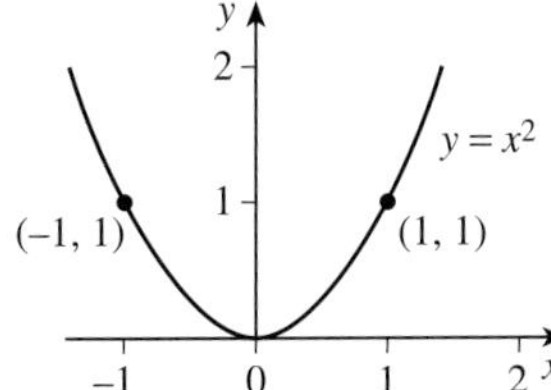

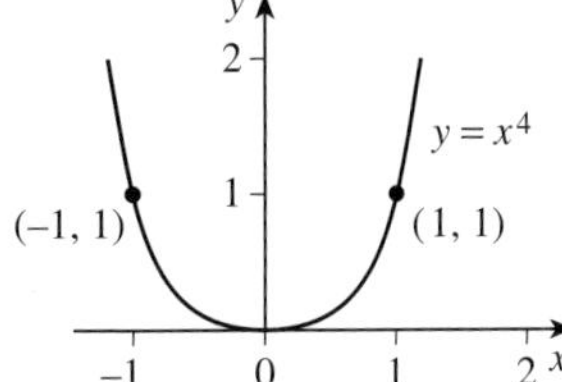

Fig. 8.5

If n is odd, $(-a)^n = -a^n$. (Think of $n = 1$ or $n = 3$.)

So for the graph $y = f(x)$ where $f(x) = x^n$,

$$\begin{aligned} f(-a) &= (-a)^n \\ &= -a^n \\ &= -f(a). \end{aligned}$$

The value of y for $x = -a$ is minus the value for $x = a$. Note that the points with coordinates (a, a^n) and $(-a, -a^n)$ are symmetrically placed on either side of the origin. This means that the whole graph is symmetrical about the origin. This is illustrated in Fig. 8.6 for the graphs of $y = x$ and $y = x^3$. Functions with the property that $f(-a) = -f(a)$ for all values of a are called **odd functions**.

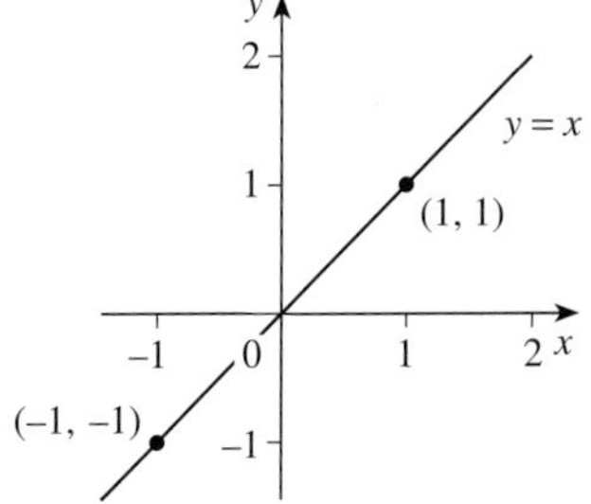

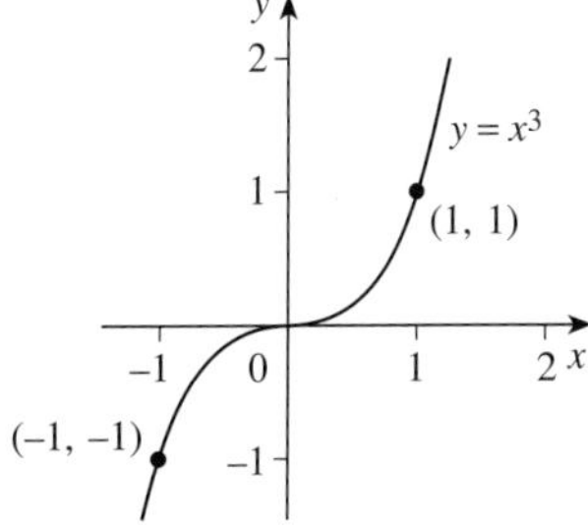

Fig. 8.6

Exercise 8B

1 Sketch the graphs of

(a) $y = x^5$, (b) $y = x^6$, (c) $y = x^{10}$, (d) $y = x^{15}$.

Use your calculator to check your sketches.

2 Given $f(x) = x^n$ and $f(3) = 81$, determine the value of n.

3 Of the following functions, one is even and two are odd. Determine which is which.

(a) $f(x) = x^7$ (b) $g(x) = x^4 + 3x^2$ (c) $h(x) = x(x^2 - 1)$

8.4 The domain of a function

Example 8.1.1 gave two functions which cannot be defined for all real numbers: $\frac{1}{x}$, which has no meaning when x is 0, and $\sqrt{x}$, which has no meaning when x is negative.

Example 8.4.1
For what values of x does $\sqrt{x(6-x)}$ have a meaning?

Since a negative number does not have a real square root, $\sqrt{x(6-x)}$ exists only if $x(6-x) \geq 0$.

For this to be true, the factors x and $6 - x$ must either be both greater than or equal to 0, or both less than or equal to 0.

If $x \geq 0$ and $6 - x \geq 0$, then $0 \leq x \leq 6$.

The alternative, that $x \leq 0$ and $6 - x \leq 0$, is impossible. The second inequality can be written as $x \geq 6$, and you can't have $x \leq 0$ and $x \geq 6$ at the same time.

So $\sqrt{x(6-x)}$ has a meaning only if $0 \leq x \leq 6$.

There are also times when you use a function which has a meaning for all real numbers x, but you are interested in it only when x is restricted in some way. For example, the formula for the volume of a cube is $V = x^3$. Although you can calculate x^3 for any real number x, you would only use this formula for $x > 0$.

Example 8.4.2

(a) One pair of sides of a rectangle is 1 metre longer than the other pair. If the length of one of the shorter sides is x metres, find a formula for the area of the rectangle in square metres.

(b) Find a formula for the sum of the first x even numbers.

(a) The sides have lengths x metres and $(x+1)$ metres, so the area in square metres is $x(x+1)$.

(b) You know from Section 2.3 that the sum of all the natural numbers from 1 to n is $\frac{1}{2}n(n+1)$. So the sum of the first x even numbers is

$$\begin{aligned} 2+4+6+...+2x &= 2(1+2+3+...+x) \\ &= 2 \times \tfrac{1}{2}x(x+1) \\ &= x(x+1). \end{aligned}$$

In both parts of this example the function is given by the same expression, but the variable x is understood in different ways. In part (a) the question makes sense if x is any positive real number. In part (b), x can only be a positive integer.

You could therefore distinguish three different functions:

$f(x) = x(x+1)$, where x is a real number ($x \in \mathbb{R}$)

$A(x) = x(x+1)$, where x is a positive real number ($x \in \mathbb{R}^+$)

$S(x) = x(x+1)$, where x is a positive integer ($x \in \mathbb{Z}^+$).

Fig. 8.7 shows part of the graphs of these three functions. Although they are all given by the same expression, they have different properties. For example, $f(x)$ has a minimum value when $x = -\frac{1}{2}$, but $A(x)$ and $S(x)$ are not defined for this value of x. It makes sense to write $f\left(1\frac{1}{2}\right) = 3\frac{3}{4}$ and $A\left(1\frac{1}{2}\right) = 3\frac{3}{4}$, but you can't find the sum of the first $1\frac{1}{2}$ even numbers.

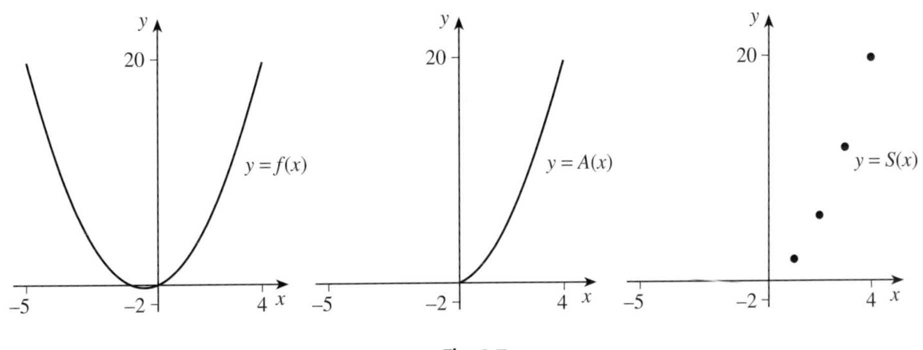

Fig. 8.7

So two possible reasons why a function $f(x)$ might not be defined for all real numbers x are

- the algebraic expression for $f(x)$ may only have meaning for some x
- only some x are relevant in the context in which the function is being used.

The set of numbers x for which a function $f(x)$ is defined is called the **domain** of the function. For example, the domain of the function in Example 8.4.1 can be taken to be the set of real numbers such that $0 \le x \le 6$; these are the only numbers for which $\sqrt{x(6-x)}$ exists. In Example 8.4.2 the domains can be taken to be the positive real numbers and the positive integers respectively; these are the only numbers which make sense in the contexts, even though the formula $x(x+1)$ has a meaning for any real number x.

8.5 The range of a function

Once you have decided the domain of a function $f(x)$, you can ask what values $f(x)$ can take. This is called the **range** of the function.

Example 8.5.1
Find the range of the function $x(6 - x)$, and interpret this geometrically.

The expression $x(6 - x)$ can be evaluated for any real number x, so the domain can be taken as the complete set of real numbers.

The simplest way to find the range is to use the graph of the function. This is shown in Fig. 8.8.

The graph looks symmetrical. If so, it will reach its highest point when $x = 3$, and y is then $3 \times (6 - 3) = 3 \times 3 = 9$. So the range consists of all real numbers less than or equal to 9.

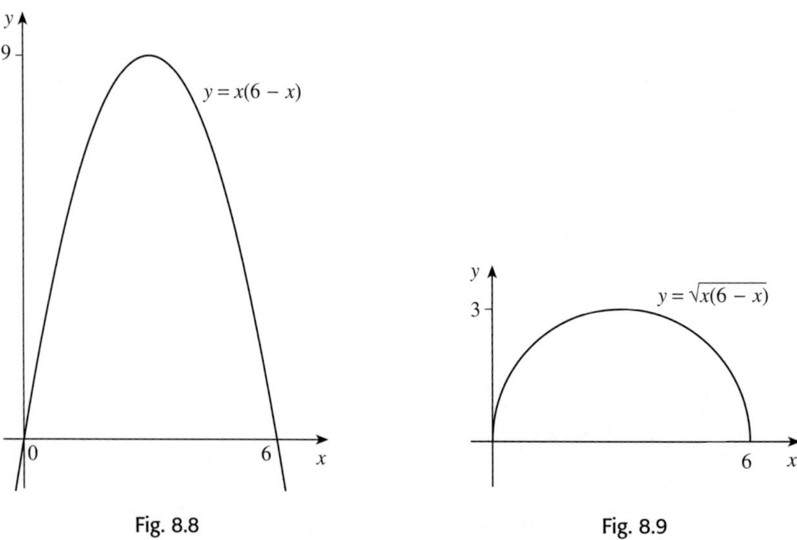

Fig. 8.8

Fig. 8.9

Example 8.5.2
Find the range of the function $\sqrt{x(6 - x)}$ taking its domain to be the set of numbers $0 \le x \le 6$.

You could use your calculator again to produce the graph in Fig. 8.9, but in fact all the information you need can be got from Fig. 8.8.

For any value of x, the y-coordinate in Fig. 8.9 is the positive square root of the corresponding y-coordinate in Fig. 8.8. This square root only exists when $y \ge 0$ in Fig. 8.8, that is when $0 \le x \le 6$; and since the maximum value in Fig. 8.8 is 9, the maximum value in Fig. 8.9 is $\sqrt{9} = 3$. So the range of $\sqrt{x(6 - x)}$ is $0 \le y \le 3$.

Example 8.5.3

A marching guardsman swings his arms so that their angle in front of the downward vertical varies from 0° to 80°. When this angle is x°, the height of his thumbnail above the ground is y metres, where $y = 1.8 - 0.8\cos x^\circ$. Find the range of this function as he marches.

In Fig. 8.10 the solid curve shows the graph of y in the domain $0 \le x \le 80$, and the dotted curves show how the graph continues outside the given domain. You can see that, on the solid curve, the graph takes values between $y = 1$ (when $x = 0$) and $y = 1.661...$ (when $x = 80$).

So the range of the function is $1 \le y \le 1.66$, correct to 3 significant figures.

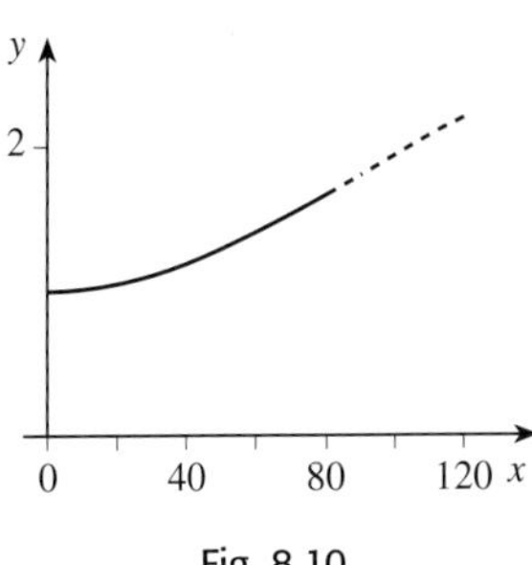

Fig. 8.10

Exercise 8C

1 Find the set of values of x for which these algebraic expressions have a meaning.

(a) $\sqrt{x}$ (b) $\sqrt{-x}$ (c) $\sqrt{x-4}$ (d) $\sqrt{4-x}$

(e) $\sqrt{x(x-4)}$ (f) $\sqrt{2x(x-4)}$ (g) $\sqrt{x^2-9}$ (h) $\sqrt{x^3-8}$

(i) $\dfrac{1}{x-2}$ (j) $\dfrac{1}{\sqrt{x-2}}$ (k) $\dfrac{1}{1+\sqrt{x}}$ (l) $\dfrac{1}{(x-1)(x-2)}$

2 The domain of each of the following functions is the set of real numbers. Find their ranges.

(a) $f(x) = x^2 + 4$ (b) $f(x) = 2(x^2 + 5)$ (c) $f(x) = (x-1)^2 + 6$

(d) $f(x) = -(1-x)^2 + 7$ (e) $f(x) = 3(x+5)^2 + 2$ (f) $f(x) = 2(x+2)^4 - 1$

3 These functions are each defined for the given domain. Display their graphs on your calculator and find their ranges.

(a) $f(x) = 2x$ for $0 \le x \le 8$ (b) $f(x) = 3 - 2x$ for $-2 \le x \le 2$

(c) $f(x) = x^2$ for $-1 \le x \le 4$ (d) $f(x) = x^2$ for $-5 \le x \le -2$

4 The domain of each of the following functions is the set of all positive real numbers. Find the range of each function.

(a) $f(x) = 2x + 7$ (b) $f(x) = -5x$ (c) $f(x) = 3x - 1$

(d) $f(x) = x^2 - 1$ (e) $f(x) = (x+2)(x+1)$ (f) $f(x) = (x-1)(x-2)$

5 The domain of each of the following functions is the set of values of x for which the algebraic expression has a meaning. Find their ranges.

(a) $f(x) = x^8$ (b) $f(x) = x^{11}$ (c) $f(x) = \dfrac{1}{x^3}$ (d) $f(x) = \dfrac{1}{x^4}$

(e) $f(x) = x^4 + 5$ (f) $f(x) = \frac{1}{4}x + \frac{1}{8}$ (g) $f(x) = \sqrt{4-x^2}$ (h) $f(x) = \sqrt{4-x}$

6 A piece of wire 24 cm long has the shape of a rectangle. Given that the width is w cm, show that the area, A cm^2, of the rectangle is given by the function $A = w(12 - w)$. Suggest a suitable domain and find the corresponding range of this function in this context.

7 Use a calculator to show the graph of $y = x(8 - 2x)(22 - 2x)$. Given that y cm^3 is the volume of a cuboid with height x cm, length $(22 - 2x)$ cm and width $(8 - 2x)$ cm, state an appropriate domain for the function given above.

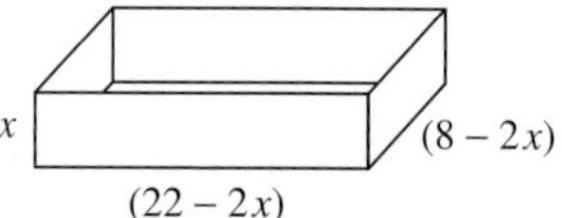

Use a graph to estimate the corresponding range.

8.6 Sequences as functions

In Section 8.4 you may have been surprised by the graph of $S(x)$ in Fig. 8.7, which is simply a set of dots. This is because the domain is the set $\mathbb{Z}^+ = \{1, 2, 3, ...\}$. The function is only defined when x is a positive integer.

In the same way, you can think of any sequence u_n as a function. To make this more obvious you could have used the notation $u(n)$ instead of the conventional notation u_n.

> If the sequence begins with u_0 rather than u_1, then the domain is the set of natural numbers $\mathbb{N} = \{0, 1, 2, ...\}$. For example, this is how the triangle numbers t_n were defined at the end of Section 2.3.

Example 8.6.1
Draw the graph of the arithmetic sequence 13, 11, 9, ... with 10 terms.

The formula for the nth term, $u_n = a + (n - 1)d$ (see Section 2.4), with $a = 13$ and $d = -2$, gives

$$\begin{aligned} u_n &= 13 - 2(n - 1) \\ &= 15 - 2n. \end{aligned}$$

Notice that u_n is positive if $1 \leq n \leq 7$, and negative if $8 \leq n \leq 10$. When $n = 10$, $u_n = 15 - 2 \times 10 = -5$.

The graph is shown in Fig. 8.11. The points all lie on a straight line with gradient -2 and y-intercept 15.

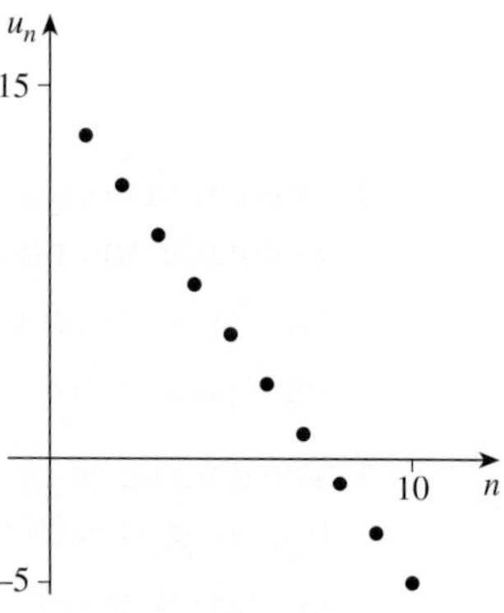

Fig. 8.11

You can produce graphs like Fig. 8.11 on your calculator. To do this, you have to put the calculator into 'sequence graphing mode'. In place of '$y = ...$' you can then enter the formula '$u_n = 15 - 2n$', and the graph will appear in the window as a line of dots.

Example 8.6.2
Sue is Don's younger sister. She was born on Don's fourth birthday; so when Sue is n years old, Don is $n + 4$. Display a graph to show the ratio of Don's age to Sue's for $1 \leq n \leq 50$. What happens to this ratio as they get older?

If the ratio is denoted by u_n, then

$$u_n = \frac{n+4}{n}.$$

You can calculate that $u_1 = 5$, so use a window of $0 \le x \le 50$, $0 \le y \le 5$. You will then get a calculator display like Fig. 8.12.

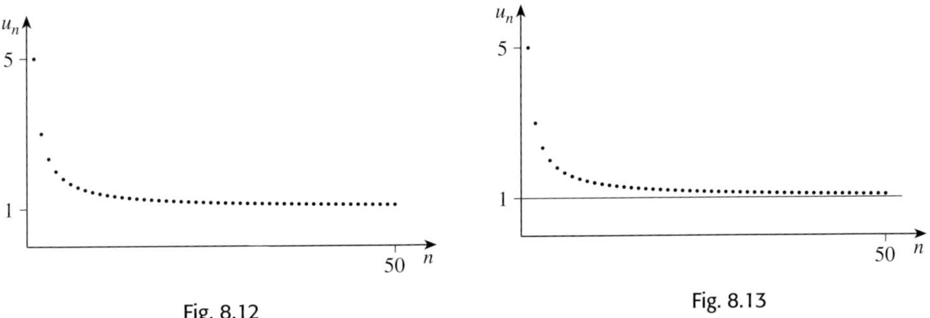

Fig. 8.12

Fig. 8.13

This shows that the ratio drops very quickly to start with, but later it changes very little from year to year. However long they live, the ratio will always be greater than 1, but it will get very close to 1 as time goes on. To show this on the graph, add a horizontal line $y = 1$ to the calculator display as shown in Fig. 8.13.

In Example 8.6.2 the sequence u_n is said to **converge** (or **tend**) **to the limit 1 as n tends to infinity**. This is written

$$u_n \to 1 \text{ as } n \to \infty,$$

or

$$\lim_{n\to\infty} u_n = 1.$$

You read the last equation as 'the limit of u_n as n tends to infinity is equal to 1.'

Exercise 8D

1 Use your calculator to display the graphs of the arithmetic sequences with the following definitions.

(a) $u_n = 3 + 2n$ for $1 \le n \le 6$

(b) $u_n = 11 - 3n$ for $1 \le n \le 5$

(c) $a = 12, d = -1$ for $1 \le n \le 20$

(d) $a = -5, d = 1.5$ for $1 \le n \le 10$

(e) $u_1 = 10, u_n = u_{n-1} - 2$ for $1 \le n \le 10$

(f) $u_1 = -8, u_n = u_{n-1} + 6$ for $1 \le n \le 5$

2 An arithmetic sequence has first term 7 and common difference –2. Show that the sum s_n of n terms of the sequence can be defined in either of two ways:

(a) $s_n = n(8 - n)$, or (b) $s_1 = 1, s_n = s_{n-1} + (9 - 2n)$.

Make graphs based on each of these definitions for $1 \le n \le 10$, and check that they are the same.

9 Linear and quadratic functions

This chapter looks in more detail at two particular types of function. When you have completed it, you should

- know what is meant by a constant function, a linear function and a quadratic function
- be able to write quadratic expressions in completed square form, and to interpret this in graphical terms
- be able to apply the theory to displacement–time and velocity–time relationships for objects moving with constant velocity and constant acceleration.

9.1 Linear functions

Example 9.1.1
A function with domain the real numbers from 0 to 5 is given by $f(x) = 3$. What is its range?

The graph of the function is shown in Fig. 9.1. The set of values taken by the function consists of the single number 3. The range of the function is therefore the set $\{3\}$.

A function whose range consists of a single number c is called a **constant function**.

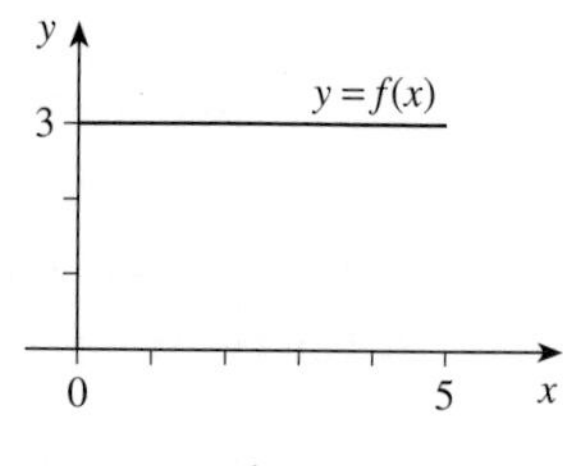

Fig. 9.1

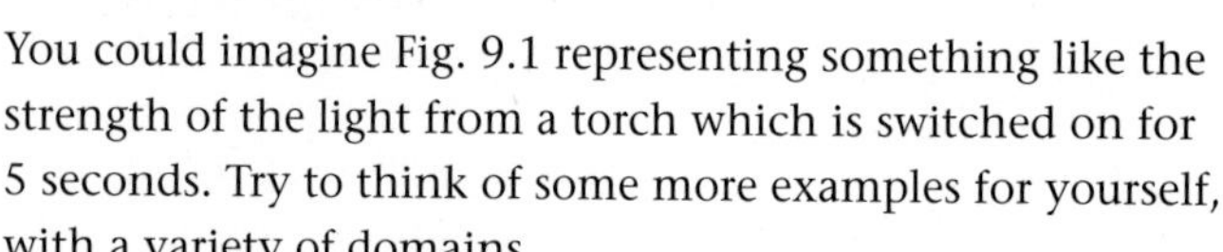

You could imagine Fig. 9.1 representing something like the strength of the light from a torch which is switched on for 5 seconds. Try to think of some more examples for yourself, with a variety of domains.

If you add to a constant a second term which is a multiple of x, you get a **linear function**, with an equation of the form $f(x) = bx + c$. (But b must not be 0, or the function would just be constant.) Try showing the graphs of functions like this for different values of b and c, such as $2x + 3$, $4x - 5$, $-x + 2$, $-3x - 1$. You know from Chapter 7 that these graphs are all straight lines, which is the reason for calling the functions 'linear'.

The numbers b and c in the equation are called **coefficients**; b is the 'coefficient of x', and c is often called the 'constant term'. From Section 7.3, the coefficient c is the y-intercept on the graph, and b corresponds to the gradient. But notice that, if different scales are used on the two axes, the gradient won't 'look right'. For example, a graph with $b = 1$ will not be at 45° to the x-axis unless the same scale is used on both axes.

If the domain of a linear function is the complete set $\mathbb{R}$ of real numbers, then the range is also $\mathbb{R}$. But in practical applications such as Example 9.1.2, the domain may be only an interval of real numbers, and then the range will also be an interval of real numbers.

Example 9.1.2

A piece of elastic 50 cm long has one end attached to a hook in the ceiling. Objects are attached to the other end and allowed to hang freely, so that the elastic stretches. For each kilogram of mass the string stretches by 8 cm, but if the mass exceeds 10 kg the elastic will break. Express the relation between the mass m kg and the length l cm as a function, and find the domain and range.

With an object of mass m kg attached the elastic stretches by $8m$ cm, so its total length is $(8m + 50)$ cm. The relation between mass and length is therefore expressed by the linear function equation

$$l = 8m + 50.$$

This equation only holds so long as the string doesn't break, so the domain is the interval $0 \le m \le 10$. In this interval the length increases from 50 cm to 130 cm, so the range is the interval $50 \le l \le 130$. This is illustrated by the graph in Fig. 9.2, which is the line segment joining the points with coordinates (0, 50) and (10, 130).

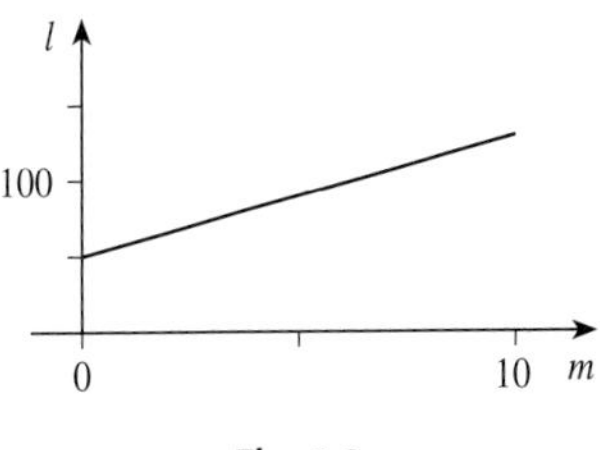

Fig. 9.2

9.2 Quadratic functions

If you add to a linear function a third term which is a multiple of x^2, you get a **quadratic function**, with an equation of the form $f(x) = ax^2 + bx + c$ (where a is not 0). The name comes from the Latin word *quadra*, meaning a square; the connection with a geometrical square is of course that a square of side x units has area x^2 units^2.

To keep things simple, most of the quadratics in this chapter have coefficients which are integers, but this is not a requirement; a, b and c can be any kind of real number.

For example, you could have $a = \frac{2}{3}$, $b = \sqrt{2}$ and $c = -\pi$, in which case the quadratic would be $f(x) = \frac{2}{3}x^2 + \sqrt{2}x - \pi$. The theory would still apply, though the arithmetic would be more complicated.

Unless stated otherwise, the domain should be assumed to be the set $\mathbb{R}$ of all real numbers.

Exercise 9A asks you to investigate the graphs of quadratic functions for various values of the coefficients, a, b and c.

Exercise 9A

1 Display, on the same set of axes, the graphs of

(a) $y = x^2 - 2x + 5$, (b) $y = x^2 - 2x + 1$,

(c) $y = x^2 - 2x$, (d) $y = x^2 - 2x - 6$.

2 Display, on the same set of axes, the graphs of

(a) $y = x^2 + x - 4$, (b) $y = x^2 + x - 1$,

(c) $y = x^2 + x + 2$, (d) $y = x^2 + x + 5$.

3 The diagram shows the graph of $y = ax^2 - bx$.
On a copy of the diagram, sketch the graphs of

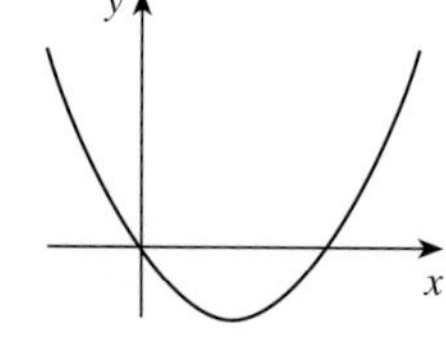

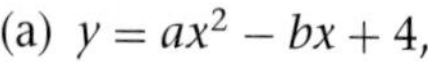

(a) $y = ax^2 - bx + 4$,

(b) $y = ax^2 - bx - 6$.

4 What is the effect on the graph of $y = ax^2 + bx + c$ of changing the value of c?

5 Display, on the same set of axes, the graphs of

(a) $y = x^2 - 4x + 1$, (b) $y = x^2 - 2x + 1$,

(c) $y = x^2 + 1$, (d) $y = x^2 + 2x + 1$.

6 Display the graph of $y = 2x^2 + bx + 4$ for different values of b. How does changing b affect the curve $y = ax^2 + bx + c$?

7 Display, on the same set of axes, the graphs of

(a) $y = x^2 + 1$, (b) $y = 3x^2 + 1$,

(c) $y = -3x^2 + 1$, (d) $y = -x^2 + 1$.

8 Display, on the same set of axes, the graphs of

(a) $y = -4x^2 + 3x + 1$, (b) $y = -x^2 + 3x + 1$,

(c) $y = x^2 + 3x + 1$, (d) $y = 4x^2 + 3x + 1$.

9 Display the graph of $y = ax^2 - 2x$ for different values of a.

10 How does changing a affect the shape of the graph of $y = ax^2 + bx + c$?

11 Which of the following could be the equation of the curve shown in the diagram?

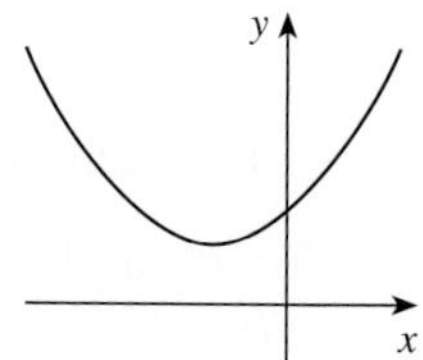

(a) $y = x^2 - 2x + 5$

(b) $y = -x^2 - 2x + 5$

(c) $y = x^2 + 2x + 5$

(d) $y = -x^2 + 2x + 5$

12 Which of the following could be the equation of the curve shown in the diagram?

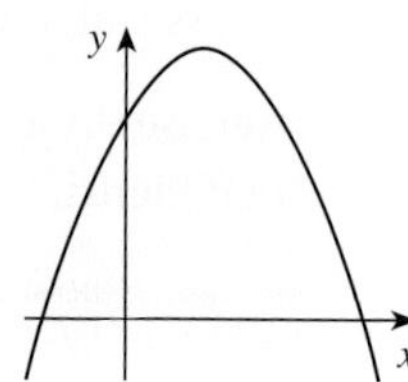

(a) $y = -x^2 + 3x + 4$

(b) $y = x^2 - 3x + 4$

(c) $y = x^2 + 3x + 4$

(d) $y = -x^2 - 3x + 4$

9.3 The shapes of graphs of the form $y = ax^2 + bx + c$

In Exercise 9A, you should have found a number of results, which are summarised below.

All the graphs have the same general shape, which is called a **parabola**. These parabolas have a vertical **axis of symmetry**. The point where a parabola meets its axis of symmetry is called the **vertex**.

Changing c moves the graph up and down in the y-direction.

Changing b also moves the axis of symmetry of the graph in the x-direction.

If a and b have the same sign the axis of symmetry is to the left of the y-axis; if a and b have opposite signs the axis of symmetry is to the right of the y-axis.

If a is positive the vertex is at the lowest point of the graph; if a is negative the vertex is at the highest point. The larger the size of $|a|$ the more the graph is elongated.

So far these are just observations based on experiments with a few particular graphs. To understand why they are true, you can use algebra to write the expression $ax^2 + bx + c$ in a different way, known as 'completed square form'. This is described in the next section.

9.4 Completed square form

Expressions like

$$f(x) = (x-2)^2 + 3, \quad g(x) = 5 - (x-1)^2, \quad h(x) = 2(x+3)^2 - 7$$

and more generally

$$F(x) = a(x-r)^2 + s$$

are said to be in **completed square form**. Multiplying out the squared brackets gives

$$\begin{aligned} f(x) &= (x^2 - 4x + 4) + 3 \\ &= x^2 - 4x + 7, \\ g(x) &= 5 - (x^2 - 2x + 1) \\ &= -x^2 + 2x + 4, \\ h(x) &= 2(x^2 + 6x + 9) - 7 \\ &= 2x^2 + 12x + 11. \end{aligned}$$

So $f(x)$, $g(x)$ and $h(x)$ are all quadratic functions.

You can use the completed square form of a function to write down the equation of the axis of symmetry and the coordinates of the vertex of its graph. The key point is that, whatever the value of x, the values of expressions such as $(x-2)^2$, $(x-1)^2$ and $(x+3)^2$ are always greater than or equal to 0. For example, for $f(x)$,

$$(x-2)^2 \geq 0, \quad \text{so that} \quad f(x) = (x-2)^2 + 3 \geq 3.$$

So the smallest possible value of $f(x)$ is 3, and it has this value when $x = 2$. This means that the vertex of the graph of $y = f(x)$ is at (2, 3).

You can take the argument further to show that the graph is symmetrical about the line $x = 2$. Fig. 9.3 shows a pair of points on the graph whose x-coordinates are symmetrical about $x = 2$. These coordinates can be written as $x = 2 - h$ and $x = 2 + h$ for some number h. Then

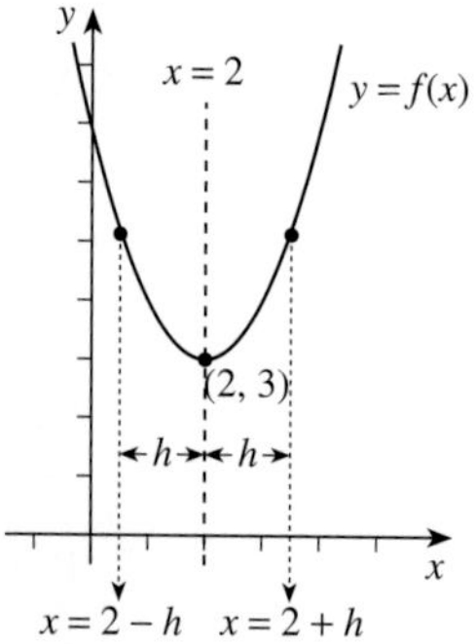

$$\begin{aligned} f(2-h) &= ((2-h)-2)^2+3 \\ &= (-h)^2+3 \\ &= h^2+3 \end{aligned}$$

Fig. 9.3

and

$$\begin{aligned} f(2+h) &= ((2+h)-2)^2+3 \\ &= h^2+3. \end{aligned}$$

So $\qquad f(2-h) = f(2+h).$

Since this is true whatever the value of h, this proves that the graph is symmetrical about $x = 2$.

Similar calculations can be carried out for $g(x)$ and $h(x)$.

$$(x-1)^2 \geq 0, \quad \text{so that} \quad g(x) = 5-(x-1)^2 \leq 5;$$

the vertex is at (1, 5) and the axis of symmetry is $x = 1$ (see Fig. 9.4).

$$(x+3)^2 \geq 0 \quad \text{so that} \quad h(x) = 2(x+3)^2 - 7 \geq -7;$$

the vertex is at $(-3, -7)$ and the axis of symmetry is $x = -3$ (see Fig. 9.5).

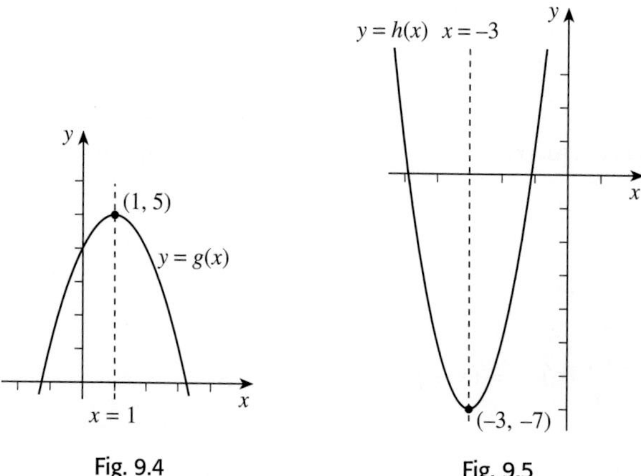

Fig. 9.4 Fig. 9.5

You will notice that the values of a for $f(x)$, $g(x)$ and $h(x)$ are 1, -1 and 2 respectively. So for $f(x)$ and $h(x)$, where a is positive, the vertex is at the lowest point; but for $g(x)$, where a is negative, the vertex is at the highest point. Also $|a| = 1$ for $f(x)$ and $g(x)$, but $|a| = 2$ for $h(x)$, so the graph of $y = h(x)$ is more elongated than the graphs of $y = f(x)$ and $y = g(x)$.

Example 9.4.1

A quadratic graph has an equation of the form $y = a(x - r)^2 + s$. Its vertex is at $(1, -3)$. The graph also contains the point $(-1, 5)$.

(a) Find the values of r, s and a.

(b) For which other value of x does $y = 5$?

(c) Write the equation in the form $y = ax^2 + bx + c$.

(a) The vertex is where $(x - r)^2$ takes its least possible value, which is 0. Since $x = 1$ at the vertex, $r = 1$.

Also, when $(x - r)^2 = 0$, $y = s$. So s is the y-coordinate of the vertex, which is -3.

The equation of the graph therefore has the form

$$y = a(x - 1)^2 - 3$$

for some value of a. And since $(-1, 5)$ is on the graph,

$$5 = a(-1 - 1)^2 - 3,$$

so $8 = 4a$, which gives $a = 2$.

(b) The axis of symmetry of the graph is $x = 1$. You are given that $y = 5$ when $x = -1$, which is 2 units to the left of the axis of symmetry. So $y = 5$ also at a point 2 units to the right of the axis of symmetry, that is when $x = 3$.

(c) The equation of the graph is

$$y = 2(x - 1)^2 - 3.$$

When multiplied out, this is

$$y = 2x^2 - 4x - 1.$$

Exercise 9B

1 Find (i) the vertex and (ii) the equation of the axis of symmetry of each of the following quadratic graphs.

(a) $y = (x - 2)^2 + 3$ (b) $y = (x - 5)^2 - 4$ (c) $y = (x + 3)^2 - 7$

(d) $y = (2x - 3)^2 + 1$ (e) $y = (5x + 3)^2 + 2$ (f) $y = (3x + 7)^2 - 4$

(g) $y = (x - 3)^2 + c$ (h) $y = (x - p)^2 + q$ (i) $y = (ax + b)^2 + c$

2 Find (i) the least or the greatest value (whichever is appropriate) of each of the following quadratic expressions and (ii) the value of x for which this occurs.

(a) $(x + 2)^2 - 1$ (b) $(x - 1)^2 + 2$ (c) $5 - (x + 3)^2$

(d) $(2x + 1)^2 - 7$ (e) $3 - 2(x - 4)^2$ (f) $(x + p)^2 + q$

(g) $(x - p)^2 - q$ (h) $r - (x - t)^2$ (i) $c - (ax + b)^2$

3 Use the given data about a quadratic graph with equation $y = a(x - r)^2 + s$ to find

(i) the equation of the axis of symmetry,

(ii) the values of r, s and a,

(iii) the equation of the graph in the form $y = ax^2 + bx + c$.

(a) The vertex is at (2, 5) and the graph also contains the point (0, 1).

(b) The graph contains the points (1, 2), (3, 2) and (2, −1).

9.5 Completing the square

In Section 9.4 the functions $f(x)$, $g(x)$ and $h(x)$ were first given in completed square form. Then, by multiplying out the squared brackets, it was shown that they were quadratic functions.

This section deals with the reverse problem: given a quadratic function $ax^2 + bx + c$, how can it be put into completed square form?

Begin with the simplest case in which $a = 1$.

When you try to write the quadratic expression $x^2 + bx + c$ in completed square form, the key point is to note that when you square $(x + \frac{1}{2}b)$ you get

$$\left(x + \tfrac{1}{2}b\right)^2 = x^2 + bx + \tfrac{1}{4}b^2, \text{ so } x^2 + bx = \left(x + \tfrac{1}{2}b\right)^2 - \tfrac{1}{4}b^2.$$

Now add c to both sides:

$$x^2 + bx + c = (x^2 + bx) + c = \left(x + \tfrac{1}{2}b\right)^2 - \tfrac{1}{4}b^2 + c.$$

Example 9.5.1
Write $x^2 + 10x + 32$ in completed square form.

$$\begin{aligned} x^2 + 10x + 32 &= (x^2 + 10x) + 32 \\ &= ((x + 5)^2 - 25) + 32 \\ &= (x + 5)^2 + 7. \end{aligned}$$

Don't try to learn the form $x^2 + bx + c = \left(x + \frac{1}{2}b\right)^2 - \frac{1}{4}b^2 + c$. Learn that you halve the coefficient of x, and write $x^2 + bx = \left(x + \frac{1}{2}b\right)^2 - \frac{1}{4}b^2$. Then add c to both sides.

If you need to write $ax^2 + bx + c$ in completed square form, but the coefficient a of x^2 is not 1, you can rewrite $ax^2 + bx + c$ by taking out the coefficient of x^2 as a factor from the first two terms:

$$ax^2 + bx + c = a\left(x^2 + \frac{b}{a}x\right) + c.$$

Then complete the square of the quadratic expression $x^2 + \dfrac{b}{a}x$ inside the bracket.

Example 9.5.2
Express $2x^2 + 10x + 7$ in completed square form. Use your result to find the axis of symmetry and the vertex of the graph of $y = 2x^2 + 10x + 7$.

Start by taking out the coefficient of x^2 as a factor from the first two terms:

$$2x^2 + 10x + 7 = 2(x^2 + 5x) + 7.$$

Dealing with the terms inside the bracket,

$$x^2 + 5x = \left(x + \tfrac{5}{2}\right)^2 - \tfrac{25}{4}.$$

So

$$\begin{aligned} 2x^2 + 10x + 7 &= 2(x^2 + 5x) + 7 \\ &= 2\left(\left(x + \tfrac{5}{2}\right)^2 - \tfrac{25}{4}\right) + 7 \\ &= 2\left(x + \tfrac{5}{2}\right)^2 - \tfrac{25}{2} + 7 \\ &= 2\left(x + \tfrac{5}{2}\right)^2 - \tfrac{11}{2}. \end{aligned}$$

It's worth checking your result mentally at this stage.

The equation of the graph can be written as $y = 2\left(x + \tfrac{5}{2}\right)^2 - \tfrac{11}{2}$.

The smallest value of this occurs when the square $\left(x + \tfrac{5}{2}\right)^2$ is 0, which is when $x = -\tfrac{5}{2}$. The smallest value is then $y = -\tfrac{11}{2}$.

So the axis of symmetry is $x = -\tfrac{5}{2}$, and the vertex is $\left(-\tfrac{5}{2}, -\tfrac{11}{2}\right)$.

If the coefficient of x^2 is negative, the technique is similar to Example 9.5.2.

Example 9.5.3
Express $3 - 4x - 2x^2$ in completed square form. Use your result to find the axis of symmetry and the vertex of the graph of $y = 3 - 4x - 2x^2$.

Start by taking out the coefficient of x^2 as a factor from the terms which involve x:

$$3 - 4x - 2x^2 = 3 - 2(x^2 + 2x).$$

Dealing with the terms inside the bracket, $x^2 + 2x = (x + 1)^2 - 1$.

So

$$\begin{aligned} 3 - 4x - 2x^2 &= 3 - 2(x^2 + 2x) \\ &= 3 - 2((x + 1)^2 - 1) \\ &= 3 - 2(x + 1)^2 + 2 \\ &= 5 - 2(x + 1)^2. \end{aligned}$$

The equation of the graph can be written as $y = 5 - 2(x + 1)^2$.

This shows that the largest value, at the vertex, is 5 when $x = -1$.

So the axis of symmetry is $x = -1$, and the vertex is $(-1, 5)$.

If you apply the procedure to the general quadratic expression $ax^2 + bx + c$, you begin by observing that $x^2 + \frac{b}{a}x$ are the first two terms of the expansion of $\left(x + \frac{b}{2a}\right)^2$, so that

$$x^2 + \frac{b}{a}x = \left(x + \frac{b}{2a}\right)^2 - \left(\frac{b}{2a}\right)^2.$$

So

$$\begin{aligned} ax^2 + bx + c &= a\left(x^2 + \frac{b}{a}x\right) + c \\ &= a\left(\left(x + \frac{b}{2a}\right)^2 - \frac{b^2}{4a^2}\right) + c \\ &= a\left(x + \frac{b}{2a}\right)^2 - \frac{b^2}{4a} + c. \end{aligned}$$

It follows that the axis of symmetry of the graph has equation $x = -\frac{b}{2a}$, and that the vertex is at $\left(-\frac{b}{2a}, c - \frac{b^2}{4a}\right)$.

It isn't worth learning this as a general formula. But it is interesting to compare the algebraic results with the observations in Section 9.3. For example, the equation of the axis of symmetry depends on a and b but not on c; and if a and b have the same sign, then $-\frac{b}{2a}$ is negative, so that the axis of symmetry is to the left of the x-axis. So these observations are not just accidental consequences of the particular numerical examples chosen in Exercise 9A, but they are generally true for the graphs of all quadratic functions.

What this also shows is that every quadratic expression $ax^2 + bx + c$ (with $a \neq 0$), without exception, can be written in completed square form as $a(x - r)^2 + s$.

Exercise 9C

1 Express the following in completed square form.

(a) $x^2 + 2x + 2$ (b) $x^2 - 8x - 3$ (c) $x^2 + 3x - 7$

(d) $5 - 6x + x^2$ (e) $x^2 + 14x + 49$ (f) $2x^2 + 12x - 5$

(g) $3x^2 - 12x + 3$ (h) $7 - 8x - 4x^2$ (i) $2x^2 + 5x - 3$

2 Use the completed square form to find as appropriate the least or greatest value of each of the following expressions, and the value of x for which this occurs.

(a) $x^2 - 4x + 7$ (b) $x^2 - 3x + 5$ (c) $4 + 6x - x^2$

(d) $2x^2 - 5x + 2$ (e) $3x^2 + 2x - 4$ (f) $3 - 7x - 3x^2$

3 By completing the square find (i) the vertex, and (ii) the equation of the axis of symmetry, of each of the following parabolas.

(a) $y = x^2 - 4x + 6$ (b) $y = x^2 + 6x - 2$ (c) $y = 7 - 10x - x^2$

(d) $y = x^2 + 3x + 1$ (e) $y = 2x^2 - 7x + 2$ (f) $y = 3x^2 - 12x + 5$

4 Find the ranges of the following quadratic functions with the given domains.

(a) $f(x) = x^2 + 10x - 3, \quad \mathbb{R}$
(b) $f(x) = 1 + 6x - 2x^2, \quad \mathbb{R}$
(c) $f(x) = x^2 - 4x - 5, \quad \mathbb{R}^+$
(d) $f(x) = x^2 + 4x + 5, \quad \mathbb{R}^+$
(e) $f(x) = 3x^2 + 2x - 1, \quad -1 \le x \le 1$
(f) $f(x) = 5 + 8x - 2x^2, \quad 0 \le x \le 3$

9.6 An application to kinematics

'Kinematics' is the theory of moving objects. This section and the next are about objects which move in a straight line, such as barges on a canal or balls thrown vertically upwards.

In Fig. 9.6 an observer O sees a walker and a jogger passing each other, 60 metres away, on a straight road. The walker is going away from her at a speed of 1 metre per second; the jogger is coming towards her at 2 metres per second.

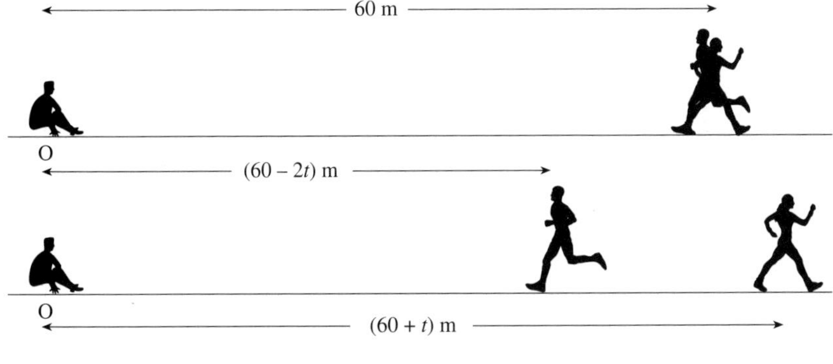

Fig. 9.6

If she looks again t seconds later, the walker will be t metres further away, and the jogger $2t$ metres closer. So the distances of the walker and the jogger from O will be $(60 + t)$ metres and $(60 - 2t)$ metres respectively.

There is one snag about this last statement. After 30 seconds the jogger will pass the observer, and the expression $(60 - 2t)$ will then become negative. So it is better not to use the word 'distance' but **displacement**, and to say that displacements are positive if made in one direction along the road, and negative in the other direction. You are already used to this when you use coordinates. The letter commonly used for displacement along a line from the origin is s. (Though x is also often used for displacement in a horizontal direction, and h, y or z for vertical displacement.) So, if s is measured in metres and t in seconds, and if displacements to the right in Fig. 9.6 are taken to be positive, you could write the equations

$$s = 60 + t$$

for the walker, and

$$s = 60 - 2t$$

for the jogger.

For a similar reason it is better to use the word **velocity**, rather than speed, and to describe velocities as positive or negative according to the direction of motion along the line. In this example the walker has velocity 1 metre per second, but the jogger's velocity is -2 metres per second. (The usual abbreviations for metres, seconds and metres per second are m, s and $\mathrm{m\,s^{-1}}$. The reason for the superscript '-1' will become clearer when you reach Chapter 13.)

You could draw two different kinds of graph to illustrate the motion. One is a **displacement–time graph**, or (t, s) graph, shown in Fig. 9.7. The second is a **velocity–time graph**, or (t, v) graph, shown in Fig. 9.8. The graphs for the walker are shown with solid lines, and those for the jogger with dotted lines.

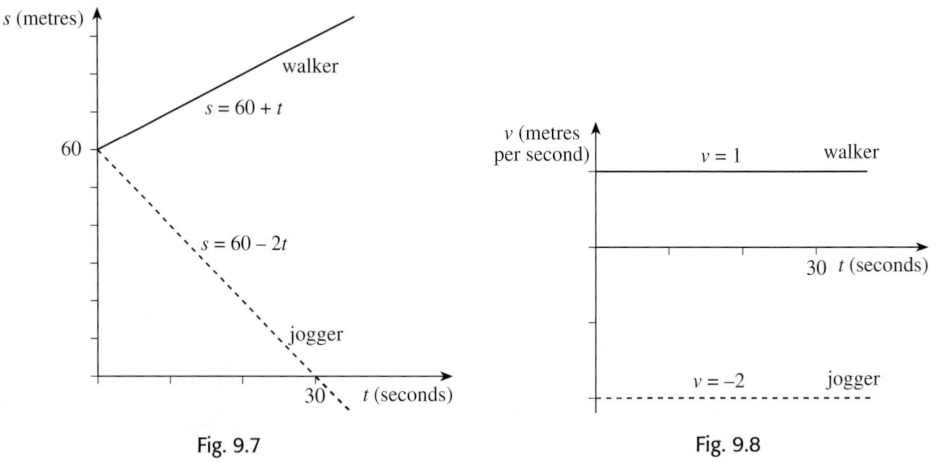

Fig. 9.7 Fig. 9.8

You can see from these graphs that:

> If the velocity is a constant function of the time, then the displacement is a linear function of the time. Also the velocity is represented by the gradient of the displacement–time graph.

(In the last statement you must, of course, take account of the fact that the graphs are drawn with unequal scales on the two axes.)

There is also a connection between the displacement and the velocity–time graph. Take a particular period of time, say 20 seconds. In that time the walker's displacement increases by 1×20 metres. The jogger's displacement decreases by 2×20 metres, which you could regard as an increase of $(-2) \times 20$ metres. How are these quantities represented on the velocity–time graph?

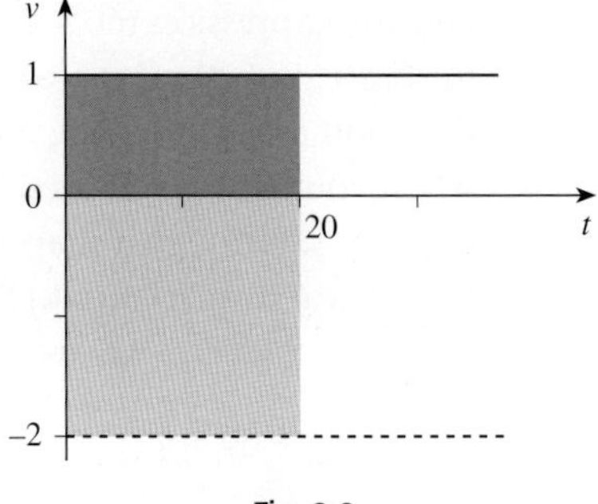

Fig. 9.9

The answer is indicated by Fig. 9.9. Over the interval $0 \le t \le 20$, the space between each graph and the t-axis is a rectangle. For the walker (with the space shaded dark grey) the product 1×20 is represented by the area of the rectangle. A similar statement is true for the jogger (with light grey shading), provided that you adopt the convention that the area of a space below the t-axis is taken to be negative.

If the velocity is constant, the increase in the displacement over an interval of time is represented by the (signed) area of the space between the velocity–time graph and the t-axis.

The importance of the statements in the blue boxes in this section is that they are true for any motion along a straight line, not just when the velocity is constant. A particular case is discussed in the next section, but the more general application must wait until Chapters 21 and 24.

9.7 Motion with constant acceleration

In Section 9.6 the walker and the jogger both moved with constant velocity, but this is a very special type of motion. In many practical applications the velocity varies with time. For example, the driver of a sports car might increase speed from 0 to 100 km per hour in 5 seconds. You would then say that the car has average **acceleration** of 20 km per hour per second.

This is not a very sensible unit for measuring acceleration, since it involves two different measures of time, the hour and the second. It would be better to change the velocity from km per hour to metres per second (m s^{-1}) and to give the acceleration in m s^{-1} per second. This is usually called 'metres per second squared', and denoted by m s^{-2}.

Example 9.7.1
Express a velocity of 100 km per hour in m s^{-1}.

Since 100 km = 100 000 metres, and 1 hour = 3600 seconds,

$$100 \text{ km per hour} = \frac{100\,000}{3600}\text{ m s}^{-1} = \frac{250}{9}\text{ m s}^{-1}.$$

So the velocity of the sports car increases by $\frac{250}{9}\text{ m s}^{-1}$ in 5 seconds, an average acceleration of $\frac{50}{9}\text{ m s}^{-2}$.

You may know that the acceleration of gravity, denoted by g, is about 10 m s^{-2}, so the driver experiences an average acceleration of about $\frac{5}{9}g$.

Like displacement and velocity, acceleration can be either positive or negative. Negative acceleration is called **deceleration**.

The next two examples are based on the assumption that the rule in Section 9.6 for calculating the displacement from the velocity–time graph, as an area, remains true even if the velocity is not constant.

Example 9.7.2

In taking off, an aircraft accelerates at a constant rate from 0 to 60 m s^{-1} in 30 seconds. Use a velocity–time graph to find

(a) the acceleration, (b) the distance the aircraft travels.

Since the acceleration is constant, the velocity–time graph is a straight line. If the time is measured from the instant when the aircraft starts to move, this line passes through the origin, as shown in Fig. 9.10.

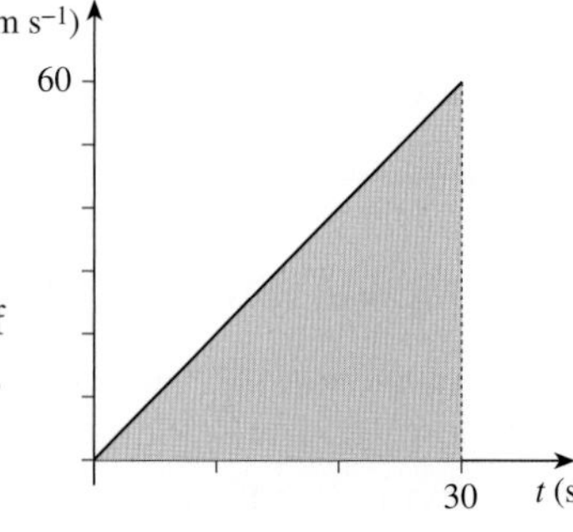

Fig. 9.10

(a) The acceleration is represented by the gradient of the line. Since the velocity is in m s^{-1} and time is in seconds, this gives the acceleration in m s^{-2}.

So the acceleration is $\frac{60}{30}$ m s^{-2}, which is 2 m s^{-2}.

(b) The space between the velocity–time graph and the t-axis has the shape of a triangle, shown shaded in Fig. 9.10. The displacement of the aircraft along the runway is represented by the area of this triangle, which is $\frac{1}{2} \times 30 \times 60 = 900$.

So the aircraft travels 900 metres along the runway before leaving the ground.

Example 9.7.3

After making a catch a cricketer throws the ball up into the air with a speed of 8 m s^{-1}. The effect of gravity is to give the ball a constant acceleration towards the ground of 10 m s^{-2}. Use a velocity–time graph to find the velocity and height of the ball after t seconds. Hence find how high the ball rises above the cricketer's hands, and how long it is in the air before he catches it again.

Taking the upward direction to be positive, and using units of metres and seconds, the velocity–time graph is a straight line with v-intercept 8 and gradient –10, so its equation is $v = -10t + 8$. Fig. 9.11 shows that, after a time $t = 0.8$, the value of v becomes negative. This means that the ball has started to descend.

The upward displacement of the ball, s metres after t seconds, is represented by the area of the shaded trapezium in Fig. 9.11. This trapezium is shown enlarged in Fig. 9.12. The area of this trapezium is

$$\tfrac{1}{2}(8 + (-10t + 8)) \times t = 8t - 5t^2.$$

The displacement–time equation is therefore $s = 8t - 5t^2$, which can be written in completed square form as

$$s = 3.2 - 5(t - 0.8)^2.$$

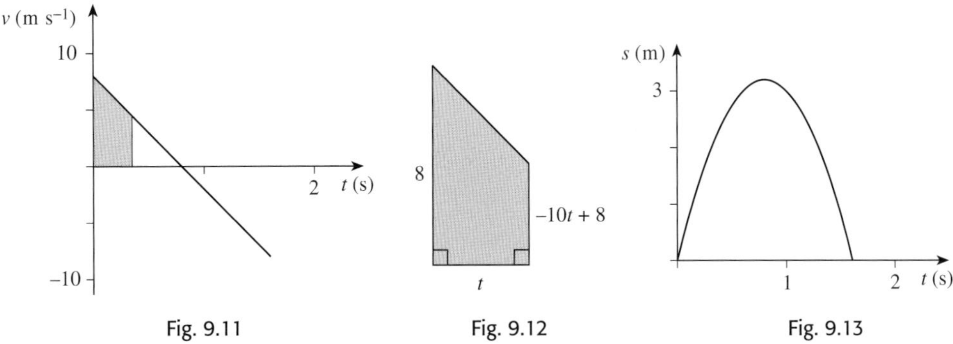

Fig. 9.11 Fig. 9.12 Fig. 9.13

So the ball reaches its greatest height of 3.2 metres after 0.8 seconds. Fig. 9.13 shows the displacement–time graph.

The ball is again at the level of the cricketer's hands when $8t - 5t^2 = 0$. Since

$$8t - 5t^2 = t(8 - 5t),$$

this occurs when $t = \frac{8}{5} = 1.6$. So he catches the ball after 1.6 seconds.

Notice that the equations in Example 9.7.3 are only valid so long as the ball is in the air, that is when $0 < t < 1.6$. So although the expressions for v and s have meaning for all real values of t, the relevant domain consists only of real numbers between 0 and 1.6.

This example illustrates a general result:

> When an object moves with constant acceleration, the velocity is a linear function of time, and the displacement is a quadratic function of time.

Exercise 9D

In questions about vertical motion, take the acceleration of gravity to be 10 m s^{-2}.

1 The straightest railway line in the world runs across the Nullarbor Plain in southern Australia, a distance of 500 kilometres. A train takes $12\frac{1}{2}$ hours to cover the distance. Model the journey by drawing

(a) a velocity–time graph, (b) a displacement–time graph.

Label your graphs to show the numbers 500 and $12\frac{1}{2}$ and to indicate the units used. Suggest some ways in which your models may not match the actual journey.

2 An aircraft flies due east at 800 km per hour from Kingston to Antigua, a displacement of about 1600 km. Model the flight by drawing

(a) a displacement–time graph, (b) a velocity–time graph.

Label your graphs to show the numbers 800 and 1600 and to indicate the units used. Can you suggest ways in which your models could be improved to describe the actual flight more accurately?

3 A stone is dropped from rest. Taking the downwards direction to be positive, sketch the velocity–time graph. Use this to find the velocity after 3 seconds, and the distance the stone has fallen in this time.

4 A machine projects a golf ball vertically upwards with a velocity of 25 m s^{-1}. The figure shows part of the velocity–time graph while it is in the air.

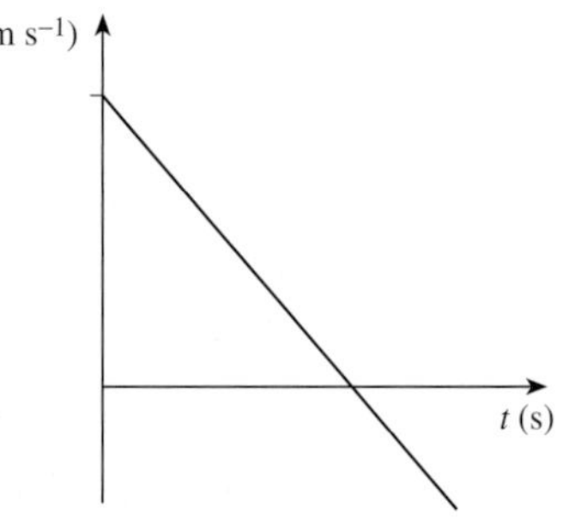

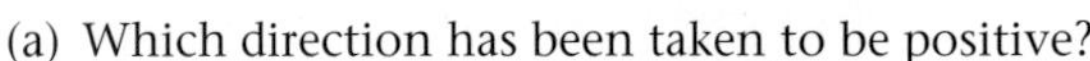

(a) Which direction has been taken to be positive?

(b) Write the equation of the velocity–time graph.

(c) When will the ball reach its highest point?

(d) What is the greatest height reached by the ball?

5 A train is travelling at 80 m s^{-1} when the driver applies the brakes. After 30 seconds the velocity has dropped to 20 m s^{-1}. The figure shows a sketch of the velocity–time graph while the train is slowing down.

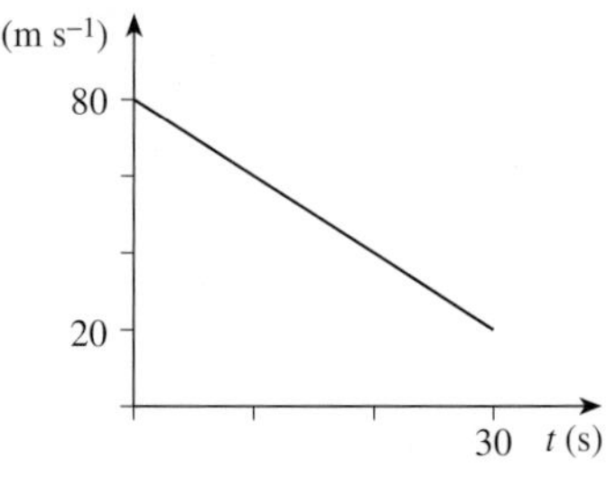

(a) Calculate the deceleration of the train.

(b) Write the equation of the velocity–time graph.

(c) How far does the train travel during this time?

6 A cyclist riding at 5 m s^{-1} accelerates at a constant rate until she reaches a speed of 7 m s^{-1}.

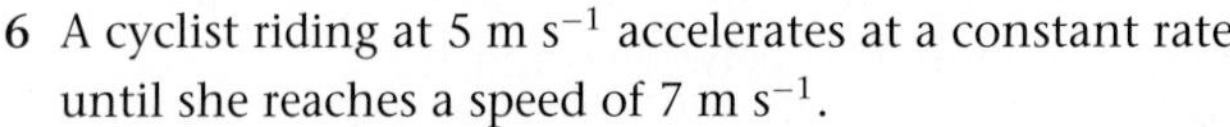

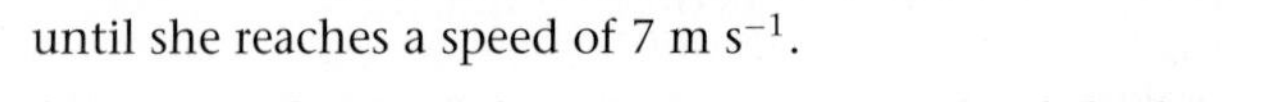

(a) Draw a sketch of the velocity–time graph while she is accelerating.

(b) If she covers a distance of 240 metres while accelerating, find the time she takes.

(c) Calculate her acceleration.

(d) Write the equation of the velocity–time graph.

(e) Find an expression for the distance she has cycled after t seconds. Use this to display the displacement–time graph on your calculator.

10 Equations and graphs

This chapter is about solving equations, and illustrating the solution with graphs. When you have completed it, you should

- interpret the solution of $f(x) = 0$ as the intersection of $y = f(x)$ with the x-axis
- be able to factorise quadratic expressions and use the factor form to solve quadratic equations
- know and be able to use the formula for solving quadratic equations
- understand the use of the discriminant to determine the number of roots of a quadratic equation
- recognise equations which become quadratic after a suitable substitution
- know how to find the points of intersection of two graphs
- be able to use a calculator to find the approximate solution of an equation which cannot be solved by exact methods.

10.1 Equations

If you use mathematics in designing a bridge or running a business, your decisions will often depend on finding the numerical solution to an equation (or a set of equations).

Any equation with a single unknown x can be arranged with all the terms on the left side, so that it has the form $f(x) = 0$ for some function f. So if you draw the graph of $y = f(x)$, solving the equation involves finding the x-coordinates of the points where the graph meets the x-axis. In Fig. 10.1 these points are P, Q and R, with x-coordinates p, q and r. These are called the **roots** of the equation. The set $\{p, q, r\}$ of all the roots is the **solution** of the equation.

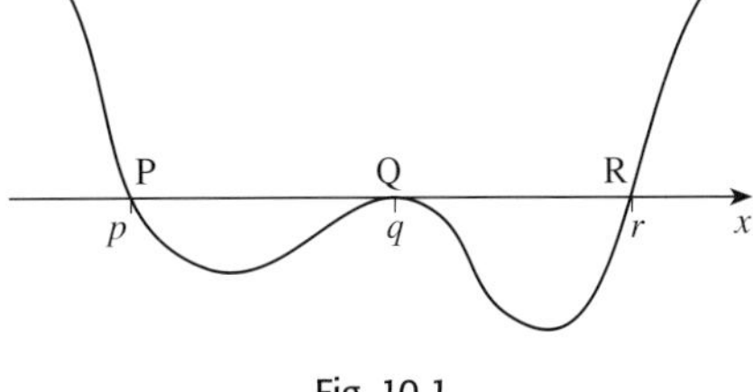

Fig. 10.1

The roots of the equation $f(x) = 0$ are sometimes called the **zeros** of the function $f(x)$.

The simplest kind of equation is when $f(x)$ is a linear function, $f(x) = bx + c$ with $b \neq 0$. The **linear equation** $f(x) = 0$ then has a single root, $-\frac{c}{b}$. This is the quantity called the x-intercept in Section 7.3.

10.2 Quadratic equations

Much more interesting is the **quadratic equation** $f(x) = 0$, where $f(x) = ax^2 + bx + c$ with $a \neq 0$.

Fig. 10.2 shows the possible ways in which the graph of a quadratic function can be related to the x-axis.

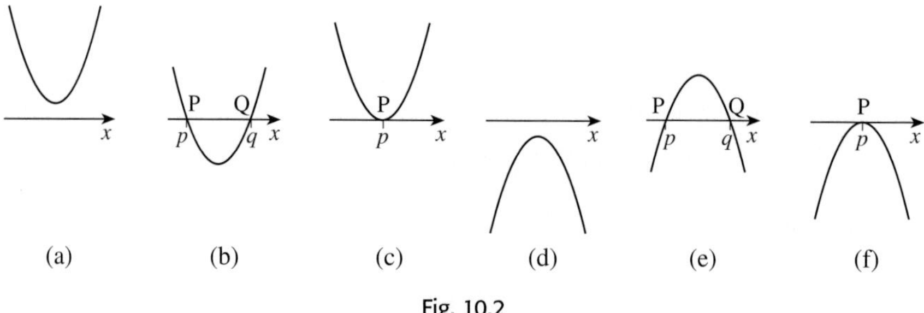

Fig. 10.2

- In (a) and (d) the graph does not meet the x-axis. The quadratic equation has no roots.
- In (b) and (e) the graph meets the x-axis at two points, P and Q, with x-coordinates p and q. The quadratic equation has two roots, p and q.
- In (c) and (f) the graph meets the x-axis at just one point P, with x-coordinate p. The quadratic equation has a single root p.

The variable x is assumed to be a real number. In more advanced mathematics a new kind of number is invented, called a complex number. If these were included, some of the statements in this chapter would have to be modified. (On some calculators it is possible for an answer to be given as a complex number.)

Example 10.2.1

Use the completed square form to show that the quadratic equation $x^2 + 6x + 10 = 0$ has no roots.

In completed square form,

$$x^2 + 6x + 10 = (x + 3)^2 + 1.$$

Since $(x + 3)^2$ can't be negative, the value of $(x + 3)^2 + 1$ is always greater than or equal to 1. Therefore $x^2 + 6x + 10$ can never equal 0.

Example 10.2.2

Verify that $(2x - 1)(x + 3) = 2x^2 + 5x - 3$. Use this to solve the quadratic equation $2x^2 + 5x - 3 = 0$.

Using the rule $(a + b)c = ac + bc$ with $(x + 3)$ for c,

$$\begin{aligned}(2x - 1)(x + 3) &= 2x(x + 3) - 1(x + 3)\\ &= 2x^2 + 6x - x - 3\\ &= 2x^2 + 5x - 3.\end{aligned}$$

So the quadratic equation $2x^2 + 5x - 3 = 0$ can be written as

$$(2x - 1)(x + 3) = 0.$$

The product of two numbers can only be 0 if one or the other is 0. So

$$\text{either } 2x - 1 = 0 \text{ or } x + 3 = 0;$$

that is,

$$\text{either } x = \tfrac{1}{2} \text{ or } x = -3.$$

The roots of the equation are $\frac{1}{2}$ and -3.

Example 10.2.3
Solve the equation $x^2 + 25 = 10x$.

Begin by rearranging the equation with all the terms on the left side, as

$$x^2 - 10x + 25 = 0.$$

You can recognise the expression $x^2 - 10x + 25$ as $(x - 5)^2$. So the equation is

$$(x - 5)^2 = 0.$$

This can be true only if $x - 5 = 0$, that is $x = 5$.

So the equation has just one root, 5.

These examples illustrate the possibilities suggested by Fig. 10.2, that a quadratic equation may have 0, 2 or 1 roots. They also show that, if there are any roots, a simple way of finding them is to write the quadratic expression as the product of linear factors, or as the square of a linear factor. The next section explains how to do this.

Some quadratic expressions $ax^2 + bx + c$ can be expressed in **factor form** as either

$$\text{(i) } a(x - p)(x - q) \quad \text{or} \quad \text{(ii) } a(x - p)^2.$$

In case (i), the quadratic equation $ax^2 + bx + c = 0$ has two roots, p and q.

In case (ii), the quadratic equation $ax^2 + bx + c = 0$ has just one root, p. This is sometimes called a **repeated root**, or a **double root** of the equation.

Notice that, in Example 10.2.2, $2x^2 + 5x - 3 = (2x - 1)(x + 3)$ is not strictly in factor form according to this definition. But since $2x - 1 = 2\left(x - \frac{1}{2}\right)$, the product can be written as $2\left(x - \frac{1}{2}\right)(x + 3)$, which is in factor form. The advantage of this form is that it shows the two roots, $\frac{1}{2}$ and -3, directly.

Example 10.2.4
A quadratic graph cuts the x-axis where $x = -1$ and $x = 2$, and it cuts the y-axis at $(0, 6)$. Find its equation.

Suppose that the equation of the graph in factor form is $y = a(x - p)(x - q)$. It cuts the x-axis where $y = 0$, that is when $x = p$ or $x = q$. So p and q are –1 and 2, and the equation has the form

$$y = a(x + 1)(x - 2).$$

The graph cuts the y-axis where $x = 0$, so $y = -2a$. You are given that $-2a = 6$, so $a = -3$. The equation of the graph is therefore

$$y = -3(x + 1)(x - 2),$$

which when multiplied out gives $y = 6 + 3x - 3x^2$.

10.3 Factorising quadratics

This section is about finding factors of quadratics like $x^2 - 2x - 3$ and $3x^2 - 2x - 5$. However, the factors in this section are restricted to those cases where the coefficients of the quadratic to be factorised, and the linear factors which make it up, are all integers. In this sense, $x^2 - 3 = (x - \sqrt{3})(x + \sqrt{3})$ will be said *not* to factorise, because the terms in the linear factors contain $\sqrt{3}$.

There are three important special cases to get out of the way quickly.

No constant term
If the constant term is zero, as in $x^2 - 2x$ and $3x^2 - 2x$, the quadratic always factorises by taking out the factor x to get

$$x^2 - 2x = x(x - 2) \quad \text{and} \quad 3x^2 - 2x = x(3x - 2).$$

Difference of two squares
If the coefficient of x is zero, and the other terms have the form of the difference of two squares such as $x^2 - 9$ and $4x^2 - 25$, then use the result from Section 1.6,

$$p^2 - q^2 = (p - q)(p + q).$$

With $p = x$ and $q = 3$ this gives

$$x^2 - 9 = (x - 3)(x + 3).$$

And putting $p = 2x$ and $q = 5$ gives

$$4x^2 - 25 = (2x - 5)(2x + 5).$$

Sum of two squares
Expressions such as $x^2 + 9$ and $4x^2 + 25$ which are the *sum* of two squares *never* factorise.

It is easy to see why. Since $x^2 \geq 0$, $x^2 + 9$ is always greater than or equal to 9, so it can never be 0. But if $x^2 + 9$ had factors $(x - p)(x - q)$, it would be 0 when $x = p$ and $x = q$. Putting these two statements together, it follows that $x^2 + 9$ doesn't factorise.

> The factors of $ax^2 + bx$ are given by
>
> $$ax^2 + bx = x(ax + b).$$
>
> The factors of $a^2x^2 - b^2$ are given by
>
> $$(ax - b)(ax + b).$$
>
> The sum of two squares, $a^2x^2 + b^2$, has no factors.

Example 10.3.1

Find the factors of (a) $3x^2 + 4x$, (b) $4x^2 - 1$.

(a) There is no constant term so

$$3x^2 + 4x = x(3x + 4).$$

(b) This has the difference of two squares form, so

$$4x^2 - 1 = (2x - 1)(2x + 1).$$

The general case

Finding the factors of other quadratics can be a hit-and-miss process. It is simple enough to factorise an expression such as $x^2 - 2x - 3$: x^2 can only split as $x \times x$, and 3 as 3×1, so if there are simple factors they must have the form $(x \ldots 3)(x \ldots 1)$ with + or − signs in place of the dots. To get a product of −3 one of these signs must be + and the other −, and a quick check produces the answer $(x - 3)(x + 1)$.

Factorising a quadratic such as $6x^2 - 7x - 10$ is a much tougher proposition. The $6x^2$ might split either as $x \times 6x$ or as $2x \times 3x$, the 10 as 1×10 or as 2×5, and in each case there are two ways of pairing the factors. Trying all the possibilities until you get the correct coefficient of x, in this case −7, can take a long time, but if you can see the factors quickly this process is the quickest way.

Example 10.3.2

Find the factors of (a) $x^2 - 8x + 12$, (b) $6x^2 - x - 2$.

(a) By inspection the factors have the form $(x - \ldots)(x - \ldots)$.

The factors of 12 are 1×12, 2×6 and 3×4, so the possibilities are $(x - 1)(x - 12)$, $(x - 2)(x - 6)$ and $(x - 3)(x - 4)$. Multiplying each of these out gives $x^2 - 13x + 12$, $x^2 - 8x + 12$ and $x^2 - 7x + 12$ respectively, so

$$x^2 - 8x + 12 = (x - 2)(x - 6).$$

(b) The possible factors of 6 are 1×6 and 2×3, and the factors of 2 are 1×2. The sign of the constant term −2 is negative, so one factor is positive and one is negative. The possible factors of $6x^2 - x - 2$ which need to be tested are

$$(x - 1)(6x + 2), \quad (x + 1)(6x - 2), \quad (x - 2)(6x + 1), \quad (x + 2)(6x - 1),$$
$$(2x + 1)(3x - 2), \quad (2x - 1)(3x + 2), \quad (2x + 2)(3x - 1), \quad (2x - 2)(3x + 1).$$

Notice that every possible combination which gives $6x^2$ as the first term and -2 as the constant term has been taken.

When you test these, you find that the correct combination is $(2x+1)(3x-2)$, so

$$6x^2 - x - 2 = (2x+1)(3x-2).$$

There is a way of shortening the work of finding the factors of $6x^2 - x - 2$. When you write out the factors, some of them, in this case, $(x-1)(6x+2)$, $(x+1)(6x-2)$, $(2x+2)(3x-1)$ and $(2x-2)(3x+1)$, have a bracket which has a factor of 2. Each of these can be factorised further to give

$$(x-1)(6x+2) = 2(x-1)(3x+1), \quad (x+1)(6x-2) = 2(x+1)(3x-1),$$
$$(2x+2)(3x-1) = 2(x+1)(3x-1), \quad (2x-2)(3x+1) = 2(x-1)(3x+1).$$

Each of these has a factor of 2, but 2 is not a factor of $6x^2 - x - 2$. So none of these four cases can possibly work. This leaves just

$$(x-2)(6x+1), \quad (x+2)(6x-1), \quad (2x+1)(3x-2), \quad (2x-1)(3x+2)$$

to be tested, which is much quicker than before.

Example 10.3.3

Find the factors of (a) $6x^2 - 5x - 4$, (b) $12x^2 - 10x - 8$.

(a) The possibilities for the factors of $6x^2 - 5x - 4$ are:

$$(x-1)(6x+4), \quad (x+1)(6x-4), \quad (x-4)(6x+1), \quad (x+4)(6x-1),$$
$$(x-2)(6x+2), \quad (x+2)(6x-2), \quad (2x+1)(3x-4), \quad (2x-1)(3x+4),$$
$$(2x+4)(3x-1), \quad (2x-4)(3x+1), \quad (2x+2)(3x-2), \quad (2x-2)(3x+2).$$

Knocking out the cases where one of the factors has a common factor leaves

$$(x-4)(6x+1), \quad (x+4)(6x-1), \quad (2x+1)(3x-4), \quad (2x-1)(3x+4),$$

to be tested.

When you test, $(2x+1)(3x-4)$ is the possibility that gives $-5x$ as the middle term, so

$$6x^2 - 5x - 4 = (2x+1)(3x-4).$$

(b) To factorise $12x^2 - 10x - 8$, first notice that you can take out the factor of 2, to get

$$12x^2 - 10x - 8 = 2(6x^2 - 5x - 4).$$

Concentrating now on $6x^2 - 5x - 4$, and using part (a),

$$12x^2 - 10x - 8 = 2(6x^2 - 5x - 4) = 2(2x+1)(3x-4).$$

If you count the number of possibilities for factors of $12x^2 - 10x - 8$ without first taking out the factor 2, you will quickly convince yourself of the benefit of taking out the numerical factor first.

Example 10.3.4

Solve the quadratic equations (a) $x^2 - 8x + 12 = 0$, (b) $6x^2 - x - 2 = 0$.

(a) From Example 10.3.2(a), $x^2 - 8x + 12 = (x-2)(x-6)$ in factor form. Therefore, from Section 10.2, the roots of $x^2 - 8x + 12 = 0$ are 2 and 6.

(b) From Example 10.3.2(b), $6x^2 - x - 2 = (2x+1)(3x-2)$.

You can complete the solution in either of two ways.

Method 1 If $(2x+1)(3x-2) = 0$, then

$$\text{either } 2x+1=0 \quad \text{or} \quad 3x-2=0,$$

so

$$\text{either } x = -\tfrac{1}{2} \quad \text{or} \quad x = \tfrac{2}{3}.$$

Method 2 Since $2x+1 = 2\left(x+\frac{1}{2}\right)$ and $3x-2 = 3\left(x-\frac{2}{3}\right)$,

$$6x^2 - x - 2 = 6\left(x+\tfrac{1}{2}\right)\left(x-\tfrac{2}{3}\right)$$

in factor form.

Therefore the roots of $6x^2 - x - 2 = 0$ are $-\frac{1}{2}$ and $\frac{2}{3}$.

Exercise 10A

1 Factorise each of the following quadratics.

(a) $x^2 + 11x + 24$ (b) $l^2 - 7l + 12$ (c) $q^2 - 12q + 35$

(d) $x^2 + x - 6$ (e) $x^2 + 5x - 24$ (f) $n^2 - 7n - 60$

(g) $r^2 - 17r + 16$ (h) $x^2 - 14x + 33$ (i) $x^2 + 4x - 21$

2 Factorise each of the following quadratics.

(a) $3x^2 - 8x + 4$ (b) $4x^2 - 12x + 5$ (c) $12x^2 + x - 1$

(d) $3x^2 - 4x - 4$ (e) $8x^2 - 15x - 2$ (f) $6x^2 + 5x - 6$

(g) $4x^2 - 8x - 5$ (h) $9x^2 - 30x + 9$ (i) $12x^2 - 10x - 8$

3 Use the 'difference of two squares' to write down the factors of the following quadratics.

(a) $x^2 - 1$ (b) $4 - 25d^2$ (c) $100 - 4z^2$

(d) $(x+1)^2 - 4x^2$ (e) $(2x+1)^2 - x^2$ (f) $(2x+1)^2 - (x-3)^2$

4 Not all quadratics have factors in which each of the coefficients is an integer. Find, where possible, factors of the following in which all the coefficients are integers.

(a) $x^2 + 2x + 2$ (b) $x^2 - 13x + 40$ (c) $x^2 + 6x - 12$

(d) $4x^2 + 16$ (e) $x^2 + 14x$ (f) $x^2 - 4x - 60$

(g) $x^2 + 16x + 12$ (h) $7 - 8x - 4x^2$ (i) $2x^2 + 5x - 3$

5 Solve the following quadratic equations.

(a) $x^2 - 2x - 35 = 0$ (b) $x^2 - 2x - 3 = 0$ (c) $x^2 + 6x - 27 = 0$

(d) $6x^2 - 5x - 6 = 0$ (e) $6 + 5x - 6x^2 = 0$ (f) $12x^2 + x - 6 = 0$

6 Find the x-coordinates of the points where the following quadratic graphs meet the x-axis.

(a) $y = x^2 + 3x - 4$ (b) $y = 2x^2 - 18$ (c) $y = 2x^2 - x - 1$

(d) $y = 2x^2 - 5x + 2$ (e) $y = x^2 - 6x + 9$ (f) $y = 1 - 9x^2$

7 A quadratic graph cuts the x-axis at $(-3, 0)$ and $(1, 0)$. It also contains the point $(2, 10)$. Find its equation in the form $y = ax^2 + bx + c$.

For what other point on the graph is the y-coordinate equal to 10?

8 A quadratic graph touches the x-axis at $(-2, 0)$. It also contains the point $(-1, 3)$. Find its equation.

10.4 The quadratic formula

All quadratic expressions can be written in completed square form, but only certain quadratics can be written in factor form. So if you have a quadratic equation to solve for which you cannot find factors, you must use another method.

Example 10.4.1
Find the roots of the quadratic equation $2x^2 + 10x + 7 = 0$.

It was shown in Example 9.5.2 that, in completed square form,

$$2x^2 + 10x + 7 = 2\left(x + \tfrac{5}{2}\right)^2 - \tfrac{11}{2}.$$

So the equation $2x^2 + 10x + 7 = 0$ can be written as

$$2\left(x + \tfrac{5}{2}\right)^2 - \tfrac{11}{2} = 0,$$

or $$\left(x + \tfrac{5}{2}\right)^2 = \tfrac{11}{4}.$$

Now there are two numbers whose square is $\frac{11}{4}$; these are $\frac{1}{2}\sqrt{11}$ and $-\frac{1}{2}\sqrt{11}$. So either

$$x + \tfrac{5}{2} = \tfrac{1}{2}\sqrt{11} \quad \text{or} \quad x + \tfrac{5}{2} = -\tfrac{1}{2}\sqrt{11}.$$

That is, either

$$x = \tfrac{1}{2}\sqrt{11} - \tfrac{5}{2} \quad \text{or} \quad x = -\tfrac{1}{2}\sqrt{11} - \tfrac{5}{2}.$$

So the exact roots of the equation are $\frac{1}{2}(\sqrt{11} - 5)$ and $-\frac{1}{2}(\sqrt{11} + 5)$. Since $\sqrt{11} = 3.3166...$, these roots are -0.842 and -4.158 correct to 3 decimal places.

The method in Example 10.4.1 can be used with any quadratic equation, whether or not it can be put into factor form. In Example 10.4.2 it is used for an equation which could also be solved using factors.

Example 10.4.2

Express $3x^2 - 8x - 3$ in completed square form, and use your result to solve the equation $3x^2 - 8x - 3 = 0$.

$$\begin{aligned} 3x^2 - 8x - 3 &= 3\left(x^2 - \tfrac{8}{3}x\right) - 3 \\ &= 3\left(\left(x - \tfrac{4}{3}\right)^2 - \tfrac{16}{9}\right) - 3 \\ &= 3\left(\left(x - \tfrac{4}{3}\right)^2 - \tfrac{16}{9} - 1\right) \\ &= 3\left(\left(x - \tfrac{4}{3}\right)^2 - \tfrac{25}{9}\right). \end{aligned}$$

The equation $3x^2 - 8x - 3 = 0$, is the same as $3\left(\left(x - \tfrac{4}{3}\right)^2 - \tfrac{25}{9}\right) = 0$.

$$\begin{aligned} 3\left(\left(x - \tfrac{4}{3}\right)^2 - \tfrac{25}{9}\right) &= 0 \\ \left(x - \tfrac{4}{3}\right)^2 - \tfrac{25}{9} &= 0 \\ \left(x - \tfrac{4}{3}\right)^2 &= \tfrac{25}{9} \end{aligned}$$

giving $x - \frac{4}{3} = \frac{5}{3}$ or $x - \frac{4}{3} = -\frac{5}{3}$.

So $x = \frac{4}{3} + \frac{5}{3} = 3$ or $x = \frac{4}{3} - \frac{5}{3} = -\frac{1}{3}$.

Check for yourself that $3x^2 - 8x - 3$ in factor form is $3(x - 3)\left(x + \frac{1}{3}\right)$.

These two examples show that this is a routine procedure, so you could apply it to the general quadratic equation and get a formula for the roots in terms of the coefficients a, b and c. The formula, which you should commit to memory, is:

The solution of $ax^2 + bx + c = 0$, where $a \neq 0$, is

$$x = \frac{-b \pm \sqrt{b^2 - 4ac}}{2a}.$$

For example, in Example 10.4.1, $a = 2$, $b = 10$ and $c = 7$, so the roots are

$$\frac{-10 + \sqrt{10^2 - 4 \times 2 \times 7}}{2 \times 2} = \frac{-10 + \sqrt{44}}{4} = \frac{-10 + 2\sqrt{11}}{4} = \frac{-5 + \sqrt{11}}{2}$$

and

$$\frac{-10 - \sqrt{10^2 - 4 \times 2 \times 7}}{2 \times 2} = \frac{-10 - \sqrt{44}}{4} = \frac{-10 - 2\sqrt{11}}{4} = \frac{-5 - \sqrt{11}}{2}.$$

You can get this formula from the result in Section 9.5 that

$$ax^2 + bx + c = a\left(x + \frac{b}{2a}\right)^2 - \frac{b^2}{4a} + c.$$

So, if $ax^2 + bx + c = 0$, then

$$a\left(x + \frac{b}{2a}\right)^2 = \frac{b^2}{4a} - c.$$

If you write the expression on the right as a single fraction,

$$\frac{b^2}{4a} - c = \frac{b^2}{4a} - \frac{4ac}{4a} = \frac{b^2 - 4ac}{4a},$$

and divide both sides by a, then the equation becomes

$$\left(x + \frac{b}{2a}\right)^2 = \frac{b^2 - 4ac}{4a^2}.$$

There are now two possibilities. Either

$$x + \frac{b}{2a} = +\sqrt{\frac{b^2 - 4ac}{4a^2}} = \frac{\sqrt{b^2 - 4ac}}{\sqrt{4a^2}} \quad \left(\text{using} \sqrt{\frac{p}{q}} = \frac{\sqrt{p}}{\sqrt{q}}, \text{ see Section 1.6}\right)$$

or $$x + \frac{b}{2a} = -\sqrt{\frac{b^2 - 4ac}{4a^2}} = -\frac{\sqrt{b^2 - 4ac}}{\sqrt{4a^2}}.$$

Since $4a^2 = (2a)^2$, $\sqrt{4a^2}$ is either $+\,2a$ (if a is positive) or $-\,2a$ (if a is negative). In either case

$$x + \frac{b}{2a} = \pm\frac{\sqrt{b^2 - 4ac}}{2a}.$$

So $$x = -\frac{b}{2a} \pm \frac{\sqrt{b^2 - 4ac}}{2a} = \frac{-b \pm \sqrt{b^2 - 4ac}}{2a}.$$

This shows that if $ax^2 + bx + c = 0$ and $a \neq 0$, then $x = \dfrac{-b \pm \sqrt{b^2 - 4ac}}{2a}$.

Example 10.4.3

Use the quadratic equation formula to solve the equations

(a) $2x^2 - 3x - 4 = 0$, (b) $2x^2 - 3x + 4 = 0$,

(c) $30x^2 - 11x - 30 = 0$, (d) $4x^2 + 4x + 1 = 0$.

(a) Comparing this with $ax^2 + bx + c = 0$, put $a = 2$, $b = -3$ and $c = -4$. Then

$$x = \frac{-(-3) \pm \sqrt{(-3)^2 - 4 \times 2 \times (-4)}}{2 \times 2} = \frac{3 \pm \sqrt{9 + 32}}{4} = \frac{3 \pm \sqrt{41}}{4}.$$

Sometimes it will be sufficient to leave the roots like this in surd form, but you may need to find the numerical values $\dfrac{3 + \sqrt{41}}{4} \approx 2.35$ and $\dfrac{3 - \sqrt{41}}{4} \approx -0.85$. Try substituting these numbers in the equation and see what happens.

(b) Putting $a = 2$, $b = -3$ and $c = 4$,

$$x = \frac{-(-3) \pm \sqrt{(-3)^2 - 4 \times 2 \times 4}}{2 \times 2} = \frac{3 \pm \sqrt{9 - 32}}{4} = \frac{3 \pm \sqrt{-23}}{4}.$$

But -23 does not have a square root. This means that the equation $2x^2 - 3x + 4 = 0$ has no roots.

Try putting $2x^2 - 3x + 4$ in completed square form; what can you deduce about the graph of $y = 2x^2 - 3x + 4$?

(c) Putting $a = 30$, $b = -11$ and $c = -30$,

$$x = \frac{-(-11) \pm \sqrt{(-11)^2 - 4 \times 30 \times (-30)}}{2 \times 30} = \frac{11 \pm \sqrt{121 + 3600}}{60}$$

$$= \frac{11 \pm \sqrt{3721}}{60} = \frac{11 \pm 61}{60}.$$

So $x = \frac{72}{60} = \frac{6}{5}$ or $x = -\frac{50}{60} = -\frac{5}{6}$.

This third example factorises, but the factors are difficult to find. But once you know the roots of the equation you can deduce that

$$30x^2 - 11x - 30 = 30(x + \tfrac{5}{6})(x - \tfrac{6}{5})$$
$$= (6x + 5)(5x - 6).$$

This can be a useful way of finding the factors of a complicated quadratic.

(d) Putting $a = 4$, $b = 4$ and $c = 1$,

$$x = \frac{-4 \pm \sqrt{4^2 - 4 \times 4 \times 1}}{2 \times 4} = \frac{-4 \pm \sqrt{16 - 16}}{8}$$

$$= \frac{-4 \pm \sqrt{0}}{8} = \frac{-4}{8} = -\tfrac{1}{2}.$$

So $x = -\frac{1}{2}$.

Exercise 10B

1 Solve the following quadratic equations. Leave your answers in surds.

(a) $(x - 3)^2 - 3 = 0$ (b) $(x + 2)^2 - 4 = 0$ (c) $2(x + 3)^2 = 5$

(d) $(3x - 7)^2 = 8$ (e) $(x + p)^2 - q = 0$ (f) $a(x + b)^2 - c = 0$

2 Use the quadratic formula to solve the following equations. Leave irrational answers in surd form. If there is no solution, say so.

(a) $x^2 + 3x - 5 = 0$ (b) $x^2 - 4x - 7 = 0$ (c) $x^2 + 6x + 9 = 0$

(d) $x^2 + 5x + 2 = 0$ (e) $x^2 + x + 1 = 0$ (f) $3x^2 - 5x - 6 = 0$

(g) $2x^2 + 7x + 3 = 0$ (h) $8 - 3x - x^2 = 0$ (i) $5 + 4x - 6x^2 = 0$

3 Factorise the following expressions by first solving the corresponding quadratic equation.

(a) $x^2 - 2x - 35$ (b) $x^2 - 14x - 176$ (c) $x^2 + 6x - 432$

(d) $6x^2 - 5x - 6$ (e) $14 + 45x - 14x^2$ (f) $12x^2 + x - 6$

10.5 The discriminant $b^2 - 4ac$

If you look back at Example 10.4.3 you will see that in part (a) the roots of the equation involved surds, in part (b) there were no roots, in part (c) the roots were fractions and in part (d) there was only one root.

You can predict which case will arise by calculating the value of the expression under the square root sign, $b^2 - 4ac$, and thinking about the effect that this value has in the quadratic equation formula $x = \dfrac{-b \pm \sqrt{b^2 - 4ac}}{2a}$.

- If $b^2 - 4ac > 0$, the equation $ax^2 + bx + c = 0$ will have two roots.
- If $b^2 - 4ac < 0$, there will be no roots.
- If $b^2 - 4ac$ is a perfect square, the equation will have solutions which are integers or fractions.
- If $b^2 - 4ac = 0$, the root has the form $x = -\dfrac{b \pm 0}{2a} = -\dfrac{b}{2a}$, and there is one root only.

  Sometimes it is said that there are two coincident roots because the root values $-\dfrac{b+0}{2a}$ and $-\dfrac{b-0}{2a}$ are equal. But it is better to describe it as one repeated root (see Section 10.2).

The expression $b^2 - 4ac$ is called the **discriminant** of the quadratic expression $ax^2 + bx + c$ because, by its value, it discriminates between the types of solution of the equation $ax^2 + bx + c = 0$. It is sometimes denoted by the Greek letter Δ (delta).

Example 10.5.1
What can you deduce from the values of the discriminants of these quadratic equations?

(a) $2x^2 - 3x - 4 = 0$ (b) $2x^2 - 3x - 5 = 0$ (c) $2x^2 - 4x + 5 = 0$ (d) $2x^2 - 4x + 2 = 0$

(a) As $a = 2$, $b = -3$ and $c = -4$, $b^2 - 4ac = (-3)^2 - 4 \times 2 \times (-4) = 9 + 32 = 41$. The discriminant is positive, so the equation $2x^2 - 3x - 4 = 0$ has two roots. Also, as 41 is not a perfect square, the roots are irrational.

(b) As $a = 2$, $b = -3$, and $c = -5$, $b^2 - 4ac = (-3)^2 - 4 \times 2 \times (-5) = 9 + 40 = 49$. The discriminant is positive, so the equation $2x^2 - 3x - 5 = 0$ has two roots. Also, as 49 is a perfect square, the roots are rational.

(c) $b^2 - 4ac = (-4)^2 - 4 \times 2 \times 5 = 16 - 40 = -24$. As the discriminant is negative, the equation $2x^2 - 4x + 5 = 0$ has no roots.

(d) $b^2 - 4ac = (-4)^2 - 4 \times 2 \times 2 = 16 - 16 = 0$. As the discriminant is zero, the equation $2x^2 - 4x + 2 = 0$ has only one (repeated) root.

Example 10.5.2
The equation $kx^2 - 2x - 7 = 0$ has two real roots. What can you deduce about the value of the constant k?

The discriminant is $(-2)^2 - 4 \times k \times (-7) = 4 + 28k$. As the equation has two real roots, the value of the discriminant is positive, so $4 + 28k > 0$, and $k > -\frac{1}{7}$.

Example 10.5.3
The equation $3x^2 + 2x + k = 0$ has a repeated root. Find the value of k.

The equation has repeated roots if $b^2 - 4ac = 0$; that is, if $2^2 - 4 \times 3 \times k = 0$. This gives $k = \frac{1}{3}$.

Notice how, in these examples, there is no need to solve the quadratic equation. You can find all you need to know from the discriminant.

Exercise 10C

1 Use the value of the discriminant $b^2 - 4ac$ to determine whether the following equations have two roots, one root or no roots.

(a) $x^2 - 3x - 5 = 0$ (b) $x^2 + 2x + 1 = 0$ (c) $x^2 - 3x + 4 = 0$

(d) $3x^2 - 6x + 5 = 0$ (e) $2x^2 - 7x + 3 = 0$ (f) $5x^2 + 9x + 4 = 0$

(g) $3x^2 + 42x + 147 = 0$ (h) $3 - 7x - 4x^2 = 0$

In parts (i) and (j), the values of p and q are positive.

(i) $x^2 + px - q = 0$ (j) $x^2 - px - q = 0$

2 The following equations have repeated roots. Find the value of k in each case. Leave your answers as integers, exact fractions or surds.

(a) $x^2 + 3x - k = 0$ (b) $kx^2 + 5x - 8 = 0$ (c) $x^2 - 18x + k = 0$

(d) $-3 + kx - 2x^2 = 0$ (e) $4x^2 - kx + 6 = 0$ (f) $kx^2 - px + q = 0$

3 The following equations have the number of roots shown in brackets. Deduce as much as you can about the value of k.

(a) $x^2 + 3x + k = 0$ (2) (b) $x^2 - 7x + k = 0$ (1) (c) $kx^2 - 3x + 5 = 0$ (0)

(d) $3x^2 + 5x - k = 0$ (2) (e) $x^2 - 4x + 3k = 0$ (1) (f) $kx^2 - 5x + 7 = 0$ (0)

(g) $x^2 - kx + 4 = 0$ (2) (h) $x^2 + kx + 9 = 0$ (0)

4 Use the value of the discriminant to determine the number of points of intersection of the following graphs with the x-axis.

(a) $y = x^2 - 5x - 5$ (b) $y = x^2 + x + 1$ (c) $y = x^2 - 6x + 9$

(d) $y = x^2 + 4$ (e) $y = x^2 - 10$ (f) $y = 3 - 4x - 2x^2$

(g) $y = 3x^2 - 5x + 7$ (h) $y = x^2 + bx + b^2$ (i) $y = x^2 - 2qx + q^2$

5 If a and c are both positive, what can be said about the graph of $y = ax^2 + bx - c$?

6 If a is negative and c is positive, what can be said about the graph of $y = ax^2 + bx + c$?

10.6 Quadratic equations in disguise

Sometimes you will come across an equation which is not quadratic, but which can be changed into a quadratic equation, usually by making a suitable substitution.

Example 10.6.1
Solve the equation $t^4 - 13t^2 + 36 = 0$.

The highest power of t in this equation is 4, so it is not a quadratic equation. It is called a quartic equation, or an equation of degree 4. But since $t^4 = (t^2)^2$, if you write t^2 as x the equation becomes $x^2 - 13x + 36 = 0$, which is a quadratic equation in x.

Then $(x-4)(x-9) = 0$, so $x = 4$ or $x = 9$.

Now recall that $x = t^2$, so $t^2 = 4$ or $t^2 = 9$, giving $t = \pm 2$ or $t = \pm 3$.

Example 10.6.2
Solve the equation $\sqrt{x} = 6 - x$.

(a) by writing $\sqrt{x}$ as y, (b) by squaring both sides of the equation.

(a) Writing $\sqrt{x} = y$, so that $x = y^2$, the equation becomes

$$y = 6 - y^2 \text{ or } y^2 + y - 6 = 0.$$

Therefore $(y+3)(y-2) = 0$, so $y = 2$ or $y = -3$.
But, as $y = \sqrt{x}$, and $\sqrt{x}$ is never negative, the only solution is $y = 2$, giving $x = 4$.

(b) Squaring both sides gives

$$x = (6-x)^2 = 36 - 12x + x^2 \text{ or } x^2 - 13x + 36 = 0.$$

Therefore $(x-4)(x-9) = 0$, so $x = 4$ or $x = 9$.

Checking the answers shows that when $x = 4$, the equation $\sqrt{x} = 6 - x$ is satisfied, but when $x = 9$, $\sqrt{x} = 3$ and $6 - x = -3$, so $x = 9$ is not a root.

Therefore $x = 4$ is the only root.

This is important. Squaring is not a reversible step, because it introduces the root or roots of the equation $\sqrt{x} = -(6-x)$ as well. Notice that $x = 9$ does satisfy this last equation, but $x = 4$ doesn't! The moral is that, when you square an equation in the process of solving it, it is essential to check your answers.

Exercise 10D

1 Solve the following equations. Give irrational answers in terms of surds.

(a) $x^4 - 5x^2 + 4 = 0$ (b) $x^4 - 10x^2 + 9 = 0$ (c) $x^4 - 3x^2 - 4 = 0$

(d) $x^4 - 5x^2 - 6 = 0$ (e) $x^6 - 7x^3 - 8 = 0$ (f) $x^6 + x^3 - 12 = 0$

2 Solve the following equations.

(a) $x - 8 = 2\sqrt{x}$ (b) $x + 15 = 8\sqrt{x}$ (c) $t - 5\sqrt{t} - 14 = 0$

(d) $t = 3\sqrt{t} + 10$ (e) $t - \sqrt{t} - 6 = 0$ (f) $x - 3\sqrt{x} = 4$

3 Solve the following equations. (In most cases, multiplication by an appropriate expression will turn the equation into a form you should recognise.)

(a) $x = 3 + \dfrac{10}{x}$ (b) $x + 5 = \dfrac{6}{x}$ (c) $2t + 5 = \dfrac{3}{t}$

(d) $x = \dfrac{12}{x+1}$ (e) $\sqrt{t} = 4 + \dfrac{12}{\sqrt{t}}$ (f) $\sqrt{t}\,(\sqrt{t} - 6) = -9$

10.7 Finding where two graphs intersect

If you draw two graphs using the same axes, it is possible that they will meet in one or more points. It is sometimes important to find the coordinates of these points.

If the graphs have equations $y = f(x)$ and $y = g(x)$, you want to find the values of x and y which satisfy both equations simultaneously. In that case you can find the values of x from the equation $f(x) = g(x)$, which can be written as $f(x) - g(x) = 0$. Having solved this equation for x, you can use either $y = f(x)$ or $y = g(x)$ to find the corresponding values of y.

Example 10.7.1
Find the point of intersection of the line $y = 2$ with the graph $y = x^2 - 3x + 4$ (see Fig. 10.3).

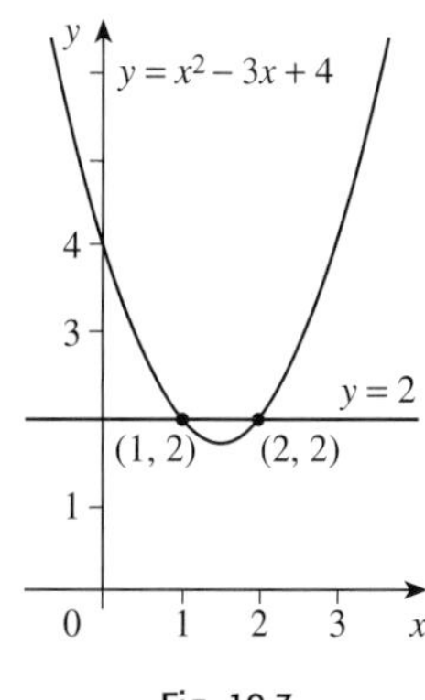

Fig. 10.3

The graphs intersect where

$$x^2 - 3x + 4 = 2,$$
$$x^2 - 3x + 2 = 0$$
$$(x-1)(x-2) = 0$$

giving $x = 1$ or $x = 2$.

Substituting these values in either equation ($y = 2$ is obviously easier!) to find y, the points of intersection are (1, 2) and (2, 2).

Example 10.7.2
Find the point of intersection of the line $y = 2x - 1$ with the graph $y = x^2$ (see Fig. 10.4).

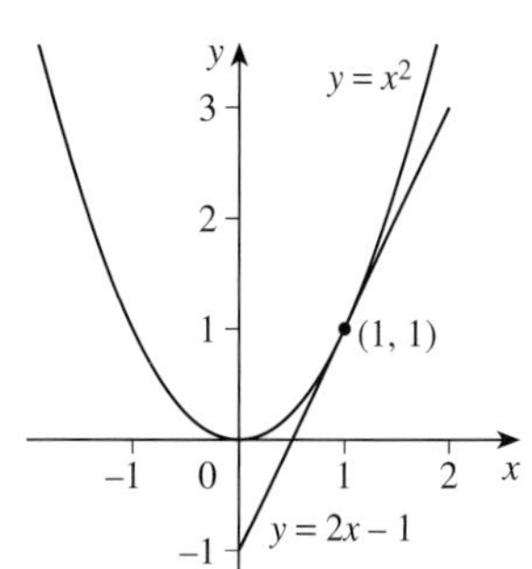

Fig. 10.4

The graphs intersect where

$$2x - 1 = x^2,$$
$$x^2 - 2x + 1 = 0$$
$$(x-1)(x-1) = 0$$

giving $x = 1$.

Substituting these values in either equation to find y gives the point of intersection as (1, 1).

The fact that there is only one point of intersection shows that this line is a tangent to the graph (see Fig. 10.4). The point (1, 1) is called the **point of contact** of the tangent and the curve.

Example 10.7.3
Find the points of intersection of the following pairs of graphs.

(a) $y = 2x + 1$ and $y = x^2 - 2x - 4$

(b) $y = x^2 - 2x + 1$ and $y = 3 + x - x^2$

(c) $y = x^3$ and $y = 4x(x - 1)$

Display the graphs on your calculator to illustrate the answers in this example.

(a) At the point of intersection

$$2x + 1 = x^2 - 2x - 4.$$

This can be written more simply as

$$x^2 - 4x - 5 = 0,$$

which can be put into factor form as

$$(x + 1)(x - 5) = 0.$$

So the graphs intersect where $x = -1$ and where $x = 5$.

Use the equation $y = 2x + 1$ to find the corresponding values of y. When $x = -1$, $y = 2 \times (-1) + 1 = -1$; when $x = 5$, $y = 2 \times 5 + 1 = 11$.

So the points of intersection are $(-1, -1)$ and $(5, 11)$.

It is often a good idea to check your answer by using the other equation. Check for yourself that these points also lie on $y = x^2 - 2x - 4$.

(b) At the point of intersection,

$$x^2 - 2x + 1 = 3 + x - x^2,$$

so

$$(2x + 1)(x - 2) = 0.$$

The graphs intersect where $x = -\frac{1}{2}$ and where $x = 2$.

Use the equation $y = x^2 - 2x + 1$, which is $y = (x - 1)^2$, to find the values of y. When $x = -\frac{1}{2}$, $y = \left(-\frac{1}{2} - 1\right)^2 = \left(-\frac{3}{2}\right)^2 = \frac{9}{4}$. When $x = 2$, $y = (2 - 1)^2 = 1$.

So the points of intersection are $\left(-\frac{1}{2}, 2\frac{1}{4}\right)$ and $(2, 1)$.

(c) At the point of intersection,

$$x^3 = 4x(x - 1),$$

so

$$x^3 - 4x^2 + 4x = 0.$$

Because the highest power of x is x^3, this is called a cubic equation. You don't have a general method for solving cubic equations, but this one is particularly simple because the terms have a common factor x. So the equation can be written as

$$x(x^2 - 4x + 4) = 0$$
$$x(x - 2)^2 = 0.$$

The product on the left is 0 if $x = 0$ or if $(x - 2)^2 = 0$, that is $x = 2$. So the graphs intersect where $x = 0$, $y = 0$ or where $x = 2$, $y = 8$.

The points of intersection are $(0, 0)$ and $(2, 8)$.

What happens at $x = 2$, where the equation has a repeated root?

10.8 Using a calculator to solve equations

However far you go in mathematics, there will always be a lot of equations that you can't solve by exact methods. But there is always the possibility of using a calculator to find approximate solutions to a high level of accuracy.

If the equation is written as $f(x) = 0$, the first step is to use the calculator to show the graph of $y = f(x)$. This will show roughly the values of x where the graph meets the x-axis.

You now need to consult your calculator manual to find how to refine these rough estimates to give solutions accurate to the required number of decimal places.

Example 10.8.1
Find the roots of the cubic equation $x^3 - 3x - 1 = 0$ correct to 4 decimal places.

Fig. 10.5 shows the graph of $y = x^3 - 3x - 1$ for $-2 \le x \le 2$. It crosses the axis in three points, at roughly $x = -1.5$, $x = -0.4$ and $x = 1.9$.

Taking each of these in turn, they can be refined using the calculator to give the roots as $-1.532\,089$, $-0.347\,296\,4$ and $1.879\,385\,2$.

Correct to 4 decimal places, these roots are -1.5321, -0.3473 and 1.8794.

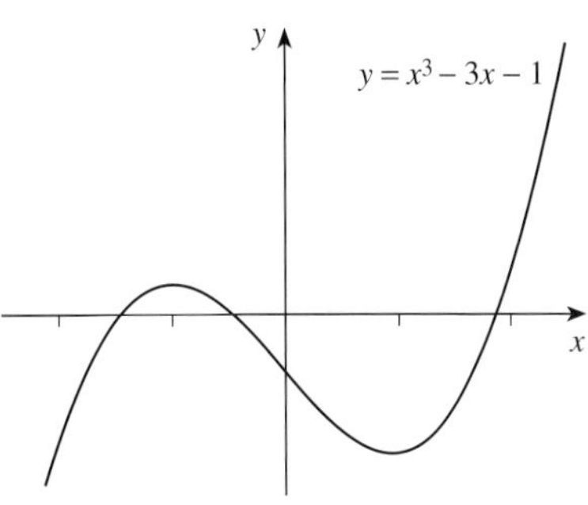

Fig. 10.5

Exercise 10E

1 Find the point or points of intersection for the following lines and curves.

(a) $x = 3$ and $y = x^2 + 4x - 7$
(b) $y = 3$ and $y = x^2 - 5x + 7$
(c) $y = 8$ and $y = x^2 + 2x$
(d) $y + 3 = 0$ and $y = 2x^2 + 5x - 6$

2 Find the points of intersection for the following lines and curves. Check your answers in each case by displaying the graphs on your calculator.

(a) $y = x + 1$ and $y = x^2 - 3x + 4$
(b) $y = 2x + 3$ and $y = x^2 + 3x - 9$
(c) $y = 3x + 11$ and $y = 2x^2 + 2x + 5$
(d) $y = 4x + 1$ and $y = 9 + 4x - 2x^2$

3 In both the following, show that the line and curve meet only once, find the point of intersection and use your calculator to check that the line touches the curve.

(a) $y = 2x + 2$ and $y = x^2 - 2x + 6$
(b) $y = -2x - 7$ and $y = x^2 + 4x + 2$

4 Find the points of intersection between the curve $y = x^2 + 5x + 18$ and the lines

(a) $y = -3x + 2$,
(b) $y = -3x + 6$.

Use your calculator to see how the lines are related to the curve.

5 Find the points of intersection between the line $y = x + 5$ and the curves

(a) $y = 2x^2 - 3x - 1$,
(b) $y = 2x^2 - 3x + 7$.

Use your calculator to see how the line and the curves are related.

6 Find the points of intersection of the following curves.

(a) $y = x^2 + 5x + 1$ and $y = x^2 + 3x + 11$
(b) $y = \frac{1}{2}x^2$ and $y = 1 - \frac{1}{2}x^2$
(c) $y = 2x^2 + 3x + 4$ and $y = x^2 + 6x + 2$
(d) $y = x^2 - 3x - 7$ and $y = x^2 + x + 1$
(e) $y = x^2 + 7x + 13$ and $y = 1 - 3x - x^2$
(f) $y = 6x^2 + 2x - 9$ and $y = x^2 + 7x + 1$

7 Use your calculator to locate roughly the roots of the following equations. Then refine the approximation to give the roots correct to 3 decimal places.

(a) $x^2 - 6x + 7 = 0$
(b) $x^3 - 9x - 2 = 0$
(c) $x^3 + 4x^2 - 4 = 0$
(d) $x^4 - 4x^3 + 10 = 0$

8 Find, correct to 2 decimal places, the points of intersection of the following pairs of graphs.

(a) $y = x^3$, $y = 12x + 20$
(b) $y = x^3$, $y = 3x^2 + 4$
(c) $y = x^2 + 1$, $y = \dfrac{10}{x + 1}$
(d) $y = 20 - x^2$, $y = \dfrac{5}{x}$

Review exercise 3

1 Show that the triangle formed by the points $(-2, 5)$, $(1, 3)$ and $(5, 9)$ is right-angled.

2 P is the point $(7, 5)$ and l_1 is the line with equation $3x + 4y = 16$.

(a) Find the equation of the line l_2 which passes through P and is perpendicular to l_1.

(b) Find the point of intersection of the lines l_1 and l_2.

(c) Find the perpendicular distance of P from the line l_1.

3 Find the equation of the perpendicular bisector of the line joining $(2, -5)$ and $(-4, 3)$.

4 The diagram shows the graph of $y = x^n$, where n is an integer. Given that the curve passes between the points $(2, 200)$ and $(2, 2000)$, determine the value of n.

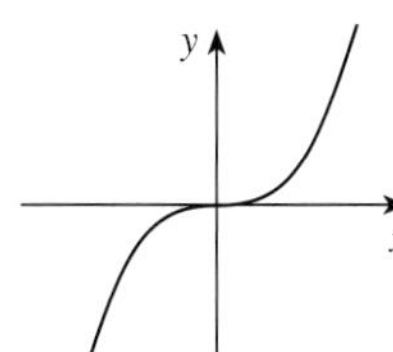

5 Find the points of intersection of the line $y = 2x + 3$ and the curve $y = 2x^2 + 3x - 7$.

6 Given that k is a positive constant, sketch the graphs of

(a) $y = (x + k)(x - 2k)$,

(b) $y = (x + 4k)(x + 2k)$,

(c) $y = x(x - k)(x - 5k)$,

(d) $y = (x + k)(x - 2k)^2$.

7 A curve with equation $y = ax^2 + bx + c$ crosses the x-axis at $(-4, 0)$ and $(9, 0)$ and also passes through the point $(1, 120)$. Where does the curve cross the y-axis?

8 Find, in surd form, the points of intersection of the curves $y = x^2 - 5x - 3$ and $y = 3 - 5x - x^2$.

9 Show that the line $y = 3x - 3$ and the curve $y = (3x + 1)(x + 2)$ do not meet.

10 Point O is the intersection of two roads which cross at right angles; one road runs from north to south, the other from east to west. Car A is 100 metres due west of O and travelling east at a speed of 20 m s^{-1}, and Car B is 80 metres due north of O and travelling south at 20 m s^{-1}.

(a) Show that after t seconds their distance apart, d metres, is given by

$$d^2 = (100 - 20t)^2 + (80 - 20t)^2.$$

(b) Show that this simplifies to $d^2 = 400((5 - t)^2 + (4 - t)^2)$.

(c) Show that the minimum distance apart of the two cars is $10\sqrt{2}$ metres.

11 The following functions are defined for all real values of x. Find their ranges.

(a) $f(x) = 9 - 2x^2$

(b) $f(x) = 5x - 7$

(c) $f(x) = x^2 + 16x - 5$

(d) $f(x) = (2x + 5)(2x - 7)$

12 The function $f(x) = 16 - 6x - x^2$ has domain all real values of x. Find the maximum value of $f(x)$ and state the range of $f(x)$.

13 Show that there exists a root, $x = \alpha$, of the equation $x^3 - 6x + 3 = 0$ such that $2 < \alpha < 3$. Find this root correct to 2 decimal places.

14 Let $f(x) = \dfrac{1}{(x-2)(x+2)}$. For what values of x is $f(x)$ positive? Write down the equations of the asymptotes of $y = f(x)$.

15 Find the equation of the straight line that passes through the points $(3, -1)$ and $(-2, 2)$. Hence find the coordinates of the point of intersection of the line and the x-axis. (OCR)

16 (a) Solve the equation $x^2 - (6\sqrt{3})x + 24 = 0$, giving your answer in terms of surds, simplified as far as possible.

(b) Find all four solutions of the equation $x^4 - (6\sqrt{3})x^2 + 24 = 0$ giving your answers correct to 2 decimal places. (OCR)

17 (a) Express $9x^2 + 12x + 7$ in the form $(ax + b)^2 + c$ where a, b, c are constants whose values are to be found.

(b) Find the set of values taken by $\dfrac{1}{9x^2 + 12x + 7}$ for real values of x. (OCR)

18 (a) Express $4x^2 - 16x + 8$ in the form $a(x + b)^2 + c$.

(b) Hence find the coordinates of the vertex of the graph of $y = 4x^2 - 16x + 8$.

(c) Sketch the graph of $y = 4x^2 - 16x + 8$, giving the x-coordinates of the points where the graph meets the x-axis. (OCR)

19 (a) Given that $\sqrt{x} = y$, show that the equation $\sqrt{x} + \dfrac{10}{\sqrt{x}} = 7$ may be written as

$$y^2 - 7y + 10 = 0.$$

(b) Hence solve the equation $\sqrt{x} + \dfrac{10}{\sqrt{x}} = 7$. (OCR)

Examination questions

1 Consider the line L with equation $y + 2x = 3$. The line L_1 is parallel to L and passes through the point $(6, -4)$.

(a) Find the gradient of L_1.

(b) Find the equation of L_1 in the form $y = mx + b$.

(c) Find the x-coordinate of the point where line L_1 crosses the x-axis. (© IBO 2005)

2 Consider the function $f(x) = 2x^2 - 8x + 5$.

(a) Express $f(x)$ in the form $a(x - p)^2 + q$, where $a, p, q \in \mathbb{Z}$.

(b) Find the minimum value of $f(x)$. (© IBO 2002)

3 (a) The first diagram shows part of the graph of a quadratic function $f(x) = x^2 + bx + c$, which intersects the x-axis at $x = 3$.

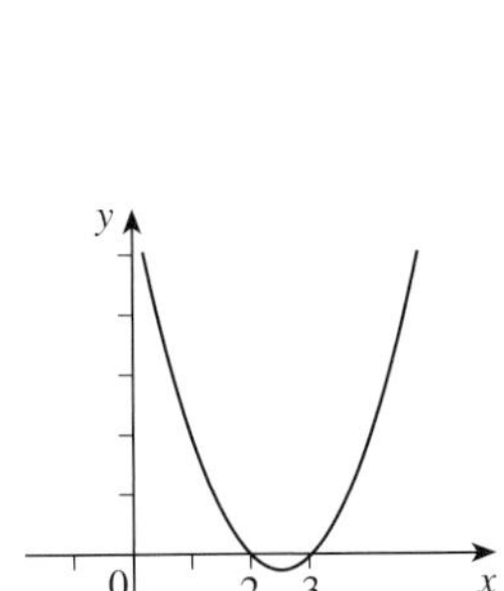

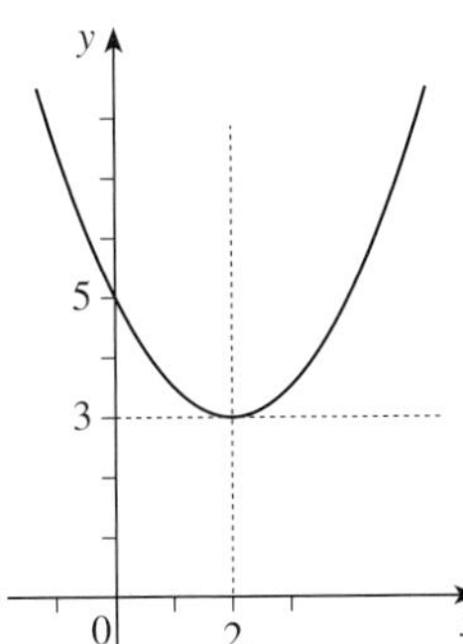

Find the value of b and of c.

(b) The second diagram shows part of the graph of another quadratic function g. It can be written in the form $g(x) = a(x - h)^2 + 3$. Its vertex is at (2, 3) and its y-intercept is 5.

(i) Write down the value of h. (ii) Find the value of a. (© IBO 2004)

4 The equation $x^2 + kx + 9 = 0$ has two distinct real roots. Find the set of all possible values of k. (© IBO 2004)

5 Two weeks after its birth, an animal weighed 13 kg. At 10 weeks this animal weighed 53 kg. The increase in weight each week is constant.

(a) Show that the relation between y, the weight in kg, and x, the time in weeks, can be written as $y = 5x + 3$.

(b) Write down the weight of the animal at birth.

(c) Write down the weekly increase in weight of the animal.

(d) Calculate how many weeks it will take for the animal to reach 98 kg. (© IBO 2005)

11 Differentiation

This chapter is about finding the gradient of the tangent at a point on a graph. When you have completed it, you should

- understand how the gradient of the tangent at a point can be obtained from the gradients of chords through the point
- know how to find the gradient at a point on a quadratic curve and certain other curves.

The first part of this chapter includes a number of experimental calculations from which the main results can be inferred. Proofs of some of these results are given at the end of the chapter.

11.1 The gradient of a curve

The gradient of the line $y = bx + c$ is b. It is easy to show this. Take two points on the line; the simplest are $(0, c)$and$(1, b + c)$. The gradient of the line joining these is $\frac{(b+c) - c}{1 - 0}$, which is $\frac{b}{1}$ or just b.

You would get the same answer if you took any other two points on the line, but the algebra would be a bit more complicated.

But how could you find the gradient of a curve? Indeed, what do you mean by the gradient of a curve? A straight line has the same direction everywhere, but a curve keeps changing direction as you move along it. So you have to think about 'the gradient of a curve at a point'. The gradient will be different at different points of the curve.

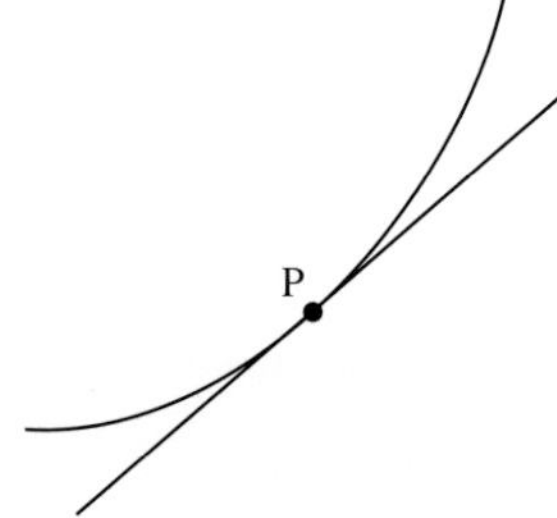

Fig. 11.1

Draw a curve and choose a particular point on it (see Fig. 11.1). Call the point P. If the curve is reasonably smooth, you can draw a tangent to the curve at P. This is a straight line, so you can find its gradient. The direction of the curve at P is the same as the direction of the tangent. So it seems natural to define the gradient of the curve at P as the gradient of the tangent.

> The **gradient of a curve** at any point is the gradient of the tangent to the curve at that point.

But the problem is how to calculate the gradient of the tangent. To find the gradient of a straight line you need to know the coordinates of two points on it. But, as Fig. 11.1 shows, the only point you know on the tangent is the point P. There is no obvious way of finding any other point on the tangent.

This difficulty doesn't occur for other lines through P. Fig. 11.2 shows several lines through P, including the tangent. The other lines meet the curve again, at points labelled M and N to the left of P, and R and S to the right of P. And the gradients of these lines can be calculated, as the gradients of the line segments [PM], [PN], [PR] and [PS]; these are called **chords** of the curve. (You are already familiar with chords when the curve is a circle.)

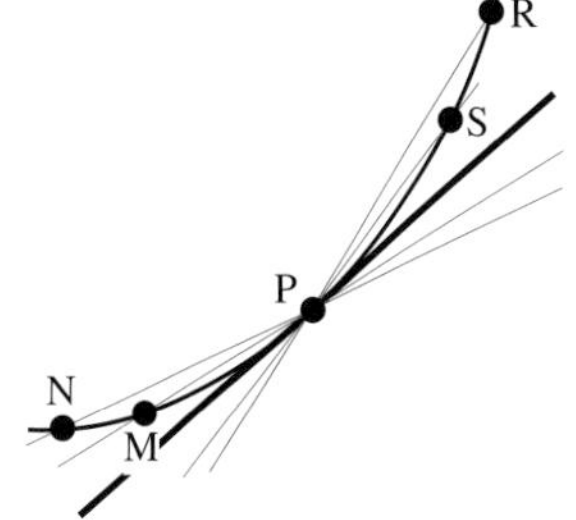

Fig. 11.2

This suggests a first step to finding the gradient of the tangent. In Fig. 11.2 the gradient of the tangent is clearly less than the gradients of [PR] and [PS], and greater than the gradients of [PN] and [PM]. So although this doesn't give the gradient of the tangent exactly, it does restrict it to a small interval of possible values.

Example 11.1.1 shows how this idea can be applied to a particular curve at a particular point.

Example 11.1.1
On the graph of $y = x^2$ take P to be the point $(0.4, 0.16)$, and let R and N be the points with x-coordinates 0.5 and 0.3 respectively. Calculate the gradients of the chords [PR] and [PN]. What can be deduced about the gradient of the tangent at P?

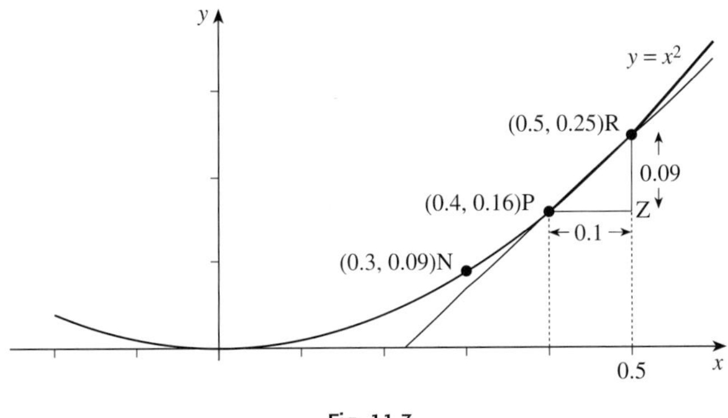

Fig. 11.3

Begin with the chord [PR], shown in Fig. 11.3. At R, with $x = 0.5$, the y-coordinate is $0.5^2 = 0.25$. To find the gradient from $P(0.4, 0.16)$ to $R(0.5, 0.25)$ calculate the x-step $0.5 - 0.4 = 0.1$ and the y-step $0.25 - 0.16 = 0.09$. These are shown in Fig. 11.3 by [PZ] and [ZR]. Then

$$\text{gradient of [PR]} = \frac{y\text{-step}}{x\text{-step}} = \frac{0.09}{0.1} = 0.9.$$

For the chord [PN] to the left of P, where N has coordinates $(0.3, 0.09)$, the x-step from P to N is $0.3 - 0.4 = -0.1$, and the y-step is $0.09 - 0.16 = -0.07$; both are negative. The gradient is then

$$\frac{-0.07}{-0.1} = 0.7.$$

You could of course take the x-step and y-step from N to P rather than from P to N in which case both would be positive. But you will see as the chapter develops why it is a good idea to take the steps from P to the point at the other end of the chord.

The gradient of the tangent at P is less than the gradient of [PR] and greater than the gradient of [PN]. So the gradient of the tangent at P is between 0.7 and 0.9.

Example 11.1.1 already gives you a useful approximation to the gradient of the curve $y = x^2$ at P, but it would be better to get a more accurate estimate. Fig. 11.2 suggests that if you take points S and M on the curve closer to P than R and N, the gradients of [PS] and [PM] will be closer to the gradient of the tangent.

Before embarking on any more calculation it is useful to introduce some new notation. The greek letter δ (delta) is used as an abbreviation for 'the increase in'. Thus 'the increase in x' is written as δx, and 'the increase in y' as δy.These are the quantities called the 'x-step' and 'y-step' in Section 7.2. Thus in the calculations for the chord [PR] in Example 11.1.1 you can write

$$\delta x = 0.5 - 0.4 = 0.1 \quad \text{and} \quad \delta y = 0.25 - 0.16 = 0.09.$$

With this notation, you can write the gradient of the chord as $\dfrac{\delta y}{\delta x}$.

Some people use the capital letter Δ rather than δ. Either is acceptable.

Notice that, in the fraction $\dfrac{\delta y}{\delta x}$, you cannot 'cancel out' the deltas. While you are getting used to the notation it is a good idea to read δ as 'the increase in', so that you are not tempted to read it as an ordinary algebraic symbol. Remember also that δx or δy could be negative, making the x-step or y-step a decrease.

Example 11.1.2

In the context of Example 11.1.1, find a better estimate for the gradient of the tangent at P by taking points S and M on the curve with x-coordinates 0.41 and 0.39.

First you need to calculate the y-coordinates of S and M. These are $0.41^2 = 0.1681$ and $0.39^2 = 0.1521$. So S is the point $(0.41, 0.1681)$, and M is $(0.39, 0.1521)$.

For the chord [PS],

$$\delta x = 0.41 - 0.4 = 0.01 \quad \text{and} \quad \delta y = 0.1681 - 0.16 = 0.0081,$$

so the gradient is $\dfrac{\delta y}{\delta x} = \dfrac{0.0081}{0.01} = 0.81$.

Fig. 11.4 is the figure corresponding to Fig. 11.3 for the chord [PS].

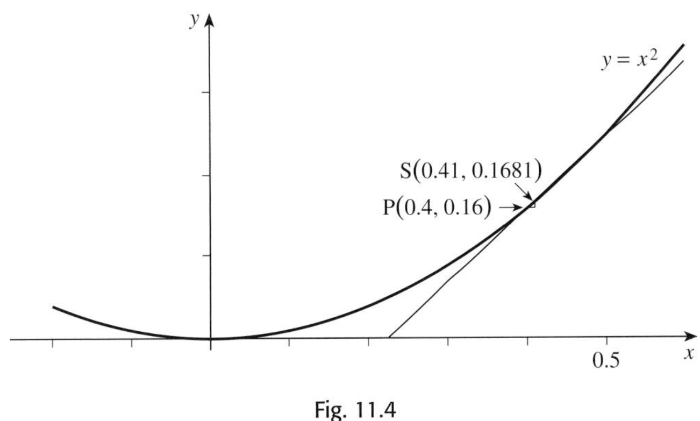

Fig. 11.4

Fig. 11.4 is not very useful as an illustration, because P and S are so close together. There is a small triangle there, like the triangle in Fig. 11.3, but you could be excused for missing it. In Fig. 11.4 it has become difficult to distinguish between the chord [PS] and the tangent at P.

For the chord [PM],

$$\delta x = 0.39 - 0.4 = -0.01 \quad \text{and} \quad \delta y = 0.1521 - 0.16 = -0.0079,$$

so the gradient is $\dfrac{\delta y}{\delta x} = \dfrac{-0.0079}{-0.01} = 0.79.$

The gradient of the tangent at P is less than the gradient of [PS] and greater than the gradient of [PM]. It is therefore between 0.79 and 0.81.

By now you are probably beginning to suspect that the gradient of the tangent at P is 0.8. But if you still have doubts, try calculating the gradients of the chords [PT] and [PL], where T is $(0.4001, 0.4001^2)$ and L is $(0.3999, 0.3999^2)$. What does this tell you about the gradient of the tangent at P?

The next example uses the method for a curve with a more complicated equation.

Example 11.1.3

Make an estimate of the gradient of the curve $y = 1 + 5x - 2x^2$ at the point P with coordinates (1, 4).

There is an important difference between this example and the previous ones. Because $1 + 5x - 2x^2$ is a quadratic with the coefficient of x^2 negative, the graph is a parabola with its vertex at the top. So if you take a point N to the left of P, the gradient of the chord PN will be greater than the gradient of the tangent at P; and if R is to the right of P, the gradient of [PR] will be less than the gradient of the tangent at P. This is illustrated in Fig. 11.5.

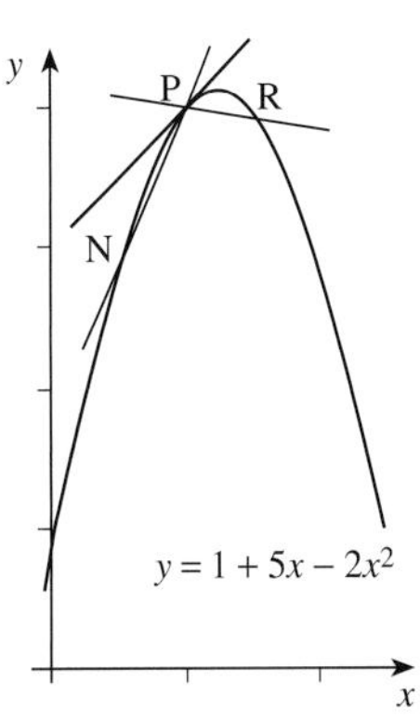

Fig. 11.5

Now that you know how the argument is going to proceed, you can take a short cut from the start by choosing points R and N very close to P. Suppose that the x-coordinates of R and N are taken to be 1.001 and 0.999. Then the y-coordinates are

$$1 + 5 \times 1.001 - 2 \times 1.001^2 = 4.000\,998$$

and $$1 + 5 \times 0.999 - 2 \times 0.999^2 = 3.998\,998.$$

So, for the chord [PR],

$$\delta x = 1.001 - 1 = 0.001 \quad \text{and} \quad \delta y = 4.000\,998 - 4 = 0.000\,998,$$

giving a gradient of $\dfrac{\delta y}{\delta x} = \dfrac{0.000\,998}{0.001} = 0.998.$

And for the chord [PN],

$$\delta x = 0.999 - 1 = -0.001 \quad \text{and} \quad \delta y = 3.998\,998 - 4 = -0.001\,002,$$

giving a gradient of $\dfrac{\delta y}{\delta x} = \dfrac{-0.001\,002}{-0.001} = 1.002.$

So the gradient of the curve at P is greater than 0.998 and less than 1.002. It is a reasonable guess that the gradient of the curve at P is 1.

This is still only a 'reasonable guess', not a proof. But it is best for the time being to work on the assumption that it is correct, and to defer the proof until you have seen how these calculations can be used.

Your calculator may be programmed to work out the gradient of a curve at a point. If you key in the equation of the curve and the value of x at the point you are interested in, the calculator will give the gradient of the curve at that point. The answer will not always be exact, but it will be a close approximation to the correct gradient. You could try using this to check your answers to the questions in Exercise 11A.

Exercise 11A

You should keep a record of your answers to this exercise. You will need to refer to them in the next section. If you are working with other students in a group, you can save time by splitting the work and pooling your results.

1 Carry out calculations similar to those in Examples 11.1.1 and 11.1.2 to find intervals within which the gradient of $y = x^2$ lies at the points

(a) $(2, 4)$, (b) $(0.6, 0.36)$, (c) $(-1, 1)$.

Use your answers to guess the gradient of the curve at these points.

2 Carry out calculations similar to those in Example 11.1.3 to find intervals within which the gradient of $y = 1 + 5x - 2x^2$ lies at the points

(a) $(0, 1)$, (b) $(-1, -6)$, (c) $(2, 3)$.

Use your answers to guess the gradient of the curve at these points.

3 For the given curves find intervals within which the gradient lies at the given points. Use your answers to guess the gradient of the curves at these points.

(a) $y = 10x^2$ at (i) $(0.5, 2.5)$, (ii) $(1.2, 14.4)$, (iii) $(-2, 40)$.

(b) $y = x^2 + 3$ at (i) $(0.4, 3.16)$, (ii) $(1.5, 5.25)$, (iii) $(-1, 4)$.

(c) $y = 3x^2 - 4x + 2$ at (i) $(1, 1)$, (ii) $(0, 2)$, (iii) $(2, 6)$.

11.2 Gradient formulae

If you collect together the results of Example 11.1.2 and Exercise 11A Question 1 for the curve $y = x^2$, the gradients at various points are set out in Table 11.6.

x-coordinate of P	-1	0.4	0.6	2
Gradient at P	-2	0.8	1.2	4

Table 11.6

It is not difficult to see a pattern! At each of the four points the gradient is twice the x-coordinate. This is unlikely to be a coincidence. If you try to find the gradient at any other point on the curve you will find that the same thing happens.

You can express this algebraically by saying that the 'gradient formula' for the curve $y = x^2$ is $2x$.

Try doing the same thing for the results of Example 11.1.3 and Exercise 11A Question 2 for the curve $y = 1 + 5x - 2x^2$. You then get the values set out in Table 11.7.

x-coordinate of P	-1	0	1	2
Gradient at P	9	5	1	-3

Table 11.7

The pattern is not quite so obvious this time, but you will notice that as you move across the table the values of x go up by 1 each time, and the values of y go down by 4. And since the gradient is 5 when $x = 0$, it is $5 - 4 \times 1$ when $x = 1$, $5 - 4 \times 2$ when $x = 2$, and so on. This suggests that the gradient formula for the curve $y = 1 + 5x - 2x^2$ is $5 - 4x$.

The process of finding the gradient formula for a curve is called **differentiation**. When you find the gradient formula, you are **differentiating**.

If the curve you are differentiating is written as $y = f(x)$, then the gradient formula for the curve is called the **derivative** of $f(x)$. It is denoted by $f'(x)$. This is pronounced 'f dashed x'.

So you can write

$$\text{if } f(x) = x^2, \text{ then } f'(x) = 2x;$$

and
$$\text{if } f(x) = 1 + 5x - 2x^2, \text{ then } f'(x) = 5 - 4x.$$

Remember that so far these formulae are just suggestions based on a few numerical experiments. They will be proved later in the chapter.

Exercise 11B

1 Use your answers to Exercise 11A Question 3 to suggest gradient formulae for the curves with equations

(a) $y = 10x^2$, (b) $y = x^2 + 3$, (c) $y = 3x^2 - 4x + 2$.

Write your conclusions using $f(x)$, $f'(x)$ notation.

11.3 Some rules for differentiation

Now that you have several examples of gradient formulae, look to see if you can find a pattern. In Table 11.8 the results are numbered as they appear in Exercise 11A.

	Equation of curve	Gradient formula
1	$y = x^2$	$2x$
2	$y = 1 + 5x - 2x^2$	$5 - 4x$
3(a)	$y = 10x^2$	$20x$
3(b)	$y = x^2 + 3$	$2x$
3(c)	$y = 3x^2 - 4x + 2$	$6x - 4$

Table 11.8

Remember also that, for the line $y = bx + c$, the gradient formula is the constant b.

You will notice at once that

- if x^2 appears in the equation (as in 1, 3(b)), it becomes $2x$ in the gradient formula
- if a multiple of x^2 appears in the equation (as in 2, 3(a), 3(c)), it becomes the same multiple of $2x$ in the gradient formula
- if a multiple of x appears in the equation (as in 2, 3(c) and the straight line), the multiplier appears as a constant term in the gradient formula
- if a constant term appears in the equation (as in 2, 3(b), 3(c) and the straight line), it disappears in the gradient formula.

These results can be summed up for any quadratic curve:

> If $f(x) = ax^2 + bx + c$, then $f'(x) = 2ax + b$.

Example 11.3.1
For the curve with equation $y = 3x^2 - 8x - 2$, find the gradient at (3, 1).

Begin by finding the gradient formula from the result in the box with $a = 3$, $b = -8$ and $c = -2$. The gradient formula is then $6x - 8$.

To find the gradient at (3, 1) substitute $x = 3$ in the gradient formula to get $6 \times 3 - 8 = 10$.

You have already used the notation $f(x)$ with a particular value substituted for x (see Section 8.1). For instance, if in Example 11.3.1 $f(x)$ is used to denote $3x^2 - 8x - 2$, then $f(3)$ gives the y-coordinate of the point on the curve where $x = 3$. This idea can be extended to the expression for the derivative. When you differentiate you get $f'(x) = 6x - 8$. You can now substitute $x = 3$ and write $f'(3) = 6 \times 3 - 8 = 10$, which gives the gradient of the curve at the point where $x = 3$.

Example 11.3.2
If $f(x) = 5 - 2x - 4x^2$, find $f(-1)$ and $f'(-1)$. What do the answers tell you about the graph of $y = 5 - 2x - 4x^2$?

$$f(-1) = 5 - 2 \times (-1) - 4 \times (-1)^2$$
$$= 5 + 2 - 4 = 3.$$

Differentiating, $f'(x) = -2 - 8x$.

So $$f'(-1) = -2 - 8 \times (-1)$$
$$= -2 + 8 = 6.$$

Graphically, this means that the curve with equation $y = 5 - 2x - 4x^2$ contains the point $(-1, 3)$ and has gradient 6 at this point.

11.4 Extending the differentiation rule

So far differentiation has been used only for quadratic curves, but exactly the same methods can be used to find the gradients of curves whose equations contain x^3, x^4 and higher powers of x. The question is how to extend the rule for differentiating x^2 to higher powers.

Begin by noticing that the gradient formula $2x$ for the curve $y = x^2$ could be written as $2 \times x^1$.

The numerical multiplier 2 in this expression is the power of x in the equation of the curve, and the new power of x is 1 less than that power, since $2 - 1 = 1$.

Try applying the same rule to the curve $y = x^3$. The power of x is now 3, so in the gradient formula you would expect the numerical multiplier to be 3, and the new power of x to be $3 - 1$, that is 2. That is, the gradient formula would be $3x^2$.

This is a very optimistic generalisation, but there are several ways of testing it out. Look back to Chapter 8 at the graph of $y = x^3$, where it is Fig. 8.6. You will see that at the origin the x-axis is a tangent to the curve, so the gradient when $x = 0$ is 0. At every other point on the curve the gradient is positive. This is just what you would expect if the gradient formula is $3x^2$.

Another way of testing the formula would be to choose a particular point and estimate the gradient by the numerical method used in Section 11.1, as in Example 11.4.1.

Example 11.4.1

Make a numerical estimate of the gradient of $y = x^3$ at the point P with coordinates (0.4, 0.064). Test whether this is the answer that you would get by using the suggested gradient formula $3x^2$.

Take points R to the right of P and N to the left of P with x-coordinates 0.401 and 0.399.

The y-coordinate of R is $0.401^3 = 0.064\,481...$, so for the chord [PR]

$$\delta x = 0.401 - 0.4 = 0.001 \quad \text{and} \quad \delta y = 0.064\,481... - 0.064 = 0.000\,481...,$$

giving

$$\frac{\delta y}{\delta x} = \frac{0.000\,481...}{0.001} = 0.481....$$

The y-coordinate of N is $0.399^3 = 0.063\,521...$, so for the chord [PN]

$$\delta x = 0.399 - 0.4 = -0.001 \quad \text{and} \quad \delta y = 0.063\,521... - 0.064 = -0.000\,478...,$$

giving

$$\frac{\delta y}{\delta x} = \frac{-0.000\,478...}{-0.001} = 0.478....$$

The gradient of the tangent at P is between 0.478... and 0.481.... It is a reasonable guess that the gradient is 0.48.

Substituting $x = 0.4$ in the suggested gradient formula $3x^2$ gives $3 \times 0.4^2 = 3 \times 0.16 = 0.48$.

With this encouragement, you could try extending the rule to $y = x^4$. The multiplier for the gradient formula would be 4, and the new power of x would be $4 - 1 = 3$. So you might expect the gradient formula to be $4x^3$. You can test this out in the same way as for $y = x^3$.

All these formulae can be summed up in a single statement by replacing the numerical powers 2, 3, 4, ... in the equations $y = x^2$, $y = x^3$, $y = x^4$, ... by the letter n:

If $f(x) = x^n$, where n is a positive integer, then $f'(x) = nx^{n-1}$.

There is one other rule for differentiation which you have probably hardly noticed, but which needs to be stated for completeness. Look back at the rule for differentiating $ax^2 + bx + c$ in Section 11.3. This is stated for a single function with three coefficients, but it could be broken down into three separate and simpler statements:

If $f(x) = x^2$, then $f'(x) = 2x$.

If $g(x) = x$, then $g'(x) = 1$.

If $h(x) = 1$, then $h'(x) = 0$.

You could then put these together and say:

The derivative of $ax^2 + bx + c$ is $a \times (2x) + b \times 1 + c \times 0$, which is $2ax + b$.

When you do this you are using a rule for combining derivatives. It is sufficient to state it for two functions $f(x)$ and $g(x)$. If there are more than two functions, you can reach the obvious extension by using the rule more than once.

> The derivative of $af(x) + bg(x)$, where a and b are constants, is $af'(x) + bg'(x)$.

Example 11.4.2
Differentiate (a) $x^5 - 4x^3 + 7x^2$, (b) $(x + 2)(2x - 3)$.

(a) The derivatives of x^5, x^3 and x^2 are $5x^4$, $3x^2$ and $2x$. So the derivative of $x^5 - 4x^3 + 7x^2$ is $5x^4 - 4(3x^2) + 7(2x)$, which is $5x^4 - 12x^2 + 14x$.

(b) None of the rules for differentiation apply directly to an expression like this. But you can multiply out the brackets to get a quadratic which you can differentiate.

Since $(x + 2)(2x - 3) = 2x^2 + x - 6$, the derivative is $2(2x) + 1 = 4x + 1$.

> If you cannot immediately differentiate a given function using the rules you know, see if you can write the function in a different form which enables you to apply one of the rules.

11.5 An alternative notation

The advantage of the $f(x)$, $f'(x)$ notation is that you can use it in two ways. With x inside the bracket it refers to the function and its derivative as a whole. But if you replace x by a particular number p, then $f(p)$, $f'(p)$ stand for the value of the function and the gradient at a single point where $x = p$.

However, if you just want to use x and y and don't need $f(x)$ notation, it is useful to have a way of writing the derivative in terms of x and y.

There is already a symbol $\frac{\delta y}{\delta x}$ which does this for the gradient of a chord. This suggests using a similar symbol for the gradient of the tangent, writing the letter 'd' instead of the greek δ.

> If y is a function of x, $\frac{\mathrm{d}y}{\mathrm{d}x}$ denotes the derivative.

But there is an important difference between $\frac{\delta y}{\delta x}$ and $\frac{\mathrm{d}y}{\mathrm{d}x}$. The symbol $\frac{\delta y}{\delta x}$ stands for a genuine fraction, the result of dividing δy by δx; $\frac{\mathrm{d}y}{\mathrm{d}x}$ is not a fraction, but a complete symbol which can't be taken apart. The separate elements $\mathrm{d}y$ and $\mathrm{d}x$ have no meaning. In speech it is pronounced (rather rapidly!) 'd y d x' with no hint that there is a fraction bar present.

Example 11.5.1

If $y = 4x^3 - 3x^4$, find $\frac{dy}{dx}$.

This is exactly the same question as 'If $f(x) = 4x^3 - 3x^4$, find $f'(x)$', or 'Differentiate $4x^3 - 3x^4$'. The answer is $\frac{dy}{dx} = 4(3x^2) - 3(4x^3) = 12x^2(1 - x)$.

The main advantages of $\frac{dy}{dx}$ notation will be seen in Chapter 21 when you come to apply differentiation to mathematical models in various real-world situations. However, there may be occasions before then when you will find it convenient, so it is worth getting used to it at this stage.

Exercise 11C

1 Write down the gradient formula for each of the following functions.

(a) x^2 (b) $x^2 - x$ (c) $4x^2$ (d) $3x^2 - 2x$

(e) $2 - 3x$ (f) $x - 2 - 2x^2$ (g) $2 + 4x - 3x^2$ (h) $\sqrt{2}x - \sqrt{3}x^2$

2 For each of the following functions $f(x)$, write down $f'(x)$. You may need to rearrange some of the functions before differentiating them.

(a) $3x - 1$ (b) $2 - 3x^2$ (c) 4 (d) $1 + 2x + 3x^2$

(e) $x^2 - 2x^2$ (f) $3(1 + 2x - x^2)$ (g) $2x(1 - x)$ (h) $x(2x + 1) - 1$

3 Find the derivative of each of the following functions $f(x)$ at $x = -3$.

(a) $-x^2$ (b) $3x$ (c) $x^2 + 3x$ (d) $2x - x^2$

(e) $2x^2 + 4x - 1$ (f) $-(3 - x^2)$ (g) $-x(2 + x)$ (h) $(x - 2)(2x - 1)$

4 For each of the following functions $f(x)$, find x such that $f'(x)$ has the given value.

(a) $2x^2$ value 3 (b) $x - 2x^2$ value -1

(c) $2 + 3x + x^2$ value 0 (d) $x^2 + 4x - 1$ value 2

(e) $(x - 2)(x - 1)$ value 0 (f) $2x(3x + 2)$ value 10

5 Repeat the numerical test in Example 11.4.1 by estimating the gradient of $y = x^3$ at the points

(a) $(1, 1)$, (b) $(-0.5, -0.125)$.

6 Make numerical estimates of the gradient of $y = x^4$ at two points of your choice, and use them to check the differentiation rule $\frac{dy}{dx} = 4x^3$.

7 Find $\frac{dy}{dx}$ for each of the following equations.

(a) $y = x^3 + 2x^2$ (b) $y = 1 - 2x^3 + 3x^2$ (c) $y = x^3 - 6x^2 + 11x - 6$

(d) $y = 2x^3 - 3x^2 + x$ (e) $y = x(1 + x^2)$ (f) $y = (2 - x^2)(2 + x^2)$

8 Find $f'(-2)$ for each of the following functions $f(x)$.

(a) $2x - x^3$ (b) $2x - x^2$ (c) $1 - 2x - 3x^2 + 4x^3$

(d) $2 - x$ (e) $x^2(1 + x)$ (f) $(3 - x^2)^2$

9 For each of the following functions find the value(s) of x such that $f'(x)$ is equal to the given number.

(a) x^3 12 (b) $x^3 - x^2$ 8 (c) $3x - 3x^2 + x^3$ 108

(d) $x^3 - 3x^2 + 2x$ -1 (e) $x(1 + x)^2$ 0 (f) $x(1 - x)(1 + x)$ 2

11.6 Proving the gradient formulae

This section shows how some of the gradient formulae found in Sections 11.1–11.4 can be proved.

In Examples 11.1.1 and 11.1.2 the gradient of $y = x^2$ at the point P with coordinates (0.4, 0.16) was guessed from the gradients of chords joining this point to points on the curve with x-coordinates 0.5, 0.3, 0.41 and 0.39. By using some simple algebra all these calculations (and many similar ones) could have been done at the same time.

The x-coordinates of the points R, S, N and M were all chosen to be close to 0.4, the x-coordinate of P. So to save time you could take a point Q with x-coordinate $0.4 + h$, work out the gradient of the chord [PQ] and then substitute various values for h such as 0.1, -0.1, 0.01 and -0.01 in this to find the gradients of the chords [PR], [PN], and so on.

Example 11.6.1
Find the gradient of the chord joining P(0.4, 0.16) to Q$(0.4 + h, (0.4 + h)^2)$

Using the delta notation,

$$\delta x = (0.4 + h) - 0.4 = h,$$

and

$$\begin{aligned}\delta y &= (0.4 + h)^2 - 0.16 \\ &= (0.16 + 0.8h + h^2) - 0.16 \\ &= 0.8h + h^2,\end{aligned}$$

so

$$\begin{aligned}\frac{\delta y}{\delta x} &= \frac{0.8h + h^2}{h} \\ &= \frac{(0.8 + h)h}{h} \\ &= 0.8 + h.\end{aligned}$$

This confirms what appeared to be happening in Examples 11.1.1 and 11.1.2. For any chord to the right of P, for which $h > 0$, the gradient is greater than 0.8; and for any chord to the left, with $h < 0$, the gradient is less than 0.8.

In fact, by taking h close enough to 0, you can make the gradient of the chord as close to 0.8 as you choose. From Example 11.6.1, the gradient of the chord is $0.8 + h$. So if you want to find a chord through (0.4, 0.16) with a gradient between, say, 0.799 999 and 0.800 001, you can do it by taking h somewhere between $-0.000\,001$ and $+0.000\,001$.

The only value that you cannot take for h is 0 itself. But you can say that 'in the limit, as h tends to 0, the gradient of the chord tends to 0.8'.

The conventional way of writing this is

$$\lim_{h\to 0}(\text{gradient of chord}) = \lim_{h\to 0}(0.8 + h) = 0.8.$$

The symbol $h \to 0$ is read 'as h tends to 0', or sometimes simply 'h tends to 0'.

This is fine as far as it goes, but that is not very far. Taking P to be the point with $x = 0.4$ was a special numerical example. In Exercise 11A Question 1 you then carried out similar calculations for points with $x = 2$, $x = 0.6$ and $x = -1$. All these calculations could have been done together by taking a more algebraic approach and taking P to be the point at which $x = p$.

Example 11.6.2
Find the gradient of the chord of $y = x^2$ joining $P(p, p^2)$ to $Q(p + h, (p + h)^2)$.

The argument is exactly the same as in Example 11.6.1.

$$\delta x = (p + h) - p = h,$$

and

$$\begin{aligned}\delta y &= (p + h)^2 - p^2\\ &= (p^2 + 2ph + h^2) - p^2\\ &= 2ph + h^2,\end{aligned}$$

so

$$\begin{aligned}\frac{\delta y}{\delta x} &= \frac{2ph + h^2}{h}\\ &= \frac{(2p + h)h}{h}\\ &= 2p + h.\end{aligned}$$

You can see that Example 11.6.1 is just a special case of this with $p = 0.4$.

Now in any particular application the value of p remains constant, but h can be varied to bring Q as close to P as you choose. Then, by the same argument as before,

$$\lim_{h\to 0}(\text{gradient of chord}) = \lim_{h\to 0}(2p + h) = 2p.$$

This shows that, as we guessed from the special cases in Section 11.2, the gradient of $y = x^2$ at any point P is double the x-coordinate of P. That is, the gradient formula for the curve $y = x^2$ is $2x$.

Example 11.6.3 uses the same method to find the derivative of the curve in Example 11.1.3.

Example 11.6.3

For the curve with equation $y = 1 + 5x - 2x^2$, prove that $\frac{dy}{dx} = 5 - 4x$.

Take any point P on the curve with coordinates $(p, 1 + 5p - 2p^2)$. Let Q be another point on the curve with x-coordinate $p + h$.

The y-coordinate of Q is

$$\begin{aligned} 1 + 5(p+h) - 2(p+h)^2 &= 1 + 5(p+h) - 2(p^2 + 2ph + h^2) \\ &= 1 + 5p + 5h - 2p^2 - 4ph - 2h^2. \end{aligned}$$

So, for the chord [PQ],

$$\begin{aligned} \delta x &= (p+h) - p = h, \\ \delta y &= (1 + 5p + 5h - 2p^2 - 4ph - 2h^2) - (1 + 5p - 2p^2) \\ &= 5h - 4ph - 2h^2 \end{aligned}$$

and

$$\begin{aligned} \frac{\delta y}{\delta x} &= \frac{5h - 4ph - 2h^2}{h} \\ &= \frac{(5 - 4p - 2h)h}{h} \\ &= 5 - 4p - 2h. \end{aligned}$$

Now, for a fixed value of p, $\frac{\delta y}{\delta x}$ can be made as close to $5 - 4p$ as you like by making h small enough. That is,

$$\lim_{h \to 0} \frac{\delta y}{\delta x} = \lim_{h \to 0} (5 - 4p - 2h) = 5 - 4p.$$

This shows that the gradient of the curve at the point where $x = p$ is $5 - 4p$, for any value of p. The gradient formula for the curve is therefore

$$\frac{dy}{dx} = 5 - 4x.$$

A similar approach can be used for any curve if you know its equation.

Fig. 11.9 shows a curve which has an equation of the form $y = f(x)$. Suppose that you want the gradient of the tangent at the point P, with coordinates $(p, f(p))$. The chord joining this point to any other point Q on the curve with coordinates $(p+h, f(p+h))$ has

$$\delta x = h, \quad \delta y = f(p+h) - f(p)$$

so that its gradient is

$$\frac{\delta y}{\delta x} = \frac{f(p+h) - f(p)}{h}.$$

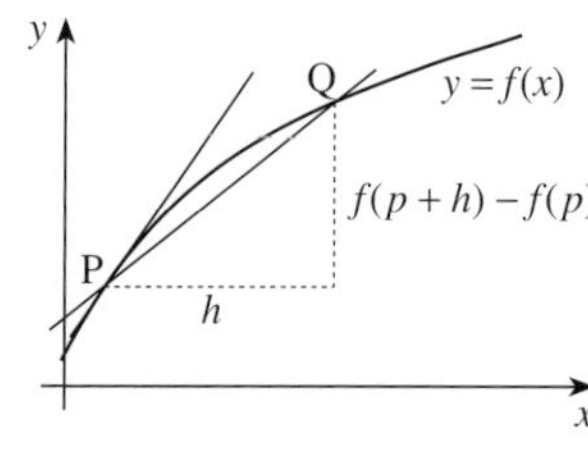

Fig. 11.9

Now let the value of h change so that the point Q takes different positions on the curve. Then, if Q is close to P, so that h is close to 0, the gradient of the chord is close to the gradient of the tangent at p. In the limit, as h tends to 0, this expression tends to $f'(p)$.

> If the curve $y = f(x)$ has a tangent at $(p, f(p))$, then its gradient is
>
> $$\lim_{h\to 0} \frac{f(p+h) - f(p)}{h}.$$
>
> This quantity is called the derivative of $f(x)$ at $x = p$; it is denoted by $f'(p)$.
>
> In general the derivative is $f'(x)$, where $f'(x) = \lim_{h\to 0} \frac{f(x+h) - f(x)}{h}$.

Example 11.6.4 uses the definition in the last line of the box to prove the result for the derivative of the general quadratic function given in Section 11.3.

Example 11.6.4

Prove that, if $f(x) = ax^2 + bx + c$, then $f'(x) = 2ax + b$.

First,

$$\begin{aligned} f(x+h) - f(x) &= (a(x+h)^2 + b(x+h) + c) - (ax^2 + bx + c) \\ &= a((x+h)^2 - x^2) + b((x+h) - x) \\ &= a(2xh + h^2) + bh \\ &= (a(2x+h) + b)h. \end{aligned}$$

Therefore

$$\begin{aligned} f'(x) &= \lim_{h\to 0} \frac{(a(2x+h) + b)h}{h} \\ &= \lim_{h\to 0}(2ax + ah + b) \\ &= 2ax + b. \end{aligned}$$

With the help of the binomial theorem, Section 3.3, you can use this method to find the derivative for higher powers of x. Example 11.6.5 shows how to do this for $f(x) = x^4$.

Example 11.6.5

Prove that, if $f(x) = x^4$, then $f'(x) = 4x^3$.

By the binomial theorem,

$$(x+h)^4 = x^4 + 4x^3h + 6x^2h^2 + 4xh^3 + h^4.$$

So

$$\begin{aligned} f(x+h) - f(x) &= (x+h)^4 - x^4 \\ &= 4x^3h + 6x^2h^2 + 4xh^3 + h^4 \\ &= (4x^3 + 6x^2h + 4xh^2 + h^3)h \end{aligned}$$

and

$$\frac{f(x+h) - f(x)}{h} = 4x^3 + 6x^2h + 4xh^2 + h^3.$$

The main differences between this and previous examples are that there are now three terms in this expression which involve h, and that in two of these the multiplying factor contains x. But since, as h varies, x remains constant, each of these terms separately tends to 0 as $h \to 0$. Their sum therefore also tends to 0, so that

$$\lim_{h\to 0} \frac{f(x+h) - f(x)}{h} = 4x^3.$$

That is, $f'(x) = 4x^3$.

Exercise 11D

1 Without using a general formula, prove that the gradient of $y = 3x^2 - 2x + 1$ at $x = 1$ is 4.

2 Prove that the gradient of $y = 4x - 3x^2$ at the point $(p,\ 4p - 3p^2)$ is $4 - 6p$.

3 Without using a general formula prove that, if $f(x) = 2x^2 + 3x + 2$, then $f'(x) = 4x + 3$.

4 Prove from first principles that the value of $\frac{\mathrm{d}y}{\mathrm{d}x}$ at the point (2, 40) on the curve $y = 5x^3$ is 60.

5 Use the definition of $f'(x)$ to prove that, if $f(x) = x^3$, then $f'(x) = 3x^2$.

12 Tangents and normals

This chapter combines results from Chapters 7 and 11. When you have completed it, you should

- be able to find the equation of the tangent to a curve at a point
- know what is meant by a normal, and be able to find the equation of the normal to a curve at a point.

12.1 Finding equations of tangents

Now that you know how to find the gradient of the tangent at a point on a curve, it is easy to find the equation of the tangent.

Example 12.1.1
Find the equation of the tangent at the point (2, 6) on the curve $y = f(x)$, where $f(x) = 2x^2 - 3x + 4$.

To find the gradient, differentiate to get $f'(x) = 4x - 3$.

The gradient of the tangent at (2, 6) is $f'(2) = 4 \times 2 - 3 = 5$.

The tangent is the line through (2, 6) with gradient 5. Using the equation of a line in the form $y - y_1 = m(x - x_1)$ (see Section 7.3), the equation of the tangent is

$$y - 6 = 5(x - 2), \quad \text{which is} \quad y = 5x - 4.$$

The important thing to remember is that, in the equation of a line, m has to be a number. You have to substitute the x-coordinate of the point into the gradient formula before you can find the equation of the line.

Example 12.1.2
Find the equation of the tangent to the graph of $y = x^2 - 4x + 2$ which is parallel to the x-axis.

From Section 7.2, a line parallel to the x-axis has gradient 0.

Let $f(x) = x^2 - 4x + 2$. Then $f'(x) = 2x - 4$.

To find when the gradient is 0 you need to solve $2x - 4 = 0$, giving $x = 2$.

When $x = 2$, $y = 2^2 - 4 \times 2 + 2 = -2$.

From Section 7.3, the equation of a line parallel to the x-axis has the form $y = c$. So the equation of the tangent is $y = -2$.

Example 12.1.3

Show that there are two points on the graph of $y = x^2(x - 2)$ at which the gradient is equal to 4. Find the equations of the tangents at these points.

Before you can differentiate, you must multiply out the brackets to get the equation in the form $y = x^3 - 2x^2$. The gradient formula is then $\frac{dy}{dx} = 3x^2 - 4x$.

This is equal to 4 if $3x^2 - 4x = 4$, that is if x is a root of the quadratic equation

$$3x^2 - 4x - 4 = 0.$$

This can be factorised as

$$(x - 2)(3x + 2) = 0,$$

so the gradient is equal to 4 if $x = 2$ or $x = -\frac{2}{3}$.

You know the gradient of the tangents, but you do not yet know the y-coordinates of the points on the curve that they have to pass through. To find these you have to substitute the values of x already found into the equation $y = x^2(x - 2)$.

When $x = 2$, $y = 2^2 \times (2 - 2) = 0$. The line through $(2, 0)$ with gradient 4 has equation

$$y - 0 = 4(x - 2), \quad \text{which is} \quad y = 4x - 8.$$

When $x = -\frac{2}{3}$, $y = \left(-\frac{2}{3}\right)^2 \times \left(-\frac{2}{3} - 2\right) = \frac{4}{9} \times \left(-\frac{8}{3}\right) = -\frac{32}{27}$. The equation of the line through $\left(-\frac{2}{3}, -\frac{32}{27}\right)$ with gradient 4 is

$$y - \left(-\tfrac{32}{27}\right) = 4\left(x - \left(-\tfrac{2}{3}\right)\right)$$

$$y + \tfrac{32}{27} = 4x + \tfrac{8}{3}$$

$$y = 4x + \tfrac{40}{27}.$$

The equations of the tangents with gradient 4 are $y = 4x - 8$ and $y = 4x + \frac{40}{27}$.

Check this by displaying the curve and the two lines on your calculator.

12.2 The normal to a curve at a point

Another line which you sometimes need to find is the line through a point of a curve at right angles to the tangent at that point. This is called the **normal** to the curve at the point.

Fig. 12.1 shows a curve with equation $y = f(x)$. The tangent and normal at the point A have been drawn.

If you know the gradient of the tangent at A, you can find the gradient of the normal by using the result in Section 7.4 for perpendicular lines. If the gradient of the tangent is m, the gradient of the normal is $-\frac{1}{m}$ provided that $m \neq 0$.

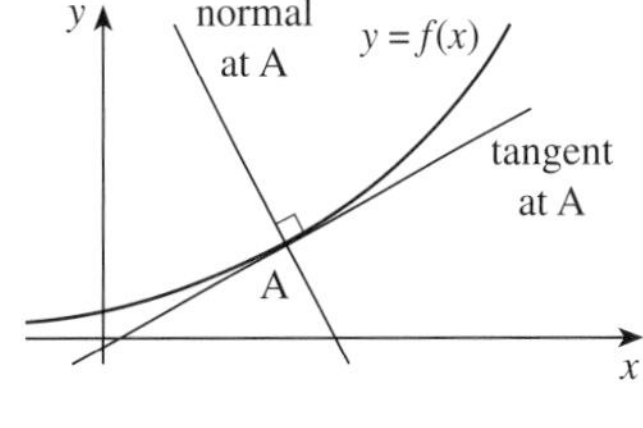

Fig. 12.1

Example 12.2.1
Find the equation of the normal to the curve at the given point in

(a) Example 12.1.1, (b) Example 12.1.2.

(a) For the curve with equation $y = 2x^2 - 3x + 4$ at the point (2, 6), the gradient of the tangent is 5. The gradient of the normal is therefore $-\frac{1}{5}$.
The equation of the normal is

$$y - 6 = -\tfrac{1}{5}(x - 2) \quad \text{which is} \quad y = -0.2x + 6.4.$$

(b) Since the tangent at (2, −2) is parallel to the x-axis, the normal is parallel to the y-axis. It therefore has equation $x = 2$.

For the curve in Examples 12.1.1 and 12.2.1(a), try plotting the curve $y = 2x^2 - 3x + 4$, the tangent $y = 5x - 4$ and the normal $y = -0.2x + 6.4$ on your calculator. You may be surprised by the results.

If you draw a curve together with its tangent and normal at a point, the normal will only appear perpendicular in your diagram if the scales are the same on both the x- and y-axes. (Or, of course, if the tangent is horizontal and the normal is vertical, as in Examples 12.1.2 and 12.2.1(b).) However, no matter what the scales are, the tangent will always appear as a tangent.

Exercise 12

1 Find the equation of the tangent to the curve at the point with the given x-coordinate.

(a) $y = x^2$ where $x = -1$
(b) $y = 2x^2 - x$ where $x = 0$
(c) $y = x^2 - 2x + 3$ where $x = 2$
(d) $y = 1 - x^2$ where $x = -3$
(e) $y = x(2 - x)$ where $x = 1$
(f) $y = (x - 1)^2$ where $x = 1$

2 Find the equation of the normal to the curve at the point with the given x-coordinate.

(a) $y = -x^2$ where $x = 1$
(b) $y = 3x^2 - 2x - 1$ where $x = 1$
(c) $y = 1 - 2x^2$ where $x = -2$
(d) $y = 1 - x^2$ where $x = 0$
(e) $y = 2(2 + x + x^2)$ where $x = -1$
(f) $y = (2x - 1)^2$ where $x = \frac{1}{2}$

3 Find the equation of the tangent to the curve $y = x^2$ which is parallel to the line $y = x$.

4 Find the equation of the tangent to the curve $y = x^2$ which is parallel to the x-axis.

5 Find the equation of the tangent to the curve $y = x^2 - 2x$ which is perpendicular to the line $2y = x - 1$.

6 Find the equation of the normal to the curve $y = 3x^2 - 2x - 1$ which is parallel to the line $y = x - 3$.

7 Find the equation of the normal to the curve $y = (x - 1)^2$ which is parallel to the y-axis.

8 Find the equation of the normal to the curve $y = 2x^2 + 3x + 4$ which is perpendicular to the line $y = 7x - 5$.

9 Find the equation of the tangent to the curve $y = x^3 + x$ at the point for which $x = -1$.

10 One of the tangents to the curve with equation $y = 4x - x^3$ is the line with equation $y = x - 2$. Find the equation of the other tangent parallel to $y = x - 2$.

11 The graphs of $y = x^2 - 2x$ and $y = x^3 - 3x^2 - 2x$ both pass through the origin. Show that they share the same tangent at the origin.

12 Find the equation of the tangent to the curve with equation $y = x^3 - 3x^2 - 2x - 6$ at the point where it crosses the y-axis.

13 The line $y = x + 2$ meets the curve $y = x^2$ at A and B.

(a) Find the coordinates of A and B.

(b) Find the equations of the tangents to the curve at A and B.

(c) Find the point of intersection of the tangents at A and B.

13 Index notation

You have already used index notation in the form of squares, cubes and other integer powers. In this chapter the notation is extended to powers which are zero, negative numbers and fractions. When you have completed it, you should

- know the rules of indices
- know the meaning of negative, zero and fractional indices
- be able to simplify expressions involving indices.

13.1 Working with indices

In the 16th century, when mathematics books began to be printed, mathematicians were finding how to solve cubic and quartic equations. They found it was more economical to write and to print the products *xxx* and *xxxx* as x^3 and x^4.

This is how index notation started. But it turned out to be much more than a convenient shorthand. The new notation led to important mathematical discoveries, and mathematics as it is today would be inconceivable without index notation.

You will already have used simple examples of this notation. In general, the symbol a^m stands for the result of multiplying m *a*s together:

$$a^m = \overbrace{a \times a \times a \times \ldots \times a}^{m \text{ of these}}.$$

The number a is called the **base**, and the number m is the **index** (plural 'indices'). Notice that, although a can be any kind of number, m must be a positive integer. Another way of describing this is 'a raised to the mth power', or more shortly 'a to the power m'. When this notation is used, expressions can often be simplified by using a few simple rules.

One of these is the **multiplication rule**,

$$a^m \times a^n = \overbrace{a \times a \times \ldots \times a}^{m \text{ of these}} \times \overbrace{a \times a \times \ldots \times a}^{n \text{ of these}} = \overbrace{a \times a \times \ldots \times a}^{m+n \text{ of these}} = a^{m+n}.$$

This is used, for example, in finding the volume of a cube of side a:

$$\text{volume} = \text{base area} \times \text{height} = a^2 \times a = a^2 \times a^1 = a^{2+1} = a^3.$$

Closely linked with this is the **division rule**,

$$\begin{aligned} a^m \div a^n &= (\overbrace{a \times a \times \ldots \times a}^{m \text{ of these}}) \div (\overbrace{a \times a \times \ldots \times a}^{n \text{ of these}}) \\ &= \overbrace{a \times a \times \ldots \times a}^{m-n \text{ of these}} \quad (\text{since } n \text{ of the } a\text{s cancel out}) \\ &= a^{m-n}, \quad \text{provided that } m > n. \end{aligned}$$

Example 13.1.1

Simplify (a) $10^3 \times 10^4 \div 10^2$, (b) $\dfrac{p^4q^5}{pq^3}$.

(a) $10^3 \times 10^4 \div 10^2 = 10^{3+4} \div 10^2 = 10^7 \div 10^2 = 10^{7-2} = 10^5$.

(b) $\dfrac{p^4q^5}{pq^3} = \dfrac{p^4}{p} \times \dfrac{q^5}{q^3} = (p^4 \div p)\times(q^5 \div q^3) = p^{4-1} \times q^{5-3} = p^3q^2$.

Another rule is the **power-on-power rule**,

$$(a^m)^n = \overbrace{\underbrace{a \times a \times \ldots \times a}_{m \text{ of these}} \times \underbrace{a \times a \times \ldots \times a}_{m \text{ of these}} \times \ldots \times \underbrace{a \times a \times \ldots \times a}_{m \text{ of these}}}^{n \text{ of these brackets}}$$

$$= \overbrace{a \times a \times \ldots \times a}^{m\times n \text{ of these}} = a^{m\times n}.$$

Example 13.1.2

Express 8^4 as a power of 2.

Since $8 = 2^3$, $8^4 = (2^3)^4 = 2^{3\times 4} = 2^{12}$.

One further rule, the **factor rule**, has two bases but just one index:

$$(a \times b)^m = \overbrace{(a \times b)\times(a \times b) \times \ldots \times (a \times b)}^{m \text{ of these brackets}} = \overbrace{a \times a \times \ldots \times a}^{m \text{ of these}} \times \overbrace{b \times b \times \ldots \times b}^{m \text{ of these}} = a^m \times b^m.$$

In explaining these rules multiplication signs have been used. But, as in other parts of algebra, they are usually omitted if there is no ambiguity. For completeness, here are the rules again:

The multiplication rule:	$a^m \times a^n = a^{m+n}$
The division rule:	$a^m \div a^n = a^{m-n}$, provided that $m > n$
The power-on-power rule:	$(a^m)^n = a^{m\times n}$
The factor rule:	$(a \times b)^m = a^m \times b^m$

Example 13.1.3

Given that $zx^4 = (x^3y)^2$, express z as simply as possible in terms of x and y.

Begin by using the factor rule to separate the powers of x and y.

$$zx^4 = (x^3)^2 \times y^2.$$

Using the power-on-power rule,

$$zx^4 = x^{3\times 2} \times y^2 = x^6y^2.$$

Divide both sides by x^4 and rearrange the factors to get the powers of x together.

$$z = x^6y^2 \div x^4 = (x^6 \div x^4) \times y^2.$$

Using the division rule,

$$z = x^{6-4} \times y^2 = x^2y^2.$$

If $zx^4 = (x^3y)^2$, then $z = x^2y^2$.

Example 13.1.4

Simplify $(2a^2b)^3 \div (4a^4b)$.

$$\begin{aligned}(2a^2b)^3 \div (4a^4b) &= \left(2^3(a^2)^3b^3\right) \div (4a^4b) && \text{factor rule}\\ &= (8a^{2\times 3}b^3) \div (4a^4b) && \text{power-on-power rule}\\ &= (8 \div 4) \times (a^6 \div a^4) \times (b^3 \div b^1) && \text{rearranging}\\ &= 2a^{6-4}b^{3-1} && \text{division rule}\\ &= 2a^2b^2.\end{aligned}$$

Exercise 13A

1 Simplify the following expressions.

(a) $a^2 \times a^3 \times a^7$ (b) $(b^4)^2$ (c) $c^7 \div c^3$

(d) $d^5 \times d^4$ (e) $(e^5)^4$ (f) $(x^3y^2)^2$

(g) $5g^5 \times 3g^3$ (h) $12h^{12} \div 4h^4$ (i) $(2a^2)^3 \times (3a)^2$

2 Simplify the following, giving each answer in the form 2^n.

(a) $2^{11} \times (2^5)^3$ (b) $(2^3)^2 \times (2^2)^3$ (c) 4^3

(d) 8^2 (e) $\dfrac{2^7 \times 2^8}{2^{13}}$ (f) $\dfrac{2^2 \times 2^3}{(2^2)^2}$

13.2 Zero and negative indices

The definition of a^m in Section 13.1, as the result of multiplying m as together, makes no sense if m is zero or a negative integer. You can't multiply -3 as or 0 as together. But extending the meaning of a^m when the index is zero or negative is possible, and useful, since it turns out that the rules still work with such index values.

Look at this sequence: $2^5 = 32,\ 2^4 = 16,\ 2^3 = 8,\ 2^2 = 4, \ldots$.

On the left sides, the base is always 2, and the indices go down by 1 at each step. On the right, the numbers are halved at each step. So you might continue the process

$$\ldots,\ 2^2 = 4,\ 2^1 = 2,\ 2^0 = 1,\ 2^{-1} = \tfrac{1}{2},\ 2^{-2} = \tfrac{1}{4},\ 2^{-3} = \tfrac{1}{8}, \ldots$$

and you can go on like this indefinitely. Now compare

$$2^1 = 2 \text{ with } 2^{-1} = \tfrac{1}{2},\quad 2^2 = 4 \text{ with } 2^{-2} = \tfrac{1}{4},\quad 2^3 = 8 \text{ with } 2^{-3} = \tfrac{1}{8}.$$

It looks as if 2^{-n} should be defined as $\dfrac{1}{2^n}$, with the special value in the middle $2^0 = 1$.

This can be standardised, for any base a (except 0), and any positive integer n, as the **negative power rule**:

$$a^{-n} = \frac{1}{a^n} \quad \text{and} \quad a^0 = 1.$$

Example 13.2.1

Write as a simple fraction (a) 2^{-5}, (b) $\left(\frac{3}{5}\right)^{-2}$, (c) $\left(1\frac{1}{2}\right)^{-1}$.

$$\text{(a)}\ 2^{-5} = \frac{1}{2^5} = \tfrac{1}{32}.$$

$$\text{(b)}\ \left(\tfrac{3}{5}\right)^{-2} = \frac{1}{\left(\frac{3}{5}\right)^2} = \frac{1}{\frac{9}{25}} = \tfrac{25}{9}.$$

$$\text{(c)}\ \left(1\tfrac{1}{2}\right)^{-1} = \left(\tfrac{3}{2}\right)^{-1} = \frac{1}{\frac{3}{2}} = \tfrac{2}{3}.$$

In handwritten work it is safer, though not strictly necessary, to insert brackets in the two-tier fraction $\dfrac{1}{\left(\frac{3}{2}\right)}$ to avoid confusing it with $\dfrac{\left(\frac{1}{3}\right)}{2}$.

Notice that in Example 13.2.1 parts (b) and (c) use the rule that $\dfrac{1}{\frac{a}{b}} = \dfrac{b}{a}$. This is because

$$\frac{b}{a} \times \frac{a}{b} = 1, \text{ so } \frac{b}{a} = 1 \div \frac{a}{b} = \frac{1}{\frac{a}{b}}.$$

Before going on to use the negative power rule, you need to be sure that the rules which were established in Section 13.1 for positive indices still work when some of the indices are negative. Here are three examples.

The multiplication rule:

$$a^3 \times a^{-7} = a^3 \times \frac{1}{a^7} = \frac{a^3}{a^7} = \frac{1}{a^7 \div a^3}$$

$$= \frac{1}{a^{7-3}} \qquad \text{using the division rule for positive indices}$$

$$= \frac{1}{a^4} = a^{-4} = a^{3+(-7)}.$$

The power-on-power rule:

$$(a^{-2})^{-3} = \left(\frac{1}{a^2}\right)^{-3} = \frac{1}{\left(\frac{1}{a^2}\right)^3} = \frac{1}{\frac{1}{(a^2)^3}}$$

$$= \frac{1}{\frac{1}{a^6}} \qquad \text{using the power-on-power rule for positive indices}$$

$$= a^6 = a^{(-2)\times(-3)}.$$

The factor rule:

$$(ab)^{-3} = \frac{1}{(ab)^3} = \frac{1}{a^3b^3} \qquad \text{using the factor rule for positive indices}$$

$$= \frac{1}{a^3} \times \frac{1}{b^3} = a^{-3}b^{-3}.$$

Try making up some more examples like these for yourself.

Example 13.2.2

Simplify (a) $2^{-3} \div 3^{-2}$, (b) $x^{-1} \times x^{-2}$, (c) $(x^{-1})^{-2}$, (d) $(p^3q^{-1})^2$.

(a) $2^{-3} \div 3^{-2} = \dfrac{1}{2^3} \div \dfrac{1}{3^2} = \frac{1}{8} \div \frac{1}{9} = \frac{1}{8} \times 9 = \frac{9}{8}$.

(b) Using the multiplication rule,

$$x^{-1} \times x^{-2} = x^{(-1)+(-2)} = x^{-3} = \frac{1}{x^3}.$$

(c) Using the power-on-power rule,

$$(x^{-1})^{-2} = x^{(-1)\times(-2)} = x^2.$$

(d) First use the factor rule, then the power-on-power rule.

$$(p^3q^{-1})^2 = (p^3)^2 \times (q^{-1})^2 = p^{3\times 2} \times q^{(-1)\times 2} = p^6 \times q^{-2} = p^6 \times \frac{1}{q^2} = \frac{p^6}{q^2}.$$

Example 13.2.3

If $a = 5$, find the value of $4a^{-2}$.

The important thing to notice is that the index -2 goes only with the a and not with the 4. So $4a^{-2}$ means $4 \times \dfrac{1}{a^2}$. When $a = 5$, $4a^{-2} = 4 \times \dfrac{1}{25} = 0.16$.

Example 13.2.4

Simplify (a) $4a^2b \times (3ab^{-1})^{-2}$, (b) $\left(\dfrac{\text{MLT}^{-2}}{\text{L}^2}\right) \div \left(\dfrac{\text{LT}^{-1}}{\text{L}}\right)$.

(a) **Method 1** Change the expression into a form where all the indices are positive.

$$4a^2b \times (3ab^{-1})^{-2} = 4a^2b \times \frac{1}{(3a \times 1/b)^2} = 4a^2b \times \frac{1}{9a^2 \times 1/b^2} = 4a^2b \times \frac{b^2}{9a^2}$$
$$= \tfrac{4}{9}b^{1+2} = \tfrac{4}{9}b^3.$$

Method 2 Use the index rules directly with positive and negative indices.

$$\begin{aligned} 4a^2b \times (3ab^{-1})^{-2} &= 4a^2b \times \left(3^{-2}a^{-2}(b^{-1})^{-2}\right) && \text{factor rule} \\ &= 4a^2b \times (3^{-2}a^{-2}b^2) && \text{power-on-power rule} \\ &= \left(4 \times \frac{1}{3^2}\right) \times (a^2a^{-2}) \times (bb^2) = \tfrac{4}{9}a^0b^3 = \tfrac{4}{9}b^3. \end{aligned}$$

(b) This is an application in mechanics: M, L, T stand for dimensions of mass, length and time in the measurement of viscosity. Taking the brackets separately,

$$\left(\frac{\text{MLT}^{-2}}{\text{L}^2}\right) = \text{ML}^{1-2}\text{T}^{-2} = \text{ML}^{-1}\text{T}^{-2}$$

and $\left(\dfrac{\text{LT}^{-1}}{\text{L}}\right) = \text{L}^{1-1}\text{T}^{-1} = \text{L}^0\text{T}^{-1} = \text{T}^{-1}$,

so $\left(\dfrac{\text{MLT}^{-2}}{\text{L}^2}\right) \div \left(\dfrac{\text{LT}^{-1}}{\text{L}}\right) = (\text{ML}^{-1}\text{T}^{-2}) \div \text{T}^{-1} = \text{ML}^{-1}\text{T}^{-2-(-1)} = \text{ML}^{-1}\text{T}^{-1}$.

This may remind you of the notation m s^{-1} and m s^{-2} used in Sections 9.6 and 9.7 for the units of velocity (metres per second) and acceleration (metres per second per second).

Example 13.2.5
Find the number x such that $2^{x+1} \div 4^{x+2} = 8^{x+3}$.

Since 4 and 8 are powers of 2, the whole equation can be written in terms of powers of 2. Using the power-on-power rule followed by the division rule,

$$2^{x+1} \div (2^2)^{x+2} = (2^3)^{x+3},$$
$$2^{x+1} \div 2^{2x+4} = 2^{3x+9},$$
$$2^{(x+1)-(2x+4)} = 2^{3x+9},$$
$$2^{-x-3} = 2^{3x+9}.$$

You can now equate the indices on the two sides of the equation to get

$$-x - 3 = 3x + 9,$$

so $4x + 12 = 0$, giving $x = -3$.

Since there are several steps in the solution, it is a good idea to check the answer. If $x = -3$, $2^{x+1} = 2^{-2} = \frac{1}{2^2} = \frac{1}{4}$, $4^{x+2} = 4^{-1} = \frac{1}{4}$ and $8^{x+3} = 8^0 = 1$. So the left side is equal to $\frac{1}{4} \div \frac{1}{4} = 1$, which agrees with the right side.

One application of negative indices is in writing down very small numbers. You probably know how to write very large numbers in standard form, or scientific notation. For example, it is easier to write the speed of light as 3.00×10^8 m s^{-1} than as 300 000 000 m s^{-1}. Similarly, the wavelength of red light, about 0.000 000 75 metres, is more easily appreciated written as 7.5×10^{-7} metres.

Computers and calculators often give users the option to work in scientific notation, and if numbers become too large (or too small) to be displayed in ordinary numerical form they will switch into standard form, for example 3.00E8 or 7.5E–7. The symbol E stands for **exponent**, yet another word for 'index'. You can write this in scientific notation by simply replacing the symbol E m by $\times\ 10^m$, for any integer m.

When you multiply or divide with numbers in standard form, the technique is to separate the powers of 10 from the rest of the expression to be evaluated, and to combine these using the rules for indices listed in Section 13.1.

At the end it may be necessary to make an adjustment to get the final answer in standard form. For example, if the calculation comes to 38.4×10^{-5}, you would write this as $(3.84 \times 10^1) \times 10^{-5}$, which is $3.84 \times (10^1 \times 10^{-5}) = 3.84 \times 10^{-4}$. If it comes to 0.093×10^{-3}, you would write it as $(9.3 \times 10^{-2}) \times 10^{-3}$, which is $9.3 \times (10^{-2} \times 10^{-3}) = 9.3 \times 10^{-5}$.

Example 13.2.6
Calculate the universal constant of gravitation, G, from $G = \frac{gR^2}{M}$ where, in SI units, $g \approx 9.81$, $R \approx 6.37 \times 10^6$ and $M \approx 5.97 \times 10^{24}$. ($R$ and M are the earth's radius and mass, and g is the acceleration due to gravity at the earth's surface.)

You can do this calculation directly with your calculator. If you enter the data in scientific mode, and key in the appropriate number of significant figures to retain, you will get the answer 6.67×10^{-11}.

The reasoning behind the calculation is as follows.

$$G \approx \frac{9.81 \times (6.37 \times 10^6)^2}{5.97 \times 10^{24}} = \frac{9.81 \times (6.37)^2}{5.97} \times \frac{(10^6)^2}{10^{24}}$$

$$\approx 66.7 \times \frac{10^{12}}{10^{24}} = 6.67 \times 10^1 \times 10^{-12} = 6.67 \times 10^{1-12} = 6.67 \times 10^{-11}.$$

Notice how, to get the correct power of 10, the number 66.7 has to be written as 6.67×10^1.

Exercise 13B

1 Express each of the following as an integer or a fraction.

(a) 2^{-3} (b) 4^{-2} (c) 5^{-1} (d) 3^{-2}

(e) 10^{-4} (f) 1^{-7} (g) $\left(\frac{1}{2}\right)^{-1}$ (h) $\left(\frac{1}{3}\right)^{-3}$

(i) $\left(2\frac{1}{2}\right)^{-1}$ (j) 2^{-7} (k) 6^{-3} (l) $\left(1\frac{1}{3}\right)^{-3}$

2 If $x = 2$, find the value of each of the following.

(a) $4x^{-3}$ (b) $(4x)^{-3}$ (c) $\frac{1}{4}x^{-3}$

(d) $\left(\frac{1}{4}x\right)^{-3}$ (e) $(4 \div x)^{-3}$ (f) $(x \div 4)^{-3}$

3 If $y = 5$, find the value of each of the following.

(a) $(2y)^{-1}$ (b) $2y^{-1}$ (c) $\left(\frac{1}{2}y\right)^{-1}$

(d) $\frac{1}{2}y^{-1}$ (e) $\dfrac{1}{(2y)^{-1}}$ (f) $\dfrac{2}{(y^{-1})^{-1}}$

4 Express each of the following in as simple a form as possible.

(a) $a^4 \times a^{-3}$ (b) $\dfrac{1}{b^{-1}}$ (c) $(c^{-2})^3$

(d) $d^{-1} \times 2d$ (e) $e^{-4} \times e^{-5}$ (f) $\dfrac{f^{-2}}{f^3}$

(g) $12g^3 \times (2g^2)^{-2}$ (h) $(3h^2)^{-2}$ (i) $(3i^{-2})^{-2}$

(j) $\left(\frac{1}{2}j^{-2}\right)^{-3}$ (k) $(2x^3y^{-1})^3$ (l) $(p^2q^4r^3)^{-4}$

(m) $(4m^2)^{-1} \times 8m^3$ (n) $(3n^{-2})^4 \times (9n)^{-1}$ (o) $(2q^{-2})^{-2} \div \left(\dfrac{4}{q}\right)^2$

5 Solve the following equations.

(a) $3^x = \frac{1}{9}$ (b) $5^y = 1$ (c) $2^z \times 2^{z-3} = 32$

(d) $7^{3x} \div 7^{x-2} = \frac{1}{49}$ (e) $4^y \times 2^y = 8^{120}$ (f) $3^t \times 9^{t+3} = 27^2$

6 The length of each edge of a cube is 3×10^{-2} metres.

(a) Find the volume of the cube. (b) Find the total surface area of the cube.

7 An athlete runs 2×10^{-1} km in 7.5×10^{-3} hours. Find her average speed in km h^{-1}.

8 The volume, V m^3, of l metres of wire is given by $V = \pi r^2 l$, where r metres is the radius of the circular cross-section.

(a) Find the volume of 80 m of wire with radius of cross-section 2×10^{-3} m.

(b) Another type of wire has radius of cross-section 5×10^{-3} m. What length of this wire has a volume of 8×10^{-3} m^3?

(c) Another type of wire is such that a length of 61 m has a volume of 6×10^{-3} m^3. Find the radius of the cross-section.

9 An equation which occurs in the study of waves is $y = \dfrac{\lambda d}{a}$.

(a) Calculate y when $\lambda = 7 \times 10^{-7}$, $d = 5 \times 10^{-1}$ and $a = 8 \times 10^{-4}$.

(b) Calculate λ when $y = 10^{-3}$, $d = 0.6$ and $a = 2.7 \times 10^{-4}$.

13.3 Fractional indices

Section 13.2 gave a meaning for the power a^m when m is any negative integer. It is possible to go further, and to find a meaning for a^m when m is any rational number.

Remember from Section 1.1 that a rational number is a number of the form $\dfrac{p}{q}$, where p and q are integers and q is not 0. For example, $\frac{3}{4}$, $\frac{8}{5}$ and $-\frac{7}{2}$ are rational numbers. The problem is to find a meaning for powers such as $a^{\frac{3}{4}}$, $a^{\frac{8}{5}}$ and $a^{-\frac{7}{2}}$.

To do this, suppose that the power-on-power rule can still be used if m is not an integer. For example, take $m = \frac{1}{2}$ and $n = 2$. Then the rule would give

$$\left(a^{\frac{1}{2}}\right)^2 = a^{\frac{1}{2}\times 2} = a^1, \quad \text{which is just } a.$$

So $a^{\frac{1}{2}}$ would be a number whose square is a.

There are only two numbers with this property, $+\sqrt{a}$ and $-\sqrt{a}$. Since in mathematics every symbol needs to have a definite meaning, a choice has to be made between these. So $a^{\frac{1}{2}}$ is defined to be the positive square root of a.

$$a^{\frac{1}{2}} = \sqrt{a}.$$

Now take $m = \frac{1}{3}$ and $n = 3$. The power-on-power rule then gives

$$\left(a^{\frac{1}{3}}\right)^3 = a^{\frac{1}{3}\times 3} = a^1 = a.$$

By the same reasoning as before, $a^{\frac{1}{3}}$ is the cube root of a. This time there is no ambiguity; each number has only one cube root.

$$a^{\frac{1}{3}} = \sqrt[3]{a}.$$

Notice that, for $a^{\frac{1}{2}} = \sqrt{a}$, the number a has to be positive or zero; $a^{\frac{1}{2}}$ has no meaning if a is negative. But for $a^{\frac{1}{3}} = \sqrt[3]{a}$, a can be positive, negative or zero; every number has a cube root.

Obviously the argument could be generalised to any rational number of the form $\frac{1}{q}$, using the power-on-power rule as

$$\left(a^{\frac{1}{q}}\right)^q = a^{\frac{1}{q}\times q} = a^1 = a.$$

So $a^{\frac{1}{q}}$ is the qth root of a. If q is even, $a^{\frac{1}{q}}$ is defined to be the positive qth root.

$$a^{\frac{1}{q}} = \sqrt[q]{a}.$$

Example 13.3.1

Express as simply as possible (a) $36^{\frac{1}{2}}$, (b) $\left(\frac{1}{8}\right)^{\frac{1}{3}}$, (c) $64^{-\frac{1}{2}}$.

(a) $36^{\frac{1}{2}} = \sqrt{36} = 6$.

(b) $\left(\frac{1}{8}\right)^{\frac{1}{3}} = \sqrt[3]{\frac{1}{8}} = \frac{1}{2}$.

(c) $64^{-\frac{1}{2}} = \dfrac{1}{64^{\frac{1}{2}}} = \frac{1}{8}$.

What about a power like $a^{\frac{2}{3}}$? You could find this by writing $\frac{2}{3}$ either as $\frac{1}{3} \times 2$ or as $2 \times \frac{1}{3}$ and using the power-on-power rule directly. This would give either

$$a^{\frac{2}{3}} = a^{\frac{1}{3}\times 2} = \left(a^{\frac{1}{3}}\right)^2 = \left(\sqrt[3]{a}\right)^2, \quad \text{or} \quad a^{\frac{2}{3}} = a^{2\times\frac{1}{3}} = (a^2)^{\frac{1}{3}} = \sqrt[3]{a^2}.$$

Both forms are equally valid. It makes no difference to the final answer whether you take the cube root first and then square, or square first and then take the cube root.

For practical calculation, the first form is the best to use if a has an exact cube root, and the second is best if it hasn't. For example, if you want to find $8^{\frac{2}{3}}$, it is slightly simpler to work out

$$8^{\frac{2}{3}} = \left(\sqrt[3]{8}\right)^2 = 2^2 = 4$$

than $8^{\frac{2}{3}} = \sqrt[3]{8^2} = \sqrt[3]{64} = 4$.

But if you want $7^{\frac{2}{3}}$,

$$7^{\frac{2}{3}} = \sqrt[3]{7^2} = \sqrt[3]{49} = 3.6593...$$

has the edge over

$$7^{\frac{2}{3}} = \left(\sqrt[3]{7}\right)^2 = (1.9129...)^2 = 3.6593....$$

By exactly the same reasoning, $a^{\frac{p}{q}}$ can be found either as

$$a^{\frac{p}{q}} = a^{\frac{1}{q}\times p} = \left(a^{\frac{1}{q}}\right)^p = \left(\sqrt[q]{a}\right)^p, \quad \text{or as} \quad a^{\frac{p}{q}} = a^{p\times\frac{1}{q}} = (a^p)^{\frac{1}{q}} = \sqrt[q]{a^p}.$$

This is the general form of the **fractional power rule**:

$$a^{\frac{p}{q}} = \left(\sqrt[q]{a}\,\right)^p = \sqrt[q]{a^p}.$$

Example 13.3.2

Simplify (a) $9^{\frac{5}{2}}$, (b) $3^{\frac{1}{2}} \times 3^{\frac{3}{2}}$, (c) $16^{-\frac{3}{4}}$.

(a) $9^{\frac{5}{2}} = \left(\sqrt{9}\right)^5 = 3^5 = 243.$

(b) $3^{\frac{1}{2}} \times 3^{\frac{3}{2}} = 3^{\frac{1}{2}+\frac{3}{2}} = 3^2 = 9.$

(c) **Method 1** $16^{-\frac{3}{4}} = (2^4)^{-\frac{3}{4}} = 2^{-3} = \frac{1}{8}.$

Method 2 $16^{-\frac{3}{4}} = \dfrac{1}{16^{\frac{3}{4}}} = \dfrac{1}{\left(\sqrt[4]{16}\right)^3} = \dfrac{1}{2^3} = \frac{1}{8}.$

There are often good alternative ways for solving problems involving indices, and you should try experimenting with them. Many people prefer to think with positive indices rather than negative ones; if you are one of them, writing $16^{-\frac{3}{4}} = \dfrac{1}{16^{\frac{3}{4}}}$, as in Method 2 of Example 13.3.2(c), makes good sense as a first step.

Example 13.3.3

Simplify (a) $\left(2\frac{1}{4}\right)^{-\frac{1}{2}}$, (b) $2x^{\frac{1}{2}} \times 3x^{-\frac{5}{2}}$, (c)$(2x^2y^{-4})^{\frac{1}{2}}$.

(a) $\left(2\frac{1}{4}\right)^{-\frac{1}{2}} = \left(\frac{9}{4}\right)^{-\frac{1}{2}} = \dfrac{1}{\left(\frac{9}{4}\right)^{\frac{1}{2}}} = \left(\frac{4}{9}\right)^{\frac{1}{2}} = \sqrt{\frac{4}{9}} = \frac{2}{3}.$

(b) $2x^{\frac{1}{2}} \times 3x^{-\frac{5}{2}} = 6x^{\frac{1}{2}-\frac{5}{2}} = 6x^{-2} = \dfrac{6}{x^2}.$

(c) Using the factor rule and then the power-on-power rule,

$$\begin{aligned}(2x^2y^{-4})^{\frac{1}{2}} &= 2^{\frac{1}{2}} \times (x^2)^{\frac{1}{2}} \times (y^{-4})^{\frac{1}{2}} \\ &= 2^{\frac{1}{2}} \times x^{2\times\frac{1}{2}} \times y^{-4\times\frac{1}{2}} \\ &= 2^{\frac{1}{2}} \times x^1 \times y^{-2} \\ &= \frac{x\sqrt{2}}{y^2}.\end{aligned}$$

In Example 13.3.3, the answer given to part (c) breaks the convention of writing numbers before letters. It is sometimes safer to write $x\sqrt{2}$ rather than $\sqrt{2}x$ to avoid possible confusion with $\sqrt{2x}$.

You will quite often need to use the fractional power rule in reverse, to convert expressions involving roots into index notation. This is illustrated by the next example.

Example 13.3.4

Write in index notation (a) $2x\sqrt{x}$, (b) $\dfrac{6}{\sqrt[3]{x}}$, (c) $\dfrac{1}{x^2\sqrt{x}}$.

(a) $2x\sqrt{x} = 2x^1 \times x^{\frac{1}{2}} = 2x^{1+\frac{1}{2}} = 2x^{\frac{3}{2}}.$

(b) $\dfrac{6}{\sqrt[3]{x}} = 6 \times \dfrac{1}{x^{\frac{1}{3}}} = 6x^{-\frac{1}{3}}.$

(c) $\dfrac{1}{x^2\sqrt{x}} = \dfrac{1}{x^2 \times x^{\frac{1}{2}}} = \dfrac{1}{x^{2+\frac{1}{2}}} = \dfrac{1}{x^{\frac{5}{2}}} = x^{-\frac{5}{2}}.$

13.4 Equations with rational indices

You have often solved equations such as $x^3 = 27$, $\sqrt{x} = 5$ and $\dfrac{1}{x} = 20$. But you probably have not realised that these are all equations of the same type, since they can all be written as $x^n = A$, with n equal to 3, $\frac{1}{2}$ and -1 respectively.

Here is a rather more complicated equation of the same type.

Example 13.4.1
Find x if $x^{\frac{3}{4}} = 27$.

If $x^{\frac{3}{4}}$ is raised to the power $\frac{4}{3}$, the power-on-power rule gives

$$\left(x^{\frac{3}{4}}\right)^{\frac{4}{3}} = x^{\frac{3}{4}\times\frac{4}{3}} = x^1 = x.$$

So the given equation can be solved by raising both sides to the power $\frac{4}{3}$. This gives

$$x = 27^{\frac{4}{3}} = \left(\sqrt[3]{27}\right)^4 = 3^4 = 81.$$

As a check, if $x = 81$, then $x^{\frac{3}{4}} = 81^{\frac{3}{4}} = \left(\sqrt[4]{81}\right)^3 = 3^3 = 27$.

The method used in this example can be used to solve any equation of the form $x^n = A$. Raising both sides to the power $\dfrac{1}{n}$ gives

$$(x^n)^{\frac{1}{n}} = A^{\frac{1}{n}}.$$

Since $(x^n)^{\frac{1}{n}} = x^{n\times\frac{1}{n}} = x^1 = x$, the solution of the equation is $x = A^{\frac{1}{n}}$.

Applying this to the three equations at the beginning of this section gives the solutions $27^{\frac{1}{3}} = 3$, $5^2 = 25$ and $20^{-1} = \frac{1}{20}$.

But you may have noticed a snag. If n is equal to 2, then $A^{\frac{1}{2}} = \sqrt{A}$ is only one of the roots of the equation $x^2 = A$; assuming that A is positive, there are two roots of the equation, $A^{\frac{1}{2}}$ and $-A^{\frac{1}{2}}$. The same happens if n is any even integer, or if it is a fraction with an even numerator such as $\frac{2}{3}$ or $\frac{4}{5}$. So to make this into a general rule it would be safer to restrict it to positive values of x and A.

> If n is a rational number and $A > 0$, the positive solution of the equation $x^n = A$ is $x = A^{\frac{1}{n}}$.

Example 13.4.2
Solve the equation $x^{\frac{3}{2}} = 10$, for $x > 0$, giving your answer correct to 3 significant figures.

If $n = \frac{3}{2}$, then $\dfrac{1}{n} = \frac{2}{3}$. The solution of the equation is therefore

$x = 10^{\frac{2}{3}} = \sqrt[3]{10^2} = \sqrt[3]{100} = 4.64$, correct to 3 significant figures.

Section 10.6 introduced some equations which were not obviously quadratic, but could be converted to quadratic form by by making a suitable substitution. For example, the equation $\sqrt{x} = 6 - x$ became $y = 6 - y^2$ after writing $\sqrt{x}$ as y.

Equations like this sometimes appear in index form. For example, $\sqrt{x} = 6 - x$ might turn up as $x^{\frac{1}{2}} = 6 - x$, You would then solve it by writing $x^{\frac{1}{2}} = y$, so that $x = y^2$.

Example 13.4.3
Solve the equation $5x^{\frac{1}{3}} = x^{\frac{2}{3}} + 4$.

The key is to notice that $x^{\frac{2}{3}} = (x^{\frac{1}{3}})^2$. So if you write $x^{\frac{1}{3}}$ as u, the equation is

$$5u = u^2 + 4,$$

a quadratic equation for u. Writing this as

$$u^2 - 5u + 4 = 0,$$
$$(u-1)(u-4) = 0,$$

the roots for u are 1 and 4.

Since the values of x are required, it is now necessary to solve for x the equations

$$x^{\frac{1}{3}} = 1 \quad \text{and} \quad x^{\frac{1}{3}} = 4.$$

This gives two roots for x,

$$x = 1^3 = 1 \quad \text{and} \quad x = 4^3 = 64.$$

13.5 Powers of negative bases

So far in this chapter it has been assumed that the base a is a positive number. This section investigates whether the negative and fractional power rules still apply if the base is a negative number.

You have often used positive integer powers with negative bases. For example,

$$(-5)^2 = (-5) \times (-5) = +5^2, (-5)^3 = (-5) \times (-5) \times (-5) = -5^3, \text{ and so on.}$$

There is no problem in extending this to negative integer indices. For example,

$$(-5)^{-2} = \frac{1}{(-5)^2} = \frac{1}{5^2} = +5^{-2}, (-5)^{-3} = \frac{1}{(-5)^3} = \frac{1}{-5^3} = -\frac{1}{5^3} = -5^{-3}, \text{ and so on.}$$

You can sum up these results in a single rule:

> If m is an integer (positive, negative or zero), and a is a positive number, then
>
> $$(-a)^m = \begin{cases} +a^m \text{ if } m \text{ is an even integer or zero,} \\ -a^m \text{ if } m \text{ is an odd integer.} \end{cases}$$

The situation is different when m is a fractional index. For example, taking a to be -64, you can write $(-64)^{\frac{1}{3}} = -4$. This is because $a^{\frac{1}{3}} = \sqrt[3]{a}$, and $(-4)^3 = -64$, so that $\sqrt[3]{-64} = -4$. But $(-64)^{\frac{1}{2}}$ has no meaning, because $a^{\frac{1}{2}} = \sqrt{a}$, and a negative number doesn't have a square root.

You can reason similarly for any index of the form $\frac{1}{q}$, and sum the results up in another rule:

If q is an integer, either positive or negative but not zero, and a is a positive number, then

$$(-a)^{\frac{1}{q}} = \begin{cases} \text{has no meaning if } q \text{ is even,} \\ -a^{\frac{1}{q}} \text{ if } q \text{ is odd.} \end{cases}$$

Example 13.5.1

Find, where possible, (a) $(-8)^{\frac{1}{3}}$, (b) $(-32)^{-\frac{1}{5}}$, (c) $(-81)^{\frac{1}{4}}$.

(a) $(-8)^{\frac{1}{3}} = \sqrt[3]{-8} = -2$, because $(-2)^3 = -8$.

(b) $(-32)^{-\frac{1}{5}} = \dfrac{1}{(-32)^{\frac{1}{5}}} = \dfrac{1}{-32^{\frac{1}{5}}} = -\frac{1}{2}$,

(c) $(-81)^{\frac{1}{4}}$ has no meaning; $\sqrt[4]{-81}$ doesn't exist, because there is no number x such that $x^4 = -81$.

What about other fractional powers? Here the situation is a bit more complicated, but a few numerical examples will illustrate the possibilities.

Example 13.5.2

Find, where possible,

(a) $(-27)^{\frac{2}{3}}$, (b) $(-16)^{\frac{3}{4}}$, (c) $(-8)^{\frac{5}{3}}$, (d) $(-32)^{-\frac{3}{5}}$, (e) $(-125)^{-\frac{2}{3}}$.

(a) $(-27)^{\frac{2}{3}}$ is $\left(\sqrt[3]{-27}\right)^2 = (-3)^2 = 9$.

(b) $(-16)^{\frac{3}{4}}$ would be $\left(\sqrt[4]{-16}\right)^3$; but since $\sqrt[4]{-16}$ does not exist, neither does $(-16)^{\frac{3}{4}}$.

(c) $(-8)^{\frac{5}{3}}$ is $\left(\sqrt[3]{-8}\right)^5 = (-2)^5 = -32$.

(d) $(-32)^{-\frac{3}{5}} = \dfrac{1}{(-32)^{\frac{3}{5}}}$, which is $\dfrac{1}{\left(\sqrt[5]{-32}\right)^3} = \dfrac{1}{(-2)^3} = \dfrac{1}{-8} = -\frac{1}{8}$.

(e) $(-125)^{-\frac{2}{3}} = \dfrac{1}{(-125)^{\frac{2}{3}}}$, which is $\dfrac{1}{\left(\sqrt[3]{-125}\right)^2} = \dfrac{1}{(-5)^2} = \frac{1}{25}$.

You can see from this example that, when the expression has a meaning, the answer is sometimes positive and sometimes negative.

Exercise 13C

1 Evaluate the following without using a calculator.

(a) $25^{\frac{1}{2}}$ (b) $8^{\frac{1}{3}}$ (c) $36^{\frac{1}{2}}$ (d) $32^{\frac{1}{5}}$

(e) $81^{\frac{1}{4}}$ (f) $9^{-\frac{1}{2}}$ (g) $16^{-\frac{1}{4}}$ (h) $49^{-\frac{1}{2}}$

(i) $32^{\frac{2}{5}}$ (j) $32^{\frac{3}{5}}$ (k) $64^{-\frac{5}{6}}$ (l) $4^{2\frac{1}{2}}$

(m) $1000^{-\frac{1}{3}}$ (n) $(-27)^{\frac{1}{3}}$ (o) $64^{\frac{2}{3}}$ (p) $(-125)^{-\frac{4}{3}}$

(q) $10\,000^{-\frac{3}{4}}$ (r) $\left(\frac{1}{125}\right)^{-\frac{4}{3}}$ (s) $\left(3\frac{3}{8}\right)^{\frac{2}{3}}$ (t) $\left(2\frac{1}{4}\right)^{-\frac{1}{2}}$

2 Evaluate the following without using a calculator.

(a) $4^{\frac{1}{2}}$ (b) $\left(\frac{1}{4}\right)^2$ (c) $\left(\frac{1}{4}\right)^{-2}$ (d) $4^{-\frac{1}{2}}$

(e) $\left(\frac{1}{4}\right)^{-\frac{1}{2}}$ (f) $\left(\frac{1}{4}\right)^{\frac{1}{2}}$ (g) $(4^4)^{\frac{1}{2}}$ (h) $\left(\left(\frac{1}{4}\right)^{\frac{1}{4}}\right)^2$

3 Simplify the following expressions.

(a) $a^{\frac{1}{3}} \times a^{\frac{5}{3}}$ (b) $3b^{\frac{1}{2}} \times 4b^{-\frac{3}{2}}$ (c) $\left(6c^{\frac{1}{4}}\right) \times (4c)^{\frac{1}{2}}$

(d) $(d^2)^{\frac{1}{3}} \div \left(d^{\frac{1}{3}}\right)^2$ (e) $(24e)^{\frac{1}{3}} \div (3e)^{\frac{1}{3}}$ (f) $\left(25p^2q^4\right)^{\frac{1}{2}}$

4 Solve the following equations, given that $x > 0$.

(a) $x^{\frac{1}{2}} = 8$ (b) $x^{\frac{1}{3}} = 3$ (c) $x^{\frac{2}{3}} = 4$ (d) $x^{\frac{3}{2}} = 27$

(e) $x^{-\frac{3}{2}} = 8$ (f) $x^{-\frac{2}{3}} = 9$ (g) $x^{\frac{3}{2}} = x\sqrt{2}$ (h) $x^{\frac{3}{2}} = 2\sqrt{x}$

5 The time, T seconds, taken by a pendulum of length l metres to complete one swing is given by $T = 2\pi l^{\frac{1}{2}} g^{-\frac{1}{2}}$ where $g \approx 9.81$ m s^{-2}.

(a) Find the value of T for a pendulum of length 0.9 metres.

(b) Find the length of a pendulum which takes 3 seconds for a complete swing.

6 The radius, r cm, of a sphere of volume V cm^3 is given by $r = \left(\frac{3V}{4\pi}\right)^{\frac{1}{3}}$. Find the radius of a sphere of volume 1150 cm^3.

7 Solve the following equations.

(a) $4^x = 32$ (b) $9^y = \frac{1}{27}$ (c) $16^z = 2$ (d) $100^x = 1000$

(e) $8^y = 16$ (f) $8^z = \frac{1}{128}$ (g) $(2^t)^3 \times 4^{t-1} = 16$

8 Solve the following equations.

(a) $x^{\frac{1}{2}} + 2x^{-\frac{1}{2}} = 3$ (b) $x + x^{\frac{1}{2}} = 12$ (c) $1 + x = 2x^{\frac{1}{2}}$

(d) $x^{\frac{2}{3}} = 2x^{\frac{1}{3}}$ (e) $x^{\frac{2}{3}} = 2x^{-\frac{1}{3}}$ (f) $2x^{\frac{1}{3}} + x^{\frac{2}{3}} = 3$

9 Rewrite the following expressions using index notation.

(a) $\frac{1}{\sqrt{x}}$ (b) $4\sqrt{x}$ (c) $\sqrt{4x}$ (d) $3x^2\sqrt{x}$ (e) $\frac{1}{\sqrt[3]{x^2}}$

10 Simplify the following by using index notation. Give your final answers in surd form.

(a) $\sqrt[3]{4} \times \sqrt[3]{6}$ (b) $\frac{\sqrt{50}}{\sqrt[3]{250}}$ (c) $\sqrt[6]{\frac{2}{3}} \times \sqrt[3]{18}$

11 (a) Without using a calculator, state which of these expressions has a value when $x = -64$. Find this value when it exists.

(i) $x^{\frac{2}{3}}$ (ii) $x^{\frac{3}{2}}$ (iii) $x^{-\frac{1}{3}}$

(iv) $\left(\frac{1}{2}x\right)^{\frac{4}{5}}$ (v) $x^{\frac{1}{6}}$ (vi) $(4x)^{\frac{3}{4}}$

(b) Investigate whether your calculator gives the answers you obtained in part (a).

(c) What can you say about p or q if $x^{\frac{p}{q}}$ has a value when x is negative?

14 Graphs of *n*th power functions

In this chapter the work of Chapters 8 and 11 is extended to include graphs with equations $y = x^n$ where n is any rational number. When you have completed it, you should

- be familiar with the shapes of these graphs, particularly when n is either a negative integer or $\frac{1}{2}$
- know that the rule for differentiating x^n is valid when n is any rational number.

14.1 Graphs of negative integer powers

In Section 8.3 you investigated the shapes of graphs with equations $y = x^n$ for positive integer values of n. You can now extend the investigation to negative values of n.

A negative integer n can be written as $-m$, where m is a positive integer. Then x^n becomes x^{-m}, or $\frac{1}{x^m}$.

It is simplest to begin with the part of the graph for which x is positive, then to use this to extend the graph for negative x.

Figure 8.4 showed the graphs of $y = x^n$ for $x \geq 0$ when n is 1, 2, 3 and 4. These graphs are reproduced here as Fig. 14.1.

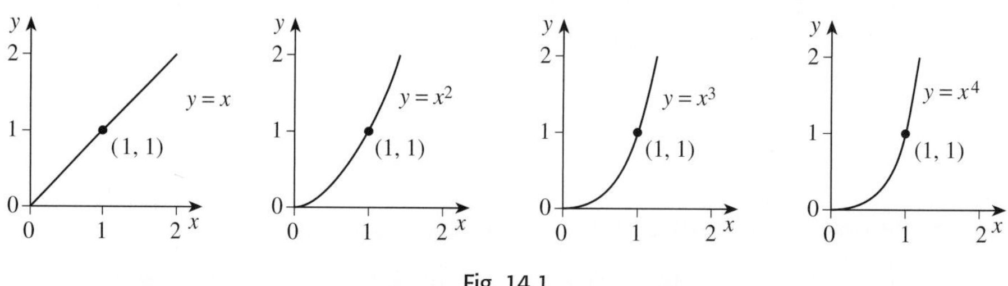

Fig. 14.1

All these graphs are in the first quadrant when $x > 0$, and they all include the origin and the point (1, 1).

When x is positive, $\frac{1}{x^m}$ is also positive, so the graphs of $y = x^{-m}$ are also in the first quadrant when $x > 0$. Also, just as when n is positive, the graphs include the point (1, 1).

But there is an important difference when $x = 0$, since then $x^m = 0$ and $\frac{1}{x^m}$ is not defined. So there is no point on these graphs for which $x = 0$.

To look at this more closely, take a value of x close to 0, say 0.01. Then for $n = -1$ the corresponding value of y is $0.01^{-1} = \frac{1}{0.01^1} = \frac{1}{0.01} = 100$; and for $n = -2$ it is $0.01^{-2} = \frac{1}{0.01^2} = \frac{1}{0.0001} = 10\,000$. Even if you use a very small scale, the graphs will disappear off the top of the page or the calculator window as x is reduced towards 0.

What happens if x is large? For example, take $x = 100$. Then for $n = -1$ the corresponding value of y is $100^{-1} = \frac{1}{100^1} = \frac{1}{100} = 0.01$; and for $n = -2$ it is $100^{-2} = \frac{1}{100^2} = \frac{1}{10\,000} = 0.0001$ So x^n becomes very small, and the graphs come very close to the x-axis.

These are the main things you need to know to draw the graphs for positive values of x. They are shown in Fig. 14.2 for $n = -1$, -2, -3 and -4.

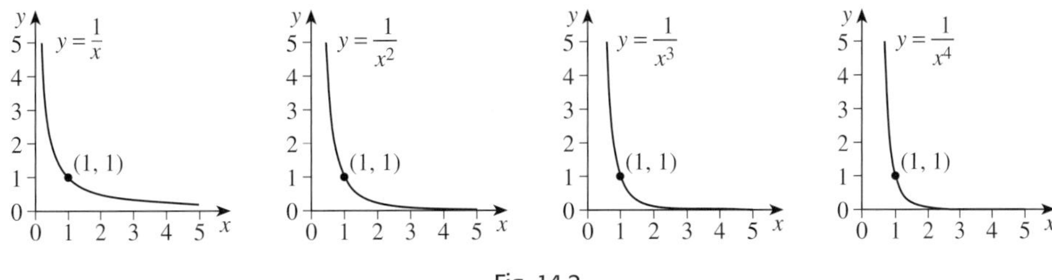

Fig. 14.2

Now consider the part of the graphs for which x is negative. You found in Chapter 8 that, for positive n, this depends on whether n is odd or even. The same is true when n is negative, and for the same reason. If n is even, x^n is an even function and its graph is symmetrical about the y-axis. If n is odd, x^n is an odd function and its graph is symmetrical about the origin.

Fig. 14.3 shows the graphs of $y = x^{-1}$ and $y = x^{-2}$ extended in this way, for all values of x except 0. Notice that, for both graphs, the x- and y-axes are asymptotes.

Try sketching for yourself the corresponding graphs of $y = x^{-3}$ and $y = x^{-4}$. Then use a calculator to check your sketches.

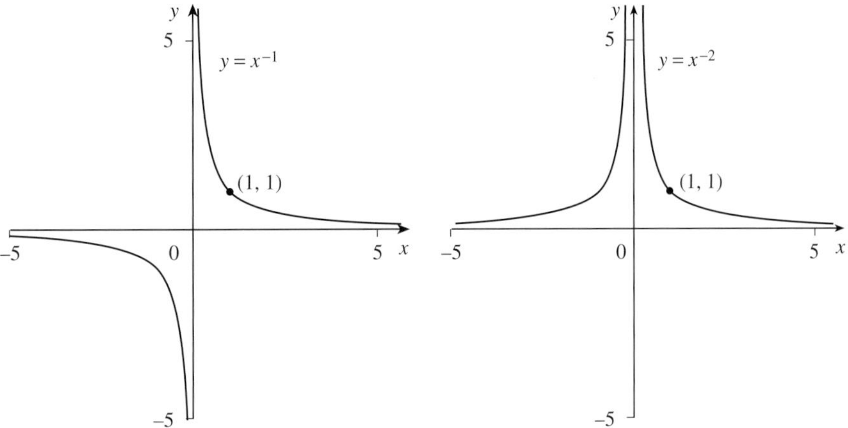

Fig. 14.3

14.2 Differentiation with negative integer indices

In Chapter 11 you found that, for positive integer powers of x, the derivative of $f(x) = x^n$ is $f'(x) = nx^{n-1}$. An obvious question to ask is whether this is still true when n is a negative integer.

You could investigate this in a number of ways:

- using the evidence of the graphs
- with a numerical check
- by algebraic proof of particular cases.

The three examples which follow illustrate each of these in turn, for the cases $n = -1$ and $n = -2$. If the rule still holds when n is negative, the derivatives would be as follows.

$$n = -1\text{: if } y = x^{-1} = \frac{1}{x}, \text{ then } \frac{dy}{dx} = -1 \times x^{-2} = -\frac{1}{x^2}.$$

$$n = -2\text{: if } y = x^{-2} = \frac{1}{x^2}, \text{ then } \frac{dy}{dx} = -2 \times x^{-3} = -\frac{2}{x^3}.$$

Example 14.2.1
Find whether the suggested differentiation rules are consistent with the graphs

(a) when $n = -1$, (b) when $n = -2$.

Some calculators are able, once you have displayed the graph of $y = f(x)$, to show with the same axes the graph of $y = f'(x)$. So for part (a), if you key in $y_1 = \frac{1}{x}$, $y_2 = \frac{dy_1}{dx}$ (consult the manual to find how to do this) and $y_3 = -\frac{1}{x^2}$, you can see whether y_2 and y_3 are the same graph. For part (b) do the same thing with $y_1 = \frac{1}{x^2}$ and $y_3 = -\frac{2}{x^3}$.

Alternatively, you can argue less precisely as follows. Note first that, for both graphs in Fig. 14.3, the gradient is very steep when x is close to 0, and very gentle when x is a long way from 0. This is in line with the expressions suggested for $\frac{dy}{dx}$ for both $n = -1$ and $n = -2$.

(a) If $y = x^{-1}$, Fig. 14.3 shows that the gradient of the graph is negative both when x is positive and when x is negative. This is consistent with the suggested derivative $\frac{dy}{dx} = -\frac{1}{x^2}$, which is negative both when $x > 0$ and when $x < 0$.

(b) If $y = x^{-2}$, Fig. 14.3 shows that the gradient of the graph is negative when x is positive, and positive when x is negative. This is consistent with the suggested derivative $\frac{dy}{dx} = -\frac{2}{x^3}$, which is negative when $x > 0$ but positive when $x < 0$.

Example 14.2.2

Make a numerical estimate of the gradient of the tangent to $y = \dfrac{1}{x^2}$ at the point $(2, 0.25)$, and check that this agrees with the value given by the rule $\dfrac{\mathrm{d}y}{\mathrm{d}x} = -\dfrac{2}{x^3}$.

From Fig. 14.3, you would expect the gradient of the tangent to be less than the gradient of a chord to the right of $(2, 0.25)$, and greater than the gradient of a chord to the left. (Note that all these gradients are negative.)

Take first the chord joining $(2, 0.25)$ to $(2.01, 0.247\,51\ldots)$. For this chord,

$$\delta x = 2.01 - 2 = 0.01, \quad \delta y = 0.247\,51\ldots - 0.25 = -0.002\,48\ldots,$$

and $$\frac{\delta y}{\delta x} = \frac{-0.002\,48\ldots}{0.01} = -0.248\ldots.$$

Now take the chord joining $(2, 0.25)$ to $(1.99, 0.252\,51\ldots)$. For this chord,

$$\delta x = 1.99 - 2 = -0.01, \quad \delta y = 0.252\,51\ldots - 0.25 = 0.002\,51\ldots,$$

and $$\frac{\delta y}{\delta x} = \frac{0.002\,51\ldots}{-0.01} = -0.251\ldots.$$

So the gradient of the tangent is less than $-0.248\ldots$ and greater than $-0.251\ldots$. A reasonable guess is that the gradient is -0.25.

When $x = 2$, the suggested derivative $-\dfrac{2}{x^3} = -\dfrac{2}{2^3} = -0.25$. So the numerical estimate supports the value given by the differentiation rule.

You could use the derivative program on a calculator to do a numerical check for some other values of x and some other negative powers.

Using the algebraic definition of $f'(x)$ given in Section 11.6 is not so easy with negative powers. Example 14.2.3 does this for the simplest case, $n = -1$, but you may leave this out if you want to.

Example 14.2.3*

Find the derivative of $f(x) = \dfrac{1}{x}$ using the definition $f'(x) = \lim\limits_{h \to 0} \dfrac{f(x+h) - f(x)}{h}$.

Begin by finding

$$f(x+h) - f(x) = \frac{1}{x+h} - \frac{1}{x}.$$

To simplify this, you must write both fractions with the same denominator.

$$\begin{aligned} \frac{1}{x+h} - \frac{1}{x} &= \frac{x}{x(x+h)} - \frac{x+h}{x(x+h)} \\ &= \frac{x-(x+h)}{x(x+h)} \\ &= \frac{-h}{x(x+h)}. \end{aligned}$$

So $$\frac{f(x+h) - f(x)}{h} = \frac{-1}{x(x+h)}.$$

You now want to find the limit of this as $h \to 0$. The only place where h appears is inside the bracket, and the limit of $x + h$ is simply x. It follows that

$$f'(x) = \lim_{h \to 0} \frac{f(x+h) - f(x)}{h}$$
$$= \frac{-1}{x \times x} = \frac{-1}{x^2}.$$

The results of these examples don't add up to a proof that the differentiation rule works with all negative integer indices, but the evidence is encouraging. It is in fact correct, but it is not possible to give a proof at this stage.

If you write $n = -m$, so that $f(x) = x^{-m} = \frac{1}{x^m}$, the rule gives $f'(x) = -mx^{-m-1} = -\frac{m}{x^{m+1}}$.

If $f(x) = \frac{1}{x^m}$, where m is a positive integer, then

$$f'(x) = -\frac{m}{x^{m+1}}.$$

There is no need to learn this as a separate rule. In any particular case you can just use $f'(x) = nx^{n-1}$ with a negative value for n. But after some practice you will probably find yourself using it without thinking.

Example 14.2.4

Find $\frac{dy}{dx}$ if (a) $y = \frac{2}{x^4}$, (b) $y = \frac{1}{5x^5}$, (c) $y = \frac{x-3}{x^2}$.

(a) Write y as $2 \times \frac{1}{x^4} = 2x^{-4}$.

Then $\frac{dy}{dx} = 2 \times (-4x^{-5}) = -8x^{-5} = -\frac{8}{x^5}$.

(b) Write y as $\frac{1}{5} \times \frac{1}{x^5} = \frac{1}{5}x^{-5}$.

Then $\frac{dy}{dx} = \frac{1}{5} \times (-5x^{-6}) = -x^{-6} = -\frac{1}{x^6}$.

(c) Split the function as $y = \frac{x}{x^2} - \frac{3}{x^2} = \frac{1}{x} - \frac{3}{x^2} = x^{-1} - 3x^{-2}$.

Then $\frac{dy}{dx} = -x^{-2} + 6x^{-3} = -\frac{1}{x^2} + \frac{6}{x^3}$.

You may sometimes want to write this as a single fraction, as in the original equation.

$$\frac{dy}{dx} = -\frac{x}{x^3} + \frac{6}{x^3} = \frac{-x+6}{x^3} = \frac{6-x}{x^3}.$$

Example 14.2.5

(a) Find the equation of the normal to $y = \dfrac{1}{x}$ at the point $\left(\frac{1}{2}, 2\right)$.

(b) Find where this normal cuts the curve again.

(a) It helps to accompany the solution with a sketch (Fig. 14.4), and to use it to give a rough check of the accuracy of the calculations as you go on.

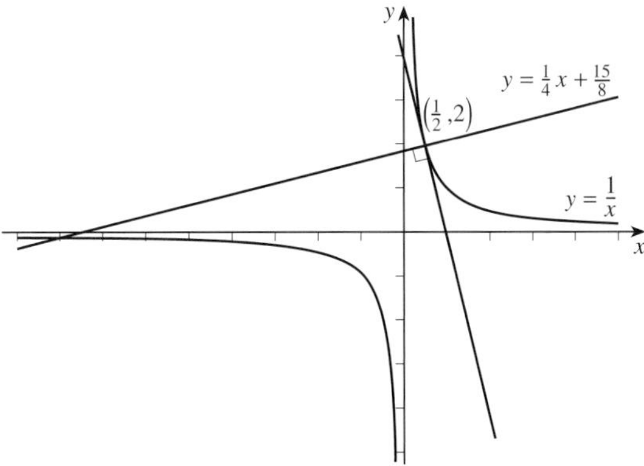

Fig. 14.4

Since $\dfrac{dy}{dx} = -\dfrac{1}{x^2}$, the gradient of the tangent at $\left(\frac{1}{2}, 2\right)$ is $-\dfrac{1}{\left(\frac{1}{2}\right)^2} = -4$. The gradient of the normal is therefore, by the rule in Section 7.4, $-\dfrac{1}{-4} = \frac{1}{4}$.

The equation of the normal is

$$y - 2 = \tfrac{1}{4}\left(x - \tfrac{1}{2}\right),$$

or more simply $y = \frac{1}{4}x + \frac{15}{8}$.

(b) To find where the normal meets the curve again, equate the values of y in the two equations to get

$$\frac{1}{x} = \tfrac{1}{4}x + \tfrac{15}{8}.$$

Multiplying this by $8x$ and rearranging the terms produces the quadratic equation

$$2x^2 + 15x - 8 = 0.$$

The factors of the left side may not be immediately obvious. But remember that you already know one root, $x = \frac{1}{2}$, because the normal certainly cuts the curve at $\left(\frac{1}{2}, 2\right)$. So $2x - 1$ must be one factor. It is then easy to see that the left side factorises to give

$$(2x - 1)(x + 8) = 0.$$

The other intersection is therefore where $x = -8$. Substituting this in $y = \dfrac{1}{x}$ gives the y-coordinate of the point of intersection as $y = \dfrac{1}{-8} = -\frac{1}{8}$. (You could equally well substitute in $y = \frac{1}{4}x + \frac{15}{8}$, but the arithmetic is harder.)

The normal meets the curve again at $\left(-8, -\frac{1}{8}\right)$.

Exercise 14A

1 Find the point(s) of intersection of these pairs of graphs. Check your answers with a calculator.

(a) $y = x^2,\ y = 8x^{-1}$ (b) $y = x^{-1},\ y = 3x^{-2}$ (c) $y = x,\ y = 4x^{-3}$

(d) $y = 8x^{-2},\ y = 2x^{-4}$ (e) $y = 9x^{-3},\ y = x^{-5}$ (f) $y = \frac{1}{4}x^4,\ y = 16x^{-2}$

2 For what values of x are these inequalities satisfied? Sketch graphs illustrating your answers.

(a) $0 < x^{-3} < 0.001$ (b) $x^{-2} < 0.0004$ (c) $x^{-4} \geq 100$ (d) $8x^{-4} < 0.000\,05$

3 Three graphs have equations (p) $y = x^{-2}$, (q) $y = x^{-3}$, (r) $y = x^{-4}$.

A line $x = k$ meets the three graphs at points P, Q and R, respectively. Give the order of the points P, Q and R on the line (from the bottom up) when k takes the following values.

(a) 2 (b) $\frac{1}{2}$ (c) $-\frac{1}{2}$ (d) -2

4 Differentiate each of the following functions. For each part, give your answer in two forms: the first using a negative index, and the second with a positive index.

(a) x^{-2} (b) x^{-5} (c) $3x^{-3}$

(d) $-2x^{-2}$ (e) $\frac{1}{4}x^{-4}$ (f) $-\frac{1}{3}x^{-6}$

5 Differentiate each of these functions $f(x)$. Give your answers $f'(x)$ in a similar form, without negative indices.

(a) $\frac{5}{x}$ (b) $\frac{1}{4x}$ (c) $\frac{3}{x^2}$

(d) x^0 (e) $\frac{3}{x} + \frac{1}{3x^3}$ (f) $\frac{x-2}{x^2}$

6 Find the equation of the tangent to the curve at the given point.

(a) $y = \frac{4}{x}$ at $(1, 4)$ (b) $y = \frac{1}{x^2}$ at $(1, 1)$ (c) $y = \frac{1}{3x^2}$ at $\left(\frac{1}{3}, 3\right)$

(d) $y = x + \frac{9}{x}$ at $(3, 6)$ (e) $y = \frac{1-x}{x^3}$ at $(1, 0)$ (f) $y = \frac{x^2-4}{x^3}$ at $(-2, 0)$

7 Find the equation of the normal to the curve at the given point.

(a) $y = \frac{4}{x^2}$ at $(2, 1)$ (b) $y = \frac{1}{2x^4}$ at $\left(1, \frac{1}{2}\right)$

(c) $y = x^2 + \frac{16}{x^2}$ at $(2, 8)$ (d) $y = \frac{x+2}{x^3}$ at $(-1, -1)$

14.3 Graphs of $y = x^n$ for fractional n

When fractional values of n are included, the graphs of $y = x^n$ have many different possible shapes. One new feature is that, when n is a fraction, the function x^n may or may not be defined for negative values of x. For example, $x^{\frac{1}{3}}$ (the cube root of x) and $x^{-\frac{4}{5}}$ have values when $x < 0$, but $x^{\frac{1}{2}}$ (the square root of x) and $x^{-\frac{3}{4}}$ do not. Even when x^n is defined for negative x, some calculators are not programmed to do the calculation. So it is simplest to concentrate on values of $x \geq 0$.

Much the most important of these graphs is that of $y = x^{\frac{1}{2}}$, or $y = \sqrt{x}$. The clue to finding the shape of this graph is to note that if $y = x^{\frac{1}{2}}$, then $x = y^2$. The graph can therefore be obtained from that of $y = x^2$ by swapping the x- and y-axes. This has the effect of tipping the graph on its side, so it faces to the right instead of upwards.

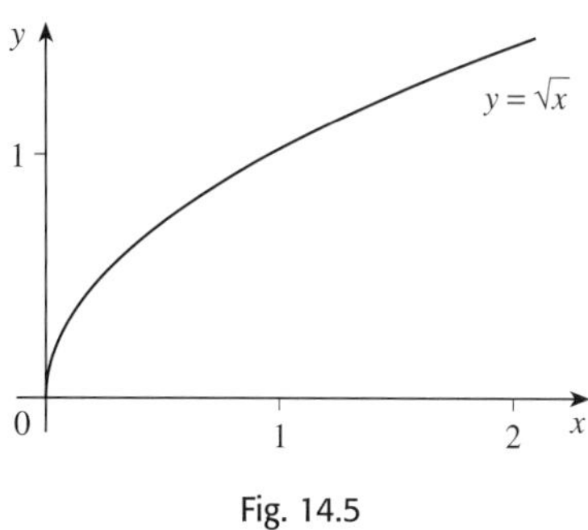

Fig. 14.5

But this is not quite the whole story. If $x = y^2$, then either $y = +\sqrt{x}$ or $y = -\sqrt{x}$. Since you want only the first of these possibilities, you must remove the part of the graph of $x = y^2$ below the x-axis, leaving only the part shown in Fig. 14.5 as the graph of $y = x^{\frac{1}{2}}$, or $y = \sqrt{x}$.

Notice that the graph exists only for $x \geq 0$, as you would expect. The tangent to the graph at the origin is the y-axis.

It is worth experimenting for yourself with various other fractional powers, using your calculator. You will find that:

- it is still true that the graph of $y = x^n$ contains the point $(1, 1)$;
- if n is positive it also contains the point $(0, 0)$;
- if $n > 1$ the x-axis is a tangent to the graph; if $0 < n < 1$ the y-axis is a tangent. (To show this convincingly you may need to zoom in to display an enlarged version of the graph close to the origin.)

To illustrate the variety of shapes which are possible when both positive and negative values of x are included, Fig. 14.6 shows six graphs with equation $y = x^n$ where n is a positive fraction.

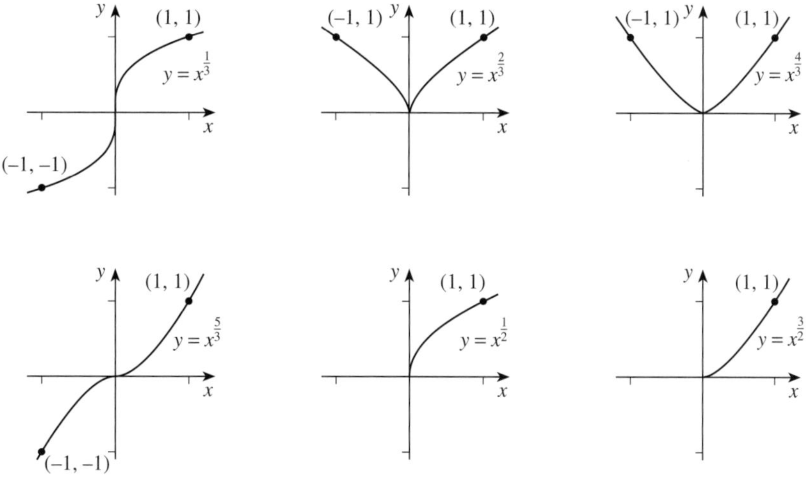

Fig. 14.6

14.4 The differentiation rule with fractional indices

You will probably not be surprised that the differentiation rule for $y = x^n$ still holds when the index n is a fraction.

Example 14.4.1

Assuming the usual differentiation rule, find $\frac{dy}{dx}$ when

(a) $y = \sqrt{x}$, (b) $y = x\sqrt{x}$, (c) $y = \frac{1}{\sqrt{x}}$.

(a) Since $\sqrt{x} = x^{\frac{1}{2}}$, the rule $\frac{dy}{dx} = nx^{n-1}$ gives $\frac{dy}{dx} = \frac{1}{2}x^{-\frac{1}{2}}$.

In surd notation, $x^{-\frac{1}{2}} = \frac{1}{x^{\frac{1}{2}}} = \frac{1}{\sqrt{x}}$. So $\frac{dy}{dx} = \frac{1}{2} \times \frac{1}{\sqrt{x}} = \frac{1}{2\sqrt{x}}$.

(b) In index notation, $x\sqrt{x} = x^1 \times x^{\frac{1}{2}} = x^{\frac{3}{2}}$.
So $\frac{dy}{dx} = \frac{3}{2}x^{\frac{1}{2}} = \frac{3}{2}\sqrt{x}$.

(c) In index notation, $\frac{1}{\sqrt{x}} = x^{-\frac{1}{2}}$.
So $\frac{dy}{dx} = -\frac{1}{2}x^{-\frac{3}{2}} = -\frac{1}{2} \times \frac{1}{x\sqrt{x}} = -\frac{1}{2x\sqrt{x}}$.

The proof of the differentiation rule with fractional indices is too difficult to give at this stage. You can, of course, check it for any particular function as in Examples 14.2.1 and 14.2.2, and it would be worth doing this using the derivative program on your calculator. But you should by now have seen enough examples to justify using the general rule for any rational power of x, positive or negative.

> If $f(x) = x^n$, where n is a rational number, then $f'(x) = nx^{n-1}$.

Compare this with the similar statement in the box in Section 11.4, which was restricted to positive integer values of n.

Example 14.4.2

Find the equation of the tangent to $y = \sqrt[3]{x}$ at the point (8, 2).

In index notation $\sqrt[3]{x} = x^{\frac{1}{3}}$. So the rule gives $\frac{dy}{dx} = \frac{1}{3}x^{(\frac{1}{3}-1)} = \frac{1}{3}x^{-\frac{2}{3}}$.

In surd notation this is $\frac{1}{3(\sqrt[3]{x})^2}$.

The gradient of the tangent at (8, 2) is therefore $\frac{1}{3(\sqrt[3]{8})^2} = \frac{1}{3 \times 2^2} = \frac{1}{12}$.

Thus the equation of the tangent is

$$y - 2 = \tfrac{1}{12}(x - 8), \text{ which is } 12y = x + 16.$$

Exercise 14B

1 Differentiate each of the following functions. Give your answer with a fractional index.

(a) $x^{\frac{1}{3}}$ (b) $x^{\frac{5}{2}}$ (c) $5x^{\frac{2}{5}}$

(d) $-5x^{-\frac{3}{5}}$ (e) $4x^{-\frac{1}{2}}$ (f) $-2x^{-\frac{3}{2}}$

2 Differentiate each of these functions $f(x)$. Give your answers $f'(x)$ in a similar form, without negative or fractional indices.

(a) $\sqrt[4]{x^3}$ (b) $6\sqrt[3]{x}$ (c) $\dfrac{4}{\sqrt{x}}$

(d) $\sqrt{16x^5}$ (e) $\dfrac{1}{\sqrt[3]{8x}}$ (f) $\dfrac{1+x}{\sqrt[4]{x}}$

3 On each of the graphs (a) $y = x^{\frac{1}{3}}$, (b) $y = x^{\frac{2}{3}}$, (c) $y = x^{-\frac{2}{3}}$, (d) $y = x^{-\frac{4}{3}}$, P is the point where $x = 8$ and Q is the point where $x = 8.1$. Find

(i) the y-coordinates of P and Q,

(ii) the gradient of the chord [PQ],

(iii) the value of $\dfrac{dy}{dx}$ at P (assuming the differentiation rule),

(iv) the equation of the tangent at P.

4 Find the equation of the tangent to the curve at the given point.

(a) $y = \sqrt{x}$ at $(9, 3)$ (b) $y = \dfrac{6}{\sqrt[3]{x}}$ at $(8, 3)$

(c) $y = 2x\sqrt{x}$ at $(1, 2)$ (d) $y = 4x + \dfrac{1}{\sqrt{x}}$ at $\left(\frac{1}{4}, 3\right)$

5 Find the coordinates of the point(s) at which the curve has the given gradient.

(a) $y = \sqrt[3]{x^2}$, gradient $\frac{1}{3}$ (b) $y = \sqrt[3]{x}$, gradient $\frac{1}{3}$

(c) $y = \dfrac{3}{\sqrt[3]{x^2}}$, gradient $\frac{1}{16}$ (d) $y = \dfrac{x^2+3}{\sqrt{x}}$, gradient 0

6 Find the equation of the tangent to $y = \sqrt[4]{x}$ with gradient 2.

7 If $n > 0$ the graph of $y = x^n$ passes through the origin. Use the fact that $\dfrac{dy}{dx} = nx^{n-1}$ to show that the x-axis is a tangent if $n > 1$, and that the y-axis is a tangent if $0 < n < 1$. What happens if $n = 1$?

Review exercise 4

1 Find the coordinates of the two points on the curve $y = 2x^3 - 5x^2 + 9x - 1$ at which the gradient of the tangent is 13.

2 Einstein's law $E = mc^2$ gives the energy of the radiation created by the destruction of a particle of mass m, where c is the velocity of light. The units for m, c and E are respectively kilograms, metres per second and joules. Given that the speed of light is 3.0×10^8 metres per second, find the energy created by a neutron of mass 1.7×10^{-27} kilograms.

3 The equation of a curve is $y = 2x^2 - 5x + 14$. The normal to the curve at the point (1, 11) meets the curve again at the point P. Find the coordinates of P.

4 A normal to the curve $y = x^2$ has gradient 2. Find where it meets the curve.

5 Evaluate the following without using a calculator.

(a) $\left(\frac{1}{2}\right)^{-1} + \left(\frac{1}{2}\right)^{-2}$ (b) $32^{-\frac{4}{5}}$ (c) $\left(4^{\frac{3}{2}}\right)^{-\frac{1}{3}}$ (d) $\left(1\frac{7}{9}\right)^{1\frac{1}{2}}$

6 Solve the equation $4^{2x} \times 8^{x-1} = 32$.

7 The table shows, for three planets in the solar system, the mean distance from the sun (r metres) and the time taken for one orbit round the sun (T seconds).

Planet	r	T
Mercury	5.8×10^{10}	7.6×10^6
Jupiter	7.8×10^{11}	3.7×10^8
Pluto	5.9×10^{12}	7.8×10^9

(a) Show that r^3T^{-2} has approximately the same value for each planet in the table.

(b) The Earth takes one year to orbit the sun. Find the mean radius of its orbit.

8 The formulae for the volume V and the surface area S of a cube are $V = x^3$ and $S = 6x^2$, where x is the length of an edge. Find expressions for

(a) S in terms of V, (b) V in terms of S,

giving each answer in the form (S or V) $= 2^m \times 3^n \times (V \text{ or } S)^p$.

9 The curve $y = x^2 - 3x - 4$ crosses the x-axis at P and Q. The tangents to the curve at P and Q meet at R. The normals to the curve at P and Q meet at S. Find the distance RS.

10 For the curve $y = \dfrac{4}{x^2}$, find the equations of

(a) the tangent at $\left(-2\sqrt{2}, \frac{1}{2}\right)$, (b) the normal at $(\sqrt{2}, 2)$.

Show that the lines in parts (a) and (b) are the same. Illustrate this with a sketch.

11 The tangents at $x = \frac{1}{4}$ to $y = \sqrt{x}$ and $y = \dfrac{1}{\sqrt{x}}$ meet at P. Find the coordinates of P.

12 The normals at $x = 2$ to $y = \dfrac{1}{x^2}$ and $y = \dfrac{1}{x^3}$ meet at Q. Find the coordinates of Q.

13 (a) Draw a sketch to show the graphs of $y = \dfrac{1}{x^2}$ and $y = \sqrt{x}$ and their point of intersection at the point P(1, 1). Find the gradient of each curve at P, and show that the tangent at P to each curve is the normal to the other curve.

(b) The graphs of $y = x^m$ and $y = x^n$ intersect at the point P(1, 1). Find the connection between m and n if the tangent at P to each curve is the normal to the other curve.

14 Express $(9a^4)^{-\frac{1}{2}}$ as an algebraic fraction in simplified form. (OCR)

15 By letting $y = x^{\frac{1}{3}}$, or otherwise, find the values of x for which $x^{\frac{1}{3}} - 2x^{-\frac{1}{3}} = 1$. (OCR)

Examination questions

1 Let $f(x) = x^3 - 2x^2 - 1$.

(a) Find $f'(x)$.

(b) Find the gradient of the curve of $f(x)$ at the point $(2, -1)$. (© IBO 2004)

2 Find the exact solution of the equation $9^{2x} = 27^{(1-x)}$. (© IBO 2005)

3 The function $f(x)$ is defined as $f(x) = -(x - h)^2 + k$. The diagram shows part of the graph of $f(x)$. The maximum point on the curve is P(3, 2).

(a) Write down the value of (i) h, (ii) k.

(b) Show that $f(x)$ can be written as $f(x) = -x^2 + 6x - 7$.

(c) Find $f'(x)$.

The point Q lies on the curve and has coordinates Q(4, 1). A straight line L, through Q, is perpendicular to the tangent at Q.

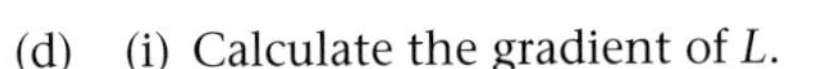

(d) (i) Calculate the gradient of L. (ii) Find the equation of L.

(iii) The line L intersects the curve again at R. Find the x-coordinate of R. (© IBO 2004)

4 The equation of a curve may be written in the form $y = a(x - p)(x - q)$. The curve intersects the x-axis at A(−2, 0) and B(4, 0). The curve of $y = f(x)$ is shown in the diagram.

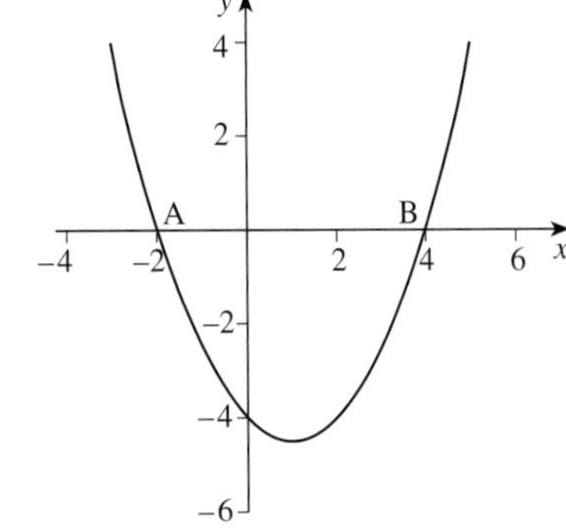

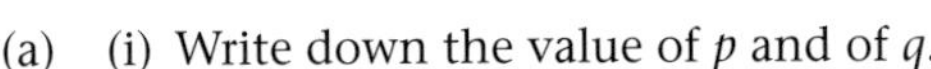

(a) (i) Write down the value of p and of q.

(ii) Given that the point (6, 8) is on the curve, find the value of a.

(iii) Write the equation of the curve in the form $y = ax^2 + bx + c$.

(b) (i) Find $\dfrac{dy}{dx}$.

(ii) A tangent is drawn to the curve at a point P. The gradient of this tangent is 7. Find the coordinates of P.

(c) The line L passes through B(4, 0), and is perpendicular to the tangent to the curve at point B.

(i) Find the equation of L.

(ii) Find the x-coordinate of the point where L intersects the curve again. (© IBO 2005)

15 Trigonometry

This chapter develops work on sines, cosines and tangents. When you have completed it, you should

- know the shapes of the graphs of sine, cosine and tangent for all angles
- know, or be able to find, exact values of the sine, cosine and tangent of certain special angles.

Letters of the Greek alphabet are often used to denote angles. In this chapter, θ (theta) and ϕ (phi) will usually be used.

15.1 The graph of cos $\theta°$

You probably first used $\cos\theta°$ in calculations with right-angled triangles, so that θ lies between 0 and 90. However, if you use a calculator, you will find that it gives a value of $\cos\theta°$ for any value of θ. This section extends the definition of $\cos\theta°$ to angles of any size, positive or negative.

Fig. 15.1 shows a circle of radius 1 unit with centre O; the circle meets the positive x-axis at A. Draw a line segment [OP] at an angle $\theta°$ to the x-axis, to meet the circle at P. Draw a perpendicular from P to meet the x-axis at N. Let ON $= x$ units and NP $= y$ units, so that the coordinates of P are (x, y).

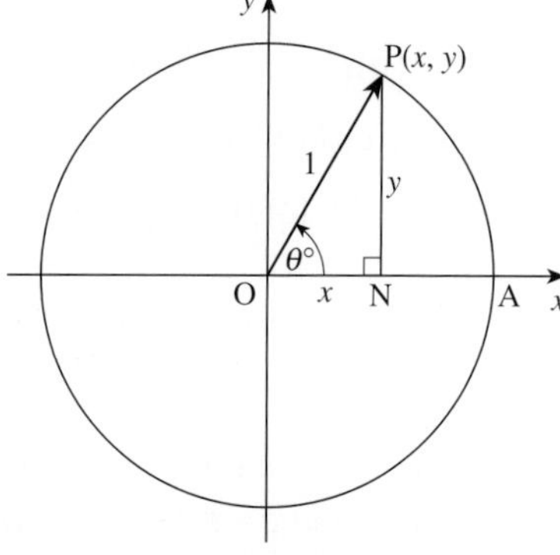

Fig. 15.1

Look at triangle ONP. Using $\cos\theta° = \dfrac{\text{adjacent}}{\text{hypotenuse}} = \dfrac{\text{ON}}{\text{OP}}$, you find that $\cos\theta° = \dfrac{x}{1} = x$.

This result, $\cos\theta° = x$, is used to define $\cos\theta°$ for all values of θ, not just acute angles.

> Referring to Fig. 15.1,
>
> $\cos\theta° = x$, for all $\theta \in \mathbb{R}$.

Example 15.1.1 investigates the consequences of this definition whenever θ is a multiple of 90.

Example 15.1.1
Find the value of $\cos\theta°$ when (a) $\theta = 180$, (b) $\theta = 270$.

(a) When $\theta = 180$, P is the point $(-1, 0)$. As the x-coordinate of P is -1, $\cos 180° = -1$. See Fig. 15.2.

(b) When $\theta = 270$, P is the point $(0, -1)$, so $\cos 270° = 0$. See Fig. 15.3.

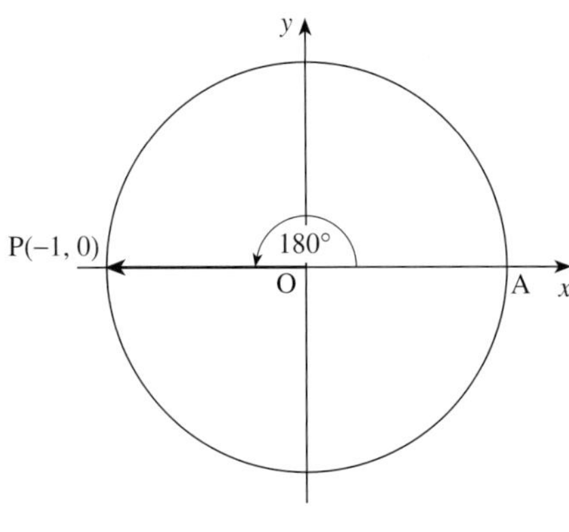

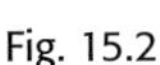
Fig. 15.2

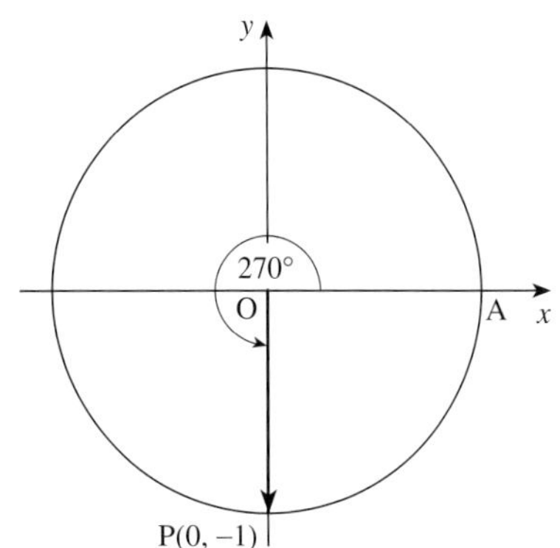

Fig. 15.3

As θ increases, the point P moves round the circle. When $\theta = 360$, P is once again at A, and as θ becomes greater than 360, the point P moves round the circle again.

For example, when [OP] has turned through 400°, P is in the same position as when $\theta = 40$; it follows that $\cos 400^\circ = \cos 40^\circ$. See Fig. 15.4.

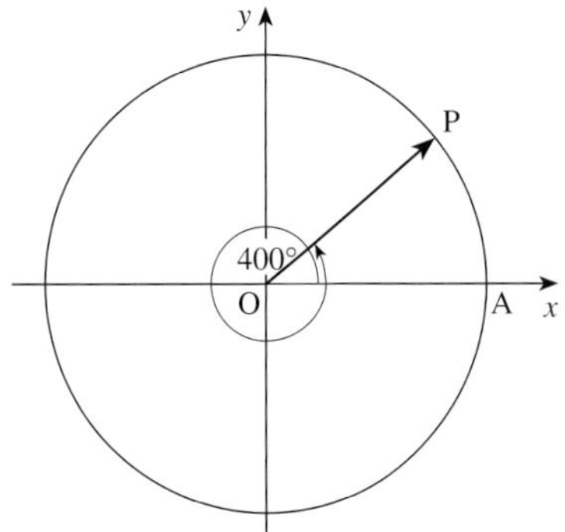

Fig. 15.4

This is a special case of a general rule that the values of $\cos\theta^\circ$ repeat themselves every time θ increases by 360. Written as an equation,

$$\cos\theta^\circ = \cos(\theta - 360)^\circ.$$

If θ is negative, P moves round the circle in the opposite (clockwise) sense, starting from A as before. Fig. 15.5 shows this with $\theta = -150$, so that P is in the third quadrant. Since the x-coordinate of P is negative, this shows that $\cos(-150)^\circ$ is negative.

In Fig. 15.5, as angle $\text{N}\hat{\text{O}}\text{P} = 30^\circ$, ON is $1 \times \cos 30^\circ = 0.866\ldots$. Therefore $\cos 150^\circ = -0.866\ldots$.

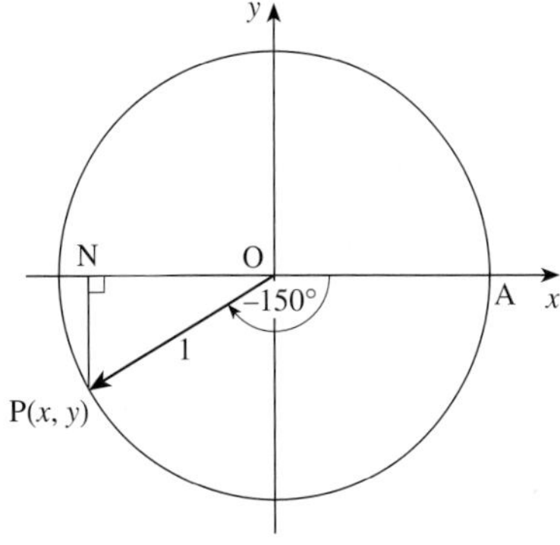

Fig. 15.5

Calculators use this definition to give values of $\cos\theta^\circ$ for all angles. Use your calculator to display the graph of $\cos\theta^\circ$, shown in Fig. 15.6.

> You will have to input the equation of the graph of $\cos\theta^\circ$ as $y = \cos x$ into the calculator, and make sure that it is in degree mode.

Note that the values taken by the cosine function are always between -1 and $+1$ (inclusive). The maximum value of 1 is taken at $\theta = \ldots, -720, -360, 0, 360, 720, \ldots$, and the minimum of -1 at $\theta = \ldots, -540, -180, 180, 540, \ldots$.

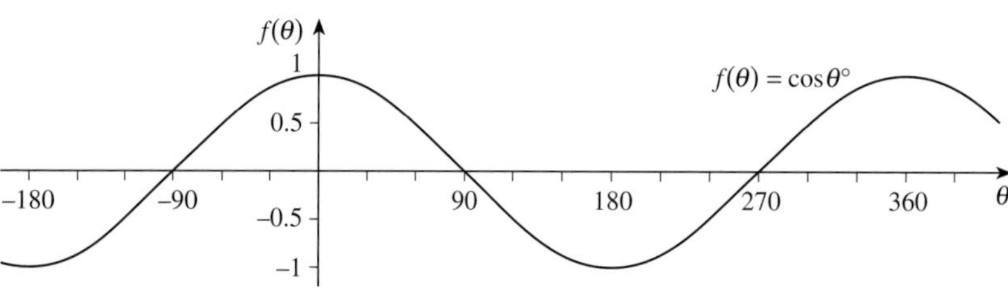

Fig. 15.6

The graph of the cosine function keeps repeating itself. Functions with this property are called **periodic**; the **period** of such a function is the smallest interval for which the function repeats itself. The period of the cosine function is therefore 360. The property that $\cos(\theta - 360)^\circ = \cos\theta^\circ$ is called the **periodic property**. Many natural phenomena have periodic properties, and cosines are often used in applications involving them.

Example 15.1.2
Find the greatest and least values of the following functions, and in each case give the smallest positive value of θ for which it occurs.

(a) $2 + \cos\theta^\circ$ (b) $3\cos 2\theta^\circ$

The greatest and least values of the cosine function are $+1$ and -1.

(a) The greatest value of $2 + \cos\theta^\circ$ is $2 + 1 = 3$, and the least value is $2 + (-1) = 1$.

The values of θ which give the value 1 are -720, -360, 0, 360, 720, etc. The smallest positive value of these is 360.

The values of θ which give the value -1 are -540, -180, 180, 540, 900, etc. The smallest positive value of these is 180.

(b) The greatest value of $3\cos 2\theta^\circ$ is $3 \times 1 = 3$, and the least value of $3\cos 2\theta^\circ$ is $3 \times (-1) = -3$.

The values of 2θ which give the value 1 for $\cos 2\theta^\circ$ are -720, -360, 0, 360, 720, etc. The smallest positive value of θ is when $2\theta = 360$, that is, $\theta = 180$.

The values of 2θ which give the value -1 for $\cos 2\theta^\circ$ are -540, -180, 180, 540, 900, etc. The smallest positive value of θ is when $2\theta = 180$, that is, $\theta = 90$.

Example 15.1.3
The height h in metres of the water in a harbour is given approximately by the formula $h = 6 + 3\cos 30t^\circ$ where t is the time in hours from noon. Find

(a) the height of the water at 9.45 p.m.,

(b) the highest and lowest water levels, and when they occur.

(a) At 9.45 p.m., $t = 9.75$, so

$$\begin{aligned} h &= 6 + 3\cos(30 \times 9.75)^\circ \\ &= 6 + 3\cos 292.5^\circ \\ &= 7.148\ldots . \end{aligned}$$

The height of the water is 7.15 metres, correct to 3 significant figures.

(b) The greatest value of h occurs when the value of the cosine function is 1, and is therefore $6 + 3 \times 1 = 9$. Similarly, the least value is $6 + 3 \times (-1) = 3$. The highest and lowest water levels are 9 metres and 3 metres. The first times that they occur after noon are when $30t = 360$ and $30t = 180$; that is, at midnight and 6.00 p.m.

15.2 The graphs of $\sin\theta°$ and $\tan\theta°$

Using the same construction as for the cosine (see Fig. 15.7 which is Fig. 15.1 again), the sine function is given by

$$\sin\theta° = \frac{\text{opposite}}{\text{hypotenuse}} = \frac{\text{NP}}{\text{OP}} = \frac{y}{1} = y,$$

so $\sin\theta° = y$ is used as the definition of $\sin\theta°$ for all values of θ.

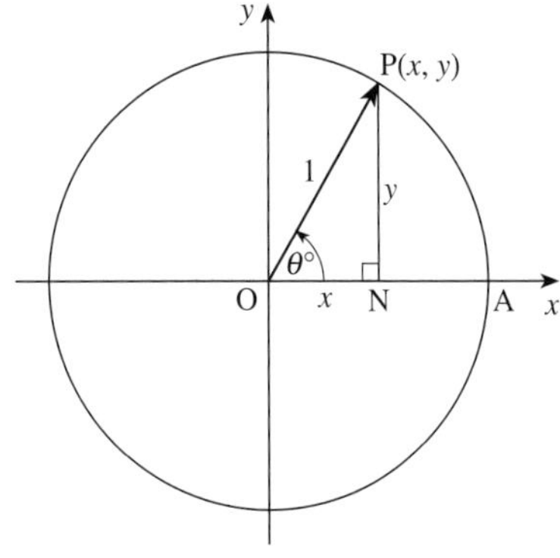

Fig. 15.7

> Referring to Fig. 15.7,
>
> $\sin\theta° = y$, for all $\theta \in \mathbb{R}$.

Like the cosine graph, the sine graph (shown in Fig. 15.8) is periodic, with period 360. It also lies between -1 and 1 inclusive.

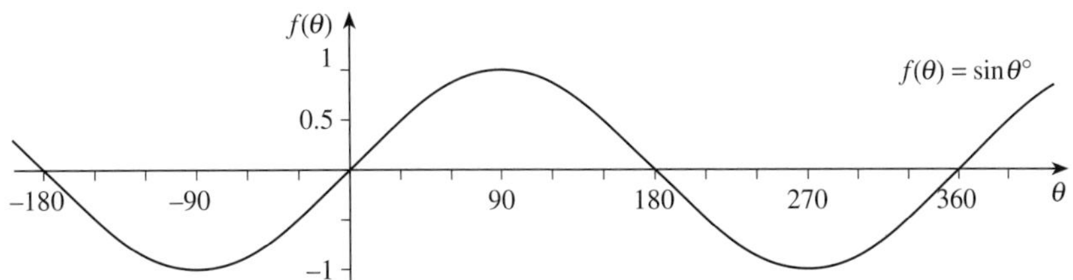

Fig. 15.8

In Fig. 15.7, you can see that $\tan\theta° = \frac{\text{NP}}{\text{ON}} = \frac{y}{x}$; this is taken as the definition of $\tan\theta°$.

> Referring to Fig. 15.7,
>
> $\tan\theta° = \frac{y}{x}$, for all $\theta \in \mathbb{R}$, provided $x \neq 0$.

The function $\tan\theta°$ is not defined for those angles for which x is zero, namely $\theta = \pm 90, \pm 270, \ldots$. Fig. 15.9 shows the graph of $\tan\theta°$, which has asymptotes at $\theta = \pm 90, \pm 270, \ldots$.

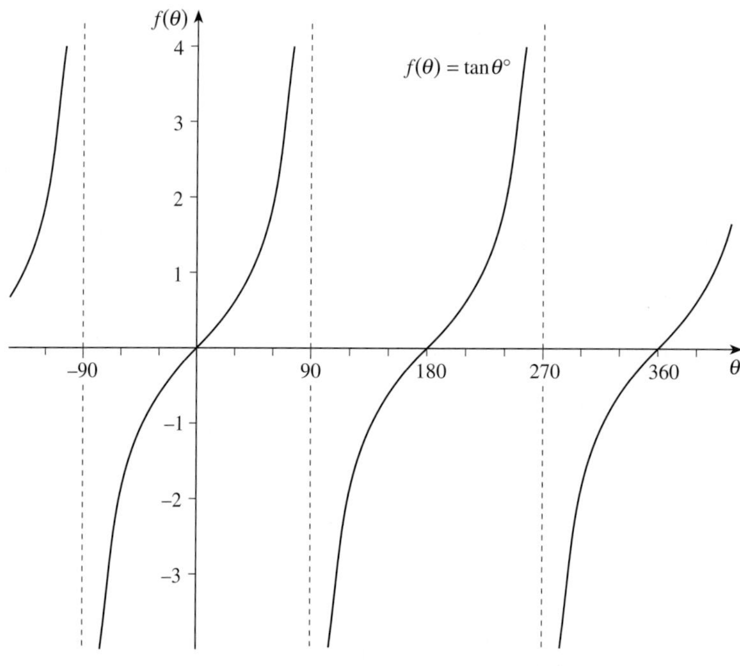

Fig. 15.9

Like the graphs of $\cos\theta°$ and $\sin\theta°$, the graph of $\tan\theta°$ is periodic, but its period is 180. Thus $\tan(\theta - 180)° = \tan\theta°$.

As $\cos\theta° = x$, $\sin\theta° = y$ and $\tan\theta° = \frac{y}{x}$, it follows that $\tan\theta° = \frac{\sin\theta°}{\cos\theta°}$. You could use this as an alternative definition of $\tan\theta°$.

Example 15.2.1

Find the greatest and least values of the following functions, and in each case give the smallest positive value of θ for which it occurs.

(a) $2\sin\theta° - 1$ (b) $\dfrac{1}{2+\sin\theta°}$

The greatest and least values of $\sin\theta°$ are 1 and -1.

(a) The greatest value of $2\sin\theta° - 1$ is therefore $2 \times 1 - 1 = 1$, and the least value is $2 \times (-1) - 1 = -3$.

The greatest occurs when $\theta = 90$, and the least when $\theta = 270$.

(b) As $\sin\theta°$ lies between -1 and 1, $2 + \sin\theta°$ lies between 1 and 3.
The greatest value of $\dfrac{1}{2+\sin\theta°}$ occurs when the denominator is 1, giving a greatest value of 1. This occurs when $\theta = 270$.
Similarly, the least value of $\dfrac{1}{2+\sin\theta°}$ occurs when the denominator is 3, giving a least value of $\frac{1}{3}$. This occurs when $\theta = 90$.

You might find it interesting to display these functions on your calculator.

Example 15.2.2
Show that for values of θ between 0 and 180, $\sin\theta^\circ = \sin(180^\circ - \theta^\circ)$.

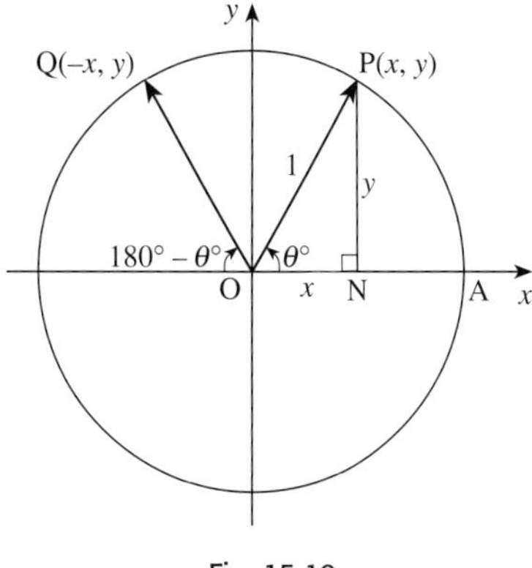

Fig. 15.10

Fig. 15.10 shows a modified version of Fig. 15.1 (or Fig 15.7).

You can see that for $0 < \theta < 180$, the y-coordinates of P and Q are always the same. It follows that $\sin\theta^\circ = \sin(180^\circ - \theta^\circ)$.

This result will be used in the next chapter. You will see later that it is actually true for all values of θ.

15.3 Exact values of some trigonometric functions

There are a few angles which have sines, cosines and tangents you can find exactly. The most important of these are 45°, 60° and 30°.

To find the cosine, sine and tangent of 45°, draw a right-angled isosceles triangle of side 1 unit, as in Fig. 15.11.

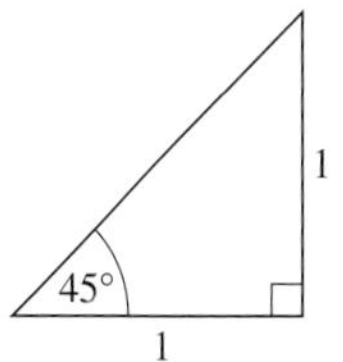

Fig. 15.11

Using Pythagoras' theorem, the length of the hypotenuse is then $\sqrt{2}$ units. Then

$$\cos 45^\circ = \frac{1}{\sqrt{2}}, \quad \sin 45^\circ = \frac{1}{\sqrt{2}}, \quad \tan 45^\circ = 1.$$

If you rationalise the denominators you get

$$\cos 45^\circ = \frac{\sqrt{2}}{2}, \quad \sin 45^\circ = \frac{\sqrt{2}}{2}, \quad \tan 45^\circ = 1.$$

To find the cosine, sine and tangent of 60° and 30°, draw an equilateral triangle of side 2 units, as in Fig. 15.12.

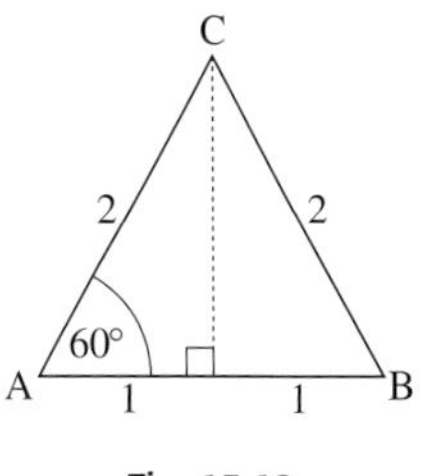

Fig. 15.12

Draw a perpendicular from one vertex, bisecting the opposite side. This perpendicular has length $\sqrt{3}$ units, and it makes an angle of 30° with [AC]. Then

$$\cos 60^\circ = \frac{1}{2}, \quad \sin 60^\circ = \frac{\sqrt{3}}{2}, \quad \tan 60^\circ = \sqrt{3};$$
$$\cos 30^\circ = \frac{\sqrt{3}}{2}, \quad \sin 30^\circ = \frac{1}{2}, \quad \tan 30^\circ = \frac{1}{\sqrt{3}} = \frac{\sqrt{3}}{3}.$$

You should be able to reproduce these results quickly.

Here is a summary of them.

θ	$\sin\theta°$	$\cos\theta°$	$\tan\theta°$
0	0	1	0
30	$\frac{1}{2}$	$\frac{\sqrt{3}}{2}$	$\frac{1}{\sqrt{3}} = \frac{\sqrt{3}}{3}$
45	$\frac{1}{\sqrt{2}} = \frac{\sqrt{2}}{2}$	$\frac{1}{\sqrt{2}} = \frac{\sqrt{2}}{2}$	1
60	$\frac{\sqrt{3}}{2}$	$\frac{1}{2}$	$\sqrt{3}$
90	1	0	undefined

Example 15.3.1
Write down the exact values of (a) $\cos 120°$, (b) $\sin 240°$, (c) $\tan 495°$.

(a) **Method 1** From the graph of $\cos\theta°$ in Fig. 15.13, the value of $\cos 120°$ is negative.

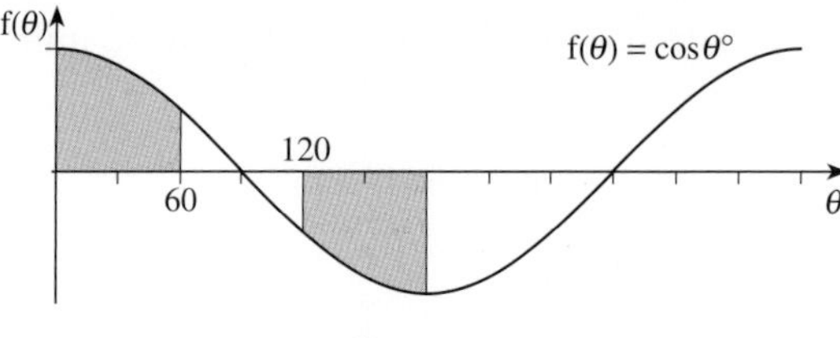

Fig. 15.13

Also from Fig. 15.13, the piece of curve between 0 and 60 is exactly the same shape as that between 120 and 180, so the numerical value (ignoring the sign) of $\cos 120°$ is the same as $\cos 60°$, which is $\frac{1}{2}$.

So $\cos 120° = -\cos 60° = -\frac{1}{2}$.

Method 2 From Fig. 15.14, 120° is a second quadrant angle, so the x-coordinate of P is negative and hence $\cos 120°$ is negative.

In Fig. 15.14, as angle $\text{N}\hat{\text{O}}\text{P} = 60°$, ON is $1 \times \cos 60° = \frac{1}{2}$.

So $\cos 120° = -\cos 60° = -\frac{1}{2}$.

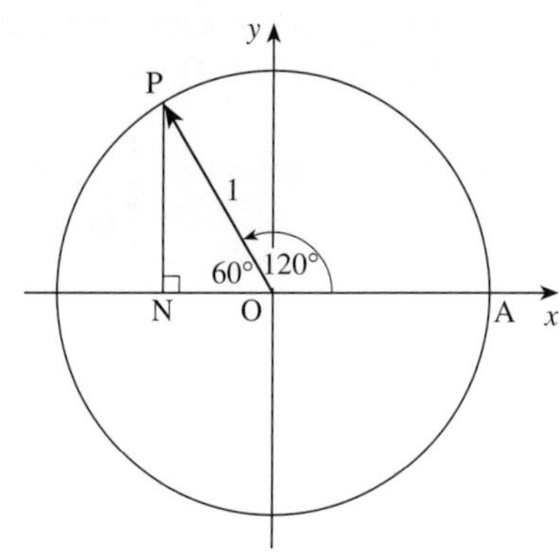

Fig. 15.14

(b) Using either Method 1 or Method 2, you first find that $\sin 240^\circ$ is negative.

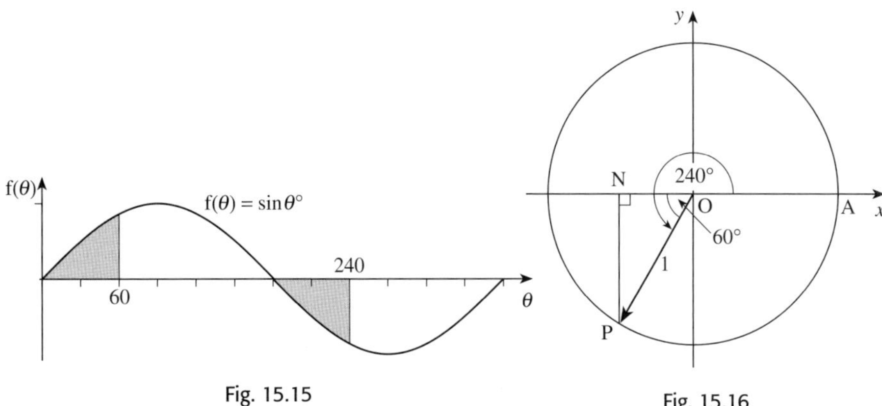

Fig. 15.15

Fig. 15.16

If you use the graph (Fig. 15.15) you see that $\sin 240^\circ = -\sin 60^\circ$, and as $\sin 60^\circ = \frac{1}{2}\sqrt{3}$, $\sin 240^\circ = -\sin 60^\circ = -\frac{1}{2}\sqrt{3}$.

If you use Fig. 15.16, then PN is $1 \times \sin 60^\circ = \frac{1}{2}\sqrt{3}$, so $\sin 240^\circ = -\frac{1}{2}\sqrt{3}$.

(c) Using either Method 1 or Method 2, you first find that $\tan 495^\circ$ is negative. Using the graph (Fig. 15.17) you see that $\tan 495^\circ = -\tan 45^\circ$, and as $\tan 45^\circ = 1$, $\tan 495^\circ = -1$.

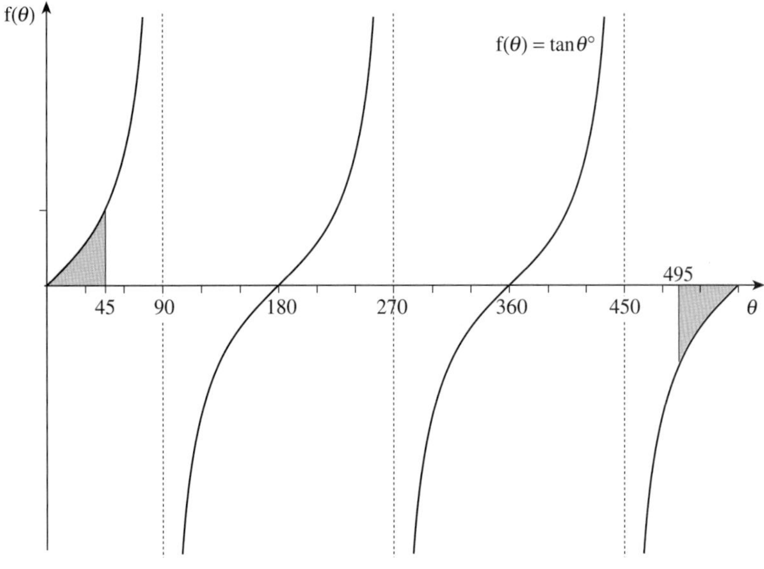

Fig. 15.17

If you use Fig. 15.18, then $\frac{PN}{ON} = \tan 45^\circ = 1$. So $\tan 495^\circ = -\tan 45^\circ = -1$.

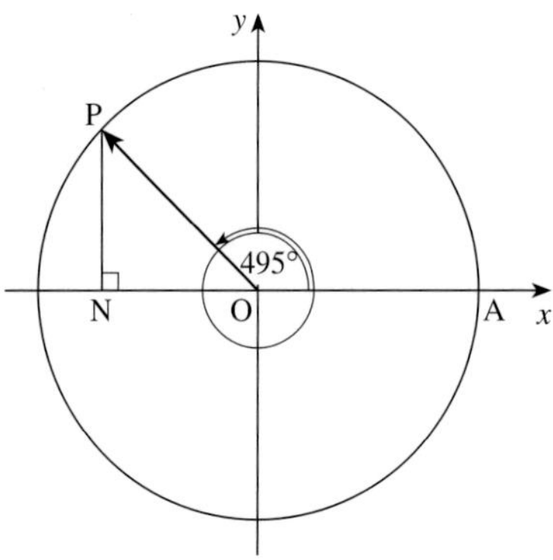

Fig. 15.18

Use either Method 1 or Method 2, whichever you prefer. But do not attempt to draw an accurate figure: a rough sketch is all that is needed.

Exercise 15

1 For each of the following values of θ find, correct to 4 decimal places, the values of (i) $\cos\theta^\circ$, (ii) $\sin\theta^\circ$, (iii) $\tan\theta^\circ$.

(a) 25 (b) 125 (c) 225 (d) 325
(e) −250 (f) 67.4 (g) 124.9 (h) 554

2 Find the greatest value and the least value of each of the following functions. In each case, give the smallest positive values of θ at which they occur.

(a) $2 + \sin\theta^\circ$ (b) $7 - 4\cos\theta^\circ$ (c) $5 + 8\cos 2\theta^\circ$
(d) $\frac{8}{3 - \sin\theta^\circ}$ (e) $9 + \sin(4\theta - 20)^\circ$ (f) $\frac{30}{2 + \cos\theta^\circ}$

3 (Do not use a calculator for this question.) In each part of the question a trigonometric function of a number is given. Find all the other numbers x, $0 \le x \le 360$, such that the same function of x is equal to the given trigonometric ratio. For example, if you are given $\sin 80^\circ$, then $x = 100$, since $\sin 100^\circ = \sin 80^\circ$.

(a) $\sin 20^\circ$ (b) $\cos 40^\circ$ (c) $\tan 60^\circ$ (d) $\sin 130^\circ$
(e) $\cos 140^\circ$ (f) $\tan 160^\circ$ (g) $\sin 400^\circ$ (h) $\cos(-30)^\circ$
(i) $\tan 430^\circ$ (j) $\sin(-260)^\circ$ (k) $\cos(-200)^\circ$ (l) $\tan 1000^\circ$

4 Without using a calculator, write down the exact values of the following.

(a) $\sin 135^\circ$ (b) $\cos 120^\circ$ (c) $\sin(-30)^\circ$ (d) $\tan 240^\circ$
(e) $\cos 225^\circ$ (f) $\tan(-330)^\circ$ (g) $\cos 900^\circ$ (h) $\tan 510^\circ$
(i) $\sin 225^\circ$ (j) $\cos 630^\circ$ (k) $\tan 405^\circ$ (l) $\sin(-315)^\circ$
(m) $\sin 210^\circ$ (n) $\tan 675^\circ$ (o) $\cos(-120)^\circ$ (p) $\sin 1260^\circ$

5 Without using a calculator, write down the smallest positive angle which satisfies each of the following equations.

(a) $\cos\theta^\circ = \frac{1}{2}$ (b) $\sin\phi^\circ = -\frac{1}{2}\sqrt{3}$ (c) $\tan\theta^\circ = -\sqrt{3}$ (d) $\cos\phi^\circ = \frac{1}{2}\sqrt{3}$

(e) $\tan\theta^\circ = \frac{1}{3}\sqrt{3}$ (f) $\tan\phi^\circ = -1$ (g) $\sin\theta^\circ = -\frac{1}{2}$ (h) $\cos\phi^\circ = 0$

(i) $\cos\theta^\circ = -\frac{1}{2}$ (j) $\tan\phi^\circ = \sqrt{3}$ (k) $\sin\theta^\circ = -1$ (l) $\cos\theta^\circ = -1$

(m) $\sin\phi^\circ = \frac{1}{2}\sqrt{3}$ (n) $\tan\theta^\circ = -\frac{1}{3}\sqrt{3}$ (o) $\sin\phi^\circ = -\frac{1}{2}\sqrt{2}$ (p) $\tan\phi^\circ = 0$

6 Without using a calculator show that

(a) $\tan 45^\circ + \sin 30^\circ = 1\frac{1}{2}$, (b) $\sin^2 60^\circ = \frac{3}{4}$,

(c) $\sin 60^\circ \cos 30^\circ + \cos 60^\circ \sin 30^\circ = 1$, (d) $\sin^2 30^\circ + \sin^2 45 = \sin^2 60^\circ$,

(e) $\dfrac{\cos 30^\circ}{\sin 30^\circ} = \tan 60^\circ$, (f) $(1 + \tan 60^\circ)^2 = 4 + 2\sqrt{3}$.

($\sin^2 60^\circ$ means $(\sin 60^\circ)^2$; similar notation applies to $\sin^2 30^\circ$ and $\sin^2 45^\circ$.)

7 The water levels in a dock follow (approximately) a twelve-hour cycle, and are modelled by the equation $D = A + B\sin 30t^\circ$, where D metres is the depth of water in the dock, A and B are positive constants, and t is the time in hours after 8 a.m.

Given that the greatest and least depths of water in the dock are 7.80 m and 2.20 m respectively, find the value of A and the value of B.

Find the depth of water in the dock at noon, giving your answer correct to the nearest cm.

16 The sine and cosine rules

This chapter shows you how to use trigonometry in triangles which are not right-angled. When you have completed it, you should

- know and be able to use the formula $\Delta = \frac{1}{2}ab\sin C$ for the area of a triangle
- know and be able to use the sine and cosine rules to find unknown sides and angles in triangles which are not right-angled.

16.1 Some notation

You have already used trigonometry to calculate lengths and angles in right-angled triangles. This chapter develops rules which you can use to calculate lengths, angles and areas in triangles which are not right-angled. To state these rules, it helps to have a standard notation.

Fig. 16.1 shows a triangle ABC. In this triangle, the length of the side [BC], which is opposite the vertex A, is denoted by a units. Similarly the lengths of the sides [CA] and [AB], which are opposite B and C respectively, are denoted by b units and c units. These units could be centimetres, miles or anything else you like. However, all the sides must be measured in the same units. That is, the units must be consistent.

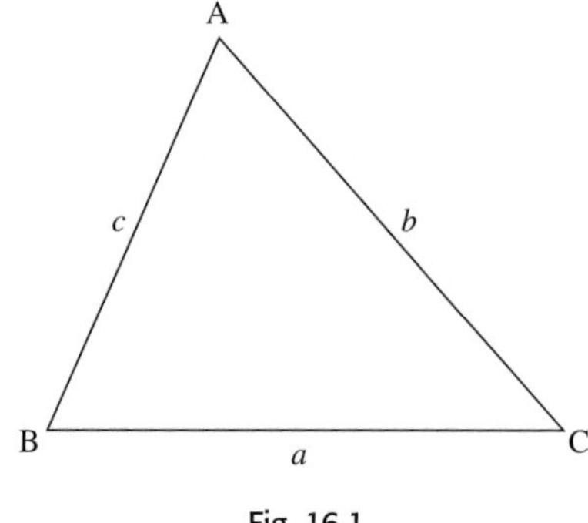

Fig. 16.1

In a practical problem, where particular units are specified, you would usually include the units when you label the sides. (See, for example, Fig. 16.4.) But where a figure might represent any triangle, such as Fig. 16.1, it is usual just to label the sides 'a, b, c' rather than 'a units, b units, c units'. You are already used to doing this when you use coordinates and write (x, y) rather than (x units, y units).

You are probably used to naming the angle at the vertex A as 'angle BAC', or perhaps '∠BAC' or BÂC. This gets rather clumsy, so when there is no ambiguity the letter $\hat{A}$ is used as an abbreviation for the size of this angle. Similarly, $\hat{B}$ and $\hat{C}$ stand for the size of the angles at the corresponding vertices. These angles will usually be measured in degrees. For example, you might write $\hat{A} = 60°$, $\hat{B} = 75°$ and $\hat{C} = 45°$. However, there is no reason why the angles could not be measured in some other units such as right angles if that were convenient. In that case $\hat{A} = \frac{2}{3}$ right angle, $\hat{B} = \frac{5}{6}$ right angle and $\hat{C} = \frac{1}{2}$ right angle.

Some triangles in this chapter will be labelled DEF, LMN, PQR, XYZ, etc. The same convention is used for these triangles, but with the letters changed. For example, the triangle PQR would have sides of length p units, q units and r units, and angles of size $\hat{P}$, $\hat{Q}$ and $\hat{R}$, where p is opposite the vertex P, and so on.

16.2 The area of an acute-angled triangle

You know the formula

$$\text{area of a triangle} = \tfrac{1}{2} \times \text{base} \times \text{height}$$

for the area of any triangle.

There are no units in this formula; however, the units of the lengths of the base and height must be the same and the unit of area must be consistent with these.

You can use trigonometry to write this formula in a different way.

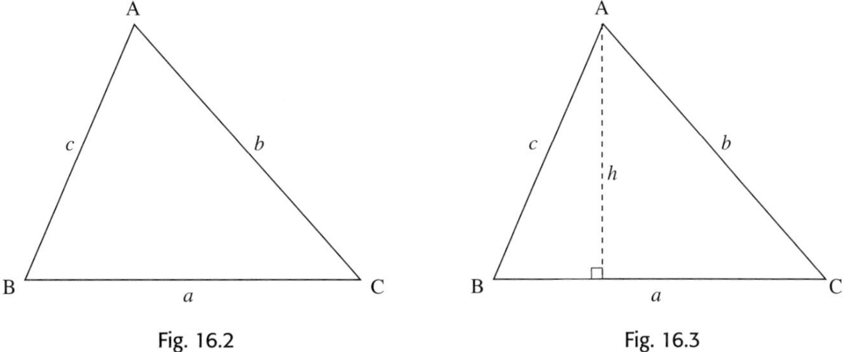

Fig. 16.2 Fig. 16.3

Suppose that you want a formula for the area of the acute-angled triangle ABC in Fig. 16.2. Then, to use the formula area $= \frac{1}{2} \times$ base $\times$ height, you need to find the height, which is shown as h in Fig. 16.3.

In the triangle on the right of Fig. 16.3, $\sin \hat{C} = \dfrac{h}{b}$, so $h = b \sin \hat{C}$.

The base of the triangle is a, so the area is given by

$$\text{area} = \tfrac{1}{2} \times \text{base} \times \text{height} = \tfrac{1}{2} \times a \times b \sin \hat{C} = \tfrac{1}{2} ab \sin \hat{C}.$$

The area of a triangle is denoted by Δ where Δ is the Greek capital 'd', called 'delta'. Then, for an acute-angled triangle,

$$\Delta = \tfrac{1}{2} ab \sin \hat{C}.$$

The units for Δ would correspond to the units for the sides of the triangle. So if the lengths were a cm and b cm, the area would be Δ cm^2.

> The symbol Δ is often used in two ways: when you write ΔABC it means 'triangle' and ΔABC is simply the triangle ABC; when you use Δ to mean the area of a triangle, it must have a unit. This ambiguity doesn't usually cause confusion.

Example 16.2.1

Calculate the area of triangle ABC in Fig. 16.4 in which BC = 5 cm, AC = 6 cm and $\hat{C} = 40^\circ$.

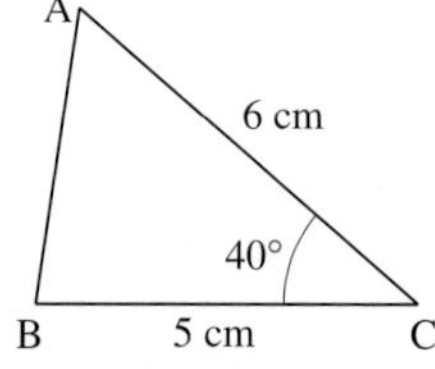

Fig. 16.4

For this triangle, $a = 5$ and $b = 6$. Substituting these into $\Delta = \frac{1}{2}ab\sin\hat{C}$ gives

$$\Delta = \tfrac{1}{2} \times 5 \times 6\sin 40^\circ = 9.641\ldots .$$

The area of triangle ABC is 9.64 cm^2, correct to 3 significant figures.

If, in Fig. 16.3, you had calculated the height h from the triangle on the left instead of the triangle on the right, you would have obtained $h = c\sin\hat{B}$ instead of $h = b\sin\hat{C}$.

Using this new expression for h gives

$$\Delta = \tfrac{1}{2} \times a \times c\sin\hat{B} = \tfrac{1}{2}ac\sin\hat{B}.$$

And, if you had drawn the perpendicular from B to the side [AC], and used [AC] as the base of the triangle you could have obtained the formula

$$\Delta = \tfrac{1}{2}bc\sin\hat{A}.$$

Therefore you have three ways of expressing the area of an acute-angled triangle,

$$\Delta = \tfrac{1}{2}bc\sin\hat{A} = \tfrac{1}{2}ca\sin\hat{B} = \tfrac{1}{2}ab\sin\hat{C}.$$

16.3 The area of an obtuse-angled triangle

Now suppose that the triangle ABC is obtuse-angled, with an obtuse angle at C, as shown in Fig. 16.5.

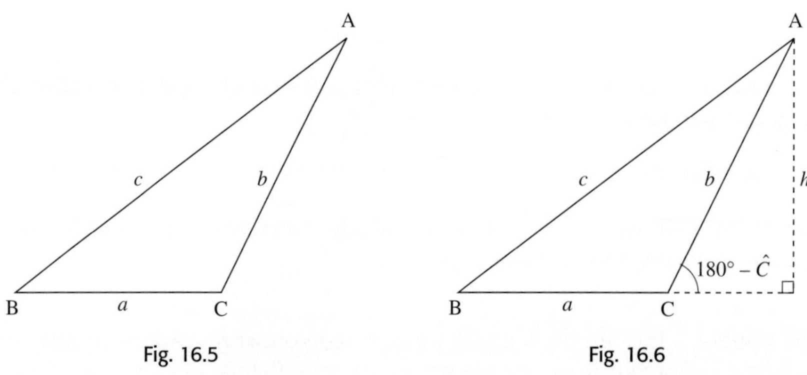

Fig. 16.5 Fig. 16.6

In Fig. 16.6, the height of the triangle ABC is shown as h; using the right-angled triangle with hypotenuse [AC] shows that $h = b\sin(180^\circ - \hat{C})$, giving

$$\begin{aligned}\Delta &= \tfrac{1}{2} \times a \times b\sin(180^\circ - \hat{C})\\ &= \tfrac{1}{2}ab\sin(180^\circ - \hat{C}).\end{aligned}$$

But from Example 15.2.2, for $0 < \theta < 180$, $\sin(180^\circ - \theta^\circ) = \sin\theta^\circ$.

So in this case $\sin(180^\circ - \hat{C}) = \sin\hat{C}$, giving

$$\Delta = \tfrac{1}{2}ab\sin\hat{C}.$$

The formula $\frac{1}{2}ab\sin\hat{C}$ can therefore be used for the area of any triangle, whether the angle at C is acute or obtuse.

What happens if the angle at C is a right angle?

The area Δ of a triangle ABC is given by

$$\Delta = \tfrac{1}{2}bc\sin A = \tfrac{1}{2}ca\sin B = \tfrac{1}{2}ab\ \sin C,$$

where the unit of area corresponds to the units for the sides.

Note that it is conventional to quote this formula without the circumflex over the angle. This will be the convention used in this book, but as soon as the formula is applied, the circumflex will be used.

A good way to remember the formula $\Delta = \frac{1}{2}bc\sin A = \frac{1}{2}ca\sin B = \frac{1}{2}ab\sin C$ is to think of it as

$$\Delta = \tfrac{1}{2} \times \text{one side} \times \text{another side} \times \text{the sine of the angle between them.}$$

This enables you to use the formula for a triangle XYZ without having to re-label it as ABC, or do mental gymnastics with the letters concerned.

The term 'included angle' is sometimes used for the angle between two sides.

Example 16.3.1
Find the areas of the triangles shown in Fig. 16.7.

Note that the triangles are not drawn accurately. Only rough sketches are needed.

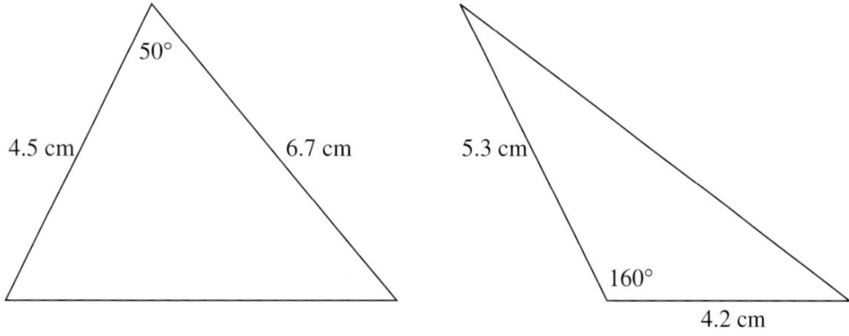

Fig. 16.7

For the left triangle, the area is given by

$$\Delta = \tfrac{1}{2} \times 4.5 \times 6.7 \times \sin 50^\circ = 11.54\ldots .$$

The area is 11.5 cm^2, correct to 3 significant figures.

For the right triangle, the area is given by

$$\Delta = \tfrac{1}{2} \times 5.3 \times 4.2 \times \sin 160^\circ = 3.806\ldots .$$

The area is 3.81 cm^2, correct to 3 significant figures.

Example 16.3.2

A triangle ABC with BC = 3.4 cm and $\hat{B} = 130^\circ$ has an area of 5.72 cm^2. Find AB.

Begin by drawing a rough sketch like Fig. 16.8.

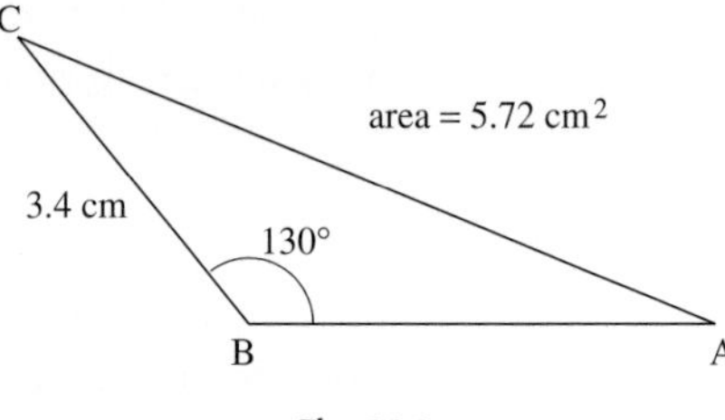

Fig. 16.8

Denoting the length of side [AB] by c cm,

$$5.72 = \tfrac{1}{2} \times 3.4 \times c \times \sin 130^\circ$$

giving

$$c = \frac{5.72}{\tfrac{1}{2} \times 3.4 \times \sin 130^\circ} = 4.392\ldots .$$

So AB is 4.39 cm, correct to 3 significant figures.

Example 16.3.3

An obtuse-angled triangle ABC with BC = 4.2 m and CA = 15 m has an area of 7.12 m^2. Find the size of the obtuse angle at C.

Fig. 16.9 shows a rough sketch of the triangle.

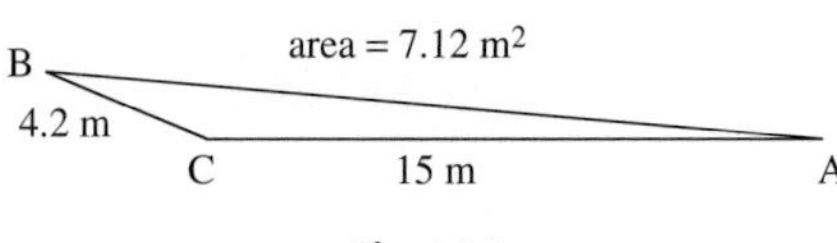

Fig. 16.9

As $7.12 = \tfrac{1}{2} \times 4.2 \times 15 \times \sin \hat{C}$,
$\sin \hat{C} = 0.2260\ldots$.

The calculator gives the acute angle whose sine is 0.2260... as 13.06...°. Using the fact that for any value of θ, $\sin(180^\circ - \theta^\circ) = \sin \theta^\circ$, the obtuse angle whose sine is 0.2260... is $(180 - 13.06\ldots)^\circ$.

Therefore $\hat{C} = 166.9^\circ$, correct to 1 decimal place.

Exercise 16A

1 In each part, the lengths of two sides of a triangle and the angle between them are given. Find the area of each triangle, giving your answer in appropriate units.

(a) 3 cm, 4 cm, 90° (b) 5 cm, 7 cm, 40° (c) 3 m, 2 m, 140°

(d) 5 cm, 3 cm, 30° (e) 4 cm, 3 cm, 123° (f) 88 cm, 1 m, 45°

2 In each part, the area of a triangle, the length of one side and an angle which is not opposite to that side are given. Find the length of the other side of the triangle which is not opposite to the given angle.

(a) 5 cm^2, 3 cm, 40° (b) 8 cm^2, 4 cm, 90° (c) 3 m^2, 4 m, 110°

(d) 23.2 cm^2, 7.1 cm, 43.3° (e) 15.1 cm^2, 1 cm, 136° (f) 1.40 m^2, 25 m, 85°

3 In each part, the length of two sides of a triangle and its area are given. Find the angle between the two sides, given that it is acute.

(a) 3 cm, 6 cm, 5 cm^2, (b) 4 cm, 5 cm, 8 cm^2, (c) 5 m, 8 m, 7 m^2,

(d) 7.5 cm, 8.3 cm, 25.9 cm^2 (e) 10 cm, 15 cm, 15.1 cm^2, (f) 3 m, 5 m, 1.40 m^2

4 With the data of Question 3, find the angle between the two sides, given that it is obtuse.

16.4 The sine rule for a triangle

In the formula $\Delta = \frac{1}{2}bc\sin\hat{A} = \frac{1}{2}ca\sin\hat{B} = \frac{1}{2}ab\sin\hat{C}$ for the area of a triangle, if you ignore the Δ and multiply all through by 2 you obtain

$$bc\sin\hat{A} = ca\sin\hat{B} = ab\sin\hat{C}$$

If you now divide each part of this equation by abc you get

$$\frac{\sin\hat{A}}{a} = \frac{\sin\hat{B}}{b} = \frac{\sin\hat{C}}{c}.$$

Just as with the formula for the area of a triangle, this formula is usually quoted without the circumflex angle signs. So

$$\frac{\sin A}{a} = \frac{\sin B}{b} = \frac{\sin C}{c}.$$

This is called the sine rule for a triangle. If you know two sides of a triangle and the angle opposite one of them, you can use it to find the angle opposite the other.

Example 16.4.1
In a triangle ABC, BC = 11 cm, CA = 15 cm and angle AB̂C = 73°. Find the angle BÂC.

Begin by drawing a rough sketch like Fig. 16.10.

You are given that $a = 11$, $b = 15$ and $\hat{B} = 73^\circ$.

So you know $\dfrac{\sin\hat{B}}{b}$ completely, and you want to find $\hat{A}$. Neither c nor $\hat{C}$ is involved, so use $\dfrac{\sin\hat{A}}{a} = \dfrac{\sin\hat{B}}{b}$.

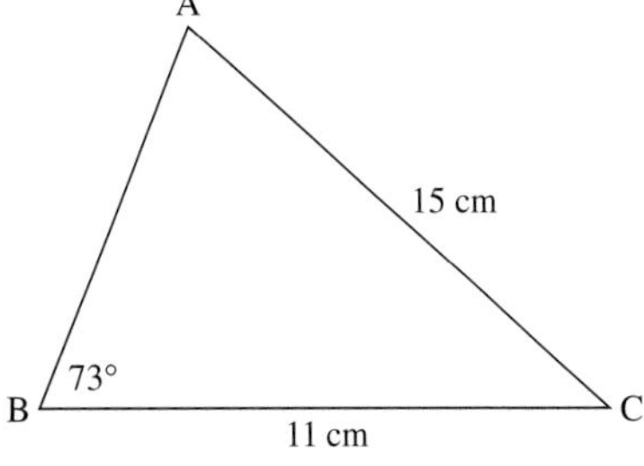

Fig. 16.10

Substituting the known values,

$$\frac{\sin \hat{A}}{11} = \frac{\sin 73^\circ}{15},$$

so $\qquad \sin \hat{A} = \dfrac{11 \times \sin 73^\circ}{15} = 0.701\ldots, \quad A = 44.53\ldots^\circ.$

The angle B$\hat{A}$C is 44.5° to the nearest 0.1°.

Notice that there is another angle, $(180 - 44.53\ldots)^\circ$, whose sine is also 0.701… . But you can't have a triangle with one angle of 73° and another of 135.46…°, since their sum is greater than 180°.

You can also use the sine rule if you know two angles of a triangle and the side opposite to one of them, and want to find the side opposite to the other. In that case the algebra is simpler if you replace each fraction by its reciprocal (that is, turn it upside down), and give the rule as

$$\frac{a}{\sin A} = \frac{b}{\sin B} = \frac{c}{\sin C}.$$

Example 16.4.2
In the triangle XYZ, angle $\hat{X} = 40^\circ$, angle $\hat{Z} = 85^\circ$ and XY = 8 cm. Calculate YZ.

The triangle is sketched in Fig. 16.11.

You know that $\hat{X} = 40^\circ$, $\hat{Z} = 85^\circ$ and $z = 8$, and want to find x. So, adapting the rule with the new letters,

$$\frac{x}{\sin 40^\circ} = \frac{8}{\sin 85^\circ}.$$

This gives $x = \dfrac{8 \sin 40^\circ}{\sin 85^\circ} = 5.161\ldots$.

Thus YZ = 5.16 cm, correct to 3 significant figures.

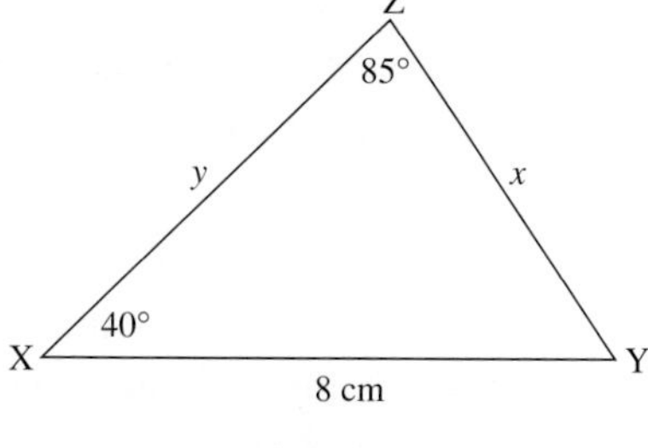

Fig. 16.11

The **sine rule** for a triangle ABC is

$$\frac{\sin A}{a} = \frac{\sin B}{b} = \frac{\sin C}{c}, \quad \text{or} \quad \frac{a}{\sin A} = \frac{b}{\sin B} = \frac{c}{\sin C}.$$

Use the formula on the left to calculate the sine of an angle if you know the lengths of two sides and one other angle, which must not be the angle between the two known sides.

Use the formula on the right to calculate a side if you know the length of another side and two of the angles of a triangle.

Example 16.4.3

In the triangle sketched in Fig. 16.12, calculate (a) the angle $\hat{Q}$, (b) PQ.

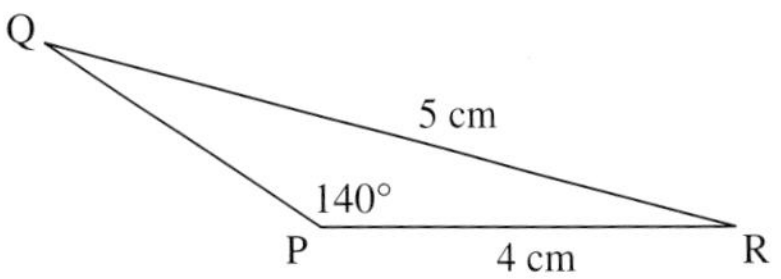

(a) You know that $p = 5$, $q = 4$ and $\hat{P} = 140°$,

so use $\dfrac{\sin \hat{P}}{p} = \dfrac{\sin \hat{Q}}{q}$.

This gives $\dfrac{\sin 140°}{5} = \dfrac{\sin \hat{Q}}{4}$, so

$$\sin \hat{Q} = \frac{4 \sin 140°}{5} = 0.5142\ldots,\ \hat{Q} = 30.94\ldots°.$$

The angle at Q is 30.9° to the nearest 0.1°.

Q, P, R, 5 cm, 140°, 4 cm

Fig. 16.12

Another angle, (180 – 30.9) °, also has the property that its sine is 0.5142... , but it should be clear that this could not be an angle of a triangle in which one of the other angles is 140°.

(b) To find r you need to know the angle $\hat{R}$. This is easy, since $\hat{P} + \hat{Q} + \hat{R} = 180°$, so $\hat{R} = 180° - 140° - 30.94\ldots° = 9.05\ldots°$.

Now use the sine rule in the form $\dfrac{p}{\sin \hat{P}} = \dfrac{r}{\sin \hat{R}}$, to give $\dfrac{5}{\sin 140°} = \dfrac{r}{\sin 9.05\ldots°}$,

$$r = \frac{5 \times \sin 9.05\ldots°}{\sin 140°} = 1.224\ldots.$$

So PQ is 1.22 cm, correct to 3 significant figures.

16.5 The longest and shortest sides of a triangle

Try drawing some sketches of triangles ABC (both acute- and obtuse-angled) with the angle at A greater than the angle at B. Is it always true that the side opposite A is longer than the side opposite B?

The answer to the question is yes:

In any triangle ABC,

if $\hat{A} > \hat{B}$, then $a > b$,

and if $a > b$, then $\hat{A} > \hat{B}$.

You can use the sine rule to prove this, but it will not be proved in this book.

It follows from this that the longest side of a triangle is the side opposite the largest angle, and the shortest side is opposite the smallest angle; it is also true that the largest angle of a triangle is opposite the longest side and the smallest angle is opposite the shortest side.

Exercise 16B

1 In each part of this question, use the sine rule to find the length of the unknown side.

(a)

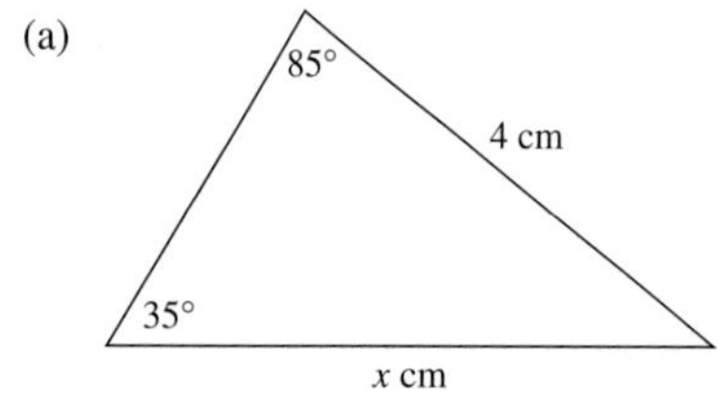

(b)

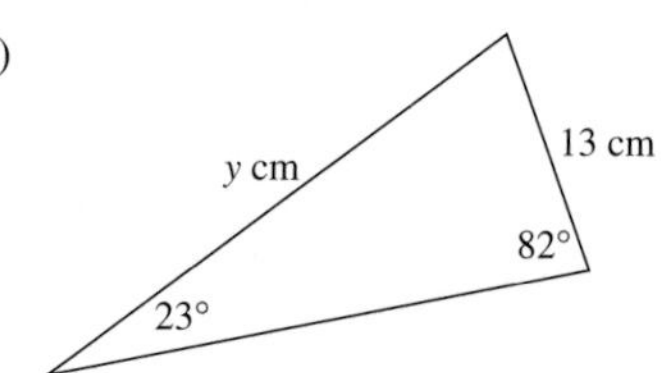

(c)

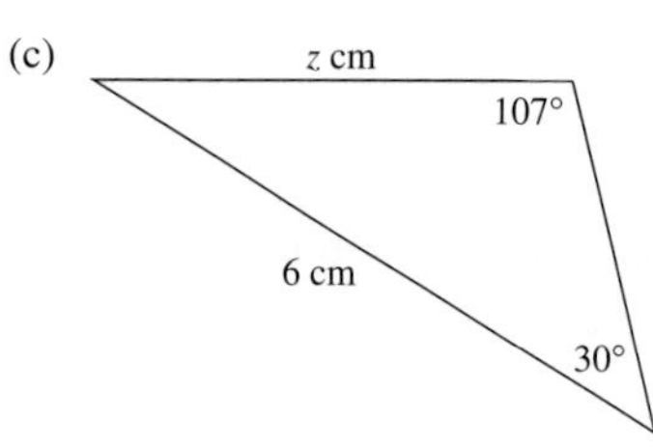

(d)

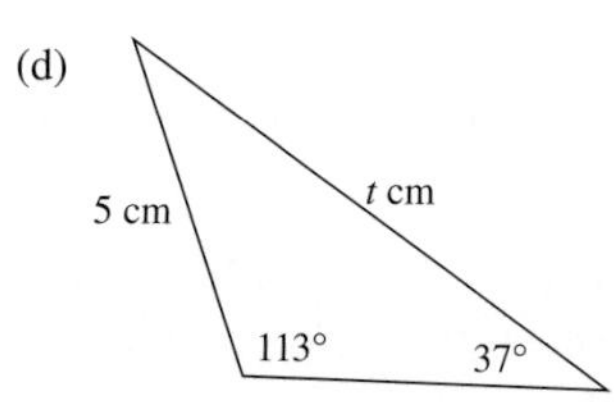

(e)

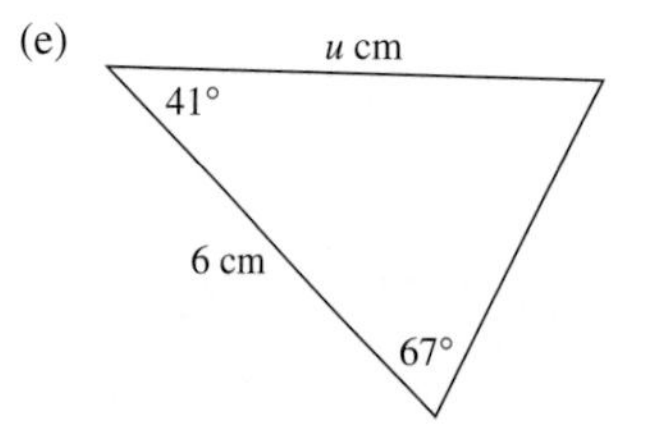

(f)

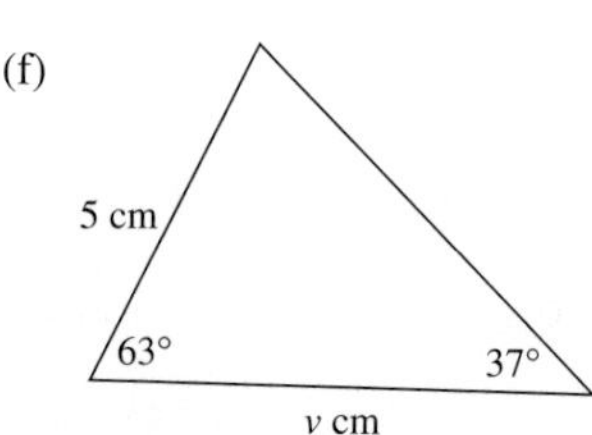

2 In each part, find the lengths of the other two sides, and the area of the triangle.

(a) In triangle ABC, $\hat{A} = 58°$, $\hat{B} = 63°$, AC = 13 cm.

(b) In triangle PQR, $\hat{Q} = 118°$, $\hat{R} = 30°$, PR = 14 cm.

(c) In triangle XYZ, $\hat{X} = 71°$, $\hat{Z} = 59°$, XZ = 12 cm.

(d) In triangle LMN, $\hat{M} = 125°$, $\hat{N} = 15°$, LN = 13.2 cm.

3 Find the remaining angles of the triangles ABC and XYZ.

(a) $\hat{B} = 91°$, BC = 11.1 cm, AC = 12.3 cm (b) $\hat{X} = 71°$, YZ = 10.1 cm, XZ = 9.2 cm

4 The triangles LMN and DEF are both obtuse-angled. Find the remaining angles.

(a) $\hat{M} = 13°$, MN = 23.1 cm, LN = 5.2 cm (b) $\hat{E} = 40°$, DF = 9 cm, DE = 13 cm

5 The following method is used to find the position of an object that you can see, but not get to, such as a tower across a river.

Let the tower be at T. Measure accurately the length of a base line [AB] on your side of the river, and measure the angles TÂB and TB̂A. Calculate

(a) AT,

(b) the perpendicular distance of the tower from the line segment [AB].

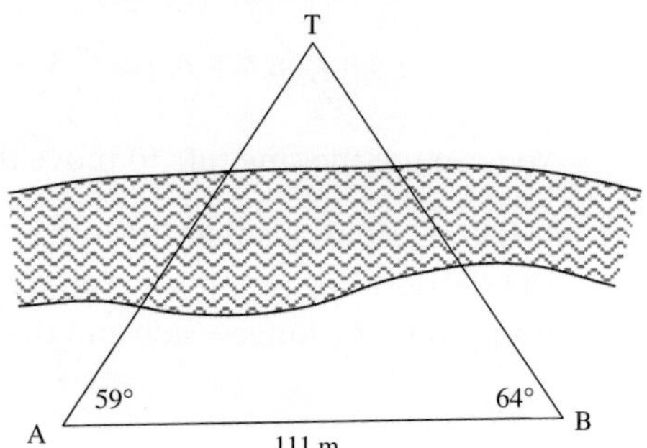

6 ABCD is a quadrilateral. The lengths of [CB] and [CD] are 4 cm and 3 cm respectively, and the diagonal CA is 5 cm. The angles at B and D are 70° and 120° respectively.

(a) Calculate angle BÂD. (b) Calculate angle BĈD.

7 If you try to find the angle $\hat{A}$ in a triangle with $\hat{B} = 120°$, $a = 15$ cm and $b = 10$ cm you get an error message. Why?

8 ABCD is a quadrilateral. BÂC = 80°, BĈA = 30°, AĈD = 50° and AD̂C = 60°. The length of [AB] is 3 cm. Calculate

(a) AC, (b) CD, (c) the area of ABCD.

16.6 The cosine rule for a triangle

You have seen that, if you know one side of a triangle and the angle opposite to it, together with one other fact, you can use the sine rule to find the other sides and angles. The extra fact can either be another side (as in Example 16.4.1) or another angle (as in Example 16.4.2).

But if you know two sides and the angle between them, the sine rule is no help. For example, suppose that $a = 5$, $b = 4$ and $\hat{C} = 60°$ and you need to find c. This is shown in Fig. 16.13.

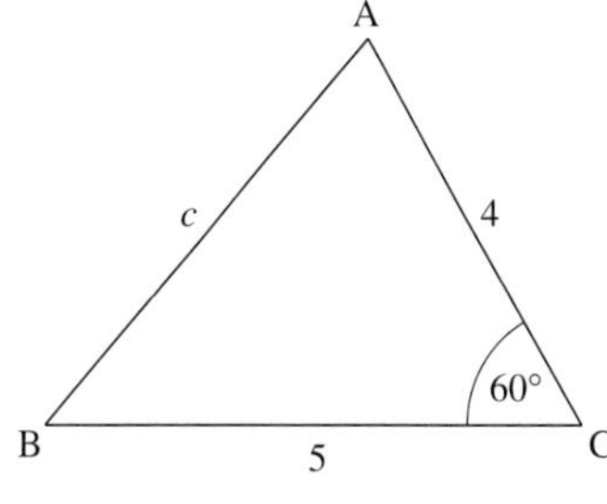

Fig. 16.13

If you try to use the sine rule, you get

$$\frac{5}{\sin \hat{A}} = \frac{4}{\sin \hat{B}} = \frac{c}{\sin 60°}.$$

There is something unknown in each of the three fractions. To find c, you would need to know either $\sin \hat{A}$ or $\sin \hat{B}$, but you don't know either. You need another method.

In general, the problem is that you know both the lengths a units and b units and the size of the angle at C, and you need to find the length c units. The angle at C may be either acute (as in Fig. 16.14) or obtuse (as in Fig. 16.15).

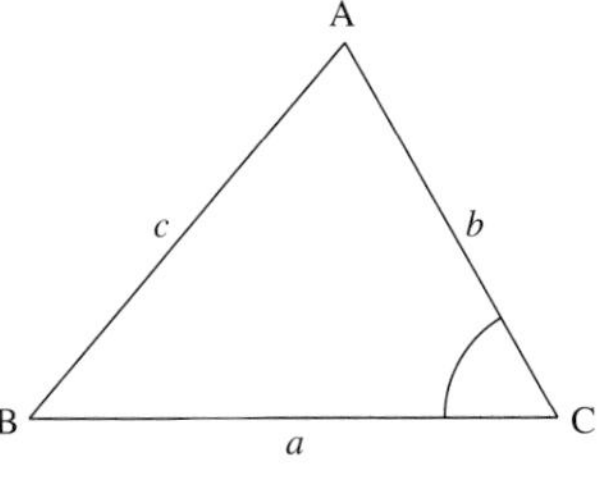

Fig. 16.14

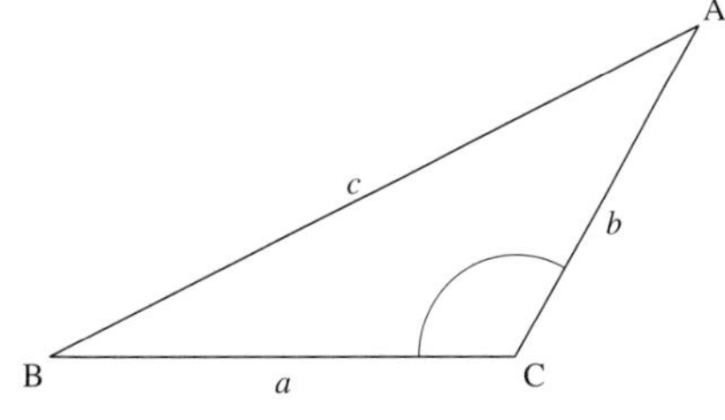

Fig. 16.15

In Sections 15.1 and 15.2 the cosine and sine of an angle were defined using coordinates. It is convenient to go back to these definitions to derive a method for solving this problem.

In Figs. 16.16 and 16.17 the triangles in Figs. 16.14 and 16.15 have been picked up and put down on a set of coordinate axes.

The vertex C is placed on the origin, and the triangle is rotated so that the vertex A is placed on the positive x-axis. The coordinates of A are therefore $(b, 0)$.

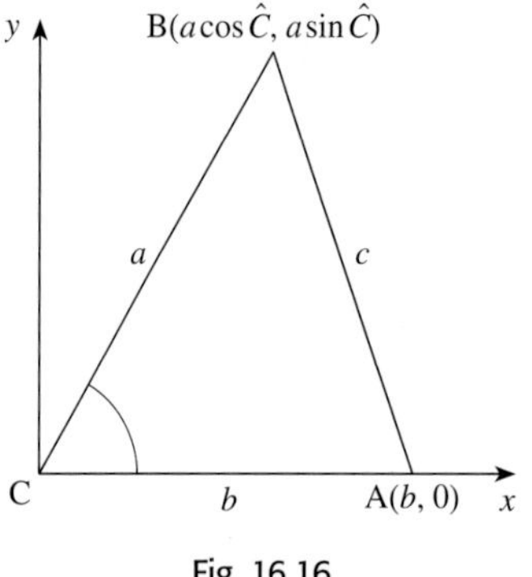

Fig. 16.16

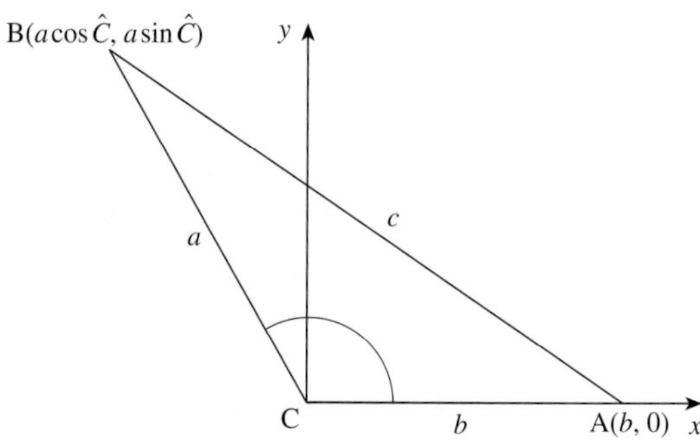

Fig. 16.17

The coordinates of the vertex B are $(a\cos\hat{C},\ a\sin\hat{C})$. This is true whether the angle ACB is acute (as in Fig. 16.16) or obtuse (as in Fig. 16.17).

The formula in Section 7.1 for AB in terms of coordinates gives

$$\begin{aligned} c^2 &= (a\cos\hat{C} - b)^2 + (a\sin\hat{C} - 0)^2 \\ &= (a\cos\hat{C})^2 - 2(a\cos\hat{C})b + b^2 + (a\sin\hat{C})^2 \\ &= a^2(\cos\hat{C})^2 - 2(a\cos\hat{C})b + b^2 + a^2(\sin\hat{C})^2. \end{aligned}$$

Conventionally, $(\cos\theta^\circ)^2$ is written as $\cos^2\theta^\circ$ and $(\sin\theta^\circ)^2$ as $\sin^2\theta^\circ$.

In this case, $(a\cos\hat{C})^2 = a^2\cos^2\hat{C}$ and $(a\sin\hat{C})^2 = a^2\sin^2\hat{C}$. Continuing with the expression for c^2,

$$\begin{aligned} c^2 &= a^2(\cos\hat{C})^2 - 2(a\cos\hat{C})b + b^2 + a^2(\sin\hat{C})^2 \\ &= a^2\cos^2\hat{C} - 2(a\cos\hat{C})b + b^2 + a^2\sin^2\hat{C} \\ &= a^2\cos^2\hat{C} + a^2\sin^2\hat{C} + b^2 - 2ab\cos\hat{C}. \end{aligned}$$

But, from Pythagoras' theorem, $a^2\cos^2\hat{C} + a^2\sin^2\hat{C}$ is the square of CB which is a^2. So

$$c^2 = a^2 + b^2 - 2ab\cos\hat{C}.$$

As with the previous formulae this formula, which is the cosine rule, is quoted without the circumflex sign over the angle.

So the cosine rule is

$$c^2 = a^2 + b^2 - 2ab\cos C.$$

Example 16.6.1 uses the cosine rule to solve the problem at the beginning of this section.

Example 16.6.1

In the triangle ABC, suppose that BC = 5 cm, CA = 4 cm and $\hat{C} = 60°$. Find the length of the side [AB] (see Fig. 16.18).

Using the cosine rule with $a = 5$, $b = 4$ and $\hat{C} = 60°$,

$$\begin{aligned} c^2 &= 5^2 + 4^2 - 2 \times 5 \times 4 \times \cos 60° \\ &= 25 + 16 - 40 \times \tfrac{1}{2} \\ &= 21, \end{aligned}$$

so $c = \sqrt{21} = 4.582\ldots$.

The side [AB] has length 4.58 cm, correct to 3 significant figures.

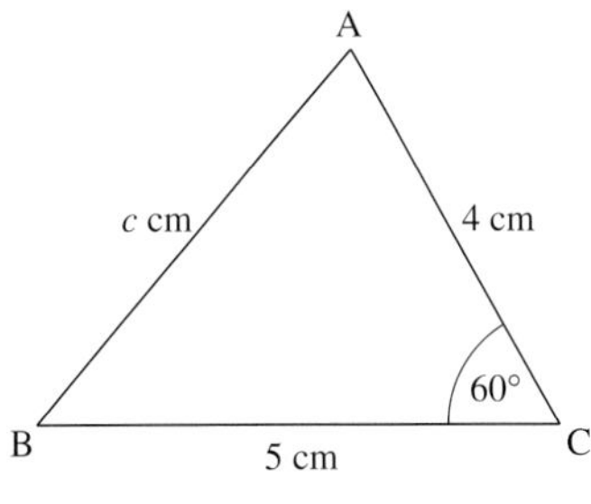

Fig. 16.18

Of course, it may happen that you are given one of the other angles of the triangle, and the lengths of the two sides which border it. In that case you will need the rule in a different form, just as with the area formula in Section 16.3.

For a triangle ABC there are three forms of the equation.

The **cosine rule** for a triangle ABC has one of the three forms:

$$a^2 = b^2 + c^2 - 2bc \cos A,$$
$$b^2 = c^2 + a^2 - 2ca \cos B,$$
$$c^2 = a^2 + b^2 - 2ab \cos C.$$

The cosine formula in one of these forms can be used to calculate the length of a side of a triangle when you know the lengths of the other two sides and the angle between them.

Don't try to learn these three forms separately. Think of the formula as being like Pythagoras' theorem but with an adjustment, and remember the form of the adjustment.

Example 16.6.2

Find the length of the third side of a triangle given that two of the sides have lengths 4.58 cm and 3.51 cm, and that the angle between them is 130°.

Fig. 16.19 shows a sketch which is not to scale.

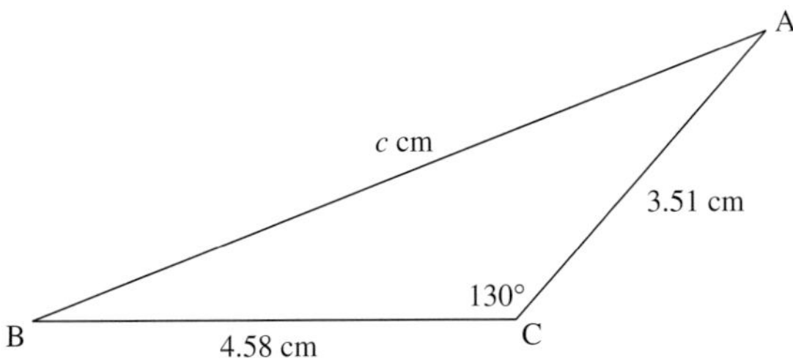

Fig. 16.19

In this case you know that $a = 4.58$, $b = 3.51$ and $\hat{C} = 130°$, so, using the cosine rule,

$$\begin{aligned} c^2 &= 4.58^2 + 3.51^2 - 2 \times 4.58 \times 3.51 \times \cos 130° \\ &= 53.963\ldots, \end{aligned}$$

giving $\quad c = 7.345\ldots$.

The length of the third side is 7.35 cm, correct to 3 significant figures.

You can also use the cosine rule when you know the lengths of all three sides of a triangle and want to find one of the angles. This is illustrated in the next example.

Example 16.6.3
Nottingham is 35 km north of Leicester. Melton Mowbray is 22 km from Leicester on the east side and 27 km from Nottingham. Find the bearing of Melton Mowbray from Leicester, giving your answer to the nearest degree.

Denoting the towns by L, M and N in Fig. 16.20, you are given that $l = 27$, $m = 35$, $n = 22$ and you want to find $N\hat{L}M$.

Substituting in the equation $l^2 = m^2 + n^2 - 2mn \cos L$,

$$729 = 1225 + 484 - 1540 \cos \hat{L},$$

so $\quad 1540 \cos \hat{L} = 1225 + 484 - 729 = 980,$

$$\cos \hat{L} = \tfrac{980}{1540} = 0.6363\ldots .$$

This gives $L = 50.47\ldots°$.

The bearing of Melton Mowbray from Leicester is 050°, to the nearest degree.

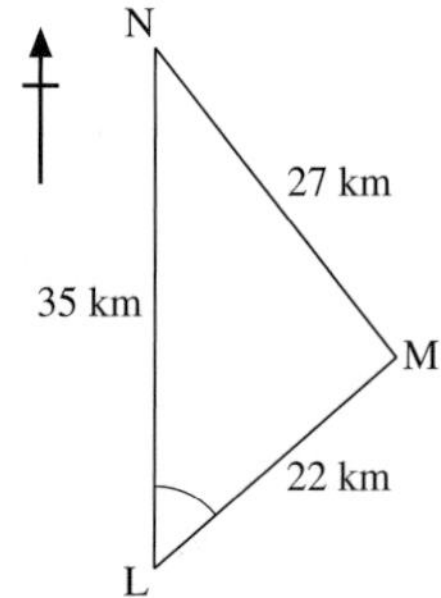

Fig. 16.20

If you put the known values of a, b and c into the formulae in the blue box earlier in this section, you get equations for the unknowns $\cos \hat{A}$, $\cos \hat{B}$ and $\cos \hat{C}$. You can then solve these equations to find $\hat{A}$, $\hat{B}$ and $\hat{C}$.

For example, if you start with $c^2 = a^2 + b^2 - 2ab \cos \hat{C}$, you can rewrite it in the form

$$2ab \cos \hat{C} = a^2 + b^2 - c^2$$

which leads to

$$\cos \hat{C} = \frac{a^2 + b^2 - c^2}{2ab}.$$

You then have three equivalent formulae for finding angles:

> The three forms of the cosine rule used for finding angles are
>
> $$\cos A = \frac{b^2 + c^2 - a^2}{2bc}, \quad \cos B = \frac{c^2 + a^2 - b^2}{2ca}$$
>
> and $\quad \cos C = \dfrac{a^2 + b^2 - c^2}{2ab}.$

Example 16.6.4
Calculate the largest angle of the triangle with sides 2 cm, 3 cm and 4 cm.

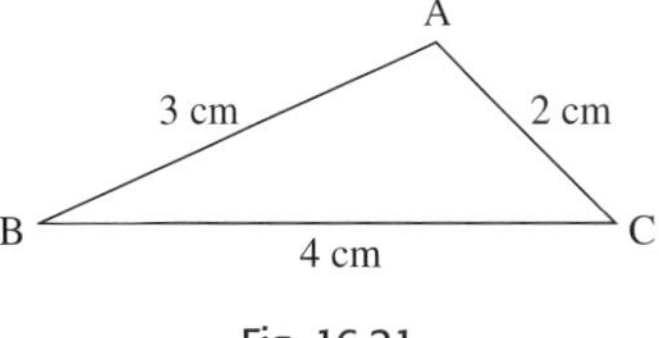

Fig. 16.21

The largest angle is at the vertex opposite the longest side. In Fig. 16.21, this is the angle at A.

Putting the values $a = 4$, $b = 2$ and $c = 3$ into the equation $\cos \hat{A} = \dfrac{b^2 + c^2 - a^2}{2bc}$ gives

$$\cos \hat{A} = \frac{2^2 + 3^2 - 4^2}{2 \times 3 \times 2}$$
$$= \frac{4 + 9 - 16}{12}$$
$$= \frac{-3}{12} = -\tfrac{1}{4} = -0.25.$$

Thus $\hat{A} = 104.47...^\circ$.

The largest angle is 104.5°, correct to 1 decimal place.

Of course, you do not need to learn the three formulae in the box because you could go back to the earlier box and use the original form of the cosine rule. It doesn't matter which you do, as long you are confident about it and use whichever form you choose accurately.

Exercise 16C

1 In each part of this question, find the length of the remaining side.

(a) BC = 10 cm, AC = 11 cm, $\hat{C} = 58^\circ$

(b) QR = 13 cm, PQ = 5 cm, $\hat{Q} = 123^\circ$

(c) XY = 15.1 cm, XZ = 14.2 cm, $\hat{X} = 23^\circ$

(d) LN = 14.8 cm, LM = 13.2 cm, $\hat{L} = 179^\circ$

2 Find the largest angle in each of the following triangles.

(a) $a = 10$, $b = 11$, $c = 12$ (b) $l = 8$, $m = 19$, $n = 13$

(c) $x = 14.1$, $y = 20.0$, $z = 15.3$ (d) $d = 9$, $e = 40$, $f = 41$

3 Find the smallest angle in each of the following triangles.

(a) $a = 10$, $b = 8$, $c = 7$ (b) $x = 9$, $y = 9$, $z = 13$

(c) $p = 8$, $q = 4$, $r = 5$ (d) $d = 4$, $e = 3$, $f = 5$

4 Find the area of the triangle with sides 8 cm, 9 cm and 10 cm.

17 Solving triangles

This chapter shows you how to use the sine and cosine rules efficiently to find unknown sides and angles of triangles. When you have completed it, you should

- know what the ambiguous case is, and be able to deal with it
- be able to use the sine and cosine rules to find all the unknown sides and angles in triangles which are not right-angled.

17.1 The ambiguous case

Suppose that you are given the following problem.

Example 17.1.1

In a triangle ABC, AB = 10 cm, $\hat{CAB} = 20^\circ$ and BC = 4 cm. Calculate $\hat{ABC}$.

As usual, start by drawing a rough sketch, shown in Fig. 17.1.

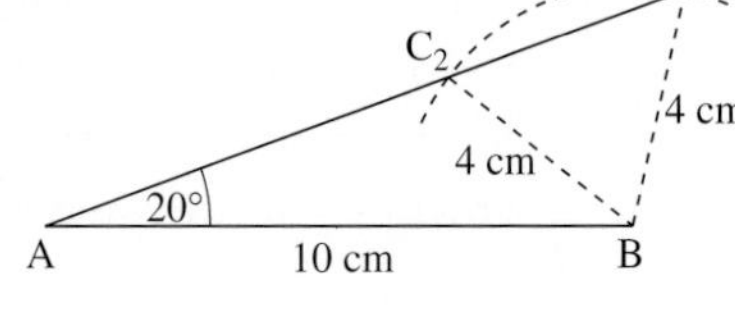

Fig. 17.1

If you draw a reasonable sketch to scale, you will see a problem. When you draw an arc with centre at B, it cuts the line at 20° to (AB) twice, giving two possible values for $\hat{ABC}$.

If you use the sine formula, you find that

$$\frac{\sin \hat{ACB}}{10} = \frac{\sin 20^\circ}{4}$$

giving

$$\sin \hat{ACB} = \frac{10 \sin 20^\circ}{4}.$$

This shows that $\hat{ACB} = 58.76...^\circ$.

It is clear that this corresponds to the point C_1. What has happened to the other point C_2?

You may have spotted the answer. The equation $\sin \hat{ACB} = \frac{10 \sin 20^\circ}{4}$ has two solutions in the interval $0^\circ < \hat{ACB} < 180^\circ$. The other solution is $180^\circ - 58.76...^\circ = 121.23...^\circ$.

So angle $\hat{ABC} = 58.8^\circ$ or 121.2°, correct to 1 decimal place.

This situation, in which the triangle is not completely specified by the information given, is called the **ambiguous case**.

It may arise when you are given two sides and one angle of a triangle, but the angle given is not the angle between the two sides.

Here is another example.

Example 17.1.2

In the triangle PQR, [PQ] has length 40 m, and $\text{P}\hat{\text{Q}}\text{R} = 40^\circ$. The length of [PR] is 30 m. Find the possible values of the angle $\text{R}\hat{\text{P}}\text{Q}$.

Start by drawing a sketch, as in Fig. 17.2.

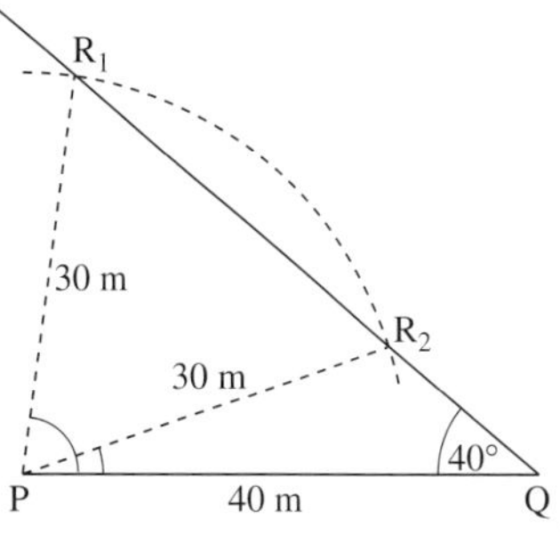

Fig. 17.2

As you can see, there are two possibilities for R: call them R_1 and R_2.

You will find that you cannot use the sine formula directly to find either of the angles R_1PQ or R_2PQ, but you can find the other angle of the triangle, and then use the angle sum of the triangle to find the third angle.

$$\frac{\sin \text{P}\hat{\text{R}}\text{Q}}{40} = \frac{\sin 40^\circ}{30}$$

giving

$$\sin \text{P}\hat{\text{R}}\text{Q} = \frac{40 \sin 40^\circ}{30},$$

so

$$\begin{aligned}\text{P}\hat{\text{R}}\text{Q} &= 58.98...^\circ \text{ or } 180^\circ - 58.98...^\circ \\ &= 58.98...^\circ \text{ or } 121.01...^\circ.\end{aligned}$$

Therefore

$$\begin{aligned}\text{R}\hat{\text{P}}\text{Q} &= 180^\circ - 40^\circ - 58.98...^\circ \text{ or } 180^\circ - 40^\circ - 121.01...^\circ \\ &= 81.01...^\circ \text{ or } 18.98...^\circ \\ &= 81.0^\circ \text{ or } 19.0^\circ, \text{ correct to 1 decimal place.}\end{aligned}$$

The next example shows another possibility when dealing with the ambiguous case.

Example 17.1.3

In the triangle XYZ, XY = 20 cm, YZ = 12 cm and angle $\text{Z}\hat{\text{X}}\text{Y} = 30^\circ$. Calculate the possible lengths of the side [XZ].

Fig. 17.3 shows the situation.

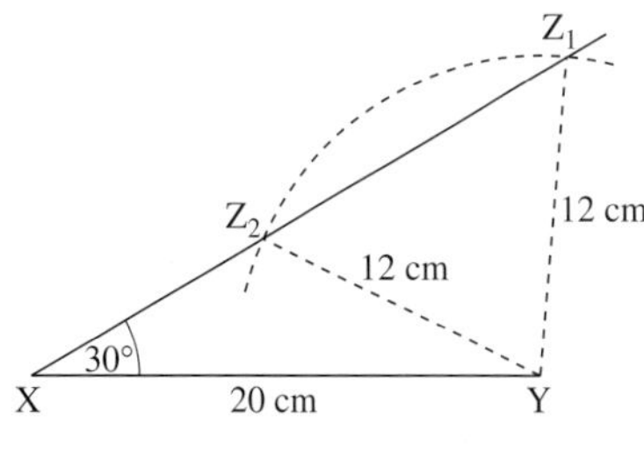

Fig. 17.3

Method 1 This method uses a direct approach.

Let the length of XZ be y cm.

Then, using the cosine formula,

$$12^2 = 20^2 + y^2 - 2 \times 20 \times y \times \cos 30^\circ$$

giving, since $\cos 30^\circ = \frac{1}{2}\sqrt{3}$,

$$y^2 - 20\sqrt{3}y + 256 = 0.$$

Solving this quadratic equation gives

$$y = \frac{20\sqrt{3} \pm \sqrt{(20\sqrt{3})^2 - 4 \times 1 \times 256}}{2}$$
$$= \frac{20\sqrt{3} \pm \sqrt{176}}{2}$$
$$= 10.68\ldots \quad \text{or} \quad 23.95\ldots .$$

So XZ is either 10.7 cm or 24.0 cm correct to 3 significant figures.

Method 2 This method uses an indirect approach.

Use the sine formula to find the angle at Z.

$$\frac{\sin \hat{Z}}{20} = \frac{\sin 30^\circ}{12},$$

giving $\hat{Z} = 56.44\ldots^\circ$ or $\hat{Z} = 180^\circ - 56.44\ldots^\circ = 123.55\ldots^\circ$.

Referring to the diagram, $X\hat{Z}_1Y = 56.44\ldots^\circ$ and $X\hat{Z}_2Y = 123.55\ldots^\circ$.

The third angle of the triangle is then $X\hat{Y}Z_1 = 180^\circ - 30^\circ - 56.44\ldots^\circ = 93.55\ldots^\circ$ or $X\hat{Y}Z_2 = 180^\circ - 30^\circ - 123.55\ldots^\circ = 26.44\ldots^\circ$.

Now use the sine formula in each case to get

$$\frac{y}{\sin 93.55\ldots^\circ} = \frac{12}{\sin 30^\circ} \quad \text{or} \quad \frac{y}{\sin 26.44\ldots^\circ} = \frac{12}{\sin 30^\circ},$$

giving $y = 23.95\ldots$ or $y = 10.68\ldots$.

So XZ is either 10.7 cm or 24.0 cm, correct to 3 significant figures.

Exercise 17A

In this exercise, there may be more than one triangle which matches the given information.

1 Find the other angles of the triangles given.

(a) In triangle ABC, $\hat{A} = 20^\circ$, AB = 10 cm, BC = 4 cm.

(b) In triangle XYZ, $\hat{Z} = 50^\circ$, ZY = 12 cm, XY = 10 cm.

(c) In triangle PQR, $\hat{Q} = 40^\circ$, PQ = 12 cm, PR = 13 cm.

2 Find the length of the third side in each of the given triangles.

(a) In triangle DEF, $\hat{D} = 25^\circ$, DE = 13 cm, EF = 6 cm.

(b) In triangle LMN, $\hat{L} = 45^\circ$, MN = 11 cm, LM = 15 cm.

(c) In triangle UVW, $\hat{U} = 80^\circ$, VW = 19 cm, UV = 18 cm.

17.2 Calculating sides and angles

If you are given information about a triangle and are asked to find all the remaining sides and angles, you are said to be **solving the triangle**.

Precisely how you do this will depend on the information you are given.

- If you know one side, the opposite angle and one other fact (a side or an angle) then begin by using the sine rule.
- If you know two sides and the angle between them, or three sides, begin by using the cosine rule.
- Once you know two angles, you can find the third by using the fact that sum of the three angles is 180°.
- Once you know three sides and an angle, you can find another angle either by using the cosine rule or by using the sine rule. If you use the sine rule, it is better to use it to find the smaller angle.
- If you know two sides and an angle which is not between the sides, it is possible that there may be more than one triangle. You could start either by using the sine rule or the cosine rule.
- Don't approximate prematurely, or you will lose accuracy; keep the full values in the calculator memory until the end of the calculation.

Example 17.2.1
In triangle ABC, $a = 9$, $b = 10$ and $\hat{B} = 20°$. Solve the triangle.

In the sketch (Fig. 17.4) side AB is labelled c.

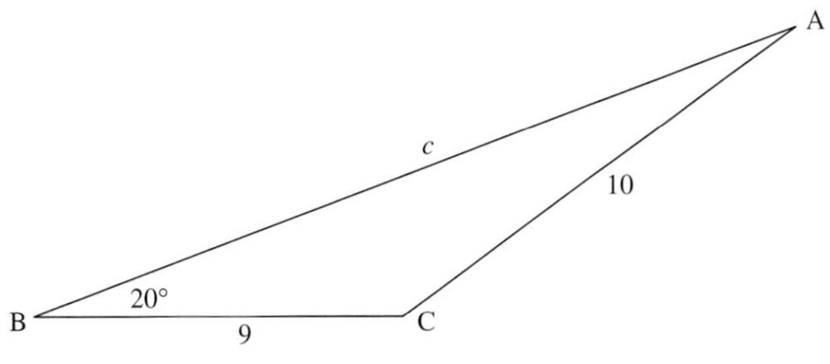

Fig. 17.4

You are given the angle $\hat{B}$ and the side b, so use the sine rule. As the other piece of information is a, use it in the form $\dfrac{\sin \hat{A}}{a} = \dfrac{\sin \hat{B}}{b}$ to get

$$\frac{\sin \hat{A}}{9} = \frac{\sin 20°}{10}$$

giving $\sin \hat{A} = \dfrac{9 \times \sin 20°}{10} = 0.307...$, so $\hat{A} = 17.92...^\circ$ or $162.07...^\circ$.

But the obtuse angle is impossible because the angle sum would be greater than 180°, so $\hat{A} = 17.92...^\circ$.

You can now find the third angle from $\hat{C} = 180^\circ - 20^\circ - 17.92...^\circ = 142.07...^\circ$.

To find c, use the sine formula.

$$\frac{10}{\sin 20^\circ} = \frac{c}{\sin 142.07...^\circ} \quad \text{gives} \quad c = \frac{10 \times \sin 142.07...^\circ}{\sin 20^\circ} = 17.97... .$$

The other two angles are 17.9° and 142.1°, correct to 1 decimal place, and $c = 18.0$, correct to 3 significant figures.

Example 17.2.2
Solve the triangle shown in Fig. 17.5.

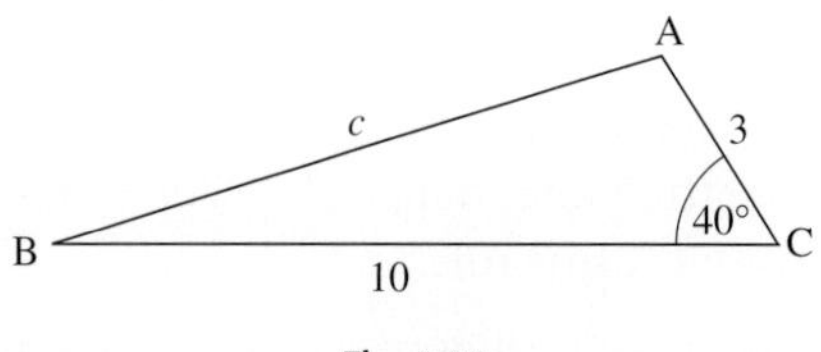

Fig. 17.5

You have no choice about how to start; use the cosine formula to find the side c.

$$c^2 = 10^2 + 3^2 - 2 \times 10 \times 3 \times \cos 40^\circ = 63.03... \quad \text{giving} \quad c = 7.939... .$$

Store this number in the calculator. You are going to need it again later.

You now have a choice: you could either use the sine rule or the cosine rule.

Method 1 Using the sine rule

Find either $\hat{A}$ or $\hat{B}$; choose the smaller angle, $\hat{B}$, because the angle at $\hat{A}$ might be obtuse.

$$\frac{\sin \hat{B}}{3} = \frac{\sin 40^\circ}{7.939...} \quad \text{giving} \quad \sin \hat{B} = \frac{3 \times \sin 40^\circ}{7.939...} = 0.2428... \text{, and}$$

B $= 14.05...^\circ$. This leaves angle $\hat{A}$ to be found by subtraction, giving

$$\hat{A} = 180^\circ - 40^\circ - 14.05...^\circ = 125.94...^\circ.$$

(Note that if you used $\dfrac{\sin \hat{A}}{10} = \dfrac{\sin 40^\circ}{7.939...}$, you would get $\sin \hat{A} = 0.809...$, giving $\hat{A} = 54.05...^\circ$, but you want $\hat{A} = 180^\circ - 54.05...^\circ$, *not* $54.05...^\circ$.)

Method 2 Using the cosine rule

Find either $\hat{A}$ or $\hat{B}$ by the cosine rule.

$$\cos \hat{A} = \frac{3^2 + 7.939...^2 - 10^2}{2 \times 3 \times 7.939...} = -0.586..., \quad \text{giving} \quad \hat{A} = 125.94...^\circ.$$

Then $\hat{B} = 180^\circ - 40^\circ - 125.94...^\circ = 14.05...^\circ$.

By either method, the angle at A is 125.9°, the angle at B is 14.1°, both correct to 1 decimal place, and the length of side c is 7.94 units, correct to 3 significant figures.

Exercise 17B

In each question solve the given triangle.

1 In triangle ABC, BC = 5 cm, $\hat{A} = 50^\circ$ and $\hat{B} = 60^\circ$.

2 In triangle XYZ, XY = 6 cm, YZ = 7 cm and $\hat{X} = 80^\circ$.

3 In triangle PQR, PQ = 3 cm, QR = 5 cm and RP = 7 cm.

4 In triangle LMN, MN = 10 cm, NL = 11 cm and $\hat{N} = 110^\circ$.

5 In triangle DEF, DE = 10 cm, EF = 6 cm and $\hat{D} = 30^\circ$.

18 Radians

This chapter introduces radians, an alternative to degrees for measuring angles. When you have completed it, you should

- know how to convert from degrees to radians and vice versa
- be able to use the formula $r\theta$ for the length of a circular arc, and the formula $\frac{1}{2}r^2\theta$ for the area of a circular sector.

18.1 Radians

Suppose that you were meeting angles for the first time, and that you were asked to suggest a unit for measuring them. It seems highly unlikely that you would suggest the degree, which was invented by the Babylonians in ancient times. The full circle, or the right angle, both seem more natural units.

However, the unit used in modern mathematics is the radian, illustrated in Fig. 18.1. This is particularly useful in differentiating trigonometric functions, as you will see when you study Chapter 40.

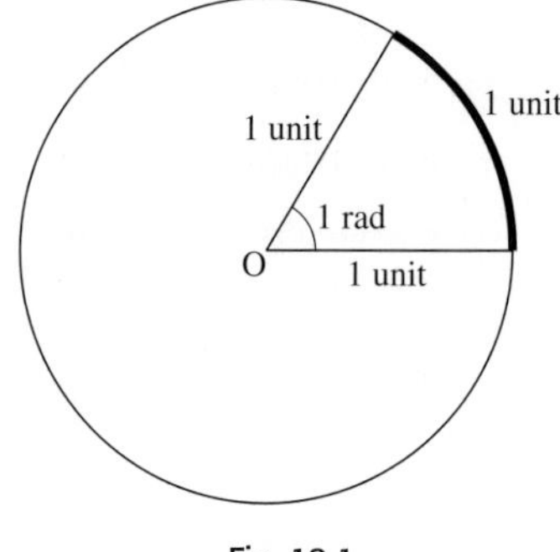

Fig. 18.1

In a circle of radius 1 unit, radii joining the centre O to the ends of an arc of length 1 unit form an angle called **1 radian**. The abbreviation for radian is **rad**.

You can see immediately from this definition that, as the circumference of the unit circle is 2π, there are 2π radians in $360°$. This leads to the following conversion rules for radians to degrees and vice versa:

> π rad $= 180°$.
>
> To convert degrees to radians, multiply by $\dfrac{\pi}{180}$.
>
> To convert radians to degrees, multiply by $\dfrac{180}{\pi}$.

You could calculate that 1 radian is equal to $57.295...°$, but no one uses this conversion. It is simplest to remember that π rad $= 180°$, and to use this to convert between radians and degrees.

> You can set your calculator to radian mode, and then work entirely in radians.
>
> You might find on your calculator another unit for angle called the 'grad'; there are 100 grads to the right angle. Grads will not be used in this course.

Example 18.1.1

Convert 40° to radians, leaving your answer as a multiple of π.

Using the conversion factor in the blue box,

$$40^\circ = 40 \times \frac{\pi}{180} \text{ rad} = \tfrac{2}{9}\pi \text{ rad}.$$

It is worthwhile learning a few common conversions, so that you can think in both radians and degrees. For example, you should know and recognise the following conversions:

$$180^\circ = \pi \text{ rad}, \qquad 90^\circ = \tfrac{1}{2}\pi \text{ rad}, \qquad 45^\circ = \tfrac{1}{4}\pi \text{ rad},$$

$$30^\circ = \tfrac{1}{6}\pi \text{ rad}, \qquad 60^\circ = \tfrac{1}{3}\pi \text{ rad}, \qquad 360^\circ = 2\pi \text{ rad}.$$

18.2 Length of arc and area of sector

Fig. 18.2 shows a circle, centre O and radius r. An arc of this circle has been drawn with a thicker line, and the two radii at the ends of the arc have been drawn. These radii have an angle θ rad between them. This is described more briefly by saying that the arc **subtends** an angle θ rad at the centre of the circle. You can calculate the length of the circular arc by noticing that the length of the arc is the fraction $\frac{\theta}{2\pi}$ of the length $2\pi r$ of the circumference of the circle.

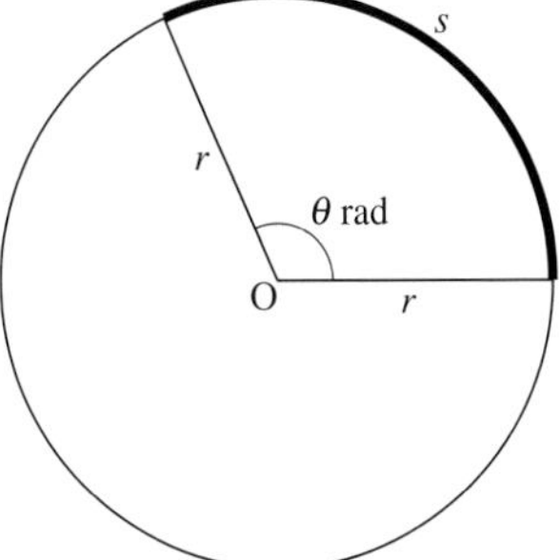

Fig. 18.2

Let s be the arc length. Then

$$s = \frac{\theta}{2\pi} \times 2\pi r = r\theta.$$

You can use a similar argument to calculate the area of a sector.

The circular sector, centre O and radius r, shown shaded in Fig. 18.3, has an angle θ rad at the centre.

The area of the circular sector is the fraction $\frac{\theta}{2\pi}$ of the area πr^2 of the full circle.

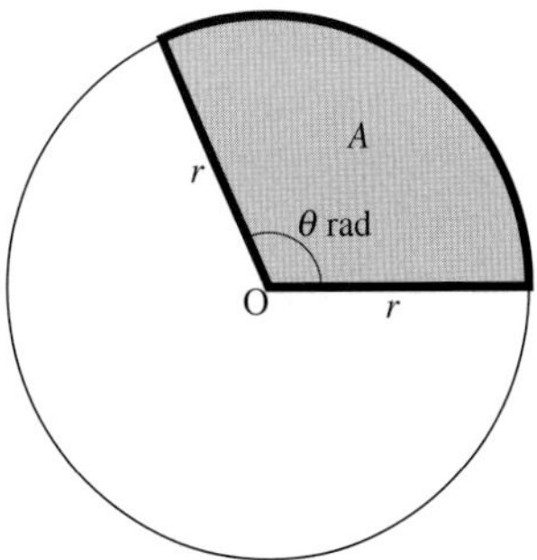

Fig. 18.3

Let A be the required area. Then

$$A = \frac{\theta}{2\pi} \times \pi r^2 = \tfrac{1}{2}r^2\theta.$$

The length of a circular arc with radius r and angle θ rad is $s = r\theta$.

The area of a circular sector with radius r and angle θ rad is $A = \tfrac{1}{2}r^2\theta$.

No units are given in the formulae above. The units are the appropriate units associated with the length; for instance, length in m and area in m^2.

Example 18.2.1

In Fig. 18.4, find the length of the arc AB and the area of the sector OAB.

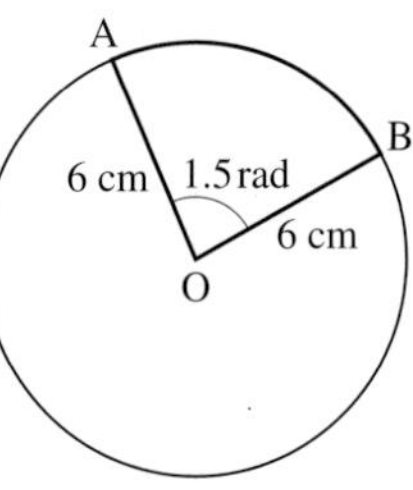

Fig. 18.4

Using the formulae in the blue box,

length of the arc AB is 6×1.5 cm $= 9$ cm,
area of sector OAB is $\frac{1}{2} \times 6^2 \times 1.5$ cm$^2 = 27$ cm^2.

Example 18.2.2

In Fig. 18.5, the area of the sector AOB is 18.4 m^2. Find A$\hat{O}$B.

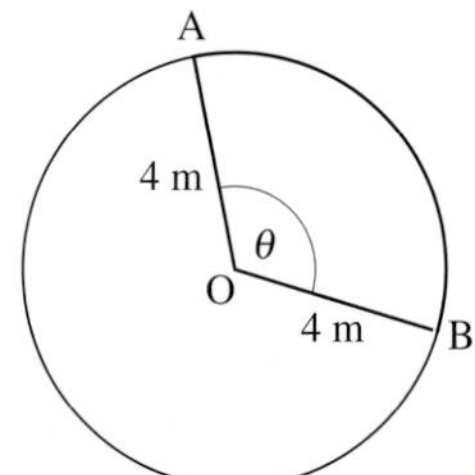

Fig. 18.5

Let A$\hat{O}$B $= \theta$ radians.

The area of the sector in m^2 is given by $\frac{1}{2} \times 4^2 \times \theta$, so

$$\tfrac{1}{2} \times 4^2 \times \theta = 18.4.$$

So $8\theta = 18.4$, giving $\theta = 2.3$.

The angle A$\hat{O}$B is 2.3 radians.

In degrees, this is $\left(\dfrac{180}{\pi} \times 2.3\right)^\circ$, which is 132° to the nearest degree.

As the radian is a measure of angle, like the degree, you can expect to need to find the sine, cosine and tangent of an angle in radians. Fortunately, your calculator enables you to do this, usually by putting it into radian mode.

Example 18.2.3

Find the perimeter and the area of the segment cut off by a chord [PQ] of length 8 cm from a circle centre O and radius 6 cm. Give your answers correct to 3 significant figures.

> In problems of this type, it is helpful to start by thinking about the complete sector OPQ, rather than just the shaded segment of Fig. 18.6.

The perimeter of the segment consists of two parts, the straight part of length 8 cm, and the curved part; to calculate the length of the curved part you need to know the angle P$\hat{O}$Q.

Call this angle θ radians. As triangle POQ is isosceles, a perpendicular drawn from O to (PQ) bisects both [PQ] and angle P$\hat{O}$Q, shown in Fig. 18.7.

$$\sin \tfrac{1}{2}\theta = \tfrac{4}{6} = 0.666\ldots, \text{ so } \tfrac{1}{2}\theta = 0.7297\ldots \text{ and } \theta = 1.459\ldots.$$

> Make sure that your calculator is in radian mode.

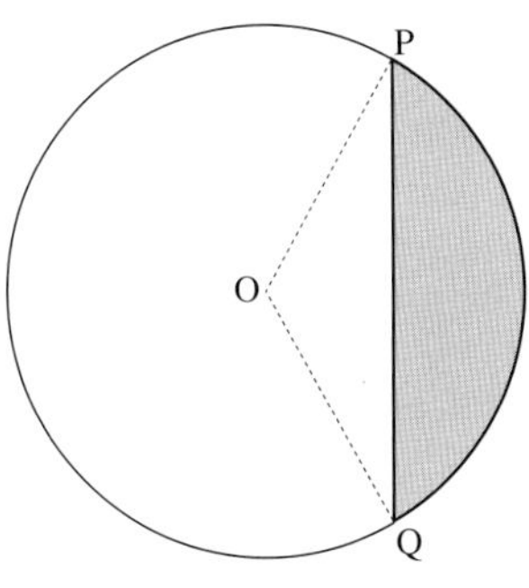

Fig. 18.6

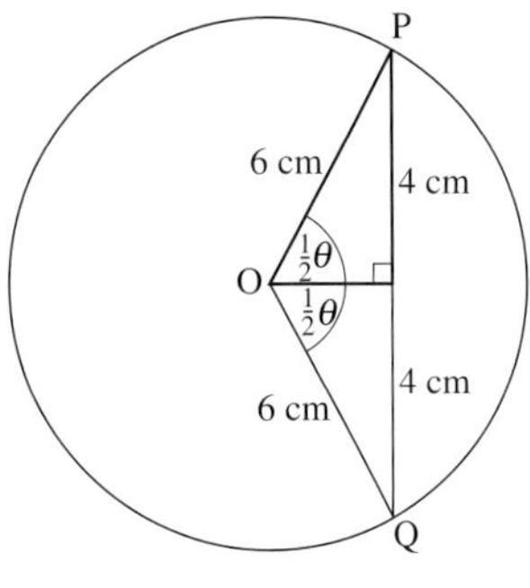

Fig. 18.7

Then the perimeter d cm is given by $d = 8 + 6\theta = 16.756...$; the perimeter is 16.8 cm, correct to 3 significant figures.

To find the area of the segment, you need to find the area of the sector OPQ, and then subtract the area of the triangle OPQ. Using the formula $\frac{1}{2}bc \sin A$ for the area of a triangle, the area of the triangle POQ is given by $\frac{1}{2}r^2 \sin\theta$. Thus the area in cm^2 of the shaded region is

$$\begin{aligned}\tfrac{1}{2}r^2(\theta - \sin\theta) &= \tfrac{1}{2} \times 6^2 \times (1.459... - \sin 1.459...)\\ &= 8.381....\end{aligned}$$

The area is 8.38 cm^2, correct to 3 significant figures.

It is worthwhile using your calculator to store the value of θ to use in the calculations. If you round θ to 3 significant figures and use the rounded value, you are liable to introduce errors.

Example 18.2.4

A chord of a circle which subtends an angle of θ radians at the centre of the circle cuts off a segment equal in area to $\frac{1}{3}$ of the area of the whole circle.

(a) Show that $\theta - \sin\theta = \frac{2}{3}\pi$.

(b) Use your calculator to solve the equation $\theta - \sin\theta = \frac{2}{3}\pi$ graphically.

(a) Let r cm be the radius of the circle in Fig. 18.8. Using a method similar to the one in Example 18.2.3, the area of the segment is

$$\tfrac{1}{2}r^2(\theta - \sin\theta).$$

This is $\frac{1}{3}$ of the area of the whole circle if

$$\tfrac{1}{2}r^2(\theta - \sin\theta) = \tfrac{1}{3}\pi r^2.$$

Multiplying by 2 and dividing by r^2 you get the required result.

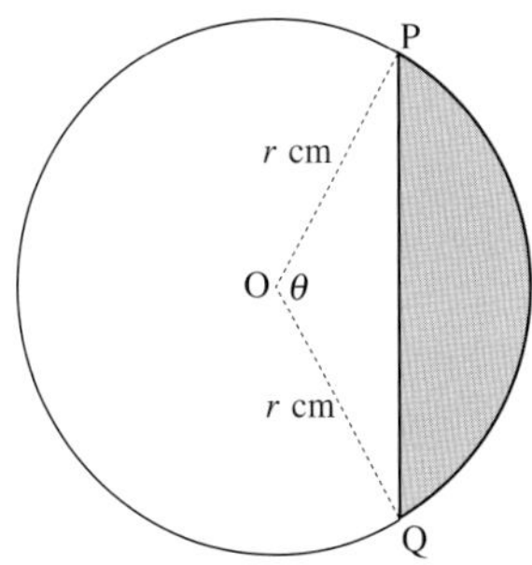

Fig. 18.8

(b) By drawing the graph of $y = \theta - \sin\theta - \frac{2}{3}\pi$ on your calculator and finding where this graph intersects the θ-axis, you find that $\theta = 2.61$ correct to 2 decimal places.

18.3 Radians or degrees?

You have probably thought up to now that degrees are the natural units for angle. However, the radian turns out to be important in differentiating and integrating trigonometric functions. For this reason, a new convention about angle will now be adopted.

In Chapter 15, when the only unit for angle that you knew was degrees, the usual way to write the cosine, sine and tangent of an angle was $\cos\theta°$, $\sin\theta°$ and $\tan\theta°$.

If the units are radians, the cosine, sine and tangent will be written without the degree sign as $\cos\theta$, $\sin\theta$ and $\tan\theta$.

If no units are given for trigonometric functions, you should assume that the units are radians, or that it doesn't matter whether the units are radians or degrees.

For example, if you see the equation $\sin\theta = 0.5$, then θ is in radians. If you are asked for the smallest positive solution of the equation, you should give $\theta = \frac{1}{6}\pi$. In this situation, where the solution is an exact multiple of π, you should express your answer as a multiple of π, but if the equation were $\sin\theta = 0.4$, you would give the answer in decimal form as 0.411... , or as 0.412, correct to 3 significant figures.

If, however, degrees are being used, then the degree sign will continue to be used. So, if you see $\sin\theta° = 0.5$, then θ is in degrees, and the smallest positive solution is $\theta = 30$.

This may seem complicated, but the context will usually make things clear.

Remember:

> $\pi \text{ rad} = 180°$.

Exercise 18

1 Write each of the following angles in radians, leaving your answer as a multiple of π.

(a) $90°$ (b) $135°$ (c) $45°$ (d) $30°$
(e) $72°$ (f) $18°$ (g) $120°$ (h) $22\frac{1}{2}°$
(i) $720°$ (j) $600°$ (k) $270°$ (l) $1°$

2 Each of the following is an angle in radians. Without using a calculator change these to degrees.

(a) $\frac{1}{3}\pi$ (b) $\frac{1}{20}\pi$ (c) $\frac{1}{5}\pi$ (d) $\frac{1}{8}\pi$
(e) $\frac{1}{9}\pi$ (f) $\frac{2}{3}\pi$ (g) $\frac{5}{8}\pi$ (h) $\frac{3}{5}\pi$
(i) $\frac{1}{45}\pi$ (j) 6π (k) $-\frac{1}{2}\pi$ (l) $\frac{5}{18}\pi$

3 The following questions refer to the diagram, where
r = radius of circle (in cm),
s = arc length (in cm),
A = area of sector (in cm^2),
θ = angle subtended at centre (in radians).

(a) $r = 7, \theta = 1.2$. Find s and A.

(b) $r = 3.5, \theta = 2.1$. Find s and A.

(c) $s = 12, r = 8$. Find θ and A.

(d) $s = 14, \theta = 0.7$. Find r and A.

(e) $A = 30, r = 5$. Find θ and s.

(f) $A = 24, r = 6$. Find s.

(g) $A = 64, s = 16$. Find r and θ.

(h) $A = 30, s = 10$. Find θ.

4 Find the area of the shaded segment in each of the following cases.

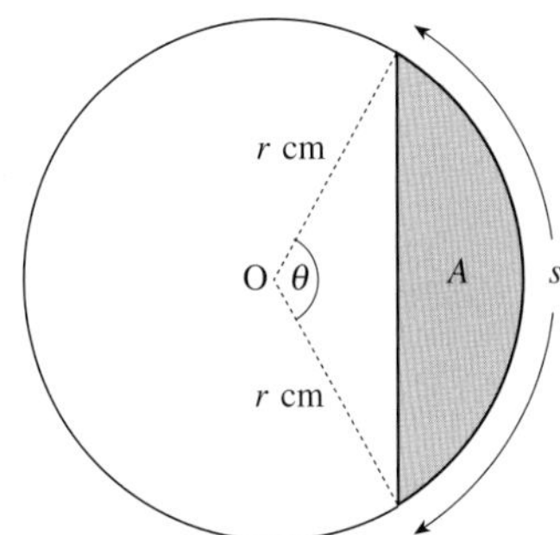

(a) $r = 5$ cm, $\theta = \frac{1}{3}\pi$

(b) $r = 3.1$ cm, $\theta = \frac{2}{5}\pi$

(c) $r = 28$ cm, $\theta = \frac{5}{6}\pi$

(d) $r = 6$ cm, $s = 9$ cm

(e) $r = 9.5$ cm, $s = 4$ cm

5 Find the area of the segment cut off by a chord of length 10 cm from a circle radius 13 cm.

6 Find the perimeter of the segment cut off by a chord of length 14 cm from a circle radius 25 cm.

7 Two circles of radii 5 cm and 12 cm are drawn, partly overlapping. Their centres are 13 cm apart. Find the area common to the two circles.

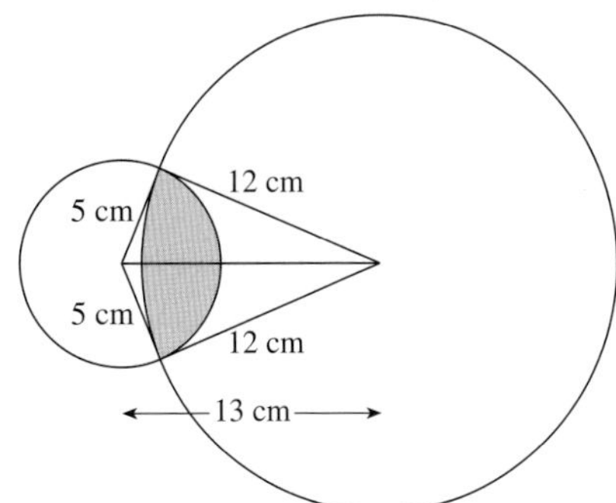

8 Two circles of radius 6 cm and 4 cm have their centres 7 cm apart. Find the perimeter and area of the region common to both circles.

9 Without the use of a calculator write down the exact values of the following.

(a) $\sin \frac{1}{3}\pi$ (b) $\cos \frac{1}{4}\pi$ (c) $\tan \frac{1}{6}\pi$ (d) $\cos \frac{3}{2}\pi$

(e) $\sin \frac{7}{4}\pi$ (f) $\cos \frac{7}{6}\pi$ (g) $\tan \frac{5}{3}\pi$ (h) $\sin^2 \frac{2}{3}\pi$

Review exercise 5

1 Write down the period of each of the following.

(a) $\sin x^\circ$ (b) $\tan 2x^\circ$ (OCR)

2 Draw the graph of $y = \cos \frac{1}{2}\theta^\circ$ for θ in the interval $-360 \le \theta \le 360$. Mark clearly the coordinates of the points where the graph crosses the θ- and y-axes.

3 A tuning fork is vibrating. The displacement, y centimetres, of the tip of one of the prongs from its rest position after t seconds is given by

$$y = 0.1 \sin(100\,000t)^\circ.$$

Find

(a) the greatest displacement and the first time at which it occurs,

(b) the time taken for one complete oscillation of the prong,

(c) the number of complete oscillations per second of the tip of the prong,

(d) the total time during the first complete oscillation for which the tip of the prong is more than 0.06 centimetres from its rest position.

4 One end of a piece of elastic is attached to a point at the top of a door frame and the other end hangs freely. A small ball is attached to the free end of the elastic. When the ball is hanging freely it is pulled down a small distance and then released, so that the ball oscillates up and down on the elastic. The depth d centimetres of the ball from the top of the door frame after t seconds is given by

$$d = 100 + 10 \cos 500t^\circ.$$

Find

(a) the greatest and least depths of the ball,

(b) the time at which the ball first reaches its highest position,

(c) the time taken for a complete oscillation,

(d) the proportion of the time during a complete oscillation for which the depth of the ball is less than 99 centimetres.

5 The shortest side of a triangle is 4.3 m long. Two of the angles are 45.1° and 51.2°. Find the length of the longest side.

6 In triangle ABC the length BC = 15.1 cm, $\mathrm{B\hat{A}C} = 56^\circ$, $\mathrm{A\hat{B}C} = 73^\circ$. Calculate the lengths of the sides AB and AC.

7 The length of the longest side of a triangle is 15 cm. Two of the angles are 39° and 48°. Find the length of the shortest side.

8 In a triangle XYZ find angle $\hat{Z}$ when YZ = 4.7 cm, XZ = 10.5 cm and XY = 8.9 cm.

9 The sides of a triangle are 7 cm, 9 cm and 12 cm. Find its angles and its area.

10 Two ships leave a harbour at the same time. The first steams on a bearing 045° at 16 km h^{-1} and the second on a bearing 305° at 18 km h^{-1}. How far apart will they be after 2 hours?

11 A sector OAB of a circle, of radius a and centre O, has $A\hat{O}B = \theta$ radians. Given that the area of the sector OAB is twice the square of the length of the arc AB, find θ. (OCR)

12 The diagram shows a sector of a circle, with centre O and radius r. The length of the arc is equal to half the perimeter of the sector. Find the area of the sector in terms of r. (OCR)

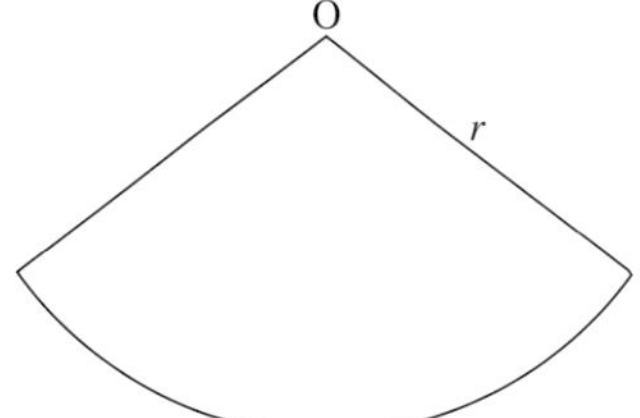

13 In the diagram, ABC is an arc of a circle with centre O and radius 5 cm. The lines [AD] and [CD] are tangents to the circle at A and C respectively. Angle $A\hat{O}C = \frac{2}{3}\pi$ radians. Calculate the area of the region enclosed by [AD], [DC] and the arc ABC, giving your answer correct to 2 significant figures. (OCR)

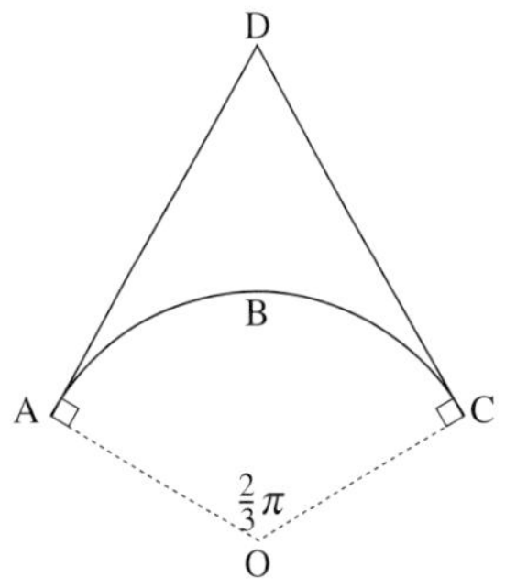

Examination questions

1 In a triangle ABC, AB = 4 cm, AC = 3 cm and the area of the triangle is 4.5 cm^2. Find the two possible values of the angle $B\hat{A}C$. (© IBO 2004)

2 In triangle ABC, AC = 5, BC = 7, $\hat{A} = 48°$, as shown in the diagram.
Find $\hat{B}$, giving your answer correct to the nearest degree. (© IBO 2002)

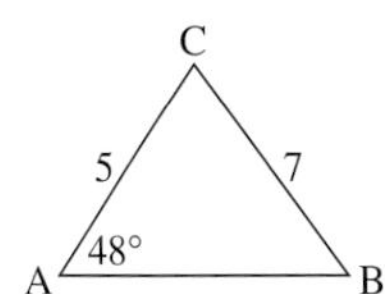

3 The points P, Q, R are three markers on level ground, joined by straight paths [PQ], [QR], [PR] as shown in the diagram. QR = 9 km, $P\hat{Q}R = 35°$, $P\hat{R}Q = 25°$.

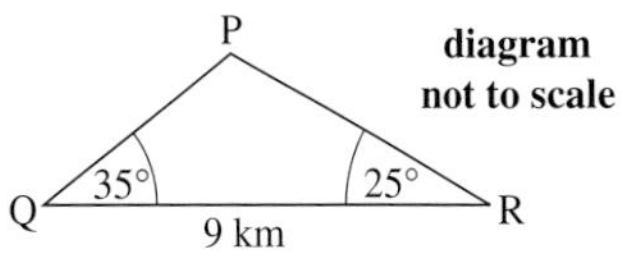

(a) Find the length PR.

(b) Tom sets out to walk from Q to P at a steady speed of 8 km h^{-1}. At the same time, Alan sets out to jog from R to P at a steady speed of a km h^{-1}. They reach P at the same time. Calculate the value of a.

(c) The point S is on [PQ], such that RS = 2QS, as shown in the diagram.

Find the length QS. (© IBO 2003)

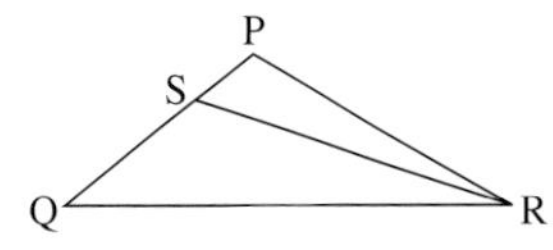

4 Two boats A and B start moving from the same point P. Boat A moves in a straight line at 20 km h^{-1} and boat B moves in a straight line at 32 km h^{-1}. The angle between their paths is 70°.

Find the distance between the boats after 2.5 hours. (© IBO 2002)

5 The diagram shows a triangular region formed by a hedge [AB], a part of a river bank [AC] and a fence [BC]. The hedge is 17 m long and BÂC is 29°. The end of the fence, point C, can be positioned anywhere along the river bank.

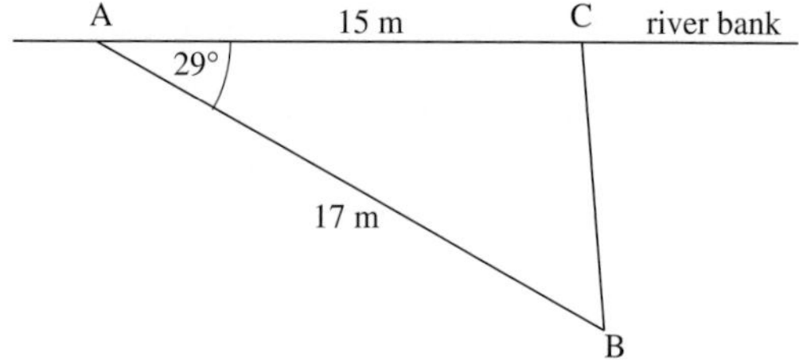

(a) Given that point C is 15 m from A, find the length of the fence [BC].

(b) The farmer has another, longer fence. It is possible for him to enclose two different triangular regions with this fence. He places the fence so that AĈB...

(i) Find the distance from A to C.

(ii) Find the area of the region ABC with the fence in this position.

(c) To form the second region, he moves the fencing so that point C is closer to point A. Find the new distance from A to C.

(d) Find the minimum length of fence [BC] needed to enclose a triangular region ABC. (© IBO 2005)

6 The diagram shows a circle of radius 5 cm with centre O. Points A and B are on the circle, and AÔB is 0.8 radians. The point N is on [OB] such that [AN] is perpendicular to [OB].

Find the area of the shaded region. (© IBO 2004)

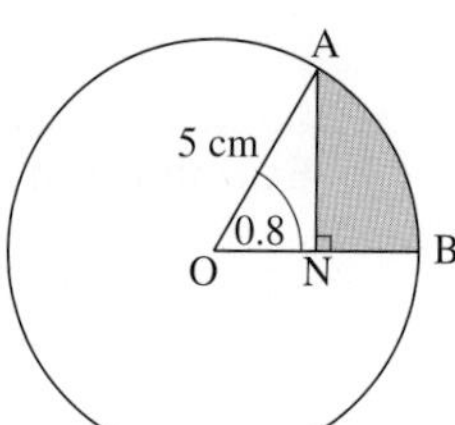

7 The diagram shows two circles which have the same centre O and radii 16 cm and 10 cm respectively. The two arcs AB and CD have the same sector angle $\theta = 1.5$ radians.

Find the area of the shaded region. (© IBO 2004)

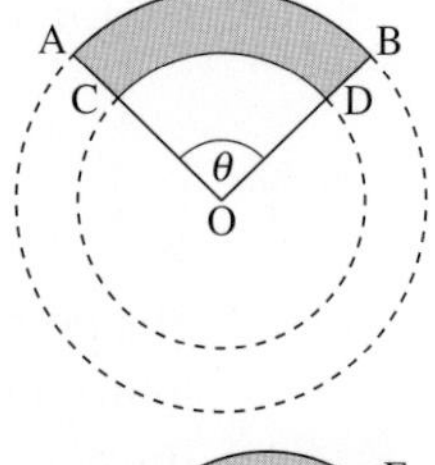

8 The diagram shows a triangle and two arcs of circles. The triangle ABC is a right-angled isosceles triangle, with AB = AC = 2. The point P is the midpoint of [BC]. The arc BDC is part of a circle with centre A. The arc BEC is part of a circle with centre P.

(a) Calculate the area of the segment BDCP.

(b) Calculate the area of the shaded region BECD. (© IBO 2003)

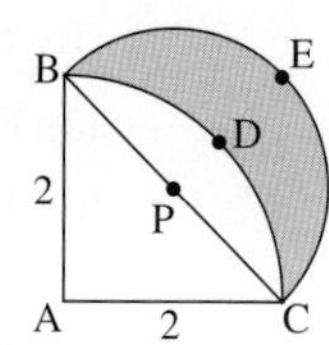

19 Investigating shapes of graphs

This chapter explains how you can use differentiation to find the shape of a graph from its equation without using a calculator. When you have completed it, you should

- understand the terms 'stationary point', 'maximum point', 'minimum point' and 'turning point'
- appreciate the significance of zero, positive and negative derivatives
- be able to locate maximum and minimum points on a graph
- use this information to investigate roots of equations.

You may wonder why this chapter is necessary. With a graphic calculator you can produce the graph of any function from its equation in a few seconds. The calculator will also give the coordinates of any maximum or minimum points to a high degree of accuracy. But now that you know about differentiation, you will be able to understand why a graph has the shape shown in the calculator display.

19.1 Stationary points

In Section 9.4 you found the coordinates of the vertex of a quadratic graph from its equation in completed square form. You used the property that the vertex of the graph is either its highest or lowest point. This is where the $(x + ...)^2$ part of the completed square expression is 0.

Another way of finding the vertex is to use differentiation. At the vertex the tangent is parallel to the x-axis, so that the gradient is 0. (See Fig. 19.1.)

Differentiation gives you the formula for the gradient. Putting this equal to 0 gives an equation for the x-coordinate of the vertex. Example 19.1.1 uses the method to find the vertex of a quadratic graph.

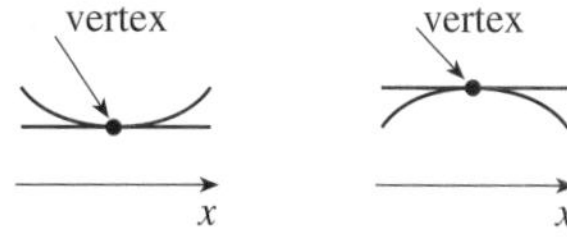

Fig. 19.1

Example 19.1.1
Locate the vertex of the parabola in Fig. 19.2 with equation $y = x^2 - 6x + 7$.

The gradient formula is $\frac{dy}{dx} = 2x - 6$. The gradient is zero when $2x - 6 = 0$, which gives $x = 3$. This is the x-coordinate of the vertex.

To find the y-coordinate of the vertex, substitute $x = 3$ in the equation, giving $y = 3^2 - 6 \times 3 + 7 = -2$. So the vertex has coordinates $(3, -2)$.

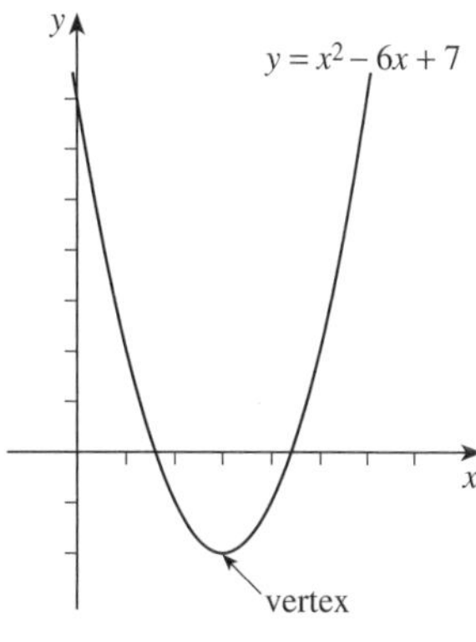

Fig. 19.2

You could of course have found the vertex in this example by writing $x^2 - 6x + 7$ as $(x - 3)^2 - 2$. But an advantage of the gradient method is that it is not restricted to quadratic graphs. Graphs with other equations do not have a 'vertex', but they may have 'peaks' or 'troughs' which occur at points where the gradient is 0.

The next two examples apply the gradient method to graphs for which $f(x)$ is a cubic and a quartic function.

Example 19.1.2
Fig. 19.3 shows part of the graph with equation $y = x^3 - 6x^2 + 9x - 1$. Find the coordinates of the peak at P and the trough at T.

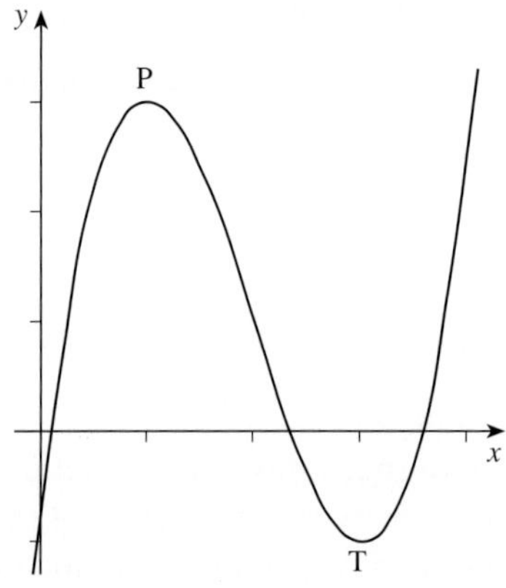

Fig. 19.3

The gradient of the curve is 0 at both P and T. Differentiating its equation gives the gradient formula

$$\frac{dy}{dx} = 3x^2 - 12x + 9.$$

So the x-coordinates of P and T satisfy the quadratic equation

$$3x^2 - 12x + 9 = 0.$$

Dividing by the common factor 3 and factorising,

$$\begin{aligned} x^2 - 4x + 3 &= 0, \\ (x - 1)(x - 3) &= 0. \end{aligned}$$

So the x-coordinates of P and T are 1 and 3.

To find the y-coordinates of P and T, substitute 1 and 3 for x in the equation $y = x^3 - 6x^2 + 9x - 1$. This gives $y = 1 - 6 + 9 - 1 = 3$ for P, and $y = 27 - 54 + 27 - 1 = -1$ for T. So the coordinates of P are $(1, 3)$, and the coordinates of T are $(3, -1)$.

Points of a graph at which the gradient is 0 are called **stationary points**. The standard method of locating stationary points is to write down the gradient formula for the graph, and to solve the equation obtained by putting this equal to 0.

Example 19.1.3
Find the stationary points on the graph with equation $y = x^4 - 4x^3 + 4x^2$.

The gradient formula is

$$\frac{dy}{dx} = 4x^3 - 12x^2 + 8x.$$

So the x-coordinates of the stationary points satisfy the equation

$$4x^3 - 12x^2 + 8x = 0.$$

Notice that $4x$ is a factor of the left side, and you can check that the other factor $x^2 - 3x + 2$ can be split into two linear factors $(x - 1)(x - 2)$. So the equation can be written as

$$4x(x - 1)(x - 2) = 0,$$

giving $x = 0$, $x = 1$ or $x = 2$.

Substituting these values of x in the equation $y = x^4 - 4x^3 + 4x^2$ gives $y = 0$, $y = 1 - 4 + 4 = 1$ and $y = 16 - 32 + 16 = 0$ respectively. The stationary points are therefore $(0, 0)$, $(1, 1)$ and $(2, 0)$.

Finding stationary points is often an important step in finding the shape of a graph. For Example 19.1.3, Fig. 19.4 shows the three stationary points with short lines indicating the horizontal tangents at these points. From this you can be sure that between $x = 0$ and $x = 2$ the curve has the form shown by the solid line in Fig. 19.5, with a peak at $(1, 1)$. You would probably guess that there are also troughs at $(0, 0)$ and $(2, 0)$, so that the graph continues as indicated by the dotted lines. You would in fact be right, but it is not so obvious. This part of the investigation is dealt with in the next section.

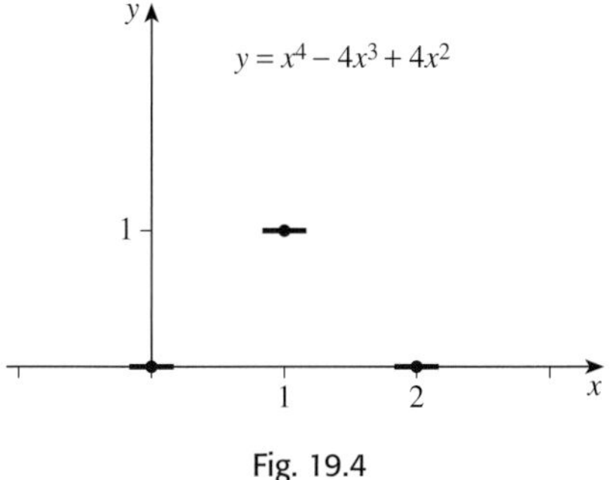

Fig. 19.4

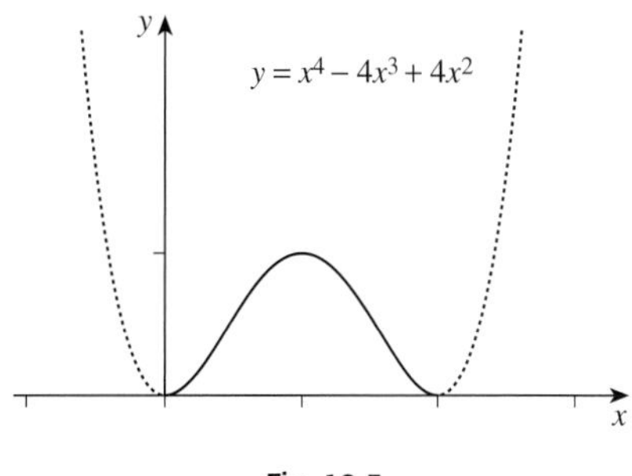

Fig. 19.5

Exercise 19A

1 Without using a calculator, find the stationary points on the graphs with the following equations.

(a) $y = 2x^2 + 4x - 5$ (b) $y = 1 + 6x - x^2$ (c) $y = x^3 + 3x^2 - 9x$

(d) $y = x^3 - 12x$ (e) $y = x^3 - 12x^2$ (f) $y = x^5 - 5x + 4$

(g) $y = (x^2 - 4)^2$ (h) $y = x(x + 1)^2$ (i) $y = x^3 - 3x^2 + 3x$

2 Find and plot the stationary points on the graphs with the following equations. Use these, and anything else you notice about the equations, to make guesses about the shape of the graphs. Then use a calculator to check your guesses.

(a) $y = 3 + 2x - x^2$ (b) $y = x^2 + x - 8$ (c) $y = (x + 5)(1 - x)$

(d) $y = (x - 2)^2$ (e) $y = 3 + x^3$ (f) $y = x^3 + 3x^2 - 2$

(g) $y = x^2(x + 1)$ (h) $y = x^3(x + 1)$ (i) $y = x^4 - 4x^3 - 20x^2$

19.2 Maximum and minimum points

The mathematical terms for the peaks and troughs of graphs are 'maximum points' and 'minimum points'. At a maximum point the value of a function $f(x)$ is higher than anywhere else on the graph in its immediate neighbourhood; it is called a 'maximum value' of the function.

But just as you can stand on top of one hill and see higher peaks across a valley, a graph may have several maximum points, each with a different maximum value. A maximum value of a function is not necessarily the greatest value it can take, but only the greatest value amongst the points on the graph in an interval around the maximum point. For this reason it is sometimes called a 'local' maximum. This is illustrated in Fig. 19.6, in which both Q and S are maximum points.

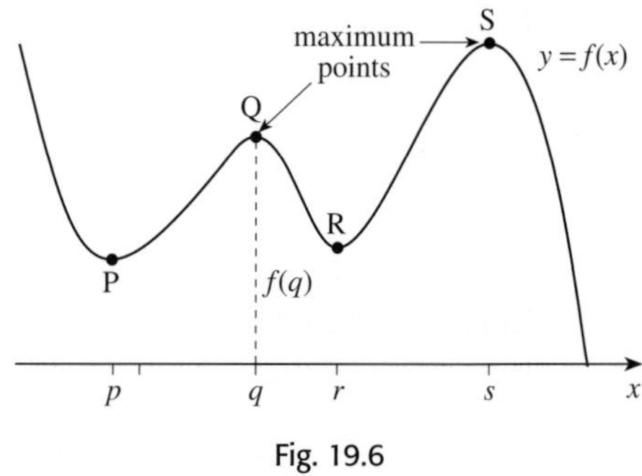

Fig. 19.6

This idea can be expressed as a precise definition:

> On the graph of $y = f(x)$ a point Q, with coordinates $(q, f(q))$, is a **(local) maximum point** if $f(q)$ is greater than the value of $f(x)$ at all the other points in an interval of values of x around q. Then $f(q)$ is called a **(local) maximum value** of $f(x)$.

The most obvious way of knowing that you have reached a peak is that you stop climbing uphill and start to walk downhill. You can use this idea to show that you are at a maximum point of a graph.

In Fig. 19.6, as you move along the curve from P to Q, the gradient $\frac{dy}{dx}$ is positive and you are gaining height the whole time. The mathematical term for this is that $f(x)$ is an **increasing function** between $x = p$ and $x = q$.

Once you are past Q the gradient is negative and you are losing height. Between $x = q$ and $x = r$, $f(x)$ is a **decreasing function**.

> If $f'(x)$ is positive in an interval of values of x, then $f(x)$ is an increasing function in that interval.
> If $f'(x)$ is negative in an interval, then $f(x)$ is a decreasing function in that interval.

> Strictly, the interval in which $f(x)$ is increasing also includes the end-points at which $f'(x) = 0$. For example, in Fig. 19.7, $f'(x) > 0$ for $p < x < q$, but $f(x)$ is increasing for $p \le x \le q$.

You can use this idea to show that Q is a maximum point on a graph with equation $y = f(x)$. Begin by finding $\frac{dy}{dx} = f'(x)$. If $\frac{dy}{dx}$ is positive in an interval to the left of $x = q$, and negative in an interval to the right, then Q is higher than any other point on the curve in an interval around it. That is, Q is a maximum point. This is illustrated in Fig. 19.7.

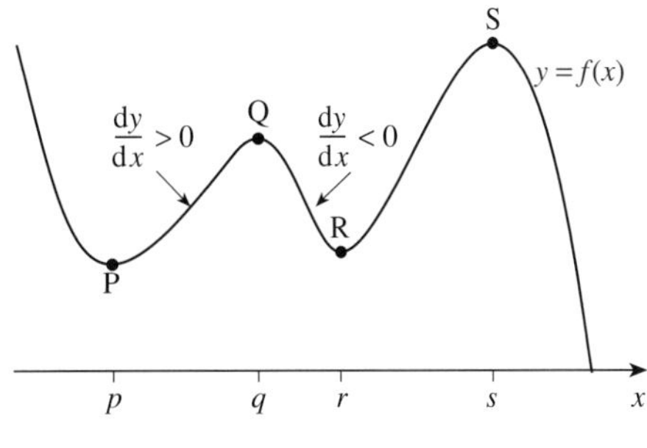

Fig. 19.7

Example 19.2.1
Find the maximum point on the graph of $y = 8 + 6x - x^2$.

The gradient formula for the graph is

$$\frac{dy}{dx} = 6 - 2x = 2(3 - x).$$

There is a stationary point where $x = 3$.

When $x < 3$, $\frac{dy}{dx}$ is positive; and when $x > 3$, $\frac{dy}{dx}$ is negative.

The stationary point at $x = 3$ is therefore a maximum point.

When $x = 3$, $y = 8 + 6 \times 3 - 3^2 = 8 + 18 - 9 = 17$.

So the maximum point has coordinates (3, 17).

Example 19.2.2
For the graph of $y = x^3 - 6x^2 + 9x - 1$ in Example 19.1.2, show that (1, 3) is a maximum point.

From Example 19.1.2,

$$\frac{dy}{dx} = 3x^2 - 12x + 9 = 3(x - 1)(x - 3).$$

You now want to know where $\frac{dy}{dx}$ is positive and where it is negative. This depends on the signs of the two factors $x - 1$ and $x - 3$; and these signs depend on whether x is greater or less than 1 and 3 respectively. These are the **critical values** for the expression. If you split the domain of the function into intervals separated by the critical values, you can produce a table of signs of $\frac{dy}{dx}$.

	$x < 1$	$x = 1$	$1 < x < 3$	$x = 3$	$x > 3$
$x - 1$	$-$	0	$+$	$+$	$+$
$x - 3$	$-$	$-$	$-$	0	$+$
$\frac{dy}{dx}$	$+$	0	$-$	0	$+$

Table 19.8

The question asked is about the point with $x = 1$. Table 19.8 shows that in the interval $x < 1$ to the left of this point the gradient is positive, so that y is increasing. In the interval $1 < x < 3$ to the right the gradient is negative, so y is decreasing. This shows that $(1, 3)$ is a maximum point.

It is useful to express this method in the form of a precise rule:

On the graph of $y = f(x)$, if $\frac{dy}{dx} > 0$ in an interval to the left of q, and $\frac{dy}{dx} < 0$ in an interval to the right of q, then $(q, f(q))$ is a maximum point.

To get the corresponding conditions for a minimum point, you have to change the direction of some of the inequalities:

On the graph of $y = f(x)$ a point Q, with coordinates $(q, f(q))$, is a **(local) minimum point** if $f(q)$ is less than the value of $f(x)$ at all the other points in an interval of values of x around q. Then $f(q)$ is called a **(local) minimum value** of $f(x)$.

If $\frac{dy}{dx} < 0$ in an interval to the left of q, and $\frac{dy}{dx} > 0$ in an interval to the right of q, then $(q, f(q))$ is a minimum point.

As an example, look back to the point R in Fig. 19.6. The gradient $\frac{dy}{dx}$ is negative when x is between q and r, and positive between r and s. So R is a minimum point on the graph.

Example 19.2.3

Find the minimum value of $f(x) = x^2 - 8x + 12$.

Differentiating,

$$f'(x) = 2x - 8 = 2(x - 4).$$

Since $f'(x)$ is negative when $x < 4$, and positive when $x > 4$, the graph of $y = f(x)$ has a minimum point where $x = 4$.

The minimum value of $f(x)$ is

$$\begin{aligned} f(4) &= 4^2 - 8 \times 4 + 12 \\ &= 16 - 32 + 12 = -4. \end{aligned}$$

Example 19.2.4
Show that the graph of $y = x^4 - 4x^3 + 4x^2$ in Example 19.1.3 has the shape predicted in Fig. 19.5.

It was shown in Example 19.1.3 that the gradient formula is $4x(x-1)(x-2)$. The critical values are $x = 0$, $x = 1$ and $x = 2$, and the table of signs is shown in Table 19.9.

	$x < 0$	$x = 0$	$0 < x < 1$	$x = 1$	$1 < x < 2$	$x = 2$	$x > 2$
$4x$	$-$	0	$+$	$+$	$+$	$+$	$+$
$x - 1$	$-$	$-$	$-$	0	$+$	$+$	$+$
$x - 2$	$-$	$-$	$-$	$-$	$-$	0	$+$
$\frac{dy}{dx}$	$-$	0	$+$	0	$-$	0	$+$

Table 19.9

This shows that, as you pass through $x = 0$ and $x = 2$ the gradient changes from negative to positive, so (0, 0) and (2, 0) are minimum points. But as you pass through $x = 1$ the gradient changes from positive to negative, so (1, 1) is a maximum point. These results agree with the graph in Fig. 19.5.

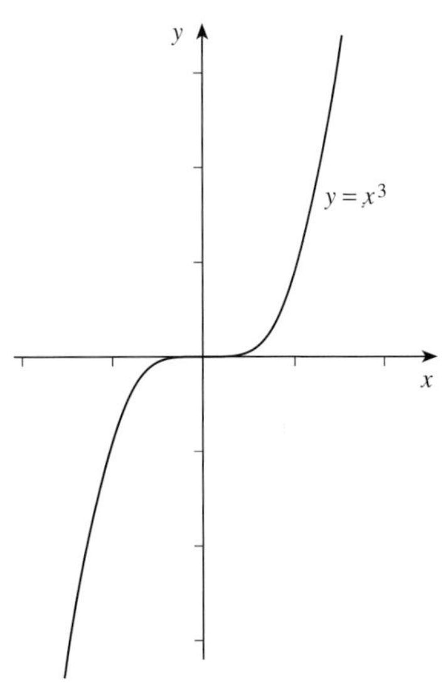

Fig. 19.10

In all the examples so far the stationary points have been either maximum or minimum points. You may be tempted to think that this is always so, but in fact you have already met exceptions.

The simplest is the graph of $y = x^3$, shown in Fig. 19.10. Since $\frac{dy}{dx} = 3x^2$, the gradient is 0 when $x = 0$. That is, the origin is a stationary point. But it is neither a maximum nor a minimum point. Since $\frac{dy}{dx}$ is positive both to the left and to the right of $x = 0$, x^3 is an increasing function for all values of x.

Example 19.2.5
Find (a) the stationary points, (b) the maximum or minimum point on the graph with equation $y = x^3(x - 4)$.

(a) Before differentiating you must multiply out the brackets to get $y = x^4 - 4x^3$. Then

$$\frac{dy}{dx} = 4x^3 - 12x^2 = 4x^2(x - 3).$$

It follows that $\frac{dy}{dx} = 0$ when $x = 0$ and when $x = 3$, where $y = 0$ and $y = 27 \times (-1) = -27$ respectively. So the stationary points are (0, 0) and (3, −27).

(b) The critical values of x are 0 and 3, giving the table of signs in Table 19.11.

	$x < 0$	$x = 0$	$0 < x < 3$	$x = 3$	$x > 3$
$4x^2$	+	0	+	+	+
$x - 3$	–	–	–	0	+
$\frac{dy}{dx}$	–	0	–	0	+

Table 19.11

This shows a sign change from – to + at $x = 3$, so $(3, -27)$ is a minimum point. But there is no sign change at $x = 0$; the gradient is negative on both sides. So this stationary point is neither a maximum nor a minimum point. This is illustrated in Fig. 19.12.

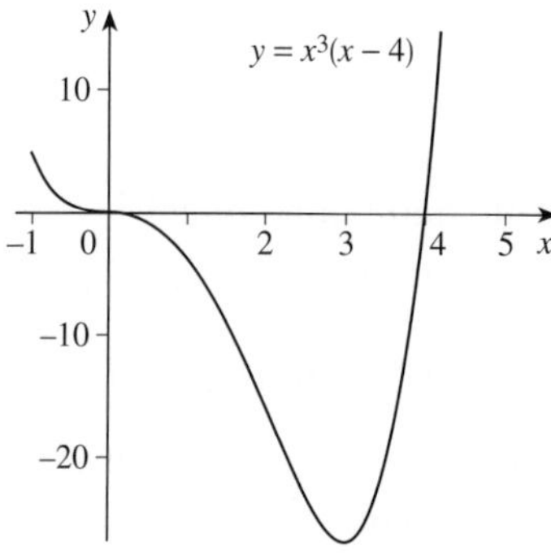

Fig. 19.12

Maximum and minimum points are sometimes also called **turning points**. A complete procedure for locating turning points, and deciding for each whether it is a maximum or a minimum, can then be summed up as follows:

To find the minimum and maximum points on the graph of $y = f(x)$:

Step 1 Find an expression for $\frac{dy}{dx} = f'(x)$.

Step 2 List the values of x for which $\frac{dy}{dx}$ is 0.

Step 3 Taking each of these values of x in turn, find the sign of $\frac{dy}{dx}$ in intervals to the left and to the right of that value.

Step 4 If these signs are – and + respectively, the graph has a minimum point. If they are + and – it has a maximum point. If the signs are the same, it has neither.

Step 5 For each value of x which gives a minimum or maximum, calculate $y = f(x)$.

Example 19.2.6

Find the turning points on the graph of $y = x^2(6 - x)$, and determine whether they are maximum or minimum points.

Step 1 $y = x^2(6 - x) = 6x^2 - x^3$, which gives $\frac{dy}{dx} = 12x - 3x^2 = 3x(4 - x)$.

Step 2 $\frac{dy}{dx} = 0$ when $x = 0$ or $x = 4$.

Step 3 Using the values of x in Step 2 as critical values, the signs of $\frac{dy}{dx}$ are shown in Table 19.13.

	$x < 0$	$x = 0$	$0 < x < 4$	$x = 4$	$x > 4$
$3x$	$-$	0	$+$	$+$	$+$
$4 - x$	$+$	$+$	$+$	0	$-$
$\frac{dy}{dx}$	$-$	0	$+$	0	$-$

Table 19.13

Step 4 There is a minimum where $x = 0$ and a maximum where $x = 4$.

Step 5 When $x = 0$, $y = 0$, so $(0, 0)$ is a minimum point on the graph.

When $x = 4$, $y = 32$, so $(4, 32)$ is a maximum point on the graph.

Exercise 19B

1 For each of the following graphs in the given interval, find whether $\frac{dy}{dx}$ is positive or negative, and state whether y is an increasing or decreasing function of x in the interval.

(a) $y = x^2 - 4x + 7, \quad x > 2$
(b) $y = 5x^2 + 7x - 3, \quad x < -0.7$
(c) $y = 3 + 8x - 2x^2, \quad x > 2$
(d) $y = 4 - 6x - 4x^2, \quad x < -\frac{3}{4}$
(e) $y = x^3 - 3x, \quad x > 1$
(f) $y = 5 - x^4, \quad x < 0$
(g) $y = 3x - 4x^2 - x^3, \quad x < -3$
(h) $y = x^3 - 3x^2, \quad 0 < x < 2$

2 For each of the following functions $f(x)$, find $f'(x)$ and any intervals in which $f(x)$ is increasing.

(a) $x^2 - 5x + 6$
(b) $x^2 + 6x - 4$
(c) $7 - 3x - x^2$
(d) $3x^2 - 5x + 7$
(e) $5x^2 + 3x - 2$
(f) $7 - 4x - 3x^2$
(g) $x^3 - 12x$
(h) $2x^3 - 18x + 5$
(i) $2x^3 - 9x^2 - 24x + 7$
(j) $x^3 - 3x^2 + 3x + 4$
(k) $x^4 - 2x^2$
(l) $x^4 + 4x^3$
(m) $3x - x^3$
(n) $2x^5 - 5x^4 + 10$
(o) $3x + x^3$

3 For each of the following functions $f(x)$, find $f'(x)$ and any intervals in which $f(x)$ is decreasing.

(a) $x^2 + 4x - 9$ (b) $5 - 3x + x^2$ (c) $4 + 7x - 2x^2$

(d) $x^3 - 27x$ (e) $x^4 + 4x^2 - 5$ (f) $x^3 - 3x^2 + 3x - 1$

(g) $3x^4 - 20x^3 + 12$ (h) $36x^2 - 2x^4$ (i) $x^5 - 5x$

4 For the graphs of each of the following functions:

(i) find the coordinates of the stationary point;

(ii) say, with reasoning, whether this is a maximum or a minimum point;

(iii) check your answer by using the method of 'completing the square' to find the vertex;

(iv) state the range of possible values of y.

(a) $y = x^2 - 8x + 4$ (b) $y = 3x^2 + 12x + 5$ (c) $y = 5x^2 + 6x + 2$

(d) $y = 4 - 6x - x^2$ (e) $y = x^2 + 6x + 9$ (f) $y = 1 - 4x - 4x^2$

5 Find the coordinates of the stationary points on the following graphs, and find whether these points are maxima or minima or neither. Use your answer to sketch the graphs, and then use your graphic calculator to check your sketch.

(a) $y = x^3 - 12x + 5$ (b) $y = 1 - 6x^2 - x^3$ (c) $y = 2x^3 - 3x^2 - 12x$

(d) $y = x^3 - 4x^2 + 5x$ (e) $y = x^4 - 2x^2 + 3$ (f) $y = 5 + 4x - x^4$

(g) $y = 2x^3 + 3x^2 - 72x + 5$ (h) $y = x^3 - 3x^2 - 45x + 7$ (i) $y = 3x^4 - 8x^3 + 6x^2$

(j) $y = 3x^5 - 20x^3 + 1$ (k) $y = 2x + x^2 - 4x^3$ (l) $y = x^3 + 3x^2 + 3x + 1$

19.3 An application to roots of equations

In Section 10.7 you saw how the points of intersection of a graph $y = f(x)$ and a line $y = k$ can be found by solving the equation $f(x) = k$. Often you want to reverse this process. Starting with an equation $f(x) = k$, drawing the graphs of $y = f(x)$ and $y = k$ will tell you something about the roots. The x-coordinates of the points of intersection are the roots of the equation. So if you know the shape of the graph $y = f(x)$, you can find how many roots there are and their approximate values. This is illustrated in Fig. 19.14.

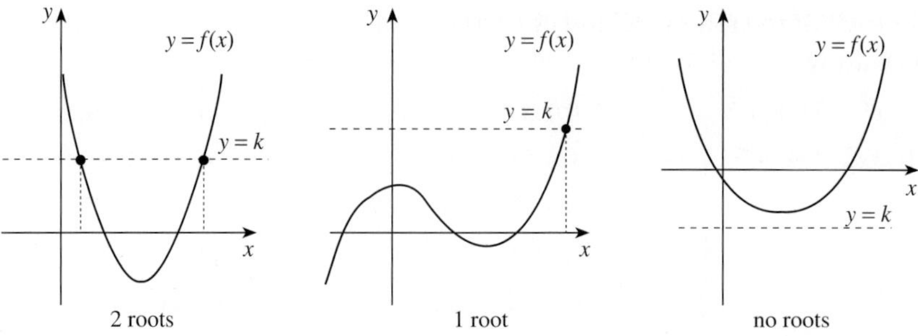

Fig. 19.14

Example 19.3.1

Show that the equation $x^3(x-4) = k$ can never have more than two roots. What can you say about the roots of the equation if k is equal to (a) 10, (b) -10, (c) -30?

The shape of the graph of $y = x^3(x-4)$ was found in Example 19.2.5, and the graph is reproduced in Fig. 19.15.

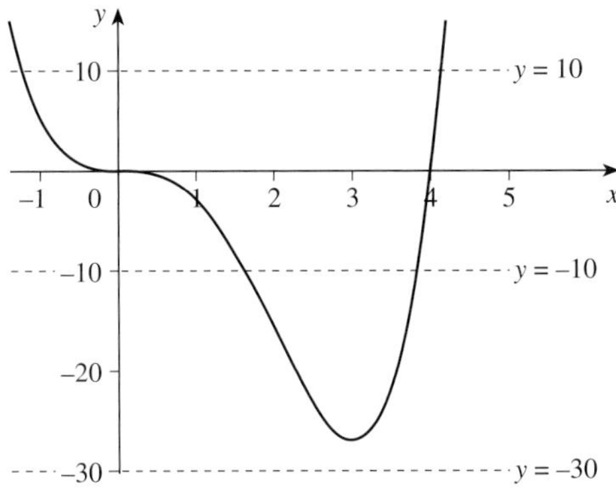

Fig. 19.15

The roots of the equation are the x-coordinates of the points of intersection of the graph with $y = k$, a line parallel to the x-axis. You can see that the largest number of points in which such a line could cut the curve is two. So the equation can never have more than two roots.

(a) If $k = 10$, the line $y = k$ is above the x-axis. One of the roots is negative and the other is greater than 4.

(b) If $k = -10$, $y = k$ is below the x-axis. Both roots are between 0 and 4.

(c) The minimum point on the graph has y-coordinate -27, so the line $y = -30$ never meets the graph. The equation with $k = -30$ has no roots.

Example 19.3.2

(a) Sketch the graph of $y = x^2(6-x)$. Verify that the point $(-2, 32)$ is on the graph.

(b) For what values of k does the equation $x^3 - 6x^2 + k = 0$ have 3 real roots? What can you then say about the values of the roots?

(c) What can you say about the roots of the equations
(i) $6x^2 - x^3 = 0$, (ii) $x^3 - 6x^2 + 32 = 0$?

(a) You often don't want to draw a graph accurately, but you need a rough idea of its general features: for example, maximum and minimum points, where the graph cuts the axes, and perhaps one or two other particular points. You can then put this information together to make a sketch of the graph.

For the graph of $y = x^2(6-x)$ you already know from Example 19.2.6 that $(0, 0)$ is a minimum point and that $(4, 32)$ is a maximum point.

To find where the graph cuts the y-axis, put $x = 0$ in the equation, which gives $y = 0$. To find where it cuts the x-axis put $y = 0$, which gives $x = 0$ or $x = 6$. So the points of the graph on the axes are $(0, 0)$ and $(6, 0)$.

When $x = -2$, $y = (-2)^2 \times (6 - (-2)) = 4 \times 8 = 32$. This verifies that $(-2, 32)$ is on the graph.

Before doing any of these calculations, it is a good idea to have drawn a pair of axes on the paper. Then, as you collect each piece of information, you can add it to the diagram. Notice that in this example it would be very awkward to get the points $(4, 32)$ and $(-2, 32)$ on the graph if you use equal scales on the two axes; so this is the time to decide to have a smaller scale on the y-axis than the x-axis. You will then have drawn something like Fig. 19.16; this should be enough to be able to sketch in the graph in Fig. 19.17.

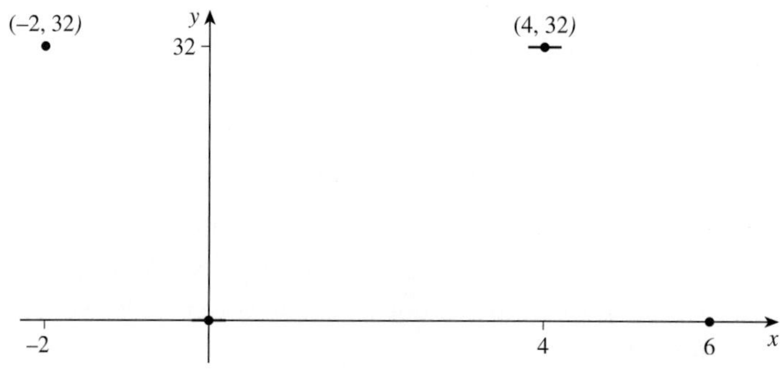

Fig. 19.16

(b) The equation $x^3 - 6x^2 + k = 0$ can be rearranged as $6x^2 - x^3 = k$, which is $x^2(6 - x) = k$. For this equation to have three real roots, the line $y = k$ must cut the graph of $y = x^2(6 - x)$ at three points. Fig. 19.17 shows that for this to happen k must be between the minimum and maximum values of the function, that is between 0 and 32. So the equation has three real roots if $0 < k < 32$.

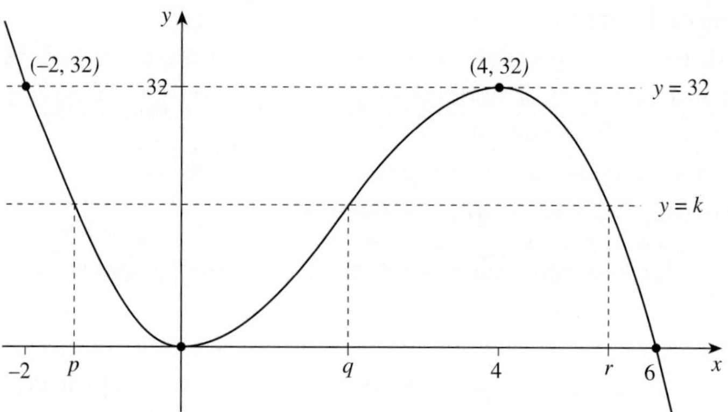

Fig. 19.17

The values of these roots are the x-coordinates of the points of intersection, which are labelled p, q and r in Fig. 19.17. The graph shows that p is between -2 and 0, q is between 0 and 4, and r is between 4 and 6.

(c) (i) The equation $6x^2 - x^3 = 0$ is $x^2(6 - x) = 0$, which is satisfied by $x = 0$ and $x = 6$.

These are just the x-coordinates of the points where the graph cuts the x-axis.

The interesting thing to notice about this equation is that the root $x = 0$ comes from a factor x^2 in the equation, and this corresponds to the point where the line $y = 0$ is a tangent to the graph. The root $x = 0$ is called a repeated root. (You will remember that in Section 10.2 a quadratic equation with only one root was said to have a repeated root. This is a similar situation for a cubic equation.)

(ii) The roots of $x^3 - 6x^2 + 32 = 0$ are the x-coordinates of the points where the graph meets the line $y = 32$. Fig. 19.17 shows that these roots are -2 and 4; and since the line touches the graph at (4, 32), you would expect 4 to be a repeated root. And taking a hint from what happened in part (i), this suggests that the cubic equation might be written in factor form as $(x + 2)(x - 4)^2 = 0$.

You can multiply this out in the usual way, using $(a + b)c = ab + ac$ with $x^2 - 8x + 16$ for c.

$$\begin{aligned}(x+2)(x-4)^2 &= (x+2)(x^2-8x+16)\\ &= x(x^2-8x+16)+2(x^2-8x+16)\\ &= (x^3-8x^2+16x)+(2x^2-16x+32)\\ &= x^3-6x^2+32,\end{aligned}$$

which is just as expected.

Exercise 19C

1 Find the minimum point on the graph of $y = x^2 - 5x$. Use your answer to find the values of k for which the equation $x^2 - 5x = k$ has two real roots.

Check your answer using the discriminant of the quadratic.

2 Use the graph of $y = 4x - 3x^2$ to find the values of k for which the equation $3x^2 - 4x + k = 0$ has no real roots.

3 Use the graph of $y = x^4 - 4x^3 + 4x^2$ (Fig. 19.5) to find the number of roots of the equations

(a) $x^4 - 4x^3 + 4x^2 = 2$,
(b) $x^4 - 4x^3 + 4x^2 = 1$,
(c) $2x^4 - 8x^3 + 8x^2 = 1$,
(d) $x^4 - 4x^3 + 4x^2 + 1 = 0$.

4 Sketch the graph of $y = x^3 - 3x$. Use it to find the number of roots of the following equations and their approximate values.

(a) $x^3 - 3x = 1$
(b) $x^3 - 3x + 2 = 0$
(c) $x^3 = 3(x + 1)$

5 Use the graph of $y = x^3 + 4x$ to show that the equation $x^3 + 4x = k$ has exactly one root for any value of k.

6 The graph of $y = x^3 + 12x^2 + 36x$ is used to find solutions of the equation $x^3 + 12x^2 + 36x = k$ for various values of k.

(a) Find the coordinates of the maximum and minimum points, and use these to sketch the graph.

(b) Verify that the point $(-8, -32)$ is on the graph.

(c) Find the number of real roots of the equation when k is

(i) 0, (ii) 20, (iii) -20, (iv) -40.

(d) For what values of k does the equation have three real roots? What can you say about these roots?

7 The graph of $y = x^4 - 2x^3 - 2x^2$ is used to find solutions of the equation $x^4 - 2x^3 - 2x^2 = k$ for various values of k.

(a) Find the coordinates of the maximum and minimum points, and sketch the graph.

(b) Find the coordinates of the points where the graph meets the x-axis.

(c) Find the number of roots of the equation when k is (i) 4, (ii) -4, (iii) -8.

(d) For what values of k does the equation have

(i) 0, (ii) 1, (iii) 2, (iv) 3, (v) 4 real roots?

(e) In case (v) of part (d), what can you say about the values of these roots?

19.4 Graphs of other functions

So far all the functions in this chapter have been **polynomials**. These are sums of terms of the form constant $\times x^r$, where r is a natural number. Although the graphs of polynomials can take many different forms, they have some features in common. For example, there are no breaks in the graphs, so that they are just a succession of peaks and troughs.

When you introduce into the equations powers of x which are not positive integers, there are some new complications. Fig. 19.18 shows three graphs which you have already met in Chapter 14. None of these could possibly be graphs of polynomials.

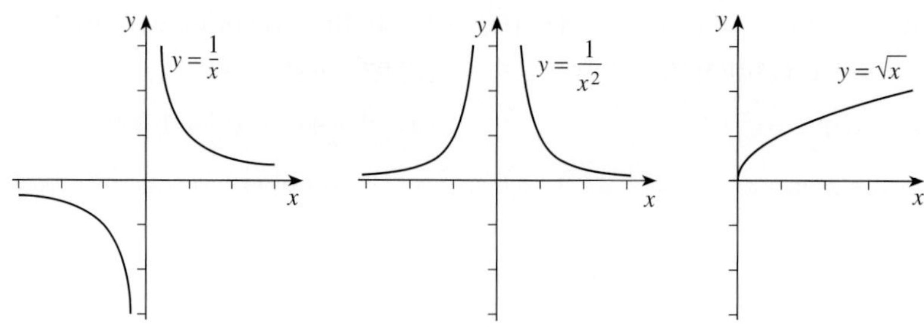

Fig. 19.18

Here are some of the new features that may appear when you draw the graph of $y = f(x)$ for functions like this.

- There may be some values of x for which $f(x)$ does not exist. For example, $\frac{1}{x}$ has no meaning if $x = 0$, and $\sqrt{x}$ has no meaning if $x < 0$. So the first thing to do in investigating the shape of the graph is to discard any values of x for which $f(x)$ has no meaning.
- When there is a break in the graph, the sign of the gradient may be different on either side of the break. For example, in the graph of $y = \frac{1}{x^2}$, $\frac{dy}{dx}$ is positive when $x < 0$ and negative when $x > 0$. So when you make a table of signs, it should be split into two parts, for values of x on either side of the break.
- There may be points on the graph at which the tangent is vertical. For example, the tangent to $y = \sqrt{x}$ at the origin is the y-axis. For this curve, $\frac{dy}{dx} = \frac{1}{2\sqrt{x}}$, and this has no meaning when $x = 0$.
- It is even possible for the graph to have a shape like Fig. 19.19. This is the graph of $y = \sqrt[3]{x^2} = x^{\frac{2}{3}}$, for which $\frac{dy}{dx} = \frac{2}{3}x^{-\frac{1}{3}} = \frac{2}{3\sqrt[3]{x}}$. This has the origin as a minimum point. But when $x = 0$, $\frac{dy}{dx}$ is not equal to 0; in fact, $\frac{dy}{dx}$ does not even exist for this value of x. So when you use the procedure for finding turning points, you need to consider values of x for which $f'(x)$ doesn't exist as well as those for which $f'(x)$ is equal to 0.

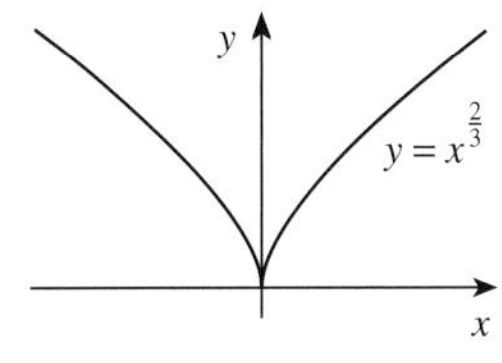

Fig. 19.19

None of these things can happen with polynomials. However, with these differences, all the results given for polynomials earlier in the chapter still apply. For example, it is still true that, if $f'(x)$ is positive in an interval of values of x, then $f(x)$ is an increasing function in that interval; you just have to be sure that the interval does not include a point where there is a break in the graph.

The similarities and differences are illustrated by the following examples.

Example 19.4.1
Find the maximum value of $f(x) = x(1 - \sqrt{x})$.

Since the function involves $\sqrt{x}$, it only exists if $x \geq 0$.

To differentiate, $f(x)$ can be expressed in terms of powers of x, as

$$f(x) = x(1 - \sqrt{x}) = x - x^{\frac{3}{2}}.$$

Then

$$f'(x) = 1 - \tfrac{3}{2}x^{\frac{1}{2}} = 1 - \tfrac{3}{2}\sqrt{x}.$$

To find where $f(x)$ takes its maximum value, put $f'(x)$ equal to 0 to get

$$\tfrac{3}{2}\sqrt{x} = 1, \quad \text{so} \quad \sqrt{x} = \tfrac{2}{3} \quad \text{and} \quad x = \tfrac{4}{9}.$$

To check that the stationary value is a maximum, note that $f'(x) > 0$ if $\frac{3}{2}\sqrt{x} < 1$, that is if $0 \le x < \frac{4}{9}$; and $f'(x) < 0$ if $\frac{3}{2}\sqrt{x} > 1$, that is if $x > \frac{4}{9}$.

The maximum value of $f(x)$ is therefore

$$\begin{aligned} f\left(\tfrac{4}{9}\right) &= \tfrac{4}{9}\left(1 - \sqrt{\tfrac{4}{9}}\right) \\ &= \tfrac{4}{9} \times \left(1 - \tfrac{2}{3}\right) \\ &= \tfrac{4}{9} \times \tfrac{1}{3} = \tfrac{4}{27}. \end{aligned}$$

This completes the solution, but it is interesting to check it by considering the shape of the graph of $f(x) = x(1 - \sqrt{x})$. Obviously $f(0) = f(1) = 0$, and the expression in the bracket is positive if $0 < x < 1$ and negative if $x > 1$. So the value of the function starts at 0 when $x = 0$, rises to a maximum value of $\frac{4}{27}$, when $x = \frac{4}{9}$, then falls to 0 again when $x = 1$. After that it becomes negative.

Example 19.4.2

Find the turning points on the graph of $y = x^2 + \dfrac{1}{x^2}$, and decide whether they are maximum or minimum points.

The expression has no meaning when $x = 0$, so there is a break in the graph.

Differentiating, write the equation as $y = x^2 + x^{-2}$ so that

$$\frac{dy}{dx} = 2x - 2x^{-3} = 2x - \frac{2}{x^3}.$$

There are stationary points where

$$2x - \frac{2}{x^3} = 0,$$

which is where $x = \dfrac{1}{x^3}$, that is, $x^4 = 1$, so $x = -1$ or $x = 1$.

To construct a table of signs it is best to write the expression for $\dfrac{dy}{dx}$ as a single fraction, and to factorise the numerator.

$$\begin{aligned} 2x - \frac{2}{x^3} &= \frac{2x^4}{x^3} - \frac{2}{x^3} \\ &= \frac{2x^4 - 2}{x^3} \\ &= \frac{2(x^2 - 1)(x^2 + 1)}{x^3} \\ &= \frac{2(x - 1)(x + 1)(x^2 + 1)}{x^3} \end{aligned}$$

Because there is a break in the domain at $x = 0$, the table of signs should be split into two parts, for $x < 0$ and $x > 0$.

	$x<-1$	$x=-1$	$-1<x<0$	$0<x<1$	$x=1$	$x>1$
$x-1$	$-$	$-$	$-$	$-$	0	$+$
$x+1$	$-$	0	$+$	$+$	$+$	$+$
x^2+1	$+$	$+$	$+$	$+$	$+$	$+$
x^3	$-$	$-$	$-$	$+$	$+$	$+$
$\frac{dy}{dx}$	$-$	0	$+$	$-$	0	$+$

Table 19.20

Table 19.20 shows that, at both stationary points, the gradient changes from negative to positive, so they are both minimum points.

Display this graph on your calculator to see how this can happen. (You might have predicted it from the fact that $x^2 + \frac{1}{x^2}$ is an even function.)

Finally, you have to find the values of y at these points, which are $(-1)^2 + \frac{1}{(-1)^2} = 2$ and $1^2 + \frac{1}{1^2} = 2$.

The graph has two minimum points, at $(-1, 2)$ and $(1, 2)$.

Exercise 19D

1 Find the stationary points on the following curves and say whether they are maximum or minimum points. Check your answers with a calculator.

(a) $y = x + \frac{1}{x}$ (b) $y = x + \frac{4}{x^2}$ (c) $y = 2\sqrt{x} - x$

(d) $y = x^2 - 4\sqrt{x}$ (e) $y = \frac{1}{x} - \frac{1}{x^2}$ (f) $y = 4x^2 - \frac{1}{x}$

(g) $y = \sqrt{x} + \frac{4}{x}$ (h) $y = \frac{1}{x} - \frac{3}{x^3}$ (i) $y = x - 12\sqrt[3]{x}$

2 Find the interval(s) of values of x for which the following functions are increasing.

(a) $y = \sqrt{x} + \frac{2}{\sqrt{x}}$ (b) $y = x^3 + \frac{3}{x}$ (c) $y = x - \frac{1}{x}$

3 Find the turning points on the following curves and say whether they are maximum or minimum points.

(a) $y = \frac{2}{x^4} - \frac{1}{x}$ (b) $y = \frac{x-3}{x^4}$ (c) $y = \frac{(x+1)^2}{x}$

(d) $y = \frac{x^4+16}{x^2}$ (e) $y = x^{\frac{4}{3}}(7 - x)$

20 Second derivatives

The last chapter showed the significance of the sign of the gradient in investigating the shape of a graph. This chapter carries the investigation further by considering the way in which the graph is bending. When you have completed it, you should

- know what is meant by the second derivative of a function
- know that the sign of the second derivative determines the way in which the graph is bending
- know what is meant by a point of inflexion, and be able to locate it
- be able to use second derivatives where appropriate to distinguish maximum and minimum points.

20.1 A measure of bending

You know that all quadratic graphs have one of the two shapes in Fig. 20.1. The parabola (a) on the left is said to 'bend upwards'; (b) on the right is said to 'bend downwards'.

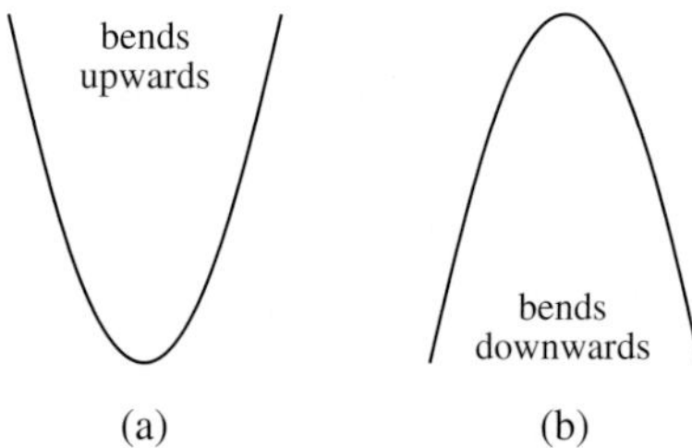

Fig. 20.1

Most of the curves in this chapter are more complicated than this. Fig. 20.2, for example, can be thought of as having two parts. In the left part, as far as the point marked I, the curve bends downwards; then, after I, it bends upwards.

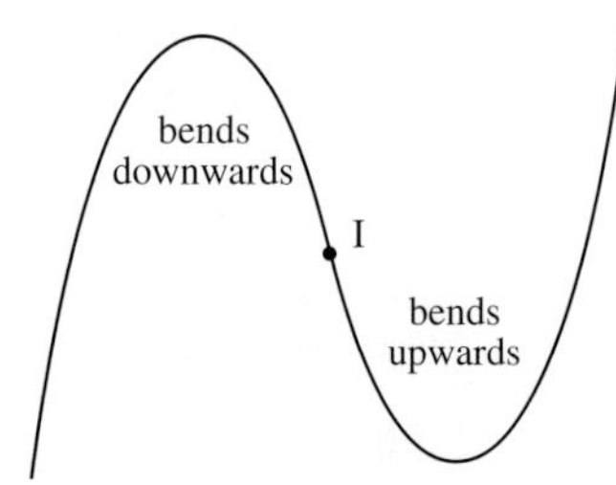

Fig. 20.2

Some curves have three parts. For example, in Fig. 19.12 in the last chapter, if you go from left to right along the curve, it bends upwards as far as the origin; then it bends downwards as far as $x = 2$, after which it bends upwards again.

Knowing whether a graph bends upwards or downwards is often useful in investigating its shape. The question is, how to tell from the equation which way it bends.

Fig. 20.3 shows the graph of a function which is bending upwards, with the tangents at several points along the curve. The gradients of the tangents at P and Q are negative; at R the gradient is 0; then at S and T the gradient is positive. All the way, as you move from left to right, the gradient increases.

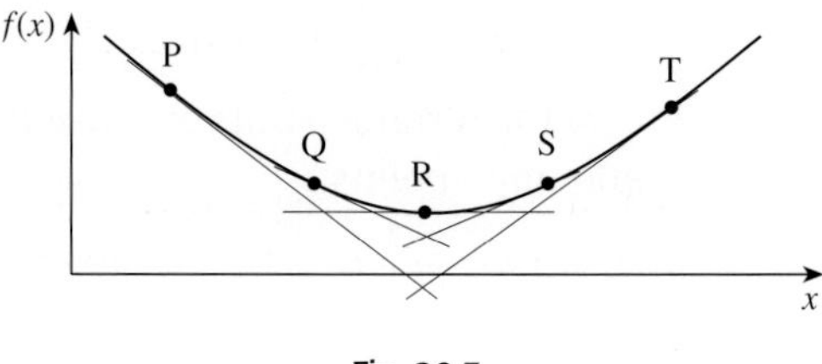

Fig. 20.3

The word 'increases' is the clue. You know that the gradient of the graph $y = f(x)$ is itself a function. It has been called the 'gradient function', and denoted by $f'(x)$. But temporarily it will help to give it a function name of its own, and to use the symbol $g(x)$ to stand for the gradient function of $f(x)$. For example, if $f(x) = x^2$, then $g(x) = 2x$.

Then Fig. 20.4 shows that $g(x)$ is an increasing function. And it was shown at the beginning of Section 19.2 that, if $g'(x) > 0$ in an interval, then $g(x)$ is an increasing function in that interval. And in that case the graph $y = f(x)$ bends upwards.

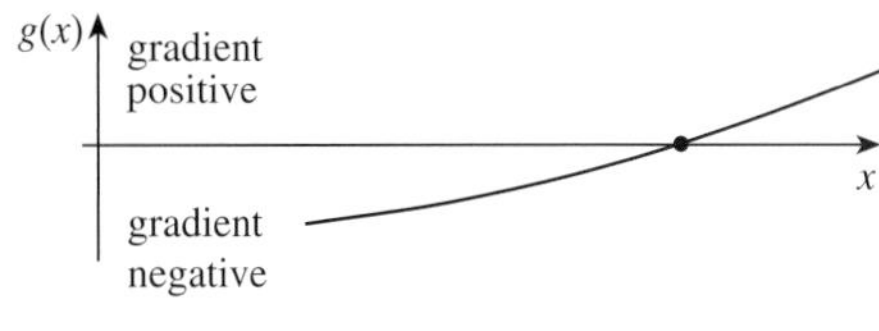

Fig. 20.4

So the way to show that the graph $y = f(x)$ bends upwards is to differentiate to get the gradient function $g(x) = f'(x)$. You then differentiate $g(x)$ to get $g'(x)$. If $g'(x)$ is positive, then the gradient function is increasing, so $y = f(x)$ bends upwards.

You will see that $g'(x)$ is what you get if you differentiate $f(x)$, and then differentiate the result a second time. This produces the 'second derivative' of $f(x)$. It is denoted by $f''(x)$. This is pronounced 'f two-dashed x', or 'f double-dashed x'.

Example 20.1.1
If $f(x) = 2x^3 + 3x^2 + 4x + 5$, find $f''(x)$.

The derivative of $f(x)$ is $f'(x) = 6x^2 + 6x + 4$.

The derivative of $f'(x)$ is $f''(x) = 12x + 6$.

Just as there are two ways of writing the derivative, either as $f'(x)$ or $\frac{dy}{dx}$, there are two ways of writing the second derivative. The derivative of $\frac{dy}{dx}$ is written as $\frac{d^2y}{dx^2}$. This is pronounced 'd squared y d x squared', or sometimes 'd two y d x squared'. The reason for this rather curious notation is explained in Section 21.5.

Example 20.1.2
Show that the graph of $y = 3x^2 + 7x - 2$ bends upwards for all values of x.

Two successive differentiations give $\frac{dy}{dx} = 6x + 7$ and $\frac{d^2y}{dx^2} = 6$.

Since $\frac{d^2y}{dx^2}$ is positive and independent of x, the graph bends upwards for all values of x.

Now draw for yourself a curve which bends downwards and draw tangents at a number of points. You will see that the gradient is decreasing as you move from left to right along the curve. If the equation is $y = f(x)$, $g(x) = f'(x)$ is a decreasing function, so that $g'(x) = f''(x)$ is negative.

A curve which bends upwards in an interval is said to be **concave up** in the interval. A curve which bends downwards is said to be **concave down**.

If $y = f(x)$, the derivative of $\frac{dy}{dx} = f'(x)$ is called the **second derivative** of $f(x)$ with respect to x, and is denoted by $f''(x)$ or $\frac{d^2y}{dx^2}$.

If $\frac{d^2y}{dx^2} = f''(x)$ is positive in an interval of values of x, the graph of $y = f(x)$ is concave up in that interval.

If $\frac{d^2y}{dx^2} = f''(x)$ is negative in an interval of values of x, the graph of $y = f(x)$ is concave down in that interval.

Example 20.1.3
For the graph of $y = x^3 - 3x^2 + 4x$,

(a) show that the gradient is always positive,

(b) find the intervals in which the graph is (i) concave down, (ii) concave up.

(a) $\frac{dy}{dx} = 3x^2 - 6x + 4$
$= 3(x-1)^2 + 1$ in completed square form.

Since $(x-1)^2$ is never negative, the gradient of the graph is greater than or equal to 1 for all values of x.

(b) $\frac{d^2y}{dx^2} = 6x - 6 = 6(x-1)$.

This is negative when $x < 1$ and positive when $x > 1$.
So the graph is

(i) concave down when $x < 1$,

(ii) concave up when $x > 1$.

These properties are illustrated in Fig. 20.5. Notice that the gradient has its smallest value of 1 at the point (1,2), which separates the part of the curve which bends downwards from the part which bends upwards.

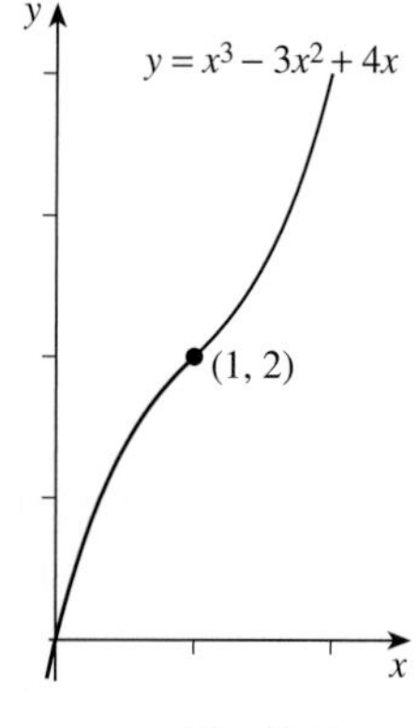

Fig. 20.5

20.2 Points of inflexion

Figure 20.2 shows a point I on a graph separating a part which is concave down from a part which is concave up. A point like this is called a **point of inflexion**.

Since the way in which a graph bends depends on the sign of the second derivative, this definition can be expressed in terms of $f''(x)$:

If, on the graph of $y = f(x)$, the sign of $f''(x)$ in an interval to the left of $x = s$ is opposite to the sign in an interval to the right of $x = s$, then the point $(s, f(s))$ is a point of inflexion.

Thus in Example 20.1.3 the point $(1, 2)$ is a point of inflexion, because $\frac{d^2y}{dx^2}$ changes sign from negative (for $x < 1$) to positive (for $x > 1$).

Example 20.2.1

Show that the graph of $y = \sqrt{x} + \frac{1}{x}$ has just one point of inflexion, and find its coordinates.

Since $\sqrt{x}$ only exists for $x \geq 0$, and $\frac{1}{x}$ does not exist when $x = 0$, the domain of the function is $\mathbb{R}^+$, the set of positive real numbers.

Writing $\sqrt{x}$ as $x^{\frac{1}{2}}$ and $\frac{1}{x}$ as x^{-1},

$$y = x^{\frac{1}{2}} + x^{-1},$$

so $$\frac{dy}{dx} = \tfrac{1}{2}x^{-\frac{1}{2}} - x^{-2}$$

and $$\frac{d^2y}{dx^2} = -\tfrac{1}{4}x^{-\frac{3}{2}} + 2x^{-3}.$$

This can be written as

$$\frac{2}{x^3} - \frac{1}{4x^{\frac{3}{2}}} = \frac{8}{4x^3} - \frac{x^{\frac{3}{2}}}{4x^3} = \frac{8 - x^{\frac{3}{2}}}{4x^3}.$$

Since $4x^3$ is always positive when $x > 0$, $\frac{d^2y}{dx^2}$ is positive when $x^{\frac{3}{2}} < 8$ and negative when $x^{\frac{3}{2}} > 8$.

Now $x^{\frac{3}{2}} = 8$ when $x = 8^{\frac{2}{3}} = 4$ (see Section 13.4), so $x^{\frac{3}{2}} < 8$ when $x < 4$ and $x^{\frac{3}{2}} > 8$ when $x > 4$. Therefore $\frac{d^2y}{dx^2}$ changes sign from positive to negative when $x = 4$, $y = \sqrt{4} + \frac{1}{4} = 2\frac{1}{4}$.

There is just one point of inflexion at $\left(4, 2\frac{1}{4}\right)$. This is shown in Fig. 20.6.

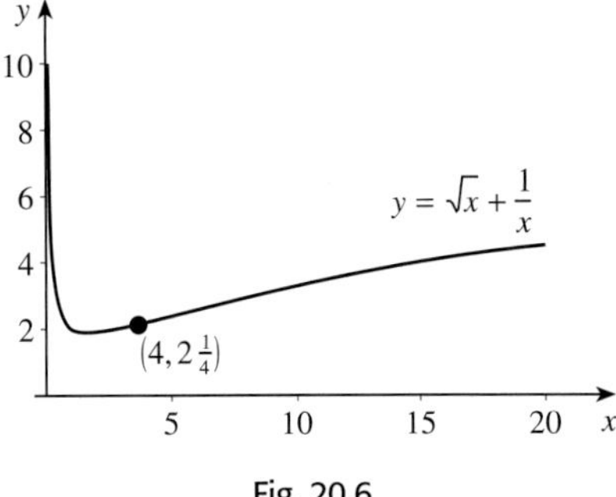

Fig. 20.6

In the solution to Example 20.2.1 you may have noticed the switch from the inequalities $x^{\frac{3}{2}} < 8$ and $x^{\frac{3}{2}} > 8$ to the equation $x^{\frac{3}{2}} = 8$. This wasn't strictly necessary, but you probably find it easier to work with the equation.

So, in the general definition, if s separates values of x for which $f''(x) < 0$ from those for which $f''(x) > 0$, what can you say about $f''(s)$?

The obvious answer to this question is that $f''(s) = 0$. However, there is another possibility (which happens much less often) that $f''(s)$ might not exist. You may never come across a function for which this occurs, but the possibility must be included in stating a general rule:

> At a point of inflexion $(s, f(s))$ on the graph of $y = f(x)$, either $f''(s) = 0$ or $f''(s)$ does not exist.

Example 20.2.2

Find the points of inflexion on the graph of $y = x^3(4 - x)$, and show these on a sketch.

If $\quad y = x^3(4 - x) = 4x^3 - x^4,$

then $\quad \dfrac{dy}{dx} = 12x^2 - 4x^3$

$= 4x^2(3 - x)$

and $\quad \dfrac{d^2y}{dx^2} = 24x - 12x^2$

$= 12x(2 - x).$

So $\dfrac{d^2y}{dx^2} = 0$ when $x = 0$ or 2. (There are no values of x for which $\dfrac{d^2y}{dx^2}$ doesn't exist.)

To check that these values of x do give points of inflexion, construct a table of signs for $\dfrac{d^2y}{dx^2}$ (Table 20.7).

	$x < 0$	$x = 0$	$0 < x < 2$	$x = 2$	$x > 2$
$12x$	$-$	0	+	+	+
$2 - x$	+	+	+	0	$-$
$\dfrac{d^2y}{dx^2}$	$-$	0	+	0	$-$

Table 20.7

This shows that $\dfrac{d^2y}{dx^2}$ has opposite signs on either side of $x = 0$ and also of $x = 2$.

When $x = 0$, $y = 0$ and when $x = 2$, $y = 2^3(4 - 2) = 16$.

So the points of inflexion on the graph are $(0, 0)$ and $(2, 16)$.

To sketch the graph you can make similar tables of signs for y and for $\dfrac{dy}{dx}$. Check for yourself that these can be summarised as Table 20.8 and Table 20.9 respectively.

	$x < 0$	$x = 0$	$0 < x < 4$	$x = 4$	$x > 4$
y	$-$	0	$+$	0	$-$

Table 20.8

	$x < 0$	$x = 0$	$0 < x < 3$	$x = 3$	$x > 3$
$\frac{dy}{dx}$	$+$	0	$+$	0	$-$

Table 20.9

Putting this information together produces the graph in Fig. 20.10.

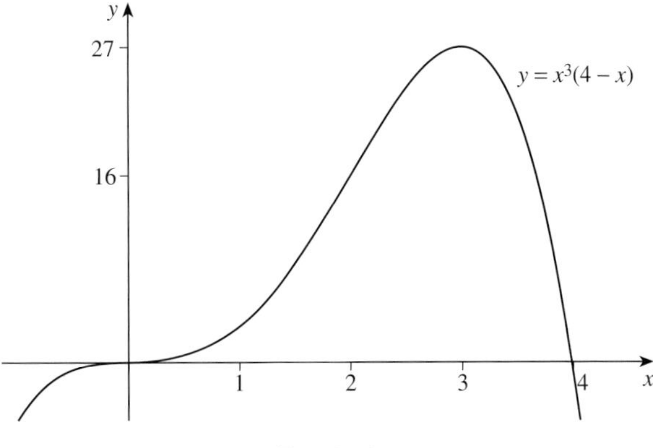

Fig. 20.10

But beware! Although points of inflexion can only occur when $f''(x)$ is 0 or undefined, it may happen that $f''(x) = 0$ where there is *not* a point of inflexion. The next example illustrates this.

Example 20.2.3
Find the points of inflexion on the graph of $y = x^4(5 - x)$.

The beginning of the solution is like that of Example 20.2.2.

If $\quad y = x^4(5 - x) = 5x^4 - x^5$

then $\quad \frac{dy}{dx} = 20x^3 - 5x^4 = 5x^3(4 - x)$

and $\quad \frac{d^2y}{dx^2} = 60x^2 - 20x^3 = 20x^2(3 - x)$

So $\frac{d^2y}{dx^2} = 0$ when $x = 0$ or 3. But the table of signs now has the form of Table 20.11.

	$x < 0$	$x = 0$	$0 < x < 3$	$x = 3$	$x > 3$
$20x^2$	$+$	0	$+$	$+$	$+$
$3 - x$	$+$	$+$	$+$	0	$-$
$\frac{d^2y}{dx^2}$	$+$	0	$+$	0	$-$

Table 20.11

So, although $\frac{d^2y}{dx^2} = 0$ when $x = 0$, the sign of $\frac{d^2y}{dx^2}$ is the same in intervals on both sides of $x = 0$. This means that $(0, 0)$ is not a point of inflexion. The only point of inflexion is at $(3, 162)$.

You can check for yourself that $(0, 0)$ is a minimum point and $(4, 256)$ is a maximum point. So the graph has the form of Fig. 20.12.

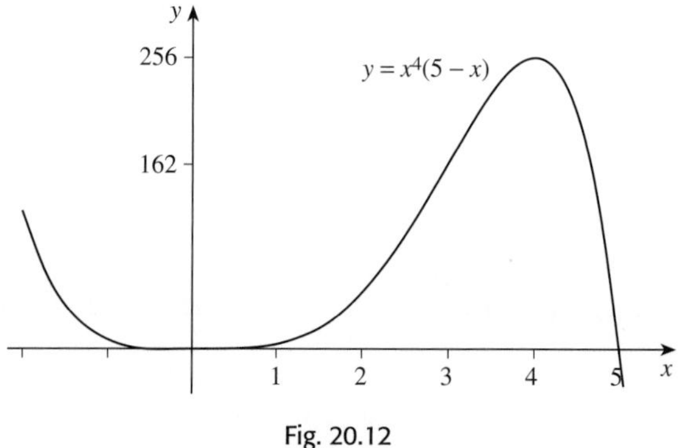

Fig. 20.12

> If $f''(s) = 0$, the point $(s, f(s))$ is not necessarily a point of inflexion of the graph of $y = f(x)$. You have to check that $f''(x)$ has opposite signs in intervals on either side of $x = s$.

20.3 Points of greatest or least gradient

Draw a curve with a point of inflexion, and lay a pencil along the tangent at the left end of the curve. Now move along the curve from left to right, keeping the pencil as a tangent. What happens as the point of contact passes through the point of inflexion?

You will find that the pencil has been rotating in one sense (clockwise or anticlockwise) and, at the point of inflexion, the sense of rotation changes.

What this shows is that, at the point of inflexion, the gradient of the curve has either a maximum or minimum value.

For example, in Example 20.1.3, the graph of $y = x^3 - 3x^2 + 4x$ has a point of inflexion where $x = 1$. And, because the gradient is $3(x - 1)^2 + 1$, this is the value of x for which the gradient has its smallest value.

It is easy to see why. If you denote the gradient function of $y = f(x)$ by $g(x)$ (as in Section 20.1), then $g(x) = f'(x)$ and $g'(x) = f''(x)$. So if $(s, f(s))$ is a point of inflexion, so that $f''(x)$ has opposite signs on either side of $x = s$, so does $g'(x)$; and this is the condition given in Section 19.2 for $g(x)$ to have a maximum or minimum at $x = s$.

Exercise 20A

1 Compare the graphs of $y = f(x)$ and $y = f'(x)$ in each of the following cases. Show that $y = f(x)$ bends upwards when $y = f'(x)$ is decreasing, and downwards when $y = f'(x)$ is increasing.

(a) $f(x) = x^2$ (b) $f(x) = 5 - x^2$ (c) $f(x) = x^2 + 4x$

(d) $f(x) = 3x^2 - 6x$ (e) $f(x) = (2 + x)(4 - x)$ (f) $f(x) = (x + 3)^2$

(g) $f(x) = x^4$ (h) $f(x) = x^2(x - 2)$ (i) $f(x) = 3 - 2x$

2 In each part of the question, the diagram shows the graph of $y = f(x)$. Sketch a graph of the gradient function $y = f'(x)$.

(a)

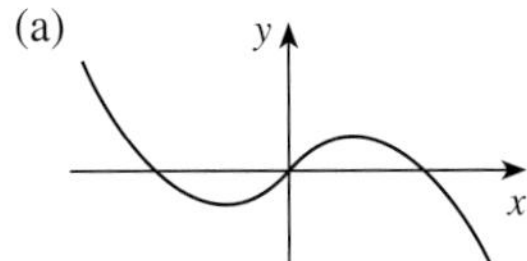

(b)

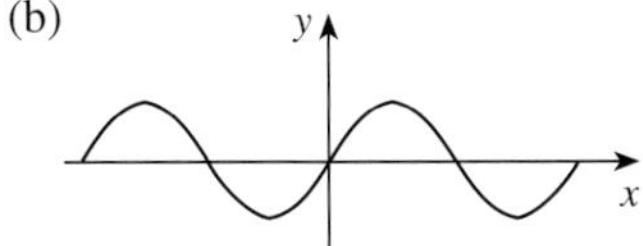

(c)

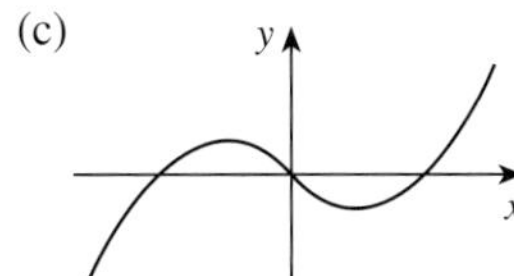

3 Write down the signs of $f'(x)$ and $f''(x)$ for the following graphs $y = f(x)$.

(a)

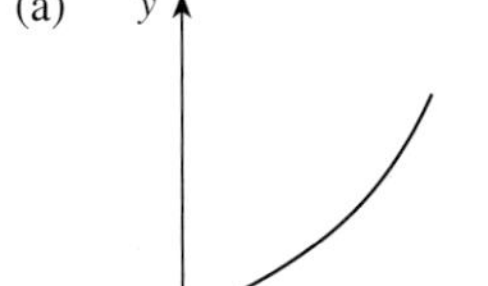

(b)

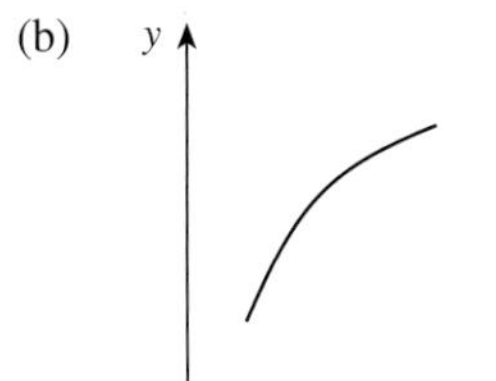

(c)

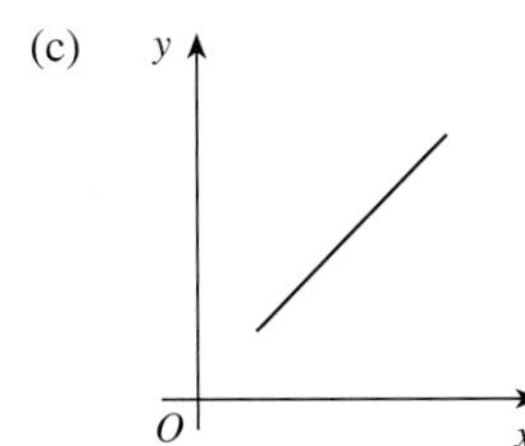

(d)

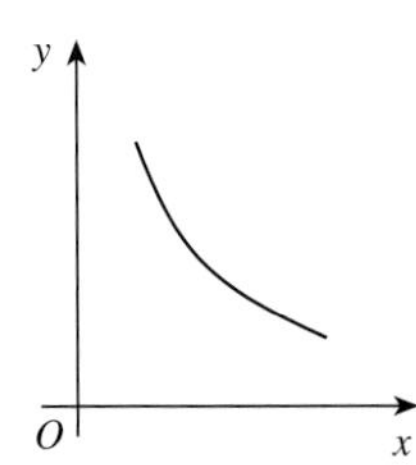

4 Find $\frac{d^2y}{dx^2}$ for the following equations.

(a) $y = 3x - 4$ (b) $y = 5 + 3x - 2x^2$

(c) $y = x^3 + 5x^2 - 2x + 13$ (d) $y = x^6$

5 Consider the graph of $y = f(x)$ where $f(x) = x^3 - x$.

(a) Use the fact that $f(x) = x(x^2 - 1) = x(x - 1)(x + 1)$ to find where the graph cuts the x-axis and hence sketch the graph.

(b) Find $f'(x)$ and sketch the graph of $y = f'(x)$.

(c) Find $f''(x)$ and sketch the graph of $y = f''(x)$.

(d) Check the consistency of your sketches: for example, check that the graph of $y = f(x)$ is concave up where $f''(x) > 0$.

6 For the graph of $y = f(x)$ where $f(x) = x^3 + x$,

(a) use factors to show that the graph crosses the x-axis once only,

(b) find $f'(x)$ and $f''(x)$,

(c) find the interval in which the graph is bending upwards,

(d) use the information gained to sketch the graph of $y = x^3 + x$,

(e) check your work using a calculator.

7 Find the intervals in which the graphs of the following equations are concave up.

(a) $y = x^3 + 4x - 7$ (b) $y = 5 + 6x^2 - x^3$ (c) $y = x^2(x + 1)$

(d) $y = \dfrac{1}{x}$ (e) $y = \dfrac{1}{x^2}$ (f) $y = \dfrac{1}{x} - \dfrac{1}{x^2}$

(g) $y = \dfrac{1}{x^2} - \dfrac{1}{x^3}$ (h) $y = x^2 + \dfrac{1}{x^2}$ (i) $y = x^2 + \sqrt{x}$

8 Find the coordinates of the points of inflexion (if any) on the following graphs. Use a calculator to check your answers.

(a) $y = x^3 - 6x^2 + 7x$ (b) $y = 3x^2 - 2x^4$ (c) $y = 2x + x^4$

(d) $y = x^4 - 6x^3 + 12x^2$ (e) $y = x^6(x - 7)$ (f) $y = \sqrt{x}(x + 3)$

(g) $y = x^2 - \dfrac{1}{x}$ (h) $y = \dfrac{x - 6}{x^4}$ (i) $y = \sqrt{x} + \dfrac{1}{\sqrt{x}}$

9 Find the point on the graph of $y = 7 - 9x^2 - x^3$ at which the gradient is greatest, and the equation of the tangent at this point. Check that this tangent does not meet the graph at any other point.

10 Find the equation of the tangent to the graph of $y = x^5 - 5x^4 + 150x$ at which the gradient has its smallest value.

11 Find the x-coordinates of the three points where the graph of $y = x^4 - 10x^3 + 24x^2$ meets the x-axis. Show that one of these points is a point of inflexion of the graph, and find the coordinates of the other point of inflexion. Find also the equations of the tangents at the two points of inflexion, and verify that they meet the graph again at $(-2, 192)$ and $(7, 147)$ respectively. Use this information to sketch the graph as accurately as you can.

20.4 Maxima and minima revisited

One of the most important uses of the second derivative is to decide whether a stationary point on a graph is a maximum or a minimum.

Look back at Figs. 20.1 and 20.2. These show graphs with maximum or minimum points. Which is which depends on whether the graph is bending upwards or downwards. Where the graph is concave up, the stationary point is a minimum; where it is concave down, the stationary point is a maximum. So whether the graph has a maximum or minimum depends on the sign of the second derivative at the stationary point.

It is often simpler to use this instead of considering the change in sign of $f'(x)$ to decide whether a point on a graph is a minimum or a maximum. The procedure described in Section 19.2 can then be amended as follows.

To find the minimum and maximum points on the graph of $y = f(x)$:

Step 1 Find an expression for $\dfrac{dy}{dx} = f'(x)$.

Step 2 List the values of x for which $\dfrac{dy}{dx}$ is 0 (or doesn't exist).

Step 3 Find an expression for $\dfrac{d^2y}{dx^2} = f''(x)$.

Step 4 For each value of x in Step 2, find the sign of $\dfrac{d^2y}{dx^2}$. If the sign is +, the graph has a minimum point; if −, a maximum. [If the value of $\dfrac{d^2y}{dx^2}$ is 0 (or doesn't exist), follow the procedure in Section 19.2.]

Step 5 For each value of x giving a minimum or maximum, calculate $y = f(x)$.

Example 20.4.1
Find the turning points on the graph of $y = x^2(6 - x)$, and determine whether they are maximum or minimum points.

Step 1 $y = x^2(6 - x) = 6x^2 - x^3$, which gives $\dfrac{dy}{dx} = 12x - 3x^2 = 3x(4 - x)$.

Step 2 $\dfrac{dy}{dx} = 0$ when $x = 0$ or $x = 4$.

Step 3 $\dfrac{d^2y}{dx^2} = 12 - 6x$.

Step 4 When $x = 0$, $\dfrac{d^2y}{dx^2} = 12 - 6 \times 0 = 12$.

When $x = 4$, $\dfrac{d^2y}{dx^2} = 12 - 6 \times 4 = -12$.

So there is a minimum point where $x = 0$ and a maximum point where $x = 4$.

Step 5 When $x = 0$, $y = 0$, so $(0, 0)$ is a minimum point on the graph.

When $x = 4$, $y = 32$, so $(4, 32)$ is a maximum point on the graph.

Example 20.4.1 is the same as Example 19.2.6, but solved by the new procedure. Steps 1, 2 and 5 are the same, but there is a different way of deciding between maximum and minimum points. You can use whichever method you prefer.

The reason for having two methods is that, although the second method is often easier, it doesn't always work. This is illustrated by the next example.

Example 20.4.2

Find the nature of the stationary points on the graphs of $y = x^3$, $y = x^4$ and $y = -x^4$,

The derivatives are $\frac{dy}{dx} = 3x^2$, $\frac{dy}{dx} = 4x^3$ and $\frac{dy}{dx} = -4x^3$. All the graphs have stationary values where $x = 0$ and nowhere else.

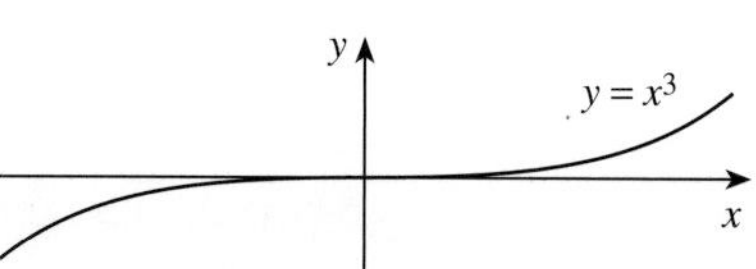

The second derivatives are $\frac{d^2y}{dx^2} = 6x$, $\frac{d^2y}{dx^2} = 12x^2$ and $\frac{d^2y}{dx^2} = -12x^2$. For each graph the value of $\frac{d^2y}{dx^2}$ where $x = 0$ is 0.

The shapes of all three graphs in the neighbourhood of the origin are shown in Fig. 20.13. One has a minimum, one has a maximum and one has neither.

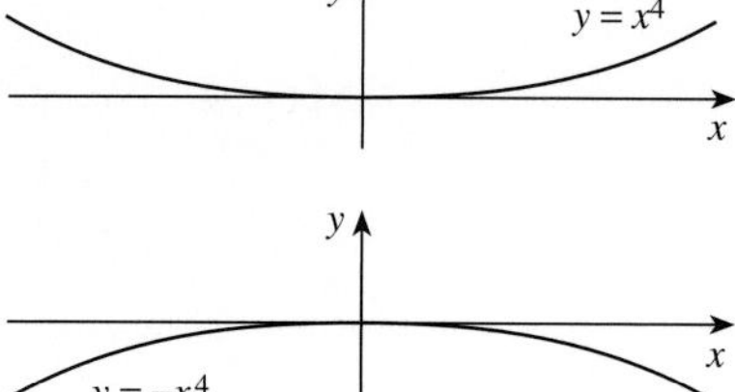

Fig. 20.13

What this example shows is that if the second derivative at a stationary point is 0, you can't use this method to decide whether it is a maximum, a minimum or neither. In that case you have to go back to the earlier method in Section 19.2.

You will also find later on that for some functions it can be very laborious to find the second derivative. In that case, it is more efficient to use the old procedure. But this will not apply to any of the functions you have met so far.

Example 20.4.3

Find the minimum and maximum points on the graph of $f(x) = x^4 + x^5$.

Step 1 $f'(x) = 4x^3 + 5x^4 = x^3(4 + 5x)$.

Step 2 $f'(x) = 0$ when $x = 0$ or $x = -0.8$.

Step 3 $f''(x) = 12x^2 + 20x^3 = 4x^2(3 + 5x)$.

Step 4 $f''(-0.8) = 4 \times (-0.8)^2 \times (3 - 4) < 0$, so $x = -0.8$ gives a maximum.

$f''(0) = 0$, so you have to use the old procedure.

	$-0.8 < x < 0$	$x = 0$	$x > 0$
x^3	$-$	0	$+$
$4 + 5x$	$+$	$+$	$+$
$f'(x)$	$-$	0	$+$

Table 20.14

Table 20.14 shows that $x = 0$ gives a minimum.

Step 5 The maximum point is $(-0.8, 0.081\,92)$; the minimum point is $(0, 0)$.

Exercise 20B

1 Use first and second derivatives to locate and describe the stationary points on the graphs of the following functions. If this method fails then you should use the change of sign of the first derivative to distinguish stationary points which are maxima, minima or neither.

(a) $f(x) = 3x - x^3$
(b) $f(x) = x^3 - 3x^2$
(c) $f(x) = 3x^4 + 1$
(d) $f(x) = 2x^3 - 3x^2 - 12x + 4$
(e) $f(x) = 2x^3 - 12x^2 + 24x + 6$

2 Find the maximum and minimum points (if any) on the following graphs.

(a) $y = 3x^4 - 4x^3 - 12x^2 - 3$
(b) $y = x^3 - 3x^2 + 3x + 5$
(c) $y = 16x - 3x^3$
(d) $y = 2x^5 - 7$
(e) $y = 3x^4 - 8x^3 + 6x^2 + 1$

21 Applications of differentiation

You have now learnt what differentiation means and how to differentiate a lot of functions. This chapter shows how you can apply these ideas to real-world problems. When you have completed it, you should

- know that you can interpret a derivative as a rate of change of one variable with respect to another
- be able to apply these techniques to real-world problems.

21.1 Derivatives as rates of change

The quantities x and y in a relationship $y = f(x)$ are often called variables, because x can stand for any number for which $f(x)$ has a meaning, and y for any value of the function. When you draw the graph you have a free choice of the values of x, and then work out y. So x is called the **independent variable** and y the **dependent variable**.

These variables often stand for physical or economic quantities, and then it is convenient to use other letters which suggest what these quantities are: for example t for time, V for volume, C for cost, P for population, and so on.

To illustrate this consider a situation familiar to deep sea divers, that pressure increases with depth below sea level. The independent variable is the depth, z metres, below the surface.

> It will soon be clear why the letter d was avoided for the depth. The letter z is often used for distances in the vertical direction.

The dependent variable is the pressure, p, measured in bars. At the surface the diver experiences only atmospheric pressure, about 1 bar, but the pressure increases as the diver descends. At offshore (coastal) depths the variables are connected approximately by the equation

$$p = 1 + 0.1z.$$

The (z, p) graph is a straight line, shown in Fig. 21.1.

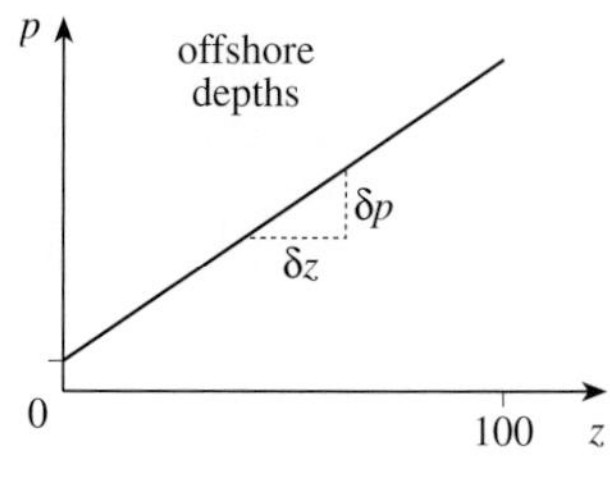

Fig. 21.1

The constant 0.1 in the equation is the amount that the pressure goes up for each extra metre of depth. This is the 'rate of change of pressure with respect to depth'.

This can be expressed algebraically using the 'delta' notation introduced in Section 11.1. If the diver descends a further distance of δz metres, the pressure goes up by δp bars; this rate of change is $\frac{\delta p}{\delta z}$. It is represented by the gradient of the graph.

But at ocean depths the (z, p) graph is no longer a straight line: it has the form of a curve which bends upwards, as in Fig. 21.2.

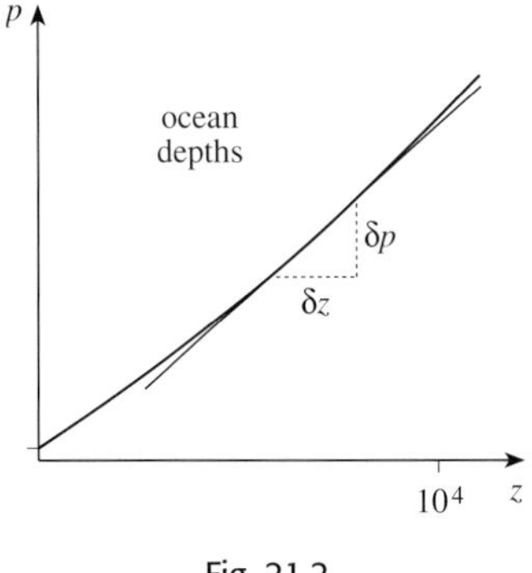

Fig. 21.2

The quantity $\frac{\delta p}{\delta z}$ now represents the average rate of change over the extra depth δz. It is represented by the gradient of the chord in Fig. 21.2.

You have already met this idea, and used this notation, in finding the gradient of the graph of $y = f(x)$. It is especially useful when you want to use different letters as variables to describe particular quantities.

In Section 11.5 the symbol $\frac{dy}{dx}$ was used to denote the gradient of the tangent, so that

$$\frac{dy}{dx} = \lim_{\delta x \to 0} \frac{\delta y}{\delta x}.$$

In just the same way you can use the symbol $\frac{dp}{dz}$, defined as

$$\frac{dp}{dz} = \lim_{\delta z \to 0} \frac{\delta p}{\delta z}.$$

It is important to understand the difference between $\frac{\delta p}{\delta z}$ and $\frac{dp}{dz}$. The symbol $\frac{\delta p}{\delta z}$ means the average rate of change of pressure with depth between one depth and another. For example, if the pressure is 125 bars at a depth of 1000 metres and 138 bars at a depth of 1100 metres, then $\delta p = 138 - 125 = 13$, $\delta z = 1100 - 1000 = 100$, so that $\frac{\delta p}{\delta z} = 0.13$. That is, the average rate of increase of pressure with depth between 1000 metres and 1100 metres is 0.13 bars per metre.

But if, for example, $\frac{dp}{dz} = 0.14$ when $z = 1100$, this means that at the particular depth of 1100 metres the pressure is increasing at a rate of 0.14 bars per metre. On a graph showing p against z, $\frac{\delta p}{\delta z}$ is the gradient of a chord and $\frac{dp}{dz}$ is the gradient of a tangent.

> If x and y are the independent and dependent variables respectively in a functional relationship, then
>
> $\frac{\delta y}{\delta x}$ represents the average rate of change of y with respect to x over an interval of values of x,
>
> $\frac{dy}{dx}$ represents the instantaneous rate of change of y with respect to x for a particular value of x.

This notation can be used in a wide variety of contexts. For example, if the area of burnt grass, t minutes after a fire has started, is A square metres, then $\frac{dA}{dt}$ measures the rate at which the fire is spreading in square metres per minute. If, at a certain point on the earth's surface, distances of x metres on the ground are represented by distances of y metres on a map, then $\frac{dy}{dx}$ represents the scale of the map at that point.

Example 21.1.1

Research into the growth of juvenile herrings suggests that after t years their mean length, l cm, is given approximately by the equation $l = 8t - \frac{1}{2}t^2$. According to this formula,

(a) find the rate of growth after 3 years,

(b) find how many years it will take the herrings to become fully grown.

The rate at which the herrings are growing is given by the derivative $\frac{dl}{dt} = 8 - t$. Since the units of length and time are centimetres and years, this equation gives the rate of growth in centimetres per year.

(a) When $t = 3$, $\frac{dl}{dt} = 8 - 3 = 5$. So after 3 years the herrings are growing at a rate of 5 centimetres per year.

(b) When the herrings are fully grown the rate of growth is zero, so $\frac{dl}{dt} = 0$. This occurs when $t = 8$. So the herrings will be fully grown after 8 years.

Notice in this example that, according to the given equation, the rate of growth becomes negative when $t > 8$. This suggests that the herrings would become shorter, which is unlikely! It is far more probable that, since the research was based on measuring juvenile herrings up to 6 years old, the formula is valid only for a certain interval of values of t. This interval will certainly not extend beyond $t = 8$.

Example 21.1.2

A boy is exactly 4 years older than his sister. Write an expression for the ratio of the boy's age to his sister's age when the sister is x years old. Find the rate at which this ratio is changing when the sister is 20 years old.

> Compare this with Example 8.6.2, in which the ratio was regarded as a sequence for positive integer values of n. In the present example, the ratio is considered as a function of a positive real number variable x. Which do you think is more appropriate?

When the sister's age is x, her brother's age is $x + 4$. So, denoting the ratio by R, $R = \frac{x+4}{x}$, which can be written as $R = 1 + \frac{4}{x} = 1 + 4x^{-1}$.

The rate at which the ratio is changing is measured by the derivative $\frac{dR}{dx}$. Differentiating,

$$\frac{dR}{dx} = -4x^{-2} = -\frac{4}{x^2}.$$

When $x = 20$, $\frac{dR}{dx} = -\frac{4}{20^2} = -0.01$. The ratio is going down at a rate of 0.01 per year.

You can check the answer to this example by calculating the actual ratios when $x = 19$, 20 and 21; thus $\frac{23}{19} = 1.2105\ldots$, $\frac{24}{20} = 1.2$ and $\frac{25}{21} = 1.1904\ldots$.

Between $x = 20$ and $x = 21$, $\delta x = 21 - 20 = 1$ and $\delta R = 1.1904... - 1.2 = -0.0095...$, so the average rate of change is $\dfrac{\delta R}{\delta x} = -0.0095...$.

Between $x = 20$ and $x = 19$, $\delta x = 19 - 20 = -1$ and $\delta R = 1.2105... - 1.2 = 0.0105...$ so the average rate of change is $\dfrac{\delta R}{\delta x} = -0.0105...$.

These average rates are approximately equal to the rate $\dfrac{dR}{dx} = -0.01$ when $x = 20$.

Draw a sketch of the (x, R) graph in the neighbourhood of $x = 20$ to illustrate these results.

Example 21.1.3

A sprinter in a women's 100-metre race reaches her top speed of 12 metres per second after she has run 36 metres. Up to that distance her speed is proportional to the square root of the distance she has run. Show that until she reaches full speed the rate of change of her speed with respect to distance is inversely proportional to her speed.

Suppose that after she has run x metres her speed is S metres per second. You are told that, up to $x = 36$, $S = k\sqrt{x}$, and also that $S = 12$ when $x = 36$. So

$$12 = k\sqrt{36}, \quad \text{giving} \quad k = \tfrac{12}{6} = 2.$$

The (x, S) relationship is therefore

$$S = 2\sqrt{x} \text{ for } 0 < x < 36.$$

The rate of change of speed with respect to distance is the derivative $\dfrac{dS}{dx}$. Since $S = 2x^{\frac{1}{2}}$,

$$\frac{dS}{dx} = 2 \times \tfrac{1}{2}x^{-\frac{1}{2}} = \frac{1}{\sqrt{x}}.$$

Since $\sqrt{x} = \dfrac{S}{2}$, $\dfrac{dS}{dx}$ can be written as $\dfrac{2}{S}$.

The rate of change is therefore inversely proportional to her speed.

If she maintains her top speed for the rest of the race, the rate of change of speed with respect to distance drops to 0 for $x > 36$. Fig. 21.3 shows that the gradient, which represents the rate of change, gets smaller as her speed increases, and then becomes zero once she reaches her top speed.

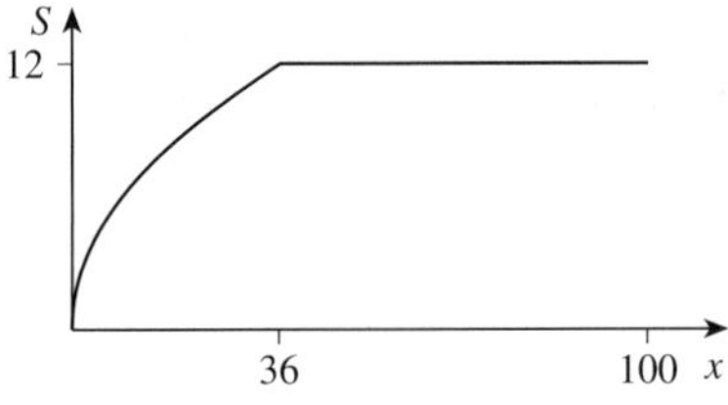

Fig. 21.3

Exercise 21A

1 In each part of this question express each derivative as 'the rate of change of . . . with respect to . . .', and say what it stands for in practice.

(a) $\dfrac{dh}{dx}$, where h is the height above sea level, and x is the distance travelled (measured horizontally), along a straight road

(b) $\dfrac{dN}{dt}$, where N is the number of people in a stadium at time t after the gates open

(c) $\dfrac{dM}{dr}$, where M is the magnetic force at a distance r from a magnet

(d) $\dfrac{dv}{dt}$, where v is the velocity of a train moving on a straight track at time t

(e) $\dfrac{dq}{dS}$, where q is the rate at which petrol is used in a car in litres per km, and S is the speed of the car in km per hour

2 Defining suitable notation and units, express each of the following as a derivative.

(a) the rate of change of atmospheric pressure with respect to height above sea level

(b) the rate of change of temperature with respect to the time of day

(c) the rate at which the tide is rising

(d) the rate at which a baby's weight increases in the first weeks of life

3 (a) Find $\dfrac{dz}{dt}$ where $z = 3t^2 + 7t - 5$.

(b) Find $\dfrac{d\theta}{dx}$ where $\theta = x - \sqrt{x}$.

(c) Find $\dfrac{dx}{dy}$ where $x = y + \dfrac{3}{y^2}$.

(d) Find $\dfrac{dr}{dt}$ where $r = t^2 + \dfrac{1}{\sqrt{t}}$.

(e) Find $\dfrac{dm}{dt}$ where $m = (t+3)^2$.

(f) Find $\dfrac{df}{ds}$ where $f = 2s^6 - 3s^2$.

(g) Find $\dfrac{dw}{dt}$ where $w = 5t$.

(h) Find $\dfrac{dR}{dr}$ where $R = \dfrac{1 - r^3}{r^2}$.

4 Devise suitable notation to express each of the following in mathematical form.

(a) The distance travelled along the motorway is increasing at a constant rate.

(b) The rate at which a savings bank deposit grows is proportional to the amount of money deposited.

(c) The rate at which the diameter of a tree increases is a function of the air temperature.

5 A hot air balloon is h metres above the ground t minutes after it is released. While it is ascending the equation connecting h with t is $h = 100t - 2t^2$.

(a) Find the average rate at which the balloon gains height during

(i) the first minute,

(ii) the 20th minute.

(b) Find the rate at which the balloon is gaining height after 10 minutes.

(c) Find how long the balloon takes to reach its greatest height.

6 The index of pollution, I, at a distance of x kilometres from a city centre is given by $I = (15 - x)^2$. The formula is valid for values of x between 0 and 10.

(a) Find the average rate of decrease of the index with respect to distance in moving from the centre of the city to a point 5 kilometres from the centre.

(b) Find the average rate of decrease of the index with respect to distance in moving from a point 5 kilometres from the centre to a point 10 kilometres from the centre.

(c) Find the rate of decrease of the index with respect to distance at a point 5 kilometres from the city centre.

7 The number of people who have completed a city marathon t hours after the start is modelled by the formula $N = 19\,200 - 21\,600t + 7200t^2 - 600t^3$ for values of t between 2 and 6. The organisers use this equation to plan how many stewards they will need to have on duty at the finishing line.

(a) How many runners are expected to have completed the course after 6 hours?

(b) What is the expected average rate per minute of arrival of runners at the finish

(i) between 2 and 3 hours after the start,

(ii) between 3 and $3\frac{1}{2}$ hours after the start?

(c) At what rate per minute are runners expected to be arriving at the finish 3 hours after the start?

8 (a) A circle of radius r has area $A = \pi r^2$. Find $\dfrac{dA}{dr}$.

(b) A sphere of radius r has volume $V = \frac{4}{3}\pi r^3$. Find $\dfrac{dV}{dr}$.

What do you notice about the answers?

9 The quantity of light received by a telescope from a star x light-years away is denoted by Q. It is known that, for stars with a given luminosity, $Q = \dfrac{C}{x^2}$, where C is a constant. Find $\dfrac{dQ}{dx}$, and deduce that $\dfrac{dQ}{dx} = -\dfrac{2Q}{x}$.

10 The pressure and volume of a quantity of air are denoted by P and V. As the air expands adiabatically, the values of P and V are related by the equation $PV^{1.4} = k$, where k is constant. Find $\dfrac{dP}{dV}$ in terms of V and k. Hence show that $\dfrac{dP}{dV} = -\dfrac{1.4P}{V}$.

11 (a) A simple pendulum consists of a small metal ball attached to a fixed point by a cord of length l centimetres. It takes T seconds to make one swing, where $T = 0.2\sqrt{l}$. Find $\dfrac{dT}{dl}$.

(b) The cord originally has length 2.5 metres. If it is lengthened by 2 millimetres, calculate what effect this will have on the time of swing

(i) by using your answer to part (a), (ii) by direct evaluation of T.

21.2 Second derivatives in practice

A local newspaper reports that 'house prices are increasing, but not as fast as they were'. This is a typical instance of a second derivative in everyday life. If p denotes the mean price of houses in the town, and t the time, then a (t, p) graph would look like Fig. 21.4.

The gradient $\frac{dp}{dt}$ represents the rate at which house prices are going up. The report says that this rate is going down, so the gradient is decreasing. The graph bends downwards, so the second derivative is negative. This second derivative is written as $\frac{d^2p}{dt^2}$.

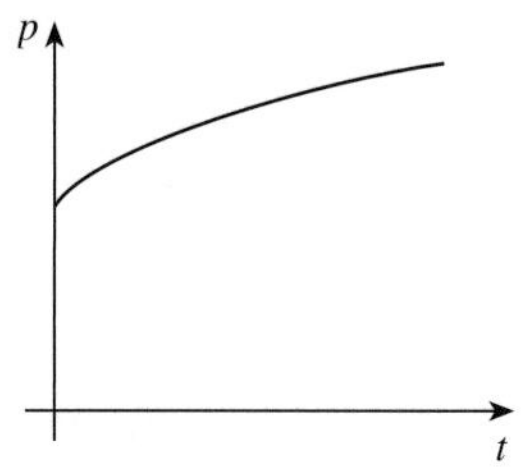

Fig. 21.4

Second derivatives are important in many applications. For example, the number of UK households possessing a DVD player has been increasing for a long time. Manufacturers will estimate the number of such households, H, in year t, and note that the graph of H against t has a positive gradient $\frac{dH}{dt}$. But to plan ahead they need to know whether this rate of increase is itself increasing (so that they should increase production of models for first-time users) or decreasing (in which case they might target existing customers to update to more sophisticated equipment). So it is the value of $\frac{d^2H}{dt^2}$ which affects strategic planning decisions.

Similarly, a weather forecaster observing the atmospheric pressure p at time t may not be too concerned if $\frac{dp}{dt}$ is negative; pressure goes up and down all the time. But if she also notices that $\frac{d^2p}{dt^2}$ is negative, it may be time to issue a warning of severe weather.

Example 21.2.1

A government plans the economy on the assumption that the population, P millions, for the next 15 years can be modelled by the equation $P = 60 + 0.02t^3 - 0.001t^4$.

(a) How large is the population expected to be in 10 years time?

(b) At what annual rate is the population expected to be increasing in 10 years time?

(c) During what period does the government expect the annual rate of increase of the population to be increasing?

(a) Substituting $t = 10$ in the equation for P gives

$$P = 60 + 0.02 \times 1000 - 0.001 \times 10\,000 = 60 + 20 - 10 = 70.$$

Since P is the population in millions, the population in 10 years time is expected to be 70 million.

(b) The rate of increase of the population is given by

$$\frac{\mathrm{d}P}{\mathrm{d}t} = 0.02 \times (3t^2) - 0.001 \times (4t^3) = 0.06t^2 - 0.004t^3.$$

When $t = 10$, the value of $\frac{\mathrm{d}P}{\mathrm{d}t}$ is

$$0.06 \times 100 - 0.004 \times 1000 = 6 - 4 = 2.$$

In 10 years time it is expected that the population will be increasing at a rate of 2 million per year.

(c) This question asks about the rate of increase of $\frac{\mathrm{d}P}{\mathrm{d}t}$, which is

$$\frac{\mathrm{d}^2P}{\mathrm{d}t^2} = 0.06 \times (2t) - 0.004 \times (3t^2) = 0.12t - 0.012t^2 = 0.012t(10 - t).$$

This is positive when $t(10 - t) > 0$, that is when $0 < t < 10$.

The rate of increase of the population is expected to increase for the next 10 years.

This is illustrated by the graph in Fig. 21.5. Between $t = 0$ and $t = 10$ the graph is concave up, which shows that the rate of increase of the population is increasing. After that, until $t = 15$, the graph is concave down; the rate of increase of the population decreases, although the population is still increasing.

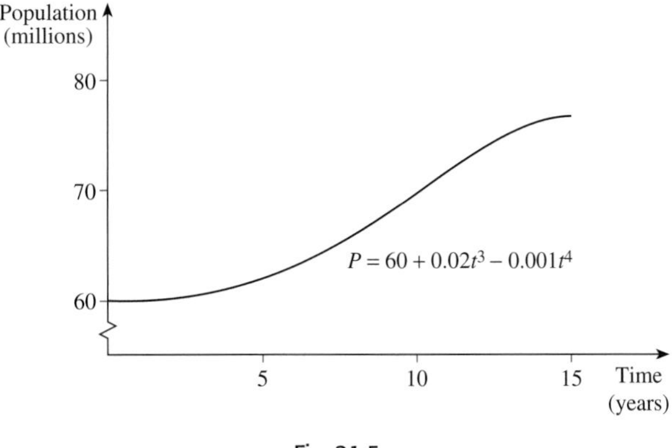

Fig. 21.5

21.3 Derivatives in kinematics

One important application of derivatives is to the motion of an object along a straight line.

In Section 9.6 it was shown that, if the velocity is constant, then the displacement is a linear function of the time, and the gradient of the displacement–time graph represents the velocity. This can now be generalised to situations in which the velocity varies with time.

Suppose that a car moving along a road has its speed checked by a radar detector at a point O (see Fig. 21.6). A pulse sent out from O locates the car at P, at a displacement s from O. A second pulse, at a time δt later, locates the car at Q, where the displacement has increased by an amount δs. Then the detector will compute the velocity of the car as $\frac{\delta s}{\delta t}$.

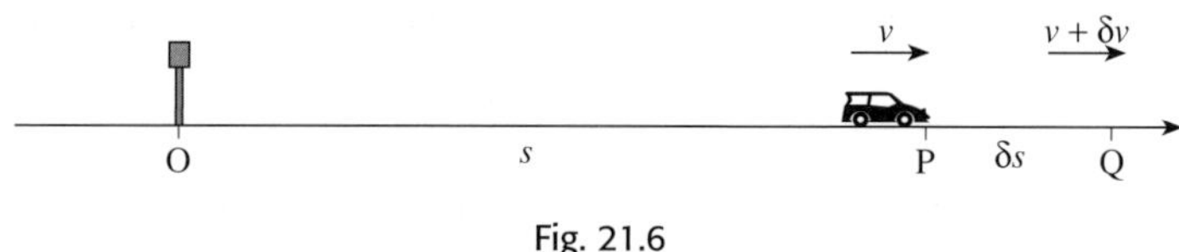

Fig. 21.6

This is not in fact the true velocity of the car, but the average velocity over the time interval δt. The advantage of using radar instead of a policeman with a stopwatch is that δt can be made much smaller. If δt is very small, the average velocity will be very close to the actual velocity at P, which is the limit of the average velocity as δt tends to 0. That is,

$$v = \lim_{\delta t \to 0} \frac{\delta s}{\delta t} = \frac{\mathrm{d}s}{\mathrm{d}t}.$$

There is a similar link between acceleration and velocity. It was stated in Section 9.7 that, if the acceleration is constant, then the velocity is a linear function of the time, and the gradient of the velocity–time graph represents the acceleration. This can be generalised to situations in which the acceleration is not constant.

If the velocity of the car in Fig. 21.6 is v when the car is at P, and if it increases by an amount δv by the time the car reaches Q, then $\frac{\delta v}{\delta t}$ measures the average acceleration of the car over the time interval δt. The actual acceleration at P is the limit of the average acceleration as δt tends to 0. That is,

$$a = \lim_{\delta t \to 0} \frac{\delta v}{\delta t} = \frac{\mathrm{d}v}{\mathrm{d}t}.$$

Since $v = \frac{\mathrm{d}s}{\mathrm{d}t}$, it follows that the acceleration can also be written as $\frac{\mathrm{d}^2 s}{\mathrm{d}t^2}$.

For an object moving in a straight line, if s denotes the displacement from a fixed point O of the line at time t, v denotes the velocity and a the acceleration, then

$$v = \frac{\mathrm{d}s}{\mathrm{d}t} \quad \text{and} \quad a = \frac{\mathrm{d}v}{\mathrm{d}t} = \frac{\mathrm{d}^2 s}{\mathrm{d}t^2}.$$

The velocity is represented by the gradient of the (t, s) graph.

The acceleration is represented by the gradient of the (t, v) graph.

Example 21.3.1

A space probe is launched by rockets. For the first stage of its ascent, which is in a vertical line and lasts for 40 seconds, the height s metres after t seconds is modelled by the equation $s = 50t^2 + \frac{1}{4}t^3$. How high is the probe at the end of the first stage, and how fast is it then moving?

To find the height, you substitute 40 for t in the equation for s, which gives

$$s = 50 \times 1600 + \tfrac{1}{4} \times 64\,000 = 96\,000.$$

To find a formula for the velocity you must differentiate, to get

$$v = \frac{ds}{dt} = 100t + \tfrac{3}{4}t^2.$$

Substituting 40 for t in this equation gives

$$v = 100 \times 40 + \tfrac{3}{4} \times 1600 = 4000 + 1200 = 5200.$$

So at the end of the first stage the probe is at a height of 96 000 m and moving at 5200 m s^{-1}. This is more conveniently expressed in kilometre units: the height is then 96 km, and the velocity is 5.2 km s^{-1}.

Example 21.3.2

A car starts to accelerate as soon as it leaves a town. After t seconds its velocity v m s^{-1} is given by the formula $v = 14 + 0.45t^2 - 0.03t^3$, until it reaches its maximum velocity. Find a formula for the acceleration. How fast is the car moving when its acceleration becomes zero?

The acceleration a is found by differentiating the formula for v, so

$$a = \frac{dv}{dt} = 0.9t - 0.09t^2.$$

This can be factorised as $a = 0.09t(10 - t)$, so the acceleration becomes zero when $t = 10$. This is when the car reaches its maximum velocity. After that the model no longer applies.

To find the maximum velocity, substitute $t = 10$ in the formula for v. This gives $v = 14 + 0.45 \times 100 - 0.03 \times 1000 = 14 + 45 - 30 = 29$.

The car reaches a maximum velocity of 29 m s^{-1} after 10 seconds.

Exercise 21B

1 (a) This graph shows prices (P) plotted against time (t). The rate of inflation, measured by $\dfrac{dP}{dt}$, is increasing. What does $\dfrac{d^2P}{dt^2}$ represent and what can be said about its value?

(b) Sketch a graph showing that prices are increasing but that the rate of inflation is slowing down with an overall increase tending to 20%.

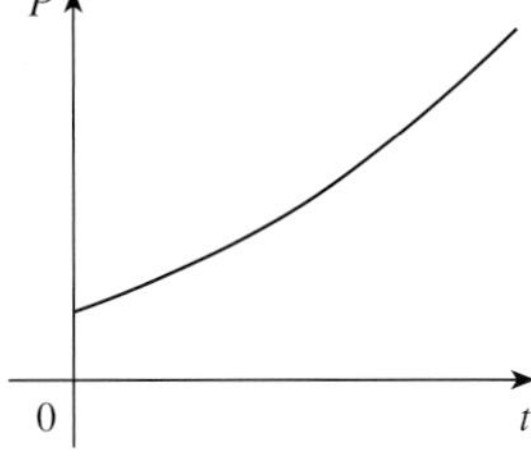

2 The graph shows the price S of shares in a certain company.

(a) For each stage of the graph comment on $\dfrac{dS}{dt}$ and $\dfrac{d^2S}{dt^2}$.

(b) Describe what happened in non-technical language.

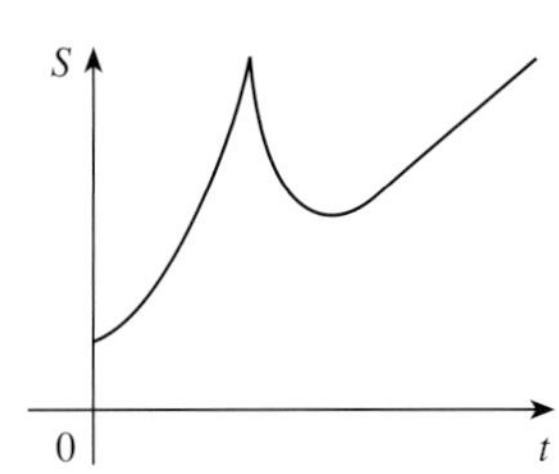

3 Colin sets off for school, which is 800 m from home. His speed is proportional to the distance he still has to go. Let x metres be the distance he has gone, and y metres be the distance that he still has to go.

(a) Sketch graphs of x against t and y against t.

(b) What are the signs of $\frac{dx}{dt}$, $\frac{d^2x}{dt^2}$, $\frac{dy}{dt}$ and $\frac{d^2y}{dt^2}$?

4 The rate of decay of a radioactive substance is proportional to the number, N, of radioactive atoms present at time t.

(a) Write an equation representing this information.

(b) Sketch a graph of N against t.

(c) What is the sign of $\frac{d^2N}{dt^2}$?

5 A weather forecaster predicts that, in t hours time, the pressure at a certain point, p millibars, will be given by the equation $p = 0.1t^3 - 1.5t^2 + 1000$, for $0 \le t \le 16$.

(a) Show that, according to this formula, the pressure will fall for the first few hours. When will it start to rise again?

(b) When will the rate at which the pressure is falling begin to decrease?

(c) When will the pressure get back to its original value? At what rate will it then be rising?

6 An economist predicts that, over the next few months, the price of oil, p dollars a barrel, in t weeks time will be given by the formula $p = 0.005t^3 - 0.3t^2 + 4.5t + 80$.

(a) What is the price at present, and how rapidly is it going up?

(b) How high does she expect the price to rise?

(c) She reckons that she will need to revise her prediction when the rate of price increase next begins to increase. When will this occur?

7 In this question, s metres is the displacement at time t seconds of particles moving in a straight line, v is the velocity in m s^{-1} and a is the acceleration in m s^{-2}. Only zero and positive values of t should be considered.

(a) Given that $s = t^3 + 5t$, find the displacement, velocity and acceleration when $t = 3$.

(b) Given that $s = 36 - \frac{4}{t}$, find the velocity and acceleration when $t = 2$.

(c) Given that $v = 3\sqrt{t}$, find the velocity and acceleration when $t = 4$.

(d) Given that $s = 120 - 15t - 6t^2 + t^3$, find the time when the velocity is zero. Find the displacement at this instant.

(e) Given that $v = t^2 - 12t + 40$, find the velocity when the acceleration is zero.

(f) Given that $s = 2t^4 + 8t$, find the displacement and the acceleration when the velocity is 35 m s^{-1}.

8 A car is accelerating from rest. At time t seconds after starting, the velocity of the car is v m s^{-1}, where $v = 6t - \frac{1}{2}t^2$, for $0 \le t \le 6$.

(a) Find the velocity of the car 6 seconds after starting.

(b) Find the acceleration of the car when its velocity is 10 m s^{-1}.

9 A train leaves a station and travels in a straight line. After t seconds the train has travelled a distance s metres, where $s = (320t^3 - 2t^4) \times 10^{-5}$. This formula is valid until the train comes to rest at the next station.

(a) Find when the train comes to rest, and hence find the distance between the two stations.

(b) Find the acceleration of the train 40 seconds after the journey begins.

(c) Find the deceleration of the train just before it stops.

(d) Find when the acceleration is zero, and hence find the maximum velocity of the train.

10 An insect flies in a straight line from one flower to another. The two flowers are 270 cm apart and the flight takes 3 seconds. At time t seconds after the flight begins, the insect is s cm from the first flower. Two alternative models are proposed:

(A) $s = 60t^2 - 10t^3$,

(B) $s = 40t^3 - 10t^4$.

For each of these models,

(a) show that the model fits the given information about the flight,

(b) find the maximum velocity of the insect,

(c) sketch the (t, v) graph.

Comment on the differences between the two models. Which do you consider to be the better model?

11 A flare is launched from a hot-air balloon and moves in a vertical line. At time t seconds, the height of the flare is x metres, where $x = 1664 - 40t - \dfrac{2560}{t}$ for $t \geq 5$.

The flare is launched when $t = 5$.

(a) Find the height and the velocity of the flare immediately after it is launched.

(b) Find the acceleration of the flare immediately after it is launched, when its velocity is zero, and when $t = 25$.

(c) Find the greatest possible downward speed of the flare.

(d) Find when the flare reaches the ground.

(e) Sketch the (t, v) graph and the (t, x) graph for the motion of the flare.

21.4 Maximum and minimum problems

In many real-world situations the aim is to find a strategy which will make some quantity as large or as small as possible. For example, a manufacturer may want to price goods so as to maximise the firm's profits, or to design a component so as to minimise the amount of raw material used. The techniques described in the last two chapters can often be useful in reaching such decisions.

The procedures are essentially similar to those for finding maximum and minimum points on graphs. But there are some differences.

One is that in practical applications you will only want to consider values of the independent variable for which the problem makes sense. For example, if the independent variable is a length x metres, you will be interested only in values of the function when $x > 0$.

Another difference is that in a practical situation it will sometimes be obvious from the nature of the problem whether the quantity has a maximum or a minimum value. Steps 3 and 4 in the procedure (in Sections 19.2 and 20.4), which are used to distinguish maximum points from minimum points, then simply serve as a check that the technique has been correctly applied.

Example 21.4.1

Fig. 21.7 shows the corner of a garden, bordered by two walls at right angles. A gardener has 30 metres of rabbit fencing. What is the largest rectangular area she can fence off?

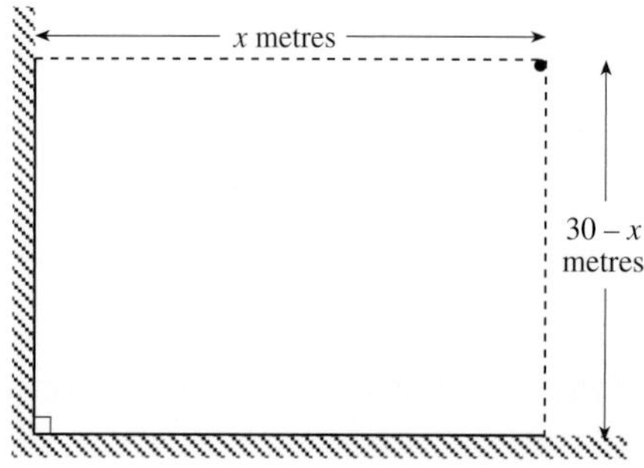

Fig. 21.7

If she makes her rectangle x metres long, she has $(30 - x)$ metres left for the other side of the rectangle. In this way she can fence off an area of A m^2, where

$$A = x(30 - x) = 30x - x^2.$$

Notice that this equation only applies if $0 < x < 30$.

The area takes its maximum value when $\frac{dA}{dx} = 0$, where

$$\frac{dA}{dx} = 30 - 2x.$$

So $\frac{dA}{dx} = 0$ when $x = 15$.

To check that this gives a maximum value of A, find

$$\frac{d^2A}{dx^2} = -2.$$

Since this is negative, $x = 15$ gives a maximum value.

To find the maximum area, substitute $x = 15$ in $A = x(30 - x)$ to get

$$A = 15 \times (30 - 15) = 15 \times 15 = 225.$$

The largest area the gardener can fence off is 225 m^2.

Example 21.4.2

Towards the end of the day a market trader has 20 boxes of peaches left unsold. By tomorrow they will be useless. He reckons that if he offers them for sale at x cents a box, he will be able to dispose of $(20 - \frac{1}{5}x)$ boxes. At what price should he offer them to make the most money?

The trader will not sell any boxes if he sets the price at 100 cents. The only values of x which are of interest are between 0 and 100.

If he sells $(20 - \frac{1}{5}x)$ boxes at x cents a box, he will make $x\,(20 - \frac{1}{5}x)$ cents. He wants to maximise this function.

Let $\quad f(x) = x\,(20 - \frac{1}{5}x) = 20x - \frac{1}{5}x^2.$

Then $\quad f'(x) = 20 - \frac{2}{5}x.$

The value of x which makes $f'(x) = 0$ is given by

$$\tfrac{2}{5}x = 20, \quad \text{that is} \quad x = 50.$$

This obviously gives a maximum rather than a minimum, but you can check this by finding $f''(x) = -\frac{2}{5}$. Since this is negative, $x = 50$ gives a maximum value of the function.

He should offer the peaches at 50 cents a box.

Example 21.4.3

A pioneer wants to build a storage shed in the shape of a cuboid with a square base, with a capacity of 32 cubic metres. To conserve materials, he wants to make the total area of the roof and the four sides as small as possible. What are the best dimensions for the shed, and what is the total area with these dimensions?

The shed is illustrated in Fig. 21.8. Suppose that the base is a square of side x metres. Then, since the volume is to be 32 cubic metres, the height must be $\dfrac{32}{x^2}$ square metres.

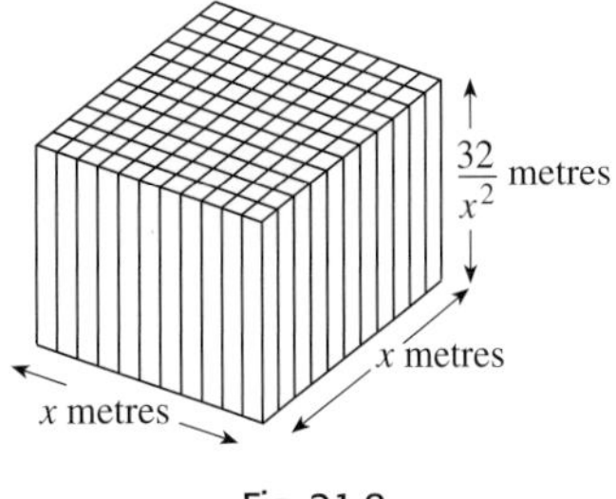

Fig. 21.8

The roof is square with area x^2 square metres. Each side is a rectangle with area $x \times \dfrac{32}{x^2}$ square metres, which is $\dfrac{32}{x}$ square metres. So, if the total area of the roof and the four sides is A square metres,

$$A = x^2 + 4 \times \frac{32}{x} = x^2 + \frac{128}{x}$$

The problem is to choose x so that A is as small as possible. To do this, follow the procedure for finding a minimum point described in Section 20.4. Note that only positive values of x are relevant in the problem.

Step 1 $\dfrac{\mathrm{d}A}{\mathrm{d}x} = 2x - \dfrac{128}{x^2}$.

Step 2 $\dfrac{\mathrm{d}A}{\mathrm{d}x} = 0$ when $2x - \dfrac{128}{x^2} = 0$, which gives $x^3 = 64$, $x = 4$.

Step 3 $\dfrac{\mathrm{d}^2 A}{\mathrm{d}x^2} = 2 + \dfrac{256}{x^3}$.

Step 4 When $x = 4$, $\dfrac{\mathrm{d}^2 A}{\mathrm{d}x^2}$ has value $2 + \dfrac{256}{4^3} = 2 + 4 = 6$, which is positive, so the stationary value is a minimum.

Step 5 When $x = 4$, $A = 4^2 + \dfrac{128}{4} = 16 + 32 = 48$.

This shows that the best dimensions for the shed are to make the base 4 metres square and the height 2 metres. This gives a total area for the roof and the sides of 48 square metres.

Notice that, in solving this problem, it was necessary to begin by choosing a suitable independent variable (in this case the length of a side of the square base). Then an equation was found for the quantity to be minimised (the area of the shed) in terms of this independent variable. Only then can you begin to use the procedure for finding the minimum point of the graph. Finally, once the procedure has been completed, the result has to be interpreted in terms of the original problem.

Example 21.4.4

A wire of length 4 metres is cut into two pieces, and each piece is bent into a square. How should this be done so that the two squares together have

(a) the smallest area, (b) the largest area?

Let the two pieces have lengths x metres and $(4 - x)$ metres. The areas of the squares are then $\left(\frac{1}{4}x\right)^2$ and $\left(\frac{1}{4}(4 - x)\right)^2$ square metres, see Fig. 21.9. So the total area, y m^2, is given by

$$\begin{aligned} y &= \tfrac{1}{16}(x^2 + (16 - 8x + x^2)) \\ &= \tfrac{1}{8}(x^2 - 4x + 8). \end{aligned}$$

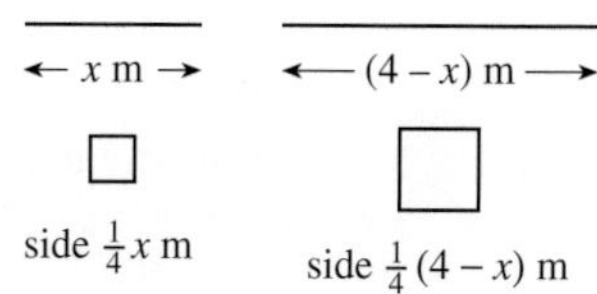

Fig. 21.9

You can evaluate this expression for any real number x, but the problem only has meaning if $0 < x < 4$. Fig. 21.10 shows the graph of the area function for this interval.

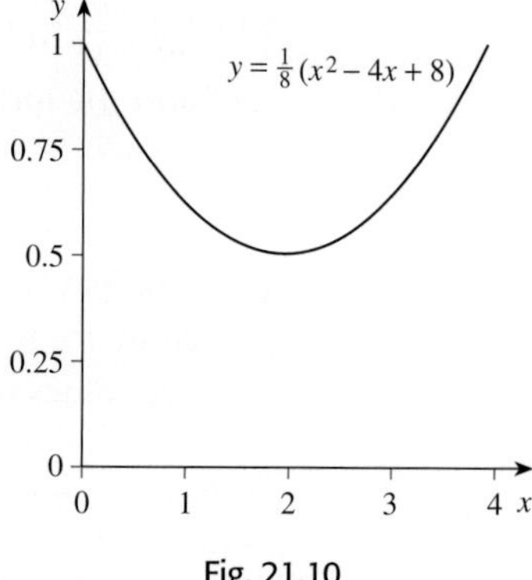

Fig. 21.10

(a) The smallest area is represented by the minimum point on the graph. Since $\frac{\mathrm{d}y}{\mathrm{d}x} = \frac{1}{8}(2x - 4) = \frac{1}{4}(x - 2)$, this is where $x = 2$. Also $\frac{\mathrm{d}^2y}{\mathrm{d}x^2} = \frac{1}{4} > 0$, which confirms that the stationary point is a minimum.

So the area is smallest when the wire is cut into two equal parts, each of length 2 metres. The area is then $\frac{1}{8}(2^2 - 4 \times 2 + 8)$ m^2, that is, $\frac{1}{2}$ m^2.

Since y is a quadratic function of x, this answer could also be found by writing y in completed square form, as $y = \frac{1}{8}((x - 2)^2 + 4)$. As $(x - 2)^2 \geq 0$, y is least when $x = 2$, and the least value of y is $\frac{1}{2}$.

(b) From the graph it looks as if the largest value of y is 1, when $x = 0$ and $x = 4$. But these values of x are excluded, since they do not produce two pieces of wire. You can get areas as near to 1 square metre as you like, but you cannot achieve this target. Strictly speaking, there is no largest area.

It is important to notice in this example that the 'largest value' is not associated with a maximum point on the graph, as defined in Section 19.2. Although largest and smallest values can often be found by using the procedure for locating maximum and minimum points, there are exceptional cases when this does not happen.

Example 21.4.5

It is found that the flow of traffic on congested roads can be improved by lowering the speed at which it travels. This is because at higher speeds vehicles travel further apart. A traffic researcher models the distance between vehicles at a speed of S metres per second as D metres, given by the equation $D = \frac{1}{10}S^2 + \frac{1}{2}S + 10$. At this speed the time interval between successive vehicles passing a checkpoint is T seconds, where $T = \frac{D}{S}$. Use this model to find the speed which minimises this time, and the number of vehicles expected to pass the checkpoint in a minute at this speed.

Note that in this situation you are only interested in positive values of S.

You want to find where $\frac{\mathrm{d}T}{\mathrm{d}S} = 0$, so write the equation for T in the form

$$T = \frac{D}{S} = \frac{\frac{1}{10}S^2 + \frac{1}{2}S + 10}{S} = \frac{\frac{1}{10}S^2}{S} + \frac{\frac{1}{2}S}{S} + \frac{10}{S} = \frac{1}{10}S + \frac{1}{2} + 10S^{-1}.$$

Then $\frac{\mathrm{d}T}{\mathrm{d}S} = \frac{1}{10} - 10S^{-2} = \frac{1}{10} - \frac{10}{S^2}$.

The minimum time interval will occur when

$$\frac{1}{10} - \frac{10}{S^2} = 0,$$

that is when $S^2 = 100$. Since only positive values of S are of interest, $S = 10$.

To check that this is a minimum, find

$$\frac{\mathrm{d}^2T}{\mathrm{d}S^2} = -10(-2S^{-3}) = \frac{20}{S^3},$$

which is certainly positive because S is positive. So $S = 10$ gives a minimum value for T.

Substituting $S = 10$ in the expression for T gives the minimum value

$$T = \tfrac{1}{10} \times 10 + \tfrac{1}{2} + \frac{10}{10} = 1 + \tfrac{1}{2} + 1 = 2\tfrac{1}{2}.$$

So at 10 metres per second a vehicle passes the checkpoint every $2\frac{1}{2}$ seconds. The number of cars passing the checkpoint in a minute is $60 \div 2\frac{1}{2}$, which is 24.

21.5 Extending $\dfrac{dy}{dx}$ notation

Although $\dfrac{dy}{dx}$ is a symbol which should not be split into smaller bits, it can usefully be adapted by separating off the y, as

$$\frac{d}{dx}y$$

so that if $y = f(x)$, you can write

$$f'(x) = \frac{d}{dx}f(x).$$

This can be used as a convenient shorthand. For example, instead of having to write

$$\text{if } y = x^4 \text{ then } \frac{dy}{dx} = 4x^3$$

you can abbreviate this to

$$\frac{d}{dx}x^4 = 4x^3.$$

In this equation $\dfrac{d}{dx}$ can be thought of as an instruction to differentiate whatever comes after it.

You may have seen calculators which do algebra as well as arithmetic. With these, you can input a function such as x^4, key in 'differentiate', and the output $4x^3$ appears in the display. The symbol $\dfrac{d}{dx}$, sometimes called the **differential operator**, is the equivalent of pressing the 'differentiate' key.

This explains the notation used for the second derivative, which is what you get by differentiating $\dfrac{dy}{dx}$; that is,

$$\frac{d}{dx}\frac{dy}{dx}.$$

If you collect the elements of this expression into a single symbol, the top line becomes d^2y, and the bottom line $(dx)^2$. Dropping the brackets, this takes the form

$$\frac{d^2y}{dx^2}.$$

Exercise 21C

1 At a speed of S km per hour a car will travel y kilometres on each litre of petrol, where

$$y = 5 + \tfrac{1}{5}S - \tfrac{1}{800}S^2.$$

Calculate the speed at which the car should be driven for maximum economy.

2 A cricket ball is thrown vertically upwards. At time t seconds its height h metres is given by $h = 20t - 5t^2$. Calculate the ball's maximum height above the ground.

3 The sum of two real numbers x and y is 12. Find the maximum value of their product xy.

4 The product of two positive real numbers x and y is 20. Find the minimum possible value of their sum.

5 The volume of a cylinder is given by the formula $V = \pi r^2 h$. Find the greatest and least values of V if $r + h = 6$.

6 A loop of string of length 1 metre is formed into a rectangle with one pair of opposite sides each x cm. Calculate the value of x which will maximise the area enclosed by the string.

7 One side of a rectangular sheep pen is formed by a hedge. The other three sides are made using fencing. The length of the rectangle is x metres; 120 metres of fencing is available.

(a) Show that the area of the rectangle is $\frac{1}{2}x(120 - x)$ m^2.

(b) Calculate the maximum possible area of the sheep pen.

8 A rectangular sheet of metal measures 50 cm by 40 cm. Equal squares of side x cm are cut from each corner and discarded. The sheet is then folded up to make a tray of depth x cm. What are the possible values of x? Find the value of x which maximises the capacity of the tray.

9 An open rectangular box is to be made with a square base, and its capacity is to be 4000 cm^3. Find the length of the side of the base when the amount of material used to make the box is as small as possible. (Ignore 'flaps'.)

10 An open cylindrical wastepaper bin, of radius r cm and capacity V cm^3, is to have a surface area of 5000 cm^2.

(a) Show that $V = \frac{1}{2}r(5000 - \pi r^2)$.

(b) Calculate the maximum possible capacity of the bin.

11* A circular cylinder is cut out of a sphere of radius 10 cm. Calculate the maximum possible volume of the cylinder. (It is probably best to take as your independent variable the height, or half the height, of the cylinder.)

Review exercise 6

1 (a) Find the stationary points and the point of inflexion on the graph of $y = 12x + 3x^2 - 2x^3$. Sketch the graph.

(b) How does your sketch show that the equation $12x + 3x^2 - 2x^3 = 0$ has exactly three real roots?

(c) Use your graph to show that the equation $12x + 3x^2 - 2x^3 = -5$ also has exactly three real roots.

(d) For what range of values of k does the equation $12x + 3x^2 - 2x^3 = k$ have

(i) exactly three real roots, (ii) only one real root?

2 Find the coordinates of the stationary points on the graph of $y = 3x^4 - 4x^3 - 12x^2 + 10$, and sketch the graph. For what values of k does the equation $3x^4 - 4x^3 - 12x^2 + 10 = k$ have

(a) exactly four roots, (b) exactly two roots?

Find the coordinates of the points of inflexion, correct to 2 decimal places.

3 The rate at which Nasreen's coffee cools is proportional to the difference between its temperature, $\theta°$, and room temperature, $\alpha°$. Sketch a graph of θ against t given that $\alpha = 20$ and that $\theta = 95$ when $t = 0$. State the signs of θ, $\frac{\mathrm{d}\theta}{\mathrm{d}t}$ and $\frac{\mathrm{d}^2\theta}{\mathrm{d}t^2}$ for $t > 0$.

4 A car accelerates to overtake a truck. Its initial speed is u. The distance x that it covers in a time t after it starts to accelerate is given by $x = ut + kt^2$, where k is a constant.

Use differentiation to show that its speed is then $u + 2kt$, and show that its acceleration is constant.

5 A car is travelling at 20 m s^{-1} when the driver applies the brakes. At a time t seconds later the car has travelled a further distance s metres, where $s = 20t - 2t^2$. Use differentiation to find expressions for the speed and the acceleration of the car at this time. For how long do these formulae apply?

6 Find the least possible value of $x^2 + y^2$ given that $x + y = 10$.

7 The sum of the two shorter sides of a right-angled triangle is 18 cm. Calculate

(a) the least possible length of the hypotenuse,

(b) the greatest possible area of the triangle.

8 A curve has equation $y = 2x^3 - 9x^2 + 12x - 5$. Show that one of the stationary points lies on the x-axis, and determine whether this point is a maximum or a minimum. Find also the coordinates of the point of inflexion.

9 Find the coordinates of the stationary points on the curve with equation $y = x(x-1)^2$. Sketch the curve.

Find the set of real values of k such that the equation $x(x-1)^2 = k^2$ has exactly one real root. (OCR, adapted)

10 Find the coordinates of the stationary points on the graph of $y = x^3 - 12x - 12$ and sketch the graph.

Find the set of values of k for which the equation $x^3 - 12x - 12 = k$ has more than one real root. (OCR)

11 (a) Find the coordinates of the stationary points on the curve $y = 2x^3 - 3x^2 - 12x - 7$.

(b) Determine whether each stationary point is a maximum point or a minimum point.

(c) It is given that $2x^3 - 3x^2 - 12x - 7$ can be written as $(x+1)^2(2x-7)$. Sketch the curve $y = (x+1)^2(2x-7)$.

(d) Write down the set of values of the constant k for which the equation $2x^3 - 3x^2 - 12x - 7 = k$ has exactly one real solution. (OCR)

12 The cross-section of an object has the shape of a quarter-circle of radius r adjoining a rectangle of width x and height r, as shown in the diagram.

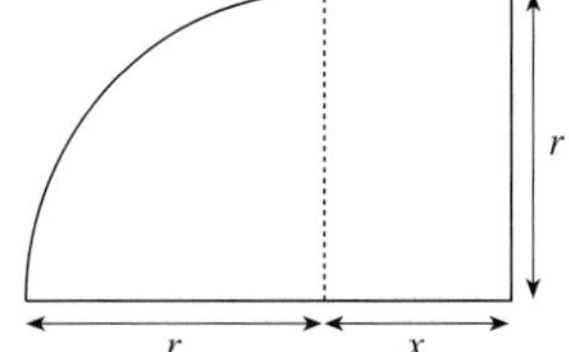

(a) The perimeter and area of the cross-section are P and A respectively. Express each of P and A in terms of r and x, and hence show that $A = \frac{1}{2}Pr - r^2$.

(b) Taking the perimeter P of the cross-section as fixed, find x in terms of r for the case when the area A of the cross-section is a maximum, and show that, for this value of x, A is a maximum and not a minimum. (OCR)

13 The costs of a firm which makes climbing boots are of two kinds:
Fixed costs (plant, rates, office expenses): \$2000 per week;
Production costs (materials, labour): \$20 for each pair of boots made.

Market research suggests that, if they price the boots at \$30 a pair they will sell 500 pairs a week, but that at \$55 a pair they will sell none at all; and between these values the graph of sales against price is a straight line.

If they price boots at \$$x$ a pair ($30 \le x \le 55$) find expressions for

(a) the weekly sales, (b) the weekly receipts,

(c) the weekly costs (assuming that just enough boots are made).

Hence show that the weekly profit, \$$P$, is given by

$$P = -20x^2 + 1500x - 24\,000.$$

Find the price at which the boots should be sold to maximise the profit. (OCR)

14* The manager of a supermarket usually adds a mark-up of 20% to the wholesale prices of all the goods he sells. He reckons that he has a loyal core of F customers and that, if he lowers his mark-up to x% he will attract an extra $k(20 - x)$ customers from his rivals. Each week the average shopper buys goods whose wholesale value is \$$A$. Show that with a mark-up of x% the supermarket will have an anticipated weekly profit of

$$\$\tfrac{1}{100}Ax\left((F + 20k) - kx\right).$$

Show that the manager can increase his profit by reducing his mark-up below 20% provided that $20k > F$. (OCR)

Examination questions

1 The displacement s metres of a car, t seconds after leaving a fixed point A, is given by $s = 10t - 0.5t^2$.

(a) Calculate the velocity when $t = 0$.

(b) Calculate the value of t when the velocity is zero.

(c) Calculate the displacement of the car from A when the velocity is zero. (© IBO 2004)

2 The graph of $y = x^3 - 10x^2 + 12x + 23$ has a maximum point between $x = -1$ and $x = 3$. Find the coordinates of this maximum point. (© IBO 2002)

3 The diagram below shows the graph of $y = f(x)$.

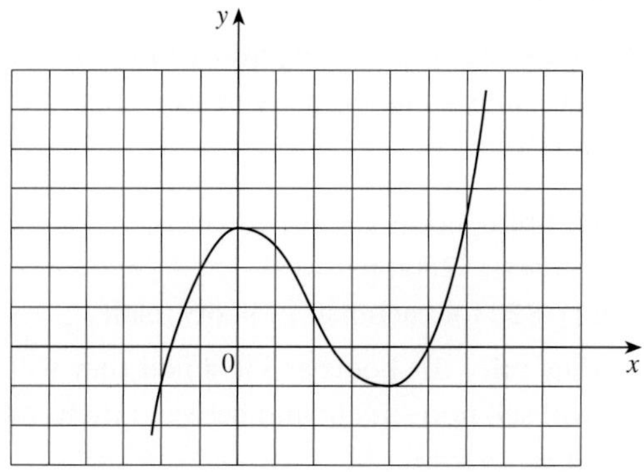

On a similar grid sketch the graph of $y = f'(x)$. (© IBO 2003)

4 Figure 1 shows the graphs of the functions f_1, f_2, f_3, f_4.
Figure 2 includes the graphs of the derivatives of the functions shown in Figure 1.

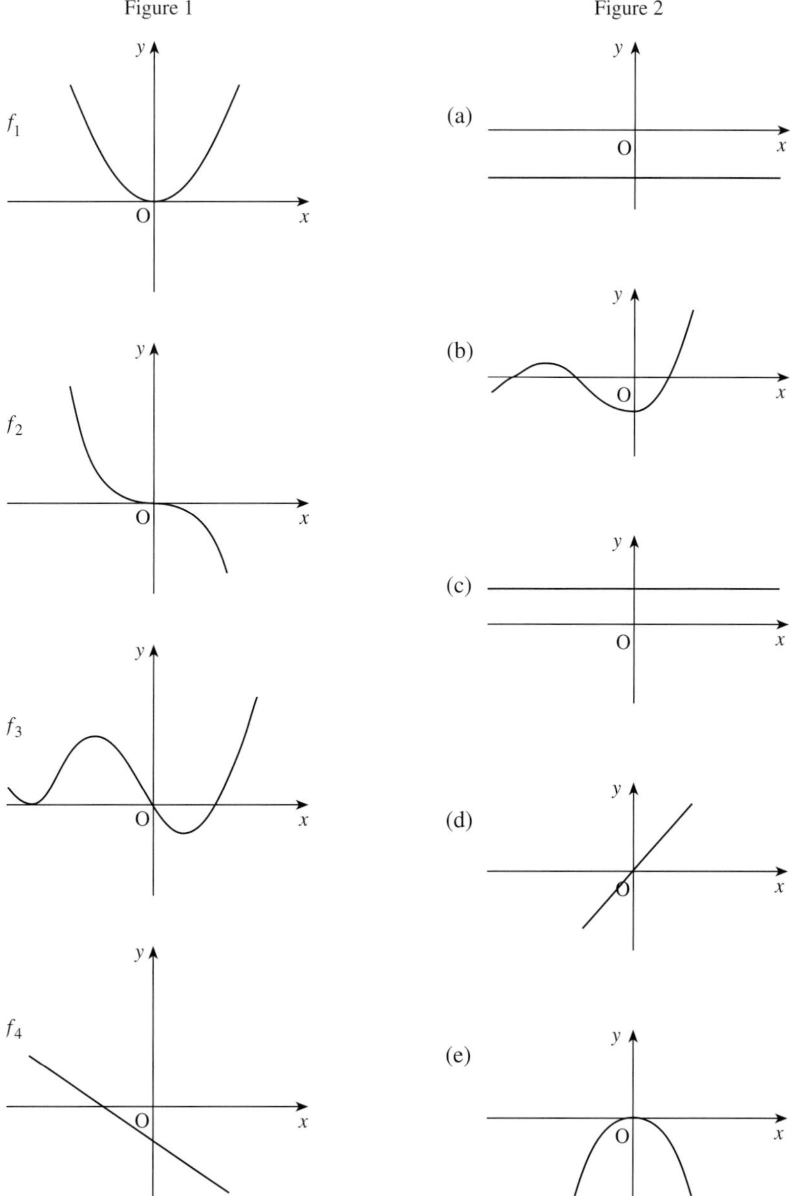

The derivative diagram (d) matches the function f_1. State which derivative diagrams match the functions f_2, f_3, f_4. (© IBO 2002)

22 Probability

In this chapter you are introduced to probabilities. When you have completed it, you should

- know what a 'sample space' is
- know the difference between an 'outcome' and an 'event' and be able to calculate the probability of an event from the probabilities of the outcomes in the sample space
- be able to use the addition law of probability
- know what is meant by mutually exclusive events.

22.1 Assigning probability

You will frequently have been unsure of the outcome of some activity or experiment, but have known what the possible outcomes were. For example, you do not know whether you will win a prize the next time you buy a raffle ticket, but you do know that you will either win or not win. You know that if you toss a coin twice, then the possible outcomes are (H, H), (H, T), (T, H) and (T, T). If you are testing a transistor to see if it is defective, then the possible outcomes are 'defective' and 'not defective'.

The list of all the possible outcomes is called the **sample space** of the experiment. The list is usually written in curly brackets, { }, and denoted by the symbol U.

Thus the sample space for buying a raffle ticket is $U = \{\text{win, not win}\}$, the sample space for tossing a coin twice is $U = \{(H, H), (H, T), (T, H), (T, T)\}$, and the sample space for testing a transistor is $U = \{\text{defective, not defective}\}$.

Notice that it is conventional when writing pairs of things like H, H to put them in brackets, like coordinates.

Each of the outcomes of an experiment has a number, called its probability, assigned to it. Sometimes you can assign the probability using symmetry. For example the sample space for throwing a dice is $\{1, 2, 3, 4, 5, 6\}$, and you would assign each outcome the probability $\frac{1}{6}$, in the belief that the dice was fair, and that each outcome was equally likely. This is the usual method for calculations about games of chance.

If the outcomes in a sample space are equally likely, then

$$\text{probability of a particular outcome} = \frac{1}{\text{number of equally likely outcomes}}.$$

From the equation in the blue box you can see that the probability must be positive, and lie between 0 and 1. You can also see that if there are n equally likely outcomes, each of the probabilities will be $\frac{1}{n}$. The total sum of all these probabilities will be $n \times \frac{1}{n} = 1$.

Now suppose that the dice is not fair, so that you cannot use symmetry for assigning probabilities. In this case you will have to carry out an experiment and throw the dice a large number of times. Suppose that you threw the dice 1000 times and the frequencies of the six possible outcomes in the sample space were as in Table 22.1.

Outcome	1	2	3	4	5	6
Frequency	100	216	182	135	170	197

Table 22.1

The probabilities you would assign would then be $\frac{100}{1000}$, $\frac{216}{1000}$, $\frac{182}{1000}$, $\frac{135}{1000}$, $\frac{170}{1000}$ and $\frac{197}{1000}$ for the outcomes 1, 2, 3, 4, 5 and 6 respectively. These are called the **relative frequencies** of the outcomes, and you can use them as estimates of the probabilities. You should realise that if you were to roll the dice another 1000 times, the results would probably not be exactly the same, but you would hope that they would not be too different. You could roll the dice more times and hope that the relative frequency would improve as an approximation to the probability. You still find that all the relative frequencies add together to give 1.

Sometimes you cannot assign a probability by using symmetry or by carrying out an experiment. For example, there is a probability that my house will be struck by lightning next year, and I could insure against this happening. The insurance company will have to have a probability in mind when it calculates the premium I have to pay, but it cannot calculate it by symmetry, or carry out an experiment for a few years. It will assign its probability using its experience of such matters and its records.

These ideas lead to the following:

When **probabilities** are assigned to the outcomes of a sample space,

- each probability is a number which must lie between 0 and 1 inclusive, and
- the sum of all the probabilities assigned must be equal to 1.

Example 22.1.1
How would you assign probabilities to the following experiments or activities?

(a) Choosing a playing card from a standard pack of cards.

(b) The combined experiment of tossing a coin and rolling a fair dice.

(c) Tossing a drawing pin on to a table to see whether it lands point down or point up.

(d) Four international football teams, Denmark, England, France and Germany, (D, E, F and G), play a knockout tournament. Who will be the winner?

(a) The sample space would consist of the list of the 52 playing cards $\{AC, 2C, \ldots, KS\}$ in some order. (A means ace, C means clubs, and so on.) Assuming that these cards are equally likely to be picked, the probability assigned to each of them is $\frac{1}{52}$.

(b) The sample space is $\left\{\begin{matrix}(H,1),(H,2),(H,3),(H,4),(H,5),(H,6),\\(T,1),(T,2),(T,3),(T,4),(T,5),(T,6)\end{matrix}\right\}$, and each of the outcomes would be assigned a probability of $\frac{1}{12}$.

(c) The sample space is {point down, point up}. You would need to carry out an experiment to assign probabilities.

(d) The sample space is $\{D$ wins, E wins, F wins, G wins$\}$. You have to assign probabilities subjectively, according to your knowledge of the game. The probabilities p_D, p_E, p_F and p_G must all be non-negative and satisfy $p_D + p_E + p_F + p_G = 1$.

22.2 Probabilities of events

Sometimes you may be interested not in one particular outcome, but in two or three or more of them. For example, suppose you toss a coin twice. You might be interested in whether the result is the same both times. The list of outcomes in which you are interested is called an **event**, and is written in brackets. The event that both tosses of the coin give the same result is $\{(H, H), (T, T)\}$. Events are often denoted by capital letters. Thus if A denotes this event, then $A = \{(H, H), (T, T)\}$. An event can be one outcome, a list of outcomes or even no outcomes.

You can find the probability of an event by looking at the sample space and adding the probabilities of the outcomes which make up the event. For example, if you were tossing a coin twice, the sample space would be $\{(H, H), (H, T), (T, H), (T, T)\}$. There are four outcomes, each equally likely, so they each have probability $\frac{1}{4}$. The event A consists of the two outcomes (H, H) and (T, T), so the probability of A is $\frac{1}{4} + \frac{1}{4}$, or $\frac{1}{2}$.

This is an example of a general rule:

> The probability, $P(A)$, of an event, A, is the sum of the probabilities of the outcomes which make up A.

Often a list of outcomes can be constructed in such a way that all of them are equally likely. If all the outcomes are equally likely then the probability of any event A can be found by finding the number of outcomes which make up event A and dividing by the total number of outcomes. Thus:

> If $n(A)$ is the number of equally likely outcomes in an event A, and $n(U)$ is the total number of equally likely outcomes in the sample space U, then
>
> $$P(A) = \frac{n(A)}{n(U)}.$$

When the outcomes are not equally likely then the probability of any event has to be found by adding the individual probabilities of all the outcomes which make up event A.

You may sometimes find it helpful to draw a Venn diagram. In a Venn diagram, the sample space is drawn, usually as a rectangle, and labelled U. The outcomes are points inside the rectangle. An event, which is a collection of outcomes, is usually depicted as a circle (or oval) with the outcomes it contains inside it.

Fig. 22.2 shows the four outcomes when the two coins above are tossed, and the event A.

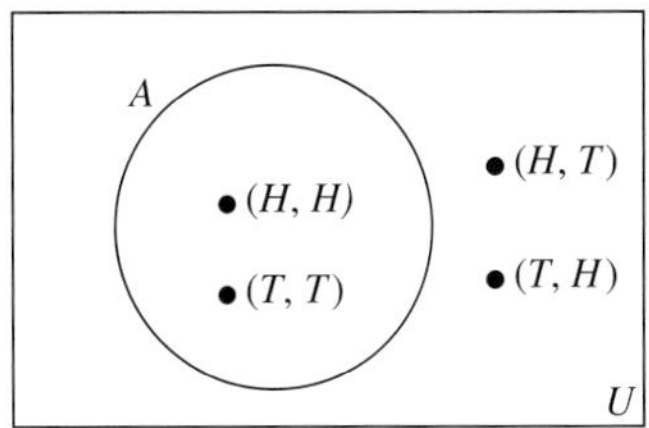

Fig. 22.2

Using the first blue box, the probability of A is given by

$$\mathrm{P}(A) = \mathrm{P}\{(H, H), (T, T)\} = \tfrac{1}{4} + \tfrac{1}{4} = \tfrac{1}{2}.$$

Using the second blue box, the probability of A is given by

$$\mathrm{P}(A) = \frac{n(A)}{n(U)} = \tfrac{2}{4} = \tfrac{1}{2}.$$

Example 22.2.1

In the USA, a roulette wheel consists of 38 sections of equal area: 18 are black, 18 are red and 2 are green. The wheel is spun and a ball is thrown onto the wheel. The ball will eventually land on one of the 38 sections.

(a) Find the probability of landing on a black colour.

Let A be the event that the ball does not land on a black section.

(b) Find the probability of A.

The number of possible outcomes for each colour are shown in Fig. 22.3.

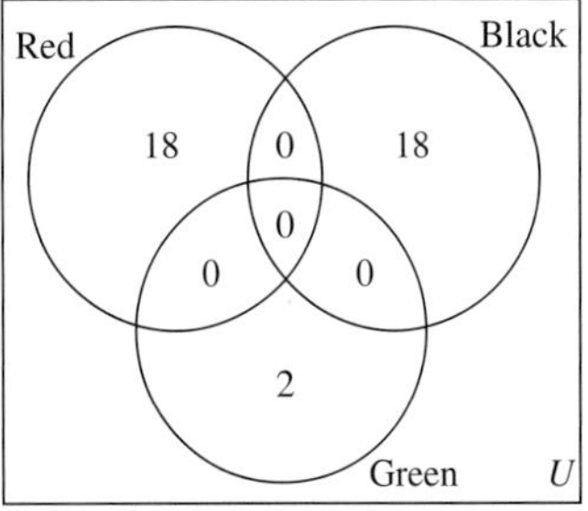

Fig. 22.3

(a) Let B be the event that the ball lands on black.

The probabilities of each section are equally likely, so each of them has probability $\frac{1}{38}$. There are 18 black sections, see Fig. 22.3, each with probability $\frac{1}{38}$, so

$$\mathrm{P}(B) = \frac{n(B)}{n(U)} = \tfrac{18}{38} = \tfrac{9}{19}.$$

(b) The number of outcomes in the event A is 20, so

$$\mathrm{P}(A) = \frac{n(A)}{n(U)} = \tfrac{20}{38} = \tfrac{10}{19}.$$

Example 22.2.2

The numbers $1, 2, \ldots, 9$ are written on separate cards. The cards are shuffled and the top one is turned over. Calculate the probability that the number on this card is prime.

The sample space for this situation is $U = \{1, 2, 3, 4, 5, 6, 7, 8, 9\}$. As each outcome is equally likely it has probability $\frac{1}{9}$.

Let B be the event that the card turned over is prime. Then $B = \{2, 3, 5, 7\}$, so

$$P(B) = \frac{n(B)}{n(U)} = \tfrac{4}{9}.$$

Example 22.2.3

A circular wheel is divided into three equal sectors, numbered 1, 2 and 3, as shown in Fig. 22.4. The wheel is spun twice. Each time, the score is the number to which the black arrow points. Calculate the probabilities of the following events:

(a) both scores are the same as each other,

(b) neither score is a 2,

(c) at least one of the scores is a 3,

(d) neither score is a 2 and both scores are the same,

(e) neither score is a 2 or both scores are the same.

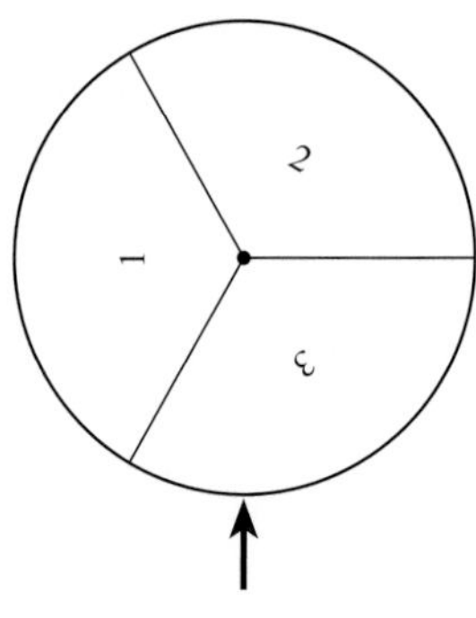

Fig. 22.4

Start by writing down the sample space, U. In this case it is helpful to write it as the **two-way table** in Table 22.5.

		Second spin		
		1	2	3
First spin	1	(1, 1)	(1, 2)	(1, 3)
	2	(2, 1)	(2, 2)	(2, 3)
	3	(3, 1)	(3, 2)	(3, 3)

Table 22.5

Each cell of the table corresponds to an outcome, each outcome has equal probability, $\frac{1}{9}$, each event corresponds to a certain number of cells and the total sample space consists of all the cells.

(a) Let A be the event that both scores are the same. The three cells corresponding to A lie on the main diagonal from top left to bottom right, so

$$P(A) = \frac{n(A)}{n(U)} = \tfrac{3}{9} = \tfrac{1}{3}.$$

(b) Let B be the event that neither score is a 2. The four cells corresponding to B lie in the corners, so

$$P(B) = \frac{n(B)}{n(U)} = \tfrac{4}{9}.$$

(c) Let C be the event that at least one of the scores is a 3. The five cells corresponding to C lie in the bottom row and the column on the right, so

$$P(C) = \frac{n(C)}{n(U)} = \tfrac{5}{9}.$$

(d) Let D be the event that neither score is a 2 *and* both scores are the same. The two cells corresponding to D lie in the top left and bottom right corners, so

$$P(D) = \tfrac{2}{9}.$$

(e) Let E be the event that neither score is a 2 *or* both scores are the same. The five cells corresponding to E lie in the corners and centre of the table, so

$$P(E) = \tfrac{5}{9}.$$

The next example shows how to modify the sample space so the outcomes are still equally likely.

Example 22.2.4

Paul has three playing cards, two queens and a king. Anya selects one of the cards at random, and returns it to Paul, who shuffles the cards. Anya then selects a second card. Anya wins if both cards selected are kings. Find the probability that Anya wins.

Imagine that the queens are different, and call them Q_1 and Q_2, and call the king K. Then the sample space is U where

$$U = \{(Q_1, Q_1), (Q_1, Q_2), (Q_1, K), (Q_2, Q_1), (Q_2, Q_2), (Q_2, K), \\ (K, Q_1), (K, Q_2), (K, K)\}.$$

Let A be the event that Anya wins. Then $A = \{(K, K)\}$ and

$$P(A) = \frac{n(A)}{n(U)} = \tfrac{1}{9}.$$

The probability that Anya wins is $\tfrac{1}{9}$.

Although the event that Anya won is a single outcome, it is still listed in curly brackets.

Sometimes it is worth using a different approach to calculating the probability of an event.

Example 22.2.5

You draw two cards from an ordinary pack. Find the probability that they are not both kings.

The problem is that the sample space has a large number of outcomes. In fact there are 52 ways of picking the first card, and then 51 ways of picking the second, so there $52 \times 51 = 2652$ possibilities. The sample space therefore consists of 2652 outcomes, each of which is assigned a probability $\frac{1}{2652}$.

To avoid counting all the outcomes which are not both kings, it is easier to look at the number of outcomes which *are* both kings.

Using an obvious notation, and writing the first card to be drawn as the first of the pair, these outcomes are (*KC*, *KD*), (*KD*, *KC*), (*KC*, *KH*), (*KH*, *KC*), (*KC*, *KS*), (*KS*, *KC*), (*KD*, *KH*), (*KH*, *KD*), (*KD*, *KS*), (*KS*, *KD*), (*KH*, *KS*) and (*KS*, *KH*).

There are thus 12 outcomes that are both kings. So the number which are not both kings is $2652 - 12 = 2640$. All 2640 of these outcomes have probability $\frac{1}{2652}$, so

$$\text{P(not both kings)} = \frac{2640}{2652} = \frac{220}{221}.$$

It is always worth looking out for this shortcut, and it is also useful to have some language for it. If A is an event, the event 'not A' is the event consisting of those outcomes in the sample space which are not in A. Since the sum of the probabilities assigned to outcomes in the sample space is 1,

$$\text{P}(A) + \text{P}(\text{not } A) = 1.$$

The event 'not A' is called the **complement** of the event A. The symbol A' is used to denote the complement of A.

If A is an event, then A' is the complement of A, and

$$\text{P}(A) + \text{P}(A') = 1.$$

22.3 Combining events

Suppose that you have two events, A and B, in a sample space U. As A and B contain outcomes, so do the events $A \cup B$ and $A \cap B$. These events are shaded in the Venn diagrams in Fig. 22.6.

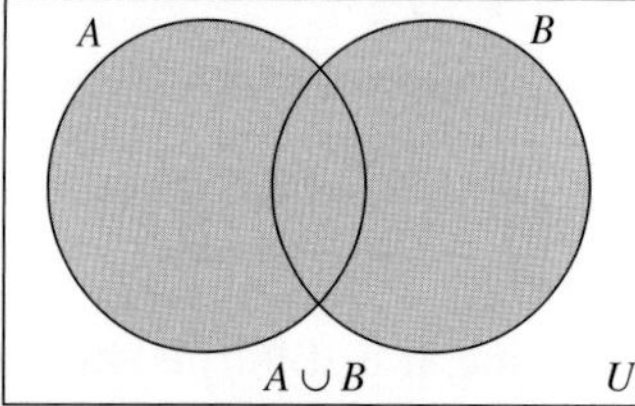

Fig. 22.6a

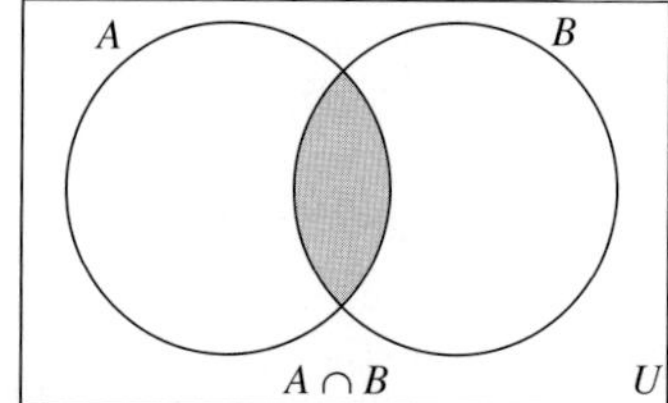

Fig. 22.6b

The event $A \cup B$, called the **union** of the events A and B and illustrated in Fig. 22.6a, consists of all those outcomes which are in A or B or both, and so is the event corresponding to A **or** B. $A \cup B$ is read as 'A union B'.

Remember, A or B means either A or B or both.

The event $A \cap B$, called the **intersection** of the events A and B and illustrated in Fig. 22.6b, consists of all those outcomes which are in both A and B, and so is the event corresponding to A **and** B. $A \cap B$ is read as 'A intersection B'.

You can see from the definitions that $A \cup B = B \cup A$ and $A \cap B = B \cap A$.

To find $\text{P}(A \cup B)$ you need to add the probabilities of the outcomes in $A \cup B$.

You can see from Fig. 22.6a that if you add the probabilities of the outcomes in A to the probabilities of those in B, that is

$$\mathrm{P}(A) + \mathrm{P}(B),$$

you have counted those outcomes in $A \cap B$ twice, once in the event A and once in the event B.

Hence

$$\mathrm{P}(A \cup B) = \mathrm{P}(A) + \mathrm{P}(B) - \mathrm{P}(A \cap B).$$

This formula is known as the addition law of probability.

The addition law of probability

If A and B are events then

$$\mathrm{P}(A \cup B) = \mathrm{P}(A) + \mathrm{P}(B) - \mathrm{P}(A \cap B).$$

Example 22.3.1

Two fair cubical dice with faces numbered 1 to 6 are thrown. A prize is won if the total is 10 or if each individual score is over 4. Find the probability of winning a prize.

The sample space U of all possible outcomes is

$$U = \left\{\begin{matrix} (1,1) & (1,2) & (1,3) & (1,4) & (1,5) & (1,6) \\ (2,1) & (2,2) & (2,3) & (2,4) & (2,5) & (2,6) \\ (3,1) & (3,2) & (3,3) & (3,4) & (3,5) & (3,6) \\ (4,1) & (4,2) & (4,3) & (4,4) & (4,5) & (4,6) \\ (5,1) & (5,2) & (5,3) & (5,4) & (5,5) & (5,6) \\ (6,1) & (6,2) & (6,3) & (6,4) & (6,5) & (6,6) \end{matrix}\right\}.$$

Each of the 36 outcomes is equally likely.

Let C be the event that the total score is 10, so $C = \{(5,5), (4,6), (6,4)\}$.

Let B be the event that each roll of the dice results in a score over 4, so $B = \{(5,5), (5,6), (6,5), (6,6)\}$.

The events B and C are illustrated in the Venn diagram in Fig. 22.7.

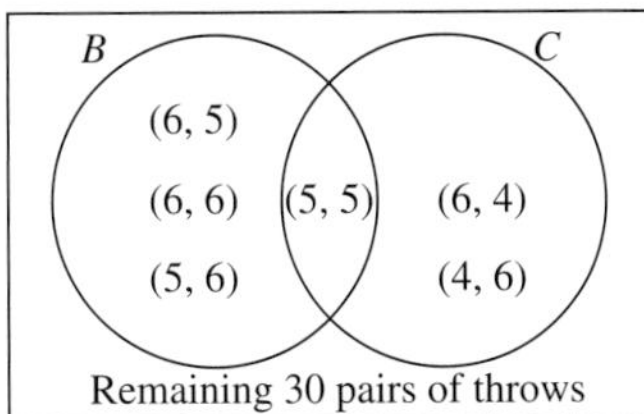

Fig. 22.7

Therefore $\mathrm{P}(B) = \frac{4}{36} = \frac{1}{9}$, $\mathrm{P}(C) = \frac{3}{36} = \frac{1}{12}$, $\mathrm{P}(B \cap C) = \frac{1}{36}$.

A prize is won if B or C (or both) occur, and the possible outcomes which comprise this event are $\{(5, 5), (4, 6), (6, 4), (5, 6), (6, 5), (6, 6)\}$.

Therefore $P(B \cup C) = \frac{6}{36} = \frac{1}{6}$.

But notice that you could have used the formula in the blue box immediately, to get

$$\begin{aligned} P(B \cup C) &= P(B) + P(C) - P(B \cap C) \\ &= \tfrac{4}{36} + \tfrac{3}{36} - \tfrac{1}{36} \\ &= \tfrac{6}{36} = \tfrac{1}{6}. \end{aligned}$$

The probability of winning a prize is $\frac{1}{6}$.

Sometimes it will occur that the events A and B cannot both occur at the same time. The next example shows such a case.

Example 22.3.2

Consider a game in which a fair cubical dice with faces numbered 1 to 6 is rolled twice. A prize is won if the total score on the two rolls is 4 or if both individual scores are over 4.

You can write the sample space U of all possible outcomes as 36 equally likely pairs, or as 36 equally likely cells in a two-way table (Table 22.8).

		Second roll					
		1	2	3	4	5	6
	1	(1, 1)	(1, 2)	(1, 3)	(1, 4)	(1, 5)	(1, 6)
	2	(2, 1)	(2, 2)	(2, 3)	(2, 4)	(2, 5)	(2, 6)
First	3	(3, 1)	(3, 2)	(3, 3)	(3, 4)	(3, 5)	(3, 6)
roll	4	(4, 1)	(4, 2)	(4, 3)	(4, 4)	(4, 5)	(4, 6)
	5	(5, 1)	(5, 2)	(5, 3)	(5, 4)	(5, 5)	(5, 6)
	6	(6, 1)	(6, 2)	(6, 3)	(6, 4)	(6, 5)	(6, 6)

Table 22.8

Each cell has probability $\frac{1}{36}$.

Let A be the event that the total score is 4 and let B be the event that both rolls of the dice give a score over 4.

Then $A = \{(1, 3), (2, 2), (3, 1)\}$, and $B = \{(5, 5), (5, 6), (6, 5), (6, 6)\}$, so

$$P(A) = \tfrac{3}{36}, \quad P(B) = \tfrac{4}{36} = \tfrac{1}{9}, \quad \text{and} \quad P(A \cap B) = 0.$$

A prize is won if A happens *or* if B happens, so

$$\begin{aligned} P(\text{a prize is won}) &= P(A \cup B) \\ &= P(A) + P(B) - P(A \cap B). \\ &= \tfrac{3}{36} + \tfrac{4}{36} - 0 = \tfrac{7}{36}. \end{aligned}$$

The probability of winning a prize is therefore $\frac{7}{36}$.

When two events A and B cannot happen together they are said to be **mutually exclusive**. If two events are mutually exclusive, then there are no outcomes in that event, so $P(A \cap B) = 0$.

Two events A and B are **mutually exclusive** if $P(A \cap B) = 0$.

If A and B are mutually exclusive, then the addition law of probability takes the form

$$P(A \cup B) = P(A) + P(B).$$

This form of the law only applies if the events A and B are mutually exclusive.

Example 22.3.3

A dice with six faces has been made from brass and aluminium, and is not fair. The probability of a 6 is $\frac{1}{4}$, the probabilities of 2, 3, 4, and 5 are each $\frac{1}{6}$, and the probability of 1 is $\frac{1}{12}$. The dice is rolled. Find the probability of (a) a 1 or a 6, (b) an even number.

(a) As the result of a single throw cannot be both 1 and 6 at the same time,

$$\begin{aligned} P(1 \text{ or } 6) &= P(1) + P(6) \\ &= \tfrac{1}{12} + \tfrac{1}{4} = \tfrac{1}{3}. \end{aligned}$$

(b) Similarly, no single throw can be 2 and 4 and 6 at the same time, so

$$\begin{aligned} P(\text{an even number}) &= P(2 \text{ or } 4 \text{ or } 6) \\ &= P(2) + P(4) + P(6) \\ &= \tfrac{1}{6} + \tfrac{1}{6} + \tfrac{1}{4} = \tfrac{7}{12}. \end{aligned}$$

Example 22.3.4

The events A and B are such that $P(B) = 2P(A) = \frac{1}{3}$ and $P(A \cap B) = \frac{1}{8}$, Find $P(A \cup B)$.

From the information given, $P(A) = \frac{1}{6}$, $P(B) = \frac{1}{3}$ and $P(A \cap B) = \frac{1}{8}$.

Using the addition law,

$$\begin{aligned} P(A \cup B) &= P(A) + P(B) - P(A \cap B) \\ &= \tfrac{1}{6} + \tfrac{1}{3} - \tfrac{1}{8} = \tfrac{9}{24} = \tfrac{3}{8}. \end{aligned}$$

Exercise 22

1 A fair dice is thrown once. Find the probabilities that the score is

(a) bigger than 3,
(b) bigger than or equal to 3,
(c) an odd number,
(d) a prime number,
(e) bigger than 3 and a prime number,
(f) bigger than 3 or a prime number or both,
(g) bigger than 3 or a prime number, but not both.

2 A card is chosen at random from an ordinary pack. Find the probability that it is

(a) red,
(b) a picture card (K, Q, J),
(c) an honour (A, K, Q, J, 10),
(d) a red honour,
(e) red, or an honour, or both.

3 Two fair dice are thrown simultaneously. Find the probability that

(a) the total is 7,
(b) the total is at least 8,
(c) the total is a prime number,
(d) neither of the scores is a 6,
(e) at least one of the scores is a 6,
(f) exactly one of the scores is a 6,
(g) the two scores are the same,
(h) the difference between the scores is an odd number.

4 A fair dice is thrown twice. If the second score is the same as the first, the second throw does not count, and the dice is thrown again until a different score is obtained. The two different scores are added to give a total.

List the possible outcomes.

Find the probability that

(a) the total is 7,
(b) the total is at least 8,
(c) at least one of the two scores is a 6,
(d) the first score is higher than the last.

5 Draw a bar-chart to illustrate the probabilities of the various total scores when two fair dice are thrown simultaneously.

6 Given that $\mathrm{P}(A) = \frac{1}{2}$, $\mathrm{P}(A \cup B) = \frac{3}{4}$ and $\mathrm{P}(A \cap B) = \frac{1}{8}$, find

(a) $\mathrm{P}(B)$,
(b) the probability that either A occurs, or B occurs, but not both.

23 Conditional probability

This chapter is about calculating with probabilities. When you have completed it, you should

- know the multiplication law of conditional probability, and be able to use tree diagrams
- know the multiplication law for independent events.

23.1 Conditional probability

Consider a class of 30 pupils, of whom 17 are girls and 13 are boys. Suppose further that 5 of the girls and 6 of the boys are left-handed, and all of the remaining pupils are right-handed. This information is shown in Fig. 23.1.

Boys	Girls	
6	5	Left-handed
7	12	Right-handed

Fig. 23.1

If a pupil is selected at random from the whole class then the chance that he or she is left-handed is $\frac{6+5}{30} = \frac{11}{30}$. However, suppose now that a pupil is selected at random from the girls in the class. The chance that this girl will be left-handed is $\frac{5}{17}$. So being told that the selected pupil is a girl alters the chance that the pupil will be left-handed. This is an example of **conditional probability**. The probability has been calculated on the basis of an extra 'condition' which you have been given.

Let L be the event that a left-handed person is chosen, and let G be the event that a girl is chosen. The symbol $\mathrm{P}(L \mid G)$ denotes the probability that the pupil chosen is left-handed *given* that the pupil chosen is a girl. So in this case $\mathrm{P}(L \mid G) = \frac{5}{17}$, although $\mathrm{P}(L) = \frac{11}{30}$.

It is useful to find a connection between conditional probabilities (where some extra information is known) and probabilities where you have no extra information. Notice that the probability $\mathrm{P}(L \mid G)$ can be written as

$$\mathrm{P}(L \mid G) = \tfrac{5}{17} = \frac{5/30}{17/30}.$$

The fraction in the numerator, $\frac{5}{30}$, is the probability of choosing a left-handed girl if you were selecting from the whole class, and the fraction in the denominator, $\frac{17}{30}$, is the probability of choosing a girl if you were selecting from the whole class. In symbols this could be written as

$$P(L \mid G) = \frac{P(L \cap G)}{P(G)}.$$

This can be generalised to any two events A and B.

If A and B are two events and $P(B) > 0$, then the **conditional probability** of A given B is

$$P(A|B) = \frac{P(A \cap B)}{P(B)}.$$

Rewriting this equation gives

$$P(A \cap B) = P(B) \times P(A \mid B),$$

which is known as the **multiplication law of probability**.

Example 23.1.1

Suppose a jar contains 7 red discs and 4 white discs. Two discs are selected without replacement. ('Without replacement' means that the first disc is not put back in the jar before the second disc is selected.) Find

(a) the probability that both of the discs are red,

(b) the probability that both the discs are the same colour.

(a) Let R_1 be the event {the first disc is red}, R_2 the event {the second disc is red}, W_1 the event {the first disc is white} and W_2 the event {the second disc is white}. To find the probability that both of the discs are red you want to find $P(R_1 \cap R_2)$.

Using the multiplication law in the blue box to find this probability,

$$P(R_1 \cap R_2) = P(R_1) \times P(R_2 \mid R_1).$$

Now $P(R_1) = \frac{7}{11}$, since there are 7 red discs in the jar and 11 discs in total. The probability $P(R_2 \mid R_1)$ appears more complicated, but it represents the probability that the second disc selected is red *given* that the first disc was red. To find this imagine that one red disc has already been removed from the jar. The jar now contains 6 red discs and 4 white discs, so the probability *now* of getting a red disc is $P(R_2 \mid R_1) = \frac{6}{10}$.

Therefore, using the multiplication law,

$$\begin{aligned} P(R_1 \cap R_2) &= P(R_1) \times P(R_2 \mid R_1) \\ &= \tfrac{7}{11} \times \tfrac{6}{10} = \tfrac{21}{55}. \end{aligned}$$

The probability that both discs are red is $\frac{21}{55}$.

(b) To find the probability that both discs are the same colour use the addition and multiplication laws together.

The event $R_1 \cap R_2$ is the event that both discs are red, and the event $W_1 \cap W_2$ is the event that both discs are white. These events cannot both be satisfied at the same time, so they are mutually exclusive. Therefore you can use the addition law in its mutually exclusive form, giving

$$\begin{aligned}\text{P(both discs are the same colour)} &= \text{P}((R_1 \cap R_2) \cup (W_1 \cap W_2)) \\ &= \text{P}(R_1 \cap R_2) + \text{P}(W_1 \cap W_2) \\ &= \text{P}(R_1) \times \text{P}(R_2 \mid R_1) + \text{P}(W_1) \times \text{P}(W_2 \mid W_1) \\ &= \tfrac{7}{11} \times \tfrac{6}{10} + \tfrac{4}{11} \times \tfrac{3}{10} \\ &= \tfrac{42}{110} + \tfrac{12}{110} = \tfrac{54}{110} = \tfrac{27}{55}.\end{aligned}$$

The probability that both discs are the same colour is $\frac{27}{55}$.

These calculations look rather forbidding, but using a tree diagram makes them easier.

23.2 Tree diagrams

Staying with Example 23.1.1, you can represent all the possible outcomes when two discs are selected from the jar in a **tree diagram**, as in Fig. 23.2.

Notice that probabilities on the first 'layer' of branches give the chances of getting a red disc or a white disc when the first disc is selected. The probabilities on the second 'layer' are the conditional probabilities. You can use the tree diagram to calculate the probabilities of the four possibilities, $R_1 \cap R_2$, $R_1 \cap W_2$, $W_1 \cap R_2$ and $W_1 \cap W_2$.

First disc
Second disc
P(R2 | R1) = 6/10
R1 ∩ R2
P(R1) = 7/11
R1
P(W2 | R1) = 4/10
R1 ∩ W2
P(R2 | W1) = 7/10
W1 ∩ R2
P(W1) = 4/11
W1
W1 ∩ W2
P(W2 | W1) = 3/10

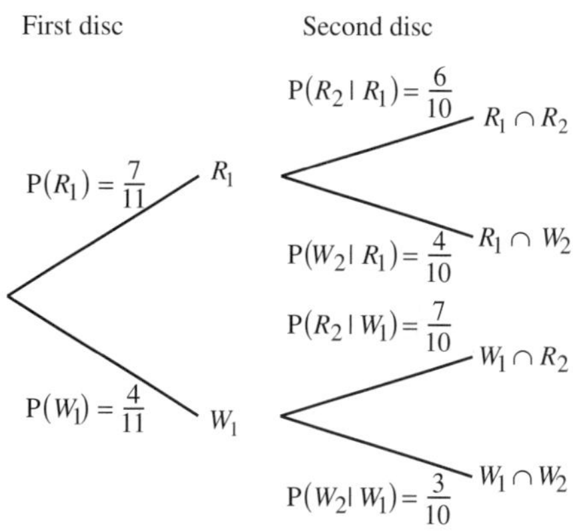

Fig. 23.2

Fig. 23.3 shows this calculation for the probability of getting a white disc followed by a red disc, $\text{P}(W_1 \cap R_2)$.

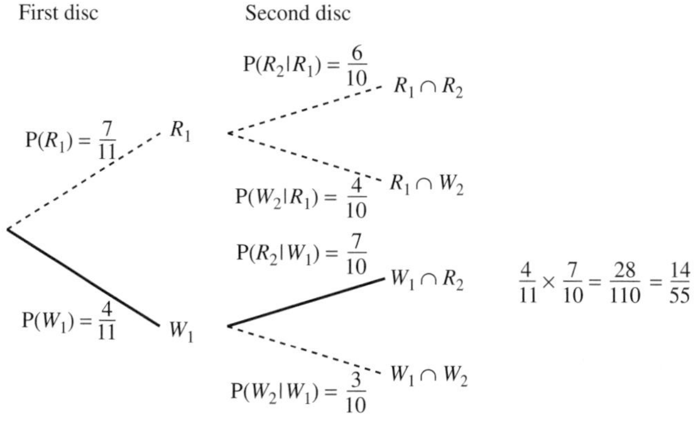

First disc
Second disc
P(R2|R1) = 6/10
R1 ∩ R2
P(R1) = 7/11
R1
R1 ∩ W2
P(W2|R1) = 4/10
P(R2|W1) = 7/10
W1 ∩ R2
4/11 × 7/10 = 28/110 = 14/55
P(W1) = 4/11
W1
W1 ∩ W2
P(W2|W1) = 3/10

Fig. 23.3

Trace the route corresponding to the event $W_1 \cap R_2$ on the tree diagram and multiply the relevant probabilities to get $\text{P}(W_1 \cap R_2) = \text{P}(W_1) \times \text{P}(R_2 \mid W_1)$.

You can also use the tree diagram for the calculation that both balls are the same colour. This time there is more than one route through the tree diagram which satisfies the event whose probability is to be found. As before, you follow the appropriate routes and multiply the probabilities. You then add all the resulting products, as in Fig. 23.4.

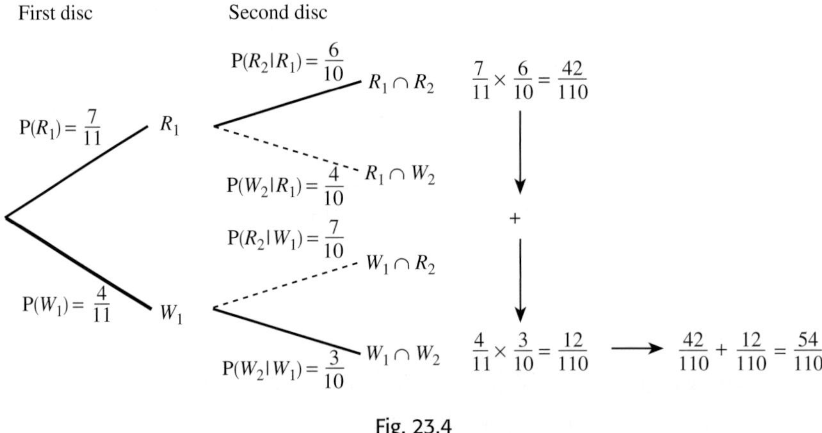

Fig. 23.4

You can use tree diagrams in any problem in which there is a clear sequence to the outcomes, including problems which are not necessarily to do with selection of objects.

Example 23.2.1

Weather records indicate that the probability that a particular day is dry is $\frac{3}{10}$. Liverton Villa is a football team whose record of success is better on dry days than on wet days. The probability that Liverton win on a dry day is $\frac{3}{8}$, whereas the probability that they win on a wet day is $\frac{3}{11}$. Liverton are due to play their next match on Saturday.

(a) What is the probability that Liverton will win?

(b) Three Saturdays ago Liverton won. What is the probability that it was a dry day?

Let D be the event that a day is dry, and let W be the event that Liverton win.

Here the sequence involves first the type of weather and then the result of the football match. The tree diagram in Fig. 23.5 illustrates the information.

Notice that some of the probabilities were not given in the statement of the question. The probability that it is not dry, $\text{P}(D')$, has been calculated using the equation $\text{P}(D) + \text{P}(D') = 1$. Then, given that it is dry, either Liverton win, or they don't. It follows that $\text{P}(W \mid D) + \text{P}(W' \mid D) = 1$. Similarly, $\text{P}(W \mid D') + \text{P}(W' \mid D') = 1$.

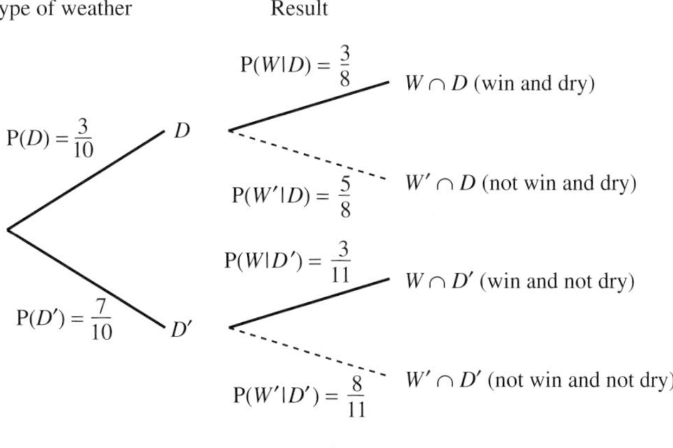

Fig. 23.5

(a) The probability that Liverton win is the sum of the probabilities at the end of the thick lines.

Using the tree diagram,

$$\begin{aligned}P(W) &= P(D) \times P(W \mid D) + P(D') \times P(W \mid D')\\ &= \tfrac{3}{10} \times \tfrac{3}{8} + \tfrac{7}{10} \times \tfrac{3}{11}\\ &= \tfrac{9}{80} + \tfrac{21}{110} = \tfrac{267}{880}.\end{aligned}$$

The probability that Liverton win is $\frac{267}{880}$.

(b) In this case you have been asked to calculate a conditional probability. However, here the sequence of events has been reversed and you want to find $P(D \mid W)$.

Remembering that $P(D \cap W) = P(W \cap D)$ and using the definition of $P(D \mid W)$ and the tree diagram, you get

$$\begin{aligned}P(D \mid W) &= \frac{P(D \cap W)}{P(W)}\\ &= \frac{P(W \cap D)}{P(W)}\\ &= \frac{9/80}{267/880} = \frac{99}{267}.\end{aligned}$$

The probability that it was a dry day given that Liverton won is $\frac{99}{267}$.

You can think of $P(D \mid W)$ as being the proportion of times that the weather is dry out of all the times that Liverton win. You may be a bit puzzled by this, because if Liverton win, the match has taken place and it is known whether or not it was a dry day. But suppose that you did not know, and had no meteorological information about the weather that day. Then the best you can do is to calculate $P(D \mid W)$.

Example 23.2.2

The probability that a person has a disease is $\frac{1}{200}$. A company is researching a test to determine whether a person has this disease. If a person has the disease then the probability that the test indicates this is $\frac{9}{10}$. If the person doesn't have the disease, then the probability that the test indicates that the person has the disease is $\frac{1}{100}$. A person, A, is chosen at random and given the test, which indicates that A has the disease. What is the probability that A has the disease?

Let D be the event that A has the disease, and let T be the event that the test is positive. The information is shown in the tree diagram in Fig. 23.6.

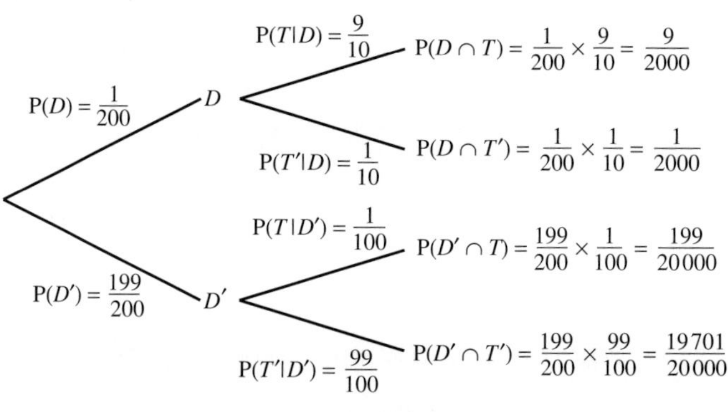

Fig. 23.6

You need to find $P(D\,|\,T)$. From the definition this is given by $\dfrac{P(D \cap T)}{P(T)}$.

From the tree diagram,

$$P(D \cap T) = \tfrac{1}{200} \times \tfrac{9}{10} = \tfrac{9}{2000},$$

and

$$\begin{aligned} P(T) &= P(D \cap T) + P(D' \cap T) \\ &= \tfrac{9}{2000} + \tfrac{199}{20\,000} = \tfrac{289}{20\,000}. \end{aligned}$$

So,

$$\begin{aligned} P(D\,|\,T) &= \frac{P(D \cap T)}{P(T)} \\ &= \tfrac{9}{2000} \Big/ \tfrac{289}{20\,000} = \tfrac{90}{289}. \end{aligned}$$

The probability that a person who tests positively has the disease is $\frac{90}{289}$.

Don't carry out all the multiplications in the tree diagram if you don't have to.

23.3 Independent events

Consider again a jar containing 7 red discs and 4 white discs. Two discs are selected, but this time with replacement. This means that the first disc is returned to the jar before the second disc is selected.

Let R_1 be the event that the first disc is red, R_2 be the event that the second disc is red, W_1 be the event that the first disc is white and W_2 be the event that the second disc is white. You can represent the selection of the two discs with Fig. 23.7, a tree diagram similar to Fig. 23.2 but with different probabilities on the second 'layer'.

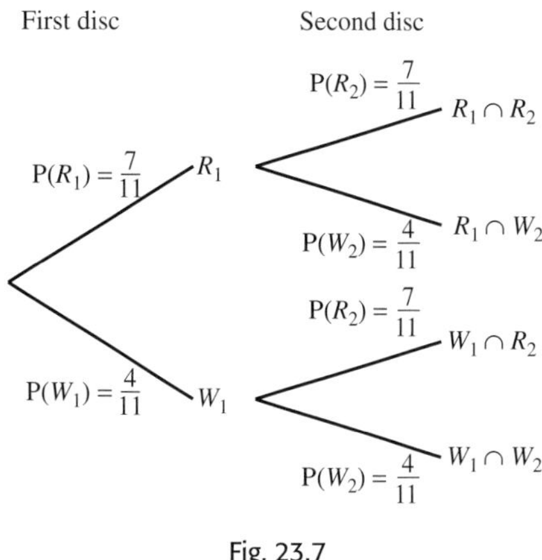

Fig. 23.7

The probability $P(R_2)$ that the second disc is red can also be found using the addition and multiplication laws.

$$\begin{aligned} P(R_2) &= P((R_1 \cap R_2) \cup (W_1 \cap R_2)) \\ &= P(R_1 \cap R_2) + P(W_1 \cap R_2) \\ &= \tfrac{7}{11} \times \tfrac{7}{11} + \tfrac{4}{11} \times \tfrac{7}{11} = \tfrac{7}{11}. \end{aligned}$$

In this case $P(R_2) = P(R_2 \mid R_1)$, which means that the first disc's being red has no effect on the chance of the second disc being red. This is what you would expect, since the first disc was replaced before the second was removed.

Recall the definition of conditional probability, $P(B \mid A) = \dfrac{P(A \cap B)}{P(A)}$. It follows that if you have $P(A \mid B) = P(A)$, as you have with $P(R_2) = P(R_2 \mid R_1)$ above, when you equate the two expressions for $P(A \mid B)$, you get

$$\frac{P(A \cap B)}{P(A)} = P(B),$$

which when rearranged gives

$$P(A \cap B) = P(A) \times P(B).$$

The fact that you can deduce that $P(A \mid B) = P(A)$, that is the probability of A is the same whether B happens or not, from $P(A \cap B) = P(A) \times P(B)$, suggests this definition.

Two events A and B are **independent** if

$$P(A \cap B) = P(A) \times P(B).$$

This result is called the **multiplication law for independent events**.

You should not be surprised that if the events A and B are independent, then the events A and B' are also independent.

For since $P(A \cap B) + P(A \cap B') = P(A)$,

$$P(A \cap B') = P(A) - P(A \cap B).$$

And if A and B are independent, $P(A \cap B) = P(A) \times P(B)$, so it follows that

$$\begin{aligned} P(A \cap B') &= P(A) - P(A) \times P(B) \\ &= P(A)(1 - P(B)). \end{aligned}$$

But, from the result at the end of Section 22.2, $P(B) + P(B') = 1$, so $1 - P(B) = P(B')$.

Hence, substituting for $1 - \mathrm{P}(B)$, you get

$$\mathrm{P}(A \cap B') = \mathrm{P}(A) \times \mathrm{P}(B'),$$

So the events A and B' are independent.

Example 23.3.1

In a carnival game, a contestant has to first spin a fair coin and then roll a fair cubical dice whose faces are numbered 1 to 6. The contestant wins a prize if the coin shows heads and the dice score is below 3. Find the probability that a contestant wins a prize.

Let W be the event that a prize is won, H be the event that the coin shows heads and let L be the event that the score is lower than 3.

Then $\mathrm{P}(W) = \mathrm{P}(H \cap L)$.

The event that the coin shows heads and the event that the dice score is lower than 3 are independent, because the score on the dice can have no effect on the result of the spin of the coin. Therefore the multiplication law for independent events can be used, so

$$\begin{aligned}\mathrm{P}(W) &= \mathrm{P}(H \cap L)\\ &= \mathrm{P}(H) \times \mathrm{P}(L)\\ &= \tfrac{1}{2} \times \tfrac{2}{6} = \tfrac{1}{6}.\end{aligned}$$

The probability that the contestant wins a prize is $\frac{1}{6}$.

The law of multiplication for independent events can be extended to more than two events, provided they are all independent of one another.

If $A_1, A_2, \ldots, A_n$ are n independent events then

$$\mathrm{P}(A_1 \cap A_2 \cap \ldots \cap A_n) = \mathrm{P}(A_1) \times \mathrm{P}(A_2) \times \ldots \times \mathrm{P}(A_n).$$

Example 23.3.2

A fair cubical dice with faces numbered 1 to 6 is thrown four times. Find the probability that three of the four throws result in a 6.

In this case you can use the addition law of mutually exclusive events and the multiplication law of independent events to break the event that 'three of the four scores are 6' down into smaller sub-events whose probabilities you can easily determine.

Let 6_1, 6_2, etc. be the events that a six is thrown on the first, second etc. throws, and let N_1, N_2, etc. be the events that a six is not thrown on the first, second etc. throws.

Let T be the event that three sixes are thrown. Then

$$\mathrm{P}(T) = \mathrm{P}\begin{pmatrix}(6_1 \cap 6_2 \cap 6_3 \cap N_4) \cup\\ (6_1 \cap 6_2 \cap N_3 \cap 6_4) \cup\\ (6_1 \cap N_2 \cap 6_3 \cap 6_4) \cup\\ (N_1 \cap 6_2 \cap 6_3 \cap 6_4)\end{pmatrix}.$$

Using the addition and multiplication laws,

$$\begin{aligned}
\mathrm{P}(T) &= \mathrm{P}(6_1 \cap 6_2 \cap 6_3 \cap N_4) + \mathrm{P}(6_1 \cap 6_2 \cap N_3 \cap 6_4) \\
&\quad + \mathrm{P}(6_1 \cap N_2 \cap 6_3 \cap 6_4) + \mathrm{P}(N_1 \cap 6_2 \cap 6_3 \cap 6_4) \\
&= \mathrm{P}(6_1) \times \mathrm{P}(6_2) \times \mathrm{P}(6_3) \times \mathrm{P}(N_4) \\
&\quad + \mathrm{P}(6_1) \times \mathrm{P}(6_2) \times \mathrm{P}(N_3) \times \mathrm{P}(6_4) \\
&\quad + \mathrm{P}(6_1) \times \mathrm{P}(N_2) \times \mathrm{P}(6_3) \times \mathrm{P}(6_4) \\
&\quad + \mathrm{P}(N_1) \times \mathrm{P}(6_2) \times \mathrm{P}(6_3) \times \mathrm{P}(6_4) \\
&= \left(\tfrac{1}{6} \times \tfrac{1}{6} \times \tfrac{1}{6} \times \tfrac{5}{6}\right) + \left(\tfrac{1}{6} \times \tfrac{1}{6} \times \tfrac{5}{6} \times \tfrac{1}{6}\right) \\
&\quad + \left(\tfrac{1}{6} \times \tfrac{5}{6} \times \tfrac{1}{6} \times \tfrac{1}{6}\right) + \left(\tfrac{5}{6} \times \tfrac{1}{6} \times \tfrac{1}{6} \times \tfrac{1}{6}\right) \\
&= 4 \times \left(\tfrac{1}{6}\right)^3 \times \tfrac{5}{6} = \tfrac{5}{324}.
\end{aligned}$$

The probability that three of the four throws result in a 6 is $\frac{5}{324}$.

Exercise 23

1 A bag contains six red and four green counters. Two counters are drawn, without replacement. Use a carefully labelled tree diagram to find the probabilities that

(a) both counters are red, (b) both counters are green, (c) just one counter is red,
(d) at least one counter is red, (e) the second counter is red.

2 Two cards are drawn, without replacement, from an ordinary pack. Find the probabilities that

(a) both are picture cards (*K*, *Q*, *J*), (b) neither is a picture card,
(c) at least one is a picture card, (d) at least one is red.

3 Events A, B and C satisfy the conditions $\mathrm{P}(A) = 0.6$, $\mathrm{P}(B) = 0.8$, $\mathrm{P}(B \mid A) = 0.45$, $\mathrm{P}(B \cap C) = 0.28$. Calculate

(a) $\mathrm{P}(A \cap B)$, (b) $\mathrm{P}(C \mid B)$, (c) $\mathrm{P}(A \mid B)$.

4 A class consists of seven boys and nine girls. Two different members of the class are chosen at random. A is the event {the first person is a girl}, and B is the event {the second person is a girl}. Find the probabilities of

(a) $B \mid A$, (b) $B' \mid A$, (c) $B \mid A'$
(d) $B' \mid A'$, (e) B.

Is it true that

(f) $\mathrm{P}(B \mid A) + \mathrm{P}(B' \mid A) = 1$, (g) $\mathrm{P}(B \mid A) + \mathrm{P}(B \mid A') = 1$?

5 A weather forecaster classifies all days as wet or dry. She estimates that the probability that June 1st next year is wet is 0.4. If any particular day in June is wet, the probability that the next day is wet is 0.6; otherwise the probability that the next day is wet is 0.3. Find the probability that, next year,

(a) the first two days of June are both wet, (b) June 2nd is wet,
(c) at least one of the first three days of June is wet.

6 A bag contains ten counters, of which six are red and four are green. A counter is chosen at random; its colour is noted and it is replaced in the bag. A second counter is then chosen at random. Find the probabilities that

(a) both counters are red, (b) both counters are green,

(c) exactly one counter is red, (d) the second counter is red.

7 Given that $\mathrm{P}(A) = 0.75$, $\mathrm{P}(B \mid A) = 0.8$ and $\mathrm{P}(B \mid A') = 0.6$, calculate $\mathrm{P}(B)$ and $\mathrm{P}(A \mid B)$.

8 A class of 30 students at an international school was asked whether they supported Argentina or Brazil or neither in a cup match. They were also asked whether they were left- or right-handed.

Twelve students were left-handed, and, of these, four supported Argentina and seven said they supported Brazil.

Of the right-handed students, one supported Argentina and ten supported Brazil.

A student, S, is picked at random from the class.

(a) Find the probability that S is left-handed.

(b) Find the probability that S prefers neither team.

(c) Given that S prefers neither team, find the probability that S is left-handed.

9 The probability that Usha wakes up early is $\frac{1}{3}$, and if she is early the probability that she gets to school on time is $\frac{3}{4}$. If she does not wake up early, the probability that she gets to school on time is $\frac{1}{5}$. On a day chosen at random she gets to school on time. Find the probability that she did not wake up early.

10 Three identical boxes A, B and C each have two drawers. Box A has a dollar in each drawer, Box B has 5 dollars in each drawer, and box C has one dollar in one drawer and 5 dollars in the other. A box is chosen at random and a drawer is opened, and found to contain 5 dollars. What is the probability that the other drawer also contains 5 dollars?

11 A family has two girls, Di and Jo, and two boys. Two are chosen at random.

(a) Find the probability that they are both girls, given that one of them is a girl.

(b) Find the probability that they are both girls, given that one of them is Jo.

Review exercise 7

1 Bag A contains 1 red ball and 1 black ball, and bag B contains 2 red balls; all four balls are indistinguishable apart from their colour. One ball is chosen at random from A and is transferred to B. One ball is then chosen at random from B and is transferred to A.

(a) Draw a tree diagram to illustrate the possibilities for the colours of the balls transferred from A to B and then from B to A.

(b) Find the probability that, after both transfers, the black ball is in bag A. (OCR)

2 The probability that an event A occurs is $\mathrm{P}(A) = 0.3$. The event B is independent of A and $\mathrm{P}(B) = 0.4$.

(a) Calculate $\mathrm{P}(A \cup B)$.

Event C is defined to be the event that neither A nor B occurs.

(b) Calculate $\mathrm{P}(C \mid A')$, where A' is the event that A does not occur. (OCR, adapted)

3 Two cubical fair dice are thrown, one red and one blue. The scores on their faces are added together. Determine which, if either, is greater:

(a) the probability that the total score will be 10 or more given that the red dice shows a 6,

(b) the probability that the total score will be 10 or more given that at least one of the dice shows a 6. (OCR)

4 Half of the A-level students in a community college study science and 30% study mathematics. Of those who study science, 40% study mathematics.

(a) What proportion of the A-level students study both mathematics and science?

(b) Calculate the proportion of those students who study mathematics but do not study science. (OCR)

5 Two events A and B are such that $\mathrm{P}(A) = \frac{3}{4}$, $\mathrm{P}(B \mid A) = \frac{1}{5}$ and $\mathrm{P}(B' \mid A') = \frac{4}{7}$. By use of a tree diagram, or otherwise, find

(a) $\mathrm{P}(A \cap B)$, (b) $\mathrm{P}(B)$, (c) $\mathrm{P}(A \mid B)$, (OCR, adapted)

6 Students have to pass a test before they are allowed to work in a laboratory. Students do not retake the test once they have passed it. For a randomly chosen student, the probability of passing the test at the first attempt is $\frac{1}{3}$. On any subsequent attempt, the probability of failing is half the probability of failing on the previous attempt. By drawing a tree diagram, or otherwise,

(a) show that the probability of a student passing the test in 3 attempts or fewer is $\frac{26}{27}$,

(b) find the conditional probability that a student passed at the first attempt, given that the student passed in 3 attempts or fewer. (OCR)

7 The probability of event A occurring is $\mathrm{P}(A) = \frac{13}{25}$. The probability of event B occurring is $\mathrm{P}(B) = \frac{9}{25}$. The conditional probability of A occurring given that B has occurred is $\mathrm{P}(A \mid B) = \frac{5}{9}$.

(a) Determine the following probabilities.

(i) $\mathrm{P}(A \cap B)$ (ii) $\mathrm{P}(B \mid A)$ (iii) $\mathrm{P}(A \cup B)$ (iv) $\mathrm{P}(A' \mid B')$

(b) Determine $\mathrm{P}(A \cup B')$ showing your working. (OCR, adapted)

8 (a) The probability that an event A occurs is $\mathrm{P}(A) = 0.4$. B is an event independent of A and $\mathrm{P}(A \cup B) = 0.7$. Find $\mathrm{P}(B)$.

(b) C and D are two events such that $\mathrm{P}(D \mid C) = \frac{1}{5}$ and $\mathrm{P}(C \mid D) = \frac{1}{4}$. Given that $\mathrm{P}(C \text{ and } D \text{ occur}) = p$, express in terms of p (i) $\mathrm{P}(C)$, (ii) $\mathrm{P}(D)$.

(c) Given also that $\mathrm{P}(C \text{ or } D \text{ or both occur}) = \frac{1}{5}$, find the value of p. (OCR, adapted)

9 A batch of forty tickets for an event at a stadium consists of ten tickets for the North stand, fourteen tickets for the East stand and sixteen tickets for the West stand. A ticket is taken from the batch at random and issued to a person, X. Write down the probability that X has a ticket for the North stand.

A second ticket is taken from the batch at random and issued to Y. Subsequently a third ticket is taken from the batch at random and issued to Z. Calculate the probability that

(a) both X and Y have tickets for the North stand,

(b) X, Y and Z all have tickets for the same stand,

(c) two of X, Y and Z have tickets for one stand and the other of X, Y and Z has a ticket for a different stand. (OCR)

10 In a lottery there are 24 prizes allocated at random to 24 prize-winners. Ann, Ben and Cal are three of the prize-winners. Of the prizes, 4 are cars, 8 are bicycles and 12 are watches. Show that the probability that Ann gets a car and Ben gets a bicycle or a watch is $\frac{10}{69}$.

Giving each answer either as a fraction or as a decimal correct to 3 significant figures, find

(a) the probability that both Ann and Ben get cars, given that Cal gets a car,

(b) the probability that either Ann or Cal (or both) gets a car,

(c) the probability that Ann gets a car and Ben gets a car or a bicycle,

(d) the probability that Ann gets a car given that Ben gets either a car or a bicycle. (OCR)

11 In a certain part of the world there are more wet days than dry days. If a given day is wet, the probability that the following day will also be wet is 0.8. If a given day is dry, the probability that the following day will also be dry is 0.6.

Given that Wednesday of a particular week is dry, calculate the probability that

(a) Thursday and Friday of the same week are both wet days,

(b) Friday of the same week is a wet day.

In one season there were 44 cricket matches, each played over three consecutive days, in which the first and third days were dry. For how many of these matches would you expect that the second day was wet? (OCR)

12 A dice is known to be biased in such a way that, when it is thrown, the probability of a 6 showing is $\frac{1}{4}$. This biased dice and an ordinary fair dice are thrown. Find the probability that

(a) the fair dice shows a 6 and the biased dice does not show a 6,

(b) at least one of the two dice shows a 6,

(c) exactly one of the two dice shows a 6, given that at least one of them shows a 6. (OCR)

Examination questions

1 A box contains 22 red apples and 3 green apples. Three apples are selected at random, one after the other, without replacement.

(a) The first two apples are green. What is the probability that the third apple is red?

(b) What is the probability that exactly two of the three apples are red? (© IBO 2002)

2 The following diagram shows a circle divided into three sectors, A, B and C. The angles at the centre are 90°, 120° and 150°. Sectors A and B are shaded as shown.

The arrow is spun. It cannot land on the lines between the sectors. Let A, B, C and S be the events defined by

A: arrow lands in sector A

B: arrow lands in sector B

C: arrow lands in sector C

S: arrow lands in a shaded region.

Find

(a) $\mathrm{P}(B)$, (b) $\mathrm{P}(S)$, (c) $\mathrm{P}(A \mid S)$. (© IBO 2004)

3 Two unbiased 6-sided dice are rolled, a red one and a black one. Let E and F be the events

E: the same number appears on both dice

F: the sum of the numbers is 10.

Find (a) $\mathrm{P}(E)$, (b) $\mathrm{P}(F)$, (c) $\mathrm{P}(E \cup F)$. (© IBO 2005)

4 In a school of 88 boys, 32 study economics (E), 28 study history (H) and 39 do not study either subject. This information is represented by the following Venn diagram.

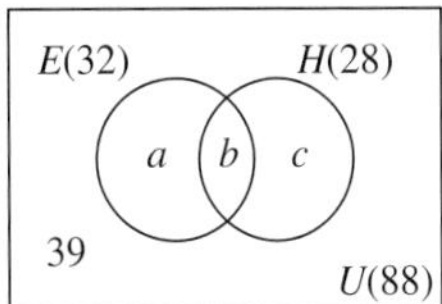

(a) Calculate the values of a, b and c.

A student is selected at random.

(b) Calculate the probability that he studies **both** economics and history.

(c) Given that he studies economics, calculate the probability that he does **not** study history.

A group of three students is selected at random from the school.

(d) Calculate the probability that none of these students studies economics.

(e) Calculate the probability that at least one of these students studies economics.

(© IBO 2003)

5 Dumisani is a student at IB World College. The probability that he will be woken by his alarm clock is $\frac{7}{8}$. If he is woken by his alarm clock the probability that he will be late for school is $\frac{1}{4}$. If he is not woken by his alarm clock the probability that he will be late for school is $\frac{3}{5}$.

Let W be the event 'Dumisani is woken by his alarm clock'.

Let L be the event 'Dumisani is late for school'.

W: L, L'
W': L, L'

(a) Copy and complete the tree diagram.

(b) Calculate the probability that Dumisani will be late for school.

(c) Given that Dumisani is late for school what is the probability that he was woken by his alarm clock? (© IBO 2004)

6 A packet of seeds contains 40% red seeds and 60% yellow seeds. The probability that a red seed grows is 0.9, and that a yellow seed grows is 0.8. A seed is chosen at random from the packet.

(a) Copy and complete the probability tree diagram below.

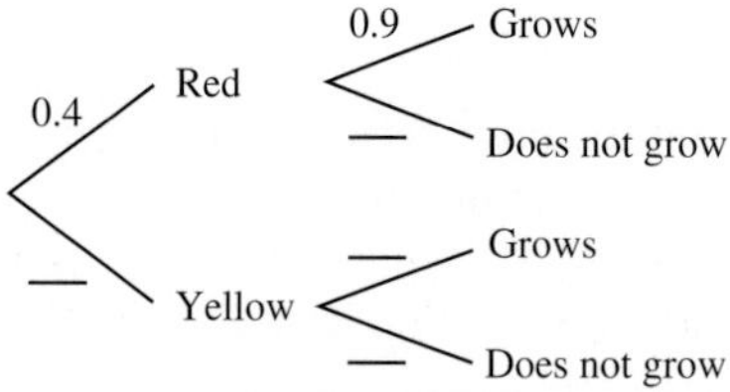

(b) Calculate the probability that the chosen seed is red and grows.

(c) Calculate the probability that the chosen seed grows.

(d) Given that the seed grows, calculate the probability that it is red. (© IBO 2004)

7 The following probabilities were found for two events R and S.

$\mathrm{P}(R) = \frac{1}{3}$, $\mathrm{P}(S \mid R) = \frac{4}{5}$, $\mathrm{P}(S \mid R') = \frac{1}{4}$.

(a) Copy and complete the tree diagram.

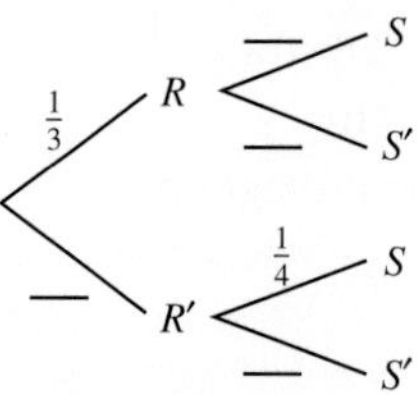

Find the following probabilities.

(b) $\mathrm{P}(R \cap S)$ (c) $\mathrm{P}(S)$ (d) $\mathrm{P}(R \mid S)$ (© IBO 2005)

24 Integration

Integration is the reverse process of differentiation. When you have completed this chapter, you should

- understand the term 'indefinite integral' and the need to add an arbitrary constant
- be able to integrate functions which can be expressed as sums of powers of x, and be aware of any exceptions
- know how to find the equation of a graph given its derivative and a point on the graph
- know how to evaluate definite integrals
- be able to use definite integrals to find areas
- be able to use integration to find displacements and velocities in kinematic problems.

24.1 Finding a function from its derivative

Example 24.1.1
Figure 24.1 shows the graph of $y = f(x)$, where $f(x) = x - \frac{1}{2}x^2 + 1$. Draw the graph of $f'(x)$, and give a geometrical description of the connection between the two graphs.

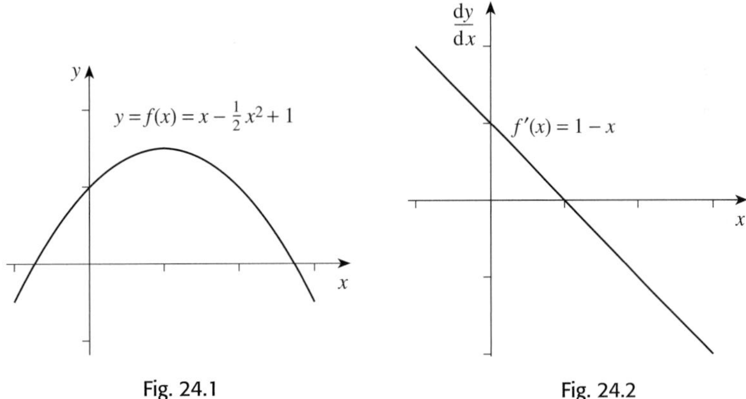

Fig. 24.1

Fig. 24.2

Since $f'(x) = 1 - \frac{1}{2}(2x) = 1 - x$, its graph is the straight line in Fig. 24.2.

For values of x to the left of 1, $f(x)$ is increasing. So the gradient $f'(x)$ is positive for $x < 1$. In Fig. 24.2, the graph of $f'(x)$ lies above the x-axis.

At $x = 1$, $f(x)$ takes its maximum value, and $f'(x) = 0$. In Fig. 24.2, the graph of $f'(x)$ crosses the x-axis.

For values of x to the right of 1, $f(x)$ is decreasing. So the gradient $f'(x)$ is negative for $x > 1$. In Fig. 24.2, the graph of $f'(x)$ lies below the x-axis.

You can add more detail to the comparison of the two graphs by noting that the graph of $f(x)$ bends downwards. That is, as you move from left to right along the curve the gradient gets smaller. This is shown in Fig. 24.2 by the fact that $f'(x)$ is a decreasing function of x.

You could make a similar comparison between the graphs of $f(x)$ and $f'(x)$ for any function you care to choose. If you know the graph of $f(x)$, then this determines the graph of $f'(x)$.

Is the reverse true? That is, if you know the graph of $f'(x)$, could you use this to draw the graph of $f(x)$?

Example 24.1.2 examines this geometrically for a graph of $f'(x)$ which is not a straight line.

Example 24.1.2

Figure 24.3 shows the graph of the derived function $f'(x)$ of some function $f(x)$. Use this to draw a sketch of the graph of $f(x)$.

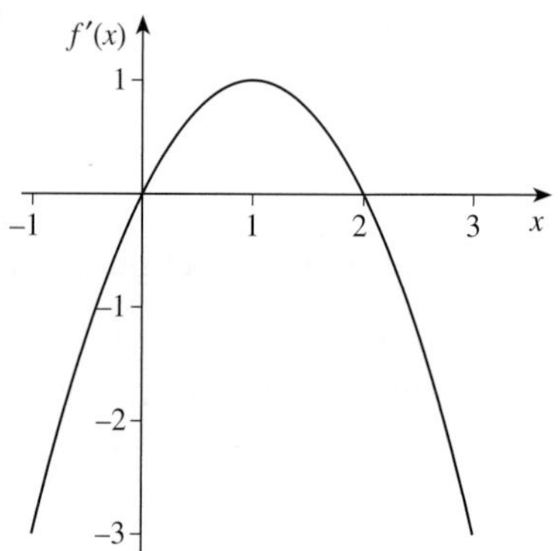

Fig. 24.3

Scanning Fig. 24.3 from left to right, you can see that:

For $x < 0$ the graph of $f'(x)$ lies below the x-axis; the gradient is negative, so $f(x)$ is decreasing.

At $x = 0$ the gradient changes from $-$ to $+$, so $f(x)$ has a minimum.

For $0 < x < 2$ the graph of $f'(x)$ lies above the x-axis; the gradient is positive, so $f(x)$ is increasing.
The gradient is greatest when $x = 1$, so that is where the graph of $f(x)$ climbs most steeply. The graph of $f'(x)$ is horizontal, so the derivative of $f'(x)$ is 0 when $x = 1$; that is $f''(1) = 0$, so the graph of $f(x)$ has a point of inflexion where $x = 1$.

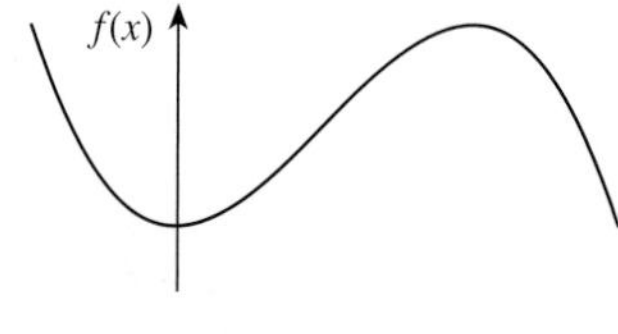

Fig. 24.4

At $x = 2$ the gradient changes from $+$ to $-$, so $f(x)$ has a maximum.

For $x > 2$ the gradient is negative, so $f(x)$ is again decreasing.

Using this information you can make a sketch like Fig. 24.4, which gives an idea of the shape of the graph of $f(x)$. But there is no way of deciding precisely where the graph is located. You could move it up and down by any amount, and it would still have the same gradient $f'(x)$. So there is no unique answer to the problem; there are many functions $f(x)$ with the given derivative.

This suggests that the answer to the question posed above is 'yes and no'. If you know the graph of $f'(x)$, this tells you the shape of the graph of $f(x)$ but not precisely where it is.

Example 24.1.3 shows this algebraically for the graphs of $f'(x)$ in Examples 24.1.1 and 24.1.2.

Example 24.1.3

What can you say about $f(x)$ if (a) $f'(x) = 1 - x$, (b) $f'(x) = 2x - x^2$?

(a) In Example 24.1.1, the derivative $f'(x) = 1 - x$ was obtained from the equation $f(x) = x - \frac{1}{2}x^2 + 1$. Working backwards, the term 1 in $f'(x)$ could only have come from a term x in $f(x)$; and the term $-x$ in $f'(x)$ could only have come from a term $-\frac{1}{2}x^2$ in $f(x)$. So if $f'(x) = 1 - x$, you can be certain that

$$f(x) = x - \tfrac{1}{2}x^2 + \text{something.}$$

But there is no reason why that 'something' has to be 1, as it was in Example 24.1.1. The equation could equally well be $f(x) = x - \frac{1}{2}x^2$, or $f(x) = x - \frac{1}{2}x^2 + 5$; both these equations give $f'(x) = 1 - x$. The best that you can say about $f(x)$ is that

$$f(x) = x - \tfrac{1}{2}x^2 + k,$$

where k is some number.

Geometrically, the graph in Fig. 24.1 could be shifted up or down by any amount in the y-direction without altering the graph of the gradient function in Fig. 24.2.

(b) This is in fact the equation of the graph in Fig. 24.3, so the question is to find the equation of the graph in Fig. 24.4.

Again there are two terms in the expression for $f'(x)$. The first term, $2x$, is easy; you will recognise this at once as the derivative of x^2. The term $-x^2$ in $f'(x)$ is a bit more tricky. You would expect it to come from an expression of the form ax^3 for some number a, which has to be found. If you differentiate ax^3 the result is $3ax^2$, so you need $3a$ to equal -1; that is, $a = -\frac{1}{3}$.

So, by the same argument as in part (a), the best that you can say is that

$$f(x) = x^2 - \tfrac{1}{3}x^3 + k,$$

where k is some number.

The process of getting from $f'(x)$ to $f(x)$ is called **integration**, and the general expression for $f(x)$ is called the **indefinite integral** of $f'(x)$. Integration is the reverse process of differentiation.

The indefinite integral always includes an added constant k, which is called an **arbitrary constant**. The word 'arbitrary' means that, in any application, you can choose its value to fit some extra condition; for example, you can make the graph of $y = f(x)$ go through some given point.

It is easy to find a rule for integrating functions which are powers of x. Because differentiation reduces the index by 1, integration must increase it by 1. So the function x^n must be derived from some multiple of x^{n+1}. But the derivative of x^{n+1} is $(n+1)x^n$; so to reduce the coefficient in the derivative to 1 you have to multiply x^{n+1} by $\dfrac{1}{n+1}$.

The rule is therefore that one integral of x^n is $\dfrac{1}{n+1}x^{n+1}$.

The extension to functions which are sums of multiples of powers of x then follows from the equivalent rules for differentiation.

Example 24.1.4

Find the indefinite integral of (a) x^4, (b) $6x - 2x^3$, (c) $\dfrac{4}{x^3}$.

(a) Putting $n = 4$, the indefinite integral of x^4 is $\dfrac{1}{4+1}x^{4+1} + k = \frac{1}{5}x^5 + k$, where k is an arbitrary constant.

(b) The term $6x$ is the derivative of $6\left(\frac{1}{2}x^2\right)$, and $-2x^3$ is the derivative of $-2\left(\frac{1}{4}x^4\right)$. So the indefinite integral of $6x - 2x^3$ is $3x^2 - \frac{1}{2}x^4 + k$.

(c) Write $\dfrac{4}{x^3}$ as $4x^{-3}$. If $n = -3$, $n + 1 = -3 + 1 = -2$, so the indefinite integral of $4x^{-3}$ is $4\left(\frac{1}{-2}x^{-2}\right) + k = -2x^{-2} + k = -\dfrac{2}{x^2} + k$.

But notice an important exception to this rule. The formula $\dfrac{1}{n+1}x^{n+1}$ has no meaning if $n+1$ is 0, so it does not give the integral of x^{-1}, or $\dfrac{1}{x}$. You will find in Chapter 32 that the integral of $\dfrac{1}{x}$ is not a power of x, but a quite different kind of function.

> The indefinite integral of a function made up of the sum of multiples of x^n, where $n \neq -1$, is the corresponding sum of multiples of $\dfrac{1}{n+1}x^{n+1}$, together with an added arbitrary constant.

Example 24.1.5

The graph of $y = f(x)$ passes through $(2, 3)$, and $f'(x) = 6x^2 - 5x$. Find its equation.

The indefinite integral is $6\left(\frac{1}{3}x^3\right) - 5\left(\frac{1}{2}x^2\right) + k$, so the graph has equation

$$y = 2x^3 - \tfrac{5}{2}x^2 + k$$

for some constant k. The coordinates $x = 2$, $y = 3$ have to satisfy this equation, so

$$3 = 2 \times 8 - \tfrac{5}{2} \times 4 + k, \quad \text{giving} \quad k = 3 - 16 + 10 = -3.$$

The equation of the graph is therefore $y = 2x^3 - \frac{5}{2}x^2 - 3$.

Example 24.1.6

A gardener is weeding a plot of land. As he gets tired he works more slowly; after t minutes he is weeding at a rate of $\dfrac{2}{\sqrt{t}}$ square metres per minute. How long will it take him to weed an area of 40 square metres?

Let A square metres be the area he has weeded after t minutes. Then his rate of weeding is measured by the derivative $\frac{dA}{dt}$. So you know that $\frac{dA}{dt} = 2t^{-\frac{1}{2}}$; in this case $n = -\frac{1}{2}$, so $n + 1 = \frac{1}{2}$ and the indefinite integral is

$$A = 2\left(\frac{1}{1/2}t^{\frac{1}{2}}\right) + k = 4\sqrt{t} + k.$$

To find k, you need to know a pair of values of A and t. Since $A = 0$ when he starts, which is when $t = 0$, $0 = 4\sqrt{0} + k$ and so $k = 0$.

The equation connecting A with t is therefore $A = 4\sqrt{t}$.

To find how long it takes to weed 40 square metres, substitute $A = 40$:

$$40 = 4\sqrt{t}, \text{ so that } \sqrt{t} = 10, \text{ and hence } t = 100.$$

It will take him 100 minutes to weed an area of 40 square metres.

24.2 Notation for indefinite integrals

You already have a short notation for differentiation, so that instead of writing

'the derivative of $3x^2 - \frac{1}{2}x^4$ is $6x - 2x^3$'

or 'if $y = 3x^2 - \frac{1}{2}x^4$, then $\frac{dy}{dx} = 6x - 2x^3$'

you can simply write without any words

$$\frac{d}{dx}(3x^2 - \tfrac{1}{2}x^4) = 6x - 2x^3.$$

The symbol $\frac{d}{dx}$ is an instruction to differentiate whatever follows it (see Section 21.5).

There is a corresponding notation for indefinite integrals, to avoid having to write

'the indefinite integral of $6x - 2x^3$ is $3x^2 - \frac{1}{2}x^4 + k$'

or 'if $\frac{dy}{dx} = 6x - 2x^3$, then $y = 3x^2 - \frac{1}{2}x^4 + k$'.

The notation used to write this without words is

$$\int (6x - 2x^3)\,dx = 3x^2 - \tfrac{1}{2}x^4 + k.$$

The symbol $\int$ is called the 'integral sign', and 'dx' tells you the letter being used as the variable. The expression $\int (\ldots)dx$ is then an instruction to integrate the expression in the brackets; it is read

'the indefinite integral of (...) with respect to x'.

The reason for this rather odd notation will become clearer when you reach Section 24.4.

If the function you are integrating is very simple, then you can leave out the brackets. For example, it would be usual to write $\int x^2\,dx$ rather than $\int (x^2)\,dx$. But if the expression has more than one term, you should put it in brackets.

Example 24.2.1

Find $\int (5x^4 + 9x^2 - 2)\,dx$.

$$\begin{aligned}\int (5x^4 + 9x^2 - 2)\,dx &= 5\left(\tfrac{1}{5}x^5\right) + 9\left(\tfrac{1}{3}x^3\right) - 2x + k\\ &= x^5 + 3x^3 - 2x + k.\end{aligned}$$

This is all you need to write. But don't forget to put in the arbitrary constant!

The notation is often used with other letters for the variable, especially when integration is used in real-world problems. If you see $\int (...)\,dt$, for example, then t is the independent variable and you have to integrate with respect to t.

Example 24.2.2

Find (a) $\int 8t^3\,dt$, (b) $\int \frac{1}{p^2}\,dp$, (c) $\int \sqrt{u}\,du$, (d) $\int (2x-1)(2x+1)\,dx$, (e) $\int \frac{y^4-4}{y^2}\,dy$.

(a) $\int 8t^3\,dt = 8\left(\tfrac{1}{4}t^4\right) + k = 2t^4 + k.$

(b) $\int \frac{1}{p^2}\,dp = \int p^{-2}\,dp = \frac{1}{-2+1}p^{-2+1} + k = -p^{-1} + k = -\frac{1}{p} + k.$

(c) $\int \sqrt{u}\,du = \int u^{\frac{1}{2}}\,du = \frac{1}{\frac{1}{2}+1}u^{\frac{1}{2}+1} + k = \frac{1}{\frac{3}{2}}u^{\frac{3}{2}} + k = \tfrac{2}{3}u\sqrt{u} + k.$

(d) You must multiply out the brackets before you can integrate.

$$\int (2x-1)(2x+1)\,dx = \int (4x^2 - 1)\,dx = 4\left(\tfrac{1}{3}x^3\right) - x + k = \tfrac{4}{3}x^3 - x + k.$$

(e) $$\begin{aligned}\int \frac{y^4-4}{y^2}\,dy &= \int \left(\frac{y^4}{y^2} - \frac{4}{y^2}\right)dy\\ &= \int (y^2 - 4y^{-2})dy = \tfrac{1}{3}y^3 - 4\left(\frac{y^{-1}}{-1}\right) + k = \tfrac{1}{3}y^3 + \frac{4}{y} + k.\end{aligned}$$

Exercise 24A

1 Find a general expression for the function $f(x)$ in each of the following cases.

(a) $f'(x) = 4x^3$ (b) $f'(x) = 6x^5$

(c) $f'(x) = 2x$ (d) $f'(x) = 3x^2 + 5x^4$

(e) $f'(x) = 10x^9 - 8x^7 - 1$ (f) $f'(x) = -7x^6 + 3x^2 + 1$

2 Find the following indefinite integrals.

(a) $\int (9x^2 - 4x - 5)\,dx$ (b) $\int (12x^2 + 6x + 4)\,dx$

(c) $\int 7dx$ (d) $\int (16x^3 - 6x^2 + 10x - 3)\,dx$

(e) $\int (2x^3 + 5x)\,dx$ (f) $\int (x + 2x^2)\,dx$

(g) $\int (2x^2 - 3x - 4)\,dx$ (h) $\int (1 - 2x - 3x^2)\,dx$

3 Find y in terms of x in each of the following cases.

(a) $\frac{dy}{dx} = x^4 + x^2 + 1$ (b) $\frac{dy}{dx} = 7x - 3$

(c) $\frac{dy}{dx} = \frac{2}{3}x^3 + \frac{1}{2}x^2 + \frac{1}{3}x + \frac{1}{6}$ (d) $\frac{dy}{dx} = \frac{1}{2}x^3 - \frac{1}{3}x^2 + x - \frac{1}{3}$

4 The graph of $y = f(x)$ passes through the origin and $f'(x) = 8x - 5$. Find $f(x)$.

5 A curve passes through $(-4, 9)$ and is such that $\frac{dy}{dx} = \frac{1}{2}x^3 + \frac{1}{4}x + 1$. Find y in terms of x.

6 Given that $f'(x) = 15x^2 - 6x + 4$ and $f(1) = 0$, find $f(x)$.

7 Each of the following diagrams shows the graph of a derivative, $f'(x)$. In each case, sketch the graph of a possible function $f(x)$.

State the x-coordinates and describe the shape of the graph at any stationary points. Give the x-coordinates of any points of inflexion.

(a)
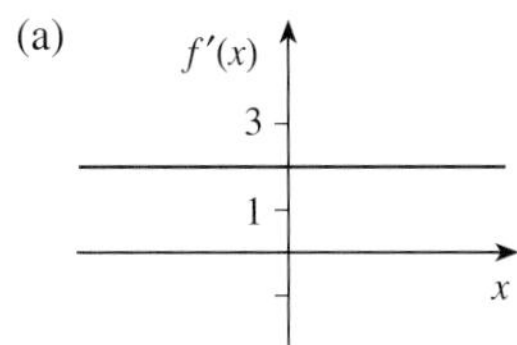

(b)
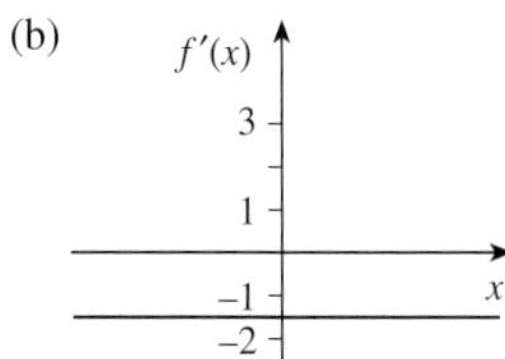

(c)
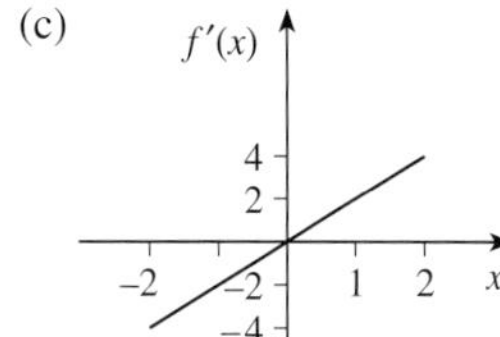

(d)
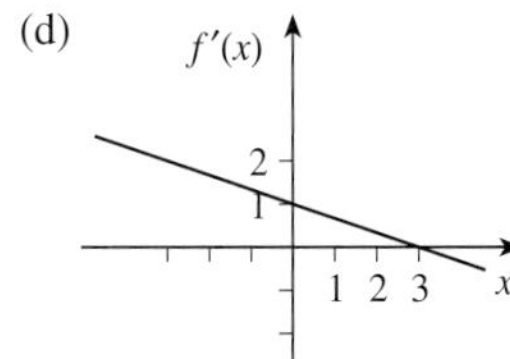

(e)
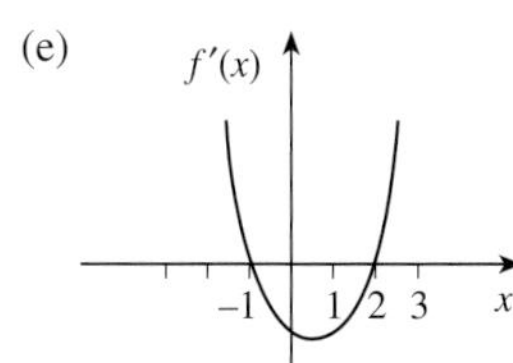

(f)
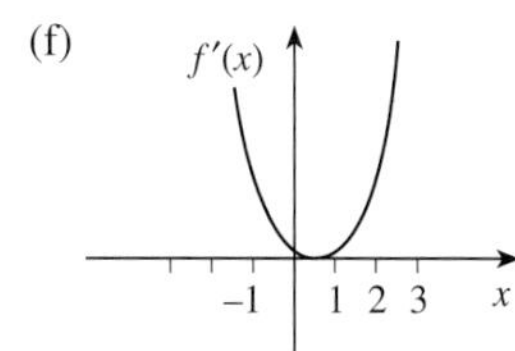

(g)
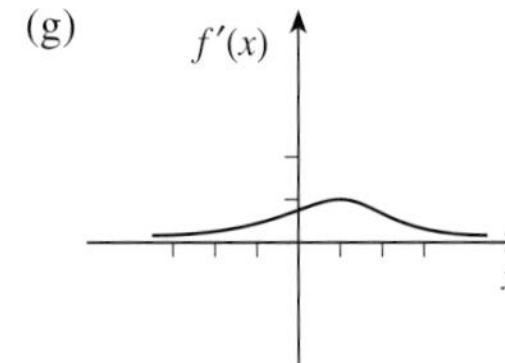

(h)
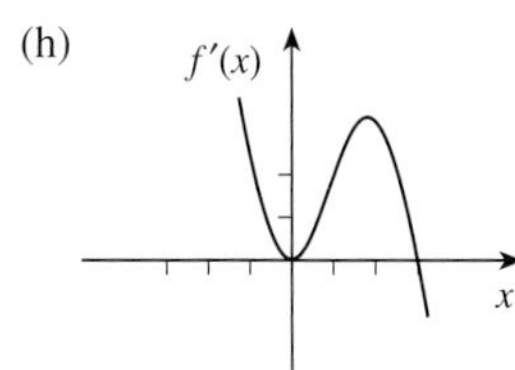

8 The graph of $y = f(x)$ passes through $(4, 25)$ and $f'(x) = 6\sqrt{x}$. Find its equation.

9 Find a general expression for the function $f(x)$ in each of the following cases.

(a) $f'(x) = x^{-2}$ (b) $f'(x) = 3x^{-4}$ (c) $f'(x) = \frac{6}{x^3}$ (d) $f'(x) = 4x - \frac{3}{x^2}$

10 Find y in terms of x in each of the following cases.

(a) $\frac{dy}{dx} = x^{\frac{1}{2}}$ (b) $\frac{dy}{dx} = 4x^{-\frac{2}{3}}$ (c) $\frac{dy}{dx} = \sqrt[3]{x}$ (d) $\frac{dy}{dx} = 2\sqrt{x} - \frac{2}{\sqrt{x}}$

11 The graph of $y = f(x)$ passes through $\left(\frac{1}{2}, 5\right)$ and $f'(x) = \frac{4}{x^2}$. Find the equation of the graph.

12 A curve passes through the point $(25, 3)$ and is such that $\frac{dy}{dx} = \frac{1}{2\sqrt{x}}$. Find the equation of the curve.

13 A curve passes through the point (1, 5) and is such that $\frac{dy}{dx} = \sqrt[3]{x} - \frac{6}{x^3}$. Find the equation of the curve.

14 In each of the following cases, find y in terms of x.

(a) $\frac{dy}{dx} = 3x(x+2)$ (b) $\frac{dy}{dx} = (2x-1)(6x+5)$ (c) $\frac{dy}{dx} = \frac{4x^3+1}{x^2}$

(d) $\frac{dy}{dx} = \frac{x+4}{\sqrt{x}}$ (e) $\frac{dy}{dx} = (\sqrt{x}+5)^2$ (f) $\frac{dy}{dx} = \frac{\sqrt{x}+5}{\sqrt{x}}$

15 Find the following indefinite integrals.

(a) $\int \left(u^2 + \frac{1}{u^2}\right) du$ (b) $\int t^5(3-t)\,dt$ (c) $\int 4(p+1)^3\,dp$

(d) $\int \frac{1}{y\sqrt{y}}\,dy$ (e) $\int \left(\sqrt[3]{z} + \frac{1}{\sqrt[3]{z}}\right)^2 dz$ (f) $\int v(1+\sqrt{v})\,dv$

16 A tree is growing so that, after t years, its height is increasing at a rate of $\frac{30}{\sqrt[3]{t}}$ cm per year. Assume that, when $t = 0$, the height is 5 cm.

(a) Find the height of the tree after 4 years.

(b) After how many years will the height be 4.1 metres?

17 A pond, with surface area 48 square metres, is being invaded by a weed. At a time t months after the weed first appeared, the area of the weed on the surface is increasing at a rate of $\frac{1}{3}t$ square metres per month. How long will it be before the weed covers the whole surface of the pond?

18 The function $f(x)$ is such that $f'(x) = 9x^2 + 4x + c$, where c is a particular constant. Given that $f(2) = 14$ and $f(3) = 74$, find the value of $f(4)$.

24.3 Calculating areas

An important application of integration is to calculate areas and volumes. Many of the formulae you have learnt, such as those for the volume of a sphere or a cone, can be proved by using integration. This chapter deals only with areas.

The particular kind of area to be investigated is illustrated in Fig. 24.5. For any function, the problem is to calculate the area bounded by the x-axis, the graph of $y = f(x)$, and the lines $x = a$ and $x = b$. This is described as **the area under the graph** from a to b.

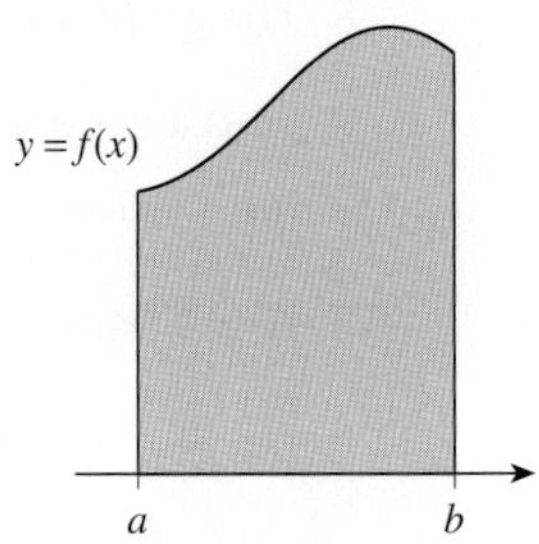

Fig. 24.5

As a start, Example 24.3.1 finds such an area for a very special case when the graph is a straight line.

Example 24.3.1

Find the area under the graph of $y = f(x)$, where $f(x) = 6x + 5$,

(a) from 0 to a, (b) from a to b,

where $b > a > 0$.

(a) In Fig. 24.6, the area under the graph from 0 to a is the area of the trapezium OAQP. This can be split into a triangle PSQ and a rectangle OASP by a line PS parallel to the x-axis. The length of the y-intercept is 5; and, since the gradient of PQ is 6, the length SQ is $6a$. So the area of the trapezium is

$$\tfrac{1}{2} \times a \times 6a + a \times 5, \text{ or more simply } 3a^2 + 5a.$$

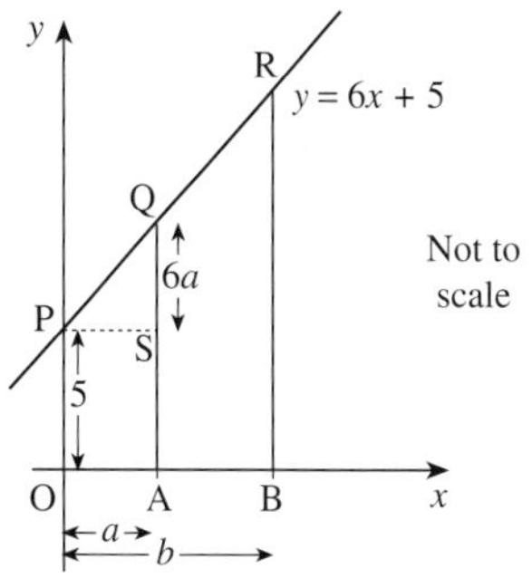

Fig. 24.6

(b) You want the area of the trapezium ABRQ, which can be found as

area OBRP − area OAQP.

Area OAQP has already been found in part (a). The trapezium OBRP is of the same kind as OAQP, but with b in place of a, so area OBRP is $3b^2 + 5b$.

It follows that the area under the graph from a to b is

$$(3b^2 + 5b) - (3a^2 + 5a).$$

Look at the form of the answer to this example. You can think of this as the difference between the values of the function $3x^2 + 5x$ when $x = b$ and $x = a$. If $I(x)$ is used to denote this function, then the area is $I(b) - I(a)$.

What is the connection between $I(x) = 3x^2 + 5x$ and $f(x) = 6x + 5$?

Obviously, in this case, $f(x)$ is the derivative of $I(x)$. Or, put another way, $I(x)$ is an integral of $f(x)$.

It has to be 'an' integral, rather than 'the' integral, because $f(x)$ has any number of integrals, as explained in Section 24.1. But $I(x)$ is the simplest of these; that is, it is the one for which the arbitrary constant is 0.

So this example suggests a procedure for finding the area under a graph.

To find the area under the graph $y = f(x)$ from $x = a$ to $x = b$:

Step 1 Find the 'simplest' integral of $f(x)$; call it $I(x)$.

Step 2 Work out $I(a)$ and $I(b)$.

Step 3 The area is $I(b) - I(a)$.

At present this is just a guess. You can't base a general theory on the result of just one example. But it can be proved that it is true for any function $f(x)$ with a continuous graph.

Example 24.3.2

Find the area between the graph of $y = 2x - x^2$ and the x-axis.

This is the graph in Fig. 24.3. It is reproduced here as Fig. 24.7. The curve cuts the x-axis when $x = 0$ and $x = 2$, so you want the area under the graph between these values of x.

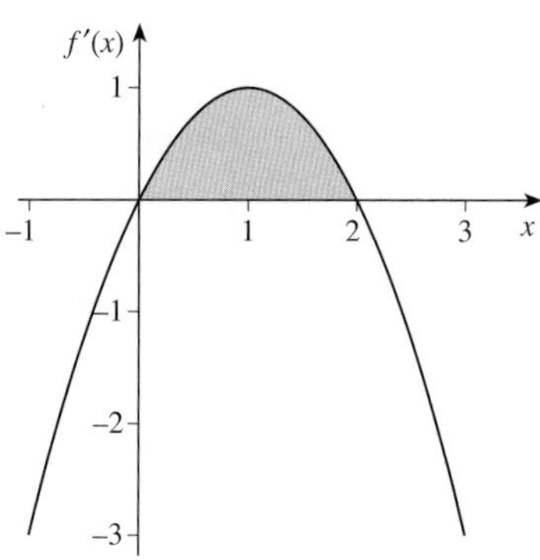

Fig. 24.7

It was shown in Example 24.1.3 that the indefinite integral of $2x - x^2$ is $x^2 - \frac{1}{3}x^3 + k$. The simplest integral has $k = 0$, so $I(x) = x^2 - \frac{1}{3}x^3$. The area is then $I(2) - I(0)$.

So calculate

$$I(2) = 4 - \tfrac{1}{3} \times 8 = \tfrac{4}{3} \quad \text{and} \quad I(0) = 0 - 0 = 0,$$

giving an area of $\frac{4}{3} - 0 = \frac{4}{3}$.

Although the procedure takes $I(x)$ to be the 'simplest' integral of $f(x)$, this is not esssential. In Example 24.3.2, if you took $I(x)$ to be $x^2 - \frac{1}{3}x^3 + k$, you would get $I(2) = \frac{4}{3} + k$ and $I(0) = k$, giving the area as $I(2) - I(0) = (\frac{4}{3} + k) - k = \frac{4}{3}$, just as before. But there is no point in making it more complicated than necessary.

Example 24.3.3

Find the area under $y = \dfrac{1}{x^2}$ from $x = 2$ to $x = 5$.

Step 1 Let $f(x) = y$. You can write $f(x)$ as x^{-2}, so $I(x)$ is $\dfrac{1}{-1}x^{-1}$, or $-\dfrac{1}{x}$.

Step 2 $I(2) = -\frac{1}{2} = -0.5, \quad I(5) = -\frac{1}{5} = -0.2.$

Step 3 The area is $I(5) - I(2) = (-0.2) - (-0.5) = -0.2 + 0.5 = 0.3$.

The answers to these examples have been given without a unit, because it is not usual to attach a unit to the variables x and y when graphs are drawn. But if in a particular application x and y each denote numbers of units, then when stating the answer a corresponding unit (the x-unit × the y-unit) should be attached to it.

24.4 Integration notation

You will carry out the procedure in Section 24.3 so often that it is worth having a special notation to describe it. This notation is an extension of that used for indefinite integrals in Section 24.2.

The 'area under $y = f(x)$ from $x = a$ to $x = b$' is denoted by

$$\int_a^b f(x)\,dx.$$

This is called a **definite integral**. Notice that a definite integral has a specific value. Unlike an indefinite integral, it is not a function of x, and it involves no arbitrary constant. For example, the result of Example 24.3.2 would be written

$$\int_0^2 (2x - x^2)\,\mathrm{d}x = \tfrac{4}{3}.$$

The numbers a and b are often called the **limits**, or the bounds, of integration. (But notice that they are not 'limits' in the sense in which the word has been used in relation to differentiation.) The function $f(x)$ is called the **integrand**.

The symbol $\int$ was originally a letter S, standing for 'sum'. Before the link with differentiation was discovered in the 17th century, attempts were made to calculate areas as the sums of areas of rectangles of height $f(x)$ and width denoted by δx, or $\mathrm{d}x$. Fig. 24.8 shows such a rectangle for the area of the region in Fig. 24.5; as δx tends to 0, and the number of rectangles increases, the rectangles fill up the whole of the area under the curve.

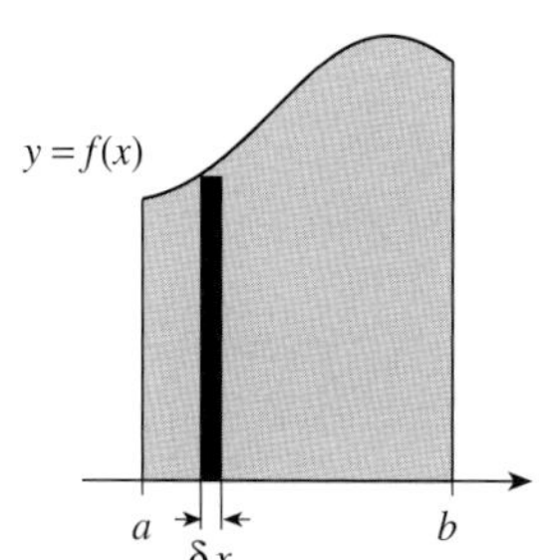

Fig. 24.8

There is also an abbreviation for $I(b) - I(a)$: it is written

$$\big[I(x)\big]_a^b.$$

So, if $I(x)$ is the simplest integral of $f(x)$, $\displaystyle\int_a^b f(x)\mathrm{d}x = \big[I(x)\big]_a^b$.

Using this notation, you would write the calculation of the area in Example 24.3.3 as

$$\begin{aligned}\text{Area} &= \int_2^5 \frac{1}{x^2}\mathrm{d}x \\ &= \left[-\frac{1}{x}\right]_2^5 \\ &= \left(-\tfrac{1}{5}\right) - \left(-\tfrac{1}{2}\right) \\ &= -0.2 + 0.5 = 0.3.\end{aligned}$$

Example 24.4.1

Find $\displaystyle\int_1^3 (3x - 2)(4 - x)\,\mathrm{d}x$.

$$\begin{aligned}\int_1^3 (3x - 2)(4 - x)\,\mathrm{d}x &= \int_1^3 (-3x^2 + 14x - 8)\,\mathrm{d}x \\ &= \big[-x^3 + 7x^2 - 8x\big]_1^3 \\ &= (-27 + 63 - 24) - (-1 + 7 - 8) \\ &= 12 - (-2) = 14.\end{aligned}$$

Example 24.4.2

Find $\displaystyle\int_{-4}^{-1}\left(x^2-\frac{1}{x^2}\right)dx$.

$$\begin{aligned}\int_{-4}^{-1}\left(x^2-\frac{1}{x^2}\right)dx &= \int_{-4}^{-1}(x^2-x^{-2})\,dx\\ &= \left[\tfrac{1}{3}x^3-(-x^{-1})\right]_{-4}^{-1}\\ &= \left[\tfrac{1}{3}x^3+\frac{1}{x}\right]_{-4}^{-1}\\ &= \tfrac{1}{3}((-1)^3-(-4)^3)+\left(\frac{1}{-1}-\frac{1}{-4}\right)\\ &= \tfrac{1}{3}(-1-(-64))+(-1+\tfrac{1}{4})\\ &= \tfrac{1}{3}\times 63+(-\tfrac{3}{4})=21-\tfrac{3}{4}=20\tfrac{1}{4}.\end{aligned}$$

Notice the different ways of completing the calculation in Examples 24.4.1 and 24.4.2. In the first case the expression in the square brackets is worked out completely for $x=3$ and $x=1$ before subtracting, following exactly the procedure described in the text. In the second the subtraction is carried out for the two terms separately, and the two results are then put together to get the answer. The second method often leads to simpler arithmetic when the integral contains fractions, or when one (or both) of the limits of integration is negative. You can use whichever method you prefer.

Example 24.4.3

Find the area under $y=\sqrt{x}$ from $x=1$ to $x=4$, shown shaded in Fig. 24.9.

$$\begin{aligned}\text{Area} &= \int_1^4 \sqrt{x}\,dx\\ &= \int_1^4 x^{\frac{1}{2}}dx\\ &= \left[\tfrac{2}{3}x^{\frac{3}{2}}\right]_1^4\\ &= \tfrac{2}{3}\times 8-\tfrac{2}{3}\times 1\\ &= \tfrac{14}{3}.\end{aligned}$$

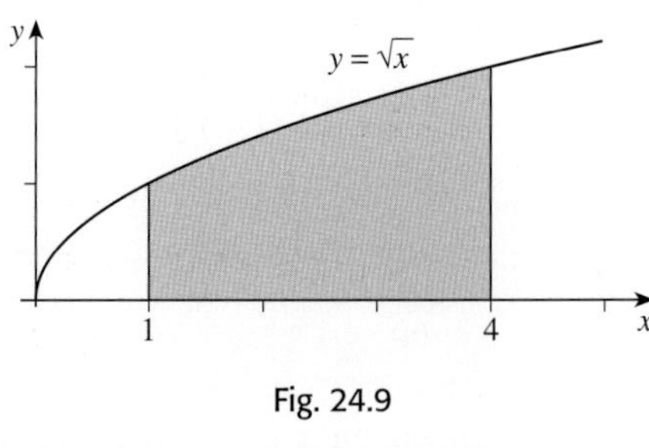

Fig. 24.9

Calculators use a version of the rectangle sum method illustrated in Fig. 24.8 to find approximate values for definite integrals of functions over a given interval, or for the areas of shaded regions under graphs. You will find details in the calculator manual. This provides a useful way of checking answers which you have found by the exact methods described in this section.

Another useful check is to find a rectangle, triangle or trapezium whose area is close to the required area. In Example 24.4.3, since $f(1)=1$ and $f(4)=2$, the shaded area is slightly larger than the area of the trapezium which you get by replacing the curve by the chord joining $(1,1)$ to $(4,2)$. The area of the trapezium is $\frac{1}{2}\times(1+2)\times 3=4\frac{1}{2}$, which can be compared with the area of $4\frac{2}{3}$ calculated in the example.

Exercise 24B

1 Evaluate the following definite integrals.

(a) $\int_1^2 3x^2\,dx$ (b) $\int_2^5 8x\,dx$ (c) $\int_0^2 x^3\,dx$

(d) $\int_{-1}^1 10x^4\,dx$ (e) $\int_0^{\frac{1}{2}} \frac{1}{2}x\,dx$ (f) $\int_0^1 2\,dx$

2 Evaluate the following definite integrals.

(a) $\int_0^2 (8x+3)\,dx$ (b) $\int_2^4 (5x-4)\,dx$ (c) $\int_{-2}^2 (6x^2+1)\,dx$

(d) $\int_0^1 (2x+1)(x+3)\,dx$ (e) $\int_{-3}^4 (6x^2+2x+3)\,dx$ (f) $\int_{-3}^3 (6x^3+2x)\,dx$

3 Find the areas under the following curves over the stated intervals. Use a calculator to check your answers.

(a) $y = x^2$ from $x = 0$ to $x = 6$ (b) $y = 4x^3$ from $x = 1$ to $x = 2$

(c) $y = 12x^3$ from $x = 2$ to $x = 3$ (d) $y = 3x^2 + 2x$ from $x = 0$ to $x = 4$

(e) $y = 3x^2 - 2x$ from $x = -4$ to $x = 0$ (f) $y = x^4 + 5$ from $x = -1$ to $x = 1$

4 The diagram shows the region under $y = 4x + 1$ between $x = 1$ and $x = 3$. Find the area of the shaded region by

(a) using the formula for the area of a trapezium,

(b) using integration.

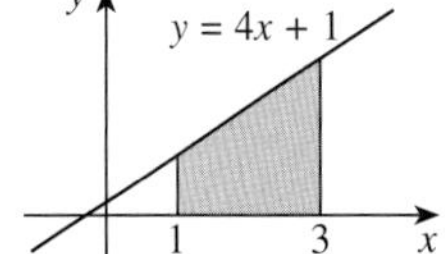

5 The diagram shows the region bounded by $y = \frac{1}{2}x - 3$, by $x = 14$ and the x-axis. Find the area of the shaded region by

(a) using the formula for the area of a triangle,

(b) using integration.

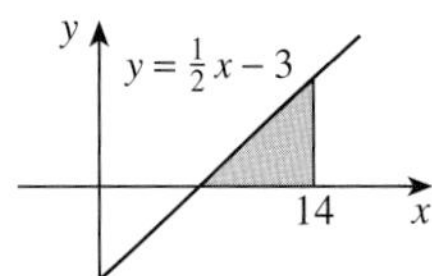

6 Find the area of the region shaded in each of the following diagrams.

(a)

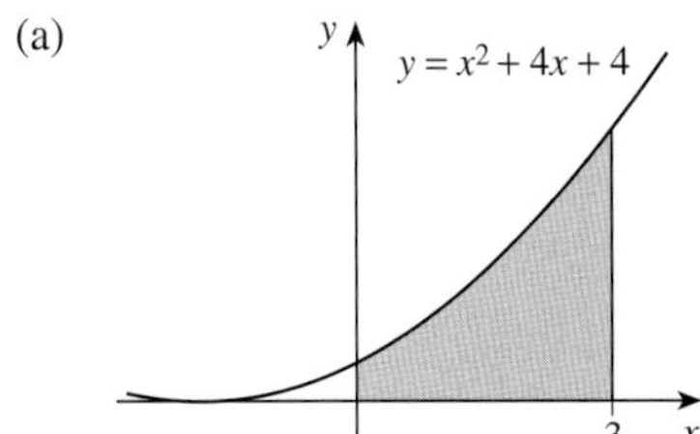

(b)

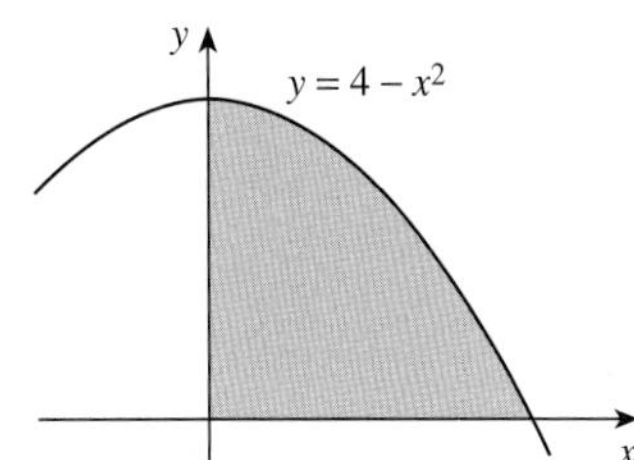

(c)

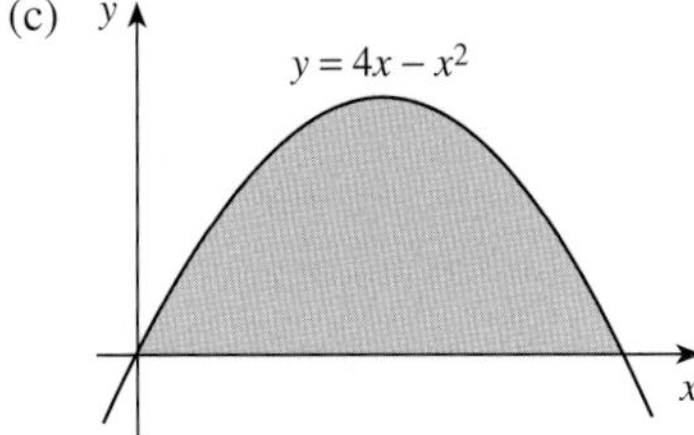

(d)

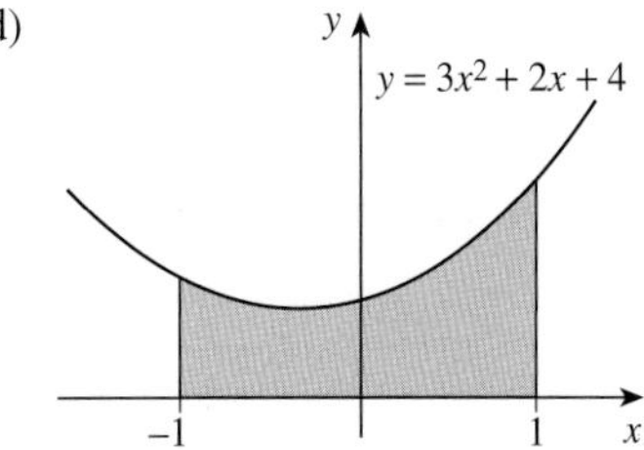

7 Evaluate the following definite integrals.

(a) $\int_0^8 12\sqrt[3]{x}\, dx$ (b) $\int_1^2 \frac{3}{x^2}\, dx$ (c) $\int_1^4 \frac{10}{\sqrt{x}}\, dx$

(d) $\int_1^2 \left(\frac{8}{x^3} + x^3\right) dx$ (e) $\int_4^9 \frac{2\sqrt{x}+3}{\sqrt{x}}\, dx$ (f) $\int_1^8 \frac{1}{\sqrt[3]{x^2}}\, dx$

8 Find the areas under the following curves over the stated intervals.

(a) $y = \frac{6}{x^4}$ between $x = 1$ and $x = 2$ (b) $y = \sqrt[3]{x}$ between $x = 1$ and $x = 27$

(c) $y = \frac{5}{x^2}$ between $x = -3$ and $x = -1$

9 Given that $\int_0^a 12x^2\, dx = 1372$, find the value of the constant a.

10 Given that $\int_0^9 p\sqrt{x}\, dx = 90$, find the value of the constant p.

11 Find the area of the shaded region in each of the following diagrams. Use a calculator to check your answers.

(a)

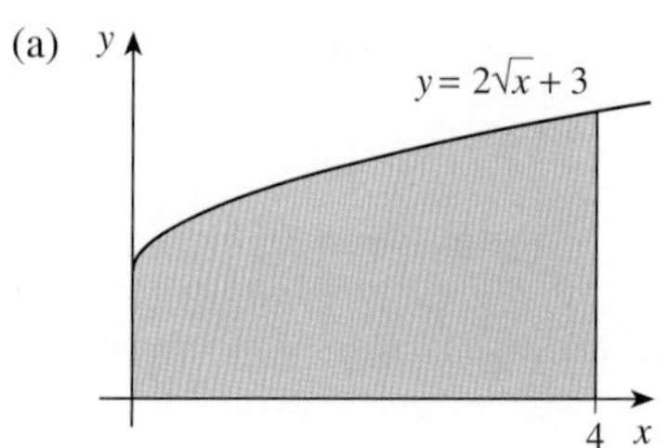

(b)

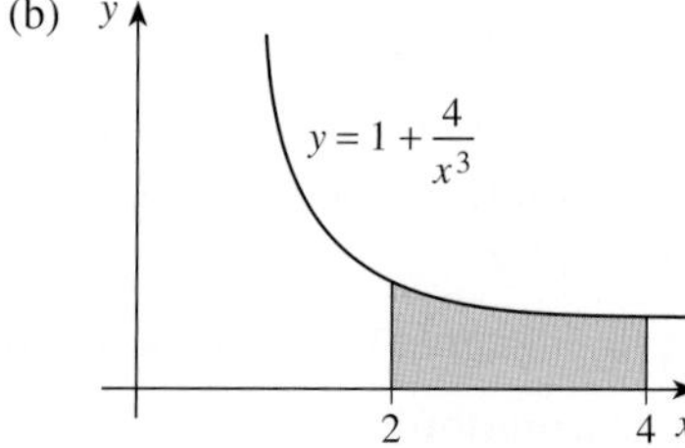

12 Find the area of the region between the curve $y = 9 + 15x - 6x^2$ and the x-axis.

24.5 Application to kinematics

One of the important applications of differentiation is to motion along a straight line. It was shown in Section 21.3 that the displacement, velocity and acceleration are connected by the equations

$$v = \frac{ds}{dt} \quad \text{and} \quad a = \frac{dv}{dt}.$$

But more often you want to work the other way round; that is, you know the acceleration and want to find how fast an object is moving, and how far it has travelled, after a given time.

For this you need to use integration rather than differentiation. The equations above can be turned round to find v and s as integrals.

For an object moving in a straight line, if a denotes the acceleration as a function of the time t,

$$v = \int a\, dt \quad \text{and} \quad s = \int v\, dt.$$

Remember that integration involves an arbitrary constant. You can usually find this by knowing the initial velocity and the initial displacement; these are the values of v and of s when $t = 0$.

Example 24.5.1
For the first few seconds of a race a horse's acceleration, a m s^{-2}, is modelled by the equation $a = 6 - 1.2t$, where t is the time in seconds from a standing start. Find an expression for the distance it covers in the first t seconds. Hence find the horse's acceleration 5 seconds after the start, how fast it is then moving and how far it has run.

Begin by finding an expression for the velocity,

$$\begin{aligned} v &= \int a\,\mathrm{d}t \\ &= \int (6 - 1.2t)\,\mathrm{d}t \\ &= 6t - 0.6t^2 + k. \end{aligned}$$

Since time is measured from a standing start, $v = 0$ when $t = 0$, so

$$0 = 6 \times 0 - 0.6 \times 0^2 + k,$$

which gives $k = 0$. The (t, v) function is therefore

$$v = 6t - 0.6t^2.$$

A second integration then gives

$$\begin{aligned} s &= \int v\,\mathrm{d}t \\ &= \int (6t - 0.6t^2)\,\mathrm{d}t \\ &= 3t^2 - 0.2t^3 + c. \end{aligned}$$

If s is measured from the starting gate, $s = 0$ when $t = 0$, so

$$0 = 3 \times 0^2 - 0.2 \times 0^3 + c.$$

This gives $c = 0$. The (t, s) function is therefore

$$s = 3t^2 - 0.2t^3.$$

Substituting $t = 5$ in the expressions for a, v and s gives the values $a = 0$, $v = 15$ and $s = 50$. So, according to this model, 5 seconds after the start the horse has stopped accelerating and has reached a speed of 15 metres per second. In this time it has run a distance of 50 metres.

Example 24.5.2
A train is travelling on a straight track at 48 m s^{-1} when the driver sees an amber light ahead. He applies the brakes for a period of 30 seconds, producing a deceleration of $\frac{1}{125}t(30 - t)$ m s^{-2}, where t is the time in seconds after the brakes are applied. Find how fast the train is moving after 30 seconds, and how far it has travelled in that time.

The train is slowing down, so the acceleration is negative. That is,

$$a = -\tfrac{1}{125}t(30 - t)$$
$$= \tfrac{1}{125}t^2 - \tfrac{6}{25}t.$$

Integrating to find v,

$$v = \int \left(\tfrac{1}{125}t^2 - \tfrac{6}{25}t\right) \mathrm{d}t$$
$$= \tfrac{1}{375}t^3 - \tfrac{3}{25}t^2 + k.$$

It is given that $v = 48$ when $t = 0$. Substituting these values gives

$$48 = 0 - 0 + k, \quad \text{so} \quad k = 48.$$

The formula for v is therefore

$$v = \tfrac{1}{375}t^3 - \tfrac{3}{25}t^2 + 48.$$

Integrating a second time to find s,

$$s = \int \left(\tfrac{1}{375}t^3 - \tfrac{3}{25}t^2 + 48\right) \mathrm{d}t$$
$$= \tfrac{1}{1500}t^4 - \tfrac{1}{25}t^3 + 48t + c.$$

If s denotes the displacement from the instant when the brakes are first applied, then $s = 0$ when $t = 0$. Substituting these values gives

$$0 = 0 - 0 + 0 + c, \quad \text{so} \quad c = 0.$$

The formula for s is therefore

$$s = \tfrac{1}{1500}t^4 - \tfrac{1}{25}t^3 + 48t.$$

To find the final speed and the distance travelled, substitute $t = 30$ in the expressions for v and s. This gives

$$v = \tfrac{27\,000}{375} - \tfrac{3 \times 900}{25} + 48$$
$$= 72 - 108 + 48 = 12$$

and

$$s = \tfrac{810\,000}{1500} - \tfrac{27\,000}{25} + 48 \times 30$$
$$= 540 - 1080 + 1440 = 900.$$

The train slows down to a speed of 12 m s^{-1}, and travels 900 metres during the time that the brakes are on.

In this example, if you only want the distance the train travels while the brakes are on, and are not interested in the (t, s) formula, you could finish off the calculation by using a definite integral. The distance is

$$\int_0^{30} \left(\tfrac{1}{375}t^3 - \tfrac{3}{25}t^2 + 48\right) \mathrm{d}t = \left[\tfrac{1}{1500}t^4 - \tfrac{1}{25}t^3 + 48t\right]_0^{30}$$
$$= (540 - 1080 + 1440) - (0 - 0 + 0) = 900.$$

Since the definite integral gives the area under the velocity–time graph, this shows that the displacement is represented by this area.

For an object moving in a straight line, with the velocity v given as a function of the time t, the displacement between times t_1 and t_2 is given by

$$\int_{t_1}^{t_2} v \, dt.$$

This displacement is represented by the area under the (t, v) graph for the interval $t_1 \leq t \leq t_2$.

Example 24.5.3
A car starts to accelerate as soon as it leaves a town. After t seconds its velocity v m s^{-1} is given by the formula $v = 14 + 0.45t^2 - 0.03t^3$, until it reaches its maximum velocity. Find the distance travelled while the car accelerates to its maximum velocity. (See Example 21.3.2.)

It was shown in Example 21.3.2 that the car reaches its maximum velocity of 29 m s^{-1} at time $t = 10$, so the distance travelled is

$$\int_0^{10} (14 + 0.45t^2 - 0.03t^3) \, dt = \left[14t + 0.15t^3 - 0.0075t^4\right]_0^{10}$$
$$= (140 + 150 - 75) - (0 + 0 - 0) = 215.$$

The car travels 215 metres in the 10 seconds that it takes to reach its maximum velocity.

Exercise 24C

1 In this question, s metres is the displacement at time t seconds of particles moving in a straight line, v is the velocity in m s^{-1} and a is the acceleration in m s^{-2}. Only zero and positive values of t should be considered.

(a) Given that $v = 3t^2 + 8$ and that the displacement is 4 m when $t = 0$, find an expression for s in terms of t. Find the displacement and the velocity when $t = 2$.

(b) Given that $v = 6\sqrt{t}$ and that the displacement is 30 m when $t = 4$, find the displacement, velocity and acceleration when $t = 1$.

(c) Given that $v = 9 - t^2$ and that the displacement is 2 m when $t = 0$, find the displacement when the velocity is zero.

(d) Given that $a = 3t - 12$, and that the velocity is 30 m s^{-1} and the displacement is 4 m when $t = 0$, find the displacement when the acceleration is zero.

(e) Given that $a = 4 - 2t$, and that the velocity is 5 m s^{-1} when $t = 0$, find the acceleration when the velocity is zero.

(f) Given that $v = 3t^2 + 4t + 3$, find the distance travelled between $t = 0$ and $t = 2$.

(g) Given that $v = \dfrac{3}{t^2}$, find the distance travelled between $t = 2$ and $t = 10$.

2 A car starts from rest and for the first 4 seconds of its motion the acceleration a m s^{-2} at time t seconds after starting is given by $a = 6 - 2t$.

(a) Find the maximum velocity of the car.

(b) Find the velocity of the car after 4 seconds, and the distance travelled up to this time.

3 A truck, with initial velocity 6 m s^{-1}, brakes and comes to rest. At time t seconds after the brakes are applied the acceleration is a m s^{-2}, where $a = -3t$. This formula applies until the truck stops.

(a) Find the time taken for the truck to stop.

(b) Find the distance travelled by the truck while it is decelerating.

(c) Find the greatest deceleration of the truck.

24.6 Some properties of definite integrals

In definite integral notation the calculation in Example 24.3.2 of the area in Fig. 24.7 would be written

$$\begin{aligned}\int_0^2 (2x - x^2)\,\mathrm{d}x &= \left[x^2 - \tfrac{1}{3}x^3\right]_0^2 \\ &= \left(\tfrac{4}{3}\right) - (0) = \tfrac{4}{3}.\end{aligned}$$

But how should you interpret the calculation

$$\begin{aligned}\int_0^3 (2x - x^2)\,\mathrm{d}x &= \left[x^2 - \tfrac{1}{3}x^3\right]_0^3 \\ &= (0) - (0) = 0?\end{aligned}$$

Clearly the area between the graph and the x-axis between $x = 0$ and $x = 3$ is not zero as the value of the definite integral suggests.

You can find the clue by calculating the integral between $x = 2$ and $x = 3$:

$$\int_2^3 (2x - x^2)\,\mathrm{d}x = \left[x^2 - \tfrac{1}{3}x^3\right]_2^3 = (0) - \left(\tfrac{4}{3}\right) = -\tfrac{4}{3}.$$

This shows that you need to be careful in identifying the definite integral as an area. In Fig. 24.10 the area of the shaded region is $\frac{4}{3}$, and the negative sign attached to the definite integral indicates that between $x = 2$ and $x = 3$ the graph lies below the x-axis.

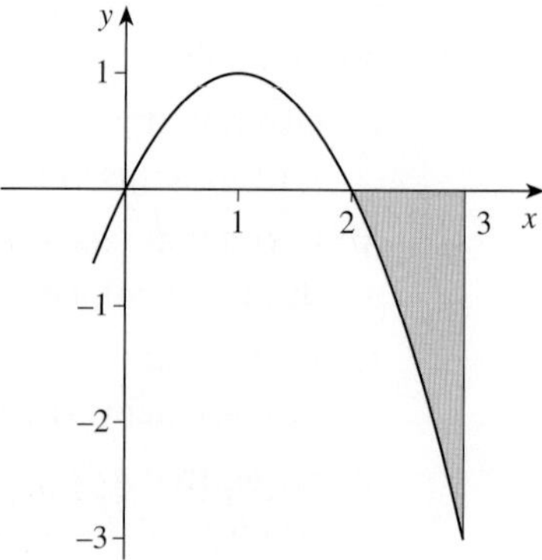

Fig. 24.10

The zero answer obtained for the integral from $x = 0$ to $x = 3$ is then explained by the fact that definite integrals are added exactly as you would expect:

$$\int_0^3 (2x - x^2)\mathrm{d}x = \int_0^2 (2x - x^2)\mathrm{d}x + \int_2^3 (2x - x^2)\mathrm{d}x = \left(\tfrac{4}{3}\right) + \left(-\tfrac{4}{3}\right) = 0.$$

This is a special case of a general rule:

$$\int_a^b f(x)\,dx + \int_b^c f(x)\,dx = \int_a^c f(x)\,dx.$$

To prove this, let $I(x)$ denote the simplest integral of $f(x)$.

Then the sum of the integrals on the left side is equal to

$$\begin{aligned}\int_a^b f(x)\,dx + \int_b^c f(x)\,dx &= [I(x)]_a^b + [I(x)]_b^c \\ &= (I(b) - I(a)) + (I(c) - I(b)), \\ &= I(c) - I(a),\end{aligned}$$

and the integral on the right side is

$$\int_a^c f(x)\,dx = I(c) - I(a).$$

Example 24.6.1

Figure 24.11 shows the graph of $y = x(x-1)(x-3)$, which crosses the x-axis at the points $(0, 0)$, $(1, 0)$ and $(3, 0)$. Find the total area between the curve and the x-axis over the interval $0 \le x \le 3$.

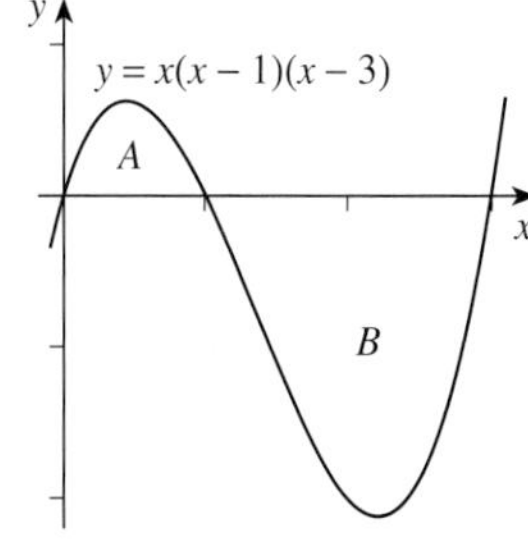

Fig. 24.11

The graph shows that there is a region A above the axis for $0 \le x \le 1$, and a region B below the axis for $1 \le x \le 3$. To find the areas of these regions you have to calculate the definite integrals

$$\begin{aligned}\int_0^1 x(x-1)(x-3)\,dx &= \int_0^1 (x^3 - 4x^2 + 3x)\,dx \\ &= \left[\tfrac{1}{4}x^4 - \tfrac{4}{3}x^3 + \tfrac{3}{2}x^2\right]_0^1 \\ &= \tfrac{1}{4} - 1\tfrac{1}{3} + 1\tfrac{1}{2} = \tfrac{5}{12}\end{aligned}$$

and

$$\begin{aligned}\int_1^3 x(x-1)(x-3)\,dx &= \left[\tfrac{1}{4}x^4 - \tfrac{4}{3}x^3 + \tfrac{3}{2}x^2\right]_1^3 \\ &= \left(20\tfrac{1}{4} - 36 + 13\tfrac{1}{2}\right) - \left(\tfrac{1}{4} - 1\tfrac{1}{3} + 1\tfrac{1}{2}\right) \\ &= -2\tfrac{2}{3}.\end{aligned}$$

The second integral is negative because the region B lies below the x-axis. In absolute value region A has area $\frac{5}{12}$ and region B has area $2\frac{2}{3}$. So the total area between the curve and the x-axis for $0 \le x \le 3$ is $\frac{5}{12} + 2\frac{2}{3}$, which is $3\frac{1}{12}$.

The question whether areas below the axis should be counted as negative or positive is well illustrated by applications to kinematics.

Example 24.6.2

A squirrel runs along a straight path, starting at a point O. Its velocity v m s^{-1} after t seconds is given by $v = t^2 - 3t$ for $0 \le t \le 5$. Find

(a) the displacement of the squirrel from O after 5 seconds,

(b) the total distance it runs in this time.

Figure 24.12 shows the velocity–time graph for the motion of the squirrel. The velocity is negative for $0 < t < 3$ and positive for $3 < t < 5$. So the squirrel runs in the negative direction along the path for 3 seconds, then turns round and runs in the positive direction.

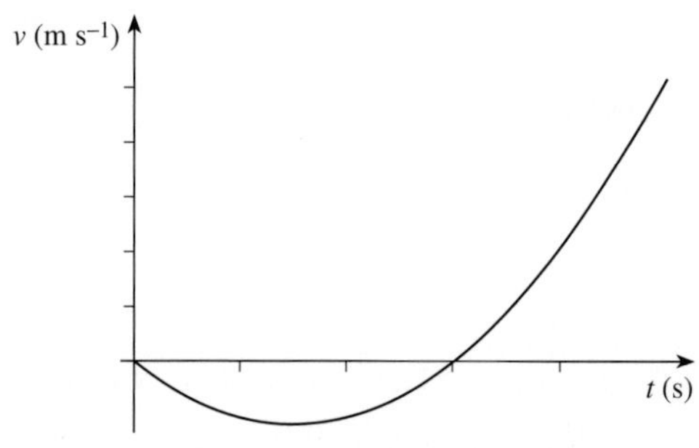

Fig. 24.12

(a) If the displacement from O after t seconds is s metres,

$$s = \int v\,\mathrm{d}t = \int (t^2 - 3t)\mathrm{d}t.$$

Since the displacement is zero when $t = 0$, the displacement after 5 seconds is given by

$$\int_0^5 (t^2 - 3t)\,\mathrm{d}t = \left[\tfrac{1}{3}t^3 - \tfrac{3}{2}t^2\right]_0^5$$
$$= \tfrac{1}{3} \times 125 - \tfrac{3}{2} \times 25 = 4\tfrac{1}{6}.$$

After 5 seconds the squirrel is $4\frac{1}{6}$ metres from O in the positive direction.

(b) To find the total distance it runs, you need to find the displacements of the squirrel in the two directions separately. These are given by

$$\int_0^3 (t^2 - 3t)\,\mathrm{d}t = \left[\tfrac{1}{3}t^3 - \tfrac{3}{2}t^2\right]_0^3$$
$$= \tfrac{1}{3} \times 27 - \tfrac{3}{2} \times 9 = -4\tfrac{1}{2}$$

and
$$\int_3^5 (t^2 - 3t)\,\mathrm{d}t = \left[\tfrac{1}{3}t^3 - \tfrac{3}{2}t^2\right]_3^5$$
$$= 4\tfrac{1}{6} - \left(-4\tfrac{1}{2}\right) = 8\tfrac{2}{3}.$$

So the squirrel runs $4\frac{1}{2}$ metres in the negative direction and then $8\frac{2}{3}$ metres in the positive direction. The total distance it runs is $\left(4\frac{1}{2} + 8\frac{2}{3}\right)$ metres, which is $13\frac{1}{6}$ metres.

This example shows that the total distance is the sum of the areas above and below the axis, counting all areas as positive. But to find the total displacement areas below the axis must be counted as negative.

Negative definite integrals can also arise when you interchange the bounds of integration. Since

$$\begin{aligned}[I(x)]_b^a &= I(a) - I(b) \\ &= -(I(b) - I(a)) \\ &= -[I(x)]_a^b,\end{aligned}$$

it follows that:

$$\int_b^a f(x)\mathrm{d}x = -\int_a^b f(x)\mathrm{d}x.$$

24.7 Calculating other areas

You sometimes want to find the area of a region bounded by the graphs of two functions $f(x)$ and $g(x)$, and by two lines $x = a$ and $x = b$, as in Fig. 24.13.

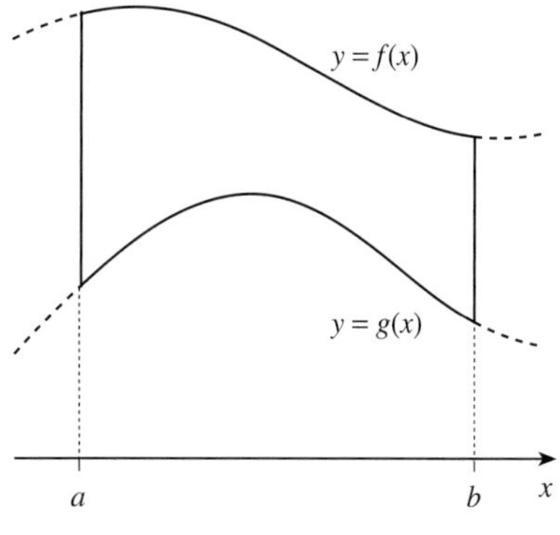

Fig. 24.13

Although you could find this as the difference of the areas of two regions of the kind illustrated in Fig. 24.5, calculated as

$$\int_a^b f(x)\,\mathrm{d}x - \int_a^b g(x)\,\mathrm{d}x,$$

it is often simpler to find it as a single integral

$$\int_a^b (f(x) - g(x))\,\mathrm{d}x.$$

Example 24.7.1
Figure 24.14 shows the graph of $y = x^2$ and the chord joining the points $(-1, 1)$ and $(2, 4)$ on the curve. Find the area of the shaded region between the curve and the chord.

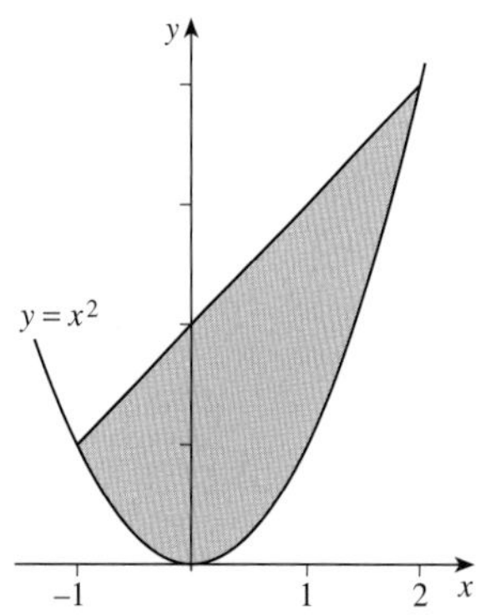

Fig. 24.14

The first step is to find the equation of the chord. Since the gradient is

$$\frac{4-1}{2-(-1)} = \tfrac{3}{3} = 1,$$

its equation is

$$y - 1 = 1(x - (-1)), \quad \text{or more simply} \quad y = x + 2.$$

To find the area, use the formula $\int_a^b (f(x) - g(x))\,dx$ with $f(x) = x + 2$, $g(x) = x^2$, $a = -1$ and $b = 2$.

$$\text{Area} = \int_{-1}^{2} (x + 2 - x^2)\,dx$$
$$= \left[\tfrac{1}{2}x^2 + 2x - \tfrac{1}{3}x^3\right]_{-1}^{2}.$$

Because of the fractions, this is a calculation where it is simpler to carry out the subtractions term-by-term, as explained in Section 24.4. This gives the area as

$$\tfrac{1}{2}(2^2 - (-1)^2) + 2(2 - (-1)) - \tfrac{1}{3}(2^3 - (-1)^3)$$
$$= \tfrac{1}{2} \times 3 + 2 \times 3 - \tfrac{1}{3} \times 9$$
$$= 1\tfrac{1}{2} + 6 - 3 = 4\tfrac{1}{2}.$$

The area of the region between the curve and the chord is $4\frac{1}{2}$.

Notice that if you had used the formula with $f(x) = x^2$ and $g(x) = x + 2$ you would have got the answer $-4\frac{1}{2}$. This is because the curve lies below the chord in the interval $-1 < x < 2$. You should always try to choose the notation so that $f(x) > g(x)$ over the interval of values of x in which you are interested.

Example 24.7.2

Show that the graphs of $y = f(x)$ and $y = g(x)$, where $f(x) = x^3 - x^2 - 6x + 8$ and $g(x) = x^3 + 2x^2 - 1$, intersect at two points, and find the area of the region enclosed between the two curves.

The graphs intersect where the two values of y are equal, so that $f(x) = g(x)$. But before writing this as an equation for x, note that it can be written as $f(x) - g(x) = 0$.

Since you are going to need $f(x) - g(x)$ in the integral later, it will save work to begin by finding

$$\begin{aligned} f(x) - g(x) &= (x^3 - x^2 - 6x + 8) - (x^3 + 2x^2 - 1) \\ &= x^3 - x^2 - 6x + 8 - x^3 - 2x^2 + 1 \\ &= -3x^2 - 6x + 9 \\ &= -3(x^2 + 2x - 3) \\ &= -3(x + 3)(x - 1). \end{aligned}$$

The graphs intersect where this is 0, that is where $x = -3$ and $x = 1$. So there are two points of intersection, $(-3, -10)$ and $(1, 2)$.

Having got this far, you may find it helpful to display the two graphs on your calculator in the interval between these values of x.

You can also use this expression for $f(x) - g(x)$ in factors to check that $f(x) > g(x)$. If $-3 < x < 1$, $x + 3$ is positive and $x - 1$ is negative, so that $f(x) - g(x) > 0$ as required.

All that remains is to calculate the area between the graphs as

$$\begin{aligned}\int_{-3}^{1}(f(x)-g(x))\,\mathrm{d}x &= \int_{-3}^{1}(-3x^2-6x+9)\,\mathrm{d}x\\ &= \left[-x^3-3x^2+9x\right]_{-3}^{1}\\ &= (-1-3+9)-(27-27-27)\\ &= 5-(-27)=32.\end{aligned}$$

The area enclosed between the two graphs is 32.

Notice that in this example, integrating $f(x)-g(x)$, rather than $f(x)$ and $g(x)$ separately, greatly reduces the amount of calculation.

Sometimes you need to find an area whose boundary includes part of a graph, but which is not the 'area under the graph' described in Section 24.3. Such areas can often be found by calculating the area under the graph and then adding or subtracting the area of some triangle or rectangle. Example 24.7.3 gives two typical calculations of this type.

Example 24.7.3

Figure 24.15 shows the part of the graph $y=3+2x-x^2$ which lies in the first quadrant. Calculate the areas of the regions labelled A and B.

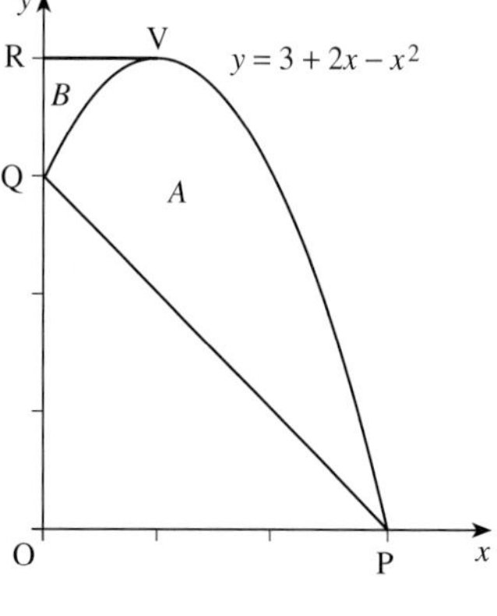

Fig. 24.15

In factor form and completed square form,

$$3+2x-x^2=(3-x)(1+x)=4-(x-1)^2.$$

Region *A* Begin by finding the coordinates of P and Q, by putting $y=0$ and $x=0$ respectively. From the factor form, when $y=0$, $x=3$ (since $x>0$). When $x=0$, $y=3$.

So P is (3, 0) and Q is (0, 3).

If you add the triangle OPQ to the region A you get the region under the graph from $x=0$ to $x=3$, whose area is

$$\begin{aligned}\int_{0}^{3}(3+2x-x^2)\,\mathrm{d}x &= \left[3x+x^2-\tfrac{1}{3}x^3\right]_{0}^{3}\\ &= (9+9-9)-(0)=9.\end{aligned}$$

The area of the triangle OPQ is $\frac{1}{2}\times 3\times 3=4\frac{1}{2}$.

So the area of region A is $9-4\frac{1}{2}=4\frac{1}{2}$.

Region *B* From the completed square form, the coordinates of the vertex V are $(1, 4)$.

Figure 24.16 shows that, if you add the region B to the region under the graph from $x = 0$ to $x = 1$, you get the rectangle ORVS, of width 1 and height 4.

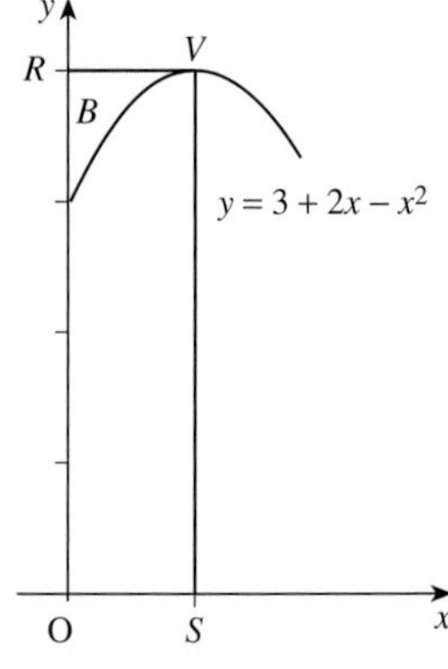

Fig. 24.16

The area under the graph from $x = 0$ to $x = 1$ is

$$\int_0^1 (3 + 2x - x^2)\,dx = \left[3x + x^2 - \tfrac{1}{3}x^3\right]_0^1$$
$$= \left(3 + 1 - \tfrac{1}{3}\right) - (0) = 3\tfrac{2}{3}.$$

The area of the rectangle is $1 \times 4 = 4$.

So the area of region B is $4 - 3\frac{2}{3} = \frac{1}{3}$.

Exercise 24D

1 Evaluate $\int_0^2 3x(x-2)\,dx$ and comment on your answer.

2 Find the total area of the region shaded in each of the following diagrams.

(a)

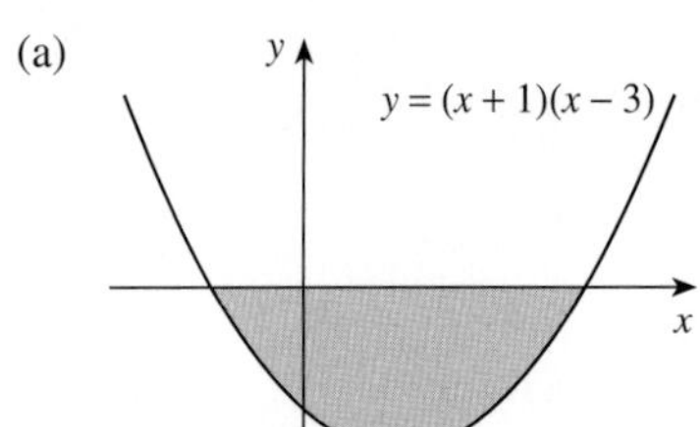

(b)

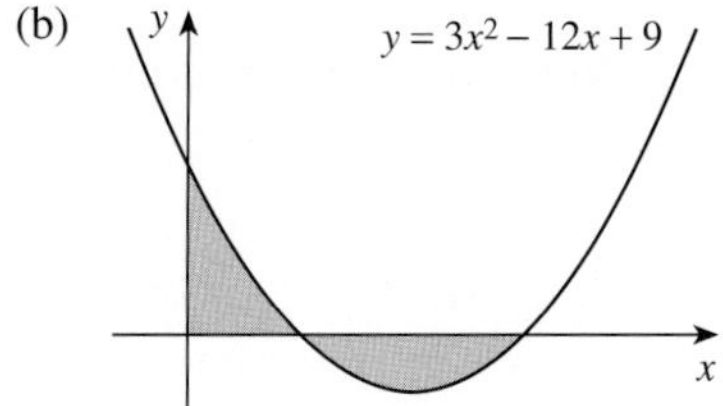

(c)

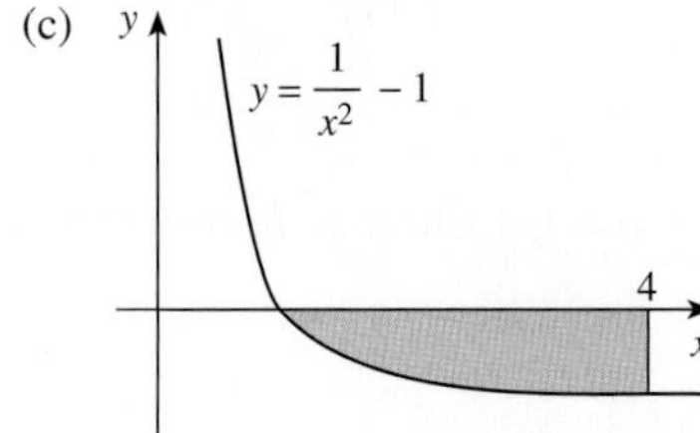

(d)

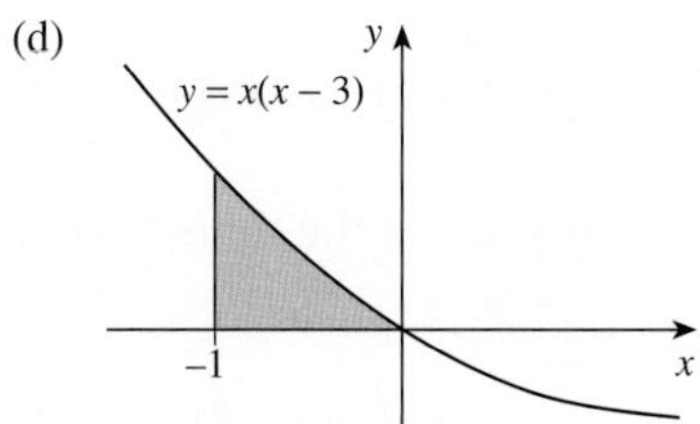

3 The diagram shows the graphs of $y = 2x + 7$ and $y = 10 - x$.

Find the area of the shaded region.

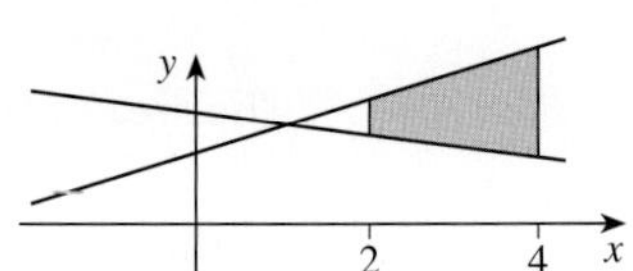

4 Find the area enclosed between the curves $y = x^2 + 7$ and $y = 2x^2 + 3$.

5 Find the area enclosed between the straight line $y = 12x + 14$ and the curve $y = 3x^2 + 6x + 5$.

6 A load is being lifted by a crane and moves in a vertical straight line. Initially the load is on the ground and after t seconds its velocity v m s^{-1} (measured upwards) is given by $v = \frac{3}{5}t(t-3)(t-4)$ for $0 \le t \le 4$.

(a) Sketch the (t, v) graph for the motion of the load.

(b) State when the magnitude of the acceleration is greatest, and calculate this greatest acceleration.

(c) State when the load is at its highest point, and find the acceleration at this instant.

(d) Find the height of the load above the ground when $t = 3$ and when $t = 4$.

(e) Sketch a graph showing the height of the load for $0 \le t \le 4$.

(f) Find the total distance moved by the load.

7 Find the area between the curves $y = (x-4)(3x-1)$ and $y = (4-x)(1+x)$.

8 The diagram shows the graph of $y = \sqrt{x}$. Given that the area of the shaded region is 72, find the value of the constant a.

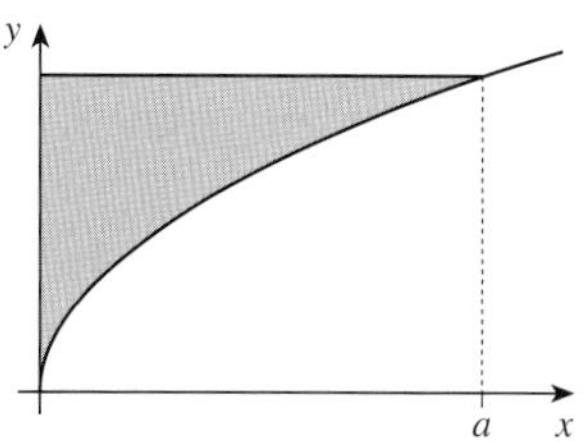

9 Parts of the graphs of $f(x) = 2x^3 + x^2 - 8x$ and $g(x) = 2x^3 - 3x - 4$ enclose a finite region. Find its area.

10 Find the area of the region shaded in each of the following diagrams.

(a)

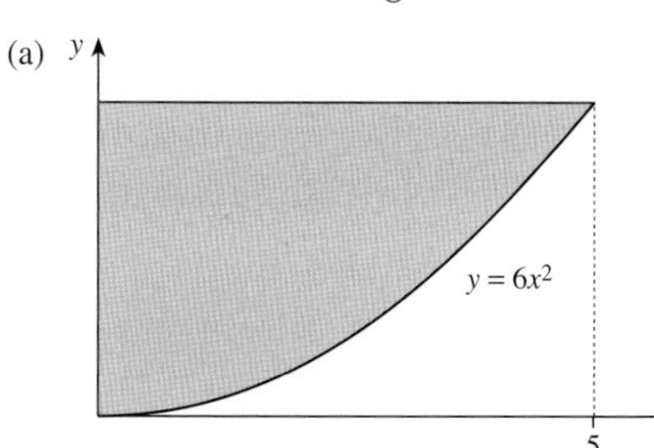

(b)

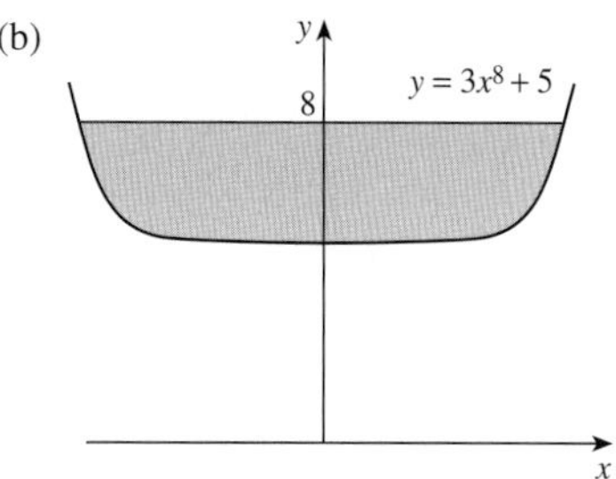

11 The diagram shows the graph of $y = 9x^2$. The point P has coordinates (4, 144). Find the area of the shaded region.

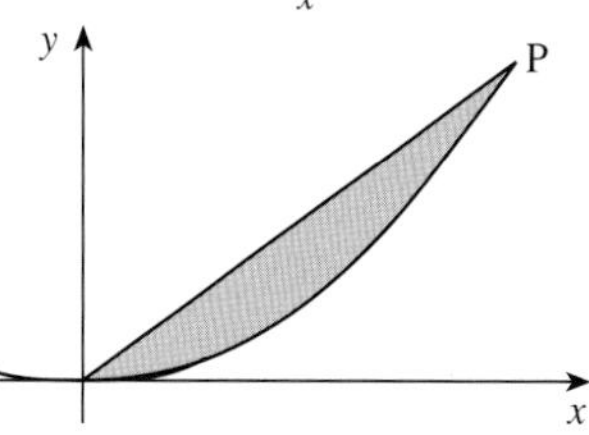

12 The diagram shows the graph of $y = \dfrac{1}{\sqrt{x}}$. Show that the area of the shaded region is $3 - \dfrac{5\sqrt{3}}{3}$.

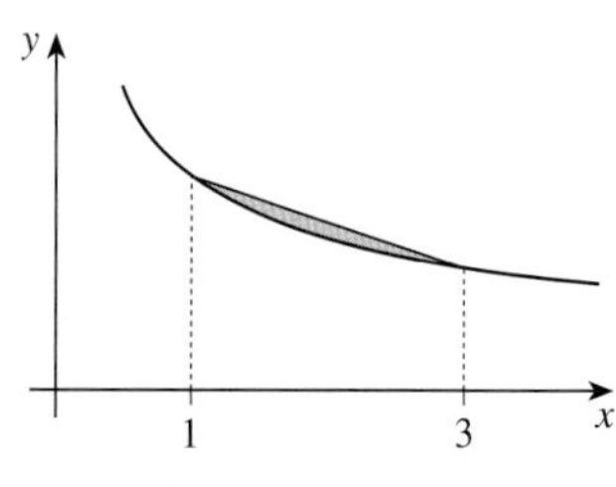

25 Geometric sequences

This chapter introduces another type of sequence, in which the ratio of successive terms is constant. When you have completed it, you should

- recognise geometric sequences and be able to do calculations on them
- know and be able to obtain the formula for the sum of a geometric series
- know the condition for a geometric series to converge, and how to find its limiting sum.

25.1 Geometric sequences

In Chapter 2 you met arithmetic sequences, in which you get from one term to the next by adding a constant. A sequence in which you get from one term to the next by multiplying by a constant is called a geometric sequence.

Example 25.1.1
Show that the numbers 4, 12, 36, 108 form a geometric sequence. If the sequence is continued, find (a) the next two terms, (b) the twentieth term.

Since $12 = 4 \times 3, \quad 36 = 12 \times 3, \quad 108 = 36 \times 3,$

there is a constant multiplying factor of 3. So the numbers form a geometric sequence.

(a) The next term is $108 \times 3 = 324$, and the term after that is $324 \times 3 = 972$.

(b) To get from the first term to the twentieth you have to multiply by 3 nineteen times. So the twentieth term is 4×3^{19}. Correct to 4 significant figures, this is 4649 million.

Example 25.1.2
The first two terms of a geometric sequence are 4, 20 and the last term is 62 500. How many terms are there altogether?

To get from the first term to the second you must multiply by $\frac{20}{4} = 5$. To get from the first term to the last you must multiply by $\frac{62\,500}{4} = 15\,625$, which is 5^6.

So, going one step at a time, you start at the first term and then multiply by 5 six times. This means that 62 500 is the seventh term of the sequence.

A general definition for this kind of sequence is:

> A **geometric sequence**, or **geometric progression**, is a sequence defined by $u_1 = a$ and $u_n = ru_{n-1}$, where $a \neq 0$, $r \neq 0$ or 1, and $n = 2,3, \ldots$.
>
> The constant r is called the **common ratio** of the sequence.

Notice that the ratios 0 and 1 are excluded. If you put $r = 0$ in the definition you get the sequence $a, 0, 0, 0, \ldots$; if you put $r = 1$ you get $a, a, a, a, \ldots$. Neither is very interesting, and some of the properties of geometric sequences break down if $r = 0$ or 1. However, r can be negative; in that case the terms are alternately positive and negative. For a similar reason $a = 0$ is excluded, since this would give you the sequence $0, 0, 0, 0, \ldots$.

It is easy to give a formula for the nth term. To get from u_1 to u_n you multiply by the common ratio $n-1$ times, so $u_n = r^{n-1} \times u_1$, which gives $u_n = ar^{n-1}$.

> The nth term of a geometric sequence with first term a and common ratio r is ar^{n-1}.

Example 25.1.3
The first two terms of a geometric sequence are 10 and 11. Show that the first term greater than 1000 is the fiftieth.

The common ratio is $11 \div 10 = 1.1$. The nth term of the sequence is therefore $10 \times 1.1^{n-1}$.

Each term of the sequence is greater than the preceding term. You therefore have to show that the 49th term is less than 1000, and that the 50th term is greater than 1000.

The 49th term is $10 \times 1.1^{49-1} = 10 \times 1.1^{48} = 970.17\ldots$.

The 50th term is $10 \times 1.1^{50-1} = 10 \times 1.1^{49} = 1067.18\ldots$.

So the first term greater than 1000 is the fiftieth.

Example 25.1.4
Show that there are two geometric sequences whose first term is 5 and whose fifth term is 80. For each of these sequences, find the tenth term.

Since the first term is given, the sequence is determined by knowing the common ratio r. The fifth term is $5 \times r^{5-1} = 5 \times r^4$.

If $5 \times r^4 = 80$, $r^4 = 16$, so $r = \pm 2$.

The two sequences are 5, 10, 20, 40, 80, ... and 5, −10, 20, −40, 80, ...

The tenth term is $5 \times r^{10-1} = 5 \times r^9$.

So when $r = 2$, the tenth term is $5 \times 2^9 = 5 \times 512 = 2560$; when $r = -2$, the tenth term is $5 \times (-2)^9 = 5 \times (-512) = -2560$.

25.2 Graphs of geometric sequences

With a calculator it is easy to produce graphs of geometric sequences, using the method described in Section 8.6. To enter the sequence you can use either the inductive definition or the formula for the nth term.

For example, to get the graph of the sequence in Example 25.1.3 you could enter either

$$u_n = 10 \times 1.1^{n-1} \quad \text{or} \quad u_1 = 10, \quad u_n = 1.1 \times u_{n-1}.$$

You would then get a graph like Fig. 25.1. You will notice that the points soon disappear off the top of the window.

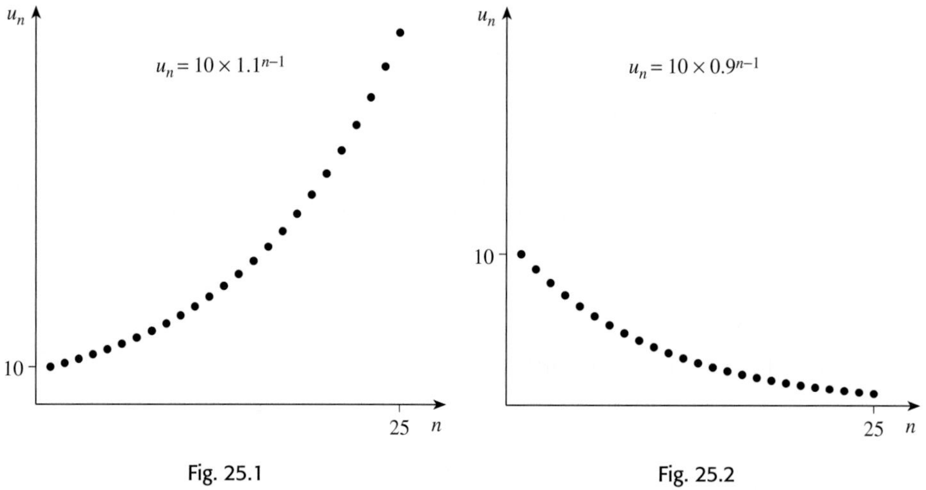

Fig. 25.1

Fig. 25.2

But this doesn't happen with all geometric sequences. If you repeat the experiment with 0.9 in place of 1.1, entering either

$$u_n = 10 \times 0.9^{n-1} \qquad \text{or} \qquad u_1 = 10, \quad u_n = 0.9 \times u_{n-1},$$

you will get a display like Fig. 25.2. These points will never disappear off the top of the window, however far you go. In fact, by making n large enough, points can be found as close as you like to the horizontal axis.

What happens if the common ratio r is negative? Try producing similar displays with -1.1 or -0.9 in place of 1.1. You will then get graphs like Fig. 25.3 and Fig. 25.4.

Comparing Fig. 25.3 with Fig. 25.1, or Fig. 25.4 with Fig. 25.2, you will see that all the points for odd values of n are the same in both graphs; but those for even values of n are reflections of each other in the horizontal axis. So the points in Fig. 25.3 soon disappear off the top or bottom of the window, but those in Fig. 25.4 approach the horizontal axis as n increases.

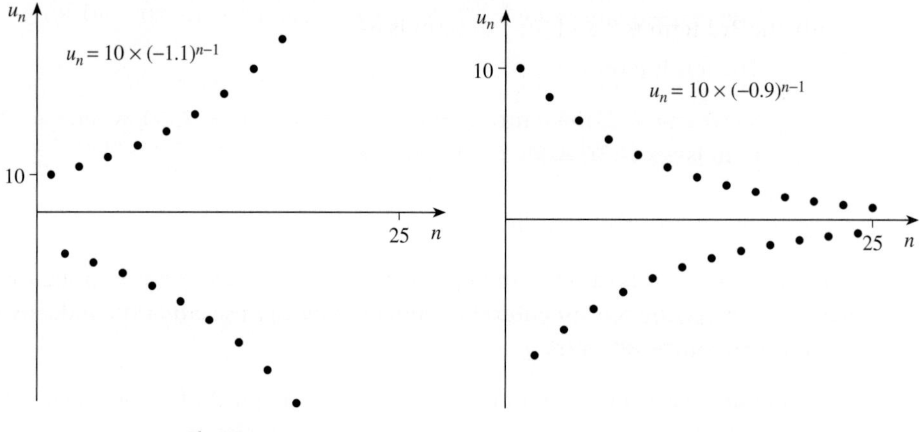

Fig. 25.3

Fig. 25.4

Try experimenting with other values of r and a for yourself. What happens if $r = -1$? Or if $r = 1$? (Look back at the definition in Section 25.1!)

The results can be summed up using the idea of convergence to a limit (see Section 8.6).

If a geometric sequence u_n has common ratio r, then

if $|r| < 1$, $\lim_{n \to \infty} u_n = 0$;

if $r > 1$ or ≤ -1, u_n does not converge to a limit as $n \to \infty$.

Exercise 25A

1 For each of the following geometric sequences find the common ratio and the next two terms.

(a) 3, 6, 12, ... (b) 2, 8, 32, ... (c) 32, 16, 8, ...

(d) 2, −6, 18, −54, ... (e) 1.1, 1.21, 1.331, ... (f) $x^2, x, 1, \ldots$

2 Find an expression for the nth term of each of the following geometric sequences.

(a) 2, 6, 18, ... (b) 10, 5, 2.5, ... (c) 1, −2, 4, ...

(d) 81, 27, 9, ... (e) $x, x^2, x^3, \ldots$ (f) $pq^2, q^3, p^{-1}q^4, \ldots$

Which of these sequences have terms which converge to 0 as $n \to \infty$?

3 Find the number of terms in each of these geometric progressions.

(a) 2, 4, 8, ..., 2048 (b) 1, −3, 9, ..., 531 441

(c) 2, 6, 18, ..., 1458 (d) 5, −10, 20, ..., −40 960

(e) 16, 12, 9, ..., 3.796 875 (f) $x^{-6}, x^{-2}, x^2, \ldots, x^{42}$

4 Find the common ratio and the first term in the geometric progressions where

(a) the 2nd term is 4 and the 5th term is 108,

(b) the 3rd term is 6 and the 7th term is 96,

(c) the 4th term is 19 683 and the 9th term is 81,

(d) the 3rd term is 8 and the 9th term is 64.

5 If x, y and z are the first three terms of a geometric sequence, show that x^2, y^2 and z^2 form another geometric sequence.

25.3 Summing geometric series

Geometric sequences have many applications in finance, biology, mechanics and probability, and you often need to find the sum of all the terms. In this context it is usual to call the sequence a **geometric series**.

The method used in Chapter 2 to find the sum of an arithmetic series does not work for geometric series. You can see this by taking a simple geometric series like

$$1 + 2 + 4 + 8 + 16$$

and placing an upside-down copy next to it, as in Fig. 25.5.

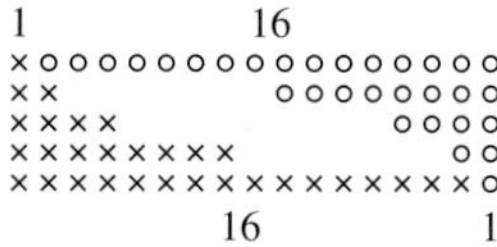

Fig. 25.5

When you did this with an arithmetic series the two sets of crosses and noughts made a perfect join (see Fig. 2.5), so they could easily be counted; but for the geometric series in Fig. 25.5 there is a gap in the middle.

For geometric series a different method is used to find the sum. If you multiply the equation

$$S = 1 + 2 + 4 + 8 + 16$$

by 2, then you get

$$2S = 2 + 4 + 8 + 16 + 32.$$

Notice that the right sides in these two equations have the terms $2 + 4 + 8 + 16$ in common. If you put all the other terms on the left sides, you get

$$S - 1 = 2 + 4 + 8 + 16$$

and

$$2S - 32 = 2 + 4 + 8 + 16.$$

So

$$S - 1 = 2S - 32, \quad \text{giving} \quad S = 31.$$

You can use this method to find the sum of any geometric series. Let S be the sum of the first n terms of the series. Then

$$S = a + ar + ar^2 + \ldots + ar^{n-2} + ar^{n-1}.$$

If you multiply this equation by r, you get

$$Sr = ar + ar^2 + ar^3 + \ldots + ar^{n-1} + ar^n.$$

The right sides in these two equations have $ar + ar^2 + \ldots + ar^{n-2} + ar^{n-1}$ in common; so

$$S - a = ar + ar^2 + \ldots + ar^{n-2} + ar^{n-1},$$

and

$$Sr - ar^n = ar + ar^2 + \ldots + ar^{n-2} + ar^{n-1}.$$

Therefore

$$S - a = Sr - ar^n,$$
$$S - Sr = a - ar^n,$$
$$S(1 - r) = a(1 - r^n).$$

That is,

$$S = \frac{a(1 - r^n)}{1 - r}.$$

The sum S of the geometric series $a + ar + ar^2 + ... + ar^{n-1}$, with n terms, is given by

$$S = \frac{a(1 - r^n)}{1 - r}.$$

Example 25.3.1
Find the sums of the geometric series having nine terms with

(a) first term 6561, common ratio $\frac{1}{3}$;
(b) first term 1, common ratio 3;
(c) first term 1, common ratio –3.

(a) Setting $a = 6561$, $r = \frac{1}{3}$ and $n = 9$ in the formula gives the sum

$$\frac{6561(1 - (\frac{1}{3})^9)}{1 - \frac{1}{3}} = \frac{6561 \times (1 - \frac{1}{19\,683})}{\frac{2}{3}} = 6561 \times \tfrac{19\,682}{19\,683} \times \tfrac{3}{2} = 9841.$$

(b) Setting $a = 1$, $r = 3$ and $n = 9$ in the formula gives the sum

$$\frac{1(1 - 3^9)}{1 - 3} = \frac{1 - 19\,683}{-2} = \frac{-19\,682}{-2} = 9841.$$

Can you see why the answers to parts (a) and (b) are the same?

(c) Setting $a = 1$, $r = -3$ and $n = 9$ in the formula gives the sum

$$\frac{1(1 - (-3)^9)}{1 - (-3)} = \frac{1 - (-19\,683)}{1 - (-3)} = \frac{1 + 19\,683}{1 + 3} = \frac{19\,684}{4} = 4921.$$

There are two points to notice in this example about the use of the formula for the sum.

- In part (c) it is used with a negative value of r. The algebraic argument used to produce the formula is equally valid whether r is positive or negative. The only value of r for which it breaks down is 1; but in the definition of a geometric sequence in Section 25.1 the value $r = 1$ is specifically excluded.
- In part (b), where r is greater than 1, both $1 - r^n$ and $1 - r$ are negative, so that when you apply the formula you get a fraction in which the top and the bottom are both negative. You could avoid the minus signs by noting that $1 - r^n = -(r^n - 1)$ and $1 - r = -(r - 1)$, so that

$$\frac{a(1 - r^n)}{1 - r} = \frac{-a(r^n - 1)}{-(r - 1)} = \frac{a(r^n - 1)}{r - 1}.$$

Some people like to use the formula in this alternative form when $r > 1$; it is one more result to remember, but you avoid the inconvenience of the minus signs. It's a matter of choice.

Example 25.3.2

A geometric series which begins $4 + 5 + \ldots$ has 15 terms. Find the sum, and compare it with the sum of the corresponding arithmetic series.

Since the first two terms are 4 and 5, the common ratio is $\frac{5}{4} = 1.25$. So the formula gives the sum of the geometric series as

$$\begin{aligned}\frac{4(1-1.25^{15})}{1-1.25} &= \frac{4(1-28.42\ldots)}{-0.25}\\ &= (-16)\times(-27.42\ldots)\\ &= 438.7\ldots = 439 \text{ to the nearest integer.}\end{aligned}$$

For the arithmetic series the common difference is 1. So the formula $S = \frac{1}{2}n(2a + (n-1)d)$ in Section 2.5 gives

$$S = \tfrac{1}{2} \times 15(2 \times 4 + 14 \times 1) = 165.$$

The sum of the geometric series is between $2\frac{1}{2}$ and 3 times as large as the sum of the arithmetic series.

If you display graphs of the terms of both series on your calculator using the same axes, you will see why the sum of the geometric series is so much greater than the sum of the arithmetic series.

Example 25.3.3

(a) The first and last terms of a geometric series are a and l, and the common ratio is r. Show that the sum of the series is $\dfrac{a - rl}{1 - r}$.

(b) Given that $5 + 15 + \ldots + 10\,935$ is a geometric series, find what proportion of the sum is contributed by the last term.

(a) From the sum formula

$$S = \frac{a(1-r^n)}{1-r} = \frac{a - ar^n}{1-r} = \frac{a - r(ar^{n-1})}{1-r}.$$

Since the last term $l = ar^{n-1}$,

$$S = \frac{a - rl}{1 - r}.$$

(b) The series has common ratio $\frac{15}{5} = 3$. Substituting $a = 5$, $r = 3$ and $l = 10\,935$ in the formula in part (a),

$$S = \frac{5 - 3 \times 10\,935}{1 - 3} = \frac{-32\,800}{-2} = 16\,400.$$

The proportion of this sum contributed by the last term is $\dfrac{10\,935}{16\,400} = 0.667\ldots$, which is just over $\frac{2}{3}$.

Example 25.3.4

A child lives 200 metres from school. He walks 60 metres in the first minute, and in each subsequent minute he walks 75% of the distance he walked in the previous minute. Show that he takes between 6 and 7 minutes to get to school.

The distances walked in the first, second, third, ... , nth minutes are 60 m, 60×0.75 m, 60×0.75^2 m, ... , $60 \times 0.75^{n-1}$ m. In the first n minutes the child walks S_n metres, where

$$\begin{aligned} S_n &= 60 + 60 \times 0.75^1 + 60 \times 0.75^2 + ... + 60 \times 0.75^{n-1} \\ &= \frac{60(1-0.75^n)}{1-0.75} = \frac{60(1-0.75^n)}{0.25} = 240(1-0.75^n). \end{aligned}$$

From this formula you can calculate that

$$S_6 = 240(1-0.75^6) = 240(1-0.177...) = 197.2...,$$

and $$S_7 = 240(1-0.75^7) = 240(1-0.133...) = 207.9.... .$$

So he has not reached school after 6 minutes, but (if he had gone on walking) he would have gone more than 200 m in 7 minutes. That is, he takes between 6 and 7 minutes to walk to school.

Example 25.3.5

Show that $\sum_{i=1}^{10} 2 \times 3^i$ is the sum of a geometric progression, and find its value.

Notice the use of the suffix i to describe the general term of the series. See Section 2.6.

To interpret an expression in $\sum$ notation, it is usually enough to write out the first three terms and the last term. In this case,

$$\begin{aligned} \sum_{i=1}^{10} 2 \times 3^i &= 2 \times 3^1 + 2 \times 3^2 + 2 \times 3^3 + ... + 2 \times 3^{10} \\ &= 6 + 18 + 54 + ... + 2 \times 3^{10}. \end{aligned}$$

To get from each term to the next you multiply by 3. So this is a geometric series with $a = 6$, $r = 3$ and $n = 10$.

Notice that 2×3^i is the same as $2 \times (3 \times 3^{i-1}) = 6 \times 3^{i-1}$. You will recognise this as the standard way of writing the ith term of a geometric sequence, ar^{i-1}, with $a = 6$ and $r = 3$.

The formula for the sum of a geometric series then gives

$$\sum_{i=1}^{10} 2 \times 3^i = \frac{6(1-3^{10})}{1-3} = \frac{-6(3^{10}-1)}{-2} = 3(3^{10}-1) = 177\,144.$$

Example 25.3.6
Find a simple expression for the sum $p^6 - p^5q + p^4q^2 - p^3q^3 + p^2q^4 - pq^5 + q^6$.

This is a geometric series of 7 terms, with first term p^6 and common ratio $-\frac{q}{p}$. Its sum is therefore

$$\frac{p^6(1-(-q/p)^7)}{1-(-q/p)} = \frac{p^6(1-(-q^7/p^7))}{1+q/p} = \frac{p^7(1+q^7/p^7)}{p(1+q/p)} = \frac{p^7+q^7}{p+q}.$$

Another way of writing the result of this example is

$$p^7 + q^7 = (p+q)(p^6 - p^5q + p^4q^2 - p^3q^3 + p^2q^4 - pq^5 + q^6).$$

You can use a similar method for any odd number n to express $p^n + q^n$ as the product of $p+q$ and another factor.

Exercise 25B

1 Find the sum, for the given number of terms, of each of the following geometric series. Give decimal answers correct to 4 places.

(a) $2 + 6 + 18 + \ldots$ 10 terms
(b) $2 - 6 + 18 - \ldots$ 10 terms
(c) $1 + \frac{1}{2} + \frac{1}{4} + \ldots$ 8 terms
(d) $1 - \frac{1}{2} + \frac{1}{4} - \ldots$ 8 terms
(e) $3 + 6 + 12 + \ldots$ 12 terms
(f) $12 - 4 + \frac{4}{3} - \ldots$ 10 terms

2 Find the sum of each of the following geometric series.

(a) $1 + 2 + 4 + \ldots + 1024$
(b) $1 - 2 + 4 - \ldots + 1024$
(c) $3 + 12 + 48 + \ldots + 196\,608$
(d) $1 + \frac{1}{2} + \frac{1}{4} + \ldots + \frac{1}{512}$
(e) $1 - \frac{1}{3} + \frac{1}{9} - \ldots - \frac{1}{19\,683}$
(f) $1 + \frac{1}{2} + \frac{1}{4} + \ldots + \frac{1}{2^n}$

3 Find the sum of each of the following geometric series. Give numerical answers as rational numbers.

(a) $\sum_{i=1}^{5} 3 \times 2^{i-1}$
(b) $\sum_{i=1}^{4} 2 \times (-2)^{i-1}$
(c) $\sum_{i=1}^{8} 16 \times (\frac{1}{2})^{i-1}$
(d) $\sum_{i=1}^{7} 4^i$

4 A well-known story concerns the inventor of the game of chess. As a reward for inventing the game it is rumoured that he was asked to choose his own prize. He asked for 1 grain of rice to be placed on the first square of the board, 2 grains on the second square, 4 grains on the third square and so on in geometric progression until all 64 squares had been covered. Calculate the total number of grains of rice he would have received. Give your answer in standard form!

5 A problem similar to that of Question 4 is posed by the child who negotiates a pocket money deal of 1 cent on 1 February, 2 cents on 2 February, 4 cents on 3 February and so on for 28 days. How much should the child receive in total during February?

6 A firm sponsors a local orchestra for seven years. It agrees to give \$2500 in the first year, and to increase its contribution by 20% each year. Show that the amounts contributed each year form a geometric sequence. How much does the firm give the orchestra altogether during the period of sponsorship?

7 An explorer sets out across the desert with 100 litres of water. He uses 6 litres on the first day. On subsequent days he rations himself to 95% of the amount he used the day before. Show that he has enough water to last for 34 days, but no more. How much will he then have left?

8 A competitor in a pie-eating contest eats one-third of his pie in the first minute. In each subsequent minute he eats three-quarters of the amount he ate in the previous minute. Find an expression for the amount of pie he has left to eat after n minutes. Show that he takes between 4 and 5 minutes to finish the pie.

9 Find expressions for the sum of n terms of the following series. Give your answer, in terms of n and x, in as simple a form as possible.

(a) $x + x^2 + x^3 + \ldots$ n terms (b) $x - x^2 + x^3 - \ldots$ n terms

25.4 Convergent geometric series

Take any sequence, such as the sequence of triangle numbers $t_1 = 1$, $t_2 = 3$, $t_3 = 6$, ... (see Section 2.3). Form a new sequence whose terms are the sums of successive triangle numbers:

$$S_1 = t_1 = 1, \quad S_2 = t_1 + t_2 = 1 + 3 = 4, \quad S_3 = t_1 + t_2 + t_3 = 1 + 3 + 6 = 10, \text{ and so on.}$$

This is called the sum sequence of the original sequence.

Notice that $S_2 = S_1 + t_2$, $S_3 = S_2 + t_3$, ...

This property can be used to give an inductive definition for the sum sequence of any sequence u_i:

For a given sequence u_i, the **sum sequence** $S_n = u_1 + \ldots + u_n$ is defined by $S_1 = u_1$ and $S_n = S_{n-1} + u_n$.

(If the original sequence begins with u_0 rather than u_1, the equation $S_1 = u_1$ in the definition is replaced by $S_0 = u_0$.)

Example 25.4.1

A sequence is given by the formula $u_n = n^3$ for $n = 1, 2, 3, \ldots$. Find the first five terms of its sum sequence.

The terms of the sequence u_n are

$$u_1 = 1, \quad u_2 = 8, \quad u_3 = 27, \quad u_4 = 64, \quad u_5 = 125, \quad \ldots .$$

So the terms of the sum sequence S_n are

$$S_1 = 1, \quad S_2 = 1 + 8 = 9, \quad S_3 = 9 + 27 = 36,$$
$$S_4 = 36 + 64 = 100, \quad S_5 = 100 + 125 = 225, \quad \ldots .$$

What general rule does this suggest?

The inductive definition for a sum sequence can be used to obtain its graph. For example, for the geometric sequence given by $u_i = 10 \times 1.1^{i-1}$, whose graph was shown in Fig. 25.1, the sum sequence is defined inductively by

$$S_1 = 10, \quad S_n = S_{n-1} + 10 \times 1.1^{n-1}.$$

Use your calculator to show the graph of the sequence S_n. You will get a display like Fig. 25.6.

This is not very interesting. But if you carry out the same procedure for the sequence whose graph was shown in Fig. 25.2, with 1.1 replaced by 0.9, the result is more surprising. The equations

$$S_1 = 10, \quad S_n = S_{n-1} + 10 \times 0.9^{n-1}$$

produce a display like Fig. 25.7.

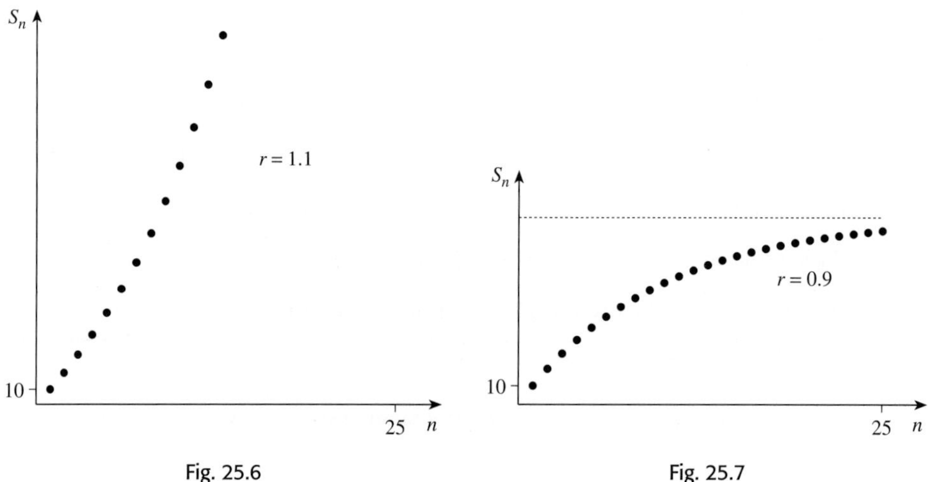

Fig. 25.6

Fig. 25.7

This looks as if it might converge to a limit. To check this, add a horizontal line to the display, and move it up the window until it appears to lie above all the points of the graph.

This is the dotted line in Fig. 25.7. What does this suggest for the limit of S_n?

You can check this by using the formula for S_n, with $a = 10$ and $r = 0.9$. This gives

$$\begin{aligned} S_n &= \frac{10\,(1 - 0.9^n)}{1 - 0.9} \\ &= \frac{10\,(1 - 0.9^n)}{0.1} \\ &= 100 - 100 \times 0.9^n. \end{aligned}$$

Now when n is a large number, 0.9^n becomes very small. (Try calculating 0.9^{1000}.) In the limit, as n tends to infinity, 0.9^n tends to 0. So

$$\lim_{n \to \infty} S_n = 100.$$

Does this agree with the estimate you made from the graph of S_n?

Something similar happens with the sequence whose graph was shown in Fig. 25.4, with common ratio -0.9. The equations

$$S_1 = 10, \quad S_n = S_{n-1} + 10 \times (-0.9)^{n-1}$$

produce a display like Fig. 25.8.

This also seems to be converging to a limit; but to find this limit you have to squeeze the horizontal line between the sequence of points for odd n and the sequence for even n. It is not so easy to guess the value of this limit.

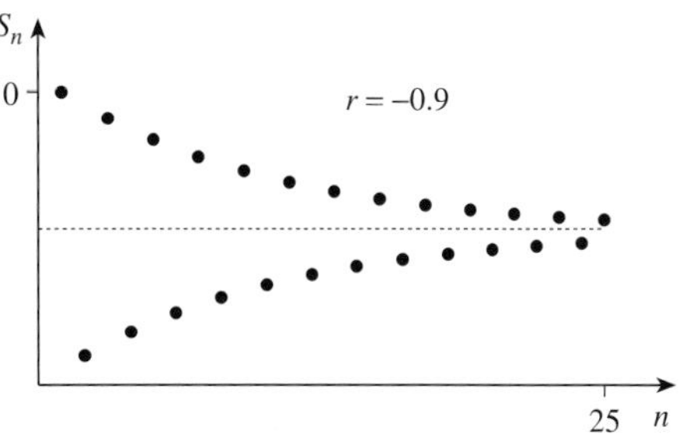

Fig. 25.8

The formula for S_n is now

$$S_n = \frac{10(1-(-0.9)^n)}{1-(-0.9)}$$
$$= \tfrac{100}{19} - \tfrac{100}{19} \times (-0.9)^n.$$

Now $(-0.9)^n$ is positive if n is even and negative if n is odd. So S_n is less than $\frac{100}{19}$ if n is even, and greater if n is odd. Also $(-0.9)^n$ tends to 0 as n tends to infinity. So

$$\lim_{n\to\infty} S_n = \tfrac{100}{19} = 5.263\ldots .$$

How close is this to your estimate from the graph?

By now you will see how the argument goes in general. The sum sequence for the general sequence $u_i = ar^{i-1}$ is given by

$$S_n = \frac{a(1-r^n)}{1-r}$$
$$= \frac{a}{1-r} - \frac{a}{1-r} \times r^n.$$

The only part of this expression which involves n is r^n. Whether or not S_n tends to a limit depends on the size of r, or more precisely on the size of $|r|$. If $|r| > 1$, then $|r^n|$ increases without limit as n increases. But if $|r| < 1$, then r^n tends to 0 as n tends to infinity. In that case,

$$\lim_{n\to\infty} S_n = \frac{a}{1-r}.$$

If $-1 < r < 1$, the sum of the geometric series with first term a and common ratio r tends to the limit $S_\infty = \dfrac{a}{1-r}$ as the number of terms tends to infinity.

The infinite geometric series is then said to be **convergent**.

S_∞ is called the **sum to infinity** of the series.

Example 25.4.2

A geometric series begins $9 + 6 + 4 + \ldots$. Find an expression for the sum of the first n terms. Show that the series is convergent, and find the sum to infinity.

The series has common ratio $\frac{6}{9} = \frac{2}{3}$. Since $a = 9$, the sum of the first n terms is

$$\frac{9(1 - (\frac{2}{3})^n)}{1 - \frac{2}{3}} = \frac{9}{\frac{1}{3}}(1 - (\tfrac{2}{3})^n) = 27(1 - (\tfrac{2}{3})^n).$$

Since the common ratio is between -1 and 1, the series is convergent. The sum to infinity is

$$\frac{9}{1 - \frac{2}{3}} = \frac{9}{\frac{1}{3}} = 27.$$

Example 25.4.3

The first term of a convergent geometric series is 20, and its sum to infinity is 15. Find the common ratio, and an expression for the sum of the first n terms.

If the common ratio is r,

$$\frac{20}{1 - r} = 15.$$

So

$$\begin{aligned} 20 &= 15 - 15r, \\ 15r &= -5, \\ r &= -\tfrac{1}{3}. \end{aligned}$$

The sum of the first n terms is therefore

$$\frac{20\,(1 - (-\frac{1}{3})^n)}{1 - (-\frac{1}{3})} = \frac{20}{\frac{4}{3}}\,(1 - (-\tfrac{1}{3})^n) = 15\,(1 - (-\tfrac{1}{3})^n).$$

Example 25.4.4

Express the recurring decimal 0.296 296 296... as a fraction.

The decimal can be written as

$$\begin{aligned} &0.296 + 0.000\,296 + 0.000\,000\,296 + \ldots \\ &\quad = 0.296 + 0.296 \times 0.001 + 0.296 \times (0.001)^2 + \ldots, \end{aligned}$$

which is a geometric series with $a = 0.296$ and $r = 0.001$. Since $-1 < r < 1$, the series is convergent with limiting sum $\frac{0.296}{1 - 0.001} = \frac{296}{999}$.

Since $296 = 8 \times 37$ and $999 = 27 \times 37$, this fraction in its simplest form is $\frac{8}{27}$.

Example 25.4.5

A beetle starts at a point O on the floor. It walks 1 m east, then $\frac{1}{2}$ m west, then $\frac{1}{4}$ m east, and so on, halving the distance at each change of direction. How far from O does it end up?

The final distance from O is $1 - \frac{1}{2} + \frac{1}{4} - \frac{1}{8} + \ldots$, which is a geometric series with common ratio $-\frac{1}{2}$. Since $-1 < -\frac{1}{2} < 1$, the series converges to a limit

$$\frac{1}{1 - (-1/2)} = \frac{1}{3/2} = \frac{2}{3}.$$

The beetle ends up $\frac{2}{3}$ m from O.

Notice that a point of trisection was obtained as the limit of a process of repeated halving.

Here is a summary of what you now know about a geometric sequence u_n. You may if you prefer use u_1 rather than a to denote the first term. The properties then take the form:

For $n = 1, 2, 3, \ldots$, the nth term is $u_n = u_1 r^{n-1}$, where $r \neq 0$ or 1.

The sum of n terms is $S_n = \dfrac{u_1(1 - r^n)}{1 - r}$.

(If $r > 1$, you may prefer to use this in the form $S_n = \dfrac{u_1(r^n - 1)}{r - 1}$.)

If $|r| < 1$, this sum converges to the limit $S_\infty = \dfrac{u_1}{1 - r}$.

25.5 Using sigma notation

Sigma notation can be used to represent a sum to infinity for a convergent series. The sum to infinity of a series with general term u_i is written as $\sum_{i=1}^{\infty} u_i$. In the case of a convergent geometric series with common ratio r such that $-1 < r < 1$, the ith term is ar^{i-1}. So the sum to infinity is

$$\sum_{i=1}^{\infty} ar^{i-1}.$$

If $-1 < r < 1$, $\sum_{i=1}^{\infty} ar^{i-1} = \dfrac{a}{1 - r}$.

Example 25.5.1
The ith term of a geometric progression is $\left(\frac{1}{4}\right)^i$. Find the first term, the common ratio and $\sum_{i=1}^{\infty} \left(\frac{1}{4}\right)^i$.

The series begins

$$\left(\tfrac{1}{4}\right)^1 + \left(\tfrac{1}{4}\right)^2 + \left(\tfrac{1}{4}\right)^3 + \ldots = \tfrac{1}{4} + \tfrac{1}{16} + \tfrac{1}{64} + \ldots.$$

The first term is $\frac{1}{4}$, and the common ratio is $\frac{1}{16} \div \frac{1}{4} = \frac{1}{4}$.

Using the formula $\sum_{i=1}^{\infty} ar^{i-1} = \dfrac{a}{1 - r}$ with $a = \frac{1}{4}$ and $r = \frac{1}{4}$,

$$\sum_{i=1}^{\infty} \left(\tfrac{1}{4}\right)^i = \frac{\frac{1}{4}}{1 - \frac{1}{4}} = \tfrac{1}{3}.$$

Exercise 25C

1 Find the sum to infinity of the following geometric series. Give your answers to parts (a) to (j) as whole numbers, fractions or exact decimals.

(a) $1+\frac{1}{2}+\frac{1}{4}+\ldots$

(b) $1+\frac{1}{3}+\frac{1}{9}+\ldots$

(c) $\frac{1}{5}+\frac{1}{25}+\frac{1}{125}+\ldots$

(d) $0.1+0.01+0.001+\ldots$

(e) $1-\frac{1}{3}+\frac{1}{9}-\ldots$

(f) $0.2-0.04+0.008-\ldots$

(g) $\frac{3}{2}+\frac{3}{4}+\frac{3}{8}+\ldots$

(h) $\frac{1}{2}-\frac{1}{4}+\frac{1}{8}-\ldots$

(i) $10-5+2.5-\ldots$

(j) $50+10+2+\ldots$

(k) $x+x^2+x^3+\ldots$, where $-1<x<1$

(l) $1-x^2+x^4-\ldots$, where $x^2<1$

(m) $1+x^{-1}+x^{-2}+\ldots$, where $x>1$

(n) $x^2-x+1-\ldots$, where $x>1$

2 Express each of the following recurring decimals as exact fractions.

(a) 0.363 636...

(b) 0.123 123 123...

(c) 0.555...

(d) 0.471 471 471...

(e) 0.142 857 142 857 142 857...

(f) 0.285 714 285 714 285 714...

(g) 0.714 285 714 285 714 285...

(h) 0.857 142 857 142 857 142...

3 Find the common ratio of a geometric series which has a first term of 5 and a sum to infinity of 6.

4 Find the common ratio of a geometric series which has a first term of 11 and a sum to infinity of 6.

5 Find the first term of a geometric series which has a common ratio of $\frac{3}{4}$ and a sum to infinity of 12.

6 Find the first term of a geometric series which has a common ratio of $-\frac{3}{5}$ and a sum to infinity of 12.

7 Identify the general term u_i for the following geometric progressions. Also find $\sum_{i=1}^{10} u_i$ and, if the series is convergent, $\sum_{i=1}^{\infty} u_i$.

(a) $1+\frac{1}{5}+\frac{1}{25}+\frac{1}{125}+\ldots$

(b) $2+4+8+16+\ldots$

(c) $4+2+1+\frac{1}{2}+\frac{1}{4}+\ldots$

(d) $1-\frac{1}{10}+\frac{1}{100}-\frac{1}{1000}+\ldots$

8 In Example 25.4.5 a beetle starts at a point O on the floor. It walks 1 m east, then $\frac{1}{2}$ m west, then $\frac{1}{4}$ m east and so on. It finishes $\frac{2}{3}$ m to the east of O. How far does it actually walk?

9 A beetle starts at a point O on the floor and walks 0.6 m east, then 0.36 m west, 0.216 m east and so on. Find its final position and how far it actually walks.

10 A 'supa-ball' is thrown upwards from ground level. It hits the ground after 2 seconds and continues to bounce. The time it is in the air for a particular bounce is always 0.8 of the time for the previous bounce. How long does it take for the ball to stop bouncing?

11 A 'supa-ball' is dropped from a height of 1 metre onto a level table. It always rises to a height equal to 0.9 of the height from which it was dropped. How far does it travel in total until it stops bouncing?

12 A frog sits at one end of a table which is 2 m long. In its first jump the frog goes a distance of 1 m along the table, with its second jump $\frac{1}{2}$ m, with its third jump $\frac{1}{4}$ m and so on.

(a) What is the frog's final position?

(b) After how many jumps will the frog be within 1 cm of the far end of the table?

26 Exponentials and logarithms

In this chapter a new type of function is introduced which has many important applications. When you have completed it, you should

- know what is meant by an exponential function, and be familiar with the shape of exponential graphs
- know what is meant by a logarithm, and be able to switch between the exponential and the logarithmic form of an equation
- know the rules for logarithms, and how they can be proved from the rules for indices
- understand the idea of a logarithmic scale
- be able to solve equations and inequalities in which the unknown appears as an index.

26.1 Exponential functions

What are the next two numbers in the sequence which begins

$$1 \qquad 1.2 \qquad 1.44 \qquad 1.728 \qquad \ldots ?$$

This looks like a geometric sequence, with first term 1 and common ratio 1.2. With this interpretation, the next two numbers would be $1.728 \times 1.2 = 2.0736$ and $2.0736 \times 1.2 = 2.488\,32$.

You could also write the sequence as

$$1.2^0 \qquad 1.2^1 \qquad 1.2^2 \qquad 1.2^3 \qquad \ldots .$$

This suggests thinking of the sequence as a function

$$f(x) = 1.2^x$$

which is defined for values of x which are positive integers or zero. Its graph is shown in Fig. 26.1. It consists of a lot of isolated points, one for each natural number.

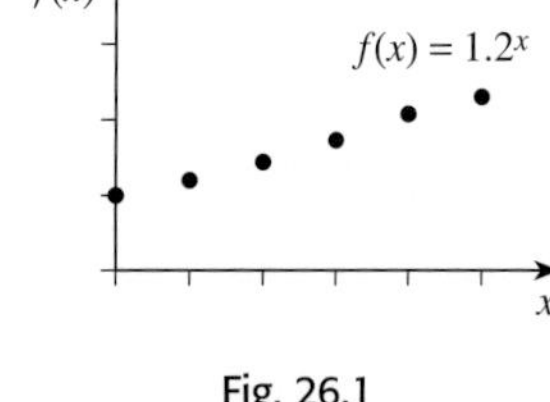

Fig. 26.1

But regarding 1.2^x as a function, there is no need to restrict x to being either an integer or positive. You know how to find 1.2^x for many other values of x. For example,

$$1.2^{\frac{1}{2}} = \sqrt{1.2} = 1.095\ldots, \qquad 1.2^{-1} = \frac{1}{1.2} = 0.833\ldots,$$

$$1.2^{0.8} = 1.2^{\frac{4}{5}} = \sqrt[5]{1.2^4} = 1.157\ldots, \qquad 1.2^{-3.5} = \frac{1}{1.2^{3.5}} = \frac{1}{1.2^3 \times \sqrt{1.2}} = 0.528\ldots, \text{ etc.}$$

In fact, the extension of index notation in Chapter 13 provides a definition of 1.2^x where x is any rational number, positive or negative. If you fill in all these additional values you get the graph in Fig. 26.2.

The only values of x for which 1.2^x doesn't yet have a meaning are the irrational numbers, like π or $\sqrt{2}$. So far you don't have a definition for powers such as 1.2^π or $1.2^{\sqrt{2}}$. This means that the graph in Fig. 26.2 has gaps in it, though you can't see them! In fact there is a way of defining expressions like b^x when x is any real number, which behave in just the same way as when x is rational. For the time being you can assume that this is true.

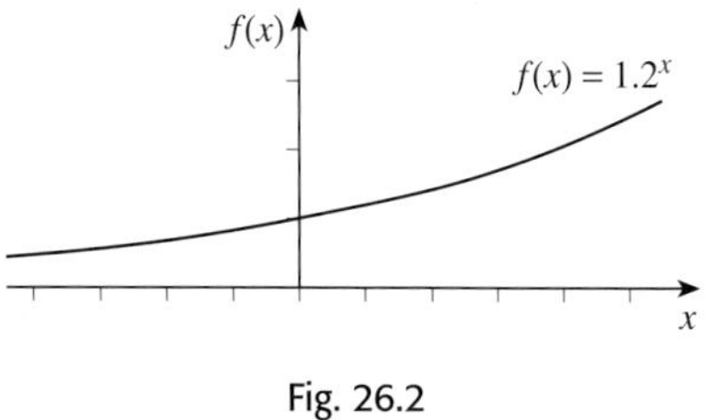

Fig. 26.2

The function 1.2^x is an example of an 'exponential function'. The reason for this name is that the variable x appears as an index, and 'exponent' is an alternative word for the index in an expression like b^x.

An **exponential function** is a function of the form $f(x) = b^x$, where b is a positive real number and $b \neq 1$. The number b is called the **base**.

Notice the restrictions on the value of b in this definition. Negative numbers are excluded because, if $b < 0$, b^x has no meaning for some values of x; for example, $b^{\frac{1}{2}} = \sqrt{b}$ does not exist if $b < 0$. Zero is excluded for a similar reason; for example $b^{-1} = \frac{1}{b}$, and $\frac{1}{0}$ does not exist. The number 1 is also excluded, but for a different reason; since $1^x = 1$ for every value of x, the function 1^x is simply the constant number 1.

Before reading on, use your calculator to display some exponential functions with different bases. Choose an interval with both negative and positive values of x. Use some values of b greater than 1, and some between 0 and 1.

Fig. 26.3 shows the graphs of some typical exponential functions for different values of b. From these you will notice that they have a number of properties in common.

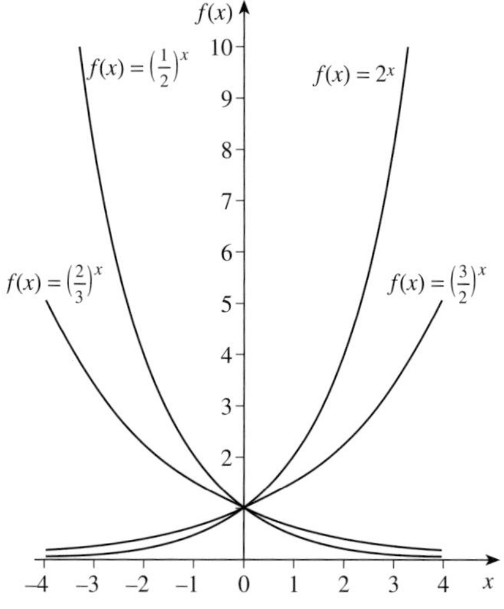

Fig. 26.3

- The point (0, 1) lies on all the graphs, because $b^0 = 1$ for all positive numbers b.
- The graph of $y = b^x$ lies entirely above the x-axis, and the x-axis is an asymptote.
- If $b > 1$ the graph of $y = b^x$ has positive gradient, so the function is increasing. If $0 < b < 1$ the graph has negative gradient, so the function is decreasing.
- The graph of $y = b^x$ is concave up both for $b > 1$ and for $0 < b < 1$.
- If $b > 1$ the graph approaches the x-axis when x is negative and numerically large; if $0 < b < 1$, the graph approaches the x-axis when x is positive and numerically large.
- The graph of $y = \left(\frac{1}{b}\right)^x$ is the reflection in the y-axis of the graph of $y = b^x$.

To prove the last statement, use the rules of indices (Chapter 13) to show that

$$b^{-h} = \frac{1}{b^h} = \left(\frac{1}{b}\right)^h.$$

So the value of $\left(\frac{1}{b}\right)^x$ when $x = h$ is the same as the value of b^x when $x = -h$. Since this is true for any number h, the reflection in the y-axis of $y = b^x$ is $y = \left(\frac{1}{b}\right)^x$.

Exercise 26A

1 If $2^{-x} < 10^{-3}$, what can you say about 2^x?

Find the smallest integer x such that 2^{-x} is less than

(a) 10^{-3}, (b) 10^{-6}, (c) 10^{-12}.

2 If $3^x < 0.0005$, what can you say about 3^{-x}?

Find the largest integer x such that 3^x is less than

(a) 0.0005, (b) 2.5×10^{-7}, (c) 10^{-7}.

3 (a) Use your calculator to display, with the same axes, the graphs of $y = 1.1^x$ and $y = 1.21^x$.

(b) Show that $1.1^h = 1.21^{\frac{1}{2}h}$. Draw a diagram to illustrate this property.

4 (a) Use your calculator to display, with the same axes, the graphs of $y = 1.25^x$ and $y = 0.8^x$.

(b) Show that $1.25^x = 0.8^{-x}$. What does this tell you about the graphs in part (a)?

26.2 Logarithms

You have seen that, if $b > 1$, then $y = b^x$ increases over all values of x; if $0 < b < 1$ it decreases. This means that in either case, if y is any positive number, there can only be one number x such that $b^x = y$. This number is called the **logarithm to base *b*** of y. It is written $x = \log_b y$.

If x is a real number and y is a positive real number, the statements

$$b^x = y \quad \text{and} \quad x = \log_b y$$

are equivalent.

In words, you can say that

$\log_b y$ is the power to which b must be raised to give y.

Example 26.2.1

Find (a) $\log_3 81$, (b) $\log_{81} 3$, (c) $\log_3\left(\frac{1}{81}\right)$, (d) $\log_{\frac{1}{3}} 81$.

(a) Since $81 = 3^4$, $\log_3 81 = 4$. The power to which 3 must be raised to give 81 is 4.

(b) $3 = 81^{\frac{1}{4}}$, so $\log_{81} 3 = \frac{1}{4}$.

(c) $\frac{1}{81} = 3^{-4}$, so $\log_3\left(\frac{1}{81}\right) = -4$.

(d) $81 = \dfrac{1}{\left(\frac{1}{3}\right)^4} = \left(\frac{1}{3}\right)^{-4}$, so $\log_{\frac{1}{3}} 81 = -4$.

It is important to notice that the logarithm exists only if y is positive, because (for any base b) the graph of $y = b^x$ lies entirely above the x-axis.

Some important results about logarithms follow from what you already know about indices. Here are some examples.

Putting $x = 0$, since $b^0 = 1$, it follows that $0 = \log_b 1$.

Putting $x = 1$ gives $b^1 = b$, so that $1 = \log_b b$.

Putting $x = 2$ gives $b^2 = y$, so that $2 = \log_b b^2$.

More generally,

putting $x = n$ gives $b^n = y$, so that $n = \log_b b^n$.

For any base b,

$$\log_b 1 = 0, \quad \log_b b = 1 \quad \text{and} \quad \log_b b^n = n.$$

The result $\log_b b^n = n$ is not restricted to integer values of n; it is true when n is any real number. If in the box at the beginning of this section you substitute b^x for y in the second statement you get

$$x = \log_b b^x.$$

And if you substitute $\log_b y$ for x in the first statement you get

$$b^{\log_b y} = y.$$

These statements are true for any number x and for any positive number. What they say, in effect, is that the processes of 'raising to a power' and 'taking logarithms' cancel each other out. If you carry out one after the other, in either order, you get back to where you started.

For any base b,

$$\log_b b^x = x \quad \text{and} \quad b^{\log_b y} = y.$$

Try this with a calculator. The key labelled [log] calculates the logarithm to base 10. Choose a number, x, calculate 10^x, then calculate log(answer). Or choose a number, y, calculate $\log(y)$ then calculate 10^{answer}.

Exercise 26B

1 Write each of the following in the form $y = b^x$.

(a) $\log_2 8 = 3$ (b) $\log_3 81 = 4$ (c) $\log_5 0.04 = -2$

(d) $\log_7 x = 4$ (e) $\log_x 5 = t$ (f) $\log_p q = r$

2 Write each of the following in the form $x = \log_b y$.

(a) $2^3 = 8$ (b) $3^6 = 729$ (c) $4^{-3} = \frac{1}{64}$

(d) $a^8 = 20$ (e) $h^9 = g$ (f) $m^n = p$

3 Evaluate the following.

(a) $\log_2 16$ (b) $\log_4 16$ (c) $\log_7 \frac{1}{49}$

(d) $\log_4 1$ (e) $\log_5 5$ (f) $\log_{27} \frac{1}{3}$

(g) $\log_{16} 8$ (h) $\log_2 2\sqrt{2}$ (i) $\log_{\sqrt{2}} 8\sqrt{2}$

4 Find the value of y in each of the following.

(a) $\log_y 49 = 2$ (b) $\log_4 y = -3$ (c) $\log_3 243 = y$

(d) $\log_{10} y = -1$ (e) $\log_2 y = 2.5$ (f) $\log_y 1296 = 4$

(g) $\log_{\frac{1}{2}} y = 8$ (h) $\log_{\frac{1}{2}} 1024 = y$ (i) $\log_y 27 = -6$

26.3 Properties of logarithms

It was shown in Section 13.1 that expressions involving indices can be simplified by applying a number of rules, such as the multiplication and division rules and the power-on-power rule. There are corresponding rules for logarithms.

The multiplication rule for indices states that $b^r \times b^s = b^{r+s}$. Using $f(x)$ to denote the function b^x, this could be written as

$$f(r) \times f(s) = f(r + s).$$

So this rule equates the *product* of values of the function for two values of x to the value of the function for their *sum*.

Logarithms do the opposite. The rule for logarithms equates the *sum* of values of the function $\log_b x$ for two values of x to the value of the function for their *product*. That is,

$$\log_b p + \log_b q = \log_b(p \times q).$$

This is the multiplication rule for logarithms. There is also a division rule and a power rule.

For any positive real numbers p and q, any real number x, and logarithms to any base:

The multiplication rule $\log_b(pq) = \log_b p + \log_b q$

The division rule $\log_b\left(\frac{p}{q}\right) = \log_b p - \log_b q$

The power rule $\log_b(p^x) = x\log_b p$

Example 26.3.1
If $\log_b 2 = r$ and $\log_b 3 = s$, express in terms of r and s

(a) $\log_b 16$, (b) $\log_b 18$, (c) $\log_b 13.5$.

(a) $\log_b 16 = \log_b 2^4 = 4\log_b 2 = 4r$.

(b) $\log_b 18 = \log_b(2 \times 3^2) = \log_b 2 + \log_b 3^2 = \log_b 2 + 2\log_b 3 = r + 2s$.

(c) $\log_b 13.5 = \log_b \frac{3^3}{2} = \log_b 3^3 - \log_b 2 = 3\log_b 3 - \log_b 2 = 3s - r$.

Example 26.3.2
Find $\log_{10} 50 + \log_{10} 8000 - 2\log_{10} 20$.

Use the power rule, then the multiplication and division rules.

$$2\log_{10} 20 = \log_{10} 20^2 = \log_{10} 400,$$

so

$$\begin{aligned}\log_{10} 50 + \log_{10} 8000 - 2\log_{10} 20 &= \log_{10} 50 + \log_{10} 8000 - \log_{10} 400\\ &= \log_{10}\left(\frac{50 \times 8000}{400}\right)\\ &= \log_{10} 1000\\ &= 3,\end{aligned}$$

since $10^3 = 1000$.

Example 26.3.3
Express $\log_b\left(\frac{p^3 q}{r^2}\right)$ in terms of $\log_b p$, $\log_b q$ and $\log_b r$.

$$\begin{aligned}\log_b\left(\frac{p^3 q}{r^2}\right) &= \log_b(p^3) + \log_b q - \log_b(r^2)\\ &= 3\log_b p + \log_b q - 2\log_b r.\end{aligned}$$

Example 26.3.4
Express as a single logarithm (a) $2\log_b x - 3\log_b y$, (b) $\frac{1}{3}\log_b 64$.

(a) $2\log_b x - 3\log_b y = \log_b(x^2) - \log_b(y^3) = \log_b\left(\frac{x^2}{y^3}\right)$.

(b) $\frac{1}{3}\log_b 64 = \log_b 64^{\frac{1}{3}} = \log_b \sqrt[3]{64} = \log_b 4$.

A useful special case of the power rule is when x is a fraction $\frac{1}{n}$ where n is a positive integer.

Then $p^x = p^{\frac{1}{n}} = \sqrt[n]{p}$, so you get:

The nth root rule $\quad \log_b \sqrt[n]{p} = \dfrac{\log_b p}{n}$

Historically logarithms were important because for many years, before calculators and computers were available, they provided the most useful form of calculating aid. With a table of logarithms students would, for example, find the cube root of 100 by looking up the value of log 100 and dividing it by 3. By the nth root rule, this gave $\log \sqrt[3]{100}$, and the cube root could then be obtained by using the logarithm table in reverse or from a table of the function 10^x.

The rules for logarithms can be proved directly from the definition of a logarithm and the rules for indices.

Proof of the multiplication and division rules

Denote $\log_b p$ by r and $\log_b q$ by s. Then, in exponential form, $p = b^r$ and $q = b^s$. So, using the multiplication and division rules for indices,

$$pq = b^r \times b^s = b^{r+s} \quad \text{and} \quad \frac{p}{q} = \frac{b^r}{b^s} = b^{r-s}.$$

Putting these back into logarithmic form gives

$$\log_b(pq) = r + s, \qquad \text{which is} \quad \log_b p + \log_b q,$$

and $$\log_b\left(\frac{p}{q}\right) = r - s, \qquad \text{which is} \quad \log_b p - \log_b q.$$

Proof of the power rule

Denote $\log_b p$ by r. Then $p = b^r$. So, using the power-on-power rule for indices,

$$p^x = (b^r)^x = b^{rx} = b^{xr}.$$

Putting this back into logarithmic form gives

$$\log_b(p^x) = xr, \qquad \text{which is} \quad x \log_b p.$$

26.4 Special bases

Although the base of a logarithm can be any real positive number except 1, only two bases are in common use. One is a number denoted by e, for which the logarithm has a number of special properties; these are explored in Chapter 32. Logarithms to base e are denoted by 'ln', and can be found using the [ln] key on your calculator.

The other base is 10, which is important because our system of writing numbers is based on powers of 10. On your calculator the key labelled [log] gives logarithms to base 10.

From now on, when you see the symbol log by itself without a base, it will mean $\log_{10}$.

When logarithms were used to do calculations, students used tables which gave $\log_{10} x$ only for values of x between 1 and 10. So to find log 3456, they would use the rules in Section 26.3 to write

$$\log 3456 = \log(3.456 \times 10^3) = \log 3.456 + \log 10^3 = \log 3.456 + 3.$$

The tables gave log 3.456 as 0.5386 (correct to 4 decimal places), so log 3456 is 3.5386. Notice that the number 3 before the decimal point is the same as the index when 3456 is written in standard form.

Logarithms to base 10 are sometimes useful in constructing logarithmic scales. As an example, suppose that you want to make a diagram to show the populations of countries which belong to the United Nations. In 1999 the largest of these was China, with about 1.2 billion people, and the smallest was San Marino, with 25 000. If you represented the population of China by a line of length 12 cm, then Nigeria would have length 1.1 cm, Malaysia just over 2 mm, and the line for San Marino would be only 0.0025 mm long!

Fig. 26.4 is an alternative way of showing the data.

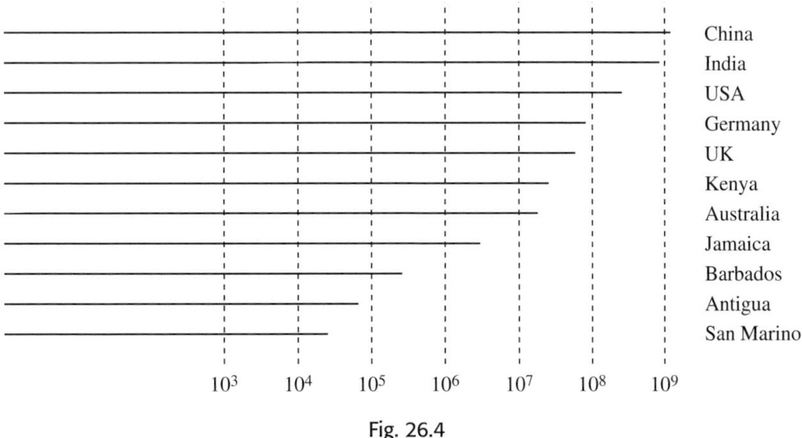

Fig. 26.4

Fig. 26.4 uses a logarithmic scale, in which a country with population P is shown by a line of length $\log_{10} P$ cm. China now has a length of just over 9 cm, and San Marino a length of between 4 and 5 cm. You have to understand the diagram in a different way; an extra centimetre in length implies a population 10 times as large, rather than 100 million larger. But the countries are still placed in the correct order, and the population of any country can be found as 10^x where x is the length of its line in centimetres.

Exercise 26C

1 Write each of the following in terms of $\log_b p$, $\log_b q$ and $\log_b r$. In parts (c), (h) and (i) the logarithms are to base 10; p, q and r are positive numbers.

(a) $\log_b pqr$ (b) $\log_b pq^2r^3$ (c) $\log 100pr^5$

(d) $\log_b \sqrt{\frac{p}{q^2r}}$ (e) $\log_b \frac{pq}{r^2}$ (f) $\log_b \frac{1}{pqr}$

(g) $\log_b \frac{p}{\sqrt{r}}$ (h) $\log \frac{qr^7p}{10}$ (i) $\log \sqrt{\frac{10p^{10}r}{q}}$

2 Express as a single logarithm, simplifying where possible. (All the logarithms have base 10, so, for example, an answer of log 100 simplifies to 2.)

(a) $2\log 5 + \log 4$ (b) $2\log 2 + \log 150 - \log 6000$

(c) $3\log 5 + 5\log 3$ (d) $2\log 4 - 4\log 2$

(e) $\log 24 - \frac{1}{2}\log 9 + \log 125$ (f) $3\log 2 + 3\log 5 - \log 10^6$

(g) $\frac{1}{2}\log 16 + \frac{1}{3}\log 8$ (h) $\log 64 - 2\log 4 + 5\log 2 - \log 2^7$

3 If $\log_b 3 = p$, $\log_b 5 = q$ and $\log_b 10 = r$, express the following in terms of p, q and r.

(a) $\log_b 2$ (b) $\log_b 45$ (c) $\log_b \sqrt{90}$

(d) $\log_b 0.2$ (e) $\log_b 750$ (f) $\log_b 60$

(g) $\log_b \frac{1}{6}$ (h) $\log_b 4.05$ (i) $\log_b 0.15$

4 Show that the rule $\log_b b^x = x$ in Section 26.2 is a special case of the power rule $\log_b(p^x) = x\log_b p$.

5 Suppose that $\log_b c = r$ and $\log_c b = s$. Write these equations in their equivalent exponential forms, and use the rules for indices to show that $rs = 1$. Write this result as an identity connecting $\log_b c$ and $\log_c b$.

6* The acidity of a substance is measured by a quantity called pH. This is defined as the value of $-\log_{10} a_{H+}$, where a_{H+} is the hydrogen ion activity in the substance. The values of pH for a cola drink and for beer are approximately 2 and 5 respectively. What does this mean in terms of the relative levels of hydrogen ion activity in the two drinks?

7* Earthquakes are recorded on a seismograph, which records surface waves whose amplitudes depend on the strength of the earthquake. The magnitude of an earthquake on the Richter scale is given by the formula $\log_{10}(k \times \text{amplitude of the surface wave})$, where k is a constant.

(a) Two earthquakes produce surface waves whose amplitudes are in the ratio 3 : 1. How do their magnitudes on the Richter scale compare?

(b) Two earthquakes have magnitudes 6.9 and 7.5 on the Richter scale. How do the amplitudes of the recorded surface waves compare?

26.5 Equations and inequalities

You know that $\log_2 2 = 1$ and $\log_2 4 = 2$, but how can you find $\log_2 3$?

Suppose that $\log_2 3 = x$. Then from the definition,

$$2^x = 3.$$

So the problem is to solve an equation where the unknown appears in the index.

The trick is to use logarithms and to write the equation as

$$\log_b 2^x = \log_b 3.$$

This is often described as 'taking logarithms of both sides of the equation'. You can now use the power rule to write this as

$$x \log_b 2 = \log_b 3.$$

In this equation you can use logarithms to any base you like. In this section base 10 will be used. The log key on the calculator gives $\log 2 = 0.301...$ and $\log 3 = 0.477....$ So

$$x \times 0.301... = 0.477...,$$

which gives $x = \log_2 3 = \dfrac{0.477...}{0.301...} = 1.58$ correct to 3 significant figures.

This type of equation arises in various applications.

Example 26.5.1
In an area of heathland the number of rabbits increases by a factor of 2.5 every year. How many years will it take for the number of rabbits to be multiplied by 100?

After t years the number of rabbits will have been multiplied by 2.5^t. So the solution to the problem is given by the equation

$$2.5^t = 100.$$

Taking logarithms to base 10 of both sides of the equation,

$$\log 2.5^t = \log 100,$$

so $$t \log 2.5 = \log 100,$$

$$t = \frac{\log 100}{\log 2.5} = \frac{2}{0.397...} = 5.025....$$

Assuming that the population increases continuously throughout the year, the number of rabbits will have multiplied by 100 after just over 5 years.

Example 26.5.2
Solve the equation $5^{3x-1} = 8$.

There is a choice of method. You can either take logarithms straight away, or begin by using the laws of indices to put the equation into the form $b^x = c$, which you know how to solve.

Method 1 Taking logarithms (to base 10) of both sides of the equation,

$$\log(5^{3x-1}) = \log 8.$$

Applying the power rule to the left side,

$$(3x - 1)\log 5 = \log 8,$$

so

$$\begin{aligned} 3x - 1 &= \frac{\log 8}{\log 5} = \frac{0.903...}{0.698...} = 1.292... \\ 3x &= 1 + 1.292... = 2.292..., \\ x &= 2.292... \div 3 = 0.764, \text{ correct to 3 significant figures.} \end{aligned}$$

If you use this method, you should keep as many figures at each stage as the calculator allows, only approximating to 3 significant figures at the end. In fact, you could if you prefer set out the solution as

$$\begin{aligned} 3x &= 1 + \frac{\log 8}{\log 5}, \\ x &= \left(1 + \frac{\log 8}{\log 5}\right) \div 3, \end{aligned}$$

and save all the calculation until the end.

Method 2 Begin by using the division and power-on-power laws for indices to give

$$5^{3x-1} = 5^{3x} \div 5^1 = (5^3)^x \div 5 = 125^x \div 5.$$

The equation can then be written as

$$\begin{aligned} 125^x \div 5 &= 8, \\ 125^x &= 5 \times 8 = 40. \end{aligned}$$

You have already met equations of this type. Taking logarithms (to base 10) of both sides and using the power law for logarithms,

$$x \log 125 = \log 40,$$

so $$x = \frac{\log 40}{\log 125} = \frac{1.602...}{2.096...} = 0.764, \text{ correct to 3 significant figures.}$$

Some applications lead to the expression of the problem as an inequality rather than an equation. So instead of an argument of the form

$$p^x = c, \quad \text{so} \quad \log_b p^x = \log_b c,$$

you have

$$p^x > c, \quad \text{so} \quad \log_b p^x > \log_b c \quad \text{(or similarly with < in place of >).}$$

For this to be valid it is necessary for the logarithm to be an increasing function: that is, for larger numbers to have larger logarithms. Is this true?

To answer this question, go back to the definition of a logarithm at the beginning of Section 26.2. This began with a positive number y, and it was stated that there is just one number x such that $b^x = y$. That number is called $\log_b y$. This is illustrated using the graph of $y = b^x$ in Fig. 26.5; the x-coordinate corresponding to each value of y is $\log_b y$. You can see that, as y gets larger the point P on the graph moves upwards and to the right, so $\log_b y$ also gets larger.

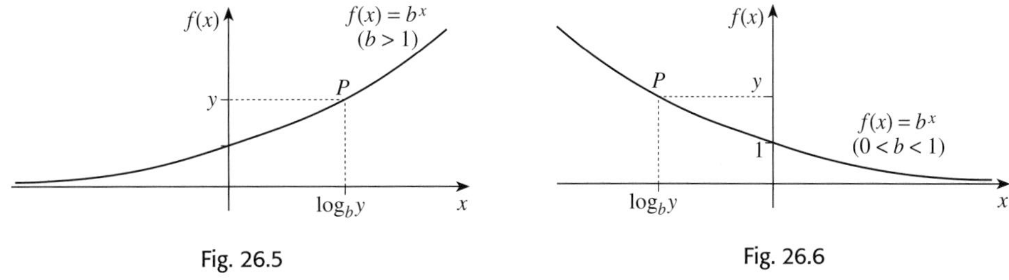

Fig. 26.5

Fig. 26.6

But this happens only because b is greater than 1. If $0 < b < 1$, you get a graph like Fig. 26.6. Now, as y gets larger, the point P moves upwards and to the left, so $\log_b y$ gets smaller.

What this implies for solving inequalities is that, if you take logarithms of both sides, then the inequality sign keeps the same direction provided that $b > 1$; but if $0 < b < 1$ you must reverse the direction of the inequality sign.

In practice, of course, nobody ever takes logarithms to a base less than 1. Both e and 10 are greater than 1. But it is still important to understand the theory on which the process is based.

> For logarithms to base $b > 1$, if $p > q$, then $\log_b p > \log_b q$.

Example 26.5.3

Iodine-131 is a radioactive isotope used in treatment of the thyroid gland. It decays so that, after t days, 1 unit of the isotope is reduced to 0.9174^t units. How many days does it take for the amount to fall to less than 0.1 units?

This requires solution of the inequality $0.9174^t < 0.1$. Since log is an increasing function, taking logarithms to base 10 gives

$$\log 0.9174^t < \log 0.1,$$

so $$t \log 0.9174 < \log 0.1.$$

Now beware! The value of $\log 0.9174$ is negative, so when you divide both sides by $\log 0.9174$ you must change the direction of the inequality:

$$t > \frac{\log 0.1}{\log 0.9174} = \frac{-1}{-0.0374...} = 26.708... .$$

The amount of iodine-131 will fall to less than 0.1 units after about 26.7 days.

Example 26.5.4
How many terms of the geometric series $1 + 1.01 + 1.01^2 + 1.01^3 + ...$ must be taken to give a sum greater than 1 million?

The sum of n terms of the series is given by the formula (see Section 25.3)

$$\frac{1 - 1.01^n}{1 - 1.01} = \frac{1 - 1.01^n}{-0.01} = 100(1.01^n - 1).$$

The problem is to find the smallest value of n for which

$$100(1.01^n - 1) > 1\,000\,000,$$

which gives $1.01^n > 10\,001$.

Taking logarithms to base 10 of both sides,

$$\log 1.01^n > \log 10\,001,$$

so

$$n \log 1.01 > \log 10\,001.$$

Since $\log 1.01$ is positive,

$$n > \frac{\log 10\,001}{\log 1.01} = \frac{4.000...}{0.004\,32...} = 925.6... .$$

The smallest integer n satisfying this inequality is 926.

26.6 Calculating logarithms to any base

The method used in the last section to find $\log_2 3$ can be generalised to find the logarithm of any positive number a to any positive base b (where $b \neq 1$).

Denote $\log_b a$ by x. Then the equation $x = \log_b a$ can be written in exponential form as

$$b^x = a.$$

Suppose that you know the logarithms of a and b to some base c. (In practice c will almost always be either 10 or e, but you don't have to assume this.) Taking logarithms of both sides to base c,

$$\log_c b^x = \log_c a.$$

Since by the power rule $\log_c b^x = x \times \log_c b$,

$$x \times \log_c b = \log_c a.$$

Therefore, dividing both sides by $\log_c b$,

$$x = \frac{\log_c a}{\log_c b}.$$

This gives the **change of base rule**, which you should either remember or be able to obtain quickly for yourself:

> If a, b and c are positive numbers (with b and $c \neq 1$),
>
> $$\log_b a = \frac{\log_c a}{\log_c b}.$$

Example 26.6.1
Calculate $\log_{27} 9$.

With $c = 3$, $\log_{27} 9 = \dfrac{\log_3 9}{\log_3 27} = \dfrac{2}{3}$.

You could of course get this directly, since $9 = 3^2 = (\sqrt[3]{27})^2 = 27^{\frac{2}{3}}$.

Example 26.6.2
Calculate $\log_6 5$.

With $c = 10$, $\log_6 5 = \dfrac{\log_{10} 5}{\log_{10} 6} = \dfrac{0.698...}{0.778...} = 0.898$, correct to 3 significant figures.

Exercise 26D

1 Solve the following equations, giving those answers which are inexact correct to 3 significant figures.

(a) $3^x = 5$ (b) $7^x = 21$ (c) $6^{2x} = 60$

(d) $5^{2x-1} = 10$ (e) $4^{\frac{1}{2}x} = 12$ (f) $2^{x+1} = 3^x$

(g) $\left(\frac{1}{2}\right)^{3x+2} = 25$ (h) $2^x \times 2^{x+1} = 128$ (i) $\left(\frac{1}{4}\right)^{2x-1} = 7$

2 Solve the following inequalities, giving your answers correct to 3 significant figures.

(a) $3^x > 8$ (b) $5^x < 10$ (c) $7^{2x+5} \le 24$

(d) $0.5^x < 0.001$ (e) $0.4^x < 0.0004$ (f) $0.2^x > 25$

(g) $4^x \times 4^{3-2x} \le 1024$ (h) $0.8^{2x+5} \ge 4$ (i) $0.8^{1-3x} \ge 10$

3 Find the number of terms in the following geometric series. In parts (c) to (f) the last terms are not exact, but are correct to the number of significant figures given.

(a) $1 + 2 + 4 + ... + 67\,108\,864$ (b) $4 + 12 + 36 + ... + 57\,395\,628$

(c) $2 + 3 + 4.5 + ... + 383\,502$ (d) $1 + 0.8 + 0.64 + ... + 0.03518$

(e) $4 + 3 + 2.25 + ... + 0.022\,55$ (f) $100 + 99 + 98.01 + ... + 36.97$

4 Find which term in the following geometric sequences is the first one greater than the number stated. Calculate the value of this term, in standard form correct to 4 significant figures.

(a) 1, 1.1, 1.21, ... ; greater than 1000 (b) 2, 2.4, 2.88, ... ; greater than 10^{12}

(c) 4, 5, 6.25, ... ; greater than 5000 (d) 5, 7, 9.8, ... ; greater than 10^7

5 Find which term in the following geometric sequences is the first one less than the number stated. Calculate the value of this term, in standard form correct to 4 significant figures.

(a) 1, 0.9, 0.81, ... ; less than 10^{-3} (b) 5, 4, 3.2, ... ; less than 10^{-6}

(c) 0.4, 0.3, 0.225, ... ; less than 10^{-4}

6 How many terms of the geometric series $1 + 2 + 4 + 8 + ...$ must be taken for the sum to exceed 10^{11}?

7 How many terms of the geometric series $2 + 6 + 18 + 54 + ...$ must be taken for the sum to exceed 3 million?

8 How many terms of the geometric series $1 + \frac{1}{2} + \frac{1}{4} + \frac{1}{8} + ...$ must be taken for its sum to differ from 2 by less than 10^{-8}?

9 How many terms of the geometric series $2 + \frac{1}{3} + \frac{1}{18} + \frac{1}{108} + ...$ must be taken for its sum to differ from its sum to infinity by less than 10^{-5}?

10 A radioactive isotope decays so that after t days an amount 0.82^t units remains. How many days does it take for the amount to fall to less than 0.15 units?

11 To say that a radioactive isotope has a half-life of 6 days means that 1 unit of isotope is reduced to $\frac{1}{2}$ unit in 6 days. So if the daily decay rate is given by r, then $r^6 = 0.5$.

(a) For this isotope, find r.

(b) How long will it take for the amount to fall to 0.25 units?

(c) How long will it take for the amount to fall to 0.1 units?

12 Find the following logarithms correct to 3 significant figures.

(a) $\log_4 12$ (b) $\log_7 100$ (c) $\log_8 2.75$

(d) $\log_{\frac{1}{2}} 250$ (e) $\log_3 \pi$ (f) $\log_{\frac{1}{4}} 0.04$

13* If $\log_{0.1} 2 = x$, show that $10^x = \frac{1}{2}$. Hence evaluate $\log_{0.1} 2$. Use a similar method to find $\log_{0.1} 3$, and verify that $\log_{0.1} 3 < \log_{0.1} 2$.

27 Exponential growth and decay

In this chapter geometric sequences and exponential functions are shown to have applications as mathematical models in everyday situations and in physical, biological and social sciences. When you have completed it, you should

- understand what is meant by exponential growth and exponential decay in both discrete and continuous models
- be able to distinguish exponential models from other models of growth and decay, and be able to calculate the constants in exponential models.

27.1 Discrete exponential growth

Geometric sequences arise in many everyday contexts. Here are two examples. The first has a common ratio greater than 1, the second has a common ratio between 0 and 1.

Example 27.1.1
A person invests \$1000 in a savings bank account which pays interest of 6% annually. Calculate the amount in the account over the next 8 years.

The interest in any year is 0.06 times the amount in the account at the beginning of the year. This is added on to the sum of money already in the account. The amount at the end of each year, after interest has been added, is 1.06 times the amount at the beginning of the year. So

Amount after 1 year = \$1000 × 1.06 = \$1060
Amount after 2 years = \$1060 × 1.06 = \$1124
Amount after 3 years = \$1124 × 1.06 = \$1191, and so on.

Continuing in this way, you get the amounts shown in Table 27.1, to the nearest whole number of dollars.

Number of years	0	1	2	3	4	5	6	7	8
Amount (\$)	1000	1060	1124	1191	1262	1338	1419	1504	1594

Table 27.1

You can see a graph of these values in Fig. 27.2.

Notice that in the first year the interest is \$60, but in the eighth year it is \$90. This is because the amount on which the 6% is calculated has gone up from \$1000 to \$1504. This is characteristic of 'exponential growth', in which the increase is proportional to the current amount. As the amount goes up, the increase goes up.

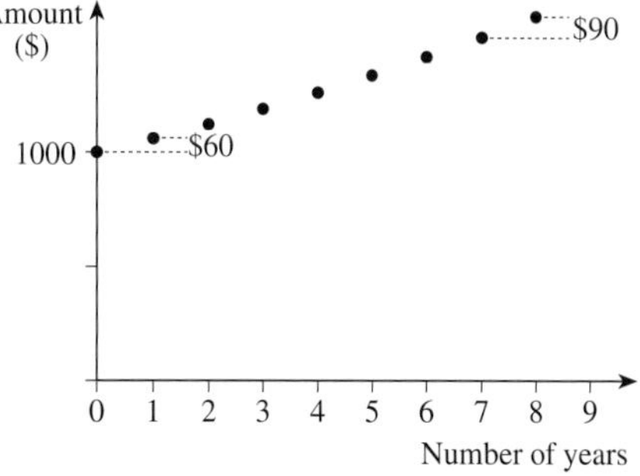

Fig. 27.2

Example 27.1.2

A car cost \$30 000 when new, and each year its value decreases by 20%. Find its value on the first five anniversaries of its purchase.

The value at the end of each year is 0.8 times its value a year earlier. The results of this calculation are given in Table 27.3.

Number of years	0	1	2	3	4	5
Value (\$)	30 000	24 000	19 200	15 360	12 288	9830

Table 27.3

These values are shown in the graph in Fig. 27.4.

The value goes down by \$6000 in the first year, but by only \$2458 in the fifth year, because by then the 20% is calculated on only \$12 288 rather than on \$30 000. This is characteristic of 'exponential decay', in which the decrease is proportional to the current value. Notice that, if the 20% rule continues, the value never becomes zero however long you keep the car.

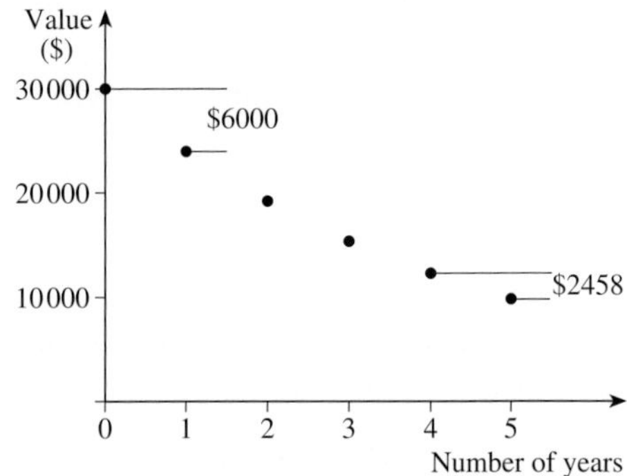

Fig. 27.4

In both these examples it is more natural to think of the first term of the sequence as u_0 rather than u_1. Also, since the values are given at regular intervals of time, it is helpful to use the letter t for the 'counting variable'. That is, $\$u_t$ stands for the amount in the account, or the value of the car, after t years.

The sequence in Example 27.1.1 then has

$$u_0 = 1000 \quad \text{and} \quad u_t = 1.06u_{t-1} \quad \text{for } 1 < t < 8.$$

From this you can deduce that $u_1 = 1000 \times 1.06$, $u_2 = 1000 \times 1.06^2$, and more generally $u_t = 1000 \times 1.06^t$.

The sequence in Example 27.1.2 has

$$u_0 = 30\,000 \quad \text{and} \quad u_t = 0.8u_{t-1} \quad \text{for } 1 < t < 5.$$

In this case $u_1 = 30\,000 \times 0.8$, $u_2 = 30\,000 \times 0.8^2$ and $u_t = 30\,000 \times 0.8^t$.

These are both examples of exponential sequences. (The reason for the name is that the variable t appears in the exponent of the formula for u_t.) An exponential sequence is a special kind of geometric sequence, in which a and r are both positive. If the first term is denoted by u_0, the sequence can be defined inductively by

$$u_0 = a \quad \text{and} \quad u_t = ru_{t-1},$$

or by the formula $\quad u_t = ar^t.$

If $r > 1$ the sequence represents exponential growth; if $0 < r < 1$ it represents exponential decay.

You saw in both examples that between any term and the next the increase or decrease is proportional to the current value. This is characteristic of any exponential sequence. Thus, for any value of t,

$$u_t - u_{t-1} = ru_{t-1} - u_{t-1},$$

which is $(r - 1)$ times u_{t-1}.

Exponential sequences

In a discrete situation, a sequence u_t represents the value of a quantity after t units of time, where t is an integer and $t \geq 0$. If

$$u_0 = a \text{ (where } a > 0\text{) and } u_t = ru_{t-1} \quad \text{for } t = 1, 2, 3, \ldots,$$

the sequence represents

exponential growth if $r > 1$

or **exponential decay** if $0 < r < 1$.

The sequence can be described by the formula

$$u_t = ar^t \quad \text{for } t = 0, 1, 2, 3, \ldots .$$

The increase or decrease in the value of the quantity between times $t - 1$ and t is $r - 1$ times the value at time $t - 1$: that is,

$$u_t - u_{t-1} = (r - 1)\, u_{t-1}.$$

Example 27.1.3

The cost of building a conservatory is made up of the cost of labour and the cost of materials. The price quoted in a firm's 2007 catalogue is based on labour costs of \$20 000 and material costs of \$16 000. In succeeding years the labour costs increase exponentially by 10% a year, and the material costs decrease exponentially by 5% a year. Find how the total costs change over the next three years, and investigate whether they change exponentially.

If the labour costs after t years are $\$L_t$, the material costs are $\$M_t$, and the total costs are $\$C_t$, then

$$L_0 = 20\,000 \quad \text{and} \quad L_t = 1.1L_{t-1};$$
$$M_0 = 16\,000 \quad \text{and} \quad M_t = 0.95M_{t-1};$$

and $$C_t = L_t + M_t.$$

These equations can be used, for $t = 1, 2, 3$ in turn, to calculate the labour and material costs in Table 27.5. These are then added to give the total costs.

Year	2007	2008	2009	2010
Labour costs	\$20 000	\$22 000	\$24 200	\$26 620
Material costs	\$16 000	\$15 200	\$14 440	\$13 718
Total costs	\$36 000	\$37 200	\$38 640	\$40 338

Table 27.5

A graph of the total costs is shown in Fig. 27.6.

You can see from the graph that the total costs increase each year, and also that the amount by which they increase goes up each year. But this is not in itself enough to show that they are growing exponentially. For this to be true, the ratio of the total costs in successive years should be constant. So calculate

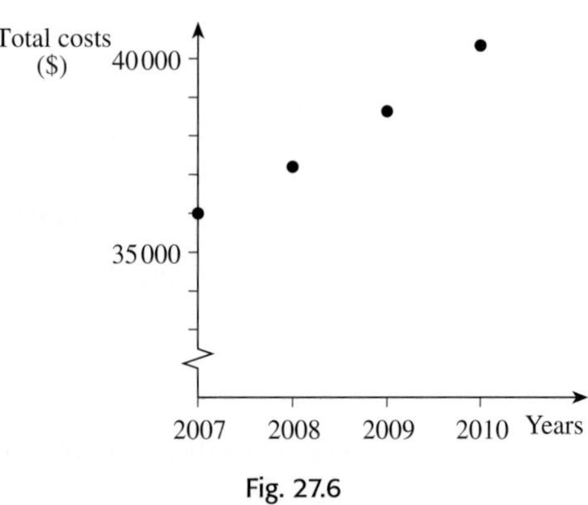

Fig. 27.6

$$\frac{C_1}{C_0} = \frac{37\,200}{36\,000} = 1.033\ldots, \quad \frac{C_2}{C_1} = \frac{38\,640}{37\,200} = 1.038\ldots, \quad \frac{C_3}{C_2} = \frac{40\,338}{38\,640} = 1.043\ldots.$$

Since these ratios are not the same, the growth in total costs is not exponential.

Although the independent variable in exponential growth and decay is usually time, this is not always the case. For example, you could construct a staircase in which the rise grows exponentially from each step to the next. In an example like this, you might choose to use a different letter for the variable instead of t.

Exercise 27A

1 There are at present 4000 houses in Growtown, and this number is growing exponentially by 10% every year. How many houses will there be in three years time?

Calculate the number of new houses which will be completed in each of the next three years. Show that this number is also growing exponentially by 10% every year.

2 A girl fills a jug with one-quarter lemon squash and three-quarters water. She fills a glass with one-tenth of the contents, drinks it and then tops up the jug with water.

(a) What proportion of the contents of the refilled jug is lemon squash?

(b) If she repeats this again and again, what proportion of the contents of the jug will be lemon squash after she has refilled it 2, 3 and 4 times?

(c) Write a formula for the proportion of lemon squash in the jug after she has refilled it t times.

3 The attendances at the last four matches played by Dudtown United were 4000, 3600, 3240 and 2916. Show that these are decreasing exponentially, and predict the attendances at the next two matches if this trend continues.

4 Each New Year's Eve Scrooge works out the value of his possessions. In 2004 it was \$50 000, and he expects it to grow exponentially by 20% a year. Find the value in each year up to 2009 on this assumption.

Find how much richer he becomes in each year, and show that these amounts also increase exponentially.

5 It is estimated that the population of sparrows on an island is decaying exponentially by 20% each decade, and that the population of sparrowhawks is growing by 20%. If there were 100 000 sparrows and 1000 sparrowhawks when recording began, calculate how many of each there will be after 1, 2 and 3 decades.

Calculate how many sparrows there will be to each sparrowhawk after 1, 2 and 3 decades. How is this ratio changing?

6 In Example 27.1.1 find an expression for the amount of interest received in the ith year. Does the amount of interest grow exponentially?

7 In Example 27.1.2 find an expression for the reduction in the value of the car in the ith year after it was purchased. Does this reduction decay exponentially?

8 The table gives the retail price index (to the nearest whole number) on 1 April for several consecutive years in a number of countries. In which countries could you say that the index is increasing or decreasing exponentially?

	Year				
Country	2000	2001	2002	2003	2004
Armensia	185	200	216	233	252
Bonvivia	135	150	165	180	195
Canadia	100	120	144	173	207
Declinia	180	169	159	150	141
Erewhon	80	69	59	50	41

9 In 1838 the Rev. H Moseley presented a paper to the Royal Society on his measurements of shells. One cone-shaped shell called *Turritella duplicata* grew in a series of whorls, whose successive widths, in inches, were 0.41, 0.48, 0.57, 0.67, 0.80, 0.94. Show that these measurements fit a model of exponential growth, and predict the width of the next two whorls.

10 Show that, if a sequence of data grows or decays exponentially, then the logarithms form an arithmetic sequence. Verify this from the data in Question 11, and estimate the common difference. What does this represent?

27.2 Continuous exponential growth

Exponential growth doesn't only occur in situations which increase by discrete steps. Rampant inflation, a nuclear chain reaction, the spread of an epidemic or the growth of cells are processes which take place in continuous time, and they need to be described by functions having the real numbers rather than the natural numbers for their domain.

For continuous exponential growth, the equation $u_t = ar^t$, where $t = 0, 1, 2, \ldots$, is replaced by

$$f(t) = ab^t, \quad \text{where } t \text{ is a real number and } t \geq 0.$$

In this equation a stands for the initial value when $t = 0$, and b is a positive constant which indicates how fast the quantity is growing. (The idea of a 'common ratio' no longer applies in the continuous case, so a different letter is used.) The graph of $f(t)$ is shown in Fig. 27.7.

For exponential growth b has to be greater than 1. If $0 < b < 1$ the graph takes the form of Fig. 27.8; for large values of t the graph gets closer to the t-axis but never reaches it. This then represents exponential decay. Examples of this are the amount of radioactive uranium in a lump of ore, and the concentration of an antibiotic in the bloodstream.

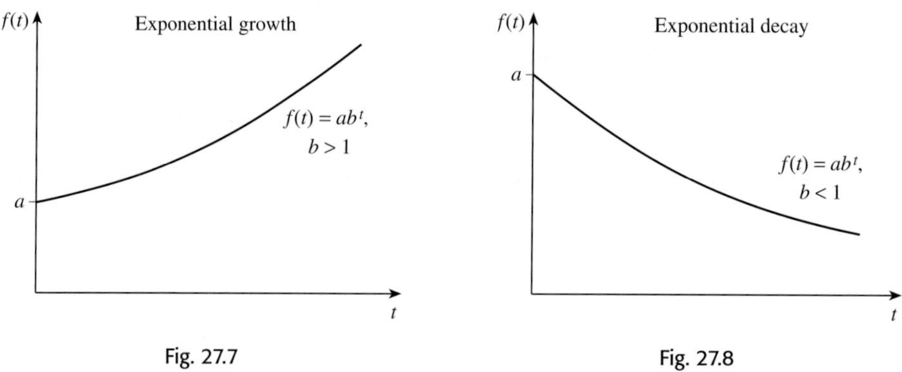

Fig. 27.7 Fig. 27.8

The letter t has again been used for the variable, since in most examples of exponential growth and decay the quantity you are measuring is a function of the time. If this is not the case (for example, the air pressure decays exponentially with the height above the earth's surface) you might use a different letter for the variable.

Exponential variation

In a continuous situation, a function $f(t)$ represents the value of a quantity after t units of time, where t is a real number and $t \geq 0$. If

$$f(t) = ab^t \quad (\text{where } a > 0),$$

the function represents

exponential growth if $b > 1$

or **exponential decay** if $0 < b < 1$.

Example 27.2.1

The population of the USA grew exponentially from the end of the War of Independence until the Civil War. It increased from 3.9 million at the 1790 census to 31.4 million in 1860. What would the population have been in 1990 if it had continued to grow at this rate?

If the population t years after 1790 is P million, and if the growth were exactly exponential, then P and t would be related by an equation of the form

$$P = 3.9b^t,$$

where $P = 31.4$ when $t = 70$. The constant b therefore satisfies the equation

$$31.4 = 3.9b^{70},$$

so
$$b^{70} = \frac{31.4}{3.9},$$
$$b = \left(\frac{31.4}{3.9}\right)^{\frac{1}{70}} = 1.030\ldots .$$

At this rate the population in 1990 would have grown to about $3.9 \times 1.030\ldots^{200}$ million, which is between 1.5 and 1.6 billion.

You can shorten this calculation as follows. In 70 years, the population multiplied by $\frac{31.4}{3.9}$. In 200 years, it therefore multiplied by $\left(\frac{31.4}{3.9}\right)^{\frac{200}{70}}$. The 1990 population can then be calculated as $3.9 \times \left(\frac{31.4}{3.9}\right)^{\frac{200}{70}}$ million, without working out b as an intermediate step.

Example 27.2.2

Carbon dating in archaeology is based on the decay of the isotope carbon-14, which has a half-life of 5715 years. By what percentage does carbon-14 decay in 100 years?

The half-life of a radioactive isotope is the time it would take half of any sample of the isotope to decay. After t years one unit of carbon-14 is reduced to b^t units, where

$$b^{5715} = 0.5 \qquad \text{(since 0.5 units are left after 5715 years)}$$

so
$$b = 0.5^{\frac{1}{5715}} = 0.999\,878\ldots .$$

When $t = 100$ the quantity left is $b^{100} \approx 0.988$ units, a reduction of 0.012 units, or 1.2%.

Again, you could shorten the calculation by expressing the multiplying factor as $0.5^{\frac{100}{5715}}$. The fraction $\frac{100}{5715}$ expresses the ratio of 100 years to the half-life of 5715 years. So the multiplying factor is $\frac{1}{2}$ raised to the power of the number of half-lives.

27.3 Graphs of exponential growth

In Section 26.5 equations of the form $p^x = c$, where the unknown appears in the index, were solved by taking logarithms of both sides. This technique can be extended to deal with economic, social or scientific data which you think might exhibit exponential growth or decay.

Suppose that a quantity y is growing exponentially, so that its value at time t is given by

$$y = ab^t,$$

where a and b are constants. Taking logarithms of both sides of this equation, to any base,

$$\log y = \log(ab^t) = \log a + \log b^t = \log a + t \log b.$$

The expression on the right increases linearly with t. So if $\log y$ is plotted against t, the graph would be a straight line with gradient $\log b$ and intercept $\log a$.

Example 27.3.1
If $\log y = 0.322 - 0.531t$, where $\log y$ denotes $\log_{10} y$, express y in terms of t.

Equating the right side to $\log a + t \log b$, $\log a = 0.322$ and $\log b = -0.531$. So, since the logarithms are to base 10, $a = 10^{0.322} = 2.10$ and $b = 10^{-0.531} = 0.294$ (both correct to 3 significant figures). In exponential form the equation for y is therefore

$$y = 2.10 \times 0.294^t.$$

If you prefer you can write this calculation in a different way, using the property that if $\log y = x$ then $y = 10^x$, so $y = 10^{\log y}$. Therefore

$$y = 10^{\log y} = 10^{0.322 - 0.531t} = 10^{0.322} \times (10^{-0.531})^t = 2.10 \times 0.294^t.$$

Example 27.3.2
An investment company claims that the price of its shares has grown exponentially over the past six years, and supports its claim with Fig. 27.9. Is this claim justified?

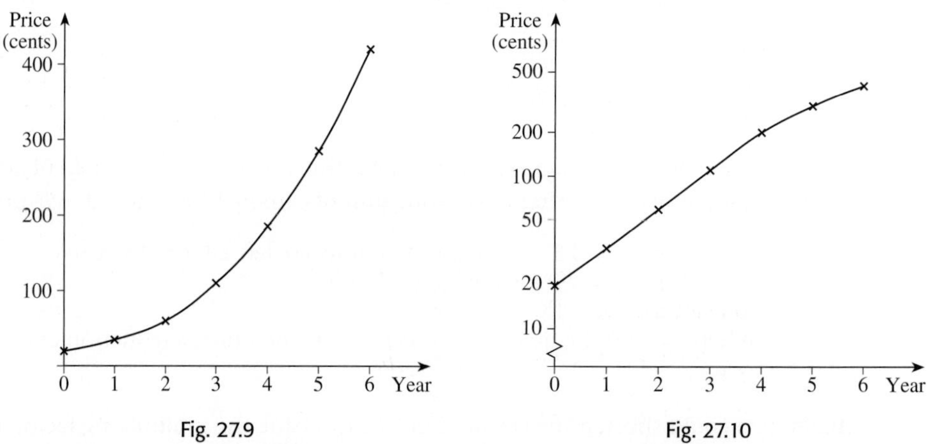

Fig. 27.9

Fig. 27.10

Fig. 27.10 shows this information with the price presented on a logarithmic scale (see Section 26.4). A price of y cents is represented by a line of length proportional to $\log y$. You can recognise this by noticing that, for example, the distance on the scale from 50 cents to 100 cents is the same as the distance from 100 cents to 200 cents; this is because $\log 100 - \log 50 = \log \frac{100}{50} = \log 2$, and $\log 200 - \log 100 = \log \frac{200}{100} = \log 2$.

If the claim were true, the graph in Fig. 27.10 would be a straight line. This seems approximately true for the first three years, but in later years the graph begins to bend downwards, suggesting that the early promise of exponential growth has not been sustained.

The ideas of the last two examples can be combined, not just to investigate whether there is an exponential relationship, but also to find the numerical constants in the equation.

Example 27.3.3

Use the census data in Table 27.11 for the USA to justify the statement in Example 27.2.1, that the population grew exponentially from 1790 to 1860.

Year	1790	1800	1810	1820	1830	1840	1850	1860
Population (millions)	3.9	5.3	7.2	9.6	12.9	17.0	23.2	31.4

Table 27.11

If you plot these figures on a graph, as in Fig. 27.12, it is clear that the points lie on a smooth curve with a steadily increasing gradient, but this doesn't by itself show that the growth is exponential.

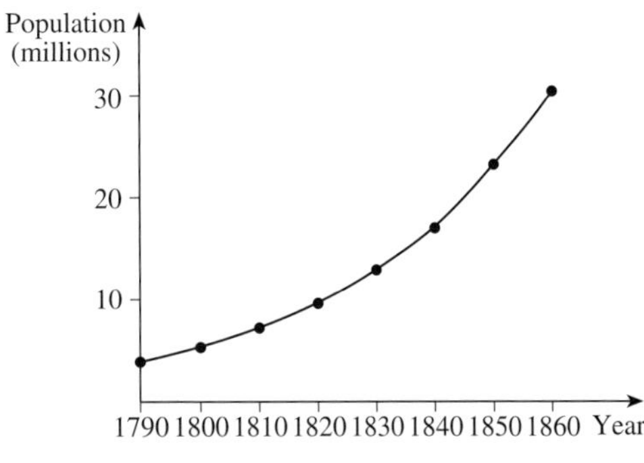

Fig. 27.12

To approach the question scientifically, the first step is to choose appropriate notation. For the population, you may as well work in millions of people, as in the table; there is no point in cluttering the data with lots of zeros, which would in any case give a false illusion of accuracy. So let P stand for the number of millions of people in the population. As for the date, since you are only interested in the period from 1790 to 1860, it is better to choose a variable t to stand for the number of years after 1790 rather than the actual year number. The theory then being investigated is that P and t are related by an equation of the form

$$P = ab^t \qquad \text{for } 0 \leq t \leq 70.$$

To convert this into a linear equation, take logarithms of both sides of the equation. You can use logarithms to any base you like; if you choose 10, the equation becomes

$$\log_{10} P = \log_{10} a + t \log_{10} b,$$

in which the independent variable is t and the dependent variable is $\log_{10} P$. So Table 27.13 contains values in terms of these variables.

t	0	10	20	30	40	50	60	70
$\log_{10} P$	0.59	0.72	0.86	0.98	1.11	1.23	1.37	1.50

Table 27.13

These values are used to plot the graph in Fig. 27.14. You can see that the points very nearly lie on a straight line, though not exactly so; you wouldn't expect a population to follow a precise mathematical relationship. However, it is quite close enough to justify the claim that the growth of the population was exponential.

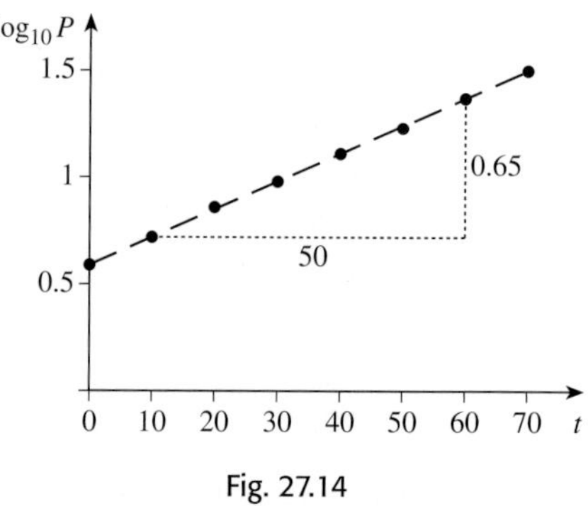

Fig. 27.14

The dashed line in Fig. 27.14 is an attempt to draw by eye a line that best fits the plotted points. By measurement, it seems that the intercept on the vertical axis is about 0.59; and, by using a suitable gradient triangle (shown with dotted lines), you can find that the gradient is about $\dfrac{0.65}{50} = 0.013$.

So the line has equation

$$\log_{10} P = 0.59 + 0.013t,$$

which is of the desired form $\log_{10} P = \log_{10} a + t \log_{10} b$ with $\log_{10} a \approx 0.59$ and $\log_{10} b \approx 0.013$.

So $\quad a \approx 10^{0.59} \approx 3.9 \quad$ and $\quad b = 10^{0.013} \approx 1.03$.

It follows that, over the period from 1790 to 1860, the growth of the population could be described to a good degree of accuracy by the law

$$P = 3.9 \times 1.03^t.$$

An equation like $P = 3.9 \times 1.03^t$ is called a **mathematical model**. It is not an exact equation giving the precise size of the population, but it is an equation of a simple form which describes the growth of the population to a very good degree of accuracy. For example, if you wanted to know the population in 1836, when $t = 46$, you could calculate $3.9 \times 1.03^{46} = 15.2...$, and assert with confidence that in that year the population of the USA was between 15 and $15\frac{1}{2}$ million.

Exercise 27B

1 A rumour spreads exponentially through a college. 100 people have heard it by noon, and 200 by 1 p.m. How many people have heard it

(a) by 3 p.m., (b) by 12.30 p.m., (c) by 1.45 p.m.?

2 A cup of coffee at 85 °C is placed in a freezer at 0 °C. The temperature of the coffee decreases exponentially, so that after 5 minutes it is 30 °C.

(a) What is its temperature after 3 minutes?

(b) Find how long it will take for the temperature to drop to 5 °C.

3 The population of Camford is increasing at a rate of 6% each year. On 1 January 1990 it was 35 200. What was its population on

(a) 1 January 2000, (b) 1 July 1990, (c) 1 January 1980?

4 The population of the UK in 1971 was 5.5615×10^7; by 1992 it was estimated to be 5.7384×10^7. Assuming a steady exponential growth estimate the population in

(a) 2003, (b) 1981.

5 The strength of a radioactive source is said to 'decay exponentially'. Explain briefly what is meant by exponential decay, and illustrate your answer by means of a sketch-graph.

After t years the strength S of a particular radioactive source, in appropriate units, is given by $S = 10\,000 \times 3^{-0.0014t}$. State the value of S when $t = 0$, and find the value of t when the source has decayed to one-half of its initial strength, giving your answer correct to 3 significant figures. (OCR, adapted)

6 An orchestra tunes to a frequency of 440, which sounds the A which is 9 semitones above middle C. Each octave higher doubles the frequency, and each of the 12 semitones in the octave increases the frequency in the same ratio.

(a) What is this ratio? (b) Find the frequency of middle C.

(c) How many semitones above the A is a note with a frequency of 600? Where is this on the scale?

7 For the following equations, express y in terms of x.

(a) $\log_{10} y = 0.4 + 0.6x$ (b) $\log_{10} y = 12 - 3x$ (c) $\log_{10} y = 0.7 + 1.7x$

(d) $\log_{10} y = 0.7 + 2\log_{10} x$ (e) $\log_{10} y = -0.5 - 5\log_{10} x$

8 Population census data for the USA from 1870 to 1910 were as follows.

Year	1870	1880	1890	1900	1910
Population (millions)	38.6	50.2	63.0	76.0	92.0

Investigate how well these figures can be described by an exponential model.

9 With the data of Example 27.1.3, graph the logarithm of the amount against t, and explain how your graph can be used to show that the amount does not grow exponentially.

10 For the data in Exercise 27A Question 10, use graphs of log(index) for each country to investigate whether the increase or decrease of the index is exponential. Where it is, give an expression for the index in the year $(2000 + t)$ in the form ar^t.

Review exercise 8

1 The diagram shows the curve $y = x^3$. The point P has coordinates (3, 27) and [PQ] is the tangent to the curve at P. Find the area of the region enclosed between the curve, [PQ] and the x-axis.

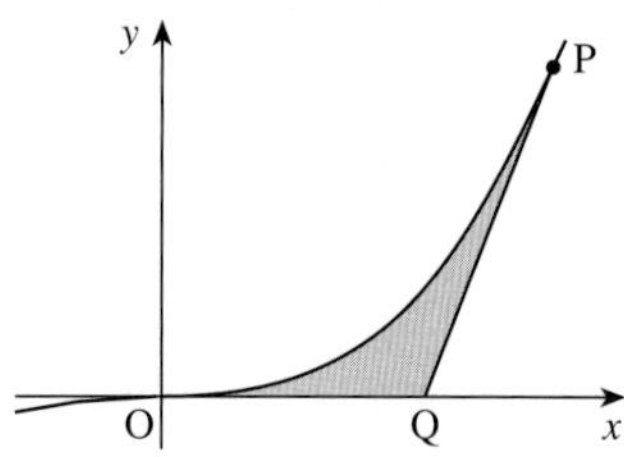

2 Given that $\int_1^p (8x^3 + 6x)\,dx = 39$, find two possible values of p. Use a graph to explain why there are two values.

3 Given that $f(x)$ and $g(x)$ are two functions such that $\int_0^4 f(x)\,dx = 17$ and $\int_0^4 g(x)\,dx = 11$ find, where possible, the value of each of the following.

(a) $\int_0^4 (f(x) - g(x))\,dx$ (b) $\int_0^4 (2f(x) + 3g(x))\,dx$ (c) $\int_0^2 f(x)\,dx$

(d) $\int_0^4 (f(x) + 2x + 3)\,dx$ (e) $\int_0^1 f(x)\,dx + \int_1^4 f(x)\,dx$ (f) $\int_4^0 g(x)\,dx$

4 Evaluate, correct to the nearest whole number,

$$0.99 + 0.99^2 + 0.99^3 + ... + 0.99^{99}.$$

5 A post is being driven into the ground by a mechanical hammer. The distance it is driven by the first blow is 8 cm. Subsequently, the distance it is driven by each blow is $\frac{9}{10}$ of the distance it was driven by the previous blow. The post is to be driven a total distance of 70 cm into the ground. Show that at least 20 blows will be needed.

Explain why the post can never be driven a total distance of more than 80 cm into the ground.

6 At the beginning of 1990, an investor decided to invest \$6000, believing that the value of the investment should increase, on average, by 6% each year. Show that, if this percentage rate of increase was in fact maintained for 10 years, the value of the investment will be about \$10 745.

The investor added a further \$6000 at the beginning of each year between 1991 and 1995 inclusive. Assuming that the 6% annual rate of increase continues to apply, show that the total value, in dollars, of the investment at the beginning of the year 2000 may be written as $6000(1.06^5 + 1.06^6 + ... + 1.06^{10})$ and evaluate this, correct to the nearest dollar.

7 The sum of the infinite geometric series $1 + r + r^2 + ...$ is k times the sum of the series $1 - r + r^2 - ...$, where $k > 0$. Express r in terms of k.

8 Prove that $\log\left(\frac{p}{q}\right) + \log\left(\frac{q}{r}\right) + \log\left(\frac{r}{p}\right) = 0$.

9 A savings account is opened with a single payment of \$2000. It attracts compound interest at a constant rate of 0.5% per month.

(a) Find the amount in the account after two complete years.

(b) Find after how many months the value of the investment will have doubled.

10 A dangerous radioactive substance has a half-life of 90 years. It will be deemed safe when its activity is down to 0.05 of its initial value. How long will it be before it is deemed safe?

11 The membership of a society has grown from 5000 to 7000 over a period of three years. If the growth in membership is exponential, what will it be after a further two years?

12 It is feared that the population of a species of finch on a remote island is endangered. At the beginning of the year 2000 it was estimated that there were 800 breeding pairs. By the beginning of 2005 this number had dropped to 640. If the size of the population is decreasing exponentially, in which year would you expect the number of breeding pairs to drop below 200?

13 (a) Find $\int x(x^2 - 2)\,dx$.

(b) The diagram shows the graph of $y = x(x^2 - 2)$ for $x \geq 0$. The value of a is such that the two shaded regions have equal areas. Find the value of a. (OCR)

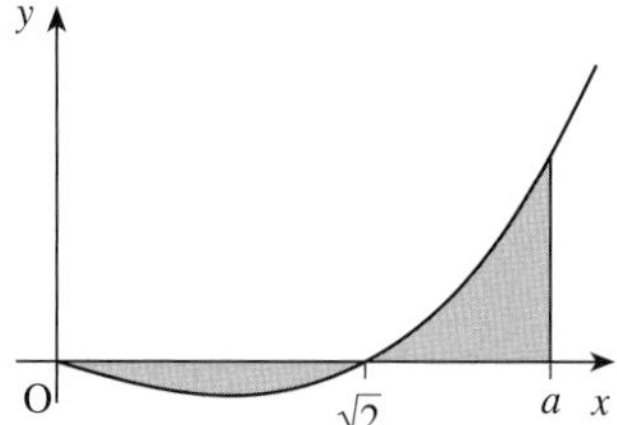

14 The diagram shows a sketch of the graph of $y = x^2$ and the normal to the curve at the point A(1, 1).

(a) Use differentiation to find the equation of the normal at A. Verify that the point B where the normal cuts the curve again has coordinates $\left(-\frac{3}{2}, \frac{9}{4}\right)$.

(b) The region which is bounded by the curve and the normal is shaded in the diagram. Calculate its area, giving your answer as an exact fraction. (OCR)

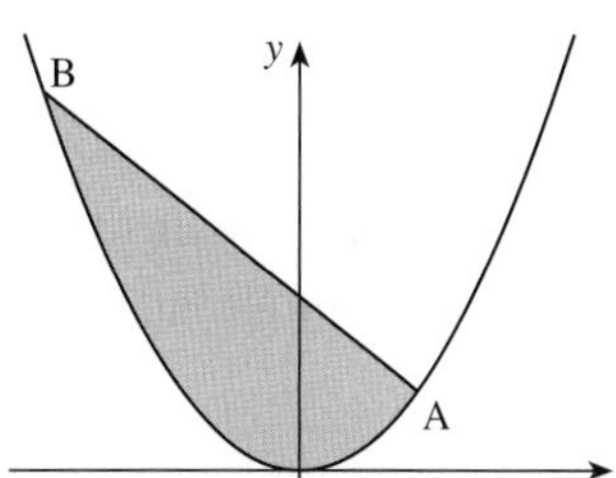

15 The diagram shows the graph of $y = \sqrt[3]{x} - x^2$. Show by integration that the area of the region (shaded in the diagram) between the curve and the x-axis is $\frac{5}{12}$. (OCR)

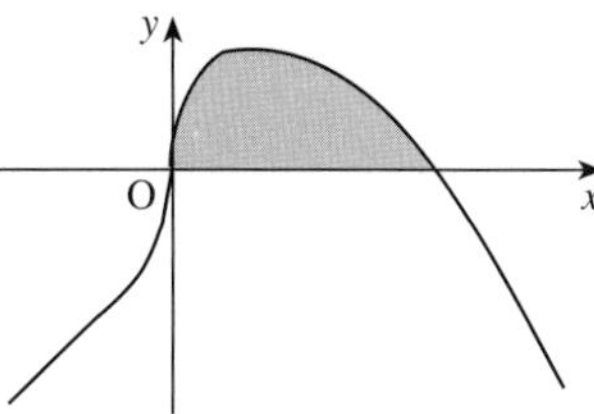

16 Solve each of the following equations to find x in terms of a where $a > 0$ and $a \neq 100$. The logarithms are to base 10.

(a) $a^x = 10^{2x+1}$ (b) $2\log(2x) = 1 + \log a$ (OCR, adapted)

17 Solve the equation $3^{2x} = 4^{2-x}$, giving your answer to 3 significant figures. (OCR)

18 Solve the inequality $8^x > 10^{30}$. (OCR)

Examination questions

1 Let $f(x) = \sqrt{x^3}$. Find

(a) $f'(x)$, (b) $\int f(x)\,dx$. (© IBO 2002)

2 Given that $\int_1^3 g(x)\,dx = 10$, deduce the value of

(a) $\int_1^3 \frac{1}{2}g(x)\,dx$, (b) $\int_1^3 (g(x) + 4)\,dx$. (© IBO 2003)

3 Solve the equation $\log_{27} x = 1 - \log_{27}(x - 0.4)$. (© IBO 2002)

4 A particle moves with a velocity v m s^{-1} given by $v = 25 - 4t^2$ where $t \geq 0$.

(a) The displacement, s metres, is 10 when $t = 3$. Find an expression for s in terms of t.

(b) Find t when s reaches its maximum value.

(c) The particle has a positive displacement for $m \leq t \leq n$. Find the value of m and the value of n. (© IBO 2005)

5 A company offers its employees a choice of two salary schemes A and B over a period of 10 years. Scheme A offers a starting salary of \$11 000 in the first year and then an annual increase of \$400 per year.

(a) (i) Write down the salary paid in the second year and in the third year.

(ii) Calculate the *total* (amount of) salary paid over ten years.

Scheme B offers a starting salary of \$10 000 dollars in the first year and then an annual increase of 7% of the previous year's salary.

(b) (i) Write down the salary paid in the second year and in the third year.

(ii) Calculate the salary paid in the tenth year.

(c) Arturo works for n complete years under scheme A. Bill works for n complete years under scheme B. Find the minimum number of years so that the total earned by Bill exceeds the total earned by Arturo. (© IBO 2004)

6 Ashley and Billie are swimmers training for a competition.

(a) Ashley trains for 12 hours in the first week. She decides to increase the amount of time she spends training by two hours each week. Find the total number of hours she spends training during the first 15 weeks.

(b) Billie also trains for 12 hours in the first week. She decides to train for 10% longer each week than in the previous week.

(i) Show that in the third week she trains for 14.52 hours.

(ii) Find the total number of hours she spends training during the first 15 weeks.

(c) In which week will the time Billie spends training first exceed 50 hours? (© IBO 2002)

7 In this question, s represents displacement in metres, and t represents time in seconds.

(a) The velocity v m s^{-1} of a moving body may be written as $v = \frac{ds}{dt} = 30 - at$ where a is a constant. Given that $s = 0$ when $t = 0$, find an expression for s in terms of a and t.

Trains approaching a station start to slow down when they pass a signal which is 200 m from the station.

(b) The velocity of Train 1 t seconds after passing the signal is given by $v = 30 - 5t$.

(i) Write down its velocity as it passes the signal.

(ii) Show that it will stop before reaching the station.

(c) Train 2 slows down so that it stops at the station. Its velocity is given by $v = \frac{ds}{dt} = 30 - at$, where a is a constant.

(i) Find, in terms of a, the time taken to stop.

(ii) Use your solutions to parts (a) and (c)(i) to find the value of a. (© IBO 2002)

8 There were 1420 doctors working in a city on 1 January 1994. After n years the number of doctors, D, working in the city is given by $D = 1420 + 100n$.

(a) (i) How many doctors were there working in the city at the start of 2004?

(ii) In what year were there first more than 2000 doctors working in the city?

At the beginning of 1994 the city had a population of 1.2 million. After n years, the population, P, of the city is given by $P = 1\,200\,000\,(1.025)^n$.

(b) (i) Find the population P at the beginning of 2004.

(ii) Calculate the percentage growth in population between 1 January 1994 and 1 January 2004.

(iii) In what year will the population first become greater than 2 million?

(c) (i) What was the average number of people per doctor at the beginning of 1994?

(ii) After how many *complete* years will the number of people per doctor first fall below 600? (© IBO 2004)

28 Circular functions

This chapter revisits sines, cosines and tangents but as functions rather than as a means of calculating lengths, angles and areas. When you have completed it, you should

- know the form of the graphs of $y = \cos x$, $y = \sin x$ and $y = \tan x$ where x is in radians
- be able to use cos and sin to model periodic variation in real-world applications.

28.1 Trigonometric functions as models

Scientists use a variety of functions as models to describe their observations. You have already used polynomials, for example in kinematics and in problems on maxima and minima; many laws depend on nth power functions, such as the inverse square law of gravitation and the relation between air resistance and speed; and exponential functions provide models for population growth and the dispersal of substances in the bloodstream.

Another type of relationship is that in which the dependent variable is a quantity which recurs periodically. The trade cycle in economics, the rise and fall of animal populations, the operation of a mechanical clock and alternating current in electricity are typical examples. The graphs of $\cos\theta^\circ$ and $\sin\theta^\circ$ appear to provide a suitable basis to describe such behaviour. But before using them for this purpose it is worth making some adjustments.

The first step is to abandon the use of degrees to measure angles. These are perfectly suitable in surveying and astronomy, for which trigonometry was originally developed, but they are inconvenient for wider scientific applications. For this purpose the natural unit is the radian.

Next, if cos and sin are to be used as functions, then it is helpful to use the letters x and y for the variables, just as you do for other functions. These must not of course be confused with the x and y in circle diagrams like Figs. 15.1 to 15.5; they have now served their purpose, and that notation won't be used again in this chapter.

It is important to understand that when you write $y = \cos x$ or $y = \sin x$, where x is in radians, then x and y are simply real numbers. Fig. 28.1 shows x, $\cos x$ and $\sin x$ as ratios of two lengths:

$$x = \frac{\text{directed arc AP}}{\text{radius OP}}, \quad \cos x = \frac{\text{directed length ON}}{\text{radius OP}}, \quad \sin x = \frac{\text{directed length NP}}{\text{radius OP}}.$$

The word 'directed' is a reminder that the measures are taken to be negative if they are made in the directions oppposite to those indicated by the arrows. So their values don't depend on the choice of unit used to measure the lengths.

The functions $y = \cos x$ and $y = \sin x$ defined in this way have for their domains the set $\mathbb{R}$ of all real numbers, and the range of each is the interval $-1 \le y \le 1$. They are called **circular functions**.

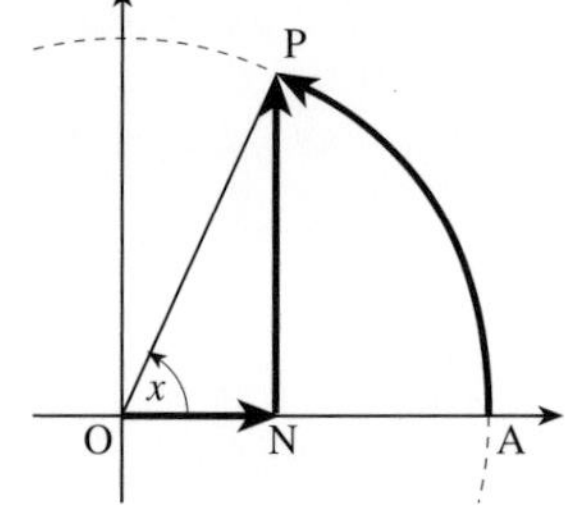

Fig. 28.1

28.2 Graphs of cos *x* and sin *x*

You know that, when radians are used to measure angles, a complete revolution has value 2π and a right angle has value $\frac{1}{2}\pi$. The graphs of $y = \cos x$ and $y = \sin x$ then have the forms shown in Fig. 28.2 and Fig. 28.3.

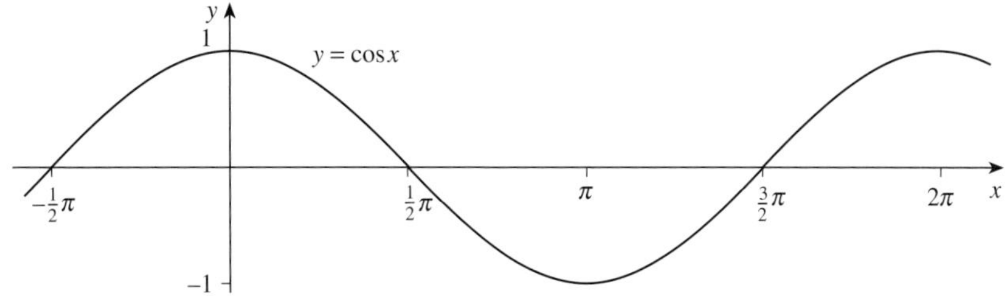

Fig. 28.2

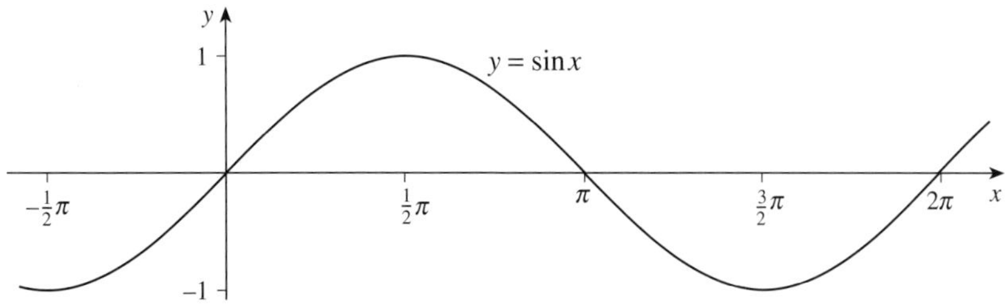

Fig. 28.3

An incidental advantage is that the graphs of the circular functions can be drawn with equal scales on the two axes. If you tried to do this for $y = \cos\theta^\circ$ and $y = \sin\theta^\circ$ you would get graphs which are far too wide and flat to be useful. You will probably have noticed that in Fig. 15.6 and Fig. 15.8 the scales on the two axes are very different.

You will often want to use a calculator to produce these graphs. Make sure that you can do this.

In Section 15.1 the word 'periodic' was used to describe $\cos\theta^\circ$ and $\sin\theta^\circ$. Changing from degrees to radians doesn't affect this. The functions $\cos x$ and $\sin x$ are also periodic, but the period is 2π rather than 360. This can be expressed by the equations

$$\cos(x - 2\pi) = \cos x \quad \text{and} \quad \sin(x - 2\pi) = \sin x,$$

which are true for all values of x.

28.3 Fitting models to numerical data

When you use circular functions to model periodic variation in real-world applications, you will usually need equations more complicated than $y = \cos x$ or $y = \sin x$. These functions have period 2π and maximum/minimum values of $+1$ and -1. In a practical application the period may be a few picoseconds or thousands of years, and the extent of the variation may be measured in nanometres or light-years. The independent variable very often represents time, but it may represent other quantities such as distance or angle. There are many possibilities for the varying quantity represented by the dependent variable, and this will often oscillate about a mean value different from zero.

So the equations may have forms such as $y = a \sin nx$ or $y = a \cos nx + c$. Also, it may be more convenient to use letters other than x and y for the variables, such as t for time. The examples in this section suggest how to determine the constants a, n and c to fit a particular application.

Which of the functions cos or sin to use often depends on the place or time from which you start to measure the dependent variable. If you start from a position of maximum displacement, use the cosine; if you start from the central position, use the sine. If the starting position is not specified, you can use either.

Example 28.3.1
In an electrical circuit the frequency of alternating current is 50 cycles per second, and the current oscillates between 5 and -5 amps. At a time t seconds after the switch is closed the current is i amps, where $i = a \sin nt$ (with $a > 0$ and $n > 0$). Find the values of a and n.

Since the maximum and minimum values of $\sin nt$ are $+1$ and -1, those of $a \sin nt$ are $+a$ and $-a$. So in this application $a = 5$.

The values of $a \sin nt$ are repeated when nt increases by 2π, so that t increases by $\frac{2\pi}{n}$. There are 50 repetitions in a second, so the period of repetition is $\frac{1}{50}$ second.

Therefore $\frac{2\pi}{n} = \frac{1}{50}$, which gives $n = 100\pi$.

The equation connecting i and t is therefore $i = 5 \sin 100\pi t$.

Example 28.3.2
The strength, S units, of a signal from a star seems to vary on a 25-day cycle, from a maximum of 10 to a minimum of 4. Suggest a possible mathematical model.

The mean between the greatest and least values is 7 units, and the variation is ± 3 units either side of this mean. So, t days after an instant of maximum strength, S might be given by an equation of the form $S = 7 + 3 \cos nt$ for some value of n.

Since 25 is very close to 8π, and values of $\cos nt$ are repeated after nt increases by 2π, $n = \frac{1}{4}$ would give a good approximation. A possible model would therefore be

$$S = 7 + 3 \cos \tfrac{1}{4}t.$$

Use your calculator to check that this equation gives a graph with the required features.

28.4 The graph of tan x

Because $\tan x = \dfrac{\sin x}{\cos x}$, the domain of $\tan x$ can't include those values of x for which $\cos x = 0$. You can see from Fig. 28.2 that these are all the odd multiples of $\frac{1}{2}\pi$, which can be written as $(2n+1) \times \frac{1}{2}\pi$, or $(n+\frac{1}{2})\pi$, where n is any integer. The domain of $\tan x$ is therefore the set of real numbers excluding $(n+\frac{1}{2})\pi$, where $n \in \mathbb{Z}$.

The graph of $y = \tan x$ is shown in Fig. 28.4. You will see that the lines $x = (n+\frac{1}{2})\pi$, where $n \in \mathbb{Z}$, are all asymptotes.

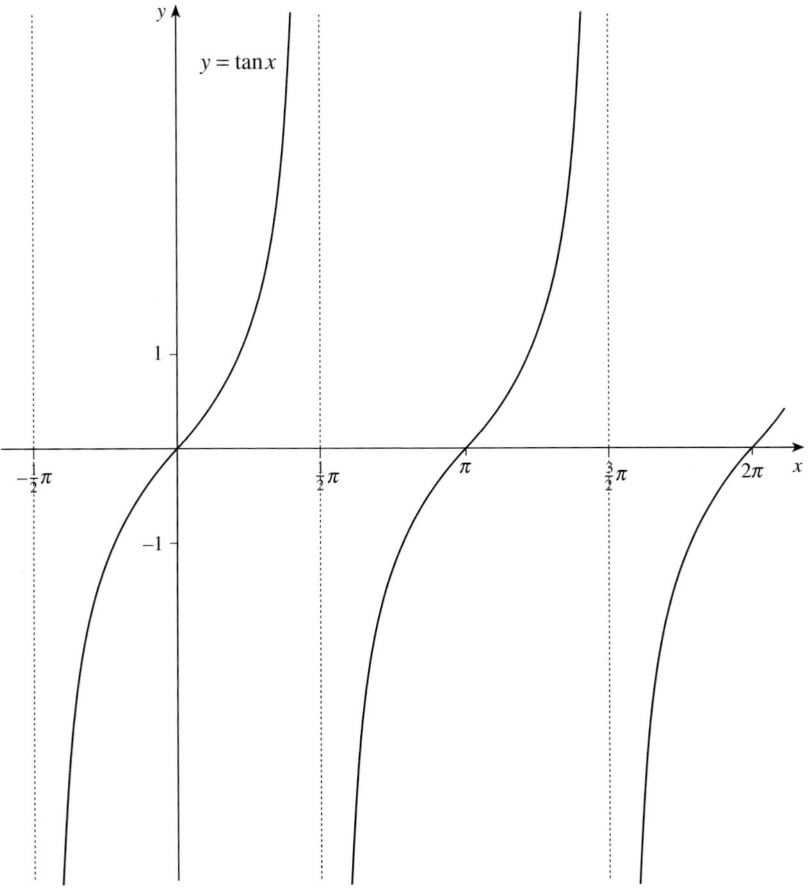

Fig. 28.4

The function $\tan x$ is also periodic, but the period after which it repeats is π rather than 2π. That is, for any value of x for which $\tan x$ is defined,

$$\tan(x - \pi) = \tan x.$$

The tan function is not often encountered as a model in applications. But it has an important role in the mathematics of circular functions, especially in connection with differentiation and integration, which will be considered in Chapter 40.

Exercise 28

1 Use your calculator to show the graphs of $y = \cos x$ and $y = \sin x$ with the same axes. Hence

(a) find the smallest positive root of the equation $\cos x = \sin x$,

(b) find a formula for all the roots of the equation $\cos x = \sin x$,

(c) find the values of x in the interval $0 \le x \le 2\pi$ for which $\cos x < \sin x$.

2 Use your calulator to show the graph of $y = \cos x + \sin x$.

(a) Show that $\cos x + \sin x$ is a periodic function, and state its period.

(b) Find all the roots of the equation $\cos x + \sin x = 1$ in the interval $0 \le x \le 2\pi$.

3 Use your calculator to show the graph of $y = \tan x - \sin x$. What is its period?

4 Use your calculator to show the graph of $f(x) = 8\sin x - \tan x$ in the interval $0 \le x \le \frac{1}{2}\pi$.

(a) You are given that $f(x)$ has a maximum point where $x = \frac{1}{3}\pi$. What is the maximum value?

(b) Calculate the x-coordinate of the point other than the origin where the graph cuts the x-axis, correct to 6 decimal places.

Use your graph to check your answers.

5 Use your calculator to show the graphs of $y = \cos x$ and $y = \tan x$ with the same axes, using equal scales on both axes.

(a) Working to 8 decimal places, verify that one root of the equation $\cos x = \tan x$ is 0.666 239 43. Find the other root in the interval $0 \le x \le 2\pi$ correct to 7 decimal places, and check your answer with a calculator.

(b) What does your display suggest about the graphs at the points where they intersect?

6 Use your calculator to show the graph of $y = (\sin x)^2$. Find

(a) the period, (b) the range.

7 Use your calculator to show the graphs of

(a) $y = (\cos x)^3$, (b) $y = \sqrt{\sin x}$.

For each function, state the domain and the range.

8 A wave travels along a straight water channel. At one instant the wave profile is described by the equation $y = 0.3\cos 0.15x$, where x metres and y metres are the horizontal and vertical coordinates of a point on the surface. Find

(a) the vertical difference between the water levels at the peaks and the troughs,

(b) the horizontal distance between successive peaks.

9 A pendulum is pulled aside from the vertical and released. After t seconds the angle θ it makes with the vertical is given by the equation $\theta = 4\cos 3t$. How long does the pendulum take to perform one complete swing to-and-fro?

10 A soprano sings a high B at a frequency of 1000 cycles a second. Her vocal cords vibrate according to an equation of the form $x = a \sin nt$. What is the value of n?

11 At a point on the equator the sun rises at 6 a.m. and sets at 6 p.m. At midday on a day in December the sun is 67° above the horizon. Suggest a simple model which might be used to calculate the angle ($\theta°$) of the sun above the horizon at a time t hours after sunrise, and use it to estimate the angle of the sun above the horizon at 9 a.m.

12 The Finance Minister bases the national economy on a model of the growth rate (g%) which oscillates between 1% and 5% over a cycle of 15 years. If time (t years) is measured from a year in which the growth rate is 5%, find an equation to fit this model.

13 A research project to investigate the variation in population of hares on an island carries out a census every second year over a 20-year period with the following result.

Year (x)	0	2	4	6	8	10	12	14	16	18	20
Population (y)	500	624	694	682	591	462	349	300	337	444	575

Draw a graph to show the data, and use it to suggest an equation connecting x and y to model the variation in population.

29 Composite and inverse functions

This chapter develops the idea of a function further, and more theoretically, than in earlier parts of the course. It introduces a kind of algebra of functions, by showing how to find a composite function. When you have completed it, you should

- be able to use correct language and notation associated with functions
- know when functions can be combined by the operation of composition, and be able to form the composite function
- know the 'one-to-one' condition for a function to have an inverse, and be able to form the inverse function
- know the relationship between the graph of a one-to-one function and the graph of its inverse function.

29.1 Function notation

When you use a calculator to do a calculation like $\sqrt{7.29}$, $\log_{10} 1000$ or $\sin 30°$ you use two different types of key:

- number keys, with which you can make up 'input numbers' such as 7.29, 1000 or 30
- function keys, such as [$\sqrt{\ }$], [log] and [sin].

(There are other keys which don't come into either of these categories, but you can ignore them in this discussion.)

> In this chapter sin, cos and tan stand for these functions as operated by your calculator in 'degree mode'. You enter a number x, and the output is $\sin x°$, $\cos x°$ or $\tan x°$. The symbol log stands for $\log_{10}$.

Different makes of calculator operate in different ways. Sometimes, to find $\sqrt{7.29}$, you begin by keying in the function $\sqrt{\ }$; the calculator 'remembers' this, and probably displays it, but can't do anything until you key in the input number 7.29.

Other calculators operate in the reverse order. You first key in 7.29, which the calculator 'remembers' and displays. Then, on keying in the function $\sqrt{\ }$, the calculation can proceed.

The details are not important. What matters is that you begin with an input number and a function; nothing can happen until both are keyed in. The function then operates on the input number to produce an output number. The process can be represented symbolically:

Input				Output
7.29	→	[$\sqrt{\ }$]	→	2.7
1000	→	[log]	→	3
30	→	[sin]	→	0.5

For any given function, the output number is called the **image** of the input number.

Not all functions can be operated with a single key. A function such as 'add 3' will use a key for the operation + and a key for 3, probably followed by a key with a label such as [=] or [ans].

But the principle is the same. The important point is that the function key sequence is the same whatever input number it is applied to. You could write

$$4 \rightarrow [\text{add } 3] \rightarrow 7.$$

You can think of a function as a kind of machine. Just as you can have a bread machine, put the ingredients in and take out a loaf, so a function takes in a number in the domain and turns it into a number in the range. For a general input number

$$x \rightarrow [\text{square}] \rightarrow x^2,$$
$$x \rightarrow [\text{add } 3] \rightarrow x+3,$$

and so on. And, for a general function,

$$x \rightarrow [f] \rightarrow f(x).$$

This course has often used phrases like 'the function x^2', 'the function $\cos x^\circ$', or 'the function $f(x)$', and you have understood what is meant. Working mathematicians do this all the time. But it is strictly wrong; x^2, $\cos x^\circ$ and $f(x)$ are symbols for the *output* when the input is x, not for the function itself. When you need to use precise language, you should refer to 'the function square', 'the function cos' or 'the function f'.

Unfortunately only a few functions have convenient names like 'square' or 'cos'. There is no simple name for a function whose output is given by an expression such as $x^2 - 6x + 4$. The way round this is to decide for the time being to call this function f (or any other letter you like). You can then write

$$f : x \mapsto x^2 - 6x + 4.$$

You read this as 'f is the function which turns any input number x in the domain into the output number $x^2 - 6x + 4$'. Notice the bar at the blunt end of the arrow; this avoids confusion with the arrow which has been used to stand for 'tends to' in finding gradients of tangents.

Example 29.1.1

If $f : x \mapsto x(5-x)$, what is $f(3)$?

The symbol $f(3)$ stands for the output when the input is 3. The function called f turns the input 3 into the output $3(5-3) = 6$. So $f(3) = 6$.

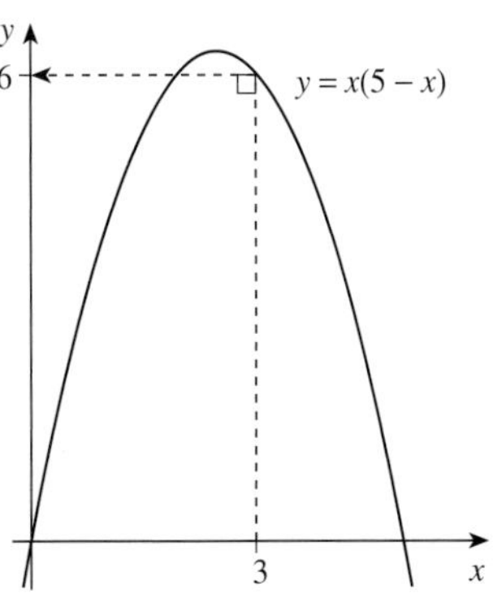

Fig. 29.1

This idea of using an arrow to show the connection between the input and the output can also be linked to the graph of the function. Fig. 29.1 shows the graph of $y = x(5-x)$, with the input number 3 on the x-axis. An arrow which goes up the page from this point and bends through a right angle when it hits the graph takes you to the output number 6 on the y-axis.

29.2 Forming composite functions

If you want to work out the value of $(x-3)^2$ when $x=8$, you say to yourself something like

'8 minus 3 equals 5, and 5 squared is 25'.

That is, you use the number 5 as a staging post between the input number 8 and the output number 25. You are in fact putting two function calculations together,

$8 \to [\text{subtract } 3] \to 5$

and $5 \to [\text{square}] \to 25.$

You could represent the whole calculation in a single chain:

$$8 \to [\text{subtract } 3] \to 5 \to [\text{square}] \to 25.$$

The output of the first function becomes the input of the second.

In this example, the complete function $x \mapsto (x-3)^2$ is called the 'composite' of the functions 'subtract 3' and 'square'.

Example 29.2.1
Find the output if the functions square and sin act in succession on inputs of
(a) 30, (b) x.

(a) $30 \to [\text{square}] \to 900 \to [\sin] \to 0.$

(b) $x \to [\text{square}] \to x^2 \to [\sin] \to \sin(x^2)^\circ.$

Notice that since in (b) the input to the function sin is x^2, not x, the output is $\sin(x^2)^\circ$, not $\sin x^\circ$. For a general input, and two general functions f and g, this would become:

$$x \to [\ f\ ] \to f(x) \to [\ g\ ] \to g(f(x)).$$

Since the output of the composite function is $g(f(x))$, the composite function itself is denoted by $g \circ f$. Notice that $g \circ f$ must be read as 'first f then g'. You must get used to reading the symbol $g \circ f$ from right to left. Writing $f \circ g$ means 'first g, then f', which is almost always a different function from $g \circ f$. For instance, if you change the order of the functions in Example 29.2.1 part (a), instead of the output 0 you get

$$30 \to [\sin] \to 0.5 \to [\text{square}] \to 0.25.$$

The **composite function** $g \circ f$ is applied by operating on an input number with the function f, then operating on the result with the function g.

That is, for any input number x,

$$g \circ f(x) = g(f(x)).$$

In general, the composite functions $g \circ f$ and $f \circ g$ are different functions.

Some books use the notation $(f \circ g)(x)$ instead of $f \circ g(x)$ to mean $f(g(x))$.

Example 29.2.2
Let $f : x \mapsto x + 3$ and $g : x \mapsto x^2$. Find $g \circ f$ and $f \circ g$. Show that there is just one number x such that $g \circ f(x) = f \circ g(x)$.

The composite function $g \circ f$ is represented by

$$x \to [\ f\ ] \to x + 3 \to [\ g\ ] \to (x + 3)^2$$

and $f \circ g$ is represented by

$$x \to [\ g\ ] \to x^2 \to [\ f\ ] \to x^2 + 3.$$

So $g \circ f : x \mapsto (x + 3)^2$ and $f \circ g : x \mapsto x^2 + 3$.

If $g \circ f(x) = f \circ g(x)$,

$$(x + 3)^2 = x^2 + 3,$$

so $\quad x^2 + 6x + 9 = x^2 + 3,$
or $\quad x = -1.$

It is worth checking the answer to Example 29.2.2 numerically. With the input number -1, 'add 3' followed by square gives

-1 plus 3 equals 2, and 2 squared is 4;

'square' followed by 'add 3' gives

-1 squared is 1, 1 plus 3 equals 4.

The final answer is 4 in both cases, but the intermediate numbers are different.

As a further check, try taking some other input number and show that this gives a different output number for the two functions.

Example 29.2.3
If $f : x \mapsto \cos x°$ and $g : x \mapsto \dfrac{1}{x}$, calculate (a) $g \circ f(60)$, (b) $g \circ f(90)$.

(a) $60 \to [\,\cos\,] \to 0.5 \to [\,\text{reciprocal}\,] \to 2$
so $g \circ f(60) = 2$.

(b) $90 \to [\,\cos\,] \to 0 \to [\,\text{reciprocal}\,] \to$!!

The problem in part (b) is that $\cos 90° = 0$ and $\frac{1}{0}$ is not defined.

Try working Example 29.2.3 with your calculator. What does it give in part (b)?

What has happened in Example 29.2.3 part (b) is that the number 0 is in the range of the function f, but it is not in the domain of g. You always need to be aware that this may happen when you find the composite of two functions. It is time to look again at domains and ranges, so that you can avoid this problem.

29.3 Domain and range revisited

In an equation such as $y = 2x - 10$, it is generally understood that x and y stand for real numbers. But sometimes it is important to be absolutely precise about this. If so you would write

$$f : x \mapsto 2x - 10, \quad x \in \mathbb{R}$$

to indicate that f is the function whose domain is the set of real numbers which turns any input x into its image $2x - 10$.

Strictly, a function is not completely defined unless you state the domain as well as the rule for obtaining the output from the input. In this case the range is also $\mathbb{R}$, although you do not need to state this in describing the function.

You know from Section 8.4 that for some functions the domain is part of $\mathbb{R}$, because the expression $f(x)$ only has meaning for some $x \in \mathbb{R}$. (Here $\in$ is read as 'belonging to' rather than 'belongs to'.) The set of real numbers for which $f(x)$ has a meaning will be called the **natural domain** of f. With a calculator, if you input a number which is not in the natural domain, the output will be an 'error' display.

For the square root function, for example, the natural domain is the set of positive real numbers and zero, so you write

$$\text{square root: } x \mapsto \sqrt{x}, \quad \text{where } x \in \mathbb{R} \text{ and } x \geq 0.$$

Example 29.3.1
Find the range of the functions

(a) sin, with natural domain $\mathbb{R}$, (b) sin, with domain $x \in \mathbb{R}$ and $0 < x < 90$.

From the graph of $y = \sin x°$ shown in Fig. 29.2 you can read off the ranges:

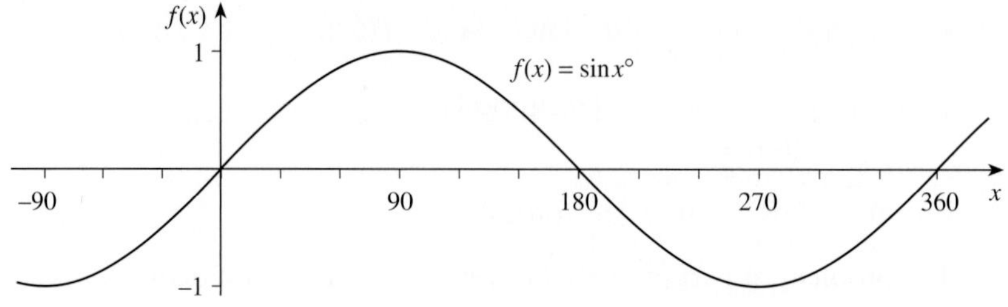

Fig. 29.2

(a) For $x \in \mathbb{R}$, the range is $y \in \mathbb{R}, -1 \leq y \leq 1$.

(b) For $x \in \mathbb{R}, 0 < x < 90$, the range is $y \in \mathbb{R}, 0 < y < 1$.

Although the letter x is usually used in describing the domain, and y for the range, this is not essential. The set of numbers $y \in \mathbb{R}, 0 < y < 1$ is the same set of numbers as $x \in \mathbb{R}, 0 < x < 1$ or $t \in \mathbb{R}, 0 < t < 1$.

It is especially important to understand this when you find composite functions. For example, in Example 29.2.3 part (a), the number 0.5 appears first as the output for the input 60 to the function $f : x \mapsto \cos x^\circ$, so you might think of this as $y = \cos 60^\circ = 0.5$. But for the input to the function $g : x \mapsto \frac{1}{x}$, it is natural to write $x = 0.5$. The number 0.5 belongs first to the range of f, then to the domain of g.

This is where Example 29.2.3 part (b) breaks down. The number 0, which appears as the output when the input to f is 90, is not in the natural domain of g. So although 90 is in the natural domain of f, it is not in the natural domain of $g \circ f$.

The general rule is:

> To form the composite function $g \circ f$, the domain D of f must be chosen so that the whole of the range of f is included in the domain of g. The function $g \circ f$ is then defined as $g \circ f : x \mapsto g(f(x)), x \in D$.

For the functions in Example 29.2.3, the domain of g is the set $\mathbb{R}$ excluding 0, so the domain of f must be chosen to exclude the numbers x for which $\cos x^\circ = 0$. These are $\ldots, -450, -270, -90, +90, +270, +450, \ldots$, all of which can be summed up by the formula $90 + 180n$, where n is an integer.

There is a neat way of writing this, using the standard symbol $\mathbb{Z}$ for the set of integers $\ldots, -3, -2, -1, 0, 1, 2, 3, \ldots$. The domain of f can then be expressed as $x \in \mathbb{R}, x \neq 90 + 180n, n \in \mathbb{Z}$.

Example 29.3.2

Find the natural domain and the corresponding range of the function $x \mapsto \sqrt{x(x-3)}$.

You can express the function as $g \circ f$, where $f : x \mapsto x(x-3)$ and $g : x \mapsto \sqrt{x}$.

The natural domain of g is $x \in \mathbb{R}, x \geq 0$, so you want the range of f to be included in $y \in \mathbb{R}, y \geq 0$. (Switching from x to y is not essential, but you may find it easier.) The solution of the inequality $y = x(x-3) \geq 0$ is $x \geq 3$ or $x \leq 0$.

The natural domain of $g \circ f$ is therefore $x \in \mathbb{R}, x \geq 3$ or $x \leq 0$.

With this domain the range of f is $y \in \mathbb{R}, y \geq 0$, so the numbers input to g are given by $x \in \mathbb{R}, x \geq 0$. With this domain, the range of g is $y \in \mathbb{R}, y \geq 0$. This is therefore the range of the combined function $g \circ f$.

Try using your calculator to plot the graph $y = \sqrt{x(x-3)}$, with a window of $-1 \leq x \leq 4$ and $0 \leq y \leq 2$. You should find that no points are plotted for the 'illegal' values of x in the interval $0 < x < 3$. If you were to input a number in this interval, such as 1, you will get as far as $1(1-3) = -2$, but the final $\sqrt{}$ key will give you an error message or some display which does not represent a real number.

Exercise 29A

1 Given $f : x \mapsto (3x+5)^2$ and $g : x \mapsto 3x^2+5$, where $x \in \mathbb{R}$, find the values of

(a) $f(2)$, (b) $f(-1)$, (c) $f(7)$,

(d) $g(2)$, (e) $g(-1)$, (f) $g(7)$.

2 Given $f : x \mapsto \dfrac{4}{x+5}$ and $g : x \mapsto \dfrac{4}{x}+5$, where $x \in \mathbb{R}$ and $x \neq -5, 0$, find the values of

(a) $f(-1)$, (b) $f(-4)$, (c) $f(3)$.

(d) $g(-1)$, (e) $g(-4)$, (f) $g(3)$.

3 Find the output if the functions 'square', 'subtract 4' act in succession on an input of

(a) 2, (b) -5, (c) $\frac{1}{2}$, (d) x.

4 Find the output if the functions 'cos', 'add 2', 'cube' act in succession on an input of

(a) 0, (b) 90, (c) 120, (d) x.

5 Find the output if the functions 'square root', 'multiply by 2', 'subtract 10', 'square', act in succession on an input of

(a) 9, (b) 16, (c) $\frac{1}{4}$, (d) x.

6 Break the following functions down into two or more components.

(a) $f : x \mapsto 4x+9$ (b) $f : x \mapsto 4(x+9)$

(c) $f : x \mapsto 2x^2-5$ (d) $f : x \mapsto 2(x-5)^2$

7 Find the natural domain and corresponding range of each of the following functions.

(a) $f : x \mapsto x^2$ (b) $f : x \mapsto \cos x^\circ$ (c) $f : x \mapsto \sqrt{x-3}$

(d) $f : x \mapsto 3^x$ (e) $f : x \mapsto \dfrac{1}{\sqrt{x}}$ (f) $f : x \mapsto x(4-x)$

(g) $f : x \mapsto \sqrt{x(4-x)}$ (h) $f : x \mapsto x^2+4x+10$ (i) $f : x \mapsto \log_2 x$

8 Given that $f : x \mapsto 2x+1$ and $g : x \mapsto 3x-5$, where $x \in \mathbb{R}$, find the value of the following.

(a) $g \circ f(1)$ (b) $g \circ f(-2)$ (c) $f \circ g(0)$ (d) $f \circ g(7)$

(e) $f \circ f(5)$ (f) $f \circ f(-5)$ (g) $g \circ g(4)$ (h) $g \circ g(2\frac{2}{9})$

9 Given that $f : x \mapsto x^2$ and $g : x \mapsto 4x-1$, where $x \in \mathbb{R}$, find the value of the following.

(a) $f \circ g(2)$ (b) $g \circ g(4)$ (c) $g \circ f(-3)$

(d) $f \circ f(\frac{1}{2})$ (e) $f \circ g \circ f(-1)$ (f) $g \circ f \circ g \circ f(2)$

10 Given that $f : x \mapsto 5-x$ and $g : x \mapsto \dfrac{4}{x}$, where $x \in \mathbb{R}$ and $x \neq 0$ or 5, find the value of the following.

(a) $f \circ f(7)$ (b) $f \circ f(-19)$ (c) $g \circ g(1)$

(d) $g \circ g(\frac{1}{2})$ (e) $g \circ g \circ g \circ g(\frac{1}{2})$ (f) $f \circ f \circ f \circ f \circ f(6)$

(g) $f \circ g \circ f \circ g(2)$ (h) $f \circ g \circ g \circ f(2)$

11 Given that $f : x \mapsto 2x + 5$, $g : x \mapsto x^2$ and $h : x \mapsto \dfrac{1}{x}$, where $x \in \mathbb{R}$ and $x \neq 0$ or $-\frac{5}{2}$, find the following composite functions.

(a) $f \circ g$ (b) $g \circ f$ (c) $f \circ h$ (d) $h \circ f$

(e) $f \circ f$ (f) $h \circ h$ (g) $g \circ f \circ h$ (h) $h \circ g \circ f$

12 Given that $f : x \mapsto \sin x°$, $g : x \mapsto x^3$ and $h : x \mapsto x - 3$, where $x \in \mathbb{R}$, find the following functions.

(a) $h \circ f$ (b) $f \circ h$ (c) $f \circ h \circ g$

(d) $f \circ g$ (e) $h \circ h \circ h$ (f) $g \circ f$

13 Given that $f : x \mapsto x + 4$, $g : x \mapsto 3x$ and $h : x \mapsto x^2$, where $x \in \mathbb{R}$, express each of the following in terms of *f*, *g*, *h* as appropriate.

(a) $x \mapsto x^2 + 4$ (b) $x \mapsto 3x + 4$

(c) $x \mapsto x^4$ (d) $x \mapsto x^2 + 8x + 16$

14 In each of the following, find the natural domain and the range of the function $g \circ f$.

(a) $f : x \mapsto \sqrt{x}$ $\quad g : x \mapsto x - 5$ (b) $f : x \mapsto x + 3$ $\quad g : x \mapsto \sqrt{x}$

(c) $f : x \mapsto x - 2$ $\quad g : x \mapsto \dfrac{1}{x}$ (d) $f : x \mapsto |x - 3|$ $\quad g : x \mapsto \sqrt{x}$

15 Given that $f : x \mapsto x^2$ and $g : x \mapsto 3x - 2$, where $x \in \mathbb{R}$, find *a*, *b* and *c* such that

(a) $f \circ g(a) = 100$, (b) $g \circ g(b) = 55$, (c) $f \circ g(c) = g \circ f(c)$.

16 The functions $f : x \mapsto 4x + 1$ and $g : x \mapsto ax + b$ are such that $f \circ g = g \circ f$ for all real values of x. Show that $a = 3b + 1$.

29.4 Inverse functions

If your sister is 2 years older than you, then you are 2 years younger than her. To get her age from yours you use the 'add 2' function; to get your age from hers you 'subtract 2'. The functions 'add 2' and 'subtract 2' are said to be **inverse functions** of each other. That is, 'subtract 2' is the inverse function of 'add 2' (and vice versa).

You know many pairs of inverse functions: 'double' and 'halve', 'cube' and 'cube root' are simple examples.

There are also some functions which are their own inverses, such as 'change sign'; to undo the effect of a change of sign, you just change sign again. Another example is 'reciprocal' $\left(x \mapsto \dfrac{1}{x}\right)$. These functions are said to be **self-inverse**.

The inverse of a function f is denoted by the symbol f^{-1}. If f turns an input number x into an output number y, then f^{-1} turns y into x. You can illustrate this graphically by reversing the arrow which symbolises the function, as in Fig. 29.3. The range of f becomes the domain of f^{-1}, and the domain of f becomes the range of f^{-1}.

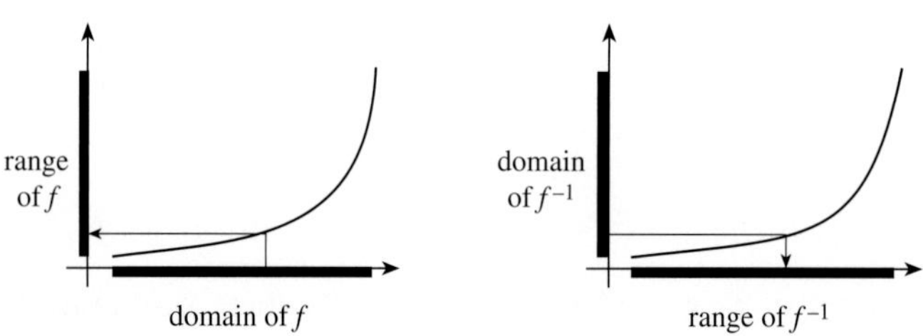

Fig. 29.3

Example 29.4.1

For the following functions with the given domains, find the inverse functions and their domains.

(a) $f : x \mapsto \sqrt{x}, \quad \mathbb{R}^+$ (b) $g : x \mapsto 2^x, \quad \mathbb{R}$ (c) $h : x \mapsto 10 - x, 0 \le x \le 10$

The graphs of these functions are shown in Fig. 29.4.

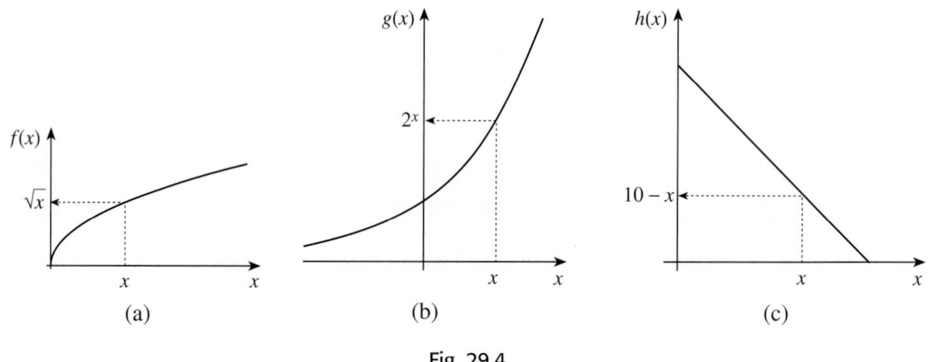

Fig. 29.4

(a) The reverse process to taking the square root is squaring. That is, $(\sqrt{x})^2 = x$.

If x is a positive real number, $\sqrt{x}$ is a positive real number (see Fig. 29.4(a)). So the inverse function is

$$f^{-1} : x \mapsto x^2, \quad \text{with domain } \mathbb{R}^+.$$

(b) If $y = 2^x$, then $x = \log_2 y$. So to get back from 2^x to x you take the logarithm to base 2.

For any real number x, 2^x is a positive real number (see Fig. 29.4(b)). So the inverse function g^{-1} is the function $\log_2$, with domain $\mathbb{R}^+$.

(c) If you start with any number x between 0 and 10, its image is $10 - x$ (see Fig. 29.4(c)), which is also between 0 and 10. To get back to the original number x you again subtract from 10, because

$$10 - (10 - x) = x.$$

So the inverse function is

$$h^{-1} : x \mapsto 10 - x, \quad \text{with domain } 0 \le x \le 10.$$

This means that the functions h and h^{-1} are the same, so h is self-inverse.

You will notice that all three graphs in Fig. 29.4 have one feature in common. That is, they are all either increasing or decreasing throughout the given domain. Because of this, you can be sure that, for any number in the range, there is just one number in the domain that it could have come from.

This would not be true for a function like $p : x \mapsto x^2$ with domain $\mathbb{R}$, or $q : x \mapsto \sin x^\circ$ with domain $0 \le x \le 180$ (see Fig. 29.5). For example, for the function p both –2 and 2 have 4 for their image; and for q both 30 and 150 have image $\frac{1}{2}$. So, when you try to find the inverse images, by tracing the arrows backwards, you can't be certain where they originated.

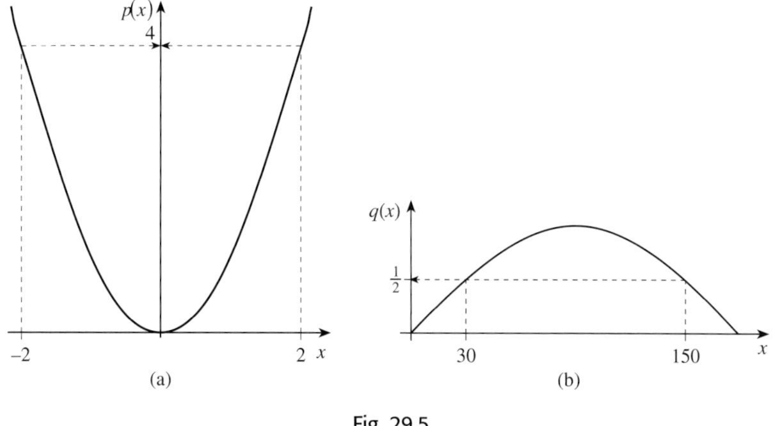

Fig. 29.5

The essential difference between the two sets of graphs is that, in Fig. 29.5, there are some numbers in the range which are the images of more than one number in the domain. In Fig. 29.4 each number in the range is the image of only one number in the domain.

The functions f, g and h in Fig. 29.4 are said to be one-to-one. This is the only kind of function for which an inverse function exists. The functions p and q in Fig. 29.5 do not have inverses.

However, the function $r : x \mapsto \sin x^\circ$ with domain $-90 \le x \le 90$ (see Fig. 29.6) does have an inverse, because over this interval $\sin x^\circ$ is an increasing function, and is therefore one-to-one. Whether a function has an inverse or not often depends on the domain over which it is defined.

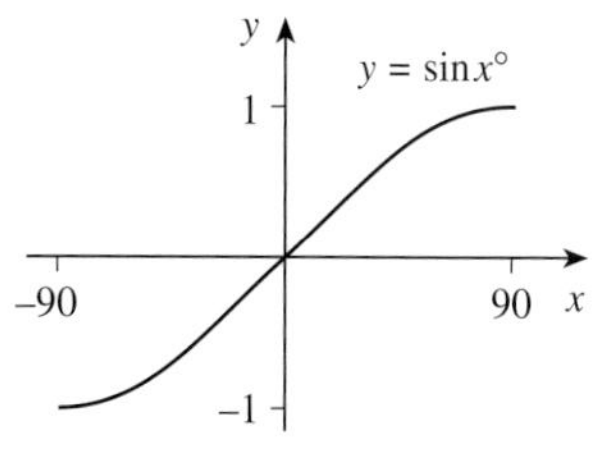

Fig. 29.6

> A function f defined for some domain D is **one-to-one** if, for each number y in the range R of f there is only one number $x \in D$ such that $y = f(x)$. The function with domain R defined by $f^{-1} : y \mapsto x$, where $y = f(x)$, is the **inverse function** of f.

This definition was illustrated above in Fig. 29.6, which was drawn to ensure that the function f was one-to-one.

Fig. 29.3 also shows that, if you combine a function with its inverse, you get back to the number you started with. That is,

$$f^{-1} \circ f(x) = x, \quad \text{and} \quad f \circ f^{-1}(y) = y.$$

The functions $f^{-1} \circ f$ and $f \circ f^{-1}$ are called **identity functions** because their inputs and outputs are identical. But there is a subtle difference between these two composite functions, since their domains may not be the same; the first has domain D and the second has domain R.

On some calculators you will find '[inv]' used to denote the inverse, so that f^{-1} becomes inv f. For example, inv log stands for the function $x \mapsto 10^x$, because $10^{\log x} = x$.

29.5 Finding inverse functions

For very simple one-step functions it is easy to write down an expression for the inverse function. The inverse of 'add 2' is 'subtract 2', so

$$f : x \mapsto x + 2, x \in \mathbb{R} \quad \text{has inverse} \quad f^{-1} : x \mapsto x - 2, x \in \mathbb{R}.$$

Notice that the inverse could equally well be written as

$$f^{-1} : y \mapsto y - 2, y \in \mathbb{R}.$$

You can sometimes break down more complicated functions into a chain of simple steps. You can then find the inverse by going backwards through each step in reverse order. (This is sometimes called the 'shoes and socks' process: you put your socks on before your shoes, but you take off your shoes before your socks. In mathematical notation, $(g \circ f)^{-1} = f^{-1} \circ g^{-1}$, where f denotes putting on your socks and g your shoes.)

However, this method does not always work, particularly if x appears more than once in the expression for the function. You can then try writing $y = f(x)$, and turn the formula round into the form $x = g(y)$. Then g is the inverse of f.

Example 29.5.1
Find the inverse of $f : x \mapsto 2x + 5, x \in \mathbb{R}$.

Note first that f is one-to-one, and that the range is $\mathbb{R}$.

Method 1 You can break the function down as

$$x \to [\text{double}] \to [\text{add } 5] \to 2x + 5.$$

To find f^{-1}, go backwards through the chain (read from right to left):

$$\tfrac{1}{2}(x - 5) \leftarrow [\text{halve}] \leftarrow [\text{subtract } 5] \leftarrow x.$$

So $f^{-1} : x \mapsto \frac{1}{2}(x - 5), x \in \mathbb{R}$.

Method 2 If $y = 2x + 5$,

$$\begin{aligned} y - 5 &= 2x \\ x &= \tfrac{1}{2}(y - 5). \end{aligned}$$

So the inverse function is $f^{-1} : y \mapsto \frac{1}{2}(y - 5), y \in \mathbb{R}$.

The two answers are the same, even though different letters are used.

Example 29.5.2

Find the inverse of the function $f : x \mapsto \dfrac{x+2}{x-2}$, where $x \in \mathbb{R}$ and $x \neq 2$.

It is not obvious that this function is one-to-one, or what its range is. However, using the second method and writing $y = \dfrac{x+2}{x-2}$,

$$\begin{aligned} y(x-2) &= x+2, \\ yx - 2y &= x+2, \\ yx - x &= 2y+2, \\ x(y-1) &= 2(y+1), \\ x &= \frac{2(y+1)}{y-1}. \end{aligned}$$

This shows that, unless $y = 1$, there is just one value of x for each value of y. So f must be one-to-one, the inverse function therefore exists, and

$$f^{-1} : y \mapsto \frac{2(y+1)}{y-1} \text{ where } y \in \mathbb{R} \text{ and } y \neq -1.$$

You may want to express this with x rather than y as the independent variable. If so, simply change y to x throughout. Then

$$f^{-1} : x \mapsto \frac{2(x+1)}{x-1} \text{ where } x \in \mathbb{R} \text{ and } x \neq -1.$$

29.6 Graphing inverse functions

Figure 29.7 shows the graph of $y = f(x)$, where f is a one-to-one function with domain D and range R. Since f^{-1} exists, with domain R and range D, you can also write the equation as $x = f^{-1}(y)$. You can regard Fig. 29.7 as the graph of both f and f^{-1}.

But you sometimes want to draw the graph in the more conventional form, as $y = f^{-1}(x)$ with the domain along the x-axis. To do this you have to swap the x- and y-axes, which you do by reflecting the graph in Fig. 29.7 in the line $y = x$. (Make sure that you have the same scale on both axes!) Then the x-axis is reflected into the y-axis and vice versa, and the graph of $x = f^{-1}(y)$ is reflected into the graph of $y = f^{-1}(x)$. This is shown in Fig. 29.8.

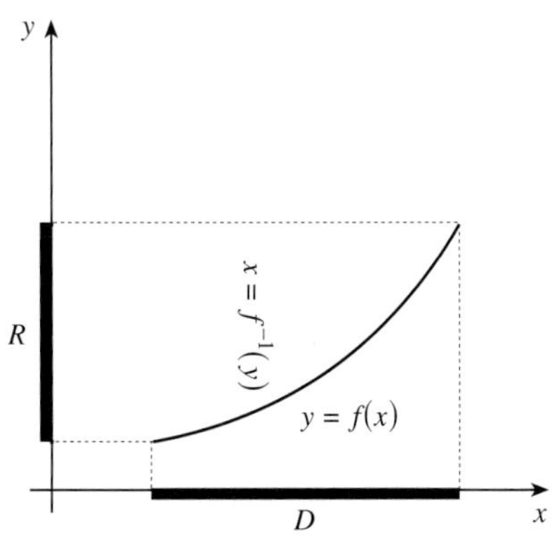

Fig. 29.7

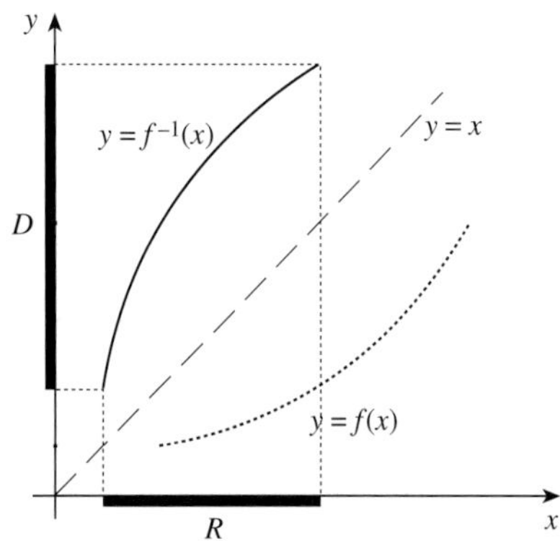

Fig. 29.8

> If f is a one-to-one function, the graphs of $y = f(x)$ and $y = f^{-1}(x)$ are reflections of each other in the line $y = x$.

Fig. 29.9 illustrates this for the three functions in Example 29.4.1, $f : x \mapsto \sqrt{x}, \mathbb{R}^+$, $g : x \mapsto 2^x, \mathbb{R}$ and $h : x \mapsto 10 - x, 0 \le x \le 10$.

Notice that, in part (c), the line segment joining (0, 10) to (10, 0) is its own reflection. This shows that the function h is self-inverse.

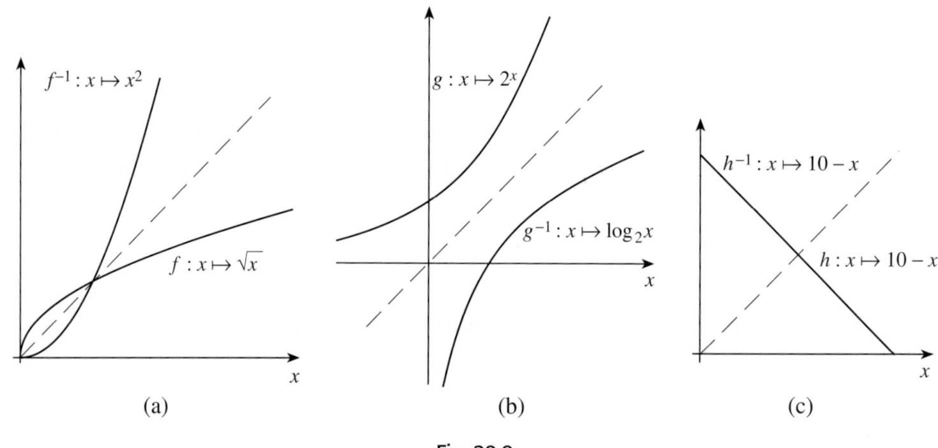

Fig. 29.9

Exercise 29B

1 Each of the following functions has domain $\mathbb{R}$. In each case use a graph to show that the function is one-to-one, and write down its inverse.

(a) $f : x \mapsto x + 4$ (b) $f : x \mapsto x - 5$ (c) $f : x \mapsto 2x$

(d) $f : x \mapsto \frac{1}{4}x$ (e) $f : x \mapsto x^3$ (f) $f : x \mapsto \sqrt[5]{x}$

2 Given the function $f : x \mapsto x - 6, x \in \mathbb{R}$, find the values of

(a) $f^{-1}(4)$, (b) $f^{-1}(1)$, (c) $f^{-1}(-3)$,

(d) $f \circ f^{-1}(5)$, (e) $f^{-1} \circ f(-4)$.

3 Given the function $f : x \mapsto 5x, x \in \mathbb{R}$, find the values of

(a) $f^{-1}(20)$, (b) $f^{-1}(100)$, (c) $f^{-1}(7)$,

(d) $f \circ f^{-1}(15)$, (e) $f^{-1} \circ f(-6)$.

4 Given the function $f : x \mapsto \sqrt[3]{x}, x \in \mathbb{R}$, find the values of

(a) $f^{-1}(2)$, (b) $f^{-1}(\frac{1}{2})$, (c) $f^{-1}(8)$,

(d) $f^{-1} \circ f(-27)$, (e) $f \circ f^{-1}(5)$.

5 Each of the following functions has domain $\mathbb{R}$. Determine which are one-to-one functions.

(a) $f: x \mapsto 3x + 4$ (b) $f: x \mapsto x^2 + 1$ (c) $f: x \mapsto x^2 - 3x$

(d) $f: x \mapsto 5 - x$ (e) $f: x \mapsto \cos x^\circ$ (f) $f: x \mapsto x^3 - 2$

(g) $f: x \mapsto \frac{1}{2}x - 7$ (h) $f: x \mapsto |x|$ (i) $f: x \mapsto x(x - 4)$

(j) $f: x \mapsto x^3 - 3x$ (k) $f: x \mapsto x^9$ (l) $f: x \mapsto \sqrt{x^2 + 1}$

6 Use your calculator to show the following functions, with the specified domains. Hence determine which of them are one-to-one.

(a) $f: x \mapsto x^2, x > 0$ (b) $f: x \mapsto \cos x^\circ, -90 < x < 90$

(c) $f: x \mapsto 1 - 2x, x < 0$ (d) $f: x \mapsto x(x - 2), 0 < x < 2$

(e) $f: x \mapsto x(x - 2), x > 2$ (f) $f: x \mapsto x(x - 2), x < 1$

(g) $f: x \mapsto \sqrt{x}, x > 0$ (h) $f: x \mapsto x^2 + 6x - 5, x > 0$

(i) $f: x \mapsto x^2 + 6x - 5, x < 0$ (j) $f: x \mapsto x^2 + 6x - 5, x > -3$

7 Each of the following functions has domain $x \geq k$. In each case, find the smallest possible value of k such that the function is one-to-one.

(a) $f: x \mapsto x^2 - 4$ (b) $f: x \mapsto (x + 1)^2$

(c) $f: x \mapsto (3x - 2)^2$ (d) $f: x \mapsto x^2 - 8x + 15$

(e) $f: x \mapsto x^2 + 10x + 1$ (f) $f: x \mapsto (x + 4)(x - 2)$

8 Use Method 1 of Example 29.5.1 to find the inverse of each of the following functions.

(a) $f: x \mapsto 3x - 1, x \in \mathbb{R}$ (b) $f: x \mapsto \frac{1}{2}x + 4, x \in \mathbb{R}$

(c) $f: x \mapsto x^3 + 5, x \in \mathbb{R}$ (d) $f: x \mapsto \sqrt{x} - 3, x > 0$

(e) $f: x \mapsto \dfrac{5x - 3}{2}, x \in \mathbb{R}$ (f) $f: x \mapsto (x - 1)^2 + 6, x \geq 1$

9 Use Method 2 of Example 29.5.1 to find the inverse of each of the following functions.

(a) $f: x \mapsto 6x + 5, x \in \mathbb{R}$ (b) $f: x \mapsto \dfrac{x + 4}{5}, x \in \mathbb{R}$

(c) $f: x \mapsto 4 - 2x, x \in \mathbb{R}$ (d) $f: x \mapsto \dfrac{2x + 7}{3}, x \in \mathbb{R}$

(e) $f: x \mapsto 2x^3 + 5, x \in \mathbb{R}$ (f) $f: x \mapsto \dfrac{1}{x} + 4, x \in \mathbb{R}$ and $x \neq 0$

(g) $f: x \mapsto \dfrac{5}{x - 1}, x \in \mathbb{R}$ and $x \neq 1$

10 For each of the following, find the inverse function and sketch the graphs of $y = f(x)$ and $y = f^{-1}(x)$.

(a) $f: x \mapsto 4x, x \in \mathbb{R}$ (b) $f: x \mapsto x + 3, x \in \mathbb{R}$

(c) $f: x \mapsto \sqrt{x}, x \in \mathbb{R}$ and $x \geq 0$ (d) $f: x \mapsto 2x + 1, x \in \mathbb{R}$

(e) $f: x \mapsto (x - 2)^2, x \in \mathbb{R}$ and $x \geq 2$ (f) $f: x \mapsto 1 - 3x, x \in \mathbb{R}$

(g) $f: x \mapsto \dfrac{3}{x}, x \in \mathbb{R}$ and $x \neq 0$ (h) $f: x \mapsto 7 - x, x \in \mathbb{R}$

(i) $f: x \mapsto 3^x, x \in \mathbb{R}$ (j) $f: x \mapsto \log_5 x, x \in \mathbb{R}^+$

11 Show that the following functions are self-inverse.

(a) $f : x \mapsto 5 - x, x \in \mathbb{R}$

(b) $f : x \mapsto -x, x \in \mathbb{R}$

(c) $f : x \mapsto \dfrac{4}{x}, x \in \mathbb{R}$ and $x \neq 0$

(d) $f : x \mapsto \dfrac{6}{5x}, x \in \mathbb{R}$ and $x \neq 0$

(e) $f : x \mapsto \dfrac{x+5}{x-1}, x \in \mathbb{R}$ and $x \neq 1$

(f) $f : x \mapsto \dfrac{3x-1}{2x-3}, x \in \mathbb{R}$ and $x \neq \frac{3}{2}$

12 Find the inverse of each of the following functions.

(a) $f : x \mapsto \dfrac{x}{x-2}, x \in \mathbb{R}$ and $x \neq 2$

(b) $f : x \mapsto \dfrac{2x+1}{x-4}, x \in \mathbb{R}$ and $x \neq 4$

(c) $f : x \mapsto \dfrac{x+2}{x-5}, x \in \mathbb{R}$ and $x \neq 5$

(d) $f : x \mapsto \dfrac{3x-11}{4x-3}, x \in \mathbb{R}$ and $x \neq \frac{3}{4}$

13 The inverse of the function $f : x \mapsto ax + b, x \in \mathbb{R}$ is $f^{-1} : x \mapsto 8x - 3$. Find a and b.

14 The function $f : x \mapsto px + q, x \in \mathbb{R}$, is such that $f^{-1}(6) = 3$ and $f^{-1}(-29) = -2$. Find $f^{-1}(27)$.

30 Transforming graphs

If you change the equation of a graph by modifying one of the variables, adding or multiplying by a constant, the graph with the new equation will have a shape similar to the original one. In this chapter, the change in the variables is linked to the change in the graph. When you have completed it, you should

- be able to modify equations of the form $y = f(x)$ so as to translate, stretch or reflect their graphs
- be able to find the result of carrying out two or more transformations in succession.

You will find your calculator especially useful in this chapter. Begin by displaying the graph of some equation (either given in the text, or of your own choice). You can then specify some change in either x or y, and produce a second graph for the modified equation. The purpose is to relate the change in the variable to the change in the graph.

30.1 Translating graphs

Use your calculator to display the graphs of $y = x^2$ and $y = x^2 + 3$. What do you notice about the graphs?

You should see that the second graph has the same shape as the first but is moved by 3 units in the y-direction.

Figure 30.1 shows a graph whose equation is $y = f(x)$. What is the graph whose equation is $y = f(x) + k$?

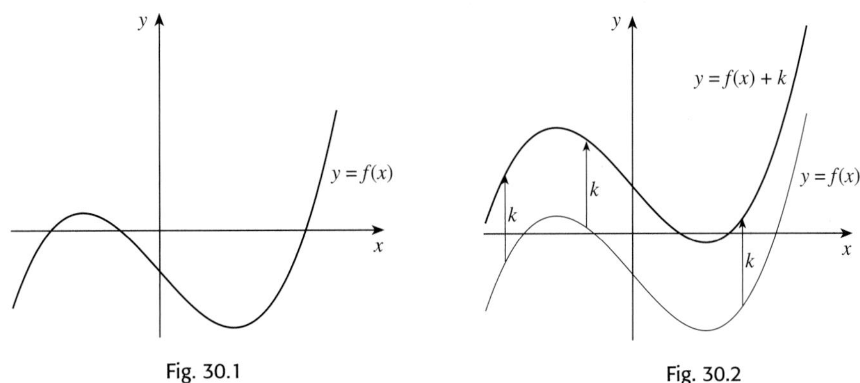

Fig. 30.1

Fig. 30.2

The answer is shown in Fig. 30.2. For each particular value of x, the y-coordinate on the second graph is k more than the y-coordinate on the first. So the whole of the second graph must lie k units higher than the first graph.

Of course, if k is negative, the second graph will be lower than the first by an amount $(-k)$ units.

The transformation which converts the first graph into the second is called a **translation**. A translation is defined by its magnitude and direction; $f(x)$ is translated into $f(x)+k$ by a translation of k units in the y-direction.

Example 30.1.1

(a) Sketch the graph of $y=\frac{1}{2}x+3$ and explain how it is related to the graph of $y=\frac{1}{2}x$.

(b) Sketch the graph of $y=x^3-4$ and explain how it is related to the graph of $y=x^3$.

(a) The graph of $y=\frac{1}{2}x$ is a straight line through the origin with gradient $\frac{1}{2}$. So $y=\frac{1}{2}x+3$ is a line parallel to this, 3 units higher, as in Fig. 30.3.

(b) The graph of $y=x^3-4$ is lower than $y=x^3$, by an amount $-(-4)$ units, that is by 4 units, as in Fig. 30.4.

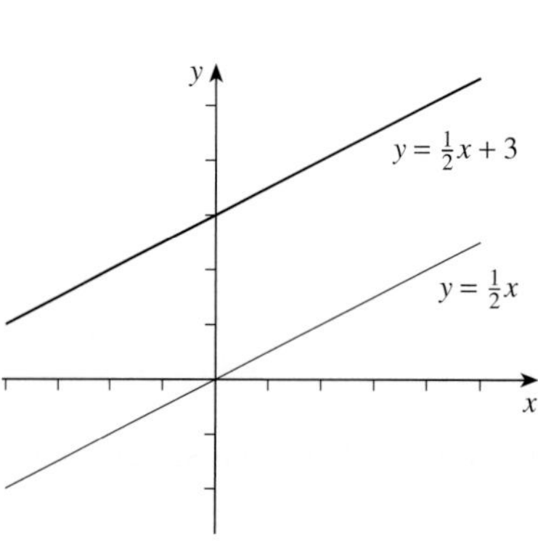

Fig. 30.3

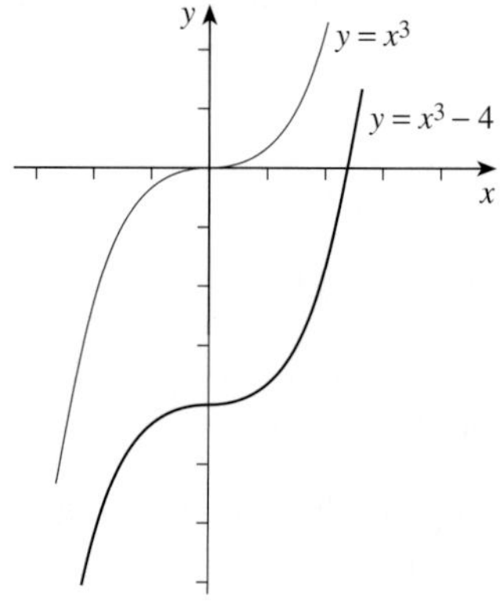

Fig. 30.4

If p is a positive number, the translation from $y=f(x)$ to $y=f(x)-p$ can be described either as a 'translation of $-p$ in the (positive) y-direction' or as a 'translation of p in the negative y-direction'.

Notice that you can write the equation $y=f(x)+k$ as $y-k=f(x)$. This shows that:

Replacing y by $y-k$ in the equation of a graph produces a translation of k units in the y-direction.

But what happens if you replace x by $x-k$?

Example 30.1.2

Use your calculator to display the graphs of

(a) $y=x^2$ and $y=(x-3)^2$,

(b) $y=x^3$ and $y=(x-3)^3$,

(c) $y=x^2$ and $y=(x+3)^2$,

(d) $y=\frac{1}{2}x$ and $y=\frac{1}{2}(x-3)$.

In parts (a) and (b) you should see that the graph has been translated by 3 units to the right.

In part (c) you should see that the curve has been translated by 3 units to the left. It is helpful in this case to think of $x+3$ as $x-(-3)$.

Part (d) is complicated by the fact that the graph is a straight line, but you should see that if you translate the original graph by 3 units to the right you get the new graph. The complication is that you can also write the equation as $y=\frac{1}{2}x-\frac{3}{2}$ and think of the graph as having been translated by $\frac{3}{2}$ in the negative y-direction.

Example 30.1.2 shows that, if you want to translate the graph of $y=f(x)$ in the x-direction, the rule is similar with y replaced by x:

> Replacing x by $x-k$ in the equation of a graph produces a translation of k units in the x-direction.

This second result is illustrated in Fig. 30.5. The graph of $y=f(x-k)$ is obtained from that of $y=f(x)$ by a shift to the right of k units.

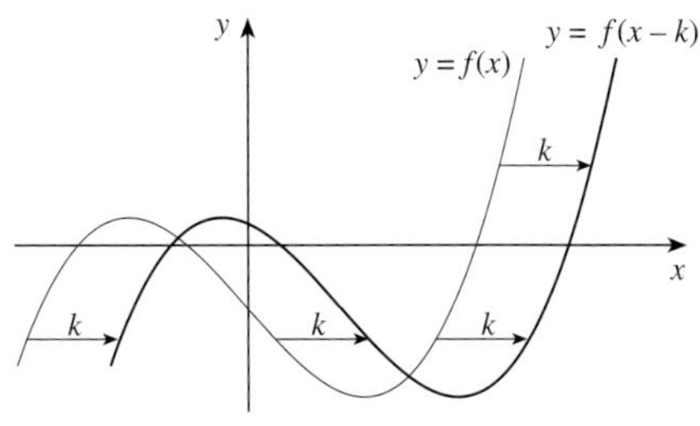

Fig. 30.5

Example 30.1.3

(a) Sketch the graph of $y=3(x-2)$ and explain how it is related to the graph of $y=3x$.

(b) Sketch the graph of $y=(x+2)^2$ and explain how it is related to the graph of $y=x^2$.

(a) The graph of $y=3x$ is a straight line through the origin with gradient 3. So $y=3(x-2)$ is a line parallel to this, 2 units to the right, as in Fig. 30.6.

(b) You can write $(x+2)^2$ as $(x-(-2))^2$. The graph of $y=(x+2)^2$ is to the left of $y=x^2$ by an amount $-(-2)$ units, that is by 2 units, as in Fig. 30.7.

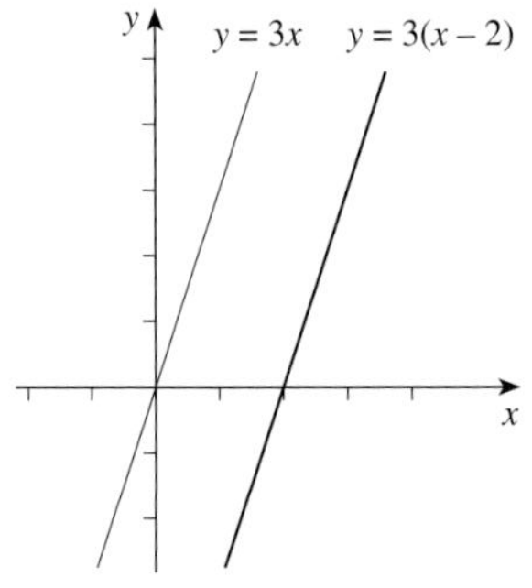

Fig. 30.6

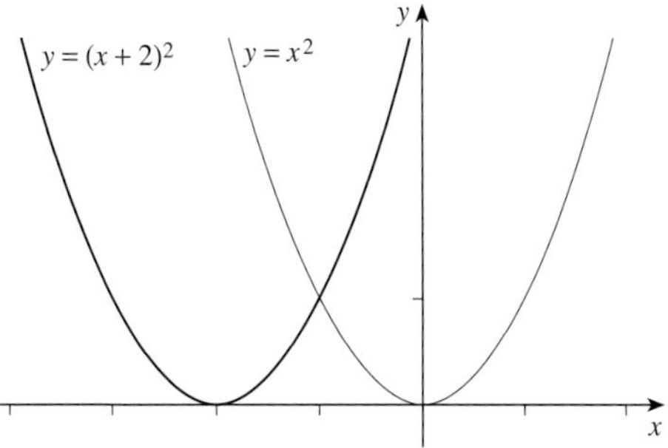

Fig. 30.7

You may be surprised by the minus sign in the equation $y = f(x - k)$, but it can easily be justified by expressing the result in the second blue box in different words:

> If the point with coordinates (r, s) lies on the graph $y = f(x)$, then the point $(r + k, s)$ lies on the graph $y = f(x - k)$.

So you have to show that, if $s = f(r)$, then $s = f((r + k) - k)$. The two equations are clearly the same, since $(r + k) - k = r$.

In the next example the graph of $y = x^2$ is modified by two translations performed one after the other, first in the x-direction and then in the y-direction.

Example 30.1.4
Describe the graph of $y = x^2 - 6x + 4$.

> In completed square form, $x^2 - 6x + 4 = (x - 3)^2 - 5$. You can get from $y = x^2$ to $y = (x - 3)^2 - 5$ via the graph of $y = (x - 3)^2$.
>
> Replacing x by $x - 3$ in the equation $y = x^2$ produces a translation of 3 units in the x-direction. Then you obtain $y = (x - 3)^2 - 5$ from $y = (x - 3)^2$ by a translation of -5 in the y-direction. The combination of the two translations is shown in Fig. 30.8.

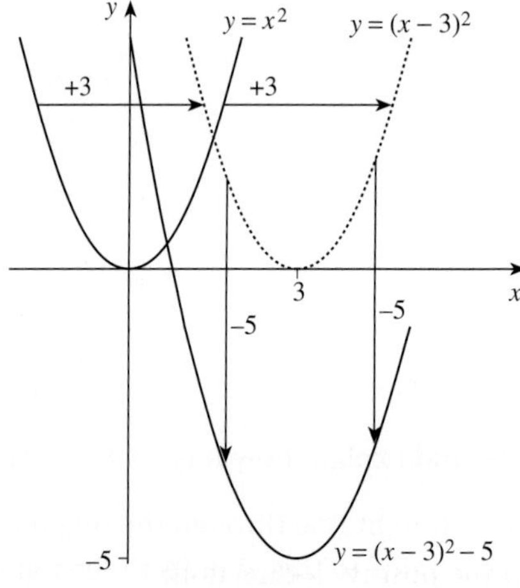

Fig. 30.8

This example takes you a stage further than Chapter 9, where the completed square form was used to find the vertex of a quadratic. Now you can see that, as the graph is obtained from $y = x^2$ by a pair of translations, the two graphs have the same shape and size.

The combination of a translation of a in the x-direction with a translation of b in the y-direction is sometimes described as a single translation of $\begin{pmatrix} a \\ b \end{pmatrix}$. Thus in Example 30.1.4 you could say that $y = x^2$ is transformed into $y = x^2 - 6x + 4$ by a translation of $\begin{pmatrix} 3 \\ -5 \end{pmatrix}$. You will make use of this notation in Chapter 42.

Exercise 30A

1 Sketch the following pairs of graphs and give the translation used to transform the first graph into the second graph.

(a) $y = -\frac{1}{2}x$ and $y = -\frac{1}{2}x + 4$ (b) $y = 2x$ and $y = 2(x + 3)$

(c) $y = x^2$ and $y = x^2 - 2$ (d) $y = x^2$ and $y = (x - 3)^2$

(e) $y = x^3$ and $y = (x + 2)^3$ (f) $y = \frac{1}{x}$ and $y = \frac{1}{x - 1}$

(g) $y = \frac{1}{x}$ and $y = \frac{1}{x + 3}$ (h) $y = \sqrt{x}$ and $y = \sqrt{x + 2}$

(i) $y = \sqrt{x}$ and $y = \sqrt{x} + 2$ (j) $y = \cos x$ and $y = \cos(x - \pi)$

(k) $y = \tan x$ and $y = \tan(x - \pi)$ (l) $y = 2^x$ and $y = 2^{x-1}$

2 (a) Show that the point (9, 3) lies on $y = \sqrt{x}$.

(b) The point (9, 3) is translated a distance 2 in the x-direction. Where does it move to?

(c) The graph $y = \sqrt{x}$ is translated a distance 2 in the x-direction. What is the equation of the new graph?

(d) Check that the point in your answer to part (b) lies on the graph in your answer to part (c).

3 The following translations are each applied to the graph of $y = x^2 + 3x$. Find the equation of each of the transformed graphs, giving your answer in as simple a form as possible.

(a) A translation of 3 units in the positive x-direction.

(b) A translation of 4 units in the positive y-direction.

(c) A translation of 3 units in the positive x-direction followed by a translation of 4 units in the positive y-direction.

(d) A translation of 4 units in the positive y-direction followed by a translation of 3 units in the positive x-direction.

4 The following translations are each applied to the graph of $y = x^2 - 5x + 7$. Find the equation of each of the transformed graphs, giving your answer in as simple a form as possible.

(a) A translation of -2 units in the positive x-direction.

(b) A translation of -5 units in the positive y-direction.

(c) A translation of -5 units in the positive y-direction followed by a translation of -2 units in the positive x-direction.

5 Give details of

(a) the translation which will convert the graph with equation $y = (x + 3)^2$ into the graph with equation $y = x^2$,

(b) the translations which will convert the graph of $y = (x - 5)^2$ into the graph with equation $y = (x - 8)^2$, and then into the graph with equation $y = (x - 8)^2 - 3$.

6 Describe the relationship of the graph of $y = x^2 + 8x + 14$ with that of the graph of $y = x^2$. Illustrate by means of a sketch graph.

7 The graph of $y = \frac{1}{x}$ is translated 2 units downwards, and the new graph is translated 1 unit to the left. Find the equations of the graph after the first translation, and of the graph in its final position.

As a check, find the coordinates of the points where the final graph cuts the x- and y-axes. From which points on the original graph did they come?

8 Display the graph of $y = \cos x$, and translate it by $\frac{1}{2}\pi$ in the x-direction. How can $\cos\left(x - \frac{1}{2}\pi\right)$ be written more simply?

30.2 Stretching graphs

What happens if you multiply a function by a constant?

Use your calculator to sketch the graphs of

(a) $y = x^2$ and $y = 3x^2$, (b) $y = x^3$ and $y = 2x^3$, (c) $y = x$ and $y = 4x$.

In each part the original graph has been subjected to a kind of stretching.

Imagine that the graph is drawn on an elastic sheet. If the sheet is held along the top and bottom edges and pulled so that the position of the new x-axis lies immediately above the old one, the y-coordinate of each point on the sheet will be increased in the same ratio.

In part (a) this ratio is 3. For parts (b) and (c) the ratios are 2 and 4 respectively.

These transformations are all examples of stretches in the y-direction.

In general, if you multiply a function by a constant c, then for each particular value of x the y-coordinate is c times as large as before. What this means geometrically depends on whether c is positive or negative. First suppose that $c > 0$.

This transformation is called a **stretch** by a factor of c in the y-direction. This is illustrated in Fig. 30.9, with a value of $c = 3$.

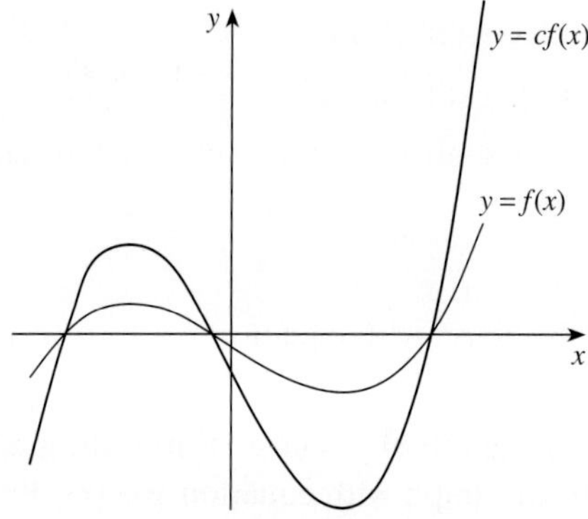

A stretch in the y-direction with $c = 3$

Fig. 30.9

The word 'stretch' is rather misleading, since if c is less than 1 the y-coordinates are reduced. But there is no mathematical advantage in separating the cases $0 < c < 1$ and $c > 1$, so even if 'stretch' appears misleading, it is always used.

Notice that you can write the equation $y = cf(x)$ as $\frac{y}{c} = f(x)$. This shows that:

Replacing y by $\frac{y}{c}$, where $c > 0$, in the equation of a graph produces a stretch of factor c in the y-direction.

But what happens if you replace x by $\frac{x}{c}$?

Example 30.2.1
Use your calculator to display the graphs of

(a) $y = x^2$ and $y = \left(\frac{x}{2}\right)^2$, (b) $y = x^3$ and $y = \left(\frac{x}{2}\right)^3$,

(c) $y = x^2$ and $y = (2x)^2$, (d) $y = x$ and $y = 2x$.

In parts (a) and (b) you should see that the curve has been stretched by a factor of 2 in the x-direction.

In part (c) you might think correctly that the curve has been stretched in the y-direction by a factor of 4, but you should also see that you can get the same result by stretching it in the x-direction by a factor of $\frac{1}{4}$. It is helpful in this case to think of $2x$ as $\frac{x}{\frac{1}{2}}$.

Part (d) is again complicated by the fact that the graph is a straight line, but you should see that if you stretch the original graph by a factor of $\frac{1}{2}$ in the x-direction you get the graph of $y = 2x$.

Example 30.2.1 shows that, if you want to stretch a graph in the x-direction, keeping the y-axis fixed:

Replacing x by $\frac{x}{c}$, where $c > 0$, in the equation of a graph produces a stretch of factor c in the x-direction.

For example, to get from the graph of $y = f(x)$ to that of $y = f(2x)$, you need to write $2x$ as $\frac{x}{\frac{1}{2}}$. So this is a stretch of factor $\frac{1}{2}$ in the x-direction; the x-coordinate of each point of the graph is halved. This is illustrated in Fig. 30.10.

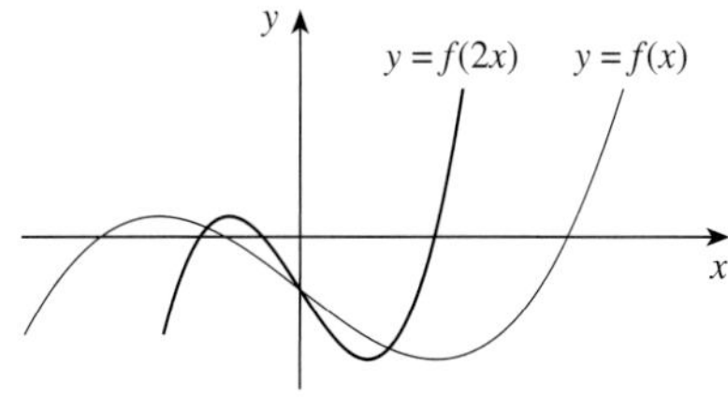

Fig. 30.10

Example 30.2.2

Find the effect of applying to the graph of $y = x$ a stretch of

(a) factor $\frac{1}{3}$ in the y-direction, (b) factor 3 in the x-direction.

(a) Replacing y by $\frac{y}{1/3}$ gives the equation $\frac{y}{1/3} = x$, or $y = \frac{1}{3}x$.

(b) Replacing x by $\frac{x}{3}$ gives the equation $y = \frac{x}{3}$, or $y = \frac{1}{3}x$.

In this example the answers to parts (a) and (b) are the same! They are illustrated in Fig. 30.11.

Try to visualise from the figure how the transformation can be achieved by either a stretch in the y-direction or a stretch in the x-direction.

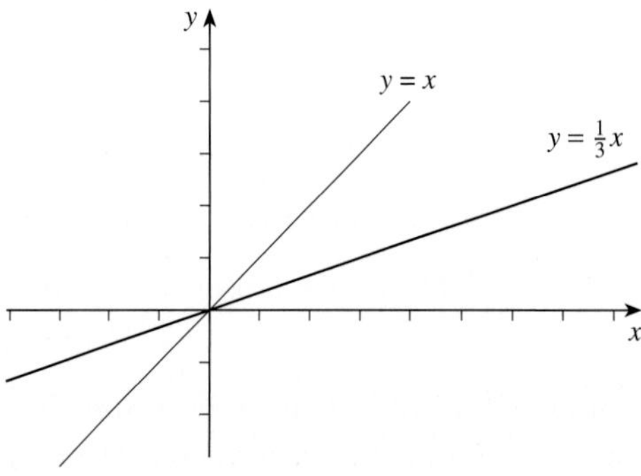

Fig. 30.11

Example 30.2.3

Find the effect of applying the stretches in Example 30.2.2 to the graph of $y = x - 3$.

Using the same methods as in Example 30.2.2, the equations are

(a) $\frac{y}{1/3} = x - 3$, or $y = \frac{1}{3}x - 1$;

(b) $y = \frac{x}{3} - 3$, or $y = \frac{1}{3}x - 3$.

These are illustrated in Fig. 30.12.

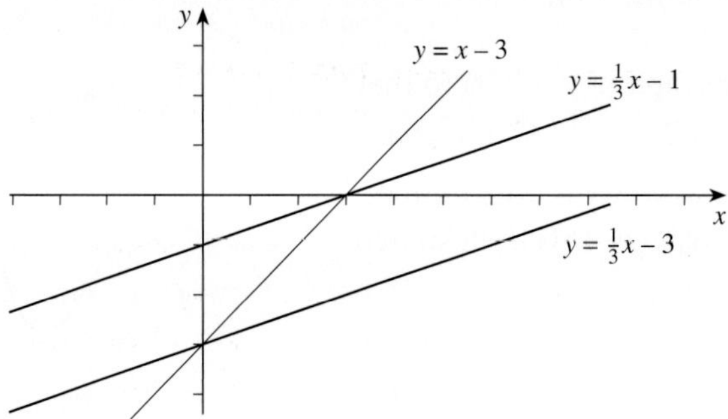

Fig. 30.12

In this example the answers to the two parts are different. Notice that a stretch in the y-direction leaves points on the x-axis unchanged, so both the original and transformed graphs pass through $(3, 0)$. A stretch in the x-direction leaves points on the y-axis unchanged, so both graphs pass through $(0, -3)$

Example 30.2.4
The graph $y = x^2$ is stretched by a factor of 4 in the y-direction, then by a factor of 4 in the x-direction. How else could you achieve the final result?

The double stretch is equivalent to an all-round enlargement of factor 4, like a photographic enlargement, which doesn't distort the shape of the graph. It is achieved by replacing y by $\frac{1}{4}y$ and x by $\frac{1}{4}x$. So the equation of the final graph is

$$\tfrac{1}{4}y = \left(\tfrac{1}{4}x\right)^2,$$

which you can write more simply as $y = \frac{1}{4}x^2$.

But you could also get $y = \frac{1}{4}x^2$ from $y = x^2$ by a stretch in the y-direction alone, in which the y-coordinate of each point on the graph is multiplied by $\frac{1}{4}$.

Also $y = \frac{1}{4}x^2$ can be written as $y = \left(\frac{1}{2}x\right)^2$. This is what you would get from $y = x^2$ by a stretch of factor 2 in the x-direction alone.

Try displaying with the same axes the graphs of $y = x^2$ and $y = \frac{1}{4}x^2$, and think how the first can be transformed into the second by each of the three transformations described in Example 30.2.4.

Finally, what happens if $c < 0$? The simplest way of dealing with this is to regard multiplication by c as a combination of multiplication by $(-c)$ and a change of sign. Since $(-c) > 0$, you already know how to deal with the first transformation. Now it is necessary to interpret the effect of changing the sign of the x- or y-coordinate. This is explained in the next section.

30.3 Reflecting graphs

If you draw with the same axes the graphs of $y = f(x)$ and $y = -f(x)$, then for each value of x the values of y on the two graphs differ only in having opposite signs, so that the corresponding points are mirror images in the x-axis. The complete graphs are therefore mirror images of each other as in Fig. 30.13.

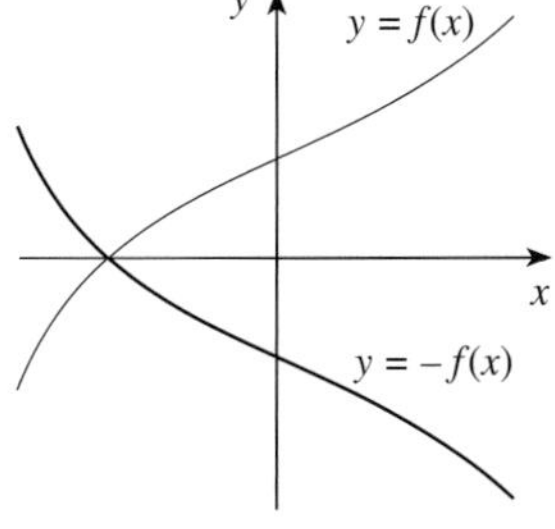

Fig. 30.13

You have to imagine a 'mathematical' mirror, capable of reflection in both directions. If $y = f(x)$ takes both positive and negative values, then the reflection converts positive to negative and negative to positive. A more practical way of doing this is to rotate the graph about the x-axis through $180°$.

Since you can write $y = -f(x)$ as $-y = f(x)$, another way of expressing this is:

Replacing y by $-y$ in the equation of a graph produces a reflection in the x-axis.

But what happens if you replace x by $-x$?

Example 30.3.1
Use your calculator to display the graphs of

(a) $y = 2x$ and $y = 2(-x)$, (b) $y = x^3$ and $y = (-x)^3$, (c) $y = x^2$ and $y = (-x)^2$.

In parts (a) and (b) you should see that the curve has been reflected in the y-axis.

In part (c) you might think correctly that the curve has not been altered, but as the curve is symmetrical about the y-axis, you could also say that the curve has been reflected in the y-axis.

Example 30.3.1 shows that, if you want to reflect a graph in the y-axis the rule is:

Replacing x by $-x$ in the equation of a graph produces a reflection in the y-axis.

Figure 30.14 shows the graph of $y = f(x)$ and its reflection in the y-axis, $y = f(-x)$.

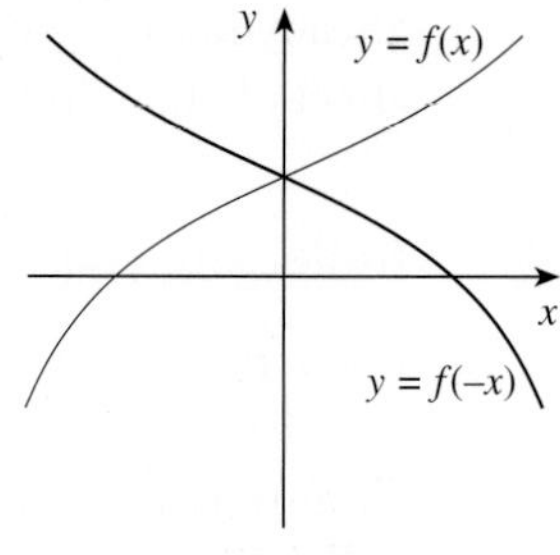

Fig. 30.14

With these results it is possible to make precise the ideas of even functions (such as x^2 or x^4) and odd functions (such as x^3) introduced in Section 8.3.

The graph of an even function is symmetrical about the y-axis, so reflection in the y-axis leaves it unchanged. This means that $y = f(x)$ and $y = f(-x)$ are the same equation, so that $f(x) = f(-x)$.

The graph of an odd function is symmetrical about the origin, so a combination of reflections in the x- and y-axes leaves it unchanged. This means that $y = f(x)$ and $-y = f(-x)$ are the same equation, so that $f(x) = -f(-x)$.

However, in using the terms 'odd' and 'even', there is an important difference between integers and functions. Every integer is either odd or even, but there are many functions, such as $x^2 + x$, which are neither odd nor even.

Example 30.3.2

Use transformations to show that the graph of

(a) $y = -x^2$ is symmetrical about the y-axis,

(b) $y = x^3 - 3x$ is symmetrical about the origin,

(c) $y = x^2 + 4x - 12$ is neither symmetrical about the y-axis nor symmetrical about the origin.

(a) The reflection of $y = -x^2$ in the y-axis is $y = -(-x)^2$. Since $(-x)^2 = x^2$, this equation can be written as $y = -x^2$.

This is the same as the original equation, so reflection in the y-axis leaves the graph unchanged. That is, the graph is symmetrical about the y-axis.

(b) If a graph is symmetrical about the origin, it is the graph of an odd function, so then $y = f(x)$ and $y = -f(-x)$ are the same equation.

If $f(x) = x^3 - 3x$, then $f(-x) = (-x)^3 - 3(-x) = -x^3 + 3x$, which is $-(x^3 - 3x)$.

So $f(x) = -f(-x)$. This means that the graph of $y = f(x)$ is symmetrical about the origin.

(c) If $f(x) = x^2 + 4x - 12$, then

$$\begin{aligned} f(-x) &= (-x)^2 + 4(-x) - 12 \\ &= x^2 - 4x - 12. \end{aligned}$$

As $x^2 + 4x - 12$ and $x^2 - 4x - 12$ are not the same function, $f(x)$ is not symmetrical about the y-axis.

As
$$\begin{aligned} -f(-x) &= -(x^2 - 4x - 12) \\ &= -x^2 + 4x + 12, \end{aligned}$$

and $x^2 + 4x - 12$ and $-x^2 + 4x + 12$ are not the same function, $f(x)$ is not symmetrical about the origin.

So $y = x^2 + 4x - 12$ is neither symmetrical about the y-axis nor symmetrical about the origin.

Example 30.3.3

A water engineer, who is studying the motion of a wave travelling at 2 metres per second along a narrow channel without change of shape, starts measurements when the wave has equation $y = f(x)$, as shown in Fig. 30.15.

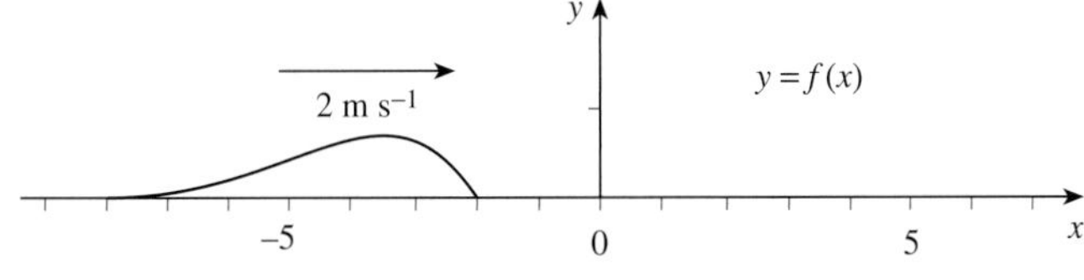

Fig. 30.15

(a) Find the equation of the wave 4 seconds later.

(b) Find the equation of the wave t seconds later.

(c) The engineer has placed a sensor on the y-axis to plot the height of the wave at this position against the time. Find the shape of the graph.

(a) The wave travels 8 metres in 4 seconds, so the graph is translated 8 metres in the x-direction (see Fig. 30.16). Its equation is then $y = f(x - 8)$.

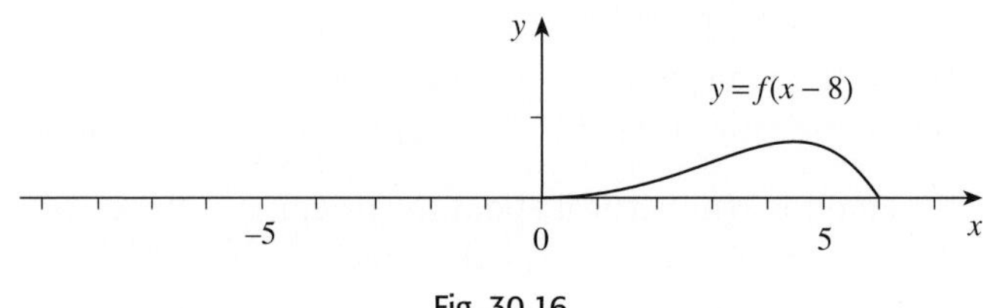

Fig. 30.16

(b) The wave travels $2t$ metres in t seconds, so its equation is then $y = f(x - 2t)$.

(c) Substituting $x = 0$ in the equation in (b) gives the equation of the height on the y-axis as $y = f(-2t)$.

Now Fig. 30.15 is shown as a graph of y against x with equation $y = f(x)$, but changing the letter x to t, and the x-axis to a t-axis, would not change the shape of the graph. To convert $y = f(t)$ into $y = f(-2t)$ you need a stretch of factor $\frac{1}{2}$ combined with a reflection in the y-axis.

This produces the graph shown in Fig. 30.17.

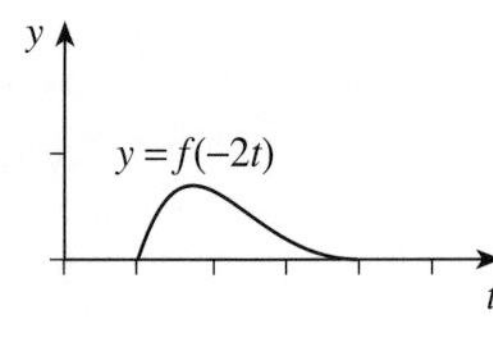

Fig. 30.17

Exercise 30B

1 Sketch the following pairs of graphs. Give the stretches and reflections used to transform the first graph into the second graph.

(a) $y = x$ and $y = 2x$

(b) $y = x$ and $y = -x$

(c) $y = x^2$ and $y = 3x^2$

(d) $y = x^2$ and $y = -x^2$

(e) $y = \sqrt{x}$ and $y = 2\sqrt{x}$

(f) $y = 2\sqrt{x}$ and $y = 2\sqrt{-x}$

(g) $y = x + 3$ and $y = 2x + 3$

(h) $y = x + 3$ and $y = 2(x + 3)$

(i) $y = x^3$ and $y = (-x)^3$

(j) $y = x - 2$ and $y = -x - 2$

(k) $y = x^2 + 1$ and $y = (-x)^2 + 1$

(l) $y = \dfrac{1}{x^2}$ and $y = -\dfrac{1}{2x^2}$

(m) $y = 2^x$ and $y = 2^{-x}$

(n) $y = \cos x$ and $y = \cos 3x$

2 (a) Show that the point $(16, 4)$ lies on $y = \sqrt{x}$.

(b) The point $(16, 4)$ is transformed by a stretch of factor $\frac{1}{2}$ in the x-direction. Where does it move to?

(c) The graph $y = \sqrt{x}$ is transformed by a stretch of factor $\frac{1}{2}$ in the x-direction. What is the equation of the new graph?

(d) Check that the point in your answer to part (b) lies on the graph in your answer to part (c).

3 The graph of $y = (2x + 1)^2$ is stretched by a factor of 2 in the x-direction. What is the equation of the new graph?

4 The graph of $y = \dfrac{1}{x^2}$ is stretched by a factor of 3 in the x-direction. Show that the same result could be achieved by a stretch in the y-direction, and find the factor of the stretch.

5 The graph $y = 2x^2$ is stretched by a factor of 2 in the y-direction. Find the equation of the new graph. The graph is then stretched by a factor of 3 in the x-direction. Find the equation of the final graph and state clearly how you could achieve the same final result with

(a) just one stretch in the x-direction, (b) just one stretch in the y-direction.

6 In which axis is the graph of $y = x^2 - 7x + 6$ reflected if its new equation is

(a) $y = x^2 + 7x + 6$, (b) $y = -x^2 + 7x - 6$?

7 The graph of $y = (x - 2)^2$ is transformed into the graph of $y = (x + 2)^2$ when it is reflected in one of the coordinate axes. Which axis is it?

8 Prove that if (r, s) lies on $y = f(x)$, then (cr, s) lies on $y = f\left(\frac{x}{c}\right)$. What property of transformations does this establish?

9 Determine if the following functions are 'even', 'odd' or 'neither even nor odd'.

(a) $f(x) = x^3 + 3x$ (b) $f(x) = 7x^2 - 8$

(c) $f(x) = (x - 1)(x - 3)$ (d) $f(x) = x^5 + 3x^3 + 1$

Find $f'(x)$ for each of the four functions and determine if it is even, odd or neither even nor odd. What does this suggest about derivatives of even and odd functions?

Can you say anything about integrals of even and odd functions?

10 Use your calculator to show that the graph of $-\sin x$ can be obtained from the graph of $\sin x$ either by a translation or by a reflection. Write this in the form of an equation.

11 Use your calculator to demonstrate that $\cos\left(x + \frac{1}{2}\pi\right) = -\sin x$.

12 Describe the transformation of the graph of $y = 2^x$ which will produce the graph of

(a) $y = 2^{x-3}$, (b) $y = 2^{-x}$, (c) $y = \left(\frac{1}{4}\right)^x$, (d) $y = 2^x + 4$.

13 The graph of $y = 2^x$ is translated by 1 in the x-direction. What other transformation applied to the graph of $y = 2^x$ would produce the same effect?

14 The graph of $y = 3^x$ is translated by -2 in the x-direction. What other transformation applied to the graph of $y = 3^x$ would have the same effect?

15 What is the relation between the graphs of $y = a^x$ and $y = b^x$

(a) if $b = a^2$, (b) if $b = a^3$, (c) if $b = \frac{1}{a}$?

16 Show that the graph of $y = \log x$ can be transformed into the graph of $y = \log(3x)$ either by a stretch in the x-direction or by a translation in the y-direction. State

(a) the factor of the stretch, (b) the magnitude of the translation.

30.4 Combining transformations

Example 30.1.4 showed the effect of combining two translations, and Example 30.2.4 showed the effect of combining two stretches. What happens if you combine a translation with a stretch?

In this section, 'x-translation' is used for a translation in the x-direction; 'x-stretch' for a stretch parallel to the x-axis; and similarly 'y-translation' and 'y-stretch'.

Example 30.4.1

The graph $y = \frac{1}{x}$ is translated by 3 in the x-direction and stretched by a factor 2 in the y-direction. What is the new equation? Draw a sketch to illustrate the situation.

After the x-translation of 3, $y = \frac{1}{x}$ becomes $y = \frac{1}{x-3}$.

After the y-stretch of factor 2, $y = \frac{1}{x-3}$ becomes $\frac{y}{2} = \frac{1}{x-3}$, which is $y = \frac{2}{x-3}$.

Fig. 30.18 shows sketches of the three graphs.

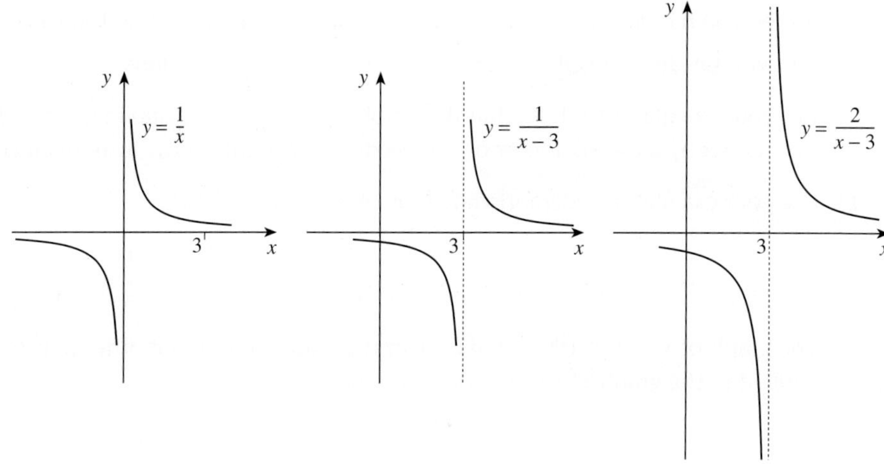

Fig. 30.18

In this example the order of the two transformations makes no difference. If you do the y-stretch first, $y = \frac{1}{x}$ becomes $y = \frac{2}{x}$. Then the x-translation transforms this to $y = \frac{2}{x-3}$. The answer is the same either way.

In the next example this doesn't happen. You get different answers by carrying out the transformations in different orders.

Example 30.4.2

The graph $y = f(x)$ is transformed by a translation of -2 in the y-direction and reflection in the x-axis. Find the equation which results from doing

(a) the translation before the reflection, (b) the reflection before the translation.

(a) After the y-translation of -2, $y = f(x)$ becomes $y - (-2) = f(x)$, which is $y = f(x) - 2$

After reflection in the x-axis, $y = f(x) - 2$ becomes $-y = f(x) - 2$, which is $y = 2 - f(x)$.

(b) After reflection in the x-axis, $y = f(x)$ becomes $-y = f(x)$, which is $y = -f(x)$.

After the y-translation, $y = -f(x)$ becomes $y - (-2) = -f(x)$, which is $y = -2 - f(x)$.

The use of sine and cosine functions to model periodic variation was described in Section 28.3. The rules for transforming graphs provide an alternative way of finding the equations.

Example 30.4.3

An equation of the form $y = a\cos nt$ is used to model an oscillation of amplitude 1.2 metres about a point O with a period of 5 seconds. Find the equation.

In Fig. 30.19 the graph on the left has equation $y = \cos t$, and the graph on the right is the graph of the oscillation to be modelled.

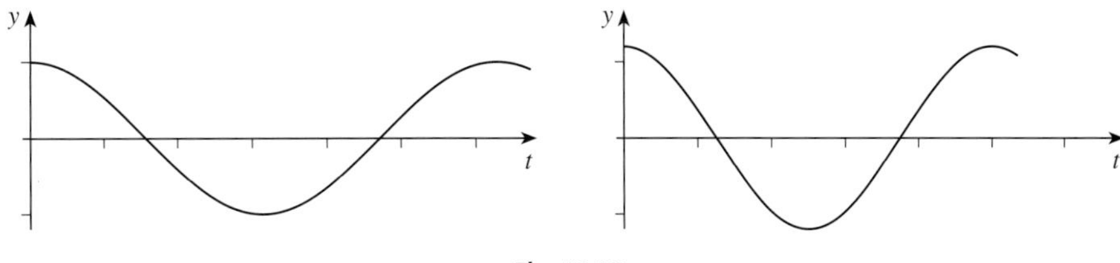

Fig. 30.19

To get from the first graph to the second you need a stretch in the t-direction of factor $\frac{5}{2\pi}$ and a stretch in the y-direction of factor 1.2.

After the t-stretch the equation becomes

$$y = \cos\left(\frac{t}{5/2\pi}\right),$$

which is

$$y = \cos \tfrac{2}{5}\pi t.$$

The y-stretch then converts this to

$$y = 1.2 \cos \tfrac{2}{5}\pi t.$$

Sometimes you want to ask the question the other way round: what transformations will convert a known simple graph into a graph with a more complicated equation?

Example 30.4.4
Find a translation and a stretch which transform the graph $y = \sin x$ to the graph $y = \sin\left(\frac{1}{2}x - \frac{1}{6}\pi\right)$, beginning with

(a) the translation, (b) the stretch.

In each case you should look for a link equation, which is the equation of the graph after the first transformation and before the second.

(a) One possible link equation is $y = \sin\left(x - \frac{1}{6}\pi\right)$.
To get from $y = \sin x$ to $y = \sin\left(x - \frac{1}{6}\pi\right)$, x-translate by $\frac{1}{6}\pi$.
To get from $y = \sin\left(x - \frac{1}{6}\pi\right)$ to $y = \sin\left(\frac{1}{2}x - \frac{1}{6}\pi\right)$, x-stretch with factor 2.

(b) Begin by noting that $\sin\left(\frac{1}{2}x - \frac{1}{6}\pi\right)$ can be written as $\sin \frac{1}{2}\left(x - \frac{1}{3}\pi\right)$, and take $y = \sin \frac{1}{2}x$ as the link equation.
To get from $y = \sin x$ to $y = \sin \frac{1}{2}x$, x-stretch with factor 2.
To get from $y = \sin \frac{1}{2}x$ to $y = \sin \frac{1}{2}\left(x - \frac{1}{3}\pi\right)$, x-translate by $\frac{1}{3}\pi$.
Both methods are illustrated in Fig. 30.20. The left chain shows method (a), the right chain method (b).

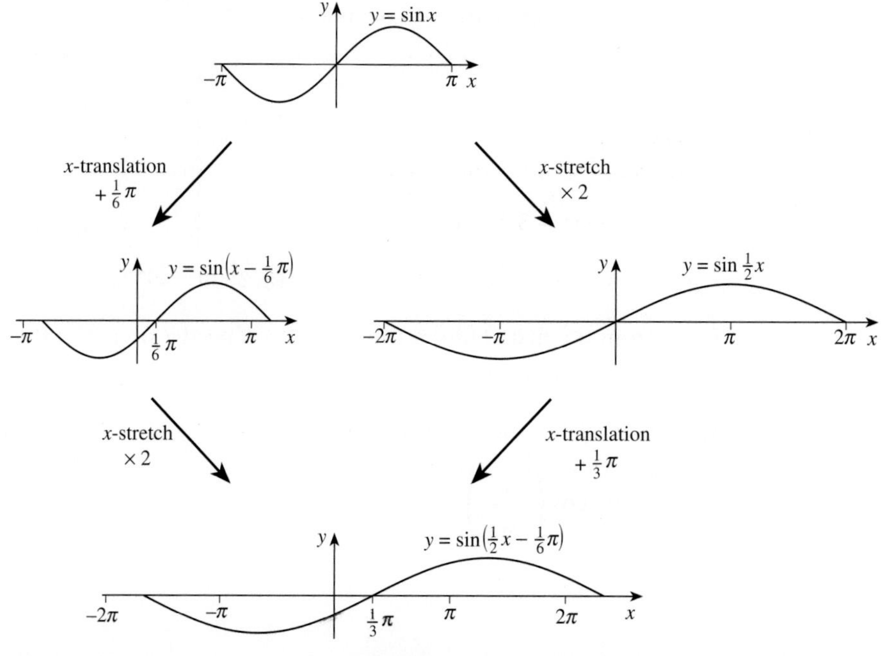

Fig. 30.20

By combining transformations it is possible to obtain the graph of any quadratic function from that of $y = x^2$.

Example 30.4.5
Find a chain of transformations to obtain the graph of $y = 4 + 12x - 2x^2$ from that of $y = x^2$.

Begin by expressing the quadratic in completed square form:

$$4 + 12x - 2x^2 = 4 - 2(x^2 - 6x) = 4 - 2(x^2 - 6x + 9) + 18 = 22 - 2(x - 3)^2.$$

To transform $y = x^2$ to $y = 22 - 2(x - 3)^2$ requires four steps in some order:

- an x-translation of 3
- a reflection in the x-axis
- a y-stretch with factor 2
- a y-translation.

Only one of these is in the x-direction, and this can be carried out at any stage. You may as well do it first, so that the first link equation is $y = (x - 3)^2$.

After that there are several solutions to the problem, depending on the order in which you carry out the reflection, the y-stretch and the y-translation. Here are two possibilities.

First solution This uses link equations

$$y = (x - 3)^2, \quad y = -(x - 3)^2, \quad y = -2(x - 3)^2.$$

An x-translation of 3 transforms $y = x^2$ to $y = (x - 3)^2$.

A reflection in the x-axis transforms $y = (x - 3)^2$ to $y = -(x - 3)^2$.

A y-stretch with factor 2 transforms $y = -(x - 3)^2$ to $y = -2(x - 3)^2$.

A y-translation of 22 transforms $y = -2(x - 3)^2$ to $y = 22 - 2(x - 3)^2$, which is $y = 4 + 12x - 2x^2$.

Second solution $y = 4 + 12x - 2x^2$ can also be written as $y = -2((x - 3)^2 - 11)$, which suggests a different sequence of link equations:

$$y = (x - 3)^2, \quad y = (x - 3)^2 - 11, \quad y = 2((x - 3)^2 - 11).$$

An x-translation of 3 transforms $y = x^2$ to $y = (x - 3)^2$.

A y-translation of -11 transforms $y = (x - 3)^2$ to $y = (x - 3)^2 - 11$.

A y-stretch with factor 2 transforms $y = (x - 3)^2 - 11$ to $y = 2((x - 3)^2 - 11)$.

A reflection in the x-axis transforms $y = 2((x - 3)^2 - 11)$ to $y = -2((x - 3)^2 - 11)$, which is $y = 4 + 12x - 2x^2$.

Exercise 30C

1 The graph of $y = x^3$ is transformed by moving it first by 1 unit in the x-direction and then by 2 units in the y-direction. Find its new equation and sketch the final graph.

2 Write down two simple transformations which will transform $y = \sin x$ into $y = 2\sin(x + \frac{1}{6}\pi)$. Sketch the final graph.

Does the order of your transformations matter? If so, give the equation of the new graph which you get if you carry out your transformations in the other order.

3 Write down two simple transformations which will transform $y = \cos x$ into $y = \cos(3x + \frac{1}{2}\pi)$. Sketch the final graph.

Does the order of your transformations matter? If so, give the equation of the new graph which you get if you carry out your transformations in the other order.

4 Each of the following graphs is stretched by a factor of 2 in both the x- and y-directions. Give their new equations.

(a) $y = x^3$ (b) $y = \dfrac{1}{x}$ (c) $y = x$ (d) $y = 2^x$

5 The graph of the straight line $y = x$ is transformed as follows:

a translation by 4 units in the positive x-direction,
followed by stretch in the y-direction with scale factor 2,
followed by reflection in the x-axis.

Find the equation of the final graph.

6 The graph of $y = \dfrac{1}{x}$ is first stretched by a factor of 3 in the x-direction and then stretched by a factor of $\frac{1}{3}$ in the y-direction. What is the effect on the original curve?

7 The function $f(x)$ is defined by $f(x) = 5(x + 2)^2 - 7$ for all real values of x.

(a) Describe clearly a sequence of transformations which will transform the graph of $y = x^2$ to the graph of $y = f(x)$.

(b) Sketch the graph of $y = f(x)$.

(c) Describe a sequence of transformations which will transform the graph of $y = f(x)$ to the graph of $y = x^2$.

(d) Find $f'(x)$ and sketch the graph of $y = f'(x)$.

(e) Describe a sequence of transformations which will transform the graph of $y = 2x$ to the graph of $y = f'(x)$.

8 Use transformations to obtain the equations

(a) $i = 5\sin 100\pi t$ in Example 28.3.1, starting with $i = \sin t$

(b) $S = 7 + 3\cos\frac{1}{4}t$ in Example 28.3.2, starting with $S = \cos t$.

Review exercise 9

1 (a) Draw sketches of the graphs of $y = \sin x$, $y = \cos x$, $y = -\sin x$ and $y = -\cos x$.

(b) Use transformations to decide which of the graphs of part (a) are the same as each of the following graphs.

(i) $y = \sin\left(x + \frac{1}{2}\pi\right)$ (ii) $y = \cos\left(x - \frac{3}{2}\pi\right)$

(iii) $y = -\cos\left(x + \frac{7}{2}\pi\right)$ (iv) $y = \sin\left(\frac{3}{2}\pi - x\right)$

2 (a) The graph of $y = 3\cos(2x + \alpha)$ can be obtained from the graph of $y = \cos x$ by a translation followed by two stretches. Describe each of these three transformations, and give the number of roots of the equation $3\cos(2x + \alpha) = k$, in the interval $0 \le x < 2\pi$, where $-3 < k < 3$.

(b) Generalise your answer to give the number of roots of the equation $a\cos(nx + \alpha) = k$ in the interval $0 \le x < 2\pi$, where $a > 0$, n is a positive integer and $-a < k < a$.

(c) How does your answer to part (c) change if n is a negative integer?

3 The curve $y = 12x^2 - 48x + 20$ is transformed by a reflection, a stretch and a translation in that order. The reflection is in the y-axis, the stretch is in the y-direction with factor $\frac{1}{4}$ and the translation is by 2 units in the positive x-direction. The equation of the final curve is $y = cx^2 + d$. Find the equation of the graph

(a) after the reflection, (b) after the stretch.

Hence find the values of c and d.

4 The functions f and g are defined by

$$f : x \mapsto x^2 + 6x,\ x \in \mathbb{R}, \quad g : x \mapsto 2x - 1,\ x \in \mathbb{R}.$$

Find the two values of x such that $f \circ g(x) = g \circ f(x)$, giving each answer in the form $p + q\sqrt{3}$.

5 Functions f and g are defined by $f : x \mapsto 4x + 5$, $x \in \mathbb{R}$ and $g : x \mapsto 3 - 2x$, $x \in \mathbb{R}$. Find

(a) f^{-1}, (b) g^{-1}, (c) $f^{-1} \circ g^{-1}$, (d) $g \circ f$, (e) $(g \circ f)^{-1}$.

6 Given the function $f : x \mapsto \dfrac{x+5}{2x-1}$, $x \in \mathbb{R}$ and $x \ne \frac{1}{2}$, find

(a) $f \circ f(x)$, (b) $f \circ f \circ f(x)$.

For $n > 3$, the notation f^n denotes $\overbrace{f \circ f \circ f \circ \ldots \circ f}^{n \text{ times}}$. Find

(c) $f^4(x)$, (d) $f^{10}(x)$, (e) $f^{351}(x)$.

7 Show that a function of the form $x \mapsto \dfrac{x+a}{x-1}$, $x \in \mathbb{R}$ and $x \ne 1$, is self-inverse for all values of the constant a except one. State the exceptional value of a.

8 The diagram shows the graph of $y = f(x)$ for $-2 \le x \le 1$. Outside this interval $f(x)$ is zero.

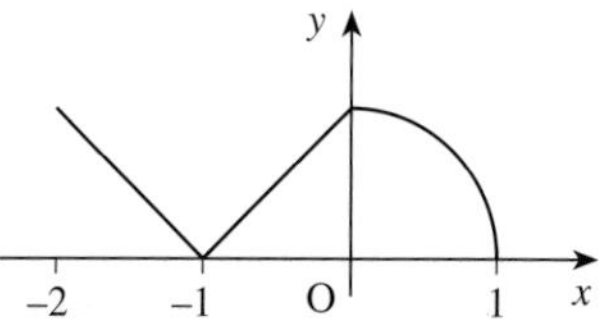

Sketch, on separate diagrams, the graphs of

(a) $y = f(x+1)$, (b) $y = -f(3x)$. (OCR)

9 The graph of $y = x^2$ can be transformed to that of $y = 2(x+1)^2$ by means of a translation and a stretch, in that order. State the magnitude and direction of the translation. State also the scale factor and direction of the stretch. (OCR, adapted)

10 Given that $f(x) = 3x^2 - 4$, $x > 0$, and $g(x) = x + 4$, $x \in \mathbb{R}$, find

(a) $f^{-1}(x), x > -4$, (b) $f \circ g(x), x > -4$. (OCR)

11 The function f is defined by $f : x \mapsto x^2 + 1, x \ge 0$. Sketch the graph of the function f and, using your sketch or otherwise, show that f is a one-to-one function. Obtain an expression in terms of x for $f^{-1}(x)$ and state the domain of f^{-1}.

The function g is defined by $g : x \mapsto x - 3, x \ge 0$. Give an expression in terms of x for $g \circ f(x)$ and state the range of $g \circ f$. (OCR)

Examination questions

1 Consider the functions $f(x) = 2x$ and $g(x) = \dfrac{1}{x-3}$, $x \ne 3$.

(a) Calculate $(f \circ g)(4)$. (b) Find $g^{-1}(x)$.

(c) Write down the domain of g^{-1}. (© IBO 2005)

2 The graph of $y = f(x)$ is shown in the diagram.

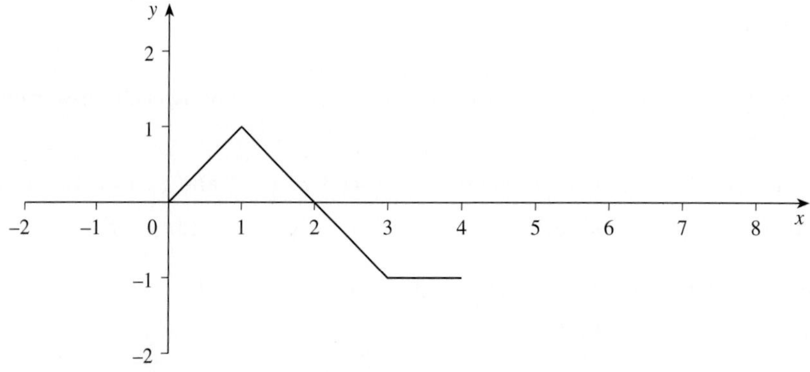

(a) Draw the graph of

(i) $y = 2f(x)$, (ii) $y = f(x-3)$.

(b) The point A$(3, -1)$ is on the graph of f. The point A′ is the corresponding point on the graph of $y = -f(x) + 1$. Find the coordinates of A′. (© IBO 2005)

3 Let $f(x) = 2x + 1$ and $g(x) = 3x^2 - 4$. Find

(a) $f^{-1}(x)$, (b) $(g \circ f)(-2)$, (c) $(f \circ g)(x)$. (© IBO 2004)

4 Let $f(x) = 2x + 1$.

(a) Draw the graph of $f(x)$ for $0 \le x \le 2$.

(b) Let $g(x) = f(x + 3) - 2$. Using the same axes, draw the graph of $g(x)$ for $-3 \le x \le -1$. (© IBO 2004)

5 Let $f(x) = \dfrac{8}{x}$ and $g(x) = x^2$.

(a) Find $f^{-1}(x)$.

(b) (i) Write down $(f^{-1} \circ g)(x)$. (ii) Solve the equation $(f^{-1} \circ g)(x) = x$. (© IBO 2004)

6 The first diagram shows a bicycle pedal.

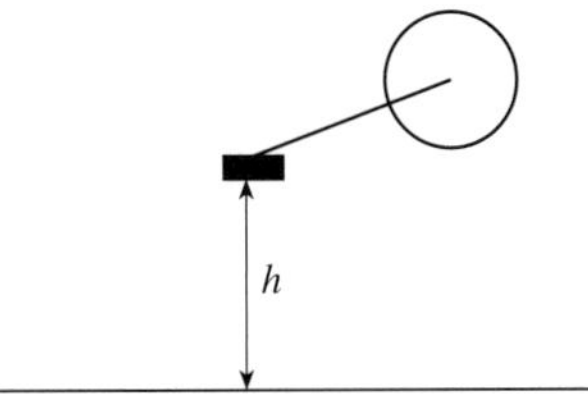

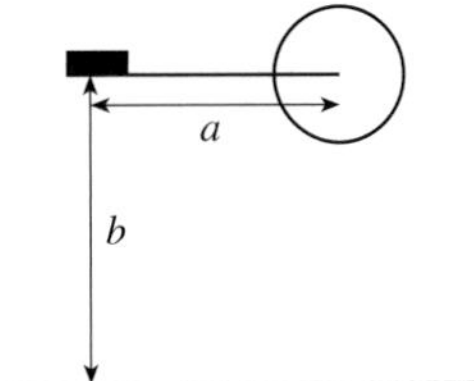

The height h cm, of the bicycle pedal above the ground after t seconds is given by $h = 24 - 14\sin 2t$.

(a) Find the height when $t = 0$.

(b) Find the maximum height of the pedal above the ground.

(c) Find the first time at which this occurs.

(d) How long does one revolution of the pedal take?

The second diagram shows the pedal in its starting position.

(e) Write down the lengths of a and b.

(f) Write down a formula for the height of the other pedal above the ground at time t seconds. (© IBO 2004)

31 Extending differentiation and integration

This chapter is about differentiating a certain kind of composite function of the form $f(ax+b)$. When you have completed it, you should

- be able to differentiate composite functions of the form $(ax+b)^n$
- be able to integrate composite functions of the form $(ax+b)^n$.

You may want to leave out Section 31.3 on a first reading, and you will find that the exercises are independent of it. You will, however, need the results stated at the end of Section 31.1 and in Section 31.2 (and proved in Section 31.3).

31.1 Differentiating $(ax+b)^n$

To differentiate a function like $(2x+1)^3$, the only method available to you at present is to use the binomial theorem to multiply out the brackets, and then to differentiate term by term.

Example 31.1.1

Find $\frac{dy}{dx}$ for (a) $y=(2x+1)^3$, (b) $y=(1-3x)^4$.

(a) Expanding by the binomial theorem,

$$\begin{aligned} y &= (2x)^3 + 3\times(2x)^2\times 1 + 3\times(2x)\times 1^2 + 1^3 \\ &= 8x^3 + 12x^2 + 6x + 1. \end{aligned}$$

So $\frac{dy}{dx} = 24x^2 + 24x + 6.$

It is useful to express the result in factors, as $\frac{dy}{dx} = 6(4x^2+4x+1) = 6(2x+1)^2$.

(b) Expanding by the binomial theorem,

$$\begin{aligned} y &= 1^4 + 4\times 1^3\times(-3x) + 6\times 1^2\times(-3x)^2 + 4\times 1\times(-3x)^3 + (-3x)^4 \\ &= 1 - 12x + 54x^2 - 108x^3 + 81x^4. \end{aligned}$$

So
$$\begin{aligned} \frac{dy}{dx} &= -12 + 108x - 324x^2 + 324x^3 \\ &= -12(1 - 9x + 27x^2 - 27x^3) \\ &= -12(1-3x)^3. \end{aligned}$$

Exercise 31A

In Question 1, see if you can predict what the result of the differentiation will be. If you can, predict the result, then check by carrying out the differentiation and factorising your result. If you can't, differentiate and factorise the result to help you to find a pattern in your answer.

1 Find $\frac{dy}{dx}$ for each of the following functions. In parts (d) and (e), a and b are constants.

(a) $(1-3x)^3$ (b) $(x+3)^2$ (c) $(2x-3)^2$ (d) $(ax+b)^3$

(e) $(b-ax)^3$ (f) $(1-x)^5$ (g) $(2x-3)^4$ (h) $(3-2x)^4$

2 Suppose that $y=(ax+b)^n$, where a and b are constants and n is a positive integer. Make a guess at a formula for $\frac{dy}{dx}$.

3 Use the formula you guessed in Question 2, after checking that it is correct, to differentiate each of the following functions.

(a) $(x+3)^{10}$ (b) $(2x-1)^5$ (c) $(1-4x)^7$ (d) $(3x-2)^5$

(e) $(4-2x)^6$ (f) $4(2+3x)^6$ (g) $(2x+5)^5$ (h) $(2x-3)^9$

In Exercise 31A, you were asked to predict how to differentiate a function of the form $(ax+b)^n$ where a and b are constants, and n is a positive integer. The result was

$$\text{If } y=(ax+b)^n,\text{ then } \frac{dy}{dx}=a\times n(ax+b)^{n-1}.$$

Now assume that the same formula works for all n, including fractional and negative values. There is a proof in Section 31.3, but you can skip this on a first reading. The result, however, is important, and you must be able to use it confidently.

> If a, b and n are constants, and $y=(ax+b)^n$,
>
> then $\frac{dy}{dx}=a\times n(ax+b)^{n-1}$.

Example 31.1.2

Find $\frac{dy}{dx}$ when (a) $y=\sqrt{3x+2}$, (b) $y=\frac{1}{1-2x}$.

(a) Writing $\sqrt{3x+2}$ in index form as $(3x+2)^{\frac{1}{2}}$ and using the result in the box,

$$\frac{dy}{dx}=3\times\tfrac{1}{2}(3x+2)^{-\frac{1}{2}}=\tfrac{3}{2}\frac{1}{(3x+2)^{\frac{1}{2}}}=\frac{3}{2\sqrt{3x+2}}.$$

(b) In index form $y=(1-2x)^{-1}$, so $\frac{dy}{dx}=-2\times(-1)(1-2x)^{-2}=\frac{2}{(1-2x)^2}$.

Example 31.1.3

Find any stationary points on the graph $y = \sqrt{2x+1} + \dfrac{1}{\sqrt{2x+1}}$, and determine whether they are maxima, minima or neither.

$\sqrt{2x+1}$ is defined for $x \geq -\frac{1}{2}$, and $\dfrac{1}{\sqrt{2x+1}}$ for $x > -\frac{1}{2}$. So the largest possible domain is $x > -\frac{1}{2}$.

$$y = (2x+1)^{\frac{1}{2}} + (2x+1)^{-\frac{1}{2}},$$

so

$$\begin{aligned}\frac{dy}{dx} &= 2 \times \tfrac{1}{2}(2x+1)^{-\frac{1}{2}} + 2 \times \left(-\tfrac{1}{2}\right)(2x+1)^{-\frac{3}{2}} \\ &= (2x+1)^{-\frac{1}{2}} - (2x+1)^{-\frac{3}{2}} \\ &= \frac{1}{(2x+1)^{\frac{1}{2}}} - \frac{1}{(2x+1)^{\frac{3}{2}}} \\ &= \frac{2x+1-1}{(2x+1)^{\frac{3}{2}}} = \frac{2x}{(2x+1)^{\frac{3}{2}}}.\end{aligned}$$

Stationary points are those for which $\dfrac{dy}{dx} = 0$, which happens when $x = 0$.

Also, using the form $\dfrac{dy}{dx} = \dfrac{1}{(2x+1)^{\frac{1}{2}}} - \dfrac{1}{(2x+1)^{\frac{3}{2}}}$,

$$\begin{aligned}\frac{d^2y}{dx^2} &= 2 \times \left(-\tfrac{1}{2}\right)(2x+1)^{-\frac{3}{2}} - 2 \times \left(-\tfrac{3}{2}\right)(2x+1)^{-\frac{5}{2}} \\ &= -(2x+1)^{-\frac{3}{2}} + 3(2x+1)^{-\frac{5}{2}} \\ &= \frac{-1}{(2x+1)^{\frac{3}{2}}} + \frac{3}{(2x+1)^{\frac{5}{2}}}.\end{aligned}$$

When $x = 0$, $\dfrac{d^2y}{dx^2} = -(1)^{-\frac{3}{2}} + 3(1)^{-\frac{5}{2}} = 2 > 0$, so y has a minimum at $x = 0$.

The rule for differentiating $y = (ax+b)^n$ is a special case of a more general rule:

> If a and b are constants, and if $\dfrac{d}{dx} f(x) = g(x)$,
>
> then $\dfrac{d}{dx} f(ax+b) = a \times g(ax+b)$.

This is the form in which it is proved in Section 31.3. Then, with $f(x) = x^n$ and $g(x) = nx^{n-1}$,

$$\begin{aligned}\frac{d}{dx}(ax+b)^n &= \frac{d}{dx} f(ax+b) \\ &= a \times g(ax+b) \\ &= an(ax+b)^{n-1}.\end{aligned}$$

Exercise 31B

1 Find $\frac{dy}{dx}$ for each of the following.

(a) $y = (4x+5)^5$ (b) $y = (2x-7)^8$ (c) $y = (2-x)^6$ (d) $y = \left(\frac{1}{2}x+4\right)^4$

2 Find $\frac{dy}{dx}$ for each of the following.

(a) $y = \dfrac{1}{3x+5}$ (b) $y = \dfrac{1}{(4-x)^2}$ (c) $y = \dfrac{1}{(2x+1)^3}$ (d) $y = \dfrac{4}{(4x-1)^4}$

3 Find $\frac{dy}{dx}$ for each of the following.

(a) $y = \sqrt{2x+3}$ (b) $y = \sqrt[3]{6x-1}$ (c) $y = \dfrac{1}{\sqrt{4x+7}}$ (d) $y = 5(3x-2)^{-\frac{2}{3}}$

4 Given that $y = (2x+1)^3 + (2x-1)^3$, find the value of $\frac{dy}{dx}$ when $x = 1$.

5 Find the coordinates of the point on the curve $y = (1-4x)^{\frac{3}{2}}$ at which the gradient is -30.

6 Find the equation of the tangent to the curve $y = \dfrac{1}{3x+1}$ at $\left(-1, -\frac{1}{2}\right)$.

7 Find the equation of the normal to the curve $y = \sqrt{6x+3}$ at the point for which $x = 13$.

8 The curve $y = (ax+b)^4$ crosses the y-axis at $(0, 16)$ and has gradient 160 there. Find the possible values of a and b.

9 Find the coordinates of the stationary point of the curve $y = \sqrt{2x+1} - \frac{1}{3}x + 7$, and determine whether the stationary point is a maximum or a minimum.

31.2 Integrating $(ax+b)^n$

You can also use the differentiation result in reverse for integration. For example, to integrate $(3x+1)^3$, you should recognise that it comes from differentiating $(3x+1)^4$.

A first guess at the integral $\int (3x+1)^3\,dx$ is $(3x+1)^4$. If you differentiate $(3x+1)^4$, you find that you get $3 \times 4(3x+1)^3 = 12(3x+1)^3$. Therefore

$$\int (3x+1)^3\,dx = \frac{1}{12}(3x+1)^4 + k.$$

You can formalise the guessing process by reversing the main result from Section 31.1.

$$\int (ax+b)^n\,dx = \frac{1}{a} \times \frac{1}{n+1}(ax+b)^{n+1} + k.$$

For a general function $g(x)$ the corresponding result is:

$$\int g(ax+b)\,dx = \frac{1}{a} \times f(ax+b) + k$$

where $f(x)$ is the simplest integral of $g(x)$.

Applying this to the example above, $g(x) = x^3$, $a = 3$ and $b = 1$. Then $f(x) = \frac{1}{4}x^4$, so

$$\begin{aligned}\int (3x+1)^3\,dx &= \int g(3x+1)\,dx \\ &= \tfrac{1}{3}f(3x+1) + k \\ &= \tfrac{1}{3} \times \tfrac{1}{4}(3x+1)^4 + k \\ &= \tfrac{1}{12}(3x+1)^4 + k.\end{aligned}$$

Example 31.2.1

Find the integrals of (a) $\sqrt{5-2x}$, (b) $\dfrac{1}{(3-x)^2}$.

(a) **Method 1** The first guess at $\int \sqrt{5-2x}\,dx = \int (5-2x)^{\frac{1}{2}}\,dx$ is $(5-2x)^{\frac{3}{2}}$.

$$\begin{aligned}\frac{d}{dx}(5-2x)^{\frac{3}{2}} &= -2 \times \tfrac{3}{2}(5-2x)^{\frac{1}{2}} \\ &= -3(5-2x)^{\frac{1}{2}}.\end{aligned}$$

Therefore

$$\int (5-2x)^{\frac{1}{2}}\,dx = -\tfrac{1}{3}(5-2x)^{\frac{3}{2}} + k.$$

Method 2 Using the result in the blue box, $g(x) = \sqrt{x} = x^{\frac{1}{2}}$, $a = -2$, $b = 5$, so

$$f(x) = \frac{x^{\frac{3}{2}}}{3/2} = \tfrac{2}{3}x^{\frac{3}{2}},$$

and

$$\begin{aligned}\int \sqrt{5-2x}\,dx &= \frac{1}{-2} \times \tfrac{2}{3}(5-2x)^{\frac{3}{2}} + k \\ &= -\tfrac{1}{3}(5-2x)^{\frac{3}{2}} + k.\end{aligned}$$

(b) First write $\dfrac{1}{(3-x)^2}$ as $(3-x)^{-2}$. Then

$$\begin{aligned}\int \frac{1}{(3-x)^2}\,dx &= \int (3-x)^{-2}\,dx \\ &= \tfrac{1}{-1} \times \tfrac{1}{-1}(3-x)^{-1} + k \\ &= \frac{1}{3-x} + k.\end{aligned}$$

Some people like to use a trial and error method of integration: guess the form of the answer, differentiate the guess, then adjust it in the light of the result. Others prefer to remember and apply a general rule. The two approaches are illustrated by Methods 1 and 2 in Example 31.2.1. With practice you might find that you can guess the correct integral at the first go, but you should always check your answer by differentiation, because it is easy to make a numerical mistake.

Example 31.2.2

Find the area between the curve $y = 16 - (2x + 1)^4$ and the x-axis. (See Fig. 31.1.)

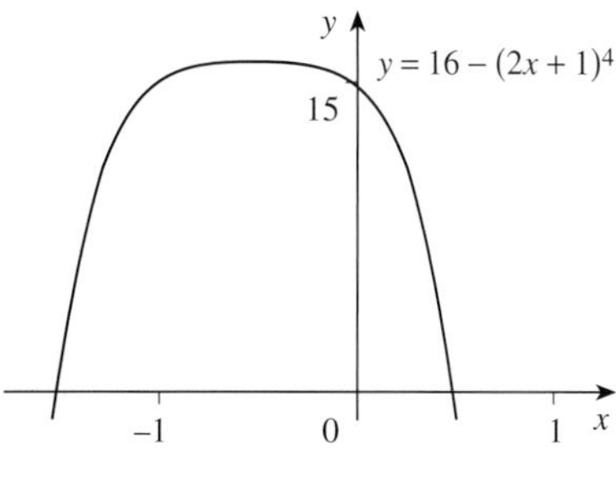

Fig. 31.1

To find where the graph cuts the x-axis, solve the equation $16 - (2x + 1)^4 = 0$.

Thus $(2x + 1)^4 = 16$, so $(2x + 1) = 2$ or $(2x + 1) = -2$, leading to the limits of integration, $x = \frac{1}{2}$ and $x = -\frac{3}{2}$.

The area is given by

$$\begin{aligned}
\int_{-\frac{3}{2}}^{\frac{1}{2}} (16 - (2x + 1)^4)\,\mathrm{d}x &= \left[16x - \tfrac{1}{10}(2x + 1)^5\right]_{-\frac{3}{2}}^{\frac{1}{2}} \\
&= \left(16 \times \tfrac{1}{2} - \tfrac{1}{10}\left(2 \times \tfrac{1}{2} + 1\right)^5\right) - \left(16 \times \left(-\tfrac{3}{2}\right) - \tfrac{1}{10}\left(2 \times \left(-\tfrac{3}{2}\right) + 1\right)^5\right) \\
&= \left(8 - \tfrac{1}{10} \times 2^5\right) - \left(-24 - \tfrac{1}{10} \times (-2)^5\right) \\
&= 4.8 - (-20.8) \\
&= 25.6.
\end{aligned}$$

The required area is then 25.6.

31.3* The reason why

This section gives an explanation of the rule for differentiating $f(ax + b)$ given in Section 31.1. You may skip it if you wish. There is no exercise on it.

You will probably find the argument easier to follow if a is written as $\dfrac{1}{c}$ and b as $-k$, since this links it with the notation used in Chapter 30. The rule is then that the derivative of $f\left(\dfrac{x}{c} - k\right)$ is equal to $\dfrac{1}{c} \times g\left(\dfrac{x}{c} - k\right)$, where $g(x) = f'(x)$.

The argument is based on the transformation of the graph of $y = f(x)$ into that of $y = f\left(\dfrac{x}{c} - k\right)$. A special case of a transformation like this was described in Example 30.4.4(a), where the graph of $y = \sin x$ was transformed into that of $y = \sin\left(\frac{1}{2}x - \frac{1}{6}\pi\right)$, using $y = \sin\left(x - \frac{1}{6}\pi\right)$ as the link equation. Generalising this, replacing sin by f, 2 by c and $\frac{1}{6}\pi$ by k, produces the chain shown in Fig. 31.2. This consists of a translation of $+k$ in the x-direction followed by a stretch parallel to the x-axis with factor c.

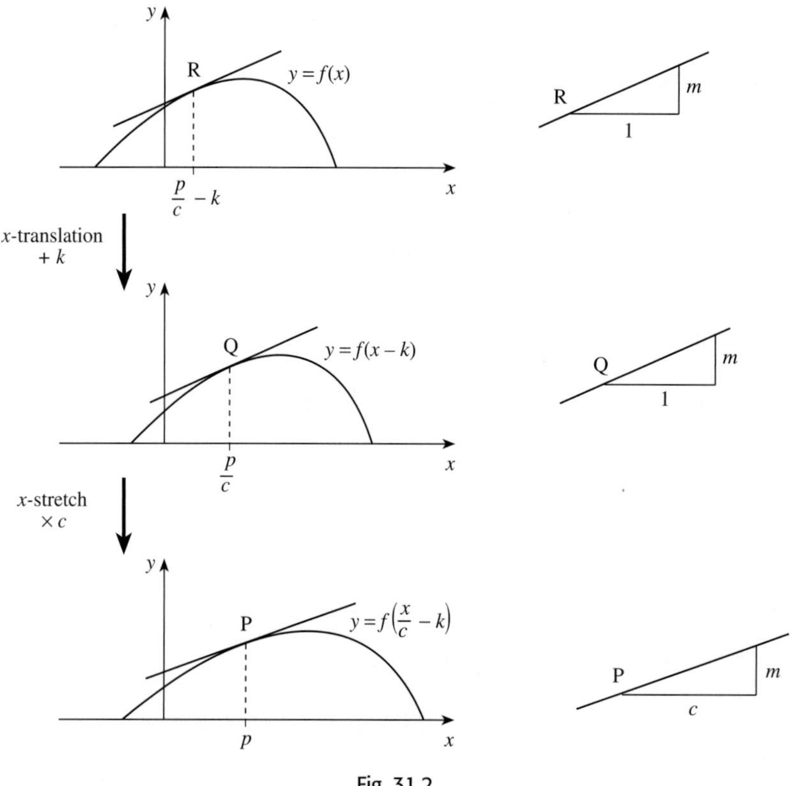

Fig. 31.2

The problem is to find the gradient of the third graph, with equation $y = f\left(\frac{x}{c} - k\right)$, at a general point P with x-coordinate p. If you follow P back through the chain, you find that it comes from a point Q on the middle graph with x-coordinate $\frac{p}{c}$, and that Q comes from a point R on the top graph with x-coordinate $\frac{p}{c} - k$. Notice that the y-coordinates of all three points are the same.

Now suppose that the tangent to $y = f(x)$ at R has gradient m, so that you can draw a gradient triangle at R with height m and width 1. (For clarity the gradient triangles in Fig. 31.2 have been drawn separate from the graphs.) The x-translation of $+k$ doesn't change the shape or size of the triangle, but the x-stretch of $\times\, c$ changes it into a triangle with height m and width c. The tangent to $y = f\left(\frac{x}{c} - k\right)$ at P therefore has gradient $\frac{m}{c}$.

The gradient function of $f(x)$ is denoted by $g(x)$, so the gradient of the tangent to $y = f(x)$ at R is $g\left(\frac{p}{c} - k\right)$. That is,

$$m = g\left(\frac{p}{c} - k\right).$$

It follows that the gradient of the tangent to $y = f\left(\frac{x}{c} - k\right)$ at P is

$$\frac{m}{c} = \frac{1}{c} \times g\left(\frac{p}{c} - k\right).$$

Since this is true for any value p of x, you can say that the gradient function of $y = f\left(\frac{x}{c} - k\right)$ is $\frac{1}{c} \times g\left(\frac{x}{c} - k\right)$. Finally, replacing $\frac{1}{c}$ by a and $-k$ by b, you can deduce that the gradient function of $y = f(ax + b)$ is $a \times g(ax + b)$.

Exercise 31C

1 Integrate the following with respect to x.

(a) $(2x + 1)^6$ (b) $(3x - 5)^4$ (c) $(1 - 7x)^3$ (d) $\left(\frac{1}{2}x + 1\right)^{10}$

2 Integrate the following with respect to x.

(a) $(5x + 2)^{-3}$ (b) $2(1 - 3x)^{-2}$ (c) $\dfrac{1}{(x + 1)^5}$ (d) $\dfrac{3}{2(4x + 1)^4}$

3 Integrate the following with respect to x.

(a) $\sqrt{10x + 1}$ (b) $\dfrac{1}{\sqrt{2x - 1}}$ (c) $\left(\frac{1}{2}x + 2\right)^{\frac{2}{3}}$ (d) $\dfrac{8}{\sqrt[4]{2 + 6x}}$

4 Evaluate the following integrals.

(a) $\displaystyle\int_1^5 (2x - 1)^3\,dx$ (b) $\displaystyle\int_1^3 \sqrt{8x + 1}\,dx$ (c) $\displaystyle\int_1^3 \frac{1}{(x + 2)^2}\,dx$ (d) $\displaystyle\int_1^3 \frac{2}{(x + 2)^3}\,dx$

5 Find the area of each of the following shaded regions.

(a)

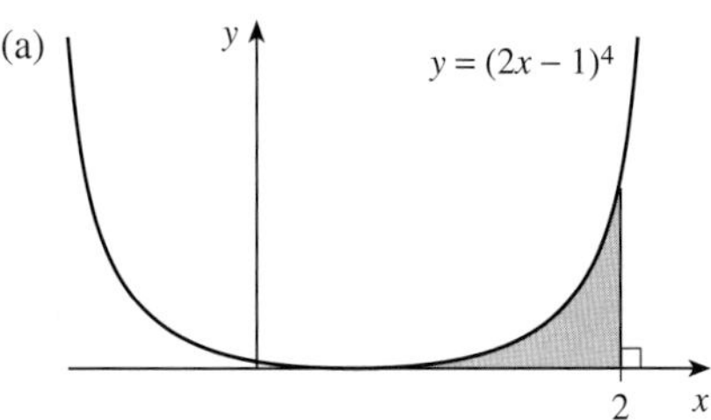

(b)

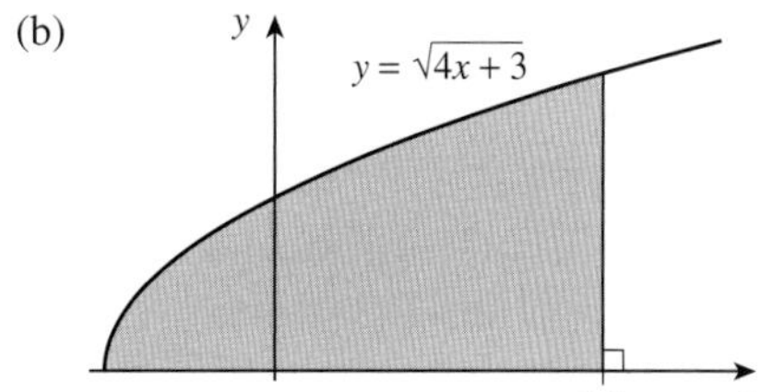

(c)

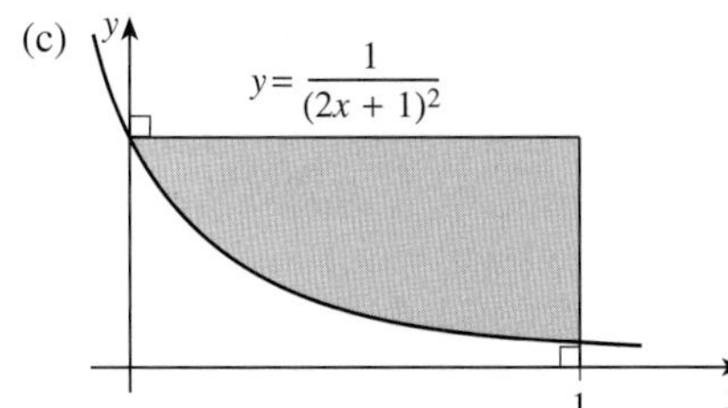

(d)

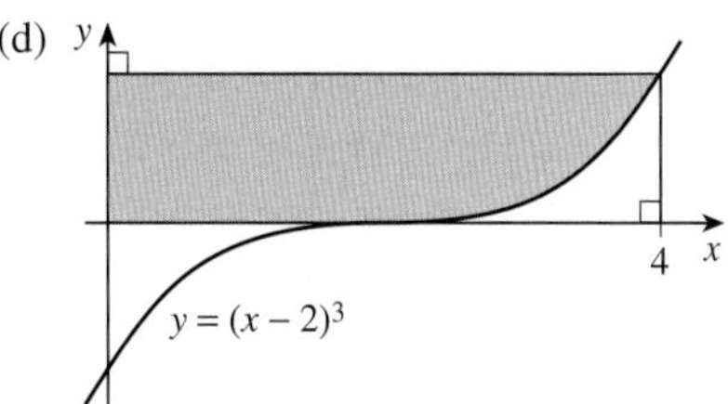

6 Given that $\displaystyle\int_{1.25}^{p} (4x - 5)^4\,dx = 51.2$, find the value of p.

7 The diagram shows the curve $y = (2x - 5)^4$. The point P has coordinates $(4, 81)$ and the tangent to the curve at P meets the x-axis at Q. Find the area of the region (shaded in the diagram) enclosed between the curve, [PQ] and the x-axis.

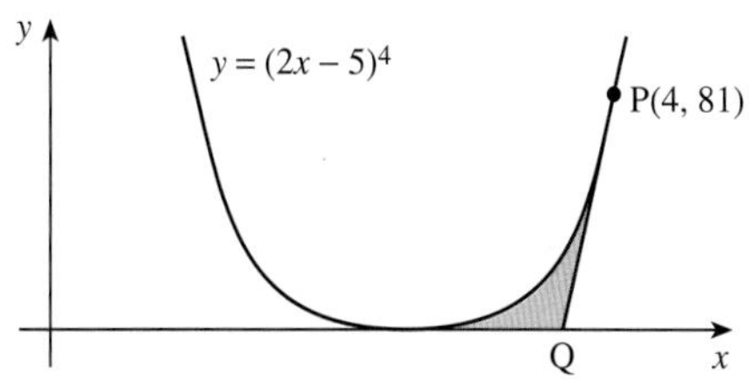

32 Differentiating exponentials and logarithms

This chapter deals with exponentials and logarithms as functions which can be differentiated and integrated. When you have completed it, you should

- understand how to find the derivative of b^x from the definition
- understand the reason for selecting e as the exponential base
- know the derivative and integral of e^x
- know that continuous exponential growth and decay can be expressed either as $y = ab^t$ or as $y = ae^{ct}$ and be able to convert either form to the other
- know the derivative of $\ln x$, and how to obtain it
- know the integral of $\frac{1}{x}$ for positive x
- be able to use the extended methods from Chapter 31 to broaden the range of such functions that you can differentiate and integrate.

32.1 Differentiating exponential functions

You saw in Section 27.1 that one of the features of exponential sequences is that the increase in the value between times t and $t + 1$ is proportional to the current value at time t. There is a corresponding property for continuous exponential variation; but in this case it is the derivative, rather than the increase over a finite unit of time, which is proportional to the current value.

To investigate this, it is necessary to find out how to differentiate the general exponential function, with equation $f(x) = b^x$, which you first met in Section 26.1. It will be simplest to begin with a particular value $b = 2$, and to consider $f(x) = 2^x$.

Fig. 32.1 shows a graph of $f(x) = 2^x$. You can see that the gradient is always positive, and also that the gradient increases as x increases. So the graph of the gradient function $f'(x)$ has a shape something like Fig. 32.2. The question is, what is the equation of this gradient function?

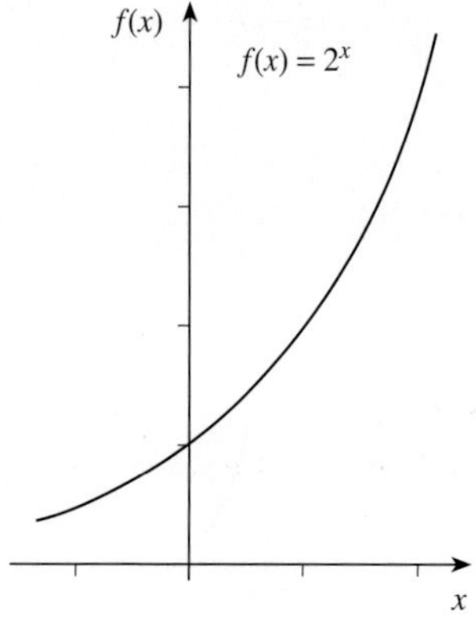

Fig. 32.1

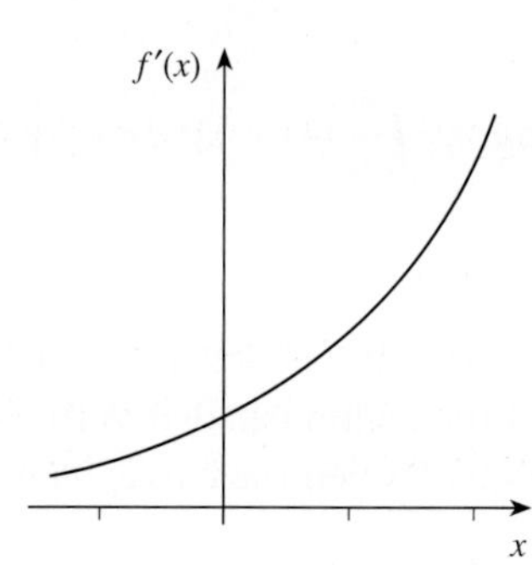

Fig. 32.2

Begin by doing a numerical experiment. It was suggested at the end of Section 11.1 that you could check your answers by using a calculator program which gives an approximation to the gradient of a given curve at a particular point. Try using this program with the function 2^x at a number of points. You will find it easier to see a pattern if you work to a small number of significant figures, as in Table 32.3.

x	-1	0	1	2
$f(x)$	0.5	1	2	4
approximate $f'(x)$	0.35	0.7	1.4	2.8

Table 32.3

It is not difficult to spot a rule from this table. For each value of x, it looks as if the value of $f'(x)$ is approximately 0.7 times the value of $f(x)$. That is,

$$\text{If } f(x) = 2^x, \quad \text{then} \quad f'(x) \approx 0.7 \times 2^x.$$

This is illustrated in Fig. 32.4, which shows the graphs of $f(x)$ and $f'(x)$ plotted using the same axes. What this experimental result suggests is that the graph of $f'(x)$ is obtained from the graph of $f(x)$ by a stretch in the y-direction of factor approximately 0.7.

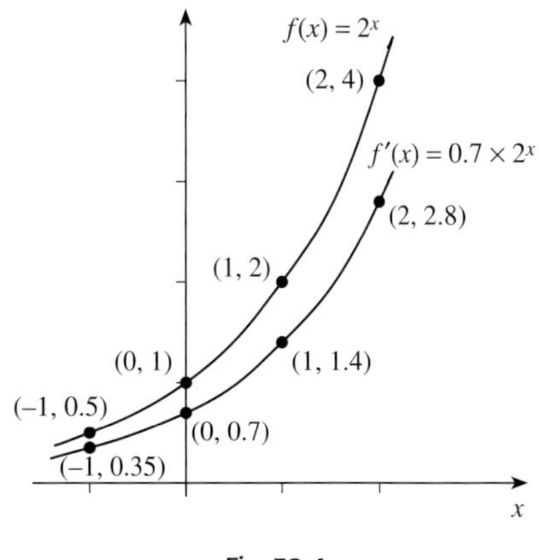

Fig. 32.4

There are two ways of going on.

With a calculator Some calculators are programmed so that, when you enter a particular function, they can produce the graphs of both $f(x)$ and $f'(x)$. So if you enter $y = 2^x$, the calculator will produce both Fig. 32.1 and Fig. 32.2. To show that $f'(x)$ is proportional to $f(x)$, you could then get the calculator to draw the graph of $\dfrac{f'(x)}{f(x)}$. This should be a horizontal line.

The instructions would be something like

$$y_1 = 2^x, y_2 = \frac{dy_1}{dx}, y_3 = \frac{y_2}{y_1},$$

but you will need to refer to the manual for precise details.

Once you have shown that $\dfrac{f'(x)}{f(x)}$ is constant, you can find the constant more accurately by using the derivative program for a particular value of x. The simplest value to use is $x = 0$, since $f(0) = 2^0 = 1$; the constant is then simply $f'(0)$. You can check for yourself that the calculator then gives $f'(0) = 0.6931...$.

So, if $f(x) = 2^x$, then $\dfrac{f'(x)}{f(x)} = 0.6931...$, so

$$f'(x) = 0.6931... \times 2^x.$$

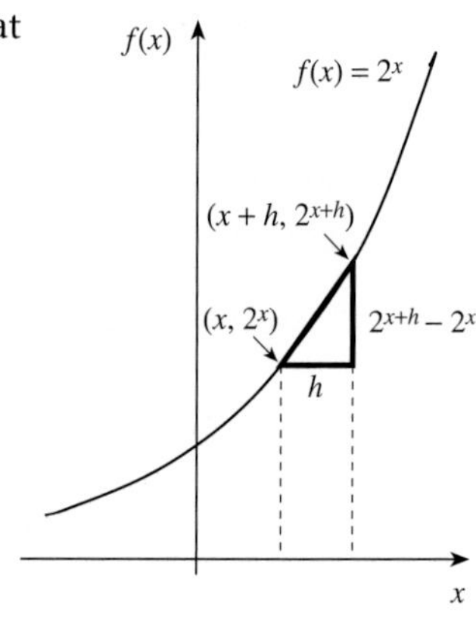

Fig. 32.5

By algebra This begins with the definition in Section 11.6, that

$$f'(x) = \lim_{h \to 0} \frac{f(x+h) - f(x)}{h}.$$

For the function 2^x, as illustrated in Fig. 32.5,

$$\begin{aligned} f(x+h) - f(x) &= 2^{x+h} - 2^x \\ &= 2^x \times 2^h - 2^x \\ &= 2^x(2^h - 1). \end{aligned}$$

So the definition becomes

$$f'(x) = \lim_{h \to 0} \frac{2^x(2^h - 1)}{h}.$$

Since 2^x does not involve h, you can write

$$f'(x) = 2^x \lim_{h \to 0} \frac{2^h - 1}{h}.$$

This shows that $f'(x)$ is the product of two factors: 2^x, which is independent of h, and a limit expression which is independent of x.

This limit expression is in fact the gradient of the tangent at the point (0, 1). This is because $\frac{2^h - 1}{h}$ is the gradient of the chord joining (0, 1) to $(h, 2^h)$, and as h tends to 0 this chord tends to the tangent. So

$$\begin{aligned} f'(x) &= 2^x \times \text{gradient of the tangent at } (0, 1) \\ &= 2^x \times f'(0); \end{aligned}$$

and since 2^x is $f(x)$, this can be written as

$$f'(x) = f(x) \times f'(0).$$

This confirms that the rate of growth of $f(x)$ is proportional to its current value.

The next step is to evaluate the limiting value $f'(0)$. You can do this with a calculator, as described above. Or you can find it to a good level of accuracy, by adapting the numerical argument that was used in Section 11.1 to find the gradient at a point of $y = x^2$. It is clear from the graph of $f(x) = 2^x$ in Fig. 32.1 that the gradient of the tangent at (0,1) is smaller than the gradient of any chord joining (0,1) to a point $(h, 2^h)$ with $h > 0$, and greater than the gradient of any such chord with $h < 0$. For example, taking h to be 0.0001 and –0.0001 in turn, you find

$$\text{gradient of chord from } (0, 1) \text{ to } (0.0001, 2^{0.0001}) \text{ is } \frac{2^{0.0001} - 1}{0.0001 - 0} = 0.693\,17\ldots$$

and

$$\text{gradient of chord from } (0, 1) \text{ to } (-0.0001, 2^{-0.0001}) \text{ is } \frac{2^{-0.0001} - 1}{-0.0001 - 0} = 0.693\,12\ldots.$$

So $0.693\,12\ldots < f'(0) < 0.693\,17\ldots.$

This shows that $f'(0) = 0.6931\ldots.$

It follows that, for the function $f(x) = 2^x$, the derivative is

$$f'(x) = \text{constant} \times 2^x, \text{ where the constant is } f'(0) = 0.6931\ldots .$$

You will see that the rule $f'(x) \approx 0.7 \times 2^x$ suggested by Table 32.3 and Fig. 32.4 fits very well with the result given by the theoretical argument.

There is nothing special about taking b to be 2. You could find the derivative for any other exponential function b^x in exactly the same way. The only difference is that the numerical value of the constant $f'(0)$ is different for different values of the base b.

For the general exponential function $f(x) = b^x$, where $b > 0$ and $b \neq 1$, the derivative is $f'(x) = \text{constant} \times b^x$, where the value of the constant, which depends on the base b, is equal to $f'(0)$.

Example 32.1.1

Show that, for any exponential function, the graph of $y = b^x$ is concave up.

If $y = b^x$,

$$\frac{dy}{dx} = f'(0)b^x$$

and

$$\frac{d^2y}{dx^2} = f'(0) \times f'(0)b^x$$
$$= (f'(0))^2 b^x.$$

Since $b \neq 1$, $f'(0)$ is not zero, so $(f'(0))^2 > 0$. Also, for all x, $b^x > 0$.

Therefore $\dfrac{d^2y}{dx^2} > 0$ for all x, so the graph is concave up.

If you look back to Chapter 26 Fig. 26.3, you can see that $f'(0)$ is positive for $b > 1$ and negative for $0 < b < 1$, but in either case the graph is concave up throughout its length.

32.2 The number e

If you carry out the limit calculation $\lim\limits_{h \to 0} \dfrac{b^h - 1}{h}$ for values of b other than 2, you get values for the constant $f'(0)$ like those in Table 32.6 below. Since the values of $f'(0)$ depend on b, they have been denoted by $L(b)$.

b	2	3	4	5	6	8	9	10
$L(b)$	0.6931	1.0986	1.3863	1.6094	1.7918	2.0794	2.1972	2.3026

Table 32.6

Before reading on, calculate one or two of these for yourself. It is also interesting to find $L(b)$ for a few values of b less than 1, such as 0.1, 0.2, 0.25 and 0.5. Look at the answers and keep a record of anything you notice for future reference.

None of these limits works out to a nice recognisable number; in fact they are all irrational numbers. But Table 32.6 suggests that between 2 and 3 there should be a number for which $L(b)$ is 1. This is the number denoted by the letter e, and it turns out to be one of the most important numbers in mathematics.

The letter e was first used for this number by the Swiss mathematician Euler in about 1727.

You can find the value of e more precisely by calculating $L(b)$ with b to more decimal places, using either the derivative program for $f'(0)$ or the algebraic method described in Section 32.1. For example, the limit calculation shows that $L(2.71) = 0.9969\ldots$, which is too small, and $L(2.72) = 1.0006\ldots$, which is too large, so $2.71 < \mathrm{e} < 2.72$. However, this is a rather tedious process, and there are far more efficient ways of calculating e to many decimal places.

Note that $L(\mathrm{e}) = 1$, and that $L(b)$ is the symbol used for the constant $f'(0)$ in the statement

$$\text{if } f(x) = b^x, \text{ then } f'(x) = f'(0)b^x.$$

This means that, if $f(x) = \mathrm{e}^x$ then $f'(0) = 1$, so

$$\text{if } f(x) = \mathrm{e}^x, \text{ then } f'(x) = \mathrm{e}^x.$$

It is this property that makes e^x so much more important than all the other exponential functions. It can be described as the 'natural' exponential function, but usually it is called '*the* exponential function' (to distinguish it from b^x for any other value of b, which is simply '*an* exponential function').

To show this, display the graphs of $f(x) = \mathrm{e}^x$ and the derivative $f'(x)$ on your calculator. What happens?

The function e^x is sometimes written as $\exp x$, so that the symbol 'exp' strictly stands for the function itself, rather than the output of the function. Thus, in formal function notation,

$$\exp : x \mapsto \mathrm{e}^x.$$

For the (natural) exponential function e^x, or $\exp x$,

$$\frac{\mathrm{d}}{\mathrm{d}x}\mathrm{e}^x = \mathrm{e}^x.$$

Many calculators have a special key labelled [exp] or [e^x], for finding values of this function. If you want to know the numerical value of e, you can use this key with an input of 1, so that the output is $\mathrm{e}^1 = \mathrm{e}$. This gives $\mathrm{e} = 2.718\,281\,828\ldots$. (But do not assume that this is a recurring decimal; e is in fact an irrational number, and the single repetition of the digits 1828 is a curious accident.)

Example 32.2.1
Find the equations of the tangents to the graph $y = e^x$ at the points (a) $(0, 1)$, (b) $(1, e)$.

(a) Since $\frac{dy}{dx} = e^x$, the gradient at $(0, 1)$ is $e^0 = 1$. The equation of the tangent is therefore $y - 1 = 1(x - 0)$, which you can simplify to $y = x + 1$.

(b) The gradient at $(1, e)$ is $e^1 = e$. The equation of the tangent is $y - e = e(x - 1)$, which you can simplify to $y = e\,x$.

It is interesting that the tangent at $(1, e)$ passes through the origin. You can demonstrate this nicely with a graphic calculator.

Example 32.2.2
Find (a) $\frac{d}{dx}e^{2x}$, (b) $\frac{d}{dx}e^{-3x}$, (c) $\frac{d}{dx}e^{2+x}$.

These are all of the form $\frac{d}{dx}f(ax + b)$, with $f(x) = e^x$. It was shown in Section 31.1 that the derivative is $a \times g(ax + b)$, where $g(x) = f'(x)$. In this case $g(x) = e^x$. The answers are therefore (a) $2e^{2x}$, (b) $-3e^{-3x}$, (c) e^{2+x}.

For (c) you could write e^{2+x} as e^2e^x. Since e^2 is constant, the derivative is e^2e^x, or e^{2+x}.

Each time you meet a new result about differentiation, you should look for a corresponding result about integration. From $\frac{d}{dx}e^x = e^x$ it follows that:

For the (natural) exponential function e^x, or $\exp x$,

$$\int e^x\,dx = e^x + k.$$

Example 32.2.3
Find the area under the graph of $y = e^{2x}$ from $x = 0$ to $x = 1$.

$\int e^{2x}dx$ is of the form $\int g(ax + b)\,dx$, with $g(x) = e^x$. The indefinite integral is therefore $\frac{1}{a}f(ax + b) + k$, where $f(x)$ is the simplest integral of $g(x)$. In this case, $f(x) = e^x$, so that

$$\int e^{2x}\,dx = \tfrac{1}{2}e^{2x} + k.$$

The area under the graph is therefore $\int_0^1 e^{2x}\,dx = \left[\tfrac{1}{2}e^{2x}\right]_0^1 = \tfrac{1}{2}e^2 - \tfrac{1}{2}e^0 = \tfrac{1}{2}(e^2 - 1)$.

In Examples 32.2.2 and 32.2.3 the rules for differentiating and integrating e^x are combined with the methods of extending differentiation and integration in Chapter 31. If you do this in general you get

$$\frac{d}{dx}e^{ax+b} = ae^{ax+b} \quad \text{and} \quad \int e^{ax+b}\,dx = \frac{1}{a}e^{ax+b} + k.$$

But it is probably better to learn the simpler rules in the blue boxes and to apply these using the methods in Chapter 31, rather than trying to remember these more complicated rules. After a little practice you will find that the process becomes almost automatic.

Exercise 32A

1 Differentiate each of the following functions with respect to x.

(a) e^{3x} (b) e^{-x} (c) $3e^{2x}$ (d) $-4e^{-4x}$

(e) e^{3x+4} (f) e^{3-2x} (g) e^{1-x} (h) $3e \times e^{2+4x}$

2 Find the gradients of the tangents to the following curves for the given values of x. Where appropriate, give your answers in terms of e.

(a) $y = 3e^x$, where $x = 2$ (b) $y = 2e^{-x}$, where $x = -1$

(c) $y = x - e^{2x}$, where $x = 0$ (d) $y = e^{6-2x}$, where $x = 3$

3 Find the equations of the tangents to the given curves for the given values of x.

(a) $y = e^x$, where $x = -1$ (b) $y = 2x - e^{-x}$, where $x = 0$

(c) $y = x^2 + 2e^{2x}$, where $x = 2$

4 Find any stationary points of the graph of $y = ex - e^x$, and determine whether they are maxima or minima.

5 Find the following indefinite integrals.

(a) $\int e^{3x}\,dx$ (b) $\int e^{-x}\,dx$ (c) $\int 3e^{2x}\,dx$ (d) $\int -4e^{-4x}\,dx$

(e) $\int e^{3x+4}\,dx$ (f) $\int e^{3-2x}\,dx$ (g) $\int e^{1-x}\,dx$ (h) $\int 3e \times e^{2+4x}\,dx$

6 Find the values of each of the following definite integrals in terms of e.

(a) $\int_1^2 e^{2x}\,dx$ (b) $\int_{-1}^1 e^{-x}\,dx$ (c) $\int_{-2}^0 2e^{1-2x}\,dx$ (d) $\int_4^5 2e^{2x}\,dx$

7 If a trapezium is used to approximate the area under the graph of $y = e^x$ for $0 \le x \le 1$, would you expect to get an overestimate or an underestimate? Use your answer to prove that $e < 3$.

32.3 Application to exponential growth and decay

The method of finding the constants in equations for exponential growth or decay, based on the equivalence of

$$y = ab^t \quad \text{and} \quad \log y = \log a + t \log b \qquad \text{(see Section 27.3)}$$

can be used with logarithms to any base. But there are some advantages in using logarithms to the base e; and a special symbol, ln, is used to denote $\log_e$. The reason for this symbol is that the letter 'n' stands for 'natural'; and the logarithm ln is called the 'natural logarithm' because the number e is based on a mathematical property (that $\frac{d}{dx}e^x = e^x$) rather than a physical accident (that mathematicians have 10 fingers).

Remember that the general definition of a logarithm (given in Section 26.2) is that

$$y = b^x \qquad \text{is equivalent to} \qquad x = \log_b y.$$

If this is applied with $b = \mathrm{e}$ you get a definition of the natural logarithm:

The **natural logarithm** function, ln, is defined by:

$$y = \mathrm{e}^x \qquad \text{is equivalent to} \qquad x = \ln y.$$

Now suppose that you have an exponential equation $y = ab^t$, and that $c = \ln b$. (Remember that by definition b is positive.) Then $b = \mathrm{e}^c$, so that

$$y = a(\mathrm{e}^c)^t = a\mathrm{e}^{ct},$$

using the power-on-power rule for indices. This is an alternative way of writing the exponential equation.

Since $c = \ln b$, it follows that $c > 0$ if $b > 1$ and $c < 0$ if $0 < b < 1$. So the constant c is positive for exponential growth and negative for exponential decay.

The continuous exponential equation can be written in the form

$$y = a\mathrm{e}^{ct}$$

where a is the initial value of y and c is constant.

This represents exponential growth if $c > 0$ and exponential decay if $c < 0$.

Example 32.3.1 (see Example 27.2.2)
Carbon dating in archaeology is based on the decay of the isotope carbon-14, which has a half-life of 5715 years. Express this property in exponential form.

Since the isotope decays exponentially, a unit of carbon-14 is reduced by a factor of e^{ct} after t years, where c is a negative constant. You are given that the reduction factor is 0.5 when $t = 5715$, so

$$\mathrm{e}^{c \times 5715} = 0.5.$$

Expressing this equation in natural logarithmic form,

$$5715c = \ln 0.5 = -0.6931\ldots,$$

$$c = \frac{-0.6931\ldots}{5715} = -0.000\,121, \quad \text{correct to 3 significant figures.}$$

So a unit of carbon-14 is reduced by a factor of $\mathrm{e}^{-0.000\,121t}$ after t years.

If you take natural logarithms of both sides of the equation $y = a\mathrm{e}^{ct}$ you get

$$\ln y = \ln a + \ln(\mathrm{e}^{ct}) = \ln a + ct$$

(because, for any number x, $\ln(\mathrm{e}^x) = \log_\mathrm{e}(\mathrm{e}^x) = x$). So if you draw a graph of $\ln y$ against t, it will be a straight line with gradient c and y-intercept $\ln a$.

This is illustrated in Example 32.3.2, in which Example 27.3.3 is re-worked using natural logarithms instead of logarithms to base 10.

Example 32.3.2 (see Example 27.3.3)
Use the census data in Table 32.7 to model the population growth in the USA from 1790 to 1860 as an equation of the form $P = ae^{ct}$.

Year	1790	1800	1810	1820	1830	1840	1850	1860
Population (millions)	3.9	5.3	7.2	9.6	12.9	17.0	23.2	31.4

Table 32.7

In Example 27.3.3 Table 32.7 was adapted to produce a table of values of $\log_{10} P$. If you take logarithms to base e instead, you get Table 32.8.

t	0	10	20	30	40	50	60	70
$\ln P$	1.36	1.67	1.97	2.26	2.56	2.83	3.14	3.45

Table 32.8

These values are plotted as a graph in Fig. 32.9, which shows that the points fit approximately on a straight line. By measurement, it seems that the intercept on the vertical axis is about 1.37; and, from the gradient triangle shown with dotted lines, the gradient is about $\frac{1.5}{50} = 0.03$. So the line has equation

$$\ln P = 1.37 + 0.03t.$$

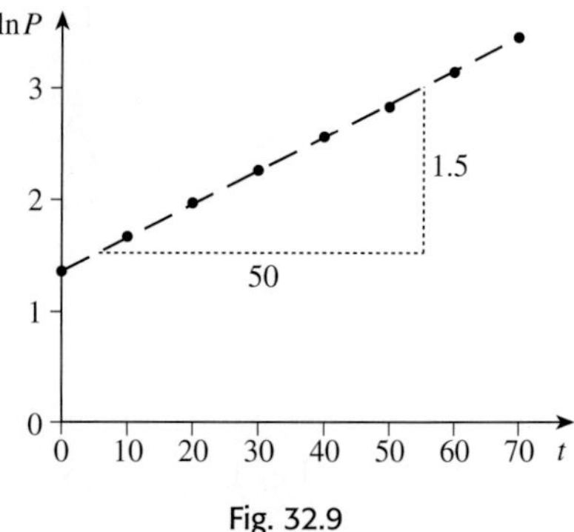

Fig. 32.9

You can finish off the calculation in one of two ways.

Method 1 Comparing the equation of the line with

$$\ln P = \ln a + ct,$$

derived from $P = ae^{ct}$, you find that $\ln a = 1.37$ and $c = 0.03$. And since

$$\ln a = 1.37 \text{ is equivalent to } a = e^{1.37} \approx 3.9,$$

the population is given approximately by the equation

$$P = 3.9e^{0.03t}.$$

Method 2 Since $\ln P = 1.37 + 0.03t$ approximately,

$$P = e^{1.37+0.03t} = e^{1.37} \times e^{0.03t} \approx 3.9e^{0.03t}.$$

Example 32.3.3

A thousand people waiting at a medical centre were asked to record how long they had to wait before they saw a doctor. Their results are summarised in Table 32.10.

Waiting time (minutes)	0 to 5	5 to 10	10 to 15	15 to 20	20 to 30	30 to 60	more than 60
Number of people	335	218	155	90	111	85	6

Table 32.10

Show that the proportion p of people who had to wait at least t minutes can be modelled by an equation of the form $p = e^{-kt}$, and find the value of k.

Obviously all of the people had to wait at least 0 minutes; all but 335, that is $1000 - 335 = 665$, had to wait at least 5 minutes; of these, $665 - 218 = 447$ had to wait at least 10 minutes; and so on. So you can make a table of p, the proportion that had to wait at least t minutes, for various values of t. This is Table 32.11.

t	0	5	10	15	20	30	60
p	1	0.665	0.447	0.292	0.202	0.091	0.006

Table 32.11

If you plot these values for yourself, you will see that they appear to fit an exponential decay graph; but to show this conclusively it is necessary to rewrite the equation so that it can be represented by a straight line.

Now if $p = e^{-kt}$ as suggested in the question, $\ln p = -kt$, so a graph of $\ln p$ against t would be a straight line through the origin with gradient $-k$. So make a table of values (Table 32.12) of $\ln p$:

t	0	5	10	15	20	30	60
$\ln p$	0	−0.41	−0.81	−1.23	−1.60	−2.40	−5.12

Table 32.12

These values are plotted in Fig. 32.13.

This example differs from Example 32.3.2 in that you know that the graph must pass through the origin. So draw the best line that you can through the origin to fit the plotted points. From Fig. 32.13 the gradient of this line is about −0.082.

So the proportion who had to wait more than t minutes is modelled by the equation $p = e^{-0.082t}$.

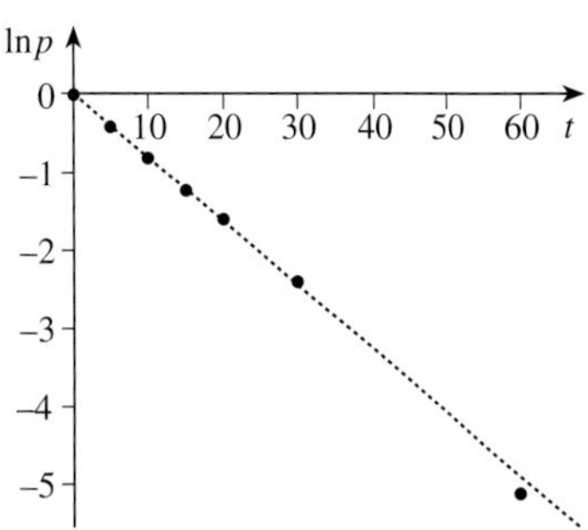

Fig. 32.13

One reason for writing the exponential equation $y = ab^t$ in the alternative form $y = ae^{ct}$, is that it is easy to differentiate, as

$$\frac{dy}{dt} = a \times ce^{ct}.$$

It follows that

$$\frac{dy}{dt} = cy.$$

That is, the quantity y grows at a rate which is c times its current value.

For example, the equation $P = 3.9e^{0.03t}$ obtained in Example 32.3.2 for the population of the USA can be differentiated to show that

$$\frac{dP}{dt} = 0.03P.$$

The interpretation of this is that the population increased at a rate of 3% of its current value. Thus when the population was 10 million, it was increasing at a rate of 300 000 per year; by the time the population had reached 20 million, the rate of increase had doubled to 600 000 per year.

A quantity Q growing (or decaying) exponentially according to the law $Q = ae^{ct}$ has a rate of growth (or decay) equal to c (or $-c$) times its current value.

Exercise 32B

1 Write the following in the form e^{cx}, giving the constant c correct to 3 significant figures.

(a) 10^x (b) 0.1^x (c) 2.5^x (d) 0.4^x

2 Write the following in the form ae^{ct}, giving the constants a and c correct to 3 significant figures.

(a) 3.6×1.1^t (b) 0.342×5.71^t (c) 7.13×0.518^t (d) 0.161×0.0172^t

3 Write the following in the form ab^t, giving the constants a and b correct to 3 significant figures.

(a) $100e^{-3t}$ (b) $2.83e^{1.46t}$ (c) $0.326e^{-0.132t}$ (d) $0.507e^{0.0123t}$

4 (a) If $\ln y = 0.4 + 0.6x$, express y in terms of x.

(b) If $\ln y = 12 - 3x$, express y in terms of x.

(c) If $\ln y = 0.7 + 1.7x$, express y in terms of x.

(d) If $\ln y = 0.7 + 2\ln x$, express y in terms of x.

(e) If $\ln y = -0.5 - 5\ln x$, express y in terms of x.

Compare your answers with the answers to Exercise 27B Question 7.

5 Justify these properties of the exponential function and the natural logarithm function.

(a) For any number x, $\ln e^x = x$.

(b) For any positive number y, $e^{\ln y} = y$.

6 Use the change of base rule in Section 26.6 to find an equation connecting $\ln a$ and $\log_{10} a$ for any positive number a.

7 (a) Verify from Table 32.6 that

(i) $L(6) = L(2) + L(3)$, (ii) $L(5) = L(10) - L(2)$,

(iii) $L(8) = 3 \times L(2)$, (iv) $L(9) = 2 \times L(3)$.

What do your results suggest?

(b) Use a calculator to make a table of values of $\ln b$ for integer values of b from 2 to 10. Compare your table with Table 32.6. What does this suggest?

(c) Deduce that $\frac{d}{dx} b^x = \ln b \times b^x$.

8 The government sets a target for the annual rate of inflation at 2% per year. This means that after t years the value of a dollar, $\$V$, would be reduced to $\$1.02^{-t}$. Express V in the form e^{ct}.

9 A sick person takes a tablet of mass 500 mg whose contents are gradually absorbed into the body. The mass not yet absorbed after t minutes is modelled by the formula $500e^{-ct}$ mg. After 30 minutes only 25 mg remains unabsorbed.

(a) Find the value of c.

(b) Find the rate at which the contents of the tablet are being absorbed

(i) when the person first takes the tablet,

(ii) when half of the tablet has been absorbed.

10 The speed of a skydiver in free fall is modelled by the equation $v = 50(1 - e^{-0.2t})$, where v is her speed in metres per second after t seconds.

(a) What speed is she certain not to exceed, however far she falls?

(b) Show that her acceleration decreases exponentially.

(c) Calculate her acceleration

(i) after 10 seconds, (ii) when her speed has reached 45 metres per second.

(d) If she continues in free fall for a minute, how far does she fall?

(e) Sketch graphs of

(i) her acceleration, (ii) her speed, (iii) the distance she has fallen.

11 An epidemic is spreading exponentially through a community, so that the total number of people who have been admitted to hospital in the first t weeks (including those who have subsequently been discharged) is modelled by the equation $y = 5e^{0.3t}$.

(a) At what rate are new patients being admitted

(i) after 5 weeks, (ii) after 200 people have already been admitted?

(b) Patients remain in hospital for 2 weeks and are then discharged. Find an expression for the number of patients in hospital after t weeks (for $t \geq 2$), and show that this number also increases exponentially.

(c) If at a certain time there are 50 patients in hospital, at what rate per week is this number increasing?

32.4 Differentiating the natural logarithm

The two statements

$$y = e^x \quad \text{and} \quad x = \ln y$$

are equivalent. So using the notation exp and ln for the exponential function and natural logarithm, the statements

$$y = \exp x \quad \text{and} \quad x = \ln y$$

are equivalent.

This shows that exp and ln are inverse functions, in the sense defined in Section 29.4. The domain of exp is the set of real numbers $\mathbb{R}$; the domain of ln is the set of positive real numbers, usually denoted by $\mathbb{R}^+$.

You are already familiar with the graphs of exponential functions of the form $y = b^x$. The graph of $y = e^x$ is the graph of this form which has gradient 1 at the point (0, 1); this is shown in Fig. 32.14. It is, of course, the same as the graph of $x = \ln y$. It was explained in Section 29.6 that, to get the graph of the inverse function $y = \ln x$, you reflect the graph of $y = e^x$ in the line $y = x$. This is also shown in Fig. 32.14. Notice from the graph that $\ln x$ exists only if $x > 0$, and that the graph passes through (1, 0), which is the reflection of (0, 1) in the line $y = x$.

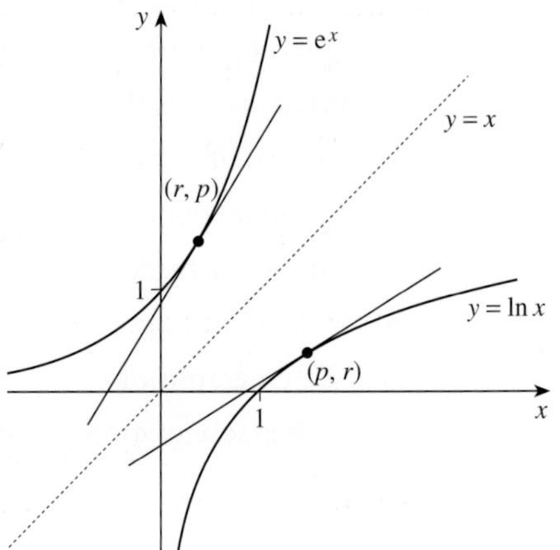

Fig. 32.14

The most important property of the natural logarithm is the derivative of $\ln x$. This can be deduced from the result $\frac{d}{dx}e^x = e^x$ in Section 32.2, but first you need a result from coordinate geometry.

Mini-theorem If a line with gradient m (where $m \neq 0$) is reflected in the line $y = x$, the gradient of the reflected line is $\frac{1}{m}$.

Proof The proof is much like that of the perpendicular line property given in Section 7.4. Fig. 32.15 shows the line of gradient m with a 'gradient triangle' ABC. Its reflection in $y = x$ is the triangle DEF. Completing the rectangle DEFG, DGF is a gradient triangle for the reflected line. GF = DE = AB = 1 and DG = EF = BC = m, so the gradient of the reflected line is $\frac{\text{GF}}{\text{DG}} = \frac{1}{m}$.

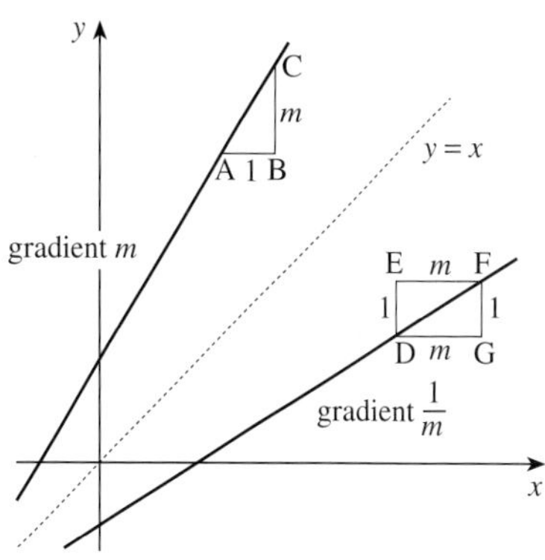

Fig. 32.15

Now consider the graphs of $y = \ln x$ and $y = e^x$ in Fig. 32.14. Since these are graphs of inverse functions, they are reflections of each other in the line $y = x$. The reflection of the tangent at the point (p, r) on $y = \ln x$ is the tangent at the point (r, p) on $y = e^x$, where $p = e^r$.

Since $\frac{d}{dx}e^x = e^x$, the gradient of the tangent at (r, p) is e^r, which is equal to p. It follows, by the mini-theorem, that the gradient of the tangent to $y = \ln x$ at (p, r) is $\frac{1}{p}$. Since this holds for any point (p, r) on $y = \ln x$, you can deduce that:

For $x > 0$, $\frac{d}{dx}\ln x = \frac{1}{x}$.

Example 32.4.1
Find the minimum value of the function $f(x) = 2x - \ln x$.

The natural domain of $f(x)$ is $x > 0$.

Since $f'(x) = 2 - \frac{1}{x}$, $f'(x) = 0$ when $x = \frac{1}{2}$.

Also $f''(x) = \frac{1}{x^2}$, so $f''(\frac{1}{2}) = 4 > 0$. So the function has a minimum when $x = \frac{1}{2}$.

The minimum value is $f(\frac{1}{2}) = 1 - \ln\frac{1}{2}$. Since $\ln\frac{1}{2} = \ln 2^{-1} = -\ln 2$, you can write the minimum value more simply as $1 + \ln 2$.

Unless you specifically need a numerical answer, it is better to leave it as $1 + \ln 2$, which is exact, than to use a calculator to convert it into decimal form.

Example 32.4.2

Find (a) $\frac{d}{dx}\ln(3x+1)$, (b) $\frac{d}{dx}\ln 3x$, (c) $\frac{d}{dx}\ln x^3$.

(a) This is of the form $f(ax+b)$, with $f(x) = \ln x$, so the derivative is

$$3 \times \frac{1}{3x+1} = \frac{3}{3x+1}.$$

(b) **Method 1** You can find the derivative as in part (a), as

$$3 \times \frac{1}{3x} = \frac{1}{x}.$$

Method 2 You can use the multiplication rule for logarithms to write

$$\ln 3x = \ln 3 + \ln x.$$

Since $\ln 3$ is constant,

$$\frac{d}{dx}\ln 3x = \frac{d}{dx}\ln x = \frac{1}{x}.$$

(c) Begin by using the power rule to write $\ln x^3$ as $3\ln x$. Then

$$\frac{d}{dx}\ln x^3 = \frac{d}{dx}(3\ln x) = 3 \times \frac{1}{x} = \frac{3}{x}.$$

In Example 32.4.2(a) the rule for differentiating $\ln x$ is combined with the method of extending differentiation in Chapter 31. If you do this in general you get

$$\frac{d}{dx}\ln(ax+b) = a \times \frac{1}{ax+b} = \frac{a}{ax+b}.$$

It is probably not worth while to learn this as a separate rule. But it is often a good idea to begin by using one of the rules for logarithms (see Section 26.3) to write the function in a form that is easier to differentiate, as illustrated by Example 32.4.2 parts (b) and (c).

Exercise 32C

1 Differentiate each of the following functions with respect to x.

(a) $\ln 2x$ (b) $\ln(2x-1)$ (c) $\ln(1-2x)$ (d) $\ln x^2$

(e) $\ln(a+bx)$ (f) $\ln\frac{1}{x}$ (g) $\ln\frac{1}{3x+1}$ (h) $\ln\frac{2x+1}{3x-1}$

(i) $3\ln x^{-2}$ (j) $\ln(x(x+1))$ (k) $\ln(x^2(x-1))$ (l) $\ln(x^2+x-2)$

2 Find the equations of the tangents to the following graphs for the given values of x.

(a) $y = \ln x$, where $x = \frac{1}{2}$ (b) $y = \ln 2x$, where $x = \frac{1}{2}$

(c) $y = \ln ex$, where $x = 1$ (d) $y = \ln 3x$, where $x = e$

3 Find any stationary points of the following curves and determine whether they are maxima or minima. Sketch the curves.

(a) $y = x - \ln x$ (b) $y = \frac{1}{2}x^2 - \ln 2x$

(c) $y = x^2 - 2\ln x$ (d) $y = x^n - n\ln x$ for $n \geq 1$

4 Prove that the tangent at the point where $x = \mathrm{e}$ to the curve with equation $y = \ln x$ passes through the origin.

5 Find the equation of the normal at $x = 2$ to the curve with equation $y = \ln(2x - 3)$.

6 Let $f(x) = \ln(x - 2) + \ln(x - 6)$. Write down the natural domain of $f(x)$.

Find $f'(x)$ and hence find the intervals for which $f'(x)$ is (i) positive, (ii) negative.

Without using a calculator, draw a sketch of the curve.

7 Repeat Question 6 for the functions

(a) $f(x) = \ln(x - 2) + \ln(6 - x)$, (b) $f(x) = \ln(2 - x) + \ln(x - 6)$.

32.5 The reciprocal integral

Now that you know that $\frac{\mathrm{d}}{\mathrm{d}x} \ln x = \frac{1}{x}$, you also know a new result about integration:

For $x > 0$, $\int \frac{1}{x}\,\mathrm{d}x = \ln x + k$.

This is an important step forward. You will recall that in Section 24.1, when giving the indefinite integral $\int x^n\,\mathrm{d}x = \frac{1}{n+1}x^{n+1} + k$, a special exception had to be made for the case $n = -1$. You can now see why: $\int \frac{1}{x}\,\mathrm{d}x$ is an entirely different kind of function, the natural logarithm.

Example 32.5.1

Find the area under the graph of $y = \frac{1}{x}$ from $x = 2$ to $x = 4$.

Before working out the exact answer, notice from Fig. 32.16 that the area should be less than the area of the trapezium formed by joining $(2, 0.5)$ and $(4, 0.25)$ with a chord. This area is

$$\tfrac{1}{2} \times 2 \times (0.5 + 0.25) = 0.75.$$

The exact area is given by the integral

$$\int_2^4 \tfrac{1}{x}\,\mathrm{d}x = \Big[\ln x\Big]_2^4 = \ln 4 - \ln 2$$
$$= \ln \tfrac{4}{2} = \ln 2.$$

The calculator gives this as 0.693 14... , which is less than 0.75, as expected.

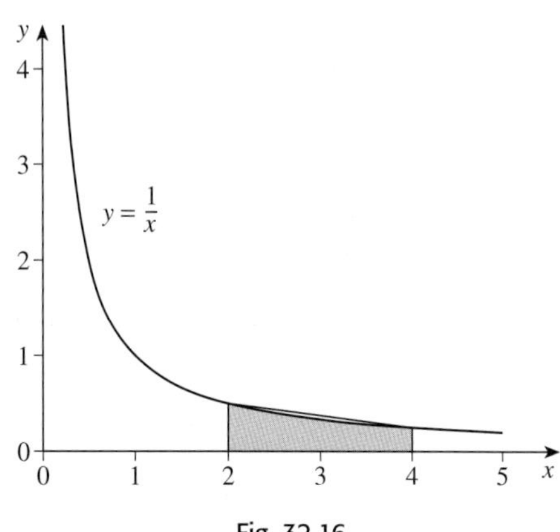

Fig. 32.16

Example 32.5.2

Find the indefinite integral $\int \frac{1}{3x-1}\,dx$.

This is of the form $\int g(ax+b)dx$, so the integral is $\frac{1}{a}f(ax+b)+k$, where $f(x)$ is the simplest integral of $g(x)$. Here, $g(x)$ is $\frac{1}{x}$, so $f(x) = \ln x$. Therefore

$$\int \frac{1}{3x-1}\,dx = \frac{1}{3}\ln(3x-1)+k.$$

Note that this integral is only valid if $x > \frac{1}{3}$, since $\ln(3x-1)$ only exists if $3x-1>0$.

Exercise 32D

1 Carry out the following indefinite integrations, and state the values of x for which your answer is valid.

(a) $\int \frac{1}{2x}\,dx$ (b) $\int \frac{1}{x-1}\,dx$ (c) $\int \frac{1}{1-x}\,dx$ (d) $\int \frac{1}{4x+3}\,dx$

(e) $\int \frac{4}{1-2x}\,dx$ (f) $\int \frac{4}{1+2x}\,dx$ (g) $\int \frac{4}{-1-2x}\,dx$ (h) $\int \frac{4}{2x-1}\,dx$

2 Calculate the area under the graph of $y = \frac{1}{x}$ from

(a) $x = 3$ to $x = 6$, (b) $x = 4$ to $x = 8$,

(c) $x = \frac{1}{2}$ to $x = 1$, (d) $x = a$ to $x = 2a$, where $a > 0$.

3 Calculate the areas under the following graphs.

(a) $y = \frac{1}{x+2}$ from $x = -1$ to $x = 0$ (b) $y = \frac{1}{2x-1}$ from $x = 2$ to $x = 5$

(c) $y = \frac{2}{3x-5}$ from $x = 4$ to $x = 6$ (d) $y = \frac{e}{ex-7}$ from $x = 4$ to $x = 5$

(e) $y = \frac{1}{-x-1}$ from $x = -3$ to $x = -2$ (f) $y = 2 + \frac{1}{x-1}$ from $x = 2$ to $x = 6$

4 Draw a sketch of $y = \frac{2}{x+1}$, and use your sketch to make a rough estimate of the area under the graph between $x = 3$ and $x = 5$. Compare your answer with the exact area.

5 Use trapeziums formed by two chords to find an approximation to the area under the graph of $y = \frac{6}{3x+4}$ between $x = 3$ and $x = 5$, indicating whether the approximation is an overestimate or an underestimate. Compare your answer with the exact area.

6 Given that $\frac{dy}{dx} = \frac{3}{2x+1}$ and that the graph of y against x passes through the point $(1, 0)$, find y in terms of x.

7 A curve has the property that $\frac{dy}{dx} = \frac{8}{4x-3}$, and it passes through $(1, 2)$. Find its equation.

Review exercise 10

1 The diagram shows parts of the curves $y = (3x - 5)^3$ and $y = \dfrac{32}{(3x-5)^2}$. Calculate the shaded area.

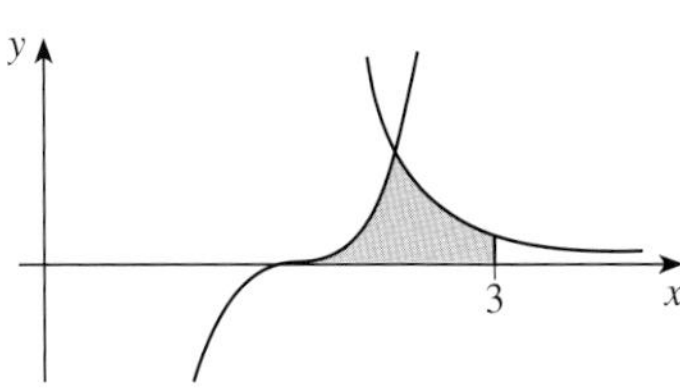

2 A bath is filled with water at a temperature of 40 °C. After t minutes the temperature has fallen to $(10 + 30e^{-0.04t})$ °C.

(a) Find the rate at which the temperature is falling

(i) initially, (ii) after 5 minutes.

(b) Find the rate at which the temperature is falling when the temperature is

(i) 38 °C, (ii) 24 °C.

(c) Sketch a graph to show how the temperature decreases with time.

3 A hospital patient requires an injection of a drug once every 12 hours. Initially Q millilitres are injected. This decays exponentially so that after t hours the quantity remaining in the bloodstream is Qe^{-ct} ml, and a further injection of $\frac{3}{4}Q$ ml is given to bring the concentration up to its initial value. This process is repeated at each subsequent injection.

(a) Draw a sketch graph to illustrate the quantity in the bloodstream over 2 days.

(b) Calculate the value of c.

(c) It is decided to increase the frequency of the injections to once every 8 hours. How large will the top-up injection need to be under this new regime?

4 Find the equation of the tangent to the curve $y = (4x + 3)^5$ at the point $(-\frac{1}{2}, 1)$, giving your answer in the form $y = mx + c$. (OCR)

5 The diagram shows the curve with equation $y = \sqrt{4x+1}$ and the normal to the curve at the point A with coordinates (6, 5).

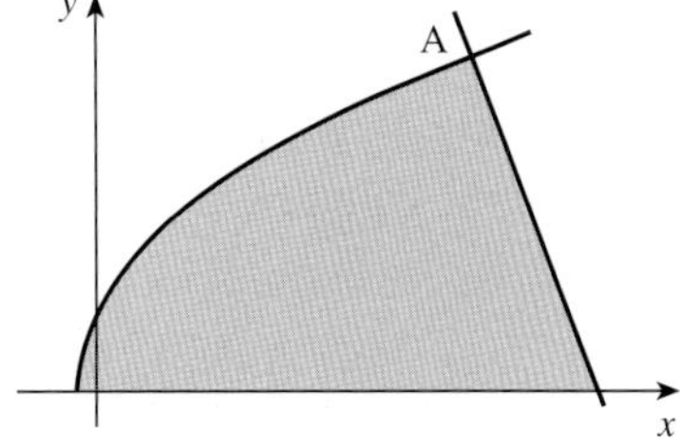

(a) Show that the equation of the normal to the curve at A is $y = -\frac{5}{2}x + 20$.

(b) Find the area of the region (shaded in the diagram) which is enclosed by the curve, the normal and the x-axis. Give your answer as a fraction in its lowest terms. (OCR)

6 The diagram shows sketches of the graphs of $y = 2 - e^{-x}$ and $y = x$. These graphs intersect at $x = a$ where $a > 0$.

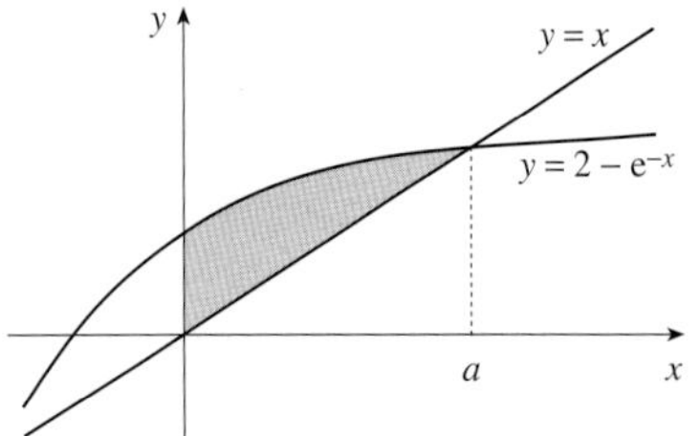

(a) Write down an equation satisfied by a.

(b) Write down an integral which is equal to the area of the shaded region.

(c) Show that the area is $1 + a - \frac{1}{2}a^2$. (OCR, adapted)

7 Use your calculator to draw a sketch of the curve $y = e^{-2x} - 3x$. The curve crosses the x-axis at A$(a, 0)$ and the y-axis at B$(0, 1)$. O is the origin.

(a) Write down an equation satisfied by a.

(b) Show that the tangent at A meets the y-axis where $y = 2ae^{-2a} + 3a$.

(c) Show that $\dfrac{d^2y}{dx^2} > 0$, and using parts (a) and (b), deduce that $6a^2 + 3a < 1$.

(d) Find, in terms of a, the area bounded by the curve and the line segments [OA] and [OB].

(e) By comparing this area with the area of the triangle OAB, show that $3a^2 + 4a > 1$. Hence show that $\frac{1}{3}\sqrt{7} - \frac{2}{3} < a < \frac{1}{12}\sqrt{33} - \frac{1}{4}$. (OCR, adapted)

Examination questions

1 Given $\displaystyle\int_3^k \frac{1}{x-2}\,dx = \ln 7$, find the value of k. (© IBO 2005)

2 Let $f(x) = 6\sin \pi x$, and $g(x) = 6e^{-x} - 3$, for $0 \le x \le 2$. The graph of f is shown on the diagram. There is a maximum value at B$(0.5, b)$.

(a) Write down the value of b.

(b) On the same diagram, sketch the graph of g.

(c) Solve $f(x) = g(x)$, for $0.5 \le x \le 1.5$. (© IBO 2005)

3 The derivative of the function f is given by $f'(x) = e^{-2x} + \dfrac{1}{1-x}$, $x \ne 1$. The graph of $y = f(x)$ passes through $(0, 4)$. Find an expression for $f(x)$. (© IBO 2004)

4 The displacement, s metres, of a car t seconds after it starts from a fixed point A is given by $s = 4t + 5 - 5e^{-t}$.

(a) Find an expression for its velocity (in m s^{-1}) after t seconds.

(b) Find the acceleration (in m s^{-2}) at A. (© IBO 2004)

5 An aircraft lands on a runway. Its velocity v m s^{-1} at time t seconds after landing is given by the equation $v = 50 + 50e^{-0.5t}$, where $0 \le t \le 4$.

(a) Find the velocity of the aircraft (i) when it lands, (ii) when $t = 4$.

(b) Write down an integral which represents the distance travelled in the first four seconds.

(c) Calculate the distance travelled in the first four seconds.

After 4 seconds, the aircraft slows down (decelerates) *at a constant rate* and comes to rest when $t = 11$.

(d) *Sketch* a graph of velocity against time for $0 \le t \le 11$. Clearly label the axes and mark on the graph the point where $t = 4$.

(e) Find the constant rate at which the aircraft is slowing down (decelerating) between $t = 4$ and $t = 11$.

(f) Calculate the distance travelled by the aircraft between $t = 4$ and $t = 11$. (© IBO 2003)

6 Write each of the following in its simplest form.

(a) $e^{\ln x}$ (b) $e^{(\ln x + \ln y)}$ (c) $\ln(e^{x+y})^2$ (© IBO 2004)

7 The derivative of the function f is given by $f'(x) = e^x + x - 5$. The point $(1, e - 2)$ lies on the graph of $f(x)$.

(a) Show that $f(x) = e^x + \frac{1}{2}x^2 - 5x + 2.5$.

(b) Sketch the graph of $y = f(x)$ for $-3 \leq x \leq 3$.

(c) Find the minimum value of $f(x)$.

(d) Find the area enclosed by the graph of $y = f(x)$, the axes and the line $x = 2$. (© IBO 2004)

8 Consider the function $f(x) = 1 + e^{-2x}$.

(a) (i) Find $f'(x)$.

(ii) Explain briefly how this shows that $f(x)$ is a decreasing function for all values of x (i.e. that $f(x)$ always decreases in value as x increases).

Let P be the point on the graph of f where $x = -\frac{1}{2}$.

(b) Find an expression in terms of e for

(i) the y-coordinate of P, (ii) the gradient of the tangent to the curve at P.

(c) Find the equation of the tangent to the curve at P, giving your answer in the form $y = ax + b$.

(d) (i) Sketch the curve of f for $-1 \leq x \leq 2$. (ii) Draw the tangent at $x = -\frac{1}{2}$.

(iii) Shade the area enclosed by the curve, the tangent and the y-axis.

(iv) Find this area. (© IBO 2003)

9 Consider functions of the form $y = e^{-kx}$.

(a) Show that $\int_0^1 e^{-kx}\,dx = \frac{1}{k}(1 - e^{-k})$.

(b) Let $k = 0.5$.

(i) Sketch the graph of $y = e^{-0.5x}$, for $-1 \leq x \leq 3$, indicating the coordinates of the y-intercept.

(ii) Shade the region enclosed by this graph, the x-axis, y-axis and the line $x = 1$.

(iii) Find the area of this region.

(c) (i) Find $\frac{dy}{dx}$ in terms of k, where $y = e^{-kx}$.

The point P(1, 0.8) lies on the graph of the function $y = e^{-kx}$.

(ii) Find the value of k in this case.

(iii) Find the gradient of the tangent to the curve at P. (© IBO 2002)

33 Probability distributions

This chapter introduces random variables. When you have completed it, you should

- understand what a random variable is and know its properties
- be able to construct a probability distribution table for a random variable
- understand the meaning of expectation.

33.1 Random variables

Most people have played board games at some time. Here is an example.

Game *A* A turn consists of throwing a dice and then moving a number of squares equal to the score on the dice.

'The number of squares moved in a turn' is a variable because it can take different numerical values, namely 1, 2, 3, 4, 5 and 6. However, the value taken at any one turn cannot be predicted, but depends on chance. For these reasons 'the number of squares moved in a turn' is called a 'random variable'.

A **random variable** is a quantity whose numerical value depends on chance.

Although you cannot predict the result of the next throw of the dice, you do know that, if the dice is fair, the probability of getting each value is $\frac{1}{6}$. A convenient way of expressing this information is to let X stand for 'the number of squares moved in a turn'. Then, for example, $P(X = 3) = \frac{1}{6}$ means 'the probability that X takes the value 3 is $\frac{1}{6}$'. Generalising, $P(X = x)$ means 'the probability that the variable X takes the value x'.

Note how the capital letter stands for the variable itself and the small letter stands for the value which the variable takes.

This notation is used in Table 33.1 to give the possible values for the number of squares moved and the probability of each value. This table is called the 'probability distribution' of X.

x	1	2	3	4	5	6	Total
$P(X = x)$	$\frac{1}{6}$	$\frac{1}{6}$	$\frac{1}{6}$	$\frac{1}{6}$	$\frac{1}{6}$	$\frac{1}{6}$	1

Table 33.1

The **probability distribution** of a random variable is a listing of the possible values x_i of the variable and the corresponding probabilities $P(X = x_i)$.

In some board games, a dice is used in a more complicated way in order to decide how many squares a person should move. Here are two different examples.

Game *B* A person is allowed a second throw of the dice if a 6 is thrown, and, in this case, moves a number Y of squares equal to the sum of the two scores obtained.

Game *C* The dice is thrown twice and the number, W, of squares moved is the sum of the two scores.

Fig. 33.2 is a tree diagram illustrating Game B.

As Y is the number of squares moved in a turn, it can take the values 1, 2, 3, 4, 5, 7, 8, 9, 10, 11 and 12. The probability of the first five values is $\frac{1}{6}$, as in the previous game. In order to score 7, you have to score 6 followed by 1. Since the two events are independent, the probability of scoring a 6 followed by a 1 is found by multiplying the two probabilities:

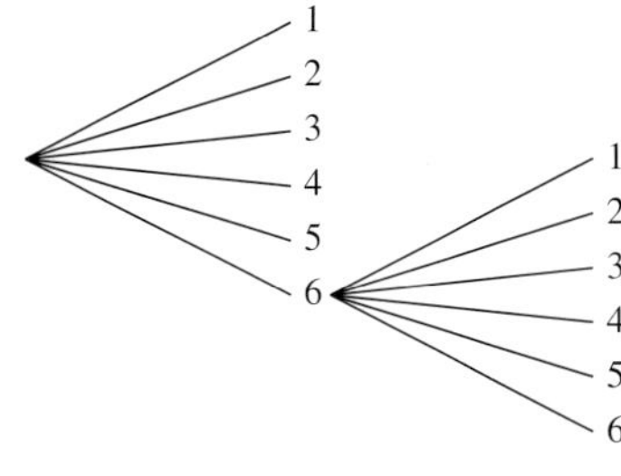

Fig. 33.2

$$\begin{aligned} P(Y = 7) &= P(6 \text{ on first throw}) \times P(1 \text{ on second throw}) \\ &= \tfrac{1}{6} \times \tfrac{1}{6} = \tfrac{1}{36}. \end{aligned}$$

The probability that Y takes each of the values 8, 9, 10, 11 and 12 will also be $\frac{1}{36}$. Table 33.3 gives the probability distribution of Y.

y	1	2	3	4	5	7	8	9	10	11	12	Total
$P(Y = y)$	$\frac{1}{6}$	$\frac{1}{6}$	$\frac{1}{6}$	$\frac{1}{6}$	$\frac{1}{6}$	$\frac{1}{36}$	$\frac{1}{36}$	$\frac{1}{36}$	$\frac{1}{36}$	$\frac{1}{36}$	$\frac{1}{36}$	1

Table 33.3

The possible values of W in Game C can be found by using a table as shown in Table 33.4.

		Second throw					
		1	2	3	4	5	6
	1	2	3	4	5	6	7
	2	3	4	5	6	7	8
First	3	4	5	6	7	8	9
throw	4	5	6	7	8	9	10
	5	6	7	8	9	10	11
	6	7	8	9	10	11	12

Table 33.4

There are 36 outcomes in the table and they are all equally likely, so, for example, $P(W = 6) = \frac{5}{36}$ and $P(W = 7) = \frac{6}{36}$. Table 33.5 gives the probability distribution of W. Some of the fractions could have been cancelled but in their present forms it is easier to see the shape of the distribution.

w	2	3	4	5	6	7	8	9	10	11	12	Total
$\text{P}(W = w)$	$\frac{1}{36}$	$\frac{2}{36}$	$\frac{3}{36}$	$\frac{4}{36}$	$\frac{5}{36}$	$\frac{6}{36}$	$\frac{5}{36}$	$\frac{4}{36}$	$\frac{3}{36}$	$\frac{2}{36}$	$\frac{1}{36}$	1

Table 33.5

Fig. 33.6 allows you to compare the probability distributions of X, Y and W.

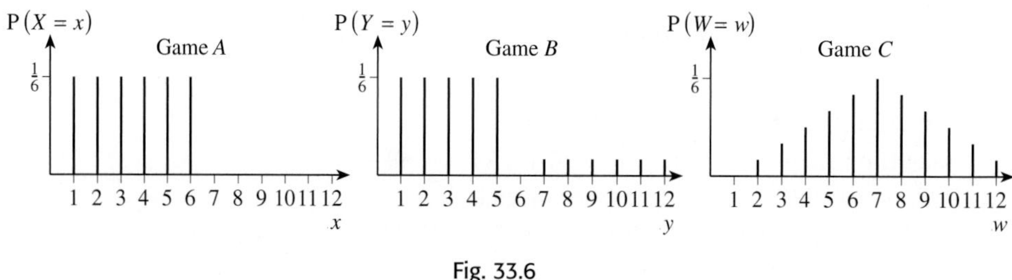

Fig. 33.6

Looking at Fig. 33.6, which method of scoring will take you round the board most quickly and which most slowly? (A method for finding the answer to this question by calculation is given in Example 33.4.1.)

Examples 33.1.1 and 33.1.2 illustrate some other probability distributions.

Example 33.1.1

A bag contains two red and three blue marbles. Two marbles are selected at random without replacement. Find the probability distribution of X, the number of blue marbles.

Fig. 33.7 is a tree diagram illustrating this situation.

R_1 denotes the event that the first marble is red and R_2 the event that the second marble is red. Similarly B_1 and B_2 stand for the events that the first and second marbles respectively are blue. X can take the values 0, 1 and 2.

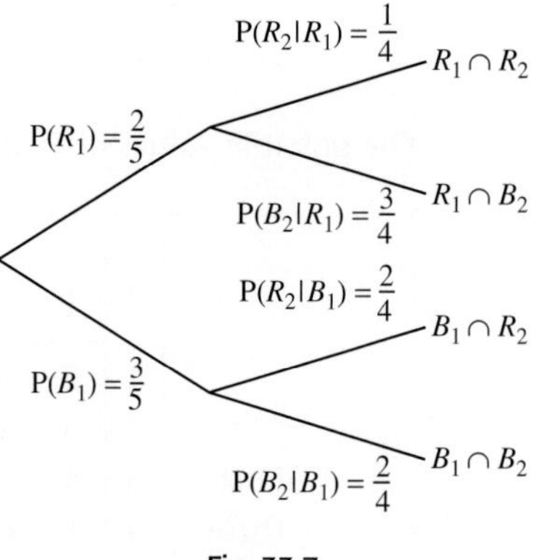

Fig. 33.7

$$\begin{aligned}\text{P}(X=0) &= \text{P}(R_1 \cap R_2)\\ &= \text{P}(R_1) \times \text{P}(R_2|R_1)\\ &= \tfrac{2}{5} \times \tfrac{1}{4} = \tfrac{2}{20} = \tfrac{1}{10}.\\ \text{P}(X=1) &= \text{P}(B_1 \cap R_2) + \text{P}(R_1 \cap B_2)\\ &= \text{P}(B_1) \times \text{P}(R_2|B_1) + \text{P}(R_1) \times \text{P}(B_2|R_1)\\ &= \tfrac{3}{5} \times \tfrac{2}{4} + \tfrac{2}{5} \times \tfrac{3}{4} = \tfrac{12}{20} = \tfrac{3}{5}.\\ \text{P}(X=2) &= \text{P}(B_1 \cap B_2)\\ &= \text{P}(B_1) \times \text{P}(B_2|B_1)\\ &= \tfrac{3}{5} \times \tfrac{2}{4} = \tfrac{6}{20} = \tfrac{3}{10}.\end{aligned}$$

Here is the probability distribution of X.

x	0	1	2	Total
$P(X = x)$	$\frac{1}{10}$	$\frac{3}{5}$	$\frac{3}{10}$	1

Example 33.1.2
A random variable, X, has the probability distribution shown below.

x	1	2	3	4
$P(X = x)$	0.1	0.2	0.3	0.4

Two observations are made of X and the random variable Y is equal to the larger minus the smaller; if the two observations are equal, Y takes the value 0. Find the probability distribution of Y. Which value of Y is most likely?

The following table gives the values for X and the corresponding values of Y. Since the two observations of X are independent, the probability of each pair is the product of the two X values, as shown in the last column of the table.

First value of X	Second value of X	Y	Probability
1	1	0	$0.1 \times 0.1 = 0.01$
1	2	1	$0.1 \times 0.2 = 0.02$
1	3	2	$0.1 \times 0.3 = 0.03$
1	4	3	$0.1 \times 0.4 = 0.04$
2	1	1	$0.2 \times 0.1 = 0.02$
2	2	0	$0.2 \times 0.2 = 0.04$
2	3	1	$0.2 \times 0.3 = 0.06$
2	4	2	$0.2 \times 0.4 = 0.08$
3	1	2	$0.3 \times 0.1 = 0.03$
3	2	1	$0.3 \times 0.2 = 0.06$
3	3	0	$0.3 \times 0.3 = 0.09$
3	4	1	$0.3 \times 0.4 = 0.12$
4	1	3	$0.4 \times 0.1 = 0.04$
4	2	2	$0.4 \times 0.2 = 0.08$
4	3	1	$0.4 \times 0.3 = 0.12$
4	4	0	$0.4 \times 0.4 = 0.16$

This table shows that Y takes the values 0, 1, 2 and 3. You can find the total probability for each value of Y by adding the individual probabilities:

$$\begin{aligned}
P(Y = 0) &= 0.01 + 0.04 + 0.09 + 0.16 = 0.30,\\
P(Y = 1) &= 0.02 + 0.02 + 0.06 + 0.06 + 0.12 + 0.12 = 0.40,\\
P(Y = 2) &= 0.03 + 0.08 + 0.03 + 0.08 = 0.22,\\
P(Y = 3) &= 0.04 + 0.04 = 0.08.
\end{aligned}$$

So Y has the probability distribution shown below.

y	0	1	2	3	Total
$P(Y = y)$	0.30	0.40	0.22	0.08	0

The most likely value of Y is 1, because it has the highest probability.

Exercise 33A

1 A fair coin is thrown four times. The random variable X is the number of heads obtained. Tabulate the probability distribution of X.

2 Two fair dice are thrown simultaneously. The random variable D is the difference between the smaller and the larger score, or zero if they are the same. Tabulate the probability distribution of D.

3 A fair dice is thrown once. The random variable X is related to the number N thrown on the dice as follows. If N is even then X is half N; otherwise X is double N. Tabulate the probability distribution of X.

4 Two fair dice are thrown simultaneously. The random variable H is the highest common factor of the two scores. Tabulate the probability distribution of H, combining together all the possible ways of obtaining the same value.

5 When a four-sided dice is thrown, the score is the number on the bottom face. Two fair four-sided dice, each with faces numbered 1 to 4, are thrown simultaneously. The random variable M is the product of the two scores multiplied together. Tabulate the probability distribution of M, combining together all the possible ways of obtaining the same value.

6 A bag contains six red and three green counters. Two counters are drawn from the bag, without replacement. Tabulate the probability distribution of the number of green counters obtained.

7 Tim picks a card at random from an ordinary pack. If the card is an ace, he stops; if not, he continues to pick cards at random, without replacement, until either an ace is picked, or four cards have been drawn. The random variable C is the total number of cards drawn. Construct a tree diagram to illustrate the possible outcomes of the experiment, and use it to calculate the probability distribution of C.

33.2 An important property of a probability distribution

You have probably noticed that, in all the probability distributions considered so far, the sum of the probabilities is 1. This must always be the case, because one of the outcomes must happen. This is an important property of a probability distribution and a useful check that you have found the probabilities correctly.

For any discrete random variable, X, the sum of the probabilities is 1; that is,

$$\sum \mathrm{P}(X = x) = 1.$$

In this case you are given no upper and lower values for the summation. It is easier to think of it simply as, the sum of the probabilities is 1.

Example 33.2.1
The table below gives the probability distribution of the random variable T.

Find (a) the value of c, (b) $\mathrm{P}(T \leq 3)$, (c) $\mathrm{P}(T > 3)$.

t	1	2	3	4	5
$\mathrm{P}(T = t)$	c	$2c$	$2c$	$2c$	c

(a) Since the probabilities must sum to 1,

$$c + 2c + 2c + 2c + c = 1, \quad \text{so } 8c = 1, \quad \text{giving} \quad c = \tfrac{1}{8}.$$

(b)
$$\begin{aligned}\mathrm{P}(T \leq 3) &= \mathrm{P}(T = 1) + \mathrm{P}(T = 2) + \mathrm{P}(T = 3)\\ &= c + 2c + 2c\\ &= 5c = \tfrac{5}{8}\end{aligned}$$

(c)
$$\begin{aligned}\mathrm{P}(T > 3) &= \mathrm{P}(T = 4) + \mathrm{P}(T = 5)\\ &= 2c + c = 3c = \tfrac{3}{8}\end{aligned}$$

Example 33.2.2
A computer is programmed to give single-digit numbers X between 0 and 9 inclusive in such a way that the probability of getting an odd digit (1, 3, 5, 7, 9) is half the probability of getting an even digit (0, 2, 4, 6, 8). Find the probability distribution of X.

Let the probability of getting an even digit be c. Then the probability of getting an odd digit is $\frac{1}{2}c$.

Since the probabilities must sum to 1,

$$\sum \mathrm{P}(X = x) = \tfrac{1}{2}c + c + \tfrac{1}{2}c + c + \tfrac{1}{2}c + c + \tfrac{1}{2}c + c + \tfrac{1}{2}c + c = 1$$

which gives $\frac{15}{2}c = 1$; that is, $c = \frac{2}{15}$.

The probability distribution of X is $P(X = x) = \frac{1}{15}$ for $x = 1, 3, 5, 7$ and 9 and $\mathrm{P}(X = x) = \frac{2}{15}$ for $x = 0, 2, 4, 6$ and 8.

Exercise 33B

1 In the following probability distribution, c is a constant. Find the value of c.

x	0	1	2	3
$P(X = x)$	$\frac{1}{4}$	$\frac{1}{5}$	$\frac{1}{2}$	c

2 In the following probability distribution, d is a constant. Find the value of d.

x	0	1	2	3
$P(X = x)$	d	0.1	0.2	0.4

3 In the following probability distribution, d is a constant. Find the value of d.

x	0	1	2	3	4
$P(X = x)$	d	0.2	0.15	0.2	$2d$

4 The score S on a spinner is a random variable with distribution given by $P(S = s) = k$ $(s = 1, 2, 3, 4, 5, 6, 7, 8)$, where k is a constant. Find the value of k.

5 A cubical dice is biased so that the probability of an odd number is three times the probability of an even number. Find the probability distribution of the score.

6 A cubical dice is biased so that the probability of any particular score between 1 and 6 (inclusive) being obtained is proportional to that score. Find the probability of scoring a 1.

7 For a biased cubical dice the probability of any particular score between 1 and 6 (inclusive) being obtained is inversely proportional to that score. Find the probability of scoring a 1.

8 In the following probability distribution, c is a constant. Find the value of c.

x	0	1	2	3
$P(X = x)$	0.6	0.16	c	c^2

33.3 Using a probability distribution as a model

So far, the discussion of probability distributions in this chapter has been very mathematical. At this point it may be helpful to point out the practical application of probability distributions. Probability distributions are useful because they provide models for experiments. Consider again the random variable X, the score on a dice, whose probability distribution was given in Table 33.1. Suppose you actually threw a dice 360 times. Since the values 1, 2, 3, 4, 5 and 6 have equal probabilities, you would expect them to occur with approximately equal frequencies of, in this case, $\frac{1}{6} \times 360 = 60$. It is very unlikely that all the observed frequencies will be exactly equal to 60. However, if the model is a suitable one, the observed frequencies should be close to the expected values.

What conclusion would you draw about the dice if the observed frequencies were not close to the expected values?

Now look at the random variable Y, whose probability distribution was given in Table 33.3. For this variable the values are not equally likely and so you would not expect to observe approximately equal frequencies. In Section 22.2 you met the idea that

$$\text{relative frequency} = \frac{\text{frequency}}{\text{total frequency}} \approx \text{probability}.$$

Rearrange this equation to give an expression for the frequencies you would expect to observe:

$$\text{frequency} \approx \text{total frequency} \times \text{probability}.$$

For 360 observations of Y, the expected frequencies will be about $360 \times \frac{1}{6} = 60$ for $y = 1, 2, 3, 4, 5$ and $360 \times \frac{1}{36} = 10$ for $y = 7, 8, 9, 10, 11$ and 12.

What will the expected frequencies be for 360 observations of the random variable W, whose probability distribution is given in Table 33.5?

Exercise 33C

1 A card is chosen at random from a pack and replaced. This experiment is carried out 520 times. State the expected number of times on which the card is

(a) a club,
(b) an ace,
(c) a picture card (K, Q, J),
(d) either an ace or a club or both,
(e) neither an ace nor a club.

2 The biased dice of Exercise 33B, Question 5, is rolled 420 times. State how many times you would expect to obtain

(a) a one,
(b) an even number,
(c) a prime number.

3 The table below gives the cumulative probability distribution for a random variable R. 'Cumulative' means that the probability given is $P(R \le r)$, not $P(R = r)$.

r	0	1	2	3	4	5
$P(R \le r)$	0.116	0.428	0.765	0.946	0.995	1.000

One hundred observations of R are made. Calculate the expected frequencies of each outcome, giving each to the nearest whole number.

4 A random variable G has a probability distribution given by the following formulae:

$$P(G = g) = \begin{cases} 0.3 \times (0.7)^g & (g = 1,\ 2,\ 3,\ 4) \\ k & (g = 5) \\ 0 & (\text{all other values of } g). \end{cases}$$

Find the value of k, and find the expected frequency of the result $G = 3$ when 1000 independent observations of G are made.

33.4 Expectation

In a game at a fund-raising event, you can pay to spin a roulette wheel. The wheel is numbered 1, 2, 3, and so on, up to 37. If the ball lands on 10, you win \$10; if it lands on a number ending in 5, you win \$5; otherwise, you win nothing. The amount, X, that you win is a random variable. If the roulette wheel is fair, X takes the values 10, 5 and 0, with probabilities

$$P(X = 10) = P(\text{ball lands on } 10) = \tfrac{1}{37},$$
$$P(X = 5) = P(\text{ball lands on } 5,\ 15,\ 25,\ 35) = \tfrac{4}{37},$$
$$P(X = 0) = 1 - P(X = 5) - P(X = 10) = 1 - \tfrac{4}{37} - \tfrac{1}{37} = \tfrac{32}{37},$$

and the probability distribution of X is given below.

x	0	5	10
$P(X = x)$	$\frac{32}{37}$	$\frac{4}{37}$	$\frac{1}{37}$

How much should the person running the game charge for a turn? Obviously the idea is to make a profit, so a starting point would be to find the charge if the game is to break even. This involves finding the mean amount won per turn. Consider the situation after 3700 turns at the game. You can calculate the frequencies you would expect using

$$\text{frequency} \approx \text{total frequency} \times \text{probability}$$

(see Section 33.3). You might expect to win nothing about $3700 \times \frac{32}{37} = 3200$ times, \$5 about $3700 \times \frac{4}{37} = 400$ times and \$10 about $3700 \times \frac{1}{37} = 100$ times. The total amount won in dollars in 3700 turns would be about $(0 \times 3200) + (5 \times 400) + (10 \times 100) = 3000$ so the mean amount per turn would be $\$\frac{3000}{3700} = \$0.8108\ldots$.

If you look at this calculation carefully, you will see that the result obtained is independent of the number of turns. For example, if you had 7400 turns, then the amount won would double but the mean amount would remain the same. This suggests that the person running the stall needs to charge at least 81.08... cents, which in practice means 82 cents.

The same result can be obtained more directly by multiplying each value by its probability and summing. Using p_i as a shortened form of $\mathrm{P}(X = x_i)$, this gives

$$\sum x_i p_i = (0 \times \tfrac{32}{37}) + (5 \times \tfrac{4}{37}) + (10 \times \tfrac{1}{37}) = \tfrac{30}{37}$$

The value which has been calculated is a theoretical mean. It is denoted by μ (which you met in Section 5.5). The symbol μ is used in order to distinguish the mean of a probability distribution from $\bar{x}$, the mean of a data set. The mean, μ, of a probability distribution does not represent the amount won at a single turn or even the mean amount won over a finite number of turns. It is the value to which the mean amount won tends as the number of turns 'tends to infinity'. In practice, it is helpful to think of μ as the mean amount you would expect to win in a very long run of turns. For this reason, μ is often called the **expectation** or **expected value** or **mean** of X and is denoted by $\mathrm{E}(X)$.

This suggests the following definition.

The expectation of a random variable X is defined by

$$\mathrm{E}(X) = \mu = \sum x_i p_i.$$

Note that the expected value is not the same as the mode. The mode is the value with the highest probability.

Example 33.4.1

Find the expected value of each of the variables X, Y and W, which have the probability distributions given below. The variables X, Y and W were discussed in Section 33.1 in connection with the number of squares moved in a turn at three different board games.

(a)

x	1	2	3	4	5	6	Total
$\mathrm{P}(X = x)$	$\frac{1}{6}$	$\frac{1}{6}$	$\frac{1}{6}$	$\frac{1}{6}$	$\frac{1}{6}$	$\frac{1}{6}$	1

(b)

y	1	2	3	4	5	7	8	9	10	11	12	Total
$\mathrm{P}(Y = y)$	$\frac{1}{6}$	$\frac{1}{6}$	$\frac{1}{6}$	$\frac{1}{6}$	$\frac{1}{6}$	$\frac{1}{36}$	$\frac{1}{36}$	$\frac{1}{36}$	$\frac{1}{36}$	$\frac{1}{36}$	$\frac{1}{36}$	1

(c)

w	2	3	4	5	6	7	8	9	10	11	12	Total
$\mathrm{P}(W = w)$	$\frac{1}{36}$	$\frac{2}{36}$	$\frac{3}{36}$	$\frac{4}{36}$	$\frac{5}{36}$	$\frac{6}{36}$	$\frac{5}{36}$	$\frac{4}{36}$	$\frac{3}{36}$	$\frac{2}{36}$	$\frac{1}{36}$	1

(a) $\mathrm{E}(X) = \sum p_i x_i = (1 \times \tfrac{1}{6}) + (2 \times \tfrac{1}{6}) + (3 \times \tfrac{1}{6}) + (4 \times \tfrac{1}{6}) + (5 \times \tfrac{1}{6}) + (6 \times \tfrac{1}{6}) = 3\tfrac{1}{2}$

You may have spotted that there is a quicker way to find the mean in this example. Since the distribution is symmetrical about $3\frac{1}{2}$, the mean must equal $3\frac{1}{2}$.

(b) This distribution is not symmetrical and so the mean has to be calculated.

$$\begin{aligned}\mathrm{E}(Y) = \sum p_i y_i &= (1 \times \tfrac{1}{6}) + (2 \times \tfrac{1}{6}) + (3 \times \tfrac{1}{6}) + (4 \times \tfrac{1}{6}) + (5 \times \tfrac{1}{6}) + (7 \times \tfrac{1}{36}) \\ &\quad + (8 \times \tfrac{1}{36}) + (9 \times \tfrac{1}{36}) + (10 \times \tfrac{1}{36}) + (11 \times \tfrac{1}{36}) + (12 \times \tfrac{1}{36}) \\ &= (1+2+3+4+5) \times \tfrac{1}{6} + (7+8+9+10+11+12) \times \tfrac{1}{36} \\ &= 15 \times \tfrac{1}{6} + 57 \times \tfrac{1}{36} = 4\tfrac{1}{12}\end{aligned}$$

(c) As in part (a), the probability distribution is symmetrical, in this case about 7, so $\mathrm{E}(W) = 7$.

This calculation shows that in the long term, you should move round the board fastest in Game *C* and slowest in Game *A*. In practice this may not happen in the short term as the actual moves depend on chance and will not necessarily follow the pattern predicted by the model.

Example 33.4.2

A random variable R has the probability distribution shown below.

r	1	2	3	4
$\mathrm{P}(R = r)$	0.1	a	0.3	b

Given that $\mathrm{E}(R) = 3$, find a and b.

Since $\sum \mathrm{P}(R = r) = 1$,

$$0.1 + a + 0.3 + b = 1, \quad \text{so} \quad a + b = 0.6.$$

Also $\mathrm{E}(R) = 3$, so $\sum r\mathrm{P}(R = r) = 3$, so

$$1 \times 0.1 + 2 \times a + 3 \times 0.3 + 4 \times b = 3, \quad \text{giving} \quad 2a + 4b = 2.$$

Solving these two equations simultaneously gives $a = 0.2$ and $b = 0.4$.

Exercise 33D

In this exercise all the variables are discrete. Give numerical answers to 4 significant figures when appropriate.

1 Find the mean of the random variables X and Y which have the following probability distributions.

(a)

x	0	1	2	3	4
$\mathrm{P}(X = x)$	$\frac{1}{8}$	$\frac{3}{8}$	$\frac{1}{8}$	$\frac{1}{4}$	$\frac{1}{8}$

(b)

y	−2	−1	0	1	2	3
$\mathrm{P}(Y = y)$	0.15	0.25	0.3	0.05	0.2	0.05

2 The random variable T has the following probability distribution. Find $\mathrm{E}(T)$.

t	1	2	3	4	5	6	7
$\mathrm{P}(T=t)$	0.1	0.2	0.1	0.2	0.1	0.2	0.1

3 Find the exact expectation of the random variable Y, which has the following probability distribution.

y	3	4	5	6	7
$\mathrm{P}(Y=y)$	$\frac{1}{18}$	$\frac{5}{18}$	$\frac{7}{18}$	$\frac{1}{18}$	$\frac{4}{18}$

4 The six faces of a fair cubical dice are numbered 1, 2, 2, 3, 3 and 3. When the dice is thrown once, the score is the number appearing on the top face. This is denoted by X.

(a) Find the mean of X.

(b) The dice is thrown twice and Y denotes the sum of the scores obtained. Tabulate the probability distribution of Y. Hence find $\mathrm{E}(Y)$.

5 A construction company can bid for one of two possible projects and the finance director has been asked to advise on which to choose. She estimates that project A will yield a profit of £150 000 with probability 0.5, a profit of £250 000 with probability 0.2 and a loss of £100 000 with probability 0.3. Project B will yield a profit of £100 000 with probability 0.6, a profit of £200 000 with probability 0.3 and a loss of £50 000 with probability 0.1. Determine which project the finance director should support, by calculating $\mathrm{E}(A)$ and $\mathrm{E}(B)$.

6 The random variable Y has the probability distribution given in the following table.

y	2	3	4	5	6	7
$\mathrm{P}(Y=y)$	0.05	0.25	a	b	0.1	0.3

Given that $\mathrm{E}(Y)=4.9$, show that $a=b$.

34 The binomial distribution

This chapter introduces you to an important probability distribution, called the binomial distribution. When you have completed it, you should

- know the conditions for a random variable to have a binomial distribution
- be able to calculate the probabilities for the binomial distribution
- know the formula for the expectation of a binomial distribution.

34.1 Routes in an American city

Imagine an American city based on a square grid, with the roads running east-west and north-south. The roads are one unit apart and the origin is at the south-west corner of the city. How many different routes of length 6 are there from (0, 0) to (4, 2)? And how many routes of length $r + s$ are there to (r, s)?

Fig. 34.1 shows part of the city with one of the routes shown.

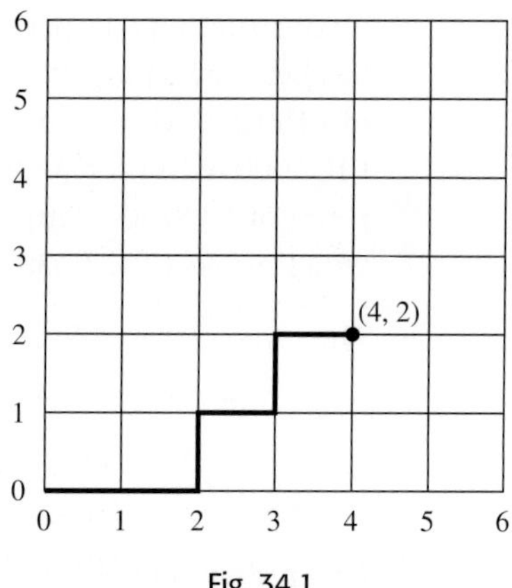

Fig. 34.1

The first problem is not difficult, but it can be tricky to keep an accurate count of the routes; and you must bear in mind the need to generalise for the second part.

A good way to proceed is to work outwards from the origin. The number of routes from (0, 0) to (1, 0) is 1, and the number from (0, 0) to (0, 1) is 1.

These numbers are shown in Fig. 34.2a where the vertices (1, 0) and (0, 1) are marked with the numbers of different routes from the origin. Similarly, Fig. 34.2b shows the numbers of different routes to (2, 0), (1, 1) and (0, 2). To avoid confusion the labels on the axes have been removed.

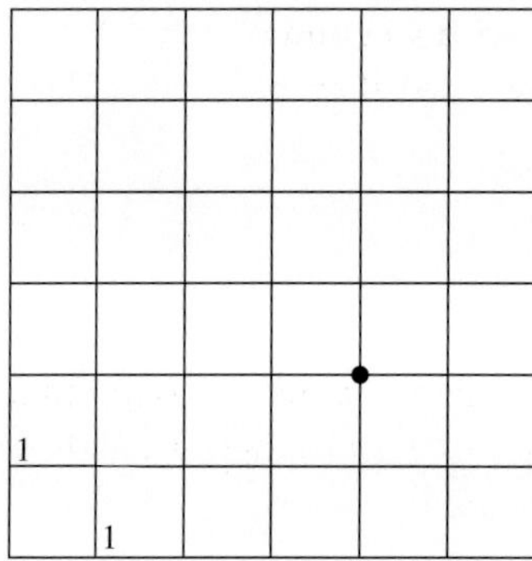

Fig. 34.2a

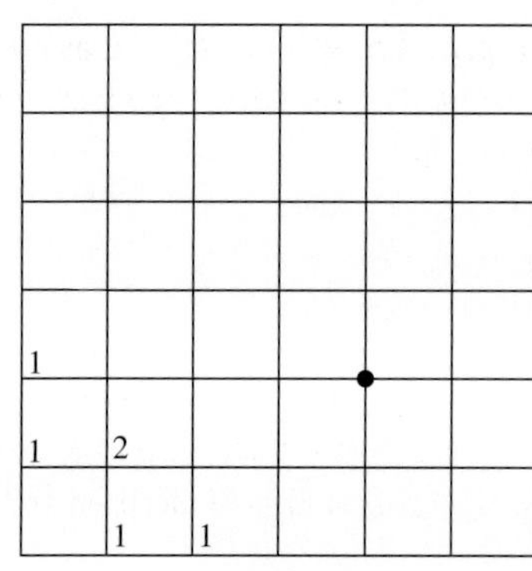

Fig. 34.2b

Moving outwards, Fig. 34.3a shows the numbers of routes of length 5. By this stage you should see that to get to (r, s) you must come from either $(r-1, s)$ or $(r, s-1)$: it follows that the number of routes to (r, s) is the sum of the routes to $(r-1, s)$ and to $(r, s-1)$. In the diagrams, this means that each number on the axes is 1 and that each number in the body of the grid is the sum of those immediately to the left and below it.

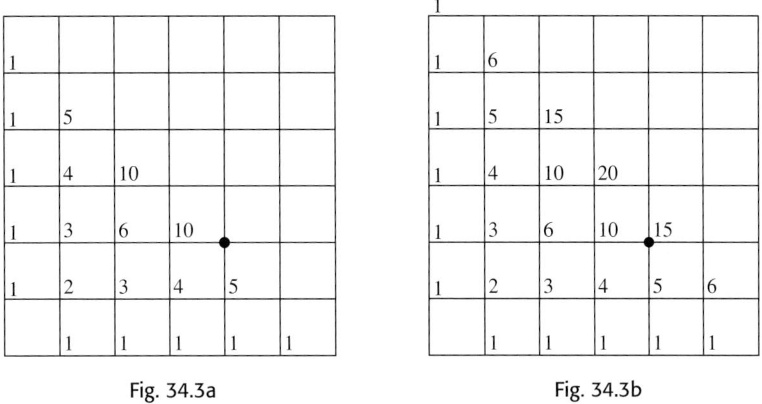

Fig. 34.3a Fig. 34.3b

Fig. 34.3b shows that the number of routes to (4, 2) is 15.

This is a pattern you have seen before. If you look at the numbers on the diagonals in the south-east direction, you will see that they are the numbers in Pascal's triangle. And if you refer back to Section 3.3, you will see how to calculate them using your calculator.

You may wonder what all this has to do with probability. The clue comes from rotating Fig 34.3b through 45° clockwise, and removing some roads, so all the routes of length 6 are shown. This gives Fig. 34.4, which shows the route highlighted in Fig. 34.1.

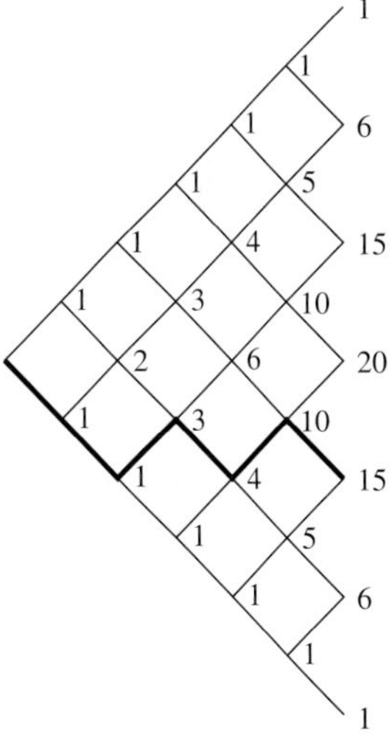

Fig. 34.4

This is now beginning to look like a tree diagram! In fact, you could denote the routes by writing them as a series of rs and ls according to whether you turn left or right at each junction. So the route highlighted might be written as $r_1r_2l_3r_4l_5r_6$, with 4 rs and 2 ls to get to (4, 2), and showing exactly what happened at each stage of the route.

34.2 The binomial distribution

The spinner in Fig. 34.5 is an equilateral triangle. When it is spun it comes to rest on one of its three edges. Two of the edges are white and one is black. In Fig. 34.5 the spinner is resting on the black edge. This will be described as 'showing black'.

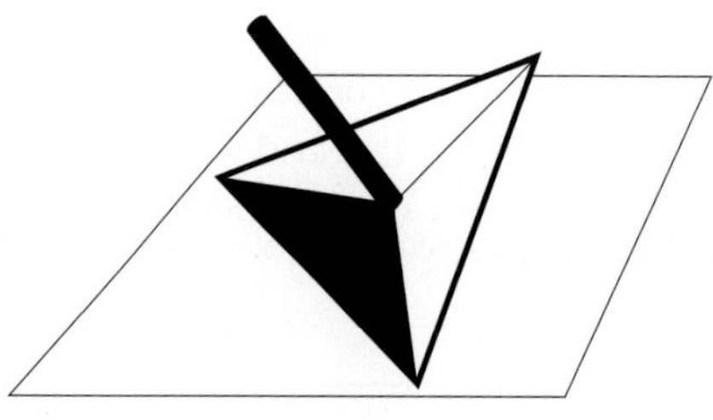

Fig. 34.5

The spinner is fair, so the probability that the spinner shows black is $\frac{1}{3}$ and the probability that it shows white is $\frac{2}{3}$.

Suppose now that the spinner is spun on 5 separate occasions. Let the random variable X be the number of times out of 5 that the spinner shows black.

To derive the probability distribution of X, it is helpful to define some terms. The act of spinning the spinner once is called a **trial**. A simple way of describing the result of each trial is to call it a **success** (s) when the spinner shows black, and a **failure** (f) when the spinner shows white. So X could now be defined as the number of successes in the 5 trials.

The event $\{X = 0\}$ would mean that the spinner did not show black on any of its 5 spins. The notation f_1 will be used to mean that the first trial resulted in a failure, f_2 will mean that the second trial resulted in a failure, and so on, giving

$$\text{P}(X = 0) = \text{P}(\text{there are 5 failures}) = \text{P}(f_1 f_2 f_3 f_4 f_5).$$

Since the outcomes of the trials are independent,

$$\begin{aligned}\text{P}(f_1 f_2 f_3 f_4 f_5) &= \text{P}(f_1) \times \text{P}(f_2) \times \text{P}(f_3) \times \text{P}(f_4) \times \text{P}(f_5)\\ &= \tfrac{2}{3} \times \tfrac{2}{3} \times \tfrac{2}{3} \times \tfrac{2}{3} \times \tfrac{2}{3} = \tfrac{32}{243}.\end{aligned}$$

The probability $\text{P}(X = 1)$ is more complicated to calculate. The event $\{X = 1\}$ means that there is one success and also four failures. One possible sequence of a success and four failures is $s_1 f_2 f_3 f_4 f_5$ (where s_1 denotes the event that the first trial was a success).

The probability that the first trial is a success and the other four trials are failures is

$$\begin{aligned}\text{P}(s_1 f_2 f_3 f_4 f_5) &= \text{P}(s_1) \times \text{P}(f_2) \times \text{P}(f_3) \times \text{P}(f_4) \times \text{P}(f_5)\\ &= \tfrac{1}{3} \times \tfrac{2}{3} \times \tfrac{2}{3} \times \tfrac{2}{3} \times \tfrac{2}{3}\\ &= \left(\tfrac{1}{3}\right)\left(\tfrac{2}{3}\right)^4 = \tfrac{16}{243}.\end{aligned}$$

However there are four other possible sequences for the event $\{X = 1\}$. They are

$$f_1 s_2 f_3 f_4 f_5 \quad f_1 f_2 s_3 f_4 f_5 \quad f_1 f_2 f_3 s_4 f_5 \quad f_1 f_2 f_3 f_4 s_5.$$

Now

$$\begin{aligned}\text{P}(s_1 f_2 f_3 f_4 f_5) &= \left(\tfrac{1}{3}\right) \times \left(\tfrac{2}{3}\right)^4.\\ \text{P}(f_1 s_2 f_3 f_4 f_5) &= \left(\tfrac{2}{3}\right) \times \left(\tfrac{1}{3}\right) \times \left(\tfrac{2}{3}\right)^3 = \left(\tfrac{1}{3}\right) \times \left(\tfrac{2}{3}\right)^4.\\ \text{P}(f_1 f_2 s_3 f_4 f_5) &= \left(\tfrac{2}{3}\right)^2 \times \left(\tfrac{1}{3}\right) \times \left(\tfrac{2}{3}\right)^2 = \left(\tfrac{1}{3}\right) \times \left(\tfrac{2}{3}\right)^4.\\ \text{P}(f_1 f_2 f_3 s_4 f_5) &= \left(\tfrac{2}{3}\right)^3 \times \left(\tfrac{1}{3}\right) \times \left(\tfrac{2}{3}\right) = \left(\tfrac{1}{3}\right) \times \left(\tfrac{2}{3}\right)^4.\\ \text{P}(f_1 f_2 f_3 f_4 s_5) &= \left(\tfrac{2}{3}\right)^4 \times \left(\tfrac{1}{3}\right) = \left(\tfrac{1}{3}\right) \times \left(\tfrac{2}{3}\right)^4.\end{aligned}$$

Therefore, summing, $\mathrm{P}(X=1) = 5 \times \left(\frac{1}{3}\right) \times \left(\frac{2}{3}\right)^4 = \frac{80}{243}$.

Notice that the probability for each individual sequence is the same as for any other sequence, namely $\left(\frac{1}{3}\right)\left(\frac{2}{3}\right)^4$, and that the 5 in the last line corresponds to the number of different sequences which give $X = 1$. These sequences are just like the routes in the north American city to $(1, 4)$: the number of different sequences is $\binom{5}{1}$ (see Section 3.3). Therefore

$$\mathrm{P}(X=1) = \binom{5}{1} \times \left(\tfrac{1}{3}\right) \times \left(\tfrac{2}{3}\right)^4.$$

Similarly you could find that for $X = 2$ there are sequences such as $s_1 s_2 f_3 f_4 f_5$ and $f_1 s_2 f_3 s_4 f_5$. To see how many of these sequences there are, it is the same as the number of routes to $(2, 3)$, which is $\binom{5}{2}$. Each of these choices has probability $\left(\frac{1}{3}\right)^2 \times \left(\frac{2}{3}\right)^3$. Using these results

$$\mathrm{P}(X=2) = \binom{5}{2} \times \left(\tfrac{1}{3}\right)^2 \times \left(\tfrac{2}{3}\right)^3.$$

Continuing in this way, you can find the distribution of X, given in Table 34.6.

x	$\mathrm{P}(X=x)$	
0	$\left(\frac{2}{3}\right)^5$	$=\frac{32}{243}$
1	$\binom{5}{1} \times \left(\frac{1}{3}\right) \times \left(\frac{2}{3}\right)^4$	$=\frac{80}{243}$
2	$\binom{5}{2} \times \left(\frac{1}{3}\right)^2 \times \left(\frac{2}{3}\right)^3$	$=\frac{80}{243}$
3	$\binom{5}{3} \times \left(\frac{1}{3}\right)^3 \times \left(\frac{2}{3}\right)^2$	$=\frac{40}{243}$
4	$\binom{5}{4} \times \left(\frac{1}{3}\right)^4 \times \left(\frac{2}{3}\right)$	$=\frac{10}{243}$
5	$\binom{5}{5} \times \left(\frac{1}{3}\right)^5$	$=\frac{1}{243}$

Table 34.6

Notice that $\sum_{x=0}^{5} \mathrm{P}(X=x)$ is 1. This is a useful check for the probabilities in any distribution table.

Notice also that as $\left(\frac{1}{3}\right)^0 = 1$ and $\left(\frac{2}{3}\right)^0 = 1$ you could write $\mathrm{P}(X=0)$ as $\binom{5}{0} \times \left(\frac{1}{3}\right)^0 \times \left(\frac{2}{3}\right)^5$, and $\mathrm{P}(X=5)$ as $\binom{5}{5} \times \left(\frac{1}{3}\right)^5 \times \left(\frac{2}{3}\right)^0$. These results enable you to write $\mathrm{P}(X=x)$ as a formula:

$$\mathrm{P}(X=x) = \binom{5}{x} \times \left(\tfrac{1}{3}\right)^x \times \left(\tfrac{2}{3}\right)^{5-x}.$$

However the formula on its own is not sufficient, because you must also give the values for which the formula is defined. In this case x can take integer values from 0 to 5 inclusive. So a more concise definition of the distribution of X than Table 34.6 would be

$$\mathrm{P}(X=x) = \binom{5}{x} \times \left(\tfrac{1}{3}\right)^x \times \left(\tfrac{2}{3}\right)^{5-x} \quad \text{for} \quad x = 0, 1, 2, \ldots, 5.$$

Although the case of the spinner is not important in itself, it is an example of an important and frequently occurring situation.

- A single trial has just two possible outcomes (often called success, s, and failure, f).
- There is a fixed number of trials, n.
- The outcome of each trial is independent of the outcome of all the other trials.
- The probability of success at each trial, p, is constant.

The random variable X, which represents the number of successes in n trials of this experiment, is said to have a **binomial distribution**.

A consequence of the last condition is that the probability of failure will also be a constant, equal to $1 - p$. This probability is usually denoted by q, which means that $q = 1 - p$.

In a binomial distribution, the random variable X has a probability distribution given by

$$\mathrm{P}(X = x) = \binom{n}{x} p^x q^{n-x} \qquad \text{for } x = 0, 1, 2, \ldots, n.$$

Provided you are given the values of n and p, you can evaluate all of the probabilities in the distribution table. The values of n and p are therefore the essential pieces of information about the probability distribution. In the example, n was 5 and p was $\frac{1}{3}$. You did not need to be told q, because its value is always $1 - p$, so in the example the value of q was $\frac{2}{3}$.

The values of n and p are called the **parameters** of the binomial distribution. You need to know the parameters of a probability distribution to calculate the probabilities numerically.

To denote that a random variable X has a binomial distribution with parameters n and p, you write $X \sim \mathrm{B}(n, p)$. So for the probability distribution in Table 34.6. you write $X \sim \mathrm{B}(5, \frac{1}{3})$.

Example 34.2.1

Given that $X \sim \mathrm{B}(8, \frac{1}{4})$, find (a) $\mathrm{P}(X = 6)$, (b) $\mathrm{P}(X \le 2)$, (c) $\mathrm{P}(X > 0)$.

(a) Using the binomial probability formula with $n = 8$ and $p = \frac{1}{4}$ you get

$$\mathrm{P}(X = 6) = \binom{8}{6} \times \left(\tfrac{1}{4}\right)^6 \times \left(\tfrac{3}{4}\right)^2 = 28 \times \left(\tfrac{1}{4}\right)^6 \times \left(\tfrac{3}{4}\right)^2 = 0.003\,85,$$

correct to 3 significant figures.

(b)
$$\begin{aligned}\mathrm{P}(X \le 2) &= \mathrm{P}(X = 0) + \mathrm{P}(X = 1) + \mathrm{P}(X = 2)\\ &= \binom{8}{0}\left(\tfrac{1}{4}\right)^0\left(\tfrac{3}{4}\right)^8 + \binom{8}{1}\left(\tfrac{1}{4}\right)^1\left(\tfrac{3}{4}\right)^7 + \binom{8}{2}\left(\tfrac{1}{4}\right)^2\left(\tfrac{3}{4}\right)^6\\ &= 0.1001\ldots + 0.2669\ldots + 0.3114\ldots\\ &= 0.6785\ldots = 0.679, \text{ correct to 3 significant figures.}\end{aligned}$$

(c) The easiest way to find $\mathrm{P}(X > 0)$ is to use the fact that $\mathrm{P}(X > 0)$ is the complement of $\mathrm{P}(X = 0)$.

So
$$\begin{aligned}\mathrm{P}(X > 0) &= 1 - \mathrm{P}(X = 0)\\ &= 1 - \binom{8}{0}\left(\tfrac{1}{4}\right)^0\left(\tfrac{3}{4}\right)^8 \qquad \text{(from part (b))}\\ &= 1 - 0.1001\ldots\\ &= 0.8998\ldots = 0.900, \text{ correct to 3 significant figures.}\end{aligned}$$

To check that the binomial formula does represent a probability distribution you must show that $\sum_{x=0}^{n} \mathrm{P}(X = x) = 1$. Consider the example involving the spinner (Fig. 34.5), but use p and q instead of $\frac{1}{3}$ and $\frac{2}{3}$ respectively. Table 34.7 shows the distribution.

x	$\mathrm{P}(X = x)$	
0	q^5	$= q^5$
1	$\binom{5}{1} \times p \times q^4$	$= 5pq^4$
2	$\binom{5}{2} \times p^2 \times q^3$	$= 10p^2q^3$
3	$\binom{5}{3} \times p^3 \times q^2$	$= 10p^3q^2$
4	$\binom{5}{4} \times p^4 \times q$	$= 5p^4q$
5	p^5	$= p^5$

Table 34.7

If you sum the probabilities in the right column you get

$$\sum_{x=0}^{5} \mathrm{P}(X = x) = q^5 + 5pq^4 + 10p^2q^3 + 10p^3q^2 + 5p^4q + p^5.$$

The right side of this equation is the binomial expansion of $(q + p)^5$ (see Section 3.3). You could check for yourself by multiplying out $(q + p)(q + p)(q + p)(q + p)(q + p)$, so

$$\sum_{x=0}^{5} \mathrm{P}(X = x) = (q + p)^5 = 1^5 = 1.$$

You can use the binomial theorem in Section 3.3 by writing $q = a$ and $p = b$ to show that

$$\begin{aligned}\sum_{x=0}^{n} \mathrm{P}(X = x) &= \sum_{x=0}^{n} \left[\binom{n}{x} \times p^x \times q^{n-x}\right] \\ &= \sum_{x=0}^{n} \left[\binom{n}{x} q^{n-x} p^x\right] \\ &= \binom{n}{0} q^n + \binom{n}{1} pq^{n-1} + \binom{n}{2} p^2q^{n-2} + \ldots + \binom{n}{n} p^n \\ &= (q + p)^n = 1^n = 1.\end{aligned}$$

The individual probabilities in the binomial distribution are the terms of the binomial expansion of $(q + p)^n$: these are two similar uses of the word 'binomial'.

Before using the binomial distribution as a model for a situation you need to convince yourself that all the conditions are satisfied. The following example illustrates some possible problems.

Example 34.2.2

A school car park has 5 parking spaces. At the same time each day, a student observes the number of spaces which are filled. Let X be the number of spaces filled at this time on a randomly chosen day. Is it reasonable to model the distribution of the random variable X with a binomial distribution?

She looks at each parking space to see whether it is occupied or not. This represents a single trial.

Are there exactly two outcomes for each trial (parking space), and are these mutually exclusive? In other words, is each parking space either occupied by a single car or not? The answer will usually be yes, but sometimes poorly parked vehicles will give the answer no.

Are there a fixed number of trials? The answer is yes. On each day there are 5 parking spaces available so the number of trials is 5 times the number of days on which observations were made.

Are the trials independent? This is not likely. Drivers may be less inclined to park in one of the centre spaces if it is surrounded by cars, because getting out of their own car may be more difficult.

Is the probability p of success (in this case a parking space being filled by a car) constant? Probably not, because people may be more likely to choose the space closest to the school entrance, for example.

You can see that, when you are proposing to model a practical situation with a binomial distribution, many of the assumptions may be questionable and some may not be valid at all. In this case, however, provided you are aware that the binomial model is far from perfect, you could still use it as a reasonable approximation. You might also have realised that you do not know the value of p in this example, so you would have to estimate it. To do this you would divide the total number of cars observed by the total number of available car parking spaces, which in this case is

$5 \times$ (the number of days for which the survey was carried out).

Example 34.2.3

State whether a binomial distribution could be used in each of the following problems. If the binomial distribution is an acceptable model, define the random variable clearly and state its parameters.

(a) A fair cubical dice is rolled 10 times. Find the probability of getting three fours, four fives and three sixes.

(b) A fair coin is spun until a head occurs. Find the probability that eight spins are necessary, including the one on which the head occurs.

(c) A jar contains 49 balls numbered 1 to 49. Six of the balls are selected at random. Find the probability that four of the six have an even score.

(a) In this case you are interested in three different outcomes: a four, a five and a six. A binomial distribution depends on having only two possible outcomes, success and failure, so it cannot be used here.

You could use the binomial distribution if you just wanted the probability of getting three fours, say. Then there would be only two outcomes: getting three fours and not getting three fours.

(b) The binomial distribution requires a fixed number of trials, n, and this is not the case here, since the number of trials is unknown. In fact, the number of trials is the random variable of interest here.

(c) Whether a binomial model is appropriate or not depends on whether the selection of the balls is done with replacement or without replacement. If the selection is without replacement, then the outcome of each trial will not be independent of all the other trials. If the selection is with replacement, then define the random variable X to be the number of balls with an even score out of six random selections. X will then have a binomial distribution with parameters 6 and $\frac{24}{49}$. You write this as $X \sim \mathrm{B}(6, \frac{24}{49})$. You are assuming, of course, that the balls are thoroughly mixed before each selection and that every ball has an equal chance of being selected.

Here is a summary of the binomial distribution:

Binomial distribution

- A single trial has exactly two possible outcomes (success and failure) and these are mutually exclusive.
- A fixed number, n, of trials takes place.
- The outcome of each trial is independent of the outcome of all the other trials.
- The probability of success at each trial is constant.

The random variable X, which represents the number of successes in the n trials of this experiment, has a probability distribution given by

$$\mathrm{P}(X = x) = \binom{n}{x} p^x q^{n-x} \quad \text{for } x = 0, 1, 2, \ldots, n,$$

where p is the probability of success and $q = 1 - p$ is the probability of failure.

When the random variable X satisfies these conditions, $X \sim \mathrm{B}(n, p)$.

34.3 Expectation of a binomial distribution

Suppose that you wanted to find the mean of the random variable X, where $X \sim \mathrm{B}(3, \frac{1}{4})$. One way would be to write out the probability distribution and calculate $\mathrm{E}(X)$ using the equation $\mathrm{E}(X) = \mu = \sum p_i x_i$.

Example 34.3.1

Calculate E(X) for $X \sim \mathrm{B}(3, \frac{1}{4})$ from the probability distribution.

The probability distribution is found using the binomial probability formula in the blue box,

$$\mathrm{P}(X = x) = \binom{n}{x} p^x (1-p)^{n-x}.$$

The distribution is shown in Table 34.8.

x	$\mathrm{P}(X = x)$	$x\mathrm{P}(X = x)$
0	$\binom{3}{0}\left(\frac{1}{4}\right)^0\left(\frac{3}{4}\right)^3 = \frac{27}{64}$	0
1	$\binom{3}{1}\left(\frac{1}{4}\right)^1\left(\frac{3}{4}\right)^2 = \frac{27}{64}$	$\frac{27}{64}$
2	$\binom{3}{2}\left(\frac{1}{4}\right)^2\left(\frac{3}{4}\right)^1 = \frac{9}{64}$	$\frac{18}{64}$
3	$\binom{3}{3}\left(\frac{1}{4}\right)^3\left(\frac{3}{4}\right)^0 = \frac{1}{64}$	$\frac{3}{64}$
Totals:	$\sum_{x=0}^{n} \mathrm{P}(X = x) = 1$	$\sum_{x=0}^{n} x\mathrm{P}(X = x) = \frac{48}{64}$

Table 34.8

The expectation E(x) is given by

$$\mathrm{E}(X) = \mu = \sum_{x=0}^{n} x\mathrm{P}(X = x) = \frac{48}{64} = \frac{3}{4}.$$

There is, however, a formula for calculating the mean of a binomial distribution directly from n and p. If you consider the general case $X \sim \mathrm{B}(n, p)$, then the mean would be given by

$$\sum_{x=0}^{n} x\mathrm{P}(X = x) = \sum_{x=0}^{n} x \binom{n}{x} p^x (1-p)^{n-x}.$$

Each term in this sum depends on the parameters n and p and so it would be reasonable to assume that E(X) also depends on n and p. Although this sum looks very complicated, it can be shown that it simplifies to np.

The expectation of a binomial distribution $X \sim \mathrm{B}(n, p)$ is given by

$$\mathrm{E}(X) = np.$$

Intuitively you might expect this result, since in n trials

$$\begin{aligned}\text{number of successes} &\approx \text{number of trials} \times \text{probability of success in each trial}\\ &= n \times p = np.\end{aligned}$$

Example 34.3.2
Calculate E(X) for $X \sim \text{B}(3, \frac{1}{4})$ using the formula $\text{E}(X) = \mu = np$.

Using the formula,

$$\text{E}(X) = \mu = np = 3 \times \tfrac{1}{4} = \tfrac{3}{4}.$$

You can see that the second method (in Example 34.3.2) is much quicker than the first (in Example 34.3.1). The formula for calculating the mean of a binomial distribution is particularly useful when n is large, as in the following example.

Example 34.3.3
Nails are sold in packets of 100. Occasionally a nail is faulty. The number of faulty nails in a randomly chosen packet is denoted by X. Assuming that faulty nails occur independently and at random, calculate the mean of X, given that the probability of any nail being faulty is 0.04.

Since faulty nails occur independently and at random and with a fixed probability, the distribution of X can be modelled by the binomial distribution with $n = 100$ and $p = 0.04$. Therefore

$$\text{E}(X) = \mu = np = 100 \times 0.04 = 4.$$

The mean number of faulty nails in a pack is 4.

To calculate μ using the equation $\mu = \text{E}(X) = \sum x_i p_i$ would involve writing out a probability distribution with 101 terms!

Example 34.3.4
Suppose that $X \sim \text{B}(10, 0.2)$. Find

(a) $\text{P}(X = 2)$, (b) $\text{P}(X \leq 2)$, (c) $\text{P}(X > 2)$. (d) Given that $(X \leq 2)$, find $\text{P}(X = 2)$.

Give your answers correct to 4 decimal places.

If your calculator has in-built routines for calculating binomial probabilities, you should use them.

(a) Using the calculator, $\text{P}(X = 2) = 0.3020$.

(b) Using the cumulative probability routine, $\text{P}(X \leq 2) = 0.6778$.

(c) Using the property that $\text{P}(X > 2) = 1 - \text{P}(X \leq 2)$,

$$\begin{aligned} \text{P}(X > 2) &= 1 - \text{P}(X \leq 2) \\ &= 1 - 0.6778 = 0.3222. \end{aligned}$$

(d) You need to find $P(X = 2|X \le 2)$. Using the defintion of conditional probability, Section 23.1,

$$\begin{aligned} P(X = 2|X \le 2) &= \frac{P((X = 2) \cap (X \le 2))}{P(X \le 2)} \\ &= \frac{P((X = 2) \cap (X = 0 \text{ or } 1 \text{ or } 2))}{P(X \le 2)} \\ &= \frac{P(X = 2)}{P(X \le 2)} \\ &= \frac{0.3020}{0.6778} = 0.4456. \end{aligned}$$

Exercise 34

In this exercise use your calculator to give probabilities correct to 4 decimal places.

1 The random variable X has a binomial distribution with $n = 6$ and $p = 0.2$. Calculate

(a) $P(X = 3)$, (b) $P(X = 4)$, (c) $P(X = 6)$, (d) $E(X)$.

2 Given that $Y \sim B(7, \frac{2}{3})$, calculate

(a) $P(Y = 4)$, (b) $P(Y = 6)$, (c) $P(Y = 0)$, (d) $E(Y)$.

3 Given that $Z \sim B(9, 0.45)$, calculate

(a) $P(Z = 3)$, (b) $P(Z = 4 \text{ or } 5)$, (c) $P(Z \ge 7)$, (d) $E(Z)$.

4 Given that $D \sim B(12, 0.7)$, calculate

(a) $P(D < 4)$, (b) the smallest value of d such that $P(D > d) < 0.90$.

5 Given that $H \sim B(9, \frac{1}{2})$, calculate the probability that H is

(a) exactly 5, (b) 5 or 6, (c) at least 8, (d) more than 2.

6 Given that $S \sim B(7, \frac{1}{6})$, find the probability that S is

(a) exactly 3, (b) at least 4.

7 Given that $Z \sim B(20, 0.3)$, find the probabillity that $Z \le 2$, given that $Z \le 4$.

8 An ordinary fair cubical die is thrown 10 times. Given that there are at least 3 threes, find the probability that the number of threes is 4 or more.

9 In a certain school, 30% of the students are in the age group 16–19.

(a) Ten students are chosen at random. Use the binomial model to calculate the probability that fewer than four of them are in the 16–19 age group.

(b) If the ten students were chosen by picking ten who were sitting together at lunch, explain why a binomial distribution might no longer have been suitable.

10 A factory makes large quantities of coloured sweets, and it is known that on average 20% of the sweets are coloured green. A packet contains 20 sweets. Assuming that the packet forms a random sample of the sweets made by the factory, calculate the probability that exactly seven of the sweets are green.

If you knew that, in fact, the sweets could have been green, red, orange or brown, would it have invalidated your calculation?

11 Eggs produced at a farm are packaged in boxes of six. Assume that, for any egg, the probability that it is broken when it reaches the retail outlet is 0.1, independent of all other eggs. A box is said to be bad if it contains at least two broken eggs. Calculate the probability that a randomly selected box is bad.

It is known that, in fact, breakages are more likely to occur after the eggs have been packed into boxes, and while they are being transported to the retail outlet. Explain why this fact is likely to invalidate the calculation.

12 On a particular tropical island, the probability that there is a hurricane in any given month can be taken to be 0.08. Use a binomial distribution to calculate the probability that there is a hurricane in more than two months of the year. State two assumptions needed for a binomial distribution to be a good model. Why may one of the assumptions not be valid?

35 The normal distribution

This chapter investigates a very commonly occurring distribution, called the normal distribution. When you have completed it, you should

- understand the use of the normal distribution to model a continuous random variable
- be able to use the cumulative normal distribution function accurately
- be able to solve problems involving the normal distribution
- be able to find a relationship between μ and σ given the value of $P(X > x)$ or its equivalent.

35.1 Comparing discrete and continuous random variables

The random variables which you studied in Chapter 33 were all discrete; that is, there were clear steps between the possible values which the variable could take. There are many variables, however, which are not discrete.

Consider the following example. The 'cars' on a ski-lift are attached at equal intervals along a cable which travels at a fixed speed. The speed of the cars is so low that people can step in and out of the cars at the station without the cars having to stop. The time interval between one car and the next arriving at the station is 5 minutes. You do not know the timetable for the cars and so you turn up at the station at a random time and wait for a car. Your waiting time, X (measured in minutes), is an example of a random variable because its value depends on chance. However, it is also a continuous variable because the waiting time can take any value in the interval 0 to 5 minutes, that is $0 \le X < 5$.

In Chapter 33 in order to describe a discrete random variable completely, you obtained a probability for each possible value of the random variable. If you try the same approach with a continuous random variable you run into difficulties: because the waiting time, X, can take an infinite number of values in the interval 0 to 5 minutes, you cannot write out a table like Table 35.1 (which is Table 33.1 again, giving the probability distribution of a discrete variable).

x	1	2	3	4	5	6	Total
$P(X = x)$	$\frac{1}{6}$	$\frac{1}{6}$	$\frac{1}{6}$	$\frac{1}{6}$	$\frac{1}{6}$	$\frac{1}{6}$	1

Table 35.1

However, you do know that if you arrive at the station at a random time, all values of X are equally likely. Would it be possible to describe the distribution by stating that all values of X between 0 and 5 are equally likely and by assigning the same non-zero probability to each one? This gives rise to another problem. The sum of the probabilities will not be one, as it should be, but will be infinite since X takes an infinite number of values. Obviously a different approach is needed in order to describe the probability distribution of a continuous random variable. This is considered in Section 35.2.

35.2 Defining the probability distribution of a continuous random variable

Although it is not possible to give the probability that X (the waiting time in Section 35.1) takes a particular value, it does make sense to talk about X taking a value within a particular range. For example, you would expect that $P(0 \le X < 2.5) = \frac{1}{2}$ since the interval from 0 to 2.5 accounts for half the values which X can take, and all values are equally likely. Extending this idea, you would expect $P(0 \le X < 1) = \frac{1}{5}$ since this interval covers $\frac{1}{5}$ of the total interval. Similarly $P(1 \le X < 2) = P(2 \le X < 3) = P(3 \le X < 4) = P(4 \le X < 5) = \frac{1}{5}$.

These probabilities could be represented on a diagram similar to a frequency histogram, as shown in Fig. 35.2. In this diagram the area of each block gives the probability that X lies in the corresponding interval. Since the width of each block is 1 its height must be 0.2 in order to make the area equal to 0.2. Notice that the total area under the graph must be 1 since the probabilities must sum to 1.

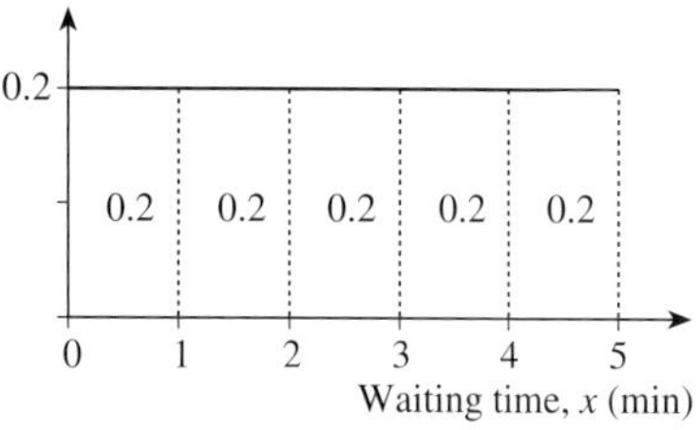

Fig. 35.2

The choice of the intervals 0 to 1, 1 to 2 and so on is arbitrary. In order to make the model more general you need to be able to find the probability that X lies within any given interval. Suppose that the divisions between the blocks in Fig. 35.2 are removed so as to give Fig. 35.3. In this diagram, probabilities still correspond to areas. For example, $P(0.5 < X \le 1)$ is given by the area under the curve between 0.5 and 1. This is shown as the shaded area in Fig. 35.4: its value is 0.1, as you would expect.

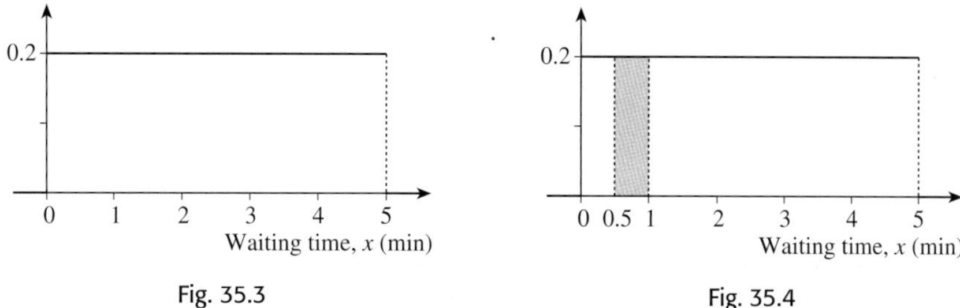

Fig. 35.3

Fig. 35.4

You should now be able to see that the probability distribution of the waiting times can be modelled by the continuous function $f(x)$ which describes Fig. 35.3. The required function is

$$f(x) = \begin{cases} 0.2 & \text{for } 0 \le x < 5, \\ 0 & \text{otherwise.} \end{cases}$$

Note that it is usual to define $f(x)$ for all real values of x.

Once $f(x)$ has been defined, you can find probabilities by calculating areas below the curve $y = f(x)$. For example, $P(1.3 \le X \le 3.5) = 0.2 \times (3.5 - 1.3) = 0.44$.

Notice that, if you want the probability that $X = 1.3$ or the probability that $X = 3.5$, the answer is zero. These are just single instants of time, and although it is theoretically possible that a car may arrive at either of those instants, the probability is actually zero. This means that $P(1.3 < X < 3.5) = P(1.3 \le X < 3.5) = P(1.3 < X \le 3.5) = P(1.3 \le X \le 3.5)$. This situation is characteristic of continuous distributions.

The function $f(x)$ is called a **probability density function**. It cannot take negative values because probabilities are never negative. It must also have the property that the total area under the curve $y = f(x)$ is equal to 1. This is because this area represents the probability that X takes any real value and this probability must be 1.

The suitability of this function as a model for actual waiting times could be tested by collecting some data and comparing a histogram of these experimental results with the shape of $y = f(x)$. Some results are given in Table 35.5.

Waiting time, x (min)	Frequency	Relative frequency
$0 \le x < 1$	107	0.214
$1 \le x < 2$	98	0.196
$2 \le x < 3$	105	0.210
$3 \le x < 4$	95	0.190
$4 \le x < 5$	95	0.190

Table 35.5

The third column gives the relative frequencies: these are found by dividing each frequency by the total frequency, in this case 500. The relative frequency gives the experimental probability that the waiting time lies in a given interval. The data are illustrated by the frequency histogram in Fig. 35.6.

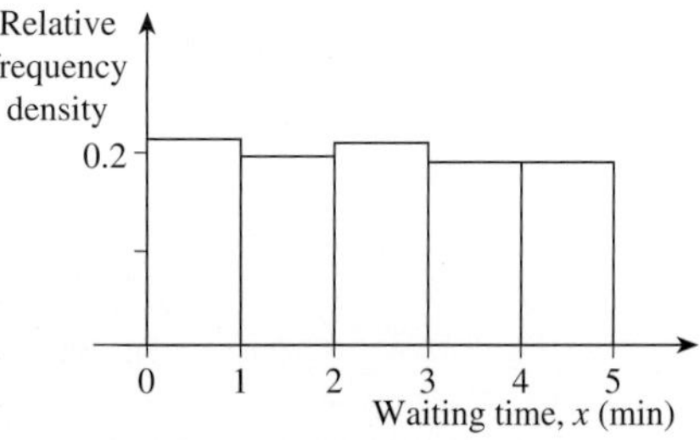

Fig. 35.6

Normally a frequency histogram is plotted with frequency density rather than *relative* frequency density on the vertical axis. The reason for using relative frequency density in this case (and others in this section) is that area then represents *relative* frequency and hence experimental probability. As a result a direct comparison can be made between this diagram and Fig. 35.3, in which area represents theoretical probability. You can see that the diagrams are very similar. The experimental probabilities are not exactly equal to the theoretical ones. For example, the experimental probability of waiting between 1 and 2 minutes is 0.196 whereas theoretically it is 0.2. This is not surprising: you saw in Section 22.1 that a probability model aims to describe what happens 'in the long run'.

The model for waiting times for a ski-lift was found by theoretical arguments and then confirmed experimentally. However, often it is not possible to predict the form of the probability density function. Instead, data are collected and the shape of the resulting frequency histogram of the relative frequency density may suggest the form of the probability density function.

Here is a summary of the properties of a probability density function:

The **probability density function**, $f(x)$, of a continuous random variable X is defined for all real values of x. It has the properties:

(a) $f(x) \geq 0$ for all x,

(b) the area under the graph is 1.

The probability that X lies in the interval $a \leq x \leq b$ is given by the area under the graph of $f(x)$ between a and b. This area can sometimes be found by using geometrical properties or it can be found from the integral

$$P(a \leq X \leq b) = \int_a^b f(x)\,\mathrm{d}x.$$

35.3 A bell-shaped distribution

In the rest of this chapter you will be considering a particular family of distributions. When you collect real, continuous data and represent the results in a frequency histogram you find that one particular pattern often occurs. Fig. 35.8 shows this sort of pattern.

The data in Table 35.7 refer to the heights of 39 people taken from the 'Brain size' datafile in Chapter 4. Fig. 35.8 is a frequency histogram for these data.

Height, h (inches)	Class boundaries	Class width	Frequency
62–63	$61.5 \leq h < 63.5$	2	4
64–65	$63.5 \leq h < 65.5$	2	5
66–67	$65.5 \leq h < 67.5$	2	8
68–69	$67.5 \leq h < 69.5$	2	9
70–71	$69.5 \leq h < 71.5$	2	4
72–73	$71.5 \leq h < 73.5$	2	3
74–75	$73.5 \leq h < 75.5$	2	2
76–77	$75.5 \leq h < 77.5$	2	4
78–79	$77.5 \leq h < 79.5$	2	0

Table 35.7

Fig. 35.8 shows some features common to many histograms.

(a) The distribution has a modal class somewhere in the middle of the range of values.

(b) The distribution is almost symmetrical (except for a blip at one end).

(c) The frequency density tails off fairly rapidly as values of the variable move further away from the modal class.

Notice that it is not true to say that the distribution shown in Fig. 35.8 is symmetrical. But remember it comes from a sample of only 39 values. You can imagine that for a larger sample the distribution might look more symmetrical, and it would not have the blip on the end. This example shows that real data do not always give you the ideal picture which you would expect.

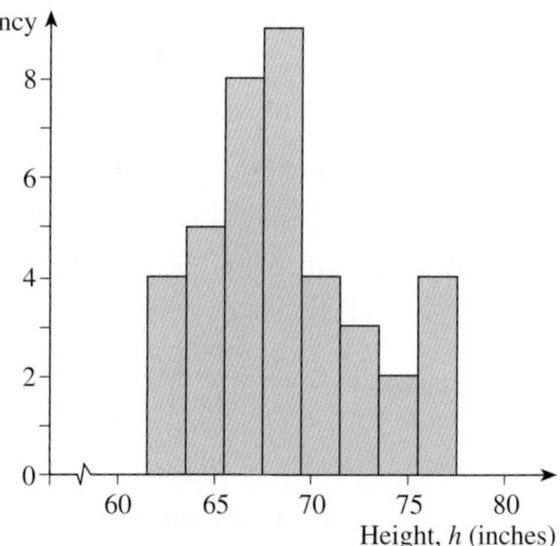

Fig. 35.8

You will have seen yourself many frequency histograms for which the distribution is almost symmetrical. If the distribution were symmetrical then the mean and median would be 'in the middle' of the distribution and would be in the centre of the modal class.

The probability density function for such an ideal distribution would have a bell shape similar to the one shown in Fig. 35.9. Many continuous distributions have probability density functions which are approximately bell-shaped.

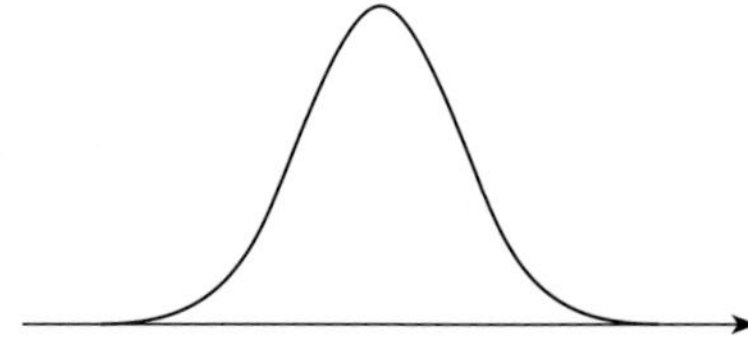

Fig. 35.9

The height and weight of living objects commonly have distributions which are approximately bell-shaped. This is not really so surprising. Consider, for example, the height of adult females. A bell-shaped distribution would suggest that most females are about 'average' in terms of height and that a few are much taller and a few are much shorter. This picture tends to be confirmed by what you see in everyday life. It would be very useful, therefore, to find a function $f(x)$ whose graph, when plotted, gives this typical bell shape.

Unfortunately it will not be enough to find one such function because, although the general bell shape applies to many situations, the precise details of the bell vary from one distribution to another. For example, the heights of adult male humans may have a mean of 172 cm but the heights of adult male chimpanzees would not be centred around the same value.

Therefore you need a family of functions which give bell-shaped curves and there needs to be some parameter that you can vary which alters the line of symmetry of the curve.

Similarly the spreads of the distributions of heights for men and chimpanzees are different. There needs to be a second parameter which allows for this fact.

Although you do not need to know or learn the formula for this family of functions it is given for your information. It is

$$f(x) = \frac{1}{\sigma\sqrt{2\pi}}\mathrm{e}^{-\frac{(x-\mu)^2}{2\sigma^2}} \qquad \text{for all real values of } x.$$

Any random variable whose distribution has this probability density function for some values of μ and σ^2 is said to have a **normal distribution** with parameters μ and σ^2. For a random variable X this is denoted by $X \sim \mathrm{N}(\mu, \sigma^2)$.

You can experiment with this function on your calculator and display the graphs for several values of μ and σ^2. You might have guessed what the symbols μ and σ^2 represent. The parameter μ gives the location of the mean of the distribution. In this case the mean is the same as the median and the mode since all three measures of location have the same value.

The line $x = \mu$ is the axis of symmetry for the curve whose equation is $y = f(x)$. Points of inflexion occur at the points on the curve where $x = \mu - \sigma$ and $x = \mu + \sigma$, so σ is a measure of the spread of the distribution. Although it is not possible to prove this at the moment, it will probably not surprise you to learn that σ^2 is the variance of the distribution.

You can see how the shape of the distribution varies with different values of μ and σ^2 by considering the diagrams in Fig. 35.10.

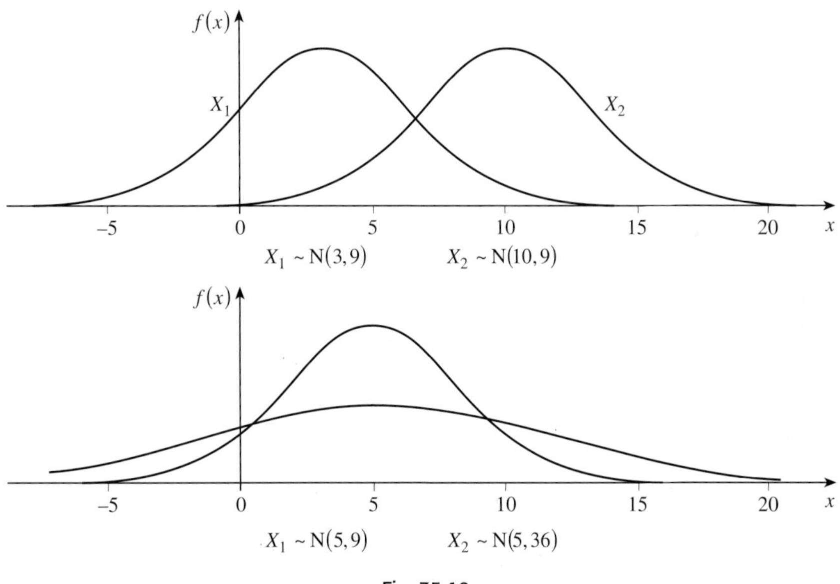

Fig. 35.10

35.4 The standard normal distribution

If the random variable $Z \sim \mathrm{N}(0, 1)$ then Z is said to have a **standard normal distribution**. In one sense this distribution has the probability density function with the 'simplest' equation. Because it is regarded as a special case, it is given its own notation. The letter Z is often reserved exclusively for a random variable with the $\mathrm{N}(0, 1)$ distribution.

The probability density function for the N(0, 1) distribution is

$$\phi(z) = \frac{1}{\sqrt{2\pi}}e^{-\frac{1}{2}z^2} \text{ for } -\infty < z < \infty.$$

where ϕ, pronounced 'fī', is the Greek letter f, and is used instead of the usual f for function.

The graph of $y = \phi(z)$ is drawn in Fig. 35.11.

Here is a summary of the properties of $\phi(z)$.

- $\phi(z)$ is symmetrical about the y-axis (the line $z = 0$),
- $\phi(z)$ has points of inflexion at $z = \pm 1$,
- $\phi(z) \to 0$ (very quickly) as $z \to \pm\infty$, and $\phi(\pm 3) \approx 0$,
- for this distribution the mean of Z is 0 and the variance of Z is 1,
- mean = median = mode = 0.

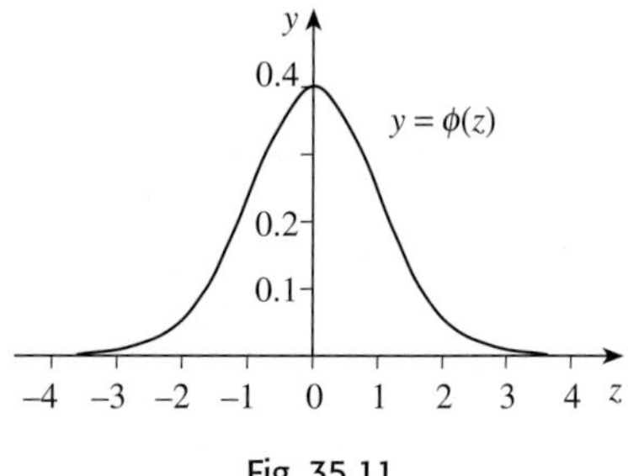

Fig. 35.11

Although you do not need to know the formula for $\phi(z)$, it is worth noting that $\frac{1}{\sqrt{2\pi}}$ is just the constant needed to ensure that the function has an area of one unit under its graph. It is not possible to show this by integration at this stage but you could verify that it is approximately true by using an approximate numerical method for integration.

Unfortunately no simple formula exists for the indefinite integral $\int \phi(z)\,dz$, so areas under the graph of $\phi(z)$ have to be found numerically and then tabulated, or found using a calculator.

The area tabulated or given by a calculator is shown by the shaded region in Fig. 35.12, and is given by p, where p is the area under the curve to the left of z.

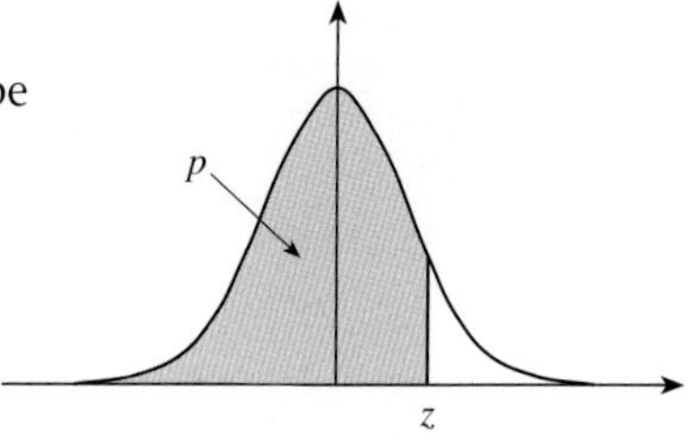

Fig. 35.12

35.5 Using normal distribution tables

> If your calculator has a routine which gives you the area under the probability density function of the standard normal distribution, you may wish to omit this section but check that you can answer questions like those in Exercise 35A. This section is included to help those who will be using normal distribution tables.

On page 612 there is a table of areas under the graph of $y = \phi(z)$.

From the table on page 612, $p = P(Z \leq 2) = 0.9773$. This means that for a random variable Z with an N(0, 1) distribution, $P(Z \leq 2) = 0.9773$. Fig. 35.13 illustrates this situation.

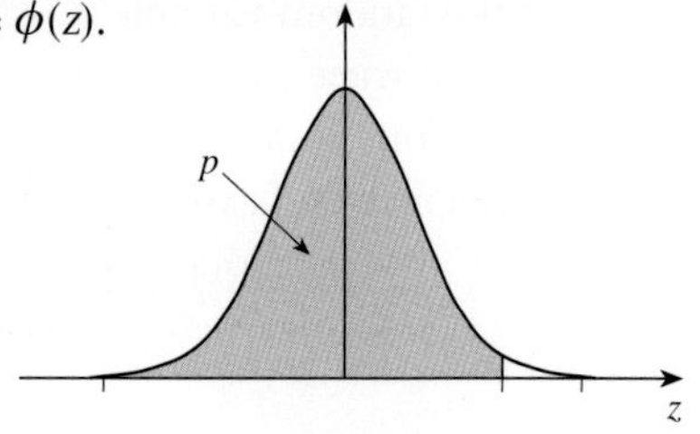

Fig. 35.13

The tables enable you to find $P(Z \le z)$ for values of z, given correct to 3 decimal places, from $z = 0$ up to $z = 3.5$. Table 35.14 is taken from the table on page 612.

z	0	0.01	0.02	0.03	0.04	0.05	0.06	0.07	0.08	0.09
0.6	0.7257	0.7291	**0.7324**	0.7357	0.7389	0.7422	0.7454	0.7486	0.7517	0.7549

Table 35.14

Suppose that you wish to find $P(Z \le 0.62)$, where $Z \sim N(0, 1)$, using the tables. The first two digits 0.6 of 0.62 indicate that you must look in the row of the z-column labelled 0.6. The digit in the second decimal place is 2 so now look at the entry in the column marked 0.02, giving the value 0.7324. Thus

$$P(Z \le 0.62) = 0.7324.$$

To find the area between two values, $z = a$ and $z = b$, use the fact that the area between $z = a$ and $z = b$ can be written as

(area between $z = a$ and $z = b$) = (area up to $z = b$) − (area up to $z = a$).

In symbols,

$$P(a < Z < b) = P(Z < b) - P(Z < a).$$

Remember, for a continuous distribution, $P(Z < b) = P(Z \le b)$ and $P(Z < a) = P(Z \le a)$.

For example,

$$\begin{aligned} P(1.20 < Z \le 2.34) &= P(Z \le 2.34) - P(Z < 1.20) \\ &= 0.9904 - 0.8849 = 0.1055. \end{aligned}$$

It is sensible to round all answers obtained from these tables to 3 decimal places since the entries are given correct to 4 decimal places. So write

$P(1.20 < Z \le 2.34) = 0.106$, correct to 3 significant figures.

Notice that the tables do not give the values of $P(Z < z)$ for negative values of z. The reason is that you can deduce the value of $P(Z < z)$ for negative z from the symmetry of the graph of $\phi(z)$. The diagrams in Fig. 35.15 show how to calculate $P(Z \le -1.2)$.

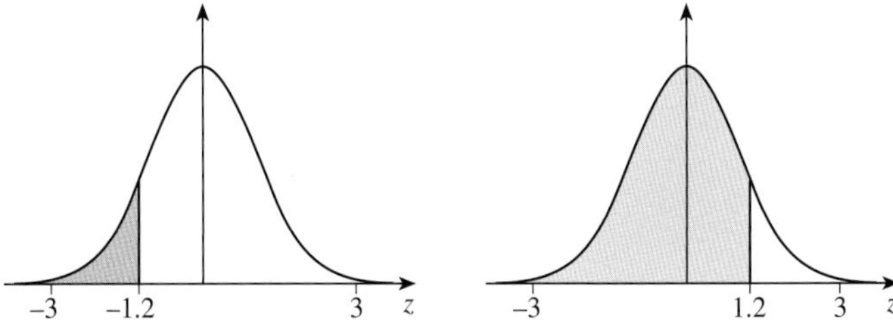

Fig. 35.15

Fig. 35.15 shows that the area shaded in the left diagram is equal to the area unshaded under the graph in the right diagram. Since the total area under the graph in each diagram, shaded and unshaded, is equal to 1,

$$\begin{aligned} P(Z \le -1.2) &= 1 - P(Z \le 1.2) \\ &= 1 - 0.8849 \\ &= 0.1151 = 0.115, \text{ correct to 3 decimal places.} \end{aligned}$$

This is an example of the identity

$$P(Z \le -z) \equiv 1 - P(Z \le z)$$

which applies for all values of z. This identity means that it is not necessary to tabulate values of $P(Z \le z)$ for negative values of z.

It will help to draw a sketch of the region whose area you are finding. Sketches will be drawn in this section, but omitted in following sections. However, you are advised always to make a sketch.

Example 35.5.1

The random variable Z is such that $Z \sim N(0, 1)$. Find the following probabilities.

(a) $P(0.7 \le Z < 1.4)$, (b) $P(Z \le -2.3)$, (c) $P(Z > 0.73)$ (d) $P(-1.4 \le Z \le 1)$

(a) $$\begin{aligned} P(0.7 \le Z < 1.4) &= P(Z < 1.4) - P(Z \le 0.7) \\ &= 0.9192 - 0.7580 \\ &= 0.1612 \\ &= 0.161, \text{ correct to 3 decimal places.} \end{aligned}$$

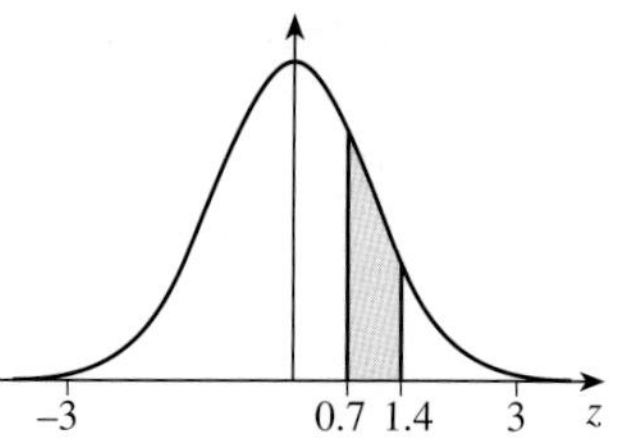

(b) Using the identity $P(Z \le -z) \equiv 1 - P(Z \le z)$,

$$\begin{aligned} P(Z \le -2.3) &= 1 - P(Z \le 2.3) \\ &= 1 - 0.9892 \\ &= 0.0108 \\ &= 0.011, \text{ correct to 3 decimal places.} \end{aligned}$$

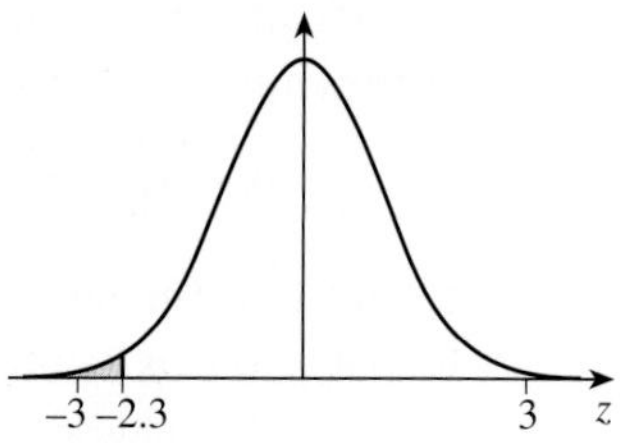

(c) $P(Z > 0.73) = 1 - P(Z \le 0.73)$
$= 1 - 0.7673$
$= 0.2327$
$= 0.233$, correct to 3 decimal places.

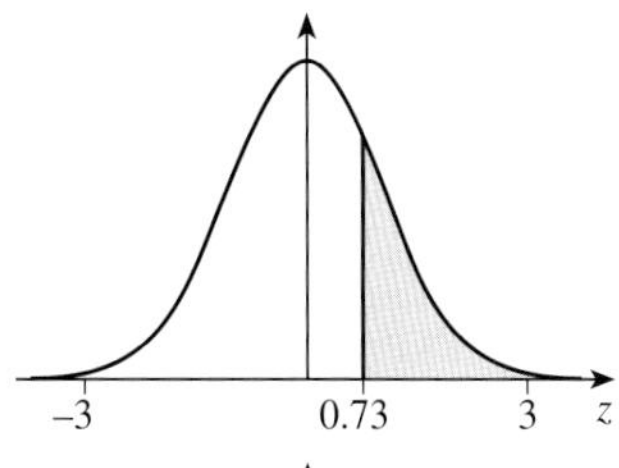

(d) $P(-1.4 \le Z \le 1) = P(Z \le 1) - P(Z \le -1.4)$
$= P(Z \le 1) - (1 - P(Z \le 1.4))$
$= P(Z \le 1) - 1 + P(Z \le 1.4)$
$= 0.8413 - 1 + 0.9192$
$= 0.7605$
$= 0.761$, correct to 3 decimal places.

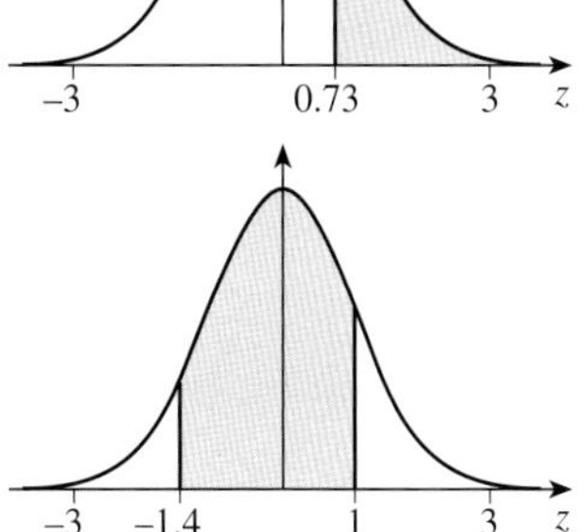

Notice how drawing a rough sketch of the graph of the N(0, 1) distribution with the ends of the sketch marked as −3 and 3 can give you some indication of whether your answer is approximately correct.

It is also sometimes necessary to use the tables or the calculator 'in reverse'. For example, if you know the probability of $P(Z \ge k)$, you may need to find the corresponding value of k.

Example 35.5.2

The random variable Z is such that $Z \sim N(0, 1)$. Use the inverse normal probabilities table to find

(a) the value of s such that $P(Z \le s) = 0.7$,

(b) the value of t such that $P(Z > t) = 0.8$.

(a) You know that $p = P(Z \le s) = 0.7$.

From the inverse normal probabilities table (pages 610–11), when $p = 0.7$, $s = 0.524$, correct to 3 decimal places.

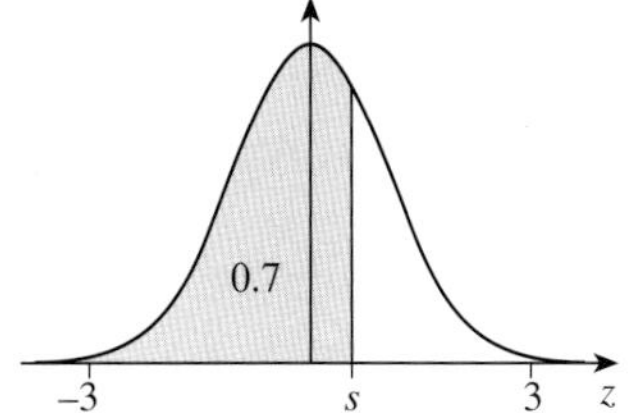

(b) From the first diagram it is clear that the value of t such that $P(Z > t) = 0.8$ is negative.

Since the value of t is negative, it cannot be found directly from the inverse normal probabilities table.

However, from the second diagram, $t = -v$ where $P(Z \le v) = 0.8$, using symmetry.

You know that $P(Z \le v) = 0.8$, so, from the table, $v = 0.842$.

Hence $t = -0.842$, correct to 3 decimal places.

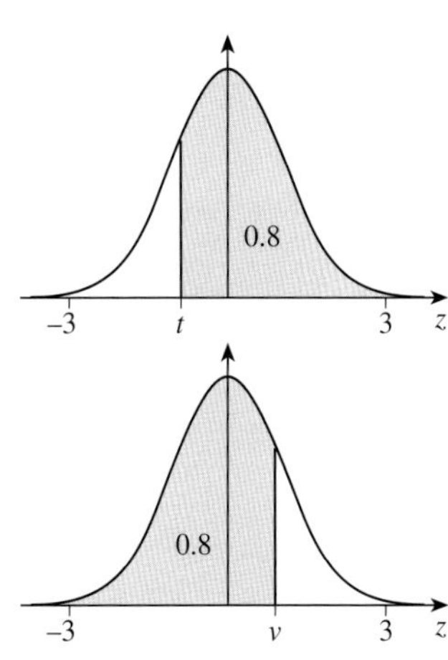

You can use your calculator to solve problems on the normal distribution, but you will need to consult the manual to find out how to access the built-in routines.

Exercise 35A

In this exercise use either your calculator or the tables on pages 610–12.

1 $Z \sim \text{N}(0, 1)$. Find the following probabilities.

(a) $\text{P}(Z < 1.23)$ (b) $\text{P}(Z \le 2.47)$ (c) $\text{P}(Z < 0.16)$

(d) $\text{P}(Z \ge 1.24)$ (e) $\text{P}(Z > 2.38)$ (f) $\text{P}(Z \ge 0.59)$

(g) $\text{P}(Z > -1.83)$ (h) $\text{P}(Z \le -2.06)$ (i) $\text{P}(Z > -0.07)$

(j) $\text{P}(Z \le -1.83)$ (k) $\text{P}(Z < -2.76)$ (l) $\text{P}(Z \le -0.21)$

2 The random variable Z is distributed such that $Z \sim \text{N}(0, 1)$. Find the following probabilities.

(a) $\text{P}(1.15 < Z < 1.35)$ (b) $\text{P}(1.11 \le Z \le 2.22)$

(c) $\text{P}(0.39 < Z < 2.42)$ (d) $\text{P}(0 \le Z < 1.55)$

(e) $\text{P}(-1.82 < Z < 2.33)$ (f) $\text{P}(-0.85 < Z \le 2.03)$

(g) $\text{P}(-2.51 < Z < 1.09)$ (h) $\text{P}(-0.55 \le Z \le 0)$

(i) $\text{P}(-2.82 < Z < -1.82)$ (j) $\text{P}(-1.75 \le Z \le -1.00)$

(k) $\text{P}(-2.57 < Z < -0.12)$ (l) $\text{P}(-1.96 \le Z < 1.96)$

3 The random variable $Z \sim \text{N}(0, 1)$. In each part, find the value of s, t, u or v.

(a) $\text{P}(Z < s) = 0.67$ (b) $\text{P}(Z < t) = 0.88$ (c) $\text{P}(Z < u) = 0.98$

(d) $\text{P}(Z < v) = 0.85$ (e) $\text{P}(Z > s) = 0.41$ (f) $\text{P}(Z > t) = 0.12$

(g) $\text{P}(Z > u) = 0.01$ (h) $\text{P}(Z > v) = 0.22$ (i) $\text{P}(Z > s) = 0.99$

(j) $\text{P}(Z > t) = 0.97$ (k) $\text{P}(Z \le u) = 0.15$ (l) $\text{P}(Z > v) = 0.5$

35.6 Standardising a normal distribution

Suppose the random variable X has a normal distribution with parameters μ and σ^2. Then the bell-shaped graph of the normal distribution is centred on μ.

Let $Y = X - \mu$. The probability density function of Y will still have the typical bell shape but it will be centred on 0 rather than on μ. (See Section 30.1.)

The spreads of the two distributions are identical, so $Y \sim \text{N}(0, \sigma^2)$. Fig. 35.16 shows the relation between the distributions of X and Y.

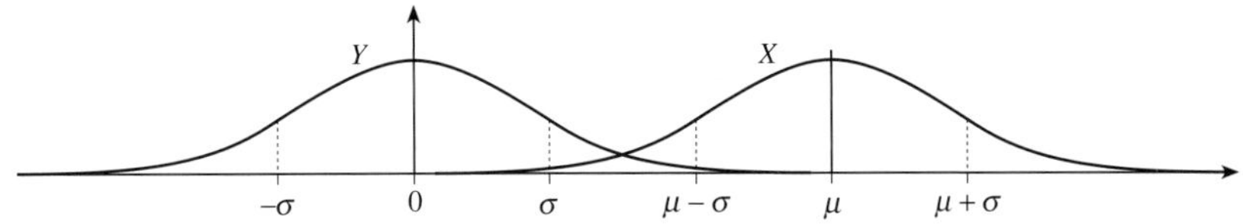

Fig. 35.16

Now let $Z = \dfrac{Y}{\sigma}$. This alters the spread of the distribution, so that when $Y = \pm\sigma$, then $Z = \pm 1$, but it does not alter the characteristic bell shape of the distribution. (See Section 30.2.) So, as Fig. 35.17 shows, the probability density function of Z is an N(0, 1) distribution.

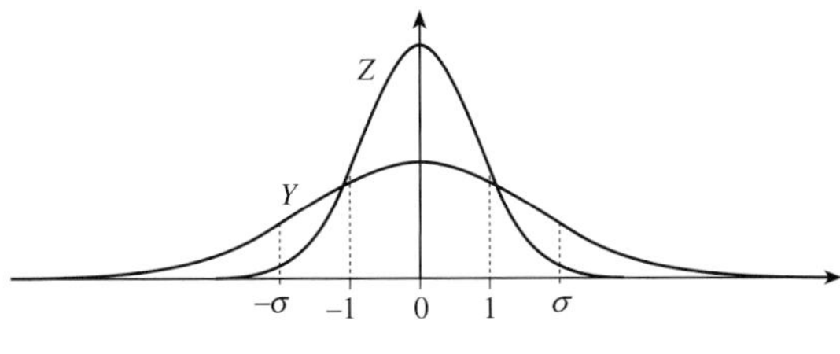

Fig. 35.17

Summarising this discussion:

> If $X \sim \mathrm{N}(\mu, \sigma^2)$ and $Z = \dfrac{X-\mu}{\sigma}$, then $Z \sim \mathrm{N}(0, 1)$.

This means that by using the transformation $Z = \dfrac{X-\mu}{\sigma}$ you can change a statement about an $\mathrm{N}(\mu, \sigma^2)$ distribution into an equivalent statement about an N(0, 1) distribution.

This process is called **standardisation** and the equation $Z = \dfrac{X-\mu}{\sigma}$ is called the **standardisation equation**.

To see how standardisation works, consider finding the probability $\mathrm{P}(X \le 230)$, where $X \sim \mathrm{N}(205, 20^2)$

Using the standardisation equation, $Z = \dfrac{X-205}{20}$, you know that $Z \sim \mathrm{N}(0, 1)$. Then

$$\begin{aligned}\mathrm{P}(X \le 230) &= \mathrm{P}\left(Z \le \frac{230-205}{20}\right)\\ &= \mathrm{P}(Z \le 1.25)\\ &= 0.8943... = 0.894,\ \text{correct to 3 decimal places.}\end{aligned}$$

Example 35.6.1

Given that $X \sim \mathrm{N}(4, 25)$, find the following probabilities.

(a) $\mathrm{P}(X < 4.5)$ (b) $\mathrm{P}(5 \le X \le 6)$ (c) $\mathrm{P}(2 \le X \le 7)$ (d) $\mathrm{P}(X > 1)$

Let $Z = \dfrac{X-4}{5}$. Then $Z \sim \mathrm{N}(0, 1)$.

(a) $$\begin{aligned}\mathrm{P}(X < 4.5) &= \mathrm{P}\left(Z < \frac{4.5-4}{5}\right)\\ &= \mathrm{P}(Z < 0.1)\\ &= 0.5398... = 0.540,\ \text{correct to 3 decimal places.}\end{aligned}$$

(b) $P(5 \le X \le 6) = P\left(\frac{5-4}{5} \le Z \le \frac{6-4}{5}\right)$
$= P(0.2 \le Z \le 0.4)$
$= P(Z \le 0.4) - P(Z \le 0.2)$
$= 0.07616... = 0.076$, correct to 3 decimal places.

(c) $P(2 \le X \le 7) = P\left(\frac{2-4}{5} \le Z \le \frac{7-4}{5}\right)$
$= P(-0.4 \le Z \le 0.6)$
$= P(Z \le 0.6) - P(Z \le -0.4)$
$= 0.3811... = 0.381$, correct to 3 decimal places.

(d) $P(X > 1) = P\left(Z > \frac{1-4}{5}\right)$
$= P(Z > -0.6)$
$= P(Z < 0.6)$ (by symmetry)
$= 0.7257... = 0.726$, correct to 3 decimal places.

Example 35.6.2

Given that $X \sim N(6, 4)$, find, correct to 3 significant figures, the values of s and t such that
(a) $P(X \le s) = 0.65$, (b) $P(X > t) = 0.82$.

Let $Z = \frac{X-6}{2}$. Then $Z \sim N(0, 1)$.

(a) The statement $P(X \le s) = 0.65$ is equivalent to $P\left(Z \le \frac{s-6}{2}\right) = 0.65$.
Using a calculator or tables, $p = 0.65$ gives $0.3853...$,
so $\frac{s-6}{2} = 0.3853...$
and $s = 6 + 2 \times 0.3853...$
$= 6.7706... = 6.77$, correct to 3 significant figures.

(b) The statement $P(X > t) = 0.82$ is equivalent to $P\left(Z > \frac{t-6}{2}\right) = 0.82$. The problem is now similar to Example 35.5.2(b).
Then

$$P\left(Z < \frac{t-6}{2}\right) = 1 - 0.82 = 0.18.$$

Using a calculator, $p = 0.18$ gives $z = -0.9153...$. (Using tables, $p = 0.82$ gives $z = 0.9154$ but you need the negative value as in Example 35.52(b)). So

$$\frac{t-6}{2} = -0.9153...$$
$$t = 6 + 2 \times (-0.9153...)$$
$$= 4.169... = 4.17, \text{ correct to 3 significant figures.}$$

Example 35.6.3
Given that $X \sim N(23, \sigma^2)$ and that $P(X < 27) = 0.83$, find σ.

Let $Z = \dfrac{X-23}{\sigma}$, so that $Z \sim N(0, 1)$.

Then $P(X < 27) = 0.83$ is equivalent to $P\left(Z < \dfrac{27-23}{\sigma}\right) = 0.83$, or

$$P\left(Z < \frac{4}{\sigma}\right) = 0.83.$$

Using the tables (or a calculator), if $p = 0.83$, then $\dfrac{4}{\sigma} = 0.9542$, so

$$\sigma = \frac{4}{0.9542} = 4.19, \text{ correct to 3 significant figures.}$$

Exercise 35B

You are strongly advised to draw rough sketches for these questions.

1 Given that $X \sim N(20, 16)$, find the following probabilities.
(a) $P(X \le 26)$ (b) $P(X > 30)$ (c) $P(X \ge 17)$ (d) $P(X < 13)$

2 Given that $X \sim N(24, 9)$, find the following probabilities.
(a) $P(X \le 29)$ (b) $P(X > 31)$ (c) $P(X \ge 22)$ (d) $P(X < 16)$

3 Given that $X \sim N(50, 16)$, find the following probabilities.
(a) $P(54 \le X \le 58)$ (b) $P(40 < X \le 44)$ (c) $P(47 < X < 57)$
(d) $P(39 \le X < 53)$ (e) $P(44 \le X \le 56)$

4 X is distributed normally with mean 3 and variance 4. Find the probability that X has a negative value.

5 The random variable X has a normal distribution. The mean is μ (where $\mu > 0$) and the variance is $\frac{1}{4}\mu^2$.
(a) Find $P(X > 1.5\mu)$. (b) Find the probability that X is negative.

6 Given that $X \sim N(44, 25)$, find s, t, u and v correct to 2 decimal places when
(a) $P(X \le s) = 0.98$, (b) $P(X \ge t) = 0.77$, (c) $P(X \ge u) = 0.05$, (d) $P(X \le v) = 0.33$.

7 Given that $X \sim N(15, 4)$, find s, t, u, v and w correct to 2 decimal places when
(a) $P(X \le s) = 0.91$, (b) $P(X \ge t) = 0.57$, (c) $P(X \le u) = 0.10$,
(d) $P(X \le v) = 0.39$, (e) $P(15 - w < X < 15 + w) = 0.9$

8 Given that $X \sim N(35.4, 12.5)$, find the values of s, t, u and v correct to 1 decimal place when
(a) $P(X < s) = 0.96$, (b) $P(X > t) = 0.94$, (c) $P(X > u) = 0.29$, (d) $P(X < v) = 0.15$.

9 X has a normal distribution with mean 32 and variance σ^2. Given that the probability that X is less than 33 is 0.64, find σ^2. Give your answer correct to 2 decimal places.

10 X has a normal distribution, and $P(X > 73) = 0.03$. Given that the variance of the distribution is 18, find the mean.

11 X is distributed normally, $P(X \geq 59) = 0.02$ and $P(X \geq 29) = 0.93$. Find the mean and standard deviation of the distribution, correct to 3 significant figures.

12 $X \sim N(\mu, \sigma^2)$, $P(X \geq 9.81) = 0.16$ and $P(X \leq 8.82) = 0.01$. Find μ and σ, correct to 3 significant figures.

35.7 Modelling with the normal distribution

The normal distribution is often used as a model for practical situations. In the following examples, you need to translate the given information into the language of the normal distribution before you can solve the problem.

Example 35.7.1

Look back to the data on heights given in Table 35.7, and to the associated frequency histogram in Fig. 35.8. Assuming that the distribution is normal, how many of the 39 people would you expect to be in the interval $61.5 \leq h < 63.5$?

You can check that the mean and the standard deviation of the data are 68.6 and 4.1. (If necessary, see Sections 5.4 and 6.6.)

Using a random variable, H, with an $N(68.6, 4.1^2)$ distribution you can calculate the expected frequency for each interval.

Given that $H \sim N(68.6, 4.1^2)$, let $Z = \dfrac{H - 68.6}{4.1}$, so that $Z \sim N(0, 1)$. Then

$$\begin{aligned} P(61.5 \leq H < 63.5) &= P\left(\frac{61.5 - 68.6}{4.1} \leq Z < \frac{63.5 - 68.6}{4.1}\right) \\ &= P(-1.73... \leq Z < -1.24...) \\ &= P(Z < -1.24...) - P(Z \leq -1.73...) \\ &= 0.0651... . \end{aligned}$$

This means that the expected frequency for the interval $61.5 \leq h < 63.5$ is $39 \times 0.0651... = 2.5$, correct to 1 decimal place.

Therefore in a group of 39 people you would expect about 2 or 3 people to have heights in the interval $61.5 \leq h < 63.5$.

The observed frequency was actually 4. Does this mean that the $N(68.9, 4.3^2)$ distribution is a poor model for these data? To answer this question sensibly, you really need to calculate the expected frequencies for all nine classes.

Using the method shown above find the expected frequencies for the remaining eight classes and then review the results to consider whether the $N(68.9, 4.3^2)$ distribution is a suitable model for these data.

Example 35.7.2

Two friends Sarah and Hannah often go to the Post Office together. They travel in Sarah's car. Sarah always drives Hannah to the Post Office and drops her off there. Sarah then drives around until she is ready to pick Hannah up some time later. Their experience has been that the time Hannah takes in the Post Office can be approximated by a normal distribution with mean 6 minutes and standard deviation 1.3 minutes. How many minutes after having dropped Hannah off should Sarah return if she wants to be at least 95% certain that Hannah will not keep her waiting?

Let T be the time Hannah takes in the Post Office on a randomly chosen trip. Then $T \sim \mathrm{N}(6, 1.3^2)$.

Let t be the number of minutes after dropping Hannah off when Sarah returns; you then need to find t such that $\mathrm{P}(T \le t) \ge 0.95$. After standardising, this becomes

$$\mathrm{P}\left(Z \le \frac{t-6}{1.3}\right) \ge 0.95.$$

Letting $p = \mathrm{P}\left(Z \le \frac{t-6}{1.3}\right) \ge 0.95$, gives

$$\frac{t-6}{1.3} \ge 1.645\ldots,$$

which, on rearranging, gives $t \ge 8.1385\ldots$.

Sarah should not return for at least 8.14 minutes, correct to 3 significant figures, if she wants to be at least 95% sure that Hannah will not keep her waiting.

Exercise 35C

1 The time spent waiting for a prescription to be prepared at a chemist's shop is normally distributed with mean 15 minutes and standard deviation 2.8 minutes. Find the probability that the waiting time, t, in minutes satisfies

(a) $t > 20$ (b) $t < 8$ (c) $10 < t < 18$.

2 The heights of a group of sixteen-year-old girls are normally distributed with mean 161.2 cm and standard deviation 4.7 cm. Find the probability that the height h cm of one of these girls will satisfy

(a) $h > 165$ (b) $h < 150$ (c) $165 < h < 170$ (d) $150 < h < 163$.

In a sample of 500 girls of this age estimate how many will have heights in each of the above four ranges.

3 The lengths of replacement car wiper blades are normally distributed with mean of 25 cm and standard deviation 0.2 cm. For a batch of 200 wiper blades estimate how many would be expected to be

(a) 25.3 cm or more in length, (b) between 24.89 cm and 25.11 cm in length,

(c) between 24.89 cm and 25.25 cm in length.

4 The time taken by a garage to replace worn-out brake pads follows a normal distribution with mean 90 minutes and standard deviation 5.8 minutes.

(a) Find the probability that the garage takes longer than 105 minutes.

(b) Find the probability that the garage takes less than 85 minutes.

(c) The garage claims to complete the replacements in 'a to b minutes'. If this claim is to be correct for 90% of the repairs, find a and b correct to 2 significant figures, based on a symmetrical interval centred on the mean.

5 The fluorescent light tubes made by the company Well-lit have lifetimes which are normally distributed with mean 2010 hours and standard deviation 20 hours. The company decides to promote its sales of the tubes by guaranteeing a minimum life of the tubes, replacing free of charge any tubes that fail to meet this minimum life. If the company wishes to have to replace free only 3% of the tubes sold, find the guaranteed minimum it must set.

6 The lengths of sweet pea flower stems are normally distributed with mean 18.2 cm and standard deviation 2.3 cm.

(a) Find the probability that the length of a flower stem is between 16 cm and 20 cm.

(b) 12% of the flower stems are longer than h cm. 20% of the flower stems are shorter than k cm. Find h and k.

(c) Stem lengths less than 14 cm are unacceptable at a florist's shop. In a batch of 500 sweet peas estimate how many would be unacceptable.

7 The T-Q company makes a soft drink sold in '330 ml' cans. The actual volume of drink in the cans is distributed normally with standard deviation 2.5 ml.

To ensure that at least 99% of the cans contain more than 330 ml, find the volume that the company should supply in the cans on average.

8 The packets in which sugar is sold are labelled '1 kg packets'. In fact the mass of sugar in a packet is distributed normally with mean mass 1.08 kg.

Sampling of the packets of sugar shows that just 2.5% are 'underweight' (that is, contain less than the stated mass of 1 kg).

Find the standard deviation of the distribution.

9 The life of the Powerhouse battery has a normal distribution with mean 210 hours. It is found that 4% of these batteries operate for more than 222 hours.

Find the variance of the distribution, correct to 2 significant figures.

10 In a statistics examination, 15% of the candidates scored more than 63 marks and 10% of the candidates scored less than 32 marks. Assuming that the marks were distributed normally find the mean mark and the standard deviation.

Review exercise 11

1 The number of times a certain factory machine breaks down each working week has been recorded over a long period. From this data, the following probability distribution for the number, X, of weekly breakdowns was produced.

x	0	1	2	3	4	5	6
$P(X = x)$	0.04	0.24	0.28	0.16	0.16	0.08	0.04

(a) Find the mean of X.

(b) What would be the expected total number of breakdowns that will occur over the next 48 working weeks?

2 An absent-minded mathematician is attempting to log on to a computer, which is done by typing the correct password. Unfortunately he can't remember his password. If he types the wrong password he tries again. The computer allows a maximum of four attempts altogether. For each attempt the probability of success is 0.4, independently of all other attempts.

(a) Calculate the probability that he logs on successfully.

(b) The total number of attempts he makes, successful or not, is denoted by X (so that the possible values of X are 1, 2, 3 or 4). Tabulate the probability distribution of X.

3 Three cards are selected at random, without replacement, from a shuffled pack of 52 playing cards. Using a tree diagram, find the probability distribution of the number of honours (A, K, Q, J, 10) obtained.

4 An electronic device produces an output of 0, 1 or 3 volts, each time it is operated, with probabilities $\frac{1}{2}$, $\frac{1}{3}$ and $\frac{1}{6}$ respectively. The random variable X denotes the result of adding the outputs for two such devices which act independently.

(a) Tabulate the possible values of X with their corresponding probabilities.

(b) In 360 independent operations of the device, state on how many occasions you would expect the outcome to be 1 volt. (OCR, adapted)

5 The probability of a novice archer hitting a target with any shot is 0.3. Given that the archer shoots six arrows, find the probability that the target is hit at least twice. (OCR)

6 Joseph and four friends each have an independent probability 0.45 of winning a prize. Find the probability that

(a) exactly two of the five friends win a prize,

(b) Joseph and only one friend win a prize. (OCR)

7 Given that $X \sim N(10, 2.25)$, find $P(X > 12)$. (OCR)

8 The lifetime of a Fotobrite light bulb is normally distributed with mean 1020 hours and standard deviation 85 hours. Find the probability that a Fotobrite bulb chosen at random has a lifetime between 1003 and 1088 hours. (OCR)

9 The manufacturers of a new model of car state that, when travelling at 56 miles per hour, the petrol consumption has a mean value of 32.4 miles per gallon with standard deviation 1.4 miles per gallon. Assuming a normal distribution, calculate the probability that a randomly chosen car of that model will have a petrol consumption greater than 30 miles per gallon when travelling at 56 miles per hour. (OCR)

10 A normally distributed random variable, X, has mean 20.0 and variance 4.15. Find the probability that $18.0 < X < 21.0$. (OCR)

11 The weights of eggs, measured in grams, can be modelled by an $X \sim \text{N}(85.0, 36)$ distribution. Eggs are classified as large, medium or small, where a large egg weighs 90.0 grams or more, and 25% of eggs are classified as small. Calculate

(a) the percentage of eggs which are classified as large,

(b) the maximum weight of a small egg. (OCR)

12 A machine cuts a very long plastic tube into short tubes. The length of the short tubes is modelled by a normal distribution with mean m cm and standard deviation 0.25 cm. The value of m can be set by adjusting the machine. Find the value of m for which the probability is 0.1 that the length of a short tube, picked at random, is less than 6.50 cm.

The machine is adjusted so that $m = 6.40$, the standard deviation remaining unchanged. Find the probability that a tube picked at random is between 6.30 and 6.60 cm long. (OCR)

13 A random variable X has an $\text{N}(m, 4)$ distribution. Its associated normal curve is shown in the diagram. Find the value of m such that the shaded area is 0.800, giving your answer correct to 3 significant figures. (OCR)

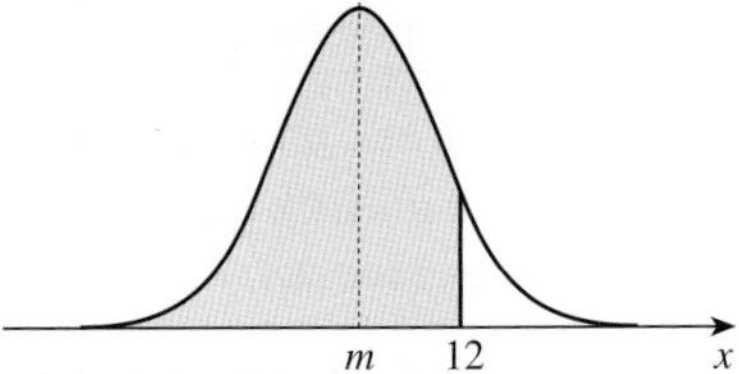

14 The mass of grapes sold per day in a supermarket can be modelled by a normal distribution. It is found that, over a long period, the mean mass sold per day is 35.0 kg, and that, on average, less than 15.0 kg are sold on one day in twenty.

(a) Show that the standard deviation of the mass of grapes sold per day is 12.2 kg, correct to 3 significant figures.

(b) Calculate the probability that, on a day chosen at random, more than 53.0 kg are sold. (OCR)

15 Two firms, Goodline and Megadelay, produce delay lines for use in communications. The delay time for a delay line is measured in nanoseconds (ns).

(a) The delay times for the output of Goodline may be modelled by a normal distribution with mean 283 ns and standard deviation 8 ns. What is the probability that the delay time of one line selected at random from Goodline's output is between 275 and 286 ns?

(b) It is found that, in the output of Megadelay, 10% of the delay times are less than 274.6 ns and 7.5% are more than 288.2 ns. Again assuming a normal distribution, calculate the mean and standard deviation of the delay times for Megadelay. Give your answers correct to 3 significant figures. (OCR)

16 The probabilities of the scores on a biased dice are shown in the table below.

Score	1	2	3	4	5	6
Probability	k	$\frac{1}{9}$	$\frac{1}{9}$	$\frac{1}{9}$	$\frac{1}{9}$	$\frac{1}{2}$

(a) Find the value of k.

Two players, Hazel and Ross, play a game with this biased dice and a fair dice. Hazel chooses one of the two dice at random and rolls it. If the score is 5 or 6 she wins a point.

(b) Calculate the probability that Hazel wins a point.

(c) Hazel chooses a dice, rolls it and wins a point. Find the probability that she chose the biased dice. (OCR)

17 The probability distribution of the random variable Y is given in the following table, where c is a constant.

y	1	2	3	4	5
$P(Y = y)$	c	$3c$	c^2	c^2	$\frac{15}{32}$

Prove that there is only one possible value of c, and state this value.

Examination questions

1 The mass of packets of a breakfast cereal is normally distributed with a mean of 750 g and standard deviation of 25 g.

(a) Find the probability that a packet chosen at random has mass

(i) less than 740 g; (ii) at least 780 g; (iii) between 740 g and 780 g.

(b) Two packets are chosen at random. What is the probability that both packets have a mass which is less than 740 g?

(c) The mass of 70% of the packets is more than x grams. Find the value of x. (© IBO 2002)

2 In a country called *Tallopia*, the height of adults is normally distributed with a mean of 187.5 cm and a standard deviation of 9.5 cm.

(a) What percentage of adults in *Tallopia* have a height greater than 197 cm?

(b) A standard doorway in *Tallopia* is designed so that 99% of adults have a space of at least 17 cm over their heads when going through a doorway. Find the height of a standard doorway in *Tallopia*. Give your answer to the nearest cm. (© IBO 2002)

3 The heights, H, of the people in a certain town are normally distributed with mean 170 cm and standard deviation 20 cm.

(a) A person is selected at random. Find the probability that his height is less than 185 cm.

(b) Given that $P(H > d) = 0.6808$, find the value of d. (© IBO 2005)

36 Relations between trigonometric functions

This chapter introduces you to a number of relations between the sine, cosine and tangent functions. When you have completed it, you should

- know Pythagoras' identity in trigonometry
- know the double angle formulae for sine and cosine, and be able to use these results for calculations and solving equations.

36.1 Relations between the trigonometric functions

In algebra you are used to solving equations, which involves finding a value of the unknown, often called x, in an equation such as $2x + 3 - x - 6 = 7$. You are also used to simplifying algebraic expressions like $2x + 3 - x - 6$, which becomes $x - 3$. You may not have realised, however, that these are quite different processes.

When you solve the equation $2x + 3 - x - 6 = 7$, you find that there is one root, $x = 10$. But the expression $x - 3$ is identical to $2x + 3 - x - 6$ for *all* values of x. Sometimes it is important to distinguish between these two situations.

If two expressions take the same values for every value of x, they are said to be **identically equal**. This is written with the symbol $\equiv$, read as 'is identically equal to'. The statement

$$2x + 3 - x - 6 \equiv x - 3$$

is called an **identity**. Thus an identity in x is a statement which is true for all values of x.

Similar ideas occur in trigonometry. In Section 15.2, it was observed that $\tan\theta^\circ = \dfrac{\sin\theta^\circ}{\cos\theta^\circ}$, provided that $\cos\theta^\circ \neq 0$. There is now no reason to use the degree sign as the statement is still true if θ is in radians. Thus

$$\tan\theta \equiv \frac{\sin\theta}{\cos\theta}.$$

The identity symbol is used even when there are some exceptional values for which neither side is defined. In the example given, neither side is defined when θ is an odd multiple of $\frac{1}{2}\pi\,(90^\circ)$, but the identity sign is still used.

There is another relationship which comes immediately from the definitions of $\cos\theta^\circ = x$ and $\sin\theta^\circ = y$ in Sections 15.1 and 15.2.

In Fig. 36.1, which is a copy of Fig. 15.1, as P lies on the circumference of a circle with radius 1 unit, Pythagoras' theorem gives $x^2 + y^2 = 1$, or $(\cos\theta^\circ)^2 + (\sin\theta^\circ)^2 \equiv 1$.

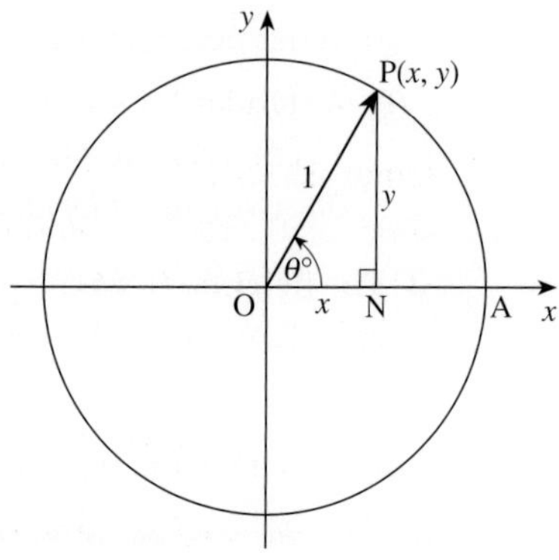

Fig. 36.1

As this is true whether the angle θ is in degrees or in radians, it is written as $(\cos\theta)^2 + (\sin\theta)^2 \equiv 1$.

Conventionally, $(\cos\theta)^2$ is written as $\cos^2\theta$ and $(\sin\theta)^2$ as $\sin^2\theta$, so for all values of θ, $\cos^2\theta + \sin^2\theta \equiv 1$. This is sometimes called Pythagoras' theorem in trigonometry.

For all values of θ:

$$\tan\theta \equiv \frac{\sin\theta}{\cos\theta}, \quad \text{provided that } \cos\theta \neq 0;$$

$$\cos^2\theta + \sin^2\theta \equiv 1.$$

The convention of using $\cos^n\theta$ to stand for $(\cos\theta)^n$ is best restricted to positive powers. In any case, it should never be used with $n = -1$, because of the danger of confusion with $\cos^{-1} x$, which is used to stand for the angle whose cosine is x. If in doubt, you should write $(\cos\theta)^n$ or $(\cos\theta)^{-n}$, which can only mean one thing.

Example 36.1.1
Simplify $1 - \cos^2\theta$.

As $\cos^2\theta + \sin^2\theta \equiv 1$, subtracting $\cos^2\theta$ from both sides gives

$$\sin^2\theta \equiv 1 - \cos^2\theta, \quad \text{so } 1 - \cos^2\theta \equiv \sin^2\theta.$$

Example 36.1.2
Show that $1 - 2\sin^2\theta \equiv 2\cos^2\theta - 1$.

To show that an identity is true, it is usually a good idea to start with one side, the more complicated one, and proceed to show that it is equal to the other side.

$$\begin{aligned} 1 - 2\sin^2\theta &\equiv 1 - 2(1 - \cos^2\theta) \qquad (\text{using } \sin^2\theta \equiv 1 - \cos^2\theta) \\ &\equiv 1 - 2 + 2\cos^2\theta \\ &\equiv 2\cos^2\theta - 1. \end{aligned}$$

Example 36.1.3
Given that $\sin\theta = \frac{3}{5}$, and that the angle θ is obtuse, find, without using a calculator, the values of $\cos\theta$ and $\tan\theta$.

Since $\cos^2\theta + \sin^2\theta \equiv 1$, $\cos^2\theta = 1 - \left(\frac{3}{5}\right)^2 = \frac{16}{25}$ giving $\cos\theta = \pm\frac{4}{5}$.

As the angle θ is obtuse, $\cos\theta$ is negative. Therefore $\cos\theta = -\frac{4}{5}$.

As $\sin\theta = \frac{3}{5}$ and $\cos\theta = -\frac{4}{5}$, $\tan\theta = \dfrac{\sin\theta}{\cos\theta} = \dfrac{3/5}{-4/5} = -\frac{3}{4}$.

Exercise 36A

1 For each triangle sketched below,

(i) use Pythagoras' theorem to find the length of the third side in an exact form,

(ii) find the exact values of $\sin\theta°$, $\cos\theta°$ and $\tan\theta°$.

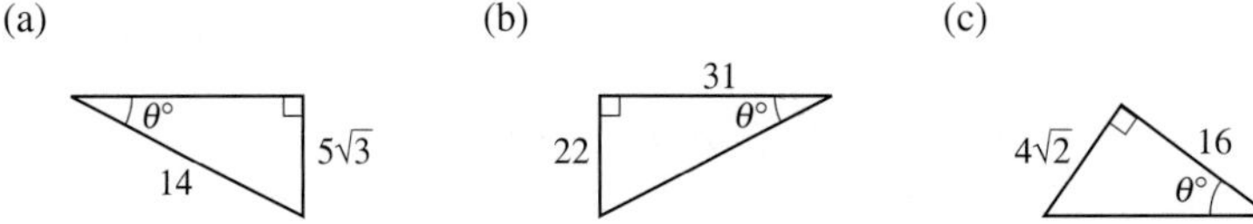

2 Simplify the following expressions, giving your answer in terms of a single trigonometric function.

(a) $\dfrac{1-\cos^2 x}{\tan^2 x}$ (b) $\dfrac{\sin^2 x}{1-\sin^2 x}$ (c) $\dfrac{1-\cos^2 x}{1-\sin^2 x}$

3 (a) Given that angle $\hat{A}$ is obtuse and that $\sin\hat{A} = \frac{5}{14}\sqrt{3}$, find the exact value of $\cos\hat{A}$.

(b) Given that $180 < \hat{B} < 360$ and that $\tan\hat{B} = -\frac{21}{20}$, find the exact value of $\cos\hat{B}$.

(c) Find all possible values of $\sin\hat{C}$ for which $\cos\hat{C} = \frac{1}{2}$.

4 Use $\tan\theta \equiv \dfrac{\sin\theta}{\cos\theta}$, $\cos\theta \neq 0$, and $\cos^2\theta + \sin^2\theta \equiv 1$ to establish the following.

(a) $\dfrac{1}{\sin\theta} - \sin\theta \equiv \dfrac{\cos^2\theta}{\sin\theta}$ (b) $\dfrac{\sin\theta°}{\tan\theta°} \equiv \cos\theta°$

(c) $(\cos\theta° + \sin\theta°)^2 + (\cos\theta° - \sin\theta°)^2 \equiv 2$ (d) $\sin\theta°\tan\theta° + \cos\theta° \equiv \dfrac{1}{\cos\theta°}$

36.2 The double angle formulae

Suppose that you know the values of $\cos\theta$ and $\sin\theta$. How could you calculate the values of $\cos 2\theta$ and $\sin 2\theta$? You could, of course, use a calculator but that would only give approximations.

In Fig. 36.2, the angles θ and $-\theta$ are drawn from the x-axis. The points P and Q then have coordinates $(\cos\theta, \sin\theta)$ and $(\cos(-\theta), \sin(-\theta))$ respectively.

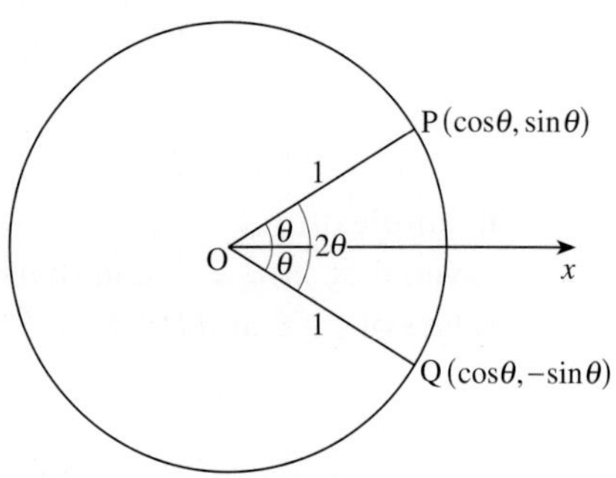

Fig. 36.2

But from the graphs of $\cos\theta$ and $\sin\theta$ (see Figs. 28.2 and 28.3, for example) you can see that $\cos(-\theta) = \cos\theta$ and $\sin(-\theta) = -\sin\theta$, so you can write the coordinates of Q as $(\cos\theta, -\sin\theta)$.

You can now write down the distance PQ, or rather an expression for PQ^2, in two ways.

First, you can use the distance formula in coordinate geometry (see Section 7.1), which gives

$$\begin{aligned}\text{PQ}^2 &= (\cos\theta - \cos\theta)^2 + (\sin\theta - (-\sin\theta))^2 \\ &= 0 + (2\sin\theta)^2 \\ &= 4\sin^2\theta.\end{aligned}$$

Secondly, you can use the cosine rule for the triangle OPQ, which gives

$$\begin{aligned}\text{PQ}^2 &= 1^2 + 1^2 - 2\times 1\times 1\times\cos 2\theta \\ &= 2 - 2\cos 2\theta.\end{aligned}$$

Comparing the two expressions for PQ^2, you will see that

$$4\sin^2\theta = 2 - 2\cos 2\theta.$$

You can divide throughout by 2 and rearrange this equation in the form

$$\cos 2\theta = 1 - 2\sin^2\theta.$$

If you use the identity $\cos^2\theta + \sin^2\theta \equiv 1$, you can replace the number 1 in the formula $\cos 2\theta = 1 - 2\sin^2\theta$ to get

$$\begin{aligned}\cos 2\theta &= \cos^2\theta + \sin^2\theta - 2\sin^2\theta \\ &= \cos^2\theta - \sin^2\theta.\end{aligned}$$

Although Fig. 36.2 is drawn with the angle θ acute, the proof is valid for all angles θ.

So

$$\cos 2\theta \equiv \cos^2\theta - \sin^2\theta.$$

Example 36.2.1

Verify the formula for $\cos 2\theta$ in the cases (a) $\theta = \frac{1}{2}\pi$, (b) $\theta = \frac{1}{6}\pi$.

(a) If $\theta = \frac{1}{2}\pi$, then

$$\cos 2\theta = \cos\pi = -1,$$

and

$$\begin{aligned}\cos^2\theta - \sin^2\theta &= \cos^2\tfrac{1}{2}\pi - \sin^2\tfrac{1}{2}\pi \\ &= 0^2 - 1^2 = -1.\end{aligned}$$

So $\cos 2\theta = \cos^2\theta - \sin^2\theta$ is true when $\theta = \frac{1}{2}\pi$.

(b) If $\theta = \frac{1}{6}\pi$, then

$$\cos 2\theta = \cos\tfrac{1}{3}\pi = \tfrac{1}{2},$$

and

$$\begin{aligned}\cos^2\theta - \sin^2\theta &= \cos^2\tfrac{1}{6}\pi - \sin^2\tfrac{1}{6}\pi \\ &= \left(\tfrac{1}{2}\sqrt{3}\right)^2 - \left(\tfrac{1}{2}\right)^2 \\ &= \tfrac{3}{4} - \tfrac{1}{4} = \tfrac{1}{2}.\end{aligned}$$

So $\cos 2\theta = \cos^2\theta - \sin^2\theta$ is true when $\theta = \frac{1}{6}\pi$.

To find a similar formula to $\cos 2\theta = \cos^2\theta - \sin^2\theta$ for $\sin 2\theta$ is not so easy, but it is not difficult to find a formula when $0 < \theta < \frac{1}{2}\pi$.

In Fig. 36.3, you can write down the area of triangle OPQ in two ways.

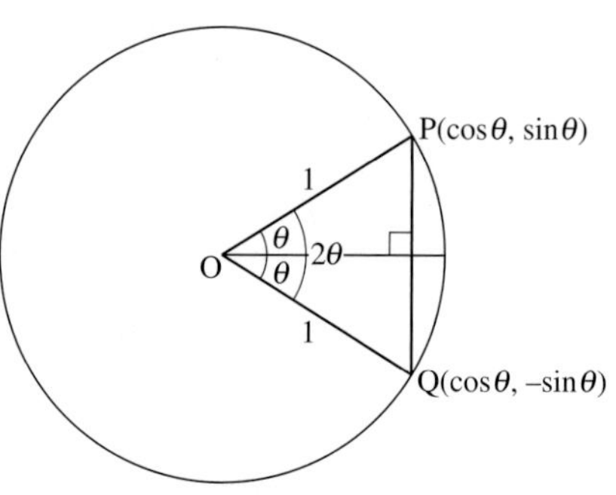

Fig. 36.3

Using the formula $\Delta = \frac{1}{2}bc\sin A$ from Section 16.3 on the whole triangle OPQ,

$$\text{area OPQ} = \tfrac{1}{2} \times 1 \times 1 \times \sin 2\theta = \tfrac{1}{2}\sin 2\theta.$$

If you look at the two right-angled triangles which make up triangle OPQ, they each have a base of $\cos\theta$ and a height of $\sin\theta$, so they each have area $\frac{1}{2} \times \cos\theta \times \sin\theta$.

And as there are two of these triangles,

$$\begin{aligned}\text{area OPQ} &= 2 \times \left(\tfrac{1}{2} \times \cos\theta \times \sin\theta\right) \\ &= \sin\theta\cos\theta.\end{aligned}$$

Equating these two expressions for area, you find $\frac{1}{2}\sin 2\theta = \sin\theta\cos\theta$, or

$$\sin 2\theta = 2\sin\theta\cos\theta.$$

Although this proof only works for values of θ which are acute, the result is true for all angles. So

$$\sin 2\theta \equiv 2\sin\theta\cos\theta.$$

These formulae are called the **double angle formulae**. You should learn them.

$$\begin{aligned}\sin 2\theta &\equiv 2\sin\theta\cos\theta, \\ \cos 2\theta &\equiv \cos^2\theta - \sin^2\theta.\end{aligned}$$

The Pythagoras' identity can be used to produce two other forms for the identity for $\cos 2\theta$, one of which you have seen already. If $\cos^2\theta$ is replaced by $1 - \sin^2\theta$, you get

$$\cos 2\theta \equiv (1 - \sin^2\theta) - \sin^2\theta,$$

that is

$$\cos 2\theta \equiv 1 - 2\sin^2\theta.$$

Alternatively, replace $\sin^2\theta$ by $1 - \cos^2\theta$, to get

$$\cos 2\theta \equiv \cos^2\theta - (1 - \cos^2\theta),$$

that is

$$\cos 2\theta \equiv 2\cos^2\theta - 1.$$

These identities are particularly useful in rearranged forms:

$$1 + \cos 2\theta \equiv 2\cos^2\theta,$$
$$1 - \cos 2\theta \equiv 2\sin^2\theta.$$

Example 36.2.2
Given that $\cos\theta = \frac{1}{3}$, find the exact value of $\cos 2\theta$.

$$\begin{aligned}\cos 2\theta &\equiv 2\cos^2\theta - 1\\ &= 2 \times \left(\tfrac{1}{3}\right)^2 - 1\\ &= 2 \times \tfrac{1}{9} - 1 = -\tfrac{7}{9}.\end{aligned}$$

Example 36.2.3
Given that $\cos\theta = \frac{1}{3}$, find the possible values of $\cos\frac{1}{2}\theta$.

Using $1 + \cos 2\theta \equiv 2\cos^2\theta$, with $\frac{1}{2}\theta$ written in place of θ, gives $1 + \cos\theta \equiv 2\cos^2\frac{1}{2}\theta$. In this case, $\frac{1}{3} + 1 = 2\cos^2\frac{1}{2}\theta$, giving $2\cos^2\frac{1}{2}\theta = \frac{4}{3}$.

This simplifies to $\cos^2\frac{1}{2}\theta = \frac{2}{3}$, so $\cos\frac{1}{2}\theta = \pm\sqrt{\frac{2}{3}} = \pm\frac{1}{3}\sqrt{6}$.

Exercise 36B

1 If $\sin\hat{A} = \frac{2}{3}$ and $\hat{A}$ is obtuse, find the exact values of $\cos\hat{A}$, $\sin 2\hat{A}$, $\cos 2\hat{A}$ and $\tan 2\hat{A}$.

2 If $\cos\hat{B} = \frac{3}{4}$, find the exact values of $\cos 2\hat{B}$ and $\cos\frac{1}{2}\hat{B}$.

3 By writing $\cos x$ in terms of $\frac{1}{2}x$, show that $\dfrac{1-\cos x}{1+\cos x} = \tan^2\frac{1}{2}x$.

4 If $\cos 2\hat{A} = \frac{7}{18}$, find the possible values of $\cos\hat{A}$ and $\sin\hat{A}$.

5 By writing $\tan 2\theta$ as $\dfrac{\sin 2\theta}{\cos 2\theta}$ and using the double angle formulae, show that $\tan 2\theta = \dfrac{2\tan\theta}{1-\tan^2\theta}$.

6 Use the result of Question 5 to find the possible values of $\tan\theta$, given that $\tan 2\theta = \frac{12}{5}$.

7 If $\tan 2\theta = 1$, find the possible values of $\tan\theta$. Hence state the exact value of $\tan 22\frac{1}{2}^\circ$.

37 Trigonometric equations

This chapter is about solving trigonometric equations, giving your solutions in either degrees or in radians. When you have completed it, you should

- be able to find the solutions of simple trigonometric equations in a finite interval
- be able to modify equations so that you can solve them.

37.1 Transforming trigonometrical graphs

You can get a lot of information about the graphs of functions like $y = \sin 2(x - \frac{1}{2}\pi)$ and $\cos 4(x - \frac{1}{4}\pi)$ by using the transformations of Chapter 30. Here is an example.

Example 37.1.1
Transform the graph of $y = \sin x$ into the graph of $y = \sin 2(x - \frac{1}{2}\pi)$.

The graph of $y = \sin x$ (between the two black blobs) has been stretched by a factor $\frac{1}{2}$ in the x-direction to convert it to $y = \sin 2x$. Then it has been translated by $\frac{1}{2}\pi$ in the x-direction to get the graph with equation $y = \sin 2(x - \frac{1}{2}\pi)$.

Fig. 37.1 shows the original graph and the stages to get the final graph.

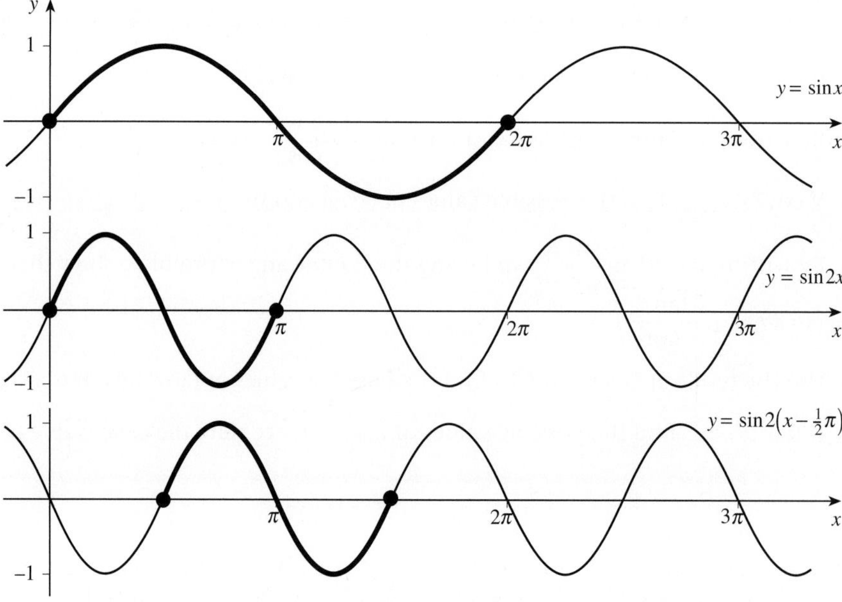

Fig. 37.1

To help you to see the stages, one complete period of the original graph between two dots has been made thicker. The corresponding pieces are also shown on the other two graphs.

Example 37.1.2
Transform the graph of $y = \cos x$ into the graph of $y = -2 + \cos \frac{1}{2}(x - \frac{1}{4}\pi)$.

The graph of $y = \cos x$ is stretched by a factor of 2 in the x-direction to convert the graph to $y = \cos \frac{1}{2}x$. This graph is then translated by $\frac{1}{4}\pi$ in the positive x-direction which converts it to $y = \cos \frac{1}{2}(x - \frac{1}{4}\pi)$. Finally it is translated by -2 in the y-direction which converts it to $y = -2 + \cos \frac{1}{2}(x - \frac{1}{4}\pi)$. Fig. 37.2 shows the original graph and the stages to get the final graph.

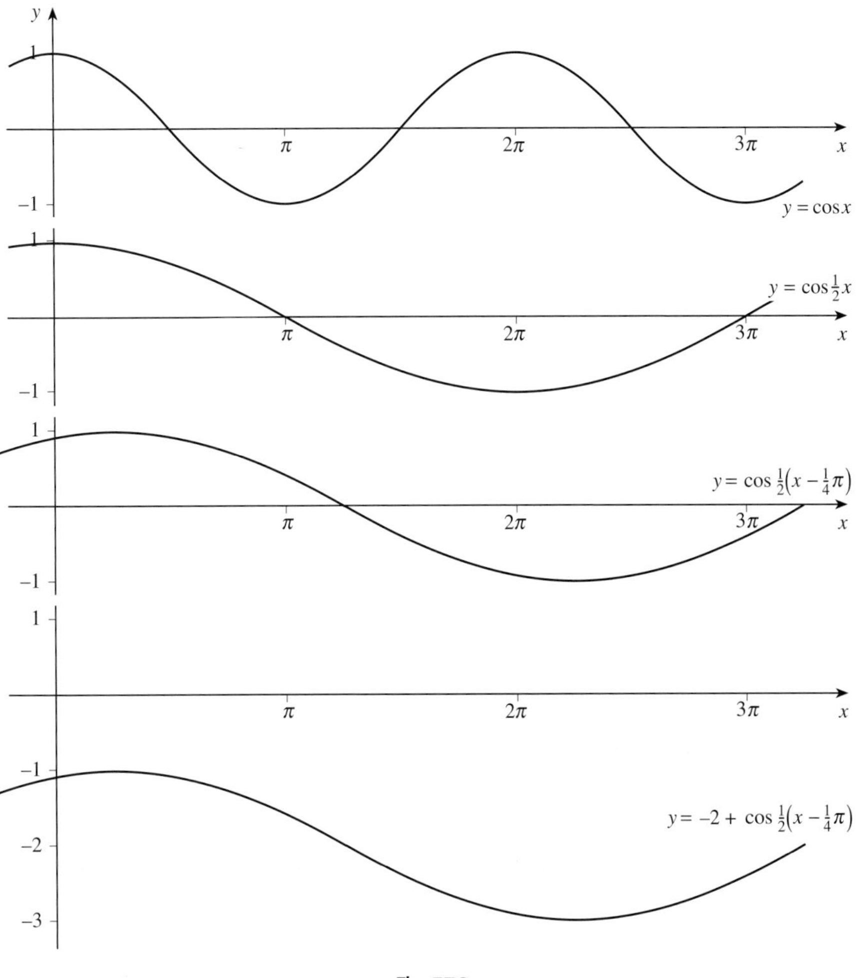

Fig. 37.2

It should not surprise you by now that the graph of $y = a\sin(b(x + c)) + d$ is simply the graph of $y = \sin x$ translated and enlarged in various ways. This gives you information about the maxima and minima of this type of graph.

To get from the graph of $y = \sin x$ to $y = a \sin b(x + c) + d$, or from $y = \cos x$ to $y = a \cos b(x + c) + d$, you carry out in turn

- an x-stretch of factor $\frac{1}{b}$, converting $y = \sin x$ to $y = \sin bx$
- an x-translation of $-c$, converting $y = \sin bx$ to $y = \sin b(x + c)$
- a y-stretch of factor a, converting $y = \sin b(x + c)$ to $y = a \sin b(x + c)$
- a y-translation of d, converting $y = a \sin b(x + c)$ to $y = a \sin b(x + c) + d$.

What can you say about the period of the graph of $y = a \sin b(x + c) + d$? The only one of the transformations which affects the period is the first. Since $y = \sin x$ has period 2π, $y = \sin bx$ has period $\frac{2\pi}{b}$.

The graph of $y = a \cos b(x + c) + d$ also has a period of $\frac{2\pi}{b}$.

The graphs of $y = a \sin b(x + c) + d$ and $y = a \cos b(x + c) + d$ have the same shapes as those of $y = \sin x$ and $y = \cos x$, but are translated and enlarged in various ways.

Their periods are $\frac{2\pi}{b}$.

If you are working in degrees, there are corresponding properties:

The graphs of $y = a \sin b(x + c)^\circ + d$ and $y = a \cos b(x + c)^\circ + d$ have the same shapes as those of $y = \sin x^\circ$ and $y = \cos x^\circ$, but are translated and enlarged in various ways.

Their periods are $\frac{360}{b}$.

Exercise 37A

Without using a calculator, sketch each of the following graphs and state their periods.

1 (a) $y = 1 + \sin x$ (b) $y = 2 \cos x$ (c) $y = 1 - \sin x$

(d) $y = 3 + 2 \cos x$ (e) $y = 2 \cos 2x$ (f) $y = 1 - 2 \sin 3x$

(g) $y = 3 \cos \tfrac{1}{2}x - 4$ (h) $y = 2 \sin 3(x - \pi) + 4$ (i) $y = 3 \cos(2x - 1) - 4$

37.2 Symmetry properties of the graphs of $\cos\theta$, $\sin\theta$ and $\tan\theta$

If you examine the graphs of $\cos\theta$, $\sin\theta$ and $\tan\theta$, you can see that they have many symmetry properties. The graph of $\cos\theta$ is shown in Fig. 37.3.

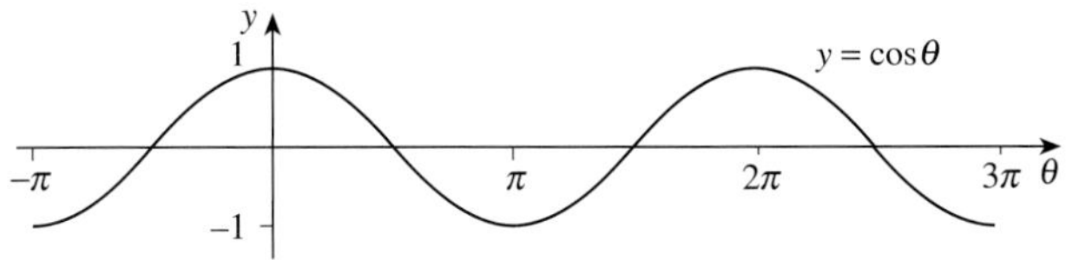

Fig. 37.3

The graph of $\cos\theta$ is symmetrical about the vertical axis. This means that if you replace θ by $-\theta$ the graph is unchanged. Therefore

$$\cos(-\theta) = \cos\theta.$$

This shows that $\cos\theta$ is an **even** function of θ (as defined in Section 8.3).

There are other symmetry properties. For example, if in Fig. 37.3 you translate the graph of $\cos\theta$ by π in the θ-direction, you get the graph of $\cos(\theta - \pi)$ in Fig. 37.4.

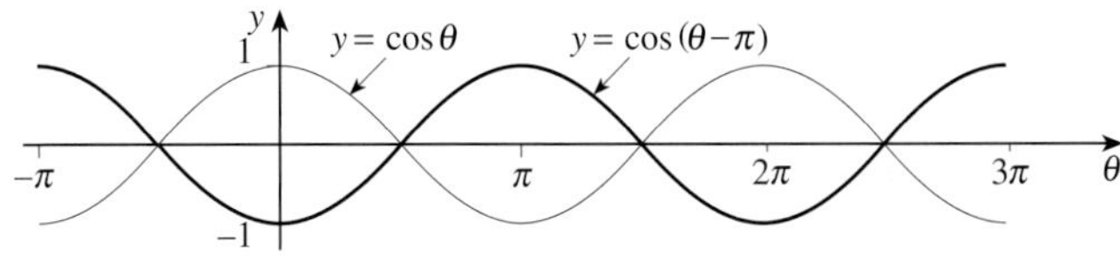

Fig. 37.4

You will notice that the result is the reflection of the $\cos\theta$ graph in the θ-axis, which is the graph of $-\cos\theta$. So

$$\cos(\theta - \pi) = -\cos\theta.$$

This is called the **translation** property.

There is one more useful symmetry property. Using the even and translation properties,

$$\begin{aligned}\cos(\pi - \theta) &= \cos(-(\theta - \pi))\\ &= \cos(\theta - \pi)\\ &= -\cos\theta.\end{aligned}$$

This is called the **supplementary** property. Angles, like θ and $\pi - \theta$, which add to π are called supplementary angles.

There are similar properties for the graph of $\sin\theta$, which is shown in Fig. 37.5.

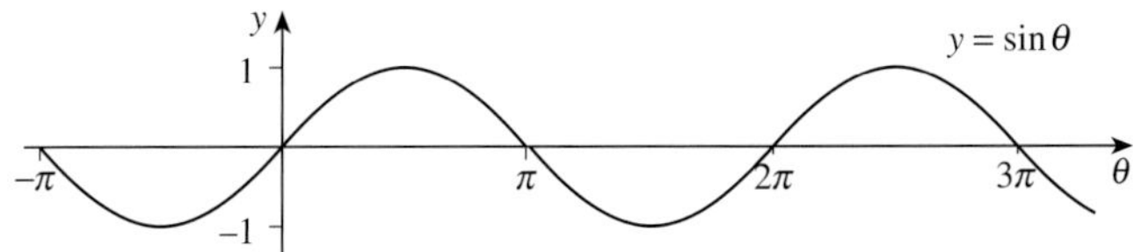

Fig. 37.5

You are asked to prove them in Exercise 37B. Their proofs are like those for the cosine.

Here are summaries of these properties, using first radians and then degrees.

The functions $\cos\theta$ and $\sin\theta$ have the following properties.

Periodic property:	$\cos(\theta - 2\pi) = \cos\theta$	$\sin(\theta - 2\pi) = \sin\theta$
Even/odd property:	$\cos(-\theta) = \cos\theta$	$\sin(-\theta) = -\sin\theta$
Translation property:	$\cos(\theta - \pi) = -\cos\theta$	$\sin(\theta - \pi) = -\sin\theta$
Supplementary property:	$\cos(\pi - \theta) = -\cos\theta$	$\sin(\pi - \theta) = \sin\theta$

The functions $\cos\theta^\circ$ and $\sin\theta^\circ$ have the following properties.

Periodic property:	$\cos(\theta - 360)^\circ = \cos\theta^\circ$	$\sin(\theta - 360)^\circ = \sin\theta^\circ$
Even/odd property:	$\cos(-\theta)^\circ = \cos\theta^\circ$	$\sin(-\theta)^\circ = -\sin\theta^\circ$
Translation property:	$\cos(\theta - 180)^\circ = -\cos\theta^\circ$	$\sin(\theta - 180)^\circ = -\sin\theta^\circ$
Supplementary property:	$\cos(180 - \theta)^\circ = -\cos\theta^\circ$	$\sin(180 - \theta)^\circ = \sin\theta^\circ$

If you refer back to the graph of $\tan\theta$ in Fig. 28.4, and think in the same way as with the cosine and sine graphs, you can obtain similar results:

The function $\tan\theta$ has the following properties.

Periodic property:	$\tan(\theta - \pi) = \tan\theta$
Odd property:	$\tan(-\theta) = -\tan\theta$
Supplementary property:	$\tan(\pi - \theta) = -\tan\theta$

The function $\tan\theta^\circ$ has the following properties.

Periodic property:	$\tan(\theta - 180)^\circ = \tan\theta^\circ$
Odd property:	$\tan(-\theta)^\circ = -\tan\theta^\circ$
Supplementary property:	$\tan(180 - \theta)^\circ = -\tan\theta^\circ$

Note that the period of the graph of $\tan\theta$ is π, and that the translation property of $\tan\theta$ is the same as the periodic property.

There are also relations between $\cos\theta$ and $\sin\theta$. One is shown in Example 37.2.1.

Example 37.2.1
Establish the property that $\cos\left(\frac{1}{2}\pi - \theta\right) = \sin\theta$.

This is easy if $0 < \theta < \frac{1}{2}\pi$: consider a right-angled triangle. But it can be shown for any value of θ.

If you translate the graph of $\cos\theta$ by $\frac{1}{2}\pi$ in the direction of the positive θ-axis, you obtain the graph of $\sin\theta$, so $\cos\left(\theta - \frac{1}{2}\pi\right) = \sin\theta$. And since the cosine is an even function, $\cos\left(\frac{1}{2}\pi - \theta\right) = \cos\left(-\left(\frac{1}{2}\pi - \theta\right)\right) = \cos\left(\theta - \frac{1}{2}\pi\right)$. Therefore $\cos\left(\frac{1}{2}\pi - \theta\right) = \sin\theta$.

Another property, which you are asked to prove in Exercise 37B, is $\sin\left(\frac{1}{2}\pi - \theta\right) = \cos\theta$.

Exercise 37B

1 Use the various symmetry properties of the sine, cosine and tangent functions to establish the following results, given in radian notation.

(a) $\sin\left(\frac{1}{2}\pi - \theta\right) = \cos\theta$ (b) $\sin\left(\frac{3}{2}\pi + \theta\right) = -\cos\theta$

(c) $\sin\left(\frac{1}{2}\pi + \theta\right) = \cos\theta$ (d) $\cos\left(\frac{1}{2}\pi + \theta\right) = -\sin\theta$

2 Use the various symmetry properties of the sine, cosine and tangent functions to establish the following results, given in degree notation.

(a) $\tan(\theta - 180)^\circ = \tan\theta^\circ$ (b) $\cos(180 - \theta)^\circ = \cos(180 + \theta)^\circ$

(c) $\tan(360 - \theta)^\circ = -\tan(180 + \theta)^\circ$ (d) $\sin(-\theta - 90)^\circ = -\cos\theta^\circ$

3 Sketch the graphs of $y = \tan\theta$ and $y = \dfrac{1}{\tan\theta}$ on the same set of axes. Show that the graph of $y = \tan\left(\theta - \frac{1}{2}\pi\right)$ can be transformed to the graph of $y = \tan\left(\frac{1}{2}\pi - \theta\right)$ by a simple transformation, which you should write down.

Hence show that $\tan\left(\frac{1}{2}\pi - \theta\right) = \dfrac{1}{\tan\theta}$.

4 Establish the symmetry properties of $\sin\theta$ by using the graph.

37.3 Solving equations involving trigonometric functions

You have two essentially different methods that you can use to solve trigonometric equations. You can use the graphical features of your calculator, but you will need to use them several times in order to get all the solutions.

The alternative is a method which does not rely on the calculator's graphical features.

In the work which follows, some of the equations will require you to work in radians, and others will be in degrees.

Solving the equation $\cos\theta = k$ or $\cos\theta^\circ = k$

The equation $\cos\theta = k$ only has a solution if k lies between -1 and 1 (inclusive). In general, there are two roots in every interval of 2π; but if $k = \pm 1$ there is only one root.

Fig. 37.6 illustrates this using the graph of $\cos\theta$ with a negative value of k.

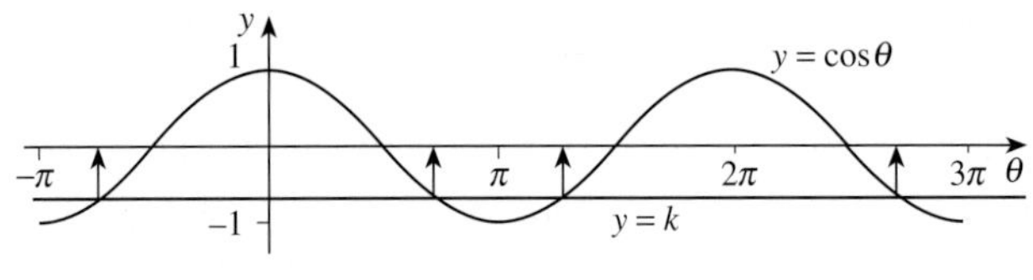

Fig. 37.6

To find an angle θ which satisfies the equation you can use the [$\cos^{-1}$] key on your calculator. Make sure that the calculator is in the appropriate mode, either degrees or radians. It then gives the simplest value of θ such that $\cos\theta = k$.

The calculator will only give you one answer. Usually you want to find all the roots of $\cos\theta = k$ in a given interval (probably one of width 2π). The problem then is how to find all the other roots in your required interval.

There are three main steps in solving the equation $\cos\theta = k$ or $\cos\theta^\circ = k$.

> Make sure your calculator is in the correct mode.
>
> **Step 1** Find $\cos^{-1} k$.
>
> **Step 2** Use the symmetry property $\cos(-\theta) = \cos\theta$ to find another root.
>
> **Step 3** Add or subtract multiples of 2π or 360 to find all the roots in the required interval.

Example 37.3.1

Solve the equation $\cos\theta = -0.7$, giving all the roots in the interval $0 \le \theta \le 2\pi$, correct to 2 decimal places.

Fig. 37.7 shows the graphs of $y = \cos\theta$ and $y = -0.7$.

Step 1 $\cos^{-1}(-0.7) = 2.346\ldots$. This gives one root in the interval $0 \le \theta \le 2\pi$.

Step 2 Use the symmetry property $\cos(-\theta) = \cos\theta$ to show that $-2.346\ldots$ is another root. Note that $-2.346\ldots$ is not in the required interval.

Step 3 Adding 2π (the period of $\cos\theta$) gives $-2.346\ldots + 2\pi = 3.936\ldots$, a root now in the required interval.

The roots of the equation $\cos\theta = -0.7$ in $0 \le \theta \le 2\pi$ are 2.35 and 3.94, correct to 2 decimal places.

From Fig. 37.7 you can see that the roots of the equation $\cos\theta = -0.7$ are just smaller and just greater than π, which suggests that the algebra is correct.

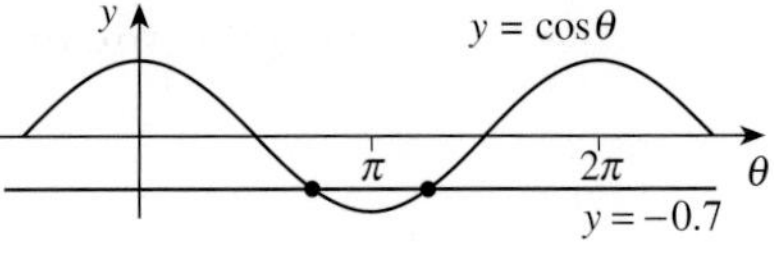

Fig. 37.7

Here is a similar example solved in degrees.

Example 37.3.2
Solve the equation $\cos\theta^\circ = \frac{1}{3}$, giving all roots in the interval $0 \le \theta \le 360$ correct to 1 decimal place.

Step 1 The calculator gives $\cos^{-1}\frac{1}{3}$ as 70.52… . This is one root in the interval.

Step 2 Use the symmetry property $\cos(-\theta)^\circ = \cos\theta^\circ$ to show that $-70.52...$ is another root. Note that $-70.52...$ is not in the required interval.

Step 3 Add 360 to obtain $-70.52... + 360 = 289.47...$, which is in $0 \le \theta \le 360$.

Therefore the roots in the interval $0 \le \theta \le 360$ are 70.5 and 289.5, correct to 1 decimal place.

There is no need to sketch the graph or to display it on your calculator, but it can be a helpful check on the final answers.

Example 37.3.3
Solve the equation $\cos 3\theta = 0.3$, giving all the roots in the interval $-\pi \le \theta \le \pi$, correct to 2 decimal places.

Let $3\theta = \phi$, so that the equation becomes $\cos\phi = 0.3$.

As θ lies in the interval $-\pi \le \theta \le \pi$, $\phi = 3\theta$ lies in the interval $-3\pi \le \phi \le 3\pi$ which is $-9.424... \le \phi \le 9.424...$.

The first part of the solution is to solve $\cos\phi = 0.3$ for $-9.424... \le \phi \le 9.424...$.

Step 1 $\cos^{-1} 0.3 = 1.266...$. This is one root in $-9.424... \le \phi \le 9.424...$.

Step 2 Using the fact that the cosine function is even, another root is $-1.266...$.

Step 3 Adding 2π to and subtracting 2π from 1.266… gives 7.549… and $-5.017...$ as the other roots, while adding and subtracting 2π to $-1.266...$ gives 5.017… and $-7.549...$ which are also in the required interval.

Since $\theta = \frac{1}{3}\phi$, the roots of the original equation are -2.52, -1.67, -0.42, 0.42, 1.67, 2.52, correct to 2 decimal places.

Fig. 37.8 shows the graphs of $y = \cos 3\theta$, which is the graph of $y = \cos\theta$ stretched by the factor $\frac{1}{3}$ in the x-direction, and $y = 0.3$. You can see that there are six roots symmetrically placed.

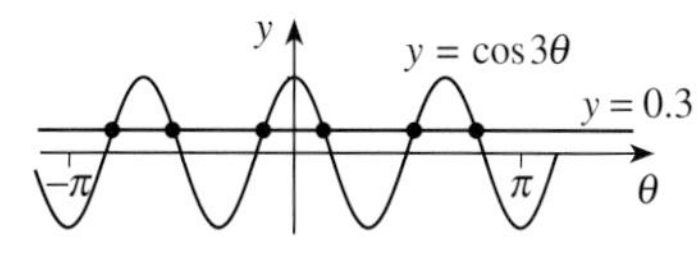

Fig. 37.8

Solving the equation $\sin\theta = k$ or $\sin\theta^\circ = k$
The equation $\sin\theta = k$, where $-1 \le k \le 1$, is solved in a way similar to that for solving $\cos\theta = k$. The only difference is that the symmetry property for $\sin\theta$ is $\sin(\pi - \theta) = \sin\theta$.

Make sure your calculator is in the correct mode.

Step 1 Find $\sin^{-1} k$.

Step 2 Use the symmetry property $\sin(\pi - \theta) = \sin\theta$ or $\sin(180 - \theta)^\circ = \sin\theta^\circ$ to find another root.

Step 3 Add or subtract multiples of 2π or 360 to find all the roots in the required interval.

Example 37.3.4
Solve the equation $\sin\theta = -0.2$, giving all the roots in the interval $-\pi \le \theta \le \pi$, correct to 2 decimal places.

Step 1 $\sin^{-1}(-0.2) = -0.201\ldots$. This is one root in the interval $-\pi \le \theta \le \pi$.

Step 2 Another root of the equation is $\pi - (-0.201\ldots) = 3.342\ldots$, but this is not in the required interval.

Step 3 Subtracting 2π gives $-2.940\ldots$, the other root in $-\pi \le \theta \le \pi$.

Therefore the roots of $\sin\theta = -0.2$ in $-\pi \le \theta \le \pi$ are -2.94 and -0.20, correct to 2 decimal places.

Example 37.3.5
Solve the equation $\sin\theta^\circ = -0.7$, giving all the roots in the interval $-180 \le \theta \le 180$ correct to 1 decimal place.

Step 1 The calculator gives $\sin^{-1}(-0.7)$ as $-44.42\ldots$. This is one root in the interval $-180 \le \theta \le 180$.

Step 2 Use the symmetry property $\sin(180 - \theta)^\circ = \sin\theta^\circ$ to show that $180 - (-44.42\ldots) = 224.42\ldots$ is another root. Unfortunately it is not in the required interval.

Step 3 Subtract 360 to obtain $224.42\ldots - 360 = -135.57\ldots$, which is in the required interval.

Therefore the roots in the interval $-180 \le \theta \le 180$ are -44.4 and -135.6, correct to 1 decimal place.

Example 37.3.6
Solve the equation $\sin \frac{1}{3}\theta^\circ = \frac{1}{2}\sqrt{3}$, giving all the roots in the interval $0 \le \theta \le 360$.

Let $\frac{1}{3}\theta = \phi$, so that the equation becomes $\sin\phi^\circ = \frac{1}{2}\sqrt{3}$, with roots required in the interval $0 \le \phi \le 120$.

Step 1 The calculator gives $\sin^{-1}\left(\frac{1}{2}\sqrt{3}\right)$ as 60. This is one root in the interval $0 \le \phi \le 120$.

Step 2 Another root is $180 - 60 = 120$, which is still in the required interval.

Step 3 Adding and subtracting multiples of 360 will not give any more roots in the interval $0 \le \phi \le 120$.

Therefore the roots of $\sin\phi^\circ = \frac{1}{2}\sqrt{3}$ in $0 \le \phi \le 120$ are 60 and 120.

Returning to the original equation, since $\theta = 3\phi$, the roots are $\theta = 180$ and 360.

Solving the equation tan $\theta = k$ or tan $\theta^\circ = k$

The equation $\tan\theta = k$ is also solved in a similar way. Note that there is generally one root for every interval of π. Other roots can be found from the periodic property, $\tan(\theta - \pi) = \tan\theta$.

> Make sure your calculator is in the correct mode.
>
> **Step 1** Find $\tan^{-1} k$.
>
> **Step 2** Add or subtract multiples of π or 180 to find the roots in the required interval.

Example 37.3.7

Solve the equation $\tan\theta = -2$, giving all the roots correct to 2 decimal places in the interval $0 \le \theta \le 2\pi$.

Step 1 The calculator gives $\tan^{-1}(-2)$ as $-1.107...$. Unfortunately, this root is not in the required interval.

Step 2 Add multiples of π to get roots in the required interval. This gives 2.034... and 5.176... .

Therefore the roots of $\tan\theta = -2$ in $0 \le \theta \le 2\pi$ are 2.03 and 5.18, correct to 2 decimal places.

Example 37.3.8

Solve the equation $\cos(\theta - 25)^\circ = -0.95$, giving all the roots correct to 1 decimal place in the interval $-180 \le \theta \le 180$.

Let $\phi = \theta - 25$, so that the equation becomes $\cos\phi^\circ = -0.95$, with roots required in the interval $-180 \le \phi + 25 \le 180$, which is $-205 \le \phi \le 155$.

Step 1 The calculator gives $\cos^{-1}(-0.95)$ as 161.8.... This root is not in the required interval for ϕ.

Step 2 Using the symmetry property $\cos(-\phi)^\circ = \cos\phi^\circ$ another root is $-161.8...$, which is in the required interval for ϕ.

Step 3 Subtracting 360 from the first root gives $161.8... - 360 = -198.1...$, which is in the required interval for ϕ.

The roots for ϕ are therefore $-198.1...$ and $-161.8...$, so the roots for θ, which is $\phi + 25$, are $-173.1...$ and $-136.8...$.

Therefore the roots of $\cos(\theta - 25)^\circ = -0.95$ in $-180 \le \theta \le 180$ are -173.2 and -136.8, correct to 1 decimal place.

Below are two examples, one in degrees and one in radians, which show applications of the trigonometric functions.

Example 37.3.9

The height in metres of the water in a harbour is given approximately by the formula $d = 6 + 3\cos 30t^\circ$ where t is the time measured in hours from noon. Find the time after noon when the height of the water is 7.5 metres for the second time.

To find when the height is 7.5 metres, solve $6 + 3\cos 30t^\circ = 7.5$. This gives $3\cos 30t^\circ = 7.5 - 6 = 1.5$, or $\cos 30t^\circ = 0.5$. After substituting $\phi = 30t$, the equation reduces to $\cos\phi^\circ = 0.5$.

Now $\cos 60^\circ = 0.5$, but 60 gives only the first root, $t = 2$. So, using the symmetry property of the cos function, another root of $\cos\phi^\circ = 0.5$ is -60. Adding 360 gives $\phi = 300$ as the second root of $\cos\phi^\circ = 0.5$. Thus $30t = 300$, and $t = 10$.

The water is at height 7.5 metres for the second time at 10.00 p.m.

Example 37.3.10

A model for the height h metres of the tide above a harbour entrance t hours after noon is given by the equation $h = 6 + 4\sin\frac{1}{2}t$. A boat can enter the harbour when the height of the tide is 8 metres. Find

(a) the first time after noon that a boat can enter the harbour,

(b) the length of time for which the boat can enter the harbour.

(a) As the sine graph is increasing the boat can enter the harbour when $h = 8$, so

$$8 = 6 + 4\sin\tfrac{1}{2}t,$$

which reduces to

$$\sin\tfrac{1}{2}t = 0.5.$$

The first positive solution of this equation is given by $\frac{1}{2}t = \frac{1}{6}\pi$, that is $t = \frac{1}{3}\pi = 1.047\ldots$.

The boat can enter the harbour at 1.05 hours, that is at 1.03 pm.

(b) The second root of the equation $8 = 6 + 4\sin\frac{1}{2}t$ is given by $\frac{1}{2}t = \pi - \frac{1}{6}\pi$, that is by $t = \frac{5}{3}\pi = 5.235\ldots$.

The boat can enter the harbour the harbour between 1.047... and 5.235... hours, that is, for 4.188... hours, or 4 hours 11 minutes.

Exercise 37C

1 Find, correct to 2 decimal places, the two smallest positive values of θ for which

(a) $\cos\theta = 0.81$, (b) $\sin\theta = 0.12$, (c) $\tan\theta = 4.1$.

2 Find, correct to 1 decimal place, the two smallest positive values of θ for which

(a) $\cos\theta^\circ = -0.84$, (b) $\sin\theta^\circ = -0.84$, (c) $\tan\theta^\circ = -0.32$.

3 Find the roots in the interval $-\pi < t \le \pi$ of each of the following equations.

(a) $\cos 3t = \frac{3}{4}$ (b) $\sin 2t = -0.42$ (c) $\tan 5t = 0.7$

4 Find the roots in the interval $-180 \le x \le 180$ of each of the following equations.

(a) $\cos 3x^\circ = \frac{2}{3}$ (b) $\tan 2x^\circ = -3$ (c) $\sin 3x^\circ = -0.2$

5 Find the roots (if there are any) in the interval $-\pi < \theta \le \pi$ of the following equations.

(a) $\cos \frac{1}{2}\theta = \frac{1}{3}$ (b) $\tan \frac{2}{3}\theta = -5$ (c) $\sin \frac{1}{5}\theta = -\frac{1}{5}$

(d) $\sin(\theta + 0.1) = 0.4$ (e) $\cos(\theta - 0.2) = 0.6$ (f) $\tan(\theta - 0.5) = 0.4$

6 Without using a calculator, find the exact roots of the following equations, if there are any, giving your answers in the interval $0 < t \le 360$.

(a) $\sin 2t^\circ = \frac{1}{2}$ (b) $\tan 2t^\circ = 0$ (c) $\cos 3t^\circ = \frac{1}{2}\sqrt{3}$

(d) $\tan \frac{3}{2}t^\circ = -\sqrt{3}$ (e) $\sin \frac{1}{2}t^\circ = 1$ (f) $\cos \frac{1}{5}t^\circ = 0$

7 At a certain latitude in the northern hemisphere, the number d of hours of daylight in each day of the year is taken to be $d = A + B\sin kt^\circ$, where A, B, k are positive constants and t is the time in days after the spring equinox.

(a) Assuming that the number of hours of daylight follows an annual cycle of 365 days, find the value of k, giving your answer correct to 3 decimal places.

(b) Given also that the shortest and longest days have 6 and 18 hours of daylight respectively, state the values of A and B. Find, in hours and minutes, the amount of daylight on New Year's Day, which is 80 days before the spring equinox.

(c) A town at this latitude holds a fair twice a year on those days having exactly 10 hours of daylight. Find, in relation to the spring equinox, which two days these are.

8 The population, P, of a certain type of bird on a remote island varies during the course of a year according to feeding, breeding, migratory seasons and predator interactions. An ornithologist doing research into bird numbers for this species attempts to model the population on the island with the annually periodic equation $P = N - C\cos\omega t$, where N, C and ω are constants, and t is the time in weeks, with $t = 0$ representing midnight on the first of January.

(a) Taking the period of this function to be 50 weeks, find the value of ω.

(b) Use the equation to describe, in terms of N and C,

(i) the number of birds of this species on the island at the start of each year,

(ii) the maximum number of these birds, and the time of year when this occurs.

37.4 Other trigonometric equations

You have already met the following identities in Sections 36.1 and 36.2.

For all values of θ:

$$\tan\theta \equiv \frac{\sin\theta}{\cos\theta}, \quad \text{provided that } \cos\theta \neq 0,$$

$$\cos^2\theta + \sin^2\theta \equiv 1,$$

$$\cos 2\theta \equiv \cos^2\theta - \sin^2\theta,$$
$$\sin 2\theta \equiv 2\sin\theta\cos\theta.$$

These identities sometimes enable you to transform an equation which contains two or more different trigonometric functions into an equation which has just one function.

Example 37.4.1
Solve the equation $\sin\theta = 2\cos\theta$, giving all the solutions in the interval $0 \leq \theta \leq 2\pi$.

As $\dfrac{\sin\theta}{\cos\theta} \equiv \tan\theta$, you can divide both sides by $\cos\theta$ to get the equation $\tan\theta = 2$.
Then, using the method of the previous section, $\theta = 1.107...$ or $4.248...$.

The roots are 1.11 and 4.25, correct to 2 decimal places.

Example 37.4.2
Solve the equation $3\cos^2\theta^\circ + 4\sin\theta^\circ = 4$, giving all the roots in the interval $-180 < \theta \leq 180$ correct to 1 decimal place.

As it stands you cannot solve this equation, but if you replace $\cos^2\theta^\circ$ by $1 - \sin^2\theta^\circ$ you obtain the equation

$$3(1 - \sin^2\theta^\circ) + 4\sin\theta^\circ = 4,$$

which reduces to $\quad 3\sin^2\theta^\circ - 4\sin\theta^\circ + 1 = 0.$
This is a quadratic equation in $\sin\theta^\circ$, which you can solve using factors:

$$(3\sin\theta^\circ - 1)(\sin\theta^\circ - 1) = 0, \text{ giving } \sin\theta^\circ = \tfrac{1}{3} \text{ or } \sin\theta^\circ = 1.$$

If $\sin\theta^\circ = \frac{1}{3}$, there are two roots. The calculator gives one root as 19.47... . The other root, obtained from the symmetry of $\sin\theta^\circ$, is $180 - 19.47... = 160.52...$. If $\sin\theta^\circ = 1$, there is only one root, $\theta = 90$.

So the roots are 19.5, 90 and 160.5, correct to 1 decimal place.

Example 37.4.3
Without using a calculator, solve the equation $\cos 2\theta + 3\sin\theta = 2$, giving all the roots in the interval $-\pi \leq \theta \leq \pi$ as multiples of π.

Using the identity $\cos 2\theta \equiv 1 - 2\sin^2\theta$ from Section 36.2, you can write the equation $\cos 2\theta + 3\sin\theta = 2$ in the form

$$1 - 2\sin^2\theta + 3\sin\theta = 2, \qquad \text{or} \qquad 2\sin^2\theta - 3\sin\theta + 1 = 0.$$

This can be factorised as $(2\sin\theta - 1)(\sin\theta - 1) = 0$.

So $\sin\theta = \frac{1}{2}$ or $\sin\theta = 1$.

If $\sin\theta = \frac{1}{2}$, $\theta = \frac{1}{6}\pi$ or $\theta = \frac{5}{6}\pi$, and if $\sin\theta = 1$, $\theta = \frac{1}{2}\pi$.

The roots are $\frac{1}{6}\pi$, $\frac{1}{2}\pi$ and $\frac{5}{6}\pi$.

Example 37.4.4
Solve the equation $2\sin 2\theta^\circ = \sin\theta^\circ$ such that $0 \le \theta \le 360$.

Using the identity $\sin 2\theta^\circ \equiv 2\sin\theta^\circ\cos\theta^\circ$,

$$\begin{aligned} 2 \times 2\sin\theta^\circ\cos\theta^\circ &= \sin\theta^\circ \\ 4\sin\theta^\circ\cos\theta^\circ &= \sin\theta^\circ \\ \sin\theta^\circ(4\cos\theta^\circ - 1) &= 0. \end{aligned}$$

At least one of these factors must be 0. Therefore either

$\sin\theta^\circ = 0$, giving $\theta = 0, 180, 360$

or $4\cos\theta^\circ - 1 = 0$, giving $\cos\theta^\circ = 0.25$, so $\theta = 75.52...$ or $284.47...$.

Therefore the required roots are $\theta = 0, 75.5, 180, 284.5, 360$ correct to 1 decimal place.

Note that if you go straight from $4\sin\theta^\circ\cos\theta^\circ = \sin\theta^\circ$ to $4\cos\theta^\circ = 1$ by dividing both sides by $\sin\theta^\circ$ you may be dividing by 0, which is not allowed. You would then miss the solutions corresponding to $\sin\theta^\circ = 0$.

Exercise 37D

1 Solve the equation $\sin^2\theta^\circ = 3\cos^2\theta^\circ$, giving all roots between 0 and 180.

2 Solve the following equations for θ, giving all the roots in the interval $0 \le \theta \le 360$ correct to the nearest 0.1, where appropriate.

(a) $4\sin^2\theta^\circ - 1 = 0$ (b) $4\sin^2\theta^\circ\cos\theta^\circ = \tan^2\theta^\circ$

(c) $4\cos^2\theta^\circ + 3\sin\theta^\circ = 4$ (d) $10\sin^2\theta^\circ - 5\cos^2\theta^\circ + 2 = 4\sin\theta^\circ$

3 Without using a calculator, solve the following equations giving your answers as exact multiples of π in the interval $0 \le \theta \le 2\pi$.

(a) $\cos^2\theta + \sin\theta + 1 = 0$ (b) $3 - 3\cos\theta = 2\sin^2\theta$

(c) $\cos^2\theta + \cos\theta = \sin^2\theta$ (d) $\sin^2\theta + 2\cos^2\theta = 2$

4 Find all values of θ, $-180 < \theta < 180$, for which $2\tan\theta^\circ - 3 = \dfrac{2}{\tan\theta^\circ}$.

5 Solve these equations for values of θ between 0 and 2π inclusive, giving non-exact answers correct to 2 decimal places. In each case use trigonometric identities and then check your results using a calculator and its 'intersect' facility.

(a) $\cos 2\theta + 3 + 4\cos\theta = 0$ (b) $2\cos 2\theta + 1 + \sin\theta = 0$

Review exercise 12

1 Write down the period of each of the following.

(a) $\sin x^\circ$ (b) $\tan 2x^\circ$ (OCR)

2 Find the roots (if there are any) in the interval $-\pi < \theta \le \pi$ of the following equations.

(a) $\tan\theta = 2\cos\theta$ (b) $\sin^2\theta = 2\cos\theta$ (c) $\sin^2\theta = 2\cos^2\theta$

3 Solve the following equations for θ, giving your answers in the interval $0 \le \theta \le 360$.

(a) $\tan\theta^\circ = 0.4$ (b) $\sin 2\theta^\circ = 0.4$ (OCR)

4 Solve the equation $3\cos 2x^\circ = 2$, giving all the solutions in the interval $0 \le x \le 180$ correct to the nearest 0.1. (OCR)

5 Find, either to 2 decimal places or an exact multiple of π, all values of x in the interval $-\pi < x \le \pi$ satisfying the following equations.

(a) $\sin x = -0.16$ (b) $\cos x(1 + \sin x) = 0$ (c) $\sin 2x = 0.23$

6 Solve $3\sin^2\theta + 4\cos\theta = 4$, giving all the roots, correct to 2 decimal places, in $0 \le \theta \le 2\pi$.

Examination questions

1 Consider the equation $3\cos 2x + \sin x = 1$.

(a) Write this equation in the form $f(x) = 0$, where $f(x) = p\sin^2 x + q\sin x + r$, and p, q and $r \in \mathbb{Z}$.

(b) Factorise $f(x)$.

(c) Write down the number of solutions of $f(x) = 0$, for $0 \le x \le 2\pi$. (© IBO 2005)

2 Consider $y = \sin\left(x + \frac{1}{9}\pi\right)$.

(a) The graph of y intersects the x-axis at point A. Find the coordinates of A, where $0 \le x \le \pi$.

(b) Solve the equation $\sin\left(x + \frac{1}{9}\pi\right) = -\frac{1}{2}$, for $0 \le x \le 2\pi$. (© IBO 2005)

3 Solve the equation $2\cos^2 x = \sin 2x$ for $0 \le x \le \pi$, giving your answers in terms of π. (© IBO 2004)

4 Let $f(x) = \sin 2x$ and $g(x) = \sin(0.5x)$.

(a) Write down (i) the minimum value of the function f, (ii) the period of the function g.

(b) Consider the equation $f(x) = g(x)$. Find the number of solutions to this equation, for $0 \le x \le \frac{3}{2}\pi$. (© IBO 2002)

5 Consider the trigonometric equation $2\sin^2 x^\circ = 1 + \cos x^\circ$.

(a) Write this equation in the form $f(x) = 0$, where $f(x) = a\cos^2 x^\circ + b\cos x^\circ + c$, and $a, b, c \in \mathbb{Z}$.

(b) Factorise $f(x)$. (c) Solve $f(x) = 0$ for $0 \le x \le 360$. (© IBO 2002)

38 The chain rule

The chain rule is a more general rule for differentiation than that described in Chapter 31. When you have completed the chapter, you should

- be able to differentiate composite functions.

38.1 Differentiating composite functions

The rule for differentiating $f(ax+b)$ given in Chapter 31 was justified by transforming the graph of $y = f(x)$ to that of $y = f(ax+b)$ (see Section 31.3). But you could also think of $x \mapsto f(ax+b)$ as a composite function:

$$x \to \text{[linear function]} \to ax+b = u \to [f] \to f(u) = y.$$

The derivative for the linear function $u = ax+b$ is $\frac{du}{dx} = a$, a constant. The derivative for the function $y = f(u)$ is $\frac{dy}{du} = f'(u)$. What the rule says is that the derivative $\frac{dy}{dx}$ is $a \times f'(ax+b)$, which is the product of $\frac{du}{dx}$ and $\frac{dy}{du}$.

In Chapter 31 $f'(u)$ was written as $g(u)$, the gradient function. The main reason for this was to make it easier to write the rule for integration. It is not necessary in this chapter, which is only about differentiation. So here the notation $f'(u)$ will be used; $f'(ax+b)$ means the value of $f'(u)$ with $ax+b$ written in place of u. The letter g has a different meaning in this chapter.

The chain rule states that $\frac{dy}{dx}$ is still the product of $\frac{du}{dx}$ and $\frac{dy}{du}$ when the linear function $u = ax+b$ is replaced by any function $u = g(x)$:

$$x \to [g] \to g(x) = u \to [f] \to f(u) = y.$$

Then the derivative of the composite function $f \circ g$ is the product of the derivatives $g'(x)$ and $f'(u) = f'(g(x))$. You will probably find this easiest to use and remember in $\frac{dy}{dx}$ notation.

The chain rule

If $y = f(u)$, where $u = g(x)$, the derivative of the composite function $f(g(x))$ (that is, $f \circ g(x)$) is

$$g'(x) \times f'(g(x)).$$

That is,

$$\frac{dy}{dx} = \frac{du}{dx} \times \frac{dy}{du}.$$

Example 38.1.1

Differentiate $y = (1 + x^2)^3$ with respect to x.

The composite function is described by the scheme

$$x \to [g] \to 1 + x^2 = u \to [f] \to u^3 = y.$$

That is, $u = 1 + x^2$ and $y = u^3$.

Then $\dfrac{du}{dx} = 2x$ and $\dfrac{dy}{du} = 3u^2 = 3(1 + x^2)^2$.

So $$\frac{dy}{dx} = \frac{du}{dx} \times \frac{dy}{du} = 2x \times 3(1 + x^2)^2 = 6x(1 + x^2)^2.$$

In Example 38.1.1 you could of course have found $\dfrac{dy}{dx}$ by using the binomial theorem to expand $(1 + x^2)^3$. This gives $y = 1 + 3x^2 + 3x^4 + x^6$.

Then $$\frac{dy}{dx} = 6x + 12x^3 + 6x^5 = 6x(1 + 2x^2 + x^4) = 6x(1 + x^2)^2.$$

But often the chain rule is the only possible method. Example 38.1.2 shows how to differentiate three such functions.

Example 38.1.2

Find $\dfrac{dy}{dx}$ when (a) $y = \ln(1 + x^2)$, (b) $y = e^{-x^2}$, (c) $y = \sqrt{1 - x^2}$.

(a) Write $u = 1 + x^2$, so $y = \ln u$.

Then $\dfrac{du}{dx} = 2x$ and $\dfrac{dy}{du} = \dfrac{1}{u} = \dfrac{1}{1 + x^2}$.

So $$\frac{dy}{dx} = \frac{du}{dx} \times \frac{dy}{du} = 2x \times \frac{1}{1 + x^2} = \frac{2x}{1 + x^2}.$$

(b) Write $u = -x^2$, so $y = e^u$.

Then $\dfrac{du}{dx} = -2x$ and $\dfrac{dy}{du} = e^u = e^{-x^2}$.

So $$\frac{dy}{dx} = \frac{du}{dx} \times \frac{dy}{du} = (-2x) \times e^{-x^2} = -2xe^{-x^2}.$$

(c) Write $u = 1 - x^2$, so $y = \sqrt{u} = u^{\frac{1}{2}}$.

Then $\dfrac{du}{dx} = -2x$ and $\dfrac{dy}{du} = \tfrac{1}{2}u^{-\frac{1}{2}} = \dfrac{1}{2\sqrt{u}} = \dfrac{1}{2\sqrt{1 - x^2}}$.

So $$\frac{dy}{dx} = \frac{du}{dx} \times \frac{dy}{du} = -2x \times \frac{1}{2\sqrt{1 - x^2}} = \frac{-x}{\sqrt{1 - x^2}}.$$

After a time you will probably find that you can write the answer down without putting in the intermediate steps.

Example 38.1.3

Differentiate $y = \dfrac{1}{1 + \sqrt{x}}$ with respect to x.

You think: 'If u is $1 + \sqrt{x}$, y is $\dfrac{1}{u}$. The derivative of $1 + \sqrt{x}$ is $\dfrac{1}{2\sqrt{x}}$ and the derivative of $\dfrac{1}{u}$ (with respect to u) is $-\dfrac{1}{u^2}$.' But probably all you will write down is

$$\frac{dy}{dx} = \frac{1}{2\sqrt{x}} \times \left(-\frac{1}{(1 + \sqrt{x})^2}\right) = -\frac{1}{2\sqrt{x}(1 + \sqrt{x})^2}.$$

But don't be in too much hurry to use this short cut. The important thing is to get the right answer, even if you have to write a bit more.

38.2* Why the chain rule works

This section presents an argument to justify the chain rule. You may skip it if you like. There is no exercise on this section.

You might be tempted to think that it is obvious that $\frac{dy}{dx} = \frac{du}{dx} \times \frac{dy}{du}$, by 'cancelling d$u$'. But $\frac{du}{dx}$ and $\frac{dy}{du}$ are not fractions. It was explained in Section 11.5 that they are complete symbols which can't be taken apart; no meaning is attached to the separate symbols dx, du and dy. So there is certainly something to prove.

The derivative $\frac{dy}{dx}$ was defined in Chapter 11 as the limit of $\frac{\delta y}{\delta x}$ as $\delta x \to 0$; and δx, δy are separate symbols, representing increases in x and y. So it is perfectly legal to 'cancel δu' to establish the equation

$$\frac{\delta y}{\delta x} = \frac{\delta u}{\delta x} \times \frac{\delta y}{\delta u} \qquad \text{(provided that } \delta u \neq 0\text{)}.$$

The situation is illustrated in Fig. 38.1. For the composite function $f \circ g$ you need two graphs, of $u = g(x)$ and $y = f(u)$. By combining these it would be possible to produce the graph of $y = f \circ g(x)$. The connection between the two graphs is that the numbers u and δu on the vertical axis of the graph on the left are the same as the u and δu on the horizontal axis of the graph on the right.

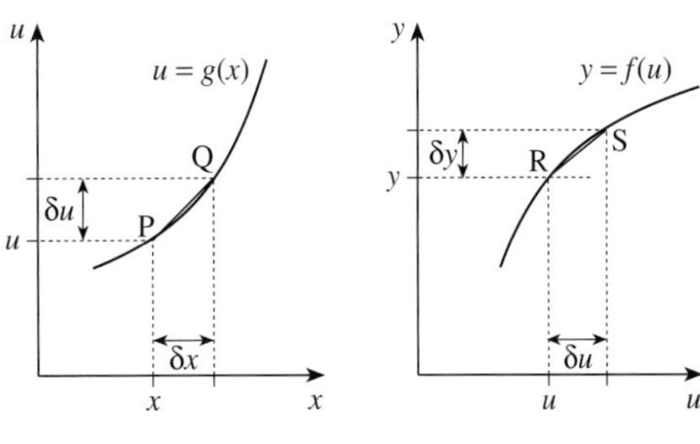

Fig. 38.1

Now let $\delta x \to 0$, so that in the graph on the left Q approaches P, and $\frac{\delta u}{\delta x}$ tends to $\frac{du}{dx}$, the gradient of the tangent at P. Also $\delta u \to 0$, so that in the graph on the right S approaches R, and $\frac{\delta y}{\delta u}$ tends to $\frac{dy}{du}$, the gradient of the tangent at R. It follows that the product $\frac{\delta u}{\delta x} \times \frac{\delta y}{\delta u}$ tends to $\frac{du}{dx} \times \frac{dy}{du}$. Therefore $\frac{\delta y}{\delta x}$ tends to this limit. That is,

$$\frac{dy}{dx} = \frac{du}{dx} \times \frac{dy}{du}.$$

There are one or two hidden assumptions in this argument. The most important is that the limit of the product of two quantities is the product of their limits. You will probably think this is a reasonable assumption, and it is in fact true, but the proof is beyond the scope of this course.

Exercise 38

1 By writing $u = 5x + 3$, differentiate with respect to x

(a) $y = (5x+3)^6$, (b) $y = (5x+3)^{\frac{1}{2}}$, (c) $y = \ln(5x+3)$.

2 By writing $u = 1 + x^3$, differentiate with respect to x

(a) $y = (1+x^3)^5$, (b) $y = (1+x^3)^{-4}$, (c) $y = \ln(1+x^3)$.

3 By writing $u = 2x^2 + 3$, differentiate with respect to x

(a) $y = (2x^2+3)^6$, (b) $y = \dfrac{1}{2x^2+3}$, (c) $y = \dfrac{1}{\sqrt{2x^2+3}}$.

4 Differentiate $y = (2x^3+1)^3$ with respect to x

(a) by using the binomial theorem to expand $y = (2x^3+1)^3$ and then differentiating term by term,

(b) by using the chain rule.

Check that your answers are the same.

5 Differentiate the following with respect to x.

(a) $y = (x^5+1)^4$ (b) $y = (2x^3-1)^8$ (c) $y = (e^{2x}+3)^6$ (d) $y = (\sqrt{x}-1)^5$

6 Differentiate the following with respect to x; try to do this without writing down the intermediate steps.

(a) $y = (x^2+6)^4$ (b) $y = (5x^3+4)^3$ (c) $y = (x^4-8)^7$ (d) $y = (2-x^9)^5$

7 Differentiate the following with respect to x.

(a) $y = (\ln x + 1)^6$ (b) $y = \left(\dfrac{1}{x}+2\right)^4$ (c) $y = \frac{1}{2}\ln(2+x^4)$ (d) $y = 3(e^{-x}+1)^5$

8 If $f(x) = \dfrac{1}{1+x^2}$, find (a) $f'(2)$, (b) the value of x such that $f'(x) = 0$.

9 If $y = \sqrt[4]{x^3+8}$, find the value of $\dfrac{dy}{dx}$ when $x = 2$.

10 If $y = \dfrac{5}{1+e^{3x}}$, find the value of $\dfrac{dy}{dx}$ when $x = 0$.

11 Find the equation of the tangent to the curve $y = (x^2-5)^3$ at the point $(2, -1)$.

12 Find the equation of the tangent to the curve $y = \dfrac{1}{\sqrt{x}-1}$ at the point $(4, 1)$.

13 Find the equation of the normal to the curve $y = \dfrac{8}{1-x^3}$ at the point $(-1, 4)$.

14 By writing $u = x^2 - 1$ and $v = \sqrt{u} + 1$ and using the chain rule in the form $\dfrac{dy}{dx} = \dfrac{du}{dx} \times \dfrac{dv}{du} \times \dfrac{dy}{dv}$, differentiate $y = (\sqrt{x^2-1}+1)^6$.

15 Find $\dfrac{d}{dx}\left(e^{\sqrt{1-x^2}}\right)$.

39 Differentiating products and quotients

This chapter extends further the range of functions which you can differentiate. When you have completed it, you should

- know and be able to apply the product and quotient rules for differentiation.

39.1 The sum and product rules

If $f(x) = x^2 + \ln x$, then $f'(x) = 2x + \frac{1}{x}$. You know this, because it has been proved that $\frac{d}{dx}x^2 = 2x$, and that $\frac{d}{dx}\ln x = \frac{1}{x}$. But the statement also depends on another property of differentiation:

> **The sum rule** If u and v are functions of x, and if $y = u + v$,
>
> then $\frac{dy}{dx} = \frac{du}{dx} + \frac{dv}{dx}$.

This was justified in Section 11.4 by means of an example. For a general proof, it is convenient to use 'delta notation'.

Take a particular value of x, and increase x by δx. There will then be corresponding increases in u, v and y of δu, δv and δy:

$$y = u + v \quad \text{and} \quad y + \delta y = (u + \delta u) + (v + \delta v).$$

Subtracting the first equation from the second gives

$$\delta y = \delta u + \delta v; \text{ and, dividing by } \delta x, \ \frac{\delta y}{\delta x} = \frac{\delta u}{\delta x} + \frac{\delta v}{\delta x}.$$

To find $\frac{dy}{dx}$, you must take the limit as $\delta x \to 0$:

$$\begin{aligned}\frac{dy}{dx} &= \lim_{\delta x \to 0} \frac{\delta y}{\delta x} \\ &= \lim_{\delta x \to 0} \left(\frac{\delta u}{\delta x} + \frac{\delta v}{\delta x} \right) \\ &= \lim_{\delta x \to 0} \frac{\delta u}{\delta x} + \lim_{\delta x \to 0} \frac{\delta v}{\delta x} \\ &= \frac{du}{dx} + \frac{dv}{dx},\end{aligned}$$

as required.

You might (rightly) object that the crucial assumption of the proof, that the limit of the sum of two terms is the sum of the limits, has never been justified. This can only be an assumption at this stage, because you don't yet have a mathematical definition of what is meant by a limit. But it *can* be justified, and for the time being you may quote the result with confidence. You may also assume the corresponding result for the limit of the product of two terms: this has already been assumed in Section 38.2, when proving the chain rule.

The rule for differentiating the product of two functions is rather more complicated than the rule for sums.

Example 39.1.1

Show that, if $y = uv$, then in general $\frac{dy}{dx}$ does *not* equal $\frac{du}{dx} \times \frac{dv}{dx}$.

The words 'in general' are put in because there might be special functions for which equality does hold. For example, if u and v are both constant functions, then y is also constant: $\frac{du}{dx}$, $\frac{dv}{dx}$ and $\frac{dy}{dx}$ are all 0, so $\frac{dy}{dx}$ does equal $\frac{du}{dx} \times \frac{dv}{dx}$.

To show that this is not always true, it is sufficient to find one case for which it is false. (This case is called a *counterexample*.)

For example, if $u = x^2$ and $v = x^3$, then $y = x^5$. In this case

$$\frac{dy}{dx} = 5x^4,$$

but $\frac{du}{dx} \times \frac{dv}{dx} = 2x \times 3x^2 = 6x^3$.

These two expressions are not the same. So in general $\frac{dy}{dx} \neq \frac{du}{dx} \times \frac{dv}{dx}$.

To find the correct rule, use the same notation as for the sum rule, but with $y = uv$. Then

$$y = uv \quad \text{and} \quad y + \delta y = (u + \delta u)(v + \delta v) = uv + (\delta u)v + u(\delta v) + (\delta u)(\delta v).$$

You could illustrate these equations by showing u and v as sides of a rectangle, so that y is the area. This is the unshaded region in Fig. 39.1. Then, if u increases by δu, and v by δv, the rectangle expands to include the shaded region as well. The area of the large rectangle is $y + \delta y$, so that the shaded region has area δy.

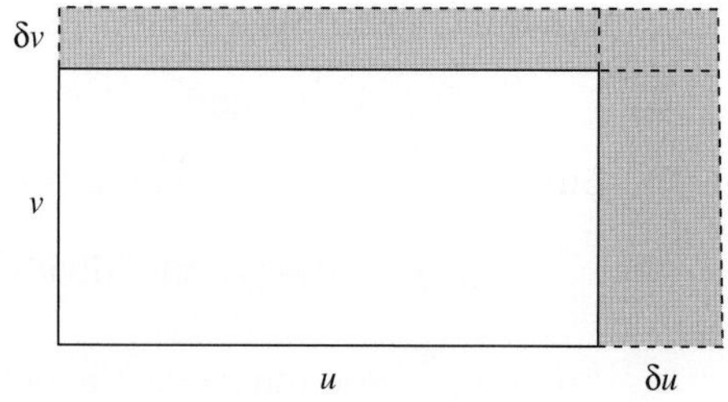

Fig. 39.1

If you subtract the equation for y from the equation for $y + \delta y$, you get

$$\delta y = (\delta u)v + u(\delta v) + (\delta u)(\delta v).$$

The three terms in the expression on the right are the areas of the three rectangles which make up the shaded region in Fig. 39.1. Notice that, if δu and δv are small, the area of the rectangle with area $(\delta u)(\delta v)$ in the top right corner is much smaller than the area of the other two shaded rectangles.

Now u and v are both functions of x, so that y is a function of x. The three increases δu, δv and δy all result from increasing x by δx. To get $\frac{dy}{dx}$, you have to find $\frac{\delta y}{\delta x}$ and then let $\delta x \to 0$. So divide the last equation by δx, to get

$$\frac{\delta y}{\delta x} = \left(\frac{\delta u}{\delta x}\right)v + u\left(\frac{\delta v}{\delta x}\right) + \left(\frac{\delta u}{\delta x}\right)(\delta v).$$

Assuming, as with the sum rule, that the limit of the sum of the terms is the sum of the limits,

$$\begin{aligned}\frac{dy}{dx} &= \lim_{\delta x\to 0}\frac{\delta y}{\delta x}\\ &= \lim_{\delta x\to 0}\left(\left(\frac{\delta u}{\delta x}\right)v\right) + \lim_{\delta x\to 0}\left(u\left(\frac{\delta v}{\delta x}\right)\right) + \lim_{\delta x\to 0}\left(\left(\frac{\delta u}{\delta x}\right)(\delta v)\right).\end{aligned}$$

Now u and v don't depend on δx, so you can write

$$\lim_{\delta x\to 0}\left(\left(\frac{\delta u}{\delta x}\right)v\right) = \lim_{\delta x\to 0}\frac{\delta u}{\delta x}\times v = \frac{du}{dx}\times v$$

and $$\lim_{\delta x\to 0}\left(u\left(\frac{\delta v}{\delta x}\right)\right) = u\times\lim_{\delta x\to 0}\frac{\delta v}{\delta x} = u\times\frac{dv}{dx}.$$

And if you assume that the limit of the product of two factors is the product of the limits,

$$\lim_{\delta x\to 0}\left(\left(\frac{\delta u}{\delta x}\right)(\delta v)\right) = \lim_{\delta x\to 0}\left(\frac{\delta u}{\delta x}\right)\times\lim_{\delta x\to 0}\delta v;$$

and this is 0 because $\lim_{\delta x\to 0}\delta v = 0$.

Putting all this together,

$$\frac{dy}{dx} = \frac{du}{dx}\times v + u\times\frac{dv}{dx}.$$

This can be stated as:

The product rule If u and v are functions of x, and if $y = uv$,

then $$\frac{dy}{dx} = \frac{du}{dx}v + u\frac{dv}{dx}.$$

In function notation, if $y = f(x)g(x)$,

then $$\frac{dy}{dx} = f'(x)g(x) + f(x)g'(x).$$

Example 39.1.2

Verify the product rule when $u = x^2$ and $v = x^3$.

The right side is $2x\times x^3 + x^2\times 3x^2 = 2x^4 + 3x^4 = 5x^4$, which is the derivative of $y = x^2\times x^3 = x^5$.

Example 39.1.3

Find the derivatives with respect to x of (a) $x^3\ln x$, (b) xe^{3x}, (c) $x^2(1+3x^2)^4$.

(a) Write $u = x^3$ and $v = \ln x$. Then $\frac{du}{dx} = 3x^2$ and $\frac{dv}{dx} = \frac{1}{x}$. So, using the product rule,

$$\begin{aligned}\frac{d}{dx}(x^3\ln x) &= 3x^2\times\ln x + x^3\times\frac{1}{x}\\ &= 3x^2\ln x + x^2\\ &= x^2(3\ln x + 1).\end{aligned}$$

You will soon find that you don't need to write this out in full. Just remember that the derivative of the product is

derivative of first factor × second factor + first factor × derivative of second factor.

(b) $$\begin{aligned}\frac{\mathrm{d}}{\mathrm{d}x}(x\mathrm{e}^{3x}) &= 1 \times \mathrm{e}^{3x} + x \times (3\mathrm{e}^{3x})\\ &= \mathrm{e}^{3x} + 3x\mathrm{e}^{3x}\\ &= (1+3x)\mathrm{e}^{3x}.\end{aligned}$$

(c) $$\begin{aligned}\frac{\mathrm{d}}{\mathrm{d}x}(x^2(1+3x^2)^4) &= 2x \times (1+3x^2)^4 + x^2(6x \times 4 \times (1+3x^2)^3)\\ &= 2x(1+3x^2)^4 + 24x^3(1+3x^2)^3\\ &= (2x(1+3x^2) + 24x^3)(1+3x^2)^3\\ &= (2x + 6x^3 + 24x^3)(1+3x^2)^3\\ &= 2x(1+15x^2)(1+3x^2)^3.\end{aligned}$$

Notice that in part (c) the chain rule is used to find $\frac{\mathrm{d}v}{\mathrm{d}x}$.

You will often find that, after you have used the product rule, the two terms in the derivative have a common factor. If so, you should write the final answer in its factorised form. This is especially important if you want to use the derivative to find stationary points on the graph.

Example 39.1.4

Find the turning point on the graph of $y = \frac{1}{x}\ln x$, and determine whether it is a maximum or minimum.

Begin by noting that the graph exists only for $x > 0$.

Differentiating by the product rule,

$$\begin{aligned}\frac{\mathrm{d}y}{\mathrm{d}x} &= \left(-\frac{1}{x^2}\right) \times \ln x + \frac{1}{x} \times \frac{1}{x}\\ &= \frac{1}{x^2}(-\ln x + 1).\end{aligned}$$

The turning point is where $\frac{\mathrm{d}y}{\mathrm{d}x} = 0$, which is where $\ln x = 1$, that is $x = \mathrm{e}$.

To find whether this is a maximum or minimum you could use the product rule again to find $\frac{\mathrm{d}^2y}{\mathrm{d}x^2}$. But in this instance it is easier to investigate the change of sign of $\frac{\mathrm{d}y}{\mathrm{d}x}$. Since the denominator x^2 is positive for $x > 0$, this depends only on the sign of $-\ln x + 1$, which is positive when $x < \mathrm{e}$ and negative when $x > \mathrm{e}$. So the turning point at $x = \mathrm{e}$ is a maximum.

When $x = \mathrm{e}$, $y = \frac{1}{\mathrm{e}}\ln \mathrm{e} = \frac{1}{\mathrm{e}} \times 1 = \frac{1}{\mathrm{e}}$. So the maximum point on the graph is $\left(\mathrm{e}, \frac{1}{\mathrm{e}}\right)$.

Example 39.1.5

Find the x-coordinates of the two points on the graph of $y = (1 - 4x)e^{-2x}$ at which the tangent passes through the origin.

To find where the tangent to a graph $y = f(x)$ passes through the origin, there is no need to find the equation of the tangent. In Fig. 39.2, P is the point on the curve with coordinates $(p, f(p))$. If the tangent at P passes through O, the gradient of OP is equal to the gradient of the tangent at P. That is, $\dfrac{f(p)}{p} = f'(p)$.

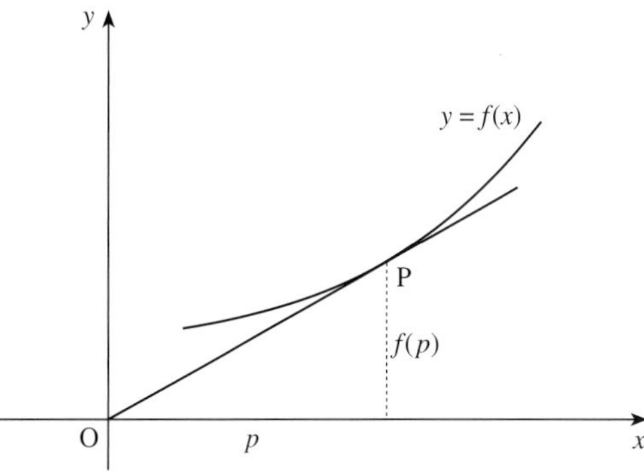

Fig. 39.2

For the graph of $y = (1 - 4x)e^{-2x}$, using the product rule gives

$$\begin{aligned}\frac{dy}{dx} &= -4e^{-2x} + (1 - 4x) \times (-2e^{-2x}) \\ &= (-4 - 2(1 - 4x))e^{-2x} \\ &= (-6 + 8x)e^{-2x}.\end{aligned}$$

The tangent at a point $P(p, (1 - 4p)e^{-2p})$ has gradient $(-6 + 8p)e^{-2p}$. This has to equal the gradient of OP, which is $\dfrac{(1 - 4p)e^{-2p}}{p}$. Therefore

$$(-6 + 8p)e^{-2p} = \frac{(1 - 4p)e^{-2p}}{p}.$$

Since e^{-2p} can't be 0, this gives

$$-6 + 8p = \frac{1 - 4p}{p}.$$

So $\quad -6p + 8p^2 = 1 - 4p,$

which reduces to $8p^2 - 2p - 1 = 0$.

The left side factorises as $(4p + 1)(2p - 1)$, so the roots are $-\frac{1}{4}$ and $\frac{1}{2}$. These are the required x-coordinates.

This is illustrated in Fig. 39.3, where the two tangents passing through the origin are drawn.

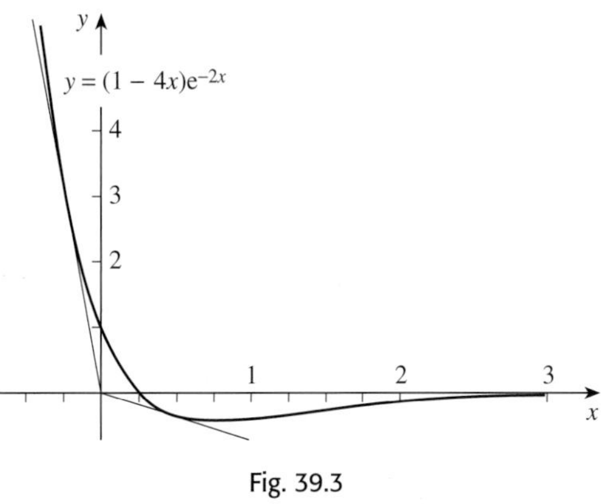

Fig. 39.3

Exercise 39A

1 Differentiate the following functions with respect to x by using the product rule. Verify your answers by multiplying out the products and then differentiating.

(a) $(x + 1)(x - 1)$ (b) $x^2(x + 2)$ (c) $(x^3 + 4)(x^2 + 3)$

(d) $(3x^2 + 5x + 2)(7x + 5)$ (e) $(x^2 - 2x + 4)(x + 2)$ (f) $x^m x^n$

2 Differentiate the following with respect to x.

(a) xe^x (b) $x^2 \ln x$ (c) $x^3(e^{-2x}+1)$

(d) $e^x \ln x$ (e) $\sqrt{x}e^{-x}$ (f) $(1+2x)e^{-2x}$

3 Find $\frac{dy}{dx}$ when

(a) $y=(x^2+3)e^x$, (b) $y=x^2(\ln 2x+e^{2x})$, (c) $y=(xe^x)^2$.

4 Find $f'(x)$ when

(a) $f(x)=x^2(2+e^x)$, (b) $f(x)=x^3e^{2x}$, (c) $f(x)=(4+3x^2)\ln x$.

5 Find the value of the gradient of the following curves when $x=2$. Give your answers in exact form.

(a) $y=xe^{-2x}$ (b) $y=e^x\ln(x-1)$ (c) $y=x\ln 3x$

6 Find the equations of the tangents to the following curves at the given points.

(a) $y=x\ln(x-1)$ when $x=2$ (b) $y=x^3\ln x$ when $x=1$

(c) $y=x\sqrt{3x+1}$ when $x=5$ (d) $y=x^3e^{-2x}$ when $x=0$

7 Find the coordinates of the turning points of the curve $y=x^2e^{-x}$.

8 When $f(x)=xe^{\sqrt{x}}$, find the exact value of $f'(4)$.

9 Find the equation of the normal to the curve $y=x\ln(2x-1)$ at the point on the curve with x-coordinate 1.

10 The volume, V, of a solid is given by $V=x^2\sqrt{8-x}$. Find the maximum value of V and the value of x at which it occurs.

11 Find the x-coordinates of the stationary points on the curve $y=x^ne^{-x}$, where n is a positive integer. Determine the nature of these stationary points, distinguishing between the cases when n is odd and when n is even.

39.2 Differentiating quotients

Functions of the form $\frac{u}{v}$ can often be written in a different form so that they can be differentiated by rules you know already, such as the product rule or the chain rule. Example 39.2.1 illustrates some of the possibilities.

Example 39.2.1

Differentiate with respect to x (a) $f(x)=\frac{x}{e^x}$, (b) $g(x)=\frac{e^x}{x}$.

(a) Since $\frac{1}{e^x}=e^{-x}$, you can write $f(x)$ as xe^{-x}. Therefore

$$\begin{aligned} f'(x) &= \frac{d}{dx}(xe^{-x}) \\ &= 1e^{-x}+x(-e^{-x}) \\ &= (1-x)e^{-x}. \end{aligned}$$

(b) **Method 1** You can write $g(x)$ as $g(x) = \mathrm{e}^x \times \frac{1}{x}$, so

$$\begin{aligned} g'(x) &= \frac{\mathrm{d}}{\mathrm{d}x}\mathrm{e}^x \times \frac{1}{x} + \mathrm{e}^x \times \frac{\mathrm{d}}{\mathrm{d}x}\left(\frac{1}{x}\right) \\ &= \mathrm{e}^x \times \frac{1}{x} + \mathrm{e}^x \times \left(\frac{-1}{x^2}\right), \end{aligned}$$

using the product rule.

You can simplify this to $g'(x) = \mathrm{e}^x\left(\frac{x-1}{x^2}\right)$.

Method 2 Since $g(x) = \frac{1}{f(x)}$, where $f(x)$ is the same as in part (a), the chain rule gives

$$g'(x) = \left(\frac{-1}{f(x)^2}\right) \times f'(x) = -\frac{f'(x)}{f(x)^2}.$$

Therefore, using the result of part (a),

$$\begin{aligned} g'(x) &= -\frac{(1-x)\mathrm{e}^{-x}}{\left(\frac{x}{\mathrm{e}^x}\right)^2} \\ &= -\mathrm{e}^{2x}\mathrm{e}^{-x}\left(\frac{1-x}{x^2}\right) \\ &= -\mathrm{e}^x\left(\frac{1-x}{x^2}\right) \\ &= \mathrm{e}^x\left(\frac{x-1}{x^2}\right). \end{aligned}$$

However, it is often useful to have a separate formula for differentiating $\frac{u}{v}$. This can be found by applying the product rule to $u \times \frac{1}{v}$, using the chain rule to differentiate $\frac{1}{v}$.

This gives

$$\begin{aligned} \frac{\mathrm{d}}{\mathrm{d}x}\left(\frac{u}{v}\right) &= \frac{\mathrm{d}}{\mathrm{d}x}\left(u \times \frac{1}{v}\right) = \frac{\mathrm{d}u}{\mathrm{d}x} \times \frac{1}{v} + u \times \left(-\frac{1}{v^2}\right)\frac{\mathrm{d}v}{\mathrm{d}x} \\ &= \frac{\mathrm{d}u}{\mathrm{d}x}\frac{1}{v} - \frac{u}{v^2}\frac{\mathrm{d}v}{\mathrm{d}x}. \end{aligned}$$

This can be conveniently written as:

> **The quotient rule** If u and v are functions of x, and if $y = \frac{u}{v}$,
>
> then $$\frac{\mathrm{d}y}{\mathrm{d}x} = \frac{\frac{\mathrm{d}u}{\mathrm{d}x}v - u\frac{\mathrm{d}v}{\mathrm{d}x}}{v^2}.$$
>
> In function notation, if $y = \frac{f(x)}{g(x)}$,
>
> then $$\frac{\mathrm{d}y}{\mathrm{d}x} = \frac{f'(x)g(x) - f(x)g'(x)}{g(x)^2}.$$

Use this formula to get the answers to Example 39.2.1.

Example 39.2.2

If $y = \frac{\sin x}{2x+1}$, find $\frac{dy}{dx}$.

In applying the quotient rule, it is important to get the two terms on the top line the right way round. It is a good idea to begin by drawing a long fraction bar, putting the square of v underneath and the derivative of u at the left on top:

$$\frac{dy}{dx} = \frac{\cos x \qquad\qquad\qquad\qquad}{(2x+1)^2}.$$

If you remember that each term has one factor differentiated and the other unchanged, it is then quite easy to remember how to fill in the rest:

$$\frac{dy}{dx} = \frac{\cos x \times (2x+1) - \sin x \times 2}{(2x+1)^2}$$

$$= \frac{(2x+1)\cos x - 2\sin x}{(2x+1)^2}.$$

Remember that the top line of the derivative is

derivative of top × bottom – top × derivative of bottom.

This is similar to the rule in Section 39.1 for differentiating a product, but with a minus in the middle instead of a plus.

Example 39.2.3

Find the minimum and maximum values of $f(x) = \frac{x-1}{x^2+3}$.

The denominator is never zero, so $f(x)$ is defined for all real numbers.

The quotient rule with $u = x - 1$ and $v = x^2 + 3$ gives

$$f'(x) = \frac{1 \times (x^2+3) - (x-1) \times 2x}{(x^2+3)^2}$$

$$= \frac{-x^2+2x+3}{(x^2+3)^2} = \frac{-(x^2-2x-3)}{(x^2+3)^2}$$

$$= \frac{-(x+1)(x-3)}{(x^2+3)^2}.$$

So $f'(x) = 0$ when $x = -1$ and $x = 3$.

You could use the quotient rule again to find $f''(x)$, but in this example it is much easier to note that $f'(x)$ is positive when $-1 < x < 3$ and negative when $x < -1$ and when $x > 3$. So there is a minimum at $x = -1$ and a maximum at $x = 3$.

The minimum value is $f(-1) = \frac{-2}{4} = -\frac{1}{2}$, and the maximum value is $f(3) = \frac{2}{12} = \frac{1}{6}$.

Applying the quotient rule sometimes involves some quite tricky algebra to get the expression for $\frac{dy}{dx}$ into its simplest form, especially when there are fractional indices present.

Example 39.2.4

Sketch the graph of $y = \frac{x+2}{\sqrt{2x+1}}$.

The expression for y only has meaning if $2x + 1 > 0$, so the domain is the set of real numbers $x > -\frac{1}{2}$. Throughout this domain y is positive. If x is just greater than $-\frac{1}{2}$, y is a large positive number, so the line $x = -\frac{1}{2}$ is an asymptote. When $x = 0$, $y = 2$.

When you use the quotient rule to find $\frac{dy}{dx}$ you will need to work out $\frac{d}{dx}\sqrt{2x+1}$, which is $2 \times \frac{1}{2\sqrt{2x+1}} = \frac{1}{\sqrt{2x+1}}$. So

$$\frac{dy}{dx} = \frac{1 \times \sqrt{2x+1} - (x+2) \times \frac{1}{\sqrt{2x+1}}}{(\sqrt{2x+1})^2}.$$

To write this more simply, multiply both top and bottom by $\sqrt{2x+1}$. Then

$$\frac{dy}{dx} = \frac{(2x+1) - (x+2)}{(2x+1)\sqrt{2x+1}}$$
$$= \frac{x-1}{(2x+1)^{\frac{3}{2}}}.$$

There is just one stationary point where $x = 1$, and $y = \frac{3}{\sqrt{3}} = \sqrt{3}$. Also $\frac{dy}{dx} > 0$ when $x > 1$ and $\frac{dy}{dx} < 0$ when $x < 1$. So $(1, \sqrt{3})$ is a minimum point on the graph.

You can investigate how the curve bends by differentiating a second time. Using the quotient rule again,

$$\frac{d^2y}{dx^2} = \frac{1 \times (2x+1)^{\frac{3}{2}} - (x-1) \times 2 \times \frac{3}{2}(2x+1)^{\frac{1}{2}}}{((2x+1)^{\frac{3}{2}})^2}.$$

To simplify this, notice that $(2x+1)^{\frac{1}{2}}$ is a factor of the top line. Dividing top and bottom by this factor,

$$\frac{d^2y}{dx^2} = \frac{(2x+1) - 3(x-1)}{(2x+1)^{\frac{5}{2}}}$$
$$= \frac{4-x}{(2x+1)^{\frac{5}{2}}}.$$

So the curve is concave up when $x < 4$ and concave down when $x > 4$. Therefore there is a point of inflexion where $x = 4$, and $y = \frac{6}{\sqrt{9}} = 2$.

Putting all this information together gives the graph in Fig. 39.4.

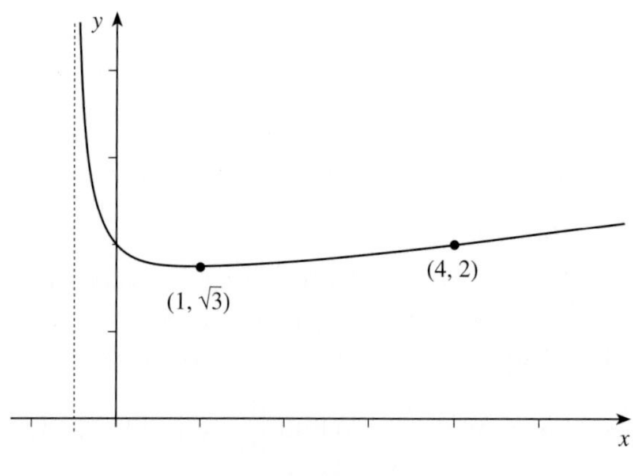

Fig. 39.4

Exercise 39B

1 Differentiate with respect to x

(a) $\dfrac{x}{1+5x}$, (b) $\dfrac{x^2}{3x-2}$, (c) $\dfrac{x^2}{1+2x^2}$,

(d) $\dfrac{e^{3x}}{4x-3}$, (e) $\dfrac{x}{1+x^3}$, (f) $\dfrac{e^x}{x^2+1}$.

2 Differentiate with respect to x

(a) $\dfrac{x}{\sqrt{x+1}}$, (b) $\dfrac{\sqrt{x-5}}{x}$, (c) $\dfrac{\sqrt{3x+2}}{2x}$.

3 Find $\dfrac{dy}{dx}$ when

(a) $y=\dfrac{e^x}{\sqrt{x}}$, (b) $y=\dfrac{e^x+5x}{e^x-2}$, (c) $y=\dfrac{\sqrt{1-x}}{\sqrt{1+x}}$,

(d) $y=\dfrac{\ln x}{x}$, (e) $y=\dfrac{\ln(x^2+4)}{x}$, (f) $y=\dfrac{\ln(3x+2)}{2x-1}$.

4 Find the equation of the tangent at the point with coordinates (1, 1) to the curve with equation $y=\dfrac{x^2+3}{x+3}$. (OCR)

5 (a) If $f(x)=\dfrac{e^x}{2x+1}$, find $f'(x)$.

(b) Find the coordinates of the turning point of the curve $y=f(x)$.

6 Find the equation of the normal to the curve $y=\dfrac{2x-1}{x(x-3)}$ at the point on the curve where $x=2$.

7 Find the x-coordinates of the turning points of the curve $y=\dfrac{x^2+4}{2x-x^2}$.

8 (a) If $f(x)=\dfrac{x^2-3x}{x+1}$, find $f'(x)$ and $f''(x)$.

(b) Find the values of x for which $f(x)$ is decreasing.

40 Differentiating circular functions

This chapter shows how to differentiate the functions $\sin x$ and $\cos x$. When you have completed it, you should

- know the derivatives and indefinite integrals of $\sin x$ and $\cos x$
- be able to differentiate a variety of functions including $\sin x$ and $\cos x$ using the chain rule and the product and quotient rules
- be able to integrate a variety of such functions, using identities where necessary.

40.1 The derivatives of sin *x* and cos *x*

Figure 40.1 is a copy of the graph of $y = \sin x$ which you have already seen as Fig. 28.3. In Chapter 28 this was used as a basis for models of quantities which vary periodically. If you want to use such a model to predict how quickly a quantity is changing, you have to differentiate. So the question is, what is the derivative of $\sin x$?

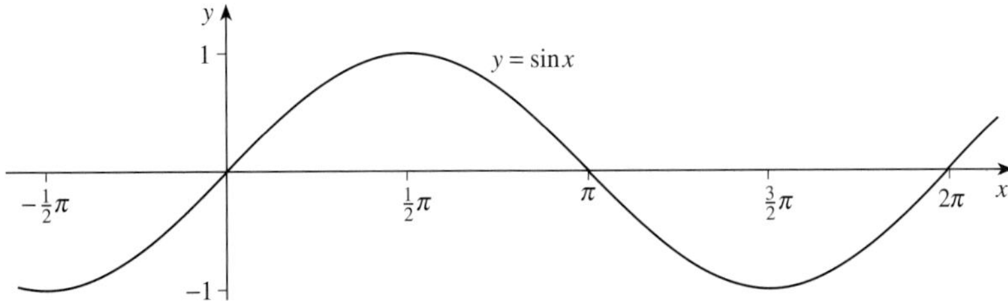

Fig. 40.1

You can guess the answer from the graph.

- Since values of $\sin x$ repeat themselves after a period of 2π, values of the derivative must also repeat themselves after this period.
- This graph is drawn with equal scales on the two axes. What does this suggest for the gradient of the graph at the origin? It certainly looks as if $\frac{dy}{dx} = 1$ where $x = 0$. (This is the great advantage of using radians. To explore this further, see Exercise 40A Question 5.)
- Obviously the gradient is 0 where $x = \frac{1}{2}\pi$ and $x = \frac{3}{2}\pi$. The gradient where $x = 2\pi$ is the same as the gradient where $x = 0$. And the gradient where $x = \pi$ is minus the gradient where $x = 0$, that is -1.

So if $y = \sin x$, $\frac{dy}{dx}$ has the values given in Table 40.2.

x	0	$\frac{1}{2}\pi$	π	$\frac{3}{2}\pi$	2π	$\frac{5}{2}\pi$	3π	...
$\frac{dy}{dx}$	1	0	-1	0	1	0	-1	...

Table 40.2

It is not difficult to guess that $\frac{dy}{dx} = \cos x$.

To check this, use your calculator to produce the graph of $y = \sin x$ (use equal scales for x and y). Then, with the same axes, show the graph of $\frac{dy}{dx}$. Finally, produce the graph of $\cos x$. If the guess is right, the second and third graphs should be the same.

You can repeat this process step-by-step for $y = \cos x$, beginning with the graph in Fig. 28.2. The values of $\frac{dy}{dx}$ are then given by Table 40.3.

x	0	$\frac{1}{2}\pi$	π	$\frac{3}{2}\pi$	2π	$\frac{5}{2}\pi$	3π	...
$\frac{dy}{dx}$	0	-1	0	1	0	-1	0	...

Table 40.3

These are not quite so easy to recognise. But if you compare them with Fig. 40.1 you will see that they are the values of $\sin x$ with all the signs changed. So the guess is that $\frac{dy}{dx} = -\sin x$.

Check this with your calculator.

These results are important, and you need to remember them:

$$\frac{d}{dx}\cos x = -\sin x, \quad \frac{d}{dx}\sin x = \cos x.$$

Now that you know the derivatives of $\sin x$ and $\cos x$, you can use the product rule and the chain rule to find the derivatives of many other trigonometric functions.

Example 40.1.1

Use the product rule to find the derivatives with respect to x of

(a) $x^3 \sin x$, (b) $\frac{1}{x}\cos x$.

(a) Writing $u = x^3$ and $v = \sin x$ in $\frac{d}{dx}(uv) = \frac{du}{dx}v + u\frac{dv}{dx}$ gives

$$\frac{d}{dx}(x^3 \sin x) = \left(\frac{d}{dx}x^3\right) \times \sin x + x^3 \times \left(\frac{d}{dx}\sin x\right) = 3x^2 \sin x + x^3 \cos x.$$

(b) $\frac{d}{dx}\left(\frac{1}{x}\cos x\right) = \left(-\frac{1}{x^2}\right) \times \cos x + \frac{1}{x} \times (-\sin x) = -\frac{1}{x^2}\cos x - \frac{1}{x}\sin x.$

Example 40.1.2

Use the chain rule to differentiate with respect to x

(a) $\sin\left(3x - \frac{1}{4}\pi\right)$, (b) $\cos^4 x$, (c) $\ln \cos x$, where $-\frac{1}{2}\pi < x < \frac{1}{2}\pi$.

(a) $\dfrac{d}{dx}\sin\left(3x - \frac{1}{4}\pi\right) = 3 \times \cos\left(3x - \frac{1}{4}\pi\right) = 3\cos\left(3x - \frac{1}{4}\pi\right).$

(b) Remember that $\cos^4 x$ is the conventional way of writing $(\cos x)^4$, so its derivative is $\dfrac{d}{dx}\cos x \times 4(\cos x)^3$.

So $\dfrac{d}{dx}\cos^4 x = -\sin x \times 4\cos^3 x = -4\cos^3 x \sin x.$

(c)
$$\frac{d}{dx}\ln \cos x = \frac{d}{dx}\cos x \times \frac{1}{\cos x} = \frac{-\sin x}{\cos x} = -\tan x.$$

The reason for the condition $-\frac{1}{2}\pi < x < \frac{1}{2}\pi$ is that $\ln u$ is only defined if $u > 0$. So $\ln \cos x$ is only defined if $\cos x > 0$.

You may find it interesting to investigate part (c) of this example with your calculator. With an interval of $-3\pi \le x \le 3\pi$ show the graph of $y = \ln \cos x$ and then the graph of $\dfrac{dy}{dx}$.

Example 40.1.3

Differentiate with respect to x (a) $\sin^2 3x$, (b) $\sin^3 x \cos x$.

(a) This is a composite function which splits into three steps:

$$x \to [\times 3] \to 3x \to [\sin] \to \sin 3x \to [\text{square}] \to \sin^2 3x.$$

Begin by dealing with the first two steps and note that

$$\frac{d}{dx}\sin 3x = 3 \times \cos 3x = 3\cos 3x.$$

Then differentiate $\sin^2 3x$, which is $(\sin 3x)^2$, as

$$\frac{d}{dx}\sin^2 3x = \frac{d}{dx}\sin 3x \times 2\sin 3x.$$

Putting the two steps together,

$$\frac{d}{dx}\sin^2 3x = 3\cos 3x \times 2\sin 3x = 6\sin 3x\cos 3x.$$

(b) This requires both the product rule and the chain rule. First use the chain rule to note that

$$\frac{\mathrm{d}}{\mathrm{d}x}\sin^3 x = \cos x \times 3\sin^2 x = 3\sin^2 x \cos x.$$

Then, by the product rule,

$$\begin{aligned}\frac{\mathrm{d}}{\mathrm{d}x}(\sin^3 x\cos x) &= \left(\frac{\mathrm{d}}{\mathrm{d}x}\sin^3 x\right)\times\cos x + \sin^3 x\times\left(\frac{\mathrm{d}}{\mathrm{d}x}\cos x\right)\\ &= 3\sin^2 x\cos x\times\cos x + \sin^3 x\times(-\sin x)\\ &= 3\sin^2 x\cos^2 x - \sin^4 x\\ &= \sin^2 x(3\cos^2 x - 3\sin^2 x).\end{aligned}$$

Example 40.1.4

Find $\frac{\mathrm{d}}{\mathrm{d}x}\tan x$.

Write $\tan x$ as $\frac{\sin x}{\cos x}$ and differentiate this by using the quotient rule.

$$\begin{aligned}\frac{\mathrm{d}}{\mathrm{d}x}\tan x = \frac{\mathrm{d}}{\mathrm{d}x}\left(\frac{\sin x}{\cos x}\right) &= \frac{\left(\frac{\mathrm{d}}{\mathrm{d}x}\sin x\right)\times\cos x - \sin x\times\left(\frac{\mathrm{d}}{\mathrm{d}x}\cos x\right)}{\cos^2 x}\\ &= \frac{\cos x\times\cos x - \sin x\times(-\sin x)}{\cos^2 x} = \frac{\cos^2 x + \sin^2 x}{\cos^2 x}.\end{aligned}$$

You can now use the identity $\cos^2 x + \sin^2 x \equiv 1$ to simplify this as $\frac{\mathrm{d}}{\mathrm{d}x}\tan x = \frac{1}{\cos^2 x}$.

The result of Example 40.1.4 is important enough to be worth remembering:

$$\frac{\mathrm{d}}{\mathrm{d}x}\tan x = \frac{1}{\cos^2 x}.$$

Exercise 40A

1 Differentiate the following with respect to x.

(a) $-\sin x$ (b) $-\cos x$ (c) $\sin 4x$ (d) $2\cos 3x$

(e) $\sin \frac{1}{2}\pi x$ (f) $\cos 3\pi x$ (g) $\cos(2x-1)$ (h) $5\sin\left(3x+\frac{1}{4}\pi\right)$

(i) $x\cos x$ (j) $\sin x\cos x$ (k) $x^3(\sin x+1)$ (l) $\mathrm{e}^{-x}\sin x$

(m) $x^2(\sin x+\cos x)$ (n) $\mathrm{e}^x(\sin x-\cos x)$

2 Differentiate the following with respect to x.

(a) $\sin^2 x$ (b) $\cos^3 x$ (c) $5\sin^2\frac{1}{2}x$ (d) $\sin x^2$

(e) $7\cos 2x^3$ (f) $\cos^3 2\pi x$ (g) $\mathrm{e}^{\cos 3x}$ (h) $5\mathrm{e}^{\sin^2 x}$

3 Differentiate the following with respect to x.

(a) $x\sin^2 x$ (b) $\frac{1}{x}\cos^2 x$ (c) $\sin x\cos^2 x$

(d) $\sin^3 x\cos^3 x$ (e) $x^2\sin^2 2x$ (f) $\sqrt{x}\cos^2\frac{1}{2}x$

4 For the following equations find an expression for $\frac{d^2y}{dx^2}$.

(a) $y = \sin 2x$ (b) $y = \cos 3x$ (c) $y = \tan x$ (d) $y = \frac{1}{\cos x}$

(e) $y = e^{\sin x}$ (f) $y = \sin^2 2x$ (g) $y = \sin^3 x$ (h) $y = x \cos \frac{1}{2}x$

5* It was shown in Section 28.1 that, in the figure,

$$\sin x = \frac{\text{directed length NP}}{\text{radius OP}} \text{ and } x = \frac{\text{directed arc AP}}{\text{radius OP}}.$$

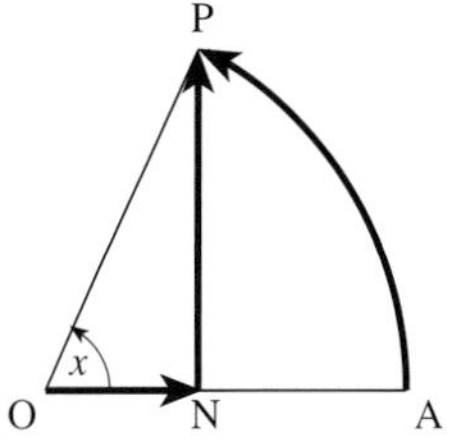

Use this to show that $\lim_{x \to 0} \frac{\sin x}{x} = 1$.

Explain how to use this to prove that, for the graph of $y = \sin x$, $\frac{dy}{dx} = 1$ where $x = 0$.

6 If $f(x) = \sin x$, sketch the graphs of $f(x)$, $f'(x)$ and $f''(x)$. Check from these graphs that

(i) $f(x)$ is increasing where $f'(x)$ is positive, and decreasing where $f'(x)$ is negative,

(ii) $f(x)$ is concave up where $f''(x)$ is positive, and concave down when $f''(x)$ is negative.

Describe the transformations which change the graph of $y = f(x)$ into $y = f'(x)$, and $y = f'(x)$ into $y = f''(x)$.

Hence show that $\frac{d}{dx} \sin x = \sin\left(x + \frac{1}{2}\pi\right)$ and that $\frac{d^2}{dx^2} \sin x = \sin(x + \pi)$.

7 Show that $\frac{d}{dx}(2\cos^2 x)$, $\frac{d}{dx}(-2\sin^2 x)$ and $\frac{d}{dx} \cos 2x$ are all the same. Explain why.

8 Find $\frac{d}{dx} \sin^2\left(x + \frac{1}{4}\pi\right)$, and write your answer in its simplest form.

40.2 Some applications

In many models of periodic variation the independent variable represents time (see Section 28.3). The derivative then measures the rate at which the quantity is changing.

Example 40.2.1

The height in metres of the water in a harbour is given approximately by the formula $h = 6 + 3\cos \frac{1}{6}\pi t$ where t is the time measured in hours from noon. Find an expression for the rate at which the water is rising at time t. When is it rising fastest, and at what rate is it then rising?

Using the chain rule, the rate at which the water is rising is

$$\frac{dh}{dt} = \tfrac{1}{6}\pi \times \left(-3\sin \tfrac{1}{6}\pi t\right) = -\tfrac{1}{2}\pi \sin \tfrac{1}{6}\pi t.$$

The water rises fastest when $\sin \frac{1}{6}\pi t = -1$, that is when $\frac{1}{6}\pi t = \frac{3}{2}\pi, \frac{7}{2}\pi, \frac{11}{2}\pi, \ldots$, so $t = 9, 21, 33, \ldots$. The water is rising fastest at 9 p.m. and again at 9 a.m. (This is exactly half-way between low and high tide.)

At these times $\frac{dh}{dt} = \frac{1}{2}\pi = 1.57\ldots$. The water is rising at a rate of 1.57 metres per hour.

Example 40.2.2
Find the minima and maxima of $f(x) = 4\cos x + \cos 2x$.

Although the domain is $\mathbb{R}$, you only need to consider the interval $0 \le x < 2\pi$. Since the period of $\cos x$ is 2π, and the period of $\cos 2x$ is π, the graph of $f(x)$ repeats itself after each interval of length 2π.

$$f'(x) = -4\sin x - 2\sin 2x.$$

Since $\sin 2x \equiv 2\sin x\cos x$,

$$\begin{aligned} f'(x) &= -4\sin x - 4\sin x\cos x \\ &= -4\sin x(1+\cos x), \end{aligned}$$

so $f'(x) = 0$ when $\sin x = 0$ or $\cos x = -1$, that is when $x = 0$ or π.

Differentiating $f'(x)$ in its original form,

$$f''(x) = -4\cos x - 4\cos 2x,$$

so $f''(0) = -4 - 4 = -8$ and $f''(\pi) = 4 - 4 = 0$.

There is therefore a maximum at $x = 0$, but the $f''(x)$ method does not work at $x = \pi$. You must instead consider the sign of $f'(x)$ below and above π.

Table 40.4 shows a table of signs.

x	$0 < x < \pi$	π	$\pi < x < 2\pi$
$-4\sin x$	$-$	0	$+$
$1+\cos x$	$+$	0	$+$
$f'(x)$	$-$	0	$+$

Table 40.4

The sign of $f'(x)$ changes from negative to positive at $x = \pi$, so this gives a minimum point on the graph.

Over the whole domain there are maxima at $0, \pm 2\pi, \pm 4\pi, \ldots$; the maximum value is $4 + 1 = 5$. There are minima at $\pm\pi, \pm 3\pi, \pm 5\pi, \ldots$, with minimum value $-4 + 1 = -3$.

Use your calculator, to check these results. Notice that, although $f(x)$ is periodic, the graph is not a simple transformation of a sine graph.

Example 40.2.3
Find the points on the graph of $y = x\sin x$ at which the tangent passes through the origin.

For the tangent at a point P to pass through the origin, its gradient must be equal to the gradient of the line joining O to P.

The product rule gives $\frac{\mathrm{d}y}{\mathrm{d}x} = \sin x + x\cos x$, so the tangent at a point P $(p, p\sin p)$ has gradient $\sin p + p\cos p$. This has to equal the gradient of OP, which is $\frac{p\sin p}{p} = \sin p$. Therefore

$$\sin p + p\cos p = \sin p,$$

giving $p\cos p = 0$.

This equation is satisfied by $p = 0$, though in fact the geometrical argument used above breaks down when $p = 0$ (can you see why?). But, it is obvious that the tangent at O passes through O.

The equation is also satisfied when $\cos p = 0$, that is by all odd multiples of $\frac{1}{2}\pi$. These points have coordinates $(0, 0)$, $(\pm\frac{1}{2}\pi, \frac{1}{2}\pi)$, $(\pm\frac{3}{2}\pi, -\frac{3}{2}\pi)$, $(\pm\frac{5}{2}\pi, \frac{5}{2}\pi)$, ... This is illustrated in Fig. 40.5.

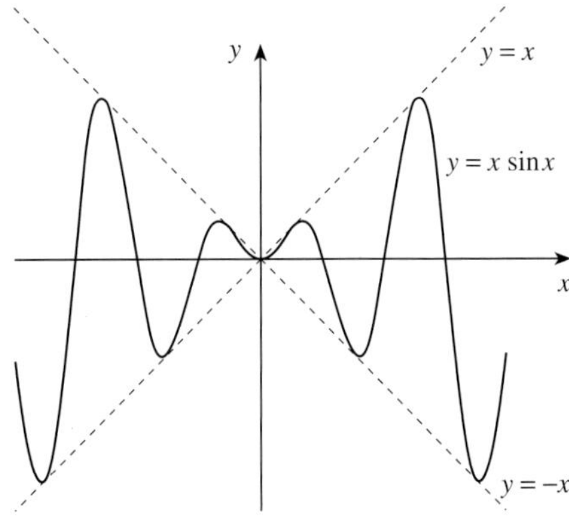

Fig. 40.5

The graph oscillates between the lines $y = x$ and $y = -x$, touching $y = x$ when $\sin x = 1$, and $y = -x$ when $\sin x = -1$.

Exercise 40B

1 The gross national product (GNP) of a country, P billion dollars, is given by the formula $P = 1 + 0.02t + 0.05\sin 0.6t$, where t is the time in years after the year 2000. At what rate is the GNP changing

(a) in the year 2000, (b) in the year 2005?

2 A tuning fork sounding A above middle C oscillates 440 times a second. The displacement of the tip of the tuning fork is given by $0.02\cos(2\pi \times 440t)$ millimetres, where t is the time in seconds after it is activated. Find

(a) the greatest velocity, (b) the greatest acceleration of the tip as it oscillates.

3 Show that, if $y = \sin nt$, where n is constant, then $\frac{\mathrm{d}^2y}{\mathrm{d}t^2} = -n^2y$. What can you deduce about the shape of the graph of $y = \sin nt$? Give a more general equation which has the same property.

4 (a) Find the equation of the tangent where $x = \frac{1}{3}\pi$ on the curve $y = \sin x$.

(b) Find the equation of the normal where $x = \frac{1}{4}\pi$ on the curve $y = \cos 3x$.

(c) Find the equation of the tangent where $x = \frac{1}{4}\pi$ on the curve $y = \ln \cos x$.

(d) Find the equation of the tangent where $x = \frac{1}{2}\pi$ on the curve $y = 3\sin^2 x$.

5 Find whether the tangent to $y = \cos x$ at $x = \frac{5}{6}\pi$ cuts the y-axis above or below the origin.

6 Find the coordinates of the point of intersection of the tangents to $y = \sin x$ and $y = \tan x$ at the points where $x = \frac{1}{3}\pi$.

7 Find any stationary points in the interval $0 \le x < 2\pi$ on each of the following curves, and find out whether they are maxima, minima or neither.

(a) $y = \sin x + \cos x$ (b) $y = x + \sin x$ (c) $y = \sin^2 x + 2\cos x$

(d) $y = \cos 2x + x$ (e) $y = \dfrac{1}{\cos x} + \dfrac{1}{\sin x}$ (f) $y = \cos 2x - 2\sin x$

8 Sketch the graphs with the following equations, and find expressions for $\dfrac{dy}{dx}$.

(a) $y = \sin\sqrt{x}$ (b) $y = \sqrt{\cos x}$ (c) $y = \sin\dfrac{1}{x}$

9* A violent oscillation, called 'resonance', can be created by forcing a system to oscillate at its natural frequency. A resonating system can be described by an equation $x = t\cos\pi t$, where $t \ge 0$.

(a) What can you say about x if t is

(i) an even integer, (ii) an odd integer, (iii) an odd multiple of $\frac{1}{2}$?

(b) Find an equation for the values of t when $\dfrac{dx}{dt} = 0$. Use graphs to show that this occurs when t is slightly greater than an integer.

(c) Sketch a graph of x against t.

(d) Find an expression for $\dfrac{d^2x}{dt^2}$, and show that $\dfrac{d^2x}{dt^2} + \pi^2 x = -2\pi\sin\pi t$.

40.3 Integrating circular functions

The results in Section 40.1 give you some new indefinite integrals. For example,

$$\text{from } \frac{d}{dx}\cos x = -\sin x \quad \text{it follows that} \quad \int \sin x \, dx = -\cos x + k,$$

$$\text{and} \quad \text{from } \frac{d}{dx}\tan x = \frac{1}{\cos^2 x} \quad \text{it follows that} \quad \int \frac{1}{\cos^2 x}\, dx = \tan x + k.$$

$$\int \cos x \, dx = \sin x + k, \quad \int \sin x \, dx = -\cos x + k,$$

$$* \int \tan x \, dx = -\ln\cos x + k, \text{ with } -\tfrac{1}{2}\pi < x < \tfrac{1}{2}\pi,$$

$$* \int \frac{1}{\cos^2 x}\, dx = \tan x + k,$$

where x is in radians.

Be very careful to get the signs correct when you differentiate or integrate sines and cosines. The minus sign appears when you differentiate $\cos x$, and when you integrate $\sin x$. If you forget which way round the signs go, draw for yourself sketches of the $\sin x$ and $\cos x$ graphs from 0 to $\frac{1}{2}\pi$. You can easily see that it is the $\cos x$ graph which has the negative gradient.

You will often need these integrals with a multiple of x. For example, since

$$\frac{\mathrm{d}}{\mathrm{d}x}\sin ax = a\cos ax \quad \text{(by the chain rule)},$$

$$\int \cos ax \,\mathrm{d}x = \frac{1}{a}\sin ax + k;$$

and similarly for the other integrals.

Example 40.3.1

Find (a) $\int \cos\left(x + \frac{1}{4}\pi\right)\mathrm{d}x$, (b)* $\int \tan \frac{1}{2}x \,\mathrm{d}x$.

(a) The simplest integral of $\cos x$ is $\sin x$. So

$$\int \cos\left(x + \tfrac{1}{4}\pi\right)\mathrm{d}x = \sin\left(x + \tfrac{1}{4}\pi\right) + k.$$

(b) You know from Example 40.1.2(c) that $\frac{\mathrm{d}}{\mathrm{d}x}\ln\cos x = -\tan x$. So

$$\frac{\mathrm{d}}{\mathrm{d}x}\ln\cos\tfrac{1}{2}x = -\tfrac{1}{2}\tan\tfrac{1}{2}x.$$

Therefore $\int \tan\frac{1}{2}x\,\mathrm{d}x = -2\ln\cos\frac{1}{2}x + k.$

Example 40.3.2

Find the area under the graph of $y = \sin\left(2x + \frac{1}{3}\pi\right)$ from $x = 0$ as far as the first point at which the graph cuts the positive x-axis.

The graph cuts the x-axis where $\sin\left(2x + \frac{1}{3}\pi\right) = 0$. That is, for positive x, where $2x + \frac{1}{3}\pi = \pi,\ 2\pi, \ldots$. The first positive root is $x = \frac{1}{3}\pi$.

$$\begin{aligned}\int_0^{\frac{1}{3}\pi}\sin\left(2x + \tfrac{1}{3}\pi\right)\mathrm{d}x &= \left[\tfrac{1}{2}\times\left(-\cos\left(2x + \tfrac{1}{3}\pi\right)\right)\right]_0^{\frac{1}{3}\pi}\\ &= \tfrac{1}{2}\times\left(-\cos\pi - \left(-\cos\tfrac{1}{3}\pi\right)\right)\\ &= \tfrac{1}{2}\times\left(1 + \tfrac{1}{2}\right) = \tfrac{3}{4}.\end{aligned}$$

So the area is $\frac{3}{4}$.

You can adapt the double angle formulae found in Section 36.2 to integrate more complicated trigonometric functions involving sines and cosines. For this you need to know the identities in the form:

$2\sin A\cos A \equiv \sin 2A.$

$2\cos^2 A \equiv 1 + \cos 2A, \quad 2\sin^2 A \equiv 1 - \cos 2A.$

Example 40.3.3

Let R be the region under the graph of $y = \sin^2 x$ in the interval $0 \le x \le \pi$. Find the area of R.

The area is given by

$$\int_0^{\pi} \sin^2 x \, dx = \int_0^{\pi} \tfrac{1}{2}(1 - \cos 2x) \, dx$$
$$= \left[\tfrac{1}{2}\left(x - \tfrac{1}{2}\sin 2x\right)\right]_0^{\pi}$$
$$= \left(\tfrac{1}{2}\pi - 0\right) - (0 - 0) = \tfrac{1}{2}\pi.$$

The area is $\frac{1}{2}\pi$.

Exercise 40C

1 Integrate the following with respect to x.

(a) $\cos 2x$ (b) $\sin 3x$ (c) $\cos(2x + 1)$

(d) $\sin(3x - 1)$ (e) $\sin(1 - x)$ (f) $\cos\left(4 - \frac{1}{2}x\right)$

(g) $\sin\left(\frac{1}{2}x + \frac{1}{3}\pi\right)$ (h) $\cos\left(3x - \frac{1}{4}\pi\right)$ (i) $-\sin \frac{1}{2}x$

2 Evaluate the following.

(a) $\displaystyle\int_0^{\frac{1}{2}\pi} \sin x \, dx$ (b) $\displaystyle\int_0^{\frac{1}{4}\pi} \cos x \, dx$ (c) $\displaystyle\int_0^{\frac{1}{4}\pi} \sin 2x \, dx$

(d) $\displaystyle\int_{\frac{1}{4}\pi}^{\frac{1}{3}\pi} \cos 3x \, dx$ (e) $\displaystyle\int_{\frac{1}{6}\pi}^{\frac{1}{3}\pi} \sin\left(3x + \tfrac{1}{6}\pi\right) dx$ (f) $\displaystyle\int_0^{\frac{1}{2}\pi} \sin\left(\tfrac{1}{4}\pi - x\right) dx$

(g) $\displaystyle\int_0^{1} \cos(1 - x) \, dx$ (h) $\displaystyle\int_0^{\frac{1}{2}} \sin\left(\tfrac{1}{2}x + 1\right) dx$ (i) $\displaystyle\int_0^{2\pi} \sin \tfrac{1}{2}x \, dx$

3* Integrate the following with respect to x.

(a) $\tan 2x$ (b) $\dfrac{1}{\cos^2 3x}$ (c) $\tan\left(\frac{1}{4}\pi - x\right)$

4* Evaluate the following.

(a) $\displaystyle\int_0^{\frac{1}{4}\pi} \tan x \, dx$ (b) $\displaystyle\int_0^{\frac{1}{12}\pi} \tan 3x \, dx$

5 Integrate the following with respect to x.

(a) $\cos^2 x$ (b) $\cos^2 \frac{1}{2}x$

(c) $\sin^2 2x$ (d) $\sin x \cos x$

6 For $-\frac{1}{2}\pi < x < \frac{1}{2}\pi$, sketch the graphs of

(a) $y = \cos x$, (b) $y = \cos^2 x$, (c)* $y = \dfrac{1}{\cos^2 x}$.

Find the area under each of these graphs over the interval $-\frac{1}{4}\pi < x < \frac{1}{4}\pi$.

7 Sketch the graph of $y = \sin \frac{1}{2}\pi x \cos \frac{1}{2}\pi x$ for $0 \le x \le 1$. Find

(a) the maximum value of y in the interval,

(b) the area enclosed between the curve and the x-axis in the interval.

41 Volumes of revolution

This chapter is about using integration to find the volume of a particular kind of solid, called a solid of revolution. When you have completed it, you should

- be able to find a volume of revolution about the x-axis.

41.1 Solids of revolution

Let O be the origin, and let OA be a line through the origin, as shown in Fig. 41.1. Consider the region between the line OA and the x-axis, shown shaded. If you rotate this region about the x-axis through 360°, it sweeps out a solid cone, shown in Fig. 41.2. A solid shape constructed in this way is called a **solid of revolution**. The volume of a solid of revolution is sometimes called a **volume of revolution**.

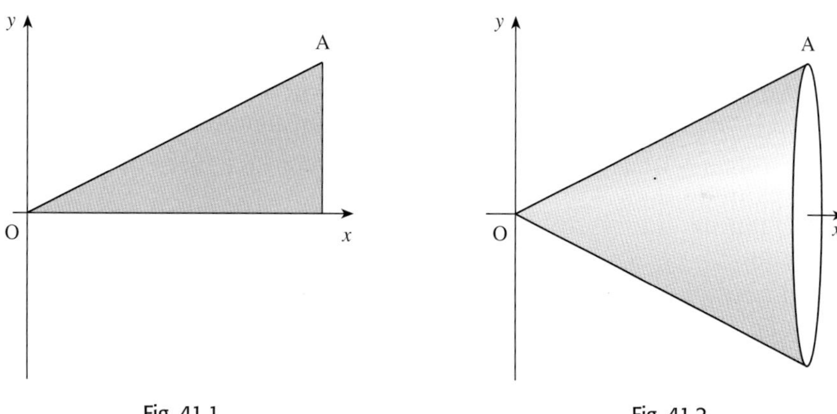

Fig. 41.1 Fig. 41.2

Calculating a volume of revolution is similar in many ways to calculating the area of a region under a curve (see Chapter 24).

An explanation of the notation $\int_a^b f(x)\,\mathrm{d}x$ for the area under a curve was given in Section 24.4. The symbol $\int$ was originally a letter S, standing for 'sum'. In Fig. 41.3 (which is a copy of Fig. 24.8) the black rectangle has area $f(x)\,\delta x$. You can imagine the region shaded grey almost filled up with rectangles like this, and the total area of these rectangles would be denoted by $\underset{x=a}{\overset{x=b}{\mathrm{S}}} f(x)\,\delta x$. The reason for the word 'almost' is that there are a few small triangle-like pieces of the region not covered. But the smaller you make the width δx of the rectangles, and the more rectangles you have, the better the coverage will be. And just as in differentiation $\frac{\delta y}{\delta x}$ becomes $\frac{\mathrm{d}y}{\mathrm{d}x}$ as $\delta x \to 0$, so in integration $\underset{x=a}{\overset{x=b}{\mathrm{S}}} f(x)\,\delta x$ becomes $\int_a^b f(x)\,\mathrm{d}x$.

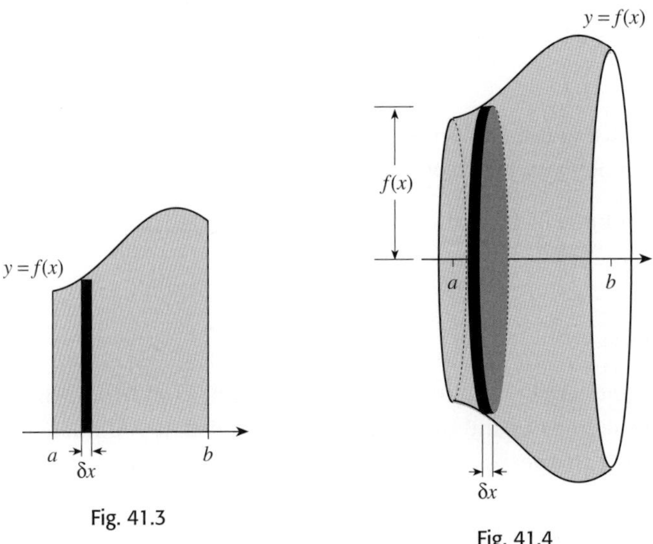

Fig. 41.3

Fig. 41.4

Now imagine the shaded region to be rotated about the x-axis through a complete revolution, to form the solid of revolution in Fig. 41.4. In place of a rectangle with height $f(x)$ and width δx you would have a thin disc with radius $f(x)$ and thickness δx. The volume of the disc would be $\pi\,(f(x))^2\,\delta x$. Now imagine the solid of revolution almost filled up with discs like this. Then the total volume would be $\mathop{\mathrm{S}}_{x=a}^{x=b} \pi\,(f(x))^2\,\delta x$. And in the limit, as $\delta x \to 0$, this would become $\int_a^b \pi\,(f(x))^2\,dx$.

Example 41.1.1

The shaded region in Fig. 41.5 is bounded by the x-axis, the lines $x = 1$ and $x = 4$, and the curve $y = \sqrt{x}$. This region is rotated through 360° about the x-axis to form a solid of revolution. Find the volume of the solid.

Figure 41.6 shows a typical disc, of radius $y = \sqrt{x}$ and thickness δx. Its volume is $\pi(\sqrt{x})^2\delta x$, which is $\pi x\,\delta x$. Imagine a large number of such discs almost making up the whole solid. Their total volume is $\mathop{\mathrm{S}}_{x=1}^{x=4} \pi x\,\delta x$.

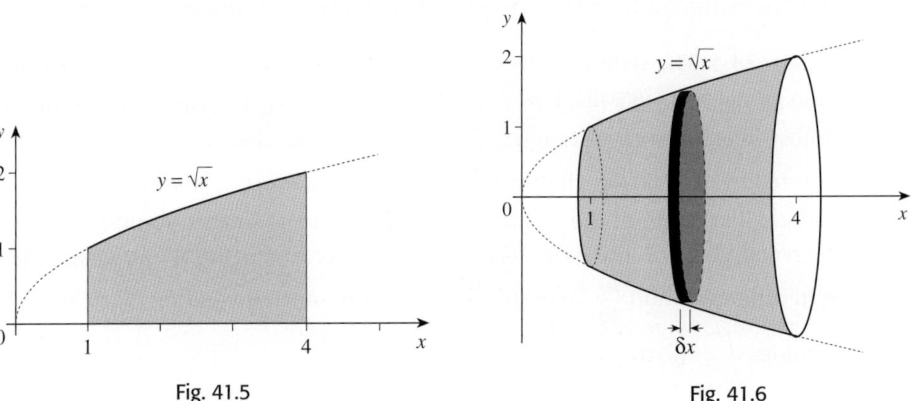

Fig. 41.5

Fig. 41.6

In the limit, as the number of discs is increased indefinitely and the thickness of the discs tends to 0, this volume becomes

$$\begin{aligned}\int_1^4 \pi x \, dx &= \left[\tfrac{1}{2}\pi x^2\right]_1^4 \\ &= \tfrac{1}{2}\pi(16-1) \\ &= \tfrac{15}{2}\pi.\end{aligned}$$

Once you have understood this argument, you needn't repeat it every time. It can be summarised in a formula.

When the region under the graph of $y = f(x)$ between $x = a$ and $x = b$ (where $a < b$) is rotated about the x-axis, the volume of the solid of revolution formed is

$$\int_a^b \pi y^2 \, dx \quad \text{or} \quad \int_a^b \pi (f(x))^2 \, dx.$$

Example 41.1.2

Find the volume generated when the region under the graph of $y = 1 + x^2$ between $x = -1$ and $x = 1$ is rotated through four right angles about the x-axis.

The phrase 'four right angles' is sometimes used in place of 360° for describing the complete rotation about the x-axis.

The required volume is V cubic units, where

$$\begin{aligned}V &= \int_{-1}^1 \pi y^2 \, dx \\ &= \int_{-1}^1 \pi (1 + x^2)^2 \, dx \\ &= \int_{-1}^1 \pi (1 + 2x^2 + x^4) \, dx \\ &= \left[\pi \left(x + \tfrac{2}{3}x^3 + \tfrac{1}{5}x^5\right)\right]_{-1}^1 \\ &= \pi\left\{\left(1 + \tfrac{2}{3} + \tfrac{1}{5}\right) - \left((-1) + \tfrac{2}{3}(-1)^3 + \tfrac{1}{5}(-1)^5\right)\right\} \\ &= \tfrac{56}{15}\pi.\end{aligned}$$

The volume of the solid is $\frac{56}{15}\pi$.

It is usual to give the result as an exact multiple of π, unless you are asked for an answer correct to a given number of significant figures or decimal places.

The answer has been given without a unit, because it is not usual to attach a unit to the variables x and y when graphs are drawn. But if in a particular situation x and y each denote numbers of units, then you should attach the corresponding unit to the value of V.

You can also use the method to obtain the formula for the volume of a cone.

Example 41.1.3

Prove that the volume V of a cone with base radius r and height h is $V = \frac{1}{3}\pi r^2 h$.

The triangle which rotates to give the cone is shown in Fig. 41.7, where the 'height' has been drawn across the page. The gradient of [OA] is $\dfrac{r}{h}$, so its equation is $y = \dfrac{r}{h}x$.

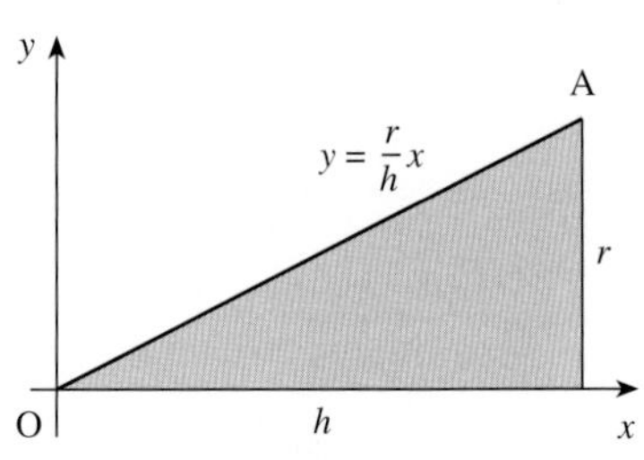

Fig. 41.7

Therefore, remembering that π, r and h are constants and do not depend on x,

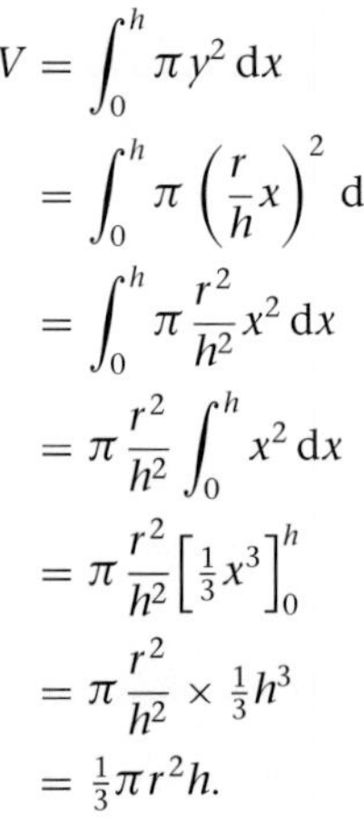

$$
\begin{aligned}
V &= \int_0^h \pi y^2 \, dx \\
&= \int_0^h \pi \left(\frac{r}{h}x\right)^2 dx \\
&= \int_0^h \pi \frac{r^2}{h^2} x^2 \, dx \\
&= \pi \frac{r^2}{h^2} \int_0^h x^2 \, dx \\
&= \pi \frac{r^2}{h^2} \left[\tfrac{1}{3}x^3\right]_0^h \\
&= \pi \frac{r^2}{h^2} \times \tfrac{1}{3}h^3 \\
&= \tfrac{1}{3}\pi r^2 h.
\end{aligned}
$$

Exercise 41

In all the questions in this exercise, leave your answers as multiples of π.

1 Find the volume of the solid generated when the region under the graph of $y = f(x)$ between $x = a$ and $x = b$ is rotated through 360° about the x-axis.

(a) $f(x) = x, \quad a = 3, \ b = 5$ (b) $f(x) = x^2, \quad a = 2, \ b = 5$

(c) $f(x) = x^3, \quad a = 2, \ b = 6$ (d) $f(x) = \dfrac{1}{x}, \quad a = 1, \ b = 4$

(e) $f(x) = e^x, \quad a = 0, \ b = 1$ (f) $f(x) = e^{-x}, \quad a = 0, \ b = 2$

2 Find the volume of the solid formed when the region under the graph of $y = f(x)$ between $x = a$ and $x = b$ is rotated through 360° about the x-axis.

(a) $f(x) = x + 3, \quad a = 3, \ b = 9$ (b) $f(x) = x^2 + 1, \quad a = 2, \ b = 5$

(c) $f(x) = \sqrt{x + 1}, \quad a = 0, \ b = 3$ (d) $f(x) = x(x - 2), \quad a = 0, \ b = 2$

(e) $f(x) = e^{\frac{1}{2}x}, \quad a = 1, \ b = 3$ (f) $f(x) = e^{-2x}, \quad a = 0, \ b = 1$

3 In each case the region enclosed between the following curves and the x-axis is rotated through 360° about the x-axis. Find the volume of the solid generated.

(a) $y = 1 - x^2$ (b) $y = x^2 - 3x$

4 The region bounded by the curve $y = \frac{1}{2}(e^x + e^{-x})$, the lines $x = -1$, $x = 1$ and the x-axis is rotated through $360°$ about the x-axis. Find the volume of the solid formed.

5 Find the area of the region between the curve $y = \cos x$ and the x-axis from $x = 0$ to $x = \frac{1}{2}\pi$.

Find also the volume generated when this area is rotated about the x-axis.

6 Find the area of the region bounded by the curve $y = 1 + \sin x$, the x-axis and the lines $x = 0$ and $x = \pi$.

Find also the volume generated when this area is rotated about the x-axis.

7 The curves $y = \sin x$, $y = \cos x$ and the x-axis enclose a region shown shaded in the sketch.

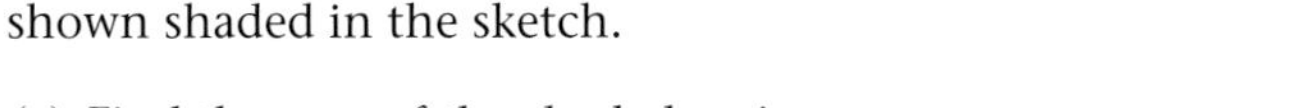

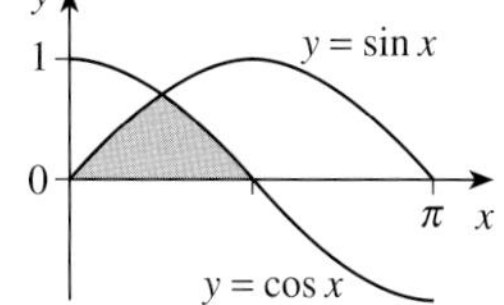

(a) Find the area of the shaded region.

(b) Find the volume generated when this region is rotated about the x-axis.

8 In the interval $0 \le x \le \pi$ the curve $y = \sin x + \cos x$ meets the y-axis at P and the x-axis at Q. Find the coordinates of P and Q.

Calculate the area of the region enclosed between the curve and the axes bounded by P and Q.

Calculate also the volume generated when this area is rotated about the x-axis.

9* The region bounded by parts of the axes, the line $x = \frac{1}{3}\pi$ and the curve $y = \dfrac{1}{\cos x}$ is denoted by R. Find the volume of the solid formed by rotating R through a complete revolution about the x-axis.

10 Sketch the curve with equation $y = \sqrt{r^2 - x^2}$. Explain why it is the equation of a semicircle with radius r.

Use this to show that the volume of a sphere with radius r is $\frac{4}{3}\pi r^3$.

Review exercise 13

1 Find the equation of the normal to the curve $y = \sqrt{2x^2 + 1}$ at the point (2, 3).

2 (a) Curve C_1 has equation $y = \sqrt{4x - x^2}$. Find $\frac{dy}{dx}$ and hence find the coordinates of the stationary point.

(b) Show that the curve C_2 with equation $y = \sqrt{x^2 - 4x}$ has no stationary point.

3 For the graph of $y = x\sqrt{3 - x}$

(a) state the values of x for which y exists, (b) find the gradient at the origin,

(c) find the coordinates of the maximum point.

Use your answers to draw a sketch of the graph.

4 Find the maximum and minimum points on the graph of $y = x(\ln x)^2$. Find also the values of x for which the graph bends downwards. Use your answers to draw a sketch of the graph.

5 Find the turning points on the graph of $y = x^2 e^{\frac{1}{2}x}$. Use your answer to sketch the graph.

Find the equation of the tangent to the graph at the point where $x = p$.

Show that there are three points on the curve at which the tangent passes through (3, 0). State their coordinates, and illustrate the property on your sketch.

6 The region under the curve with equation $y = \frac{1}{\sqrt{2x - 1}}$ is rotated through 4 right angles about the x-axis to form a solid. Find the volume of the solid between $x = 3$ and $x = 8$.

7 A metal napkin ring is modelled by rotating the part of the graph of $y = 5 - x^2$ cut off by the line $y = 4$ about the x-axis. Find the volume of the solid of revolution formed.

8 Find the equation of the tangent at (2, 1) on the curve $y = \sqrt{x^2 - 3}$. (OCR)

9 Differentiate $\frac{x}{\sqrt{x + 3}}$ simplifying your answer as far as possible. (OCR)

10 A curve has equation $y = \frac{x}{\sqrt{2x^2 + 1}}$.

(a) Show that $\frac{dy}{dx} = (2x^2 + 1)^{-\frac{3}{2}}$.

(b) Hence show that the curve has no turning points. (OCR)

11 The region R is bounded by the part of the curve $y = (x - 2)^{\frac{3}{2}}$ for which $2 \le x \le 4$, the x-axis, and the line $x = 4$. Find, in terms of π, the volume of the solid obtained when R is rotated through four right angles about the x-axis. (OCR)

12 A function f is defined by $f(x) = e^x \cos x$ $(0 \le x \le 2\pi)$.

(a) Find $f'(x)$.

(b) State the values of x between 0 and 2π for which $f'(x) < 0$.

(c) What does the fact that $f'(x) < 0$ in this interval tell you about the shape of the graph of $y = f(x)$? (OCR)

13 The motion of an electric train on the straight stretch of track between two stations is given by $x = 11\left(t - \frac{45}{\pi}\sin\left(\frac{\pi}{45}t\right)\right)$, where x metres is the distance covered t seconds after leaving the first station. The train stops at these two stations and nowhere between them.

(a) Find the velocity, v m s^{-1} in terms of t. Hence find the time taken for the journey between the two stations.

(b) Calculate the distance between the two stations. Hence find the average velocity of the train.

(c) Find the acceleration of the train 30 seconds after leaving the first station. (OCR)

14 (a) By first expressing $\cos 4x$ in terms of $\cos 2x$, show that

$$\cos 4x = 8\cos^4 x - 8\cos^2 x + 1,$$

and hence show that

$$8\cos^4 x = \cos 4x + 4\cos 2x + 3.$$

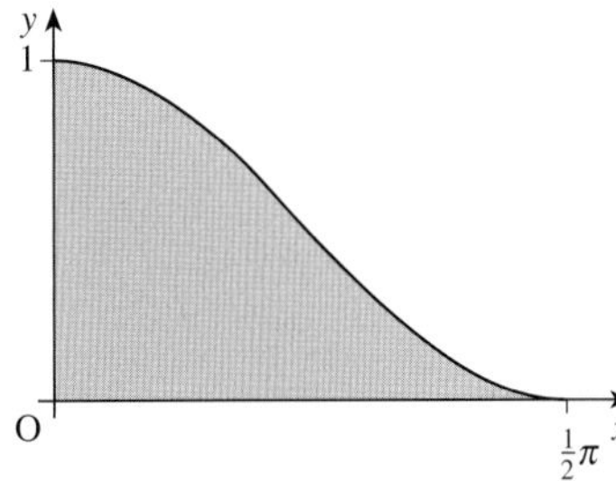

(b) The region R, shown shaded in the diagram, is bounded by the part of the curve $y = \cos^2 x$ between $x = 0$ and $x = \frac{1}{2}\pi$ and by the x- and y-axes. Show that the volume of the solid formed when R is rotated completely about the x-axis is $\frac{3}{16}\pi^2$. (OCR)

15 A curve C has equation $y = \frac{\sin x}{x}$, where $x > 0$. Find $\frac{dy}{dx}$, and hence show that the x-coordinate of any stationary point of C satisfies the equation $x = \tan x$. (OCR)

16 In each of the following, construct a formula involving a trigonometric function which could be used to model the situations described.

(a) Water depths in a canal vary between a minimum of 3.6 metres and a maximum of 6 metres over 24-hour periods.

(b) Petroleum refining at a chemical plant is run on a 10-day cycle, with a minimum production of 15 000 barrels per day and a maximum of 28 000 barrels per day.

(c) At a certain town just south of the Arctic circle, the number of hours of daylight varies between 2 and 22 hours during a 360-day year.

Examination questions

1 Let $f(x) = e^{\frac{1}{3}x} + 5\cos^2 x$. Find $f'(x)$. (© IBO 2003)

2 The derivative of the function f is given by $f'(x) = \frac{1}{x+1} - 0.5\sin x$, for $x \neq -1$. The graph of f passes through $(0, 2)$. Find an expression for $f(x)$. (© IBO 2002)

3 (a) Find $\int (1 + 3\sin(x + 2))\,dx$.

(b) The diagram shows part of the function $f(x) = 1 + 3\sin(x + 2)$. The area of the shaded region is given by $\int_0^a f(x)\,dx$. Find the value of a.

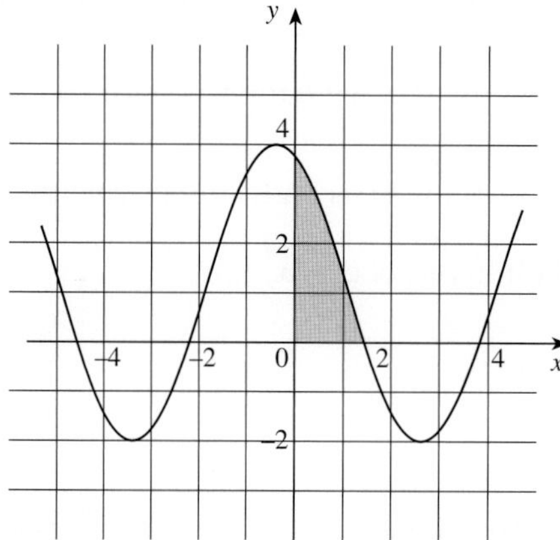

(© IBO 2003)

4 Consider the function f given by $f(x) = \dfrac{2x^2 - 13x + 20}{(x - 1)^2}$. A part of the graph of f is given.

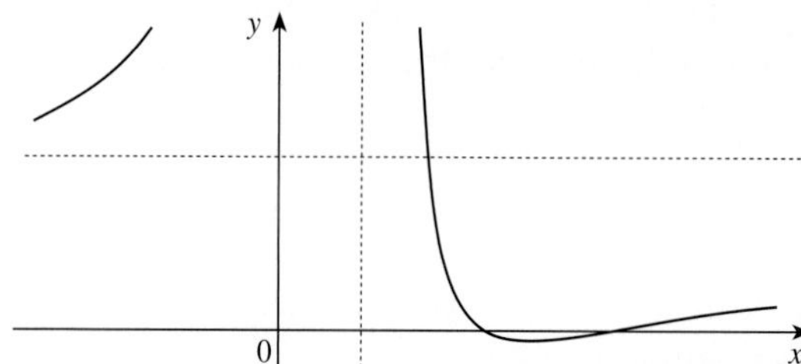

The graph has a vertical asymptote and a horizontal asymptote, as shown.

(a) Write down the *equation* of the vertical asymptote.

(b) $f(100) = 1.91$, $f(-100) = 2.09$, $f(1000) = 1.99$.

(i) Evaluate $f(-1000)$.

(ii) Write down the *equation* of the horizontal asymptote.

(c) Show that $f'(x) = \dfrac{9x - 27}{(x - 1)^3}$, $x \neq 1$.

The second derivative is given by $f''(x) = \dfrac{72 - 18x}{(x - 1)^4}$, $x \neq 1$.

(d) Using values of $f'(x)$ and $f''(x)$, explain why a minimum must occur at $x = 3$.

(e) There is a point of inflexion on the graph of f. Write down its coordinates. (© IBO 2003)

5 The graph of $y = \sin 2x$ for $0 \le x \le \pi$ is shown. The area of the shaded region is 0.85. Find the value of k.

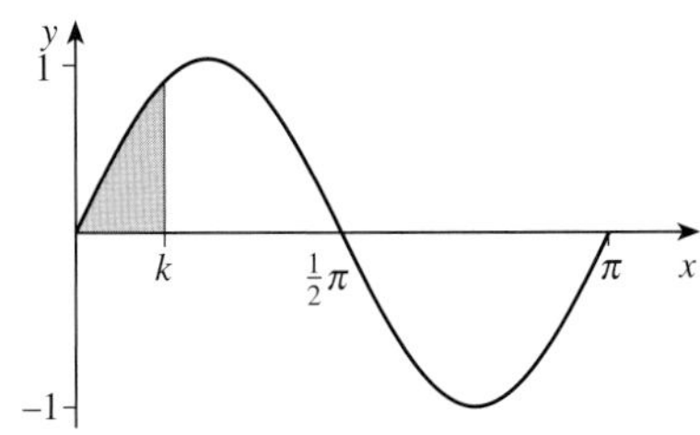

(© IBO 2005)

6 Consider the function $f(x) = \cos x + \sin x$.

(a) (i) Show that $f\left(-\frac{1}{4}\pi\right) = 0$.

(ii) Find, in terms of π, the smallest *positive* value of x which satisfies $f(x) = 0$.

The diagram below shows the graph of $f(x) = e^x(\cos x + \sin x)$, $-2 \le x \le 3$. The graph has a maximum turning point at C(a, b) and a point of inflexion at D.

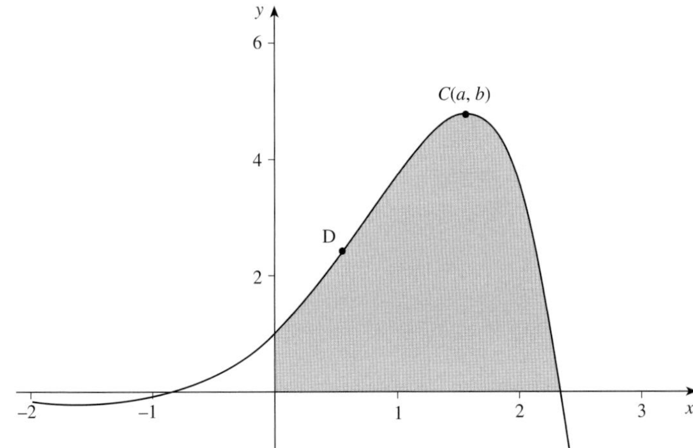

(b) Find $\frac{dy}{dx}$.

(c) Find the *exact* value of a and of b.

(d) Show that at D, $y = \sqrt{2}e^{\frac{1}{4}\pi}$.

(e) Find the area of the shaded region.

(© IBO 2003)

7 The diagram shows a sketch of the graph of the function $y = \sin(e^x)$ where $-1 \le x \le 2$, and x is in *radians*. The graph cuts the y-axis at A, and the x-axis at C and D. It has a maximum point at B.

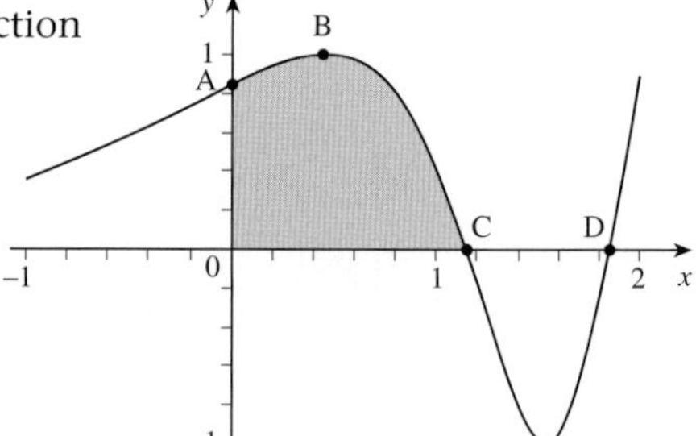

(a) Find the coordinates of A.

(b) The coordinates of C may be written as $(\ln k, 0)$. Find the *exact* value of k.

(c) (i) Write down the y-coordinate of B.

(ii) Find $\dfrac{dy}{dx}$. (iii) Hence, show that at B, $x = \ln \frac{1}{2}\pi$.

(d) (i) Write down the integral which represents the shaded area.

(ii) Evaluate this integral.

(e) (i) Copy the above diagram, and, on it, sketch the graph of $y = x^3$.

(ii) The two graphs intersect at P. Find the x-coordinate of P. (© IBO 2002)

8 Let $f(x) = \frac{1}{2}\sin 2x + \cos x$, for $0 \le x \le 2\pi$.

(a) (i) Find $f'(x)$.

One way of writing $f'(x)$ is $-2\sin^2 x - \sin x + 1$.

(ii) Factorise $2\sin^2 x + \sin x - 1$. (iii) Hence or otherwise, solve $f'(x) = 0$.

The graph of $y = f(x)$ is shown below.

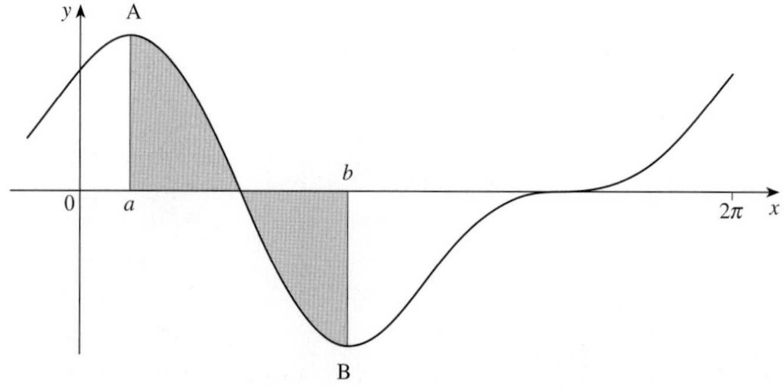

There is a maximum point at A and a minimum point at B.

(b) Write down the x-coordinate of point A.

(c) The region bounded by the graph, the x-axis and the lines $x = a$ and $x = b$ is shaded in the diagram above.

(i) Write down an expression that represents the area of this shaded region.

(ii) Calculate the area of this shaded region. (© IBO 2005)

42 Vectors

This chapter introduces the idea of vectors as a way of doing geometry in two or three dimensions. When you have completed it, you should

- understand the idea of a translation, and how it can be expressed either in column form or in terms of basic unit vectors
- know and be able to use the rules of vector algebra
- understand the idea of displacement and position vectors, and use these to prove geometrical results.

42.1 Translations of a plane

In Section 30.1 you saw how to translate a graph through distance k in the x- or y-direction: $y = f(x)$ becomes respectively $y = f(x - k)$ or $y = f(x) + k$. A practical way of doing this is to draw the graph on a transparent sheet placed over a coordinate grid, and then to move this sheet across or up the grid by k units.

The essential feature of a translation is that the sheet moves over the grid without turning. A more general translation would move the sheet k units across and l units up the grid. This is shown in Fig. 42.1, where several points move in the same direction through the same distance. Such a translation is called a **vector** and is written $\begin{pmatrix} k \\ l \end{pmatrix}$.

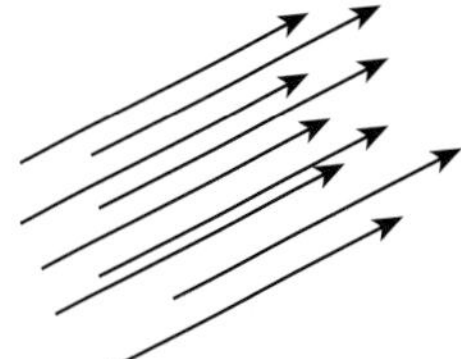

Fig. 42.1

For example, the translations of $y = f(x)$ described above would be performed by the vectors $\begin{pmatrix} k \\ 0 \end{pmatrix}$ and $\begin{pmatrix} 0 \\ k \end{pmatrix}$ respectively. A vector like $\begin{pmatrix} k \\ l \end{pmatrix}$ is often called a **column vector**.

In practice, drawing several arrows, as in Fig. 42.1, is not a convenient way of representing a vector. It is usual to draw just a single arrow, as in Fig. 42.2. But you must understand that the position of the arrow in the (x, y)-plane is of no significance. This arrow is just one of infinitely many that could be drawn to represent the vector.

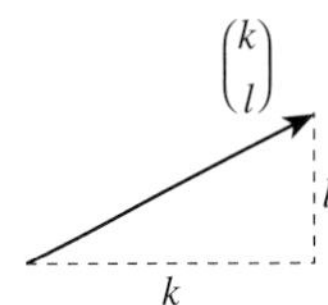

Fig. 42.2

Later you may meet other uses of vectors. For example, mechanics uses velocity vectors, momentum vectors, force vectors, and so on. When you need to make the distinction, the vectors described here are called **translation vectors**. These are the only vectors used in this book.

42.2 Vector algebra

It is often convenient to use a single letter to stand for a vector. In print, bold type is used to distinguish vectors from numbers. For example, in $\boldsymbol{p} = \begin{pmatrix} k \\ l \end{pmatrix}$, $\boldsymbol{p}$ is a vector but k and l are numbers, called the **components** of the vector $\boldsymbol{p}$ in the x- and y-directions.

In handwriting vectors are indicated by a wavy line underneath the letter: $\underset{\sim}{p} = \begin{pmatrix} k \\ l \end{pmatrix}$. It is important to get into the habit of writing vectors in this way, so that it is quite clear in your work which letters stand for vectors and which for numbers.

If s is any number and $\boldsymbol{p}$ is any vector, then $s\boldsymbol{p}$ is another vector. If $s > 0$, the vector $s\boldsymbol{p}$ is a translation in the same direction as $\boldsymbol{p}$ but s times as large; if $s < 0$ it is in the opposite direction and $|s|$ times as large. A number such as s is often called a **scalar**, because it usually changes the scale of the vector.

The similar triangles in Fig. 42.3 show that $s\boldsymbol{p} = \begin{pmatrix} sk \\ sl \end{pmatrix}$. In particular, $(-1)\boldsymbol{p} = \begin{pmatrix} -k \\ -l \end{pmatrix}$, which is a translation of the same length as $\boldsymbol{p}$ but in the opposite direction. It is denoted by $-\boldsymbol{p}$, and illustrated in Fig. 42.4.

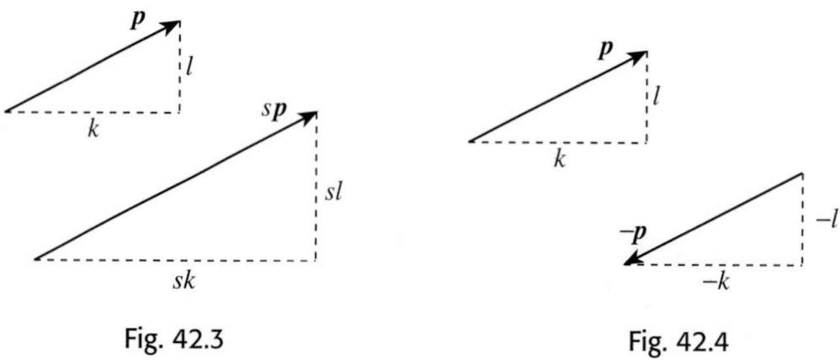

Fig. 42.3

Fig. 42.4

Vectors are added by performing one translation after another. In Fig. 42.5, $\boldsymbol{p}$ and $\boldsymbol{q}$ are two vectors. To form their sum, you want to represent them as a pair of arrows by which you can trace the path of a particular point of the moving sheet. In Fig. 42.6, $\boldsymbol{p}$ is shown by an arrow from U to V, and $\boldsymbol{q}$ by an arrow from V to W. Then when the translations are combined, the point of the sheet which was originally at U would move first to V and then to W. So the sum $\boldsymbol{p} + \boldsymbol{q}$ is represented by an arrow from U to W.

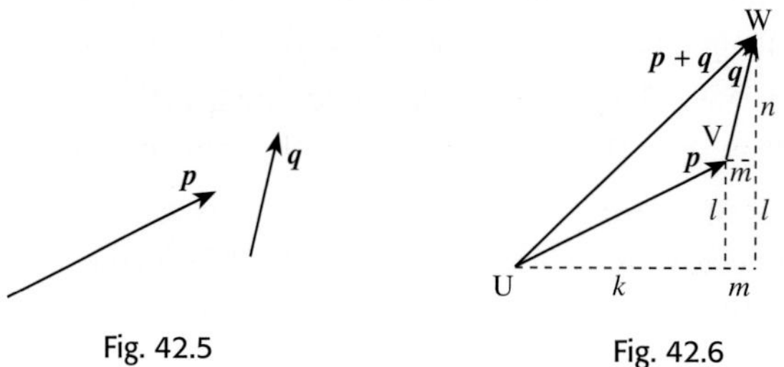

Fig. 42.5

Fig. 42.6

Fig. 42.6 also shows that:

$$\text{If } \boldsymbol{p} = \begin{pmatrix} k \\ l \end{pmatrix} \text{ and } \boldsymbol{q} = \begin{pmatrix} m \\ n \end{pmatrix}, \text{ then } \boldsymbol{p} + \boldsymbol{q} = \begin{pmatrix} k+m \\ l+n \end{pmatrix}.$$

To form the sum $\boldsymbol{q} + \boldsymbol{p}$ the translations are performed in the reverse order. In Fig. 42.7, $\boldsymbol{q}$ is now represented by the arrow from U to Z; and since UVWZ is a parallelogram $\boldsymbol{p}$ is represented by the arrow from Z to W. This shows that

$$\boldsymbol{p} + \boldsymbol{q} = \boldsymbol{q} + \boldsymbol{p}.$$

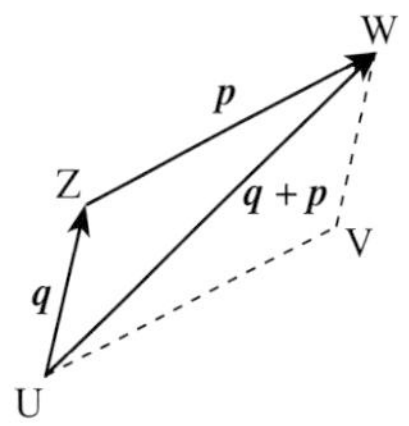

This is called the **commutative rule for addition** of vectors.

Fig. 42.7

Example 42.2.1

If $\boldsymbol{p} = \begin{pmatrix} 3 \\ -1 \end{pmatrix}$ and $\boldsymbol{q} = \begin{pmatrix} 2 \\ 3 \end{pmatrix}$, calculate (a) $\boldsymbol{p} + \boldsymbol{p}$, (b) $\boldsymbol{p} + \boldsymbol{q}$.

(a) $\boldsymbol{p} + \boldsymbol{p} = \begin{pmatrix} 3 \\ -1 \end{pmatrix} + \begin{pmatrix} 3 \\ -1 \end{pmatrix} = \begin{pmatrix} 3+3 \\ (-1)+(-1) \end{pmatrix} = \begin{pmatrix} 6 \\ -2 \end{pmatrix}.$

(b) $\boldsymbol{p} + \boldsymbol{q} = \begin{pmatrix} 3 \\ -1 \end{pmatrix} + \begin{pmatrix} 2 \\ 3 \end{pmatrix} = \begin{pmatrix} 3+2 \\ (-1)+3 \end{pmatrix} = \begin{pmatrix} 5 \\ 2 \end{pmatrix}.$

Example 42.2.2

If $\boldsymbol{p} = \begin{pmatrix} 2 \\ -3 \end{pmatrix}$, $\boldsymbol{q} = \begin{pmatrix} 1 \\ 2 \end{pmatrix}$ and $\boldsymbol{r} = \begin{pmatrix} 5 \\ 3 \end{pmatrix}$, show that there is a number s such that $\boldsymbol{p} + s\boldsymbol{q} = \boldsymbol{r}$.

You can write $\boldsymbol{p} + s\boldsymbol{q}$ in column vector form as

$$\begin{pmatrix} 2 \\ -3 \end{pmatrix} + s\begin{pmatrix} 1 \\ 2 \end{pmatrix} = \begin{pmatrix} 2 \\ -3 \end{pmatrix} + \begin{pmatrix} s \\ 2s \end{pmatrix} = \begin{pmatrix} 2+s \\ -3+2s \end{pmatrix}.$$

If this is equal to $\boldsymbol{r}$, then both the x- and y-components of the two vectors must be equal. This gives the two equations

$$2 + s = 5 \quad \text{and} \quad -3 + 2s = 3.$$

Both these equations are satisfied by $s = 3$, so it follows that $\boldsymbol{p} + 3\boldsymbol{q} = \boldsymbol{r}$. You can check this for yourself using squared paper, showing arrows representing $\boldsymbol{p}$, $\boldsymbol{q}$, $\boldsymbol{p} + 3\boldsymbol{q}$ and $\boldsymbol{r}$.

The idea of addition can be extended to three or more vectors. But when you write $\boldsymbol{p} + \boldsymbol{q} + \boldsymbol{r}$ it is not clear whether you first add $\boldsymbol{p}$ and $\boldsymbol{q}$ and then add $\boldsymbol{r}$ to the result, or whether you add $\boldsymbol{p}$ to the result of adding $\boldsymbol{q}$ and $\boldsymbol{r}$. Fig. 42.8 shows that it doesn't matter, since the outcome is the same either way. That is,

$$(\boldsymbol{p} + \boldsymbol{q}) + \boldsymbol{r} = \boldsymbol{p} + (\boldsymbol{q} + \boldsymbol{r}).$$

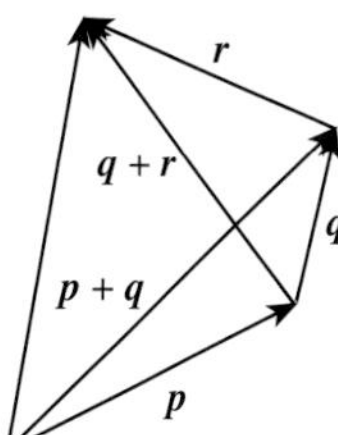

Fig. 42.8

This is called the **associative rule for addition** of vectors.

To complete the algebra of vector addition, the symbol **0** is needed for the **zero vector**, the 'stay-still' translation, which has the properties that, for any vector $\boldsymbol{p}$,

$$0\boldsymbol{p} = \mathbf{0}, \quad \boldsymbol{p} + \mathbf{0} = \boldsymbol{p}, \quad \text{and} \quad \boldsymbol{p} + (-\boldsymbol{p}) = \mathbf{0}.$$

Vector addition and multiplication by a scalar can be combined according to the two **distributive rules** for vectors:

$$s(\boldsymbol{p}+\boldsymbol{q}) = s\boldsymbol{p}+s\boldsymbol{q} \qquad \text{(from the similar triangles in Fig. 42.9)}$$

and $$(s+t)\boldsymbol{p} = s\boldsymbol{p}+t\boldsymbol{p} \qquad \text{(see Fig. 42.10).}$$

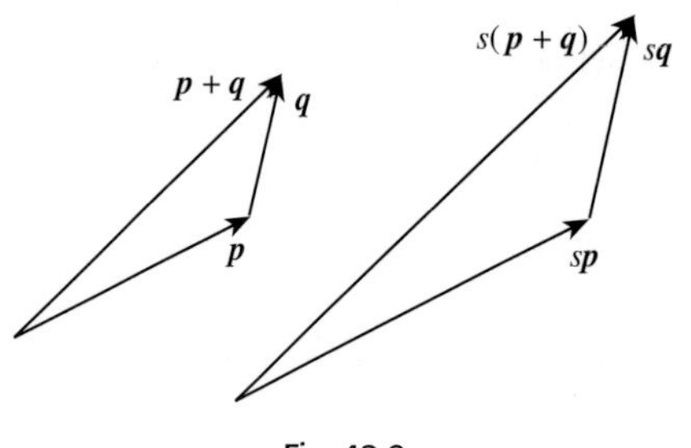

Fig. 42.9

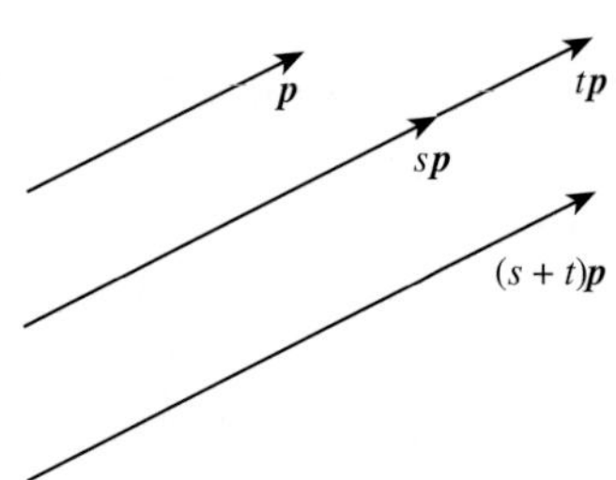

Fig. 42.10

Subtraction of vectors is defined by

$$\boldsymbol{p}+\boldsymbol{x}=\boldsymbol{q} \quad \text{means} \quad \boldsymbol{x}=\boldsymbol{q}-\boldsymbol{p} \quad \text{(and vice versa).}$$

This is illustrated in Fig. 42.11. Notice that to show $\boldsymbol{q}-\boldsymbol{p}$ you represent $\boldsymbol{p}$ and $\boldsymbol{q}$ by arrows which both start at the same point; this is different from addition, where the arrow representing $\boldsymbol{q}$ starts where the $\boldsymbol{p}$ arrow ends. Comparing Fig. 42.11 with Fig. 42.12 shows that

$$\boldsymbol{q}-\boldsymbol{p}=\boldsymbol{q}+(-\boldsymbol{p}).$$

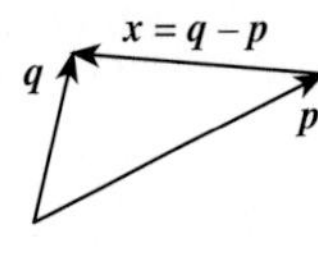

Fig. 42.11

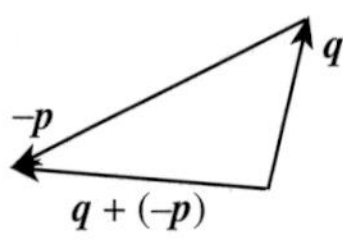

Fig. 42.12

In summary, the rules of vector addition, subtraction and multiplication by scalars look very similar to the rules of number addition, subtraction and multiplication. But the diagrams show that the rules for vectors are interpreted differently from the rules for numbers.

42.3 Basic unit vectors

If you apply the rules of vector algebra to a vector in column form, you can see that

$$\boldsymbol{p}=\begin{pmatrix}k\\l\end{pmatrix}=\begin{pmatrix}k+0\\0+l\end{pmatrix}=\begin{pmatrix}k\\0\end{pmatrix}+\begin{pmatrix}0\\l\end{pmatrix}=k\begin{pmatrix}1\\0\end{pmatrix}+l\begin{pmatrix}0\\1\end{pmatrix}.$$

The vectors $\begin{pmatrix}1\\0\end{pmatrix}$ and $\begin{pmatrix}0\\1\end{pmatrix}$ which appear in this last expression are called **basic unit vectors** in the x- and y-directions. They are denoted by the letters $\boldsymbol{i}$ and $\boldsymbol{j}$, so

$$\boldsymbol{p}=k\boldsymbol{i}+l\boldsymbol{j}.$$

This is illustrated by Fig. 42.13. The equation shows that any vector in the plane can be constructed as the sum of multiples of the two basic vectors $\boldsymbol{i}$ and $\boldsymbol{j}$.

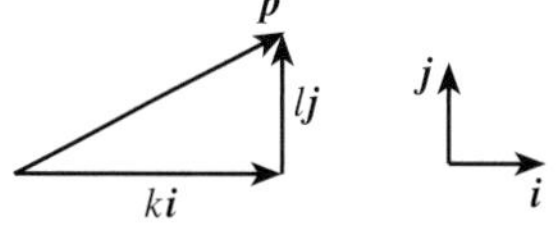

Fig. 42.13

The vectors $k\boldsymbol{i}$ and $l\boldsymbol{j}$ are called the **component vectors** of $\boldsymbol{p}$ in the x- and y-directions.

You now have two alternative notations for doing algebra with vectors. For example, if you want to find $3\boldsymbol{p} - 2\boldsymbol{q}$, where $\boldsymbol{p}$ is $\begin{pmatrix} 2 \\ 5 \end{pmatrix}$ and $\boldsymbol{q}$ is $\begin{pmatrix} 1 \\ -3 \end{pmatrix}$, you can write either

$$3\begin{pmatrix} 2 \\ 5 \end{pmatrix} - 2\begin{pmatrix} 1 \\ -3 \end{pmatrix} = \begin{pmatrix} 6 \\ 15 \end{pmatrix} - \begin{pmatrix} 2 \\ -6 \end{pmatrix} = \begin{pmatrix} 6-2 \\ 15-(-6) \end{pmatrix} = \begin{pmatrix} 4 \\ 21 \end{pmatrix}$$

or

$$3(2\boldsymbol{i} + 5\boldsymbol{j}) - 2(\boldsymbol{i} - 3\boldsymbol{j}) = (6\boldsymbol{i} + 15\boldsymbol{j}) - (2\boldsymbol{i} - 6\boldsymbol{j}) = 6\boldsymbol{i} + 15\boldsymbol{j} - 2\boldsymbol{i} + 6\boldsymbol{j} = 4\boldsymbol{i} + 21\boldsymbol{j}.$$

You will find that sometimes one of these forms is more convenient than the other, but more often it makes no difference which you use.

42.4 Vectors in three dimensions

The power of vector methods is best appreciated when they are used to do geometry in three dimensions. This requires setting up axes in three directions, as in Fig. 42.14. The usual convention is to take x- and y-axes in a horizontal plane (shown shaded), and to add a z-axis pointing vertically upwards.

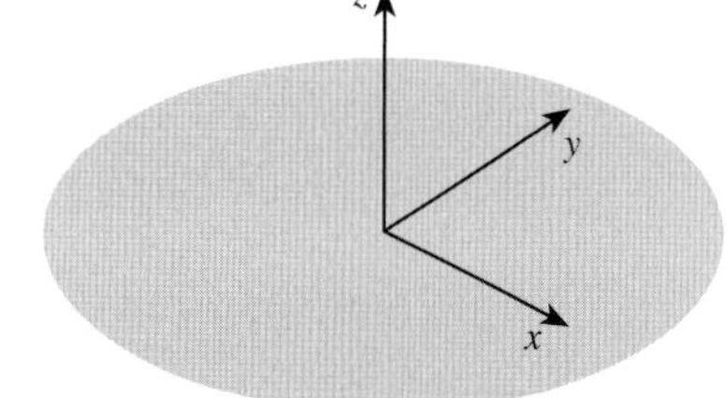

Fig. 42.14

These axes are said to be 'right-handed': if the outstretched index finger of your right hand points in the x-direction, and you bend your middle finger to point in the y-direction, then your thumb can naturally point up in the z-direction.

A vector $\boldsymbol{p}$ in three dimensions is a translation of the whole of space relative to a fixed coordinate framework. (You could imagine Fig. 42.1 as a blizzard, with the arrows showing the translations of the individual snowflakes.)

It is written as $\begin{pmatrix} l \\ m \\ n \end{pmatrix}$, which is a translation of l, m and n units in the x-, y- and z-directions. It can also be written in the form $l\boldsymbol{i} + m\boldsymbol{j} + n\boldsymbol{k}$, where $\boldsymbol{i} = \begin{pmatrix} 1 \\ 0 \\ 0 \end{pmatrix}$, $\boldsymbol{j} = \begin{pmatrix} 0 \\ 1 \\ 0 \end{pmatrix}$, $\boldsymbol{k} = \begin{pmatrix} 0 \\ 0 \\ 1 \end{pmatrix}$ are basic unit vectors in the x-, y- and z-directions.

Exercise 42A

When you are asked to illustrate a vector equation geometrically, you should show vectors as arrows on a grid of squares, either on paper or on screen.

1 Illustrate the following equations geometrically.

(a) $\begin{pmatrix}4\\1\end{pmatrix}+\begin{pmatrix}-3\\2\end{pmatrix}=\begin{pmatrix}1\\3\end{pmatrix}$ (b) $3\begin{pmatrix}1\\-2\end{pmatrix}=\begin{pmatrix}3\\-6\end{pmatrix}$

(c) $\begin{pmatrix}0\\4\end{pmatrix}+2\begin{pmatrix}1\\-2\end{pmatrix}=\begin{pmatrix}2\\0\end{pmatrix}$ (d) $\begin{pmatrix}3\\1\end{pmatrix}-\begin{pmatrix}5\\1\end{pmatrix}=\begin{pmatrix}-2\\0\end{pmatrix}$

(e) $3\begin{pmatrix}-1\\2\end{pmatrix}-\begin{pmatrix}-4\\3\end{pmatrix}=\begin{pmatrix}1\\3\end{pmatrix}$ (f) $4\begin{pmatrix}2\\3\end{pmatrix}-3\begin{pmatrix}3\\2\end{pmatrix}=\begin{pmatrix}-1\\6\end{pmatrix}$

(g) $\begin{pmatrix}2\\-3\end{pmatrix}+\begin{pmatrix}4\\5\end{pmatrix}+\begin{pmatrix}-6\\-2\end{pmatrix}=\begin{pmatrix}0\\0\end{pmatrix}$ (h) $2\begin{pmatrix}3\\-1\end{pmatrix}+3\begin{pmatrix}-2\\3\end{pmatrix}+\begin{pmatrix}0\\-7\end{pmatrix}=\begin{pmatrix}0\\0\end{pmatrix}$

2 Rewrite each of the equations in Question 1 using unit vector notation.

3 Express each of the following vectors as column vectors, and illustrate your answers geometrically.

(a) $\mathbf{i}+2\mathbf{j}$ (b) $3\mathbf{i}$ (c) $\mathbf{j}-\mathbf{i}$ (d) $4\mathbf{i}-3\mathbf{j}$

4 Show that there is a number s such that $s\begin{pmatrix}1\\2\end{pmatrix}+\begin{pmatrix}-3\\1\end{pmatrix}=\begin{pmatrix}-1\\5\end{pmatrix}$. Illustrate your answer geometrically.

5 If $\mathbf{p}=5\mathbf{i}-3\mathbf{j}$, $\mathbf{q}=2\mathbf{j}-\mathbf{i}$ and $\mathbf{r}=\mathbf{i}+5\mathbf{j}$, show that there is a number s such that $\mathbf{p}+s\mathbf{q}=\mathbf{r}$. Illustrate your answer geometrically.

Rearrange this equation so as to express $\mathbf{q}$ in terms of $\mathbf{p}$ and $\mathbf{r}$. Illustrate the rearranged equation geometrically.

6 Find numbers s and t such that $s\begin{pmatrix}5\\4\end{pmatrix}+t\begin{pmatrix}-3\\-2\end{pmatrix}=\begin{pmatrix}1\\2\end{pmatrix}$. Illustrate your answer geometrically.

7 If $\mathbf{p}=4\mathbf{i}+\mathbf{j}$, $\mathbf{q}=6\mathbf{i}-5\mathbf{j}$ and $\mathbf{r}=3\mathbf{i}+4\mathbf{j}$, find numbers s and t such that $s\mathbf{p}+t\mathbf{q}=\mathbf{r}$. Illustrate your answer geometrically.

8 Show that it isn't possible to find numbers s and t such that $\begin{pmatrix}4\\-2\end{pmatrix}+s\begin{pmatrix}3\\1\end{pmatrix}=\begin{pmatrix}-6\\3\end{pmatrix}$ and $\begin{pmatrix}3\\4\end{pmatrix}+t\begin{pmatrix}-1\\2\end{pmatrix}=\begin{pmatrix}1\\1\end{pmatrix}$. Give geometrical reasons.

9 If $\mathbf{p}=2\mathbf{i}+3\mathbf{j}$, $\mathbf{q}=4\mathbf{i}-5\mathbf{j}$ and $\mathbf{r}=\mathbf{i}-4\mathbf{j}$, find a set of numbers f, g and h such that $f\mathbf{p}+g\mathbf{q}+h\mathbf{r}=\mathbf{0}$. Illustrate your answer geometrically. Give a reason why there is more than one possible answer to this question.

10 If $\mathbf{p}=3\mathbf{i}-\mathbf{j}$, $\mathbf{q}=4\mathbf{i}+5\mathbf{j}$ and $\mathbf{r}=2\mathbf{j}-6\mathbf{i}$,

(a) can you find numbers s and t such that $\mathbf{q}=s\mathbf{p}+t\mathbf{r}$,

(b) can you find numbers u and v such that $\mathbf{r}=u\mathbf{p}+v\mathbf{q}$?

Give a geometrical reason for your answers.

11 Write the vectors $\boldsymbol{a} = \begin{pmatrix} 1 \\ -2 \\ 1 \end{pmatrix}$ and $\boldsymbol{b} = \begin{pmatrix} -3 \\ 1 \\ 2 \end{pmatrix}$ in $\boldsymbol{i}$, $\boldsymbol{j}$, $\boldsymbol{k}$ notation, and calculate $3\boldsymbol{a} - 2\boldsymbol{b}$ giving your answer in $\boldsymbol{i}$, $\boldsymbol{j}$, $\boldsymbol{k}$ notation.

12 If $\boldsymbol{v} = \boldsymbol{i} - 8\boldsymbol{j} - \boldsymbol{k}$ and $\boldsymbol{w} = -2\boldsymbol{i} + 3\boldsymbol{j} - \boldsymbol{k}$, find $2\boldsymbol{v} - 3\boldsymbol{w}$ giving your answer in column form.

42.5 Position vectors

If E and F are two points on a grid, there is a unique translation which takes you from E to F. This translation can be represented by the arrow which starts at E and ends at F, and it is denoted by the symbol $\overrightarrow{\mathrm{EF}}$.

(Some books use **EF** in bold type rather than $\overrightarrow{\mathrm{EF}}$ to emphasise that it is a vector.)

However, although this translation is unique, its name is not. If G and H are two other points on the grid such that the line segments [EF] and [GH] are parallel and equal in length (so that EFHG is a parallelogram, see Fig. 42.15), then the translation $\overrightarrow{\mathrm{EF}}$ also takes you from G to H, so that it could also be denoted by $\overrightarrow{\mathrm{GH}}$. In a vector equation $\overrightarrow{\mathrm{EF}}$ could be replaced by $\overrightarrow{\mathrm{GH}}$ without affecting the truth of the statement.

Vectors written like this are sometimes called **displacement vectors**. But they are not a different kind of vector, just translation vectors written in a different way.

There is, however, one displacement vector which is especially important. This is the translation that starts at the origin O and ends at a point A where (in Fig. 42.15) $\overrightarrow{\mathrm{OA}} = \overrightarrow{\mathrm{EF}} = \overrightarrow{\mathrm{GH}}$. The translation which takes you from O to A is called the **position vector** of A.

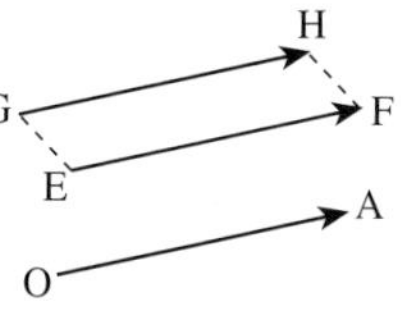

Fig. 42.15

There is a close link between the coordinates of A and the component form of its position vector. If A has coordinates (u, v), then to get from O to A you must move u units in the x-direction and v units in the y-direction, so that the vector $\overrightarrow{\mathrm{OA}}$ has components u and v.

The position vector of the point A with coordinates (u, v) is

$$\overrightarrow{\mathrm{OA}} = \begin{pmatrix} u \\ v \end{pmatrix} = u\boldsymbol{i} + v\boldsymbol{j}.$$

A useful convention is to use the same letter for a point and its position vector. For example, the position vector of the point A can be denoted by $\boldsymbol{a}$. This 'alphabet convention' will be used wherever possible in this book. It has the advantages that it economises on letters of the alphabet and avoids the need for repetitive definitions.

42.6 Algebra with position vectors

Multiplication by a scalar has a simple interpretation in terms of position vectors. If the vector $s\boldsymbol{a}$ is the position vector of a point D, then:

- If $s > 0$, D lies on the directed line OA (produced (extended) if necessary) such that $\text{OD} = s\text{OA}$.
- If $s < 0$, D lies on the directed line AO produced such that $\text{OD} = |s|\,\text{OA}$.

This is shown in Fig. 42.16 for $s = \frac{3}{2}$ and $s = -\frac{1}{2}$.

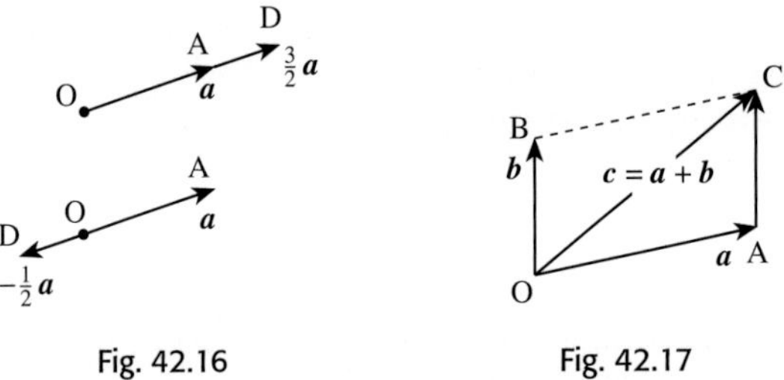

Fig. 42.16

Fig. 42.17

To identify the point with position vector $\boldsymbol{a} + \boldsymbol{b}$ is not quite so easy, because the arrows from O to A and from O to B are not related in the way needed for addition (see Fig. 42.6). It is therefore necessary to complete the parallelogram OACB, as in Fig. 42.17.

Then

$$\boldsymbol{a} + \boldsymbol{b} = \overrightarrow{\text{OA}} + \overrightarrow{\text{OB}} = \overrightarrow{\text{OA}} + \overrightarrow{\text{AC}} = \overrightarrow{\text{OC}}.$$

This is called the **parallelogram rule of addition** for position vectors.

Subtraction can be shown in either of two ways. If you compare Fig. 42.18 with Fig. 42.11, you will see that $\boldsymbol{b} - \boldsymbol{a}$ is the displacement vector $\overrightarrow{\text{AB}}$. To interpret this as a position vector, draw a line segment [OE] equal and parallel to [AB], so that $\overrightarrow{\text{OE}} = \overrightarrow{\text{AB}}$. Then E is the point with position vector $\boldsymbol{b} - \boldsymbol{a}$.

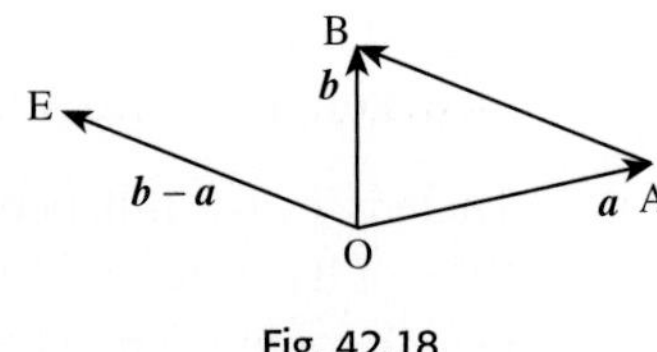

Fig. 42.18

Alternatively, you can write $\boldsymbol{b} - \boldsymbol{a}$ as $\boldsymbol{b} + (-\boldsymbol{a})$, and then apply the parallelogram rule of addition to the points with position vectors $\boldsymbol{b}$ and $-\boldsymbol{a}$. By comparing Figs. 42.18 and 42.19 you can see that this leads to the same point E.

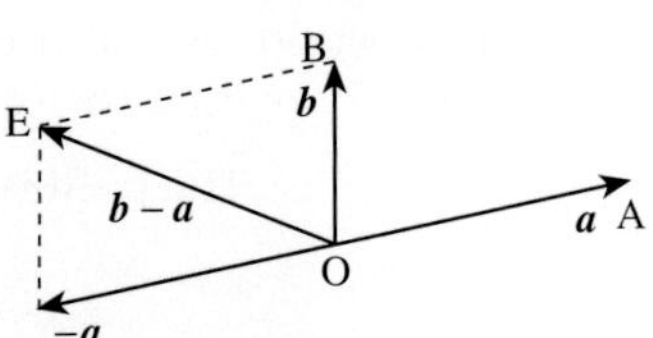

Fig. 42.19

You will use the following relation often; it is worth remembering:

> The displacement vector $\overrightarrow{\text{AB}}$ is given by
>
> $$\overrightarrow{\text{AB}} = \overrightarrow{\text{OB}} - \overrightarrow{\text{OA}} = \boldsymbol{b} - \boldsymbol{a}.$$

Example 42.6.1

Points A and B have position vectors $\boldsymbol{a}$ and $\boldsymbol{b}$. Find the position vectors of

(a) the mid-point M of [AB], (b) the point of trisection T such that AT $= \frac{2}{3}$AB.

(a) **Method 1** The displacement vector $\overrightarrow{\mathrm{AB}} = \boldsymbol{b} - \boldsymbol{a}$, so $\overrightarrow{\mathrm{AM}} = \frac{1}{2}(\boldsymbol{b} - \boldsymbol{a})$. Therefore

$$\begin{aligned}\boldsymbol{m} &= \overrightarrow{\mathrm{OM}} \\ &= \overrightarrow{\mathrm{OA}} + \overrightarrow{\mathrm{AM}} \\ &= \boldsymbol{a} + \tfrac{1}{2}(\boldsymbol{b} - \boldsymbol{a}) = \tfrac{1}{2}\boldsymbol{a} + \tfrac{1}{2}\boldsymbol{b}.\end{aligned}$$

Method 2 If the parallelogram OACB is completed (see Fig. 42.17) then $\boldsymbol{c} = \boldsymbol{a} + \boldsymbol{b}$. Since the diagonals of OACB bisect each other, the mid-point M of [AB] is also the mid-point of [OC]. Therefore

$$\begin{aligned}\boldsymbol{m} &= \tfrac{1}{2}\boldsymbol{c} \\ &= \tfrac{1}{2}(\boldsymbol{a} + \boldsymbol{b}) = \tfrac{1}{2}\boldsymbol{a} + \tfrac{1}{2}\boldsymbol{b}.\end{aligned}$$

(b) The first method of (a) can be modified. $\overrightarrow{\mathrm{AT}} = \frac{2}{3}\overrightarrow{\mathrm{AB}} = \frac{2}{3}(\boldsymbol{b} - \boldsymbol{a})$, so

$$\begin{aligned}\boldsymbol{t} &= \boldsymbol{a} + \tfrac{2}{3}(\boldsymbol{b} - \boldsymbol{a}) \\ &= \tfrac{1}{3}\boldsymbol{a} + \tfrac{2}{3}\boldsymbol{b}.\end{aligned}$$

The position vector of the mid-point M of [AB] is given by

$$\boldsymbol{m} = \tfrac{1}{2}(\boldsymbol{a} + \boldsymbol{b}).$$

The results of Example 42.6.1 can be used to prove an important theorem about triangles.

Example 42.6.2

In triangle ABC the mid-points of [BC], [CA] and [AB] are D, E and F. Prove that the line segments [AD], [BE] and [CF] (called the **medians**) meet at a point G, which is a point of trisection of each of the medians (see Fig. 42.20).

From Example 42.6.1, $\boldsymbol{d} = \frac{1}{2}\boldsymbol{b} + \frac{1}{2}\boldsymbol{c}$, and the point of trisection on the median [AD] closer to D has position vector

$$\begin{aligned}\tfrac{1}{3}\boldsymbol{a} + \tfrac{2}{3}\boldsymbol{d} &= \tfrac{1}{3}\boldsymbol{a} + \tfrac{2}{3}\left(\tfrac{1}{2}\boldsymbol{b} + \tfrac{1}{2}\boldsymbol{c}\right) \\ &= \tfrac{1}{3}\boldsymbol{a} + \tfrac{1}{3}\boldsymbol{b} + \tfrac{1}{3}\boldsymbol{c}.\end{aligned}$$

This last expression is symmetrical in $\boldsymbol{a}$, $\boldsymbol{b}$ and $\boldsymbol{c}$. It therefore also represents the point of trisection on the median [BE] closer to E, and the point of trisection on [CF] closer to F.

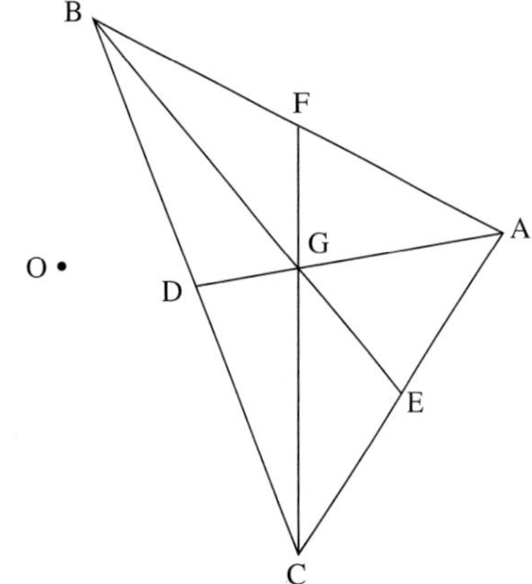

Fig. 42.20

Therefore the three medians meet each other at a point G, with position vector $\boldsymbol{g} = \frac{1}{3}(\boldsymbol{a} + \boldsymbol{b} + \boldsymbol{c})$. This point is called the **centroid** of the triangle.

Exercise 42B

In this exercise the alphabet convention is used, that $\boldsymbol{a}$ stands for the position vector of the point A, and so on.

1 The points A and B have coordinates (3, 1) and (1, 2). Plot on squared paper the points C, D, ... , H defined by the following vector equations, and state their coordinates.

(a) $\boldsymbol{c} = 3\boldsymbol{a}$ (b) $\boldsymbol{d} = -\boldsymbol{b}$ (c) $\boldsymbol{e} = \boldsymbol{a} - \boldsymbol{b}$

(d) $\boldsymbol{f} = \boldsymbol{b} - 3\boldsymbol{a}$ (e) $\boldsymbol{g} = \boldsymbol{b} + 3\boldsymbol{a}$ (f) $\boldsymbol{h} = \frac{1}{2}(\boldsymbol{b} + 3\boldsymbol{a})$

2 Points A and B have coordinates (2, 7) and (−3, −3) respectively. Use a vector method to find the coordinates of C and D, where

(a) C is the point such that $\overrightarrow{AC} = 3\,\overrightarrow{AB}$, (b) D is the point such that $\overrightarrow{AD} = \frac{3}{5}\,\overrightarrow{AB}$.

3 C is the point on [AB] produced such that $\overrightarrow{AB} = \overrightarrow{BC}$. Express C in terms of $\boldsymbol{a}$ and $\boldsymbol{b}$. Check your answer by using the result of Example 42.6.1(a) to find the position vector of the mid-point of [AC].

4 C is the point on [AB] such that AC : CB = 4 : 3. Express $\boldsymbol{c}$ in terms of $\boldsymbol{a}$ and $\boldsymbol{b}$.

5 If C is the point on [AB] such that $\overrightarrow{AC} = t\,\overrightarrow{AB}$, prove that $\boldsymbol{c} = t\boldsymbol{b} + (1 - t)\boldsymbol{a}$.

6 Write a vector equation connecting $\boldsymbol{a}$, $\boldsymbol{b}$, $\boldsymbol{c}$ and $\boldsymbol{d}$ to express the fact that $\overrightarrow{AB} = \overrightarrow{DC}$. Deduce from your equation that

(a) $\overrightarrow{DA} = \overrightarrow{CB}$,

(b) if E is the point such that OAEC is a parallelogram, then OBED is a parallelogram.

7 ABC is a triangle. D is the mid-point of [BC], E is the mid-point of [AC], F is the mid-point of [AB] and G is the mid-point of [EF]. Express the displacement vectors $\overrightarrow{AD}$ and $\overrightarrow{AG}$ in terms of $\boldsymbol{a}$, $\boldsymbol{b}$ and $\boldsymbol{c}$. What can you deduce about the points A, D and G?

8 A and B are points with coordinates (2, 1, 4) and (5, −5, −2). Find the coordinates of the point C such that $\overrightarrow{AC} = \frac{2}{3}\,\overrightarrow{AB}$.

9 Four points A, B, C and D with position vectors $\boldsymbol{a}$, $\boldsymbol{b}$, $\boldsymbol{c}$ and $\boldsymbol{d}$ are vertices of a tetrahedron. The mid-points of [BC], [CA], [AB], [AD], [BD], [CD] are denoted by P, Q, R, U, V, W. Find the position vectors of the mid-points of [PU], [QV] and [RW].

What do you notice about the answer? State your conclusion as a geometrical theorem.

10 If E and F are two points with position vectors $\boldsymbol{e}$ and $\boldsymbol{f}$, find the position vector of the point H such that $\overrightarrow{EH} = \frac{3}{4}\,\overrightarrow{EF}$.

With the notation of Question 9, express in terms of $\boldsymbol{a}$, $\boldsymbol{b}$, $\boldsymbol{c}$ and $\boldsymbol{d}$ the position vectors of G, the centroid of triangle ABC, and of H, the point on [DG] such that DH : HG = 3 : 1.

43 Scalar products of vectors

This chapter shows how vectors can be used to find results about lengths and angles. When you have completed it, you should

- know the definition of the scalar product, and its expression in components
- be able to find the lengths of vectors and the angle between them
- be able to use the rules of vector algebra which involve scalar products.

43.1 The magnitude of a vector

Any translation can be described by giving its length and direction. The length is usually called the **magnitude** of the vector. The notation used for the magnitude of a vector $\boldsymbol{v}$, ignoring its direction, is $|\boldsymbol{v}|$.

If you have two vectors $\boldsymbol{v}$ and $\boldsymbol{w}$ which are not equal, but which have equal magnitudes, then you can write $|\boldsymbol{v}| = |\boldsymbol{w}|$.

If s is a scalar multiple of $\boldsymbol{v}$, then it follows from the definition of $s\boldsymbol{v}$ (see Section 42.2) that $|s\boldsymbol{v}| = |s| \times |\boldsymbol{v}|$. This is true whether s is positive or negative (or zero).

The symbol for the magnitude of a vector is the same as the one for the modulus of a real number, but this does not present a problem. In fact, a real number x behaves just like the vector $x\boldsymbol{i}$ in one dimension, where $\boldsymbol{i}$ is a basic unit vector. This can be used to represent a displacement on the number line, and the modulus $|x|$ then measures the magnitude of the displacement, whether it is in the positive or the negative direction.

A vector of magnitude 1 is called a **unit vector**. The basic unit vectors $\boldsymbol{i}$, $\boldsymbol{j}$, $\boldsymbol{k}$ defined in Chapter 42 are examples of unit vectors: there is a unit vector in every direction.

43.2 Scalar products

In Chapter 42 vectors were added, subtracted and multiplied by scalars, but they were not multiplied together. The next step is to define the product of two vectors:

The **scalar product**, or **dot product**, or **inner product** of vectors $\boldsymbol{v}$ and $\boldsymbol{w}$ is the number (or scalar) $|\boldsymbol{v}| \times |\boldsymbol{w}| \cos\theta$, where θ is the angle between the directions of $\boldsymbol{v}$ and $\boldsymbol{w}$. It is written $\boldsymbol{v} \cdot \boldsymbol{w}$ and pronounced 'v dot w'.

The angle θ may be acute or obtuse, but it is important that it is the angle between $\boldsymbol{v}$ and $\boldsymbol{w}$, and not (for example) the angle between $\boldsymbol{v}$ and $-\boldsymbol{w}$. It is best to show θ in a diagram in which the vectors are represented by arrows with their tails at the same point, as in Fig. 43.1.

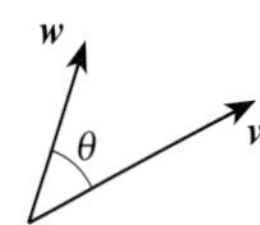

Fig. 43.1

The reason for calling this the 'scalar product', rather than simply the product, is that mathematicians also use another product, called the 'vector product'. But it is important to distinguish the scalar product from 'multiplication by a scalar', which you met in Chapter 42. To avoid confusion, many people prefer to use the alternative name 'dot product'.

You must always insert the 'dot' between $\mathbf{v}$ and $\mathbf{w}$ for the scalar product, but you must *not* insert a dot between s and $\mathbf{v}$ when multiplying a vector by a scalar.

For example, you can never have a scalar product of three vectors, $\mathbf{u} \cdot \mathbf{v} \cdot \mathbf{w}$. You will remember from Section 42.2 that the sum of these three vectors can be regarded as $(\mathbf{u} + \mathbf{v}) + \mathbf{w}$ or as $\mathbf{u} + (\mathbf{v} + \mathbf{w})$, and that these expressions are equal. But $(\mathbf{u} \cdot \mathbf{v}) \cdot \mathbf{w}$ has no meaning: $\mathbf{u} \cdot \mathbf{v}$ is a scalar, and you cannot form a dot product of this scalar with the vector $\mathbf{w}$. Similarly, $\mathbf{u} \cdot (\mathbf{v} \cdot \mathbf{w})$ has no meaning.

However, $s\,(\mathbf{v} \cdot \mathbf{w})$, where s is scalar, does have a meaning; as you would expect, $s\,(\mathbf{v} \cdot \mathbf{w})$ is equal to $(s\mathbf{v}) \cdot \mathbf{w}$. The proof depends on whether s is positive (see Fig. 43.2) or negative (see Fig. 43.3).

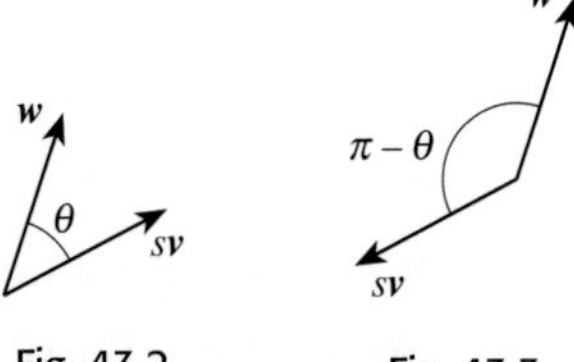

Fig. 43.2 Fig. 43.3

If $s > 0$, then the angle between $s\mathbf{v}$ and $\mathbf{w}$ is θ, so

$$\begin{aligned}(s\mathbf{v}) \cdot \mathbf{w} &= |s\mathbf{v}| \times |\mathbf{w}| \cos\theta \\ &= |s| \times |\mathbf{v}| \times |\mathbf{w}| \cos\theta \\ &= |s| \times (|\mathbf{v}| \times |\mathbf{w}| \cos\theta) \\ &= s\,(\mathbf{v} \cdot \mathbf{w}).\end{aligned}$$

If $s < 0$, then the angle between $s\mathbf{v}$ and $\mathbf{w}$ is $\pi - \theta$, and $s = -|s|$, so

$$\begin{aligned}(s\mathbf{v}) \cdot \mathbf{w} &= |s\mathbf{v}| \times |\mathbf{w}| \cos(\pi - \theta) \\ &= |s| \times |\mathbf{v}| \times |\mathbf{w}| (-\cos\theta) \\ &= -|s| \times (|\mathbf{v}| \times |\mathbf{w}| \cos\theta) \\ &= s\,(\mathbf{v} \cdot \mathbf{w}).\end{aligned}$$

Another property of the scalar product is that $\mathbf{v} \cdot \mathbf{w} = \mathbf{w} \cdot \mathbf{v}$, which follows immediately from the definition. This is called the **commutative rule for scalar products**.

There are three important special cases in the definition of the scalar product. They provide ways of using vectors to find lengths, to identify right angles and to identify parallel vectors.

- Take $\theta = 0$ and put $\mathbf{w} = \mathbf{v}$. Then

  $\mathbf{v} \cdot \mathbf{v} = |\mathbf{v}|^2$ ($\mathbf{v} \cdot \mathbf{v}$ is sometimes written as $\mathbf{v}^2$).

- Take $\theta = \frac{1}{2}\pi$. Then, if neither $\mathbf{v}$ nor $\mathbf{w}$ is the zero vector,

  $\mathbf{v} \cdot \mathbf{w} = 0$ is the same as saying $\mathbf{v}$ and $\mathbf{w}$ are in perpendicular directions.

- Take $\theta = 0$ or $\theta = \pi$. Then, if neither $\mathbf{v}$ nor $\mathbf{w}$ is the zero vector,

  $\mathbf{v} \cdot \mathbf{w} = \pm|\mathbf{v}|\,|\mathbf{w}|$ is the same as saying that $\mathbf{v}$ and $\mathbf{w}$ are in parallel directions.

43.3 The distributive rule

The rules in the last section suggest that algebra with scalar products is much like ordinary algebra, except that some expressions (such as the scalar product of three vectors) have no meaning. You need one more rule to be able to use vectors to get geometrical results. This is the **distributive rule** for multiplying out brackets:

$$(\boldsymbol{u}+\boldsymbol{v})\cdot\boldsymbol{w}=\boldsymbol{u}\cdot\boldsymbol{w}+\boldsymbol{v}\cdot\boldsymbol{w}.$$

This rule is absolutely vital for the scalar product to be useful, but unfortunately it is difficult to prove properly – you will be relieved to know that the property will be assumed!

43.4 Scalar products in component form

In the special cases at the end of Section 43.2, take $\boldsymbol{v}$ and $\boldsymbol{w}$ to be basic unit vectors. You then get:

> For the basic unit vectors $\boldsymbol{i}$, $\boldsymbol{j}$, $\boldsymbol{k}$,
> $$\boldsymbol{i}\cdot\boldsymbol{i}=\boldsymbol{j}\cdot\boldsymbol{j}=\boldsymbol{k}\cdot\boldsymbol{k}=1,$$
> and $\boldsymbol{j}\cdot\boldsymbol{k}=\boldsymbol{k}\cdot\boldsymbol{i}=\boldsymbol{i}\cdot\boldsymbol{j}=0.$

In the previous chapter vectors p and q were written as $\mathrm{k}i+\mathrm{l}j$ and $\mathrm{m}i+\mathrm{n}j$. You will see that this has already used eight letters of the alphabet, even in two dimensions. To economise on letters you can use a suffix notation, writing a general vector v as $\mathrm{v}_1 i+\mathrm{v}_2 j+\mathrm{v}_3 k$ and w as $\mathrm{w}_1 i+\mathrm{w}_2 j+\mathrm{w}_3 k$. Then

$$\begin{aligned}\boldsymbol{v}\cdot\boldsymbol{w}&=(v_1\boldsymbol{i}+v_2\boldsymbol{j}+v_3\boldsymbol{k})\cdot(w_1\boldsymbol{i}+w_2\boldsymbol{j}+w_3\boldsymbol{k})\\&=v_1w_1\boldsymbol{i}\cdot\boldsymbol{i}+v_1w_2\boldsymbol{i}\cdot\boldsymbol{j}+v_1w_3\boldsymbol{i}\cdot\boldsymbol{k}+v_2w_1\boldsymbol{j}\cdot\boldsymbol{i}+v_2w_2\boldsymbol{j}\cdot\boldsymbol{j}+v_2w_3\boldsymbol{j}\cdot\boldsymbol{k}\\&\qquad+v_3w_1\boldsymbol{k}\cdot\boldsymbol{i}+v_3w_2\boldsymbol{k}\cdot\boldsymbol{j}+v_3w_3\boldsymbol{k}\cdot\boldsymbol{k}\\&=v_1w_1\times1+v_1w_2\times0+v_1w_3\times0+v_2w_1\times0+v_2w_2\times1+v_2w_3\times0\\&\qquad+v_3w_1\times0+v_3w_2\times0+v_3w_3\times1\\&=v_1w_1+v_2w_2+v_3w_3.\end{aligned}$$

> In component form, the scalar product is
> $$\begin{aligned}\begin{pmatrix}v_1\\v_2\\v_3\end{pmatrix}\cdot\begin{pmatrix}w_1\\w_2\\w_3\end{pmatrix}&=(v_1\boldsymbol{i}+v_2\boldsymbol{j}+v_3\boldsymbol{k})\cdot(w_1\boldsymbol{i}+w_2\boldsymbol{j}+w_3\boldsymbol{k})\\&=v_1w_1+v_2w_2+v_3w_3.\end{aligned}$$

Combining the definition of scalar product with the component form gives

> $$|\boldsymbol{v}|\,|\boldsymbol{w}|\cos\theta=v_1w_1+v_2w_2+v_3w_3.$$

These results have many applications. In particular, $\boldsymbol{v}\cdot\boldsymbol{v}=v_1^2+v_2^2+v_3^2$, showing that $\boldsymbol{v}\cdot\boldsymbol{v}$ is the square of the length of the vector $\boldsymbol{v}$.

Thus, $|\boldsymbol{v}|^2=v_1^2+v_2^2+v_3^2$, so that $|\boldsymbol{v}|=\sqrt{v_1^2+v_2^2+v_3^2}$.

Also, if you know the components of two non-zero vectors, you can easily find out if the vectors are perpendicular by testing to see if $\cos\theta = 0$. So, using $|\boldsymbol{v}|\,|\boldsymbol{w}|\cos\theta = v_1w_1 + v_2w_2 + v_3w_3$, if $v_1w_1 + v_2w_2 + v_3w_3 = 0$ then $\cos\theta = 0$ and the vectors are perpendicular.

The non-zero vectors $\boldsymbol{v}$ and $\boldsymbol{w}$ are perpendicular if and only if $\boldsymbol{v} \cdot \boldsymbol{w} = 0$.

Similarly if you know the components of two non-zero vectors, you can find out whether the vectors are parallel by testing to see if the angle between them is $0°$ or $180°$, that is to see whether $\cos\theta = \pm 1$.

Finally, you can turn the formula $|\boldsymbol{v}|\,|\boldsymbol{w}|\cos\theta = v_1w_1 + v_2w_2 + v_3w_3$ round to find the angle between two vectors.

The angle θ between two non-zero vectors $\boldsymbol{v}$ and $\boldsymbol{w}$ is given by

$$\cos\theta = \frac{v_1w_1 + v_2w_2 + v_3w_3}{|\boldsymbol{v}|\,|\boldsymbol{w}|}.$$

Example 43.4.1

Prove that the vectors $3\boldsymbol{i} - 2\boldsymbol{j} + 4\boldsymbol{k}$ and $-4\boldsymbol{i} - 8\boldsymbol{j} - \boldsymbol{k}$ are perpendicular.

The scalar product of these vectors is

$$\begin{aligned}(3\boldsymbol{i} - 2\boldsymbol{j} + 4\boldsymbol{k}) \cdot (-4\boldsymbol{i} - 8\boldsymbol{j} - \boldsymbol{k}) &= 3 \times (-4) + (-2) \times (-8) + 4 \times (-1) \\ &= -12 + 16 - 4 = 0\end{aligned}$$

As the scalar product is 0, the vectors are perpendicular.

Example 43.4.2

Find the angle between the vectors $\boldsymbol{v} = \begin{pmatrix} 1 \\ 2 \\ 3 \end{pmatrix}$ and $\boldsymbol{w} = \begin{pmatrix} -4 \\ 2 \\ 1 \end{pmatrix}$.

Substituting in the equation $\cos\theta = \dfrac{v_1w_1 + v_2w_2 + v_3w_3}{|\boldsymbol{v}|\,|\boldsymbol{w}|}$ where θ is the angle between $\boldsymbol{v}$ and $\boldsymbol{w}$ requires some initial work.

$$|\boldsymbol{v}| = \sqrt{1^2 + 2^2 + 3^2} = \sqrt{14} \quad \text{and} \quad |\boldsymbol{w}| = \sqrt{(-4)^2 + 2^2 + 1^2} = \sqrt{21}.$$

Then

$$\begin{aligned}\cos\theta &= \frac{1 \times (-4) + 2 \times 2 + 3 \times 1}{\sqrt{14} \times \sqrt{21}} \\ &= \frac{3}{\sqrt{14} \times \sqrt{21}}. \\ \theta &= 1.39 \text{ (or } 79.9°\text{)}.\end{aligned}$$

The angle is 1.39 radians or $79.9°$.

Example 43.4.3
Find a unit vector in the same direction as $3\boldsymbol{i}+2\boldsymbol{j}-\boldsymbol{k}$.

Let the unit vector be $\boldsymbol{v}$.

Then as $\boldsymbol{v}$ is in the same direction as $3\boldsymbol{i}+2\boldsymbol{j}-\boldsymbol{k}$, it must be a scalar multiple of $3\boldsymbol{i}+2\boldsymbol{j}-\boldsymbol{k}$, and so is of the form $\boldsymbol{v}=\lambda(3\boldsymbol{i}+2\boldsymbol{j}-\boldsymbol{k})$, where $\lambda>0$.

Using the result in Section 43.1,

$$\begin{aligned}|\boldsymbol{v}| &= \lambda\,|3\boldsymbol{i}+2\boldsymbol{j}-\boldsymbol{k}|\\ &= \lambda\sqrt{3^2+2^2+(-1)^2}\\ &= \lambda\sqrt{9+4+1}=\lambda\sqrt{14},\end{aligned}$$

and since $\boldsymbol{v}$ is a unit vector $\lambda\sqrt{14}=1$, so $\lambda=\dfrac{1}{\sqrt{14}}$.

So $\boldsymbol{v}=\dfrac{1}{\sqrt{14}}(3\boldsymbol{i}+2\boldsymbol{j}-\boldsymbol{k})$.

Exercise 43

1 Let $\boldsymbol{a}=\begin{pmatrix}3\\2\end{pmatrix}$, $\boldsymbol{b}=\begin{pmatrix}-4\\2\end{pmatrix}$ and $\boldsymbol{c}=\begin{pmatrix}1\\4\end{pmatrix}$. Calculate $\boldsymbol{a}\cdot\boldsymbol{b}$, $\boldsymbol{a}\cdot\boldsymbol{c}$ and $\boldsymbol{a}\cdot(\boldsymbol{b}+\boldsymbol{c})$, and verify that $\boldsymbol{a}\cdot(\boldsymbol{b}+\boldsymbol{c})=\boldsymbol{a}\cdot\boldsymbol{b}+\boldsymbol{a}\cdot\boldsymbol{c}$.

2 Let $\boldsymbol{a}=2\boldsymbol{i}-\boldsymbol{j}$, $\boldsymbol{b}=4\boldsymbol{i}-3\boldsymbol{j}$ and $\boldsymbol{c}=-2\boldsymbol{i}-\boldsymbol{j}$. Calculate $\boldsymbol{a}\cdot\boldsymbol{b}$, $\boldsymbol{a}\cdot\boldsymbol{c}$ and $\boldsymbol{a}\cdot(\boldsymbol{b}+\boldsymbol{c})$, and verify that $\boldsymbol{a}\cdot(\boldsymbol{b}+\boldsymbol{c})=\boldsymbol{a}\cdot\boldsymbol{b}+\boldsymbol{a}\cdot\boldsymbol{c}$.

3 Let $\boldsymbol{u}=\begin{pmatrix}3\\-1\\4\end{pmatrix}$, $\boldsymbol{v}=\begin{pmatrix}-1\\-9\\3\end{pmatrix}$ and $\boldsymbol{w}=\begin{pmatrix}33\\-13\\-28\end{pmatrix}$. Calculate $\boldsymbol{u}\cdot\boldsymbol{v}$, $\boldsymbol{u}\cdot\boldsymbol{w}$ and $\boldsymbol{v}\cdot\boldsymbol{w}$. What can you deduce about the vectors $\boldsymbol{u}$, $\boldsymbol{v}$ and $\boldsymbol{w}$?

4 Which of the following vectors are perpendicular to each other?

(a) $2\boldsymbol{i}-3\boldsymbol{j}+6\boldsymbol{k}$ (b) $2\boldsymbol{i}-3\boldsymbol{j}-6\boldsymbol{k}$ (c) $-3\boldsymbol{i}-6\boldsymbol{j}+2\boldsymbol{k}$ (d) $6\boldsymbol{i}-2\boldsymbol{j}-3\boldsymbol{k}$

5 Let $\boldsymbol{p}=\boldsymbol{i}-2\boldsymbol{k}$, $\boldsymbol{q}=3\boldsymbol{j}+2\boldsymbol{k}$ and $\boldsymbol{r}=2\boldsymbol{i}-\boldsymbol{j}+5\boldsymbol{k}$. Calculate $\boldsymbol{p}\cdot\boldsymbol{q}$, $\boldsymbol{p}\cdot\boldsymbol{r}$ and $\boldsymbol{p}\cdot(\boldsymbol{q}+\boldsymbol{r})$ and verify that $\boldsymbol{p}\cdot(\boldsymbol{q}+\boldsymbol{r})=\boldsymbol{p}\cdot\boldsymbol{q}+\boldsymbol{p}\cdot\boldsymbol{r}$.

6 Find the magnitude of each of the following vectors.

(a) $\begin{pmatrix}-3\\4\end{pmatrix}$ (b) $\begin{pmatrix}-2\\1\end{pmatrix}$ (c) $\begin{pmatrix}-1\\-2\end{pmatrix}$ (d) $\begin{pmatrix}0\\-1\end{pmatrix}$

(e) $\begin{pmatrix}1\\-2\\2\end{pmatrix}$ (f) $\begin{pmatrix}4\\-3\\12\end{pmatrix}$ (g) $\begin{pmatrix}0\\-3\\4\end{pmatrix}$ (h) $\begin{pmatrix}2\\-1\\1\end{pmatrix}$

(i) $\boldsymbol{i}-2\boldsymbol{k}$ (j) $3\boldsymbol{j}+2\boldsymbol{k}$ (k) $2\boldsymbol{i}-\boldsymbol{j}+5\boldsymbol{k}$ (l) $2\boldsymbol{k}$

7 Let $\boldsymbol{a}=\begin{pmatrix}4\\-3\end{pmatrix}$. Find the magnitude of $\boldsymbol{a}$, and find a unit vector in the same direction as $\boldsymbol{a}$.

8 Find unit vectors in the same directions as $\begin{pmatrix} 1 \\ -2 \\ 2 \end{pmatrix}$ and $2\boldsymbol{i} - \boldsymbol{j} + 2\boldsymbol{k}$.

9 Let A and B be points with position vectors $\boldsymbol{a} = \begin{pmatrix} 3 \\ 1 \end{pmatrix}$ and $\boldsymbol{b} = \begin{pmatrix} 3 \\ 2 \end{pmatrix}$ respectively. Draw a diagram showing the points O, A and B. Calculate the angle $A\hat{O}B$.

10 Use a vector method to calculate the angles between the following pairs of vectors, giving your answers in degrees to one place of decimals, where appropriate.

(a) $\begin{pmatrix} 2 \\ 1 \end{pmatrix}$ and $\begin{pmatrix} 1 \\ 3 \end{pmatrix}$ (b) $\begin{pmatrix} 4 \\ -5 \end{pmatrix}$ and $\begin{pmatrix} -5 \\ 4 \end{pmatrix}$ (c) $\begin{pmatrix} 4 \\ -6 \end{pmatrix}$ and $\begin{pmatrix} -6 \\ 9 \end{pmatrix}$

(d) $\begin{pmatrix} -1 \\ 4 \\ 5 \end{pmatrix}$ and $\begin{pmatrix} 2 \\ 0 \\ -3 \end{pmatrix}$ (e) $\begin{pmatrix} 1 \\ 2 \\ -3 \end{pmatrix}$ and $\begin{pmatrix} 2 \\ 3 \\ -4 \end{pmatrix}$ (f) $\begin{pmatrix} 2 \\ -1 \\ 3 \end{pmatrix}$ and $\begin{pmatrix} 5 \\ -2 \\ -4 \end{pmatrix}$

11 Let $\boldsymbol{r}_1 = \begin{pmatrix} x_1 \\ y_1 \end{pmatrix}$ and $\boldsymbol{r}_2 = \begin{pmatrix} x_2 \\ y_2 \end{pmatrix}$. Calculate $|\boldsymbol{r}_2 - \boldsymbol{r}_1|$ and interpret your result geometrically.

12 Find the angle between the line joining (1, 2) and (3, −5) and the line joining (2, −3) to (1, 4).

13 Find the angle between the line joining (1, 3, −2) and (2, 5, −1) and the line joining (−1, 4, 3) to (3, 2, 1).

14 Find the angle between the diagonals of a cube.

15 ABCD is the base of a square pyramid of side 2 units, and V is the vertex. The pyramid is symmetrical, and of height 4 units. Calculate the acute angle between [AV] and [BC], giving your answer in degrees correct to 1 decimal place.

16 Two aeroplanes are flying in directions given by the vectors $300\boldsymbol{i} + 400\boldsymbol{j} + 2\boldsymbol{k}$ and $-100\boldsymbol{i} + 500\boldsymbol{j} - \boldsymbol{k}$. A person from the flight control centre is plotting their paths on a map. Find the acute angle between their paths on the map.

44 Vector equations of lines

This chapter shows how vectors can be used to find whether and where lines in three dimensions intersect. When you have completed it, you should

- know how to write the equation of a line in vector form
- be able to distinguish between coincident lines and parallel lines
- be aware that non-parallel lines in three dimensions may not meet
- be able to find the coordinates of the point of intersection of lines which do meet.

44.1 The vector equation of a line in two dimensions

Figure 44.1 shows the origin O and a line through a point A in the direction of a non-zero vector $\boldsymbol{b}$. If R is any point on the line, the displacement vector $\overrightarrow{AR}$ is a scalar multiple of $\boldsymbol{b}$. The position vector $\boldsymbol{r}$ of R, that is, the vector $\overrightarrow{OR}$, is given by

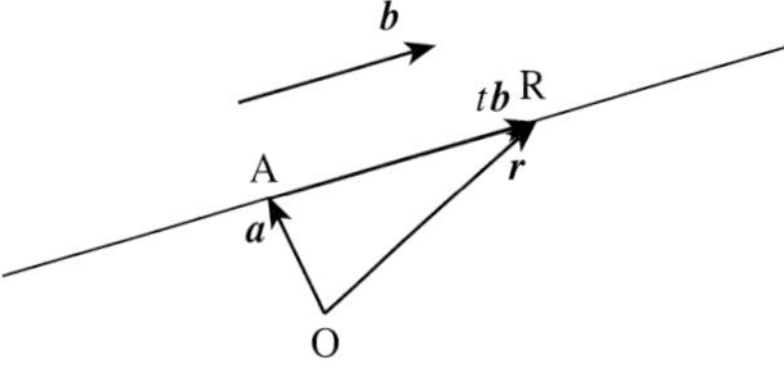

Fig. 44.1

$$\boldsymbol{r} = \overrightarrow{OR} = \overrightarrow{OA} + \overrightarrow{AR} = \boldsymbol{a} + t\boldsymbol{b},$$

where t is a scalar. The value of t measures the ratio of the displacement $\overrightarrow{AR}$ to $\boldsymbol{b}$, and so takes a different value for each point R on the line.

> Points on a line through A in the direction of $\boldsymbol{b}$ have position vectors $\boldsymbol{r} = \boldsymbol{a} + t\boldsymbol{b}$, where t is a variable scalar. This is called the **vector equation** of the line.

The variable scalar t is often called a **parameter**.

The following examples show how vector equations can be used in two dimensions as an alternative to Cartesian equations. The first example will be solved by using vectors in column form, and the second by using the basic unit vectors.

Example 44.1.1
Find a vector equation for the line through $(2, -1)$ with gradient $\frac{3}{4}$, and deduce its Cartesian equation.

The position vector of the point $(2, -1)$ is $\begin{pmatrix} 2 \\ -1 \end{pmatrix}$. There are many vectors with gradient $\frac{3}{4}$, but the simplest is the vector which goes 4 units across the grid and 3 units up, that is, $\begin{pmatrix} 4 \\ 3 \end{pmatrix}$. So a vector equation for the line is

$$\boldsymbol{r} = \begin{pmatrix} 2 \\ -1 \end{pmatrix} + t\begin{pmatrix} 4 \\ 3 \end{pmatrix}.$$

If R has coordinates (x, y), the position vector $\boldsymbol{r}$ is $\begin{pmatrix} x \\ y \end{pmatrix}$, so this can be written

$$\begin{pmatrix} x \\ y \end{pmatrix} = \begin{pmatrix} 2+4t \\ -1+3t \end{pmatrix}.$$

This is equivalent to the two equations

$$x = 2 + 4t, \quad y = -1 + 3t.$$

You can see that each of these equations can be solved for the parameter t.

$$t = \frac{x-2}{4} \quad \text{and} \quad t = \frac{y+1}{3}.$$

If you eliminate t you get $\dfrac{x-2}{4} = \dfrac{y+1}{3}$

from which $3(x-2) = 4(y+1)$ and $4y = 3x - 10$.

You can check that $4y = 3x - 10$ has gradient $\frac{3}{4}$ and contains the point $(2, -1)$.

To find the Cartesian equation of a line from the vector equation, eliminate the parameter (variable scalar) of the line.

Example 44.1.2

Find a vector equation for the line through (3, 1) parallel to the y-axis, and deduce its Cartesian equation.

A vector parallel to the y-axis is $\boldsymbol{j}$, and the position vector of (3, 1) is $3\boldsymbol{i} + \boldsymbol{j}$, so a vector equation for the line is

$$\boldsymbol{r} = (3\boldsymbol{i} + \boldsymbol{j}) + t\boldsymbol{j}.$$

Writing $\boldsymbol{r}$ as $x\boldsymbol{i} + y\boldsymbol{j}$, this is

$$x\boldsymbol{i} + y\boldsymbol{j} = (3\boldsymbol{i} + \boldsymbol{j}) + t\boldsymbol{j}.$$

This is equivalent to the two equations $x = 3$, $y = 1 + t$.

No elimination is necessary this time: the first equation does not involve t, so the Cartesian equation is just $x = 3$.

Example 44.1.3

Find the points common to the pairs of lines

(a) $\boldsymbol{r} = \begin{pmatrix} 1 \\ 2 \end{pmatrix} + s\begin{pmatrix} 1 \\ 1 \end{pmatrix}$ and $\boldsymbol{r} = \begin{pmatrix} 3 \\ -2 \end{pmatrix} + t\begin{pmatrix} 1 \\ 4 \end{pmatrix}$,

(b) $\boldsymbol{r} = \begin{pmatrix} 3 \\ 1 \end{pmatrix} + s\begin{pmatrix} 4 \\ -2 \end{pmatrix}$ and $\boldsymbol{r} = \begin{pmatrix} 1 \\ 2 \end{pmatrix} + t\begin{pmatrix} -6 \\ 3 \end{pmatrix}$.

Notice that different letters are used for the variable scalars on the two lines.

(a) Position vectors of points on the two lines can be written as

$$\boldsymbol{r} = \begin{pmatrix} 1+s \\ 2+s \end{pmatrix} \quad \text{and} \quad \boldsymbol{r} = \begin{pmatrix} 3+t \\ -2+4t \end{pmatrix}.$$

If these are the same point,

$$1+s = 3+t \quad \text{and} \quad 2+s = -2+4t,$$

that is $s - t = 2$ and $s - 4t = -4$.

This is a pair of simultaneous equations for s and t, with solution $s = 4$, $t = 2$. Substituting these values into the equation of one of the lines gives $\boldsymbol{r} = \begin{pmatrix} 5 \\ 6 \end{pmatrix}$. So the point common to the two lines has coordinates (5, 6).

(b) You can check for yourself that the procedure used in (a) leads to the equations

$$3+4s = 1-6t \quad \text{and} \quad 1-2s = 2+3t,$$

that is $2s + 3t = -1$ and $2s + 3t = -1$.

The two equations are the same! So there is really only one equation to solve, and this has infinitely many solutions in s and t. If you take any value for s, say $s = 7$, and calculate the corresponding value $t = -5$, then you have a solution of both vector equations. You can easily check that $s = 7$, $t = -5$ gives the position vector $\begin{pmatrix} 31 \\ -13 \end{pmatrix}$ in both lines. (Try some other pairs of values for yourself.)

The reason for this is that the direction vectors of the two lines are $\begin{pmatrix} 4 \\ -2 \end{pmatrix} = 2\begin{pmatrix} 2 \\ -1 \end{pmatrix}$ and $\begin{pmatrix} -6 \\ 3 \end{pmatrix} = -3\begin{pmatrix} 2 \\ -1 \end{pmatrix}$. This means that the lines have the same direction, so they are either parallel or the same line. Also the position vectors of the given points on the two lines are $\begin{pmatrix} 3 \\ 1 \end{pmatrix}$ and $\begin{pmatrix} 1 \\ 2 \end{pmatrix}$, and $\begin{pmatrix} 3 \\ 1 \end{pmatrix} - \begin{pmatrix} 1 \\ 2 \end{pmatrix} = \begin{pmatrix} 2 \\ -1 \end{pmatrix}$; so the line joining these points is also in the same direction. The lines are therefore identical. This is illustrated in Fig. 44.2.

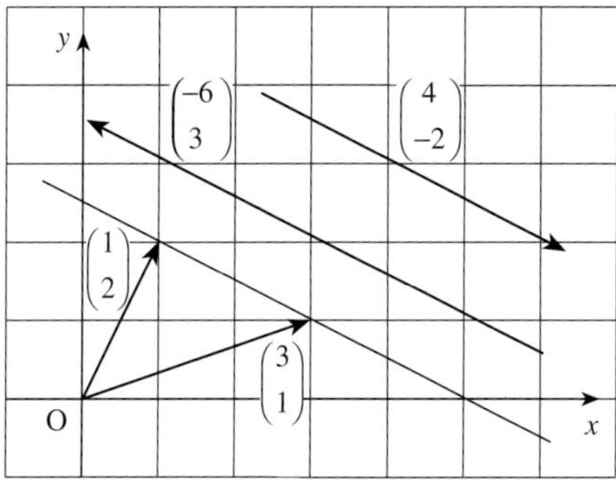

Fig. 44.2

The general result demonstrated in Example 44.1.3(b) is:

> The lines with vector equations $\boldsymbol{r} = \boldsymbol{a} + s\boldsymbol{p}$ and $\boldsymbol{r} = \boldsymbol{b} + t\boldsymbol{q}$ have the same direction if $\boldsymbol{p}$ is a multiple of $\boldsymbol{q}$. If in addition $\boldsymbol{b} - \boldsymbol{a}$ is a multiple of $\boldsymbol{q}$, the lines are the same; otherwise the lines are parallel.

This also shows that lines do not have unique vector equations. Two equations may represent the same line even though the vectors $\boldsymbol{a}$ and $\boldsymbol{b}$, and the vectors $\boldsymbol{p}$ and $\boldsymbol{q}$, are different.

Example 44.1.4
Show that the lines with vector equations $\boldsymbol{r} = 2\boldsymbol{i} - 3\boldsymbol{j} + s(-\boldsymbol{i} + 3\boldsymbol{j})$ and $\boldsymbol{r} = 4\boldsymbol{i} + t(2\boldsymbol{i} - 6\boldsymbol{j})$ are parallel, and find a vector equation for the parallel line through (1, 1).

The direction vectors of the two lines are $-\boldsymbol{i} + 3\boldsymbol{j}$ and $2\boldsymbol{i} - 6\boldsymbol{j}$.

As $2\boldsymbol{i} - 6\boldsymbol{j} = -2(-\boldsymbol{i} + 3\boldsymbol{j})$, $2\boldsymbol{i} - 6\boldsymbol{j}$ is a scalar multiple of $-\boldsymbol{i} + 3\boldsymbol{j}$, so the lines are in the same or, in this case, opposite directions. The lines are therefore parallel.

The position vector of (1, 1) is $\boldsymbol{i} + \boldsymbol{j}$, so an equation for the parallel line through (1, 1) is $\boldsymbol{r} = \boldsymbol{i} + \boldsymbol{j} + s(-\boldsymbol{i} + 3\boldsymbol{j})$. Or, alternatively, you could use $\boldsymbol{r} = \boldsymbol{i} + \boldsymbol{j} + t(2\boldsymbol{i} - 6\boldsymbol{j})$.

Example 44.1.5
Find a vector equation for the line with Cartesian equation $2x + 5y = 1$.

The gradient of the line is $-\frac{2}{5}$, so the direction vector could be taken as $\begin{pmatrix} 5 \\ -2 \end{pmatrix}$. A point on the line is $(-2, 1)$, with position vector $\begin{pmatrix} -2 \\ 1 \end{pmatrix}$. So a possible vector equation is $\boldsymbol{r} = \begin{pmatrix} -2 \\ 1 \end{pmatrix} + t\begin{pmatrix} 5 \\ -2 \end{pmatrix}$.

But in this example the direction vector could have been taken as $\begin{pmatrix} 10 \\ -4 \end{pmatrix}$ and the point on the line as $(3, -1)$, giving $\boldsymbol{r} = \begin{pmatrix} 3 \\ -1 \end{pmatrix} + t\begin{pmatrix} 10 \\ -4 \end{pmatrix}$. It is not immediately obvious from these two equations that they represent the same line.

Exercise 44A

1 Write down vector equations for the line through the given point in the specified direction. Then eliminate t to obtain the Cartesian equation.

(a) $(2, -3)$, $\begin{pmatrix} 1 \\ 2 \end{pmatrix}$

(b) $(4, 1)$, $\begin{pmatrix} -3 \\ 2 \end{pmatrix}$

(c) $(5, 7)$, parallel to the x-axis

(d) $(0, 0)$, $\begin{pmatrix} 2 \\ -1 \end{pmatrix}$

2 Find vector equations for lines with the following Cartesian equations.

(a) $x = 2$ (b) $x + 3y = 7$ (c) $2x - 5y = 3$

3 Find the coordinates of the point where the line with vector equation $\boldsymbol{r} = \begin{pmatrix} -3 \\ 4 \end{pmatrix} + t\begin{pmatrix} 2 \\ -1 \end{pmatrix}$ intersects the line with Cartesian equation $2x + y = 7$.

4 Find the coordinates of the points common to the following pairs of lines, if any.

(a) $\boldsymbol{r} = \begin{pmatrix} 2 \\ 0 \end{pmatrix} + s\begin{pmatrix} 5 \\ 3 \end{pmatrix}$, $\boldsymbol{r} = \begin{pmatrix} 3 \\ -1 \end{pmatrix} + t\begin{pmatrix} 1 \\ 1 \end{pmatrix}$

(b) $\boldsymbol{r} = \begin{pmatrix} 5 \\ 1 \end{pmatrix} + s\begin{pmatrix} -1 \\ 2 \end{pmatrix}$, $\boldsymbol{r} = \begin{pmatrix} 3 \\ -5 \end{pmatrix} + t\begin{pmatrix} 1 \\ 0 \end{pmatrix}$

(c) $\boldsymbol{r} = \begin{pmatrix} 2 \\ -1 \end{pmatrix} + s\begin{pmatrix} 1 \\ -3 \end{pmatrix}$, $\boldsymbol{r} = \begin{pmatrix} 4 \\ 0 \end{pmatrix} + t\begin{pmatrix} -2 \\ 6 \end{pmatrix}$

(d) $\boldsymbol{r} = \begin{pmatrix} 2 \\ -2 \end{pmatrix} + s\begin{pmatrix} 3 \\ 4 \end{pmatrix}$, $\boldsymbol{r} = \begin{pmatrix} 1 \\ 5 \end{pmatrix} + t\begin{pmatrix} -4 \\ 3 \end{pmatrix}$

5 Which of the following points lie on the line through (2, 0) to (4, 3)?

(a) (8, 9) (b) (12, 13) (c) (−4, −1) (d) (−6, −12)

6 Find vector equations for the lines joining the following pairs of points.

(a) (3, 7), (5, 4) (b) (2, 3), (2, 8) (c) (−1, 2), (5, −1)

7 Find a vector in the direction of the line l with Cartesian equation $3x - y = 8$. Write down a vector equation for the line through P(1, 5) which is perpendicular to l. Hence find the coordinates of the foot of the perpendicular from P to l.

44.2 The vector equation of a line in three dimensions

Almost everything in Section 44.1 about the equation of a straight line in two dimensions in vector form carries over to three dimensions. There are two important points to note.

- The idea of the gradient of a line does not carry over into three dimensions. However, you can still use a vector to describe the direction of a line. This is one of the main reasons why vectors are especially useful in three dimensions.
- In three dimensions lines which are not parallel may or may not meet. (Think of a railway crossing a road. They may either intersect, at a level crossing, or not intersect, where there is a bridge or a viaduct.) Non-parallel lines which do not meet are said to be **skew**.

Example 44.2.1
Points A and B have coordinates (−5, 3, 4) and (−2, 9, 1). Find a vector equation for the line (AB).

The displacement vector $\overrightarrow{AB}$ is

$$\boldsymbol{b} - \boldsymbol{a} = \begin{pmatrix} -2 \\ 9 \\ 1 \end{pmatrix} - \begin{pmatrix} -5 \\ 3 \\ 4 \end{pmatrix} = \begin{pmatrix} 3 \\ 6 \\ -3 \end{pmatrix} = 3\begin{pmatrix} 1 \\ 2 \\ -1 \end{pmatrix}.$$

So $\begin{pmatrix} 1 \\ 2 \\ -1 \end{pmatrix}$ can be taken as a direction vector for the line. A vector equation for the line (AB) is therefore $\boldsymbol{r} = \begin{pmatrix} -5 \\ 3 \\ 4 \end{pmatrix} + t\begin{pmatrix} 1 \\ 2 \\ -1 \end{pmatrix}$, or $\boldsymbol{r} = \begin{pmatrix} -5 + t \\ 3 + 2t \\ 4 - t \end{pmatrix}$.

Example 44.2.2

Do the lines $\boldsymbol{r} = \begin{pmatrix} 1 \\ 4 \\ -2 \end{pmatrix} + s \begin{pmatrix} 2 \\ -3 \\ 1 \end{pmatrix}$ and $\boldsymbol{r} = \begin{pmatrix} 4 \\ 2 \\ 4 \end{pmatrix} + t \begin{pmatrix} -1 \\ 4 \\ 5 \end{pmatrix}$ intersect?

If the point with parameter s on the first line is the same as the point with parameter t on the second, then

$$\begin{pmatrix} 1 \\ 4 \\ -2 \end{pmatrix} + s \begin{pmatrix} 2 \\ -3 \\ 1 \end{pmatrix} = \begin{pmatrix} 4 \\ 2 \\ 4 \end{pmatrix} + t \begin{pmatrix} -1 \\ 4 \\ 5 \end{pmatrix}.$$

Equating the components gives

$$\begin{aligned} 1 + 2s &= 4 - t & & 2s + t = 3 \\ 4 - 3s &= 2 + 4t & \text{or} \quad & 3s + 4t = 2 \\ -2 + s &= 4 + 5t & & s - 5t = 6. \end{aligned}$$

Solving the first two equations simultaneously gives $s = 2$ and $t = -1$.

It is important to check whether these values satisfy the third equation: substituting $s = 2$ and $t = -1$ gives

$$\text{left side} = 2 - 5 \times (-1) = 7.$$

As the right side is 6, there are no values of s and t which satisfy all these equations, so there is no solution to the set of equations. The lines do not intersect.

Example 44.2.3

Find the value of u for which the lines $\boldsymbol{r} = (\boldsymbol{j} - \boldsymbol{k}) + s(\boldsymbol{i} + 2\boldsymbol{j} + \boldsymbol{k})$ and $\boldsymbol{r} = (\boldsymbol{i} + 7\boldsymbol{j} - 4\boldsymbol{k}) + t(\boldsymbol{i} + u\boldsymbol{k})$ intersect.

Points on the lines can be written as $s\boldsymbol{i} + (1 + 2s)\boldsymbol{j} + (-1 + s)\boldsymbol{k}$ and $(1 + t)\boldsymbol{i} + 7\boldsymbol{j} + (-4 + ut)\boldsymbol{k}$. If these are the same point, then

$$s = 1 + t, \quad 1 + 2s = 7, \quad \text{and} \quad -1 + s = -4 + ut.$$

The first two equations give $s = 3$ and $t = 2$. Putting these values into the third equation gives $-1 + 3 = -4 + 2u$, so $u = 3$.

You can easily check that, with these values, both equations give $\boldsymbol{r} = 3\boldsymbol{i} + 7\boldsymbol{j} + 2\boldsymbol{k}$, so the point of intersection has coordinates $(3, 7, 2)$. For every other value of u the lines are skew.

Example 44.2.4

Two airliners take off simultaneously from different airports. As they climb, their positions relative to an air traffic control centre t minutes later are given by the vectors

$\boldsymbol{r}_1 = \begin{pmatrix} 5 \\ -30 \\ 0 \end{pmatrix} + t \begin{pmatrix} 8 \\ 2 \\ 0.5 \end{pmatrix}$ and $\boldsymbol{r}_2 = \begin{pmatrix} 13 \\ 26 \\ 0 \end{pmatrix} + t \begin{pmatrix} 6 \\ -3 \\ 0.6 \end{pmatrix}$, the units being kilometres. Find the coordinates of the point on the ground over which both airliners pass. Find also the difference in heights, and the difference in the times, when they pass over that point.

The airliners are directly over the same point when their x- and y-coordinates are equal, but the times will be different for each aircraft. Let t_1 and t_2 be the times for the two aircraft to be over this point.

This occurs when

$$5 + 8t_1 = 13 + 6t_2 \quad \text{and} \quad -30 + 2t_1 = 26 - 3t_2,$$

which are the same equations as

$$4t_1 - 3t_2 = 4 \quad \text{and} \quad 2t_1 + 3t_2 = 56.$$

Solving these equations simultaneously gives $t_1 = 10$, $t_2 = 12$.

Substituting these values of t_1 and t_2 into the vector equations of the lines gives the points with coordinates $(85, -10, 5)$ and $(85, -10, 7.2)$.

So the point on the ground over which both aeroplanes pass is $(85, -10, 0)$. The difference in the times is 2 minutes. The difference in heights is 2.2 kilometres.

44.3 An important application

Suppose that in the vector equation of a line, $\boldsymbol{r} = \boldsymbol{a} + t\boldsymbol{p}$, in either two or three dimensions, the scalar t represents time. Let P be the point whose position vector is $\boldsymbol{r}$. How can you calculate how fast P is moving along the line?

In Section 21.3 it was shown that, if s is the displacement of a point from the origin, and t is time, then the velocity v is given by

$$v = \lim_{\delta t \to 0} \frac{\delta s}{\delta t} = \frac{\mathrm{d}s}{\mathrm{d}t}.$$

A similar approach is adopted here.

Example 44.3.1
A chair in a chair lift has position vector $\boldsymbol{r} = (2\boldsymbol{i} + 3\boldsymbol{j} + \boldsymbol{k}) + t(2\boldsymbol{i} - 2\boldsymbol{j} + \boldsymbol{k})$, where t is the time in minutes and the unit vectors are in metres. Find its velocity and its speed.

The position P of the chair at time t is given by

$$\boldsymbol{r} = (2\boldsymbol{i} + 3\boldsymbol{j} + \boldsymbol{k}) + t(2\boldsymbol{i} - 2\boldsymbol{j} + \boldsymbol{k}).$$

At time $t + \delta t$, the position vector is given by $\boldsymbol{r} + \delta\boldsymbol{r}$, where

$$\boldsymbol{r} + \delta\boldsymbol{r} = (2\boldsymbol{i} + 3\boldsymbol{j} + \boldsymbol{k}) + (t + \delta t)(2\boldsymbol{i} - 2\boldsymbol{j} + \boldsymbol{k}).$$

By subtraction

$$\begin{aligned}\delta\boldsymbol{r} &= (2\boldsymbol{i} + 3\boldsymbol{j} + \boldsymbol{k}) + (t + \delta t)(2\boldsymbol{i} - 2\boldsymbol{j} + \boldsymbol{k}) - (2\boldsymbol{i} + 3\boldsymbol{j} + \boldsymbol{k}) + t(2\boldsymbol{i} - 2\boldsymbol{j} + \boldsymbol{k}) \\ &= \delta t(2\boldsymbol{i} - 2\boldsymbol{j} + \boldsymbol{k}),\end{aligned}$$

so $$\frac{\delta\boldsymbol{r}}{\delta t} = 2\boldsymbol{i} - 2\boldsymbol{j} + \boldsymbol{k}.$$

If δt is very small, the average velocity will be very close to the actual velocity at P, which is the limit of the average velocity as δt tends to 0. That is,

$$\boldsymbol{v} = \lim_{\delta t \to 0} \frac{\delta \boldsymbol{r}}{\delta t} = \frac{\mathrm{d}\boldsymbol{r}}{\mathrm{d}t}.$$

In this case, $\dfrac{\delta \boldsymbol{r}}{\delta t}$ is a constant, so $\boldsymbol{v} = 2\boldsymbol{i} - 2\boldsymbol{j} + \boldsymbol{k}$.

The speed is the magnitude of the velocity, and so is given by

$$\begin{aligned} \text{speed} &= |\boldsymbol{v}| \\ &= |2\boldsymbol{i} - 2\boldsymbol{j} + \boldsymbol{k}| \\ &= \sqrt{2^2 + (-2)^2 + 1^2} \\ &= \sqrt{9} = 3. \end{aligned}$$

The speed of the chair is 3 metres per minute.

In general, similar reasoning leads to the following:

> If a point is moving with position vector $\boldsymbol{r} = \boldsymbol{a} + t\boldsymbol{p}$, the velocity, in appropriate units, is $\boldsymbol{p}$ and the speed is $|\boldsymbol{p}|$.

Example 44.3.2

A car is moving on a straight level road with velocity vector given by $\boldsymbol{v} = \begin{pmatrix} 16 \\ 30 \end{pmatrix}$, where the units are metres and seconds. Its position at time $t = 0$ is $(2, -1)$. Find the speed of the car, and a vector equation of its path.

The speed of the car is $|\boldsymbol{v}|$, so

$$\begin{aligned} |\boldsymbol{v}| &= \left| \begin{pmatrix} 16 \\ 30 \end{pmatrix} \right| \\ &= \sqrt{16^2 + 30^2} \\ &= \sqrt{256 + 900} \\ &= \sqrt{1156} = 34. \end{aligned}$$

The speed is $34\,\mathrm{m\,s^{-1}}$.

Using the result in the blue box, the equation of its path is $\boldsymbol{r} = \begin{pmatrix} 2 \\ -1 \end{pmatrix} + t\begin{pmatrix} 16 \\ 30 \end{pmatrix}$.

Exercise 44B

1 Write down vector equations for the line through the given point in the specified direction.

(a) $(2, -3, 5)$, $\begin{pmatrix} 1 \\ 2 \\ -6 \end{pmatrix}$

(b) $(4, -1, 1)$, $\begin{pmatrix} 4 \\ -2 \\ -3 \end{pmatrix}$

(c) $(5, 7, 4)$, parallel to the x-axis

(d) $(0, 0, 0)$, $\begin{pmatrix} 2 \\ -3 \\ 1 \end{pmatrix}$

2 Investigate whether or not it is possible to find numbers s and t which satisfy the following vector equations.

(a) $s\begin{pmatrix}3\\4\\1\end{pmatrix}+t\begin{pmatrix}2\\-1\\0\end{pmatrix}=\begin{pmatrix}0\\11\\2\end{pmatrix}$ (b) $\begin{pmatrix}-1\\-2\\3\end{pmatrix}+s\begin{pmatrix}1\\2\\-1\end{pmatrix}+t\begin{pmatrix}3\\-1\\1\end{pmatrix}=\begin{pmatrix}5\\3\\1\end{pmatrix}$

(c) $s\begin{pmatrix}1\\2\\-3\end{pmatrix}+t\begin{pmatrix}5\\1\\1\end{pmatrix}=\begin{pmatrix}1\\-7\\11\end{pmatrix}$

3 Find if the following pairs of lines intersect. If they do, give the point of intersection.
(a) $\mathbf{r}=\mathbf{i}+s(\mathbf{i}+\mathbf{j}+\mathbf{k})$ and $\mathbf{r}=8\mathbf{i}+3\mathbf{j}+3\mathbf{k}+t\mathbf{i}$
(b) $\mathbf{r}=3\mathbf{i}-2\mathbf{j}-\mathbf{k}+s(-2\mathbf{i}+3\mathbf{j}-5\mathbf{k})$ and $\mathbf{r}=8\mathbf{i}+4\mathbf{j}+\mathbf{k}+t(-\mathbf{i}-3\mathbf{j}+\mathbf{k})$
(c) $\mathbf{r}=-3\mathbf{i}+5\mathbf{j}+2\mathbf{k}+s(-\mathbf{i}-2\mathbf{j}-4\mathbf{k})$ and $\mathbf{r}=8\mathbf{i}+5\mathbf{j}+\mathbf{k}+t(-\mathbf{i}-3\mathbf{j}+3\mathbf{k})$

4 Find vector equations for the lines joining the following pairs of points.
(a) (8, 7, 5), (−1, 2, −1) (b) (2, −2, 0), (2, −1, 0) (c) (4, 5, −2), (−2, −3, 4)

5 If $\mathbf{p}=2\mathbf{i}-\mathbf{j}+3\mathbf{k}$, $\mathbf{q}=5\mathbf{i}+2\mathbf{j}$ and $\mathbf{r}=4\mathbf{i}+\mathbf{j}+\mathbf{k}$, find a set of numbers f, g and h such that $f\mathbf{p}+g\mathbf{q}+h\mathbf{r}=0$. What does this tell you about the translations represented by $\mathbf{p}$, $\mathbf{q}$ and $\mathbf{r}$?

6 For each of the following sets of points A, B, C and D, determine whether the lines (AB) and (CD) are parallel, intersect each other, or are skew.
(a) A(3, 2, 4), B(−3, −7, −8), C(0, 1, 3), D(−2, 5, 9)
(b) A(3, 1, 0), B(−3, 1, 3), C(5, 0, −1), D(1, 0, 1)
(c) A(−5, −4, −3), B(5, 1, 2), C(−1, −3, 0), D(8, 0, 6)
(d) A(2, 0, 3), B(−1, 2, 1), C(4, −1, 5), D(10, −5, 1)

7 Find a vector equation for the line l through (3, 2, 6) parallel to the line with vector equation $\mathbf{r}=\begin{pmatrix}4\\0\\5\end{pmatrix}+t\begin{pmatrix}-3\\1\\2\end{pmatrix}$. Find also the coordinates of the points where l meets the xy-plane and the xz-plane.

8 A student displays her birthday cards on strings which she has pinned to opposite walls of her room, whose floor measures 3 metres by 4 metres. Relative to one corner of the room, the coordinates of the ends of the first string are (0, 3.3, 2.4) and (3, 1.3, 1.9) in metre units. The coordinates of the ends of the second string are (0.7, 0, 2.3) and (1.5, 4, 1.5). Find the difference in the heights of the two strings where one passes over the other.

9 A balloon flying over flat fenland reports its position at 7.40 a.m. as (7.8, 5.4, 1.2), the coordinates being given in kilometres relative to a checkpoint on the ground. By 7.50 a.m. its position has changed to (9.3, 4.4, 0.7). Find its speed and, assuming that it continues to descend at the same speed along the same line, find the coordinates of the point where it would be expected to land, and the time when this would occur.

Review exercise 14

1 Two lines have equations $\mathbf{r} = \begin{pmatrix} 1 \\ 3 \\ 2 \end{pmatrix} + \lambda \begin{pmatrix} 4 \\ -2 \\ 1 \end{pmatrix}$ and $\mathbf{r} = \begin{pmatrix} 3 \\ 8 \\ 7 \end{pmatrix} + \mu \begin{pmatrix} 2 \\ -3 \\ -1 \end{pmatrix}$. Show that the lines intersect, and find the position vector of the point of intersection. (OCR)

2 (a) A straight line, l_1, has vector equation $\mathbf{r} = \begin{pmatrix} 4 \\ 2 \end{pmatrix} + t \begin{pmatrix} 1 \\ 4 \end{pmatrix}$ where $\mathbf{r} = \begin{pmatrix} x \\ y \end{pmatrix}$. Find the Cartesian equation of this line.

(b) Another straight line, l_2, has equation $2x - 3y + 3 = 0$. Find a vector equation for it.

(c) Find, in Cartesian or vector form, an equation of the line through $(-1, 5)$ parallel to l_2. (OCR)

3 Investigate the intersection of the following pairs of lines, one given by a vector equation and the other by a cartesian equation.

(a) $\mathbf{r} = \begin{pmatrix} 2 \\ 0 \end{pmatrix} + t \begin{pmatrix} 1 \\ -3 \end{pmatrix}$, $3x + y = 8$

(b) $\mathbf{r} = \begin{pmatrix} -1 \\ 4 \end{pmatrix} + t \begin{pmatrix} 2 \\ 5 \end{pmatrix}$, $x - 4y = 1$

(c) $\mathbf{r} = \begin{pmatrix} 0 \\ 3 \end{pmatrix} + t \begin{pmatrix} 2 \\ -1 \end{pmatrix}$, $2y + x = 6$

4 Show that the two lines with equations $\mathbf{r} = -2\mathbf{i} + 3\mathbf{j} - \mathbf{k} + s(4\mathbf{i} - 2\mathbf{j} + \mathbf{k})$ and $\mathbf{r} = 2\mathbf{i} + 4\mathbf{j} + 3\mathbf{k} + t(-4\mathbf{i} + \mathbf{j} - 2\mathbf{k})$ intersect, and find the position vector of the point of intersection.

5 Find whether or not the line passing through the points $(1, 5, 1)$ and $(3, 7, -2)$ meets

$$\mathbf{r} = \begin{pmatrix} 6 \\ -2 \\ 1 \end{pmatrix} + t \begin{pmatrix} -3 \\ 5 \\ 1 \end{pmatrix}.$$

6 A tunnel is to be excavated through a hill. In order to define position, coordinates (x, y, z) are taken relative to an origin O such that x is the distance east from O, y is the distance north and z is the vertical distance upwards, with one unit equal to 100 m. The tunnel starts at point A(2, 3, 5) and runs in the direction $\begin{pmatrix} 1 \\ 1 \\ -0.5 \end{pmatrix}$.

(a) Write down the equation of the tunnel in the form $\mathbf{r} = \mathbf{u} + \lambda \mathbf{t}$.

(b) An old tunnel through the hill has equation $\mathbf{r} = \begin{pmatrix} 4 \\ 1 \\ 2 \end{pmatrix} + \mu \begin{pmatrix} 7 \\ 15 \\ 0 \end{pmatrix}$. Show that the point P on the new tunnel where $x = 7\frac{1}{2}$ is directly above a point Q in the old tunnel. Find the vertical separation PQ of the tunnels at this point. (MEI)

7 An airliner climbs so that its position relative to the airport control tower t minutes after take-off is given by the vector $\boldsymbol{r} = \begin{pmatrix} 1 \\ 2 \\ 0 \end{pmatrix} + t\begin{pmatrix} 4 \\ 5 \\ 0.6 \end{pmatrix}$, the units being kilometres. The x- and y-axes point towards the east and the north respectively.

(a) Find the position of the airliner when it reaches its cruising height of 9 km.

(b) With reference to (x, y) coordinates on the ground, the coastline has equation $x + 3y = 140$. How high is the aircraft flying as it crosses the coast?

(c) Calculate the speed of the airliner over the ground in kilometres per hour, and the bearing on which it is flying.

(d) Calculate the speed of the airliner through the air, and the angle to the horizontal at which it is climbing.

8 Point A has coordinates $(2, -1, 3)$ and point B has coordinates $(1, 0, 5)$.

(a) Write down the equation of the line (AB) in the form $\boldsymbol{r} = \boldsymbol{a} + t\boldsymbol{u}$.

(b) Find the angle between the line (AB) and the line $\begin{pmatrix} x \\ y \\ z \end{pmatrix} = \begin{pmatrix} 1 \\ 3 \\ 4 \end{pmatrix} + \lambda\begin{pmatrix} -4 \\ 7 \\ 6 \end{pmatrix}$, giving your answer to the nearest degree. (MEI, adapted)

9 Find which pairs of the following vectors are perpendicular to each other.

$\boldsymbol{a} = 2\boldsymbol{i} + \boldsymbol{j} - 2\boldsymbol{k}$ $\quad \boldsymbol{b} = 2\boldsymbol{i} - 2\boldsymbol{j} + \boldsymbol{k}$ $\quad \boldsymbol{c} = \boldsymbol{i} + 2\boldsymbol{j} + 2\boldsymbol{k}$ $\quad \boldsymbol{d} = 3\boldsymbol{i} + 2\boldsymbol{j} - 2\boldsymbol{k}$

10 The points A, B and C have position vectors $\boldsymbol{a} = \begin{pmatrix} 2 \\ 1 \\ 2 \end{pmatrix}$, $\boldsymbol{b} = \begin{pmatrix} -3 \\ 2 \\ 5 \end{pmatrix}$ and $\boldsymbol{c} = \begin{pmatrix} 4 \\ 5 \\ -2 \end{pmatrix}$ respectively, with respect to a fixed origin. The point D is such that ABCD, in that order, is a parallelogram.

(a) Find the position vector of D.

(b) Find the position vector of the point at which the diagonals of the parallelogram intersect.

(c) Calculate the angle BÂC, giving your answer to the nearest tenth of a degree. (OCR)

11 The points A, B and C have position vectors given respectively by $\boldsymbol{a} = 7\boldsymbol{i} + 4\boldsymbol{j} - 2\boldsymbol{k}$, $\boldsymbol{b} = 5\boldsymbol{i} + 3\boldsymbol{j} - 3\boldsymbol{k}$, $\boldsymbol{c} = 6\boldsymbol{i} + 5\boldsymbol{j} - 4\boldsymbol{k}$.

(a) Find the angle BÂC. (b) Find the area of the triangle ABC. (OCR)

Examination questions

1 A boat B moves with constant velocity along a straight line. Its velocity vector is given by $\boldsymbol{v} = \begin{pmatrix} 4 \\ 3 \end{pmatrix}$. At time $t = 0$ it is at the point $(-2, 1)$.

(a) Find the magnitude of $\boldsymbol{v}$. (b) Find the coordinates of B when $t = 2$.

(c) Write down a vector equation representing the position of B, giving your answer in the form $\boldsymbol{r} = \boldsymbol{a} + t\boldsymbol{b}$. (© IBO 2005)

2 Points A, B and C have position vectors $4\boldsymbol{i} + 2\boldsymbol{j}$, $\boldsymbol{i} - 3\boldsymbol{j}$ and $-5\boldsymbol{i} - 5\boldsymbol{j}$. Let D be a point on the x-axis such that ABCD forms a parallelogram.

(a) (i) Find $\overrightarrow{BC}$. (ii) Find the position vector of D.

(b) Find the angle between $\overrightarrow{BD}$ and $\overrightarrow{AC}$.

The line L_1 passes through A and is parallel to $\boldsymbol{i} + 4\boldsymbol{j}$. The line L_2 passes through B and is parallel to $2\boldsymbol{i} + 7\boldsymbol{j}$. A vector equation of L_1 is $\boldsymbol{r} = (4\boldsymbol{i} + 2\boldsymbol{j}) + s(\boldsymbol{i} + 4\boldsymbol{j})$.

(c) Write down a vector equation of L_2 in the form $\boldsymbol{r} = \boldsymbol{b} + t\boldsymbol{q}$.

(d) The lines L_1 and L_2 intersect at the point P. Find the position vector of P.

(© IBO 2004)

3 The points A and B have position vectors $\begin{pmatrix} 4 \\ -3 \end{pmatrix}$ and $\begin{pmatrix} -1 \\ -2 \end{pmatrix}$ respectively.

(a) (i) Find the vector $\overrightarrow{AB}$. (ii) Find $|\overrightarrow{AB}|$.

The point D has position vector $\begin{pmatrix} d \\ 22 \end{pmatrix}$.

(b) Find the vector $\overrightarrow{AD}$ in terms of d.

The angle $\text{B}\hat{\text{A}}\text{D}$ is $90°$.

(c) (i) Show that $d = 9$.

(ii) Write down the position vector of the point D.

The quadrilateral ABCD is a rectangle.

(d) Find the position vector of the point C.

(e) Find the area of the rectangle ABCD. (© IBO 2004)

4 The vector equations of two lines are given below.

$$\boldsymbol{r}_1 = \begin{pmatrix} 5 \\ 1 \end{pmatrix} + \lambda \begin{pmatrix} 3 \\ -2 \end{pmatrix}, \quad \boldsymbol{r}_2 = \begin{pmatrix} -2 \\ 2 \end{pmatrix} + t \begin{pmatrix} 4 \\ 1 \end{pmatrix}.$$

The lines intersect at the point P. Find the position vector of P. (© IBO 2003)

45 Matrices

This chapter explains why and how matrices are defined, and how to add, subtract and multiply them. When you have completed it, you should

- be able to carry out operations of matrix addition, subtraction, multiplication and multiplication by a scalar
- know what is meant by the terms 'zero matrix' and 'identity matrix'.

45.1 What is a matrix?

Suppose that you wanted to program a computer to solve a pair of simultaneous linear equations such as

$$\left.\begin{aligned} x + 2y &= 3 \\ 2x + 3y &= 4 \end{aligned}\right\}.$$

What are the essential ingredients of this pair of equations? What information do you need to give to the computer?

Notice that the equations $\left.\begin{aligned} x + 2y &= 3 \\ 2x + 3y &= 4 \end{aligned}\right\}$ are essentially the same as $\left.\begin{aligned} p + 2q &= 3 \\ 2p + 3q &= 4 \end{aligned}\right\}.$

You would not change the way that you solve the equations just because the unknowns are labelled p and q instead of x and y. This suggests that all the necessary information is held by the array of coefficients and symbols

$$\begin{array}{cccc} 1 & 2 & = & 3 \\ 2 & 3 & = & 4 \end{array}$$

You don't even need the equals signs, provided that you remember what the array means and what the symbols in it stand for. Thus all the information is held by the array

$$\begin{array}{ccc} 1 & 2 & 3 \\ 2 & 3 & 4 \end{array}$$

It turns out to be useful to think of a rectangular array of numbers like this as a single object, called a **matrix**. It is usual to write a matrix in brackets, and to denote it by a single letter written in bold-faced italic type. Thus $\boldsymbol{A} = \begin{pmatrix} 1 & 2 & 3 \\ 2 & 3 & 4 \end{pmatrix}$.

A matrix has **rows** and **columns**. In this example, $\boldsymbol{A}$ has 2 rows and 3 columns and is called a '2 by 3' matrix. The matrix $\boldsymbol{A}$ is said to have **order** 2×3. If the number of rows is equal to the number of columns, the matrix is **square**. The individual numbers in the matrix are called **elements**. A matrix with just one column, such as $\begin{pmatrix} 2 \\ 4 \end{pmatrix}$, is sometimes called a **column matrix**. Similarly a matrix with just one row, such as $(1 \quad 2 \quad 3)$, is called a **row matrix**.

> A **matrix** $\boldsymbol{A}$ is a rectangular array of numbers, called **elements**.
>
> A matrix $\boldsymbol{A}$ with m rows and n columns is called an $m \times n$ matrix and has **order** $m \times n$. If $m = n$, $\boldsymbol{A}$ is said to be a **square** matrix.
>
> A matrix with n rows and 1 column is called a **column matrix**.
>
> A matrix with 1 row and n columns is called a **row matrix**.

Matrices can arise from many sources other than simultaneous equations. For example, suppose that Amy and Bob go to a baker's shop to buy cakes, doughnuts and eclairs. The numbers of each that they buy is given by the array of numbers in Table 45.1.

	Cakes	Doughnuts	Eclairs
Amy	2	1	1
Bob	4	0	2

Table 45.1

The array of numbers in Table 45.1 is another example of a matrix. You could strip it of its headings and simply use the numbers in a 'purchase matrix'

$$\boldsymbol{P} = \begin{pmatrix} 2 & 1 & 1 \\ 4 & 0 & 2 \end{pmatrix}.$$

Suppose that on the next day they make purchases represented by the matrix

$$\boldsymbol{Q} = \begin{pmatrix} 3 & 0 & 1 \\ 1 & 3 & 1 \end{pmatrix}.$$

Then on the two days together they will have bought $\begin{pmatrix} 5 & 1 & 2 \\ 5 & 3 & 3 \end{pmatrix}$, and it is natural to denote this by $\boldsymbol{P} + \boldsymbol{Q}$. Thus

$$\boldsymbol{P} + \boldsymbol{Q} = \begin{pmatrix} 2 & 1 & 1 \\ 4 & 0 & 2 \end{pmatrix} + \begin{pmatrix} 3 & 0 & 1 \\ 1 & 3 & 1 \end{pmatrix} = \begin{pmatrix} 5 & 1 & 2 \\ 5 & 3 & 3 \end{pmatrix}.$$

If they make the same purchase $\boldsymbol{P}$ on five days the total bought will be

$$5\boldsymbol{P} = \begin{pmatrix} 10 & 5 & 5 \\ 20 & 0 & 10 \end{pmatrix}.$$

These examples suggest the general definitions of sums and multiples of matrices given in the next section.

45.2 Addition and multiplication by a scalar

Two $m \times n$ matrices $\boldsymbol{A}$ and $\boldsymbol{B}$ are defined to be **equal** if all the elements in corresponding positions are equal. Two matrices of different orders cannot be equal.

Thus if you are given that $\begin{pmatrix} a & b \\ c & d \end{pmatrix} = \begin{pmatrix} 0 & 1 \\ 2 & -1 \end{pmatrix}$ you can deduce that $a = 0$, $b = 1$, $c = 2$ and $d = -1$. But $\begin{pmatrix} 1 & 2 \\ 3 & 4 \end{pmatrix} \neq \begin{pmatrix} 1 & 3 \\ 2 & 4 \end{pmatrix}$ and $\begin{pmatrix} 1 & 2 \\ 3 & 4 \end{pmatrix} \neq \begin{pmatrix} 1 & 2 & 0 \\ 3 & 4 & 0 \end{pmatrix}$.

Addition

Addition of two $m \times n$ matrices $\boldsymbol{A}$ and $\boldsymbol{B}$ is performed by adding the corresponding elements. Thus, if $\boldsymbol{A} = \begin{pmatrix} 1 & 2 \\ 3 & 4 \end{pmatrix}$ and $\boldsymbol{B} = \begin{pmatrix} 1 & 3 \\ 2 & 4 \end{pmatrix}$, then their sum

$$\boldsymbol{A} + \boldsymbol{B} = \begin{pmatrix} 1 & 2 \\ 3 & 4 \end{pmatrix} + \begin{pmatrix} 1 & 3 \\ 2 & 4 \end{pmatrix} = \begin{pmatrix} 1+1 & 2+3 \\ 3+2 & 4+4 \end{pmatrix} = \begin{pmatrix} 2 & 5 \\ 5 & 8 \end{pmatrix}.$$

You cannot add matrices if they are of different orders.

The zero matrix

The matrix $\boldsymbol{O}$, of any order, in which all the elements are 0, is called the **zero matrix**, or null matrix.

Notice that the 2×2 matrix $\boldsymbol{O}$, that is $\begin{pmatrix} 0 & 0 \\ 0 & 0 \end{pmatrix}$, is different from the 2×3 matrix $\boldsymbol{O}$, that is $\begin{pmatrix} 0 & 0 & 0 \\ 0 & 0 & 0 \end{pmatrix}$. In practice, there is no confusion about the fact that they are both called $\boldsymbol{O}$.

An important property of the zero matrix is that for any matrix $\boldsymbol{A}$, and the zero matrix $\boldsymbol{O}$ which is the same order as $\boldsymbol{A}$,

$$\boldsymbol{A} + \boldsymbol{O} = \boldsymbol{O} + \boldsymbol{A} = \boldsymbol{A}.$$

> In some books the matrix $\boldsymbol{O}$ is denoted by $\boldsymbol{Z}$ (for zero) or by $\mathbf{0}$.

Scalar multiples

You can also multiply a matrix by a number. For example, it seems natural to write $\boldsymbol{A} + \boldsymbol{A}$ as $2\boldsymbol{A}$. If $\boldsymbol{A} = \begin{pmatrix} 1 & 2 \\ 3 & 4 \end{pmatrix}$, then

$$2\boldsymbol{A} = \boldsymbol{A} + \boldsymbol{A} = \begin{pmatrix} 1 & 2 \\ 3 & 4 \end{pmatrix} + \begin{pmatrix} 1 & 2 \\ 3 & 4 \end{pmatrix} = \begin{pmatrix} 2 & 4 \\ 6 & 8 \end{pmatrix}.$$

If s is any number and $\boldsymbol{A}$ is any $m \times n$ matrix, the product $s\boldsymbol{A}$ is the $m \times n$ matrix formed by multiplying every element of $\boldsymbol{A}$ by s. The process is called **multiplying by a scalar**.

Subtraction

Subtraction of two matrices $\boldsymbol{A}$ and $\boldsymbol{B}$ is defined by

$$\boldsymbol{X} = \boldsymbol{A} - \boldsymbol{B} \quad \text{means} \quad \boldsymbol{B} + \boldsymbol{X} = \boldsymbol{A} \quad \text{and vice versa.}$$

You can easily show that $\boldsymbol{A} - \boldsymbol{B} = \boldsymbol{A} + (-1)\boldsymbol{B}$. This shows that the elements of $\boldsymbol{A} - \boldsymbol{B}$ are simply the elements of $\boldsymbol{B}$ subtracted from those of $\boldsymbol{A}$.

For these properties of addition and multiplication by a scalar, matrices behave just like numbers. Properties that you expect to hold, do hold.

Example 45.2.1

Let $\boldsymbol{A} = \begin{pmatrix} -1 & -2 \\ 3 & 1 \end{pmatrix}$ and $\boldsymbol{B} = \begin{pmatrix} 2 & 6 \\ -3 & 4 \end{pmatrix}$.

Calculate (a) $\boldsymbol{A} + \boldsymbol{B}$, (b) $2\boldsymbol{A} + 3\boldsymbol{B}$, (c) $\boldsymbol{A} - \boldsymbol{B}$.

$$\text{(a)}\ \boldsymbol{A} + \boldsymbol{B} = \begin{pmatrix} -1 & -2 \\ 3 & 1 \end{pmatrix} + \begin{pmatrix} 2 & 6 \\ -3 & 4 \end{pmatrix} = \begin{pmatrix} -1+2 & -2+6 \\ 3+(-3) & 1+4 \end{pmatrix} = \begin{pmatrix} 1 & 4 \\ 0 & 5 \end{pmatrix}.$$

$$\begin{aligned} \text{(b)}\ 2\boldsymbol{A} + 3\boldsymbol{B} &= 2\begin{pmatrix} -1 & -2 \\ 3 & 1 \end{pmatrix} + 3\begin{pmatrix} 2 & 6 \\ -3 & 4 \end{pmatrix} = \begin{pmatrix} -2 & -4 \\ 6 & 2 \end{pmatrix} + \begin{pmatrix} 6 & 18 \\ -9 & 12 \end{pmatrix} \\ &= \begin{pmatrix} -2+6 & -4+18 \\ 6+(-9) & 2+12 \end{pmatrix} = \begin{pmatrix} 4 & 14 \\ -3 & 14 \end{pmatrix}. \end{aligned}$$

$$\begin{aligned} \text{(c)}\ \boldsymbol{A} - \boldsymbol{B} &= \begin{pmatrix} -1 & -2 \\ 3 & 1 \end{pmatrix} + (-1)\begin{pmatrix} 2 & 6 \\ -3 & 4 \end{pmatrix} = \begin{pmatrix} -1 & -2 \\ 3 & 1 \end{pmatrix} + \begin{pmatrix} -2 & -6 \\ 3 & -4 \end{pmatrix} \\ &= \begin{pmatrix} -1+(-2) & -2+(-6) \\ 3+3 & 1+(-4) \end{pmatrix} = \begin{pmatrix} -3 & -8 \\ 6 & -3 \end{pmatrix}. \end{aligned}$$

In practice you will usually shorten such calculations by omitting some of the steps.

Example 45.2.2

Solve for $\boldsymbol{X}$ the matrix equation $\boldsymbol{A} + 3\boldsymbol{X} = 4\boldsymbol{B}$.

In this example, you must assume that all the matrices are the same order, say $m \times n$, otherwise addition would not be defined.

$$\begin{aligned} \boldsymbol{A} + 3\boldsymbol{X} &= 4\boldsymbol{B} \\ 3\boldsymbol{X} &= 4\boldsymbol{B} - \boldsymbol{A} \\ \boldsymbol{X} &= \tfrac{1}{3}(4\boldsymbol{B} - \boldsymbol{A}). \end{aligned}$$

45.3 Multiplying two matrices

The rules for adding two matrices and multiplying a matrix by a scalar were rather obvious. The rule for multiplying two matrices is not at all obvious.

Return to Amy and Bob at the baker's shop (Section 45.1). Recall that what they bought was given by the matrix $\boldsymbol{P} = \begin{pmatrix} 2 & 1 & 1 \\ 4 & 0 & 2 \end{pmatrix}$. Suppose now that there are actually two shops, X and Y, that they could buy at, and that these shops charge prices in pence given by Table 45.2.

	Shop X	Shop Y
Cakes	40	45
Doughnuts	30	25
Eclairs	50	40

Table 45.2

Stripping out the headings gives a cost matrix $\boldsymbol{C} = \begin{pmatrix} 40 & 45 \\ 30 & 25 \\ 50 & 40 \end{pmatrix}$.

Now suppose that Amy and Bob want to compare how much they would spend in each shop.

Amy would spend $2 \times 40 + 1 \times 30 + 1 \times 50 = 160$ pence in shop X.

Amy would spend $2 \times 45 + 1 \times 25 + 1 \times 40 = 155$ pence in shop Y.

Bob would spend $4 \times 40 + 0 \times 30 + 2 \times 50 = 260$ pence in shop X.

Bob would spend $4 \times 45 + 0 \times 25 + 2 \times 40 = 260$ pence in shop Y.

You could now put these results in a table, as in Table 45.3.

	Shop X	Shop Y
Amy	160	155
Bob	260	260

Table 45.3

The corresponding matrix, $\begin{pmatrix} 160 & 155 \\ 260 & 260 \end{pmatrix}$, obtained by 'multiplying' purchases by costs, is called the product matrix $\boldsymbol{PC}$. Thus

$$\begin{aligned} \boldsymbol{PC} &= \begin{pmatrix} 2 & 1 & 1 \\ 4 & 0 & 2 \end{pmatrix} \begin{pmatrix} 40 & 45 \\ 30 & 25 \\ 50 & 40 \end{pmatrix} \\ &= \begin{pmatrix} 2 \times 40 + 1 \times 30 + 1 \times 50 & 2 \times 45 + 1 \times 25 + 1 \times 40 \\ 4 \times 40 + 0 \times 30 + 2 \times 50 & 4 \times 45 + 0 \times 25 + 2 \times 40 \end{pmatrix} \\ &= \begin{pmatrix} 160 & 155 \\ 260 & 260 \end{pmatrix}. \end{aligned}$$

Notice how the individual elements of $\boldsymbol{PC}$ are calculated. The process of calculating

$$\begin{pmatrix} 2 & 1 & 1 \\ . & . & . \end{pmatrix} \begin{pmatrix} 40 & . \\ 30 & . \\ 50 & . \end{pmatrix} = \begin{pmatrix} 2 \times 40 + 1 \times 30 + 1 \times 50 & . \\ . & . \end{pmatrix}$$

the first row and first column of $\boldsymbol{PC}$ will be called the 'product' of the first row of $\boldsymbol{P}$ and the first column of $\boldsymbol{C}$.

More generally, the element in the ith row and jth column of $\boldsymbol{PC}$ is the product of the ith row of $\boldsymbol{P}$ and the jth column of $\boldsymbol{C}$. Check this for yourself.

This idea of taking the product of rows from the left matrix with columns from the right matrix is central to the multiplication of two matrices. Here are some examples.

Example 45.3.1

Find $\boldsymbol{AB}$ and $\boldsymbol{BA}$ when $\boldsymbol{A} = \begin{pmatrix} 1 & 2 \\ 3 & 4 \end{pmatrix}$ and $\boldsymbol{B} = \begin{pmatrix} 5 & 6 \\ 7 & 8 \end{pmatrix}$.

$$\boldsymbol{AB} = \begin{pmatrix} 1 & 2 \\ 3 & 4 \end{pmatrix}\begin{pmatrix} 5 & 6 \\ 7 & 8 \end{pmatrix} = \begin{pmatrix} 1\times 5 + 2\times 7 & 1\times 6 + 2\times 8 \\ 3\times 5 + 4\times 7 & 3\times 6 + 4\times 8 \end{pmatrix} = \begin{pmatrix} 19 & 22 \\ 43 & 50 \end{pmatrix};$$

$$\boldsymbol{BA} = \begin{pmatrix} 5 & 6 \\ 7 & 8 \end{pmatrix}\begin{pmatrix} 1 & 2 \\ 3 & 4 \end{pmatrix} = \begin{pmatrix} 5\times 1 + 6\times 3 & 5\times 2 + 6\times 4 \\ 7\times 1 + 8\times 3 & 7\times 2 + 8\times 4 \end{pmatrix} = \begin{pmatrix} 23 & 34 \\ 31 & 46 \end{pmatrix}.$$

An important fact emerges from this example. You cannot assume that $\boldsymbol{AB}$ and $\boldsymbol{BA}$ are equal. In fact, for matrices in general, $\boldsymbol{AB} \neq \boldsymbol{BA}$.

In general, the product of the matrices $\begin{pmatrix} a & b \\ c & d \end{pmatrix}$ and $\begin{pmatrix} e & f \\ g & h \end{pmatrix}$ is

$$\begin{pmatrix} a & b \\ c & d \end{pmatrix}\begin{pmatrix} e & f \\ g & h \end{pmatrix} = \begin{pmatrix} ae + bg & af + bh \\ ce + dg & cf + dh \end{pmatrix}.$$

Example 45.3.2

Find the products $\boldsymbol{AB}$ and $\boldsymbol{BA}$ when $\boldsymbol{A} = \begin{pmatrix} 2 & -3 & 1 \\ -5 & 2 & -2 \end{pmatrix}$ and $\boldsymbol{B} = \begin{pmatrix} 1 & 3 \\ 2 & 4 \\ 3 & 6 \end{pmatrix}$.

Although $\boldsymbol{A}$ and $\boldsymbol{B}$ are not square matrices, you can still use the principle that the element in the ith row and jth column of the product matrix is the product of the ith row of the left matrix with the jth column of the right matrix.

$$\begin{aligned} \boldsymbol{AB} &= \begin{pmatrix} 2 & -3 & 1 \\ -5 & 2 & -2 \end{pmatrix}\begin{pmatrix} 1 & 3 \\ 2 & 4 \\ 3 & 6 \end{pmatrix} \\ &= \begin{pmatrix} 2\times 1 + (-3)\times 2 + 1\times 3 & 2\times 3 + (-3)\times 4 + 1\times 6 \\ (-5)\times 1 + 2\times 2 + (-2)\times 3 & (-5)\times 3 + 2\times 4 + (-2)\times 6 \end{pmatrix} \\ &= \begin{pmatrix} -1 & 0 \\ -7 & -19 \end{pmatrix}, \end{aligned}$$

$$\begin{aligned} \text{and}\quad \boldsymbol{BA} &= \begin{pmatrix} 1 & 3 \\ 2 & 4 \\ 3 & 6 \end{pmatrix}\begin{pmatrix} 2 & -3 & 1 \\ -5 & 2 & -2 \end{pmatrix} \\ &= \begin{pmatrix} 1\times 2 + 3\times(-5) & 1\times(-3) + 3\times 2 & 1\times 1 + 3\times(-2) \\ 2\times 2 + 4\times(-5) & 2\times(-3) + 4\times 2 & 2\times 1 + 4\times(-2) \\ 3\times 2 + 6\times(-5) & 3\times(-3) + 6\times 2 & 3\times 1 + 6\times(-2) \end{pmatrix} \\ &= \begin{pmatrix} -13 & 3 & -5 \\ -16 & 2 & -6 \\ -24 & 3 & -9 \end{pmatrix}. \end{aligned}$$

You can see from this example that $\boldsymbol{AB}$ and $\boldsymbol{BA}$ are not always the same order. The next example shows that sometimes it is not even possible to multiply two matrices.

Example 45.3.3

Let $\boldsymbol{A} = \begin{pmatrix} -1 & 2 \\ -3 & -7 \end{pmatrix}$, $\boldsymbol{B} = \begin{pmatrix} 3 \\ -1 \end{pmatrix}$ and $\boldsymbol{C} = \begin{pmatrix} 2 & 5 \end{pmatrix}$. Determine which of the products $\boldsymbol{A}^2$, $\boldsymbol{AB}$, $\boldsymbol{AC}$, $\boldsymbol{BA}$, $\boldsymbol{B}^2$, $\boldsymbol{BC}$, $\boldsymbol{CA}$, $\boldsymbol{CB}$ and $\boldsymbol{C}^2$ exist and calculate those which do.

> Why might a matrix product not exist? The product rule for rows and columns relies on the length of the rows of the left matrix matching the length of the columns of the right matrix, otherwise you cannot carry out the multiplication to obtain the product.

$$\boldsymbol{A}^2 = \begin{pmatrix} -1 & 2 \\ -3 & -7 \end{pmatrix}\begin{pmatrix} -1 & 2 \\ -3 & -7 \end{pmatrix} = \begin{pmatrix} -5 & -16 \\ 24 & 43 \end{pmatrix}; \quad \boldsymbol{AB} = \begin{pmatrix} -1 & 2 \\ -3 & -7 \end{pmatrix}\begin{pmatrix} 3 \\ -1 \end{pmatrix} = \begin{pmatrix} -5 \\ -2 \end{pmatrix};$$

$$\boldsymbol{AC} = \begin{pmatrix} -1 & 2 \\ -3 & -7 \end{pmatrix}\begin{pmatrix} 2 & 5 \end{pmatrix} \text{ does not exist;} \qquad \boldsymbol{BA} = \begin{pmatrix} 3 \\ -1 \end{pmatrix}\begin{pmatrix} -1 & 2 \\ -3 & -7 \end{pmatrix} \text{ does not exist;}$$

$$\boldsymbol{B}^2 = \begin{pmatrix} 3 \\ -1 \end{pmatrix}\begin{pmatrix} 3 \\ -1 \end{pmatrix} \text{ does not exist;} \qquad \boldsymbol{BC} = \begin{pmatrix} 3 \\ -1 \end{pmatrix}\begin{pmatrix} 2 & 5 \end{pmatrix} = \begin{pmatrix} 6 & 15 \\ -2 & -5 \end{pmatrix};$$

$$\boldsymbol{CA} = \begin{pmatrix} 2 & 5 \end{pmatrix}\begin{pmatrix} -1 & 2 \\ -3 & -7 \end{pmatrix} = \begin{pmatrix} -17 & -31 \end{pmatrix}; \qquad \boldsymbol{CB} = \begin{pmatrix} 2 & 5 \end{pmatrix}\begin{pmatrix} 3 \\ -1 \end{pmatrix} = (1);$$

$$\boldsymbol{C}^2 = \begin{pmatrix} 2 & 5 \end{pmatrix}\begin{pmatrix} 2 & 5 \end{pmatrix} \text{ does not exist.}$$

The product rule for multiplying matrices implies that you can only multiply two matrices if they are **conformable** for multiplication. That is, if $\boldsymbol{A}$ is an $m \times n$ matrix and $\boldsymbol{B}$ is a $p \times q$ matrix, then the product $\boldsymbol{AB}$ exists if, and only if, $n = p$. The order of this product is $m \times q$.

Thus multiplying matrices of orders $m \times n$ and $n \times q$ results in a $m \times q$ matrix.

There are a number of rules concerning the algebra of matrices. Questions 12 to 16 in Exercise 45 suggest (correctly) that the following are true.

> For matrices $\boldsymbol{A}$, $\boldsymbol{B}$ and $\boldsymbol{C}$, and for scalars s:
>
> $$\begin{aligned} &\boldsymbol{A}(\boldsymbol{B}+\boldsymbol{C}) = \boldsymbol{AB}+\boldsymbol{AC}, && (\boldsymbol{B}+\boldsymbol{C})\boldsymbol{A} = \boldsymbol{BA}+\boldsymbol{CA}, \\ &\boldsymbol{A}(\boldsymbol{BC}) = (\boldsymbol{AB})\boldsymbol{C}, && s(\boldsymbol{AB}) = (s\boldsymbol{A})\boldsymbol{B} = \boldsymbol{A}(s\boldsymbol{B}), \\ &\boldsymbol{AO} = \boldsymbol{O}, && \boldsymbol{OA} = \boldsymbol{O}, \end{aligned}$$
>
> provided that the various sums and products exist.
>
> In general, $\boldsymbol{AB} \neq \boldsymbol{BA}$.

45.4 A matrix corresponding to the number 1

The important characteristic of the number 1 in multiplication is that it has the property that

$$1 \times x = x, \text{ for every } x \in \mathbb{R}.$$

Is there a matrix $\begin{pmatrix} p & q \\ r & s \end{pmatrix}$ with the property that $\begin{pmatrix} p & q \\ r & s \end{pmatrix}\boldsymbol{X} = \boldsymbol{X}$ for every 2×2 matrix $\boldsymbol{X}$?

Example 45.4.1

Find the matrix $\begin{pmatrix} p & q \\ r & s \end{pmatrix}$ such that $\begin{pmatrix} p & q \\ r & s \end{pmatrix}\begin{pmatrix} 1 & 2 \\ 3 & 5 \end{pmatrix} = \begin{pmatrix} 1 & 2 \\ 3 & 5 \end{pmatrix}$.

If $\begin{pmatrix} p & q \\ r & s \end{pmatrix}\begin{pmatrix} 1 & 2 \\ 3 & 5 \end{pmatrix} = \begin{pmatrix} 1 & 2 \\ 3 & 5 \end{pmatrix}$, then $\begin{pmatrix} p+3q & 2p+5q \\ r+3s & 2r+5s \end{pmatrix} = \begin{pmatrix} 1 & 2 \\ 3 & 5 \end{pmatrix}$.

Looking at the elements in the top row, $p + 3q = 1$ and $2p + 5q = 2$.

From the first equation, $p = 1 - 3q$.

Substituting this in the second equation gives

$$\begin{aligned} 2(1-3q) + 5q &= 2 \\ 2 - 6q + 5q &= 2 \\ -q &= 0 \\ q &= 0. \end{aligned}$$

Substituting $q = 0$ in the first equation gives $p = 1$.

Similarly, looking at the second row elements, $r + 3s = 3$ and $2r + 5s = 5$. Then solving these equations simultaneously gives $r = 0$, $s = 1$.

So the matrix $\begin{pmatrix} p & q \\ r & s \end{pmatrix}$ is $\begin{pmatrix} 1 & 0 \\ 0 & 1 \end{pmatrix}$.

$\begin{pmatrix} 1 & 0 \\ 0 & 1 \end{pmatrix}$ also has the property that $\begin{pmatrix} 1 & 0 \\ 0 & 1 \end{pmatrix}\begin{pmatrix} a & b \\ c & d \end{pmatrix} = \begin{pmatrix} a & b \\ c & d \end{pmatrix}$, for any matrix $\begin{pmatrix} a & b \\ c & d \end{pmatrix}$.

In addition, it also has the property that $\begin{pmatrix} a & b \\ c & d \end{pmatrix}\begin{pmatrix} 1 & 0 \\ 0 & 1 \end{pmatrix} = \begin{pmatrix} a & b \\ c & d \end{pmatrix}$.

The matrix $\begin{pmatrix} 1 & 0 \\ 0 & 1 \end{pmatrix}$ is called the **2 × 2 identity matrix**, and is denoted by $\boldsymbol{I}$. Similarly the **3 × 3 identity matrix** is $\begin{pmatrix} 1 & 0 & 0 \\ 0 & 1 & 0 \\ 0 & 0 & 1 \end{pmatrix}$, and is also denoted by $\boldsymbol{I}$. When you write a matrix statement such as

$$\boldsymbol{IX} = \boldsymbol{XI} = \boldsymbol{X}$$

then the order of the identity matrix $\boldsymbol{I}$ has to be correct for multiplication by $\boldsymbol{X}$.

This means that if $\boldsymbol{X}$ is 2×2 then $\boldsymbol{I}$ will be 2×2, and if $\boldsymbol{X}$ is 3×3 then $\boldsymbol{I}$ is 3×3.

However, if $\boldsymbol{X}$ is not square, and is, say, $m \times n$, then the two $\boldsymbol{I}$s in the equation $\boldsymbol{IX} = \boldsymbol{XI} = \boldsymbol{X}$ have different orders. The left $\boldsymbol{I}$ will be $m \times m$ and the right $\boldsymbol{I}$ $n \times n$. This sounds confusing, but it is never a problem in practice.

If you wish to specify the order of the identity matrix, then it is usual to write $\boldsymbol{I}_n$ for the $n \times n$ identity matrix.

A useful way of describing where the 1s occur in the identity matrix is to say that they appear on the **leading diagonal**, which, for a square matrix, runs from the top left corner to the bottom right.

> An **identity matrix** is a square matrix consisting of 1s on the leading diagonal and 0s everywhere else. The identity matrix with n rows and n columns is denoted by $\boldsymbol{I}_n$.
>
> If $\boldsymbol{X}$ is any square matrix with n rows and n columns, then
>
> $$\boldsymbol{I}_n\boldsymbol{X} = \boldsymbol{X}\boldsymbol{I}_n = \boldsymbol{X}.$$
>
> There is no such thing as a non-square identity matrix.

Example 45.4.2

Let $\boldsymbol{A} = \begin{pmatrix} 1 & 3 \\ 0 & 2 \end{pmatrix}$. Find a 2×2 matrix $\boldsymbol{C}$ such that $\boldsymbol{CA} = \boldsymbol{I}$. Verify that $\boldsymbol{AC} = \boldsymbol{I}$.

Let $\boldsymbol{C} = \begin{pmatrix} a & b \\ c & d \end{pmatrix}$.

Then if $\boldsymbol{CA} = \boldsymbol{I}$, $\begin{pmatrix} a & b \\ c & d \end{pmatrix}\begin{pmatrix} 1 & 3 \\ 0 & 2 \end{pmatrix} = \begin{pmatrix} 1 & 0 \\ 0 & 1 \end{pmatrix}$, so $\begin{pmatrix} a & 3a+2b \\ c & 3c+2d \end{pmatrix} = \begin{pmatrix} 1 & 0 \\ 0 & 1 \end{pmatrix}$.

Then, as the two matrices are equal, their elements are equal, so

$$a = 1, 3a + 2b = 0, c = 0 \text{ and } 3c + 2d = 1.$$

Solving these equations gives

$$a = 1, \quad b = -\tfrac{3}{2}, \quad c = 0 \quad \text{and} \quad d = \tfrac{1}{2}.$$

Therefore $\boldsymbol{C} = \begin{pmatrix} 1 & -\frac{3}{2} \\ 0 & \frac{1}{2} \end{pmatrix}$.

Then $\boldsymbol{AC} = \begin{pmatrix} 1 & 3 \\ 0 & 2 \end{pmatrix}\begin{pmatrix} 1 & -\frac{3}{2} \\ 0 & \frac{1}{2} \end{pmatrix} = \begin{pmatrix} 1 & -\frac{3}{2} + 3 \times \frac{1}{2} \\ 0 & 2 \times \frac{1}{2} \end{pmatrix} = \begin{pmatrix} 1 & 0 \\ 0 & 1 \end{pmatrix} = \boldsymbol{I}$.

Example 45.4.3

(a) Find the product of the matrices $\begin{pmatrix} a & 1 \\ 2 & 3 \end{pmatrix}$ and $\begin{pmatrix} b & -1 \\ -2 & a \end{pmatrix}$.

(b) If the product is equal to the identity matrix, find a and b.

(a) The product of $\begin{pmatrix} a & 1 \\ 2 & 3 \end{pmatrix}$ and $\begin{pmatrix} b & -1 \\ -2 & a \end{pmatrix}$ is

$$\begin{pmatrix} a & 1 \\ 2 & 3 \end{pmatrix}\begin{pmatrix} b & -1 \\ -2 & a \end{pmatrix} = \begin{pmatrix} ab-2 & -a+a \\ 2b-6 & -2+3a \end{pmatrix}.$$

(b) The identity matrix is $\begin{pmatrix} 1 & 0 \\ 0 & 1 \end{pmatrix}$, so if $\begin{pmatrix} ab-2 & -a+a \\ 2b-6 & -2+3a \end{pmatrix} = \begin{pmatrix} 1 & 0 \\ 0 & 1 \end{pmatrix}$, then, by equating the corresponding entries, you get the four equations

$$ab-2=1, \quad -a+a=0,$$
$$2b-6=0, \quad -2+3a=1.$$

From the last two equations, $b=3$ and $a=1$. Substituting these values in the first equation shows that the left side is $1 \times 3 - 2 = 1$, which is the same as the right side.

So $a=1$ and $b=3$.

Your calculator will enable you to carry out matrix algebra involving numbers. However, it would not be able to carry out the calculations in Example 45.4.3.

Exercise 45

1 Let $\boldsymbol{A} = \begin{pmatrix} 1 & 2 \\ 3 & 4 \end{pmatrix}$ and $\boldsymbol{B} = \begin{pmatrix} 2 & 3 \\ 4 & -1 \end{pmatrix}$. Calculate the matrices

(a) $\boldsymbol{A}+\boldsymbol{B}$, (b) $\boldsymbol{A}-\boldsymbol{B}$, (c) $3\boldsymbol{A}+2\boldsymbol{B}$, (d) $4\boldsymbol{A}-3\boldsymbol{B}$.

2 Solve for $\boldsymbol{X}$ the matrix equation $2\boldsymbol{X}+3\boldsymbol{A}=4\boldsymbol{X}-3\boldsymbol{B}$. What do you need to assume about the orders of $\boldsymbol{A}$, $\boldsymbol{B}$ and $\boldsymbol{X}$?

3 Prove that, for matrices $\boldsymbol{A}$, $\boldsymbol{B}$ and $\boldsymbol{C}$ of the same order, $\boldsymbol{A}+(\boldsymbol{B}+\boldsymbol{C})=(\boldsymbol{A}+\boldsymbol{B})+\boldsymbol{C}$.

4 Find the products $\boldsymbol{AB}$ and $\boldsymbol{BA}$ where $\boldsymbol{A} = \begin{pmatrix} 1 & 2 \\ 3 & 4 \end{pmatrix}$ and $\boldsymbol{B} = \begin{pmatrix} 2 & 3 \\ 4 & -1 \end{pmatrix}$.

5 Let $\boldsymbol{A} = \begin{pmatrix} 2 & 3 & -1 \\ 1 & 3 & 5 \\ -3 & -2 & 2 \end{pmatrix}$ and $\boldsymbol{B} = \begin{pmatrix} 4 & -2 & -3 \\ 5 & 1 & 2 \\ 2 & -4 & 1 \end{pmatrix}$. Calculate $\boldsymbol{AB}$ and $\boldsymbol{BA}$.

6 Let $\boldsymbol{A} = \begin{pmatrix} -3 & 2 & 6 \\ 2 & -1 & 2 \end{pmatrix}$ and $\boldsymbol{B} = \begin{pmatrix} 6 & 2 \\ 3 & 2 \\ 2 & -1 \end{pmatrix}$. Calculate $\boldsymbol{AB}$ and $\boldsymbol{BA}$.

7 Although in general, it is true that $\boldsymbol{AB} \neq \boldsymbol{BA}$, there are matrices $\boldsymbol{A}$ and $\boldsymbol{B}$ such that $\boldsymbol{AB}=\boldsymbol{BA}$. Find such a pair $\boldsymbol{A}$ and $\boldsymbol{B}$ in which none of the elements is 0.

8 Let $\boldsymbol{A}=\begin{pmatrix}1\\-1\\1\end{pmatrix}$, $\boldsymbol{B}=\begin{pmatrix}-4 & 2 & 3\\-2 & 3 & -3\end{pmatrix}$ and $\boldsymbol{C}=(2\quad 3\quad 1)$. Calculate those of the following matrix products which exist.

(a) $\boldsymbol{AB}$ (b) $\boldsymbol{BA}$ (c) $\boldsymbol{AC}$ (d) $\boldsymbol{CA}$

(e) $\boldsymbol{BC}$ (f) $\boldsymbol{CB}$ (g) $(\boldsymbol{CA})\boldsymbol{B}$ (h) $\boldsymbol{C}(\boldsymbol{AB})$

9 Find a matrix $\boldsymbol{X}=\begin{pmatrix}a & b\\c & d\end{pmatrix}$ such that $\boldsymbol{X}\begin{pmatrix}1 & 2\\3 & 7\end{pmatrix}=\begin{pmatrix}1 & 0\\0 & 1\end{pmatrix}$. Calculate the product $\begin{pmatrix}1 & 2\\3 & 7\end{pmatrix}\boldsymbol{X}$. Try to do the same calculations with $\begin{pmatrix}1 & 2\\3 & 6\end{pmatrix}$ in place of $\begin{pmatrix}1 & 2\\3 & 7\end{pmatrix}$.

10 Let $\boldsymbol{A}=\begin{pmatrix}a & b\\c & d\end{pmatrix}$, $\boldsymbol{X}=\begin{pmatrix}x\\y\end{pmatrix}$ and $\boldsymbol{P}=\begin{pmatrix}p\\q\end{pmatrix}$. Show that solving the matrix equation $\boldsymbol{AX}=\boldsymbol{P}$ is equivalent to solving the simultaneous equations $\left.\begin{matrix}ax+by=p\\cx+dy=q\end{matrix}\right\}$ and that this is equivalent to solving the vector equation $x\begin{pmatrix}a\\c\end{pmatrix}+y\begin{pmatrix}b\\d\end{pmatrix}=\begin{pmatrix}p\\q\end{pmatrix}$.

11 Find the matrix $\boldsymbol{X}$ such that $\begin{pmatrix}1 & 2 & 2\\1 & 3 & -1\\2 & 4 & 5\end{pmatrix}\boldsymbol{X}=\begin{pmatrix}1 & 0 & 0\\0 & 1 & 0\\0 & 0 & 1\end{pmatrix}$. Calculate $\boldsymbol{X}\begin{pmatrix}1 & 2 & 2\\1 & 3 & -1\\2 & 4 & 5\end{pmatrix}$.

12 Verify that $\boldsymbol{A}(\boldsymbol{B}+\boldsymbol{C})=\boldsymbol{AB}+\boldsymbol{AC}$, $(\boldsymbol{B}+\boldsymbol{C})\boldsymbol{A}=\boldsymbol{BA}+\boldsymbol{CA}$ and $(\boldsymbol{AB})\boldsymbol{C}=\boldsymbol{A}(\boldsymbol{BC})$ for the following matrices:

$$\boldsymbol{A}=\begin{pmatrix}3 & 2\\6 & -2\end{pmatrix},\quad \boldsymbol{B}=\begin{pmatrix}1 & -1\\2 & 0\end{pmatrix}\quad\text{and}\quad \boldsymbol{C}=\begin{pmatrix}2 & -1\\1 & 3\end{pmatrix}.$$

13 Let $\boldsymbol{A}=(2\quad -3)$, $\boldsymbol{B}=\begin{pmatrix}3 & 2\\-4 & 1\end{pmatrix}$ and $\boldsymbol{C}=\begin{pmatrix}4\\-1\end{pmatrix}$. Verify that $(\boldsymbol{AB})\boldsymbol{C}=\boldsymbol{A}(\boldsymbol{BC})$.

14 Establish results similar to those in the blue box in Section 45.4 for $\boldsymbol{I}$ for the products $\boldsymbol{AO}$ and $\boldsymbol{OA}$.

15 Prove for 2×2 matrices $\boldsymbol{A}$ and $\boldsymbol{B}$ and a scalar s that $(s\boldsymbol{A})\boldsymbol{B}=s(\boldsymbol{AB})$.

16 Prove that $\boldsymbol{A}(\boldsymbol{B}+\boldsymbol{C})=\boldsymbol{AB}+\boldsymbol{AC}$ when $\boldsymbol{A}$, $\boldsymbol{B}$ and $\boldsymbol{C}$ are 2×2 matrices.

17 Find a matrix $\boldsymbol{X}$ such that $\boldsymbol{X}\begin{pmatrix}5 & 3\\3 & 2\end{pmatrix}=\begin{pmatrix}1 & 0\\0 & 1\end{pmatrix}$.

18 Find a matrix $\boldsymbol{X}$ such that $\boldsymbol{X}\begin{pmatrix}5 & 2\\7 & 3\end{pmatrix}=\begin{pmatrix}1 & 0\\0 & 1\end{pmatrix}$.

19 Let $\boldsymbol{M}=\begin{pmatrix}1 & 2 & -1\\2 & 1 & 2\\1 & 0 & 1\end{pmatrix}$. Show that $\boldsymbol{M}^3-3\boldsymbol{M}^2=2\boldsymbol{I}$.

46 Inverse matrices

This chapter shows how and when matrices can be divided. When you have completed it, you should

- be able to find an inverse matrix, if it exists, for a 2×2 matrix
- be able to find an inverse matrix, if it exists, for a 3×3 matrix, using a calculator.

46.1 A matrix problem

In Section 45.4 you saw that the 2×2 matrix $\boldsymbol{I} = \begin{pmatrix} 1 & 0 \\ 0 & 1 \end{pmatrix}$ behaves like the number 1 in the sense that, for any other 2×2 matrix $\boldsymbol{A}$

$$\boldsymbol{IA} = \boldsymbol{AI} = \boldsymbol{A}.$$

But how can you divide using matrices? Exercise 46A will show the first steps of the way.

Exercise 46A

1 Find the matrix $\begin{pmatrix} p & q \\ r & s \end{pmatrix}$ which has the property that $\begin{pmatrix} p & q \\ r & s \end{pmatrix}\boldsymbol{A} = \boldsymbol{I}$ in each of the following cases. In each case test whether $\boldsymbol{A}\begin{pmatrix} p & q \\ r & s \end{pmatrix} = \boldsymbol{I}$.

(a) $\boldsymbol{A} = \begin{pmatrix} 5 & -7 \\ -2 & 3 \end{pmatrix}$ (b) $\boldsymbol{A} = \begin{pmatrix} -3 & 8 \\ -2 & 5 \end{pmatrix}$ (c) $\boldsymbol{A} = \begin{pmatrix} 7 & 3 \\ 9 & 4 \end{pmatrix}$

Use your answers to make and write down a generalisation.

2 Using the generalisation that you made in Question 1, write down what you think is the matrix $\begin{pmatrix} p & q \\ r & s \end{pmatrix}$ which has the property that $\begin{pmatrix} p & q \\ r & s \end{pmatrix}\boldsymbol{A} = \boldsymbol{I}$ in each of the following cases. In each case test your answer and, if necessary, refine it. In each case test whether $\boldsymbol{A}\begin{pmatrix} p & q \\ r & s \end{pmatrix} = \boldsymbol{I}$.

(a) $\boldsymbol{A} = \begin{pmatrix} -5 & -3 \\ 2 & 1 \end{pmatrix}$ (b) $\boldsymbol{A} = \begin{pmatrix} 3 & 2 \\ 1 & 4 \end{pmatrix}$ (c) $\boldsymbol{A} = \begin{pmatrix} 5 & 2 \\ 4 & 3 \end{pmatrix}$

Use your answers to make and write down a refined generalisation.

3 (a) Write down in terms of a, b, c and d the matrix $\begin{pmatrix} p & q \\ r & s \end{pmatrix}$ which has the property that

$\begin{pmatrix} p & q \\ r & s \end{pmatrix}\begin{pmatrix} a & b \\ c & d \end{pmatrix} = \boldsymbol{I}.$

(b) Check that your matrix also satisfies $\begin{pmatrix} a & b \\ c & d \end{pmatrix}\begin{pmatrix} p & q \\ r & s \end{pmatrix} = \boldsymbol{I}.$

(c) It is not always possible to find such a matrix. Write down a condition on a, b, c and d for your matrix to fail to satisfy $\begin{pmatrix} a & b \\ c & d \end{pmatrix}\begin{pmatrix} p & q \\ r & s \end{pmatrix} = \boldsymbol{I}.$

46.2 Inverse of a 2 × 2 matrix

Suppose that you are given a 2×2 matrix $\boldsymbol{A}$. Then, if there exists a matrix $\boldsymbol{C}$ such that

$$\boldsymbol{AC} = \boldsymbol{CA} = \boldsymbol{I},$$

where $\boldsymbol{I}$ is the 2×2 identity matrix, then $\boldsymbol{C}$ is called the **inverse** of $\boldsymbol{A}$ and written as $\boldsymbol{A}^{-1}$. Then the equation above can be written in the form

$$\boldsymbol{AA}^{-1} = \boldsymbol{A}^{-1}\boldsymbol{A} = \boldsymbol{I}.$$

The work of Exercise 46A should have convinced you that:

the inverse of $\begin{pmatrix} a & b \\ c & d \end{pmatrix}$ is $\dfrac{1}{ad-bc}\begin{pmatrix} d & -b \\ -c & a \end{pmatrix}$, provided that $ad - bc \neq 0$.

It is also true, but won't be proved here, that if $ad - bc = 0$, the matrix $\begin{pmatrix} a & b \\ c & d \end{pmatrix}$ has no inverse.

The inverse of the matrix $\boldsymbol{A} = \begin{pmatrix} a & b \\ c & d \end{pmatrix}$ is given by

$$\boldsymbol{A}^{-1} = \frac{1}{ad-bc}\begin{pmatrix} d & -b \\ -c & a \end{pmatrix}$$

provided that $ad - bc \neq 0$.

The inverse $\boldsymbol{A}^{-1}$ of $\boldsymbol{A}$ has the property that

$$\boldsymbol{AA}^{-1} = \boldsymbol{A}^{-1}\boldsymbol{A} = \boldsymbol{I}.$$

If $ad - bc = 0$, then $\boldsymbol{A}$ has no inverse.

The expression $ad - bc$ is important. It is called the determinant of the matrix $\boldsymbol{A}$, and its properties are taken further in the next chapter.

Note that a 2×2 matrix $\boldsymbol{A}$ cannot have more than one inverse. For suppose that there are two distinct inverses, called $\boldsymbol{B}$ and $\boldsymbol{C}$, with the property that $\boldsymbol{AB} = \boldsymbol{BA} = \boldsymbol{I}$ and $\boldsymbol{AC} = \boldsymbol{CA} = \boldsymbol{I}$.

Then

$$\begin{aligned} \boldsymbol{B} &= \boldsymbol{BI} && \text{(definition of } \boldsymbol{I}\text{)} \\ &= \boldsymbol{B}(\boldsymbol{AC}) && \text{(since } \boldsymbol{AC} = \boldsymbol{I}\text{)} \\ &= (\boldsymbol{BA})\boldsymbol{C} && \text{(rule of matrix multiplication)} \\ &= \boldsymbol{IC} && \text{(definition of } \boldsymbol{I}\text{)} \\ &= \boldsymbol{C}. \end{aligned}$$

This shows that the supposition that $\boldsymbol{B}$ and $\boldsymbol{C}$ are different has led to a contradiction, so $\boldsymbol{B}$ and $\boldsymbol{C}$ must be the same.

To return to the question 'How can you divide using matrices?', the answer is 'You can't!'. But if the inverse of a matrix exists, then you can multiply by this inverse, and it has the effect of division. So for example, if you have a matrix equation of the form $\boldsymbol{AX} = \boldsymbol{B}$, where $\boldsymbol{A}$, $\boldsymbol{X}$ and $\boldsymbol{B}$ are 2×2 matrices, and $\boldsymbol{A}$ has an inverse, you can immediately say

$$\begin{aligned} \boldsymbol{AX} &= \boldsymbol{B} \\ \boldsymbol{A}^{-1}\boldsymbol{AX} &= \boldsymbol{A}^{-1}\boldsymbol{B} && \text{(multiply on the left by } \boldsymbol{A}^{-1}\text{)} \\ \boldsymbol{IX} &= \boldsymbol{A}^{-1}\boldsymbol{B} && \text{(simplify } \boldsymbol{A}^{-1}\boldsymbol{A}\text{)} \\ \boldsymbol{X} &= \boldsymbol{A}^{-1}\boldsymbol{B} \end{aligned}$$

and you have effectively divided by the matrix $\boldsymbol{A}$.

> You may think that matrices are special in the sense that an inverse may not exist, but numbers have the same property. The number a has an inverse $\frac{1}{a}$ provided $a \neq 0$.

46.3 Using the inverse matrix

The inverse matrix can be used to solve two simultaneous equations with two unknowns. But first you need to think of the equations in a different way, which you saw first in Exercise 45 Question 10.

Consider the set of equations $\left.\begin{aligned} 2x + 3y &= 9 \\ 3x - 4y &= 5 \end{aligned}\right\}$. You can write these in the form

$$\begin{pmatrix} 2x + 3y \\ 3x - 4y \end{pmatrix} = \begin{pmatrix} 9 \\ 5 \end{pmatrix}, \quad \text{which in turn you can write as} \quad \begin{pmatrix} 2 & 3 \\ 3 & -4 \end{pmatrix}\begin{pmatrix} x \\ y \end{pmatrix} = \begin{pmatrix} 9 \\ 5 \end{pmatrix}.$$

If you write $\boldsymbol{A} = \begin{pmatrix} 2 & 3 \\ 3 & -4 \end{pmatrix}$, then the equations become $\boldsymbol{A}\begin{pmatrix} x \\ y \end{pmatrix} = \begin{pmatrix} 9 \\ 5 \end{pmatrix}$.

Using the result in the blue box, the inverse $\boldsymbol{A}^{-1}$ of $\boldsymbol{A}$ is given by

$$\boldsymbol{A}^{-1} = \frac{1}{2 \times (-4) - 3 \times 3}\begin{pmatrix} -4 & -3 \\ -3 & 2 \end{pmatrix} = -\frac{1}{17}\begin{pmatrix} -4 & -3 \\ -3 & 2 \end{pmatrix}.$$

Now see what happens when you multiply both sides of the equation by $\boldsymbol{A}^{-1}$.
On the left side you get

$$\boldsymbol{A}^{-1}\boldsymbol{A}\begin{pmatrix}x\\y\end{pmatrix}=\boldsymbol{I}\begin{pmatrix}x\\y\end{pmatrix}=\begin{pmatrix}x\\y\end{pmatrix}.$$

On the right side you get

$$\begin{aligned}\begin{pmatrix}x\\y\end{pmatrix}&=\boldsymbol{A}^{-1}\begin{pmatrix}9\\5\end{pmatrix}\\&=-\frac{1}{17}\begin{pmatrix}-4&-3\\-3&2\end{pmatrix}\begin{pmatrix}9\\5\end{pmatrix}=-\frac{1}{17}\begin{pmatrix}-4\times 9-3\times 5\\-3\times 9+2\times 5\end{pmatrix}\\&=-\frac{1}{17}\begin{pmatrix}-36-15\\-27+10\end{pmatrix}=-\frac{1}{17}\begin{pmatrix}-51\\-17\end{pmatrix}=\begin{pmatrix}3\\1\end{pmatrix}.\end{aligned}$$

The solution of the equations is then $x=3$, $y=1$.

What has happened is that the equation $\boldsymbol{A}\begin{pmatrix}x\\y\end{pmatrix}=\begin{pmatrix}9\\5\end{pmatrix}$ has been transformed by the inverse $\boldsymbol{A}^{-1}$ of $\boldsymbol{A}$ to the equation $\begin{pmatrix}x\\y\end{pmatrix}=\boldsymbol{A}^{-1}\begin{pmatrix}9\\5\end{pmatrix}$. At this stage all you need to do is multiply the matrices $\boldsymbol{A}^{-1}$ and $\begin{pmatrix}9\\5\end{pmatrix}$ to find the solution.

In practice, you would not write the solution in such a long-winded way.

Example 46.3.1

Solve the equations $\left.\begin{aligned}4x-5y&=10\\x-3y&=13\end{aligned}\right\}$.

Write the equations $\left.\begin{aligned}4x-5y&=10\\x-3y&=13\end{aligned}\right\}$ as $\boldsymbol{A}\begin{pmatrix}x\\y\end{pmatrix}=\begin{pmatrix}10\\13\end{pmatrix}$, where $\boldsymbol{A}=\begin{pmatrix}4&-5\\1&-3\end{pmatrix}$.

The inverse of $\boldsymbol{A}$ is given by $\boldsymbol{A}^{-1}=\dfrac{1}{4\times(-3)-(-5)\times 1}\begin{pmatrix}-3&5\\-1&4\end{pmatrix}=-\frac{1}{7}\begin{pmatrix}-3&5\\-1&4\end{pmatrix}$.

The solution is

$$\begin{aligned}\begin{pmatrix}x\\y\end{pmatrix}&=\boldsymbol{A}^{-1}\begin{pmatrix}10\\13\end{pmatrix}=-\frac{1}{7}\begin{pmatrix}-3&5\\-1&4\end{pmatrix}\begin{pmatrix}10\\13\end{pmatrix}\\&=-\frac{1}{7}\begin{pmatrix}-3\times 10+5\times 13\\-1\times 10+4\times 13\end{pmatrix}=-\frac{1}{7}\begin{pmatrix}35\\42\end{pmatrix}=\begin{pmatrix}-5\\-6\end{pmatrix}.\end{aligned}$$

So $x=-5$, $y=-6$.

Example 46.3.2

Find the inverse of $\begin{pmatrix}4&-5\\3&7\end{pmatrix}$, and use it to solve the equations $\left.\begin{aligned}4x-5y&=3\\3x+7y&=13\end{aligned}\right\}$.

The inverse of $\begin{pmatrix}4&-5\\3&7\end{pmatrix}$ is $\frac{1}{43}\begin{pmatrix}7&5\\-3&4\end{pmatrix}$.

Writing the equations $\left.\begin{aligned} 4x - 5y &= 3 \\ 3x + 7y &= 13 \end{aligned}\right\}$ as $\begin{pmatrix} 4 & -5 \\ 3 & 7 \end{pmatrix}\begin{pmatrix} x \\ y \end{pmatrix} = \begin{pmatrix} 3 \\ 13 \end{pmatrix}$, the solution is

$$\begin{pmatrix} x \\ y \end{pmatrix} = \begin{pmatrix} 4 & -5 \\ 3 & 7 \end{pmatrix}^{-1}\begin{pmatrix} 3 \\ 13 \end{pmatrix} = \tfrac{1}{43}\begin{pmatrix} 7 & 5 \\ -3 & 4 \end{pmatrix}\begin{pmatrix} 3 \\ 13 \end{pmatrix} = \tfrac{1}{43}\begin{pmatrix} 21+65 \\ -9+52 \end{pmatrix} = \begin{pmatrix} 2 \\ 1 \end{pmatrix}.$$

Therefore the solution is $x = 2$, $y = 1$.

Example 46.3.3

Solve for $\boldsymbol{M}$ the matrix equation $\boldsymbol{M}\begin{pmatrix} 2 & 1 \\ 1 & 1 \end{pmatrix} = \begin{pmatrix} 1 & 3 \\ 3 & 2 \end{pmatrix}$.

To solve, multiply on the right by $\begin{pmatrix} 2 & 1 \\ 1 & 1 \end{pmatrix}^{-1} = \tfrac{1}{1}\begin{pmatrix} 1 & -1 \\ -1 & 2 \end{pmatrix} = \begin{pmatrix} 1 & -1 \\ -1 & 2 \end{pmatrix}$. Thus

$$\begin{aligned} \boldsymbol{M}\begin{pmatrix} 2 & 1 \\ 1 & 1 \end{pmatrix}\begin{pmatrix} 2 & 1 \\ 1 & 1 \end{pmatrix}^{-1} &= \begin{pmatrix} 1 & 3 \\ 3 & 2 \end{pmatrix}\begin{pmatrix} 2 & 1 \\ 1 & 1 \end{pmatrix}^{-1} \\ \boldsymbol{MI} &= \begin{pmatrix} 1 & 3 \\ 3 & 2 \end{pmatrix}\begin{pmatrix} 1 & -1 \\ -1 & 2 \end{pmatrix} \\ \boldsymbol{M} &= \begin{pmatrix} 1 & 3 \\ 3 & 2 \end{pmatrix}\begin{pmatrix} 1 & -1 \\ -1 & 2 \end{pmatrix} = \begin{pmatrix} -2 & 5 \\ 1 & 1 \end{pmatrix}. \end{aligned}$$

Therefore $\boldsymbol{M} = \begin{pmatrix} -2 & 5 \\ 1 & 1 \end{pmatrix}$.

It is important in Example 46.3.3 to multiply by the inverse of $\begin{pmatrix} 2 & 1 \\ 1 & 1 \end{pmatrix}$ on the correct side of $\boldsymbol{M}\begin{pmatrix} 2 & 1 \\ 1 & 1 \end{pmatrix}$. The reason why the method works is that, when you multiply on the right by $\begin{pmatrix} 2 & 1 \\ 1 & 1 \end{pmatrix}^{-1}$, you get $\boldsymbol{M}\begin{pmatrix} 2 & 1 \\ 1 & 1 \end{pmatrix}\begin{pmatrix} 2 & 1 \\ 1 & 1 \end{pmatrix}^{-1}$, and the product of the last two factors is $\begin{pmatrix} 2 & 1 \\ 1 & 1 \end{pmatrix}\begin{pmatrix} 2 & 1 \\ 1 & 1 \end{pmatrix}^{-1} = \boldsymbol{I}$. If you multiply on the left, you get $\begin{pmatrix} 2 & 1 \\ 1 & 1 \end{pmatrix}^{-1}\boldsymbol{M}\begin{pmatrix} 2 & 1 \\ 1 & 1 \end{pmatrix}$ which you cannot simplify. This does not apply in the same way to Example 46.3.2, because you cannot multiply $\begin{pmatrix} 3 \\ 13 \end{pmatrix}$ on the right by the inverse of $\begin{pmatrix} 4 & -5 \\ 3 & 7 \end{pmatrix}$. Try it!

Example 46.3.4

Let $\boldsymbol{M} = \begin{pmatrix} 4 & 5 \\ 2 & 3 \end{pmatrix}$. Show that $\boldsymbol{M}^2 - 7\boldsymbol{M} + 2\boldsymbol{I} = \boldsymbol{O}$. Use this to show that $\boldsymbol{M}^{-1} = \tfrac{1}{2}\begin{pmatrix} 3 & -5 \\ -2 & 4 \end{pmatrix}$.

$$\boldsymbol{M}^2 = \begin{pmatrix} 4 & 5 \\ 2 & 3 \end{pmatrix}\begin{pmatrix} 4 & 5 \\ 2 & 3 \end{pmatrix} = \begin{pmatrix} 4\times4+5\times2 & 4\times5+5\times3 \\ 2\times4+3\times2 & 2\times5+3\times3 \end{pmatrix} = \begin{pmatrix} 26 & 35 \\ 14 & 19 \end{pmatrix}, \text{ so}$$

$$\boldsymbol{M}^2 - 7\boldsymbol{M} + 2\boldsymbol{I} = \begin{pmatrix} 26 & 35 \\ 14 & 19 \end{pmatrix} - \begin{pmatrix} 28 & 35 \\ 14 & 21 \end{pmatrix} + \begin{pmatrix} 2 & 0 \\ 0 & 2 \end{pmatrix} = \begin{pmatrix} 0 & 0 \\ 0 & 0 \end{pmatrix} = \boldsymbol{O}.$$

You can now rearrange this formula to give an expression for $\boldsymbol{M}^{-1}$.

As $\boldsymbol{M}^2 - 7\boldsymbol{M} + 2\boldsymbol{I} = \boldsymbol{O}$,

$$2\boldsymbol{I} = 7\boldsymbol{M} - \boldsymbol{M}^2 = \boldsymbol{M}(7\boldsymbol{I} - \boldsymbol{M}),$$

so $\quad \boldsymbol{I} = \boldsymbol{M}\left(\frac{1}{2}(7\boldsymbol{I} - \boldsymbol{M})\right)$.

As $\boldsymbol{M}$ multiplied by the matrix $\left(\frac{1}{2}(7\boldsymbol{I} - \boldsymbol{M})\right)$ is equal to the identity matrix $\boldsymbol{I}$,

$$\boldsymbol{M}^{-1} = \tfrac{1}{2}(7\boldsymbol{I} - \boldsymbol{M}).$$

Hence $\boldsymbol{M}^{-1} = \frac{1}{2}\left(\begin{pmatrix} 7 & 0 \\ 0 & 7 \end{pmatrix} - \begin{pmatrix} 4 & 5 \\ 2 & 3 \end{pmatrix}\right) = \frac{1}{2}\begin{pmatrix} 3 & -5 \\ -2 & 4 \end{pmatrix}$.

Example 46.3.5

$\boldsymbol{A}$, $\boldsymbol{B}$, $\boldsymbol{C}$ and $\boldsymbol{X}$ are 2×2 matrices and $3\boldsymbol{X} - \boldsymbol{C}\boldsymbol{X} = \boldsymbol{A} + \boldsymbol{B}$. Solve this equation for $\boldsymbol{X}$ in terms of $\boldsymbol{A}$, $\boldsymbol{B}$ and $\boldsymbol{C}$.

At first sight it looks as though it is difficult to factorise the left side, but if you write $3\boldsymbol{X}$ as $3\boldsymbol{I}\boldsymbol{X}$, the equation then becomes

$$3\boldsymbol{I}\boldsymbol{X} - \boldsymbol{C}\boldsymbol{X} = \boldsymbol{A} + \boldsymbol{B}.$$

Factorising the left side gives $(3\boldsymbol{I} - \boldsymbol{C})\boldsymbol{X} = \boldsymbol{A} + \boldsymbol{B}$, so multiplying on the left by $(3\boldsymbol{I} - \boldsymbol{C})^{-1}$ gives

$$\boldsymbol{X} = (3\boldsymbol{I} - \boldsymbol{C})^{-1}(\boldsymbol{A} + \boldsymbol{B}).$$

Exercise 46B

1 Find the inverses (if they exist) of the following matrices.

(a) $\begin{pmatrix} 1 & -1 \\ 1 & 1 \end{pmatrix}$ (b) $\begin{pmatrix} 4 & 9 \\ 3 & 7 \end{pmatrix}$ (c) $\begin{pmatrix} 3 & -5 \\ -4 & 7 \end{pmatrix}$

(d) $\begin{pmatrix} 2 & -1 \\ -5 & 4 \end{pmatrix}$ (e) $\begin{pmatrix} 2 & -6 \\ -3 & 9 \end{pmatrix}$ (f) $\begin{pmatrix} 5 & -3 \\ 10 & -5 \end{pmatrix}$

2 By finding the appropriate inverse matrices, find the solutions of the following equations.

(a) $\left.\begin{aligned} 2x + 3y &= -1 \\ 3x - 2y &= 18 \end{aligned}\right\}$ (b) $\left.\begin{aligned} -3x + 2y &= 13 \\ -5x + 4y &= 23 \end{aligned}\right\}$ (c) $\left.\begin{aligned} 2x + 5y &= 9 \\ -5x + 2y &= -8 \end{aligned}\right\}$

3 Solve for $\boldsymbol{X}$ the following matrix equations.

(a) $\begin{pmatrix} 1 & 3 \\ 2 & 4 \end{pmatrix}\boldsymbol{X} = \begin{pmatrix} -2 & 9 \\ -2 & 14 \end{pmatrix}$ (b) $\boldsymbol{X}\begin{pmatrix} 1 & 3 \\ 2 & 4 \end{pmatrix} = \begin{pmatrix} -2 & 9 \\ -2 & 14 \end{pmatrix}$

(c) $\begin{pmatrix} 1 & 3 \\ 2 & 4 \end{pmatrix}\boldsymbol{X}^{-1} = \begin{pmatrix} -2 & 9 \\ -2 & 14 \end{pmatrix}$

4 Let $\boldsymbol{X} = \dfrac{1}{\sqrt{2}}\begin{pmatrix} 1 & -1 \\ 1 & 1 \end{pmatrix}$. Calculate the matrix $\boldsymbol{A}$ where $\boldsymbol{X}\begin{pmatrix} 2 & 3 \\ 4 & 1 \end{pmatrix}\boldsymbol{X}^{-1} = \boldsymbol{A}$.

5 If $\boldsymbol{A}$ is the matrix $\begin{pmatrix} 7 & 4 \\ 6 & 3 \end{pmatrix}$, show that $\boldsymbol{A}^2 - 10\boldsymbol{A} - 3\boldsymbol{I} = \boldsymbol{O}$. Hence find $\boldsymbol{A}^{-1}$.

6 It is given that $\boldsymbol{A}$, $\boldsymbol{B}$, $\boldsymbol{C}$ and $\boldsymbol{X}$ are 2×2 matrices.

(a) In each part solve the equation for $\boldsymbol{X}$ in terms of $\boldsymbol{A}$, $\boldsymbol{B}$ and $\boldsymbol{C}$, assuming that all the necessary inverses exist.

(i) $\boldsymbol{A} + \boldsymbol{BX} = \boldsymbol{C}$ (ii) $\boldsymbol{XA} + \boldsymbol{B} = \boldsymbol{C}$ (iii) $\boldsymbol{X}(\boldsymbol{A} + \boldsymbol{B}) = \boldsymbol{C}$

(iv) $\boldsymbol{A} + \boldsymbol{BX} = \boldsymbol{CX}$ (v) $\boldsymbol{X} + \boldsymbol{AX} = \boldsymbol{B}$ (vi) $2\boldsymbol{X} - \boldsymbol{XA} = \boldsymbol{C}$

(b) Given that $\boldsymbol{A} = \begin{pmatrix} 1 & 2 \\ 3 & 4 \end{pmatrix}$, $\boldsymbol{B} = \begin{pmatrix} 1 & 3 \\ 0 & 1 \end{pmatrix}$ and $\boldsymbol{C} = \begin{pmatrix} 1 & 0 \\ 2 & 1 \end{pmatrix}$, evaluate $\boldsymbol{X}$ for each part of (a).

46.4 Inverse of a 3 × 3 matrix

Finding the inverse of a 3×3 matrix is more difficult than finding the inverse of a 2×2 matrix. Fortunately, your calculator can do it for you.

As for a 2×2 matrix, there are certain conditions for which a 3×3 matrix has no inverse.

The inverse of the matrix $\boldsymbol{A} = \begin{pmatrix} a & b & c \\ d & e & f \\ g & h & k \end{pmatrix}$ exists provided that

$$aek - afh + bfg - bdk + cdh - ceg \neq 0$$

If $aek - afh + bfg - bdk + cdh - ceg = 0$, then $\boldsymbol{A}$ has no inverse.

At this stage, ignore the expression $aek - afh + bfg - bdk + cdh - ceg$. You will learn more about it in Section 47.3.

Example 46.4.1

Find the inverse of the matrix $\boldsymbol{A} = \begin{pmatrix} 4 & 1 & -1 \\ 3 & -1 & 2 \\ 4 & 0 & -3 \end{pmatrix}$.

Using your calculator, $\boldsymbol{A}^{-1} = \begin{pmatrix} 0.12 & 0.12 & 0.04 \\ 0.68 & -0.32 & -0.44 \\ 0.16 & 0.16 & -0.28 \end{pmatrix}$.

If you notice it, you can take out the factor $\frac{1}{25}$ and write

$$\boldsymbol{A}^{-1} = \frac{1}{25}\begin{pmatrix} 3 & 3 & 1 \\ 17 & -8 & -11 \\ 4 & 4 & -7 \end{pmatrix}$$

Note that you may have to 'guess' the divisor 25, because your calculator may give you decimal entries in your inverse matrix. In Chapter 47 you will see how to find this factor.

Example 46.4.2

Solve the equations $\left.\begin{aligned} 4x + y - z &= 12 \\ 3x - y + 2z &= -1 \\ 4x \phantom{{}+y} - 3z &= 17 \end{aligned}\right\}$.

You can write these equations as $\mathbf{A}\begin{pmatrix} x \\ y \\ z \end{pmatrix} = \begin{pmatrix} 12 \\ -1 \\ 17 \end{pmatrix}$, with $\mathbf{A} = \begin{pmatrix} 4 & 1 & -1 \\ 3 & -1 & 2 \\ 4 & 0 & -3 \end{pmatrix}$.

Then multiplying on the left of both sides of the equation by $\mathbf{A}^{-1}$ (which exists since $\mathbf{A}$ is the matrix of Example 46.4.1) you get

$$\begin{aligned} \mathbf{A}^{-1}\mathbf{A}\begin{pmatrix} x \\ y \\ z \end{pmatrix} &= \mathbf{A}^{-1}\begin{pmatrix} 12 \\ -1 \\ 17 \end{pmatrix} \\ \mathbf{I}\begin{pmatrix} x \\ y \\ z \end{pmatrix} &= \mathbf{A}^{-1}\begin{pmatrix} 12 \\ -1 \\ 17 \end{pmatrix}, \\ \begin{pmatrix} x \\ y \\ z \end{pmatrix} &= \mathbf{A}^{-1}\begin{pmatrix} 12 \\ -1 \\ 17 \end{pmatrix}. \end{aligned}$$

$$\text{So } \begin{pmatrix} x \\ y \\ z \end{pmatrix} = \tfrac{1}{25}\begin{pmatrix} 3 & 3 & 1 \\ 17 & -8 & -11 \\ 4 & 4 & -7 \end{pmatrix}\begin{pmatrix} 12 \\ -1 \\ 17 \end{pmatrix}$$
$$= \tfrac{1}{25}\begin{pmatrix} 36 - 3 + 17 \\ 204 + 8 - 187 \\ 48 - 4 - 119 \end{pmatrix} = \tfrac{1}{25}\begin{pmatrix} 50 \\ 25 \\ -75 \end{pmatrix} = \begin{pmatrix} 2 \\ 1 \\ -3 \end{pmatrix}.$$

Therefore $x = 2$, $y = 1$, $z = -3$.

Example 46.4.3

Find the matrix $\boldsymbol{M}$ such that $\boldsymbol{M}\begin{pmatrix} 1 & 4 & 3 \\ 2 & 1 & 4 \\ 3 & 2 & -1 \end{pmatrix} = \begin{pmatrix} 4 & 6 & 2 \\ 8 & 1 & 8 \\ 5 & 3 & 3 \end{pmatrix}$.

Using your calculator,

$$\begin{pmatrix} 1 & 4 & 3 \\ 2 & 1 & 4 \\ 3 & 2 & -1 \end{pmatrix}^{-1} = \begin{pmatrix} -0.18 & 0.2 & 0.26 \\ 0.28 & -0.2 & 0.04 \\ 0.02 & 0.2 & -0.14 \end{pmatrix},$$

$$\text{giving } \boldsymbol{M} = \begin{pmatrix} 4 & 6 & 2 \\ 8 & 1 & 8 \\ 5 & 3 & 3 \end{pmatrix} \times \begin{pmatrix} -0.18 & 0.2 & 0.26 \\ 0.28 & -0.2 & 0.04 \\ 0.02 & 0.2 & -0.14 \end{pmatrix} = \begin{pmatrix} 1 & 0 & 1 \\ -1 & 3 & 1 \\ 0 & 1 & 1 \end{pmatrix}.$$

Exercise 46C

1 Find the inverse, if it exists, of each of the following matrices.

(a) $\begin{pmatrix} 1 & -2 & 3 \\ 1 & -1 & 2 \\ -2 & 4 & -5 \end{pmatrix}$ (b) $\begin{pmatrix} 1 & 1 & 1 \\ -1 & 0 & 1 \\ -2 & -2 & 0 \end{pmatrix}$ (c) $\begin{pmatrix} 1 & -2 & -1 \\ 2 & -1 & -1 \\ 1 & -2 & 1 \end{pmatrix}$

(d) $\begin{pmatrix} 1 & -2 & -3 \\ 2 & -1 & -4 \\ 3 & -3 & -5 \end{pmatrix}$ (e) $\begin{pmatrix} 1 & -2 & -1 \\ 2 & 1 & 5 \\ 3 & -2 & 3 \end{pmatrix}$ (f) $\begin{pmatrix} 2 & -1 & 3 \\ 1 & 2 & 1 \\ 3 & -4 & 5 \end{pmatrix}$

2 By finding the appropriate inverse matrices, find the solutions of the following equations.

(a) $\left.\begin{aligned} 2x - y - z &= 4 \\ x + 2y \quad &= 10 \\ y - z &= 2 \end{aligned}\right\}$ (b) $\left.\begin{aligned} x + \ y - z &= 3 \\ 3x - 2y - z &= 1 \\ 2x + 3y - z &= 9 \end{aligned}\right\}$ (c) $\left.\begin{aligned} 2x - 3y + 4z &= 7 \\ x - 2y + 3z &= 5 \\ 3x - 5y + 2z &= 2 \end{aligned}\right\}$

3 Solve for $\boldsymbol{X}$ the following matrix equations.

(a) $\begin{pmatrix} 1 & 3 & 2 \\ 4 & 0 & -1 \\ 2 & 3 & -3 \end{pmatrix} \boldsymbol{X} = \begin{pmatrix} 0 & -6 & 3 \\ 21 & 6 & -9 \\ -9 & 5 & -4 \end{pmatrix}$ (b) $\boldsymbol{X} \begin{pmatrix} 3 & -1 & 5 \\ 2 & 4 & -2 \\ 1 & 2 & 0 \end{pmatrix} = \begin{pmatrix} 18 & 29 & -3 \\ 7 & 0 & 12 \\ 7 & 0 & 10 \end{pmatrix}$

4 $\boldsymbol{A} = \begin{pmatrix} 1 & 3 & 0 \\ 2 & 1 & 2 \\ 3 & 2 & 3 \end{pmatrix}$ and $\boldsymbol{B}^{-1} = \begin{pmatrix} 4 & 2 & 2 \\ 1 & 0 & 1 \\ 0 & 1 & 0 \end{pmatrix}$. Calculate $\boldsymbol{BA}^{-1}$.

5 Find the matrix $\boldsymbol{M}$ such that $\begin{pmatrix} 1 & 2 & 3 \\ 2 & 3 & 4 \\ 1 & -1 & 0 \end{pmatrix} + \boldsymbol{M} \begin{pmatrix} 0 & 1 & 1 \\ 1 & 0 & 1 \\ 1 & 1 & 0 \end{pmatrix} = \begin{pmatrix} 3 & 5 & 6 \\ 3 & 3 & 3 \\ 2 & 0 & 2 \end{pmatrix}$.

47 Determinants

This chapter discusses a condition for an inverse matrix to exist. When you have completed it, you should

- know how to evaluate determinants of 2×2 and 3×3 matrices.

47.1 The determinant of a 2×2 matrix

Let $A = \begin{pmatrix} a & b \\ c & d \end{pmatrix}$ be a 2×2 matrix. Then the determinant of $\mathbf{A}$, abbreviated to $\det \mathbf{A}$, is defined to be the number

$$\det \mathbf{A} = ad - bc.$$

Sometimes the notation $\begin{vmatrix} a & b \\ c & d \end{vmatrix}$ is used instead of $\det \mathbf{A}$. Then

$$\det \mathbf{A} = \begin{vmatrix} a & b \\ c & d \end{vmatrix} = ad - bc.$$

In the previous chapter you saw that the inverse of the matrix $\mathbf{A} = \begin{pmatrix} a & b \\ c & d \end{pmatrix}$ is given by

$$\mathbf{A}^{-1} = \frac{1}{ad - bc}\begin{pmatrix} d & -b \\ -c & a \end{pmatrix}$$

provided that $ad - bc \neq 0$ which can be written as $ad \neq bc$.

It follows from the definition of $\det \mathbf{A}$ that

$$\mathbf{A}^{-1} = \frac{1}{\det \mathbf{A}}\begin{pmatrix} d & -b \\ -c & a \end{pmatrix}, \text{ provided that } \det \mathbf{A} \neq 0.$$

If $\det \mathbf{A} = 0$, then $\mathbf{A}$ has no inverse. (This is true, but has not been proved.)

In fact, the determinant $\det \begin{pmatrix} a & b \\ c & d \end{pmatrix} = ad - bc$ determines, by being not equal to 0, whether the matrix $A = \begin{pmatrix} a & b \\ c & d \end{pmatrix}$ has an inverse.

Example 47.1.1

Find $\det \begin{pmatrix} 2 & 4 \\ 3 & 7 \end{pmatrix}$.

$$\det \begin{pmatrix} 2 & 4 \\ 3 & 7 \end{pmatrix} = 2 \times 7 - 4 \times 3$$
$$= 14 - 12 = 2.$$

Example 47.1.2

(a) Find $\det\begin{pmatrix} 1 & 2 \\ 3 & a \end{pmatrix}$ in terms of a.

(b) Solve the simultaneous equations $\left.\begin{aligned} x + 2y &= 3 \\ 3x + ay &= b \end{aligned}\right\}$ in terms of a and b, given that $a \neq 6$.

(a) $\det\begin{pmatrix} 1 & 2 \\ 3 & a \end{pmatrix} = 1 \times a - 2 \times 3 = a - 6.$

(b) If you subtract 3 times the top equation from the bottom equation you get the new set of equations

$$\left.\begin{aligned} x + \quad 2y &= 3 \\ (a-6)\,y &= b - 9. \end{aligned}\right\}$$

Then, from the second equation, provided $a \neq 6$, you can divide to get

$$y = \frac{b-9}{a-6}.$$

Substituting in the first equation to find x gives

$$x = \frac{3a-2b}{a-6}.$$

In general, you can solve the simultaneous equations

$$\left.\begin{aligned} ax + by &= p \\ cx + dy &= q \end{aligned}\right\}$$

provided that the inverse of the matrix $A = \begin{pmatrix} a & b \\ c & d \end{pmatrix}$ exists, that is, provided $\det \mathbf{A} \neq 0$.

You can write this result as:

> The simultaneous equations $\left.\begin{aligned} ax + by &= p \\ cx + dy &= q \end{aligned}\right\}$ have a unique solution
>
> if and only if $\det\begin{pmatrix} a & b \\ c & d \end{pmatrix} = ad - bc \neq 0.$

Example 47.1.3

Find the values of a for which the equations $\left.\begin{aligned} (2-a)\,x + \quad y &= 0 \\ 3x + (5-2a)\,y &= 0 \end{aligned}\right\}$ do not have a unique solution.

From the result in the blue box the equations $\left.\begin{aligned}(2-a)x + \quad y &= 0\\ 3x + (5-2a)y &= 0\end{aligned}\right\}$ do not have a unique solution if $\det\begin{pmatrix}2-a & 1\\ 3 & 5-2a\end{pmatrix} = 0$. So

$$\begin{aligned}\det\begin{pmatrix}2-a & 1\\ 3 & 5-2a\end{pmatrix} &= (2-a)(5-2a) - 1\times 3\\ &= 10 - 9a + 2a^2 - 3\\ &= 2a^2 - 9a + 7\\ &= (a-1)(2a-7)\end{aligned}$$

and this is zero when $a = 1$ and when $a = 3\frac{1}{2}$.

Notice that when $a = 1$ the equations become $\left.\begin{aligned}x + y &= 0\\ 3x + 3y &= 0\end{aligned}\right\}$, and when $a = 3\frac{1}{2}$ they become $\left.\begin{aligned}-1\tfrac{1}{2}x + y &= 0\\ 3x - 2y &= 0\end{aligned}\right\}$. In both cases the second equation is a multiple of the first.

47.2 Calculators and determinants

Your calculator will find the value of a determinant when all the entries are numbers rather than unknowns. The procedure is not always straightforward, so it is worth practising finding determinants, even 2×2 determinants, on your calculator.

Exercise 47A

1 Write down the value of the determinants of the following matrices, where $a \in \mathbb{R}$.

(a) $\begin{pmatrix}1 & 4\\ 1 & 3\end{pmatrix}$ (b) $\begin{pmatrix}2 & 1\\ a & 7\end{pmatrix}$ (c) $\begin{pmatrix}2 & a\\ a & 8\end{pmatrix}$

2 Use your calculator to find the value of the following determinants.

(a) $\begin{pmatrix}3 & -1\\ 1 & 3\end{pmatrix}$ (b) $\begin{pmatrix}-4 & -2\\ 4 & 2\end{pmatrix}$ (c) $\begin{pmatrix}3 & -9\\ -1 & 3\end{pmatrix}$

3 (a) Find the values of a such that $\det\begin{pmatrix}a & 2a+3\\ 1 & a\end{pmatrix} = 0$.

(b) Write down the inverse of the matrix $\begin{pmatrix}a & 2a+3\\ 1 & a\end{pmatrix}$, giving any restrictions on the value of a.

4 Let $\boldsymbol{A} = \begin{pmatrix}a & b\\ c & d\end{pmatrix}$. Prove that $\det \boldsymbol{A}^{-1} = \dfrac{1}{\det \boldsymbol{A}}$, provided that $\det \boldsymbol{A} \neq 0$.

47.3 The determinant of a 3 × 3 matrix

The determinant of the 3 × 3 matrix $\mathbf{A} = \begin{pmatrix} a & b & c \\ d & e & f \\ g & h & k \end{pmatrix}$ is given by

$$\det \mathbf{A} = aek - afh + bfg - bdk + cdh - ceg.$$

The 3 × 3 determinant has the same properties, for 3 × 3 matrices and for three simultaneous equations with three unknowns, as the 2 × 2 determinant has for 2 × 2 matrices and two simultaneous equations with two unknowns. These properties will be stated and used but not proved.

> If $\mathbf{A} = \begin{pmatrix} a & b & c \\ d & e & f \\ g & h & k \end{pmatrix}$, the inverse matrix $\mathbf{A}^{-1}$ exists if
>
> $\det \mathbf{A} = aek - afh + bfg - bdk + cdh - ceg \neq 0.$

Unfortunately the expression $aek - afh + bfg - bdk + cdh - ceg$ for the determinant is almost impossible to remember. The next section shows you how to work with it.

47.4 Organising 3 × 3 determinants

When dealing with three equations it is helpful to use a different notation from $\mathbf{A} = \begin{pmatrix} a & b & c \\ d & e & f \\ g & h & k \end{pmatrix}$ because it simply uses too many letters to be clear about what is happening. For example, if you see the letter h there is nothing about h which tells you which row or column it is in. You have to look back at the original equations.

It is better to use the notation $\mathbf{A} = \begin{pmatrix} a_1 & b_1 & c_1 \\ a_2 & b_2 & c_2 \\ a_3 & b_3 & c_3 \end{pmatrix}$ where the letters a, b and c are attached to the first, second and third columns respectively and the suffix attached to a, b and c tells you which row it comes from.

The determinant $aek - afh + bfg - bdk + cdh - ceg$ then takes the form

$$a_1b_2c_3 - a_1c_2b_3 + b_1c_2a_3 - b_1a_2c_3 + c_1a_2b_3 - c_1b_2a_3,$$

so $$\det \begin{pmatrix} a_1 & b_1 & c_1 \\ a_2 & b_2 & c_2 \\ a_3 & b_3 & c_3 \end{pmatrix} = a_1b_2c_3 - a_1c_2b_3 + b_1c_2a_3 - b_1a_2c_3 + c_1a_2b_3 - c_1b_2a_3.$$

> Already there is more organisation. Every term in the determinant has one of the letters a, b and c, and one of the numbers 1, 2 and 3.

If you look at the determinant $a_1b_2c_3 - a_1c_2b_3 + b_1c_2a_3 - b_1a_2c_3 + c_1a_2b_3 - c_1b_2a_3$ and rewrite it in the form

$$a_1(b_2c_3 - c_2b_3) + b_1(c_2a_3 - a_2c_3) + c_1(a_2b_3 - b_2a_3),$$

you can then think of it in a different way.

If you start with the matrix $\begin{pmatrix} a_1 & b_1 & c_1 \\ a_2 & b_2 & c_2 \\ a_3 & b_3 & c_3 \end{pmatrix}$ and cross out the row and column containing a_1 you get

$$\begin{pmatrix} \cancel{a_1} & \cancel{b_1} & \cancel{c_1} \\ \cancel{a_2} & b_2 & c_2 \\ \cancel{a_3} & b_3 & c_3 \end{pmatrix},$$

whose determinant is $\det\begin{pmatrix} b_2 & c_2 \\ b_3 & c_3 \end{pmatrix}$ with value $b_2c_3 - c_2b_3$.

If you now cross out the row and column containing b_1 you get $\begin{pmatrix} \cancel{a_1} & \cancel{b_1} & \cancel{c_1} \\ a_2 & \cancel{b_2} & c_2 \\ a_3 & \cancel{b_3} & c_3 \end{pmatrix}$, where the determinant of what remains is $\det\begin{pmatrix} a_2 & c_2 \\ a_3 & c_3 \end{pmatrix} = a_2c_3 - c_2a_3$.

(Notice the sign of this expression compared with the middle bracket of the original 3×3 determinant.)

Finally if you cross out the row and column containing c_1 you get $\begin{pmatrix} \cancel{a_1} & \cancel{b_1} & \cancel{c_1} \\ a_2 & b_2 & \cancel{c_2} \\ a_3 & b_3 & \cancel{c_3} \end{pmatrix}$, where the determinant of what remains is $\det\begin{pmatrix} a_2 & b_2 \\ a_3 & b_3 \end{pmatrix} = a_2b_3 - b_2a_3$.

Thus,

$$\det\begin{pmatrix} a_1 & b_1 & c_1 \\ a_2 & b_2 & c_2 \\ a_3 & b_3 & c_3 \end{pmatrix} = a_1 \det\begin{pmatrix} b_2 & c_2 \\ b_3 & c_3 \end{pmatrix} + b_1\left(-\det\begin{pmatrix} a_2 & c_2 \\ a_3 & c_3 \end{pmatrix}\right) + c_1 \det\begin{pmatrix} a_2 & b_2 \\ a_3 & b_3 \end{pmatrix}.$$

This is called the **expansion of the determinant** $\det\begin{pmatrix} a_1 & b_1 & c_1 \\ a_2 & b_2 & c_2 \\ a_3 & b_3 & c_3 \end{pmatrix}$ **by the first row**.

Using the original notation, this formula can be rewritten in the form

$$\det\begin{pmatrix} a & b & c \\ d & e & f \\ g & h & k \end{pmatrix} = a\begin{vmatrix} e & f \\ h & k \end{vmatrix} - b\begin{vmatrix} d & f \\ g & k \end{vmatrix} + c\begin{vmatrix} d & e \\ g & h \end{vmatrix}$$

It is possible to expand determinants by other rows and columns, but they will not be discussed in this book.

Example 47.4.1

Find the value of $\det\begin{pmatrix} 0 & 3 & 0 \\ 1 & 4 & 2 \\ 3 & 1 & 5 \end{pmatrix}$.

Expanding by the first row,

$$\det\begin{pmatrix} 0 & 3 & 0 \\ 1 & 4 & 2 \\ 3 & 1 & 5 \end{pmatrix} = 0 \times \det\begin{pmatrix} 4 & 2 \\ 1 & 5 \end{pmatrix} + 3 \times \left(-\det\begin{pmatrix} 1 & 2 \\ 3 & 5 \end{pmatrix}\right) + 0 \times \det\begin{pmatrix} 1 & 4 \\ 3 & 1 \end{pmatrix}$$
$$= 3 \times \left(-\det\begin{pmatrix} 1 & 2 \\ 3 & 5 \end{pmatrix}\right) = 3\,(-(1 \times 5 - 2 \times 3)) = 3\,(-5 + 6) = 3.$$

Example 47.4.2

Find the value of k such that the matrix $\boldsymbol{A} = \begin{pmatrix} 1 & 2 & 4 \\ 3 & 1 & 2 \\ 8 & 1 & k \end{pmatrix}$ has no inverse.

The matrix $\boldsymbol{A} = \begin{pmatrix} 1 & 2 & 4 \\ 3 & 1 & 2 \\ 8 & 1 & k \end{pmatrix}$ has no inverse if $\det\begin{pmatrix} 1 & 2 & 4 \\ 3 & 1 & 2 \\ 8 & 1 & k \end{pmatrix} = 0$.

Expanding the determinant by the first row,

$$\det\begin{pmatrix} 1 & 2 & 4 \\ 3 & 1 & 2 \\ 8 & 1 & k \end{pmatrix} = 1 \times \det\begin{pmatrix} 1 & 2 \\ 1 & k \end{pmatrix} + 2 \times \left(-\det\begin{pmatrix} 3 & 2 \\ 8 & k \end{pmatrix}\right) + 4 \times \det\begin{pmatrix} 3 & 1 \\ 8 & 1 \end{pmatrix}$$
$$= 1 \times (k - 2) + 2 \times (-3k + 16) + 4 \times (3 - 8)$$
$$= k - 2 - 6k + 32 - 20$$
$$= -5k + 10.$$

So the matrix $\boldsymbol{A}$ has no inverse if $-5k + 10 = 0$, that is, when $k = 2$.

Example 47.4.3

Find the values of k such that $\det\begin{pmatrix} 1 & k & 0 \\ 3 & 0 & k \\ k & 1 & 1 \end{pmatrix} = 0$. Interpret your solution in terms of the matrix $\boldsymbol{A} = \begin{pmatrix} 1 & k & 0 \\ 3 & 0 & k \\ k & 1 & 1 \end{pmatrix}$.

Expanding by the first row, the value of the determinant is

$$1 \times \left(\det\begin{pmatrix} 0 & k \\ 1 & 1 \end{pmatrix}\right) + k \times \left(-\det\begin{pmatrix} 3 & k \\ k & 1 \end{pmatrix}\right) + 0 \times \det\begin{pmatrix} 3 & 0 \\ k & 1 \end{pmatrix}$$
$$= 1 \times (-k) + k \times (-3 + k^2) + 0$$
$$= k^3 - 4k.$$

Thus the determinant is zero when $k^3 - 4k = 0$, that is when $k = 0$ or ± 2.

This shows that the matrix $\boldsymbol{A} = \begin{pmatrix} 1 & k & 0 \\ 3 & 0 & k \\ k & 1 & 1 \end{pmatrix}$ has no inverse if $k = 0$ or ± 2.

Example 47.4.4

Find the exact inverse of the matrix $\begin{pmatrix} 2 & 4 & 1 \\ 6 & -1 & 4 \\ 3 & -7 & 1 \end{pmatrix}$.

Using your calculator, you get

$$\boldsymbol{A}^{-1} = \begin{pmatrix} 0.692... & -0.282... & 0.435... \\ 0.153... & -0.025... & -0.051... \\ -1 & 0.666... & -0.666... \end{pmatrix}.$$

This needs to be given in exact form. The problem is that it is difficult to identify the decimals as fractions.

However, guessing from the result for the inverse of a 2×2 matrix (in the first blue box in Section 47.1), where you divide by the determinant of the matrix, calculate $\det \boldsymbol{A}$, which is 39.

Then, removing the factor $\frac{1}{39}$ gives

$$\boldsymbol{A}^{-1} = \tfrac{1}{39}\begin{pmatrix} 27 & -11 & 17 \\ 6 & -1 & -2 \\ -39 & 26 & -26 \end{pmatrix}.$$

Example 47.4.5

$\boldsymbol{A}$, $\boldsymbol{B}$, $\boldsymbol{C}$, $\boldsymbol{D}$ and $\boldsymbol{X}$ are 3×3 matrices which satisfy the matrix equation $\boldsymbol{AX} + \boldsymbol{B} = \boldsymbol{CX} + \boldsymbol{D}$.

(a) Solve the equation for $\boldsymbol{X}$ in terms of the other matrices, assuming that any necessary matrix inverse exists.

(b) Given $\boldsymbol{A} = \begin{pmatrix} 1 & 4 & 0 \\ 2 & 1 & 4 \\ 1 & 6 & 2 \end{pmatrix}$, $\boldsymbol{B} = \begin{pmatrix} 1 & 4 & 6 \\ 1 & 3 & 2 \\ -1 & 3 & 0 \end{pmatrix}$, $\boldsymbol{C} = \begin{pmatrix} 3 & -7 & 4 \\ -1 & 1 & -4 \\ 2 & -4 & 7 \end{pmatrix}$ and $\boldsymbol{D} = \begin{pmatrix} -1 & 2 & -3 \\ 4 & -1 & 9 \\ 1 & 0 & -1 \end{pmatrix}$, find $\boldsymbol{X}$, giving your answer in exact form.

(a) The matrix equation is solved almost like a linear equation.

$$\begin{aligned} \boldsymbol{AX} + \boldsymbol{B} &= \boldsymbol{CX} + \boldsymbol{D} \\ \boldsymbol{AX} - \boldsymbol{CX} &= \boldsymbol{D} - \boldsymbol{B} \\ (\boldsymbol{A} - \boldsymbol{C})\boldsymbol{X} &= \boldsymbol{D} - \boldsymbol{B} \\ \boldsymbol{X} &= (\boldsymbol{A} - \boldsymbol{C})^{-1}(\boldsymbol{D} - \boldsymbol{B}) \end{aligned}$$

(b) Working out the matrices in the solution, you get

$$\boldsymbol{A} - \boldsymbol{C} = \begin{pmatrix} -2 & 11 & -4 \\ 3 & 0 & 8 \\ -1 & 10 & -5 \end{pmatrix} \text{ and } \boldsymbol{D} - \boldsymbol{B} = \begin{pmatrix} -2 & -2 & -9 \\ 3 & -4 & 7 \\ 2 & -3 & -1 \end{pmatrix}.$$

Using your calculator,

$$\begin{aligned} \boldsymbol{X} &= (\boldsymbol{A} - \boldsymbol{C})^{-1}(\boldsymbol{D} - \boldsymbol{B}) \\ &= \begin{pmatrix} -2 & 11 & -4 \\ 3 & 0 & 8 \\ -1 & 10 & -5 \end{pmatrix}^{-1} \begin{pmatrix} -2 & -2 & -9 \\ 3 & -4 & 7 \\ 2 & -3 & -1 \end{pmatrix}, \\ &= \begin{pmatrix} 3.25... & -1.40... & 6.29... \\ 0.10... & -0.42... & -0.21... \\ -0.85... & 0.02... & -1.48... \end{pmatrix}. \end{aligned}$$

This solution is not in exact form. From your calculator, det $(\boldsymbol{A} - \boldsymbol{C}) = 117$, and then using the property in the first blue box in Section 47.1,

$$\boldsymbol{X} = \frac{1}{117}\begin{pmatrix} 381 & -164 & 737 \\ 12 & -50 & -25 \\ -99 & 3 & -174 \end{pmatrix}.$$

Exercise 47B

1 Find the values of the following determinants.

(a) $\det\begin{pmatrix} 1 & 2 & 3 \\ 4 & 5 & 6 \\ 7 & 8 & 9 \end{pmatrix}$ (b) $\det\begin{pmatrix} 1 & 2 & 3 \\ 4 & 5 & 6 \\ 7 & 8 & 10 \end{pmatrix}$ (c) $\det\begin{pmatrix} 4 & 5 & 7 \\ 4 & 5 & 3 \\ 4 & 6 & 2 \end{pmatrix}$

2 Find the value or values of k for which each of the following determinants is zero.

(a) $\det\begin{pmatrix} 4 & 3 & 4 \\ -3 & -2 & -1 \\ 2 & 1 & k \end{pmatrix}$ (b) $\det\begin{pmatrix} 5 & k & 8 \\ 2 & 6 & 3 \\ -1 & 4 & -2 \end{pmatrix}$ (c) $\det\begin{pmatrix} k & 1 & 1 \\ 1 & k & 1 \\ 1 & 1 & k \end{pmatrix}$

3 Find the value of k for which each of the following sets of equations does not have a unique solution. Do not solve the equations.

(a) $\left.\begin{aligned} 3x + 4y + 2z &= 0 \\ 2x + 3y + 5z &= 0 \\ 3x + 5y + kz &= 0 \end{aligned}\right\}$ (b) $\left.\begin{aligned} 4x - 2y + 6z &= 0 \\ x + ky - 3z &= 0 \\ 3x - 5y + 9z &= 0 \end{aligned}\right\}$ (c) $\left.\begin{aligned} kx + y - z &= 0 \\ x + 3y - 2z &= 0 \\ 5x \qquad + z &= 0 \end{aligned}\right\}$

4 Find the value of k such that the equations $\left.\begin{aligned} x+2y+3z&=0\\ x+3y-2z&=0\\ x+4y+kz&=0 \end{aligned}\right\}$ do not have a unique solution.

5 Find the value of k such that the equations $\left.\begin{aligned} 3x-\ \ y+6z&=4\\ 2x+4y+5z&=-2\\ 4x-6y+kz&=r \end{aligned}\right\}$ do not have a unique solution.

6 Find the exact inverse of the matrix $\begin{pmatrix} 1 & -4 & 7 \\ 6 & -1 & -4 \\ -3 & 2 & -2 \end{pmatrix}$.

7 Given that $\boldsymbol{A}=\begin{pmatrix} 3 & 2 & 3 \\ 4 & -2 & -3 \\ 1 & 0 & 1 \end{pmatrix}$, $\boldsymbol{B}=\begin{pmatrix} 2 & 1 & 2 \\ 1 & -2 & 1 \\ 1 & 4 & 3 \end{pmatrix}$ and $\boldsymbol{C}=\begin{pmatrix} 0 & 4 & 3 \\ 2 & -1 & 1 \\ 0 & 3 & 1 \end{pmatrix}$, solve each of the following equations for $\boldsymbol{X}$, giving your answers in exact form.

(a) $\boldsymbol{AX}=\boldsymbol{B}+\boldsymbol{CX}$ (b) $2\boldsymbol{X}+\boldsymbol{XB}=\boldsymbol{A}$

Review exercise 15

1 Calculate $\boldsymbol{AB}$ and $\boldsymbol{BA}$ where $\boldsymbol{A} = \begin{pmatrix} 1 & 3 \\ a & 1 \end{pmatrix}$ and $\boldsymbol{B} = \begin{pmatrix} 1 & a \\ 1 & 1 \end{pmatrix}$. Find the two values of a for which $\boldsymbol{AB} = \boldsymbol{BA}$.

2 $\boldsymbol{P}$ is a 2×2 matrix for which $\boldsymbol{P}\begin{pmatrix} 1 \\ 0 \end{pmatrix} = \begin{pmatrix} 3 \\ 2 \end{pmatrix}$ and $\boldsymbol{P}\begin{pmatrix} 0 \\ 1 \end{pmatrix} = \begin{pmatrix} -2 \\ 2 \end{pmatrix}$.

(a) Find $\boldsymbol{P}$. (b) Find det $\boldsymbol{P}$. (c) Find $\boldsymbol{P}^{-1}$.

3 (a) $\boldsymbol{E}_1 = \boldsymbol{PQ}$, where $\boldsymbol{P} = \begin{pmatrix} 1 & 0 \\ 0 & -1 \end{pmatrix}$ and $\boldsymbol{Q} = \begin{pmatrix} 1 & 0 \\ 0 & 5 \end{pmatrix}$. Calculate $\boldsymbol{E}_1$.

(b) $\boldsymbol{M} = \boldsymbol{E}_3\boldsymbol{E}_2\boldsymbol{E}_1$, where $\boldsymbol{M} = \begin{pmatrix} 1 & 3 \\ 3 & 4 \end{pmatrix}$ and $\boldsymbol{E}_3 = \begin{pmatrix} 1 & 0 \\ 3 & 1 \end{pmatrix}$. Find $\boldsymbol{E}_2$.

4 Prove that the matrix $\begin{pmatrix} k+1 & k \\ -k & k+1 \end{pmatrix}$ has an inverse for all real values of k.

5 Let $\boldsymbol{X} = \dfrac{1}{\sqrt{2}}\begin{pmatrix} 1 & -1 \\ 1 & 1 \end{pmatrix}$. Calculate the matrix $\boldsymbol{A}^{-1}$ where $\boldsymbol{X}\begin{pmatrix} 2 & 1 \\ 4 & 3 \end{pmatrix}\boldsymbol{X}^{-1} = \boldsymbol{A}$.

6 The matrix $\boldsymbol{A} = \begin{pmatrix} 3 & 1 & -3 \\ 2 & 4 & 3 \\ -4 & 2 & -1 \end{pmatrix}$.

(a) (i) Show that $\boldsymbol{A}^2 = \boldsymbol{A} + 20\boldsymbol{I}$ where $\boldsymbol{I}$ is the 3×3 identity matrix.

(ii) Use this equation to deduce the inverse matrix, $\boldsymbol{A}^{-1}$, of $\boldsymbol{A}$.

(b) Determine the unique solution of the system of equations

$$\left.\begin{aligned} 3x + y - 3z &= 9 \\ 2x + 4y + 3z &= 11 \\ -4x + 2y - z &= 23 \end{aligned}\right\}.$$

(OCR)

7 The matrices $\boldsymbol{A}$ and $\boldsymbol{B}$ are given by $\boldsymbol{A} = \begin{pmatrix} 2 & 3 & -1 \\ 3 & -1 & 2 \\ 5 & 3 & 0 \end{pmatrix}$ and $\boldsymbol{B} = \begin{pmatrix} -6 & -3 & 5 \\ 10 & 5 & -7 \\ 14 & 9 & -11 \end{pmatrix}$.

(a) Calculate the matrix $\boldsymbol{AB}$, and hence find $\boldsymbol{A}^{-1}$.

(b) Use the matrix $\boldsymbol{A}^{-1}$ to solve the equations $\left.\begin{aligned} 2x + 3y - z &= 11 \\ 3x - y + 2z &= 19 \\ 5x + 3y &= 23 \end{aligned}\right\}.$

8 (a) Calculate the matrix product $(x \quad 1)\begin{pmatrix} a & b \\ b & c \end{pmatrix}\begin{pmatrix} x \\ 1 \end{pmatrix}$.

(b) Show that the equation $(x \quad 1)\begin{pmatrix} a & b \\ b & c \end{pmatrix}\begin{pmatrix} x \\ 1 \end{pmatrix} = (0)$ has distinct real roots if, and only if, $\det\begin{pmatrix} a & b \\ b & c \end{pmatrix} < 0$.

9 $\boldsymbol{A} = \begin{pmatrix} 2 & 4 & 7 \\ 2 & 3 & 2 \\ 3 & -1 & 0 \end{pmatrix}$ and $\boldsymbol{B} = \begin{pmatrix} -2 & 1 & -3 \\ -3 & -7 & 2 \\ 1 & 3 & 4 \end{pmatrix}$.

(a) Calculate det $\boldsymbol{A}$ and det $\boldsymbol{B}$.

(b) Find $\boldsymbol{A}^{-1}$ and $\boldsymbol{B}^{-1}$, giving your answers in exact form.

Use your answers to solve the following equations for $\boldsymbol{X}$ and $\boldsymbol{Y}$.

(c) $\boldsymbol{AX} = \boldsymbol{B}$

(d) $\boldsymbol{BY} = \boldsymbol{A}$

(e) Calculate $\boldsymbol{XY}$.

Examination questions

1 Consider the matrix $\boldsymbol{A} = \begin{pmatrix} 5 & -2 \\ 7 & 1 \end{pmatrix}$.

(a) Write down the inverse, $\boldsymbol{A}^{-1}$.

$\boldsymbol{B}$, $\boldsymbol{C}$ and $\boldsymbol{X}$ are also 2×2 matrices.

(b) Given that $\boldsymbol{XA} + \boldsymbol{B} = \boldsymbol{C}$, express $\boldsymbol{X}$ in terms of $\boldsymbol{A}^{-1}$, $\boldsymbol{B}$ and $\boldsymbol{C}$.

(c) Given that $\boldsymbol{B} = \begin{pmatrix} 6 & 7 \\ 5 & -2 \end{pmatrix}$, and $\boldsymbol{C} = \begin{pmatrix} -5 & 0 \\ -8 & 7 \end{pmatrix}$, find $\boldsymbol{X}$. (© IBO 2003)

2 Let $\boldsymbol{C} = \begin{pmatrix} -2 & 4 \\ 1 & 7 \end{pmatrix}$ and $\boldsymbol{D} = \begin{pmatrix} 5 & 2 \\ -1 & a \end{pmatrix}$. The 2×2 matrix $\boldsymbol{Q}$ is such that $3\boldsymbol{Q} = 2\boldsymbol{C} - \boldsymbol{D}$.

(a) Find $\boldsymbol{Q}$. (b) Find $\boldsymbol{CD}$. (c) Find $\boldsymbol{D}^{-1}$. (© IBO 2005)

Inverse normal probabilities

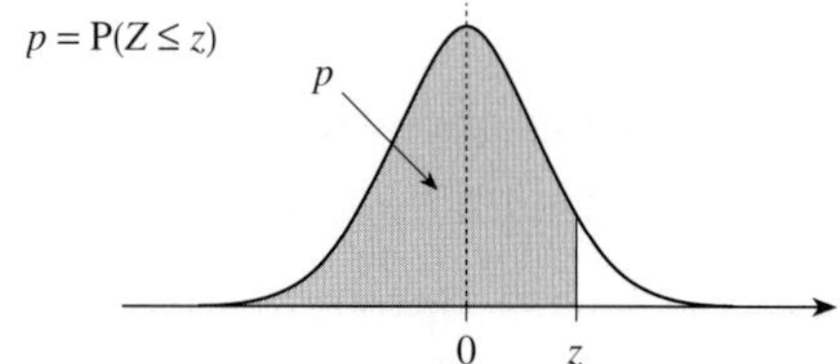

p	0	0.001	0.002	0.003	0.004	0.005	0.006	0.007	0.008	0.009
0.50	0.0000	0.0025	0.0050	0.0075	0.0100	0.0125	0.0150	0.0176	0.0201	0.0226
0.51	0.0251	0.0276	0.0301	0.0326	0.0351	0.0376	0.0401	0.0426	0.0451	0.0476
0.52	0.0502	0.0527	0.0552	0.0577	0.0602	0.0627	0.0652	0.0677	0.0702	0.0728
0.53	0.0753	0.0778	0.0803	0.0828	0.0853	0.0878	0.0904	0.0929	0.0954	0.0979
0.54	0.1004	0.1030	0.1055	0.1080	0.1105	0.1130	0.1156	0.1181	0.1206	0.1231
0.55	0.1257	0.1282	0.1307	0.1332	0.1358	0.1383	0.1408	0.1434	0.1459	0.1484
0.56	0.1510	0.1535	0.1560	0.1586	0.1611	0.1637	0.1662	0.1687	0.1713	0.1738
0.57	0.1764	0.1789	0.1815	0.1840	0.1866	0.1891	0.1917	0.1942	0.1968	0.1993
0.58	0.2019	0.2045	0.2070	0.2096	0.2121	0.2147	0.2173	0.2198	0.2224	0.2250
0.59	0.2275	0.2301	0.2327	0.2353	0.2379	0.2404	0.2430	0.2456	0.2482	0.2508
0.60	0.2534	0.2559	0.2585	0.2611	0.2637	0.2663	0.2689	0.2715	0.2741	0.2767
0.61	0.2793	0.2819	0.2845	0.2872	0.2898	0.2924	0.2950	0.2976	0.3002	0.3029
0.62	0.3055	0.3081	0.3107	0.3134	0.3160	0.3186	0.3213	0.3239	0.3266	0.3292
0.63	0.3319	0.3345	0.3372	0.3398	0.3425	0.3451	0.3478	0.3505	0.3531	0.3558
0.64	0.3585	0.3611	0.3638	0.3665	0.3692	0.3719	0.3745	0.3772	0.3799	0.3826
0.65	0.3853	0.3880	0.3907	0.3934	0.3961	0.3989	0.4016	0.4043	0.4070	0.4097
0.66	0.4125	0.4152	0.4179	0.4207	0.4234	0.4262	0.4289	0.4316	0.4344	0.4372
0.67	0.4399	0.4427	0.4454	0.4482	0.4510	0.4538	0.4565	0.4593	0.4621	0.4649
0.68	0.4677	0.4705	0.4733	0.4761	0.4789	0.4817	0.4845	0.4874	0.4902	0.4930
0.69	0.4959	0.4987	0.5015	0.5044	0.5072	0.5101	0.5129	0.5158	0.5187	0.5215
0.70	0.5244	0.5273	0.5302	0.5331	0.5359	0.5388	0.5417	0.5446	0.5476	0.5505
0.71	0.5534	0.5563	0.5592	0.5622	0.5651	0.5681	0.5710	0.5740	0.5769	0.5799
0.72	0.5828	0.5858	0.5888	0.5918	0.5948	0.5978	0.6008	0.6038	0.6068	0.6098
0.73	0.6128	0.6158	0.6189	0.6219	0.6250	0.6280	0.6311	0.6341	0.6372	0.6403
0.74	0.6434	0.6464	0.6495	0.6526	0.6557	0.6588	0.6620	0.6651	0.6682	0.6714
0.75	0.6745	0.6776	0.6808	0.6840	0.6871	0.6903	0.6935	0.6967	0.6999	0.7031
0.76	0.7063	0.7095	0.7128	0.7160	0.7192	0.7225	0.7257	0.7290	0.7323	0.7356
0.77	0.7389	0.7421	0.7455	0.7488	0.7521	0.7554	0.7588	0.7621	0.7655	0.7688
0.78	0.7722	0.7756	0.7790	0.7824	0.7858	0.7892	0.7926	0.7961	0.7995	0.8030
0.79	0.8064	0.8099	0.8134	0.8169	0.8204	0.8239	0.8274	0.8310	0.8345	0.8381
0.80	0.8416	0.8452	0.8488	0.8524	0.8560	0.8596	0.8633	0.8669	0.8706	0.8742
0.81	0.8779	0.8816	0.8853	0.8890	0.8927	0.8965	0.9002	0.9040	0.9078	0.9116
0.82	0.9154	0.9192	0.9230	0.9269	0.9307	0.9346	0.9385	0.9424	0.9463	0.9502
0.83	0.9542	0.9581	0.9621	0.9661	0.9701	0.9741	0.9782	0.9822	0.9863	0.9904
0.84	0.9945	0.9986	1.0027	1.0069	1.0110	1.0152	1.0194	1.0237	1.0279	1.0322

Inverse normal probabilities (*cont.*)

p	0	0.001	0.002	0.003	0.004	0.005	0.006	0.007	0.008	0.009
0.85	1.0364	1.0407	1.0451	1.0494	1.0537	1.0581	1.0625	1.0669	1.0714	1.0758
0.86	1.0803	1.0848	1.0894	1.0939	1.0985	1.1031	1.1077	1.1123	1.1170	1.1217
0.87	1.1264	1.1311	1.1359	1.1407	1.1455	1.1504	1.1552	1.1601	1.1651	1.1700
0.88	1.1750	1.1800	1.1850	1.1901	1.1952	1.2004	1.2055	1.2107	1.2160	1.2212
0.89	1.2265	1.2319	1.2372	1.2426	1.2481	1.2536	1.2591	1.2646	1.2702	1.2759
0.90	1.2816	1.2873	1.2930	1.2988	1.3047	1.3106	1.3165	1.3225	1.3285	1.3346
0.91	1.3408	1.3469	1.3532	1.3595	1.3658	1.3722	1.3787	1.3852	1.3917	1.3984
0.92	1.4051	1.4118	1.4187	1.4255	1.4325	1.4395	1.4466	1.4538	1.4611	1.4684
0.93	1.4758	1.4833	1.4909	1.4985	1.5063	1.5141	1.5220	1.5301	1.5382	1.5464
0.94	1.5548	1.5632	1.5718	1.5805	1.5893	1.5982	1.6073	1.6164	1.6258	1.6352
0.95	1.6449	1.6546	1.6646	1.6747	1.6849	1.6954	1.7060	1.7169	1.7279	1.7392
0.96	1.7507	1.7624	1.7744	1.7866	1.7991	1.8119	1.8250	1.8384	1.8522	1.8663
0.97	1.8808	1.8957	1.9110	1.9268	1.9431	1.9600	1.9774	1.9954	2.0141	2.0335
0.98	2.0538	2.0749	2.0969	2.1201	2.1444	2.1701	2.1973	2.2262	2.2571	2.2904
0.99	2.3264	2.3656	2.4089	2.4573	2.5121	2.5758	2.6521	2.7478	2.8782	3.0902

Area under the standard normal curve

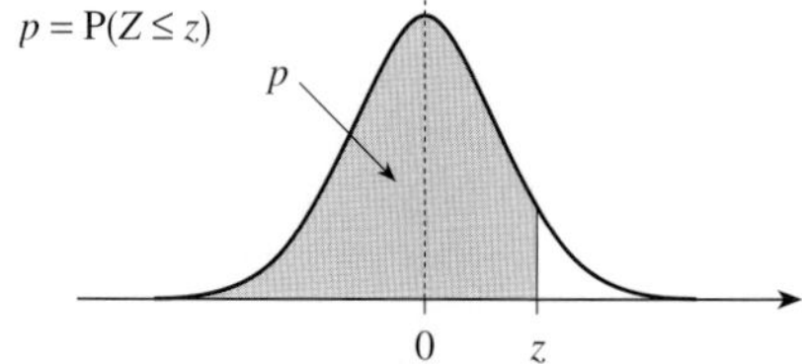

z	0	0.01	0.02	0.03	0.04	0.05	0.06	0.07	0.08	0.09
0.0	0.5000	0.5040	0.5080	0.5120	0.5160	0.5199	0.5239	0.5279	0.5319	0.5359
0.1	0.5398	0.5438	0.5478	0.5517	0.5557	0.5596	0.5636	0.5675	0.5714	0.5753
0.2	0.5793	0.5832	0.5871	0.5910	0.5948	0.5987	0.6026	0.6064	0.6103	0.6141
0.3	0.6179	0.6217	0.6255	0.6293	0.6331	0.6368	0.6406	0.6443	0.6480	0.6517
0.4	0.6554	0.6591	0.6628	0.6664	0.6700	0.6736	0.6772	0.6808	0.6844	0.6879
0.5	0.6915	0.6950	0.6985	0.7019	0.7054	0.7088	0.7123	0.7157	0.7190	0.7224
0.6	0.7257	0.7291	0.7324	0.7357	0.7389	0.7422	0.7454	0.7486	0.7517	0.7549
0.7	0.7580	0.7611	0.7642	0.7673	0.7704	0.7734	0.7764	0.7794	0.7823	0.7852
0.8	0.7881	0.7910	0.7939	0.7967	0.7995	0.8023	0.8051	0.8079	0.8106	0.8133
0.9	0.8159	0.8186	0.8212	0.8238	0.8264	0.8289	0.8315	0.8340	0.8365	0.8389
1.0	0.8413	0.8438	0.8461	0.8485	0.8508	0.8531	0.8554	0.8577	0.8599	0.8621
1.1	0.8643	0.8665	0.8686	0.8708	0.8729	0.8749	0.8770	0.8790	0.8810	0.8830
1.2	0.8849	0.8869	0.8888	0.8907	0.8925	0.8944	0.8962	0.8980	0.8997	0.9015
1.3	0.9032	0.9049	0.9066	0.9082	0.9099	0.9115	0.9131	0.9147	0.9162	0.9177
1.4	0.9192	0.9207	0.9222	0.9236	0.9251	0.9265	0.9279	0.9292	0.9306	0.9319
1.5	0.9332	0.9345	0.9357	0.9370	0.9382	0.9394	0.9406	0.9418	0.9429	0.9441
1.6	0.9452	0.9463	0.9474	0.9484	0.9495	0.9505	0.9515	0.9525	0.9535	0.9545
1.7	0.9554	0.9564	0.9573	0.9582	0.9591	0.9599	0.9608	0.9616	0.9625	0.9633
1.8	0.9641	0.9649	0.9656	0.9664	0.9671	0.9678	0.9686	0.9693	0.9699	0.9706
1.9	0.9713	0.9719	0.9726	0.9732	0.9738	0.9744	0.9750	0.9756	0.9761	0.9767
2.0	0.9773	0.9778	0.9783	0.9788	0.9793	0.9798	0.9803	0.9808	0.9812	0.9817
2.1	0.9821	0.9826	0.9830	0.9834	0.9838	0.9842	0.9846	0.9850	0.9854	0.9857
2.2	0.9861	0.9864	0.9868	0.9871	0.9875	0.9878	0.9881	0.9884	0.9887	0.9890
2.3	0.9892	0.9896	0.9898	0.9901	0.9904	0.9906	0.9909	0.9911	0.9913	0.9916
2.4	0.9918	0.9920	0.9922	0.9925	0.9927	0.9929	0.9931	0.9932	0.9934	0.9936
2.5	0.9938	0.9940	0.9941	0.9943	0.9945	0.9946	0.9948	0.9949	0.9951	0.9952
2.6	0.9953	0.9955	0.9956	0.9957	0.9959	0.9960	0.9961	0.9962	0.9963	0.9964
2.7	0.9965	0.9966	0.9967	0.9968	0.9969	0.9970	0.9971	0.9972	0.9973	0.9974
2.8	0.9974	0.9975	0.9976	0.9977	0.9977	0.9978	0.9979	0.9979	0.9980	0.9981
2.9	0.9981	0.9982	0.9983	0.9983	0.9984	0.9984	0.9985	0.9985	0.9986	0.9986
3.0	0.9987	0.9987	0.9988	0.9988	0.9988	0.9989	0.9989	0.9989	0.9990	0.9990
3.1	0.9990	0.9991	0.9991	0.9991	0.9992	0.9992	0.9992	0.9992	0.9993	0.9993
3.2	0.9993	0.9993	0.9994	0.9994	0.9994	0.9994	0.9994	0.9995	0.9995	0.9995
3.3	0.9995	0.9995	0.9996	0.9996	0.9996	0.9996	0.9996	0.9996	0.9996	0.9997
3.4	0.9997	0.9997	0.9997	0.9997	0.9997	0.9997	0.9997	0.9997	0.9997	0.9998
3.5	0.9998	0.9998	0.9998	0.9998	0.9998	0.9998	0.9998	0.9998	0.9998	0.9998

Answers

1 Numbers

Exercise 1A (page 7)

1 (a) all (b) $\mathbb{Q}, \mathbb{R}, \mathbb{Q}^+, \mathbb{R}^+$
(c) $\mathbb{Q}, \mathbb{R}, \mathbb{Q}^+, \mathbb{R}^+$ (d) all
(e) $\mathbb{R}, \mathbb{R}^+$ (f) $\mathbb{N}, \mathbb{Z}, \mathbb{Q}, \mathbb{R}$
(g) $\mathbb{R}$ (h) $\mathbb{Z}, \mathbb{Q}, \mathbb{R}$

2 (a) $\{1, 2, 3\}$ (b) $\{0, 1, 2, 3, 4\}$
(c) $\{-2, -1, 0, 1\}$ (d) $\{0, 1\}$
(e) $\{1, 2, 3\}$ (f) $\{0, 1, 2\}$

3 (a) $x > 14$ (b) $x \le 2.5$ (c) $x \le -3.2$
(d) $x \le -4$ (e) $x \ge -4$ (f) $x \le 4$
(g) $x \le 22$ (h) $x \le 6$ (i) $x > -2$
(j) $x \ge -2$ (k) $x \ge \frac{1}{3}$ (l) $x < 1$
(m) $x > 3$ (n) $x \ge -9$ (o) $x > 6$
(p) $x \le \frac{6}{7}$ (q) $x \ge -1$

Exercise 1B (page 10)

1 (a) 6 (b) 2 (c) 28

2 $0 < \dfrac{1}{x^2} < 0.0001$

3 (a) $4.755 \le m \le 4.765$ (b) $|m - 4.76| \le 0.005$

4 (a) $16.6 \le P \le 17$ (b) $|P - 16.8| \le 0.2$

5 (a) $16.8625 \le A \le 17.7025$
(b) $|A - 17.2825| \le 0.42$

6 (a) $2 < x < 4$ (b) $-2.1 \le x \le -1.9$
(c) $1.4995 \le x \le 1.5005$
(d) $-1.25 \le x \le 2.75$

7 (a) $|x - 1.5| \le 0.5$ (b) $|x - 1| < 2$
(c) $|x + 3.65| \le 0.15$ (d) $|x - 2.85| < 0.55$

8 $|x| \in \mathbb{N}$

Exercise 1C (page 12)

1 (a) 3 (b) 10 (c) 4 (d) 8
(e) 6 (f) 15 (g) 30 (h) 60
(i) 28 (j) 27 (k) 5 (l) 48

2 (a) $3\sqrt{2}$ (b) $2\sqrt{5}$ (c) $2\sqrt{6}$ (d) $4\sqrt{2}$
(e) $2\sqrt{10}$ (f) $3\sqrt{5}$ (g) $4\sqrt{3}$ (h) $5\sqrt{2}$

3 (a) $5\sqrt{2}$ (b) $3\sqrt{3}$ (c) $\sqrt{5}$
(d) $2\sqrt{2}$ (e) 0 (f) $13\sqrt{5}$

4 (a) 2 (b) 3 (c) 2 (d) 5
(e) 5 (f) 3 (g) $\frac{1}{4}$ (h) $\frac{1}{2}$

5 (a) 1 (b) 7 (c) 4 (d) 7
(e) 46 (f) 5 (g) 107 (h) -3

Exercise 1D (page 15)

1 (a) $\frac{1}{3}\sqrt{3}$ (b) $\frac{1}{5}\sqrt{5}$ (c) $2\sqrt{2}$ (d) $\sqrt{6}$
(e) $\sqrt{11}$ (f) $\frac{1}{2}\sqrt{2}$ (g) $4\sqrt{3}$ (h) $2\sqrt{7}$
(i) $\sqrt{3}$ (j) $\frac{1}{3}\sqrt{3}$ (k) $\sqrt{15}$ (l) $\frac{4}{5}\sqrt{30}$

2 (a) $20\sqrt{2}$ cm^2 (b) $3\sqrt{10}$ cm

3 (a) 10.198 039 027 2
(b) 25.495 097 568 0
(c) 2.549 509 756 8

4 (a) $4\sqrt{13}$ cm (b) $5\sqrt{11}$ cm
(c) $2\sqrt{15}$ cm (d) $3\sqrt{5}$ cm

2 Sequences

Exercise 2A (page 18)

1 (a) 7, 14, 21, 28, 35
(b) 13, 8, 3, −2, −7
(c) 4, 12, 36, 108, 324
(d) 6, 3, 1.5, 0.75, 0.375
(e) 2, 7, 22, 67, 202
(f) 1, 4, 19, 364, 132 499

2 (a) $u_1 = 2, u_n = u_{n-1} + 2$
(b) $u_1 = 11, u_n = u_{n-1} - 2$
(c) $u_1 = 2, u_n = u_{n-1} + 4$
(d) $u_1 = 2, u_n = 3u_{n-1}$
(e) $u_1 = \frac{1}{3}, u_n = \frac{1}{3}u_{n-1}$
(f) $u_1 = \frac{1}{2}a, u_n = \frac{1}{2}u_{n-1}$
(g) $u_1 = 1, u_n = -u_{n-1}$
(h) $u_1 = 1, u_n = (1 + x)u_{n-1}$

3 (a) 5, 7, 9, 11, 13; $u_1 = 5, u_n = u_{n-1} + 2$
(b) 1, 4, 9, 16, 25; $u_1 = 1, u_n = u_{n-1} + 2n - 1$
(c) 1, 3, 6, 10, 15; $u_1 = 1, u_n = u_{n-1} + n$
(d) 1, 5, 14, 30, 55; $u_1 = 1, u_n = u_{n-1} + n^2$
(e) 6, 18, 54, 162, 486; $u_1 = 6, u_n = 3u_{n-1}$
(f) 3, 15, 75, 375, 1875; $u_1 = 3, u_n = 5u_{n-1}$

4 (a) $u_n = 10 - n$ (b) $u_n = 2 \times 3^n$
(c) $u_n = n^2 + 3$ (d) $u_n = 2n(n + 1)$
(e) $u_n = \dfrac{2n - 1}{n + 3}$ (f) $u_n = \dfrac{n^2 + 1}{2^n}$

Exercise 2B (page 20)

1 (a) 820 (b) 610 (c) 420 (d) 400

3 (a) n (c) $1^3 = t_1^2 - t_0^2, 2^3 = t_2^2 - t_1^2,$
$3^3 = t_3^2 - t_2^2, \ldots, n^3 = t_n^2 - t_{n-1}^2$

Exercise 2C (page 29)

1 (a), (d), (f), (h); 3, -2, q, x respectively

2 (a) $12, 2n$ (b) $32, 14+3n$
(c) $-10, 8-3n$ (d) $3.3, 0.9+0.4n$
(e) $3\frac{1}{2}, \frac{1}{2}+\frac{1}{2}n$ (f) $43, 79-6n$
(g) $x+10, x-2+2n$
(h) $1+4x, 1-2x+xn$

3 (a) 14 (b) 88 (c) 36 (d) 11

4 (a) 610 (b) 795 (c) -102
(d) $855\frac{1}{2}$ (e) -1025 (f) 998 001

5 (a) 54, 3132 (b) 20, 920
(c) 46, 6532 (d) 28, -910
(e) 28, 1120 (f) 125, 42 875
(g) 1000, 5 005 000 (h) 61, -988.2

6 (a) $a=3, d=4$ (b) $a=2, d=5$
(c) $a=1.4, d=0.3$ (d) $a=12, d=-2.5$
(e) $a=25, d=-3$ (f) $a=-7, d=2$

7 (a) 20 (b) 12 (c) 16

8 (a) 62 (b) 25

9 (a) \$76 (b) \$1272

10 (a) 5050 (b) 15 050 (c) $\frac{1}{2}n(3n+1)$

11 \$1 626 000

Exercise 2D (page 34)

1 (a) $2+3$ (b) $2+2+2$
(c) $1+\frac{1}{2}+\frac{1}{3}+\frac{1}{4}$ (d) $1+4+9+16$
(e) $5+7+9+11$ (f) $u_0+u_1+u_2$

2 (a) $\sum_{i=2}^{4} i$ (b) $\sum_{i=1}^{4} i^2$ (c) $\sum_{i=3}^{7} i^3$
(d) $\sum_{i=1}^{3} \frac{1}{2i}$ (e) $\sum_{i=1}^{4} (2i+1)$ (f) $\sum_{i=1}^{5} (3i-1)$

3 (b) 41 230, 637 336, 716 946

3 The binomial theorem

Exercise 3A (page 38)

1 (a) x^3+3x^2+3x+1
(b) $8x^3+12x^2+6x+1$
(c) $64+48p+12p^2+p^3$
(d) x^3-3x^2+3x-1
(e) $x^3+6x^2+12x+8$
(f) $8p^3+36p^2q+54pq^2+27q^3$
(g) $1-12x+48x^2-64x^3$
(h) $1+2x+\frac{3}{2}x^2+\frac{1}{2}x^3+\frac{1}{16}x^4$
(i) $x^6+6x^4+12x^2+8$
(j) $1-15x^2+75x^4-125x^6$
(k) $x^6+3x^4y^3+3x^2y^6+y^9$
(l) $1-3x^3+3x^6-x^9$

2 (a) 12 (b) 150

3 (a) 240 (b) 54

4 (a) 270 (b) -1000

5 $m^3+12m^2+48m+64$;
$m^4+13m^3+60m^2+112m+64$

6 $24r^4+124r^3+234r^2+189r+54$

7 7

8 $a^9+9a^8b+36a^7b^2+84a^6b^3+126a^5b^4$
$+126a^4b^5+84a^3b^6+36a^2b^7+9ab^8+b^9$

9 8064

Exercise 3B (page 42)

1 (a) 35 (b) 28 (c) 126 (d) 715
(e) 15 (f) 45 (g) 11 (h) 1225

2 (a) 10 (b) -56 (c) 165 (d) -560

3 (a) 84 (b) -1512 (c) 4032 (d) $-\frac{99}{4}$

4 (a) 3003 (b) 192 192
(c) 560 431 872 (d) 48 048

5 (a) $1+13x+78x^2+286x^3$
(b) $1-15x+105x^2-455x^3$
(c) $1+30x+405x^2+3240x^3$
(d) $128-2240x+16\,800x^2-70\,000x^3$

6 (a) $1+22x+231x^2$
(b) $1-30x+435x^2$
(c) $1-72x+2448x^2$
(d) $1+114x+6156x^2$

7 $1+16x+112x^2$; 1.17

8 $4096+122\,880x+1\,689\,600x^2$; 4220.57

9 $2+56x^2+140x^4+56x^6+2x^8$; $x=0.01$;
2.005 601 400 056 000 2

Review exercise 1 (page 43)

1 (a) $4\sqrt{3}$ (b) $\sqrt{7}$
(c) $111\sqrt{10}$ (d) $3\sqrt[3]{2}$

2 (a) $\frac{3}{2}\sqrt{3}$ (b) $\frac{1}{25}\sqrt{5}$
(c) $\frac{1}{3}\sqrt{2}$ (d) $\frac{2}{15}\sqrt{30}$

4 (a) 14 cm^2

5 (a) $12\sqrt{3}$ (b) 48

6 $x>\frac{4}{3}$

7 1444

8 $128-448x+672x^2-560x^3$; 123.59

9 (a) 1683 (b) 3367

10 $a^{10}+10a^7+40a^4+80a+\frac{80}{a^2}+\frac{32}{a^5}$

11 71 240

12 $n(2n+3)$

13 168

14 167 167; 111 445

15 (b) 22

16 (a) 5 (b) $\frac{1}{2}$

Examination questions (page 44)

1 (a) 90 (b) 34

2 2 345 625

3 $16\,800x^{10}$

4 (a) 1730 metres (b) 50 180 metres

5 (a) 7 (b) 4 (c) 19

6 3

7 (a) 10 (b) 2268

4 Representation of statistical data

Exercise 4A (page 51)

B means 'class boundaries', F means 'frequency'.

1 B: 30 40 50 60 70 80 90
F: 12 32 56 72 20 8

2 B: 4.5 9.5 14.5 19.5 24.5 29.5 34.5 39.5
F: 2 5 8 14 17 11 3

3 (a) 6 cm (b) 7

4 B: −0.5 9.5 19.5 29.5 39.5 49.5 59.5
F: 6 21 51 84 82 31

5 Assuming data correct to 1 decimal place
B: 8.95 9.95 10.95 11.95 12.95 13.95 14.95 15.95 16.95
F: 1 4 7 6 9 8 7 3

6 (a) F: 3, 4, 6, 7, 10, 4 (b) 2.875, 3.875
(c) B: 2.875 3.875 4.875 5.875 6.875 7.875 8.875
F: 3 4 6 7 10 4

7 (a), (b) B: 10 20 30 40 50 60 70 80
F: 12 40 44 47 32 15 10

Exercise 4B (page 53)

1 Plot at (30, 0), (40, 12), (50, 44), (60, 100), (70, 172), (80, 192), (100, 200).
(a) About 32% (b) About 52 m.p.h.

2 Plot at (−0.5, 0), (9.5, 6), (19.5, 27), (29.5, 78), (39.5, 162), (49.5, 244), (59.5, 275).
(a) About 27% (b) 20

3 (a) Plot at (0, 0), (16, 14.3), (40, 47.4), (65, 82.7), (80, 94.6), (100, 100).
(b) 10.2 million

4 Plot at (0, 0), (2, 15), (3, 42), (4, 106), (5, 178), (6, 264), (7, 334), (8, 350), (9, 360). About 55 poor days and 12 good days.

5 Plot at (0, 0), (4.5, 12), (9.5, 41), (14.5, 104), (19.5, 117), (24.5, 129), (29.5, 132).
(a) About 8.3 miles
(b) About 14 miles

5 Measures of location

Exercise 5A (page 58)

1 5.4 kg; 5.7 kg

2 (a) 27.5 m.p.h. (b) 1.1 hours

3 13.5

4 £500 approximately

5 (a) F: 13, 16, 18, 15, 6, 8, 2, 2
(b) Plot at (0.95, 0), (2.45, 13), (3.95, 29), (5.45, 48), (6.95, 62), (8.45, 68), (9.95, 76), (11.45, 78), (12.95, 80)
4.85 s
(c) 5.0 s; Data not evenly spread over interval 4.0–5.4.

6 34

7 (a) 70.5 inches (b) 66.0 inches
On average the men are taller than the women.

Exercise 5B (page 63)

1 10.5

2 71.43 inches. Students appear taller, on average than the population. This can be explained by the large values 75.5, 75.5, 76.5 and 77.0.

3 (a) 11.3 (b) 105.5

4 0.319

5 3.59

6 24.3

7 59.2 m.p.h.

8 (a) −0.5, 2.5, 5.5, 8.5, 11.5, 14.5
(b) 3.54 minutes.

9 \$12.89; \$12.39

10 95 kg

11 117 kg

Exercise 5C (page 67)

1 (a) 0 (b) No mode. (c) 2–3 (d) Brown

2 (a) Mode (b) Mean (c) Median

3 It could be true for mean or mode, not the median.

4 (a) Roughly symmetrical
(b) Skewed
(c) Skewed
(d) Roughly symmetrical

5 (a) Mean 4.875, median 5, mode 6
(b) It has a 'tail' of low values.

6 Measures of spread

Exercise 6A (page 76)

1 (a) 17, 9.5 (b) 9.1, 2.8

2 (a) 2.3 (b) About 5

3 Monday: $Q_1 = 105$, $Q_2 = 170$, $Q_3 = 258$
Wednesday: $Q_1 = 240$, $Q_2 = 305$, $Q_3 = 377$
Audienees larger on Wednesday, with less variation.

4 (a) Negative skew
(b) Positive skew
(c) Roughly symmetrical

5 (a) £38.73, £43.23, £49.24, £54.15, £58.42.
(c) Slight negative skew

6 Box and whisker plots are preferred since they give visual comparison of the shapes of distributions, the quartiles, IQRs and ranges. Histograms will indicate the general shape of the distributions and will give only a rough idea of quartiles and so on. However, means and standard deviations can be estimated from a histogram but not a box and whisker plot.

Exercise 6B (page 79)

1 (a) 4, 2 (b) 5, 4.899

2 (a) 3.489 (b) 4.278

3 50.728 g, 10.076 g^2; g^2

4 (a) Anwar is better; his mean of 51.5 is greater than Brian's 47.42 (Anwar scores more runs than Brian).
(b) Brian is more consistent since his standard deviation of 27.16 is less than Anwar's 34.13.

Exercise 6C (page 82)

1 0.740, 1.13

2 1.58 ≈ 1.5

3 797.4 min^2

4 250.77(5) g, 3.51 g
Increase the number of classes; weigh more accurately; use more packets.

5 Mid-class values are 18.5, 23.5, 28.5, 33.5, 38.5, 45.5, 55.5, 65.5. Mean 37.3 years, SD 11.68 years. In the second company the general age is lower and with smaller spread.

Review exercise 2 (page 83)

1 (a) F: 17, 11, 10, 9, 3, 4, 2, 2, 1, 1
(b) B: −0.5 9.5 19.5 29.5 39.5 49.5 59.5 69.5 79.5 89.5 99.5
FD: 1.7, 1.1, 1.0, 0.9, 0.3, 0.4, 0.2, 0.2, 0.1, 0.1
(c) Plot at (−0.5, 0), (9.5, 17), (19.5, 28), (29.5, 38), (39.5, 47), (49.5, 50), (59.5, 54), (69.5, 56), (79.5, 58), (89.5, 59), (99.5, 60); 44

2 (a) Both 22.0–23.9
(b) Not supported since modal classes the same. Either mean_1 (23.21 °C) is greater than mean_2 (22.43 °C) or median_1 (≈23 °C) is greater than median_2 (≈22 °C).

3 (a) \$0.62; \$0.717; modes: \$0.50, \$0.52, \$0.59
(b) Median, since it is not affected by extreme values or mean, since it involves all values.
(c) \$0.336

4 23.16 cm, 1.32 cm; 22.89 cm, 1.13 cm
House sparrows have smaller variability; little difference in means.

5 (a) 2.825, 2.941, 3.000, 3.020, 3.175
(b) 0.060 cm
(c) 1.32 approx.; close to 1.3

6 Mean and standard deviation of the sample are 64.6 kg and 8.36 kg, correct to three significant figures.
These are also estimates of the mean and standard deviation of the population.

Examination questions (page 84)

1 8, 9

2 3, 3, 4, 5, 10; 3, 3, 4, 6, 9; 3, 3, 4, 7, 8

3 (a) 6 (b) 4.7 (c) 2.6

4 3

5 (a) (i) \$24 (ii) 154
(b) 40 (c) 93

6 (a) Plot at (0, 0), (100, 12), (200, 58), (300, 87), (400, 94), (500, 10)
(b) About 116 (c) 7, 6 (d) \$199 000
(e) About 8

7 3, 7, 11, 11

8 (a) 49.56 (b) 48.87

7 Coordinates, points and lines

Exercise 7A (page 93)

1 (a) 13; $(4\frac{1}{2}, 11)$ (b) 5; $(4, 3\frac{1}{2})$
(c) 10; (7, 5) (d) 5; $(-1, \frac{1}{2})$
(e) $5\sqrt{2}$; $(1\frac{1}{2}, -2\frac{1}{2})$ (f) $2\sqrt{13}$; $(-5, 0)$

3 (4, −6)

4 (a) 2 (b) −3 (c) $\frac{1}{2}$ (d) $-\frac{3}{4}$

5 $\frac{1}{2}$, $\frac{1}{2}$; points lie on a straight line

6 No

7 (a) Gradients PQ and RS both −1, QR and SP both $\frac{3}{5}$
(b) $PQ = RS = 4\sqrt{2}$, $QR = SP = \sqrt{34}$
(c) Both $(3\frac{1}{2}, -1\frac{1}{2})$
(d) Parallelogram

Exercise 7B (page 98)

1 (a) Yes (b) No

2 (a) $y = 5x - 7$ (b) $y = -3x + 1$
(c) $2y = x + 8$ (d) $8y = -3x + 2$
(e) $y = -3x$ (f) $y = 8$
(g) $4y = -3x - 19$ (h) $2y = x + 3$
(i) $8y = 3x + 1$ (j) $2y = -x + 11$
(k) $y = -2x + 3$ (l) $y = 3x + 1$
(m) $y = 7x - 4$ (n) $y = -x + 2$

3 (a) $y = 3x + 1$ (b) $y = 2x - 3$
(c) $3y = -2x + 12$ (d) $x = 3$
(e) $5y = 3x - 45$ (f) $y = -3x + 8$
(g) $y = -3$ (h) $3y = -x + 2$
(i) $3y = -5x - 14$ (j) $7y = -2x - 11$
(k) $x = -3$ (l) $y = -x - 1$
(m) $y = 3x + 1$ (n) $3y = -5x - 13$
(o) $y = -\frac{3}{5}x$ (p) $py = qx$

4 (a) −1, −3, −3 (b) 3, −4, 12
(c) $-2\frac{1}{2}, -\frac{3}{5}, -1\frac{1}{2}$ (d) 0, none, 5
(e) $1\frac{1}{2}, -1\frac{1}{3}, 2$ (f) Undefined, $1\frac{2}{5}$, none
(g) $-2, 3\frac{1}{2}, 7$ (h) $\frac{3}{4}, 2\frac{2}{3}, -2$
(i) $-\frac{1}{2}, 7, 3\frac{1}{2}$

5 $y = \frac{1}{2}x + 2$

6 $y = -2x + 5$

Exercise 7C (page 100)

1 (a) $-\frac{1}{2}$ (b) $\frac{1}{3}$ (c) $-1\frac{1}{3}$
(d) $1\frac{1}{5}$ (e) 1 (f) $-\frac{4}{7}$
(g) m (h) $-1/m$ (i) $-q/p$
(j) Undefined (k) $1/m$ (l) $(c - b)/a$

2 (a) $4y = -x + 14$ (b) $y = 2x + 7$
(c) $5y = x - 27$ (d) $x = 7$
(e) $2y = 3x + 11$ (f) $3y = -5x + 29$
(g) $y = -3$ (h) $2y = -x + 6$

3 $2y = -x + 8$

8 Functions and graphs

Exercise 8A (page 105)

1 (a) 11 (b) 5 (c) −3 (d) 0

2 (a) 50 (b) 5 (c) 29 (d) 29

3 (a) 15 (b) $5\frac{1}{4}$ (c) 0 (d) 0

4 (a) 17 (b) 9

5 $\frac{1}{2}$

6 4, 2

7 Semicircle

8 $x = -1, x = 1, y = 1$

9 $-1 \le x \le 3, 0 \le y \le 4$ would do

10 $x = 3, y = -2$

Exercise 8B (page 108)

2 4

3 (a) and (c) are odd; (b) is even.

Exercise 8C (page 111)

1 (a) $x \ge 0$ (b) $x \le 0$
(c) $x \ge 4$ (d) $x \le 4$
(e) $x \le 0$ and $x \ge 4$ (f) $x \le 0$ and $x \ge 4$
(g) $x \le -3$ and $x \ge 3$ (h) $x \ge 2$
(i) All real numbers except 2
(j) $x > 2$ (k) $x \ge 0$
(l) All real numbers except 1 and 2

2 (a) $f(x) \ge 4$ (b) $f(x) \ge 10$ (c) $f(x) \ge 6$
(d) $f(x) \le 7$ (e) $f(x) \ge 2$ (f) $f(x) \ge -1$

3 (a) $0 \le f(x) \le 16$ (b) $-1 \le f(x) \le 7$
(c) $0 \le f(x) \le 16$ (d) $4 \le f(x) \le 25$

4 (a) $f(x) > 7$ (b) $f(x) < 0$ (c) $f(x) > -1$
(d) $f(x) > -1$ (e) $f(x) > 2$ (f) $f(x) \ge -\frac{1}{4}$

5 (a) $f(x) \ge 0$ (b) all real numbers
(c) all real numbers except 0
(d) $f(x) > 0$ (e) $f(x) \ge 5$
(f) all real numbers
(g) $0 \le f(x) \le 2$ (h) $f(x) \ge 0$

6 $0 < w < 12, 0 < A \leq 36$

7 $0 < x < 4, 0 < y \leq 145.7...$

9 Linear and quadratic functions

Exercise 9A (page 115)

4 Changing c moves the graph parallel to the y-axis.

6 Changing b moves the graph parallel to both axes, but the shape stays the same.

10 Changing a makes the graph narrower and steeper.

11 (c)

12 (a)

Exercise 9B (page 119)

1 (a) (i) $(2, 3)$ (ii) $x = 2$
(b) (i) $(5, -4)$ (ii) $x = 5$
(c) (i) $(-3, -7)$ (ii) $x = -3$
(d) (i) $(\frac{3}{2}, 1)$ (ii) $x = \frac{3}{2}$
(e) (i) $(-\frac{3}{5}, 2)$ (ii) $x = -\frac{3}{5}$
(f) (i) $(-\frac{7}{3}, -4)$ (ii) $x = -\frac{7}{3}$
(g) (i) $(3, c)$ (ii) $x = 3$
(h) (i) (p, q) (ii) $x = p$
(i) (i) $(-b/a, c)$ (ii) $x = -b/a$

2 (a) (i) -1 (ii) -2 (b) (i) 2 (ii) 1
(c) (i) 5 (ii) -3 (d) (i) -7 (ii) $-\frac{1}{2}$
(e) (i) 3 (ii) 4 (f) (i) q (ii) $-p$
(g) (i) $-q$ (ii) p (h) (i) r (ii) t
(i) (i) c (ii) $-b/a$

3 (a) (i) $x = 2$ (ii) 2, 5, -1
(iii) $y = -x^2 + 4x + 1$
(b) (i) $x = 2$ (ii) 2, -1, 3
(iii) $y = 3x^2 - 12x + 11$

Exercise 9C (page 122)

1 (a) $(x+1)^2 + 1$ (b) $(x-4)^2 - 19$
(c) $\left(x + 1\frac{1}{2}\right)^2 - 9\frac{1}{4}$ (d) $(x-3)^2 - 4$
(e) $(x+7)^2$ (f) $2(x+3)^2 - 23$
(g) $3(x-2)^2 - 9$ (h) $11 - 4(x+1)^2$
(i) $2\left(x + 1\frac{1}{4}\right)^2 - 6\frac{1}{8}$

2 (a) 3 when $x = 2$ (b) $2\frac{3}{4}$ when $x = 1\frac{1}{2}$
(c) 13 when $x = 3$ (d) $-1\frac{1}{8}$ when $x = 1\frac{1}{4}$
(e) $-4\frac{1}{3}$ when $x = -\frac{1}{3}$ (f) $7\frac{1}{12}$ when $x = -1\frac{1}{6}$

3 (a) (i) $(2, 2)$ (ii) $x = 2$
(b) (i) $(-3, -11)$ (ii) $x = -3$
(c) (i) $(-5, 32)$ (ii) $x = -5$
(d) (i) $\left(-1\frac{1}{2}, -1\frac{1}{4}\right)$ (ii) $x = -1\frac{1}{2}$
(e) (i) $\left(1\frac{3}{4}, -4\frac{1}{8}\right)$ (ii) $x = 1\frac{3}{4}$
(f) (i) $(2, -7)$ (ii) $x = 2$

4 (a) $f(x) \geq -28$ (b) $f(x) \leq 5\frac{1}{2}$
(c) $f(x) \geq -9$ (d) $f(x) > 5$
(e) $-1\frac{1}{3} \leq f(x) \leq 4$ (f) $5 \leq f(x) \leq 13$

Exercise 9D (page 127)

3 30 m s^{-1}, 45 m

4 (a) Upwards (b) $v = 25 - 10t$
(c) After 2.5 seconds (d) 31.25 m

5 (a) 2 m s^{-2} (b) $v = 80 - 2t$ (c) 1500 m

6 (a) A straight line from (0, 5) reaching height 7
(b) 40 s (c) $\frac{1}{20}$ m s^{-2}
(d) $v = 5 + \frac{1}{20}t$ (e) $5t + \frac{1}{40}t^2$

10 Equations and graphs

Exercise 10A (page 135)

1 (a) $(x+3)(x+8)$ (b) $(l-3)(l-4)$
(c) $(q-5)(q-7)$ (d) $(x-2)(x+3)$
(e) $(x-3)(x+8)$ (f) $(n-12)(n+5)$
(g) $(r-1)(r-16)$ (h) $(x-3)(x-11)$
(i) $(x-3)(x+7)$

2 (a) $(x-2)(3x-2)$ (b) $(2x-1)(2x-5)$
(c) $(3x+1)(4x-1)$ (d) $(x-2)(3x+2)$
(e) $(x-2)(8x+1)$ (f) $(3x-2)(2x+3)$
(g) $(2x-5)(2x+1)$ (h) $3(x-3)(3x-1)$
(i) $2(3x-4)(2x+1)$

3 (a) $(x-1)(x+1)$ (b) $(2-5d)(2+5d)$
(c) $4(5-z)(5+z)$ (d) $(1-x)(1+3x)$
(e) $(x+1)(3x+1)$ (f) $(x+4)(3x-2)$

4 (a) No factors (b) $(x-5)(x-8)$
(c) No factors (d) No factors
(e) $x(x+14)$ (f) $(x-10)(x+6)$
(g) No factors (h) No factors
(i) $(2x-1)(x+3)$

5 (a) $-5, 7$ (b) $-1, 3$ (c) $-9, 3$
(d) $-\frac{2}{3}, \frac{3}{2}$ (e) $-\frac{2}{3}, \frac{3}{2}$ (f) $-\frac{3}{4}, \frac{2}{3}$

6 (a) $-4, 1$ (b) $-3, 3$ (c) $-\frac{1}{2}, 1$
(d) $\frac{1}{2}, 2$ (e) 3 (f) $-\frac{1}{3}, \frac{1}{3}$

7 $y = 2x^2 + 4x - 6$, $(-4, 10)$

8 $y = 3x^2 + 12x + 12$

Exercise 10B (page 139)

1 (a) $3 \pm \sqrt{3}$ (b) $0, -4$ (c) $-3 \pm \frac{1}{2}\sqrt{10}$
(d) $\frac{1}{3}(7 \pm 2\sqrt{2})$ (e) $-p \pm \sqrt{q}$ (f) $-b \pm \sqrt{\frac{c}{a}}$

2 (a) $\frac{1}{2}(-3 \pm \sqrt{29})$ (b) $2 \pm \sqrt{11}$
(c) -3 (repeated) (d) $\frac{1}{2}(-5 \pm \sqrt{17})$
(e) No solution (f) $\frac{1}{6}(5 \pm \sqrt{97})$
(g) -3 and $-\frac{1}{2}$ (h) $\frac{1}{2}(-3 \pm \sqrt{41})$
(i) $\frac{1}{6}(2 \pm \sqrt{34})$

3 (a) $(x-7)(x+5)$ (b) $(x-22)(x+8)$
(c) $(x+24)(x-18)$ (d) $(3x+2)(2x-3)$
(e) $(2+7x)(7-2x)$ (f) $(4x+3)(3x-2)$

Exercise 10C (page 141)

1 (a) 2 (b) 1 (c) 0 (d) 0 (e) 2
(f) 2 (g) 1 (h) 2 (i) 2 (j) 2

2 (a) $-\frac{9}{4}$ (b) $-\frac{25}{32}$ (c) 81
(d) $\pm 2\sqrt{6}$ (e) $\pm 4\sqrt{6}$ (f) $p^2/4q$

3 (a) $k < \frac{9}{4}$ (b) $k = \frac{49}{4}$ (c) $k > \frac{9}{20}$
(d) $k > -\frac{25}{12}$ (e) $k = \frac{4}{3}$ (f) $k > \frac{25}{28}$
(g) $k > 4$ or $k < -4$ (h) $-6 < k < 6$

4 (a) 2 (b) 0 (c) 1 (d) 0 (e) 2
(f) 2 (g) 0 (h) 0 (i) 1

5 Intersects x-axis twice, faces up.

6 Intersects x-axis twice, faces down.

Exercise 10D (page 142)

1 (a) $\pm 1, \pm 2$ (b) $\pm 1, \pm 3$ (c) ± 2
(d) $\pm\sqrt{6}$ (e) $-1, 2$ (f) $\sqrt[3]{3}, -\sqrt[3]{4}$

2 (a) 16 (b) 25, 9 (c) 49
(d) 25 (e) 9 (f) 16

3 (a) $-2, 5$ (b) $-6, 1$ (c) $-3, \frac{1}{2}$
(d) $-4, 3$ (e) 36 (f) 9

Exercise 10E (page 146)

1 (a) $(3, 14)$ (b) $(1, 3), (4, 3)$
(c) $(-4, 8), (2, 8)$ (d) $(-3, -3), (\frac{1}{2}, -3)$

2 (a) $(1, 2), (3, 4)$ (b) $(-4, -5), (3, 9)$
(c) $(-1\frac{1}{2}, 6\frac{1}{2}), (2, 17)$ (d) $(-2, -7), (2, 9)$

3 (a) $(2, 6)$ (b) $(-3, -1)$

4 (a) $(-4, 14)$ (b) $(-6, 24), (-2, 12)$

5 (a) $(-1, 4), (3, 8)$ (b) $(1, 6)$

6 (a) $(5, 51)$ (b) $(-1, \frac{1}{2}), (1, \frac{1}{2})$
(c) $(1, 9), (2, 18)$ (d) $(-2, 3)$
(e) $(-3, 1), (-2, 3)$ (f) $(-1, -5), (2, 19)$

7 (a) 1.586, 4.414
(b) $-2.882, -0.223, 3.105$
(c) $-3.709, -1.194, 0.903$
(d) 1.612, 3.821

8 (a) $(4.11, 69.29)$
(b) $(3.36, 37.77)$ (c) $(1.66, 3.76)$
(d) $(-4.59, -1.09), (0.25, 19.94), (4.34, 1.15)$

Review exercise 3 (page 147)

2 (a) $3y = 4x - 13$ (b) $(4, 1)$ (c) 5

3 $4y = 3x - 1$

4 9

5 $(-2\frac{1}{2}, -2), (2, 7)$

7 $(0, 108)$

8 $(\sqrt{3}, -5\sqrt{3}), (-\sqrt{3}, 5\sqrt{3})$

11 (a) $f(x) \le 9$ (b) All real values
(c) $f(x) \ge -69$ (d) $f(x) \ge -36$

12 25; $f(x) \le 25$

13 2.15

14 $|x| > 2$; $x = -2$, $x = 2$, $y = 0$

15 $y = -\frac{3}{5}x + \frac{4}{5}$; $(1\frac{1}{3}, 0)$

16 (a) $2\sqrt{3}, 4\sqrt{3}$ (b) $\pm 1.86, \pm 2.63$

17 (a) $(3x+2)^2 + 3$ (b) $0 < f(x) \le \frac{1}{3}$

18 (a) $4(x-2)^2 - 8$ (b) $(2, -8)$
(c) $2 - \sqrt{2}, 2 + \sqrt{2}$

19 (b) 4, 25

Examination questions (page 148)

1 (a) -2 (b) $y = -2x + 8$ (c) 4

2 (a) $2(x-2)^2 - 3$ (b) -3

3 (a) $-5, 6$ (b) (i) 2 (ii) $\frac{1}{2}$

4 $|k| > 6$

5 (b) 3 kg (c) 5 kg (d) 19

11 Differentiation

Exercise 11A (page 154)

1 (a) 4 (b) 1.2 (c) -2

2 (a) 5 (b) 9 (c) -3

3 (a) (i) 10 (ii) 24 (iii) -40
(b) (i) 0.8 (ii) 3 (iii) -2
(c) (i) 2 (ii) -4 (iii) 8

Exercise 11B (page 156)

1 (a) $20x$ (b) $2x$ (c) $6x - 4$

Exercise 11C (page 160)

1 (a) $2x$ (b) $2x - 1$ (c) $8x$
(d) $6x - 2$ (e) -3 (f) $1 - 4x$
(g) $4 - 6x$ (h) $\sqrt{2} - 2\sqrt{3}x$

2 (a) 3 (b) $-6x$ (c) 0
(d) $2 + 6x$ (e) $-2x$ (f) $6 - 6x$
(g) $2 - 4x$ (h) $4x + 1$

3 (a) 6 (b) 3 (c) -3 (d) 8
(e) -8 (f) -6 (g) 4 (h) -17

4 (a) $\frac{3}{4}$ (b) $\frac{1}{2}$ (c) $-\frac{3}{2}$
(d) -1 (e) $\frac{3}{2}$ (f) $\frac{1}{2}$

5 (a) 3 (b) 0.75

7 (a) $3x^2 + 4x$ (b) $-6x^2 + 6x$
(c) $3x^2 - 12x + 11$ (d) $6x^2 - 6x + 1$
(e) $1 + 3x^2$ (f) $-4x^3$

8 (a) -10 (b) 6 (c) 58
(d) -1 (e) 8 (f) -8

9 (a) $-2, 2$ (b) $-\frac{4}{3}, 2$ (c) $-5, 7$
(d) 1 (e) $-1, -\frac{1}{3}$ (f) No values

12 Tangents and normals

Exercise 12 (page 168)

1 (a) $y = -2x - 1$ (b) $y = -x$
(c) $y = 2x - 1$ (d) $y = 6x + 10$
(e) $y = 1$ (f) $y = 0$

2 (a) $2y = x - 3$ (b) $4y = -x + 1$
(c) $8y = -x - 58$ (d) $x = 0$
(e) $2y = x + 9$ (f) $x = \frac{1}{2}$

3 $4y = 4x - 1$

4 $y = 0$

5 $y = -2x$

6 $12y = 12x - 17$

7 $x = 1$

8 $7y = -x + 64$

9 $y = 4x + 2$

10 $y = x + 2$

12 $y = -2x - 6$

13 (a) $(-1, 1), (2, 4)$
(b) $y = -2x - 1, y = 4x - 4$ (c) $(\frac{1}{2}, -2)$

13 Index notation

Exercise 13A (page 172)

1 (a) a^{12} (b) b^8 (c) c^4
(d) d^9 (e) e^{20} (f) x^6y^4
(g) $15g^8$ (h) $3h^8$ (i) $72a^8$

2 (a) 2^{26} (b) 2^{12} (c) 2^6
(d) 2^6 (e) 2^2 (f) 2^1

Exercise 13B (page 176)

1 (a) $\frac{1}{8}$ (b) $\frac{1}{16}$ (c) $\frac{1}{5}$
(d) $\frac{1}{9}$ (e) $\frac{1}{10000}$ (f) 1
(g) 2 (h) 27 (i) $\frac{2}{5}$
(j) $\frac{1}{128}$ (k) $\frac{1}{216}$ (l) $\frac{27}{64}$

2 (a) $\frac{1}{2}$ (b) $\frac{1}{512}$ (c) $\frac{1}{32}$
(d) 8 (e) $\frac{1}{8}$ (f) 8

3 (a) $\frac{1}{10}$ (b) $\frac{2}{5}$ (c) $\frac{2}{5}$
(d) $\frac{1}{10}$ (e) 10 (f) $\frac{2}{5}$

4 (a) a (b) b (c) c^{-6}
(d) 2 (e) e^{-9} (f) f^{-5}
(g) $3g^{-1}$ (h) $\frac{1}{9}h^{-4}$ (i) $\frac{1}{9}i^4$
(j) $8j^6$ (k) $8x^9y^{-3}$
(l) $p^{-8}q^{-16}r^{-12}$ (m) $2m$
(n) $9n^{-9}$ (o) $\frac{1}{64}q^6$

5 (a) $x = -2$ (b) $y = 0$ (c) $z = 4$
(d) $x = -2$ (e) $y = 120$ (f) $t = 0$

6 (a) 2.7×10^{-5} m^3 (b) 5.4×10^{-3} m^2

7 26.7 km h^{-1} (to 1 decimal place)

8 (a) 1.0×10^{-3} m^3 (to 2 significant figures)
(b) 101.9 m (to 1 decimal place)
(c) 5.6×10^{-3} m (to 2 significant figures)

9 (a) 4.375×10^{-4} (b) 4.5×10^{-7}

Exercise 13C (page 182)

1 (a) 5 (b) 2 (c) 6 (d) 2
(e) 3 (f) $\frac{1}{3}$ (g) $\frac{1}{2}$ (h) $\frac{1}{7}$
(i) 4 (j) 8 (k) $\frac{1}{32}$ (l) 32
(m) $\frac{1}{10}$ (n) -3 (o) 16 (p) $\frac{1}{625}$
(q) $\frac{1}{1000}$ (r) 625 (s) $2\frac{1}{4}$ (t) $\frac{2}{3}$

2 (a) 2 (b) $\frac{1}{16}$ (c) 16 (d) $\frac{1}{2}$
(e) 2 (f) $\frac{1}{2}$ (g) 16 (h) $\frac{1}{2}$

3 (a) a^2 (b) $12b^{-1}$ (c) $12c^{3/4}$
(d) 1 (e) 2 (f) $5pq^2$

4 (a) 64 (b) 27 (c) 8 (d) 9
(e) $\frac{1}{4}$ (f) $\frac{1}{27}$ (g) 2 (h) 2

5 (a) 1.9 (to 1 decimal place)
(b) 2.2 m (to 1 decimal place)

6 6.5 cm (to 1 decimal place)

7 (a) $x = \frac{5}{2}$ (b) $y = -\frac{3}{2}$ (c) $z = \frac{1}{4}$ (d) $x = \frac{3}{2}$
(e) $y = \frac{4}{3}$ (f) $z = -\frac{7}{3}$ (g) $t = \frac{6}{5}$

8 (a) $1, 4$ (b) 9 (c) 1
(d) $0, 8$ (e) 2 (f) $1, -27$

9 (a) $x^{-\frac{1}{2}}$ (b) $4x^{\frac{1}{2}}$ (c) $2x^{\frac{1}{2}}$
(d) $3x^{\frac{5}{2}}$ (e) $x^{-\frac{2}{3}}$

10 (a) $2\sqrt[3]{3}$ (b) $\sqrt[6]{2}$ (c) $\sqrt{6}$

11 (a) (i) 16 (iii) $-\frac{1}{4}$ (iv) 16
(ii), (v), (vi) No value
(c) q must be odd

14 Graphs of *n*th power functions

Exercise 14A (page 190)

1 (a) $(2, 4)$
(b) $(3, \frac{1}{3})$
(c) $(\sqrt{2}, \sqrt{2}), (-\sqrt{2}, -\sqrt{2})$
(d) $(\frac{1}{2}, 32), (-\frac{1}{2}, 32)$
(e) $(\frac{1}{3}, 243), (-\frac{1}{3}, -243)$
(f) $(2, 4), (-2, 4)$

2 (a) $x > 10$
(b) $x < -50$ or $x > 50$
(c) $-\frac{1}{10}\sqrt{10} \le x \le \frac{1}{10}\sqrt{10}, x \ne 0$
(d) $x < -20$ or $x > 20$

3 (a) RQP (b) PQR (c) QPR (d) QRP

4 (a) $-2x^{-3}, -\dfrac{2}{x^3}$ (b) $-5x^{-6}, -\dfrac{5}{x^6}$
(c) $-9x^{-4}, -\dfrac{9}{x^4}$ (d) $4x^{-3}, \dfrac{4}{x^3}$
(e) $-x^{-5}, -\dfrac{1}{x^5}$ (f) $2x^{-7}, \dfrac{2}{x^7}$

5 (a) $-\dfrac{5}{x^2}$ (b) $-\dfrac{1}{4x^2}$ (c) $-\dfrac{6}{x^3}$
(d) 0 (e) $-\dfrac{3}{x^2} - \dfrac{1}{x^4}$ (f) $\dfrac{4-x}{x^3}$

6 (a) $y = -4x + 8$ (b) $y = -2x + 3$
(c) $y = -18x + 9$ (d) $y = 6$
(e) $y = -x + 1$ (f) $2y = x + 2$

7 (a) $y = x - 1$ (b) $y = \frac{1}{2}x$
(c) $x = 2$ (d) $4y = x - 3$

Exercise 14B (page 193)

1 (a) $\frac{1}{3}x^{-\frac{2}{3}}$ (b) $\frac{5}{2}x^{\frac{3}{2}}$ (c) $2x^{-\frac{3}{5}}$
(d) $3x^{-\frac{8}{5}}$ (e) $-2x^{-\frac{3}{2}}$ (f) $3x^{-\frac{5}{2}}$

2 (a) $\dfrac{3}{4\sqrt[4]{x}}$ (b) $\dfrac{2}{\sqrt[3]{x^2}}$ (c) $-\dfrac{2}{\sqrt{x^3}}$
(d) $10\sqrt{x^3}$ (e) $-\dfrac{1}{6\sqrt[3]{x^4}}$ (f) $\dfrac{3x-1}{4\sqrt[4]{x^5}}$

3 (a) (i) 2, 2.008 298 8... (ii) 0.082 988...
(iii) $\frac{1}{12}$ (iv) $12y = x + 16$
(b) (i) 4, 4.033 264 2... (ii) 0.332 642...
(iii) $\frac{1}{3}$ (iv) $3y = x + 4$
(c) (i) 0.25, 0.247 938 1... (ii) −0.020 618...
(iii) $-\frac{1}{48}$ (iv) $48y = -x + 20$
(d) (i) 0.0625, 0.061 473 3...
(ii) −0.010 266...
(iii) $-\frac{1}{96}$
(iv) $96y = -x + 14$

4 (a) $6y = x + 9$ (b) $8y = -x + 32$
(c) $y = 3x - 1$ (d) $y = 3$

5 (a) $(8, 4)$ (b) $(-1, -1), (1, 1)$
(c) $(-8, \frac{3}{4})$ (d) $(1, 4)$

6 $y = 2x + \frac{3}{8}$

7 The line $y = x$ bisects the angle between the axes.

Review exercise 4 (page 194)

1 $(-\frac{1}{3}, -4\frac{17}{27}), (2, 13)$

2 1.5×10^{-10} joules

3 $(2, 12)$

4 $(-\frac{1}{4}, \frac{1}{16}), (2\frac{1}{4}, 5\frac{1}{16})$

5 (a) 6 (b) $\frac{1}{16}$ (c) $\frac{1}{2}$ (d) $2\frac{10}{27}$

6 $x = \frac{8}{7}$

7 (b) 1.5×10^{11} m (to 2 significant figures)

8 (a) $S = 2^1 \times 3^1 \times V^{\frac{2}{3}}$
(b) $V = 2^{-\frac{3}{2}} \times 3^{-\frac{3}{2}} \times S^{\frac{3}{2}}$

9 13

10 (a), (b) $2\sqrt{2}y = x + 3\sqrt{2}$

11 $(\frac{11}{20}, \frac{4}{5})$

12 $(\frac{67}{32}, \frac{5}{8})$

13 (a) −2 and $\frac{1}{2}$ (b) $mn = -1$

14 $\dfrac{1}{3a^2}$

15 −1 and 8

Examination questions (page 195)

1 (a) $3x^2 - 4x$ (b) 4

2 $\frac{3}{7}$

3 (a) (i) 3 (ii) 2
(c) $-2x + 6$
(d) (i) $\frac{1}{2}$ (ii) $2y = x - 2$ (iii) $1\frac{1}{2}$

4 (a) (i) −2, 4 (ii) $\frac{1}{2}$
(iii) $y = \frac{1}{2}x^2 - x - 4$
(b) (i) $x - 1$ (ii) $(8, 20)$
(c) (i) $3y = -x + 4$ (ii) $-2\frac{2}{3}$

15 Trigonometry

Exercise 15 (page 204)

1 (a) (i) 0.9063 (ii) 0.4226 (iii) 0.4663
(b) (i) −0.5736 (ii) 0.8192
(iii) −1.4281

(c) (i) −0.7071 (ii) −0.7071 (iii) 1

(d) (i) 0.8192 (ii) −0.5736 (iii) −0.7002

(e) (i) −0.3420 (ii) 0.9397 (iii) −2.7475

(f) (i) 0.3843 (ii) 0.9232 (iii) 2.4023

(g) (i) −0.5721 (ii) 0.8202 (iii) −1.4335

(h) (i) −0.9703 (ii) −0.2419 (iii) 0.2493

2 (a) greatest 3 at $x = 90$, least 1 at $x = 270$
(b) greatest 11 at $x = 180$, least 3 at $x = 360$
(c) greatest 13 at $x = 180$, least −3 at $x = 90$
(d) greatest 4 at $x = 90$, least 2 at $x = 270$
(e) greatest 10 at $x = 27\frac{1}{3}$, least 8 at $x = 72\frac{1}{3}$
(f) greatest 30 at $x = 180$, least 10 at $x = 360$

3 (a) 160 (b) 320 (c) 240
(d) 50 (e) 220 (f) 340
(g) 40, 140 (h) 30, 330 (i) 70, 250
(j) 80, 100 (k) 160, 200 (l) 100, 280

4 (a) $\frac{1}{2}\sqrt{2}$ (b) $-\frac{1}{2}$ (c) $-\frac{1}{2}$ (d) $\sqrt{3}$
(e) $-\frac{1}{2}\sqrt{2}$ (f) $\frac{1}{3}\sqrt{3}$ (g) −1 (h) $-\frac{1}{3}\sqrt{3}$
(i) $-\frac{1}{2}\sqrt{2}$ (j) 0 (k) 1 (l) $\frac{1}{2}\sqrt{2}$
(m) $-\frac{1}{2}$ (n) −1 (o) $-\frac{1}{2}$ (p) 0

5 (a) 60 (b) 240 (c) 120 (d) 30
(e) 30 (f) 135 (g) 210 (h) 90
(i) 120 (j) 60 (k) 270 (l) 180
(m) 60 (n) 150 (o) 225 (p) 180

7 $A = 5$, $B = 2.8$; 7.42 m

16 The sine and cosine rules

In this chapter, angles are given correct to 1 decimal place (unless they are exact), and lengths and areas correct to 3 significant figures.

Exercise 16A (page 210)

1 (a) 6 cm^2 (b) 11.2 cm^2 (c) 1.93 m^2
(d) 3.75 cm^2 (e) 5.03 cm^2 (f) 0.311 m^2

2 (a) 5.19 cm (b) 4 cm (c) 1.60 m
(d) 9.53 cm (e) 43.5 cm (f) 11.2 m

3 (a) 33.7° (b) 53.1° (c) 20.5°
(d) 56.3° (e) 11.6° (f) 10.8°

4 (a) 146.3° (b) 126.9° (c) 159.5°
(d) 123.7° (e) 168.4° (f) 169.2°

Exercise 16B (page 214)

1 (a) 6.95 cm (b) 32.9 cm
(c) 3.14 cm (d) 7.65 cm
(e) 5.81 cm (f) 8.18 cm

2 (a) $a = 12.4$ cm, $c = 12.5$ cm, 68.9 cm^2
(b) $p = 8.40$ cm, $r = 7.93$ cm, 29.4 cm^2
(c) $x = 14.8$ cm, $z = 13.4$ cm, 76.2 cm^2
(d) $l = 10.4$ cm, $n = 4.17$ cm, 17.7 cm^2

3 (a) $\hat{A} = 64.5°$, $\hat{C} = 24.5°$
(b) $\hat{Y} = 59.5°$, $\hat{Z} = 49.5°$

4 (a) $\hat{L} = 92.1°$, $\hat{N} = 74.9°$
(b) $\hat{D} = 28.2°$, $\hat{F} = 111.8°$

5 (a) 119 m (b) 102 m

6 (a) 80.0° (b) 90.0°

7 The largest side, a, must be opposite the largest angle which is therefore $\hat{A}$; but $\hat{B}$ is the largest angle.

8 (a) 5.64 cm (b) 6.12 cm (c) 21.5 cm^2

Exercise 16C (page 219)

1 (a) 10.2 cm (b) 16.3 cm
(c) 5.91 cm (d) 28.0 cm

2 (a) 69.5° (b) 128.0° (c) 85.6° (d) 90°

3 (a) 44.0° (b) 43.8° (c) 24.1° (d) 36.9°

4 34.2 cm^2

17 Solving triangles

Exercise 17A (page 222)

1 (a) 58.8°, 100.2° or 121.2°, 38.8°
(b) 66.8°, 63.2° or 113.2°, 16.8°
(c) 36.4°, 103.6°

2 (a) 9.37 cm or 14.2 cm
(b) 7.69 cm or 13.5 cm
(c) 9.96 cm

Exercise 17B (page 225)

1 $\hat{C} = 70°$, $b = 5.65$ cm, $c = 6.13$ cm

2 $\hat{Y} = 42.4°$, $\hat{Z} = 57.6°$, $y = 4.79$ cm

3 $\hat{P} = 38.2°$, $\hat{Q} = 120°$, $\hat{R} = 21.8°$

4 $\hat{L} = 33.1°$, $\hat{M} = 36.9°$, $n = 17.2$ cm

5 $\hat{E} = 93.6°$, $\hat{F} = 56.4°$, $e = 12.0$ cm or
$\hat{E} = 26.4°$, $\hat{F} = 123.6°$, $e = 5.34$ cm

18 Radians

Exercise 18 (page 230)

1 (a) $\frac{1}{2}\pi$ (b) $\frac{3}{4}\pi$ (c) $\frac{1}{4}\pi$ (d) $\frac{1}{6}\pi$
(e) $\frac{2}{5}\pi$ (f) $\frac{1}{10}\pi$ (g) $\frac{2}{3}\pi$ (h) $\frac{1}{8}\pi$
(i) 4π (j) $\frac{10}{3}\pi$ (k) $\frac{3}{2}\pi$ (l) $\frac{1}{180}\pi$

2 (a) $60°$ (b) $9°$ (c) $36°$ (d) $22\frac{1}{2}°$
(e) $20°$ (f) $120°$ (g) $112\frac{1}{2}°$ (h) $108°$
(i) $4°$ (j) $1080°$ (k) $-90°$ (l) $50°$

3 (a) $s = 8.4, A = 29.4$ (b) $s = 7.35, A = 12.9$
(c) $\theta = 1.5, A = 48$ (d) $r = 20, A = 140$
(e) $\theta = 2.4, s = 12$ (f) $s = 8$
(g) $r = 8, \theta = 2$ (h) $\theta = \frac{5}{3}$

4 (a) $2.26\,\text{cm}^2$ (b) $1.47\,\text{cm}^2$ (c) $830\,\text{cm}^2$
(d) $9.05\,\text{cm}^2$ (e) $0.556\,\text{cm}^2$

5 $6.72\,\text{cm}^2$

6 28.2 cm

7 $26.3\,\text{cm}^2$

8 15.5 cm, $14.3\,\text{cm}^2$

9 (a) $\frac{1}{2}\sqrt{3}$ (b) $\frac{1}{2}\sqrt{2}$ (c) $\frac{1}{3}\sqrt{3}$ (d) 0
(e) $-\frac{1}{2}\sqrt{2}$ (f) $-\frac{1}{2}\sqrt{3}$ (g) $-\sqrt{3}$ (h) $\frac{3}{4}$

Review exercise 5 (page 232)

1 (a) 360 (b) 90

2 $(0, 1), (\pm 180, 0)$

3 (a) 0.1 cm, 0.0009 seconds
(b) 0.0036 seconds
(c) 278 (d) 0.002 13 seconds

4 (a) 110 cm and 90 cm (b) 0.36 seconds
(c) 0.72 seconds (d) 0.468

5 6.03 m

6 14.2 cm, 17.4 cm

7 9.45 cm

8 $57.4°$ (or 1 radian)

9 $35.4°, 48.2°, 96.4°$, $31.3\,\text{cm}^2$

10 52.2 km

11 $\frac{1}{4}$

12 r^2

13 $17\,\text{cm}^2$

Examination questions (page 233)

1 $48.6°, 131.4°$

2 $32°$

3 (a) 5.96 km (b) $10.9\,\text{km}\,\text{h}^{-1}$ (c) 3.29 km

4 78.5 km

5 (a) 8.29 m
(b) (i) 18.5 m (ii) $76.4\,\text{m}^2$
(c) 11.2 m (d) 8.24 m

6 $3.75\,\text{cm}^2$

7 $117\,\text{cm}^2$

8 (a) $1.14\,\text{cm}^2$ (b) $2\,\text{cm}^2$

19 Investigating shapes of graphs

Exercise 19A (page 238)

1 (a) $(-1, -7)$ (b) $(3, 10)$
(c) $(-3, 27), (1, -5)$ (d) $(-2, 16), (2, -16)$
(e) $(0, 0), (8, -256)$ (f) $(-1, 8), (1, 0)$
(g) $(-2, 0), (0, 16), (2, 0)$
(h) $(-1, 0), \left(-\frac{1}{3}, -\frac{4}{27}\right)$ (i) $(1, 1)$

2 (a) $(1, 4)$ (b) $\left(-\frac{1}{2}, -8\frac{1}{4}\right)$
(c) $(-2, 9)$ (d) $(2, 0)$
(e) $(0, 3)$ (f) $(-2, 2), (0, -2)$
(g) $\left(-\frac{2}{3}, \frac{4}{27}\right), (0, 0)$ (h) $\left(-\frac{3}{4}, -\frac{27}{256}\right), (0, 0)$
(i) $(-2, -32), (0, 0), (5, -375)$

Exercise 19B (page 243)

1 (a) +, increasing (b) −, decreasing
(c) −, decreasing (d) +, increasing
(e) +, increasing (f) +, increasing
(g) −, decreasing (h) −, decreasing

2 (a) $2x - 5, x \geq \frac{5}{2}$ (b) $2x + 6, x \geq -3$
(c) $-3 - 2x, x \leq -\frac{3}{2}$ (d) $6x - 5, x \geq \frac{5}{6}$
(e) $10x + 3, x \geq -\frac{3}{10}$ (f) $-4 - 6x, x \leq -\frac{2}{3}$
(g) $3x^2 - 12, x \leq -2$ and $x \geq 2$
(h) $6x^2 - 18, x \leq -\sqrt{3}$ and $x \geq \sqrt{3}$
(i) $6x^2 - 18x - 24, x \leq -1$ and $x \geq 4$
(j) $3x^2 - 6x + 3$, all x
(k) $4x - 4x, -1 \leq x \leq 0$ and $x \geq 1$
(l) $4x^3 + 12x^2, x \geq -3$
(m) $3 - 3x^2, -1 \leq x \leq 1$
(n) $10x^4 - 20x^3, x \leq 0$ and $x \geq 2$
(o) $3(1 + x^2)$, all x

3 (a) $2x + 4, x \leq -2$ (b) $-3 + 2x, x \leq \frac{3}{2}$
(c) $7 - 4x, x \geq \frac{7}{4}$ (d) $3x^2 - 27, -3 \leq x \leq 3$
(e) $4x^3 + 8x, x \leq 0$ (f) $3x^2 - 6x + 3$, none
(g) $12x^3 - 60x^2, x \leq 5$
(h) $72x - 8x^3, -3 \leq x \leq 0$ and $x \geq 3$
(i) $5x^4 - 5, -1 \leq x \leq 1$

4 (a) (i) $(4, -12)$ (ii) minimum (iv) $y \geq -12$
(b) (i) $(-2, -7)$ (ii) minimum (iv) $y \geq -7$
(c) (i) $\left(-\frac{3}{5}, \frac{1}{5}\right)$ (ii) minimum (iv) $y \geq \frac{1}{5}$
(d) (i) $(-3, 13)$ (ii) maximum (iv) $y \leq 13$
(e) (i) $(-3, 0)$ (ii) minimum (iv) $y \geq 0$
(f) (i) $\left(-\frac{1}{2}, 2\right)$ (ii) maximum (iv) $y \leq 2$

5 (a) $(-2, 21)$ maximum, $(2, -11)$ minimum
(b) $(-4, -31)$ minimum, $(0, 1)$ maximum
(c) $(-1, 7)$ maximum, $(2, -20)$ minimum
(d) $(1, 2)$ maximum, $\left(1\frac{2}{3}, 1\frac{23}{27}\right)$ minimum
(e) $(-1, 2)$ mimimum, $(0, 3)$ maximum, $(1, 2)$ minimum
(f) $(1, 8)$ maximum
(g) $(-4, 213)$ maximum, $(3, -130)$ minimum
(h) $(-3, 88)$ maximum, $(5, -168)$ minimum
(i) $(0, 0)$ minimum, $(1, 1)$ neither
(j) $(-2, 65)$ maximum, $(0, 1)$ neither, $(2, -63)$ minimum
(k) $\left(-\frac{1}{3}, -\frac{11}{27}\right)$ minimum, $\left(\frac{1}{2}, \frac{3}{4}\right)$ maximum
(l) $(-1, 0)$ neither

Exercise 19C (page 247)

1 $\left(2\frac{1}{2}, -6\frac{1}{4}\right)$; $k > -6\frac{1}{4}$; $\Delta = 25 + 4k$

2 $k > 1\frac{1}{3}$

3 (a) 2 (b) 3 (c) 4 (d) 0

4 (a) 3; one between $-\sqrt{3}$ and -1, one between -1 and 0, one greater than $\sqrt{3}$.
(b) 2; 1, and one less than $-\sqrt{3}$ (in fact, -2)
(c) 1; greater than $\sqrt{3}$.

5 If $f(x) = x^3 + 4x$, $f'(x) = 3x^2 + 4 > 0$, so y is an increasing function of x for all x.

6 (a) $(-6, 0)$ maximum, $(-2, -32)$ minimum
(c) (i) 2 (ii) 1 (iii) 3 (iv) 1
(d) $-32 < k < 0$; between -8 and -6, between -6 and -2, between -2 and 0

7 (a) $\left(-\frac{1}{2}, -\frac{3}{16}\right)$ minimum, $(0, 0)$ maximum, $(2, -8)$ minimum
(b) $(1 - \sqrt{3}, 0)$, $(0, 0)$, $(1 + \sqrt{3}, 0)$
(c) (i) 2 (ii) 2 (iii) 1
(d) (i) $k < -8$ (ii) $k = -8$
(iii) $-8 < k < -\frac{3}{16}$ and $k > 0$
(iv) $k = -\frac{3}{16}$ and $k = 0$ (v) $-\frac{3}{16} < k < 0$
(e) Roots lie between $-(\sqrt{3} - 1)$ and $-\frac{1}{2}$, between $-\frac{1}{2}$ and 0, between 0 and 2, and between 2 and $1 + \sqrt{3}$.

Exercise 19D (page 251)

1 (a) $(-1, -2)$ maximum, $(1, 2)$ minimum
(b) $(2, 3)$ minimum
(c) $(1, 1)$ maximum
(d) $(1, -3)$ minimum
(e) $\left(2, \frac{1}{4}\right)$ maximum
(f) $\left(-\frac{1}{2}, 3\right)$ minimum
(g) $(4, 3)$ minimum
(h) $\left(-3, -\frac{2}{9}\right)$ minimum, $\left(3, \frac{2}{9}\right)$ maximum
(i) $(-8, 16)$ maximum, $(8, -16)$ minimum

2 (a) $x \geq 2$ (b) $x \leq -1$, $x \geq 1$
(c) $x < 0$, $x > 0$

3 (a) $\left(2, -\frac{3}{8}\right)$ minimum
(b) $\left(4, \frac{1}{256}\right)$ maximum
(c) $(-1, 0)$ maximum, $(1, 4)$ minimum
(d) $(-2, 8)$ minimum, $(2, 8)$ minimum
(e) $(0, 0)$ minimum, $(4, 19.0\ldots)$ maximum

20 Second derivatives

Exercise 20A (page 259)

3 (a) $+, +$ (b) $+, -$ (c) $+, 0$ (d) $-, +$

4 (a) 0 (b) -4 (c) $6x + 10$ (d) $30x^4$

5 (a) $(-1, 0)$, $(0, 0)$, $(1, 0)$ (b) $3x^2 - 1$ (c) $6x$

6 (b) $3x^2 + 1$, $6x$ (c) $x > 0$

7 (a) $x > 0$ (b) $x < 2$
(c) $x > -\frac{1}{3}$ (d) $x > 0$
(e) $x < 0$, $x > 0$ (f) $x > 3$
(g) $x < 0$, $x > 2$ (h) $x < 0$, $x > 0$
(i) $x > \frac{1}{4}$

8 (a) $(2, -2)$ (b) $\left(-\frac{1}{2}, \frac{5}{8}\right)$, $\left(\frac{1}{2}, \frac{5}{8}\right)$
(c) None (d) $(1, 7)$, $(2, 16)$
(e) $(5, -31\,250)$ (f) $(1, 4)$
(g) $(1, 0)$ (h) $(10, 0.0004)$
(i) $\left(3, \frac{4}{3}\sqrt{3}\right)$

9 $(-3, -47)$, $y = 27x + 34$

10 $y = 15x + 243$

11 0, 4, 6; $(1, 15)$; $y = -32x + 128$, $y = 22x - 7$

Exercise 20B (page 263)

1 (a) $(-1, -2)$ minimum, $(1, 2)$ maximum
(b) $(0, 0)$ maximum, $(2, -4)$ minimum
(c) $(0, 1)$ minimum
(d) $(-1, 11)$ maximum, $(2, -16)$ minimum
(e) $(2, 22)$ neither

2 (a) $(-1, -8)$ minimum, $(0, -3)$ maximum, $(2, -35)$ minimum
(b) None
(c) $\left(-\frac{4}{3}, -14\frac{2}{9}\right)$ minimum, $\left(\frac{4}{3}, 14\frac{2}{9}\right)$ maximum
(d) None (e) $(0, 1)$ minimum

21 Applications of differentiation

Exercise 21A (page 268)

1 (a) Gradient of road
(b) Rate of increase of crowd inside the stadium
(c) Rate of change of magnetic force with respect to distance

(d) Acceleration of train
(e) Rate of increase of petrol consumption with respect to speed

2 (a) $\frac{dp}{dh}$, p in millibars, h in metres
(b) $\frac{d\theta}{dt}$, θ in degrees C, t in hours
(c) $\frac{dh}{dt}$, h in metres, t in hours
(d) $\frac{dW}{dt}$, W in kilograms, t in weeks

3 (a) $6t+7$ (b) $1-\frac{1}{2\sqrt{x}}$
(c) $1-\frac{6}{y^3}$ (d) $2t-\frac{1}{2t\sqrt{t}}$
(e) $2t+6$ (f) $12s^5-6s$
(g) 5 (h) $-\frac{2}{r^3}-1$

4 (a) $\frac{dx}{dt}=c$
(b) $\frac{dA}{dt}=kA$; A stands for the amount deposited
(c) $\frac{dx}{dt}=f(\theta)$; x stands for diameter, θ for air temperature

5 (a) (i) 98 metres per minute
(ii) 22 metres per minute
(b) 60 metres per minute
(c) 25 minutes

6 (a) 25 per km (b) 15 per km (c) 20 per km

7 (a) 19 200
(b) (i) 50 per minute (ii) 102.5 per minute
(c) 90 per minute

8 (a) $2\pi r$ (b) $4\pi r^2$
$\frac{dA}{dr}$ is the circumference of the circle,
$\frac{dV}{dr}$ is the surface area of the sphere.

9 $-\frac{2C}{x^3}$

10 $-\frac{1.4k}{V^{2.4}}$

11 (a) $\frac{0.1}{\sqrt{l}}$
(b) It will increase by 0.001 26 seconds

Exercise 21B (page 273)

1 (a) Rate of increase of inflation, positive

2 (a) Both positive, sudden change (drop in S), then $\frac{dS}{dt}$ is negative changing to positive with $\frac{d^2S}{dt^2}$ positive.
(b) Price rose sharply, sudden 'crash', price continued to drop but less quickly and then recovered to give steadier growth.

3 (b) $+, -, -, +$

4 (a) $\frac{dN}{dt}=-kN, k>0$ (c) $+$

5 (a) After 10 hours (b) After 5 hours
(c) After 15 hours, 22.5 mb per hour

6 (a) \$80 a barrel, \$4.50 a barrel per week
(b) \$100 a barrel (c) After 20 weeks

7 (a) 42 m, 32 m s^{-1}, 18 m s^{-2}
(b) 1 m s^{-1}, -1 m s^{-2}
(c) 6 m s^{-1}, $\frac{3}{4}\text{ m s}^{-2}$
(d) 5 s; 20 m
(e) 4 m s^{-1}
(f) $22\frac{1}{8}$ m, 54 m s^{-2}

8 (a) 18 m s^{-1} (b) 4 m s^{-2}

9 (a) 120 s, 1380 m (b) 0.384 m s^{-2}
(c) 1.15 m s^{-2} (d) 80 s, 20.5 m s^{-1}

10 (b) (A) 120 cm s^{-1}, (B) 160 cm s^{-1}
(B), because $v=0$ when $r=3$.

11 (a) 952 m, 62.4 m s^{-1}
(b) -41.0 m s^{-2}, -10 m s^{-2}, -0.328 m s^{-2}
(c) 40 m s^{-1} (d) 40 s

Exercise 21C (page 281)

1 80 km h^{-1}

2 20 m

3 36

4 $4\sqrt{5}$

5 Greatest $V=32\pi$ when $r=4$, least $V=0$ when $r=0$ or $h=0$

6 $x=25$

7 (b) 1800 m^2

8 $0<x<20$, 7.36

9 20 cm

10 (b) $38\,400\text{ cm}^3$ (to 3 significant figures)

11 2420 cm^3 (to 3 significant figures)

Review exercise 6 (page 282)

1 (a) $(-1,-7)$, $(2,20)$; $(\frac{1}{2}, 6\frac{1}{2})$
(b) The graph crosses the x-axis 3 times.
(c) The graph has 3 intersections with the line $y=-5$.
(d) (i) $-7<k<20$ (ii) $k<-7$ and $k>20$

2 $(-1, 5)$, $(0, 10)$, $(2, -22)$
(a) $5 < k < 10$
(b) $-22 < k < 5$ and $k > 10$
$(-0.54, 7.32)$, $(1.22, -8.36)$
3 $+, -, +$
5 $(20 - 4t)$ m s^{-1}, -4 m s^{-2}; for $0 \le t \le 5$
6 50
7 (a) $9\sqrt{2}$ cm (b) $40\frac{1}{2}$ cm^2
8 Maximum; $(1\frac{1}{2}, -\frac{1}{2})$
9 $(\frac{1}{3}, \frac{4}{27})$, $(1, 0)$; $k < -\frac{2}{9}\sqrt{3}$ and $k > \frac{2}{9}\sqrt{3}$
10 $(-2, 4)$, $(2, -28)$; $-28 \le k \le 4$
11 (a) $(-1, 0)$, $(2, -27)$
(b) $x = -1$ maximum, $x = 2$ minimum
(d) $k < -27$ and $k > 0$
12 (a) $P = 2x + 2r + \frac{1}{2}\pi r$, $A = \frac{1}{4}\pi r^2 + rx$
(b) $x = \frac{1}{4}r(4 - \pi)$
13 (a) $1100 - 20x$ (b) $\$x(1100 - 20x)$
(c) $\$(24\,000 - 400x)$
$37.50

Examination questions, (page 284)
1 (a) 10 m s^{-1} (b) 10 (c) 50 m
2 $(\frac{2}{3}, 26\frac{23}{27})$
4 $f_2 \to$ (e), $f_3 \to$ (b), $f_4 \to$ (a)

22 Probability

Exercise 22 (page 295)
1 (a) $\frac{1}{2}$ (b) $\frac{2}{3}$ (c) $\frac{1}{2}$ (d) $\frac{1}{2}$
(e) $\frac{1}{6}$ (f) $\frac{5}{6}$ (g) $\frac{2}{3}$
2 (a) $\frac{1}{2}$ (b) $\frac{3}{13}$ (c) $\frac{5}{13}$ (d) $\frac{5}{26}$ (e) $\frac{9}{13}$
3 (a) $\frac{1}{6}$ (b) $\frac{5}{12}$ (c) $\frac{5}{12}$ (d) $\frac{25}{36}$
(e) $\frac{11}{36}$ (f) $\frac{5}{18}$ (g) $\frac{1}{6}$ (h) $\frac{1}{2}$
4 (1, 2), (1, 3), (1, 4), (1, 5), (1, 6), (2, 1), (2, 3), (2, 4), (2, 5), (2, 6), (3, 1), (3, 2), (3, 4), (3, 5), (3, 6), (4, 1), (4, 2), (4, 3), (4, 5), (4, 6), (5, 1), (5, 2), (5, 3), (5, 4), (5, 6), (6, 1), (6, 2), (6, 3), (6, 4), (6, 5)
(a) $\frac{1}{5}$ (b) $\frac{2}{5}$ (c) $\frac{1}{3}$ (d) $\frac{1}{2}$
6 (a) $\frac{3}{8}$ (b) $\frac{5}{8}$

23 Conditional probability

Exercise 23 (page 305)
1 (a) $\frac{1}{3}$ (b) $\frac{2}{15}$ (c) $\frac{8}{15}$ (d) $\frac{13}{15}$ (e) $\frac{3}{5}$
2 (a) $\frac{11}{221}$ (b) $\frac{10}{17}$ (c) $\frac{7}{17}$ (d) $\frac{77}{102}$
3 (a) 0.27 (b) 0.35 (c) 0.3375
4 (a) $\frac{8}{15}$ (b) $\frac{7}{15}$ (c) $\frac{3}{5}$ (d) $\frac{2}{5}$ (e) $\frac{9}{16}$
(f) Yes (g) No
5 (a) 0.24 (b) 0.42 (c) 0.706
6 (a) $\frac{9}{25}$ (b) $\frac{4}{25}$ (c) $\frac{12}{25}$ (d) $\frac{3}{5}$
7 0.75, 0.8
8 (a) $\frac{2}{5}$ (b) $\frac{4}{15}$ (c) $\frac{1}{8}$
9 $\frac{8}{23}$
10 $\frac{2}{3}$
11 (a) $\frac{1}{5}$ (b) $\frac{1}{3}$

Review exercise 7 (page 307)

1 (a) After first draw:
P(A Red) $= \frac{1}{2}$, P(A Black) $= \frac{1}{2}$
After second draw:
P(A 1Red, 1Black) $= \frac{1}{2} + \frac{1}{6} = \frac{2}{3}$
P(A 2Red) $= \frac{1}{3}$
(b) $\frac{2}{3}$
2 (a) 0.58 (b) 0.6
3 (a) $\frac{1}{2}$ (b) $\frac{5}{11}$
4 (a) 0.2 (b) 0.1
5 (a) $\frac{3}{20}$ (b) $\frac{9}{35}$ (c) $\frac{7}{12}$
6 (b) $\frac{9}{26}$
7 (a) (i) $\frac{1}{5}$ (ii) $\frac{5}{13}$ (iii) $\frac{17}{25}$ (iv) $\frac{1}{2}$
(b) $\frac{21}{25}$
8 (a) $\frac{1}{2}$ (b) (i) $5p$ (ii) $4p$ (c) $\frac{1}{40}$
9 $\frac{1}{4}$; (a) 0.0577 (b) 0.1057 (c) 0.6676
10 (a) $\frac{3}{253}$ (b) $\frac{43}{138}$ (c) $\frac{11}{138}$ (d) $\frac{11}{69}$
11 (a) 0.32 (b) 0.56; 8
12 (a) $\frac{1}{8}$ (b) $\frac{3}{8}$ (c) $\frac{8}{9}$

Examination questions (page 309)
1 (a) $\frac{22}{23}$ (b) $\frac{693}{2300}$
2 (a) $\frac{1}{3}$ (b) $\frac{7}{12}$ (c) $\frac{3}{7}$
3 (a) $\frac{1}{6}$ (b) $\frac{1}{12}$ (c) $\frac{2}{9}$
4 (a) 21, 11, 17
(b) $\frac{1}{8}$ (c) $\frac{21}{32}$ (d) $\frac{315}{1247}$ (e) $\frac{932}{1247}$
5 (a) Reading downwards, $\frac{7}{8}$, $\frac{1}{8}$; $\frac{1}{4}$, $\frac{3}{4}$, $\frac{3}{5}$, $\frac{2}{5}$
(b) $\frac{47}{160}$ (c) $\frac{35}{47}$
6 (a) Reading downwards, 0.6; 0.1, 0.8, 0.2
(b) 0.36 (c) 0.84 (d) $\frac{3}{7}$
7 (a) Reading downwards, $\frac{2}{3}$; $\frac{4}{5}$, $\frac{1}{5}$, $\frac{3}{4}$
(b) $\frac{4}{15}$ (c) $\frac{13}{30}$ (d) $\frac{8}{13}$

24 Integration

Exercise 24A (page 316)

1 (a) $x^4 + k$ (b) $x^6 + k$
(c) $x^2 + k$ (d) $x^3 + x^5 + k$
(e) $x^{10} - x^8 - x + k$ (f) $-x^7 + x^3 + x + k$

2 (a) $3x^3 - 2x^2 - 5x + k$
(b) $4x^3 + 3x^2 + 4x + k$
(c) $7x + k$
(d) $4x^4 - 2x^3 + 5x^2 - 3x + k$
(e) $\frac{1}{2}x^4 + \frac{5}{2}x^2 + k$
(f) $\frac{1}{2}x^2 + \frac{2}{3}x^3 + k$
(g) $\frac{2}{3}x^3 - \frac{3}{2}x^2 - 4x + k$
(h) $x - x^2 - x^3 + k$

3 (a) $y = \frac{1}{5}x^5 + \frac{1}{3}x^3 + x + k$
(b) $y = \frac{7}{2}x^2 - 3x + k$
(c) $y = \frac{1}{6}x^4 + \frac{1}{6}x^3 + \frac{1}{6}x^2 + \frac{1}{6}x + k$
(d) $y = \frac{1}{8}x^4 - \frac{1}{9}x^3 + \frac{1}{2}x^2 - \frac{1}{3}x + k$

4 $4x^2 - 5x$

5 $y = \frac{1}{8}x^4 + \frac{1}{8}x^2 + x - 21$

6 $5x^3 - 3x^2 + 4x - 6$

7 (a) No stationary points, no inflexions
(b) No stationary points, no inflexions
(c) Minimum at $x = 0$, no inflexions
(d) Maximum at $x = 3$, no inflexions
(e) Maximum at $x = -1$, minimum at $x = 2$, inflexion at $x = \frac{1}{2}$
(f) Stationary inflexion at $x = \frac{1}{2}$
(g) No stationary points, inflexion at $x = 1$
(h) Stationary inflexion at $x = 0$, maximum at $x = 3$, inflexion at $x = 2$

8 $y = 4x\sqrt{x} - 7$

9 (a) $-\dfrac{1}{x} + k$ (b) $-\dfrac{1}{x^3} + k$
(c) $-\dfrac{3}{x^2} + k$ (d) $2x^2 + \dfrac{3}{x} + k$

10 (a) $y = \frac{2}{3}x^{\frac{3}{2}} + k$ (b) $y = 12x^{\frac{1}{3}} + k$
(c) $y = \frac{3}{4}x^{\frac{4}{3}} + k$
(d) $y = \frac{4}{3}x\sqrt{x} - 4\sqrt{x} + k$

11 $y = -4x^{-1} + 13$

12 $y = \sqrt{x} - 2$

13 $y = \frac{3}{4}x^{\frac{4}{3}} + 3x^{-2} + \frac{5}{4}$

14 (a) $y = x^3 + 3x^2 + k$
(b) $y = 4x^3 + 2x^2 - 5x + k$
(c) $y = 2x^2 - \dfrac{1}{x} + k$
(d) $y = \frac{2}{3}x\sqrt{x} + 8\sqrt{x} + k$
(e) $y = \frac{1}{2}x^2 + \frac{20}{3}x\sqrt{x} + 25x + k$
(f) $y = x + 10\sqrt{x} + k$

15 (a) $\frac{1}{3}u^3 - \dfrac{1}{u} + k$
(b) $\frac{1}{2}t^6 - \frac{1}{7}t^7 + k$
(c) $p^4 + 4p^3 + 6p^2 + 4p + k$
(d) $-\dfrac{2}{\sqrt{y}} + k$
(e) $\frac{3}{5}z^{\frac{5}{3}} + 2z + 3z^{\frac{1}{3}} + k$
(f) $v^2\left(\frac{1}{2} + \frac{2}{5}\sqrt{v}\right) + k$

16 (a) 118 cm (to 3 s.f.) (b) 27

17 17 months (to the nearest month)

18 192

Exercise 24B (page 323)

1 (a) 7 (b) 84 (c) 4
(d) 4 (e) $\frac{1}{16}$ (f) 2

2 (a) 22 (b) 22 (c) 36
(d) $7\frac{1}{6}$ (e) 210 (f) 0

3 (a) 72 (b) 15 (c) 195
(d) 80 (e) 80 (f) $10\frac{2}{5}$

4 18

5 16

6 (a) 39 (b) $5\frac{1}{3}$ (c) $10\frac{2}{3}$ (d) 10

7 (a) 144 (b) $1\frac{1}{2}$ (c) 20
(d) $6\frac{3}{4}$ (e) 16 (f) 3

8 (a) $1\frac{3}{4}$ (b) 60 (c) $3\frac{1}{3}$

9 7

10 5

11 (a) $22\frac{2}{3}$ (b) $2\frac{3}{8}$

12 $42\frac{7}{8}$

Exercise 24C (page 327)

1 (a) $s = t^3 + 8t + 4$; 28 m, 20 m s^{-1}
(b) 2 m, 6 m s^{-1}, 3 m s^{-2}
(c) 20 m (d) 60 m (e) -6 m s^{-2}
(f) 22 m (g) 1.2 m

2 (a) 9 m s^{-1} (b) 8 m s^{-1}, $26\frac{2}{3}$ m

3 (a) 2 s (b) 8 m (c) 6 m s^{-2}

Exercise 24D (page 334)

1 -4; the graph lies below the x-axis for $0 < x < 2$.

2 (a) $10\frac{2}{3}$ (b) 8 (c) $2\frac{1}{4}$ (d) $1\frac{5}{6}$

3 12

4 $10\frac{2}{3}$

5 32

6 (b) 0 s, $7.2\,\text{m s}^{-2}$ (c) 3 s, $-1.8\,\text{m s}^{-2}$
(d) 6.75 m, 6.4 m (f) 7.1 m

7 $42\frac{2}{3}$

8 36

9 $4\frac{1}{2}$

10 (a) 500 (b) $5\frac{1}{3}$

11 96

25 Geometric sequences

Exercise 25A (page 339)

1 (a) 2; 24, 48 (b) 4; 128, 512
(c) $\frac{1}{2}$; 4, 2 (d) -3; 162, -486
(e) 1.1; 1.4641, 1.610 51
(f) $\frac{1}{x}$; $\frac{1}{x}$, $\frac{1}{x^2}$

2 (a) $2 \times 3^{n-1}$ (b) $10 \times \left(\frac{1}{2}\right)^{n-1}$
(c) $(-2)^{n-1}$ (d) $81 \times \left(\frac{1}{3}\right)^{n-1}$
(e) x^n (f) $p^{2-n}q^{n+1}$
(b), (d), (e) if $|x| < 1$, (f) if $|q| < |p|$

3 (a) 11 (b) 13 (c) 7
(d) 14 (e) 6 (f) 13

4 (a) 3; $1\frac{1}{3}$ (b) 2; $1\frac{1}{2}$ or -2; $1\frac{1}{2}$
(c) $\frac{1}{3}$; 531 441 (d) $\pm\sqrt{2}$; 4

Exercise 25B (page 344)

1 (a) 59 048 (b) $-29\,524$ (c) 1.9922
(d) 0.6641 (e) 12 285 (f) 8.9998

2 (a) 2047 (b) 683 (c) 262 143
(d) $\frac{1023}{512}$ (e) $\frac{14\,762}{19\,683}$ (f) $2 - \left(\frac{1}{2}\right)^n$

3 (a) 93 (b) -10 (c) $31\frac{7}{8}$ (d) 21 844

4 $2^{64} - 1 \approx 1.84 \times 10^{19}$

5 $2 684 354.55

6 $32 289.76

7 0.979 litres

8 $\left(\frac{3}{4}\right)^{n-1} - \frac{1}{3}$

9 (a) $\frac{x(1-x^n)}{1-x}$ (b) $\frac{x(1-(-x)^n)}{1+x}$

Exercise 25C (page 350)

1 (a) 2 (b) $\frac{3}{2}$ (c) $\frac{1}{4}$
(d) $\frac{1}{9}$ (e) $\frac{3}{4}$ (f) $\frac{1}{6}$
(g) 3 (h) $\frac{1}{3}$ (i) $\frac{20}{3}$
(j) 62.5 (k) $\frac{x}{1-x}$ (l) $\frac{1}{1+x^2}$
(m) $\frac{x}{x-1}$ (n) $\frac{x^3}{x+1}$

2 (a) $\frac{4}{11}$ (b) $\frac{41}{333}$ (c) $\frac{5}{9}$ (d) $\frac{157}{333}$
(e) $\frac{1}{7}$ (f) $\frac{2}{7}$ (g) $\frac{5}{7}$ (h) $\frac{6}{7}$

3 $\frac{1}{6}$

4 $-\frac{5}{6}$

5 3

6 19.2

7 (a) $\left(\frac{1}{5}\right)^{i-1}$, $\frac{2\,441\,406}{1\,953\,125}$, $1\frac{1}{4}$
(b) 2^i, 2046, not convergent
(c) 8×2^{-i}, $\frac{1023}{128}$, 8
(d) $\left(-\frac{1}{10}\right)^{i-1}$, $\frac{909\,090\,909}{1\,000\,000\,000}$, $\frac{10}{11}$

8 2 m

9 0.375 m east of O, 1.5 m

10 10 seconds

11 19 m

12 (a) Edge of table (b) 8

26 Exponentials and logarithms

Exercise 26A (page 354)

1 $2^x > 1000$ (a) 10 (b) 20 (c) 40

2 $3^{-x} > 2000$ (a) -7 (b) -14 (c) -15

4 (b) They are reflections of each other in the y-axis.

Exercise 26B (page 356)

1 (a) $8 = 2^3$ (b) $81 = 3^4$
(c) $0.04 = 5^{-2}$ (d) $x = 7^4$
(e) $5 = x^t$ (f) $q = p^r$

2 (a) $3 = \log_2 8$ (b) $6 = \log_3 729$
(c) $-3 = \log_4 \frac{1}{64}$ (d) $8 = \log_a 20$
(e) $9 = \log_h g$ (f) $n = \log_m p$

3 (a) 4 (b) 2 (c) -2
(d) 0 (e) 1 (f) $-\frac{1}{3}$
(g) $\frac{3}{4}$ (h) $\frac{3}{2}$ (i) 7

4 (a) 7 (b) $\frac{1}{64}$ (c) 5
(d) $\frac{1}{10}$ (e) $4\sqrt{2}$ (f) 6
(g) $\frac{1}{256}$ (h) -10 (i) $\frac{1}{3}\sqrt{3}$

Exercise 26C (page 360)

1 (a) $\log_b p + \log_b q + \log_b r$
(b) $\log_b p + 2\log_b q + 3\log_b r$
(c) $2 + \log p + 5\log r$
(d) $\frac{1}{2}(\log_b p - 2\log_b q - \log_b r)$
(e) $\log_b p + \log_b q - 2\log_b r$
(f) $-(\log_b p + \log_b q + \log_b r)$

(g) $\log_b p - \frac{1}{2}\log_b r$
(h) $\log p + \log q + 7\log r - 1$
(i) $\frac{1}{2}(1 + 10\log p - \log q + \log r)$

2 (a) 2 (b) −1 (c) $\log 30\,575$ (d) 0
(e) 3 (f) −3 (g) $\log 8$ (h) 0

3 (a) $r - q$ (b) $2p + q$ (c) $p + \frac{1}{2}r$
(d) $-q$ (e) $p + 2q + r$
(f) $p - q + 2r$ (g) $q - p - r$
(h) $4p + q - 2r$ (i) $p + q - 2r$

5 $c = b^r$, $b = c^s$; $\log_b c \times \log_c b = 1$

6 The hydrogen ion activity of cola is about 1000 times that of beer.

7 (a) The magnitudes differ by 0.477.
(b) The ratio of the amplitudes is 1:3.98.

Exercise 26D (page 365)

1 (a) 1.46 (b) 1.56 (c) 1.14
(d) 1.22 (e) 3.58 (f) 1.71
(g) −2.21 (h) 3 (i) −0.202

2 (a) $x > 1.89$ (b) $x < 1.43$ (c) $x \le -1.68$
(d) $x > 9.97$ (e) $x > 8.54$ (f) $x < -2$
(g) $x \ge -2$ (h) $x \le -5.61$ (i) $x \ge 3.77$

3 (a) 27 (b) 16 (c) 31
(d) 16 (e) 19 (f) 100

4 (a) 74, 1.051×10^3 (b) 149, 1.047×10^{12}
(c) 33, 5.049×10^3 (d) 45, 1.345×10^7

5 (a) 67, 9.550×10^{-4} (b) 71, 8.228×10^{-7}
(c) 30, 9.524×10^{-5}

6 37

7 14

8 28

9 7

10 9.56

11 (a) 0.891 (b) 12 days (c) 19.9 days

12 (a) 1.79 (b) 2.37 (c) 0.486
(d) −7.97 (e) 1.04 (f) 2.32

13 −0.301, −0.477

27 Exponential growth and decay

Exercise 27A (page 370)

1 5324; 400, 440, 484,

2 (a) $\frac{9}{40}$ (b) $\frac{81}{400}, \frac{729}{4000}, \frac{6561}{40\,000}$
(c) $\frac{1}{4} \times \left(\frac{9}{10}\right)^t$

3 2624, 2362

4 \$60 000, \$72 000, \$86 400, \$103 680, \$124 416; \$10 000, \$12 000, \$14 400, \$17 280 \$20 736

5 80 000, 64 000, 51 200; 1200, 1440, 1728; 100, 66.6..., 44.4..., 29.6... ; decreases by one-third each decade

6 $\$\dfrac{60}{1.06} \times 1.06^t$; yes

7 $\$7500 \times 0.8^t$; yes

8 Armensia, Canadia, Declinia

9 1.11 inches, 1.31 inches

10 0.072; the $\log_{10}$ of the growth factor

Exercise 27B (page 376)

1 (a) 800 (b) 141 (c) 336

2 (a) 45.5 °C (b) 13.6 minutes

3 (a) 63 000 (b) 36 200 (c) 19 700

4 (a) 5.83×10^7 (b) 5.65×10^7

5 10 000, 451

6 (a) $\sqrt[12]{2} \approx 1.059$ (b) 262
(c) between 5 and 6; between D and D sharp

7 (a) $y = 2.51 \times 3.98^x$ (b) $y = 10^{12} \times 0.001^x$
(c) $y = 5.01 \times 50.1^x$ (d) $y = 5.01x^2$
(e) $y = \frac{0.316}{x^5}$

8 $p = 39.7 \times 1.022^x$ gives $p = 39.7, 49.4, 61.3, 76.3, 94.8$. The exponential model does not fit so well in this period.

9 The points do not lie in a straight line.

10 Armensia: 185×1.08^t
Canadia: 100×1.20^t
Declinia: 180×0.94^t

Review exercise 8 (page 378)

1 $6\frac{3}{4}$

2 ±2

3 (a) 6 (b) 67 (c) —
(d) 45 (e) 17 (f) −11

4 62

5 The sum of the infinite series is only 80 cm.

6 \$56 007

7 $r = \dfrac{k-1}{k+1}$

9 (a) \$2254.32 (b) 139

10 389 years

11 8760

12 2031

13 (a) $\frac{1}{4}x^4 - x^2 + k$ (b) 2

14 (a) $y = -\frac{1}{2}x + \frac{3}{2}$ (b) $2\frac{29}{48}$

16 (a) $\dfrac{1}{\log a - 2}$ (b) $\sqrt{\dfrac{5a}{2}}$

17 0.774

18 $x > 33.2$

Examination questions (page 380)

1 (a) $\frac{3}{2}\sqrt{x}$ (b) $\frac{2}{5}\sqrt{x^5} + k$

2 (a) 5 (b) 18

3 5.4

4 (a) $s = 25t - \frac{4}{3}t^3 - 29$
(b) $2\frac{1}{2}$ (c) 1.27, 3.55

5 (a) (i) \$11 400, \$11 800 (ii) \$128 000
(b) (i) \$10 700, \$11 449 (ii) \$18 384.59
(c) 7 years

6 (a) 390 hours (b) (ii) 381 hours
(c) 16th week

7 (a) $s = 30t - \frac{1}{2}at^2$ (b) (i) 30 m s^{-1}
(c) (i) $\dfrac{30}{a}$ seconds (ii) 2.25

8 (a) (i) 2420 (ii) 1999
(b) (i) 1 540 000 (ii) 28.0% (iii) 2014
(c) (i) 845 (ii) after 15 years

28 Circular functions

Exercise 28 (page 386)

1 (a) $\frac{1}{4}\pi$ (b) $\frac{1}{4}\pi + n\pi, n \in \mathbb{Z}$
(c) $\frac{1}{4}\pi < x < \frac{5}{4}\pi$

2 (a) 2π (b) $0, \frac{1}{2}\pi, 2\pi$

3 2π

4 (a) $3\sqrt{3}$ (b) 1.445 468

5 (a) 2.475 353 2
(b) They are at right angles to each other.

6 (a) π (b) $0 \le y \le 1$

7 (a) $\mathbb{R}, -1 \le y \le 1$
(b) $2n\pi \le x \le (2n+1)\pi$ for each $n \in \mathbb{Z}$, $0 \le y \le 1$

8 (a) 0.6 m (b) 41.9 m

9 2.09 seconds

10 2000π

11 $\theta = 67 \sin \frac{1}{12}\pi t$; 47°

12 $g = 3 + 2\cos \frac{2}{15}\pi t$

13 $y = 500 + 200 \sin \frac{1}{3}x$

29 Composite and inverse functions

Exercise 29A (page 394)

1 (a) 121 (b) 4 (c) 676
(d) 17 (e) 8 (f) 152

2 (a) 1 (b) 4 (c) $\frac{1}{2}$
(d) 1 (e) 4 (f) $6\frac{1}{3}$

3 (a) 0 (b) 21
(c) $-3\frac{3}{4}$ (d) $x^2 - 4$

4 (a) 27 (b) 8
(c) $3\frac{3}{8}$ (d) $(\cos x° + 2)^3$

5 (a) 16 (b) 4
(c) 81 (d) $(2\sqrt{x} - 10)^2$

6 (a) $q \circ p$, where $p : x \mapsto 4x$, $q : x \mapsto x + 9$
(b) $p \circ q$ with p, q as in (a)
(c) $r \circ q \circ p$ with $p : x \mapsto x^2$, $q : x \mapsto 2x$, $r : x \mapsto x - 5$
(d) $q \circ p \circ r$, with p, q, r as in (c)

7 (a) $\mathbb{R}, f(x) \ge 0$ (b) $\mathbb{R}, -1 \le f(x) \le 1$
(c) $x \ge 3, f(x) \ge 0$ (d) $\mathbb{R}, f(x) > 0$
(e) $x > 0, f(x) > 0$ (f) $\mathbb{R}, f(x) \le 4$
(g) $0 \le x \le 4, 0 \le f(x) \le 2$
(h) $\mathbb{R}, f(x) \ge 6$ (i) $x > 0, \mathbb{R}$

8 (a) 4 (b) −14 (c) −9 (d) 33
(e) 23 (f) −17 (g) 16 (h) 0

9 (a) 49 (b) 59 (c) 35
(d) $\frac{1}{16}$ (e) 9 (f) 899

10 (a) 7 (b) −19 (c) 1 (d) $\frac{1}{2}$
(e) $\frac{1}{2}$ (f) −1 (g) $3\frac{2}{3}$ (h) 2

11 (a) $x \mapsto 2x^2 + 5$ (b) $x \mapsto (2x + 5)^2$
(c) $x \mapsto \dfrac{2}{x} + 5$ (d) $x \mapsto \dfrac{1}{2x + 5}$
(e) $x \mapsto 4x + 15$ (f) $x \mapsto x$
(g) $x \mapsto \left(\dfrac{2}{x} + 5\right)^2$ (h) $x \mapsto \dfrac{1}{(2x + 5)^2}$

12 (a) $x \mapsto \sin x° - 3$ (b) $x \mapsto \sin(x - 3)°$
(c) $x \mapsto \sin(x^3 - 3)°$ (d) $x \mapsto \sin(x^3)°$
(e) $x \mapsto x - 9$ (f) $x \mapsto (\sin x°)^3$

13 (a) $f \circ h$ (b) $f \circ g$ (c) $h \circ h$ (d) $h \circ f$

14 (a) $x \ge 0, g \circ f(x) \ge -5$
(b) $x \ge -3, g \circ f(x) \ge 0$
(c) $x \ne 2, g \circ f(x) \ne 0$
(d) $\mathbb{R}, g \circ f(x) \ge 0$

15 (a) $-2\frac{2}{3}$ or 4 (b) 7 (c) 1

Exercise 29B (page 400)

1 (a) $x \mapsto x - 4$ (b) $x \mapsto x + 5$
(c) $x \mapsto \frac{1}{2}x$ (d) $x \mapsto 4x$
(e) $x \mapsto \sqrt[3]{x}$ (f) $x \mapsto x^5$

2 (a) 10 (b) 7 (c) 3
(d) 5 (e) −4

3 (a) 4 (b) 20 (c) $\frac{7}{5}$
(d) 15 (e) −6

4 (a) 8 (b) $\frac{1}{8}$ (c) 512
(d) −27 (e) 5

5 a, d, f, g, k

6 a, c, e, f, g, h, j

7 (a) 0 (b) −1 (c) $\frac{2}{3}$
(d) 4 (e) −5 (f) −1

8 (a) $x \mapsto \frac{1}{3}(x+1)$ (b) $x \mapsto 2(x-4)$
(c) $x \mapsto \sqrt[3]{x-5}$ (d) $x \mapsto (x+3)^2, x > -3$
(e) $x \mapsto \frac{1}{5}(2x+3)$ (f) $x \mapsto 1+\sqrt{x-6}, x \geq 6$

9 (a) $y \mapsto \frac{1}{6}(y-5)$ (b) $y \mapsto 5y-4$
(c) $y \mapsto \frac{1}{2}(4-y)$ (d) $y \mapsto \frac{1}{2}(3y-7)$
(e) $y \mapsto \sqrt[3]{\frac{1}{2}(y-5)}$ (f) $y \mapsto \dfrac{1}{y-4}, y \neq 4$
(g) $y \mapsto \dfrac{5}{y}+1, y \neq 0$

10 (a) $x \mapsto \frac{1}{4}x$ (b) $x \mapsto x-3$
(c) $x \mapsto x^2, x \geq 0$ (d) $x \mapsto \frac{1}{2}(x-1)$
(e) $x \mapsto \sqrt{x}+2, x \geq 0$ (f) $x \mapsto \frac{1}{3}(1-x)$
(g) $x \mapsto \dfrac{3}{x}, x \neq 0$ (h) $x \mapsto 7-x$
(i) $x \mapsto \log_3 x, x \in \mathbb{R}^+$ (j) $x \mapsto 5^x$

12 (a) $y \mapsto \dfrac{2y}{y-1}, y \neq 1$
(b) $y \mapsto \dfrac{4y+1}{y-2}, y \neq 2$
(c) $y \mapsto \dfrac{5y+2}{y-1}, y \neq 1$
(d) $y \mapsto \dfrac{3y-11}{4y-3}, y \neq \frac{3}{4}$

13 $a = \frac{1}{8}, b = \frac{3}{8}$

14 6

30 Transforming graphs

Exercise 30A (page 407)

1 (a) 4 in the y-direction
(b) −3 in the x-direction
(c) −2 in the y-direction
(d) 3 in the x-direction
(e) −2 in the x-direction
(f) 1 in the x-direction
(g) −3 in the x-direction
(h) −2 in the x-direction
(i) 2 in the y-direction
(j) π in the x-direction
(k) π in the x-direction
(l) 1 in the x-direction

2 (b) (11, 3) (c) $y = \sqrt{x-2}$

3 (a) $y = x^2 - 3x$ (b) $y = x^2 + 3x + 4$
(c) $y = x^2 - 3x + 4$ (d) $y = x^2 - 3x + 4$

4 (a) $y = x^2 - x + 1$ (b) $y = x^2 - 5x + 2$
(c) $y = x^2 - x - 4$

5 (a) 3 units in the x-direction
(b) 3 units in the x-direction then −3 units in the y-direction

6 If $y = x^2$ is translated by −4 units in the x-direction and −2 units in the y-direction, in either order, the equation becomes $y = x^2 + 8x + 14$.

7 $y = \dfrac{1}{x} - 2$, $y = \dfrac{1}{x+1} - 2$;
$(-\frac{1}{2}, 0)$, $(0, -1)$; $(\frac{1}{2}, 2)$, $(1, 1)$

8 $\cos\left(x - \frac{1}{2}\pi\right) = \sin x$

Exercise 30B (page 414)

The answers to Question 1 are not all unique.

1 (a) Stretch by 2 in the y-direction
(b) Reflection in the y-axis
(c) Stretch by 3 in the y-direction
(d) Reflection in the x-axis
(e) Stretch by 2 in the y-direction
(f) Reflection in the y-axis
(g) Stretch by $\frac{1}{2}$ in the x-direction
(h) Stretch by 2 in the y-direction
(i) Reflection in the y-axis
(j) Reflection in the y-axis
(k) Reflection in the y-axis
(l) Stretch by $-\frac{1}{2}$ in the y-direction
(m) Reflection in the y-axis
(n) Stretch by $\frac{1}{3}$ in the x-direction

2 (b) (8, 4) (c) $y = \sqrt{2x}$

3 $y = (x+1)^2$

4 9

5 $y = 4x^2$, $y = \frac{4}{9}x^2$
(a) Use a factor of $\frac{3}{2}\sqrt{2}$.
(b) Use a factor of $\frac{2}{9}$.

6 (a) y-axis (b) x-axis

7 y-axis

8 Replacing x by $\dfrac{x}{c}$ in the equation of a graph produces a stretch of factor c in the x-direction.

9 (a) odd; $3x^2 + 3$, even
(b) even; $14x$, odd
(c) neither; $2x - 4$, neither

(d) neither; $5x^4 + 9x^2$, even

The derivative of an even function is odd, and the derivative of an odd function is even.

The integral of an odd function is even, but the integral of an even function need not be either even or odd.

10 $\sin(x - \pi) = -\sin x$

12 (a) Translation of 3 in the positive x-direction, or a stretch in the y-direction with factor $\frac{1}{8}$
(b) Reflection in the y-axis.
(c) Reflection in the y-axis and a stretch in the x-direction of factor $\frac{1}{2}$, in either order.
(d) Translation of 4 in the y-direction.

13 A stretch of factor $\frac{1}{2}$ in the y-direction

14 A stretch of factor 9 in the y-direction

15 (a) From b^x to a^x is a stretch of factor 2 in the x-direction.
(b) From b^x to a^x is a stretch of factor 3 in the x-direction.
(c) They are reflections of each other in the y-axis.

16 (a) $\frac{1}{3}$ (b) $\log 3$

Exercise 30C (page 420)

1 $y = (x - 1)^3 + 2$

2 Stretch factor 2 in the y-direction and translation of $-\frac{1}{6}\pi$ in the x-direction, in either order.

3 One possible answer is 'Translation of $-\frac{1}{2}\pi$ in the x-direction followed by a stretch with factor $\frac{1}{3}$ in the x-direction.
Order matters:
$y = \cos\left(3\left(x + \frac{1}{2}\pi\right)\right) = \cos\left(3x + \frac{3}{2}\pi\right)$

4 (a) $y = \frac{1}{4}x^3$ (b) $y = \dfrac{4}{x}$
(c) $y = x$ (d) $y = 2^{\frac{1}{2}x+1}$

5 $y = -2x + 8$

6 The curve remains the same.

7 (a) Translation by 2, in negative x-direction
Stretch, y-direction, factor 5
Translation by 7, in negative y-direction
(c) Translation by 7, in y-direction
Stretch, y-direction, factor $\frac{1}{5}$
Translation by 2, in x-direction
(d) $10x + 20$
(e) Translation by 2, in negative x-direction
Stretch, y-direction, factor 5

8 (a) From graph of $i = \sin t$: t-stretch factor $\dfrac{1}{100\pi}$, i-stretch factor 5, in either order
(b) From graph of $S = \cos t$: t-stretch factor 4, S-stretch factor 3 in either order, then S-translation of 7

Review exercise 9 (page 421)

1 (b) (i) $y = \cos x$ (ii) $y = -\sin x$
(iii) $y = -\sin x$ (iv) $y = -\cos x$

2 (a) Translate by α in the negative x-direction, stretch by 3 in the y-direction and by $\frac{1}{2}$ in the x-direction; 4 roots
(b) $2n$ roots (c) $2|n|$ (or $-2n$) roots

3 (a) $y = 12x^2 + 48x + 20$
(b) $y = 3x^2 + 12x + 5$
$c = 3, d = -7$

4 $1 \pm \sqrt{3}$

5 (a) $x \mapsto \frac{1}{4}(x - 5)$ (b) $x \mapsto \frac{1}{2}(3 - x)$
(c) $x \mapsto -\frac{1}{8}(7 + x)$ (d) $x \mapsto -8x - 7$
(e) $x \mapsto -\frac{1}{8}(7 + x)$

6 (a) x (b) $\dfrac{x+5}{2x-1}$ (c) x
(d) x (e) $\dfrac{x+5}{2x-1}$

7 -1

8 (a) (b)

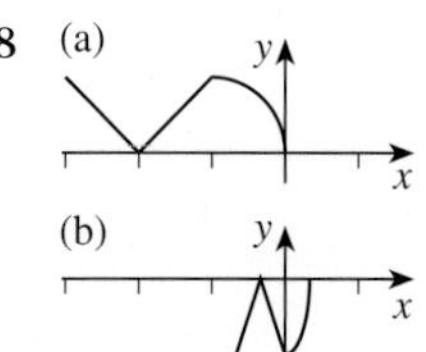

9 Translation by 1, in negative x-direction
Stretch, y-direction, factor 2

10 (a) $\sqrt{\frac{1}{3}(x + 4)}$ (b) $3x^2 + 24x + 44$

11 $f^{-1}(x) = \sqrt{x - 1}, x \geq 1$;
$g \circ f(x) = x^2 - 2, g \circ f(x) \geq -2$

Examination questions (page 422)

1 (a) 2 (b) $\dfrac{1}{x} + 3$ (c) $\mathbb{R}, x \neq 0$

2 (a) (i)

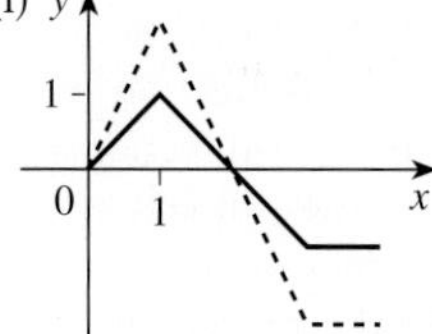

(ii)

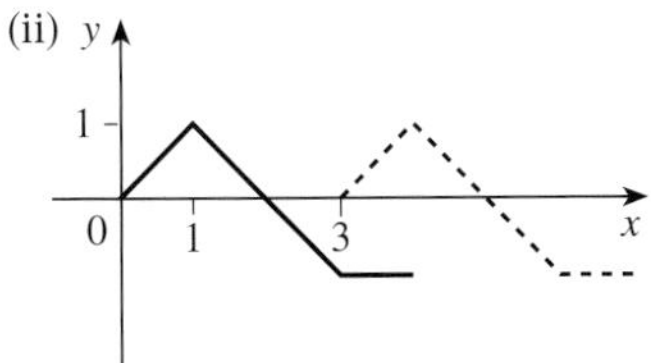

(b) (3, 2)

3 (a) $\frac{1}{2}(x-1)$ (b) 23 (c) $6x^2-7$

5 (a) $\frac{8}{x}$ (b) (i) $\frac{8}{x^2}$ (ii) 2

6 (a) 24 cm (b) 38 cm (c) $\frac{3}{4}\pi$ s (d) π s
(e) $a=14, b=24$ (f) $h=24+14\sin 2t$

31 Extending differentiation and integration

Exercise 31A (page 425)

1 (a) $-9(1-3x)^2$ (b) $2(x+3)$
(c) $4(2x-3)$ (d) $3a(ax+b)^2$
(e) $-3a(b-ax)^2$ (f) $-5(1-x)^4$
(g) $8(2x-3)^3$ (h) $-8(3-2x)^3$

2 $an(ax+b)^{n-1}$

3 (a) $10(x+3)^9$ (b) $10(2x-1)^4$
(c) $-28(1-4x)^6$ (d) $15(3x-2)^4$
(e) $-12(4-2x)^5$ (f) $72(2+3x)^5$
(g) $10(2x+5)^4$ (h) $18(2x-3)^8$

Exercise 31B (page 427)

1 (a) $20(4x+5)^4$ (b) $16(2x-7)^7$
(c) $-6(2-x)^5$ (d) $2\left(\frac{1}{2}x+4\right)^3$

2 (a) $\frac{-3}{(3x+5)^2}$ (b) $\frac{2}{(4-x)^3}$
(c) $\frac{-6}{(2x+1)^4}$ (d) $\frac{-64}{(4x-1)^5}$

3 (a) $\frac{1}{\sqrt{2x+3}}$ (b) $\frac{2}{\sqrt[3]{(6x-1)^2}}$
(c) $\frac{-2}{(4x+7)\sqrt{4x+7}}$ (d) $-10(3x-2)^{-\frac{5}{3}}$

4 60

5 (−6, 125)

6 $y=-\frac{3}{4}x-\frac{5}{4}$

7 $y=-3x+48$

8 $a=-5, b=-2$ or $a=5, b=2$

9 $(4, 8\frac{2}{3})$, maximum

Exercise 31C (page 431)

1 (a) $\frac{1}{14}(2x+1)^7+k$ (b) $\frac{1}{15}(3x-5)^5+k$
(c) $-\frac{1}{28}(1-7x)^4+k$ (d) $\frac{2}{11}\left(\frac{1}{2}x+1\right)^{11}+k$

2 (a) $\frac{-1}{10(5x+2)^2}+k$ (b) $\frac{2}{3(1-3x)}+k$
(c) $\frac{-1}{4(x+1)^4}+k$ (d) $\frac{-1}{8(4x+1)^3}+k$

3 (a) $\frac{1}{15}(10x+1)^{\frac{3}{2}}+k$ (b) $\sqrt{2x-1}+k$
(c) $\frac{6}{5}\left(\frac{1}{2}x+2\right)^{\frac{5}{3}}+k$ (d) $\frac{16}{9}(2+6x)^{\frac{3}{4}}+k$

4 (a) 820 (b) $8\frac{1}{6}$ (c) $\frac{2}{15}$ (d) $\frac{16}{225}$

5 (a) $24\frac{3}{10}$ (b) $4\frac{1}{2}$ (c) $\frac{2}{3}$ (d) 28

6 2.25

7 9.1125

32 Differentiating exponentials and logarithms

Exercise 32A (page 438)

1 (a) $3e^{3x}$ (b) $-e^{-x}$ (c) $6e^{2x}$
(d) $16e^{-4x}$ (e) $3e^{3x+4}$ (f) $-2e^{3-2x}$
(g) $-e^{1-x}$ (h) $12e^{3+4x}$

2 (a) $3e^2$ (b) $-2e$ (c) −1 (d) −2

3 (a) $ey=x+2$ (b) $y=3x-1$
(c) $y=(4+4e^4)x-(4+6e^4)$

4 (1, 0), maximum

5 (a) $\frac{1}{3}e^{3x}+k$ (b) $-e^{-x}+k$
(c) $\frac{3}{2}e^{2x}+k$ (d) $e^{-4x}+k$
(e) $\frac{1}{3}e^{3x+4}+k$ (f) $-\frac{1}{2}e^{3-2x}+k$
(g) $-e^{1-x}+k$ (h) $\frac{3}{4}e^{3+4x}+k$

6 (a) $\frac{1}{2}(e^4-e^2)$ (b) $e-\frac{1}{e}$
(c) e^5-e (d) $e^{10}-e^8$

7 An overestimate

Exercise 32B (page 442)

1 (a) $e^{2.30x}$ (b) $e^{-2.30x}$
(c) $e^{0.916x}$ (d) $e^{-0.916x}$

2 (a) $3.6e^{0.0953t}$ (b) $0.342e^{1.74t}$
(c) $7.13e^{-0.658t}$ (d) $0.161e^{-4.06t}$

3 (a) 100×0.0498^t (b) 2.83×4.31^t
(c) 0.326×0.876^t (d) 0.507×1.01^t

4 (a) $y=1.49e^{0.6x}=1.49\times 1.82^x$
(b) $y=1.63\times 10^5e^{-3x}=1.63\times 10^5\times 20.1^{-x}$
(c) $y=2.01e^{1.7x}=2.01\times 5.47^x$
(d) $y=2.01x^2$
(e) $y=\frac{0.607}{x^5}$

6 $\ln a = 2.302\,585... \times \log_{10} a$ or
$\log_{10} a = 0.434\,294... \times \ln a$

8 $V=e^{-0.0198t}$

9 (a) 0.0999
(b) (i) 49.9 mg per minute
(ii) 25.0 mg per minute

10 (a) 50 m s^{-1}
(c) (i) 1.35 m s^{-2} (ii) 1 m s^{-2}
(d) 2750 m

11 (a) (i) about 7 per week (ii) 60 per week
(b) $2.26e^{0.3t}$ (c) 15 per week

Exercise 32C (page 446)

1 (a) $\frac{1}{x}$ (b) $\frac{2}{2x-1}$ (c) $\frac{-2}{1-2x}$
(d) $\frac{2}{x}$ (e) $\frac{b}{a+bx}$ (f) $-\frac{1}{x}$
(g) $-\frac{3}{3x+1}$ (h) $\frac{2}{2x+1}-\frac{3}{3x-1}$
(i) $-\frac{6}{x}$ (j) $\frac{1}{x}+\frac{1}{x+1}$
(k) $\frac{2}{x}+\frac{1}{x-1}$ (l) $\frac{1}{x-1}+\frac{1}{x+2}$

2 (a) $y=2x-\ln 2-1$ (b) $y=2x-1$
(c) $y=x$ (d) $ey=x+e\ln 3$

3 (a) (1, 1), minimum
(b) $\left(1, \frac{1}{2}-\ln 2\right)$, minimum
(c) (1, 1), minimum
(d) (1, 1), minimum

5 $2y=2-x$

6 $x>6$, $\frac{1}{x-2}+\frac{1}{x-6}$
(i) $x>6$ (ii) None

7 (a) $2<x<6$, $\frac{1}{x-2}-\frac{1}{6-x}$
(i) $2<x<4$ (ii) $4<x<6$
(b) There are no points in the domain.

Exercise 32D (page 448)

1 (a) $y=\frac{1}{2}\ln x+k, \quad x>0$
(b) $y=\ln(x-1)+k, \quad x>1$
(c) $y=-\ln(1-x)+k, \quad x<1$
(d) $y=\frac{1}{4}\ln(4x+3)+k, \quad x>-\frac{3}{4}$
(e) $y=-2\ln(1-2x)+k, \quad x<\frac{1}{2}$
(f) $y=2\ln(1+2x)+k, \quad x>-\frac{1}{2}$
(g) $y=-2\ln(-1-2x)+k, \quad x<-\frac{1}{2}$
(h) $y=2\ln(2x-1)+k, \quad x>\frac{1}{2}$

2 (a) ln 2 (b) ln 2 (c) ln 2 (d) ln 2

3 (a) ln 2 (b) $\frac{1}{2}\ln 3$ (c) $\frac{2}{3}\ln\frac{13}{7}$
(d) $\ln\frac{5e-7}{4e-7}$ (e) ln 2 (f) $8+\ln 5$

4 $2\ln\frac{3}{2}$; the trapezium formed by the chord gives $\frac{5}{6}=0.833...$; exact answer $2\ln\frac{3}{2}=0.810....$

5 $\frac{1509}{1976}=0.763...$, overestimate, $2\ln\frac{19}{13}=0.758....$

6 $y=\frac{3}{2}\ln\left(\frac{1}{3}(2x+1)\right)$

7 $y=2\ln(4x-3)+2$

Review exercise 10 (page 449)

1 4

2 (a) (i) 1.2 °C per min (ii) 0.982 °C per min
(b) (i) 1.12 °C per min (ii) 0.56 °C per min

3 (b) 0.116 (c) about $\frac{3}{5}Q$ ml

4 $y=20x+11$

5 (b) $25\frac{5}{6}$

6 (a) $2-e^{-a}=a$ (b) $\int_0^a (2-e^{-x}-x)\,dx$

7 (a) $e^{-2a}-3a=0$ (d) $\frac{1}{2}-\frac{3}{2}a^2-\frac{1}{2}e^{-2a}$

Examination questions (page 450)

1 9

2 (a) 6 (c) 1.05

3 $-\frac{1}{2}e^{-2x}-\ln(1-x)+4\frac{1}{2}$

4 (a) $4+5e^{-t}$ (b) -5 m s^{-2}

5 (a) (i) 100 m s^{-1} (ii) 56.8 m s^{-1}
(b) $\int_0^4 50(1-e^{-05t})\,dt$ (c) 286 m
(e) 8.11 m s^{-2} (f) 199 m

6 (a) x (b) xy (c) $2(x+y)$

7 (c) 0.514 (d) 2.72

8 (a) (i) $-2e^{-2x}$ (ii) $f'(x)<0$ for all x
(b) (i) $1+e$ (ii) $-2e$
(c) $y=1-2ex$
(d) (iv) $\frac{1}{4}e-\frac{1}{2}$

9 (b) (i) (0, 1) (iii) 0.787
(c) (i) $-ke^{-kx}$ (ii) 0.223 (iii) -0.179

33 Probability distributions

Exercise 33A (page 456)

1

x	0	1	2	3	4
$P(X=x)$	$\frac{1}{16}$	$\frac{4}{16}$	$\frac{6}{16}$	$\frac{4}{16}$	$\frac{1}{16}$

2

d	0	1	2	3	4	5
$P(D=d)$	$\frac{6}{36}$	$\frac{10}{36}$	$\frac{8}{36}$	$\frac{6}{36}$	$\frac{4}{36}$	$\frac{2}{36}$

3

x	1	2	3	6	10
$P(X=x)$	$\frac{1}{6}$	$\frac{2}{6}$	$\frac{1}{6}$	$\frac{1}{6}$	$\frac{1}{6}$

4

h	1	2	3	4	5	6
$P(H=h)$	$\frac{23}{36}$	$\frac{7}{36}$	$\frac{3}{36}$	$\frac{1}{36}$	$\frac{1}{36}$	$\frac{1}{36}$

5

m	1	2	3	4	6
$P(M=m)$	$\frac{1}{16}$	$\frac{2}{16}$	$\frac{2}{16}$	$\frac{3}{16}$	$\frac{2}{16}$

	8	9	12	16
	$\frac{2}{16}$	$\frac{1}{16}$	$\frac{2}{16}$	$\frac{1}{16}$

6

Number	0	1	2
Probability	$\frac{5}{12}$	$\frac{1}{2}$	$\frac{1}{12}$

7

c	1	2	3	4
$P(C=c)$	$\frac{1}{13}$	$\frac{16}{221}$	$\frac{376}{5525}$	$\frac{4324}{5525}$

Exercise 33B (page 458)

1 $\frac{1}{20}$

2 0.3

3 0.15

4 $\frac{1}{8}$

5

x	1	2	3	4	5	6
$P(X=x)$	$\frac{1}{4}$	$\frac{1}{12}$	$\frac{1}{4}$	$\frac{1}{12}$	$\frac{1}{4}$	$\frac{1}{12}$

6 $\frac{1}{21}$

7 $\frac{20}{49}$

8 0.2

Exercise 33C (page 459)

1 (a) 130 (b) 40 (c) 120 (d) 160 (e) 360

2 (a) 105 (b) 105 (c) 245

3 12, 31, 34, 18, 5, 0 (0 is better than 1 because it makes the total 100)

4 0.468, 103

Exercise 33D (page 462)

1 (a) $1\frac{7}{8}$ (b) 0.05

2 4

3 $5\frac{1}{9}$

4 (a) $\frac{7}{3}$

(b)

y	2	3	4	5	6
$P(Y=y)$	$\frac{1}{36}$	$\frac{1}{9}$	$\frac{5}{18}$	$\frac{1}{3}$	$\frac{1}{4}$

$\frac{14}{3}$

5 $E(A) = £95\,000$, $E(B) = £115\,000$; choose B.

6 $a = b = 0.15$

34 The binomial distribution

Exercise 34 (page 474)

1 (a) 0.0819 (b) 0.0154 (c) 0.0001 (d) 1.2

2 (a) 0.2561 (b) 0.2048 (c) 0.0005 (d) $\frac{14}{3}$

3 (a) 0.2119 (b) 0.4728 (c) 0.0498 (d) $\frac{81}{20}$

4 (a) 0.0017 (b) 6

5 (a) 0.2461 (b) 0.4102 (c) 0.0195 (d) 0.9102

6 (a) 0.0781 (b) 0.0176

7 0.1494

8 0.3102

9 (a) 0.6496
(b) The students are not chosen independently.

10 0.0545; no (the outcomes are still green and not-green).

11 0.1143; breakages are not independent of each other (if one egg in a box is broken, it is more likely that others will be).

12 0.0652; for example, P(hurricane) is constant for each month, it is clear when there is a hurricane as opposed to a very brisk wind. In practice, hurricanes tend to appear in summer months.

35 The normal distribution

The answers might change in the fourth figure, depending on whether you use a calculator or tables.

Exercise 35A (page 486)

1 (a) 0.8907 (b) 0.9933 (c) 0.5636
(d) 0.1075 (e) 0.0087 (f) 0.2776
(g) 0.9664 (h) 0.0197 (i) 0.5279
(j) 0.0336 (k) 0.0029 (l) 0.4168

2 (a) 0.0366 (b) 0.1203 (c) 0.3405
(d) 0.4394 (e) 0.9557 (f) 0.7816
(g) 0.8561 (h) 0.2088 (i) 0.0320
(j) 0.1186 (k) 0.4472 (l) 0.9500

3 (a) 0.4399 (b) 1.1750 (c) 2.0537
(d) 1.0364 (e) 0.2275 (f) 1.1750
(g) 2.3263 (h) 0.7722 (i) −2.326
(j) −1.8808 (k) −1.0365 (l) 0

Exercise 35B (page 489)

1 (a) 0.9332 (b) 0.0062
(c) 0.7734 (d) 0.0401

2 (a) 0.9522 (b) 0.0098
(c) 0.7475 (d) 0.0038

3 (a) 0.1359 (b) 0.0606 (c) 0.7333
(d) 0.7704 (e) 0.8664

4 0.0668

5 (a) 0.1587 (b) 0.0228

6 (a) 54.27 (b) 40.31 (c) 52.22 (d) 41.80

7 (a) 17.68 (b) 14.65 (c) 12.44
(d) 14.44 (e) 3.29

8 (a) 41.6 (b) 29.9 (c) 37.4 (d) 31.7

9 7.78

10 65.0

11 41.5, 8.50

12 9.51, 0.298

Exercise 35C (page 491)

1 (a) 0.0371 (b) 0.0062 (c) 0.8209

2 (a) 0.2094 (b) 0.0086 (c) 0.1788
(d) 0.6405 105, 4, 89, 320

3 (a) 13 (b) 84 (c) 121

4 (a) 0.0048 (b) 0.1943 (c) 80, 100

5 1972

6 (a) 0.614 (b) 20.9, 16.3 (c) 17

7 336 ml

8 0.041 kg

9 47 h^2

10 49.1, 13.4

Review exercise 11 (page 493)

1 (a) 2.56 (b) 122.9

2 (a) 0.8704

(b)

x	1	2	3	4
$P(X = x)$	0.4	0.24	0.144	0.216

3

Number	0	1	2	3
Probability	$\frac{248}{1105}$	$\frac{496}{1105}$	$\frac{304}{1105}$	$\frac{57}{1105}$

4 (a)

x	0	1	2	3	4	6
$P(X = x)$	$\frac{1}{4}$	$\frac{1}{3}$	$\frac{1}{9}$	$\frac{1}{6}$	$\frac{1}{9}$	$\frac{1}{36}$

(b) 120

5 0.420

6 (a) 0.337 (b) 0.135

7 0.0912

8 0.3674

9 0.9568

10 0.5251

11 (a) 20.2 (b) 81.0 g

12 6.82; 0.444

13 10.3

14 (b) 0.069

15 (a) 0.488 (b) 281, 5.00

16 (a) $\frac{1}{18}$ (b) $\frac{17}{36}$ (c) $\frac{11}{17}$

17 $\frac{1}{8}$

Examination questions (page 495)

1 (a) (i) 0.345 (ii) 0.115 (iii) 0.540
(b) 0.119 (c) 737

2 (a) 15.9 (b) 227 cm

3 (a) 0.773 (b) 160.6

36 Relations between trigonometric functions

Exercise 36A (page 498)

1 (a) (i) 11 (ii) $\frac{5}{14}\sqrt{3}, \frac{11}{14}, \frac{5}{11}\sqrt{3}$
(b) (i) $17\sqrt{5}$ (ii) $\frac{22}{85}\sqrt{5}, \frac{31}{85}\sqrt{5}, \frac{22}{31}$
(c) (i) $12\sqrt{2}$ (ii) $\frac{1}{3}, \frac{2}{3}\sqrt{2}, \frac{1}{4}\sqrt{2}$

2 (a) $\cos^2 x$ (b) $\tan^2 x$ (c) $\tan^2 x$

3 (a) $-\frac{11}{14}$ (b) $\frac{20}{29}$ (c) $\pm\frac{1}{2}\sqrt{3}$

Exercise 36B (page 501)

1 $-\frac{1}{3}\sqrt{5}, -\frac{4}{9}\sqrt{5}, \frac{1}{9}, -4\sqrt{5}$

2 $\frac{1}{8}, \pm\frac{1}{4}\sqrt{14}$

4 $\pm\frac{5}{6}, \pm\frac{1}{6}\sqrt{11}$

6 $\frac{2}{3}, -\frac{3}{2}$

7 $\pm\sqrt{2} - 1, \sqrt{2} - 1$

37 Trigonometric equations

Exercise 37A (page 504)

1 (a) 2π (b) 2π (c) 2π
(d) 2π (e) π (f) $\frac{2}{3}\pi$
(g) 4π (h) $\frac{2}{3}\pi$ (i) π

Exercise 37B (page 507)

3 Reflection in $x = \frac{1}{4}\pi$

Exercise 37C (page 513)

1 (a) 0.63, 5.66 (b) 0.12, 3.02
(c) 1.33, 4.47

2 (a) 147.1, 212.9 (b) 237.1, 302.9
(c) 162.3, 342.3

3 (a) −2.34, −1.85, −0.24, 0.24, 1.85, 2.34
(b) −1.35, −0.22, 1.79, 2.92
(c) −3.02, −2.39, −1.76, −1.13, −0.51, 0.12, 0.75, 1.38, 2.01, 2.64

4 (a) ±16.1, ±103.9, ±136.1
(b) −125.8, −35.8, 54.2, 144.2
(c) −176.2, −123.8, −56.2, −3.8, 63.8, 116.2

5 (a) −2.46, 2.46 (b) −2.06, 2.65
(c) −1.01 (d) 0.31, 2.63
(e) −0.72, 1.12 (f) −2.26, 0.88

6 (a) 15, 75, 195, 255
(b) 90, 180, 270, 360
(c) 10, 110, 130, 230, 250, 350
(d) 80, 200, 320
(e) 180
(f) none

7 (a) 0.986
(b) $A = 12$, $B = 6$, 6 hours 7 minutes
(c) Days 202, 345

8 (a) 0.126
(b) (i) $N - C$
(ii) $N + C$, after 25 weeks

Exercise 37D (page 515)

1 60, 120

2 (a) 30, 150, 210, 330
(b) 0, 51.0, 180, 309.0, 360
(c) 0, 48.6, 131.4, 180, 360
(d) 36.9, 143.1, 199.5, 340.5

3 (a) $\frac{3}{2}\pi$ (b) $0, \frac{1}{3}\pi, \frac{5}{3}\pi, 2\pi$
(c) $\frac{1}{3}\pi, \pi, \frac{5}{3}\pi$ (d) $0, \pi, 2\pi$

4 −116.6, −26.6, 63.4, 153.4

5 (a) π (b) $\frac{1}{2}\pi$, 3.99, 5.44

Review exercise 12 (page 516)

1 (a) 360 (b) 90

2 (a) 0.90, 2.25 (b) −1.14, 1.14
(c) −2.19, −0.96, 0.96, 2.19

3 (a) 21.8, 201.8
(b) 11.8, 78.2, 191.8, 258.2

4 24.1, 155.9

5 (a) −2.98, −0.16 (b) $-\frac{1}{2}\pi, \frac{1}{2}\pi$
(c) −3.03, −1.69, 0.12, 1.45

6 0, 1.23, 5.05, 2π

Examination questions (page 516)

1 (a) $6\sin^2 x - \sin x - 2 = 0$
(b) $(3\sin x - 2)(2\sin x + 1)$
(c) 4

2 (a) $(\frac{8}{9}\pi, 0)$ (b) $\frac{19}{18}\pi, \frac{31}{18}\pi$

3 $\frac{1}{4}\pi, \frac{1}{2}\pi$

4 (a) (i) −1 (ii) 4π (b) 4

5 (a) $2\cos^2 x + \cos x - 1 = 0$
(b) $(2\cos x - 1)(\cos x + 1)$
(c) 60, 180, 300

38 The chain rule

Exercise 38 (page 520)

1 (a) $30(5x+3)^5$ (b) $\frac{5}{2}(5x+3)^{-\frac{1}{2}}$
(c) $\dfrac{5}{5x+3}$

2 (a) $15x^2(1+x^3)^4$ (b) $-12x^2(1+x^3)^{-5}$
(c) $\dfrac{3x^2}{1+x^3}$

3 (a) $24x(2x^2+3)^5$ (b) $-4x(2x^2+3)^{-2}$
(c) $-2x(2x^2+3)^{-\frac{3}{2}}$

4 (a) $72x^8 + 72x^5 + 18x^2$ (b) $18x^2(2x^3+1)^2$

5 (a) $20x^4(x^5+1)^3$ (b) $48x^2(2x^3-1)^7$
(c) $12e^{2x}(e^{2x}+3)^5$ (d) $\frac{5}{2}x^{-\frac{1}{2}}(\sqrt{x}-1)^4$

6 (a) $8x(x^2+6)^3$ (b) $45x^2(5x^3+4)^2$
(c) $28x^3(x^4-8)^6$ (d) $-45x^8(2-x^9)^4$

7 (a) $\dfrac{6}{x}(\ln x + 1)^5$ (b) $-\dfrac{4}{x^2}\left(\dfrac{1}{x}+2\right)^3$
(c) $\dfrac{2x^3}{2+x^4}$ (d) $-15e^{-x}(e^{-x}+1)^4$

8 (a) $-\frac{4}{25}$ (b) 0

9 $\frac{3}{8}$

10 $-3\frac{3}{4}$

11 $y = 12x - 25$

12 $4y = -x + 8$

13 $6y = -x + 23$

14 $6x(x^2 - 1)^{-\frac{1}{2}}(\sqrt{x^2 - 1} + 1)^5$

15 $-x(1 - x^2)^{-\frac{1}{2}} e^{\sqrt{1-x^2}}$

39 Differentiating products and quotients

Exercise 39A (page 525)

1 (a) $2x$ (b) $3x^2 + 4x$
(c) $5x^4 + 9x^2 + 8x$ (d) $63x^2 + 100x + 39$
(e) $3x^2$ (f) $(m+n)x^{m+n-1}$

2 (a) $(x + 1)e^x$ (b) $x(2\ln x + 1)$
(c) $3x^2(e^{-2x} + 1) - 2x^3e^{-2x}$
(d) $e^x \ln x + \dfrac{e^x}{x}$
(e) $\dfrac{1}{2\sqrt{x}}e^{-x} - \sqrt{x}\,e^{-x} = \dfrac{(1 - 2x)\,e^{-x}}{2\sqrt{x}}$
(f) $-4xe^{-2x}$

3 (a) $(x^2 + 2x + 3)e^x$
(b) $x(2\ln 2x + 2e^{2x} + 1 + 2xe^{2x})$
(c) $2x(1 + x)e^{2x}$

4 (a) $4x + (2x + x^2)e^x$
(b) $x^2(3 + 2x)e^{2x}$
(c) $6x \ln x + \dfrac{4}{x} + 3x$

5 (a) $-3e^{-4}$ (b) e^2 (c) $1 + \ln 6$

6 (a) $y = 2x - 4$
(b) $y = x - 1$
(c) $8y = 47x - 75$
(d) $y = 0$

7 $(2, 4e^{-2}), (0, 0)$

8 $2e^2$

9 $x + 2y = 1$

10 $V \approx 51.8, x = 6.4$

11 When n is even, there is a maximum at $x = n$, and a minimum at $x = 0$. When n is odd, there is a maximum at $x = n$; if $n > 1$, there is also a point of inflexion at $x = 0$.

Exercise 39B (page 530)

1 (a) $\dfrac{1}{(1 + 5x)^2}$ (b) $\dfrac{3x^2 - 4x}{(3x - 2)^2}$
(c) $\dfrac{2x}{(1 + 2x^2)^2}$ (d) $\dfrac{(12x - 13)e^{3x}}{(4x - 3)^2}$
(e) $\dfrac{1 - 2x^3}{(1 + x^3)^2}$ (f) $\dfrac{(x - 1)^2e^x}{(x^2 + 1)^2}$

2 (a) $\dfrac{x + 2}{2(x + 1)^{\frac{3}{2}}}$ (b) $\dfrac{10 - x}{2x^2\sqrt{x - 5}}$
(c) $-\dfrac{3x + 4}{4x^2\sqrt{3x + 2}}$

3 (a) $\dfrac{e^x(2x - 1)}{2x\sqrt{x}}$ (b) $\dfrac{3e^x - 10 - 5xe^x}{(e^x - 2)^2}$
(c) $\dfrac{-1}{(1 + x)^{\frac{3}{2}}(1 - x)^{\frac{1}{2}}}$ (d) $\dfrac{1 - \ln x}{x^2}$
(e) $\dfrac{2}{x^2 + 4} - \dfrac{\ln(x^2 + 4)}{x^2}$
(f) $\dfrac{3}{(3x + 2)(2x - 1)} - \dfrac{2\ln(3x + 2)}{(2x - 1)^2}$

4 $4y = x + 3$

5 (a) $\dfrac{(2x - 1)e^x}{(2x + 1)^2}$ (b) $\left(\frac{1}{2}, \frac{1}{2}e^{\frac{1}{2}}\right)$

6 $14y = 8x - 37$

7 $2(\sqrt{2} - 1), -2(1 + \sqrt{2})$

8 (a) $\dfrac{x^2 + 2x - 3}{(x + 1)^2}, \dfrac{8}{(x + 1)^3}$
(b) $-3 \le x < -1, -1 < x \le 1$

40 Differentiating circular functions

Exercise 40A (page 534)

1 (a) $-\cos x$ (b) $\sin x$
(c) $4\cos 4x$ (d) $-6\sin 3x$
(e) $\frac{1}{2}\pi \cos \frac{1}{2}\pi x$ (f) $-3\pi \sin 3\pi x$
(g) $-2\sin(2x - 1)$ (h) $15\cos\left(3x + \frac{1}{4}\pi\right)$
(i) $\cos x - x\sin x$
(j) $\cos^2 x - \sin^2 x\,(= \cos 2x)$
(k) $3x^2(\sin x + 1) + x^3 \cos x$
(l) $e^{-x}(\cos x - \sin x)$
(m) $2x(\sin x + \cos x) + x^2(\cos x - \sin x)$
(n) $2e^x \sin x$

2 (a) $2\cos x \sin x$ (b) $-3\cos^2 x \sin x$
(c) $5\sin \frac{1}{2}x \cos \frac{1}{2}x$ (d) $2x \cos x^2$
(e) $-42x^2 \sin 2x^3$ (f) $-6\pi \cos^2 2\pi x \sin 2\pi x$
(g) $-3\sin 3x\, e^{\cos 3x}$ (h) $10 \sin x \cos x\, e^{\sin^2 x}$

3 (a) $\sin^2 x + 2x\cos x \sin x$
(b) $-\dfrac{1}{x^2}\cos^2 x - \dfrac{2}{x}\sin x \cos x$
(c) $\cos^3 x - 2\sin^2 x \cos x$
(d) $3\sin^2 x \cos^2 x(\cos^2 x - \sin^2 x)$
(e) $2x \sin 2x(\sin 2x + 2x\cos 2x)$
(f) $\dfrac{1}{\sqrt{x}} \cos \frac{1}{2}x\left(\frac{1}{2}\cos \frac{1}{2}x - x \sin \frac{1}{2}x\right)$

4 (a) $-4\sin 2x$
(b) $-9\cos 3x$
(c) $2\dfrac{\sin x}{\cos^3 x}$

(d) $\dfrac{1}{\cos x} + \dfrac{2\sin^2 x}{\cos^3 x}$
(e) $e^{\sin x}(\cos^2 x - \sin x)$
(f) $8\cos 4x$
(g) $3\sin x(2\cos^2 x - \sin^2 x)$
(h) $-\sin \frac{1}{2}x - \frac{1}{4}x\cos\frac{1}{2}x$

5 The gradient of the chord joining (0, 0) to $(h, \sin h)$ is $\dfrac{\sin h}{h}$. As $h \to 0$, the gradient of the chord tends to the gradient of the tangent at (0, 0).

6 Both are x-translations of $-\frac{1}{2}\pi$.

7 As $2\cos^2 x - 1 = 1 - 2\sin^2 x = \cos 2x$, they all differ by only a constant, and therefore have the same derivative.

8 $\cos 2x$

Exercise 40B (page 537)

1 (a) Growing at 50 million dollars per year
(b) Falling at 9.7 million dollars per year

2 (a) $55.3\,\text{mm s}^{-1}$ (b) $153\,\text{m s}^{-2}$

3 The curve is concave down when $y > 0$, and concave up when $y < 0$; $y = \sin(nt + \alpha)$.

4 (a) $2y = x + \sqrt{3} - \frac{1}{3}\pi$
(b) $3y = \sqrt{2}(x - \frac{3}{2} - \frac{1}{4}\pi)$
(c) $y = -x - \frac{1}{2}\ln 2 + \frac{1}{4}\pi$
(d) $y = 3$

5 Above, at $y = \cos\frac{5}{6}\pi + \frac{5}{12}\pi \approx 0.443$

6 $(\frac{1}{3}\pi - \frac{1}{7}\sqrt{3}, \frac{3}{7}\sqrt{3})$

7 (a) $(\frac{1}{4}\pi, \sqrt{2})$ maximum,
$(\frac{5}{4}\pi, -\sqrt{2})$ minimum
(b) (π, π) neither
(c) (0, 2) maximum, $(\pi, -2)$ minimum
(d) $(\frac{1}{12}\pi, \frac{1}{2}\sqrt{3} + \frac{1}{12}\pi)$ maximum,
$(\frac{5}{12}\pi, -\frac{1}{2}\sqrt{3} + \frac{5}{12}\pi)$ minimum,
$(\frac{13}{6}\pi, \frac{1}{2}\sqrt{3} + \frac{13}{12}\pi)$ maximum,
$(\frac{17}{12}\pi, -\frac{1}{2}\sqrt{3} + \frac{17}{12}\pi)$ minimum
(e) $(\frac{1}{4}\pi, 2\sqrt{2})$ minimum,
$(\frac{5}{4}\pi, -2\sqrt{2})$ maximum
(f) $(\frac{1}{2}\pi, -3)$ minimum, $(\frac{7}{6}\pi, \frac{3}{2})$ maximum,
$(\frac{3}{2}\pi, 1)$ minimum, $(\frac{11}{6}\pi, \frac{3}{2})$ maximum

8 (a) $\dfrac{\cos\sqrt{x}}{2\sqrt{x}}$ (b) $\dfrac{-\sin x}{2\sqrt{\cos x}}$ (c) $-\dfrac{1}{x^2}\cos\dfrac{1}{x}$

9 (a) (i) $x = t$ (ii) $x = -t$ (iii) $x = 0$
(b) $\tan \pi t = \dfrac{1}{\pi t}$
(d) $-2\pi\sin\pi t - \pi^2 t\cos\pi t$

Exercise 40C (page 540)

1 (a) $\frac{1}{2}\sin 2x + k$ (b) $-\frac{1}{3}\cos 3x + k$
(c) $\frac{1}{2}\sin(2x+1) + k$ (d) $-\frac{1}{3}\cos(3x-1) + k$
(e) $\cos(1-x) + k$ (f) $-2\sin(4 - \frac{1}{2}x) + k$
(g) $-2\cos(\frac{1}{2}x + \frac{1}{3}\pi) + k$
(h) $\frac{1}{3}\sin(3x - \frac{1}{4}\pi) + k$ (i) $2\cos\frac{1}{2}x + k$

2 (a) 1 (b) $\frac{1}{2}\sqrt{2}$ (c) $\frac{1}{2}$
(d) $-\frac{1}{6}\sqrt{2}$ (e) $\frac{1}{6}(\sqrt{3} - 1)$ (f) 0
(g) $\sin 1$ (h) $2\cos 1 - 2\cos\frac{5}{4}$ (i) 4

3 (a) $-\frac{1}{2}\ln\cos 2x + k$ (b) $\frac{1}{3}\tan 3x + k$
(c) $\ln\cos(\frac{1}{4}\pi - x) + k$

4 (a) $\frac{1}{2}\ln 2$ (b) $\frac{1}{6}\ln 2$

5 (a) $\frac{1}{2}(x + \frac{1}{2}\sin 2x) + k$ (b) $\frac{1}{2}(x + \sin x) + k$
(c) $\frac{1}{2}(x - \frac{1}{4}\sin 4x) + k$ (d) $-\frac{1}{4}\cos 2x + k$

6 (a) $\sqrt{2}$ (b) $\frac{1}{2} + \frac{1}{4}\pi$ (c) 2

7 (a) $\frac{1}{2}$ (b) $\dfrac{1}{\pi}$

41 Volumes of revolution

Exercise 41 (page 544)

1 (a) $\frac{98}{3}\pi$ (b) $\frac{3093}{5}\pi$
(c) $\frac{279\,808}{7}\pi$ (d) $\frac{3}{4}\pi$
(e) $\frac{1}{2}\pi(e^2 - 1)$ (f) $\frac{1}{2}\pi\left(1 - \dfrac{1}{e^4}\right)$

2 (a) 504π (b) $\frac{3498}{5}\pi$
(c) $\frac{15}{2}\pi$ (d) $\frac{16}{15}\pi$
(e) $\pi(e^3 - e)$ (f) $\frac{1}{4}\pi\left(1 - \dfrac{1}{e^4}\right)$

3 (a) $\frac{16}{15}\pi$ (b) $\frac{81}{10}\pi$

4 $\frac{1}{4}\pi\left(4 + e^2 - \dfrac{1}{e^2}\right)$

5 1; $\frac{1}{4}\pi^2$

6 $\pi + 2$; $\frac{1}{2}\pi(8 + 3\pi)$

7 (a) $2 - \sqrt{2}$ (b) $\frac{1}{4}\pi(\pi - 2)$

8 (0, 1), $(\frac{3}{4}\pi, 0)$; $1 + \sqrt{2}$; $\frac{1}{4}\pi(3\pi + 2)$

9 $\pi\sqrt{3}$

Review exercise 13 (page 546)

1 $4y = -3x + 18$

2 (a) $\dfrac{2 - x}{\sqrt{4x - x^2}}$, (2, 2)

3 (a) $x \le 3$ (b) $\sqrt{3}$ (c) (2, 2)

4 $\left(\dfrac{1}{e^2}, \dfrac{4}{e^2}\right)$ maximum, (1, 0) minimum;
$0 < x < \dfrac{1}{e}$

5 (0, 0) minimum, $\left(-4, \frac{16}{e^2}\right)$ maximum;

$y - p^2 e^{\frac{1}{2}p} = (2p + \frac{1}{2}p^2)e^{\frac{1}{2}p}(x - p)$;

$\left(-3, \frac{9}{e^{\frac{3}{2}}}\right)$, (0, 0), (4, 16e^2)

6 $\frac{1}{2}\pi \ln 3$

7 $\frac{176}{15}\pi$

8 $y = 2x - 3$

9 $\dfrac{x+6}{2(x+3)^{\frac{3}{2}}}$

11 4π

12 (a) $e^x(\cos x - \sin x)$ (b) $\frac{1}{4}\pi < x < \frac{5}{4}\pi$
(c) The gradient is negative for these values of x.

13 (a) $v = 11\left(1 - \cos\left(\frac{\pi}{45}t\right)\right)$, 90 seconds
(b) 990 metres, 11 m s^{-1}
(c) 0.665 m s^{-2}

15 $\dfrac{dy}{dx} = \dfrac{x\cos x - \sin x}{x^2}$

16 (a) $4.8 \pm 1.2 \sin \frac{1}{12}\pi t$ or $4.8 \pm 1.2 \cos \frac{1}{12}\pi t$
(b) $21\,500 \pm 6500 \sin \frac{1}{5}\pi t$ or $21\,500 \pm 6500 \cos \frac{1}{5}\pi t$
(c) $12 \pm 10 \sin \frac{1}{180}\pi t$ or $12 \pm 10 \cos \frac{1}{180}\pi t$

Examination questions (page 547)

1 $\frac{1}{3}e^{\frac{1}{3}x} - 10 \sin x \cos x$

2 $\ln(x+1) + 0.5 \cos x + 1.5$

3 (a) $x - 3\cos(x+2) + k$ (b) 1.48

4 (a) $x = 1$ (b) (i) 2.009 (ii) $y = 2$
(e) (4, 0)

5 1.17

6 (a) (ii) $\frac{3}{4}\pi$ (b) $2e^x \cos x$
(c) $\frac{1}{2}\pi$, $e^{\frac{1}{2}\pi}$ (e) $\frac{1}{\sqrt{2}}e^{\frac{3}{4}\pi}$

7 (a) (0, sin 1) (b) π
(c) (i) 1 (ii) $e^x \cos e^x$
(d) (i) $\int_0^{\ln \pi} \sin e^x \, dx$ (ii) 0.906
(e) (ii) 0.877

8 (a) (i) $\cos 2x - \sin x$
(ii) $(2\sin x - 1)(\sin x + 1)$
(iii) $\frac{1}{6}\pi$, $\frac{5}{6}\pi$, $\frac{3}{2}\pi$
(b) $\frac{1}{6}\pi$
(c) (i) $\int_{\frac{1}{6}\pi}^{\frac{1}{2}\pi} f(x)\,dx - \int_{\frac{1}{2}\pi}^{\frac{5}{6}\pi} f(x)\,dx$
(ii) $1\frac{3}{4}$

42 Vectors

Exercise 42A (page 556)

2 (a) $(4\boldsymbol{i} + \boldsymbol{j}) + (-3\boldsymbol{i} + 2\boldsymbol{j}) = \boldsymbol{i} + 3\boldsymbol{j}$
(b) $3(\boldsymbol{i} - 2\boldsymbol{j}) = 3\boldsymbol{i} - 6\boldsymbol{j}$
(c) $4\boldsymbol{j} + 2(\boldsymbol{i} - 2\boldsymbol{j}) = 2\boldsymbol{i}$
(d) $(3\boldsymbol{i} + \boldsymbol{j}) - (5\boldsymbol{i} + \boldsymbol{j}) = -2\boldsymbol{i}$
(e) $3(-\boldsymbol{i} + 2\boldsymbol{j}) - (-4\boldsymbol{i} + 3\boldsymbol{j}) = \boldsymbol{i} + 3\boldsymbol{j}$
(f) $4(2\boldsymbol{i} + 3\boldsymbol{j}) - 3(3\boldsymbol{i} + 2\boldsymbol{j}) = -\boldsymbol{i} + 6\boldsymbol{j}$
(g) $(2\boldsymbol{i} - 3\boldsymbol{j}) + (4\boldsymbol{i} + 5\boldsymbol{j}) + (-6\boldsymbol{i} - 2\boldsymbol{j}) = \boldsymbol{0}$
(h) $2(3\boldsymbol{i} - \boldsymbol{j}) + 3(-2\boldsymbol{i} + 3\boldsymbol{j}) + (-7\boldsymbol{j}) = \boldsymbol{0}$

3 (a) $\begin{pmatrix} 1 \\ 2 \end{pmatrix}$ (b) $\begin{pmatrix} 3 \\ 0 \end{pmatrix}$
(c) $\begin{pmatrix} -1 \\ 1 \end{pmatrix}$ (d) $\begin{pmatrix} 4 \\ -3 \end{pmatrix}$

4 $s = 2$

5 $s = 4$; $\boldsymbol{q} = \frac{1}{4}(\boldsymbol{r} - \boldsymbol{p})$

6 2, 3

7 $1\frac{1}{2}$, $-\frac{1}{2}$

8 $\begin{pmatrix} 4 \\ -2 \end{pmatrix}$ and $\begin{pmatrix} -6 \\ 3 \end{pmatrix}$ are parallel, $\begin{pmatrix} 3 \\ 1 \end{pmatrix}$ is in a different direction;
$\begin{pmatrix} -1 \\ 2 \end{pmatrix}$ is not parallel to $\begin{pmatrix} 1 \\ 1 \end{pmatrix} - \begin{pmatrix} 3 \\ 4 \end{pmatrix}$

9 Any multiple of 1, −1, 2. If $f\boldsymbol{p} + g\boldsymbol{q} + h\boldsymbol{r} = \boldsymbol{0}$, then any multiple of f, g and h will also give 0.

10 (a) no (b) −2, 0;
$\boldsymbol{p}$ is parallel to $\boldsymbol{r}$, but $\boldsymbol{q}$ is in a different direction.

11 $\boldsymbol{a} = \boldsymbol{i} - 2\boldsymbol{j} + \boldsymbol{k}$, $\boldsymbol{b} = -3\boldsymbol{i} + \boldsymbol{j} + 2\boldsymbol{k}$;
$9\boldsymbol{i} - 8\boldsymbol{j} - \boldsymbol{k}$

12 $\begin{pmatrix} 8 \\ -25 \\ 1 \end{pmatrix}$

Exercise 42B (page 560)

1 (a) (9, 3) (b) (−1, −2)
(c) (2, −1) (d) (−8, −1)
(e) (10, 5) (f) $(5, 2\frac{1}{2})$

2 (a) (−13, −23) (b) (−1, 1)

3 $\boldsymbol{c} = 2\boldsymbol{b} - \boldsymbol{a}$

4 $\frac{3}{7}\boldsymbol{a} + \frac{4}{7}\boldsymbol{b}$

6 $\boldsymbol{b} - \boldsymbol{a} = \boldsymbol{c} - \boldsymbol{d}$

7 $\frac{1}{2}(\boldsymbol{b} + \boldsymbol{c} - 2\boldsymbol{a})$, $\frac{1}{4}(\boldsymbol{b} + \boldsymbol{c} - 2\boldsymbol{a})$; G is the mid-point of [AD].

8 (4, −3, 0)

9 They are all $\frac{1}{4}(\boldsymbol{a}+\boldsymbol{b}+\boldsymbol{c}+\boldsymbol{d})$.
The line segments joining the mid-points of opposite edges of a tetrahedron meet and bisect one another.

10 $\frac{1}{4}\boldsymbol{e}+\frac{3}{4}\boldsymbol{f}$, $\frac{1}{3}(\boldsymbol{a}+\boldsymbol{b}+\boldsymbol{c})$, $\frac{1}{4}(\boldsymbol{a}+\boldsymbol{b}+\boldsymbol{c}+\boldsymbol{d})$

43 Scalar products of vectors

Exercise 43 (page 565)

1 −8, 11, 3

2 11, −3, 8

3 18, 0, 0; $\boldsymbol{w}$ is perpendicular to both $\boldsymbol{u}$ and $\boldsymbol{v}$.

4 (a) and (d) are perpendicular; so are (b) and (c).

5 −4, −8, −12

6 (a) 5 (b) $\sqrt{5}$ (c) $\sqrt{5}$ (d) 1
(e) 3 (f) 13 (g) 5 (h) $\sqrt{6}$
(i) $\sqrt{5}$ (j) $\sqrt{13}$ (k) $\sqrt{30}$ (l) 2

7 $5, \begin{pmatrix} \frac{4}{5} \\ -\frac{3}{5} \end{pmatrix}$

8 $\begin{pmatrix} \frac{1}{3} \\ -\frac{2}{3} \\ \frac{2}{3} \end{pmatrix}, \frac{2}{3}\boldsymbol{i}-\frac{1}{3}\boldsymbol{j}+\frac{2}{3}\boldsymbol{k}$

9 15.3°

10 (a) 45° (b) 167.3° (c) 180°
(d) 136.7° (e) 7.0° (f) 90°

11 $\sqrt{(x_2-x_1)^2+(y_2-y_1)^2}$; the distance between the points with position vectors $\boldsymbol{r}_1$ and $\boldsymbol{r}_2$.

12 172.2° (or 7.8°)

13 99.6° (or 80.4°)

14 70.5°

15 76.4°

16 48.2°

44 Vector equations of lines

Exercise 44A (page 570)

Note that, since vector equations are not unique, other correct answers are sometimes possible.

1 (a) $\boldsymbol{r}=\begin{pmatrix} 2 \\ -3 \end{pmatrix}+t\begin{pmatrix} 1 \\ 2 \end{pmatrix}, y=2x-7$

(b) $\boldsymbol{r}=\begin{pmatrix} 4 \\ 1 \end{pmatrix}+t\begin{pmatrix} -3 \\ 2 \end{pmatrix}, 2x+3y=11$

(c) $\boldsymbol{r}=\begin{pmatrix} 5 \\ 7 \end{pmatrix}+t\begin{pmatrix} 1 \\ 0 \end{pmatrix}, y=7$

(d) $\boldsymbol{r}=t\begin{pmatrix} 2 \\ -1 \end{pmatrix}, x+2y=0$

2 (a) $\boldsymbol{r}=\begin{pmatrix} 2 \\ 0 \end{pmatrix}+t\begin{pmatrix} 0 \\ 1 \end{pmatrix}$

(b) $\boldsymbol{r}=\begin{pmatrix} 1 \\ 2 \end{pmatrix}+t\begin{pmatrix} 3 \\ -1 \end{pmatrix}$

(c) $\boldsymbol{r}=\begin{pmatrix} -1 \\ -1 \end{pmatrix}+t\begin{pmatrix} 5 \\ 2 \end{pmatrix}$

3 (3, 1)

4 (a) (7, 3) (b) (8, −5)
(c) No common points (d) (5, 2)

5 (a), (d)

6 (a) $\boldsymbol{r}=\begin{pmatrix} 3 \\ 7 \end{pmatrix}+t\begin{pmatrix} 2 \\ -3 \end{pmatrix}$

(b) $\boldsymbol{r}=\begin{pmatrix} 2 \\ 3 \end{pmatrix}+t\begin{pmatrix} 0 \\ 1 \end{pmatrix}$

(c) $\boldsymbol{r}=\begin{pmatrix} -1 \\ 2 \end{pmatrix}+t\begin{pmatrix} 2 \\ -1 \end{pmatrix}$

7 $\begin{pmatrix} 1 \\ 3 \end{pmatrix}, \boldsymbol{r}=\begin{pmatrix} 1 \\ 5 \end{pmatrix}+t\begin{pmatrix} -3 \\ 1 \end{pmatrix}$; (4, 4)

Exercise 44B (page 574)

1 (a) $\boldsymbol{r}=\begin{pmatrix} 2 \\ -3 \\ 5 \end{pmatrix}+t\begin{pmatrix} 1 \\ 2 \\ -6 \end{pmatrix}$

(b) $\boldsymbol{r}=\begin{pmatrix} 4 \\ -1 \\ 1 \end{pmatrix}+t\begin{pmatrix} 4 \\ -2 \\ -3 \end{pmatrix}$

(c) $\boldsymbol{r}=\begin{pmatrix} 5 \\ 7 \\ 4 \end{pmatrix}+t\begin{pmatrix} 1 \\ 0 \\ 0 \end{pmatrix}$

(d) $\boldsymbol{r}=\begin{pmatrix} 0 \\ 0 \\ 0 \end{pmatrix}+t\begin{pmatrix} 2 \\ -3 \\ 1 \end{pmatrix}$

2 (a) 2, −3 (b) 3, 1 (c) No solution

3 (a) They meet at (4, 3, 3).
(b) They meet at (5, −5, 4).
(c) They do not intersect.

4 (a) $\boldsymbol{r}=\begin{pmatrix} 8 \\ 7 \\ 5 \end{pmatrix}+t\begin{pmatrix} -9 \\ -5 \\ -6 \end{pmatrix}$

(b) $\boldsymbol{r}=\begin{pmatrix} 2 \\ -2 \\ 0 \end{pmatrix}+t\begin{pmatrix} 0 \\ 1 \\ 0 \end{pmatrix}$

(c) $\boldsymbol{r}=\begin{pmatrix} 4 \\ 5 \\ -2 \end{pmatrix}+t\begin{pmatrix} -6 \\ -8 \\ 6 \end{pmatrix}$

5 Any multiple of 1, 2, −3; the translations are all parallel to the same plane.

6 (a) Intersect at (1, −1, 0) (b) Parallel
(c) Intersect at (−7, −5, −4) (d) Skew

7 $\boldsymbol{r} = \begin{pmatrix} 3 \\ 2 \\ 6 \end{pmatrix} + t \begin{pmatrix} -3 \\ 1 \\ 2 \end{pmatrix}$; $(12, -1, 0)$, $(9, 0, 2)$

8 0.4 m

9 $3\sqrt{14}$ km h^{-1}, $(11.4, 3, 0)$ at 8.04 a.m.

Review exercise 14 (page 576)

1 $\begin{pmatrix} 9 \\ -1 \\ 4 \end{pmatrix}$

2 (a) $y = 4x - 14$ (b) $\boldsymbol{r} = \begin{pmatrix} 0 \\ 1 \end{pmatrix} + t \begin{pmatrix} 3 \\ 2 \end{pmatrix}$

(c) $2x - 3y + 17 = 0$, or $\boldsymbol{r} = \begin{pmatrix} -1 \\ 5 \end{pmatrix} + t \begin{pmatrix} 3 \\ 2 \end{pmatrix}$

3 (a) No intersection (b) $(-3, -1)$

(c) Same line

4 $-10\boldsymbol{i} + 7\boldsymbol{j} - 3\boldsymbol{k}$

5 The lines do not meet.

6 (a) $\boldsymbol{r} = \begin{pmatrix} 2 \\ 3 \\ 5 \end{pmatrix} + \lambda \begin{pmatrix} 1 \\ 1 \\ -0.5 \end{pmatrix}$ (b) 25 m

7 (a) Above (61, 77) on the ground

(b) 4200 m

(c) 384 km h^{-1}, 38.7°

(d) 386 km h^{-1}, 5.35°

8 (a) $\boldsymbol{r} = \begin{pmatrix} 2 \\ -1 \\ 3 \end{pmatrix} + t \begin{pmatrix} -1 \\ 1 \\ 2 \end{pmatrix}$

(b) 21°

9 $\boldsymbol{a}$ and $\boldsymbol{b}$, $\boldsymbol{a}$ and $\boldsymbol{c}$, $\boldsymbol{b}$ and $\boldsymbol{c}$, $\boldsymbol{b}$ and $\boldsymbol{d}$

10 (a) $\boldsymbol{d} = \begin{pmatrix} 9 \\ 4 \\ -5 \end{pmatrix}$ (b) $\begin{pmatrix} 3 \\ 3 \\ 0 \end{pmatrix}$ (c) 120.5°

11 (a) 60° (b) $\frac{3}{2}\sqrt{3}$

Examination questions (page 577)

1 (a) 5 (b) (6, 7)

(c) $\boldsymbol{r} = \begin{pmatrix} -2 \\ 1 \end{pmatrix} + t \begin{pmatrix} 4 \\ 3 \end{pmatrix}$

2 (a) (i) $-6\boldsymbol{i} - 2\boldsymbol{j}$ (ii) $-2\boldsymbol{i}$

(b) 97.1°

(c) $\boldsymbol{r} = \boldsymbol{i} - 3\boldsymbol{j} + t(2\boldsymbol{i} + 7\boldsymbol{j})$

(d) $15\boldsymbol{i} + 46\boldsymbol{j}$

3 (a) (i) $\begin{pmatrix} -5 \\ 1 \end{pmatrix}$ (ii) $\sqrt{26}$

(b) $\begin{pmatrix} d-4 \\ 25 \end{pmatrix}$ (c) (ii) $\begin{pmatrix} 9 \\ 22 \end{pmatrix}$

(d) $\begin{pmatrix} 4 \\ 23 \end{pmatrix}$ (e) 130

4 $\begin{pmatrix} 2 \\ 3 \end{pmatrix}$

45 Matrices

Exercise 45 (page 588)

1 (a) $\begin{pmatrix} 3 & 5 \\ 7 & 3 \end{pmatrix}$ (b) $\begin{pmatrix} -1 & -1 \\ -1 & 5 \end{pmatrix}$

(c) $\begin{pmatrix} 7 & 12 \\ 17 & 10 \end{pmatrix}$ (d) $\begin{pmatrix} -2 & -1 \\ 0 & 19 \end{pmatrix}$

2 $\boldsymbol{X} = \frac{3}{2}(\boldsymbol{A} + \boldsymbol{B})$; they are all the same order.

4 $\begin{pmatrix} 10 & 1 \\ 22 & 5 \end{pmatrix}$, $\begin{pmatrix} 11 & 16 \\ 1 & 4 \end{pmatrix}$

5 $\begin{pmatrix} 21 & 3 & -1 \\ 29 & -19 & 8 \\ -18 & -4 & 7 \end{pmatrix}$, $\begin{pmatrix} 15 & 12 & -20 \\ 5 & 14 & 4 \\ -3 & -8 & -20 \end{pmatrix}$

6 $\begin{pmatrix} 0 & -8 \\ 13 & 0 \end{pmatrix}$, $\begin{pmatrix} -14 & 10 & 40 \\ -5 & 4 & 22 \\ -8 & 5 & 10 \end{pmatrix}$

7 For example, $\begin{pmatrix} 1 & -2 \\ -2 & 1 \end{pmatrix}$ and $\begin{pmatrix} 2 & -3 \\ -3 & 2 \end{pmatrix}$.

8 (a) Does not exist. (b) $\begin{pmatrix} -3 \\ -8 \end{pmatrix}$

(c) $\begin{pmatrix} 2 & 3 & 1 \\ -2 & -3 & -1 \\ 2 & 3 & 1 \end{pmatrix}$ (d) (0)

(e) Does not exist. (f) Does not exist.

(g) Does not exist. (h) Does not exist.

9 $\begin{pmatrix} 7 & -2 \\ -3 & 1 \end{pmatrix}$, $\begin{pmatrix} 1 & 0 \\ 0 & 1 \end{pmatrix}$; no such matrix.

11 $\begin{pmatrix} 19 & -2 & -8 \\ -7 & 1 & 3 \\ -2 & 0 & 1 \end{pmatrix}$, $\begin{pmatrix} 1 & 0 & 0 \\ 0 & 1 & 0 \\ 0 & 0 & 1 \end{pmatrix}$

14 $\boldsymbol{OA} = \boldsymbol{AO} = \boldsymbol{O}$

17 $\begin{pmatrix} 2 & -3 \\ -3 & 5 \end{pmatrix}$

18 $\begin{pmatrix} 3 & -2 \\ -7 & 5 \end{pmatrix}$

46 Inverse matrices

Exercise 46A (page 590)
No answers are given for this exercise.

Exercise 46B (page 595)
Answers from a calculator are given in decimal form. These answers are given as fractions; you may need to convert them to decimals if you have used a calculator.

1 (a) $\frac{1}{2}\begin{pmatrix}1 & 1\\ -1 & 1\end{pmatrix}$ (b) $\begin{pmatrix}7 & -9\\ -3 & 4\end{pmatrix}$

(c) $\begin{pmatrix}7 & 5\\ 4 & 3\end{pmatrix}$ (d) $\frac{1}{3}\begin{pmatrix}4 & 1\\ 5 & 2\end{pmatrix}$

(e) No inverse (f) $\frac{1}{5}\begin{pmatrix}-5 & 3\\ -10 & 5\end{pmatrix}$

2 (a) $x = 4, y = -3$ (b) $x = -3, y = 2$
(c) $x = 2, y = 1$

3 (a) $\begin{pmatrix}1 & 3\\ -1 & 2\end{pmatrix}$ (b) $\begin{pmatrix}13 & -\frac{15}{2}\\ 18 & -10\end{pmatrix}$

(c) $\begin{pmatrix}\frac{2}{5} & -\frac{3}{5}\\ \frac{1}{5} & \frac{1}{5}\end{pmatrix}$

4 $\begin{pmatrix}-2 & 0\\ 1 & 5\end{pmatrix}$

5 $\frac{1}{3}\begin{pmatrix}-3 & 4\\ 6 & -7\end{pmatrix}$

6 (a) (i) $\boldsymbol{B}^{-1}(\boldsymbol{C}-\boldsymbol{A})$ (ii) $(\boldsymbol{C}-\boldsymbol{B})\boldsymbol{A}^{-1}$
(iii) $\boldsymbol{C}(\boldsymbol{A}+\boldsymbol{B})^{-1}$ (iv) $(\boldsymbol{C}-\boldsymbol{B})^{-1}\boldsymbol{A}$
(v) $(\boldsymbol{I}+\boldsymbol{A})^{-1}\boldsymbol{B}$ (vi) $\boldsymbol{C}(2\boldsymbol{I}-\boldsymbol{A})^{-1}$

(b) (i) $\begin{pmatrix}3 & 7\\ -1 & -3\end{pmatrix}$ (ii) $\frac{1}{2}\begin{pmatrix}-9 & 3\\ -8 & 4\end{pmatrix}$

(iii) $\frac{1}{5}\begin{pmatrix}-5 & 5\\ -7 & 8\end{pmatrix}$ (iv) $\frac{1}{6}\begin{pmatrix}9 & 12\\ -2 & -4\end{pmatrix}$

(v) $\frac{1}{4}\begin{pmatrix}5 & 13\\ -3 & -7\end{pmatrix}$ (vi) $\frac{1}{8}\begin{pmatrix}2 & -2\\ 1 & -5\end{pmatrix}$

Exercise 46C (page 598)

1 (a) $\begin{pmatrix}-3 & 2 & -1\\ 1 & 1 & 1\\ 2 & 0 & 1\end{pmatrix}$ (b) $\begin{pmatrix}1 & -1 & \frac{1}{2}\\ -1 & 1 & -1\\ 1 & 0 & \frac{1}{2}\end{pmatrix}$

(c) $\begin{pmatrix}-\frac{1}{2} & \frac{2}{3} & \frac{1}{6}\\ -\frac{1}{2} & \frac{1}{3} & -\frac{1}{6}\\ -\frac{1}{2} & 0 & \frac{1}{2}\end{pmatrix}$ (d) $\begin{pmatrix}-\frac{7}{6} & -\frac{1}{6} & \frac{5}{6}\\ -\frac{1}{3} & \frac{2}{3} & -\frac{1}{3}\\ -\frac{1}{2} & -\frac{1}{2} & \frac{1}{2}\end{pmatrix}$

(e) $\begin{pmatrix}\frac{13}{2} & 4 & -\frac{9}{2}\\ \frac{9}{2} & 3 & -\frac{7}{2}\\ -\frac{7}{2} & -2 & \frac{5}{2}\end{pmatrix}$ (f) No inverse

2 (a) $x = 4, y = 3, z = 1$
(b) $x = 2, y = 2, z = 1$
(c) $x = 1, y = 1, z = 2$

3 (a) $\begin{pmatrix}6 & 1 & -2\\ -4 & -1 & 1\\ 3 & -2 & 1\end{pmatrix}$ (b) $\begin{pmatrix}1 & 4 & 7\\ 2 & -1 & 3\\ 2 & 0 & 1\end{pmatrix}$

4 $\frac{1}{2}\begin{pmatrix}3 & 29 & -20\\ -2 & -14 & 10\\ -3 & -35 & 24\end{pmatrix}$

5 $\begin{pmatrix}2 & 1 & 1\\ -1 & 0 & 1\\ 1 & 1 & 0\end{pmatrix}$

47 Determinants

Exercise 47A (page 601)

1 (a) -1 (b) $14 - a$ (c) $16 - a^2$

2 (a) 10 (b) 0 (c) 0

3 (a) $-1, 3$

(b) $\dfrac{1}{(a+1)(a-3)}\begin{pmatrix}a & -2a-3\\ -1 & a\end{pmatrix}$,
$a \neq -1, 3$

Exercise 47B (page 606)

1 (a) 0 (b) -3 (c) 16

2 (a) -2 (b) 8 (c) $-2, 1$

3 (a) 13 (b) 3 (c) $-\frac{4}{3}$

4 -7

5 7

6 $\frac{1}{23}\begin{pmatrix}-10 & -6 & -23\\ -24 & -19 & -46\\ -9 & -10 & -23\end{pmatrix}$

7 (a) $\frac{1}{28}\begin{pmatrix}16 & -20 & 0\\ -4 & -44 & -28\\ 2 & 15 & 0\end{pmatrix}$

(b) $\frac{1}{12}\begin{pmatrix}8 & 0 & 4\\ 20 & -21 & -11\\ 0 & 12 & 0\end{pmatrix}$

Review exercise 15 (page 608)

1 $\begin{pmatrix}4 & a+3\\ a+1 & a^2+1\end{pmatrix}, \begin{pmatrix}1+a^2 & a+3\\ a+1 & 4\end{pmatrix}; \pm\sqrt{3}$

2 (a) $\begin{pmatrix}3 & -2\\ 2 & 2\end{pmatrix}$ (b) 10 (c) $\frac{1}{10}\begin{pmatrix}2 & 2\\ -2 & 3\end{pmatrix}$

3 (a) $\begin{pmatrix}1 & 0\\ 0 & -5\end{pmatrix}$ (b) $\begin{pmatrix}1 & -\frac{3}{5}\\ 0 & 1\end{pmatrix}$

5 $\frac{1}{2}\begin{pmatrix}5 & 2\\ -1 & 0\end{pmatrix}$

6 (a) (ii) $\frac{1}{20}\begin{pmatrix} 2 & 1 & -3 \\ 2 & 3 & 3 \\ -4 & 2 & 2 \end{pmatrix}$

(b) $x = -2, y = 6, z = -3$

7 (a) $4\boldsymbol{I}, \boldsymbol{A}^{-1} = \frac{1}{4}\boldsymbol{B} = \frac{1}{4}\begin{pmatrix} -6 & -3 & 5 \\ 10 & 5 & -7 \\ 14 & 9 & -11 \end{pmatrix}$

(b) $x = -2, y = 11, z = 18$

8 (a) $(ax^2 + 2bx + c)$

9 (a) $-49, 88$

(b) $\boldsymbol{A}^{-1} = \frac{1}{49}\begin{pmatrix} -2 & 7 & 13 \\ -6 & 21 & -10 \\ 11 & -14 & 2 \end{pmatrix}$

$\boldsymbol{B}^{-1} = \frac{1}{88}\begin{pmatrix} -34 & -13 & -19 \\ 14 & -5 & 13 \\ -2 & 7 & 17 \end{pmatrix}$

(c) $\boldsymbol{X} = \frac{1}{49}\begin{pmatrix} -4 & -12 & 72 \\ -61 & -183 & 20 \\ 22 & 115 & -53 \end{pmatrix}$

(d) $\boldsymbol{Y} = \frac{1}{88}\begin{pmatrix} -151 & -156 & -264 \\ 57 & 28 & 88 \\ 61 & -4 & 0 \end{pmatrix}$

(e) $\boldsymbol{I}$

Examination questions (page 609)

1 (a) $\frac{1}{19}\begin{pmatrix} 1 & 2 \\ -7 & 5 \end{pmatrix}$ (b) $\boldsymbol{X} = (\boldsymbol{C} - \boldsymbol{B})\boldsymbol{A}^{-1}$

(c) $\begin{pmatrix} 2 & -3 \\ -4 & 1 \end{pmatrix}$

2 (a) $\begin{pmatrix} -3 & 2 \\ 1 & \frac{1}{3}(14 - a) \end{pmatrix}$

(b) $\begin{pmatrix} -14 & 4a - 4 \\ -2 & 7a + 2 \end{pmatrix}$ (c) $\dfrac{1}{5a + 2}\begin{pmatrix} a & -2 \\ 1 & 5 \end{pmatrix}$

Index

The page numbers refer to the first mention of each term, or the box if there is one.